# Encyclopedia
## of the
## American Constitution

# Original 1986 Editorial Board

# Encyclopedia
## of the
# American Constitution

## SECOND EDITION

Edited by
**LEONARD W. LEVY**
and
**KENNETH L. KARST**

ADAM WINKLER, Associate Editor for the Second Edition

DENNIS J. MAHONEY, Assistant Editor for the First Edition
JOHN G. WEST, JR., Assistant Editor for Supplement I

MACMILLAN REFERENCE USA
*An imprint of the Gale Group*
New York

Copyright © 2000 by Macmillan Reference USA

Macmillan Library Reference USA
1633 Broadway
New York, NY 10019

Printed in the United States of America

Printing Number
10 9 8 7 6 5 4 3 2 1

**Library of Congress Cataloging-in-Publication Data**
Encyclopedia of the American Constitution / edited by Leonard W. Levy and Kenneth L.
Karst.—2nd ed. / Adam Winkler, associate editor for the second edition.
    p. cm.
    Includes bibliographical references and indexes.
    ISBN 0-02-864880-3 (hard cover : alk. paper)
        1. Constitutional law—United States—Encyclopedias.   I. Levy, Leonard Williams,
1923–   II. Karst, Kenneth L.   III. Winkler, Adam.
    KF4548 .E53   2000
    342.73—dc21
                                                                                    00-029203

This paper meets the requirements of ANSI-NISO Z39.48-1992 (Permanence of Paper).

# TAFT, ROBERT A.
## (1889–1953)

Senator Robert Alphonso Taft, the son of President and Chief Justice WILLIAM HOWARD TAFT, was a leader of Republican opposition to the NEW DEAL policies of FRANKLIN D. ROOSEVELT. A graduate of Yale University and Harvard Law School, Taft served in the Ohio legislature from 1921 to 1933. His public crusade against the Roosevelt revolution began in 1935; in 1938 he was elected to the United States SENATE, sworn to do battle against "the mistaken belief that government can remove all poverty, redistribute all wealth, and bestow happiness on every citizen."

An advocate of STRICT CONSTRUCTION of constitutional provisions that confer power on government, Taft severely criticized Roosevelt's appointees to the Supreme Court for acting as if "constitutional principles are weak as water" by abdicating their duty to keep the government within the limits set by the Constitution. He strongly urged that Congress become the locus of responsible CONSTITUTIONALISM, and he opposed, both in peacetime and wartime, DELEGATIONS OF POWER to the executive branch.

Taft continued to oppose expansion of the executive power after HARRY S. TRUMAN became President. During the STEEL SEIZURE CONTROVERSY Taft argued that if the President could increase his own powers by simply declaring a national emergency the Constitution would become a dead letter. Taft used his position as chairman of the Senate Labor Committee to sponsor a comprehensive reform of federal labor law, now known as the TAFT-HARTLEY ACT.

After a decade and a half of being "Mr. Republican," Taft felt entitled to his party's presidential nomination in 1952. However, the nomination, and election to the presidency, went to General DWIGHT D. EISENHOWER, hero of WORLD WAR II. Nevertheless, Taft had a major share in formulating the domestic policy of the new administration during its first year in office.

DENNIS J. MAHONEY
(1986)

Bibliography

KIRK, RUSSEL and MCCLELLAN, JAMES 1967 *The Political Principles of Robert A. Taft.* New York: Fleet Press Corporation.

# TAFT, WILLIAM HOWARD
## (1857–1930)

William Howard Taft's life was amazing both for length of public service (1881–1930) and for the variety of his activities: prosecuting attorney in his native state of Ohio, superior court judge in Cincinnati, SOLICITOR GENERAL of the United States, federal circuit court judge, governor general of the Philippine Islands, cabinet member, President of the United States (1908–1912), professor of law at Yale, and CHIEF JUSTICE of the United States (1921–1930).

Taft appeared to be almost the prototype of a Chief Justice. Large of frame and good-natured, weighing well over 350 pounds, he filled out the popular image. His gallantry was famous. "I heard recently," Justice DAVID J. BREWER reported, "that he arose in a street car and gave his seat to three women."

Taft idolized Chief Justice JOHN MARSHALL. One day, passing by the west entrance to the Capitol, he paused in front of the bronze statue of Marshall. "Would you rather have been Marshall than President?" a friend asked. "Of course," Taft answered, "I would rather have been Marshall than any other American unless it had been Washington, and I am inclined to think I would rather have been Marshall than Washington. He made this country." Taft himself became the only man in history to occupy both the White House and the Supreme Court's center chair.

During THEODORE ROOSEVELT's administration Taft rejected two opportunities to join the Supreme Court as associate justice. As successor to Roosevelt in the White House, Taft thought longingly about the future and pined to succeed aging Chief Justice MELVILLE W. FULLER. "If the Chief Justice would only retire," Taft lamented, "how simple everything would become!"

As President Taft signed Associate Justice EDWARD D. WHITE's commission as Chief Justice, he grieved: "There is nothing I would have liked more than being Chief Justice of the United States. I can't help seeing the irony in the fact that I, who desired that office so much, should now be signing the commission of another man." Rating Supreme Court appointments as among his most important presidential functions, Taft had the opportunity to appoint five associate Justices as well as the Chief—WILLIS VAN DEVANTER, HORACE H. LURTON, JOSEPH R. LAMAR, CHARLES EVANS HUGHES, and MAHLON PITNEY. Each appointment was a continuing source of pride to Taft, who at every opportunity underscored the importance of the judiciary.

Taft's cordial relations with Roosevelt did not last. Differences developed during Taft's presidency over questions of policy and administration. Finally the clash led to a split in the Republican Party. As a result, when Taft ran for reelection in 1912 Roosevelt ran as a Progressive. The upshot was a Democratic victory and the election of WOODROW WILSON as President.

After Justice Lamar died, rumor began to spread that the new President might, rising above party politics, follow the example of his predecessor's high-mindedness when in 1910 Taft had selected as Chief Justice a southern Democrat and Roman Catholic, Associate Justice Edward D. White. But Wilson appointed LOUIS D. BRANDEIS instead, and Taft, outraged by that appointment, declared that Brandeis was "not a fit person to be a member of the Court."

In 1919, Taft was off the public payroll for the first time. Soon he took a position at Yale, teaching constitutional law. Meanwhile, the chief justiceship seemed a remote possibility. Prospects brightened in 1920 with the smashing Republican victory of WARREN G. HARDING. Shortly after Harding's election the unblushing aspirant made the pilgrimage to Marion, Ohio. Taft was "nearly struck dumb" when the President-elect broached a Supreme Court ap-

pointment. Of course, the former President was available, but he made it clear that, having appointed three of the present bench and three others and, having vigorously opposed Brandeis's appointment in 1916, he would accept only the chief justiceship.

Taft's opportunity to achieve his ambition was not altogether accidental. During his presidency, when Chief Justice Fuller died, two choices loomed as possibilities— CHARLES EVANS HUGHES and Edward D. White. The latter, seventeen years Hughes's senior, received the nod. Had Taft chosen Hughes, instead of White, his lifelong ambition would not have been realized.

The office of Chief Justice carries scant inherent power. He manages the docket, presents the cases in conference, and guides discussion. When in the majority, he assigns the writing of opinions. In 1921 Taft remarked: "The Chief Justice goes into a monastery." Yet it is difficult to think of a Chief Justice who more frequently violated the American Bar Association's canons of judicial propriety on so many fronts. During the presidency of CALVIN COOLIDGE he was often a White House visitor. His political activities ranged widely over legislation and judicial appointments at all levels. In his choice of judges his alleged purpose was competence. But Taft even opposed selection of the eminent New York Judge BENJAMIN N. CARDOZO, fearful lest he "herd with [OLIVER WENDELL] HOLMES and Brandeis." At the outset, he had kind words for HARLAN F. STONE, indeed claimed credit for his appointment to the Court. But when Stone began to join Holmes and Brandeis, the Chief Justice became increasingly critical.

As institutional architect, Taft ranks second only to OLIVER ELLSWORTH, the third Chief Justice, who originally devised the judicial system. Taft's best known extrajudicial achievement, "The Judges' Bill" of 1925, giving the Supreme Court control over its docket, passed with only token opposition. Soon Congress authorized other procedural changes Taft had long advocated. To achieve these reforms Taft lobbied Presidents and members of Congress and sought press support. The most striking example of his effectiveness as a lobbyist was his campaign for the marble palace in which the Court now sits. At the cornerstone ceremony, in October 1932, Chief Justice Hughes declared: "For this enterprise progressing to completion we are indebted to the late Chief Justice William Howard Taft more than anyone else. The building is the result of his intelligent persistence."

Taft's goals as Chief Justice were efficiency, prompt dispatch of the Court's business, and harmonious relations among his colleagues. His overwhelming desire was to "mass" the Court. For the ex-President, Brandeis's appointment had been "one of the deepest wounds that I have had as an American and a lover of the constitution and a believer in progressive conservatism." Naturally Taft anticipated strained relations with his new colleague. To smooth this possible difficulty he wrote Brandeis long letters on the desirability of taking prompt steps to make the Court more efficient. Such friendly appeals moved his brother Horace to predict: "I expect to see you and Brandeis hobnobbing together with the utmost good will." Taft's strategy worked. Soon he was able to write: "I've come to like Brandeis very much." The feeling was mutual. Brandeis thought of Taft as "a cultivated man" and enjoyed talking with him. The Chief Justice's brother thought Brandeis "had been taken into camp." Justice JOHN H. CLARKE resigned because he believed that Brandeis could no longer be counted on to uphold the liberal stance.

"Things go happily in the CONFERENCE room with Taft," Brandeis commented. "The judges go home less tired emotionally and less weary physically than in White's day. When we differ, we agree to differ without any ill feelings." It seems likely that certain of Brandeis's unpublished opinions reflect his high regard for the Chief Justice. In one decision in particular, the second child labor case, BAILEY V. DREXEL FURNITURE CO. (1922), Taft writing for the Court invoked the authority of HAMMER V. DAGENHART (1918), a singularly conservative ruling. Yet, Brandeis went along with the majority, explaining: "I can't always dissent. I sometimes endorse an opinion with which I do not agree. I acquiesce." Brandeis's silence may have been the measure of Taft's gift for leadership.

In ALEXANDER BICKEL's volume, *The Unpublished Opinions of Mr. Justice Brandeis* (1957), eight out of eleven were prepared during less than ten years of Taft's chief justiceship. Taft went to great pains to create esprit de corps. Seemingly trivial personal considerations—the sending of a salmon to Justice WILLIS VAN DEVANTER, the customary ride he gave Holmes and Brandeis after the Saturday conference, the Christmas card that always went out to Justice JOSEPH MCKENNA—all such thoughtful attention to highly dissimilar human beings contributed immeasurably to judicial teamwork.

Justice Van Devanter posed a unique problem. He was indispensable in conference where Taft was not always acquainted with judicial technicalities or even facts of the cases. But Van Devanter was "opinion shy." This, however, evoked no complaint from the Chief Justice, even if he wrote no opinions at all. Taft regarded him as "the mainstay of the Court" and dubbed him "my Lord Chancellor."

Taft was determined to make the Court's promptness "a model for the courts of the country." His colleagues, as Holmes said, approved the Chief's "way of conducting business . . . especially his disinclination to put cases over." To accelerate the Court's work, Taft urged cutting vacations from seventeen to twelve weeks and using various time-saving devices.

Taft's first major opinion, TRUAX V. CORRIGAN (1921), involved the constitutionality of an Arizona statute barring state courts from issuing injunctions in LABOR cases, except under special conditions. Owners of a restaurant sought an injunction against a BOYCOTT and PICKETING of their place of business. A majority of five Justices, concluding that the bar against injunctions denied DUE PROCESS OF LAW and EQUAL PROTECTION OF THE LAW, declared the act unconstitutional. "A law which operates to make lawful such a wrong as described in the plaintiff's complaint," the Chief Justice observed, "deprives the owner of the business and the premises of his property without due process of law and cannot be held valid under the FOURTEENTH AMENDMENT. . . . The Constitution was intended, its very purpose was to prevent experimentation with the fundamental rights of the individual."

Taft's next major opinion, STAFFORD V. WALLACE (1922), upheld broad federal power under the COMMERCE CLAUSE, announcing that Congress had a "wide area of discretion, free from judicial second guessing." At issue was the PACKERS AND STOCKYARD ACT of 1929, regulating the business of packers done in INTERSTATE COMMERCE. The "chief evil" Congress aimed at was the monopoly of packers, "enabling them unduly and arbitrarily to lower prices to the shipper who sells, and unduly and arbitrarily to increase the price to the consumer who buys." In deciding *Stafford* Taft relied mainly on Holmes's majority opinion in SWIFT V. UNITED STATES (1905). "That case," wrote the Chief Justice, "was a milestone in the interpretation of the Commerce Clause of the Constitution. It recognized the great changes and development in the business of this vast country and drew again the dividing line between interstate and intrastate commerce where the Constitution intended it to be. It refused to permit local incidents of great interstate movements which, taken alone, were intrastate, to characterize the movement as such. The *Swift* case merely fitted the Commerce Clause to the real and practical essence of modern business growth."

Another example of Taft's effort to keep the Court "consistent with itself" was ADKINS V. CHILDREN'S HOSPITAL (1923) involving an act of Congress fixing the minimum wage for women and minors. Speaking for the Court, Justice Sutherland invalidated the act, relying primarily on Justice RUFUS PECKHAM's reactionary decision in LOCHNER V. NEW YORK (1905). Refusing to endorse *Lochner,* Taft and Holmes dissented: "It is impossible," the Chief Justice explained, "for me to reconcile the *Bunting* [*v. Oregon*] case of 1917 and the *Lochner* case and I have always supposed that the *Lochner* case was thus overruled *sub silentio.*" Although Sutherland and Taft disagreed in *Adkins,* Taft could not bring himself to endorse Holmes's dissent because of its irreverent treatment of the FREEDOM OF CONTRACT doctrine. And in *Wolff Packing Co. v. Court of*

*Industrial Relations* (1923) Taft for the Court approvingly cited Sutherland's *Adkins* opinion on that doctrine.

The year 1926 witnessed a significant decision in American constitutional history: the 6–3 ruling in MYERS V. UNITED STATES upholding the President's power to remove a postmaster without the consent of the Senate. Said Taft: "I never wrote an opinion that I felt to be so important in its effect." The Chief Justice's unqualified appraisal reflects his White House experience. There were three dissenters—Holmes, JAMES C. MCREYNOLDS, and Brandeis. Brandeis wrote: "The separation of powers of government did not make each branch completely autonomous. It left each in some measure dependent on the other. . . . The doctrine of SEPARATION OF POWERS was adopted by the [CONSTITUTIONAL] CONVENTION OF 1787, not to promote efficiency but to preclude the exercise of arbitrary power. The purpose was not to avoid friction, but by means of the inevitable friction incident to the distribution of governmental powers among the departments, to save the people from autocracy."

Taft did not live to see the Court's later qualification of the President's power to remove executive officers. In HUMPHREY'S EXECUTOR V. UNITED STATES (1935) the President was denied executive power to remove a federal trade commissioner, appointed for seven years with the ADVICE AND CONSENT of the Senate, on the score of inefficiency or neglect of duty. Speaking for the Court in that later case, Justice Sutherland, who had enjoyed most cordial relations with Taft, went out of his way to say that the authority of the *Myers* case remained intact. The Court did not adopt the views of the *Myers* dissenters, but shifted emphasis from the "simple logic" of Article II of the Constitution—that the removal power is inherently "executive"—to the theory that a postmaster "is merely one of the units in the executive department and hence inherently subject to the exclusive and illimitable power of removal by the Chief Executive whose subordinate and aide he is."

As Taft's tenure drew to a close, dissents came more frequently and vehemently. Holmes and Brandeis, who had dissented from Taft's first major opinion in *Truax*, dissented from his last major opinion in OLMSTEAD V. UNITED STATES (1928). Justice Stone and even Justice PIERCE BUTLER joined the dissenters. Taft, a crusader for stricter enforcement of the criminal law, narrowly construed the FOURTH AMENDMENT's ban on unreasonable searches and seizures by ruling that evidence obtained by wiretapping could be introduced at a criminal trial. In the face of hostile criticism of his *Olmstead* opinion, Taft declared privately, "If they think we are going to be frightened in our effort to stand by the law and give the public a chance to punish criminals, they are mistaken, even though we are condemned for lack of high ideals." Taft thought that

Holmes's dissent was sentimental in declaring that "it is a lesser evil that some criminals should escape than that the Government should play an ignoble part."

Near the end, Taft winced nervously whenever he contemplated his probable successor. Knowing that President HERBERT C. HOOVER's attachment to Stone was "very great," Taft feared the worst: "I have no doubt that if I were to retire or die, the President would appoint Stone head of the Court." Once in the Chief Justice's good graces, Stone had fallen into profound disfavor. "He definitely has ranged himself with Brandeis and with Holmes in a good many of our constitutional differences." Nor was Stone's "herding" with the Court's "kickers" his only shortcoming. He was "not a great leader and would have a great deal of trouble in massing the Court." The Chief was not entirely without hope: "With Van and Mac and Sutherland and you and Sanford," he wrote to Justice Butler in 1929, "there will be five to steady the boat. So there would be a great deal of difficulty in working through reversals of present positions, even if I either had to retire or were gathered to my fathers, so that we must not give up at once."

Taft's triumphant march continued to the end, but the future was clouded with uncertainty. By 1929 the world he had known and the people on whom he relied were in eclipse. As the economy slid rapidly toward the abyss, government intervention was openly advocated. To combat these forces, Taft's determination stiffened. "As long as things continue as they are and I am able to answer in my place," he resolved to "stay on the Court in order to prevent the Bolsheviki from getting control." President Hoover, Taft thought, "would put in some rather extreme destroyers of the Constitution. . . ."

None of Taft's predecessors, with the possible exception of Marshall, entertained so expansive a view of the chief justiceship, or used it so effectively on so many fronts. Taft was a great administrator, a great judicial architect, a skillful harmonizer of human relations. Yet he is not commonly considered a great Chief Justice.

ALPHEUS THOMAS MASON
(1986)

Bibliography

MASON, ALPHEUS THOMAS 1930 The Labor Decisions of Chief Justice Taft. *University of Pennsylvania Law Review* 78:585–625.
—— 1964 *William Howard Taft: Chief Justice.* New York: Simon & Schuster.
—— 1979 *The Supreme Court from Taft to Burger.* Baton Rouge: Louisiana State University Press.
MCHALE, FRANCIS 1931 *President and Chief Justice: The Life and Public Services of William Howard Taft.* Philadelphia: Dorrance.
MURPHY, W. F. 1961 In His Own Image: Mr. Justice Taft and

Supreme Court Appointments. *Supreme Court Review* 1961: 159–193.

——— 1962 Chief Justice Taft and the Lower Court Bureaucracy. *Journal of Politics* 24:453–476.

PRINGLE, H. F. 1939 *The Life and Times of William Howard Taft.* New York: Farrar & Rinehart.

# TAFT COURT
## (1921–1930)

WILLIAM HOWARD TAFT became Chief Justice of the United States on June 30, 1921. Never before or since has any person brought such a range of distinguished experience in public affairs and professional qualifications to the bench. Taft presided over a court that included Justices of highly varied abilities and achievements. In 1921, OLIVER WENDELL HOLMES, already a great figure of the law, had served nineteen years on the Supreme Court. He remained on the Court throughout Taft's tenure and beyond. Holmes's only equal on the Court was LOUIS D. BRANDEIS, who had been on the Court barely five years at Taft's accession. Taft, a private citizen in 1916, had vigorously opposed the appointment of Brandeis to the High Court. Although they remained ideological opponents and although some mistrust persisted on both sides, they maintained cordial relations, carrying on their opposition in a highly civil manner.

The rest of the Court that Taft inherited lacked the stature or ability of Holmes and Brandeis. Three Justices, JOHN H. CLARKE, MAHLON PITNEY, and WILLIAM R. DAY would retire within the first two years of Taft's tenure. Their retirements gave President WARREN C. HARDING a chance to reconstitute the Court. The President appointed his former Senate colleague GEORGE H. SUTHERLAND to one of the vacancies. The other two spots were filled by men strongly recommended by Taft: PIERCE BUTLER and EDWARD T. SANFORD.

The other Justices on the Court in 1921 were WILLIS VAN DEVANTER, JAMES C. MCREYNOLDS, and JOSEPH MCKENNA. Van Devanter had been appointed to the bench by Taft when he was President. He, like Butler and Sanford, continued to be strongly influenced by the Chief Justice. During the Taft years, he served the Chief Justice in the performance of many important institutional tasks outside the realm of decision making and opinion writing. For example, Van Devanter led the drive to revamp the JURISDICTION of the Supreme Court in the "Judges' Bill," the JUDICIARY ACT OF 1925. McReynolds, a Wilson appointee, was an iconoclastic conservative of well-defined prejudices.

Finally, Taft inherited Joseph McKenna, whose failing health impaired his judicial performance. In 1925, Taft,

after consulting the other justices, urged McKenna to retire. McKenna was succeeded by HARLAN F. STONE. Though deferential to Taft at the outset, by the end of the decade Stone became increasingly identified with the dissenting positions of Holmes and Brandeis. From early 1923 through Taft's resignation only that one change took place.

Because of the substantial continuity of personnel the Taft Court can be thought of as an institution with a personality and with well-defined positions on most critical issues that came before it. Outcomes were as predictable as they ever can be, and the reasoning, persuasive or not, was consistent.

Taft was a strong Chief Justice. He lobbied powerfully for more federal judges, for a streamlined federal procedure, for reorganization of the federal judiciary, and for greater control by the Supreme Court over the cases it would decide. The most concrete of Taft's reforms was a new building for the Court itself, though the building was not completed until after his death.

A second major institutional change was completed during Taft's term. In 1925 Congress passed the "Judges' Bill." The Supreme Court's agenda is one of the most important factors in determining the evolution of constitutional law. Until 1891 that agenda had been determined largely at the initiative of litigants. In 1891 the Court received authority to review certain classes of cases by the discretionary WRIT OF CERTIORARI. However, many lower court decisions had continued to be reviewable as of right in the Supreme Court even after 1891. The 1925 act altered the balance by establishing the largely discretionary certiorari jurisdiction of the Supreme Court as it has remained for six decades. The act was one of Taft's major projects. It relieved the docket pressure occasioned by the press of obligatory jurisdiction, and placed agenda control at the very center of constitutional politics.

The successful initiatives of the Court in seizing control of its own constitutional agenda and constructing a new home should not obscure the fact that the Court's institutional position was, as always, under attack during the 1920s. A spate of what were perceived as antilabor decisions in 1921–1922 led to calls from the labor movement and congressional progressives to circumscribe the Court's powers. In the 1924 election ROBERT LA FOLLETTE, running as a third-party candidate on the Progressive ticket, called for a constitutional amendment to limit JUDICIAL REVIEW. Both the Republican incumbent, CALVIN COOLIDGE, and the 1924 Democratic candidate, JOHN W. DAVIS, defended the Court against La Follette. The upshot of the unsuccessful La Follette campaign was a heightened sensitivity to judicial review as an issue and a firm demonstration of the consensus as to its legitimacy and centrality in the American constitutional system.

Much of the labor movement had supported La Follette's initiatives against judicial review, but labor specifically sought limitations on federal court labor INJUNCTIONS. Labor's campaign against injunctions peaked in 1927 after the Supreme Court simultaneously declined to review a series of controversial injunctions in the West Virginia coal fields and approved an injunction in BEDFORD CUT STONE COMPANY V. JOURNEYMAN STONECUTTERS, holding that a union's nationwide refusal to handle nonunion stone should be enjoined as an agreement in RESTRAINT OF TRADE. Between 1928 and 1930 the shape of what was to become the NORRIS-LAGUARDIA ACT OF 1932 emerged in Congress. The impetus behind that law, the politics of it, indeed, the language and theory of the statute itself are rooted in the Taft years.

A description of the Court's institutional role must consider the relations between CONGRESS AND THE COURT in shaping constitutional law and constitutional politics. During the Taft years a dialogue between Court and Congress persisted on a variety of crucial constitutional issues. The decision of the Court striking down the first Child Labor Act in HAMMER V. DAGENHART (1918) led to congressional interest in using the taxing power to circumvent apparent limitations on the direct regulatory authority of Congress under the COMMERCE CLAUSE. The second Child Labor Act imposed an excise tax on the profits of firms employing child labor. That act was struck down as unconstitutional in 1922.

From 1922 on Congress had before it various versions of antilynching legislation—most notably the Dyer Bill, which had actually passed the House. Opponents of the antilynching legislation argued that it was an unconstitutional federal usurpation of state functions. In *Moore v. Dempsey* (1923), decided shortly after the Dyer Bill had nearly succeeded in passage, the Court held that a state criminal trial dominated by a mob constituted a denial of DUE PROCESS OF LAW, appropriately redressed in a federal HABEAS CORPUS proceeding. *Moore v. Dempsey* did not establish that an antilynching law would be constitutional. Yet a conclusion that mob domination of a criminal trial did *not* deny due process surely would have been a constitutional nail in the coffin of antilynching laws. And, prior to *Moore v. Dempsey* the relatively recent PRECEDENT of FRANK V. MANGUM (1915) had pointed toward just such a conclusion. Considerations concerning the response of Congress regularly influenced the constitutional decision making of the Taft Court. When Taft was appointed, three important labor cases were pending that had been argued but not decided by the WHITE COURT. The Court had reached an impasse. Two of the cases presented questions about the use of injunctions to restrain labor picketing. Section 20 of the Clayton Act appeared to deny the federal courts the power to issue such injunctions subject to certain exceptions, most notably the power to use the injunc-

tion to protect property from damage. *American Steel Foundries v. Tri-City Labor Council* presented questions of construction of this section, and TRUAX V. CORRIGAN, involving a state law, presented a constitutional variant of the Clayton Act problem.

In *American Steel Foundries*, Taft's first significant opinion as Chief Justice, the Court read section 20 to encompass protection of the property interest in an ongoing business from unreasonable or intimidating picketing or from illegal BOYCOTTS or strikes. Statutory construction thus preserved the injunction as a restraint on labor.

But not all state courts saw the issue as the Taft Court did. The Arizona Supreme Court read its statute to bar injunctions in labor disputes, at least where actual destruction of physical property was not threatened. In *Truax v. Corrigan*, decided a week after *American Steel Foundries*, Taft wrote for a majority of five, holding that Arizona had unconstitutionally denied employers the injunction in labor disputes. *Truax* in effect created a constitutional *right* to a labor injunction. It did so on two grounds. First, it held that employers were denied the EQUAL PROTECTION OF THE LAWS insofar as their particular type of property interest was denied the same protection afforded other property interests. Second, it held that the failure to protect the interest in the continued operation of a business deprived the business owner of property without due process of law. *Truax v. Corrigan* was the cornerstone of the Taft Court edifice of industrial relations. Not only did the decision suggest that Congress could not constitutionally prevent the federal courts from granting labor injunctions, but it also ushered in a decade of the most intensive use of the labor injunction the country had ever seen. A desperate battle was fought to save the unionized sector of coal from competition from the newer, largely nonunion, southern mines. That union campaign was broken by dozens of labor injunctions upheld by the Fourth Circuit in a consolidated appeal. The Supreme Court's refusal to review those decisions in 1927 attracted larger headlines than all but the most significant of Supreme Court opinions ever get. The Fourth Circuit opinion later cost Circuit Judge John J. H. Parker a seat on the Supreme Court. In fact, however, his conclusion was an all but inevitable consequence of the Supreme Court's position in *Truax v. Corrigan*.

The industrial order that the Taft Court sought to protect from labor insurgency was itself built upon uncertain constitutional foundations. The Taft Court was not committed, unambiguously, to a laissez-faire market. The Court distinguished sharply between legislation regulating the price (wage or rent) terms of a contract and laws regulating other terms. Thus, in the best known of its apparent inconsistencies, the Taft Court held void a District of Columbia law prescribing a minimum wage for women, although only a year later it upheld a New York law establishing maximum hours for women. The Court also struck down a state statute regulating fees or commissions for employment brokers while intimating that other reasonable regulatory measures directed at employment brokerage would be upheld.

Sutherland, in his peculiar majority opinion in the minimum wage case—ADKINS V. CHILDREN'S HOSPITAL (1923)—seemed preoccupied with the redistributive aspects of the minimum wage law. There was nothing wrong with a legislative preference for a living (minimum) wage; the problem lay in imposing an obligation on the employer to pay it. One person's need, he argued, could not, in itself, justify another's obligation to satisfy it. The regulation of non-price terms need not be redistributive in effect, for the costs of any such regulation could be recaptured by negotiated changes in price. If the Court was seeking to protect bargains against regulation with redistribution effect, then shielding price terms from governmental interference was the most visible and easily understood way to accomplish its purpose.

In general the Taft Court sought to maintain principled distinctions among three forms of economic activity. Government enterprise was subject to the usual constitutional constraints upon government. This form of economic activity was relatively unimportant in the 1920s, although in cases involving municipal utilities the Court had some opportunity to address such issues as contractual rate structure. The Court spoke more frequently to the problem of transition from private to public or from public to private enterprise. WORLD WAR I had seen government control of the railroads, shipping, coal, and, to a lesser degree, labor relations generally. The Court had to develop principles of compensation to govern the takeover and return of such large-scale enterprises.

More important than the dichotomy between governmental and private economic activity was the distinction drawn between private activity AFFECTED WITH A PUBLIC INTEREST and the more general run of private economic endeavor. Upon this distinction turned the constitutionality of public regulation—including price regulation in some circumstances—of various forms of economic activity. Although the category of business affected with a public interest had been part of the Court's rhetorical stock in trade for almost half a century when Taft took his seat, it assumed particular significance through the decade beginning with a case from Kansas. In 1920, having survived the effects of a bitter coal strike, Kansas passed its Industrial Court Act, declaring all production and distribution of food, clothing, shelter, and fuel for human consumption or use to be business affected with a public interest. Public transportation and public utilities were also so labeled. The act forbade strikes, lockouts, and plant closings in all

such industries except by order of the Kansas Court of Industrial Relations. Moreover, that court upon its own motion or upon the petition of virtually any person could adjudicate the fitness or adequacy of wages and prices in any such business. The act contemplated a form of compulsory arbitration to replace labor bargaining against a background of strikes and lockouts.

In a series of unanimous opinions the Supreme Court struck down one after another of these innovative aspects of the Kansas act. Taft, in the leading opinion, WOLFF PACKING CORPORATION V. COURT OF INDUSTRIAL RELATIONS (1923) held that the state could not, by legislative fiat, declare businesses to be affected with a public interest for purposes so comprehensive as to include supervision of their wage and price structures. Taft's opinion wholly failed to state a principled distinction between those businesses traditionally subject to price regulation (such as grain elevators), on the one hand, and meat packing, on the other. In OBITER DICTUM he suggested that the competitive structure of the industry was not determinative of the legislature's power to regulate. But the opinion did acknowledge that long-established law permitted regulation of publicly conferred monopolies and of common carriers or inns even if not monopolies.

The Taft Court thus rejected a generalization, based on the war experience, that all basic economic activity could be defined as affected with a public interest. But the Court was not unmindful of the war's lessons. Unanimously it upheld the recapture provisions of the [Railroad] Transportation Act of 1920 despite the overt redistributive effect of the law. The act required the payment into a federal trust fund of half the profits earned by strong railroads, for redistribution to failing ones. The Chief Justice, at least, understood the recapture provisions as justified in part because the alternative to such a scheme might have to be nationalization. Furthermore, the Court had already gone to great lengths to uphold other, seemingly inevitable, characteristics of rate regulation in an integrated transportation system. The Interstate Commerce Commission (ICC), if it were to be effective at all, needed power to regulate joint rates over hauls using more than one line for a single journey. It was apparent that the apportionment of joint rates could be used to redistributive effect. In the *New England Divisions Case* (1923) the Court had already upheld the ICC's explicit consideration of the need to strengthen the weaker New England lines when it apportioned revenues from joint rates. It was a short step from such use of joint rates to the recapture provisions.

The Court's willingness to accept some qualifications of vested property rights in the interest of planning was not confined to such traditional areas of regulation as transportation and public utilities. The Court decided its first cases challenging general ZONING ordinances in the 1920s and, on the whole, upheld the power, though not without significant dissent and important qualifications.

Despite the Court's upholding of zoning and of regulatory initiatives, the Taft Court has long been considered to have been ardent in imposing constitutional limits upon legislation that restricted vested property interests. That reputation is soundly based, although the extent to which the Taft Court differed from predecessor and successor Courts has been substantially exaggerated by FELIX FRANKFURTER and his followers.

Perhaps the best known of the Taft Court pronouncements on the constitutional protection of property is Justice Holmes's opinion for the Court in *Pennsylvania Coal Company v. Mahon* (1923). Pennsylvania's Kohler Act required anthracite coal mining to be done so as to avoid subsidence of surface areas at or near buildings, streets, and other structures used by human beings. The Court held unconstitutional the application of the law to mining in an area where the mining company had conveyed surface rights, expressly reserving to itself and to its successors the subsurface mining rights.

Despite Brandeis's dissenting opinion, Holmes's opinion was moderate in tone and antithetical to the sort of dogmatics that characterized Sutherland's opinions in the wage and price regulation area. Indeed, Holmes's methodology was explicitly one that reduced the takings-regulation distinction to a matter of degree—as Holmes himself once recognized in a flippant reference to "the petty larceny of the police power." Moreover, the Court that decided *Pennsylvania Coal* decided the case of *Miller v. Schoene* (1928) five years later, upholding a Virginia law providing for the uncompensated (or less than fully compensated) destruction of cedar trees infected with cedar rust, a condition harmful only to neighboring apple trees.

The Court also had to face the implications of the constitutional protection of property in considering the methodology of public utility rate regulation. In a series of cases beginning in 1923 and proceeding throughout the Taft period, Justice Brandeis posed a major challenge to the "fair value" methodology of SMYTH V. AMES (1895). Industry during the 1920s argued that the rate base—the "property" upon which the Constitution guaranteed a reasonable rate of permissible return—should be valued according to the replacement cost of capital items—despite a general inflationary trend, accelerated by World War I. Brandeis formulated a comprehensive critique both of this particular windfall calculation and of the rule that produced it. Brandeis first reformulated the problem in a characteristically daring way. The issue was not so much a vested right to a return on capital as it was the necessity for a level of profit that could attract the new capital required for effective operation of the public utility. Brandeis lost the battle for

a new approach to rate-making. Yet here, no less than in other arenas for disputes over the constitutional protection of property, doctrinal lines had been drawn that anticipated the issues of the New Deal.

Traditional, genteel conservativism is neither overtly ideological in content nor strident in manner. In most respects the Taft Court was traditionally conservative. The Court was hostile to labor and to any insurgency from the left, but the hostility usually took the form of a neutral defense of civil order. That neutrality, though it almost always worked against the left, was not explicitly one-sided and was, in fact, applied occasionally against rightist militant politics and street activity as well.

The constitutional defense of civil order entailed a strong commitment to ratify the acts of local government and of the national political branches so long as their power and authority were used to put down militant politics and especially politics of the street. Thus, the Court consistently upheld CRIMINAL SYNDICALISM LAWS, even while recognizing, in GITLOW V. NEW YORK (1925), that the FIRST AMENDMENT limited state as well as federal legislative power. Moreover, in a theoretically interesting, though practically less significant case, the Court upheld a New York law requiring the registration and disclosure of names of members of certain secret societies—a measure directed against the Ku Klux Klan. Brandeis and Holmes repeatedly dissented in the criminal syndicalism cases, sketching an alternative version of the political process far more hospitable to insurgent initiatives for change.

A second pillar of the defense of civic order was the reliance upon independent courts as guarantors of vested property rights against street politics. To this end the injunction was elevated to a constitutional pedestal. *Truax v. Corrigan*, which constitutionalized capital's right to a labor injunction, must be seen not only as a part of a larger antilabor *corpus* but also as the link between that work and the principle of civic order.

For traditional conservatives the injunction had much to commend it. It was in the hands of politically independent judges, who were less susceptible than other officials to mass pressure. It was governed—or supposed to be governed—by neutral principles rather than special interests; it permitted the adaptation of principle to local needs and adjusted the level of intervention to that necessary to shore up appropriately sound local elites. No wonder, then, that the issue of the injunction pervaded the constitutional politics of the 1920s.

If Taft was committed to the courts' playing a dominant role in labor discipline and the guarantee of civic order, he was at the same time committed to an efficient, unintimidated, and uncorrupted judiciary to do the job. In *Tumey v. Ohio* (1927) he wrote for a unanimous Court striking down as a denial of due process an Ohio scheme through which a public official judging traffic violations was paid a percentage of the fines collected. Of greater significance was MOORE V. DEMPSEY (1923), in which a divided Court upheld the power of a federal district court in federal HABEAS CORPUS proceedings to go behind the record of a state court murder conviction to determine whether the trial had been dominated by a mob.

Racist justice was a deeply rooted problem, not high on the conservative agenda for reform. Taft was, however, very concerned with the potential for corruption of the courts inherent in the great national experiment of the decade, prohibition. The Chief Justice realized that there were many opportunities for organized crime in the liquor business to buy friendly judges and other officials, especially in states where prohibition was unpopular. The Court refused to extend the protection of the DOUBLE JEOPARDY principle to cases of successive prosecutions under state and federal law for substantially the same conduct. Part of the reason for this limit upon the double jeopardy principle was the potential under any contrary rule of insulating conduct from federal prosecution by securing a state conviction and paying a small fine. The Court's interpretation of FEDERALISM to tolerate structural redundancy was thus a major prophylactic against the dangers of local corruption of courts.

Like all its predecessors, however conservative, the Taft Court paid lip service to the idea that the people are sovereign and, consequently, that popular government is a pervasive and overriding principle in constitutional interpretation. Even though dissenters within the court (Holmes and Brandeis) and critical commentators without (Frankfurter, EDWARD S. CORWIN, and THOMAS REED POWELL) claimed that the Justices ignored the presumption of constitutionality that ought to attach to the work of the popular branches, the simple fact is that no Justice denied, as an abstract principle, either the presumption of constitutionality or the deference that ought to be paid to legislative judgments. It was the application of the principle that divided the Court.

Most of the Justices were skeptical of the capacity of the masses intelligently to exercise the rights and discharge the obligations of participatory, popular government. Taft himself welcomed a leading role for elites in suppressing, or at least damping, the demands of the rabble and in representing the "better class" of citizens. But Taft's views in these matters were not very different from those of Holmes. Holmes doubted the capacity of the masses and considered a dominant role for elites in politics to be almost a natural law. Brandeis, the only real contrast, was considerably more committed to reform and to its promise. But he, in his own way, also distrusted the masses. He saw hope for change in a shift from a propertied oligarchy to a technically trained meritocracy. At the same time Brandeis understood the limits of this vision. His support of STATES' RIGHTS and localism in politics and his hostility to concentration in industry had common roots: the recognition of limits to techniques of effective organization; the affirmation of political principles limiting concentrations of power; and the affirmation of the principles of maximum participation in public affairs. Chiefly in this last respect, Brandeis stood committed to a principle that the other Justices ignored or rejected.

In what ways did the general attitudes of the Justices to popular government affect the work of the Court? Perhaps the most direct effect was visible in the great, perennial debate over the power of judicial review. The Justices appear to have been unanimous in their private opposition to schemes such as that of LaFollette to limit the power of judicial review by statute or constitutional amendment. Even Brandeis, who was personally close to LaFollette and who supported the Wisconsin senator's positions on many substantive issues, opposed initiatives to curb the Court.

In at least one important area the Taft Court initiated a significant reform in the mechanics of popular government itself. The Court struck down the first version of the Texas system of white primaries which, through official state action, denied blacks the right to vote in statewide PRIMARY ELECTIONS. NIXON V. HERNDON (1927) was the first in a line of cases that ultimately destroyed the white primary device.

The Court upheld the power of Congress to conduct LEGISLATIVE INVESTIGATIONS and to use COMPULSORY PROCESS to that end. The Court also appeared to uphold an enlarged vision of an exclusive PRESIDENTIAL POWER to remove executive officers. A special constitutional status for government of TERRITORIES was approved. Finally, the Court struggled mightily but produced no satisfactory or consistent principles in the area of STATE TAXATION OF COMMERCE and STATE REGULATION OF COMMERCE.

The 1920s saw a determined attack upon the ethnic pluralism, the cultural and ethical relativism, and the absence of traditional controls that characterized a newly emergent urban America. The prohibition movement, resurgent religious fundamentalism, virulent nativism, and racism gave rise to a reactionary program for legal reform. In the area of prohibition the Court did more than give full effect to a constitutional amendment and its implementing legislation. The Justices also decided a host of criminal procedure issues in such a way as to arm the enforcers against what was perceived as a concerted attack on law and order themselves.

But the Court was actively hostile to groups like the "new" Ku Klux Klan. It not only upheld a Klan registration statute but also, in PIERCE V. SOCIETY OF SISTERS (1925), held invalid an Oregon statute that had effectively outlawed private schools. The law was the product of a popular initiative organized and vigorously supported by the Klan as part of its nativist and anti-Catholic crusade. The decision in MEYER V. NEBRASKA (1923) striking down laws forbidding the teaching of German in the schools also reflected the Justices' unwillingness to permit nativist sentiment to cut too deeply into the social fabric.

But the Court did uphold state ALIEN land ownership laws directed principally against Asian immigrants and upheld the disgraceful national discrimination against Asian immigration in the face of constitutional attack. The Court also permitted the continuation of restrictive covenants in housing (CORRIGAN V. BUCKLEY, 1926) and segregation in public schools (GONG LUM V. RICE, 1927), though in each instance it avoided an explicit articulation of constitutional approval for these practices.

The constitutional work of the Taft Court extended over the customary broad area of national life, but it was dominated by the motif of conflict between property and labor. Civil strife, policies toward insurgency, free or regulated markets, confiscation—all were issues that arose principally from the overarching conflict. It is a measure of the Taft Court's achievement that, through Brandeis on the one hand and Taft on the other, a measure of clarity was achieved in articulating the implications of this conflict for constitutional structure and doctrine over a wide range of subjects. It was Taft's vision alone, however, that dominated the Court's action—consistently hostile to labor and its interests. The traditional conservative structure of property and order was one legacy of Taft's Court to the era of the Great Depression; Brandeis's vision—as yet wholly unrealized—was the other.

ROBERT M. COVER
(1986)

Bibliography

BERNSTEIN, IRVING 1960 The Lean Years: A History of the American Worker, 1920–1933. Boston: Houghton Mifflin.

BICKEL, ALEXANDER M. 1957 The Unpublished Opinions of Mr. Justice Brandeis: The Supreme Court at Work. Cambridge, Mass.: Belknap Press of Harvard University Press.

DANELSKI, DAVID J. 1964 A Supreme Court Justice Is Appointed. New York: Random House.

FRANKFURTER, FELIX and GREENE, NATHAN 1930 The Labor Injunction. New York: Macmillan.

MASON, ALPHEUS THOMAS 1946 Brandeis: A Free Man's Life. New York: Viking.

——— 1956 Harlan Fiske Stone: Pillar of the Law. New York: Viking.

——— 1964 William Howard Taft: Chief Justice. New York: Simon & Schuster.

MURPHY, WALTER F. 1964 Elements of Judicial Strategy. Chicago: University of Chicago Press.

PRINGLE, HENRY F. 1939 The Life and Times of William Howard Taft. New York: Farrar & Rinehart.

RABBAN, DAVID M. 1983 The Emergence of Modern First Amendment Doctrine. University of Chicago Law Review 50: 1205–1355.

# TAFT-HARTLEY LABOR RELATIONS ACT
## 61 Stat. 136 (1947)

Passed over President HARRY S. TRUMAN's veto, the Taft-Hartley Act represented Republican hostility to the power of labor unions and the National Labor Relations Board (NLRB); its provisions limit the authority and conduct of unions and their officials and curtail the Board's authority.

In amending the WAGNER (NATIONAL LABOR RELATIONS) ACT, the measure banned the CLOSED SHOP; permitted employers to sue unions for strike-incurred damages; forbade union contributions to political campaigns; required public disclosure of union finances; required unions to give sixty days notice before inaugurating strikes; and allowed the President to halt a major strike by seeking a court INJUNCTION for an eighty-day "cooling off" period. Although the right to COLLECTIVE BARGAINING was further guaranteed, section 14b permitted states to adopt RIGHT-TO-WORK LAWS, forbidding any requirement that workers join unions to hold jobs. Most constitutionally suspect were provisions requiring labor union officials, in order to use the facilities of the NLRB, to sign affidavits denying communist party membership or belief. These noncommunist oath provisions were unsuccessfully challenged in the courts in AMERICAN COMMUNICATIONS ASSOCIATION V. DOUDS (1950).

PAUL L. MURPHY
(1986)

Bibliography

SUTHERLAND, ARTHUR E. 1948 The Constitutionality of the Taft-Hartley Law. Industrial and Labor Relations Review 1: 177–205.

# TAKAHASHI v. FISH AND GAME COMMISSION
## 334 U.S. 410 (1948)

Under California law, ALIENS ineligible for CITIZENSHIP (mainly Asians) could not hold commercial fishing licenses. Citing the broad power of Congress to regulate aliens, the Supreme Court held, 7–2, that the PREEMPTION DOCTRINE barred the law. The CIVIL RIGHTS ACT OF 1866 was taken to protect the rights of aliens to pursue their livelihoods under nondiscriminatory state laws. The OPINION also conveyed overtones of FOURTEENTH AMENDMENT reasoning.

KENNETH L. KARST
(1986)

# TAKING OF PROPERTY

The authority of government to acquire private PROPERTY from an involuntary owner (usually called the power of EMINENT DOMAIN) is recognized in the Fifth Amendment to the Constitution, which provides: "nor shall private property be taken for public use, without JUST COMPENSATION." The public use and compensation requirements of the Constitution apply not only to acquisitions by the federal government but—by INCORPORATION in the FOURTEENTH AMENDMENT—to acquisitions by the states as well. Similar provisions appear in the state constitutions, and the state and federal requirements are usually identically interpreted. It is, however, possible that a taking would pass muster under the federal Constitution and still be held to violate the state constitutional provision (or vice versa).

The requirement of PUBLIC USE has been liberally interpreted by the courts, which rarely find that a taking is not for a public use. For example, property may be taken for resale to private developers in an urban renewal project, or for the development of an industrial park. Indeed, the courts have permitted authority to take private property to be vested by LEGISLATION in privately owned public utilities, such as water companies. The test is not ultimate public ownership, or even direct public benefit, but rather the general benefit to the public from projects that are publicly sponsored or encouraged to promote the economy or the public welfare. The only clear limits on the broad interpretation of "public use" would be (1) the grant of the taking authority to a private company simply to improve its private economic position; or (2) the use of the taking power by the government if government itself were simply seeking to make money by engaging in strictly entrepreneurial activities.

The requirement of "just compensation" has been interpreted to mean the amount a willing seller would get from a willing buyer in the absence of the government's desire to acquire the property. The owner is not entitled to receive more for the property simply because the government has an urgent need for it—as for a military base. Neither may the owner receive less compensation because the government's plan for the area—to install a garbage dump, for example, has depressed neighborhood values. Nor is the owner entitled to increased compensation merely because the property has special value to him, such

as sentimental or family value, or because he would not sell the property at any price. Compensation must be given in cash immediately upon the taking; government cannot oblige the owner to accept future promises of payment which may be unmarketable, or marketable only at a discount from the just compensation value.

Ordinarily there is no ambiguity about whether a property has been taken. Nor is there any ambiguity about the principle of takings law, stated at the most general level: if the public wants something, it should pay for it and not coerce private owners into contributing their property to the public. If government wants a site for a post office, for example, it is obliged to institute condemnation proceedings in court, leading to an involuntary transfer of title and possession, at which time it will pay the owner just compensation. But in many instances government legislates or behaves in a way that reduces or destroys the value of private property without formally taking title or possession and without instituting condemnation proceedings. If the owner complains, seeking just compensation for a taking, government may reply that it has simply regulated under the POLICE POWER, but has not "taken" the property and thus need not compensate. The great bulk of all legal controversies over the taking of property turn on the question whether there has been a "taking" at all.

Plainly government sometimes gets the benefits of a taking without any of the formal incidents of ownership. A celebrated case, *Causby v. United States* (1946), involved the flight of military planes just above the surface of privately owned farmland adjacent to a military airport. As a result of noise from the overflights the farm was made virtually worthless for agricultural purposes. The farmer claimed that his farm had in practical effect been taken, that government was using it as a sort of extension of the runway, and that government should have to pay for it as it had for the rest of the airport. The Supreme Court agreed that this use of the farmland was a taking in effect, if not in form, and that the farmer was entitled to just compensation for what is called INVERSE CONDEMNATION.

This ruling does not mean that the neighbors of a public airport or highway subjected to noise that reduces their property values will always be compensated. In general such disadvantaged neighbors are not viewed by the courts as having had their property taken in the constitutional sense. The reason is that although a nearly total loss (such as the farmer sustained) is judicially viewed as a taking, some modest diminution of value resulting from neighboring public activities is viewed as one of the disadvantages of modern life that must be accepted by property owners.

The judicial focus on the quantum of loss as a test of a taking is called the diminution of value theory and was put forward many years ago by Justice OLIVER WENDELL HOL-

MES in *Pennsylvania Coal Co. v. Mahon* (1922). There is no clear line, Holmes believed, between the formal taking of property by government (in which title and possession are acquired) and the various forms of government regulation (such as zoning and pollution control), which do not transfer ownership formally, but restrict private owners' uses and values for the benefit of the general public. In both cases, according to Holmes, the traditional rights of private owners are being restricted for the benefit of the public. If there were no legal limits on such restrictions, he said, private property would be worthless and wholly at the mercy of government. On the other hand, Holmes said, if every value-diminishing regulation were viewed as a compensable taking of property, government would be unable to function, for essentially all of its regulatory activities (speed limits, liquor control, safety standards, rent control) disadvantage property owners to some degree.

He thus devised a practical test. We must all accept some impairment of property values so that society can function in a civilized way, and government must be permitted to make regulations requiring such impairments. If, however, the losses from such regulations become extreme—nearing total destruction of the property's value for any owner—then the society should compensate the owner and bear the losses of the regulation commonly. Thus, under the Holmesian theory, the amount of the loss and the ability of the owner to continue to earn some return from his property after the regulation has been imposed become the critical determinants of the constitutional question: has there been a taking for which compensation must be paid?

Although Holmes's test continues to dominate taking cases, there are a number of other theories that are widely found in the literature and in judicial opinions. One theory holds that prohibitions of certain socially undesirable uses do not qualify as compensable takings despite considerable loss to the owners, because one cannot be viewed as having a property right to engage in "noxious" conduct, and losses flowing from prohibition of such conduct is not a taking away of property. The illegalization of manufacture and sale of a dangerous drug, or of polluting activity, has been so categorized.

Another theory sometimes advanced is that certain government restrictions imposed on property owners are not a taking of property from the owners by the government, but are the merely regulation by the government of activities by which it mediates between various private uses in conflict with each other. Under this theory compensation is required only when the government as an enterprise itself benefits directly from the regulation (it gets additional space for its military airport, for example). The enterpriseregulation theory has sometimes been used to justify ZONING and other LAND USE controls that restrict the amount or type of building permitted to a landowner on his land. Modern historic preservation ordinances as well as safety and environmental controls are sometimes justified on this theory.

Still another view suggests that government may, without compensation, impose much greater restrictions to prevent future additional exploitation of property, while leaving existing uses, than it may cut back on existing uses. Thus, in PENN CENTRAL TRANSPORTATION CO. V. NEW YORK (1978), an important case, the Supreme Court upheld a historic preservation ordinance prohibiting the owners of Grand Central Station in New York from building a high rise office tower above the railroad station, noting that the existing station did produce some economic return to the owners. The claimed "taking" of a property right to build a bigger building was rejected.

Although no single theory wholly dominates taking law, two guidelines permit safe prediction about the great majority of cases. Courts will find a taking and require just compensation if (1) the government acquires physical possession of the property; or if (2) regulation so reduces the owner's values that virtually no net economic return is left to the proprietor.

JOSEPH L. SAX
(1986)

(SEE ALSO: *Dames & Moore v. Regan; Hawaii Housing Authority v. Midkiff.*)

### Bibliography

ACKERMAN, BRUCE A. 1977 *Private Property and the Constitution.* New Haven, Conn.: Yale University Press.
BOSSELMAN, FRED et al. 1973 *The Taking Issue.* Washington, D.C.: Council on Environmental Quality.
MICHELMAN, FRANK I. 1967 Property, Utility and Fairness: Comments on the Ethical Foundations of "Just Compensation" Law. *Harvard Law Review* 80:1165–1258.
SAX, JOSEPH L. 1971 Taking and the Police Power. *Yale Law Journal* 74:36–76.
——— 1971 Takings, Private Property and Public Rights. *Yale Law Journal* 81:149–186.

# TAKING OF PROPERTY
## (Update 1)

Recent historical scholarship indicates that the taking clause was something of an innovation. Only two of the state constitutions adopted between 1776 and 1780 required the government to pay compensation when private PROPERTY was taken for a public use. The lack of constitutional protection for PROPERTY RIGHTS was consistent with the republican ethos of the period. BENJAMIN FRANKLIN, for example, once said that "Private Property . . . is a

Creature of Society, and is subject to the Calls of that Society, whenever its Necessities shall require it, even to its last Farthing; its contributions therefore to the public Exigencies are . . . to be considered . . . the Return of an obligation previously received, or the Payment of a just Debt." The taking clause seems to represent a victory of Lockean liberalism over this earlier republican philosophy.

The Supreme Court has recently used the taking clause to strike down a variety of government regulations. In one case, the federal government claimed that the public had the right to use a marina that a private developer had connected with a public waterway. The Court held that giving the public access to the marina would be an unconstitutional taking of the developer's property. In another case, Congress was concerned because certain lands belonging to American Indians had so many owners that managing the lands had become impractical. As a way of consolidating landholdings, a federal statute mandated that some of the tiniest interests would revert to the tribe on the owners' deaths. This, too, was an unconstitutional taking. The Court also found a taking when New York required landlords to give their tenants access to cable television. The reason was that the cable box would "take" some of the space on the building's roof.

A 1987 case, *Nollan v. California Coastal Commission*, exemplifies the Court's revived interest in protecting property rights. The case involved a couple who wanted to build a larger beach house. As a condition for receiving a permit, the California Coastal Commission required them to allow the public to walk along the beach. The majority opinion was written by Justice ANTONIN SCALIA, who had quickly emerged as the strongest guardian of property rights on the REHNQUIST COURT. Scalia was willing to concede, at least for the purposes of argument, that California could have banned the construction entirely as a means of preserving the public's right to see the ocean from the street. Alternatively, he conceded, the Nollans could have been required to allow the public to walk from the street around to the back of their house. But because the government had chosen to give the public direct access laterally along the beach, rather than from the street, Justice Scalia held the permit condition unconstitutional.

The Court's rationale in *Nollan* was that lateral access was not closely enough related to the government's right to protect the view of the ocean. Justice Scalia seemed suspicious of the government's motives in imposing the permit condition, at one point referring to similar permit conditions as a form of "extortion."

In contrast to *Nollan*, another 1987 case rather surprisingly failed to find a taking. *Keystone Bituminous Coal Association v. DeBenedictus* was a replay of *Pennsylvania Coal Co. v. Mahon* (1922), the classic decision of Justice OLIVER WENDELL HOLMES, JR. Holmes had struck down a Pennsylvania statute that required underground coal mines to maintain adequate support for surface structures. The *DeBenedictus* Court, however, found a similar but more recently enacted Pennsylvania statute to be constitutional. The Court distinguished *Mahon* on the ground that the newer statute had a broader public purpose. No taking was found, because the statute required mining companies to leave only a small fraction of their coal in the ground.

It is often difficult to predict whether a given government regulation will be found to be a taking, but two factors seem particularly significant. First, if the regulation takes away the owner's right to control physical access to the property, it is much more likely to be found a taking—and almost sure to be found a taking if there is a permanent physical occupation of the property. Second, unless physical access is involved, the owner probably will not be able to claim a taking unless the regulation virtually destroys the value of the property.

At present, takings doctrine is in flux. Under Chief Justices HARLAN F. STONE and EARL WARREN, the Court took little interest in the taking clause. The BURGER COURT began to take a renewed interest in the area, but did not aggressively use the taking clause as a means of attacking important government regulations. It remains to be seen whether the Rehnquist Court will introduce a greater degree of activism.

Most of the current scholarship on the taking clause may be divided into three camps. One group argues for minimal judicial scrutiny of economic regulations, so that very few government actions would be held a taking. In contrast, a second group argues for vigorous scrutiny under the auspices of the taking clause—reminiscent of the era of LOCHNER V. NEW YORK (1905). A third group argues for renewed judicial protection, but limited to a particular category of property, that of peculiar personal significance to individuals, as opposed to ordinary business interests. It is uncertain whether any of these groups of scholars will succeed in influencing the Justices. At present, the Court seems content to muddle through taking cases without the benefit of a broad theoretical perspective.

DANIEL A. FARBER
(1992)

Bibliography

EPSTEIN, RICHARD A. 1985 *Takings: Private Property and the Power of Eminent Domain.* Cambridge, Mass.: Harvard University Press.

LEVY, LEONARD W. 1988 Property as a Human Right. *Constitutional Commentary* 5:169–184.

NOTE 1985 The Origins and Original Significance of the Just

Compensation Clause of the Fifth Amendment. *Yale Law Journal* 94:694–716.

# TAKING OF PROPERTY
## (Update 2)

The Fifth Amendment includes the command, "nor shall private property be taken for public use, without just compensation."

Putting aside the perhaps puzzling fact that the PUBLIC USE limitation has been largely read out of existence— the government can take PROPERTY for almost any reason, including the improvement of "slums" or the conveyance of clear title to tenants—the so-called takings clause has been easy enough to apply in most cases. If the government wants property, it can assert its right of EMINENT DOMAIN and take it. But then it must pay JUST COMPENSATION. The hard cases arise when government has not simply appropriated property outright but instead has taken a legislative or regulatory action that lessens the value of private property.

The fountainhead for so-called REGULATORY TAKINGS cases is the Supreme Court's opinion in *Pennsylvania Coal Co. v. Mahon* (1922), credited as the first to apply the takings clause to government regulation short of complete appropriation. Pennsylvania law prohibited coal companies from mining subsurface coal "in such a way as to cause the subsidence of, among other things, any structure used as a human habitation." Justice OLIVER WENDELL HOLMES, JR., first held that the law was a proper exercise of the POLICE POWER. "Government could hardly go on if to some extent values incident to property could not be diminished without paying for every such change in the law." But Holmes also found that such power "must have its limits." Therein lies the rub, for Holmes could not pin down what those limits were to be. "The general rule at least is, that while property may be regulated to a certain extent, if regulation goes too far it will be recognized as a taking." How far is too far? Four years later, the Court held that ZONING was not necessarily a taking in EUCLID V. AMBLER REALTY CO. (1926), even though the regulation caused the private owner to lose three-quarters of the property's value.

Holmes's majority opinion in *Mahon* is famous. Far less attention has been paid to the dissent of LOUIS D. BRANDEIS. Brandeis noted that every law affects private values. He would thus emphasize the nature of the government action more than the private party's loss. "[R]estriction imposed to protect the public health, safety or morals from dangers threatened is not a taking."

The Holmes–Brandeis fault line has played itself out over the ensuing decades. It is often hard to understand the law of regulatory takings except in fairly bald, political terms. Liberal advocates of the NEW DEAL, such as Brandeis and, later, WILLIAM J. BRENNAN, JR., have tended to find no government taking, a trend that reached its high point in PENN CENTRAL TRANSPORTATION CO. V. NEW YORK CITY (1978).

Conservative and libertarian commentators have long been critical of the takings jurisprudence of the WARREN COURT, as epitomized in *Penn Central.* If government has to pay in order to act, it often will not act. The BURGER COURT and REHNQUIST COURT have aimed to stem the tide of government expanse, in part by putting teeth in Holmes's takings test.

One front in the battle has been the articulation of per se rules to give greater clarity to the field. One such rule is that any regulation that effects a "permanent physical occupation" will be considered a compensable taking, regardless of how slight the physical intrusion may be. In LORETTO V. TELEPROMPTER, INC. (1982), New York City required landlords to install cable for tenants' televisions. The just compensation for the resulting "taking" of the air space occupied by the cable wires was held to be $1 per building. A second per se takings rule, formalized in LUCAS V. SOUTH CAROLINA COASTAL COUNCIL (1992), is triggered whenever a governmental act deprives a landowner of "all economically beneficial or productive use" of land.

The tightening of the takings clause has gone beyond per se rules. The Court in *Nollan v. California Coastal Commission* (1987) required an "essential nexus" between the harms associated with development and the conditions that government can place on granting a building permit. In DOLAN V. CITY OF TIGARD (1994), the Court added a prong to the *Nollan* test, ruling that such conditional exactions must also satisfy a "rough proportionality" test—the burden on the private party must be loosely in keeping with the impact of the proposed development.

Application of the takings clause has always depended on an understanding of what "property" is in the first place, a point noted by Brandeis in his *Mahon* dissent. In *Phillips v. Washington Legal Foundation* (1998), the Court, in a 5–4 decision with Chief Justice WILLIAM H. REHNQUIST writing for the majority, held that the interest accrued on lawyer trust-fund accounts was "property" of the client for purposes of the Fifth Amendment. As with *Loretto, Phillips* may foreshadow another move to tighten the takings clause by finding even relatively minor government actions to be covered in its sweep.

These recent cases have brought with them divided courts, vigorous DISSENTING OPINIONS, and a plethora of scholarly commentary. Critics charge the majorities of resurrecting *Lochner*-era SUBSTANTIVE DUE PROCESS to invalidate government regulations that are normally accorded only RATIONAL BASIS review. Practical politicians have leapt in to fill what they perceive as a void, advancing legislative proposals to require the government to pay whenever a regulation diminishes private property values by more than a given, objective limit—say one-third. Such proposals have both practical and theoretical difficulties, of course, and have been criticized by legal scholars and others.

Paraphrasing Sigmund Freud, sometimes a question of degree is just a question of degree. Seven decades have not fleshed out Holmes's vague pronouncements in *Mahon*. Absent some major shift in the political landscape, we may just have to live with uncertainty in the contours of regulatory takings law.

EDWARD J. McCAFFERY
(2000)

Bibliography

BEEN, VICKI 1991 "Exit" as a Constraint on Land Use Exactions: Rethinking the Unconstitutional Conditions Doctrine. *Columbia Law Review* 91:473–545.

FISCHEL, WILLIAM A. 1995 *Regulatory Takings.* Cambridge, Mass.: Harvard University Press.

MICHELMAN, FRANK I. 1995 A Skeptical View of "Property Rights" Legislation. *Fordham Environmental Law Journal* 6: 409–421.

RUBENFELD, JED 1993 Usings. *Yale Law Journal* 102:1077–1163.

TREANOR, WILLIAM MICHAEL 1995 The Original Understanding of the Takings Clause and the Political Process. *Columbia Law Review* 95:782–887.

# TANEY, ROGER BROOKE
## (1777–1864)

Roger B. Taney, CHIEF JUSTICE of the United States from 1836 until his death in 1864, profoundly shaped American constitutional development in cases dealing with states' regulatory powers, CORPORATIONS, SLAVERY, and the JURISDICTION of federal courts. His reputation long suffered from invidious and inappropriate comparisons with his predecessor Chief Justice JOHN MARSHALL and because of his disastrous opinion in DRED SCOTT V. SANDFORD (1857). But his influence has been enduring and, on balance, beneficial.

Taney was born in 1777 in Calvert County, Maryland. His father, a well-to-do planter, destined him for a career in law. After graduation from Dickinson College (Pennsylvania), he was admitted to the bar in 1799 and began a thirty-six-year career of politics and law practice in Maryland. He served intermittently in both houses of the state legislature until 1821, at first as a Federalist. But finding that affiliation intolerable because of the conduct of New

England Federalists during the War of 1812, he assumed leadership of a local faction known as Coodies and then after 1825 supported ANDREW JACKSON. Practicing first in Frederick, where he maintained his lifelong residence, and then in Baltimore, he became a preeminent member of the Maryland bar, state attorney general from 1827 to 1831, and then attorney general of the United States, a position he held until 1833, when he served for a year as secretary of the treasury.

Taney urged President Jackson to veto the bill to recharter the Bank of the United States and contributed that part of JACKSON'S VETO OF THE BANK BILL in which the President denied that the Supreme Court's opinion on constitutional matters bound the President. As treasury secretary, Taney ordered removal of the federal deposits from the Bank and their distribution to certain "pet banks." In these bank matters, Taney was not the mere pliant tool of Jackson; rather, he acted in accord with his own deep suspicions of centralized and monopolistic economic power.

As attorney general, Taney also had occasion to explore issues involving slavery and free blacks. Upholding South Carolina's Negro Seamen's Act, which prohibited black seamen from disembarking from their vessels while in Carolina waters, Taney insisted that the state's sovereign right to control slaves and free blacks overrode any inconsistent exercise of federal treaty and commerce powers. Presaging his *Dred Scott* opinion, he maintained that blacks were "a separate and degraded people," incapable of being citizens. He also expressed doubt that a Supreme Court decision holding the statute unconstitutional would bind the states.

As Chief Justice of the United States after 1836, Taney left an enduring imprint on the American Constitution. Most of the landmark cases coming before the Court in the first decade of his tenure involved questions of the power of the states to regulate the economic behavior of persons or corporations within their jurisdictions. In CHARLES RIVER BRIDGE V. WARREN BRIDGE (1837) Taney employed a paradigmatic balance between investors' demands for autonomy and the states' insistence on public control of that new legal creature, the private corporation. Refusing to read into a bridge company's charter an implicit grant of a transportation monopoly, Taney held that "in charters, . . . no rights are taken from the public, or given to the corporation, beyond those which the words of the charter, by their natural and proper construction, purport to convey." (See RESERVED POLICE POWERS.)

Subsequent decisions of the Taney Court confirmed the *Charles River Bridge* DOCTRINE: where the state had explicitly conveyed monopoly rights or otherwise conferred valuable privileges, a majority of the Court honored the grant and held the state to it under CONTRACT CLAUSE doctrines deriving from FLETCHER V. PECK (1810). On the other hand, the Court refused to infer monopoly grants or other restrictions on state regulatory power if they were not explicitly conferred in a corporate charter. Thus in BANK OF AUGUSTA V. EARLE (1839) Taney held that states could regulate the activities of foreign corporations within their jurisdictions, or exclude them altogether, but that such regulations would have to be explicit. Absent express declarations of state policy, the TANEY COURT refused to hold that banking corporations could not enter into contracts outside the state that chartered them.

Yet Taney entertained an instinctive sympathy for states' efforts to control economic activity within their jurisdictions. In another case from his maiden term, BRISCOE V. BANK OF KENTUCKY (1837), Taney supported the majority's holding that a state was not precluded from creating a bank wholly owned by it and exercising note-issuing powers, so long as the state did not pledge its credit to back the notes. Such notes would have been a subterfuge form of the state BILLS OF CREDIT that had been struck down in CRAIG V. MISSOURI (1830). In BRONSON V. KINZIE (1843), however, Taney invalidated state statutes that restricted foreclosure sales and granted mortgagors rights to redeem foreclosed property. Even here, however, he emphasized that states could modify contractual remedies so long as they did not tamper with the substance of existing contracts.

Taney's opinions dealing with the jurisdiction of federal courts proved to be among his most significant. Some of these restricted the autonomy of the states in the interests of protecting the national market. Thus in SWIFT V. TYSON (1842) the Court unanimously supported an opinion by Justice JOSEPH STORY holding that in commercial law matters, federal courts need not look to the forum state's COMMON LAW for rules of decision, but instead might formulate commercial law doctrines out of "the general principles and doctrines of commercial jurisprudence," a principle that survived until *Swift* was overruled in ERIE RAILROAD V. TOMPKINS (1938). (See FEDERAL COMMON LAW.) In PROPELLER GENESEE CHIEF V. FITZHUGH (1851), Taney discarded the English tidewater rule of ADMIRALTY JURISDICTION that Story had imported into American law, and held instead that the inland jurisdiction of federal courts in admiralty matters extended to all navigable waters, tidal or not, thus expanding the reach of federal admiralty jurisdiction to the Great Lakes and the interior rivers. But in LUTHER V. BORDEN (1849), he reasserted the POLITICAL QUESTION doctrine, holding that a challenge to the legitimacy of Rhode Island's government after the Dorr Rebellion of 1842 was to be resolved only by the legislative and executive branches of the national government, not the judicial.

It might be expected that Taney would have been warmly sympathetic to the emerging doctrine of the PO-

LICE POWER, first fully articulated by Massachusetts Chief Justice LEMUEL SHAW in *Commonwealth v. Alger* (1851). But Taney held unspoken reservations about the police power doctrine, fearing that if the states' regulatory powers were defined too explicitly or couched under a rubric, they might somehow be restricted by the federal Constitution. He thus preferred to avoid an explicit definition of the police power, and instead emphasized the states' inherent powers of SOVEREIGNTY over persons and things within their jurisdiction, believing that if the issue were framed in terms of sovereignty rather than regulatory power, the states' autonomy from external interference might be more secure.

This issue of state regulatory power remained sensitive throughout Taney's tenure and was prominent in cases arising out of the attempt of Democratic majorities in the Ohio legislature to levy taxes on banks that had been exempted from certain forms of taxation by their charters. In *Ohio Life Insurance & Trust Co. v. Debolt* (1854) Taney held, in accordance with the *Charles River Bridge* paradigm, that the Court would not read into bank charters an implicit exemption from taxes. But in DODGE V. WOOLSEY (1856), Taney joined a majority in defending an explicit charter exemption against a state constitutional amendment empowering the state to tax exempted banks. Taney was not hostile to banks and corporations as such; he had an alert appreciation of the role that they would play in developing the national market.

Another issue—indeed, the critical one—that kept Taney and his colleagues sensitized to issues of state regulatory power was the protean matter of slavery and black people. This issue, deep in the background, skewed all but one of the Taney Court's COMMERCE CLAUSE decisions. In his first term, the Court skirted slavery complications in a case, MAYOR OF NEW YORK V. MILN (1837), challenging the right of a state to impose some measure of control over the ingress of foreign passengers, by holding that the challenged authority was not a regulation of commerce but rather an exercise of the police power. But this evasion would not dispose of subsequent cases challenging the power of the state to control the importation of liquor or the immigration of persons. In the LICENSE CASES (1847), the Court rendered six opinions, including one by Taney who was with the majority for the result, sustaining the efforts of three New England states to prohibit the importation and sale of liquor. But in the PASSENGER CASES (1849), raising issues similar to *Miln*, the court produced eight opinions, this time with Taney in the minority, striking down state laws regulating or taxing the influx of ALIENS. Taney was consistent throughout, insisting that no federal constitutional restraints existed on the power of the states to control persons or objects coming into their borders. His brush with the controversy over the Negro

Seamen's Act as United States attorney general had left him hostile to any constitutional restraints that might inhibit the power of the slave states to control the ingress of free blacks, slaves, abolitionists, or antislavery propaganda.

The Taney Court did manage to filter slavery complications out of one major commerce clause case, thereby producing another paradigm of state regulatory power. In COOLEY V. BOARD OF WARDENS OF PHILADELPHIA (1851) the Court, with Taney in the majority, held that the commerce clause did not restrain the states from regulating matters essentially local in nature (such as, in this case, pilotage fees or harbor regulations) even if they had some impact on interstate or foreign commerce.

Curiously, the Court was more successful, in the short run, in disposing of cases where the question of slavery was overt rather than implicit. Taney, deeply dedicated to the welfare of his state and region, and anxious above all to protect the slave states from external meddling that would threaten their control of the black population, free or slave, or that would promote widespread emancipation, adopted passionate and extremist postures in slavery cases. In GROVES V. SLAUGHTER (1841), which involved the validity of a contract for sale of a slave under a state constitution that prohibited the commercial importation of slaves, Taney was provoked to a sharp reiteration of his attorney general's opinion, insisting that the power of a state to control blacks within its borders was exclusive of all federal power, including that under the commerce clause.

In PRIGG V. PENNSYLVANIA (1842) Taney was again prodded into another concurrence. Though he agreed with most of Justice Joseph Story's opinion for the majority holding unconstitutional a Pennsylvania PERSONAL LIBERTY LAW, he firmly disavowed Story's dic-1860tum that states need not participate in the recapture and rendition of fugitive slaves. Taney rejected Story's assertion that states could not enact legislation supplemental to the federal Fugitive Slave Act, and maintained that states must do so; his colleagues PETER V. DANIEL and SMITH THOMPSON merely asserted that a state could adopt such laws.

In STRADER V. GRAHAM (1851) Taney spoke for the Court in a case raising American variants of issues earlier canvassed in SOMERSET'S CASE (1772), a doctrinally seminal English decision that had passed into the mainstream of American constitutional thought. Appellant sought to have the Court overturn a Kentucky Court of Appeals decision that slaves permitted by their master to sojourn in a free state who then returned to their slave domicile did not become liberated because of their free-state sojourn. Taney held that the state court determination of the slaves' status was conclusive on federal courts (a point consistent with his emphasis on state control of blacks and a doctrinal

opportunity for evading the issues of *Dred Scott* later). But Taney uttered OBITER DICTA disturbing to the free states. He suggested that the power of states over persons in their jurisdictions was unfettered "except in so far as the powers of the states in this respect are restrained . . . by the Constitution of the United States," thus hinting that there might be some federal constitutional impediment to the abolition statutes of the free states. He further insisted, needlessly, that the antislavery provisions of the NORTHWEST ORDINANCE were defunct, no longer an effective prohibition of the introduction of slavery in the states that had been carved out of the Northwest Territory.

*Dred Scott* (1857) was Taney's definitive utterance on the slavery question. His opinion, though one of nine, was taken by contemporaries to be for the Court, and Taney himself so considered it. Taney first excluded blacks descended from slaves from the status of "Citizens" as that term was used both in the Article III diversity clause and the Article IV PRIVILEGES AND IMMUNITIES clause. In order to support this conclusion, Taney asserted, incorrectly, that blacks in 1787 had been "considered as a subordinate and inferior class of beings, who . . . had no rights which the white man was bound to respect." Taney further insisted that the meaning of the Constitution does not change over time, so that the connotations of its words in 1787 remained rigid and static, unalterable except by formal amendment.

In the second half of his long opinion, Taney held that the federal government lacked power to exclude slavery from the territories, thus holding the MISSOURI COMPROMISE unconstitutional (even though it had already been declared void by the KANSAS-NEBRASKA ACT of 1854). He grounded this lack of federal power not in the territories clause of Article IV, but in its textual sibling, the new states clause, insisting that Congress could not impose conditions on the admission of new states that would put them in a position inferior to those already admitted. Taney also suggested in passing that the DUE PROCESS clause of the Fifth Amendment prohibited Congress from interfering with the property rights of slaveholders. But the significance of this utterance as a source of the later doctrine of SUBSTANTIVE DUE PROCESS has been overrated. Taney was not a devotee of HIGHER LAW doctrines, such as those enunciated by Justice SAMUEL CHASE in CALDER V. BULL (1798), by Justice Story in cases like TERRETT V. TAYLOR (1815) and *Wilkinson v. Leland* (1829), and by numerous state court judges, most recently in the landmark case of WYNEHAMER V. NEW YORK (1856).

In his *Dred Scott* opinion Taney also adopted three points of proslavery constitutional thought previously voiced in Southern legislatures and doctrinal writings: the federal government had no power over slavery except to protect the rights of slaveholders; the federal government was the "trustee" of the states for the territories, and as such must protect the interests of all of them there; and the territorial legislature could not exclude slavery during the territorial period. His performance in the *Dred Scott* case was widely condemned. Justice BENJAMIN R. CURTIS effectively controverted it in his scholarly dissent in *Dred Scott;* northern legislators, political leaders, attorneys, and polemicists poured forth innumerable rebuttals; and the Vermont legislature and the Maine Supreme Judicial Court flatly rejected its doctrines. ABRAHAM LINCOLN insisted that *Dred Scott's* doctrine must be overruled.

Taney remained unmoved by such criticism, insisting in private correspondence that his position would be validated in time. Though aged and in intermittent ill health, he continued his judicial labors unabated. In ABLEMAN V. BOOTH (1859), a magisterial treatise on the role of the federal judiciary in the American federal system, Taney held that state courts could not interfere with the judgment of a federal court through use of the writ of HABEAS CORPUS. He adumbrated the doctrine of dual sovereignty: the federal and state governments "are yet separate and distinct sovereignties, acting separately and independently of each other." (See DUAL FEDERALISM.) But he insisted on the unfettered independence of federal courts in their execution of federal laws. In *dictum,* he asserted that the Fugitive Slave Act of 1850 was constitutional.

Taney produced significant published and unpublished opinions during the CIVIL WAR. In private communications, he supported SECESSION and condemned Lincoln's resort to force to save the Union. In keeping with such views, he drafted opinions, probably to be incorporated into conventional judicial opinions when the opportunity arose, condemning the EMANCIPATION PROCLAMATION, CONSCRIPTION, and the Legal Tender Acts. He also extended the first half of his *Dred Scott* opinion to exclude all blacks, not just those descended from slaves, from CITIZENSHIP; and he reasserted the obligation of the free states to return fugitive slaves. In an official opinion on circuit he condemned Lincoln's suspension of the writ of *habeas corpus* in EX PARTE MERRYMAN (1861), an opinion Lincoln refused to honor. He also joined the dissenters in the PRIZE CASES (1863), who insisted that because only Congress can declare war, Lincoln's military response to secession and southern military actions was "private" and of no legal effect. His death in 1864 relieved him from the painful necessity of seeing his vision of the constitutional and social order destroyed by the victory of Union arms.

Taney's lasting contributions consisted of his reinforcement of the political question doctrine, his strong defense of the states' regulatory powers, and his vigorous aggrandizement of the jurisdiction of the federal courts. More than his colleagues, he keenly appreciated the role of technological change in American law, a sensitivity apparent

in *Charles River Bridge* and *Genesee Chief.* His defense of regional autonomy and his hostility to the power of concentrated capital retain a perennial relevance. His instinct for dynamic balance in the formulation of enduring rules of law, as in the *Charles River Bridge* paradigm, evinced judicial statesmanship of the first rank.

Constitutional problems related to slavery combined with Taney's personal failings to blight his reputation and eclipse his real achievements. *Dred Scott* remains a monument to judicial hubris, and all the slavery cases that came before the Taney Court bear the impress of Taney's determination to bend the Constitution to the service of sectional interest. Though he manumitted nearly all his own slaves and was in his personal relations a kind and loving man, Taney as Chief Justice was immoderate and willful when the times called for judicial caution. His tolerance of multiple opinions permitted dissents and concurrences to proliferate, blurring the clarity of doctrine in commerce clause cases. In any case touched directly or indirectly by slavery, Taney's sure instincts for viable doctrine, as well as his nobler personal qualities, deserted him and gave way to a blind and vindictive sectionalism unworthy of the Chief Justice of the United States.

It is the tragic irony of Taney's career that his virtues were so closely linked to his faults, especially in their results. He fully merited FELIX FRANKFURTER's warm appreciation of his role in shaping the American federal system: "the intellectual power of his opinions and their enduring contribution to a workable adjustment of the theoretical distribution of authority between two governments for a single people, place Taney second only to Marshall in the constitutional history of our country." Yet no other Justices have so gravely damaged the federal system because of sectional bias, and the real merits of Taney's defense of localist values have been obscured by his racial antipathies and sectional dogmatism.

WILLIAM M. WIECEK
(1986)

Bibliography

FEHRENBACKER, DON E.  1979  *The Dred Scott Case: Its Significance in American Law and Politics.* New York: Oxford University Press.

HARRIS, ROBERT J.  1957 (1966)  Chief Justice Taney: Prophet of Reform and Reaction. Pages 93–118 in Leonard W. Levy, ed., *American Constitutional Law: Historical Essays.* New York: Harper & Row.

LEWIS, WALKER  1965  *Without Fear or Favor: A Biography of Chief Justice Roger Brooke Taney.* Boston: Houghton Mifflin.

SWISHER, CARL B.  1935  *Roger B. Taney.* New York: Macmillan.

——— 1974  The Taney Period, 1835–64. Volume 5 of The Oliver Wendell Holmes Devise History of The Supreme Court of the United States. New York: Macmillan.

# TANEY COURT
## (1836–1864)

The Supreme Court under Chief Justice ROGER B. TANEY (1836–1864) has not been a favorite among historians, perhaps because it defies easy generalization. There were few great constitutional moments and no dramatic law-making DECISIONS comparable to those handed down by the MARSHALL COURT. The fifteen Justices who served with Taney (not counting ABRAHAM LINCOLN's CIVIL WAR appointees) varied immensely in ability—from JOSEPH STORY of Massachusetts who was the leading scholar on the bench until his death in 1845 to JOHN MCKINLEY of Alabama whose twenty-five years on the Court left barely a trace. Institutional unity and efficiency were often disrupted by abrasive personalities like HENRY BALDWIN (who became mentally unstable shortly after his appointment in 1830) and PETER V. DANIEL (whose passion for STATES' RIGHTS drove him into chronic dissent). Division was constant and bitter as the Justices disagreed openly over corporation, banking, and slavery questions—all of which tended to be seen from a sectional point of view. Fortunately for the ongoing work of the Court, most of its members shared a respect for the Constitution and had a common commitment to economic progress and property rights that cut across ideological and sectional differences. All were Democrats, too, except Story, JOHN MCLEAN, and BENJAMIN R. CURTIS. Most of the Court respected the Chief Justice—whose legal mind was of a high order—and responded well to his patient, democratic style of leadership. Still the Court under Taney did not quite cohere. There was no "leading mind," as DANIEL WEBSTER complained, and no clear-cut doctrinal unity.

Clearly the Taney Court was not the Marshall Court—but then again it was not the age of Marshall. The society that conditioned the Taney Court and defined the perimeters within which it made law was democratic in its politics, pluralistic in social composition, divided in ideology, and shaped by capitalist forces which increasingly sought freedom from traditional governmental restraints. Most threatening to judicial unity, because it was directly reflected in the opinions of the Court, was the intensification of sectional rivalry. As northern states committed themselves to commerce and manufacturing, they came to see themselves—taking their cultural cues from the abolitionists—as a section united in defense of liberty and freedom. The South found ideological conservatism an ideal umbrella for an expansive social-economic system based on cotton and organized around plantation slavery. As the sections competed for political power and control of the new West, each came to think of itself as the last best hope of mankind. And each insisted that the Constitution accommodate its policy preferences—a demand that the Supreme Court could satisfy only by compromising doctrinal purity and finally could not satisfy at all.

In short, the political and economic problems of the new age became constitutional problems just as ALEXIS DE TOCQUEVILLE had said they would. Whether the Supreme Court would be the primary agency to resolve those problems was, of course, a matter of debate. ANDREW JACKSON, armed with a mandate from the people, did not believe that the Court had a monopoly of constitutional wisdom. Newly organized POLITICAL PARTIES stood ready to dispute judicial decisions that offended their constituencies. States armed with JOHN C. CALHOUN's theory of NULLIFICATION insisted that they, not the Court, had the final word on the Constitution. Accordingly, the margin of judicial error was drastically reduced. The Court was obliged to make the Constitution of 1787 work for a new age; the high nationalism of the Marshall Court, along with its Augustan style of judging, would have to be toned down. Changes would have to come. The question—and it was as yet a new one in American constitutional law—was whether they could be made without disrupting the continuity upon which the authority of the law and the prestige of the Court rested.

The moment of testing came quickly. Facing the Court in its 1837 term were three great constitutional questions dealing with state banking, the COMMERCE CLAUSE, and corporate contracts. Each had been argued before the Marshall Court and each involved a question of FEDERALISM which pitted new historical circumstances against a precedent from the Marshall period. The Court's decisions in these cases would set the constitutional tone for the new age.

In BRISCOE V. BANK OF KENTUCKY the challenge was simple and straightforward. The issue was whether notes issued by the state-owned Commonwealth Bank were prohibited by Article I, section 10, of the Constitution, which prevented states from issuing BILLS OF CREDIT. The Marshall Court had ruled broadly against state bills of credit in CRAIG V. MISSOURI (1830), but the new Jacksonian majority ruled for the state bank. Justice McLean's opinion paid deference to legal continuity by distinguishing *Briscoe* from *Craig*, but political and economic expediency controlled the decision as Story's bitter dissent made clear. The fact was that, after the demise of the second Bank of the United States, state bank notes were the main currency of the country. To rule against the bank would put such notes in jeopardy, a risk the new Court refused to take.

Policy considerations of a states' rights nature also overwhelmed doctrinal consistency in commerce clause litigation, the Court's primary means of drawing the line between national and state power. Marshall's opinion in

GIBBONS V. OGDEN (1824) had conceded vast power over INTERSTATE COMMERCE to Congress, although the Court had not gone so far as to rule that national power automatically excluded states from passing laws touching FOREIGN and INTERSTATE COMMERCE. The new age needed a flexible interpretation of the commerce clause that would please states' rights forces in both the North and the South and at the same time encourage the growth of a national market.

In MAYOR OF NEW YORK V. MILN, the second of the trio of great cases in 1837, the Court struggled toward such a reinterpretation. A New York law required masters of all vessels arriving at the port of New York to make bond that none of their passengers should become wards of the city. The practical need for such a law seemed clear enough; the question was whether it encroached unconstitutionally on federal power over interstate commerce as laid out in the *Gibbons* decision. The Chief Justice assigned the opinion to Justice SMITH THOMPSON who was prepared to justify the New York law as a police regulation and as a legitimate exercise of concurrent commerce power. His narrow definition of STATE POLICE POWER displeased some of his brethren, however, and even more so his position on CONCURRENT POWER. When he refused to compromise, the opinion was reassigned to PHILIP P. BARBOUR, who upheld the state regulation as a valid exercise of state police power. Barbour's contention that police power was "unqualified and exclusive" far exceeded anything that precedent could justify, however, as Story pointed out in his dissent. Indeed, Barbour's opinion, so far as it ruled that states could regulate interstate passengers, went beyond the position agreed upon in CONFERENCE and lacked the full concurrence of a majority.

The *Miln* case settled little except that the New York regulation was constitutional. The Court remained sharply divided over the basic questions: whether congressional power over foreign and interstate commerce was exclusive of the states or concurrent with them and, if it was concurrent, how much congressional action would be necessary to sustain national predominance. The doctrine of state police power had taken a tentative step toward maturity, but its relation to the commerce clause remained unsettled. That the states reserved some power to legislate for the health and welfare of their citizens seemed clear enough, but to establish an enclave of state power prior to, outside the scope of, and superior to powers delegated explicitly to Congress was to beg, not settle the crucial constitutional question.

The uncertainty regarding the questions generated by *Miln* continued throughout the 1840s in such cases as GROVES V. SLAUGHTER (1841) where the Court refused to rule on whether the provision of the Mississippi Constitution of 1832 touching the interstate slave trade was a

violation of national commerce power. Confusion increased in the LICENSE CASES (1847) and the PASSENGER CASES (1849), which dealt with state regulation of alcohol and immigration respectively. The Justices upheld state authority in the first and denied it in the second, but in neither did they clarify the relation of state police power to federal authority over interstate commerce.

Not until COOLEY V. BOARD OF WARDENS (1852), which considered the constitutionality of a Pennsylvania law regulating pilotage in the port of Philadelphia, did the Court supply guidelines for commerce clause litigation. Congress had twice legislated on pilotage, but in neither case was there any conflict with the Pennsylvania law. The issue came, therefore, precisely and unavoidably to focus on EXCLUSIVE POWER versus concurrent power: whether the constitutional grant of commerce power to Congress automatically prohibited STATE REGULATION OF COMMERCE or whether the states could regulate commerce as long as such regulations did not actually conflict with congressional legislation.

Justice Curtis's majority opinion upheld the state law and in the process salvaged some doctrinal regularity. Starting from the undeniable premise that the commerce power granted to Congress did not expressly exclude the states from exercising authority over interstate commerce, he ruled that exclusive congressional JURISDICTION obtained only when the subject matter itself required it. The SUBJECTS OF COMMERCE, however, were vast and varied and did not require blanket exclusiveness. Some matters, he said, needed a "single uniform rule, operating equally on the commerce of the United States in every port." Some just as certainly admitted of local regulation. Power, in other words, followed function: if the subject matter required uniform regulation, the power belonged to Congress; if it did not, the states might regulate it. State police power remained to be settled, but the pressure to do so was lessened because the concurrent commerce power of the states was now clearly recognized.

SELECTIVE EXCLUSIVENESS, as the Court's approach in *Cooley* came to be called, was not a certain and final answer to the problem of allocating commerce power between the national government and the states, however. The rule was clear enough but how to apply it was not, which is to say that Curtis gave no guidelines for determining which aspects of commerce required uniform regulation or which permitted diversity. What was clear was that the Court had retreated from the constitutional formalism of the Marshall period. The opinion was short, only ten pages long; it made no reference to precedent, not even *Gibbons*. The Justices now willed to do what they had previously done unwillingly: they decided cases without a definitive pronouncement of DOCTRINE. The important difference in *Cooley* was that the Court devised a rule of thumb recognizing the judicial interest-balancing that previously had been carried on covertly in the name of formal distinctions. Ordered process, not logical categories, would be the new order of the day.

The Court's flexibility also signaled a shift of power in the direction of the states. The constitutional legacy of the Marshall Court had been altered to fit Jacksonian priorities. Still, national authority had not been destroyed. The Taney Court had refused to extend the nationalist principles of MCCULLOCH V. MARYLAND (1819) and *Gibbons*, to be sure, but the principles stood. The Court's new federalism did not rest on new states' rights constitutional doctrine. Neither did the new federalism threaten economic growth, as conservatives had predicted. Agrarian capitalism, for example, fared as well under the Taney Court as it had under its predecessor. The Justices did sometimes resist the most exorbitant demands of land speculators, and occasionally a dissenting Justice spoke for the little man as did Daniel in *Arguello v. United States* (1855). But the majority took their cue from FLETCHER V. PECK (1810), which is to say that plungers in the land market mostly got free rein, as for example in *Cervantes v. United States* (1854) and *Fremont v. United States* (1855). That slaveholding agrarian capitalists were to benefit from this judicial largess was clear from the decision in DRED SCOTT V. SANDFORD (1857).

The Court's promotion of commercial-industrial-corporate capitalism proved more difficult because of the sectional disagreements among the Justices. But there is no doubt that the Taney Court served as a catalyst for the release of American entrepreneurial energies. Its plan for a democratic, nonmonopolistic capitalism, Jacksonian style, was unveiled in CHARLES RIVER BRIDGE V. WARREN BRIDGE, the last of the three landmark decisions of the 1837 term. Here the question was whether the toll-free Warren Bridge, chartered and built in 1828 a few hundred feet from the Charles River Bridge, destroyed the property rights of the old bridge, in violation of its charter as protected by DARTMOUTH COLLEGE V. WOODWARD (1819). The difficulty was that the charter of 1785, although granting the Charles River Bridge the right to collect tolls, had not explicitly granted a monopoly. The fate of the old bridge depended, therefore, on the willingness of the Taney Court to extend the principle of *Dartmouth College* by implication.

Taney, who spoke for the new Jacksonian majority on the Court, refused to do so. The Chief Justice agreed that "the rights of private property are sacredly guarded," but he insisted "that the community also have rights, and that the happiness and well-being of every citizen depends on their faithful preservation." The Court should not venture into the no-man's land of inference and construction when the public interest rested in the balance, Taney argued.

He cleverly supported this position by citing Marshall's opinion in PROVIDENCE BANK V. BILLINGS (1830). And the public interest, as Taney saw it, lay in extending equality of economic opportunity. "Modern science," he said with an eye on new railroad corporations, would be throttled and transportation set back to the last century if turnpike and canal companies could turn charter rights into monopoly grants.

The *Bridge* decision, like the Court's decisions in banking and commerce, revealed a distinct instrumentalist tone as well as a new tolerance for state legislative discretion. The Court also showed its preference for dynamic over static capital. Still, property rights were not generally threatened. To be sure, in WEST RIVER BRIDGE COMPANY V. DIX (1848) the Court recognized the power of state legislatures to take property for public purposes with JUST COMPENSATION, but conservatives themselves were willing to recognize that power. The Court also took a liberal view of state debtor's relief legislation, especially laws applying to mortgages for land, but even here the Court could claim the Marshall Court's decision in OGDEN V. SAUNDERS (1827) as its guide. There was no doubt, on the other hand, as BRONSON V. KINZIE (1843) showed, that state relief laws that impaired substantial contractual rights would not be tolerated.

Corporate property also remained secure under the *Bridge* ruling. Indeed, corporate expansion was strongly encouraged by the Taney Court despite the resistance of some of the southern agrarian Justices. After 1837 the Court consistently refused to extend charter rights by implication, but it also upheld corporate charters that explicitly granted monopoly rights even though in some cases such rights appeared hostile to community interest. Corporations also greatly profited from BANK OF AUGUSTA V. EARLE (1839), which raised the question whether corporations chartered in one state could do business in another. Taney conceded that the legislature could prohibit foreign corporations from doing business in the state and some such laws were subsequently passed. But such prohibitions, he went on to say, had to be explicit; practically speaking, this limitation assured corporations the right to operate across state lines. Hardly less important to corporate expansion was *Louisville Railroad v. Letson* (1844) which held that corporations could be considered citizens of the states in which they were chartered for purposes of DIVERSITY JURISDICTION—Thus removing the increasingly unworkable fiction created in *Bank of United States v. Deveaux* (1809) and assuring corporate access to federal courts where the bias in favor of local interests would be minimized.

The Court's promotion of capitalism showed the basic continuity between the Marshall and Taney periods and the fact that antebellum law followed the contours of economic development. Acknowledgment of this continuity, however, should not obscure the real changes in constitutional federalism as the Taney Court deferred more to state power and legislative discretion. Overall the Court spoke more modestly, too, readily acknowledging former errors and generally toning down its rhetoric. In LUTHER V. BORDEN (1849), it went so far as to promise judicial self-restraint regarding POLITICAL QUESTIONS, though that promise ought not to be confused with a hard-and-fast doctrine, which it clearly was not. Although the Court avoided stridency, it did not claim less power. The constitutional nationalism which the Taney Court reduced was not the same as the judicial nationalism which it actually extended. In short, the Court did things differently, but it did not surrender its power to do them. Although the *Bridge* case conceded new power to state legislatures and promised judicial restraint, the Court still monitored the federal system in corporate contract questions. The Court's commerce clause decisions worked to make the federal system more flexible. But in every case from *Miln* through *Cooley*, the Court retained the right to judge—and often, as in *Cooley*, by vague constitutional standards. This judicial authority, moreover, was used throughout the Taney period to expand the jurisdiction of the Court, often at the expense of state judiciaries which the Court claimed to respect.

Never was federal judicial expansion more striking than in SWIFT V. TYSON (1842), a commercial law case which arose under federal diversity jurisdiction. For a unanimous Court, Story held that, in matters of general commercial law, state "laws," which section 34 of the JUDICIARY ACT OF 1789 obliged the federal courts to follow in diversity cases, did not include state court decisions. In the absence of controlling state statutes, then, federal courts were free to apply general principles of commercial law, which they proceeded to do until *Swift* was overruled in 1938. Almost as expansive was Taney's opinion in PROPELLER GENESEE CHIEF V. FITZHUGH (1851), which bluntly overturned the tidewater limitation imposed by the Marshall Court and extended the admiralty jurisdiction of the federal courts over the vast network of inland lakes and rivers.

Both these decisions were part of the Court's consistent effort to establish a system of uniform commercial principles conducive to the interstate operation of business. Both paved the way for federal judicial intrusion into state judicial authority. When state courts objected to this judicial nationalism, as the Wisconsin Supreme Court did in the slave rendition case of ABLEMAN V. BOOTH (1859), Jacksonian Roger Taney put them in their place with a ringing defense of federal judicial authority that was every bit as unyielding as was Federalist John Marshall's in COHENS V. VIRGINIA (1821). *Ableman* was an assertion of power that would have astonished conservative critics in 1837 who

predicted the imminent decline and fall of the Court. Instead, by 1850 the Taney Court was even more popular than the Marshall Court had been and the Chief Justice was praised by men of all political persuasions. All this would change when the Court confronted the issue of SLAVERY.

Adjudicating the constitutional position of slavery fell mainly to the Taney Court; there was no escape. Slavery was the foundation of the southern economy, a source of property worth billions, a social institution that shaped the cultural values of an entire section and the politics of the whole nation. Moreover, it was an integral part of the Constitution, which the Court had to interpret. At the same time, it was, of all the issues facing the antebellum Court, least amenable to a rational legal solution—and in this respect, it foreshadowed social issues like abortion and AFFIRMATIVE ACTION which have troubled the contemporary Court. No other single factor so much accounts for the divisions on the Taney Court or its inability to clearly demarcate power in the federal system.

Given the slavery question's explosive nature, the Justices not surprisingly tried to avoid confronting it directly. Thus the obfuscation in *Groves v. Slaughter* (1841), where the issue was whether a provision in the Mississippi Constitution prohibiting the importation of slaves for sale after 1833 illegally encroached upon federal power over interstate commerce. The Court circumvented this issue by ruling that the state constitutional clause in question was not self-activating—a position that, while avoiding trouble for the Court, also guaranteed the collection of millions of dollars of outstanding debts owed slave traders and in effect put the judicial seal of approval on the interstate slave trade. The Court also dodged the substantive issue in STRADER V. GRAHAM (1851), which raised the question whether slaves who resided in Kentucky had become free by virtue of their temporary residence in the free state of Ohio. The Court refused jurisdiction on the ground that Kentucky law reasserted itself over the slaves on their return, so that no federal question was involved.

Where the substantive question could not be side-stepped, the Court aimed to decide cases on narrow grounds and in such a way as to please both North and South. Thus in *The Amistad* (1841), Justice Story ruled that Africans on their way to enslavement who escaped their Spanish captors were free by virtue of principles of international law and a close reading of the Treaty of 1794 with Spain. Extremists in neither section were pleased. Even less were they content with Story's efforts to juggle sectional differences, morality, and objective adjudication in PRIGG V. PENNSYLVANIA (1842). There the question was whether and to what extent states were allowed to pass PERSONAL LIBERTY LAWS protecting the rights of free Negroes in rendition cases. The South was pleased when

Story declared the Pennsylvania liberty law of 1826 to be a violation of the constitutional and statutory obligation to return fugitive slaves. He went on to say, with his eye on northern opinion (and with doubtful support from a majority on the Court), that the power over fugitives belonged exclusively to the federal government and that states were not obliged to cooperate in their return. The decision encouraged northern states to pass personal liberty laws but also necessitated the more stringent federal fugitive slave law of 1850. Both developments fueled sectional conflict. (See FUGITIVE SLAVERY.)

The Court's strategy of avoidance aimed to keep slavery on the state level where the Constitution had put it, but the slavery question would not stay put. What brought it forth politically and legally as a national question was SLAVERY IN THE TERRITORIES, a problem which confronted the Court and the nation in *Dred Scott*. The nominal issue in that famous case was whether a Negro slave named Scott, who had resided in the free state of Illinois and the free territory of Minnesota (made free by the MISSOURI COMPROMISE of 1820) and who returned to the slave state of Missouri, could sue in the federal courts. Behind this jurisdictional issue lay the explosive political question of whether Congress could prohibit slavery in the territories, or to put it another way, whether the Constitution guaranteed it there. The future of slavery itself was on the line.

The first inclination of the Justices when they confronted the case early in 1856 was to continue the strategy of avoidance by applying *Strader v. Graham* (1851); by that precedent Scott would have become a slave on his return to Missouri with no right to sue in the federal courts. This compromise was abandoned: in part because of pressure from President JAMES BUCHANAN and Congress; in part because northern Justices McLean and Curtis planned to confront the whole issue in dissent; in part because the proslave, pro-South wing of the Court (led by Taney and Wayne) wanted to silence the abolitionists by putting the Constitution itself behind slavery in the territories; in part because the Justices pridefully believed they could put the troublesome question to rest and save the Union.

Taney's was the majority opinion so far as one could be gleaned from the cacophony of separate opinions and dissents. It was totally prosouthern and brutally racist: Scott could not sue in the federal courts because he was not a citizen of the United States. He was not a citizen because national CITIZENSHIP followed state citizenship, and in 1787 the states had looked upon blacks as racially inferior (which the states in fact did) and unqualified for citizenship (which several states did not). Scott's argument that he was free by virtue of residence in a free state was wrong, said Taney, because of *Strader* (which had been relied upon by the Supreme Court of Missouri); Scott's

argument that residence in a free territory made him free carried no weight because Congress had no authority to prohibit slavery in the territories—an assertion that ignored seventy years of constitutional practice and permitted Taney to set forth the SUBSTANTIVE DUE PROCESS theory of the Fifth Amendment against the TAKING OF PROPERTY. Scott was still a slave. Congress could not prohibit slavery in the territories, because the Constitution guaranteed it there; neither, as the creatures of Congress, could territorial legislatures prohibit slavery as claimed by proponents of the doctrine of POPULAR SOVEREIGNTY. Taney's Constitution was for whites only.

Instead of saving the Union the decision brought it closer to civil war and put the Court itself in jeopardy. In effect, the decision outlawed the basic principle of the Republican party (opposition to the extension of slavery in the territories), forcing that party to denounce the Court. The Democratic party, the best hope for political compromise, was now split between a southern wing (which in 1860 chose the certainty of *Dred Scott* over the vagueness of popular sovereignty) and northern antislavery forces who, if they did not defect to the Republicans, went down to defeat with STEPHEN DOUGLAS and popular sovereignty. Sectional hatred intensified and the machinery of political compromise was seriously undercut—along with the prestige of the Court. From its peak of popularity in 1850 the Taney Court descended to an all-time low. After SECESSION it served only the section of the Union that ignored *Dred Scott* entirely, condemned the Court as a tool of southern expansionism, and looked upon the Chief Justice as an arch-traitor to liberty and national union.

Fortunately, these disabilities were not permanent. Northern hatred focused less on the Court as an institution and more on the particular decision of *Dred Scott*, which was obliterated by the THIRTEENTH and FOURTEENTH AMENDMENTS. *Dred Scott* seemed less important, too, after President Lincoln "Republicanized" the Court with new appointments (five, including a new Chief Justice who had been an abolitionist). More important, the Court brought itself into harmony with the northern war effort by doing what the Supreme Court has always done in wartime: deferring to the political branches of government and bending law to military necessity. Sometimes the Court deferred by acting (as in the PRIZE CASES of 1863 where it permitted the President to exercise WAR POWERS and still not recognize the belligerent status of the Confederacy) and sometimes it deferred by not acting (as when it refused to interfere with the broad use of martial law during the war).

The Taney Court not only survived but it also salvaged its essential powers—and with time even a grudging respect from historians. The memory of *Dred Scott* could not be totally exorcised, of course, but it diminished along with the idealism of the war years and with the recognition that the racism of the opinion was shared by a majority of white Americans. In any case, the reform accomplishments of the Taney Court helped to balance the reactionary ones. Its modest style of judging fit the new democratic age. Through its decisions ran a new appreciation of the democratic nature and reform potential of state action and a tacit recognition as well of the growing maturity of legislative government. The Court's pragmatic federalism, while it could support the evil of slavery, also embodied a tradition of cultural pluralism, local responsibility, and suspicion of power. This it did without destroying the foundations of constitutional nationalism established by the Marshall Court. Change is the essence of American experience. The Taney Court accepted this irresistible premise and accommodated the Constitution to it. The adjustment was often untidy, but the Court's preference for process over substance looked to the modern age and prefigured the main direction of American constitutional law.

R. KENT NEWMYER
(1986)

Bibliography

COVER, ROBERT M.   1975   *Justice Accused: Antislavery and the Judicial Process.* New Haven: Yale University Press.

FEHRENBACHER, DON E.   1978   *The Dred Scott Case: Its Significance in American Law and Politics.* New York: Oxford University Press.

FRANKFURTER, FELIX   1937   *The Commerce Clause under Marshall, Taney and Waite.* Chapel Hill: University of North Carolina Press.

HARRIS, ROBERT J.   1957   Chief Justice Taney: Prophet of Reform and Reaction. *Vanderbilt Law Review* 10:227–257.

KUTLER, STANLEY   1971   *Privilege and Creative Destruction: The Charles River Bridge Case.* Philadelphia: J. B. Lippincott.

SWISHER, CARL B.   1974   *The Taney Period, 1836–1864.* Volume V of *The Oliver Wendell Holmes Devise History of the Supreme Court of the United States.* New York: Macmillan.

WARREN, CHARLES   1926   *The Supreme Court in United States History,* Vol. 2. New and revised ed. Boston: Little, Brown.

## TARIFF ACT
### 4 Stat. 270 (1828)

Known as the "Tariff of Abominations," this act was designed to embarrass JOHN QUINCY ADAMS and help ANDREW JACKSON win the Presidency. Jacksonians controlling the House Committee on Manufactures wrote a tariff with excessively high duties for iron, hemp, flax, and numerous other raw materials. The bill's authors believed Adams's New England supporters would have to oppose the bill,

and that the failure to pass a tariff would cost Adams the Middle States and the election. When New Englanders tried to amend the bill they were voted down by a coalition of southern and Middle State representatives organized by MARTIN VAN BUREN. The plan ultimately failed when representatives from everywhere but the South voted for the bill. Legislatures in South Carolina, Georgia, Mississippi, and Virginia denounced the act. JOHN C. CALHOUN anonymously wrote the South Carolina EXPOSITION AND PROTEST which laid out a theory of state NULLIFICATION of federal laws. While not adopting the Exposition, the South Carolina legislature printed 5,000 copies for distribution and declared the tariff unconstitutional. Although nullification was defeated at this juncture, and the tariff was amended in 1832, the 1828 act set the stage for the nullification crisis of 1832–1833.

PAUL FINKELMAN
(1986)

Bibliography

FREEHLING, WILLIAM W.   1965   *Prelude to Civil War: The Nullification Controversy in South Carolina, 1816–1836.* New York: Harper & Row.

## TAXATION

See: State and Local Government Taxation; State Taxation of Commerce; State Tax Incentives and Subsidies to Business; Taxing and Spending Powers

## TAXATION WITHOUT REPRESENTATION

Taxation without representation was the primary underlying cause of the AMERICAN REVOLUTION. Taxation by consent, through representatives chosen by local electors, is a fundamental principle of American CONSTITUTIONALISM. From the colonial period, REPRESENTATION had been actual: a legislator was the deputy of his local electors. He represented a particular geographic constituency, and like his electors he had to meet local residence requirements. Thus, representation of the body politic and government by consent of the governed were structurally connected in American thought.

Taxation without representation deprived one of his property contrary to the first principles of the SOCIAL COMPACT and of the British constitution. No Englishmen endorsed the constitutionality of taxation without representation; that it violated FUNDAMENTAL LAW was the teaching of the CONFIRMATIO CARTARUM, the PETITION OF RIGHT, and the BILL OF RIGHTS. Englishmen claimed, however, that

Parliament "virtually" represented the colonies—every member of Parliament represented the English nation, not a locality—and therefore could raise a revenue in America. Rejecting the concept of virtual representation, Americans insisted that they were not and could not be represented in Parliament. The argument of virtual representation implicitly conceded the American contention that taxation was the function of a representative body, not merely a legislative or sovereign body. American legislatures, facing parliamentary taxation for the first times in 1764 and 1765, resolved that Parliament had no constitutional authority to raise a revenue in America. Pennsylvania's assembly, for example, resolved "that the taxation of the people of this province, by any other . . . than . . . their representatives in assembly is unconstitutional." Similarly, the STAMP ACT CONGRESS resolved that the colonies could not be constitutionally taxed except by their own assemblies. The resolutions of the colonies, individually and collectively, claimed an exemption from all parliamentary taxation including customs duties and trade regulations whose purpose was to raise revenue.

The American claims were not simply concocted to meet the unprecedented taxation levied by Parliament in 1764 and after. The experience of Virginia, the first colony, was typical. Its charter guaranteed the rights of Englishmen, which Virginia assumed included the exclusive right of its own representative assembly to tax its inhabitants; the assembly so declared in a statute of 1624. In 1652 planters in a county not represented in the assembly protested the imposition of a tax. In 1674, when Virginia sought confirmation from the crown of its exclusive right to tax its inhabitants, the crown's attorney in England endorsed "the right of Virginians, as well as other Englishmen, not to be taxed but by their consent, expressed by their representatives." The Committee for Foreign Plantations and the Privy Council approved, too, but the king withheld approval because of Bacon's Rebellion. Virginia nevertheless persisted in its position. In 1717 the imposition of a royal postal fee produced, in the words of the colony's royal governor, "a great clamor. . . . The people were made to believe that Parliament could not levy any tax (for so they called the rates of postage) here without consent of the General Assembly." In 1753, when Virginia's governor imposed a trivial fee for the use of his seal on each land patent, the assembly lectured him on the theme that subjects cannot be "deprived of the least part of their property but by their own consent: Upon this excellent principle is our constitution funded." The history of any colony would yield similar incidents, showing how entrenched were the claims that Americans advanced when Parliament first sought to tax the colonies.

When the Declaratory Act of 1766 claimed for Parliament a power to "legislate" for America "in all cases whatsoever," some members of Parliament argued the American position that Parliament could tax only in its representative capacity and therefore could not tax America. WILLIAM PITT and Lord Camden (CHARLES PRATT) endorsed that position. Pitt denounced virtual representation as a contemptible idea and declared that taxation "is no part of the governing or legislative power"; he also distinguished taxes levied for revenue from trade regulations that incidentally but not deliberately produced some revenue. The dominant British position, however, assumed that because taxation was inseparable from SOVEREIGNTY, Parliament as the sovereign legislature in the empire had the power to tax in matters of imperial concern, even though the tax fell on unrepresented members of the empire. That position provoked Americans to distinguish the powers belonging to local governments (the idea of FEDERALISM); to develop the concepts of LIMITED GOVERNMENT, fundamental law, and a CONSTITUTION as supreme law over all government; and to frame written constitutions that enumerated the powers of government.

LEONARD W. LEVY
(1986)

Bibliography

BAILYN, BERNARD 1967 The Ideological Origins of the American Revolution. Cambridge, Mass.: Harvard University Press.
MORGAN, EDMUND S. 1976 The Challenge of the American Revolution. Chap. 1. New York: W. W. Norton.
MORTON, RICHARD L. 1960 Colonial Virginia, 2 vols. Chapel Hill: University of North Carolina Press.

# TAX COURT OF THE UNITED STATES

When the Internal Revenue Service determines a deficiency, a taxpayer who disagrees can either pay the additional tax and sue for a refund in a federal district court or withhold payment and petition the Tax Court to set aside the deficiency. Tax Court decisions are reviewed in the UNITED STATES COURTS OF APPEALS.

The Tax Court, until 1942 called the Board of Tax Appeals, was declared by Congress in 1970 to be a "court." It is not, however, a CONSTITUTIONAL COURT created under Article III, but a LEGISLATIVE COURT. Its members do not have life tenure but serve for fifteen-year terms.

KENNETH L. KARST
(1986)

# TAX CREDITS AND RELIGIOUS SCHOOLS

See: Government Aid to Religious Institutions

# TAXING AND SPENDING POWERS

A principal weakness of the ARTICLES OF CONFEDERATION was that Congress had no power of taxation. It could request the states to contribute their fair shares to the national treasury but it had no power to collect when, as often happened, the states did not pay. Hence, the first grant of power to Congress in the Constitution was to "have Power to Lay and collect Taxes, Duties, Imposts and Excises, to pay the Debts and provide for the common Defense and general Welfare of the United States; but all Duties, Imposts and Excises shall be uniform throughout the United States." The Constitution also imposed two other limitations. Congress could not tax exports nor lay a "Capitation, or other direct, Tax" unless "in Proportion to the Census or Enumeration herein before directed to be taken."

The direct limitations on taxing power pose few problems. Congress does not impose capitation or property taxes, which would be direct taxes and require apportionment among the states in accordance with population. Other taxes must be uniform—which means that the same subject or activity must be taxed at the same rate wherever it is found. Congress, like the states, cannot tax exports to foreign countries.

More difficult problems have risen because taxes not only raise revenue but also regulate. A tax on liquor may be designed to raise money but also to discourage consumption. A deduction for interest in computing income tax encourages home ownership. A tax may be high enough to virtually stop the production and sale of a particular product. Before the Civil War the federal government derived most of its revenue from the customs and in many years had no internal revenue beyond that. But beginning with the Civil War, Congress expanded the scope of federal taxation at a time when the Supreme Court had fairly restrictive views as to congressional powers to regulate local activities. The question became how far Congress could use taxation to achieve policies that were forbidden to it through direct regulation.

When Congress imposed a ten percent tax on local banknotes for the purpose of achieving a federal government monopoly in the issuing of currency, the Court in VEAZIE BANK V. FENNO (1869) indicated that the tax was constitutional but said that in any event no regulatory problem was presented; Congress did have an independent MONETARY POWER, and the tax was merely a means of implementing it. Thirty-five years later the Court faced the problem more directly. Congress had imposed a ten cents per pound tax on oleomargarine that was colored and only one-quarter cent per pound if it was white. The Court in MCCRAY V. UNITED STATES (1904) said that even though Congress did not have the power to pass a statute forbidding the sale of colored oleomargarine, it could still tax it and the courts would not interfere merely on the grounds that the tax was too high. And the Court also held that Congress could impose a tax on distributing narcotic drugs and include in the same statute regulations as to how such drugs were to be distributed. The Court in UNITED STATES V. DOREMUS (1919) said that a tax was not invalid just because it had regulatory as well as taxation purposes and that the regulations attached to the tax were constitutional as facilitating the collection of the tax.

But in the Child Labor Tax Case (1922) the Court concluded that a tax might really be a regulation and thus invalid. A federal statute prohibiting interstate transportation of goods made by child labor had been held to exceed Congress's power under the COMMERCE CLAUSE in HAMMER V. DAGENHART (1918). So Congress imposed a tax of ten percent of the net profits for the year for any manufacturing business that employed children within certain age limits. Here, the court said, the challenge was not merely that the tax was too high. Rather, Congress had imposed a regulation and used the tax as a penalty for violation. "[A] court must be blind not to see that the so-called tax is imposed to stop the employment of children within the age limits prescribed. Its prohibitory and regulatory effect and purpose are palpable." In *United States v. Constantine* (1935) the Court similarly held invalid a special tax of $1,000 upon anyone dealing in liquor in a state or locality where such dealing was illegal. The Court said that the law clearly was not a tax but rather a penalty for violating state law.

In a series of later cases, however, the Court upheld the taxes. A heavy tax on sale of special weapons such as sawed-off shotguns was upheld in SONZINSKY V. UNITED STATES (1937). In *United States v. Sanchez* (1950) and *United States v. Kahriger* (1953) the Court upheld taxes on narcotics and gambling in which taxpayers were required to register with the federal government, even though that registration would make it easier for the states to enforce their gambling and narcotics laws. In *Sanchez* the Court said: "It is beyond serious question that a tax does not cease to be valid merely because it regulates, discourages, or even definitely deters the activities taxed. . . . The principle applies even though the revenue obtained is obviously negligible, . . . or the revenue purpose of the tax may be secondary. . . . Nor does a statute necessarily fall because it touches on activities which Congress might not otherwise regulate. . . . These principles are controlling here. The tax in question is a legitimate exercise of the taxing power despite its collateral regulatory purpose and effect." Later, in MARCHETTI V. UNITED STATES (1968), the Court eliminated the use of the taxing power to compel violators of state laws to register with the federal government on the grounds that it violates the

RIGHT AGAINST SELF-INCRIMINATION. And since the power of the federal government to regulate has received such major expansion in modern times, there is little need to use the taxing power to expand federal powers. Even though the Child Labor Tax Case may still be good law in defining when a tax ceases to be a tax and becomes a regulation, it is of minor importance. Congress will almost always have power to regulate and can cast its regulation in the form of a tax.

The SPENDING POWER has also raised constitutional questions. Before the early 1900s, Congress spent money chiefly to defray its routine powers of government. It made a few grants to the states to encourage the construction of roads and universities, granting the money outright with no matching requirements or federal supervision. In 1902 the grants amounted to only seven million dollars per year. Soon, however, Congress began to see that grants could be used to encourage states to take action meeting federal standards even with respect to parts of the economy then thought to be outside congressional power.

The SHEPPARD-TOWNER MATERNITY ACT of 1921 provided for federal grants to states that would agree to spend the money for reducing maternal and infant mortality. Massachusetts, which had refused the grants, and Frothingham, a citizen and taxpayer, brought suits. The Supreme Court in *Massachusetts v. Mellon* and FROTHINGHAM V. MELLON (1923) held that neither had STANDING to litigate the issue. Massachusetts had no real interest at stake, for it had refused the grant. Frothingham had no standing as a taxpayer because her interest in the funds spent was miniscule and shared with all other federal taxpayers. The result of this suit was to make most government spending programs impossible to challenge in court.

As a result, it was not until 1936 that a major question as to the scope of the spending power was settled. Congress has power to levy taxes "to pay the Debts and provide for the common Defence and general Welfare of the United States." What does the GENERAL WELFARE CLAUSE mean? JAMES MADISON had argued that money could be spent only to carry out the other powers given to Congress—that there was not, in essence, any additional power granted by the general welfare language. ALEXANDER HAMILTON had said that the clause granted a substantive power to tax and spend so long as it was for the general welfare of the United States.

The Court finally had an opportunity to decide the issue in 1936 in UNITED STATES V. BUTLER. The AGRICULTURE ADJUSTMENT ACT OF 1933 had provided for agreements between the secretary of agriculture and farmers to reduce acreage in exchange for benefit payments. The money for the payments came from a tax levied on the processors of the commodity concerned with all of the tax proceeds directed to that purpose. The Court held first that the pro-

cessors upon whom the tax was levied did have standing to challenge the expenditure, because they paid a substantial tax earmarked for that expenditure. Next, the Court adopted the Hamilton position that the power to spend might be exercised for the general welfare and was not limited to the other direct grants of legislative power. Finally, the Court said it did not have to decide whether the expenditure in this case was for the general welfare, because this law was a regulation, not an expenditure, and invalid as going beyond congressional regulatory power.

The *Butler* interpretation of the spending power, however, soon became the basis to uphold expenditures. In HELVERING V. DAVIS (1937) the Court upheld the SOCIAL SECURITY ACT, concluding that expenditures for old age pensions were expenditures for the general welfare. And in BUCKLEY V. VALEO (1976) the Court held that expenditures of funds to finance campaigns of presidential candidates was valid as an expenditure for the general welfare. (See CAMPAIGN FINANCING.) The Court said: "Congress was legislating for the "general welfare'—to reduce the deleterious influence of large contributions on our political process, to facilitate communication by candidates with the electorate, and to free candidates from the rigors of fundraising. . . . Congress has concluded that the means are "necessary and proper' to promote the general welfare, and we thus decline to find this legislation without the grant of power in Art. I, § 8."

The use of grants to states as a means of federal regulation has proceeded apace, almost totally free of challenge by the courts. Only where the challenge is based on the ESTABLISHMENT OF RELIGION has the Court recognized standing to challenge by taxpayers. And that holding, in FLAST V. COHEN (1968), is not absolute, as was shown by VALLEY FORGE CHRISTIAN COLLEGE V. AMERICANS UNITED FOR SEPARATION OF CHURCH AND STATE (1982). The seven million dollars of such grants in 1902 had risen to seven billion in 1960 and to over one hundred billion in the early 1980s— about one-third percent of state and local receipts from their own sources. Again, however, the constitutional issues have lost their former importance. If the expenditure can be said to be for the general welfare, the intrusion of the federal government into a local area does not matter. Because congressional powers to spend for the general welfare and to regulate under the commerce clause are so broad, there is little prospect of a successful constitutional challenge to federal spending.

Both as to taxation and as to expenditure, no major constitutional problems remain. Congress has such broad regulatory powers that it no longer needs to attempt to get around power limitations by using taxation and expenditure. These methods of regulation are used today as convenient devices for accomplishing goals within congressional power. The major limitations on them are political. If the increase in federal grants to states appears to be slowing and if some recent Presidents have talked about a New Federalism policy to decrease such federal spending, the reasons lie not in constitutional limitations but in governmental policy.

EDWARD L. BARRETT, JR.
(1986)

(SEE ALSO: *Direct and Indirect Taxes; Economic Regulation; Import-Export Clause; Impoundment of Funds; National Police Power.*)

Bibliography

GRANT, J. A. C. 1936 Commerce, Production, and the Fiscal Powers of Congress. *Yale Law Journal* 45:751–778.
POWELL, THOMAS R. 1922 Child Labor, Congress and the Constitution. *North Carolina Law Review* 1:61–81.
TRIBE, LAURENCE H. 1978 *American Constitutional Law.* Pages 225–227, 244–250. Mineola, N.Y.: Foundation Press.

# TAXING AND SPENDING POWERS
## (Update)

The distinction between real and sham taxes (so-called taxes that, in substance, are really punishments) was used in BAILEY V. DREXEL FURNITURE CO. (1922) (also known as the Child Labor Tax Case) and *United States v. Constantine* (1935) to vindicate the principle of enumerated federal powers. The Supreme Court applied this distinction again in *Department of Revenue of Montana v. Kurth Ranch* (1994) to invalidate a state's assessment of a tax on possession of prohibited drugs after the possessor had been separately prosecuted for the crime of possession. Holding the "tax" really a penalty, the Court held that assessing it after the possession had already been the subject of criminal prosecution violated the guarantee against DOUBLE JEOPARDY.

To mark the always debatable boundary between real and sham taxes, the Court in *Kurth Ranch* employed some of the same factors used in *Constantine* and the Child Labor Tax Case. Montana's drug possession "tax" was extremely high in amount (a factor not determinative by itself), and the "tax" was conditioned on the possession's being a crime. This was different from "mixed-motive taxes," imposed not only to raise revenue but also to discourage the activity taxed. With cigarette taxes, for example, deterrence of smoking might be a goal, but that goal is moderated not only by the desire to raise revenue but also by other objectives, such as permitting satisfaction of consumer demand and avoiding severe detriment to tobacco industry employment. The Court said, however, that "when the taxed activity is completely forbidden" the

evident motivation is not so mixed, and the so-called tax ceases to be justifiable as a revenue measure because "the legitimate revenue-raising purpose that might support such a tax could be equally well served by increasing the fine imposed upon conviction." When a government "taxes" an activity that is completely unlawful, the "tax" is not a revenue device, but rather a penalty to enforce the prohibition.

The Court in *Kurth Ranch* also deemed it significant that the "tax" was for possessing property that could not be possessed lawfully and that had been confiscated and destroyed before the tax was assessed. "A tax on 'possession' of goods that no longer exist and that the taxpayer never lawfully possessed has an unmistakable punitive character," the Court said.

In the past, one could remark that this distinction between real taxes and "taxes" that amount to regulatory penalties is "of minor importance," given Congress's LEGISLATIVE POWER over INTERSTATE COMMERCE. However, the Court began reemphasizing the federal government's ENUMERATED POWERS limitations in UNITED STATES V. LÓPEZ (1995). If this emphasis continues, the distinction between real and sham taxes might become important for federal laws again. Even though *Kurth Ranch* involved only state LEGISLATION, it is notable for reinforcing the Justice ROBERT H. JACKSON description of a tax in *United States v. Kahriger* (1953) as a "good-faith revenue measure," in contrast to what Justice FELIX FRANKFURTER characterized in the same case as regulation "merely . . . wrapped . . . in the verbal celophane of a revenue measure."

Spending power DOCTRINE has continued to mature as the ramifications of ALEXANDER HAMILTON's classic view of that power have gradually been recognized. For example, in PENNHURST STATE SCHOOL V. HALDERMAN (1981) the Court observed that "legislation enacted pursuant to the spending power is much in the nature of a contract: as consideration for federal funds, the States [or other grantees] agree to comply with federally imposed conditions." Spending conditions thus are enforcible not as legislation (by virtue of some lawmaking power), but rather as contracts (by virtue of consideration and consent). Hamilton understood the very practical point that Congress may spend even for things beyond the scope of its powers to legislate: Because "money talks," federal payments (and promises made in exchange for federal payments) can strongly influence things that the federal government has no power to govern. JAMES MADISON's mistake was his failure to distinguish between governing behavior and inducing it by payment.

Even the 1937 decisions upholding the SOCIAL SECURITY ACT, including STEWARD MACHINE COMPANY V. DAVIS (1937) and HELVERING V. DAVIS (1937), repeated Madison's mistake by assuming that in order to uphold social welfare spending, relief of the elderly or unemployed (for example) must be considered an "end legitimately national," one "within the scope of national policy and power." Not until the following decade did the Court fully grasp the point of Hamilton's spending power thesis: The Justices held in *Oklahoma v. United States Civil Service Commission* (1947) that by grant condition Congress could influence something outside the scope of any national power, a grantee's policy regarding its own employees.

In the *Pennhurst* case, the contract character of spending conditions led the Court to conclude that in order to be enforcible, conditions must be clear enough in advance "that we can fairly say that the State [or other grantee] could make an informed choice." Where the condition is clear, however, the recipient's acceptance makes it contractually binding regardless of whether Congress would have constitutional power to impose it legislatively. Thus in *South Dakota v. Dole* (1987) the Supreme Court upheld a condition curtailing highway funds to states refusing to raise the drinking age, "[e]ven if Congress might lack the power to impose a national minimum drinking age directly." However, the Court has explained that because their force derives from contract rather than legislative competence, spending conditions are enforcible only against "those who are in a position to accept or reject those obligations as a part of the decision whether or not to 'receive' federal funds."

Persisting confusion about the spending power can produce anomalous results. For example, because they depend on contract rather than legislative power, spending conditions cannot evoke the SUPREMACY CLAUSE; yet as late as 1988 the Court was uncritically assuming that conditions in grants to individuals and local governments could trump laws of states that were not contracting parties.

Similarly, sometimes a "germaneness" restriction on spending conditions has been asserted. Following her DISSENTING OPINION in *South Dakota v. Dole*, Justice SANDRA DAY O'CONNOR wrote for six Justices in NEW YORK V. UNITED STATES (1992) that "conditions must . . . bear some relationship to the purpose of the federal spending." If this statement means that conditions must relate to some enumerated power, it reiterates Madison's error. On the other hand, if this germaneness rule means that every condition must pertain to an objective of the particular spending program involved (even though, as Hamilton understood, spending objectives need not pertain to any enumerated power), it is supported neither by constitutional text nor by logic or PRECEDENT, and it imperils conditions like those against RACIAL DISCRIMINATION and SEX DISCRIMINATION, which Congress has attached to all spending programs regardless of program objectives. Calls for germaneness disclose a spending power doctrine that is not fully coherent.

One perennial source of confusion is misattributing the spending power to the taxing clause (which contains the "GENERAL WELFARE" phrase). Congress may spend not only tax proceeds, but also the proceeds of fines, sales, gifts, and investments. Money is property, and power to dispose of federal property resides in the legislative branch by virtue of the Constitution's Article IV. This power, however, is a prerogative of ownership, not of SOVEREIGNTY; the history of land grants has much to contribute toward full understanding of the spending power.

DAVID E. ENGDAHL
(2000)

(SEE ALSO: *Child Labor Tax Act.*)

Bibliography

ENGDAHL, DAVID E. 1994 The Spending Power. *Duke Law Journal* 44:1–109.

McCOY, THOMAS R. and FRIEDMAN, BARRY 1988 Conditional Spending: Federalism's Trojan Horse. *Supreme Court Review* 1988:85–127.

ROSENTHAL, ALBERT J. 1987 Conditional Federal Spending and the Constitution. *Stanford Law Review* 39:1103–1164.

# TAXPAYERS' AND CITIZENS' SUITS

Federal courts will rule on the merits of a legal claim only at the request of one with a "personal stake in the outcome of the controversy." As a corollary of this central, entrenched STANDING doctrine, the federal judiciary turns away attacks on the legality of government behavior by citizens suing only as such. The rule stems from a SEPARATION OF POWERS premise: that federal judges should not review conduct of Congress or the Executive absent the need to protect a plaintiff from distinct personal injury. The rule has been applied mostly to reject challenges by United States citizens to acts of the political branches of the federal government, although it also appears to bar federal court suits by state or local citizens against acts of their governments. In essence, the citizen interest in lawful governance is viewed as an ideological, not a personal, interest, an interest best left to political rather than judicial resolution. Nonetheless, if a plaintiff can show concrete individual injury, as in SIERRA CLUB V. MORTON (1972), the public interest may then be argued in behalf of the personal claim, even if the primary motive for suing is not the personal but the citizen interest.

The law of taxpayer standing is more elaborate, because taxpayers' suits are sometimes deemed sufficiently personal to permit standing and sometimes rejected as disguised citizens' suits. Taxpayers contesting their own tax liability have a "personal stake," of course, but such an individualized interest is less clear for taxpayers disputing how tax revenues are spent. In FROTHINGHAM V. MELLON

(1923) the Supreme Court found the pecuniary interest of a federal taxpayer in federal spending too remote to justify JUDICIAL REVIEW of congressional appropriations, but it re-affirmed its previous approval of federal court suits by local taxpayers attacking local spending programs. In FLAST V. COHEN (1968) the Court created an exception, allowing federal taxpayers to challenge congressional spending as an ESTABLISHMENT OF RELIGION because the establishment clause gives taxpayers a special interest in challenging the use of tax dollars to support religion. The dissent objected that the Court was recognizing standing to bring a "public action" having no effect on the suing taxpayer's financial interest.

Since *Flast*, the Court has denied standing to federal taxpayers who raised other constitutional objections in *United States v. Richardson* (1974) and *Schlesinger v. Reservists Committee* (1974). And in VALLEY FORGE CHRISTIAN COLLEGE V. AMERICANS UNITED (1982), a decision that substantially undermines the premise of *Flast*, the Court denied standing to taxpayers who raised establishment clause objections, but challenged federal distribution of surplus property rather than congressional appropriations of money. Even at the state taxpayer level, invoking the establishment clause will not suffice if the claim is not of government financial support of religion but of regulatory support, as in DOREMUS V. BOARD OF EDUCATION (1952). In short, a federal court will recognize taxpayer standing only when there is a tangible financial connection between a local or state taxpayer's interest and government spending, or when a local, state, or federal taxpayer challenges legislative appropriations on establishment clause grounds.

The federal judiciary's rejection of citizen suits and most taxpayer attacks on spending reflects a view that the power of judicial review is only a by-product of the need to apply law, including constitutional law, to decide the rights of those claiming injury. To entertain public actions would be to expand judicial scrutiny of acts of the elected branches of government—usurpation that might bring retaliation, in the eyes of those who take this view. For those who think judicial review is founded on a broader obligation to assure government adherence to the Constitution, such an expanded scrutiny would be desirable. If Congress were to authorize the federal courts to take jurisdiction over public actions, the Supreme Court probably would not find Article III's "case" or "controversy" requirement an insurmountable barrier. But the Court has always been reluctant to entertain public actions on its own authority.

JONATHAN D. VARAT
(1986)

Bibliography

WRIGHT, CHARLES A.; MILLER, ARTHUR R.; and COOPER, EDWARD H. 1984 *Federal Practice and Procedure.* Vol. 13:634–663. St. Paul, Minn.: West Publishing Co.

# TAYLOR, JOHN
## (1753–1824)

John Taylor of Caroline read law in the office of his uncle, EDMUND PENDLETON. He became involved early in Virginia revolutionary politics and was a delegate to the FIRST CONTINENTAL CONGRESS. He served as an Army officer and almost continuously as a member of the House of Delegates (1779–1785). In the legislature he supported a measure to end ESTABLISHMENT OF RELIGION in Virginia.

As a delegate to the state convention in 1788 Taylor opposed RATIFICATION OF THE CONSTITUTION, which lacked a BILL OF RIGHTS, gave too much power to the general government, and was insufficiently republican. Even so, he involved himself immediately in the politics of the new government, becoming the foremost publicist of Jeffersonian democracy. Both in the SENATE (1792–1794) and in the public press he was a leading opponent of the economic policies of ALEXANDER HAMILTON. In the controversy over the ALIEN AND SEDITION ACTS, Taylor introduced the Virginia Resolutions (written by JAMES MADISON) in the state legislature. (See VIRGINIA AND KENTUCKY RESOLUTIONS.)

An ardent supporter of THOMAS JEFFERSON, Taylor returned briefly to the Senate in 1803. He supported the TWELFTH AMENDMENT and defended the constitutionality of the LOUISIANA PURCHASE when even the President doubted it. Taylor broke with the Republican party over the War of 1812 and the renomination of President Madison, but he did not deviate from its principles. In his final term in the Senate (1822–1824) and in his last books Taylor denounced the growing power of the federal judiciary, JOHN MARSHALL's decision in MCCULLOCH V. MARYLAND (1819), and HENRY CLAY'S AMERICAN SYSTEM, with its INTERNAL IMPROVEMENTS and protective tariff. He advocated STRICT CONSTRUCTION of constitutional grants of power to the federal government.

Taylor saw himself as the defender of a liberty in constant danger and a republic in perpetual crisis. He thought that, in every generation, the American people were presented with a choice between the political principles and practice of Thomas Jefferson and those of JOHN ADAMS—the former conducive to, and the latter destructive of, self-government and public happiness. He believed that the civic virtue of farmers, tradesmen, and professional persons was the indispensable basis of free institutions; and for him banks and corporations raised the specter of economic oligarchy, undermining both that virtue and those institutions. Big government was the creature and ally of big business; and bigness was the enemy of liberty and equality. Incongruously, for all his concern with liberty and equality he unqualifiedly supported black slavery. Taylor is probably best known as a theorist of STATES' RIGHTS: his ideas bridged the gap between the Virginia and Kentucky Resolutions and JOHN C. CALHOUN's doctrine of NULLIFICATION.

Taylor's most important books are *An Enquiry into the Principles and Policies of the Government of the United States* (1814), a comprehensive statement of the political theory of agrarian democracy, and *Construction Construed and Constitutions Vindicated* (1820), an attack on the expansion of federal court JURISDICTION and the use of JUDICIAL REVIEW to reduce the independence of the states.

DENNIS J. MAHONEY
(1986)

Bibliography

HILL, CHARLES W.   1977   *The Political Theory of John Taylor of Caroline.* Rutherford, N.J.: Fairleigh Dickinson University Press.

LLOYD, THOMAS GORDON   1973   *The Danger Not Yet Over: The Political Thought and Practice of John Taylor of Caroline.* Ph.D. dissertation, Claremont Graduate School.

## TAYLOR, ZACHARY
### (1784–1850)

A professional soldier and hero of the Mexican War, Zachary Taylor was elected President as a WHIG in 1848. A moderate on most issues, Taylor was a Louisiana slaveholder who was politically close to New Yorkers Thurlow Weed and WILLIAM SEWARD. Taylor opposed any interference with slavery in the South but also opposed opening the Mexican Cession to slavery. Similarly, he opposed the WILMOT PROVISO but advocated immediate admission of California and New Mexico as free states. He opposed the COMPROMISE OF 1850 and would probably have vetoed most of its provisions, had he not died in July 1850.

PAUL FINKELMAN
(1986)

Bibliography

HAMILTON, HOLMAN   1941   *Zachary Taylor: Soldier of the Republic.* Indianapolis: Bobbs-Merrill.

## *TAYLOR v. LOUISIANA*
### 419 U.S. 522 (1975)

Under Louisiana law women were selected for jury service only when they explicitly volunteered for duty; men were selected irrespective of their desires. In *Hoyt v. Florida* (1961), the Supreme Court had employed a RATIONAL BASIS standard of review to uphold a similar law against DUE PROCESS and EQUAL PROTECTION attacks. In *Taylor,* however, the Court invalidated this jury selection system as a denial of the Sixth Amendment right of the accused to "a jury drawn from a fair cross section of the community." That the accused was male was irrelevant to this claim. The vote was 8–1; Justice WILLIAM H. REHNQUIST dissented, and Chief Justice WARREN E. BURGER concurred only in the result.

Writing for the other seven Justices, Justice BYRON R. WHITE declined to follow *Hoyt;* if the fair cross section requirement ever "permitted the almost total exclusion of women, this is not the case today." Women had entered the work force in large numbers, undermining their exemption "solely on their sex and the presumed role in the home." *Taylor* is not only an important JURY DISCRIMINATION precedent but also a strong judicial rejection of laws resting on stereotypical assumptions about "woman's role."

KENNETH L. KARST
(1986)

## TELEVISION

See: Broadcasting

## TEMPORAL LIMITS ON LAWMAKING POWERS

A republic derives its power from the people, and as JAMES MADISON declared in THE FEDERALIST #39 and #53, the persons elected to administer it hold office only "for a limited period" and enjoy no license to extend the length of their terms. Although in contemporary America such a concept seems almost beyond dispute, Madison's pronouncement marked a radical departure from English tradition.

By the Triennial Act of 1694 the English Parliament limited the term of Parliament to three years. In 1716, however, the members of Parliament, in their final year of service and concerned that elections might be perilous to the ruling party, repealed the Triennial Act. In its place they enacted the Septennial Act, by which the legal duration of the sitting Parliament was immediately extended to seven years. The powers of the incumbent members of the House of Commons were thus prolonged by four years. Although the English might have regarded this exercise of legislative authority as contemptuous or extravagant, they did not consider it ULTRA VIRES in a system constructed on the concept of parliamentary supremacy.

The United States Constitution rejects the cornerstone of legislative supremacy. The recognition of the citizenry as an external force from which all power originates severed the umbilical connection with English tradition. The Preamble's opening phrase, "We the people," is more than flashy prose. The legislators were transformed from the masters of the electorate to their servants. The people are the source of all power; the legislators are merely designated agents.

There is, as ALEXANDER HAMILTON pronounced in *The Federalist* #78, "no position which depends on clearer principles, than that every act of a delegated authority, contrary to the tenor of the commission under which it is exercised, is void." Agency may be limited in duration as well as scope. The Framers devoted considerable attention to the appropriate length of a representative's term of office. The decision to limit the terms of the members of the HOUSE OF REPRESENTATIVES to two years was prompted by a recognition that in order to ensure liberty, government must have an immediate dependence on, and intimate sympathy with, the people. Frequent elections, warned Madison in *The Federalist* #53, are "the only policy by which this dependence and sympathy can be effectively secured." Although the longer six-year term for senators was a concession to the need for some continuity and stability in government, the expiration of the terms of one-third of the body every two years provides a reminder of accountability (the dependence factor) and permits infusions of new directions from the electorate (the sympathy factor) at more frequent intervals.

Just as American legislatures lack the power to extend their terms beyond those set by their constitutive documents, they may not undermine the spirit of that document by "entrenching" their legislative efforts. Each election furnishes the electorate with an opportunity to provide new directions for its representatives. The process would be reduced to an exercise in futility were newly elected representatives bound by the policy choices of a prior generation of voters. The fundamental, although often debatable, assumption of American political life—that legislative action reflects current majoritarian preferences—could be finally laid to rest if shifting majorities were unable to alter prior majoritarian preferences.

Instances of legislative entrenchment rarely are the subjects of judicial decision. To begin with, most legislators share an understanding of the temporal limits of their authority. Of equal import, successor legislators usually find ways to outflank entrenched restrictions, but if they cannot, they may simply choose to ignore their predecessors' directives, safe in the knowledge that courts are unlikely to void their efforts. Nonetheless, the prohibition against entrenchment has been at the heart of numerous congressional debates.

The CLOTURE rule of the Senate requires the assent of a supermajority (sixty members) to terminate a filibuster. On more than eighty occasions since this rule's adoption, a majority of senators have unsuccessfully attempted to cut off debate and bring an issue to a vote. Such failures have often been followed by efforts to amend the cloture rule; but the supermajority requirement has been entrenched. Rule 32(2) of the Senate's Standing Rules explicitly mandates, "The rules of the Senate shall continue from one Congress to the next Congress unless they are changed *as provided in these rules*." Thus, any effort to change the cloture rule may itself be blocked by a filibuster. The defenders of this entrenchment argue that because each biennial election only affects one-third of the Senate's membership, the Senate is a continuing body capable of binding itself. Periodically, senators mount constitutional attacks against Rule 32(2) on the ground that no legislative body can so limit its successors. In 1957, Vice-President RICHARD M. NIXON, the Senate's presiding officer, announced his personal opinion that a rule limiting the right of the Senate's current majority to promulgate its own rules was unconstitutional. In the end, however, Nixon and his successors have left the ultimate issue of constitutionality with the membership of the Senate itself. Numerous votes of that body have rejected Nixon's constitutional assessment. Today an overwhelming majority of the senators are of the view that the "continuous" nature of the Senate permits this narrow exception to the rule against entrenchment.

Entrenchment issues also surround much of the constitutional AMENDING PROCESS. Thus, the binding power of legslative bodies has been at the heart of debates about (1) the power of Congress to extend time limits for RATIFICATION placed on a proposed constitutional amendment by a prior Congress; (2) the right of state legislature to rescind its predecessor's ratification vote; and (3) Congress's ability, by legislation, to establish the rules of operation for futrue constitutional conventions that might occur.

One of the few entrenchment issues to have received a judicial airing concerns the extent to which contractual commitments made by legislatures bind subsequent legislatures. The CONTRACT CLAUSE of the Constitution prohibits states from impairing the OBLIGATION OF CONTRACTS. There exists no evidence, however, that the Framers intended or expected the contract clause to be applied to obligations involving the state itself. In spite of this unequivocal history, Chief Justice JOHN MARSHALL, in FLETCHER V. PECK (1810), extended the reach of the contract clause to legislatively created obligations, finding it sufficient that the words of the Constitution drew no distinction between private and public contracts. The tension between *Fletcher's* extension of the contract clause and the temporal nature of lawmaking power was first clearly articulated by ROGER BROOKE TANEY during his tenure as ATTORNEY GENERAL. Legislatures, said Taney, "cannot bind the state by contract . . . beyond the scope of the authority granted them by their constituents." The power to limit contractually the legislative powers of successors, Taney asserted, is one that the agent cannot enjoy consistent with "the principles upon which our political institutions are founded." Even Marshall was mindful of the entrenchment implications of his interpretation. Recognizing that his reading potentially allowed legislatures to limit the power of their successors, he endeavored to draw a distinction between "general legislation" (which could not bind successor legislators) and "contracts" (which could). Marshall therefore concluded that when a law is in its nature a contract, vesting absolute rights, "a repeal of the law cannot devest those rights."

The dichotomy Marshall posited between general legislation and contracts matured in later years into a judicial understanding that at least some state action was beyond the reach of the contracting power. No body of representatives can bargain away the so-called POLICE POWER of the state. Thus, in STONE V. MISSISSIPPI (1880), the Supreme Court sustained a legislative revocation of its predecessor's grant of a twenty-five-year charter to operate a lottery, noting that the police power must remain a continuing power to be exercised "as the special exigencies of the moment may require." This limitation ultimately proved the contract clause's undoing as the exception swallowed the rule, and the contract clause faded from the judicial scene following the 1930s.

In the 1970s the Supreme Court temporarily resurrected the specter of contractual entrenchment. New Jersey and New York issued bonds in 1962 to construct bridges and tunnels, and promised bondholders that none of the tolls pledged to secure such bonds would be used for "any railroad purpose." By 1974, the public call for increased mass transit made such a commitment unwieldy. Massive toll increases were announced. A reserve fund was established for the bondholders, but in 1974 the commitment not to spend any surplus toll money for mass transit was repealed. There was no evidence of a diminution in the value of the bonds as a result of this broken promise. Nonetheless, the Court, in UNITED STATES TRUST CO. OF NEW YORK V. NEW JERSEY (1977), ruled that the state legislature had impaired the bondholders' contractual rights. Justice WILLIAM J. BRENNAN, in dissent, reminded his colleagues that "one of the fundamental premises of our popular democracy is that each generation of representatives can and will remain responsive to the needs and desires of those whom they represent." Nothing, he summed up, so jeopardized the "legitimacy of a system of government that relies on the ebbs and flow of politics to clean out the rascals than the possibility that those same rascals might perpetuate their polices simply by locking them into binding contracts." Justice Brennan may have struck a resonant chord. Since *United States Trust,* no legislative commitment has been enforced against a recalcitrant successor legislature. It is ordinarily in a legislature's

best interest to maintain a reputation for honoring its word. On those occasions, however, when the public interest leads a legislature to abandon a prior commitment, it will be rare for courts to enforce the promise.

JULIAN N. EULE
(1992)

Bibliography

EULE, JULIAN N.   1987   Temporal Limits on the Legislative Mandate: Entrenchment and Retroactivity. *American Bar Foundation Research Journal* 1987:379–459.

HOCHMAN, CHARLES B.   1960   The Supreme Court and the Constitutionality of Retroactive Legislation. *Harvard Law Review* 73:692–727.

KAHN, PAUL W.   1987   Gramm-Rudman and the Capacity of Congress to Control the Future. *Hastings Constitutional Law Quarterly* 13:185–231.

# TEN BROEK, JACOBUS
## (1911–1968)

The major contribution of Jacobus ten Broek to American constitutional scholarship was *The Antislavery Origins of the Fourteenth Amendment* (1951; rev. ed., *Equal under Law,* 1965), in which he described the influence of the abolitionist movement on the drafting and ratification of the FOURTEENTH AMENDMENT. Ten Broek argued that the abolitionists identified the NATURAL RIGHTS of human beings as constitutional rights requiring a national constitutional power of enforcement. He maintained that the PRIVILEGES AND IMMUNITIES clause of the amendment protected these natural rights and the auxiliary rights necessary to their enjoyment; that the EQUAL PROTECTION clause required the states to supply full legal protection to natural rights and authorized Congress to protect these rights if the states failed to do so; and that the amendment applied to the states those provisions of the federal Bill of Rights guaranteeing natural rights, as well as those natural rights not mentioned in the Bill of Rights. Ten Broek, a lawyer, was a political scientist at the University of California, Berkeley.

RICHARD B. BERNSTEIN
(1986)

# *TENNESSEE v. GARNER*
## 471 U.S. 1 (1985)

At the time of this case a majority of police departments in the nation prohibited the use of deadly force against nonviolent suspects, and the Supreme Court sought by its decision to stimulate a uniformity of that practice. Justice BYRON R. WHITE for a 6–3 majority held unconstitutional on FOURTH AMENDMENT grounds a state act authorizing an officer to shoot to kill in order to prevent an escape after he gave notice of an intent to arrest. The DOCTRINE of the case is that to kill a fleeing, unarmed felon as a last resort in order to prevent his getaway constitutes an unreasonable seizure unless the officer believes that failure to use deadly force will result in serious harm to himself or others. Justice SANDRA DAY O'CONNOR, for the dissenters, would have permitted deadly force at least against residential burglars who resist arrest by attempting to flee the scene of the crime.

LEONARD W. LEVY
(1986)

(SEE ALSO: *Unreasonable Search.*)

## TENNESSEE v. SCOPES
### 289 SW 363 (1925)

In 1925 Dayton, Tennessee, authorities arrested a local high school teacher, John T. Scopes, for violating the state's Butler Act, which prohibited public school instructors from teaching "any theory that denies the story of the Divine Creation of man as taught in the Bible, and to teach instead that man has descended from a lower order of animals." Scopes admitted to teaching about evolution from George Hunter's *Civic Biology*, a book approved by Tennessee's textbook commission. The Scopes trial, soon known throughout the nation as "the monkey trial," came in the middle of a decade punctuated by the Red Scare, increased urban-rural tensions, and the resurgence of the Ku Klux Klan. The Dayton courtroom soon became an arena of cultural and political conflict between fundamentalist Christians and civil libertarians.

The former, led by William Jennings Bryan, a three-time presidential candidate and ardent prohibitionist who joined the prosecution staff, argued that the Butler Act was a traditional exercise of STATE POLICE POWER with respect to public education, little different from mandating other curricula and fixing the qualifications of teachers. They also saw the statute as a defense of traditional folk values against the moral relativism of modern science and other contemporary religious beliefs. Scopes's defenders, including the AMERICAN CIVIL LIBERTIES UNION (ACLU) and the celebrated criminal lawyer Clarence Darrow, saw in the Butler Act a palpable threat to several constitutional guarantees, including SEPARATION OF CHURCH AND STATE and FREEDOM OF SPEECH.

The trial judge, John T. Raulston, rejected all constitutional attacks against the statute; he also declined to permit testimony by scientific and religious experts, many of whom hoped to argue the compatibility between evolution

and traditional religious values, including the belief in a supreme being. The only issue for the jury, Raulston noted, was the narrow one of whether or not John Scopes had taught his class that man had descended from a lower form of animals. Because Scopes has already admitted doing so, the jury's verdict was never in doubt. Darrow and the defense gained a public relations triumph by putting Bryan on the stand to testify as an expert about the Bible. The Great Commoner, who collapsed and died several days after the trial ended, affirmed his faith in biblical literalism, including the story of Jonah and the whale. The jury, however, found Scopes guilty and Raulston fined him the statutory minimum of $100.

Darrow and the ACLU encountered only frustration when they attempted to APPEAL the conviction. The state supreme court, with one judge dissenting, upheld the constitutionality of the Butler Act. However, they reversed Scopes's conviction on a technicality, holding that the Tennessee constitution prohibited trial judges from imposing fines in excess of $50 without a jury recommendation. The state supreme court also urged Tennessee officials to cease further prosecution of John Scopes—advice which the attorney general followed. The Butler Act remained on the Tennessee statute books but was not enforced against other educational heretics.

MICHAEL E. PARRISH
(1986)

(SEE ALSO: *Creationism.*)

Bibliography

GINGER, RAY   1958   *Six Days or Forever? Tennessee v. John Thomas Scopes.* New York: Oxford University Press.

## TENNESSEE VALLEY AUTHORITY ACT
### 48 Stat. 58 (1933)

A debate over the best use for an uncompleted defense plant site at Muscle Shoals—in the heart of a chronically depressed region—emerged after WORLD WAR I, ending with passage of the Tennessee Valley Authority Act. In 1933, President FRANKLIN D. ROOSEVELT urged creation of "a corporation clothed with the power of government but possessed of the flexibility and initiative of a private enterprise" to rehabilitate and develop the resources of the Tennessee River valley.

The resultant act, largely written by Senator GEORGE W. NORRIS, encompassed a variety of objectives including national defense; flood control and the improvement of navigation; the development of agriculture, industry, and electric power; and even reforestation. To accomplish these goals, Congress created the Tennessee Valley Authority (TVA), granting it the power to construct dams and power works in the valley and to increase production of badly needed fertilizers. The act also authorized the TVA to sell any energy produced in excess of its needs, giving preference to publicly owned organizations; the TVA further received authority to build power lines to facilitate sales and transmission of power. A series of amendments in 1935 and 1939 sought to liquidate the system's costs by providing for sales of electric power, producing "gross revenues in excess of the costs of production," to acquire major utility properties, and even to issue credit to assist the distribution of its power.

Supporters of the act relied on arguments including the GENERAL WELFARE CLAUSE, the commerce power, and the WAR POWERS. The Supreme Court sustained a TVA contract for the sale of surplus power in ASHWANDER V. TENNESSEE VALLEY AUTHORITY (1936), thus effectively sustaining the act's constitutionality.

DAVID GORDON
(1986)

## TENNEY v. BRANDHOVE
### 341 U.S. 367 (1951)

This decision established the absolute immunity of state legislative officials from damages actions, brought under SECTION 1983, TITLE 42, UNITED STATES CODE, alleging violations of constitutional rights. William Brandhove claimed that Senator Jack B. Tenney and other members of a California state legislative committee had violated his constitutional rights by conducting hearings to intimidate and silence him. In an opinion by Justice FELIX FRANKFURTER, the Supreme Court noted the history of parliamentary immunity in England, and cited the SPEECH OR DEBATE CLAUSE as a recognition of the need for a fearless and independent legislature. It held that, despite the unequivocal language of section 1983, Congress had not meant to "impinge on a tradition so well grounded in history and reason." (See LEGISLATIVE IMMUNITY.)

THEODORE EISENBERG
(1986)

## TEN POUND ACT CASES
### N.H. (1786–1787)

These cases, about which little is known (not even the names of the litigants are known), are notable as the first instances in our history of a state court's holding unconstitutional an act of a state legislature. The Inferior Court of Common Pleas of Rockingham County, sitting in Ports-

mouth, New Hampshire, in 1786 and 1787, voided the "Ten Pound Act," which had been passed in 1785 for the speedy recovery of small debts. Our scanty knowledge of the cases derives from newspaper reports and legislative records. The act of 1785 allowed justices of the peace to try certain civil cases, involving sums less than ten pounds, without juries. The state constitutional guarantee of TRIAL BY JURY extended to all civil cases except those which juries customarily did not try. New Hampshire practice had previously allowed a justice of the peace to try a case without a jury if the sum amounted to less than two pounds. After the court ruled that the act conflicted with the right to trial by jury, petitions to the state House of Representatives demanded IMPEACHMENT of the judges. The house, by a 3–1 majority, voted that the act was constitutional, but the judges stood by their initial decision or reaffirmed it in another case. Following the failure of a motion to impeach the judges, the house capitulated and repealed the Ten Pound Act.

LEONARD W. LEVY
(1986)

## TENTH AMENDMENT

Adopted in 1791 as part of the BILL OF RIGHTS, the Tenth Amendment declares that "powers not delegated to the United States by the Constitution . . . are reserved to the States respectively, or to the people." This language was an attempt to satisfy the public that the new constitution would not make a reality of that most repeated of Anti-Federalist fears: a completely centralized or "consolidated" government. But while the Tenth Amendment reminded Congress that its concerns were limited, the Constitution envisioned the effective exercise of national power, as the NECESSARY AND PROPER CLAUSE and the SUPREMACY CLAUSE indicated. The inevitable question was to be: what happens when Congress's responsibilities require measures the states say are beyond Congress's powers? JOHN MARSHALL attempted the Supreme Court's first answer to this question in MCCULLOCH V. MARYLAND (1819). *McCulloch* is best interpreted as advancing the following propositions: by granting and enumerating powers, the Constitution envisions the pursuit of a limited number of ends (see ENUMERATED POWERS); the framers did not and could not have enumerated all the legislative means appropriate to achieving constitutional ends in changing historical circumstances; Congress can select appropriate means to authorized national ends without regard for state prerogatives; the states, by contrast, cannot enact measures conflicting with lawful congressional policies.

To reach these conclusions Marshall observed that in drafting the Tenth Amendment the First Congress had refused to limit national powers to those "expressly granted," as the ARTICLES OF CONFEDERATION had done, and that a STRICT CONSTRUCTION of national powers would defeat the vital purposes for which the Constitution had been established. By rejecting a rigid line between state and national powers *McCulloch* opened the way to the future assumption of state responsibilities by the national government as needed to achieve national ends. Critics charged that Marshall would consolidate all power in the national government by permitting unlimited means to an ostensibly limited number of national ends. Marshall defended his theory by insisting that judges should invalidate pretextual congressional acts, that is, congressional acts cloaked in the commerce power and other national powers but actually aimed at state concerns, not at the free flow of commerce or other authorized national ends. The Court did not always conform to this view of *McCulloch* in upholding the expansions of national power in the twentieth century. The SOCIAL SECURITY ACT, the FAIR LABOR STANDARDS ACT, and the CIVIL RIGHTS ACT of 1964 were good faith exercises of national power because they were plausible as means to the nation's economic health or the ends of the Civil War amendments. The same cannot be said for the MANN ACT, the Little Lindbergh Act, and other uses of national power for POLICE POWER purposes. (See GENERAL WELFARE CLAUSE.)

From the late 1840s to the late 1930s judges unfriendly either to national power or to government generally lapsed into a static conception of state-federal powers that exempted "state instrumentalities" from federal taxation (see INTERGOVERNMENTAL IMMUNITIES) and removed aspects of the nation's economic life (such as labor relations and other incidents of manufacturing) from Congress's reach. (See COMMERCE CLAUSE.) Scholars have imputed a theory of DUAL FEDERALISM to many of the decisions of this period because the Court seemed to say that the RESERVED POWERS of the states constituted a line Congress could not cross in exercising its admitted powers. The most infamous of dual federalist decisions, HAMMER V. DAGENHART (1918), prevented Congress from using its power over INTERSTATE COMMERCE to combat child labor, a practice then considered reserved to state control. After the Depression changed attitudes toward federal power, the Court all but eliminated the tax immunity doctrine, leaving only hypothetical protection from federal taxes that might interfere with "essential state functions," as might a federal tax on a statehouse. And in the landmark case of UNITED STATES V. DARBY (1941) the Court overruled *Hammer,* holding that Congress, regardless of its underlying purposes, could stop any goods from moving in interstate commerce, even though they were produced in conformity to state policies toward child labor and other conditions of manufacturing. For the *Darby* majority Justice HARLAN FISKE STONE said

that the Tenth Amendment declared the "truism" that Congress could only exercise granted powers but that it had no effect on the question of what powers had actually been granted. Stone thus returned the Court to Marshall's view that Congress could disregard state prerogatives in the pursuit of what it saw as the nation's economic health in changing circumstances. But by disavowing judicial inquiries into underlying legislative purposes, Stone rejected the view that judges should invalidate pretextual uses of power—the essence of Marshall's defense of *McCulloch* as a decision compatible with the concept of a national government with limited concerns. Time had run out on this concept by the mid-1940s as Congress had advanced far in the use of its commerce, taxing, and spending powers for purposes of admitted state concern. (See NATIONAL POLICE POWER.)

Such was the general picture in the postwar constitutional law of state-federal power until a surprise decision in 1976 invalidated federal wage and hour standards for state employees. A plurality opinion in NATIONAL LEAGUE OF CITIES V. USERY (1976) likened STATES' RIGHTS "regarding the conduct of integral governmental functions" to the rights of individuals protected by the Bill of Rights. Here was an even clearer statement of dual federalism than *Hammer,* and critics charged that this radical departure from *McCulloch* threatened federal standards in areas such as CIVIL RIGHTS and environmental protection. But after evading extension of *Usery* for a decade the Court overruled *Usery* in GARCIA V. SAN ANTONIO METROPOLITAN TRANSIT AUTHORITY (1985), on the theory that representation of state governmental interests in Congress, as opposed to judicial vindication of states' rights, is the constitutionally preferred way to protect state prerogatives. *Garcia* thus abandoned *Usery* without returning to the theory of *McCulloch.*

Beyond fluctuations in judicial doctrine one can attribute the decline of the Tenth Amendment to the social and economic interdependencies of an industrial society and an enhanced public commitment to minority and other fundamental rights with which states' rights historically clashed.

SOTIRIOS A. BARBER
(1986)

Bibliography

CORWIN, EDWARD S.   1950   The Passing of Dual Federalism. *Virginia Law Review* 36:1–24.

FLAX, KAREN H.   1983   In the Wake of National League of Cities v. Usery: A "Derelict" Makes Waves. *South Carolina Law Review* 34:649–686.

WECHSLER, HERBERT   1954   The Political Safeguards of Federalism: The Role of the States in the Composition and Selection of the National Government. *Columbia Law Review* 54:543–560.

# TENURE OF OFFICE ACT
## 14 Stat. 430 (1867)

After a complete political rupture between President AN-DREW JOHNSON and congressional Republicans over RECON-STRUCTION policy, Congress enacted the Tenure of Office Act in March 1867, providing that all officials of the executive branch, except cabinet officers whose appointment had required Senate confirmation, would hold office until their successors had likewise been confirmed. Cabinet officers were to hold office only during the term of the president appointing them plus one month. The act also provided for interim appointments while the SENATE was not in session.

In February 1868, President Johnson removed Secretary of War EDWIN M. STANTON, who was hostile to his Reconstruction policies, and appointed General Lorenzo Thomas in his place. The House promptly voted to impeach Johnson. Though Republicans sought to remove him from office because of his stubborn obstruction of their Reconstruction program, debates in his Senate trial turned on the constitutionality of the statute. The President's counsel maintained that it was unconstitutional as an interference with the president's removal power, a prerogative distinct from the appointive power. The Senate could not muster the two-thirds vote necessary for conviction. Congress repealed the act in 1887.

WILLIAM M. WIECEK
(1986)

(SEE ALSO: *Appointing and Removal Power, Presidential.*)

Bibliography

BENEDICT, MICHAEL LES 1973 *The Impeachment and Trial of Andrew Johnson.* New York: Norton.

# TERM
## (Supreme Court)

As prescribed by congressional statute, the Supreme Court holds a regular annual term of court, beginning on the first Monday in October. The term usually concludes in late June or early July of the following year. The Court is also authorized to hold special terms outside the normal October terms but does so only infrequently, in urgent circumstances (EX PARTE QUIRIN, 1942, German saboteurs convicted by military commission; O'BRIEN V. BROWN, 1972, seating of delegates to Democratic National Convention).

Although Congress manipulated the Court's terms to postpone decision of MARBURY V. MADISON (1803) for nearly a year, modern times have seen no similar stratagems.

KENNETH L. KARST
(1986)

# *TERMINIELLO v. CHICAGO*
## 337 U.S. 1 (1949)

Terminiello was convicted of disorderly conduct after a meeting in a private hall outside of which a thousand persons violently protested his anti-Semitic, antiblack, and anticommunist harangue. The Court reversed because the jury had been instructed that it might convict on a finding that Terminiello's speech "invite[d] dispute." This instruction failed to require a finding of CLEAR AND PRESENT DANGER of violence. *Terminiello* frequently is coupled with FEINER V. NEW YORK (1951) as illustrations of the HOSTILE AUDIENCE problem.

MARTIN SHAPIRO
(1986)

# TERM LIMITS

After the 1994 elections, twenty-two states had acted to limit the terms of office of their federal legislators. Term limits supporters hope to rid Congress of professional politicians because they believe that such lawmakers inevitably act in ways contrary to the public interest. They seek to replace the professionals with amateurs who have little experience in politics but a great deal of experience as ordinary citizens. The democratic theories prompting support for term limits are diverse. Some advocates argue that lawmakers will become more responsive to the demands of the electorate. Others contend that term limits will insulate lawmakers from reelection pressures and allow them to fulfill a Madisonian vision of representative democracy. All believe that this reform will eliminate unseemly close relationships between elected officials and special INTEREST GROUPS.

Some analysts are skeptical that term limits will result in positive change. For example, a study of the political opportunities that remain open to term-limited lawmakers suggests that political careers will remain possible, although a careerist will be forced to adopt a strategy of "progressive" political ambition by moving periodically to a new political job. Even those who enter the legislature intending to leave after a short time will often decide to pursue longer political careers so that they can continue to benefit from the skills they have developed as lawmakers. Once legislators have developed the human capital to perform political functions, they may find the benefits of holding similar office are greater than the benefits of pursuing unrelated careers.

Some critics object to term limits because they will deprive legislatures of their most experienced members, thereby reducing Congress's ability to pass controversial or complex LEGISLATION. Reduced legislator effectiveness also may shift the balance of power between the branches of government. In the federal system, bureaucrats will represent a source of expertise for congressional amateurs, strengthening the executive branch relative to Congress. Similarly, term-limited politicians may rely more heavily on staff or on lobbyists. Finally, some opponents argue that interest groups will continue to influence representatives disproportionately by giving campaign money either to them or to POLITICAL PARTIES, and that term limits will provide special interests with an even more powerful tool for influence: post-service jobs for term-limited representatives.

At the same time that voters adopted term limits on federal legislators, they also voted in most cases to reelect incumbents. Einer Elhauge argues that this seeming inconsistency in voter behavior disappears when one understands the collective action problems facing voters. "Incumbents . . . have more seniority than challengers, and this seniority gives them more legislative clout. Any individual district that ousts its incumbent is thus penalized by a smaller share of legislative power and governmental benefits unless the other districts also oust their incumbents." Voters might prefer the ideological views of a challenger, but they will continue to vote for the incumbent who has more power in an institution like Congress that is organized according to seniority. On balance, voters will choose the more influential representative, who can send constituents a greater share of benefits. If, however, voters can be sure that no district can vote for incumbents because of term limits, the penalty of electing a challenger is greatly reduced.

As the debate about state-imposed term limits on federal lawmakers heated up, the Supreme Court declared them to be unconstitutional in *U.S. Term Limits, Inc. v. Thornton* (1995). The petitioner challenged a popularly enacted amendment to the Arkansas state constitution that prohibited the name of an otherwise eligible candidate for Congress from appearing on the ballot if the candidate had already served three terms in the U.S. HOUSE OF REPRESENTATIVES or two terms in the U.S. SENATE. The Court applied the reasoning of POWELL V. MCCORMACK (1969) where it had held that Congress lacked the power to impose qualifications for federal legislators other than those set forth in Article I, section 5. State-imposed qualifications similarly undermine the "fundamental principle of our representative democracy" identified in *Powell*—the

idea that "the people should choose whom they please to govern them."

The dissent by Justice CLARENCE THOMAS found the Court's use of democratic principles "ironic" because the majority invalidated a provision that 60 percent of voters in a statewide election had supported. Moreover, he stated, "the authority to narrow the field of candidates . . . may be part and parcel of the right to elect Members of Congress. That is, the right to choose may include the right to winnow." The restriction on incumbents might actually increase the electorate's choices by leveling the political playing field and improving the chances that a challenger could mount a successful campaign for office. "The voters of Arkansas evidently believe that incumbents would not enjoy such overwhelming success if electoral contests were truly fair" and the advantages incumbents enjoy (such as greater name recognition) were balanced by the handicap of running as a write-in candidate.

The dissent contended that the Constitution's silence concerning the ability of states to add to the constitutional qualifications meant that the power was reserved to them under the TENTH AMENDMENT. The majority's notion of reserved powers was different. Relying on Justice JOSEPH STORY's treatise on constitutional law, the Court determined that the only powers reserved to the states under the Tenth Amendment were those that they had possessed before the Constitution was ratified and that they had retained. The states did not have an "original power" to appoint a national official; thus, the power to set qualifications for such offices cannot be a reserved power. Furthermore, the majority's reading of the history of the drafting and ratification of the Constitution as well as early congressional practice convinced it that "the Qualifications Clauses were intended to preclude the States from exercising [the power to adopt qualifications] and to fix as exclusive" the constitutional qualifications.

Importantly, the Arkansas amendment was phrased as a BALLOT ACCESS provision. Long-time incumbents could run for federal office but only as write-in candidates. The Court held that this phrasing was "an indirect attempt to accomplish what the Constitution prohibits [the state] from accomplishing directly." Because the state provision had the "avowed purpose and obvious effect" of evading the qualifications clauses, it was unconstitutional.

The majority acknowledged the intensity and importance of the debate concerning the merits of term limits, a debate that began at the time of ratification, when some argued in favor of a rotation requirement so that lawmakers would be forced to return to private life occasionally. Noting that a constitutional amendment had imposed term limits on the presidency, the Court concluded that such a "fundamental change in the constitutional framework" must come through Article V's AMENDING PROCE-

DURES. Interest groups supporting legislative term limits at the federal level have responded to that challenge. For example, some states have tried to increase the pressure on federal legislators to propose a constitutional amendment by requiring that the election ballot reflect a candidate's opposition to term limits through designations like "Disregarded Voters' Instructions on Term Limits." Challenges to these "scarlet letter" amendments have been successful, with courts holding that the designations interfere with the deliberative process or violate candidates' First Amendment rights.

Term limitations are common in state and local government. Nearly half of the states place limitations on state legislators; forty states limit the number of terms of their governors; and many local officials face term limits. State term limits on legislators have generally been upheld. In the leading case, *Legislature of the State of California v. Eu* (1991), the California Supreme Court balanced the interests of incumbents to stay in office and of voters to have the choice of reelecting them against the state's interest in ending the advantage of incumbency. The court found that voters have no FUNDAMENTAL RIGHT to vote for a particular candidate and that the state's interest in structuring its own government was considerable. In some states, term limits have very little effect on the political dynamics because legislators did not tend to serve for long periods of time before the limitations were imposed. In states like California, however, where legislatures were full of career politicians, term limits have caused significant, and sometimes complete, turnover, helped bring to power new leaders, and may have affected the ability of legislators to pass controversial or significant laws. Such states are just beginning to feel the impact of limitations; with more experience over the next few years, researchers will be able to draw firmer conclusions based on empirical evidence about the consequences of legislative term limitations.

ELIZABETH GARRETT
(2000)

(SEE ALSO: *Initiative; Referendum.*)

Bibliography

ELHAUGE, EINER 1997 Are Term Limits Undemocratic? *University of Chicago Law Review* 64:83–201.
GARRETT, ELIZABETH 1996 Term Limitations and the Myth of the Citizen-Legislator. *Cornell Law Review* 81:623–697.
GROFMAN, BERNARD, ed. 1996 *Legislative Term Limits: Public Choice Perspectives.* Boston: Kluwer Academic Publishers.

## *TERRETT v. TAYLOR*
### 9 Cranch 43 (1815)

This was the first case and one of the very few in which the Supreme Court relied exclusively upon the concept of a HIGHER LAW as the sole basis for holding a state act unconstitutional. After adopting THOMAS JEFFERSON's statute of religious liberty, which separated church and state in Virginia, the legislature confiscated certain Episcopal glebe lands and sold them, using the proceeds for charity. The lands in question having been donated to the church by private persons, no contract and therefore no CONTRACT CLAUSE issue existed. Justice JOSEPH STORY for the Court held the confiscation act void, offering as grounds: "we think ourselves standing upon the principles of natural justice, upon the fundamental laws of every free government, upon the spirit and letter of the constitution. . . ." Story did not mention *which* letter. Usually the Court applied the DOCTRINE OF VESTED RIGHTS in a way that absorbed the higher law within express provisions of the Constitution.

LEONARD W. LEVY
(1986)

## TERRITORIAL COURT

From the beginning the United States has held TERRITORIES outside the existing states. Some territories have been destined for statehood, others for independence, and still others for "permanent" territorial status. (See COMMONWEALTH STATUS.) Early in our history Congress established courts to serve the territories, but it did not give their judges the life tenure and salary guarantees demanded by Article III for judges of CONSTITUTIONAL COURTS. The constitutional status of these territorial courts was thus uncertain.

Chief Justice John Marshall sought to resolve the uncertainty in AMERICAN INSURANCE CO. V. CANTER (1828) by inventing a new category called LEGISLATIVE COURTS. Such a court, Marshall said, is not created under Article III, which provides for the establishment of constitutional courts to exercise the JUDICIAL POWER of the United States. Rather it is created by Congress in carrying out its general legislative powers under Article I, including the power to provide for the government of the territories. Although the case at hand was one of ADMIRALTY AND MARITIME JURISDICTION, plainly within the federal judicial power, the fact that it arose in a territory made it appropriate for disposition by such a "legislative" territorial court. The result made good sense in a territory (Florida) that was to become a state; upon statehood, most of the work of the territorial courts would be taken over by the state courts, and there would be no place for a large body of life-tenured judges in the new federal courts. Furthermore, independence from the President and Congress receded in importance in a territorial government that had essentially the same power as a state to discard the principle of SEPARATION OF POWERS.

Today legislative courts continue to serve in territories such as Guam and the Virgin Islands. In the Commonwealth of PUERTO RICO, Congress has created a dual court system matching that of the DISTRICT OF COLUMBIA: one set of constitutional courts, operating wholly within the terms of Article III, and one set of commonwealth courts roughly equivalent to state courts.

KENNETH L. KARST
(1986)

Bibliography

WRIGHT, CHARLES ALAN　1983　*The Law of Federal Courts*, 4th ed. Pages 14–15, 40–42, 49, 139–140. St. Paul, Minn.: West Publishing Co.

# TERRITORIES OF
# THE UNITED STATES

The United States has five permanent territories. PUERTO RICO, in the Caribbean, and Guam, in the Western Pacific, were acquired as a result of the Spanish-American War in 1899. American Samoa, the only U.S. TERRITORY south of the equator, was ceded to the United States by the *matai* (the chiefs) of the islands in 1900 and 1904. The U.S. Virgin Islands, in the Caribbean east of Puerto Rico, were purchased from Denmark in 1917. The people of what is now the Commonwealth of the Northern Mariana Islands (CNMI), formerly a part of the Trust Territory of the Pacific Islands, voted in a 1976 plebiscite to become a part of the United States. Residents of each of the territories, except American Samoa, enjoy United States CITIZENSHIP at birth. Residents of American Samoa are United States nationals at birth, and may obtain immediate United States citizenship upon establishing a domicile in a U.S. state (which they, along with other territorials, have an absolute right to do). Official and unofficial REFERENDA indicate that large majorities in each of the territories favor continued affiliation with the United States.

The United States has had territories from its inception. The Northwest Territory was a part of the nation when the Constitution was ratified. That the Framers of the Constitution contemplated the existence of nonstate territories is demonstrated by Article IV, Section 3, Clause 2, commonly called the "territorial clause." It provides, "The Congress Shall have Power to dispose of and make all needful Rules and Regulations respecting the Territory or other Property belonging to the United States."

In 1826, Chief Justice JOHN MARSHALL held, in *American Insurance Co. v. 356 Bales of Cotton* (David Canter, claimant), that Congress, acting under this clause, could treat territories differently from states and could create courts in territories that combine the functions of Article III federal courts and state courts.

So far as the rest of the Constitution is concerned, early cases seemed to follow the "ex proprio vigore" (by its own force) DOCTRINE, which was summed up in the phrase "the Constitution follows the flag." In the INSULAR CASES (1901) (especially *Downes v. Bidwell*), the Supreme Court moved toward the "incorporation doctrine," which was clearly accepted law by the time of *Balzac v. Porto Rico* (1922). Under the incorporation doctrine, the Constitution is not fully applicable in a territory unless that territory has been "incorporated into and made a part of the United States." (Modern examples of incorporation are Alaska and Hawai'i.) Although Congress has granted U.S. citizenship to the residents of most of the territories, none of the current territories are deemed to be incorporated.

The Supreme Court has not OVERRULED the "incorporation" doctrine, but lower courts have considered it modified by decisions such as REID V. COVERT (1957), which held that the Sixth Amendment right to TRIAL BY JURY applied to a civilian on a U.S. Air Force base in Great Britain. At least two federal CIRCUIT COURTS—in *King v. Morton* (1975) and *Wabol v. Villacrusis* (1992)— have adopted a rule of construction which holds that in any given case there is a presumption that the Constitution applies. However, that presumption can be rebutted by proof that a particular application is "impractical" (i.e., that it would not work because of cultural differences) or that it would be "anomalous" (i.e., that it would be destructive of the indigenous culture).

In addition to the distinction between incorporated and unincorporated territories, there is a distinction between organized and unorganized territories. An organized territory has an organic act, an act of Congress that establishes its local government. An unorganized territory was traditionally governed under the authority of the President of the United States. Today, American Samoa is the only territory with a substantial indigenous population that is "unorganized." However, American Samoa has some protection for its local self-government in that federal law now provides that no changes can be made in the Samoan constitution without the approval of the U.S. Congress. Thus the distinction between organized and unorganized territories has become less significant.

Puerto Rico and the CNMI are designated "commonwealths." The principal identifying characteristic of a commonwealth is that the organic act is in the form of a covenant or compact between the U.S. government and the people of the territory. In general, Congress has respected these agreements. However, the courts have held that Congress, acting under the territorial clause, can enact valid LEGISLATION that is inconsistent with the covenants.

The United States is in a relationship of "free association" with the Federated States of Micronesia, the Republic of the Marshall Islands, and the Republic of Palau. These island nations, along with what is now the CNMI, were formerly the Trust Territory of the Pacific Islands, for which the United States was trustee. The relationship between the United States and these islands is close. The U.S. government is pledged to defend these nations as if they were part of the United States, and has a veto over any action of any of their governments if the United States considers such action inconsistent with its obligation to defend them. Nevertheless, the three are recognized as sovereign and independent nations by the UNITED NATIONS, and hence the U.S. Constitution has no application to them (except perhaps as to U.S. government officials acting in their official capacities there).

STANLEY K. LAUGHLIN, JR.
(2000)

Bibliography

LAUGHLIN, STANLEY K.  1995  *The Law of United States Territories and Affiliated Jurisdictions* (with 1997 supplement). New York: Lawyers Cooperative-West Group.

# TERRITORY

At the time of independence several states had extensive claims to territory on the western frontier. A dispute over whether such territories were to be administered by the claimant states or by and for the United States long delayed ratification of the ARTICLES OF CONFEDERATION. In 1780 Congress passed a resolution urging the states to cede their claims to the United States. The resolution contained three promises which became the basic principles of American CONSTITUTIONALISM as extended to the territories: that the territories would be "disposed of for the common benefit of the United States"; that they would be "settled and formed into distinct republican states"; and that they would eventually "become members of the federal union and have the same rights of SOVEREIGNTY, freedom, and independence as the other states." After the cession was complete and the western boundary was settled by the Treaty of Paris (1783), Congress embodied these three principles in measures for the temporary government of the territories: the ORDINANCE OF 1784 and the NORTHWEST ORDINANCE OF 1787. The same principles were reaffirmed by the CONSTITUTIONAL CONVENTION OF 1787. Although some delegates advocated maintaining the western lands as a federal colony to be exploited and governed permanently by the existing states, the Constitution provided for the admission of new states on an equal basis with the original states.

The first acquisition of territory beyond the original borders of the nation was the LOUISIANA PURCHASE. After brief debate about the constitutional propriety of such territorial expansion, Congress proceeded to organize the Louisiana Territory following the model of the Northwest Ordinance. Exploration, purchase, and cession, as well as the conquests of the Mexican War, resulted in further territorial expansion.

Congress's power to make rules and regulations for the territories derives from the second clause of Article IV, section 3. In the first important case on territories to be decided by the Supreme Court, AMERICAN INSURANCE COMPANY V. CANTER (1828), Chief Justice JOHN MARSHALL suggested that the power to govern the territories was also implied in the power to acquire them through the use of the TREATY POWER or the WAR POWERS. He added that, whatever its source, Congress's power over the territories was plenary, whether exercised directly or through a local legislature, and extended even to creation of TERRITORIAL COURTS with JURISDICTION beyond the JUDICIAL POWER of the United States.

In the early nineteenth century the question of SLAVERY IN THE TERRITORIES divided the country and sparked new controversy over the constitutional status of territories. Southerners maintained that the federal government held the territories in trust for the states and that Congress could not properly prohibit slavery in them, while northern Whigs such as ABRAHAM LINCOLN maintained that the territories were national possessions and failure to prohibit slavery in them would constitute a national endorsement of the institution. STEPHEN A. DOUGLAS proposed to avoid the issue by leaving it to a vote of the settlers in each territory. Congress sought to allay sectional contention in the MISSOURI COMPROMISE by permitting slavery in one part of the Louisiana Purchase while prohibiting it in the rest. In the COMPROMISE OF 1850, Douglas's formula (which he called POPULAR SOVEREIGNTY) was adopted for the territory acquired in the Mexican War (except California). In DRED SCOTT V. SANDFORD (1857) the Supreme Court held that Congress did not have the power to exclude slavery from the territories. The CIVIL WAR, by eliminating the slavery issue, ended the sectional dispute over the status of territories.

By 1869 American territorial acquisition on the mainland of North America was complete. A new debate about the status of territories began when, at the end of the nineteenth century, the United States started to acquire overseas possessions, not a part of the continent and apparently not destined for statehood. The place of this "colonial empire" in the constitutional system was a subject of political dispute in the 1900 elections; but it was not resolved until the Supreme Court decided the INSULAR CASES. In these cases the Court formulated the doctrine of INCORPORATION OF TERRITORIES, according to which territorial possessions do not become part of the United

States until Congress, by some positive action, makes them so.

Territories may be either incorporated or unincorporated, and either organized or unorganized. The former refers to the degree of constitutional protection enjoyed by inhabitants and to Congress's ultimate intention to confer statehood or not; the latter refers to the provision Congress has made for government of the territory. There are now no incorporated territories, but there are both organized and unorganized unincorporated territories. In 1934 the special status of "commonwealth" was created for the Philippines, which became independent after WORLD WAR II; PUERTO RICO and the Northern Marianas currently have COMMONWEALTH STATUS and enjoy virtually complete internal self-government. After World War II the United States accepted a mandate over the Trust Territory of the Pacific Islands. Authority over that territory was exercised by virtue of the UNITED NATIONS CHARTER until the trusteeship ended in 1981.

DENNIS J. MAHONEY
(1986)

Bibliography

BLOOM, JOHN PORTER, ed. 1973 *The American Territorial System.* Athens: Ohio University Press.

LIEBOWITZ, A. H. 1979 United States Federalism: States and Territories. *American University Law Review* 28:449–482.

PERKINS, WHITNEY T. 1962 *Denial of Empire.* Leyden, Netherlands: A. W. Sythoff.

# TERRORISM CONTROL AND THE CONSTITUTION

Terrorism inspires fear, politically charged rhetoric, and, too often, official overreaction. Much like Communism in the 1950s, terrorism today raises a number of constitutional issues. One reason it does so is that it is an inevitably politically loaded term of art, used more often to divide our enemies from our friends that to describe a particular form of conduct. Thus, in the 1980s the U.S. State Department routinely labeled the African National Congress and the Irish Republican Army as terrorist organizations, but did not assign that term to the Nicaraguan Contras or the Afghanistan Mujahedin, organizations that engaged in similar military tactics to further their insurrections, but whose battles the United States supported.

The most common definition of terrorism—the use of force against noncombatants in a manner designed to instill fear for political ends—would apply to virtually any bombing of an urban or residential area, and thus would cover the military activities of most nations that have been at war, including the United States. Under U.S. IMMIGRA-TION law, "terrorist activity" is defined even more broadly, to encompass any unlawful use of a firearm to endanger person or PROPERTY (except for personal monetary gain), a definition that would encompass injuries inflicted in a lovers' quarrel. Because of its almost limitless applicability, the term is almost always used selectively; when that selectivity is enacted into law, serious constitutional questions under the FIRST AMENDMENT are implicated.

Government responses to terrorism thus far have raised two principal constitutional issues: (1) the extent to which those who associate with or support terrorist organizations may be punished; and (2) the extent to which the threat of terrorism justifies departures from DUE PROCESS.

As with Communism, the fear associated with terrorism has induced governments to act not only against those who actually engage in terrorism, but also against those who are merely associated in some way with groups that engage in terrorism. For example, the U.S. government has sought to expel and deny visas to foreign citizens for associating with so-called terrorist organizations, and has criminalized the provision of material support to such organizations, even where the support is intended to further (and in fact furthers) only the groups' wholly nonviolent and lawful activities.

These efforts repeat the excesses of MCCARTHYISM. The anticommunist laws of the McCarthy Era presumed that anyone working with or assisting the Communists was guilty of the Communist Party's illegal ends, even if the individual cooperated only for legal purposes, such as LABOR organizing or CIVIL RIGHTS activism. The injustices of that experiment with guilt by association led the Supreme Court to rule that where the government seeks to hold someone accountable for her connection to a group, it must prove that the individual specifically intended to further the group's unlawful ends. The requirement of "specific intent" distinguishes individual culpability from associational guilt.

Under the ANTITERRORISM AND EFFECTIVE DEATH PENALTY ACT OF 1996, however, persons who support the wholly lawful ends of designated groups face prison sentences. Under the law, the U.S. Secretary of State may designate any foreign group that uses unlawful force as "terrorist," and it then becomes a crime, punishable by ten years in prison, to support that group's lawful activities. The Secretary's designation is for all practical purposes unreviewable. If this law had been in place in the 1980s, the thousands of Americans who supported the lawful antiapartheid work of the African National Congress in South Africa would have faced ten-year prison sentences. Congress justified the law on the theory that any support for a terrorist organization will free up resources that the organization can use for terrorist ends, but if that argument were accepted, guilt by association would be permissible wherever an organization had engaged in any unlawful activity, whether it be the African National Congress or the Democratic Party.

The terrorist threat has also induced the federal government to dispense with the most basic requisite of due process—the right to confront evidence against oneself. Citing NATIONAL SECURITY concerns, the 1996 antiterrorism law authorizes the government to expel immigrants accused of connections to terrorism on the basis of secret evidence that neither the immigrant nor his attorney would ever see. The government may submit evidence behind closed doors to a judge, and may make secret arguments and take secret appeals outside the immigrant's presence. The government has not yet invoked this particular provision, but in other immigration settings the government has increasingly used secret evidence against immigrants.

The only two federal courts to address the issue in the past decade have ruled that the use of secret evidence against immigrants residing here violates due process. As Justice FELIX FRANKFURTER said in a related setting, "Secrecy is not congenial to truth-seeking. . . . No better instrument has been devised for arriving at truth than to give a person in jeopardy of serious loss notice of the case against him and opportunity to meet it."

The government argues that secret evidence procedures are needed because it sometimes has classified information that it would like to use without having to reveal its source. But the government faces this situation every day in criminal courts across the country, where it must choose between revealing the source and not using the evidence. This rule applies in criminal court no matter how heinous the crime, no matter how sensitive the information, and no matter how serious the threat to national security. There simply is no other way in a fair system of justice, because it is impossible to defend oneself against secret evidence.

Proponents of the measures described above warn that America's open society makes it especially vulnerable to terrorist attack. But one of the principal benefits of an open society with substantial political freedoms is that it provides peaceful ways to express opposition and to work for political change. Repressive governments tend to breed rather than contain violence. Empowering government to blacklist disfavored groups and use secret evidence plays into the hands of zealots; it feeds their paranoia. At the same time, it is likely to drive extremists underground, where they will be more difficult to track. The United States has until now been relatively free of terrorism, and arguably that is because of, not in spite of, our political freedoms.

DAVID COLE
(2000)

Bibliography

DEMPSEY, JAMES X. and COLE, DAVID 1999 *Terrorism and the Constitution: Sacrificing Civil Liberties in the Name of National Security.* Los Angeles: First Amendment Foundation.
HEYMANN, PHILIP B. 1998 *Terrorism and America: A Commonsense Strategy for a Democratic Society.* Cambridge, Mass.: MIT Press.

## TERRY v. ADAMS
### 345 U.S. 461 (1953)

With confidence, we can call *Terry* the last of the series of "Texas primary cases" beginning with NIXON V. HERNDON (1927). The decision is also a clear modern example of the "public function" strand of STATE ACTION doctrine. In a Texas county, a group called the Jaybird Democratic Association conducted pre-PRIMARY ELECTIONS, from which black voters were excluded. The winners of these elections consistently won both the Democratic primaries and the general elections. The Supreme Court held that black plaintiffs were entitled to a DECLARATORY JUDGMENT that their exclusion from the Jaybird election amounted to state action in violation of the FIFTEENTH AMENDMENT. There was no MAJORITY OPINION. Three Justices said that the state could not constitutionally permit a racial exclusion from the only election that mattered in the county. The electoral process was inescapably public, subject to the Fifteenth Amendment's commands. Four other Justices said the Jaybirds were an auxiliary of the local Democratic party organization, and thus included within the doctrine of SMITH V. ALLWRIGHT (1944). Justice FELIX FRANKFURTER found state action in the participation of state election officials as voters in the Jaybird election. Justice SHERMAN MINTON dissented, calling the Jaybirds nothing but a "pressure group."

KENNETH L. KARST
(1986)

## TERRY v. OHIO
### 392 U.S. 1 (1968)
## SIBRON v. NEW YORK
### 392 U.S. 40 (1968)

*Terry v. Ohio* marked the first attempt by the Supreme Court to deal with a pervasive type of police conduct known as STOP AND FRISK. Where an individual's suspicious conduct gives rise to an apprehension of danger, but PROBABLE CAUSE for an arrest does not exist, it is common police practice to stop the suspect for questioning and to pat down (frisk) his outer clothing in a search for concealed weapons. While this may be an effective way to deter crime it is susceptible to abuse. Though far less intrusive on privacy and security than formal arrest and thorough search, a stop and, especially, a frisk can be a frightening and humiliating experience.

It was this consideration that led the Court in *Terry* to hold that stop and frisk is subject to limitations established by the FOURTH AMENDMENT. Chief Justice EARL WARREN declared that the forcible restraint of an individual, however temporary, is a "seizure," and a frisk, though limited in scope, is a "search," within the meaning of the Fourth Amendment. However, the imperative of sound law enforcement, as well as the need of the police to assure their own safety and that of the citizenry, requires that the amendment's reasonableness clause—rather than the probable cause standard of the warrant clause—should govern this type of police conduct. Balancing individual freedom against community needs, Warren concluded that if "a reasonably prudent [officer] in the circumstances [is] warranted in the belief that his safety or that of others [is] in danger," he is, under the reasonableness clause, entitled to stop and frisk the suspect in order to avoid the threatened harm. Any weapon thus seized is admissible at trial. However, in *Terry*'s companion case, *Sibron v. New York* the Court held that where the motivation for the frisk is the discovery of EVIDENCE rather than the confiscation of weapons, the evidence seized is inadmissible.

The officer's apprehension of danger must be based on articulable facts rather than mere hunch; the difference between probable cause and the less strict standard authorized in *Terry* is a difference between reasonable belief and reasonable suspicion. Paradoxically, the case both significantly limited and momentously expanded the police search power: it placed "on the street" police-citizen encounters under the protection of the Fourth Amendment even as it allowed, for the first time, a standard less exacting than probable cause to meet the requirement of reasonableness for searches made in EXIGENT CIRCUMSTANCES.

JACOB W. LANDYNSKI
(1986)

# TEST CASE

Whenever a unit of government, or an interest in the private sector, wants a favorable constitutional DECISION on a point in question, a test case is often organized to gain a ruling from the Supreme Court. The Court has not defined the term, and need not, as there is no judicial criterion for "test case" under the CASES AND CONTROVERSIES clause of Article III. Scholarship on the judicial process provides the best understanding of the term as a strategy employed by different interests, for differing ends.

FLETCHER V. PECK (1810) showed that systematically plotting a test case, so framing it as to elicit particular answers based on prediction concerning how the Justices are likely to respond, and then using the judicial decision for political advantage is not a strategy unique to recent CIVIL RIGHTS cases but a durable aspect of constitutional litigation since the early years of the Republic.

Organizers of test cases sometimes look upon victory in the Supreme Court as a secondary goal. For example, the arguments of the National Woman Suffrage Association that women, as citizens, were already enfranchised by terms of the FOURTEENTH AMENDMENT breathed new life into the organization through publicity of test cases. MINOR V. HAPPERSETT (1875) and two other cases failed but they produced national news.

The Department of Justice took little initiative in enforcing new legislation in the nineteenth century, largely because Congress intended enforcement to come through complaints of individuals entitled to sue violators. An example of this is the CIVIL RIGHTS CASES (1883). Individuals challenged about a hundred violations of the CIVIL RIGHTS ACT OF 1875. Eventually, five came to the Supreme Court as test cases, where they were unsuccessfully argued by the SOLICITOR GENERAL. These test cases were not managed; they simply happened as individual blacks complained.

Business interests may bring test cases to prevent enforcement of new regulatory legislation, as in 1917 when David Clark for the Southern Cotton Manufacturers sought to invalidate the KEATING-OWEN ACT which prohibited shipment in INTERSTATE COMMERCE of designated products manufactured in plants employing children. Stephen Wood reports the advice of a Philadelphia lawyer to the manufacturers:

> No legal proceeding will lie until the [Keating-Owen] bill is in operation. Some action must be taken under some provision of the bill so that a real and not a moot question is raised. A court, in order to pass upon any phase of it, must have before it an actual case, and if the measure is to be contested, the case should not only be carefully selected in order that the constitutional principle desired to be raised may be clearly presented, but I believe then that when the issue is raised, if possible, a judicial district should be selected in which the judge is a man of known courage. This is no case to try before a weak character [1968: 87–88].

Clark proceeded to raise money, select suitable counsel, identify Judge James Edmund Boyd as courageous, and locate cotton companies in the western district of North Carolina ready to cooperate. After searching for the "perfect combination of factors," Clark worked up four possible test cases to submit to the attorneys in New York. There the *Dagenhart* case was selected as the best. The

Dagenharts, a father and two minor sons, and the company "were mere figureheads" whom Clark persuaded to set up the case. First, the company posted notices that under-age employees would be dismissed when the Keating-Owen law went into effect. The attorneys employed by Clark then prepared a complaint for Dagenhart asserting that this threat would deprive him of his VESTED RIGHTS, because he was entitled to the services of his minor sons and the compensation arising from their labors. By moving before the law became effective, the cotton manufacturers put the Department of Justice on the defensive, trapped within the confines of their test case. Judge Boyd, who ruled the Keating-Owen Act invalid under the FIFTH and TENTH AMENDMENTS, was upheld by the Supreme Court in 1918 in HAMMER V. DAGENHART.

Success in managing constitutional litigation requires understanding of both substantive law and litigation practice. Following enactment of the WAGNER ACT in 1935, lawyers for the National Labor Relations Board combined these talents in impressive fashion, gaining a stunning triumph from the Supreme Court in *NLRB v. Jones & Laughlin* in March 1937. (See WAGNER ACT CASES.) Against hostile attacks by the National Lawyers' Committee of the American Liberty League, NLRB lawyers carefully developed cases running the gamut of size and type to make the first tests establishing wide congressional power to regulate labor practices in businesses affecting interstate commerce.

NLRB lawyers, even before the Wagner Act was signed, had designed a "master plan" envisioning test cases built around COMMERCE CLAUSE issues stressing the type of industry, characteristics of individual businesses, the degree of actual or threatened obstruction of commerce, and the type of unfair labor practices charged. In Peter Irons's words, this "master plan" gave clear directions for "sifting through their massive case loads in search of ideal test cases, charting a clear path from the picket line to the Supreme Court." The NLRB staff functioned as legal craftsmen, "as much meticulous technicians as partisan advocates," who "winnowed and selected cases with care; scrutinized records with a fine-tooth comb; chose courts with a shopper's discriminating eye; wrote briefs to draw the issues narrowly and precisely."

Although numerous voluntary associations with litigation programs, such as the Anti-Saloon League of America, the National Consumers' League, and the AMERICAN JEWISH CONGRESS, have sponsored test cases as a way of influencing public policy, the organizations most noted for this practice have been the National Association for the Advancement of Colored People (NAACP), formed in 1909, and the NAACP LEGAL DEFENSE FUND, Inc., organized in 1939.

Modern test cases by associations, public interest law firms, or lawyers working *pro bono publico* are often cast as CLASS ACTIONS under the FEDERAL RULES OF CIVIL PROCEDURE. Although they may attack conditions that are widespread, these cases rest on particularized explorations of fact, often through discovery and expert testimony. In attacking school segregation in the five cases styled as BROWN V. BOARD OF EDUCATION, the NAACP sought to develop full factual records, building upon the experience of THURGOOD MARSHALL and others as counsel in the earlier white primary cases and racial RESTRICTIVE COVENANT cases. Widespread test cases will continue because both government and private counsel can approach the Supreme Court only by representing particular parties with particular concrete claims.

CLEMENT E. VOSE
(1986)

Bibliography

CORTNER, RICHARD C.   1964   *The Wagner Act Cases.* Pages 106–141. Knoxville: University of Tennessee Press.
FREUND, PAUL A.   1951   *On Understanding the Supreme Court.* Pages 77–116. Boston: Little, Brown.
IRONS, PETER   1982   *The New Deal Lawyers.* Pages 234–289. Princeton, N.J.: Princeton University Press.
KLUGER, RICHARD   1975   *Simple Justice: The History of Brown v. Board of Education and Black America's Struggle for Equality.* Pages 256–540. New York: Vintage Books.
VOSE, CLEMENT E.   1959   Caucasians Only: The Supreme Court, the Naacp, and the Restrictive Covenant Cases. Pages 50–73, 151–176. Berkeley: University of California Press.
WOOD, STEPHEN B.   1968   *Constitutional Politics in the Progressive Era.* Pages 81–110. Chicago: University of Chicago Press.

# TESTIMONIAL AND NONTESTIMONIAL COMPULSION

In the 1960s the Supreme Court ruled that the RIGHT AGAINST SELF-INCRIMINATION was not infringed when police compelled the driver of an accident vehicle to give a blood sample for analysis of its alcoholic content, compelled a suspect in a LINEUP to utter before witnesses the words used by a bank robber, and compelled another suspected bank robber to submit a sample of his handwriting for comparison with a note given to a bankteller. In the 1970s the Court held that the right against self-incrimination did not protect a person from the compulsory production of business and tax records in the possession of his or her accountant or lawyer, and did not protect a person from a court order to make a voice recording for a federal GRAND JURY seeking to identify a criminal by the sound of a voice on a legally intercepted telephone conversation. All these decisions shared a thorny problem: if a person is compelled to provide the state with evidence to incriminate him, is he necessarily a witness against himself in the Fifth Amendment sense?

The Court prefers a different formulation: does nontestimonial compulsion force a person to be a witness against himself criminally? The consistent answer has been "no," even if there was a testimonial dimension to the forced admissions. If that testimonial dimension loomed too large, the Court loosened its distinction between testimonial and nontestimonial compulsion and relied on some other distinction. Thus, when the driver of a vehicle involved in an accident was required by state law to stop and identify himself, though doing so subjected him to criminal penalties, the Court saw no Fifth Amendment issue, only a regulation promoting the satisfaction of civil liabilities. Similarly, when a lawyer or accountant was forced to turn over a client's incriminating records, the client had not been compelled at all, though he paid the criminal penalty and lost the chance to make a Fifth Amendment plea. And when the police during the course of a lawful search found incriminating business records, the records were introduced in evidence, although they could not have been subpoenaed directly from the businessman. In these cases, where the compulsion was communicative or testimonial in character, the Court inconsistently discoursed on the need to decide as it did in order to avoid a decision against the introduction of nontestimonial evidence that had been compelled.

More often the Court relied on a supposed distinction between forcing a person to furnish evidence against himself of a testimonial nature and forcing him to be the source of nontestimonial or physical evidence against himself, usually derived from his body. The word "witness" implies giving testimony based on one's knowledge, not displaying one's person. Compulsion to reveal information other than one's physical characteristics is generally unconstitutional, especially if the information is derived directly from the party himself, though not if the police lawfully find his records. The Court's distinction between testimonial and nontestimonial compulsion is obviously a bit porous. That distinction derived from the realistic need to prevent the Fifth Amendment from disabling police identifications based on fingerprints, handwriting, photographs, blood samples, voice exemplars, and lineups. The distinction had its origin in a passing remark by Justice OLIVER WENDELL HOLMES in 1910, when he dismissed as "an extravagant extension of the Fifth Amendment" the claim that requiring a defendant to model a shirt for identification purposes breached the right against self-incrimination.

The trouble with the distinction, apart from the Court's own inconsistency, is that physical or identifying evidence can be communicative in character, as when a laboratory report, the result of a drunken driver's blood sample, is introduced against him, or when a grand jury indicts one whose voice identifies him as the culprit. Whether by writing, speaking, or giving blood involuntarily, an individual has been compelled to furnish evidence against himself. That he has not been forced to "testify" is a distinction less persuasive than semantically catchy. However, some such distinction seems necessary. The fundamental meaning of the Fifth Amendment is that a person need not be the unwilling instrument of his own undoing and that the state must find its own evidence against him without his involuntary cooperation, and a literal reading of the amendment would prevent the police from fingerprinting a suspect or making him stand in a lineup for identification purposes. Thus the Court must find ways around the amendment.

A minority of Justices have sought a compromise by permitting as nontestimonial that evidence which does not require volition or affirmative cooperation; thus, the lineup and taking blood, photographs, and fingerprints require merely passive conduct. If, however, incriminating evidence can be secured only by the active volition of one asked to repeat certain words, model clothing, or give a handwriting sample, these minority Justices would sustain a Fifth Amendment plea. But their distinction between volitional and passive acts is as hairsplitting as the majority's between testimonial and nontestimonial compulsion. Anyone overpowered to give a sample of his blood would scarcely think he affirmatively cooperated.

The Justices in the majority also make unreal distinctions, as between the physical properties of one's voice and the testimonial content of what he says: "This is a stickup" communicates more than pitch and resonance. If the right against self-incrimination protects a defendant at his trial from having to speak up for the benefit of witnesses, why does it not protect him in the grand jury room, the interrogation room, or the lineup?

The distinction between testimonial and nontestimonial compulsion derives from the needs of law enforcement and seems to be a permanent addition to constitutional law. The Court, which can reach whatever results it desires, probably will add to the roster of nontestimonial evidence that can be compelled and will narrow the meaning of testimonial compulsion or find exceptions to it.

LEONARD W. LEVY
(1986)

Bibliography

BAUER, W. J.  1977  Formalism, Legal Realism, & Constitutionally Protected Privacy under the Fourth & Fifth Amendments. *Harvard Law Review* 90:945–991.

KOONTZ, HAL and STODEL, JEFFREY 1973 The Scope of Testimonial Immunity under the Fifth: *Kastigar v. United States.* *Loyola* (Los Angeles) *Law Review* 6:350–383.

# TESTIMONIAL IMMUNITY

See: Immunity Grant

# TEST OATH CASES
*Cummings v. Missouri*
4 Wallace 277 (1867)
*Ex Parte Garland*
4 Wallace 333 (1867)

Historically test oaths were weapons to inflict penalties and punishments on obnoxious minorities and were enemies of freedom of political and religious thought. A test or LOYALTY OATH should not be confused with an oath of allegiance, which is a promissory oath by which one swears to support the government and, if assuming office, to discharge its duties faithfully. An oath of allegiance concerns future conduct. A test oath is retroactive and purgative, because it is a disclaimer of specific beliefs, associations, and behavior deemed criminal or disloyal.

Missouri by its constitution prescribed a series of disavowals of belief and past conduct in the form of oaths to be taken by all voters, jurors, state officers, clergymen, lawyers, teachers, and corporation officers. All must swear as a condition of voting, holding office, teaching, and the like, that they had never been in armed hostility to the United States, had never by word or deed manifested adherence to the enemies of the country or desired their victory, had never been connected with any organization inimical to the United States, and had never been a Southern sympathizer. Anyone teaching, preaching, voting, or engaging in any of the specified activities without first taking the oaths was subject to fine and imprisonment. Cummings, a Roman Catholic priest, carried on his religious duties without taking the oath and was convicted.

The test oath prescribed by Congress was a disclaimer of having served the Confederacy and applied only to federal officials until extended in 1865 to members of the federal bar. It could be construed as a wartime qualification for office until it was extended to peacetime and to members of the federal bar. Until then it was not passed to inflict punishment for past offenses. The oath disqualified AUGUSTUS H. GARLAND, who had spent the war as a member of the Confederate Congress, from resuming his prewar practice before the Supreme Court, although he had been given a presidential pardon.

The Supreme Court, Justice STEPHEN J. FIELD writing for a bare majority, held unconstitutional both the Missouri requirement of a test oath and the federal requirement of 1865. Field reasoned that each violated the bans against EX POST FACTO laws and BILLS OF ATTAINDER. To conclude that they constituted ex post facto laws, Field had to demonstrate that they retroactively imposed punishment for acts not criminal when committed. Missouri's dragnet covered not only hostile acts against the government but "words, desires, and sympathies also," and some of the acts were not even blameworthy. The federal statute reached acts that under certain circumstances might not have been offenses, such as assisting persons in armed hostility to the United States, serving in innocuous positions in the South, or reluctantly obeying the existing order. Persons who were incapable of truthfully taking the oaths suffered disabilities that constituted punishment, such as the deprivation of civil and political rights, disqualifications from office and from the pursuit of lawful professions, and, in the case of Garland, disbarment. Justice SAMUEL F. MILLER for the dissenters replied that an ex post facto law punished only in a criminal sense by imposing fines and imprisonment, not civil disabilities.

Field described a bill of attainder as a legislative act that inflicts punishment without a judicial trial. Attainders, he insisted, could be directed against whole classes, not just named individuals, and might inflict punishments conditionally, as in these cases. Cummings the priest and Garland the lawyer were presumed guilty until they removed that presumption by their expurgatory oaths; if it was not removed, they faced the punishment of being deprived of their professions without trial and conviction. Miller could see no attainder because the required oaths designated no criminal by name or description, declared no guilt, and inflicted neither sentence nor punishment. He saw merely a qualification for office, a position that Field savaged. Miller accurately argued, however, that Field stretched the conventional meanings of ex post facto laws and bills of attainder to cover the cases before the Court. For that reason, these decisions are today considered triumphs for CIVIL LIBERTIES; in their time, however, they exposed the Court to accusations of sympathizing with the Confederate cause, opposing Reconstruction, and assisting enemies of the Union.

LEONARD W. LEVY
(1986)

Bibliography

FAIRMAN, CHARLES 1939 *Mr. Justice Miller and the Supreme Court.* Pages 129–136. Cambridge, Mass.: Harvard University Press.

SWISHER, CARL BRENT (1930) 1963 *Stephen J. Field: Craftsman of the Law.* Pages 138–154. Hamden, Conn.: Archon Books.

## TEXAS v. BROWN
### 460 U.S. 730 (1983)

This case is significant for Justice WILLIAM H. REHNQUIST's exposition of the scope and applicability of the PLAIN VIEW DOCTRINE, which had emerged in COOLIDGE V. NEW HAMPSHIRE (1971) as an exception to the warrant requirement for a SEARCH AND SEIZURE. According to Rehnquist, the answer to the question whether property in plain view may be seized depends on the lawfulness of the intrusion that allows the police to see that property. Plain view therefore provides the basis for seizure if an officer's access to the object has a prior FOURTH AMENDMENT justification. The police may seize a suspicious object if they are engaged in a lawful activity; they do not have to know at once that the object inadvertently exposed to their sight is EVIDENCE of a crime. Reasonable suspicion on PROBABLE CAUSE is sufficient even if the property seized was not immediately apparent as evidence of crime. No Justice dissented in this case, but Rehnquist spoke for a mere plurality, and a mere plurality had announced the plain view doctrine in *Coolidge.* Accordingly, judicial controversy about the doctrine will continue, as will controversy about its application to particular facts.

LEONARD W. LEVY
(1986)

## TEXAS v. JOHNSON

See: Flag Desecration

## TEXAS v. WHITE
### 7 Wallace 700 (1869)

In 1867 the Court accepted ORIGINAL JURISDICTION of *Texas v. White* because one party was a state (Article III, section 2). So doing, the Court raised again, as in EX PARTE MILLIGAN (1866) and the TEST OATH cases, a possibility of judicial intervention into military reconstruction. Some decision on the state-status question was needed. Democrats insisted that the nation was not empowered to answer the state-status question and that the South's states, like bottom-weighted dolls, had sprung up, fully restored, with prevailing race hierarchies intact, in the wake of Union Army advances. Almost all Republicans assumed that the South's states, by attempting to secede, had twisted themselves out of their proper federal relations; that the Constitution (Article IV, section 4) imposed a duty on the

nation to guarantee every state a REPUBLICAN FORM OF GOVERNMENT; and that the nation also possessed temporary "grasp of war" dominion over the defeated states.

Post-Appomattox Texas wished to recover possession of state bonds that secessionist Texas had sold. Counsel for bond buyers argued in 1869, when the Supreme Court heard *Texas v. White,* that Texas was always a state and the sales were valid. Special counsel for Texas, Unionist George Washington Paschal, author of a recent treatise on the Constitution, insisted that though Texas remained a state, its acts adverse to federal responsibilities invalidated the bond sales; the state should recover the bonds.

Chief Justice SALMON P. CHASE, for the majority of the Court, accepted and restated Paschal's position. The Constitution "looks to an indestructible Union composed of indestructible States." SECESSION was void. Texas's acts supportive of rebellion, performed while seceded, were unsupportable.

Justices ROBERT C. GRIER, SAMUEL F. MILLER, and NOAH SWAYNE insisted that Texas was as much out of the Union in 1869 as in 1861. Therefore the original jurisdiction clause of the Constitution did not apply.

Both the majority and the minority stressed Congress's primacy in defining a state's status. Chase, though insisting that he was not pronouncing upon military reconstruction, by implication approved its constitutional bases and reinforced Court pretensions to at least an equal share, if not more, in implementation of policy, through its review authority.

HAROLD M. HYMAN
(1986)

## TEXAS ANNEXATION

See: Annexation of Texas

## TEXAS MONTHLY, INC. v. BULLOCK
### 489 U.S. 1 (1989)

The decision in this case affected the fifteen states whose statutes on sales and use taxes exempted religious publications. Texas exempted periodicals that consisted entirely of writings promulgating a religious faith. Voting 6–3, the Court held the act unconstitutional. Justice BYRON R. WHITE believed that because the statute discriminated on the basis of the content of publication, it violated the free-press clause. A bare majority believed that the statute violated the ESTABLISHMENT CLAUSE. Justice WILLIAM J. BRENNAN, for the Court, concluded that the statute failed to serve the secular purpose of maintaining the SEPARATION OF CHURCH AND STATE, but rather, had the purpose of advancing the religious mission of a particular faith. The exemption of the religious periodical in effect subsidized its teachings at the expense of taxpayers who were not exempt from the tax.

Brennan went further, thereby losing Justices HARRY A. BLACKMUN and SANDRA DAY O'CONNOR, when he also declared the statute violative of the free-exercise clause. Blackmun and O'Connor preferred to rest exclusively on the establishment clause, believing that Brennan's free-exercise argument subordinated RELIGIOUS LIBERTY to the establishment clause. In dissent, Justices ANTONIN SCALIA, WILLIAM H. REHNQUIST, and ANTHONY M. KENNEDY protested that the Court had mangled its own PRECEDENTS and diminished the free-exercies clause. Their views, however would have altered the constitutional law of the subject.

LEONARD W. LEVY
(1992)

# TEXTUALISM

Textualism denotes the opinion that whenever possible, judges resolving questions of constitutional law should rely primarily on the language of the Constitution itself. The text should guide decision and the text itself, rather than other considerations such as ORIGINAL INTENT, ratifier intent, history, principles inferred from the text, altered circumstances, judicial readings of societal values, or even judicial precedents. Justice OWEN J. ROBERTS, for the Court in UNITED STATES V. BUTLER (1936), manifested an allegiance to textualism when he declared that the constitutionality of a contested statute should be squared against the appropriate language of the text to see if they match.

This view of the best way to determine constitutionality was the most prevalent one at the time of the making of the Constitution. THOMAS JEFFERSON and ALEXANDER HAMILTON differed on the question as to whether an act of Congress incorporating a bank was constitutional; but, as Hamilton said, Jefferson would agree "that whatever may have been the intention of the framers of a constitution, or of a law, that intention is to be sought for in the instrument itself, according to the usual established rules of construction." Hamilton accurately stated the truth of the matter to the founding generation.

Despite near unanimity on the propriety of interpreting the Constitution according to established rules of construction, the Framers arrived at contradictory results when applying those rules to numerous important constitutional issues. Their belief in textualism did not prevent them from dividing on the removal power, the power to charter a corporation, the power to declare neutrality, the scope of executive powers, the power to enact excise and use taxes without apportioning them on population, the

power of a treaty to obligate the House to appropriate money, the power of JUDICIAL REVIEW, the power to deport aliens, the power to pass an act against SEDITIOUS LIBEL, the power to abolish judicial offices of life tenure, and the jurisdiction of the Supreme Court to decide suits against states without their consent or to issue writs of MANDAMUS against executive officers.

Rules of constitutional construction by which to construe the text are comparable to those of statutory construction, which a current federal judge, Frank Easterbrook, called "a total jumble." For every rule, as Karl Llewellyn demonstrated in his *Common Law Tradition*, "there is an equal and opposite rule." A master commentator, Justice JOSEPH STORY, discoursed on the rules of construction for some sixty pages in his *Commentaries on the Constitution*, yet he failed completely to convince his Jacksonian colleagues on the bench. Rules of construction in effect free, rather than fetter, judicial discretion. The fact remains, however, that textualism should be the bedrock of judicial review; as Story said, "Nothing but the text itself was adopted by the whole people." Whenever the fair or plain meaning of the Constitution can be ascertained, it should guide judgment.

The problem is that the Constitution is a brief elliptical document framed by common lawyers trained to believe that a few comprehensive and expansive principles supplementing a structural description will be infinitely adaptable and will provide guides that can serve to answer virtually any question that might arise on a case-to-case basis. In some crucial respects, the Constitution resembles Martin Chuzzlewit's grandnephew, who, Dickens said, "had no more than the first idea and sketchy notion of a face." The Framers had a genius for studied imprecision and calculated ambiguity. They relied on many general terms because common lawyers expressed themselves that way out of conviction and because politics required compromise, and compromise required ambiguity and vagueness.

The text, even with twenty-six amendments that have been added in two centuries, is scarcely 7,000 words long, and only about two percent of the verbiage possesses any significance in constitutional law. Almost without exception, these are the purposefully or unavoidably general terms: commerce among the states, OBLIGATION OF CONTRACTS, NECESSARY AND PROPER, BILLS OF CREDIT, REPUBLICAN FORM OF GOVERNMENT, DUE PROCESS OF LAW, PRIVILEGES AND IMMUNITIES, direct taxes, GENERAL WELFARE, liberty, UNREASONABLE SEARCHES, EQUAL PROTECTION, and the like.

For the most part, the CONSTITUTIONAL CONVENTION OF 1787 designed the Constitution with the utmost diligence and attention to detail. The Convention usually chose words with craft and craftsmanship. This is the reason that constitutional law does not involve the bulk of the Constitution. It does not have to be litigated because it is clear and understandable. Consequently, the vagueness and ambiguities found in the Constitution were probably deliberate. In THE FEDERALIST #37, JAMES MADISON replied to the Anti-Federalist criticism that the Constitution's lack of clarity on some matters threatened the states and liberty. Obscure and equivocal language was inevitable, he contended, but its meaning would be clarified in time by adjudications. ABRAHAM BALDWIN of Georgia, another Framer, declared that some subjects were left "a little ambiguous and uncertain" for political reasons and would be settled in time by practice or by amendments. Some textual language remained open-ended to avoid giving offense by explicitness. Treaty powers, judicial powers, and rival powers of legislation fell into these categories, according to Baldwin.

Ambiguity and vagueness arise in the nonstructural sections. Ambiguous words permit different understandings; vague words do not allow for much understanding. The exceptions clause of Article III is a good example of ambiguity. It might mean that Congress may switch APPELLATE JURISDICTION to ORIGINAL JURISDICTION, thereby adding to the Supreme Court's original jurisdiction, as counsel in MARBURY V. MADISON (1803) argued, or it might mean that the original jurisdiction of the Court is fixed, as JOHN MARSHALL held. If the exceptions clause means that Congress may make exceptions to the Court's jurisdiction by diminishing its appellate jurisdiction, how far can Congress go? And how can the Court exercise the jurisdiction specified in Article III as belonging to the JUDICIAL POWER OF THE UNITED STATES if it is dependent on Congress's will?

The text of Article I, section 8, poses problems too. Congress may pass no capitation or "other direct tax" unless apportioned among the states on the basis of population. Although the Framers probably regarded direct taxes as only taxes imposed on people per capita and on land, they did not say so. They left "other direct taxes" open to interpretation. Article I, section 8, on the tax power is all the more puzzling because it is not known whether the tax power connotes an equally expansive power to spend, and the meaning of the "general welfare" is equally mystifying. Constitutional government as the Framers understood it cannot survive a national power to legislate for the general welfare, nor can the federal system survive a national power authorized to spend for the general welfare, yet the text gives credibility to these views.

The term "in pursuance of" in Article VI (the SUPREMACY CLAUSE) is also ambiguous. Usually this term is taken to mean that in order for acts of Congress to be constitutional, they must be consistent with the Constitution. The "in pursuance of" clause is a mainstay of the argument that the Supreme Court may exercise judicial review over

acts of Congress. Yet at the time of the framing, the text of the ARTICLES OF CONFEDERATION showed that "in pursuance of" meant "under authority of" or "done in prosecution of."

The EXECUTIVE POWER with which the President is endowed is ambiguous too. It is not known what is meant by the executive power, apart from an obligation to execute the laws faithfully. Moreover, the text indicates that the President can call on the armed forces to suppress rebellions or repel attacks, but not whether he can engage in military hostilities without either congressional support or a congressional DECLARATION OF WAR. In the case of EXECUTIVE AGREEMENTS, there is not even a vague provision of the Constitution to construe. Nothing in the document authorizes treaty-making by the President without the ADVICE AND CONSENT of the Senate. Nothing in the document authorizes the Congress to empower the President to make international agreements that have the force of the supreme law of the land or authorizes such agreements to have this force when both branches of Congress retroactively or subsequently approve of an international agreement made by the President on the President's own initiative. Nevertheless, Presidents have been making executive agreements with foreign nations throughout U.S. history and on major matters, without successful constitutional challenge. Moreover, the text of the Constitution does not provide for the device of the JOINT CONGRESSIONAL RESULTION. By this device, Congress has considerably augmented its powers in foreign affairs, as when it annexed Texas and then Hawaii to circumvent the requirement of a two-thirds vote of the Senate to approve treaties.

Three major provisions of the Constitution are among the vaguest: Congress has the power to regulate commerce among the states; neither the national government nor a state may take life, liberty, or property without due process of law; and no state may deny to any person the equal protection of the laws. These are the most litigated clauses in U.S. constitutional history because they are among the muddiest and most important.

Even the seemingly specific injunctions and provisions of the BILL OF RIGHTS are vague or ambiguous, offering little guidance for interpretation. A good example of such ambiguity is the term ESTABLISHMENT OF RELIGION in the FIRST AMENDMENT. James Madison, its author, mistakenly used the term interchangeably with "religious establishment," which denotes an institution of religion such as a church or sectarian school. "Religious establishment" carries no implication of government aid to religion or government involvement with it, as does "establishment of religion." When Madison misquoted the clause as if it outlawed religious establishment, he meant that the government had no authority to legislate on religion or its institutions. Nevertheless, the term itself has no self-evident meaning. History supplies that meaning, and historians differ.

The term FREEDOM OF THE PRESS constitutes another ambiguity. In Anglo-American thought and law, it meant an exemption from PRIOR RESTRAINT; it did not exclude liability under the criminal law for seditious, obscene, or blasphemous LIBEL. In contrast, the Framers, who did not adopt or reject the definition of a free press under the COMMON LAW, knew only a rasping, corrosive, and licentious press. They did not likely use the term "freedom of the press" without intending to protect the freedom that in fact existed and that they knew. The text itself surely lacks clarity. It declares in absolute terms that Congress shall make no law abridging the freedom of speech or press, but the COPYRIGHT clause of the Constitution authorizes Congress to make laws that do abridge the freedom of speech and press of those who would infringe copyrights.

This same clause, in Article I, section 8, refers only to "authors and inventors," making a literal interpretation of it fail to protect artists, sculptors, composers, computer-software designers, television programmers, and many others who come under its protection. If only authors and inventors benefited from the clause, they could not even assign a copyright to others. The problem with the copyright clause is not that it is ambiguous or vague; it is utterly clear. But, it possesses inappropriate specificity and therefore cannot mean what it says.

The First Amendment exhibits the same problem. Assuming that its framers chose their language carefully, the fact that they failed to give adequate protection to the free exercise of religion must be confronted. The text declares that the freedom of the press may not be abridged, but by contrast, only says that freedom of religion may not be prohibited. This is a comparatively diminished protection because freedom of religion may be abridged in many ways without being prohibited. The same amendment also suffers from terminological exactitude: Congress shall make "no law" abridging freedom of the press. A reliance on textualism would mean that neither PORNOGRAPHY nor direct and successful verbal incitements to crime can be abridged. Yet the absolute of "no law" cannot apply to copyright laws, which can constitute abridgments.

The Fifth Amendment's self-incrimination clause cannot be taken literally either. If the text meant what it says, it meant little when framed because defendants then had no right to give sworn testimony for or against themselves. Moreover, the clause protected the right only in criminal cases, but the right existed in civil as well as criminal cases and in nonjudicial proceedings such as grand jury and legislative investigations. Finally, a person may be compelled to be a witness against himself or herself in noncriminal ways; at the time of the adoption of the Bill of Rights, the

Fifth Amendment right protected persons from being forced to expose themselves to public infamy. In 1892, the Supreme Court acknowledged that the text does not mean what it says; the Court declared, "It is impossible that the meaning of the constitutional provision can only be that a person shall not be compelled to be a witness against himself in a criminal prosecution against himself."

Other examples of the text not meaning what it says appear in the Sixth Amendment, which enumerates a variety of RIGHTS OF THE CRIMINALLY ACCUSED available to them "in all criminal prosecutions." "All" is an absolute that admits of no exceptions. Yet the Framers did not intend to extend the right of TRIAL BY JURY to misdemeanants; persons accused of petty crimes were tried in a more summary manner than trial by jury. In this regard, the Sixth Amendment reinforced the provision in Article III, section 2: "The trial of all crimes, except in cases of impeachment, shall be by jury. . . ." "All crimes" here means merely all felonies; the exception for impeachments really extended to misdemeanors also. Misdemeanants are still not entitled to trial by jury unless they can be imprisoned for more than six months. The text misleads.

Similarly, the right to the assistance of counsel in all criminal prosecutions does not mean what it says: "In all criminal prosecutions, the accused . . . shall have the assistance of counsel." "Shall" conveys an imperative; but the amendment merely meant that one might have counsel if he or she could afford it. Not until 1932 did indigents receive the benefit of court-appointed counsel in capital cases in state courts; not until 1938 did all federal defendants receive the right to court-appointed counsel in any criminal prosecution. Juveniles have long been deprived of the right to trial by jury, and no one is entitled to be represented by counsel before a GRAND JURY, which initiates a criminal prosecution. Furthermore, the text does not mean what it says in the provision that in all criminal prosecutions the accused shall be confronted with the witnesses against them; the exceptions to this, in fact, are numerous.

The problem of inappropriate specificity appears in the DOUBLE JEOPARDY clause of the Fifth Amendment: "Nor shall any person be subject for the same offense to be twice put in jeopardy of life or limb." Here the Constitution neither means what it says, nor says what it means. It means "life or liberty," not "life or limb." The reference to "limb" is meaningless because we have long ceased to tear people apart or crop their ears. One cannot be put in jeopardy of loss of limb even if convicted by due process of law at a single trial. The double jeopardy clause implies, however, that a conviction can result in loss of limb. This would surely constitute a violation of the Eighth Amendment's guarantee against CRUEL AND UNUSUAL PUNISHMENT. The text also leads to a logical puzzle. Life may be taken if one receives due process and is not exposed to double jeopardy. But if limb may not be taken, why may life be taken?

The SECOND AMENDMENT is both vague and ambiguous. Some think it upholds the collective right of state militias to bear arms, while others argue that it protects the right of individuals to bear arms. But this right existed only to maintain militias. If a standing army, even in peacetime, has succeeded militias, and if the armed forces provides weapons to those in the service, the reason for the right to bear arms may no longer be as apparent as it once was. "Arms" once meant a flintlock rifle. Does the right to bear arms include a right to bear a Saturday-night special, an assault rifle, or a bazooka?

Vagueness, not ambiguity, saturates the FOURTH AMENDMENT, which prohibits "unreasonable" SEARCH AND SEIZURE and provides that no warrants shall issue "but on probable cause." "Unreasonable" and "probable" rank high on any list of indefinite terms. It is possible, similarly, to parse every provision of the Bill of Rights and be bewildered by the meaning of the text. Terms such as SPEEDY TRIAL, JUST COMPENSATION, PUBLIC USE, "impartial jury," "excessive bail," "excessive fines," and "cruel and unusual" simply do not permit a constitutional jurisprudence to be based securely on textualism. To speak of STRICT CONSTRUCTION is faintly ridiculous given the imprecision of the provisions of the Bill of Rights and of the FOURTEENTH AMENDMENT. Ambiguity cannot be strictly construed. Strictly construing vagueness as well as inappropriately specific terms can equally lead to ludicrous, tragic, or unjust results.

The Constitution is, indeed, as Jefferson once said in exasperation, "a thing of wax that the Judiciary may twist and shape into any form they please." Unlike Humpty Dumpty, the Framers of the Constitution were unable to make words mean what they wanted them to mean. Perhaps they sensed that America would change beyond their grasp, and they did not think they could master the future. Perhaps they understood, with JAMES WILSON, that they were representatives "not merely of the present age, but of future times; not merely of the territory along the seacoast, but of regions immensely extended westward." This is the reason the Constitutional Convention accepted the advice of EDMUND RANDOLPH to keep the Constitution focused on "essential principles" so it can "be accomodated [sic] to times and events." The text is merely a point of departure; textualism as constitutional gospel is as impractical as original intent. Like original intent, however, textualism is entitled to serious attention, within its distinct limits, because Story was right: the people of the United States ratified the text, only the text, and it is the fundamental and supreme law of the land.

LEONARD W. LEVY
(1992)

Bibliography

LAYCOCK, DOUGLAS. 1984 Taking Constitutions Seriously: A Theory of Judicial Review. *Texas Law Review* 59:343–394.

LEVY, LEONARD W. 1988 *Original Intent and the Framers' Constitution.* New York: Macmillan.

SCHAUER, FREDERICK 1985 Easy Cases. *Southern California Law Review* 58:399–440.

TUSHNET, MARK V. 1985 A Note on the Revival of Textualism in Constitutional Theory. *Southern California Law Review* 58:683–700.

# THAYER, JAMES BRADLEY
## (1831–1902)

American jurist, Harvard law professor, and author of a masterful treatise on EVIDENCE. Thayer is important in constitutional studies for his powerful advocacy of judicial self-restraint, or deference to legislation challenged as unconstitutional. He influenced Justices LOUIS D. BRANDEIS, FELIX FRANKFURTER, and OLIVER WENDELL HOLMES, and Judge LEARNED HAND.

Thayer invoked a supposedly established judicial rule which, recognizing that the Constitution admitted of different interpretations and allowed legislatures a vast range of permissible choice, required that all rational legislative choices be adjudged constitutional. Properly holding legislation unconstitutional only in cases clear beyond REASONABLE DOUBT, courts should not consider their own views on unconstitutionality, but should consider instead whether the legislature could reasonably have thought its actions constitutional. (See RATIONAL BASIS.)

Thayer regarded JUDICIAL REVIEW as a legitimate outgrowth of American experience and as a valuable conservative admixture in popular government. But he warned that this "outside" corrective threatened to curtail the people's political education. His strictures against JUDICIAL ACTIVISM were published just as the Supreme Court was embarking on a course of active defense of FREEDOM OF CONTRACT against ECONOMIC REGULATION. In a later era, when the Court's activism turned to personal liberties of another kind, Thayer's rule came under criticism: it was not an "established rule," but a policy preference; its reasonable doubt standard either would enfeeble judicial review or would be too flexible to restrain courts effectively; its applicability in Supreme Court review of state legislation was unclear; it was particularly inappropriate for legislation affecting specific BILL OF RIGHTS guarantees. Regrettably, Thayer himself had not adequately explored either the strengths and weaknesses of his rule or the broader underlying problem—how to square JUDICIAL REVIEW AND DEMOCRACY.

HOWARD E. DEAN
(1986)

Bibliography

THAYER, JAMES BRADLEY 1893 The Origin and Scope of the American Doctrine of Constitutional Law. *Harvard Law Review* 7:129–156.

# THEORIES OF THE UNION

Political unions are organizations of states possessing specific powers for carrying out purposes of mutual interest to constituent polities. Unions are formed by means of confederation or federation, and by definition are combinative or compound in nature rather than unitary or homogeneous. In American history the Union refers to the general structure of political authority created during the Revolution by the American people, acting through their colonial and state governments, for the pursuit of common purposes as an expression of their incipient nationality. Theories of the Union are explanations of the American state system, descriptive and normative in purpose, which have been formulated to guide political action and resolve controversies among the member states. Especially important in the period from 1789 to 1868, theories of the Union have been concerned with four principal issues: the origin and nature of statehood; the nature and extent of state powers; the origin, nature, and extent of the powers of the central government; and the manner of resolving conflicts between the states and the central authority.

Although intercolonial cooperation occurred intermittently before the Revolution, in an effective political sense the formation by the colonies in 1774 of an assembly to deal with imperial matters of common concern marked the beginning of the American Union. In 1776 this assembly, the CONTINENTAL CONGRESS, issued the DECLARATION OF INDEPENDENCE, proclaiming that the colonies "are, and of right ought to be, free and independent states." Yet the Declaration also referred to the people in the colonies as "one people," and to the colonies as "the United States of America." The practical effect was to announce the existence of a national Union comprising thirteen state governments and a central body, Congress, which, although not constituted as a government and incapable of legislating for individuals in the states, was more than merely the agent of the states. Although theory and principle to explain this new compound political organization were yet to be formulated, the fact of a division of SOVEREIGNTY characterized the American Union from the outset.

The Union thus existed as political reality before it was rationalized in a formal instrument of government, the ARTICLES OF CONFEDERATION (1781). Asserting that "[e]ach State retains its sovereignty, freedom and independence, and every Power, JURISDICTION, and right which is not by this confederation expressly delegated to the United States," the Articles conformed to the model of a league of autonomous states. However, the language of state sovereignty notwithstanding, the states were not perfect states. And Congress, although empowered only to make resolutions and recommendations rather than to make law, in matters submitted to its consideration acted as a real government. In practical effect the Union resembled the operation of the British empire, in which sovereignty had been divided between the colonial governments managing local affairs and the authority of Parliament regulating matters of general interest in the empire.

Theory of the Union was relevant to territorial problems of the 1780s, which raised the question of the origin and nature of statehood. The original colonies based their claim to statehood on their COLONIAL CHARTERS and the fact of succession to previously existing political establishments. This theory of the creation of states implied a fixed or determinate Union, and was useless to those people—either in existing states or outside them—who desired to form new states and join the Union. An alternative approach was to claim a revolutionary right of self-government; Vermont may be said to have employed this principle in its struggle to separate from New York and achieve statehood. A third method of state making was to form a political community and secure recognition from the other states. This technique was developed in the 1780s when Virginia and other states with extensive land claims, desiring to confirm their sovereignty, ceded some of their lands to Congress and secured in return approval of their claims and state boundaries. Implicit in these transactions was an expansive rather than static conception of the Union: although states might proclaim their sovereignty, the determination of statehood—the very existence of the states—depended on the sanction of the other states acting through Congress.

The CONSTITUTIONAL CONVENTION OF 1787 altered the nature and structure of the Union by creating a central government, capable of making law and regulating individuals, in place of the noncoercive authority of the Confederation. Precisely how much and in what ways the restructured Union differed from the Confederation was debated during the process of RATIFICATION OF THE CONSTITUTION. These debates gave rise to the classic theories of the Union expounded by statesmen of the early national period.

In providing for a government based on the SEPARATION OF POWERS and comprising a legislature elected in part by the people, the Framers of the Constitution applied republican principles to the problem of organizing the American Union. They did not, however, completely reject the essential principle of the Confederation, the idea that the states were the constituent power. This principle was retained in the provisions for equal state representation in the Senate and for the contingency plan for electing the President in the House of Representatives, where each state was to have had one vote. The result, as JAMES MADISON wrote in THE FEDERALIST #39, was a government partly national and partly federal in respect of the source, operation, and extent of its powers; the constituent basis on which it was established; and the nature of the amending authority. Some of these functions embodied the idea that the American people as a single national community were the constituent power; others, the idea that the states as separate political communities were constituting the central government.

In contemporary usage the term "federal" referred to a confederation of sovereign states, and the word "national" to a unitary government operating directly on individuals. Accordingly, the Articles of Confederation were described as a federal government. But the supporters of the new government, combining elements of both a confederation and a unitary national government, called *it* a federal government. In doing so they gave a new definition to FEDERALISM as the division of sovereignty among a central government and separate state governments operating on the same population in the same area.

In the ratification controversy Federalists and Anti-Federalists combined arguments from history, the constitutional text, and political theory to fashion competing theories of the Union in pursuit of their divergent political goals. Denying that sovereignty could be divided, Anti-Federalists warned that the proposed central government would transform the Union into a consolidated state. The Federalists, in order to allay STATES' RIGHTS apprehensions, stressed the division of authority between the states and the central government and the ultimate sovereignty of the people. Although the Federalists glossed over conflicts that were bound to arise in a governmental system based on a division of sovereign authority, their constitutional theory confirmed the main tendencies in the operation of the American Union from its inception.

Perhaps the single most important formulation of Unionist theory was contained in the VIRGINIA AND KENTUCKY RESOLUTIONS of 1798–1799, written by JAMES MADISON and THOMAS JEFFERSON. Seeking a constitutionally legitimate way to prevent the enforcement of the ALIEN AND SEDITION ACTS, the Republican party leaders advanced the compact theory of the Union. On this theory were based all subsequent assertions of states' rights and state sovereignty, including those supporting SECESSION in 1861.

Jefferson and Madison argued that the Union was a compact made by the states, which as the constituent parties retained the right to judge whether the central government had violated the compact. Exercising this right by the accepted practices for implementing compacts, the states, according to Madison, could "interpose" their authority to stop unconstitutional acts of the central govern-

ment. In the Kentucky Resolutions of 1799 Jefferson declared that a NULLIFICATION by the sovereign states of all unauthorized acts of the federal government was "the rightful remedy." The theory thus propounded held that the states created the Union; the federal government could exercise only delegated powers, not including regulation of speech and press, which were reserved to the states; and the states had authority to question the exercise of central authority and by implication to settle constitutional disputes over federal-state relations.

Whether Madison and Jefferson contemplated peaceful concerted action by the states, or single-state defiance of federal authority (possibly by force, as was later proposed in South Carolina), their action served as precedent and model for one of the basic strategies of constitutional politics throughout the antebellum period. From the standpoint of constitutional law the most significant feature of the compact theory was the proposition that the states had created the Constitution and the Union. The argument could mean any number of things depending on how a state was defined. A state could be considered to be the territory occupied by a political community, the governing institutions and officers of the community, or the people forming the community. In his report to the Virginia legislature in 1800, Madison used the third of these definitions to explain how the states, through the ratification process, had made the Constitution. On this theory, the TENTH AMENDMENT expressed the equivalence of state and people, reserving powers not delegated to the federal government "to the States respectively or to the people." A fixed feature of later states' rights and state sovereignty teaching, this popular conception of statehood enabled compact theorists to define the nation as self-governing political communities founded on common republican principles.

An alternative theory of the Union was propounded by the Federalist party. Federalists held that the Constitution and the Union had been made by the people of the United States, who as the constituent power had divided sovereignty between the states and the central government. The government of the United States possessed limited powers, but within its sphere of action it was supreme. Federalists, and their Whig political descendants in the 1830s, further reasoned that according to the original constitutional design conflicts in federal-state relations were to be resolved by the federal judiciary. In his debate with Robert Y. Hayne of South Carolina in 1830 on the nature of the Union, DANIEL WEBSTER said the judicial article and the SUPREMACY CLAUSE were the "key-stone of the arch" of Union. "With these," he declared, "it is a constitution; without them, it is a confederacy."

Distrusting localism, Federalists identified the nation with the central government, and theirs is often referred to as the nationalist theory of the Union. This reference is misleading, however, insofar as it implies that the compact theory was not a valid expression of American nationality. Properly regarded, the Federalist-Whig doctrine is the central supremacy theory of the Union. Acknowledging divided sovereignty and the limited nature of federal authority, Federalists and Whigs recognized states' rights as essential to the Union. But, believing the nation could act only through the central government, they insisted on the supremacy of federal power when it conflicted with an otherwise legitimate state power. The supremacy clause of the Constitution was the positive expression of the principle of federal paramountcy that its proponents believed was intended to guide national development.

In refuting the compact theory, central supremacy theorists made the popular origins of the Union their most distinctive tenet. They insisted that the Constitution was not a compact made by the states but an instrument of government made by "the people of the United States." The meaning of this term is not self-evident. It might be taken to mean that the American people constituted and could act as a single political community. Webster seemed to have this conception in mind when in the debate with Hayne he argued that the Constitution "pronounces that it is established by the people of the United States in the aggregate," not by the states or even by the people of the several states. JOHN MARSHALL stated the popular-origins thesis more carefully in MCCULLOCH V. MARYLAND (1819). Marshall observed that the Constitution was "submitted to the people" for ratification, and they acted on it "by assembling in Convention." In a sense Marshall conceded the compact theorists' main point—that the Constitution had been ratified by the people acting as separate political communities. "It is true," he wrote, "they assembled in their several States." But he discounted the significance of this fact, adding: "and where else should they have assembled? No political dreamer was ever wild enough to think of breaking down the lines which separate the States, and of compounding the American people into one common mass. Of consequence, when they act they act in their States." Thus the same facts on which the compact theorists based their conclusion that the Union was made by the states supported the central supremacy contention that the Union was made by the people of the United States.

From 1830 to 1860 theories of the Union continued to have political significance as Americans expanded territorially and struggled with the slavery question. Two variations of the compact theory were developed to protect slavery within the state system: DUAL FEDERALISM and the nullification theory of JOHN C. CALHOUN of South Carolina. Within the central supremacy theory, meanwhile, the idea of the Union as perpetual and indissoluble was elaborated.

Although formally accepting divided sovereignty, dual federalists in a practical sense sought to remove actual or potential central government restraints on state power, including the power to protect slavery. Insisting that the reserved powers of the states constituted a limitation on the federal government, they regarded the Tenth Amendment as a kind of supremacy clause for the states. Accordingly, in cases such as NEW YORK V. MILN (1837) the Supreme Court under Chief Justice ROGER B. TANEY, reversing the effect of Marshall's central supremacy unionism, held that state powers over matters of "police" had not been surrendered to federal authority.

Calhoun's doctrine of nullification, employed in South Carolina's fight against the tariff in 1832, was a more radical extension of the compact theory of the Union. Calhoun held that federal powers were granted in trust by the states, which he defined as the people exercising indivisible sovereignty in separate political communities. He thus rejected the principle of divided sovereignty. Picking up where Madison and Jefferson had left off, Calhoun sought to devise a constitutional means of obstructing unconstitutional acts of the central government. His ingenious, if ultimately perverse, solution was to transform the creative constituent power of the states, identified in the Article V amending power, into an instrument of negation. Calhoun reasoned that a state, acting in popular convention, might interpose its authority to nullify a federal measure. The states would then be consulted, and if three-fourths of them did not approve the objectionable measure it would be withdrawn. If, however, the states upheld the central government, the nullifying state could secede from the Union.

Placed on the defensive by the nullificationists, central supremacy advocates were moved to insist on the perpetuity of the Union. This idea was implicit in the very creation of the Constitution. The fact that the Articles of Confederation referred to the Union as "perpetual" did not prevent men from believing that a state might withdraw its membership; by the same token the omission from the Constitution of the language of perpetuity did not mean that the Framers considered the Union to be anything less than a permanent government. It is nevertheless significant that while the terms disunion and secession were employed in the early nineteenth century, not until the nullification crisis did central supremacy theorists like Webster and JOHN QUINCY ADAMS explicate the perpetuity idea. Their argument may be described as declaratory in nature. But it was not only Whig keepers of the central supremacy tradition but also Democrats who met the South Carolina challenge by asserting perpetual Unionism. In his Proclamation to South Carolina (1832) President ANDREW JACKSON condemned secession as unconstitutional and affirmed the Constitution as a binding obligation on the states.

Changing little as constitutional doctrine, the central supremacy theory of the Union formed part of a nationalist ideology that emerged in the North in the pre-Civil War period. In contrast to the universalistic, democratic, and decentralized nationalism associated with the compact school, northern nationalism, based on New England Federalist sources and developed by Whig and Republican politicians, was historical, ethnic, cultural, and religious in nature. Whereas President GEORGE WASHINGTON in his Farewell Address had said it was the "unity of government which constitutes you one people," central supremacy theorists such as FRANCIS LIEBER turned the equation around by regarding the American people as forming a sovereign national community, from which emanated the Constitution and the Union. In this sectionally sponsored nationalism, the Union, without ceasing to be a means of securing liberty, became as well an end in itself: an organically rooted thing of absolute and intrinsic value.

Theories of the Union had a configurative as well as causative effect on the Civil War and Reconstruction. The existence of the compact theory—and the reiteration of this theory from 1798 to 1860 as the basis for states' rights, nullification, and disunionist demands—provided an arguably constitutional course of action for Southerners to follow in seceding from the Union in response to the antislavery threat. In the North the tradition of central supremacy constitutionalism was available to rationalize and sustain the Republican party's decision to resist secession. Pronouncing secession "the essence of anarchy," President ABRAHAM LINCOLN in 1861 affirmed the perpetuity of the Union, declared its primacy over the states, and asserted that "the States have their *status* in the Union, and they have no other *legal status.*" The war would be fought, Congress resolved in 1861, "to defend and maintain the supremacy of the Constitution and to preserve the Union, with all the dignity, equality, and rights of the several States unimpaired."

Applying central supremacy tenets, the United States government between 1861 and 1868 regarded the Union as unbroken in a constitutional sense. It denied any legal effect to secession, treated the rebellious states as disorganized communities, and adopted measures to form loyal state governments capable of resuming their place in the Union. Acknowledging at most that the seceded states were out of their proper practical relation with the Union, federal authorities were forced to consider the fundamental question in Unionist theory: the origin, nature, and meaning of statehood.

Was a state to be defined as territory, population, governmental institutions and officers, or political community? Federal reconstruction policy held that a state was a body of people constituting a political community whose existence was dependent on and qualified by the Union. Implicit in the history of the state system, this relationship was explicitly rationalized in Article IV, section 4, of the Constitution, which states: "The United States shall guarantee to every State in this Union a Republican Form of Government." In choosing the guarantee clause as a reconstruction basis, Congress rejected the idea that a state was mere territory, or population, or governmental institutions and officers whose acts of disloyalty could destroy the state and cause it to revert to a territorial condition, subject to the plenary power of Congress. The progression to statehood out of the territorial condition, if not a constitutional right enjoyed by the people as a political community, was at least irreversible.

Although compact theorists had long feared the transformation of the Union into a consolidated government, when political conditions in the 1860s were most favorable for this development, reconstruction policymakers evinced a concern for states' rights and divided sovereignty as essential to Unionism. The Supreme Court expressed this outlook in TEXAS V. WHITE (1869), confirming the congressional view of statehood as an irreversible condition. The Court declared that a "State, in the ordinary sense of the Constitution, is a political community of free citizens, occupying a territory of defined boundaries." Without the states in the Union, the Court reasoned, there could be no such political body as the United States. The conclusion therefore followed that "the preservation of the States, and the maintenance of their governments, are as much within the design and care of the Constitution as the preservation of the Union and the maintenance of the National government. The Constitution, in all its provisions, looks to an indestructible Union, composed of indestructible States."

The triumph of the central government in the Civil War signified the rejection of the compact theory of the Union as a framework for national development. Although aspects of the theory continued to be used in political and constitutional debate, it was repudiated in relation to the practical question that made it a vital element in antebellum politics: the mounting of single or concerted state resistance to central authority, including the possibility of secession. After the war secession was no longer a constitutionally conceivable or politically practical course of action. The central supremacy theory prevailed as the framework for constitutional development.

Although it is doubtful whether the American people, to use John Marshall's formulation, could in a constitutional sense be described as having been compounded into a single common mass as a result of the war, nevertheless in a political and ideological sense the idea of the people as a single national community, rather than as similar yet separate political communities, gained wider acceptance. Moreover, within the central supremacy theory the adoption of the THIRTEENTH, FOURTEENTH, and FIFTEENTH AMENDMENTS greatly altered federal-state relations. The nature and extent of federal and state powers of course continued to be a major issue in constitutional law and politics. But the nature of statehood, the nature of the Union, and the propriety of federal resolution of conflicts in the operation of the state system were now settled issues. Theories of the Union, associated with fundamentally different conceptions of nationalism, ceased to be relevant to basic political choices as Americans entered the period of industrialization.

HERMAN BELZ
(1986)

Bibliography

ARIELI, YEHOSHUA  1966  *Individualism and Nationalism in American Ideology.* Baltimore: Penguin Books.

BENNETT, WALTER HARTWELL  1964  *American Theories of Federalism.* University: University of Alabama Press.

CARPENTER, JESSE T.  1930  *The South as a Conscious Minority 1789–1861: A Study in Political Thought.* New York: New York University Press.

DAVIS, S. RUFUS  1978  *The Federal Principle: A Journey through Time in Quest of Meaning.* Berkeley: University of California Press.

DIAMOND, MARTIN  1974  What the Framers Meant by Federalism. In R. A. Goldwin, ed., *A Nation of States: Essays on the American Federal System.* Chicago: Rand McNally.

ONUF, PETER S.  1983  *The Origins of the Federal Republic: Jurisdictional Controversies in the United States, 1775–1787.* Philadelphia: University of Pennsylvania Press.

STAMPP, KENNETH M.  1978  The Concept of a Perpetual Union. *Journal of American History* 65:5–33.

# THIRD AMENDMENT

Quartering of troops in private houses, except in cases of military necessity, has long been regarded as contrary to British political traditions. Illegal quartering figured in important controversies between the king and the people, and it was condemned in the PETITION OF RIGHT (1628) and the English BILL OF RIGHTS (1689).

The British government sent regular troops to America in 1765 to discourage resistance to parliamentary taxation. Parliament, in the Quartering Act, required that the soldiers be housed at the expense of the province to which they were sent, and provided that, if existing barracks were insufficient, private buildings would be commandeered for the purpose. This measure was one of the specific grievances cited in the DECLARATION OF INDEPENDENCE.

During the debates over RATIFICATION OF THE CONSTITUTION several state conventions suggested a prohibition against quartering of troops. It was among JAMES MADISON's original proposals for the BILL OF RIGHTS, and the First Congress approved it unanimously and virtually without

change. The amendment affirms the sanctity of private property in our constitutional system: the refusal of an individual property owner is an absolute bar to quartering in peacetime. The amendment represents a principle so fundamental that no act of Congress has ever been seriously challenged under it.

DENNIS J. MAHONEY
(1986)

# THIRD-PARTY CONSENT

When someone invites the police into his or her home, the police need neither PROBABLE CAUSE nor a warrant to accept the invitation. Acting on one person's invitation or consent to search, however, the police may uncover evidence that incriminates some other person. For example, a spouse or child may consent to a search that uncovers evidence against another spouse or a parent; a landlord may permit a search that reveals evidence useful in prosecuting the landlord's tenant; a common carrier may authorize the police to open a package shipped by a suspected drug dealer; or a school principal may authorize the police to search a student's locker. In litigation under the FOURTH AMENDMENT, the issues raised by cases of this sort have been treated under the rubric "third-party consent." Courts have held that the consent of someone other than the person against whom evidence is offered can sometimes justify seizure of this evidence despite the lack of probable cause or a SEARCH WARRANT.

No unitary theory explains when third-party consent justifies a search under the Fourth Amendment. In some cases, courts have invoked concepts of agency. In an extreme and unlikely case, the agency might be express; a person might execute a document authorizing an agent to admit the police to his or her premises at the agent's unfettered discretion. In these circumstances, a court could easily conclude that the principal himself or herself had authorized the search. Agency principles appear to justify both holdings that a manager of business premises may consent to a search that uncovers evidence against the owner of the business and rulings that the consent of a secretary or maintenance worker to a search of areas not open to casual visitors is ordinarily insufficient.

Courts also have upheld third-party consent searches that could not have been justified on agency principles. For example, a husband may assault his wife, and the wife may admit the police to the home that she owns with her husband to reveal the location of the assault weapon. In this case, the husband may be present and may inform the police that his wife has no authority to waive his Fourth Amendment rights. When the wife admits the police, however, she does not act as the agent of her husband, and she does not waive his rights. Instead, she exercises her own PROPERTY RIGHTS. As in other cases of third-party consent, the husband's Fourth Amendment rights are limited by the authority of others to control premises in which he otherwise would have a reasonable expectation of privacy. Whether the authority of others is grounded in agency, PROPERTY, license, contract, or something else does not matter.

The general rule articulated in *United States v. Matlock* (1974) is that when two or more people have joint access to or control over premises that the police wish to search, "any of the co-inhabitants has the right to permit inspection." The Supreme Court cautioned that "the authority which justifies third-party consent does not rest upon the law of property, with its attendant historical and legal refinements." In practice, the consenting party's authority is determined largely by general cultural understandings, and as in other situations in which courts consider expectations of privacy, these understandings may be ad hoc, changing, and difficult to assess.

For example, an inhabitant ordinarily may invite a guest to enter the house that he or she shares with another, but the inhabitant may not invite his or her guest surreptitiously to observe the inhabitant's housemate in the shower. Even sole ownership of a house does not confer a privilege to invade the privacy of a guest or to permit others to do so. Similarly, a lease may give a landlord authority to inspect the leased premises, but the landlord would exceed his or her authority if he or she invited the television crew of "Lifestyles of the Rich and Famous" to participate in the inspection. (Courts have in fact held the consent of a landlord insufficient to justify a police search of leased premises.) In *Stoner v. California* (1964), although a hotel clerk had authorized the search of a hotel room, the Supreme Court held the search invalid. Maids and other hotel employees might legitimately have entered the room, but they could not properly have brought along their friends, their relatives, or the police.

Whether a person should have greater or lesser authority to permit the police to search than he or she would have to authorize a search by someone other than a police officer may be a difficult question. A wife whose husband has permitted a police search might protest, "I have no reasonable expectation that my husband will not invite guests to our home; but in most situations I do expect that he will not invite the police to enter for reasons hostile to my interests." On this view, a person's consent to a search by a police officer might be invalid, although consent to a similar inspection by a nonpolice officer would be permissible.

A person is likely to have stronger legitimate reasons to cooperate with the police than to permit inspection by others, however, and courts have upheld police searches based on third-party consent when consent to inspection by anyone else—even by a close friend—probably would have been unauthorized. For example, a husband probably would violate customary norms of privacy by permitting a friend to rummage through a dresser used not only by him but by his wife. In *Matlock* and in *Frazier v. Cupp* (1969), however, the Supreme Court upheld searches in which the police had opened closets and luggage used in common by consenting and nonconsenting parties. To consider what authority a consenting party would have had to permit inspection by someone other than a police officer may be helpful as a starting point, but courts cannot avoid fact-specific assessments of expectations of privacy in particular situations. Because most police searches lack close analogues in everyday experience, this task is often difficult.

Under the Supreme Court's decision in *Illinois v. Rodriguez* (1990), courts judge the authority of a third party to consent to a search from the perspective of a reasonable police officer; they do not require that the consenting party have authority in fact. This approach may seem harsh when a thief who pretends to be the owner of luggage that he or she has stolen gives the police permission to open it—with the result that the police uncover evidence against the owner. This owner may be incriminated by evidence that the police obtained without his or her consent and without probable cause.

Nevertheless, the Constitution guards almost exclusively against governmental abuse, and the Fourth Amendment proscribes only UNREASONABLE SEARCHES and seizures. When the police act on the basis of reasonable appearances, the objectives of the amendment seem satisfied. These objections do not include protection against all unjustified invasions of privacy but only against improper invasions of privacy by the government. Permitting the police to rely on a consenting party's apparent authority seems especially appropriate when the police might have conducted their search with a warrant had a seemingly valid consent not been given.

The third party's consent must reasonably appear to the police to be voluntary. When the police coerce a person to consent to a search that reveals evidence against another, the incriminated person has the same power to object to the search that he or she would have had if the police had not obtained the third party's consent at all.

This principle applies to cases of ELECTRONIC EAVESDROPPING just as it does to cases in which the police have seized tangible evidence. Although state statutes sometimes forbid electronic monitoring even when one party to a conversation has consented to it, the Fourth Amendment as construed by the Supreme Court permits electronic monitoring so long as any party to a conversation has agreed to it. The Court has concluded that this monitoring is indistinguishable from the disclosure of a conversation by one of the participants after it has occurred.

If consensual electronic monitoring is indistinguishable from a participant's later disclosure of a conversation, however, any party who could assert that another's consent to electronic monitoring was involuntary also should be allowed to object to an informant's involuntary disclosure of a conversation after the fact. Yet he or she is not. Although the question has been litigated raely, no one other than the informant himself or herself has been permitted to challenge the voluntariness of the informant's disclosure. The rule that a person lacks STANDING to object to the violation of another person's rights has been thought to foreclose a challenge o the voluntariness of an informant's statements by a person othe than the informant.

The principles that courts have developed in cases of third-party consent thus have not been consistently applied, and these principles might work important changes in the police informant system. Permitting others to challenge the use of coercive tactics against informants would subject some common police practices to new judicial scrutiny (for example, the practice of threatening to charge potential informants with crimes and to hold them on high bond). The coercion of third-party informants may invade the reasonable expectations of privacy of people whom the informants incriminate. This coercion can violate the rights of these people along with the rights of the informants themselves.

ALBERT W. ALSCHULER
(1992)

Bibliography

ALSCHULER, ALBERT W. 1983 Interpersonal Privacy and the Fourth Amendment. *Northern Illinois University Law Review* 4:1–57.

LAFAVE, WAYNE R. 1987 *Search and Seizure: A Treatise on the Fourth Amendment*, 2nd ed, Vol. 3, pp. 235–331.

# THIRTEENTH AMENDMENT
## (Framing)

Scholars and jurists have virtually ignored the Thirteenth Amendment, the Constitution's first formal addition in sixty-one years. Reasons for this indifference seem, initially, to be both obvious and adequate. The Thirteenth Amendment, ratified in December 1865, appears to be a simple, brief statement of the noble, limited effect of the CIVIL WAR.

Its succinct text, written by Illinois Senator LYMAN TRUMBULL, echoed clauses of the NORTHWEST ORDINANCE. In the Civil War's last weeks, during the closing session of the 38th Congress, Senator CHARLES SUMNER tried to substitute for the proposed Amendment's second section one specifying that every person was equal before both national and state laws. Trumbull, a constitutional specialist, favored section 2 in its present form. Sumner and many other congressmen assumed that all parts of the Constitution, including amendments, implicitly authorized enforcement; Trumbull wished to have the amendment empower enforcement explicitly. There was almost no other discussion on the amendment. In a sense, abolition had been before the congressmen and the nation since 1861.

Persons who celebrated abolition's arrival in 1865 did not foresee that race problems and derivative strains in federal relations were to require a FOURTEENTH and a FIFTEENTH AMENDMENT plus enforcement legislation, and would lead to the first IMPEACHMENT of a President. Celebrants of 1865 stressed the "war-gulf" that separated the ratified Thirteenth Amendment from one in early 1861 that Congress had proposed and three states had ratified in a desperate effort to seduce the South from seceding. The aborted Thirteenth Amendment would have forbidden the nation perpetually from curtailing SLAVERY in states where it existed. Thereafter the nation steadily raised both its sense of self-interest and its moral sights. Union troops in the South reported that the only trustworthy residents were black. Though few Negroes lived outside the South, most Northern states had long been racist in laws and customs, if never so fiercely as in the slave states. During the war Northern racism softened, partially as a result of pro-Negro reports from Union soldiers and partly from the diffusion of ABOLITIONIST CONSTITUTIONAL THEORY. Before the war, abolitionists, long hard-pressed even in the North, had come to scorn the Constitution, for it did not protect them against unpunished harassments. But once the war started, Union and abolition became identified. Gradually, Congress and ABRAHAM LINCOLN caught up to Union soldiers' needs, constituents' altering race sentiments, and abolitionists' aspirations and perceptions.

In 1861 and 1862, CONFISCATION ACTS threatened disloyal individuals with the loss of their title to property, including slaves, after individual prosecutions in federal courts. In September 1862, Lincoln's EMANCIPATION PROCLAMATION, an executive, war-power order, offered slaveowners ninety days in which to give up the rebellion or lose their slaves. That grace period having expired, Lincoln in January 1863 ordered also the recruitment of Negroes, most of whom lived in the South, into the Union's armies. In December 1863 and July 1864 respectively, Reconstruction policies issued by the President and the Congress provided for emancipation as a prerequisite for state restorations. The fall 1864 election proved the growth of a Northern consensus in favor of irreversible emancipation as a war result, though, save for abolitionists, it had not been an original war aim. Therefore the 38th Congress, with Lincoln's warm support, prepared the present Thirteenth Amendment, and when the war ended it sent it to the states for ratification.

Despite its simplicity, the Thirteenth Amendment was a momentous, perhaps revolutionary change in constitutional relationships. It prohibited not only the national or state governments or officials but every American institution and person from allowing slavery or involuntary servitude to exist, and it specifically authorized Congress to enforce the prohibition. If states, the traditional parents of slavery, did not comply with the prohibition and allowed individuals to hold other people in a slave status, the nation now had authority to punish directly either the oppressing persons or the states.

Democrats strongly opposed ratification. Even before the Civil War, most Democrats rejected a view of the Constitution as an adaptable, organic instrument. The amendment's enforcement clause allowed Congress to initiate changes in race relationships beyond abolition. Some Democrats insisted that abolition was illicit even by means of an amendment; that slave property remained totally a state's right to define; and that the unrepresented Southern states could not properly be asked to ratify the amendment.

Republicans argued for the amendment's ratification, in part because Lincoln's Emancipation Proclamation might have left slavery alive in the unseceded border states and in some Confederate areas earlier reconquered. It was clear also that individual confiscation trials could never reach the millions of slaveholders and slaves. Republicans also worried because the amendment voided the Constitution's THREE-FIFTHS CLAUSE. The South's Negroes were now to count as whole persons in determining the size of a state's congressional representation. Ironically, the South, after initiating and carrying on a civil war for four years, would substantially increase its strength in the House of Representatives. "Radical" Republicans looked at the Thirteenth Amendment as the culmination of abolitionist constitutional theory. Radicals asserted that the amendment, freeing slaves, also equalized all Americans in the protections due to them in their states for the exercise of both public and private rights. The DECLARATION OF INDEPENDENCE and the BILL OF RIGHTS defined the duties all states owed to every resident; the nation's duty was to see to state performance. State justice, down to the remotest hamlet, must protect every resident equally against hurtful positive acts or discriminatory nonacts by public officers and private persons, in both civil and criminal relationships.

No Republicans advocated centralization; all Republi-

cans were STATES' RIGHTS nationalists. State sovereignty was dead but state rights flourished. State wrongs that diminished individuals' rights as defined by state laws, were, however, unacceptable; they again threatened the nation's stability. Republicans assumed that the ex-rebel states would emulate, in their formal law at least, the lessened racism of the rest of the nation, and afford Negroes the same protections that whites enjoyed. But it became apparent from evidence such as the BLACK CODES that the South would not behave as expected.

All through 1865, Democrats criticized the fact that President ANDREW JOHNSON required the reconstructing states to ratify the Thirteenth Amendment, and they insisted that those states were entitled to be represented in Congress. The Johnson provisional states, excepting Florida and Texas where reconstruction proceeded slowly, did ratify the Thirteenth Amendment, though reluctantly, with spokesmen expressing special distaste for the enforcement clause. Johnson pressured recalcitrant states with threats of indefinite military rule if ratification failed; Secretary of State WILLIAM SEWARD calmed Southerners by asserting that the amendment restricted Congress to enforcing only a prohibition of formal slavery, a dubious interpretation. On December 15, 1865, Seward proclaimed the amendment to be in effect. Were the southern states truly states for the purposes of ratification? The question asked in 1865 and again in 1868 and 1870 when the Fourteenth and Fifteenth Amendments were ratified, and repeated endlessly since, has a metaphysical quality. Ratification was a mandate to the nation by a clear majority of the American people, not an act of the national government. Lincoln's insight that the South's states were still states, although out of their proper relationship to the Union of states, neither supported immediate restorations of those states nor diminished their capacities to perform certain state functions including ratification of amendments. In 1865 the southern states ratified in number beyond the Constitution's requirement (Article V) that three-fourths of the states approve an amendment. Additional states ratified subsequently to end all doubts as to the amendment's validity. But in 1865, those doubts existed and enhanced the doubts that Democrats spread, and Republicans also felt, about President Johnson's unlimited authority over the South.

The 39th Congress assembled in December 1865 for its first postwar session. Its Republican members, upon examination of the Black Codes and other evidence from the South of lingering vestiges of servitude, resorted immediately to the just-ratified Thirteenth Amendment's enforcement clause. Sharing a mobile, organic view of the Constitution, Republicans were ready to confirm that the nation had an interest in and a duty to personal equality in states, as defined by state law and customs; their readiness is evident in the quick formulation of the CIVIL RIGHTS BILL (the world's first), the second FREEDMAN'S BUREAU BILL, and the Fourteenth Amendment. Republicans created these measures in light of the Thirteenth Amendment, a far more complex and inclusive statement than most accounts suggest.

HAROLD M. HYMAN
(1986)

Bibliography

BUCHANAN, SIDNEY G.   1976   *The Quest for Freedom: A Legal History of the Thirteenth Amendment.* Houston: Reprint from *Houston Law Review.*

HOWE, MARK A. DeWOLFE   1965   Federalism and Civil Rights. [Massachusetts Historical Society] *Proceedings* 77:15–67.

HYMAN, HAROLD M. and WIECEK, WILLIAM M.   1982   *Equal Justice under Law: Constitutional Development 1835–1875.* Chaps. 10–11. New York. Harper & Row.

TEN BROEK, JACOBUS   1951   *The Antislavery Origins of the Fourteenth Amendment.* Chap. 13. Berkeley: University of California Press.

# THIRTEENTH AMENDMENT
## (Judicial Interpretation)

Ratification of the Thirteenth Amendment in 1865 not only diminished the urgency of the debate over the constitutionality of the EMANCIPATION PROCLAMATION but also wrote a new substantive value into the Constitution. The amendent's first section abolished SLAVERY and involuntary servitude throughout the nation, and its second section empowered Congress to enforce abolition. If any of the amendment's framers expected it to end the system of racial dominance and dependence, they were soon divested of that illusion. The persistence of a plantation economy and the adoption in southern states of the BLACK CODES kept blacks in a position of subordination that was not only economic but political and social as well.

The question thus arose whether section 2 of the Thirteenth Amendment gave Congress the power to do more than provide sanctions against slavery or involuntary servitude, narrowly defined. Over a presidential veto, Congress adopted the CIVIL RIGHTS ACT OF 1866, which not only declared the CITIZENSHIP of the freed slaves but also protected them against the sort of RACIAL DISCRIMINATION that had been embodied in the Black Codes, such as disqualification to own property, to make contracts, or to serve on juries. President ANDREW JOHNSON had explained his veto of the bill partly on the ground that the Thirteenth Amendment had not empowered Congress to adopt legislation aimed at such purposes. Reacting to this argument, Congress proposed the FOURTEENTH AMENDMENT as a means of assuring the validity of the 1866 Act and placing beyond doubt the power of Congress to enforce the CIVIL RIGHTS of the freed slaves.

From the beginning it was arguable that the abolition of slavery implied that the persons so freed would take on the status of free citizens—that the amendment should be read broadly as a response to the whole social system of racial subordination associated with slavery. But in the early years, this view did not prosper in the Supreme Court; it was found mainly in OBITER DICTA and in dissenting opinions. All agreed that section 1 of the amendment was self-executing: slavery and involuntary servitude were abolished, whether or not Congress enacted civil or criminal sanctions to enforce the abolition. Because the amendment contained no STATE ACTION limitation, it operated directly, of its own force, against either public or private conduct that imposed slavery. But the Court limited the notion of "involuntary servitude" to personal servitude, refusing to extend it (by analogy to feudal servitudes) to cover the granting of monopolies or other similar privileges. (See SLAUGHTERHOUSE CASES). By the end of the nineteenth century, the Court was saying that slavery implied no more than "a state of bondage," and the lack of "a legal right to the disposal of [one's] own person, property, and services"; thus the Thirteenth Amendent standing alone did not even forbid a state to impose racial segregation on seating in railroad cars. (See PLESSY V. FERGUSON.)

This narrow view of the Thirteenth Amendment's self-executing reach was reflected in the Supreme Court's treatment of the power granted to Congress by section 2. In the CIVIL RIGHTS CASES (1883) the Court, in the face of a powerful dissenting opinion by Justice JOHN MARSHALL HARLAN, held invalid the CIVIL RIGHTS ACT OF 1875, a congressional statute forbidding racial discrimination in such PUBLIC ACCOMMODATIONS as hotels, theaters, and railroads. Both the majority and the dissent agreed that the Thirteenth Amendment was designed to put an end to the "incidents" of slavery as well as slavery itself. The question was whether racially based refusals of access to public accommodations amounted to "badges of slavery and servitude," and the majority held that they did not. This severely restrictive interpretation of the power of Congress to enforce the Thirteenth Amendment culminated in 1906, when the Court decided HODGES V. UNITED STATES. Congress could prohibit no more than the "entire subjection" of one person to another, as in laws forbidding PEONAGE; Congress was not empowered by section 2 to go further in erasing "badges" or "incidents" of slavery.

So matters stood for six decades. The Thirteenth Amendment, like the Fourteenth Amendment's guarantee of the EQUAL PROTECTION OF THE LAWS, lay dormant, offering no effective protection against racial discrimination. The judicial interpretation of the Thirteenth Amendment mirrored the nation's political history; Congress adopted no civil rights legislation from the time of Reconstruction to the late 1950s. The first modern civil rights law of major importance was the CIVIL RIGHTS ACT OF 1964; its public accommodations provisions were upheld by the Supreme Court, but on the basis of the COMMERCE CLAUSE, not the Thirteenth or Fourteenth Amendments. (See HEART OF ATLANTA MOTEL V. UNITED STATES; KATZENBACH V. MCCLUNG.) The Court seemed determined to uphold congressional legislation aimed at establishing racial equality, and in UNITED STATES V. GUEST (1966) six Justices agreed in two separate opinions that Congress could reach even private conduct that interfered with the exercise of Fourteenth Amendment rights. The state action limitation, in other words, would not bar congressional enforcement of the equal protection clause of the Fourteenth Amendment's prohibition on private discrimination.

The reach of the equal protection clause, of course, is not limited to racial inequalities. Perhaps some of the Justices were reluctant to pursue the line of doctrinal development suggested by the separate opinions in *Guest*, for fear of giving Congress an invitation without apparent limitation. The solution to this puzzle—if it was a puzzle—came only two years after the *Guest* decision, in the form of a complete turnabout in the interpretation of the power of Congress to enforce the Thirteenth Amendment.

The turnabout came in JONES V. ALFRED H. MAYER CO. (1968), when the Court interpreted the 1866 Civil Rights Act to prohibit all racial discrimination in the sale of property and upheld the act as so construed. The Court overruled the *Hodges* decision and essentially adopted the dissenting views of Justice Harlan in the *Civil Rights Cases.* The Thirteenth Amendment was held to empower Congress not only to eliminate slavery but also to eliminate slavery's "badges and incidents." Furthermore, said the Court, it is for Congress itself "rationally to determine what are the badges and incidents of slavery," and to enact laws to eradicate any such "relic of slavery" it might find.

This broad language is not limited to racial discrimination. Commentators have asked whether the Court, in seeking to avoid an open-ended interpretation of congressional power under the Fourteenth Amendment, has offered Congress a different set of constitutional bootstraps. In the quoted passage from the *Jones* opinion, the Court appears to authorize Congress to define a given right—any right—as one that is essential to freedom, to define its impairment as an incident of slavery, and to enact a law protecting the right against both public and private interference.

When the right in question is a right to be free from racial discrimination, this line of reasoning accords not only with the language of the *Jones* opinion but also with the decision's place in the historical process of constitutional validation of modern civil rights legislation. Outside the racial context, however, the reasoning is unlikely to be adopted by the Supreme Court. Of course the Thirteenth Amendment prohibits the enslavement of anyone, of any race. And the Court has upheld an application of the 1866 act to a case of racial discrimination against whites, evidently (but without discussion) on the basis of Congress's power to enforce the Thirteenth Amendment, in *McDonald v. Santa Fe Trail Transportation Co.* (1976). The decision is defensible, despite the lack of historic links between slavery and discrimination against whites. There is a basis in experience for a congressional conclusion that discrimination against one racial group affects attitudes toward race generally and promotes discrimination against other races. It would be much harder to justify a similar conclusion about the effects of discrimination on the basis of gender, or sexual preference, or physical handicap. Even if the analogy were stronger, the doctrinal context of the *Jones* decision cautions against a prediction that its "badges and incidents" reasoning will be extended beyond cases of racial discrimination. The Thirteenth Amendment seems to have had its main appeal as a basis for congressional power precisely because that power could be contained within the confines of remedies for racial discrimination. The "badges and incidents of slavery" which justify congressional intervention are to be found in racial discrimination if they are to be found at all.

The power of Congress to enforce the Thirteenth Amendment, like any other congressional power, is subject to the limitations of the BILL OF RIGHTS. Without question, the amendment empowers Congress to prohibit racial discrimination in all the public areas of life, including commercial dealings. In RUNYON V. MCCRARY (1976), for example, the Supreme Court relied on the Thirteenth Amendment to uphold application of the 1866 act to a private school that accepted applicants from children in the public at large but excluded blacks. The potential limitations of the Bill of Rights found expression in that case. Justice LEWIS F. POWELL, concurring, cautioned that some hypothetical congressional enforcements of the Thirteenth Amendment might violate constitutional rights of PRIVACY or associational freedom, as when a litigant might seek application of the 1866 act to a case of racial discrimination in the selection of a home tutor or babysitter.

The expansion of the power of Congress to enforce the Thirteenth Amendment has not been accompanied by a corresponding expansion of the amendment's reach as a self-executing provision. The *Jones* opinion left open the question whether the amendment "by its own terms did anything more than abolish slavery," and although MEMPHIS V. GREENE (1981) raised the issue, the Court did not reach it. Thus, even though a great many forms of private racial discrimination may constitute "badges and incidents of slavery" justifying congressional action to secure their elimination, if Congress has not acted, these same "badges and incidents" are insufficient to trigger the operation of the amendment's section 1. The practical significance of this difference, however, is slight. The Supreme Court has construed existing civil rights legislation broadly enough to prohibit a wide range of private acts of racial discrimination.

Even assuming that the Thirteenth Amendment's self-executing force is limited to cases of bondage to personal service, there is room for debate about the kinds of compulsion that constitute involuntary servitude. Debt bondage—the requirement that a person work in discharge of a debt—is a classic case of peonage and is plainly forbidden by the amendment. However, compulsory military service (or alternative service for CONSCIENTIOUS OBJECTORS), hard labor for persons imprisoned for crime, and restrictions on the right to strike all have been sustained against Thirteenth Amendment attacks.

KENNETH L. KARST
(1986)

Bibliography

CASPER, GERHARD 1968 Jones v. Mayer: Clio, Bemused and Confused Muse. *Supreme Court Review* 1968:89–132.
FAIRMAN, CHARLES 1971 *Reconstruction and Reunion: 1864–1888, Part One.* Chapter XIX. New York: Macmillan Company.
NOTE 1969 The "New" Thirteenth Amendment: A Preliminary Analysis. *Harvard Law Review* 82:1294–1321.

# THOMAS, CLARENCE
## (1948–   )

In 1991, President GEORGE H. W. BUSH nominated Clarence Thomas to fill the U.S. Supreme Court seat vacated in the retirement of Justice THURGOOD MARSHALL. Thomas's qualifications that appealed to Bush were not those of legal accomplishment and judicial experience. At the time of his nomination, Thomas was at forty-three a young man whose experience consisted largely of service in the administration of President RONALD REAGAN. By 1991, Thomas had served for little more than one year as a judge on the U.S. Court of Appeals for the District of Columbia Circuit. Because Marshall was the Supreme Court's first and only African American Justice, Bush apparently wanted to have an African American replacement to avoid being blamed for creating an all-white Supreme Court once again. With virtually no experienced federal African American judges whose decisions were sufficiently conservative to satisfy Bush, the President selected Thomas, who had expressed his commitment to conservative doctrines.

Thomas's confirmation hearings before the SENATE JUDICIARY COMMITTEE caught the nation's attention when Anita Hill, a law professor who had previously worked as Thomas's assistant in the Reagan administration, accused Thomas of sexual harassment. In the aftermath of the controversy, Thomas's nomination was confirmed by the narrowest of margins—fifty-two to forty-eight—in a nationally televised vote in the U.S. SENATE. During his confirmation testimony, Thomas consistently distanced himself from the many speeches he had made endorsing controversial conservative positions, such as opposition to ABORTION and AFFIRMATIVE ACTION, during his years as a Reagan administration official. Although Thomas portrayed himself to the Judiciary Committee as open-minded and moderate, his subsequent performance as a Justice casts him as a confident, doctrinaire jurist whose opinions seek to make significant changes in constitutional law.

Thomas aspires to follow a coherent theory of CONSTITUTIONAL INTERPRETATION. Rather than reacting to individual issues as they arise, Thomas consistently expresses a commitment to interpret the Constitution according to the ORIGINAL INTENT of the Framers who wrote the document. Thomas seeks to eliminate what he sees as JUDICIAL ACTIVISM, interfering in the policies established by legislators and other elected officials. Thomas claims that by following the intentions of the Framers he avoids the pitfall of applying his own values and policy preferences in judicial decisions. Nonetheless, the legal conclusions he designates as dictated by the Framers' intentions consistently produce conservative results that apparently fit his values and policy preferences. Unlike other scholars and jurists who debate whether the intentions of the Framers can be determined for each provision of the Constitution and whether original intent should be based on the understandings of the authors or the ratifiers of each provision, Thomas manifests confidence about the certainty of his historical knowledge. That confidence is often translated into strident opinions that show little respect for alternative interpretations. Thomas's tone may deter Chief Justice WILLIAM H. REHNQUIST, with whom Thomas agrees on the outcomes of nearly all cases, from giving Thomas the responsibility for writing important majority opinions. Although Thomas receives his fair share of majority opinion assignments, his assignments nearly always concern either taxation and other statutory issues, or unanimous constitutional decisions. Thomas's first assignment to write the majority opinion in a controversial constitutional-rights case came in *Kansas v. Hendricks* (1997), in which the Court rejected DUE PROCESS, EX POST FACTO, and DOUBLE JEOPARDY claims to permit states to detain sex offenders indefinitely after they have already served out their entire criminal sentences. Thomas's uncompromising positions may limit his potential for shaping constitutional law on behalf of the Supreme Court majority. Often he finds himself writing CONCURRING and DISSENTING OPINIONS to express views with which no Justice other than ANTONIN SCALIA agrees.

Thomas's views, if adopted by majority, would change constitutional law significantly. In a dissenting opinion in *Helling v. McKinney* (1993), joined only by Scalia, Thomas argued that the drafters of the Eighth Amendment never intended for the prohibition against "CRUEL AND UNUSUAL PUNISHMENTS" to protect convicted offenders inside prisons. Thomas concluded that the Eighth Amendment only prevents a judge from announcing a cruel and unusual punishment as a sentence for a crime. If Thomas's views had governed the Eighth Amendment, federal judges never would have been able to order correctional institutions to end the brutal practices and inhuman conditions that were characteristic of prisons in several states prior to the 1980s.

Thomas's concurring opinion in UNITED STATES V. LÓPEZ (1995) argued that the Framers' original intentions for the COMMERCE CLAUSE preclude congressional regulation of manufacturing, agriculture, and mining. This argument contradicted sixty years of development in constitutional law. Carried to its logical conclusion, it would require a return to nineteenth-century constitutional DOCTRINES that forbade the federal government from regulating most areas of business endeavor. However, Thomas recognized that adherence to PRECEDENT "may convince us that we cannot wipe the slate clean" of the Court's more recent decisions. Thus, he does not seem to anticipate that the Court will follow his preferred theory by invalidating a wide range of federal laws affecting minimum wages, EMPLOYMENT DISCRIMINATION, consumer protection, and a variety of other areas in which the federal government has actively regulated economic activities since the 1930s.

Because Thomas believes that his originalist theory of interpretation holds the answers to virtually all constitutional questions presented to courts, he is critical of courts' reliance on what he calls "the easy answers" of SOCIAL SCIENCE. But relying on formal legal theory rather than empirical evidence often leads to unrealistic assumptions about difficult constitutional problems. In a concurring opinion in *Graham v. Collins* (1993), for example, Thomas suggested that mandatory CAPITAL PUNISHMENT for all offenders convicted of first-degree murder would cure problems of RACIAL DISCRIMINATION in capital SENTENCING. Thomas has been criticized for not recognizing that mandatory sentences cannot eliminate the discriminatory impact of discretionary decisions occurring throughout the criminal process, such as decisions by prosecutors about which defendants to charge with first-degree murder and

the discretion of juries in convicting offenders of lesser homicide offenses.

Drawing on his mistrust of social science, Thomas appears implicitly to criticize the Court's revered decision in BROWN V. BOARD OF EDUCATION (1954) for relying on social science evidence indicating that school SEGREGATION was harmful to African American children. In his concurring opinion in MISSOURI V. JENKINS (1995), Thomas suggested that such conclusions rest on "an assumption of black inferiority." In light of Thomas's belief in limiting the authority of judges to remedy social problems as well as historical evidence that the Framers of the EQUAL PROTECTION clause did not intend to end racial segregation, it is difficult to square Thomas's theory of constitutional interpretation with *Brown*.

Thomas's consistent adherence to his version of original intent jurisprudence has established him as the most conservative Justice of the REHNQUIST COURT. Although his colleagues Scalia and Rehnquist reject individuals' constitutional claims with similar frequency, Thomas's approach to constitutional interpretation has the most dramatic implications for changing constitutional law.

CHRISTOPHER E. SMITH
(2000)

(SEE ALSO: *Appointment of Supreme Court Justices; Confirmation Process*.)

### Bibliography

BAUGH, JOYCE and SMITH, CHRISTOPHER E. 1996 Doubting Thomas: Confirmation Veracity Meets Performance Reality. *Seattle University Law Review* 19:455–496.

MAYER, JANE and ABRAMSON, JILL 1994 *Strange Justice: The Selling of Clarence Thomas.* Boston: Houghton Mifflin Co.

ROSEN, JEFFREY 1996 Moving On. *The New Yorker*, April 29 & May 6, pp. 66–73.

SMITH, CHRISTOPHER E. 1996 Bent on Original Intent. *American Bar Association Journal* 82(October):48–52.

—— 1997 Clarence Thomas: A Distinctive Justice. *Seton Hall Law Review* 28:1–28.

## *THOMAS v. REVIEW BOARD*
### 450 U.S. 707 (1981)

Reaffirming its decision in SHERBERT V. VERNER (1963), the Supreme Court, 8–1, invalidated Indiana's refusal of unemployment compensation to a Jehovah's Witness who, for religious reasons, had quit his job rather than work on weapons production. The state had not shown that denying benefits was the LEAST RESTRICTIVE MEANS of achieving a COMPELLING STATE INTEREST.

KENNETH L. KARST
(1986)

## THOMAS v. UNION CARBIDE AGRICULTURAL PRODUCTS CO.
### 473 U.S. 568 (1985)

The Supreme Court's decision in NORTHERN PIPELINE CON-STRUCTION CO. V. MARATHON PIPE LINE CO. (1982) left considerable confusion about the power of Congress to confer JURISDICTION on administrators or LEGISLATIVE COURTS over cases falling within the judicial power of the United States. *Thomas* provided some useful clarification.

The Federal Insecticide, Fungicide, and Rodentcide Act (FIFRA) requires a manufacturer, as a condition on registering a pesticide, to supply research data on the pesticide's health, safety, and environmental effects to the Environmental Protection Agency (EPA). These data may be used in evaluating a second manufacturer's registration of a similar product, provided that the second manufacturer offers to compensate the first. If the two manufacturers cannot agree on the compensation, FIFRA requires binding arbitration of the dispute. An arbitrator's decision is reviewable by a court only for "fraud, misrepresentation or other misconduct."

Various pesticide manufacturers sued the EPA administrator challenging the constitutionality of the scheme of binding arbitration with limited court review. The federal district court held that the scheme violated Article III of the Constitution; on direct APPEAL, the Supreme Court unanimously reversed, upholding the law.

Justice SANDRA DAY O'CONNOR, writing for the Court, recognized a broad policy in Article III "that federal judicial power shall be vested in courts whose judges enjoy life tenure and fixed compensation." *Marathon* effectuated a part of that policy but was distinguishable here. Considering the origin of the claims to compensation in federal law, along with the reasons of public policy that persuaded Congress to impose binding arbitration, the manufacturers' claimed rights were properly considered "public rights," the adjudication of which Congress could place in administrative hands. Cases involving "public rights" were not limited to those in which the government itself was a party. Nor, said the Court in an important OBITER DICTUM, is Article III's requirement of independent judges irrelevant merely because the government is a party. Here the assignment of decision to nonjudicial arbitrators was softened somewhat by FIFRA's provision of some minimal review by CONSTITUTIONAL COURTS of arbitrators' decisions. (In some cases, the Court noted, DUE PROCESS considerations might independently require further court review.)

*Thomas* thus adopted a flexible approach to Article III's limitations on Congress's employment of nonjudicial tribunals—the very approach urged by the *Marathon* dis-senters. Justice WILLIAM J. BRENNAN, for three Justices, concurred separately on the basis of his PLURALITY OPINION in *Marathon*. Justice JOHN PAUL STEVENS concurred, saying the manufacturers lacked STANDING to challenge the law's validity.

KENNETH L. KARST
(1986)

## THOMPSON, SMITH
### (1763–1843)

Smith Thompson was among the most experienced judges ever appointed to the Supreme Court, and his tenure on the bench (1823–1843) linked the constitutional doctrines of the MARSHALL COURT and the TANEY COURT. After sixteen years on the New York Supreme Court (1802–1818), four years as chief justice, Thompson had been secretary of the navy (1818–1823). His experience in JAMES MONROE's cabinet made Monroe feel so comfortable with Thompson, presumably including his constitutional views, that the President insisted that the New Yorker fill the seat vacated by the death of a fellow New Yorker, H. BROCKHOLST LIVINGSTON.

Thompson did not change his jurisprudence significantly during his twenty years on the Court. He remained a black-letter lawyer, whose most interesting contributions to constitutional jurisprudence can be traced to his New York judicial and cabinet experiences. Besides adhering to precedent, Thompson concerned himself with maintaining judicial independence while showing a willingness to let the legislature have free rein. Having served in an era when Congress was relatively inactive, Thompson appears today as a STATES' RIGHTS advocate, or more precisely an adherent to states' responsibilities. Yet his values did not differ greatly from those of his nationalistic brethren on the Marshall Court. He was, for example, aware of the business community's needs. Unlike Livingston, his predecessor on the Marshall Court, Thompson was more willing to express his differences with the rest of the Court.

He was absent when GIBBONS V. OGDEN (1824) was argued, but in *Livingston v. Van Ingen* (1812), decided by the New York court, he had resolved some of the questions involved in *Gibbons* in favor of the steamboat monopoly. Although Thompson's *Van Ingen* opinion did not consider the commerce clause question, that of his colleague, JAMES KENT, did and commerce clause cases subsequent to *Gibbons* show that Thompson subscribed to Kent's doctrine of concurrent powers to regulate commerce. JOHN MARSHALL's language in *Gibbons* was, moreover, sufficiently broad to allow Thompson to render lip service to *Gibbons* while taking a contrary position. In BROWN V. MARYLAND

(1827), Thompson dissented from Marshall's majority opinion holding that Maryland's law imposing license taxes on wholesalers of imported goods violated both the import and export and the COMMERCE CLAUSE. Like Kent, Thompson did not examine the nature of the power underlying state regulations. Whether the state regulated commerce or not was immaterial so long as the statute did not conflict with a congressional act. In rejecting Marshall's ORIGINAL PACKAGE DOCTRINE in *Brown*, Thompson set forth the position that goods became subject to a state's jurisdiction upon crossing its borders. Thompson continued his adherence to the doctrine of concurrent commerce powers in MAYOR OF NEW YORK V. MILN (1837), to the extent that he wrote separately rather than subscribe to the majority's reasoning that regulation of immigrant passengers was simply a valid exercise of the STATE POLICE POWER. Subsequently, the concurrent powers doctrine became an integral part of ROGER B. TANEY's constitutional thought. Taney had not advanced that doctrine while arguing for the state in *Brown*, and it is reasonable to assume that he borrowed it from Thompson.

On the slavery question, Thompson assumed the doughface position later followed by his replacement on the Court, SAMUEL NELSON, of providing support for the peculiar institution, while striving to confine the question at hand and giving the appearance of sticking rigidly to precedent. Typical, in this respect, was GROVES V. SLAUGHTER (1841), where Thompson, speaking for the Court's majority, was able to avoid the question whether Mississippi's constitutional ban on uncontrolled slave shipments from other states violated the commerce clause. In PRIGG V. PENNSYLVANIA (1842), Thompson differed from JOSEPH STORY's opinion that the fugitive slave clause did not prohibit state laws designed "faithfully" to enforce the clause. In contrast with Thompson's adherence to legal formalism in slavery cases was his activism in *Cherokee Nation v. Georgia* (1831). Dissenting, in the most elaborate opinion of his career, he asserted that regardless of their relative weakness to their white neighbors, the Cherokees constituted an independent, foreign, sovereign, nation. The following year, Thompson's dissent became the majority position in WORCESTER V. GEORGIA. (See CHEROKEE INDIAN CASES.)

Thompson's conservative attitude toward government and business sometimes put him at odds with both Marshall and Taney. Perhaps none of his contemporaries had more concern for protecting VESTED RIGHTS than did Thompson. He joined Story's CHARLES RIVER BRIDGE dissent (1837), and in his own *Wheaton v. Peters* (1834) dissent he said that as a matter of "sound reason and abstract morality" the COMMON LAW provided COPYRIGHT protection. It was his concern for vested rights alone with his administrative experience that caused Thompson to distinguish

between cabinet officers' political and ministerial duties. Only the latter functions were "subject to the control of the law, and the direction of the president," he said in *United States ex rel. Stokes et al. v. Kendall* (1838). Thompson's conservatism meshed with his adherence to states' responsibilities in interpreting the CONTRACT CLAUSE. In his view contracts were subject to the existing law of a place, including insolvency laws. Such laws, like the long-standing New York system, were also good for business. These beliefs explain Thompson's opposition to Marshall in OGDEN V. SAUNDERS (1837), and partially explains his CRAIG V. MISSOURI dissent (1830). Thompson's impact on constitutional law was slight, and only a few Whig politicians lamented his death.

DONALD M. ROPER
(1986)

Bibliography
DUNNE, GERALD T.  1969  Smith Thompson. In Leon Friedman and Fred L. Israel, eds., *The Justices of the United States Supreme Court*. Pages 475–492. New York: Chelsea House.

## *THOMPSON v. OKLAHOMA*
### 487 U.S. 815 (1988)

The Court held that the CRUEL AND UNUSUAL PUNISHMENT clause of the Eighth Amendment, applicable to the states by the INCORPORATION DOCTRINE, prohibited the death sentence against a first-degree murderer who committed the offense at the age of fifteen. Justice JOHN PAUL STEVENS spoke for a four-member plurality in whose JUDGMENT Justice SANDRA DAY O'CONNOR joined. Stevens asserted that the execution of the juvenile would "offend civilized standards of decency" and be "abhorrent to the conscience of the community."

O'Connor discerned no such consensus from the EVIDENCE adduced by the plurality. Indeed, the Court divided 4–4 on the question as to whether such a consensus existed. O'Connor believed that the sentence must be set aside because of the risk that the state did not realize that its CAPITAL PUNISHMENT statute might apply to fifteen-year-olds.

Stevens had a second string to his bow. He declared that the execution of the minor did not contribute to the purposes underlying the death penalty. O'Connor and the dissenters believed that the plurality Justices failed to understand that some fifteen-year-olds were as blameworthy as adults.

Justice ANTONIN SCALIA, for the three dissenters (Justice ANTHONY M. KENNEDY did not participate), believed that a consensus existed showing that the execution of juveniles under fifteen years of age did not offend community standards and therefore did not violate the Eighth Amendment. In STANDFORD V. PENRY (1988) the Court ruled that the execution of juveniles who murdered at sixteen years of age was constitutional.

LEONARD W. LEVY
(1992)

## THORNBURGH v. AMERICAN COLLEGE OF OBSTETRICIANS AND GYNECOLOGISTS
### 476 U.S. 747 (1986)

Although this 5–4 decision struck down a series of Pennsylvania laws restricting ABORTION, it also showed that support within the Supreme Court for the principles of ROE V. WADE (1973) had eroded. The invalidated restrictions covered a wide range: (1) a twenty-four-hour waiting period; (2) a requirement that a doctor provide a woman seeking an abortion with literature and oral statements, including warnings about medical risks, an estimate of the fetus's gestational age, a description of the probable physical characteristics of the fetus at two-week gestational increments, information about possible medical benefits for childbirth, and a reminder of a father's responsibility for child support; (3) detailed reporting requirements for doctors, including a statement of the basis for the doctor's finding that the fetus was not viable; and (4) a second-physician requirement. Justice HARRY A. BLACKMUN wrote for the Court, reaffirming *Roe v. Wade* and concluding that all of the challenged requirements subordinated women's interest in privacy "in an effort to deter a woman from a decision that, along with her physician, is hers to make."

Chief Justice WARREN E. BURGER dissented, noting his willingness to "reexamine *Roe.*" Justice BYRON R. WHITE, joined by Justice WILLIAM H. REHNQUIST, filed a lengthy and vigorous dissent that called for *Roe* to be overruled and specifically challenged the majority's rulings on each of the provisions invalidated here. Justice SANDRA DAY O'CONNOR, the fourth dissenter, reasserted what she had said in an earlier opinion, that was unworkable and should be replaced by a principle that would uphold a law unless it were "unduly burdensone" on a woman's decision to have an abortion. Justice JOHN PAUL STEVENS concurred in a long opinion, taking issue with Justice White's attack on *Roe.* The White-Stevens debate encapsulates many of the main points made in the debate over the proper role of the judiciary in the field of abortion.

KENNETH L. KARST
(1992)

## THORNHILL v. ALABAMA
### 310 U.S. 88 (1940)

This case involved a FIRST AMENDMENT challenge to convictions under an Alabama antipicketing statute. Normally one has STANDING only to plead one's own constitutional rights. In *Thornhill,* however, the Supreme Court did not ask whether the particular activity in which the pickets had engaged was constitutionally protected. Instead it asked whether the statute itself, rather than its application to these particular persons, violated the First Amendment. Because the statute was INVALID ON ITS FACE, it could be challenged, even by a union that itself might have engaged in violent picketing not protected by the First Amendment. The theory was that the statute's general ban on all labor dispute picketing would threaten peaceful picketers as well, even though no peaceful picketers had even been prosecuted.

Justice FRANK MURPHY acknowledged that the state legislature legitimately might have written a narrowly drawn statute that condemned only violent or mass picketing. Instead it wrote a general ban on all picketing in labor-management disputes. "The existence of such a statute . . . which does not aim specifically at evils within the allowable area of state control but, on the contrary, sweeps within its ambit other activities that in ordinary circumstances constitute an exercise of freedom of speech . . . readily lends itself to . . . discriminatory enforcement by local prosecuting officials [and] results in a continuous and pervasive unconstitutional restraint on all freedom of discussion." Subsequently the Court was to speak of the unconstitutional CHILLING EFFECT of such "facially overbroad" statutes.

MARTIN SHAPIRO
(1986)

## THORNTON v. CALDOR, INC.
### 472 U.S. 703 (1985)

The Supreme Court held unconstitutional, on establishment clause grounds, a state act authorizing employees to designate a sabbath day and not work that day. Applying the three-part test of LEMON V. KURTZMAN (1971), Chief Justice WARREN E. BURGER found that by vesting in employees an "absolute and unqualified" right not to work on the sabbath of one's choice, and by forcing employers to adjust work schedules to the religious practices of employees, the act constituted a law respecting an ESTABLISHMENT OF RELIGION. In purpose and effect it advanced religion, preferring those who believe in not working on the sabbath to those who hold no such belief. By implication, a statute giving employers some leeway would be constitutional. Only Justice WILLIAM H. REHNQUIST dissented, without opinion. No member of the Court defended the statute as a state effort to prevent discrimination against sabbath believers by preventing the imposition of employment penalties on those acting in obedience to conscience by refusing to work. (See SHERBERT V. VERNER.)

LEONARD W. LEVY
(1986)

# THORPE, FRANCIS N.
## (1857–1926)

Francis Newton Thorpe, professor of history at the University of Pennsylvania, edited seven volumes of *American Charters and Constitutions*. He also wrote several books on political and constitutional history from a post-CIVIL WAR nationalist viewpoint. He emphasized the UNWRITTEN CONSTITUTION by which the written Constitution is continually extended and adapted.

DENNIS J. MAHONEY
(1986)

# THREE-FIFTHS CLAUSE

Article I, section 2, clause 3, of the United States Constitution originally provided that members of the HOUSE OF REPRESENTATIVES would be apportioned among the states on a formula that added to "free Persons" (including indentured servants but excluding untaxed Indians) "three fifths of all other Persons." The 1840 publication of JAMES MADISON's notes of debates in the CONSTITUTIONAL CONVENTION OF 1787 revealed that the euphemism "all other Persons" referred to slaves.

The clause originated in an unsuccessful 1783 proposal in the Confederation Congress to amend the ARTICLES OF CONFEDERATION by changing the method of apportioning taxes among the states to a per capita basis that would include all free persons and "three-fifths of all other persons." At the Philadelphia convention, JAMES WILSON, a Pennsylvania delegate, resurrected the three-fifths formula as an amendment to the VIRGINIA PLAN and thereby touched off heated debates on counting slaves for apportionment purposes. The underlying conflict of interests between slave and free states provoked a great crisis of the convention. The deadlock was resolved by a complex formula that was part of the GREAT COMPROMISE basing both representation and DIRECT TAXES on the three-fifths formula and, for good measure, making the direct-tax provisions of Article I, section 9, unamendable (Article V).

Madison in THE FEDERALIST #54 defended the clause as an arbitrary but reasonable compromise that roughly reflected the anomalous legal status of a slave, a human for certain purposes and a chattel for others. The slave was "debased by servitude below the equal level of free inhabitants, which regards the slave as divested of two-fifths of the man." NATHANIEL GORHAM of Massachusetts had earlier agreed, accepting the clause as "pretty near the just proportion."

The three-fifths formula gave the slave states an additional political weight in Congress quite close to what they would have enjoyed if they had counted all slaves for purposes of apportionment. In 1811 this produced eighteen slave-state representatives more than the southern states would have had if slaves had been excluded altogether from apportionment. The clause therefore rankled New England and middle-state Federalists, who used the clause as a vehicle to voice their resentment at the Virginia Dynasty and the rising political power of the west. Reviving arguments of 1787 that if Virginia counted its slaves Massachusetts should be able to count its cattle, New Englanders complained with JOHN QUINCY ADAMS that "slave representation has governed the union." The HARTFORD CONVENTION demanded in 1814 that the clause be abrogated.

Later debates during the abolition controversy renewed this dispute. Abolitionists either disingenuously tried to construe the clause as referring to persons other than slaves (indentured servants or ALIENS) or demanded that the clause be expunged. Defenders of SLAVERY and Garrisonian abolitionists both cited the clause as an explicit assurance of the privileged constitutional status of that unique form of property, human chattels.

Though the abolitionist debates proved inconclusive, the clause bedeviled Republicans during Reconstruction. After the abolition of slavery, all blacks became "free Persons" and thus the congressional representation of the former Confederate states would be augmented by perhaps a dozen congressmen, endangering the Republicans' objectives for the war and Reconstruction. To forestall this, Republicans first temporarily excluded ten of the former seceded states from representation in Congress, then forced ratification of the FOURTEENTH AMENDMENT, whose section 2 provides that representatives shall be apportioned simply on "the whole number of persons in each State," and that a state's representation should be reduced in proportion to its denial of the vote to male citizens over twenty-one years old, except for participation in rebellion or crime.

WILLIAM M. WIECEK
(1986)

Bibliography

OHLINE, HOWARD A. 1971 Republicanism and Slavery: Origins of the Three-Fifths Clause in the United States Constitution. *William and Mary Quarterly* 28:563–594.

SIMPSON, ALBERT F. 1941 The Political Significance of Slave Representation, 1787–1821. *Journal of Southern History* 7: 315–342.

## THREE-JUDGE COURT

The Supreme Court's decision in EX PARTE YOUNG (1908) made it possible for one federal judge to tie up an entire state legislative program by granting preliminary injunctive relief. In 1910 Congress required certain applications for federal-court INTERLOCUTORY injunctions against state officers to be heard by three judges. Such a court's order was made directly appealable to the Supreme Court. A similar statutory scheme had been devised earlier for certain ANTITRUST and railroad regulation cases. The 1948 revision of the JUDICIAL CODE made clear that the three-judge requirement applied to all hearings on applications for interlocutory or permanent INJUNCTIONS against state officers.

A considerable body of law developed out of this statute. Applications for DECLARATORY JUDGMENTS were not subject to the requirement, although injunctive relief is authorized to enforce a declaratory judgment. Three-judge courts were required only for actions seeking to enjoin state officers in carrying out statutes of general and statewide application, not local ordinances. While three judges were ordinarily necessary to deny injunctive relief as well as grant it, a single judge could dismiss such an action when it was "insubstantial."

The system of three-judge courts was enormously burdensome, both on the lower federal courts and on the Supreme Court. In 1976, Congress drastically limited the three-judge requirement, retaining it only in certain cases involving legislative REAPPORTIONMENT or VOTING RIGHTS and some cases under the CIVIL RIGHTS ACT OF 1964.

KENNETH L. KARST
(1986)

Bibliography

WRIGHT, CHARLES ALAN 1983 *The Law of Federal Courts*, 4th ed. Pages 295–299, 728–729. St. Paul, Minn.: West Publishing Co.

## "THREE STRIKES" LAWS

See: Career Criminal Sentencing Laws

## TIEDEMAN, CHRISTOPHER G.
### (1857–1903)

Christopher G. Tiedeman, a professor of law, published *A Treatise on the Limitations of Police Power in the United States* (1886). Second only to THOMAS COOLEY's *Constitu-*

*tional Limitations* in its influence on American constitutional law, Tiedeman's book spurred the conversion of the FOURTEENTH AMENDMENT into a bulwark of VESTED RIGHTS. He believed that liberty found its highest expression in laissez-faire economics and that the POLICE POWER, which he sought to reduce to the role of policeman, was making "socialism, communism, and anarchism . . . rampant in America." He found evidence for that claim in the advocacy of prolabor legislation and state protection of the weak against the strong. CONSERVATISM, he wrote, feared "the advent of an absolutism more tyrannical and more unreasoning than any before experienced by man, the absolutism of a democratic majority." JUDICIAL REVIEW in support of written constitutions that limited government provided the only hope, and Tiedeman's exposition of cases was calculated to assist courts in their task of thwarting invasions of private rights. In 1900, in the preface to a revised second edition, Tiedeman expressed gratification that "the first edition of this book has been quoted by the courts in hundreds of cases."

LEONARD W. LEVY
(1986)

## TILTON v. RICHARDSON

See: *Lemon v. Kurtzman*

## TIMBER CULTURE ACT

See: Environmental Regulation and the Constitution

## TIMES-MIRROR CO. v. CALIFORNIA

See: *Bridges v. California*

## TIMMONS v. TWIN CITIES AREA NEW PARTY
### 520 U.S. 351 (1997)

Beginning with *Williams v. Rhodes* (1968), the Supreme Court rebuffed attempts by state legislatures to justify BALLOT ACCESS restrictions or other election laws favoring the Democratic and Republican parties on grounds that such laws favored the "two-party system." Though the *Williams* Court did not reject the idea that a state in theory could defend an election law on these grounds, the Court struck down Ohio's ballot access law because it favored "two particular parties—the Republicans and the Democrats—and in effect tends to give them a complete monopoly."

The 6–3 *Timmons* decision, in which the Court for the first time accepted the two-party rationale, suggests a major shift in favor of allowing state legislatures to protect the Democratic and Republican parties. The Twin Cities Area New Party, a minor political party, wished to nominate Andy Dawkins as its candidate for state representative in the Minnesota legislature. Dawkins was already the candidate of the Democratic Party (known in Minnesota as the Democratic–Farmer–Labor Party, or DFL). Though neither Dawkins nor the DFL objected to this multiple-party or "fusion" candidacy, Minnesota officials refused to accept the New Party's nominating petitions because Minnesota law prohibits fusion. A majority of states similarly ban fusion, though a few states, most notably New York, allow the practice.

The New Party challenged Minnesota's antifusion law as unconstitutional under the FIRST and FOURTEENTH AMENDMENTS. The Court, in an opinion by Chief Justice WILLIAM H. REHNQUIST, upheld the law's constitutionality. In ballot access and similar election law cases, the Court does not use a single level of scrutiny (or "litmus-paper test") to judge a challenged law's constitutionality. Instead, the Court calibrates the scrutiny to the severity of the law's burden on First Amendment rights; the greater the burden, the higher the scrutiny. The *Timmons* majority first held that the burden on the New Party was not severe, though it recognized that the law slightly burdened the party by reducing the universe of potential party nominees and by limiting the ability of the party to send a message to voters and to its preferred candidates through its nomination process.

Nonetheless, the Court held that three "sufficiently weighty" state interests justified the burden. First, the fusion ban prevented parties from joining with sham parties with popular catch phrases, like the "No New Taxes" party. Second, the ban prevented a minor party from capitalizing on the popularity of another party's candidate, rather than its own appeal to the voters, in order to secure access to the ballot. Finally, the Court agreed that states "have a strong interest in the stability of their political systems" and therefore they may "enact reasonable regulations that may, in practice, favor the traditional two-party system."

The first two reasons hardly seem "sufficiently weighty" to overcome even a minor burden on the New Party's First Amendment rights. As for the first interest, reasonable ballot access laws can prevent the formation of sham parties, and the Court expressly denied it was concerned about voter confusion. The second argument ignores the ability of the state to list candidates on the ballots once under each party and then count only the votes cast for the candidate under the minor party label to meet that minor party's future ballot access requirements. This leaves the state's interest in promoting the two-party system, which the Court stated "temper[s] the destabilizing effects of party-splintering and excessive factionalism."

Unfortunately, the *Timmons* majority failed to examine with care the propositions that the two-party system deserves or needs the Court's protection. Proponents of a strong two-party system have argued that it promotes political stability, decreases interest-group politics, and provides a valuable voting cue to busy voters. But these proponents have not been able to demonstrate that the existence of only two major political parties actually promotes stability or decreases factionalism; and increasing the number of parties may enhance the voting cue by increasing the salience of differences among parties and candidates. Moreover, even if the two-party system is a valuable institution, the Court need not uphold antifusion and similar laws in order to preserve it; instead, the predominant first-past-the-post, single-member district voting mechanism appears to drive a political system with only two viable political parties.

Three Justices dissented in *Timmons.* Justice JOHN PAUL STEVENS, for himself and Justice RUTH BADER GINSBURG, found the risk to political stability engendered by fusion politics "speculative at best," but Justice DAVID H. SOUTER rejected the two-party system argument only on the ground that the state had failed to raise it.

Given the lack of evidence that the two-party system deserves or needs protection, and given the agency problem that stems from having these laws passed by legislatures made up almost exclusively of Democrats and Republicans, the Court should be wary of such flimsy justifications for infringing First Amendment rights.

RICHARD L. HASEN
(2000)

(SEE ALSO: *Political Parties and the Constitution.*)

Bibliography

ARGERSINGER, PETER H.   1980   "A Place on the Ballot": Fusion Politics and Antifusion Laws. *American Historical Review* 85: 287–306.
HASEN, RICHARD L.   1998   Entrenching the Duopoly: Why the Supreme Court Should Not Allow the States to Protect the Democrats and Republicans from Political Competition. *Supreme Court Review* 1997:331–371.
ISSACHAROFF, SAMUEL and PILDES, RICHARD H.   1998   Politics as Markets: Partisan Lockups of the Democratic Process. *Stanford Law Review* 50:643–717.

# TINKER v. DES MOINES INDEPENDENT COMMUNITY SCHOOL DISTRICT
### 393 U.S. 503 (1969)

*Tinker* is a leading modern decision on the subjects of SYMBOLIC SPEECH and CHILDREN'S RIGHTS. A group of adults and students in Des Moines planned to protest the VIET-NAM WAR by wearing black armbands during the 1965 holiday season. On learning of this plan, the public school principals adopted a policy to forbid the wearing of armbands. Two high school students and one junior high school student wore armbands to school, refused to remove them, and were suspended until they might return without armbands. They sued in federal court to enjoin enforcement of the principals' policy and for nominal damages. The district court dismissed the complaint, and the court of appeals affirmed by an equally divided court. The Supreme Court reversed, 7–2, in an opinion by Justice ABE FORTAS.

The wearing of these armbands was "closely akin to "pure speech" and protected by the FIRST AMENDMENT. The school environment did imply limitations on the freedom of expression, but here the principals lacked justification for imposing any such limitations. The authorities' "undifferentiated fear" of disturbance was insufficient. While student expression could be forbidden when it materially disrupted school work or school discipline, these students had undertaken "a silent, passive expression of opinion, unaccompanied by any disorder or disturbance." Furthermore, only this "particular symbol . . . was singled out for prohibition"; political campaign buttons had been allowed, and even "the Iron Cross, traditionally a symbol of Nazism." (Justice Fortas may have been unaware of the vogue among surfers and their inland imitators.)

Justice HUGO L. BLACK dissented, accusing the majority of encouraging students to defy their teachers and arguing that the wearing of the armbands had, in fact, diverted other students' minds from their schoolwork. He did not ask how much the principals' reaction to the planned protest might have contributed to that diversion.

KENNETH L. KARST
(1986)

## TITLES OF NOBILITY

In the twentieth century, the idea of a hereditary ruling elite using titles of nobility as a device for maintaining its authority seems a bit frivolous. To the founding generation, however, the threat was only too real. Moreover, the threat that a foreign potentate might suborn an American citizen or official by proffering such a title was also perceived as significant. The ARTICLES OF CONFEDERATION forbade the acceptance of foreign titles by any person holding federal or state office and forbade the granting of titles by the United States or by any state. The prohibitions were carried over into the Constitution, except that there is no longer a ban on state officers accepting foreign titles, and Congress may authorize acceptance of titles by federal

officers. In both documents, titles of nobility are treated, along with gifts and offices, as items of value that foreign governments might offer in exchange for favors, and Governor EDMUND RANDOLPH, at the CONSTITUTIONAL CONVENTION, asserted that the provision was designed to guard against corruption.

As it appears in the Constitution, the prohibition against accepting foreign titles applies only to those holding a federal office of trust or profit. On the eve of the War of 1812, Congress proposed to the states a constitutional amendment extending the prohibition to every citizen of the United States. Under the proposed amendment, acceptance of a title of nobility would have caused automatic forfeiture of United States CITIZENSHIP and permanent disqualification from holding federal or state office. The titles-of-nobility amendment was one of only six constitutional amendments ever proposed by Congress to fall short of ratification by the states.

DENNIS J. MAHONEY
(1986)

## TOCQUEVILLE, ALEXIS DE
### (1805–1859)

The French magistrate and political theorist Alexis Clerel de Tocqueville spent nine months of 1831 and 1832 in the United States. He believed that democracy was the inescapable destiny of all nations and that America, as the first avowedly democratic nation in the modern world, offered an opportunity for the student of politics to observe democracy in action. One product of Tocqueville's sojourn on our shores was *Democracy in America*.

Tocqueville thought that the main problem of democracy was a tendency toward radical equality of condition which was destructive of the liberty necessary for excellence in human endeavors. He perceived in America two undesirable developments: a pervasive tyranny of the majority and a centrifugal individualism. He proposed, as a solution to democracy's problems, a "new science of politics" based on enlightened self-interest. He emphasized the utility, rather than the beauty or nobility, of virtue and public-spiritedness.

A shrewd observer of political affairs, Tocqueville was one of the first to discern the American tendency toward JUDICIAL SUPREMACY. American judges, he noted, although confined to deciding particular cases, and only those presenting justiciable controversies, possess immense political power. This is possible because "scarcely any political question arises in the United States which is not resolved, sooner or later, into a judicial question," and because of the simple fact that the Americans have acknowledged the right of judges to found their decisions on the Constitution rather than on the laws, or, in other words, they have permitted them not to apply such laws as may appear to them to be unconstitutional. The political power of the judges, arising out of the exercise of JUDICIAL REVIEW, appeared to Tocqueville a salutary check on potential legislative excess. Tocqueville's observation, made when the Supreme Court had voided only a single federal law as unconstitutional, seems all the more perceptive today.

Tocqueville also recognized the unique status of the Constitution in American political life. The English constitution was alterable by ordinary legislation and the constitutions of continental monarchies were immutable save by violent revolution; only in America was the Constitution regarded as an expression of the SOVEREIGNTY of the people, not subject to change at the whim of legislators, but amendable by the common consent of the citizens in accordance with established rules.

Not all of Tocqueville's observations remain valid. For example, he wrote that the states were more powerful than the national government and that Congress was more powerful than the President. In each case, however, he identified the factors that have caused those relationships to be reversed in our own day.

Tocqueville's purpose in writing *Democracy in America* was not merely to describe American institutions. He addressed himself to the universal problems of modern politics—economic and social, as well as governmental. America provided illustrations and examples, and from the American experience he made generalizations applicable to all modern nations. In America Tocqueville learned how to make democracy safe for the world.

DENNIS J. MAHONEY
(1986)

Bibliography

PIERSON, G. W.   1959   *Tocqueville in America.* New York: Basic Books.
ZETTERBAUM, MARVIN   1965   *Tocqueville and the Problem of Democracy.* New York: Basic Books.

## TODD, THOMAS
### (1765–1826)

Thomas Todd served as a Justice of the United States Supreme Court for nearly nineteen years, but he had only a small impact on the Court's decisions. Born into a fairly prominent Virginia family, he was orphaned at an early age. Because the bulk of his father's estate went to his eldest brother, he was forced to fend for himself. Following a short enlistment in the army during the Revolutionary War he went to Liberty Hall in Lexington, Virginia (later Washington and Lee University), where he studied the classics and mathematics. Todd then entered the household of his cousin Harry Innes, an accomplished lawyer and respected member of the Virginia legislature, where he served as a tutor in return for room and board. In 1784 Innes and his family removed to Kentucky where he became a judge, and Todd accompanied them. Through his cousin's political connections Todd quickly became involved in the movement to make Kentucky a separate state, serving as secretary and clerk for the various conventions that were called, and helped to write Kentucky's first CONSTITUTION in 1792.

Admitted to the bar in 1788, Todd developed a lucrative law practice, with a specialty in land titles. During the 1790s he served as secretary to the Kentucky legislature and as clerk to the federal district court. In 1799 he was appointed judge of that court, and five years later he became chief judge. In 1807 Congress increased the number of United States Supreme Court Justices from five to six in order to accommodate the newly created western circuit (Ohio, Kentucky, and Tennessee) and to resolve the special problems in land law arising there. As this was Todd's area of expertise and because Todd was popular with the congressmen from the western states, President THOMAS JEFFERSON appointed him to the newly created post.

Although a Republican, Todd invariably supported the strongly nationalist and probusiness decisions of the MARSHALL COURT. Reportedly he was opposed to the Supreme Court's ruling in DARTMOUTH COLLEGE V. WOODWARD (1819), but he was absent when it was handed down. In fact, bad health combined with the difficulties of riding the western circuit forced him to miss many of the Supreme Court sessions. He wrote only fourteen decisions, eleven for the majority, two concurring, and one dissenting in the relatively unimportant case of *Finley v. Lynn* (1810). With the exception of his last opinion, *Riggs v. Taylor* (1824), which dealt with an evidentiary problem, all his opinions dealt with problems involving land titles. He remained active in various local and state civic affairs until his death.

RICHARD E. ELLIS
(1986)

Bibliography

ISRAEL, FRED L.   1969   Thomas Todd. Pages 407–412 in Leon Friedman and Fred L. Israel, eds., *Justices of the Supreme Court, 1789–1969. New York: Chelsea House.*

## TOLERATION ACT
### 1 William & Mary ch. 18 (1689)

The principle of RELIGIOUS LIBERTY denies that the state has any legitimate authority over the individual's religion or irreligion; the principle of toleration insists that a state which maintains an ESTABLISHMENT OF RELIGION indulge the existence of nonconformist religious groups. Toleration is a step between persecution and liberty. The Toleration Act, which accompanied the Glorious Revolution of 1688–1689, was a political necessity that restored peace to a religiously pluralistic England and ended a period of persecution during which thousands of nonconformist Protestant ministers had died in jail.

The act, entitled "A Bill of Indulgence," exempted most nonconformists from the penalties of the persecutory laws of the Restoration, leaving those laws in force but inapplicable to persons qualifying for indulgence. Subjects who took the requisite oaths to support the new king and reject the authority of the pope might have the privilege of worshipping as they pleased, because they were exempted from the penalties that had suppressed them. Baptists and Quakers received special indulgences. Thus the act had the effect of permitting the existence of lawful nonconformity, though nonconformists still had to pay tithes to the established church and endure many civil disabilities. One section of the act excluded from its benefits Roman Catholic recusants and Protestant antitrinitarians. England still regarded the former as political subversives, the latter as virtual atheists. For all its faults the statute of 1689 ushered in an era of toleration under the established church and ultimately benefited dissenters in those American colonies that maintained establishments of religion.

LEONARD W. LEVY
(1986)

Bibliography

SEATON, A. (1911) 1972 *The Theory of Toleration under the Later Stuarts.* Pages 92–236. New York: Octagon Books.

# TONKIN GULF RESOLUTION

See: Gulf of Tonkin Resolution

# TOOMBS, ROBERT A.
## (1810–1885)

A Georgia attorney educated at Schenectady's Union College, Robert Augustus Toombs was a congressman (1843–1853) and senator (1853–1861) before becoming a SECESSION leader. Initially a conservative WHIG and an ally of ALEXANDER STEPHENS, Toombs became a Democrat, but not a fire-eater, after the COMPROMISE OF 1850. In 1856 he supported the admission of Kansas without SLAVERY, if the settlers there voted for statehood on that basis. In 1860

Toombs worked for a united Democratic Party, but despite this goal and his previous support for STEPHEN A. DOUGLAS in the SENATE, Toombs opposed Douglas's presidential aspirations. After ABRAHAM LINCOLN's election Toombs supported the Crittenden Compromise, and he also offered his own. When compromise failed, he returned to Georgia as a secession leader, writing a report for the Georgia Secession Convention explaining why disunion was necessary. Appointed Confederate secretary of state, Toombs resigned after five months to accept a rebel army commission. When he was denied a promotion after Antietam, Toombs left the army and became a critic of JEFFERSON DAVIS's economic inefficiency, confederate violations of CIVIL LIBERTIES, and CONSCRIPTION. In 1865 he escaped to England; he returned in 1867 to lead Georgia's anti-RECONSTRUCTION forces. He dominated Georgia's 1877 CONSTITUTIONAL CONVENTION, which paved the way for black disfranchisement, and, at Toombs's insistence, severely limited corporate charters and railroad development. Toombs never petitioned for CITIZENSHIP, and although a successful attorney, never again held public office.

PAUL FINKELMAN
(1986)

Bibliography

THOMPSON, ROBERT Y. 1966 *Robert Toombs of Georgia.* Baton Rouge: Louisiana State University Press.

# TOOMER v. WITSELL
## 334 U.S. 385 (1948)

South Carolina required state residents to pay a $25-per-boat license fee to gather shrimp in state waters; for nonresidents, the fee was $2,500. The Supreme Court, speaking through Chief Justice FRED M. VINSON, held that this discrimination violated both the PRIVILEGES AND IMMUNITIES clause of Article IV and the COMMERCE CLAUSE. (See STATE REGULATION OF COMMERCE.) The commerce ground was easy and unanimously supported by the Justices. The decision's main importance lay in its approach to the privileges and immunities clause; on this issue the Court divided, 6–3. Earlier decisions had suggested that the clause protected only "fundamental rights." *Toomer* redirected the inquiry: discrimination against nonresidents was permissible only if it bore a substantial relation to solving a problem distinctively presented by nonresidents. South Carolina's discriminatory tax failed this test.

KENNETH L. KARST
(1986)

## *TORCASO v. WATKINS*
### 367 U.S. 488 (1961)

The Maryland Constitution provided: "No RELIGIOUS TEST ought ever to be required as a qualification to any office . . . other than a declaration of belief in the existence of God. . . ." For Justice HUGO L. BLACK, speaking for the Supreme Court, the Maryland requirement contravened the ESTABLISHMENT OF RELIGION clause of the FIRST AMENDMENT. Black, quoting his own opinion for the Court in EVERSON V. BOARD OF EDUCATION (1947), repeated that government may not "force a person to profess a belief . . . in any religion."

RICHARD E. MORGAN
(1986)

## TORT CLAIMS ACT

See: Federal Tort Claims Act

## TORT LIABILITY AND JOURNALISTIC PRACTICES

See: Journalistic Practices, Tort Liability, and Freedom of the Press

## TORTS

The Constitution intersects with tort law, broadly conceived, in various ways. Most basically, the DUE PROCESS clauses of the Fifth Amendment and FOURTEENTH AMENDMENT require that in any legal proceeding enforced by public authority in which a property interest is at stake, as it almost invariably is in a tort suit, the parties must be accorded PROCEDURAL DUE PROCESS and the EQUAL PROTECTION OF THE LAWS. These requirements, however, are not cumbersome. As the Supreme Court said in *Snyder v. Massachusetts* (1934), a state remains "free to regulate procedure of [its] courts in accordance with [its] own conception of policy and fairness unless in so doing it offends some principle of justice so rooted in the traditions and conscience of our peoples as to be ranked as fundamental." Moreover, due process of law does not always require a proceeding in court. The states are free, for example, to replace the traditional COMMON LAW approach to employee injuries with an administrative workers' compensation system, as all states have now done.

Beyond these rudimentary requirements of procedural due process, which apply to all state-enforced proceedings, the interactions between the Constitution and tort law become considerably more complex. To begin with, the Constitution sometimes functions as a sword, that is, as a source of rights that may be protected by tortlike civil action and damage remedies, and sometimes functions as a shield, that is, as an obstacle to civil actions and remedies that would otherwise be available under state or federal law. Moreover, the Constitution interacts with tort law as a sword and as a shield both directly and obliquely. We begin with the Constitution's more indirect interactions.

By virtue of the SUPREMACY CLAUSE (Article VI, clause 2), the Constitution is the ultimate source of congressional authority. Thus, the Constitution is indirectly the source of all tortlike civil causes of action created by federal statutes. Where a statute explicitly creates a private cause of action, this area of law raises few problems. However, many federal regulatory and criminal statutes specify standards of conduct without expressly authorizing suits for money DAMAGES. Not surprisingly, individuals injured by violations of these laws often ask the federal courts to create private causes of action with damages as a remedy. All agree that the issue of whether the federal courts should infer such a cause of action is a matter of statutory construction and that what must ultimately be determined is whether Congress intended to create the private remedy asserted. Yet, the question of what constitutes sufficient evidence of congressional intent and how restrictive or liberal the Court should be in finding implied private causes of action is highly controversial and has sharply divided the Court. It is clear, however, that during the twenty-five years since its 1964 decision in *J. I. Case Co. v. Borak*, where the Court seemed willing to create a private right of action wherever doing so would help effectuate the purpose of the statute, the Court has generally grown increasingly hostile toward implied causes of action. The prevailing view on the Court now seems to be that first expressed by Justice LEWIS F. POWELL in his dissent in *Cannon v. University of Chicago* (1979): "absent the most compelling evidence of affirmative congressional intent, a federal court should not infer a private cause of action."

The Constitution is also the ultimate source of authority for the FEDERAL TORT CLAIMS ACT, which provides that the "United States shall be liable . . . to tort claims in the same manner and to the same extent as a private individual under like circumstances" (28 U.S.C. 2674). The act does not create new causes of action. Rather, it constitutes a waiver of SOVEREIGN IMMUNITY by the United States for negligent acts by its employees that would constitute torts in states where the conduct occurs. The act has many important express exceptions (such as an exception for intentional acts and for "discretionary functions") and the Supreme Court has inferred additional exceptions (such as the bar to suits by members of the ARMED FORCES for injuries they incur while in the military). Nevertheless, the act, which was not passed until 1946, remains the only basis for recovery of damages from the United States for the torts of its employees.

Not only is the Constitution the ultimate source of authority for federal statutes that create or permit tortlike causes of action, but it is also the ultimate source of authority for federal statutes that preclude state tort remedies that would otherwise be available. In this case, too, the issue is one of statutory interpretation (did Congress intend to displace state laws dealing with the same subject matter as the federal statute?), and here, also, the issue is easily resolved where Congress made it clear that the federal statute is intended to preempt the relevant state law. For example, in *Duke Power Co. v. Carolina Environmental Study Group*, the Court upheld the Price-Anderson Act, which expressly limited aggregate liability for a single nuclear power plant accident to $560 million, thereby limiting the tort remedies that might otherwise be available to plaintiffs in state courts. The Court rejected the claim that the statute resulted in an unconstitutional deprivation of the property rights of potential accident victims.

More difficult issues arise where Congress's intent with respect to state law is unclear. For example, the Federal Cigarette Label and Advertising Act requires that cigarette packages be marked with certain specified warning labels. Although the act forbids states to require additional warnings of any kind, the act does not make it clear whether, or to what extent, state courts are precluded from allowing tort actions by smokers who claim to have been harmed by smoking cigarettes sold with the requisite federal warnings. This issue is now being widely litigated in state and lower federal courts.

Although there are limits to generalizations that can be drawn, it seems that the Supreme Court has been unwilling to find PREEMPTION of state tort remedies in the absence of clear legislative intent to displace state law. For example, in *Silkwood v. Kerr-McGee Corp.* (1984), the Court held that state laws awarding punitive damages for injuries resulting from the escape of plutonium from a nuclear plant were not preempted by the extensive federal regulatory scheme governing the safety of nuclear plants.

Both the implied-cause-of-action cases and the preemption cases raise issues of statutory interpretation. Unquestionably, Congress has broad constitutional power to create new tortlike causes of action or, instead, to abolish or replace existing causes of action. In recent years, however, the Supreme Court has tended to construe federal statutes narrowly, leaving things as they are in the absence of a clear indication of an intent by Congress to change them. Thus, the Court has been reluctant either to infer private causes of action from federal statutes or to find that state law has been preempted by federal statutes.

The Constitution not only affects tort law indirectly through the commands of federal statutes, but bears directly on tort law as a source of tortlike causes of action against governmental officials and entities and as an obstacle to tort actions and remedies that would otherwise be available. We begin with the constitution as a sword.

The idea that compensatory and punitive-damage actions could be premised on the Constitution itself took some time to develop, particularly where the defendant was an official of the federal government. The common-law courts tended to treat an official who invaded the protected interests of another without legal authority simply as a private individual who had committed a tort. The BILL OF RIGHTS, which originally applied only to the federal government, incorporated some common-law norms against unjustified official invasions of person and property. For example, it forbids federal officials from making unreasonable SEARCHES AND SEIZURES, forbids issuance of SEARCH WARRANTS without probable cause, and forbids deprivations of life, liberty, or property without due process of law.

Until the CIVIL WAR, the Constitution played only an indirect role in tort actions against federal officials. A person who believed that his or her person or property had been wrongfully invaded by a federal officer would bring a common-law trespass action against him. The official pleaded justification—that he or she had been acting within his or her constitutional and statutory authority, so the action was not tortious. For example, an official might argue that a seizure of the plaintiff's property was reasonable. The issue of reasonableness could have been characterized as a question of whether the plaintiff's FOURTH AMENDMENT rights had been violated. But neither the parties, nor the courts it seems, perceived the action as different from an ordinary tort action because the constitutional and preexisting common-law standards were largely coextensive.

The constitutional amendments and legislation of the RECONSTRUCTION era increased the interplay of tort law and the Constitution, particularly in actions against state and local officials. With the Fourteenth Amendment, the common-law protections against unjustified invasions of liberty or property were now constitutionalized as against state and local officials rather than only against federal officials. And new rights that were not recognized at common law, such as the right to equal protection of the laws, were added to the Constitution.

In addition, the 1871 Civil Rights Act recognized under COLOR OF STATE LAW a cause of action for invasion of rights secured by the Constitution, and the JUDICIARY ACT OF 1875 extended FEDERAL COURT JURISDICTION to FEDERAL QUESTION cases generally. Before the Civil War, plaintiffs had brought suits against government officers as tort claims, and the constitutional issues arose by way of answer and reply. The Reconstruction legislation, however, offered the plaintiffs a federal forum if they pleaded a constitutional violation in their complaints. Over time these "constitutional" torts came to be viewed as separate from the common-law tort actions from which they derived. This separation occurred in part because constitutional rights came to include some rights that had not received protection in common-law actions, such as rights to free speech. In addition, the demise of the concept of a general nationwide common law made lawyers look for federal or state positive-law sources for interests that the courts would protect and look to the source of constitutional tort actions as the Constitution rather than general tort law.

Today federal court actions against state and local officials for constitutional invasions are primarily brought under SECTION 1983 of the 1871 Civil Rights Act. Suits against LOCAL GOVERNMENT entities—although not states, which are usually shielded from federal court liability by the ELEVENTH AMENDMENT—can also be brought in federal courts under section 1983. (Local governments are liable, however, only for their own unconstitutional policies, not for the unauthorized tortious acts of their employees.) There is no counterpart to section 1983 for suits against federal officials. Therefore, a claim against a federal official, such as the claim that an FBI agent violated the plaintiff's Fourth Amendment rights, must be rooted in the Constitution itself. Although the general federal-question statute empowers federal courts to adjudicate cases arising under the Constitution, neither that statute nor the Constitution itself expressly creates a cause of action for money damages. It was not until 1971, in the landmark case of BIVENS V. SIX UNKNOWN NAMED AGENTS, that the Supreme Court ruled that a federal official can be sued for money damages as a cause of action implied from the Constitution itself—in this case, from the Fourth Amendment. *Bivens* made clear that the constitutional claim was not tied to the niceties of state tort law: "The federal question becomes not merely a possible defense to the State Law action, but an independent claim both necessary and sufficient to make out the . . . cause of action."

Since *Bivens*, the Court has recognized other constitutional provisions, such as the Eighth Amendment's proscription on CRUEL AND UNUSUAL PUNISHMENT, as bases for damage actions. *Bivens*, however, leaves many open questions, most crucially, whether the availability of a cause of action against federal officers for money damages is required by the Constitution itself or is federal common law that Congress could abolish by statute. In recent years the Court has rejected a variety of constitutional damage claims either because, in the Court's view, Congress had provided an alternative remedy or, more broadly, because the Court perceived "special factors" counseling caution in inferring a constitutional cause of action for damages.

Moreover, the Supreme Court has ruled that both state officials sued under section 1983 and federal officials sued in a *Bivens* action possess some degree of immunity from liability (municipalities sued under section 1983 do not). Some officials, such as judges and prosecutors performing their official duties, enjoy absolute immunity from suit, but most officials are accorded only a "qualified," or "good faith," immunity. This form of immunity, which has little support in the common law and is not mentioned either in section 1983 or in the Constitution itself, must be claimed as an affirmative defense. Although this partial immunity is often called good-faith immunity, the Supreme Court's most recent formulation in *Harlan v. Fitzgerald* (1982) makes clear that the test is an objective one: "[G]overnment officials performing discretionary functions generally are shielded from liability for civil damages insofar as their conduct does not violate clearly established statutory or constitutional rights of which a reasonable person would have known."

Although the rights litigated in these "section 1983" and *Bivens* suits are rights secured by the Constitution and the various immunity doctrines are peculiar to suits against governmental officials, these actions are still seen in some respects as in the nature of tort actions, as shown by the borrowing of state-tort statutes of limitation. In addition, many such constitutional actions, for example, those seeking damages for illegal searches or arrests, resemble common-law actions that may be brought under state tort law or, in limited cases, under the Federal Tort Claims Act if the violator is a federal law enforcement official. Other "constitutional tort" actions go beyond the common law—for example, an action under the 1871 Act claiming that one was dismissed from public employment for exercising one's FIRST AMENDMENT rights. Actions for official negligence typically are relegated to traditional tort remedies, as are some intentional torts, such as libel.

If it took a surprisingly long time for the Court to rule that the Constitution could itself be the source for tortlike causes of action for damages, it took almost as long for it to rule that the Constitution could be an obstacle to tort remedies otherwise available. The primary constitutional limit on common-law private tort actions is the First Amendment's prohibition against "law[s] . . . abridging the freedom of speech or of the press." Originally, this prohibition applied only to Congress, but with the INCORPORATION of the Bill of Rights into the Fourteenth Amendment, it became applicable to state governments as well. Nevertheless, it was not until NEW YORK TIMES V. SULLIVAN (1964) that the Supreme Court interpreted the First Amendment as a limitation on damage remedies in private suits brought under the states' common law of libel. Although it might seem anomalous that constitutional language securing rights against the government would also come into play in legal actions between private parties, by the time of *Sullivan* it had become clear that a state could infringe constitutionally protected interests by enforcing a legal judgment as well as by enacting a statute.

In *Sullivan*, a city commissioner of Montgomery, Alabama, brought a libel action in state court against the *New York Times* and four black ministers who had advertised in the *Times*, appealing for contributions to a legal-defense fund for MARTIN LUTHER KING, JR., who had recently been arrested in Alabama on a perjury charge. The ad, which had not mentioned Sullivan, made several assertions about the conduct of the Montgomery police that were largely, though not entirely, accurate. Sullivan claimed that because his duties included supervision of the Montgomery police, the allegations against the police defamed him personally. An Alabama jury awarded him $500,000. By the time the case reached the Supreme Court, it was but one of eleven LIBEL claims totaling $5,600,000 pending against the *Times* in Alabama; it was obvious that the *Sullivan* litigation was part of a concerted effort to discourage the press from supporting the CIVIL RIGHTS MOVEMENT in the South and to silence the movement's leaders. This effort, moreover, seemed likely to succeed, for under the common law of Alabama and most other states it was difficult to defeat these libel claims. Under standard common-law rules governing libel actions, truth was an affirmative defense, but the evident inability of civil rights advocates to prove to hostile juries the "truth" of statements criticizing popularly elected officials posed the clear danger that speech would be stifled by the threat of crushing civil liability. And in most states the common-law rule of strict liability for defamation recognized no privilege of "fair comment" for statements of fact that were false. To combat this danger to First Amendment values, the Court in *Sullivan* ruled that a statement criticizing a public official and relating to matters of public concern could be actionable under state libel law only if the statement were defamatory, false, and made with actual malice'—that is, with knowledge that it was false or with reckless disregard of whether it was false or not."

In subsequent years, the Court recognized that "the establishment" against which caustic political speech was often addressed encompassed more individuals than merely those who actually held public office. Indeed, there are many people, such as labor leaders or prominent business leaders, who may be so powerful or influential that their actions clearly affect the outcome of political controversies. Acknowledging this reality, the Court, in the cases of *Associated Press v. Walker* and *Curtis Publishing Company v. Butts* (1967), extended the *Sullivan* rules to libel actions brought by PUBLIC FIGURES. However, in GERTZ V. ROBERT WELCH, INC. (1974), the Court recognized that there are other people who, although perhaps well known, have not so injected themselves into public controversy as to become public figures for purposes of the First Amendment's limitations on libel actions. Where such a nonpublic figure brings a libel suit, there is much less likelihood that a libel action is a state-supported attempt to silence unpopular speech. Moreover, such private individuals have a correspondingly lesser opportunity than public figures or public officials to obtain access to the media to rebut the allegedly defamatory statements. Thus, the Court ruled in *Gertz* that private plaintiffs in such cases need only to show whatever standard of fault the state requires, although some level of fault (at the least negligence) is a constitutional requirement for recovery.

First Amendment concerns ebb as the public status of the plaintiff decreases, but the status of the plaintiff is not the only factor that determines whether the challenged speech is entitled to special constitutional protection. In DUN & BRADSTREET V. GREENMOSS BUILDERS, INC. (1985) the Supreme Court ruled that special First Amendment protection extends only to speech relating to matters of public concern. If the challenged statement touches only matters of private concern, there is little danger that state libel law is being used to silence unpopular political speech, and so the states are free to apply whatever libel law they choose. It is possible, in theory, that public officials or public figures might thus succeed in silencing the speech of unpopular critics. But it is clear that a given topic of interest may change categories as the social status of the plaintiff changes, so that matters that are "private" in the context of statements about private citizens may be of public concern in the context of statements about public officials or public figures.

The Court's First Amendment libel jurisprudence has become extremely—some would say unduly—complex and has required extensive revamping of not only substantive libel law, but procedural and remedial libel law as well. For example, in a "public concern" case the defendant no longer bears the burden of persuasion on the issue of the truth of the alleged defamation. Now, in a departure from the common law, it is the plaintiff who must prove that the challenged statement contains an untrue assertion before any liability will exist. And although falsehood may be established by the common-law standard of a preponderance of the evidence, "actual malice" (in the case of a "public official" or "public figure" plaintiff) or negligence (in the case of a "private individual" plaintiff) must now be established by clear and convincing evidence. In addition to these changes in trial procedure, the Court has effected a change in appellate procedure in libel actions, ruling in *Bose Corporation v. Consumers Union of United States, Inc.* (1984) that a reviewing court is not to accord trial court findings the normal "clearly erroneous" standard of deference. Instead, said the Court, the First

Amendment requires that an appellate court independently evaluate the evidence in the record to determine whether there is clear and convincing evidence of "actual malice" or the appropriate level of fault.

With respect to remedies for libel and defamation, the law is also complex and, perhaps, in a state of flux. But in essence, the current rule is the following: where the speech relates to matters of public concern, regardless of the social status of the target of the speech, presumed and punitive damages may be awarded only upon a showing of actual malice (of course, where the plaintiff is a public official or public figure, no damages at all will lie, absent a showing of actual malice); but where the subject matter of the speech is purely private, the First Amendment places no limitation on any type of damages.

Many libel plaintiffs also allege that they are entitled to recover on some other basis, such as invasion of privacy or intentional infliction of emotional distress. Like libel, these other causes of action also present the risk of state-supported attempts to silence controversial or unpopular speech. Not surprisingly, when the Court in HUSTLER MAGAZINE V. FALWELL (1988) considered whether the First Amendment places any limitations on actions for intentional infliction of emotional distress, it held that a public official or a public-figure plaintiff in such an action must prove that the statement at issue contains a false assertion made with actual malice. The Court did not discuss the public concern/private concern distinction of *Dun & Bradstreet*, but its reasoning suggests that emotional distress actions, as well as other tort actions based on defendant's speech, must be analyzed in light of the same First Amendment principles as libel actions.

Until now, the First Amendment has been by far the most important source of constitutionally based limitations on tort law. But the Court will soon consider whether the due-process clause of the Fourteenth Amendment places some limits on the award of punitive damages under state law, not only for speech related torts, such as libel and slander, but for all torts. As punitive-damage awards have skyrocketed in recent years, business interests have argued for some constitutionally based limits on the size of punitive awards. In *Browning-Ferris Industries of Vermont Inc. v. Kelco Disposal Inc.* (1989) the Court ruled that the Eighth Amendment's EXCESSIVE FINES clause applies only to criminal cases and not to awards of punitive damages in civil suits between private parties. However, the Court expressly left open the possibility that the due-process clause regulates in some way the imposition of punitive damages in such suits.

SILAS WASSERSTROM
ANNE WOOLHANDLER
(1992)

Bibliography

JEFFRIES, JOHN C. 1989 Compensation for Constitutional Torts: Reflections on the Significance of Fault. *Michigan Law Review* 88:82–103.

NICHOLS, GENE 1989 *Bivens, Chilicky,* and Constitutional Damages Claims. *Virginia Law Review* 75:1117–1154.

SMOLLA, RODNEY 1987 *Dun & Bradstreet, Hepps,* and *Liberty Lobby:* A New Analytic Primer on the Future Course` of Defamation. *Georgetown Law Journal* 75:1519–1573.

## TOTH, UNITED STATES EX REL., v. QUARLES
### 350 U.S. 11 (1955)

Five months after his honorable discharge from the Air Force, Toth was charged with committing murder while on active duty in Korea. Taken to Korea for trial by court martial, Toth sought HABEAS CORPUS in a DISTRICT OF COLUMBIA court. On APPEAL, the Supreme Court held, 6–3, that a civilian was entitled to TRIAL BY JURY in a civilian court established under Article III; court-martial JURISDICTION was constitutionally limited to actual members of the armed forces.

KENNETH L. KARST
(1986)

(SEE ALSO: *Judicial Power; Military Justice.*)

## TOWNSEND v. SAIN
### 372 U.S. 29 (1963)

When a state prisoner seeks federal HABEAS CORPUS review of a constitutional error in his or her case, the federal court must decide what weight to give the state court fact findings that are relevant to the prisoner's claim. The fairness and accuracy of such findings are crucial to the proper adjudication of federal constitutional rights, because most habeas corpus petitions raise mixed questions of law and fact, such as the VOLUNTARINESS of a WAIVER OF CONSTITUTIONAL RIGHTS, or the suggestiveness of a LINE-UP identification. In *Townsend*, a unanimous Supreme Court held that a federal court in a habeas corpus proceeding always has the power to try the facts anew, and that it must do so if the defendant did not receive a full and fair evidentiary hearing in any state court proceeding. The Court split 5–4 over the need for more specific directives concerning mandatory hearings, with Chief Justice EARL WARREN setting forth the majority's view that a hearing is required in six particular circumstances.

In 1966, Congress enacted a modified form of the

*Townsend* criteria in an amendment to the JUDICIAL CODE, specifying eight circumstances when the validity of state court findings may not be presumed. In other circumstances, the habeas corpus petitioner bears the burden of proving that the state fact findings were erroneous.

CATHERINE HANCOCK
(1986)

# TOWNSHEND ACTS
## (1767)

The Townshend Acts imposed duties upon American imports of glass, lead, paint, paper, and tea and authorized WRITS OF ASSISTANCE as one means of enforcing payment. Although "external" in form, the duties were not levied to regulate trade but to raise revenue to help pay for maintaining British soldiers and officials in America. The colonists protested that the levies constituted TAXATION WITHOUT REPRESENTATION. The Townshend Act duties (except that on tea) were repealed in 1770.

DENNIS J. MAHONEY
(1986)

# TRADE UNIONS

See: Labor and the Constitution

# TRAFFIC STOPS

Although traffic stops are not the most burdensome seizures regulated by the FOURTH AMENDMENT, they have become among the most controversial—partly because they are so common. Most Americans have never been arrested, but the vast majority have been pulled over. More importantly, traffic enforcement is highly discretionary. Vehicle codes are so widely breached that the police can stop almost any car if they follow it with a modicum of patience. This discretion is a boon for law enforcement; police departments increasingly have found vehicle codes a useful tool for finding and apprehending violators of more serious laws.

But the discretionary nature of traffic enforcement also has a worrisome side. Because vehicle codes give police officers authority to stop practically any motorist, they present some of the same risks of arbitrariness posed in colonial America by GENERAL WARRANTS and WRITS OF ASSISTANCE, the very instruments against which the Fourth Amendment was most clearly aimed. And a growing body of evidence suggests that the police are far more likely to pull over cars driven by members of racial minorities, particularly African Americans, and that minority motorists stopped by the police are more likely to be verbally or physically abused.

Recent decisions by the Supreme Court have exacerbated these dangers. In the most important of these decisions, *Whren v. United States* (1996), the Court held unanimously that the police can stop a car whenever they have PROBABLE CAUSE to believe that the driver has violated traffic laws, regardless of the officers' true motivation, and regardless of whether the violation would prompt a reasonable officer to pull the car over. *Whren* put to rest a persistent ambiguity in constitutional CRIMINAL PROCEDURE, ruling that "[s]ubjective intentions play no role in ordinary, probable-cause Fourth Amendment analysis." The decision also rejected the reasoning of some scholars and lower courts that a traffic stop should be deemed unconstitutionally pretextual if it departed so sharply from usual police practices that a reasonable officer would not have made the stop for the reasons given. Writing for the Court, Justice ANTONIN SCALIA saw this alternative approach as an unwieldy and unjustifiable attempt to bring subjective intentions back into the analysis through the back door.

In other recent cases the Court has broadened the power that the police can exercise once they pull over a car. Having held in *Pennsylvania v. Mimms* (1977) that during any lawful traffic stop the police can order the driver out of the car, the Court in *Maryland v. Wilson* (1997) extended the *Mimms* rule to passengers. In *Ohio v. Robinette* (1996), the Court ruled that the police can seek consent to search a car without first explaining that the traffic stop has ended; *Robinette* built on SCHNECKLOTH V. BUSTAMONTE (1973), which held that a suspect can validly consent to a search without knowing he or she has the right to refuse.

In all these cases the Court demonstrated a commendable regard for law enforcement necessities and the considerable hazards faced by officers carrying out traffic stops. What the decisions unfortunately lack is similar attention to ways in which traffic stops lend themselves to particularly troubling forms of police harassment.

DAVID A. SKLANSKY
(2000)

(SEE ALSO: *Search and Seizure.*)

Bibliography

DAVIS, ANGELA J. 1997 Race, Cops, and Traffic Stops. *University of Miami Law Review* 51:425–443.
SALKEN, BARBARA C. 1989 The General Warrant of the Twentieth Century? A Fourth Amendment Solution to Unchecked

Discretion to Arrest for Traffic Offenses. *Temple Law Review* 62:221–275.

SKLANSKY, DAVID A.  1998  Traffic Stops, Minority Motorists, and the Future of the Fourth Amendment. *Supreme Court Review* 1997:271–329.

# TRANSACTIONAL IMMUNITY

See: Immunity Grant

# TRANSFORMATION OF CONSTITUTIONAL LAW

Over the past two hundred years, American CONSTITUTIONAL INTERPRETATION has undergone a transformation from its early static and TEXTUALIST tradition to a modern, dynamic approach wherein a "LIVING CONSTITUTION" changes to accommodate the needs of the times. Two pivotal periods in constitutional thought have catalyzed this shift away from ORIGINALISM, initially starting with the Progressive reaction to the excesses of the *Lochner* Court, and later continuing with the WARREN COURT and its broad constitutional reforms.

For the first hundred years, American constitutional interpretation firmly adhered to what historian Michael Kammen describes as a Newtonian conception of the Constitution. Constitutional concepts and principles were static and unchanging, akin to the timeless scientific truths of Newtonian mechanics. Indeed, so firmly entrenched was this originalist approach to judicial thinking that the Supreme Court all but ignored Chief Justice JOHN MARSHALL's statement in MCCULLOCH V. MARYLAND (1819) that "[the] constitution was intended to endure for ages to come, and, consequently, to be adapted to the various crises of human affairs." The passage was cited only once in a Court opinion during the entire nineteenth century, and only a total of six times by 1945.

The dominance of literal constitutional interpretation was not entirely surprising given the strong influence of Protestant thought early in American history. Protestants rejected the priestly interpretations of the Bible espoused by Catholics, supporting instead textualist interpretations that were more freely available to laypersons. Indeed, at the time of the writing of the Constitution, the only established competitor to originalism was the COMMON LAW methodology, which by the early eighteenth century had been recognized as changing and evolutionary. Nonetheless, despite the Framers' acceptance of the dynamic nature of the common law, they largely held to the originalist view. For instance, when constructing the Virginia code, THOMAS JEFFERSON would entertain only ancient, "timeless" English common law rules, excluding the "uncertain"

reforms proffered in the then-recent common law jurisprudence of Lord Mansfield.

The originalist approach had internal conflicts and difficulties. One problem was the degree of literalness to be applied. Were judges to interpret the Constitution on its face, considering only express terms, or were they to consider historical context and implied meaning as well? The former, the plain meaning approach, faced semiotic difficulties, since as JAMES MADISON suggested, "no language is so copious as to supply words and phrases for every complex idea. . . ." The preference for the letter of the Constitution over the spirit also clashed with early Christian foundations, which militated against extreme literalism. "[F]or the letter killeth, but the spirit giveth life" (2 *Corinthians* 3:6). The historical context approach suffered its own interpretative problems, for the Constitution and its amendments had been adopted through a process of debate, representing a multitude of often contradictory intentions. Intent was not just difficult to discover; oftentimes a unified intent did not even exist. These deficiencies led Justice WILLIAM J. BRENNAN, JR., later to criticize historical analysis as "arrogance cloaked as humility." It was plainly arrogant, if not unbelievable, to think that a court could accurately guess the intent of the Framers decades or centuries later.

The high-water mark for a static conception of constitutional meaning centered around LOCHNER V. NEW YORK (1905), where the Court struck down a maximum hour law for bakers as a violation of FREEDOM OF CONTRACT. *Lochner*'s holding, however, demonstrated the great deficiency of static, originalist constitutional interpretation; it was simply incapable of adapting to a changing world. Abstract legal concepts such as freedom of contract had grown out of touch with the practical realities of an increasingly exploitative industrial society, and originalist thinking provided no easy alternative. *Lochner* thus provoked a fervent reaction from the Progressives, who sought to transform the conception of constitutional law from static to dynamic to meet the rapidly changing needs of twentieth-century society.

The stage for a dynamic conception of constitutional law was set by Darwin's theory of evolution, which served to undermine the static Newtonian model of constitutionalism while concurrently suggesting that law, like science, might change over time. Progressives argued for an organic Constitution premised on Justice OLIVER WENDELL HOLMES, JR.'s, classic maxim from *The Common Law* (1881): "The life of the law has not been logic; it has been experience." Constitutional principles were not to be derived solely from the text, but rather were changed by customs and common experiences over time. Justice THOMAS M. COOLEY of the Michigan Supreme Court similarly supported this organic conception of constitutional interpretation, suggesting that the Constitution's "peculiar excellence is that it is forever adapted to the people, and expands to accommodate new circumstances and new and higher conditions of society." By the turn of the century, then-Professor WOODROW WILSON summarized PROGRESSIVE CONSTITUTIONAL THOUGHT most markedly: "government is not a machine, but a living thing. . . . It is accountable to Darwin, not to Newton."

To introduce a dynamic, orgainc concept of a "living Constitution" into a still predominantly originalist legal community, the Progressives used the justification of "changed circumstances." This DOCTRINE, pioneered by future-Justice LOUIS D. BRANDEIS's brief to the Court in MULLER V. OREGON (1908), created a fiction by which the Court could maintain the aura of originalism. The Constitution remained static and unchanging; instead, the factual situation was the novelty, requiring a new, but still originalist interpretation of the Constitution. In *Muller*, despite the foreboding PRECEDENT of *Lochner*, the "BRANDEIS BRIEF", as it became commonly known, successfully argued the constitutionality of an Oregon maximum hour law for women by using the "changed circumstances" argument, daringly submitting 110 pages of sociological and economic data on the modern situation of working women.

The originalist underpinning of the changed circumstances doctrine was tenuous, and failed to confine the doctrine for very long. Quickly, the doctrine became a key point of departure from static originalism. Justice BENJAMIN N. CARDOZO soon expanded the doctrine to embrace the idea of a "living Constitution," advocating in *The Nature of the Judicial Process* (1921) that "[t]he great generalities of the constitution have a content and significance that vary from age to age." No longer was a court applying a previously fixed rule to new facts. Indeed, as Cardozo suggested, the meaning of the rule itself could not be determined independently of its times or its specific applications. Cardozo's theory of a dynamic Constitution was poignantly expressed in his unpublished CONCURRING OPINION in the *Minnesota Mortgage Moratorium Case* (1934):

> [The Framers] did not see the changes in the relation between states and nation or in the play of social forces that lay hidden in the womb of time. It may be inconsistent with things that they believed or took for granted. Their beliefs to be significant must be adjusted to the world they knew.

Cardozo withdrew his concurrence, however, when his charge was boldly echoed in the MAJORITY OPINION by Chief Justice CHARLES EVANS HUGHES:

> It is no answer to say that this public need was not apprehended a century ago, or to insist that what the provision of the Constitution meant to the vision of that day it must

mean to the vision of our time. . . . It was to guard against such a narrow conception that Chief Justice Marshall uttered the memorable warning—'We must never forget, that it is *a constitution* we are expounding'—'a constitution intended to endure for ages to come, and consequently, to be adapted to the various *crises* of human affairs.'

Among its multitude of reforms and constitutional reinterpretations, the Warren Court's treatment of the FOURTEENTH AMENDMENT, specifically the EQUAL PROTECTION clause, best evinced its commitment to a dynamic and changing Constitution. Shortly after the ratification of the Fourteenth Amendment, the RECONSTRUCTION Court had sought to limit and narrow the amendment's scope. In the twenty-eight years between the ratification of the Fourteenth Amendment and PLESSY V. FERGUSON (1896), which legalized "SEPARATE BUT EQUAL" SEGREGATION, the Court did not once rule in favor of blacks seeking protection against RACIAL DISCRIMINATION. The Court instead consistently struck down or narrowly construed CIVIL RIGHTS LEGISLATION. As Justice LEWIS F. POWELL, JR., suggested in REGENTS OF UNIVERSITY OF CALIFORNIA V. BAKKE (1978), the equal protection clause was "[v]irtually strangled in infancy by post-civil-war reactionism." The Warren Court endeavored to revisit and rewrite Fourteenth Amendment jurisprudence, notably in BROWN V. BOARD OF EDUCATION (1954), HARPER V. VIRGINIA STATE BOARD OF ELECTIONS (1966), and REYNOLDS V. SIMS (1964).

The theory under which the Court reached its decision in *Brown*, which held school segregation unconstitutional, remains ambiguous. Was *Plessy* incorrect from the day it was decided, or had *Plessy* been previously correct but changed circumstances mandated a reevaluation? Chief Justice EARL WARREN's opinion hinted at both theories. On one hand, it held that "[s]eparate educational facilities are inherently unequal," suggesting timeless, originalist principles. On the other hand, the Court also stated that it could not "turn the clock back to 1868 when the Amendment was adopted," but instead had to "consider public education in the light of its full development and its present place in American life," implying changed circumstances.

*Brown*'s theoretical basis proves particularly difficult to grasp because the Court desired unanimity due to legitimacy concerns. Consequently, Warren was forced to draft the opinion to avoid any specter of moral superiority that might alienate the Southern members of the Court. A suggestion that *Plessy* had always been incorrect would have disparaged "the Southern way of life" as it had been widely practiced for the previous fifty years.

Law clerk (and future professor) ALEXANDER M. BICKEL's memo to Justice FELIX FRANKFURTER on the eve of *Brown* offered an alternative theory of a changing Constitution.

Examining legislative history, Bickel concluded that the drafters of the Fourteenth Amendment had not intended to invalidate segregation at the time it was drafted. However, they had used broad language, anticipating and intending that the Court might adapt and change the interpretation in the future.

In *Harper*, the Court struck down a Virginia POLL TAX as violative of the equal protection clause, OVERRULING a PRECEDENT of thirty years. The ensuing exchange in *Harper* between Justices WILLIAM O. DOUGLAS and HUGO BLACK depicts the victory of the dynamic theory over the static. Douglas, writing for the majority, espoused a living Constitution, holding that "the Equal Protection Clause is not shackled to the political theory of a particular era." He further cited *Brown* for the proposition that the concept of equality changes with changed circumstances. This reasoning, however, provoked a bitter dissent from Black, who unequivocally denied "hold[ing] segregation in public schools unconstitutional on any such theory." For Black, who had grown increasingly disenchanted with dynamic constitutional theory, *Plessy* had been wrong the day it had been decided.

*Reynolds* further demonstrated the Court's shift to a living Constitution. In *Reynolds*, the Court held that the equal protection clause required equal ELECTORAL DISTRICTING for both houses of state legislatures, to which Warren applied the maxim "ONE PERSON, ONE VOTE". Given that the U.S. SENATE is comprised of two senators per state regardless of population, the *Reynolds* holding could scarcely have derived from an original understanding. Its only justification was that democratic principles had evolved to mandate the "one person, one vote" principle, irrespective of ORIGINAL INTENT. After the WORLD WAR II, democracy had become a desirable ideal, no longer confined and feared as leading to a "tyranny of the majority," but rather nurtured by JUDICIAL REVIEW to further inclusiveness in a pluralistic society.

The Warren Court's expansive view of judicial power and dynamic constitutional interpretation provoked a backlash from conservatives in the early 1980s. Focusing on judicial restraint and yearning for a truer and simpler past, Attorney General Edwin Meese proposed a return to originalism, a view often adopted by the REHNQUIST COURT.

A major departure from the Rehnquist Court's originalist tendencies, however, occurred in PLANNED PARENTHOOD V. CASEY (1992). In *Casey*, the Court considered whether to overrule the case that legalized abortion, ROE V. WADE (1973). Writing to reaffirm *Roe*, Justice DAVID H. SOUTER in his part of a joint plurality opinion suggested a standard under which the Court can overrule prior precedent and disregard the traditional, conservative doctrine of STARE DECISIS. Examining the cases overruling *Lochner*

and *Plessy*, the plurality opinion concluded that overruling decisions are based primarily on changing circumstances. "[T]he decisions were . . . defensible, not merely as the victories of one doctrinal school over another by dint of numbers (victories though they were), but as applications of constitutional principle to facts as they had not been seen by the Court before." Despite the recent emphasis on a static Constitution, the dynamic conception had resurfaced yet again.

MORTON J. HORWITZ
(2000)

Bibliography

BARRON, DAVID J. 1999 The Promise of Cooley's City: Traces of Local Constitutionalism. *University of Pennsylvania Law Review* 147:487–612.
BICKEL, ALEXANDER M. 1955 The Original Understanding and the Segregation Decision. *Harvard Law Review* 69:1–65.
CARDOZO, BENJAMIN N. 1921 *The Nature of the Judicial Process.* New Haven Conn.: Yale University Press.
FRIEDMAN, BARRY and SMITH, SCOTT B. 1998 The Sedimentary Constitution. *University of Pennsylvania Law Review* 147:1–90.
HOLMES, OLIVER W., JR. 1881 *The Common Law.* Boston: Little, Brown.
HORWITZ, MORTON J. 1993 The Constitution of Change: Legal Fundamentality Without Fundamentalism. *Harvard Law Review* 107:30–117.
——— 1998 *The Warren Court and the Pursuit of Justice.* New York: Hill and Wang.
KAMMEN, MICHAEL G. 1986 *A Machine That Would Go of Itself: The Constitution and American Culture.* New York: Knopf.
MEESE, EDWIN, III 1985 Address Before the D.C. Chapter of the Federalist Society Lawyers Division. *UC Davis Law Review.* 19:22–30.
RAKOVE, JACK N. 1996 *Original Meanings: Politics and Ideas in the Making of the Constitution.* New York: Knopf.

## *TRANS-MISSOURI FREIGHT ASSOCIATION v. UNITED STATES*
### 166 U.S. 290 (1897)

A 5–4 Supreme Court, holding that the SHERMAN ANTITRUST ACT extended to railroads, rejected the RULE OF REASON advanced by Justice EDWARD D. WHITE in dissent. In 1889, eighteen railroads had combined to form the Trans-Missouri Freight Association "for the purpose of mutual protection, by establishing and maintaining reasonable rates, rules and regulations [over their mutual] freight traffic." Any member's proposed rate reduction for a route shared with another member needed Association approval.

Justice RUFUS PECKHAM, the Court's spokesman, found

two questions: Did the Sherman Act apply to railroads and, if so, was the Freight Association agreement a violation of that act? He dismissed the railroads' claim of exemption on two grounds. Their business was commerce, and the lower courts and the dissenters had relied on a mistaken belief that the Sherman Act could not apply to railroads because the INTERSTATE COMMERCE ACT already regulated carriers. He refused "to read into the act by way of judicial legislation an exception that is not placed there [by Congress]." Policy matters were not questions for judicial determination; any alteration of the law was for Congress to undertake. Peckham concluded that the Sherman Act prohibited all restraints of INTERSTATE COMMERCE; adopting the rule of reason would "substantially . . . leave the question of reasonableness to the companies themselves." Endorsing free competition, the Court declared that intent need not be proved: the Association agreement clearly restrained commerce.

DAVID GORDON
(1986)

# TRAVEL

See: Right to Travel

# TREASON

Treason is the only crime defined in the United States Constitution. Article III, section 3, declares that

> Treason against the United States shall consist only in levying war against them, or in adhering to their enemies, giving them aid and comfort. No person shall be convicted of treason unless on the testimony of two witnesses to the same overt act, or on confession in open court. The Congress shall have power to declare the punishment of treason, but no ATTAINDER OF TREASON shall work corruption of blood, or forfeiture except during the life of the person attainted.

State constitutions contain similar limiting definitions of treason against a state. However, since national independence there has been little action or development of doctrine under the state provisions. The notable exceptions are the trials of Thomas Wilson Dorr (1844) and of John Brown (1859) which ended in convictions of treason by levying war against the states of Rhode Island and Virginia, respectively. State histories include a few abortive attempts to employ treason INDICTMENTS against people who incurred the wrath of powerful elements in the community. Thus indictments were brought against Mormon leaders in Missouri in 1838 and in Illinois in 1844; for political reasons the Missouri charge was not pressed and

the defendants escaped jail; a mob murdered Joseph Smith shortly after his arrest on the Illinois indictment. Such isolated instances aside, the law of treason in the United States has been almost wholly the product of debates over making the national Constitution and decisions of federal courts under Article III, section 3.

As it has developed under the Constitution, the law regarding treason has strikingly mingled concern for the security of government and the legal order and concern for the freedom of private individuals and groups. The crime deals with the most serious threats to the existence of the state. In adopting the Constitution everyone took for granted that, since the people were creating a new SOVEREIGNTY, it must have authority to protect itself. Congress has reflected this judgment of the gravity of the matter by prescribing penalties that may extend to life imprisonment, or perhaps even to execution. Where charges have fallen fairly within the constitutional definition of the offense, judges have not hesitated to make firm application of the law. However, on its face the Constitution takes a limiting approach to the crime. Treason, says Article III, section 3, shall consist "only" in two named types of conduct; Congress is thus barred from adding new categories of treason, as it is also explicitly limited in fixing penalties. Moreover, the treason clause puts a stringent limit on the executive in prosecuting the crime; absent a confession in open court, by constitutional mandate the prosecution must muster testimony of two witnesses to the same overt act that the accused committed in seeking to carry out the treason. Federal judges in cases arising under the treason clause have followed a restrictive approach in marking the outer boundaries of the crime. Thus in one aspect the treason clause guards the security of the government. But in another dimension it sets limitations that make it functionally analogous to provisions of the BILL OF RIGHTS, protecting CIVIL LIBERTIES of private individuals and groups.

The constitutional emphasis on restricting the scope of the crime of treason is a marked departure from the main directions the law had taken in England and in this country before 1789. Before the eighteenth century, in practice, official policy had given clear primacy to the security of government, often more obviously to serve the interests of particular powerholders than to serve the common good.

From the fourteenth to the eighteenth century, English political history included aggressive use of charges of treason as weapons of partisan conflict; prosecution was usually vindictive and pressed with scant regard to fair procedure or careful insistence on clear proof or reliable evidence. The only counterweight to this abusive trend was the continuance of the statute of 25 Edward III (1350), stating seven categories of high treason—notably those of levying war, adhering to enemies, or seeking "to compass or imagine the death of our lord the King"—and asserting that only Parliament might enlarge the definitions of treason, thus forbidding judges to extend the offense by interpretation. The restrictive emphasis of the statute of Edward III was stressed by the English treatise writers from whom lawmakers in the new United States got most of their knowledge of the course of English policy regarding treason. In particular, EDWARD COKE, Matthew Hale, and WILLIAM BLACKSTONE spoke of abuse of vague, extended definitions of the crime as instruments of partisan combat, imperiling the general liberty. Thus Hale warned, "How dangerous it is by construction and analogy to make treasons, where the letter of the law has not done it; for such a method admits of no limits or bounds, but runs as far as the wit and invention of accusers, and the odiousness and detestation of persons accused will carry men." Offsetting such warnings, however, the English treatises also brought to the knowledge of lawmakers in North America a considerable range of decisions in which English judges had, despite the limit declared in Edward III's statute, greatly enlarged the offense of treason by construction.

Security in the most elemental sense was at stake for the English colonies in North America under the threat of French and Indian wars and in the new states torn through the AMERICAN REVOLUTION by bitter divisions between those loyal to the Crown and those asserting independence. Thus in the colonies and in the new states during the years of the Revolutionary War, statute books included many broadly and sometimes vaguely defined offenses of subversion, in dramatic contrast to the limited definition of treason later written into the national Constitution and thereafter typically included in constitutions of the states. Though colonial and early state legislation sometimes borrowed the language of the act of Edward III, we must realize that at least by the late eighteenth century lawyers here would be familiar, through the standard English treatises, with the expansive readings which English courts had given the old statute.

With adoption of the national Constitution we encounter introduction of a restrictive emphasis to balance the security concerns previously dominant in the law of treason. There is not a great deal about the treason clause in the records of the framing and RATIFICATION OF THE CONSTITUTION. But what there is shows sensitivity to lessons that policymakers here felt they should draw from English experience of the dangers to individual and political liberty of loose resort to treason prosecutions. JAMES WILSON was probably the ablest lawyer on the CONSTITUTIONAL CONVENTION's Committee of Detail, which took the responsibility of adopting a restrictive rather than an extensive approach to defining treason. In the Pennsylvania ratifying convention, Wilson twice—on his own initiative and without any criticisms of the provision voiced by an alert and suspicious opposition—praised the treason clause as including protection of civil liberty along with protection of government. In his law lectures delivered at the College of Philadelphia in 1790 and 1791, Wilson emphasized the constitutional provision by devoting an entire lecture to it. He made the centerpoint of his analysis the importance of carefully bounding the crime: "It is the observation of the celebrated Montesquieu, that if the crime of treason be indeterminate, this alone is sufficient to make any government degenerate into arbitrary power." Two fears were prominent in the limited attention given the treason clause in adopting the Constitution: that holders of official power would use the treason charge to suppress legitimate, peaceful political opposition and to destroy those who were out of official favor, and that popular fear and emotion might be stirred under the dread charge to produce convictions without additional evidence. Subsequent federal court opinions recognized this restrictive background, in decisions limiting extension of the offense. Speaking for the Supreme Court in EX PARTE BOLLMAN AND SWARTWOUT (1807) in a matter indirectly involving a treason charge, Chief Justice JOHN MARSHALL declared that "to prevent the possibility of those calamities which result from the extension of treason to offences of minor importance, that great fundamental law which defines and limits the various departments of our government, has given a rule on the subject both to the legislature and the courts of America, which neither can be permitted to transcend." In the first treason case to reach the Supreme Court, CRAMER V. UNITED STATES (1945), the Court reaffirmed the propriety of this approach, quoting with approval Marshall's further admonition that "It is, therefore, more safe, as well as more consonant to the principles of our constitution, that the crime of treason should not be extended by construction to doubtful cases; and that crimes not clearly within the constitutional definition, should receive such punishment as the legislature in its wisdom may provide."

Three key elements enter into the crime of treason: an obligation of allegiance to the legal order, and intent and action to violate that obligation. First, treason is a breach of allegiance. A citizen owes loyal support to the sovereignty within which he lives or from which he derives his citizen's status. There are circumstances under which by the law of a foreign state an individual may owe it allegiance at the same time that he owes fealty to the United States; thus an individual may be a citizen of the United States because he was born here, and also be a citizen of another nation because he was born to nationals of that country. But dual nationality does not relieve an individual of obligation to refrain from volunteering aid or comfort to the foreign nation when it is at war with the United

States. The restrictive tone attending treatment of treason charges had an analogy in WORLD WAR II decisions which put on the government the burden of proving by clear and convincing evidence that citizens of the United States who had been lawfully present in an enemy country at the outbreak of war and were conscripted into enemy military service on the basis of their dual nationality had not complied under duress. However, in 1961 Congress amended the governing legislation to put the burden of proving duress on the individual claiming to hold United States CITIZENSHIP. The change from the court decisions to Congress's amendment revealed the persistence of tension between values placed on governmental security and on individual security, familiar in the treatment of the treason offense. One other facet of the allegiance element deserves note. Though the matter has not been presented to a court in this country, a resident alien enjoying the nation's protection owes it obedience to its laws while he is a resident. Such an individual is probably guilty of treason if he commits acts that would constitute the offense if done by a citizen.

To convict one of treason, the government must prove that the accused had a treasonable intent to levy war or to adhere to an enemy and to give aid and comfort to that enemy. Since betrayal of allegiance is at the heart of the offense, the requisite wrongful intent must be specific— a focused purpose to bring about a betrayal. In many crimes requiring proof of a guilty mind, the law holds an individual responsible as intending the reasonably foreseeable consequences of his conduct, even though he pleads that he did not intend to bring about the particular outcome for which he is charged. In *Cramer v. United States* the Supreme Court opinion included some incautious language which appeared to adopt that position. But the weight of authority in earlier federal court decisions and in rulings after *Cramer* indicates that the prosecution must prove that the defendant did intend to challenge the full authority of government at home (levy war) or to deliver aid to an enemy, as a substantial, independent element in his purpose, whatever other ends he may have had in mind. To this extent it appears that the prosecution must prove that the accused had a specific intent to levy war or to aid enemies. However, this requirement does not necessitate proof of guilty purpose by explicit statement or direct admission; the prosecution may prove the guilty intent by strong inference from the context of the accused's behavior.

The calculated limitations of the treason clause of the Constitution offer persuasive evidence that proof of the crime should require showing a specific intent. The Constitution obviously narrows the prior scope of treason by omitting any analogue to the offense of "compassing" or "imagining" the death of the king. Under that head, old English doctrine erected "constructive" treasons by inferring the wrongful intent from speech or writings that complaisant judges ruled might have the "natural consequences" of stirring popular discontent out of which violence might erupt to endanger the state. The weight of authority in federal court decisions has recognized that the policy of Article III, section 3, is to prevent expansion of the offense by building upon loose inferences of intention.

The character of the requisite wrongful intent varies according to which of the two heads of the offense is in issue. To be guilty of levying war against the United States, the individual must intend to use organized force to overthrow the government. Under the older English law treason existed if there was intent by collective force to prevent enforcement of a particular statute or other lawful order, or to obtain some particular benefit for a group, contrary to law. This English doctrine was followed in two early instances involving violent group resistance to enforcing particular federal laws—collection of a federal excise on whiskey (the WHISKEY REBELLION in western Pennsylvania in 1794) and collection of a federal property tax (the FRIES' REBELLION, also in Pennsylvania, 1799). However, the later weight of authority is that nothing short of intention to overthrow the government suffices to make out the offense. Significant of this trend was the disposition of a late nineteenth-century effort to revive the old English doctrine. Following the Homestead Riot of 1892, several strike leaders were indicted for levying war against the state of Pennsylvania. But the indictments were later quietly dropped, while use of the treason charge met with prompt criticism even from conservative legal commentators. Violent group actions short of challenge to the existence of the government are now treated under heads of INCITEMENT, riot, or unlawful assembly.

Adhering to an enemy requires intent to render the enemy tangible support ("aid and comfort"). Established doctrine has defined "enemies" as only those against whom a legally declared STATE OF WAR exists. However, in the twentieth century, experience of such undeclared shooting hostilities as the Korean POLICE ACTION has raised the question of the continued vitality of the older limitation. The accused does not rebut the existence of the requisite intent for treason by pleading that he acted for mixed purposes, as to make money by selling goods to an enemy, if one of his purposes was in fact to render performance useful to the enemy. However, the accused may seek to persuade the court that he acted solely for a nontreasonable purpose, as when out of parental affection a father gave shelter to his son who was present in the country in wartime as an enemy agent. So, too, one whom the outbreak of war finds in a hostile country probably will not be found to have had treasonable intent merely because he took a job there to meet the necessities of earning a living, though the employment may have made some contributions to the enemy's strength.

In addition to proving wrongful intent, the government must prove that the accused committed some overt act to carry out his treasonable purpose. The calculated omission from the constitutional definition of treason of any counterpart of the English charge of compassing the death of the king underlines the requirement of proving overt action. The function of the overt act element, said the Supreme Court in *Cramer v. United States*, is to ensure "that mere mental attitudes or expression should not be treason." However, the Court's opinion in *Cramer* clouded definition of the requirement thus put on the prosecution; the Court seemed to say that the act must be of such character as itself to be evidence of the treasonable intent—a position apparently contrary to the emphasis common in other court rulings that the intent and the act elements are distinct. But in HAUPT V. UNITED STATES (1947) the Court somewhat clarified the matter: the behavior of the accused proved by the required testimony of two witnesses need not on its face evidence treasonable intent; an act apparently innocent, such as a transfer of money, might suffice if, in the light of other evidence of the context of the action, what the accused did could fairly be understood to aid an enemy. However, *Haupt* indicated that evidence of the context illuminating the significance of the overt act must also be supplied by two witnesses to the same circumstances. On the other hand, by the weight of authority, to prove the offense the prosecution need not establish that the accused succeeded in delivering aid to the enemy; it is enough that he took overt action to attempt delivery, though the *Cramer* opinion also contains language suggesting that effective delivery of aid should be shown. Mindful of abuses of charges of treason to suppress peaceful political opposition, English doctrine, adopted by judges in the United States, declares that a meeting to plan against the government is not a sufficient overt act to establish treason; conspiracy to levy war is not the levy of war, said Coke. But there is no comparable line of authority that a meeting to plan giving aid to an enemy is insufficient as an overt act of adherence to the enemy.

About the constitutional requirement of "testimony of two witnesses to the same overt act" hangs the uncertainty earlier noted, created by the Supreme Court opinion in *Cramer*, whether the act so proved must itself evidence treasonable intent or constitute actual delivery of aid to the enemy. Otherwise, rulings under the two-witness requirement have been straightforward. Courts have shown care to enforce the substance of the requirement, but not with doctrinaire rigidity. Two witnesses must testify directly to the act charged in the indictment; it will not suffice that there is two-witness evidence of a separate act from which it might be inferred that the charged act occurred. Two-witness testimony to the accused's admissions of an act does not meet the requirement of two-witness evidence to the act itself. However, the testimony of the two witnesses need not be identical or precise as to all aspects of the behavior cited as the overt act, nor need the testimony minutely cover every element into which an episode of behavior might be analyzed; the evidence is sufficient if it joins in identifying what reasonable jurors can regard as a connected transaction. Thus in *Haupt* the Supreme Court held that it was not fatal to the government's case that two-witness testimony did not show the enemy agent entering the accused's apartment, where it did show that he entered the building in which the accused had an apartment, and entered only as the accused's licensee, since the prosecution showed by other two-witness testimony that no other tenant in the building sheltered the agent.

This record suggests regard for the restrictive policy embodied in the constitutional history of treason. However, probably in large measure it also indicates that through most of its history the country has enjoyed substantial political stability. In any event the record shows little vindictive resort to the charge and few cases carrying politically controversial tones. Most actions taken against Loyalists in the American Revolution were to confiscate property. Because of the scale of the CIVIL WAR and the de facto belligerent status which events assigned the Confederacy, there was no material resort to treason prosecutions in that contest, though clearly those who took arms in behalf of the seceded states levied war against the United States. JEFFERSON DAVIS, President of the Confederacy, was indicted for treason. But the government faced strong arguments that it improperly charged treason against those conducting a rebel government which had achieved the status of a recognized belligerent. Though the government did not formally concede the point, neither did it bring Davis to trial on the indictment. Treason cases arising out of the Whiskey Rebellion (1795), the Fries disturbance (1799–1800), the Burr conspiracy (1807), THOMAS JEFFERSON's embargo (1808), and resistance to enforcement of the Fugitive Slave Law (1850), grew out of difficult domestic political issues but were of limited practical impact. Treason prosecutions by state authorities incident to the Dorr Rebellion in Rhode Island (1844) and John Brown's raid in Virginia (1859) were exceptional for their broad political bearing. Some cases carried tones of domestic ideological disputes over the country's entry into WORLD WAR I. But this cast was notably absent from treason prosecutions incident to World War II.

By its terms the constitutional definition of treason puts some limits on governmental agencies in dealing with subversion. Congress may not increase the categories of conduct which the government may prosecute under the name of treason, nor may it extend the reach of the offense by including under the heads of adherence to enemies or levying war conduct lacking the historic elements of those crimes, or by mandating an extensive view of the evidence deemed relevant to establishing the elements of such treasons. The treason clause pointedly restricts Congress's authority to fixing penalties for the crime, and the position of the clause in Article III (establishing the JUDICIAL POWER of the United States) underlines the implication that problems of applying the law of treason are ultimately for the courts. In their turn, federal judges have generally found in the language and history of Article III, section 3, a mandate against extending the range of the offense in doubtful cases. The two-witness requirement implies a further limitation on Congress. In light of that strict limitation on the prosecution's case, Congress should not have authority to avoid the two-witness requirement simply by changing labels and legislating under other names against offenses that involve all the elements of treason within the constitutional definition. However, the Supreme Court's decision in EX PARTE QUIRIN (1942) cast doubt on the validity of this analysis. One of several Nazi agents landed secretly on the east coast of the United States to sabotage war production plants was an American citizen. The Court rejected the argument that he must be prosecuted for treason by adhering to the enemy, and not for an offense against the laws of war incorporated in an act of Congress. Clearly the accused had committed treason. But the Court focused on the fact that the offense under the laws of war included another element—that the accused, having the status of an enemy belligerent, had passed the country's defenses in civilian dress with a hostile purpose.

Though it approaches the borderline of propriety, the Court's decision in *Quirin* might find support in analogues that date from the First Congress. There is no evidence that those who adopted the limiting constitutional definition of "treason" meant thereby to bar legislators from creating other crimes of subversion, the elements of which did not turn on the distinctive character of levying war or adhering to enemies. Congress in fact has defined and provided for punishment of other offenses of subversive or hostile activity against the security of the government, and federal courts have sustained such statutes. *United States v. Rosenberg* (1953) presented charges of conspiracy to violate the Federal ESPIONAGE ACT, which provides penalties for "whoever, with intent or reason to believe that it is to be used to the injury of the United States or to the advantage of a foreign nation," communicates or delivers to any foreign government or its agents information relating to the national defense. The federal court of appeals held that the treason clause did not bar creation of this offense, because "in the Rosenbergs' case, an essential element of treason, giving aid to an 'enemy' is irrelevant

to the espionage offense." In *United States v. Drummond* (1965) the same appeals court dealt with a charge of conspiracy to violate the same statute by a serviceman in the United States Navy who between 1957 and 1962 delivered classified military materials to Soviet agents. Reaffirming that the treason clause did not bar creation of the espionage offense, the court found it "unnecessary" to invoke the difference relied on in *Rosenberg*, because it found differences in the required mental element in the crimes of treason and espionage. It pointed out that the espionage act required a showing only (1) that the defendant transmitted information with intent "or reason to believe" that it would be used for a forbidden result; and (2) with intent or reason to believe that it would be used either "to the injury of the United States or to the advantage of a foreign nation." In contrast, the court implied, treason requires proof of a specific intent, and a specific intent both to aid an enemy and to injure the United States.

Though the constitutional definition of treason may do no more formally than limit the kinds of conduct that may be prosecuted under the name of treason, there are respects in which it may have broader practical effect in restricting action of official agencies. The Constitution abolished the barbarous or oppressive penalties that were once a distinguishing mark of the crime. But legislation still allows heavy penalties for the offense; in light of Supreme Court limitations put on resort to the death penalty in other crimes there may be doubt whether a court may order execution of a convicted traitor, but the law still permits imposing a life sentence. Thus it may be of consequence whether the prosecutor can make out a case of "treason" or is limited to another charge which may carry a lesser penalty. Political history teaches that the mere accusation of treason, rather than of another crime, carries peculiar intimidation and stigma. Federalist treason prosecutions arising out of the Whiskey Rebellion (1794) were designed to stain supporters of Jefferson and JAMES MADISON with the imputation of subversive intent. The Jefferson administration sought to use the charge of treason (1808) to make examples against widespread opposition to the Embargo imposed to press England to respect rights of neutral use of the high seas. Democratic accusations of treason against the HARTFORD CONVENTION protesting the conduct of war with England (1814–1815) helped that venture to weaken a tottering Federalist party structure. A prosecution for treason undertook to discredit opposition to enforcement of the Fugitive Slave Law (1850). To break rank-and-file morale, Pennsylvania authorities brought treason indictments against leaders of the Homestead Strike (1892). In the cold war emotions of the 1950s, epithets of "treason" were employed in reckless attacks on the record of Democratic administrations in conducting relations with communist Russia and China. Such episodes validate the cautions expressed among those who adopted the national Constitution, that the definition of treason be limited so that this country would not repeat the old English experience of using the charge to destroy legitimate, peaceful political competition. Adoption of the FIRST AMENDMENT guarantees of free speech, press, assembly, and petition provided more direct and comprehensive declarations of the values of free political processes, and eventually these guarantees found substantial enforcement in decisions of the Supreme Court. That the First Amendment tended to preempt the field was early indicated when it became the prime reliance of those who attacked the constitutionality of the Sedition Act of 1798. (See ALIEN AND SEDITION ACTS.) However, given the extent to which concern for safeguarding peaceful public policy debate and activity figured in adopting a restrictive definition of treason, constitutional history here offers as yet unrealized possibilities for safeguarding First Amendment values.

JAMES WILLARD HURST
(1986)

Bibliography

ABRAMS, STUART E.   1976   Threats to the President and the Constitutionality of Constructive Treason. *Columbia Journal of Law and Social Problems* 12:351–392.

CHAPIN, BRADLEY   1964   *The American Law of Treason: Revolutionary and Early National Origins.* Seattle: University of Washington Press.

HILL, L. M.   1968   The Two-Witness Rule in English Treason Trials. *American Journal of Legal History* 12:95–111.

HURST, JAMES WILLARD   1971   *The Law of Treason in the United States.* Westport, Conn.: Greenwood Press.

SIMON, WALTER G.   1961   The Evolution of Treason. *Tulane Law Review* 35:667–704.

STILLMAN, ARTHUR M. and ARNER, FREDERICK R.   1954   *Federal Case Law Concerning the Security of the United States.* 83rd Congress, 2d session. Printed for the use of the Senate Committee on Foreign Relations. Washington, D.C.: Government Printing Office.

WIENER, FREDERICK BERNAYS   1962   Uses and Abuses of Legal History. *The Law Society's Gazette* 59:311–315.

# TREATY OF GUADALUPE HIDALGO
## 9 Stat. 922 (1850)

In 1821 Mexico, having declared its independence from Spain, took control of the territory that now includes all of California, Arizona, New Mexico, and Texas, and parts of Nevada, Utah, and Colorado. But within twenty-five years, present-day Texas had been annexed by the United States, and at the end of the Mexican War the remaining areas were ceded to the United States under the Treaty of Guadalupe Hidalgo.

The treaty, signed in 1848, was not ratified by the Senate until 1850; the delay was caused by the unsuccessful efforts of Republicans to attach to the treaty the WILMOT PROVISO, banning SLAVERY in the newly acquired territory. For more than a decade an important constitutional issue was debated but not resolved: the question whether the treaty's provisions preserving Spanish or Mexican local law in the territory were themselves sufficient to abolish slavery.

The Treaty of Guadalupe Hidalgo gave all inhabitants of the affected territory the option of becoming United States citizens or of relocating within the new Mexican borders. Although some moved to Mexico, the overwhelming majority remained at home in what had become United States territory. As a result, for the first time in the nation's history United States CITIZENSHIP was conferred on people who were not citizens of any state. This action added fuel to a constitutional debate about the relation of national citizenship to state citizenship, a debate that continued until the FOURTEENTH AMENDMENT was ratified in 1868.

The international border remained unmarked and for most purposes unreal. Until 1894 there was no formal control over the border; United States IMMIGRATION statistics recorded the arrival of Mexicans only at seaports. Many border areas remained integrated economic regions, with workers traveling in both directions to fill fluctuating labor demands. Many Mexicans, especially those in direct conflict with Americans in the border region, continued to think of the southwest as "lost" territory that was rightfully Mexico's. These views, long expressed by the Mexican government, are echoed among today's Chicanos in support of diffuse if underdeveloped positions concerning the legal (including constitutional) effects of the Treaty of Guadalupe Hidalgo: for example, that the territory rightfully belongs to Mexicans or Chicanos, or that United States violations of the treaty have voided its effects. Whatever one may think of such claims, one should appreciate the collective sense of group identification reflected in their public assertion.

GERALD P. LÓPEZ
KENNETH L. KARST
(1986)

(SEE ALSO: *Compromise of 1850; Slavery in the Territories.*)

# TREATY ON THE EXECUTION OF PENAL SENTENCES
## 24 U.S.T. 7399 (1977)

The Mexican American Treaty on the Execution of Penal Sentences was signed on November 25, 1976. Legislation implementing the treaty became law on October 28, 1977.

Since that time, thousands of prisoners have been exchanged under its provisions.

The treaty, a model for later agreements with countries such as Canada, responded to concerns about the treatment of Americans imprisoned in Mexican jails, concerns that became increasingly acute as the two countries in the 1970s began a crackdown on drug traffic from Mexico to the United States. Preexisting procedures for monitoring and improving the conditions of Americans incarcerated in Mexico, mainly action taken by United States consular offices, had proven unsatisfactory.

Under the treaty, any American imprisoned in Mexico can, with his consent and the consent of Mexico and the United States, be sent to serve his sentence in the American prison system. Mexican prisoners can similarly be transferred from the United States to Mexico. Once transferred, the prisoner's sentence can be reduced by any procedures such as parole or conditional release applicable in the receiving country. The treaty covers only acts criminal in both countries, and does not extend to political crimes or to infractions of IMMIGRATION laws or "purely military" laws.

The attorney general administers the obligations of the United States under the treaty. The implementing legislation requires the attorney general to verify the prisoner's consent to transfer, and also provides a right to appointed counsel during the verification proceedings should the prisoner be unable to pay.

Lower federal courts have held that the treaty does not violate the Constitution despite the fact that under it the United States incarcerates United States citizens whose trials may not have complied with the BILL OF RIGHTS.

GERALD L. LÓPEZ
(1986)

(SEE ALSO: *Prisoners' Rights.*)

# TREATY POWER

To enhance the pledged word of the United States in foreign relations, the Framers of the Constitution granted to the President, in cooperation with the Senate, the power to make and enter into treaties. They also provided that this power should vest exclusively in the federal government. The Framers neglected to define the term "treaty," however, leaving its meaning to subsequent clarification. Today, under international law, the term is used for all manner of formal instruments of agreement between or among nations that, regardless of the titles used, create relationships of reciprocal rights and obligations. Under United States law, the term "treaty" usually denotes only those international agreements that are concluded by the federal government and ratified by the President upon re-

ceiving the ADVICE AND CONSENT of the SENATE. All other international agreements—EXECUTIVE AGREEMENTS, for example—are brought into force for the United States upon a constitutional basis other than senatorial advice and consent.

The process of treaty making involves negotiation, signature, ratification, exchange of instruments of ratification, publication, and proclamation; but, other than prescribing that two-thirds of the senators present must give their advice and consent to the ratification of a treaty, the Constitution is silent on the subject. In the early days of the Republic, it was thought that the Senate would participate with the President by giving its advice and consent at every negotiating juncture. Today, it is the accepted practice for the President to solicit the advice and consent of the Senate only after a treaty has been negotiated and signed, although in many—especially important—instances, Senate and even House committees play active roles in advance of the conclusion of a treaty, sometimes on their own initiative, sometimes at the behest of the executive branch.

Once the negotiation of a treaty is complete, the President decides whether to sign the treaty and, if so, whether to submit it to the Senate for advice and consent to ratification. If the Senate is perceived as hostile, the President may choose to let the treaty die rather than suffer defeat. If the Senate receives the treaty, it refers the treaty to the Committee on Foreign Relations, which may or may not report the treaty to the full Senate for its advice and consent. Committee inaction is the usual method for withholding consent to controversial treaties. Sometimes the executive branch will request that the committee withhold or suspend action. Few treaties are defeated by direct vote of the full Senate.

After the Senate gives its advice and consent to ratification, often subject to "reservations," "understandings," and "declarations" initiated by the Senate or the executive branch itself (to clarify, alter, or amend the treaty), the treaty is returned to the President for ratification. The President may choose to ratify the treaty or to return it to the Senate for further consideration. The President also may choose not to ratify the treaty at that time.

After a treaty is ratified, which is a national act, some international act—typically the exchange or deposit of instruments of ratification—usually is required to bring the treaty into force. Also upon ratification, the President issues a proclamation making the treaty officially public. There is disagreement over whether proclamation of a treaty is constitutionally required before the treaty takes effect domestically, but it is the norm to issue such a proclamation which, in any event, is useful in determining the date on which the treaty enters into force.

The Constitution does not limit the treaty power explicitly. Moreover, no treaty or treaty provision has ever been held unconstitutional. Nevertheless, it is generally agreed that such limitations exist. For example, the Supreme Court held, in REID V. COVERT (1957), that treaties may not contravene any constitutional prohibition, such as those in the BILL OF RIGHTS or in the THIRTEENTH, FOURTEENTH, and FIFTEENTH AMENDMENTS. Further, although MISSOURI V. HOLLAND (1920) largely disposed of the argument that the subject matter of treaties is limited by the TENTH AMENDMENT, it remains possible, as the Court hinted in *DeGeofroy v. Riggs* (1890), that the treaty power may be limited by "restraints . . . arising from the nature . . . of the states."

Beyond these limitations, however, the treaty power is perceived as a broad power, extending to all matters of "international concern," a phrase that some claim limits the treaty power, but that the courts have used to illustrate the power's broad scope. Ordinarily it is difficult to show that a treaty matter is not of international concern even in the presence of domestic effects.

In addition to granting the power to make and enter into treaties, the Framers of the Constitution provided that resulting treaties, together with the duly enacted laws of the United States, should constitute part of the "supreme law of the land." Thus, as well as giving rise to international legal obligations, treaties have force as domestic law, to be applied as federal statutes and consequently to prevail at all times over inconsistent state laws (assuming no conflict with the Constitution).

Still, not all treaties are automatically binding on American courts. Aside from the general constitutionality requirement, two additional conditions must obtain for treaties to have domestic effect. First, a treaty must not conflict with a subsequent act of Congress. This is in keeping with the judiciary's interpretation of the SUPREMACY CLAUSE, ranking treaties and acts of Congress equally and therefore ruling that the law later in time prevails. With the sole exception of *Cook v. United States* (1933), cases in this area have involved conflicts between an earlier treaty and a later statute, with the latter prevailing. The courts presume, however, that Congress does not intend to supersede treaties, and consequently the courts are disposed toward interpretations that will achieve compatibility between treaties and federal statutes on the same subject.

Second, for a treaty to bind courts it must be "self-executing" or, alternatively, "non-self-executing" but supported by enabling legislation. Such was the holding in *Foster v. Neilson* (1829). Judicial decisions vary widely in their application of this requirement, however. The distinction between "self-executing" and "non-self-executing" treaties is more easily stated than applied. A determination that a treaty fits one category or the other often may be shown to depend on subjective, at times political, considerations.

Although the Constitution is silent on the question of who has the power to suspend or terminate treaties and under what circumstances, it is generally accepted that the President has such power, *without* the advice and consent of the Senate, based on the President's established constitutional authority to conduct the foreign affairs of the United States. A challenge to the President's authority in this connection has thus far arisen only in the one case of GOLDWATER V. CARTER (1979), and that case was decided, on purely jurisdictional grounds, against the challenge. Were the Senate to consent to a treaty on the condition that its advice and consent would be required for the treaty's suspension or termination, however, such a condition might be binding on the President. Also, based on the power of Congress to declare war, it is arguable that the entire Congress (not just the Senate) might legitimately claim a voice in the termination of a treaty where such termination might threaten war.

BURNS H. WESTON
(1986)

Bibliography

AMERICAN LAW INSTITUTE  1965  *Restatement of the Law, Second—Foreign Relations Law of the United States.* Pages 361–448. St. Paul, Minn.: American Law Institute.

———  1980  *Restatement of the Law—Foreign Relations Law of the United States (Revised), Tentative Draft No. 1.* Pages 71–144. Philadelphia: American Law Institute.

FOSTER, J.  1901  The Treaty-Making Power under the Constitution. *Yale Law Journal* 11:69–79.

HENKIN, LOUIS  1972  *Foreign Affairs and the Constitution.* Mineola, N.Y.: Foundation Press.

MCLAUGHLIN, C. H.  1958  The Scope of the Treaty Power in the United States. *Minnesota Law Review* 42:709–771; 43: 651–725.

WRIGHT, QUINCY  1919  The Constitutionality of Treaties. *American Journal of International Law* 13:242–266.

# TRENCHARD, JOHN

See: Cato's Letters

# TRESPASS

A person commits trespass when he or she enters or remains on the property of another without the permission of the property owner. Violation of trespass laws may result in civil action by the property owner or criminal prosecution. Constitutional issues arise in civil or criminal trespass actions when a defendant claims that the basis for his or her exclusion from the property violates the Constitution. A defendant may assert that she was excluded from the property because she engaged in an activity protected by the Constitution (such as the FREEDOM OF SPEECH protected by the FIRST AMENDMENT) or because she is a member of a constitutionally protected class (such as a racial group) disfavored by the property owner.

If a property owner uses the property to perform a public function or if the property owner has become associated with the government in the operation of a business located on the property, the owner may not exclude persons on a basis that is incompatible with constitutional values. A public function is an activity that traditionally has been within the exclusive province of government, such as the operation of a municipality. When a state allowed a private company to own and operate a company town, which included residential and business districts, the First Amendment protection for freedom of speech prohibited exclusion of a woman who wished to distribute religious literature within the town. Operation of a store or SHOPPING CENTER on privately owned property is not held to be a public function. Thus, the First Amendment is not violated when a shopping center owner relies on trespass laws to exclude persons from the shopping mall who wish to engage in speech, PICKETING, or distribution of leaflets.

The Supreme Court will not allow trespass laws to be used to exclude persons from private property because of their race or political activity if the property owner has been directed or encouraged by the government to use the trespass laws in such a discriminatory manner. The Court has held that statutes requiring or specifically allowing a restaurant owner to provide separate areas for customers of different races encouraged racial segregation so that the owner could not use the trespass laws to exclude persons seeking service on a race neutral, integrated basis. Similarly, the owner of a restaurant operated in a government building could not exclude persons from the premises because of their race.

Federal statutes or state law may also limit the use of trespass laws. The National Labor Relations Board, for example, may order store or shopping center owners to allow labor picketers to walk on privately owned sidewalks or parking lots adjacent to businesses involved in a labor dispute. A state supreme court may interpret its state constitution to prohibit shopping center owners from excluding persons who wish to engage in political speech. These state and federal limitations on property owners' use of the trespass laws to exclude persons from their property do not violate any right guaranteed the property owners by the United States Constitution.

JOHN E. NOWAK
(1986)

Bibliography

NOWAK, JOHN E.; ROTUNDA, RONALD D.; and YOUNG, J. NELSON 1983 *Constitutional Law.* Pages 497–525. St. Paul, Minn.: West Publishing Co.

VAN ALSTYNE, WILLIAM W. and KARST, KENNETH L. 1961 State Action. *Stanford Law Review* 14:3–58.

# TREVETT v. WEEDEN
## (Rhode Island, 1786)

A Rhode Island case of 1786, this is the best known of the alleged state precedents for JUDICIAL REVIEW. The Superior Court of Judicature, the state's highest tribunal, did not hold a state act unconstitutional but it did construe it in a manner that left it inoperative. The case arose under a force act passed by the legislature to compel observance of the state paper-money laws; anyone refusing to accept paper money at par with specie was triable without a jury or right of appeal "according to the laws of the land" and on conviction was subject to a 100 pound fine and costs or be committed "till sentence be performed." Trevett filed an INFORMATION before the state chief justice charging that Weeden refused tender of paper money at face value. James Varnum, representing Weeden, argued that the force act violated the right to TRIAL BY JURY, guaranteed by the unwritten state constitution, which was FUNDAMENTAL LAW that limited legislative powers; the legislature could make law "not repugnant to the constitution" and the judiciary had "the sole power of judging those laws . . . but cannot admit any act of the legislative as law, which is against the constitution."

The court refused to decide the issue, ruling that it lacked JURISDICTION. Its JUDGMENT was simply that Trevett's complaint "does not come under the cognizance of the Justices . . . and it is hereby dismissed." Orally, however, some of the judges, according to the newspaper accounts, declared the force act "to be repugnant and unconstitutional," and one of them pointed out that its phrase, "without trial by jury, according to the laws of the land," was self-contradictory and thus unenforceable.

The governor called the legislature into special session, and the legislature summoned the high court judges to explain their reasons, the legislature said, for holding an act "unconstitutional, and so absolutely void," an "unprecedented" judgment that tended "to abolish the legislative authority." Judge David Howell, the court's main spokesman, defended judicial review and judicial independence. Although he summarized Varnum's argument that the act was unconstitutional, Howell insisted that the legislature had confused the argument, for the judgment was just that the complaint was "cognizable."

The legislature, unconvinced by the court's technical distinction, recognized that the judgment made the paper money laws unenforceable; in effect the court had exercised judicial review, which the legislature deemed subversive of its supremacy. Howell, by contrast, had claimed that if the legislature could pass on the court's judgment, "the Legislature would become the supreme judiciary—a perversion of power totally subversive of civil liberty." Anticipating a motion to unseat them, the judges presented a memorial demanding DUE PROCESS OF LAW. Varnum and the attorney general supported them, arguing that they could not be removed except on a criminal charge. The motion to remove the judges failed, and the legislature even repealed the force act, but it revenged itself on the judges by failing to reelect four of the five members when their annual terms expired, and by ousting Congressman Varnum and the state attorney general. Varnum published a one-sided pamphlet on the case, giving it publicity even in Philadelphia while the CONSTITUTION CONVENTION OF 1787 met. Although the pamphlet popularized the doctrine of judicial review, in Rhode Island no judge endorsed it for seventy years after.

LEONARD W. LEVY
(1986)

# TRIAL BY JURY

The right to jury trial is provided in three clauses of the Constitution of the United States. Jury trial in federal criminal cases is required by Article III, which is otherwise given to defining the role of the federal judiciary: "The Trial of all Crimes, except in Cases of IMPEACHMENT, shall be by Jury." This provision is repeated in the Sixth Amendment, which is otherwise given to the rights of the accused: "In all criminal prosecutions, the accused shall enjoy the right to a speedy and PUBLIC TRIAL, by an impartial jury. . . ." The BILL OF RIGHTS also included a provision for jury trial in civil matters; this right is embodied in the SEVENTH AMENDMENT: "In Suits at common law, where the value in controversy shall exceed twenty dollars, the right of trial by jury shall be preserved. . . ."

The federal Constitution makes no explicit provision regarding the right to trial by jury in proceedings in state courts. State constitutions contain many similar provisions, although the interpretations of the right in state courts have varied significantly from the standards applied in federal courts. Substantial variation survived the enactment of the FOURTEENTH AMENDMENT, which for the first time subjected the state courts to the strictures of the DUE PROCESS clause. It was early held, and appears still to be the law, that the Fourteenth Amendment does not incorporate the Seventh, that there is no federal constitutional requirement of a right to jury trial in *civil* cases in state court. (See WALKER V. SAUVINET.) More recently, the Supreme Court has held that due process does require some form of access to a jury in major criminal prosecutions in state courts. (See DUNCAN V. LOUISIANA.)

Although the institution of jury trial has been known to American and English courts for a millennium, there have been significant changes in its form and nature over that period. Indeed, the origins of the institution are shrouded in the uncertainties of prehistory. Germanic tribes, like most stable societies, made early use of laymen in official resolution of disputes. Such practices were well known to Saxons and their neighbors at the time of the Norman Conquest in 1066. Nevertheless, at that time and place, more common resort was made to various ordeals, which were essentially religious services purporting to reveal the will of the deity. One variation on trial by ordeal was trial by battle, in which the Saxon disputants, or their champions, waged a ritual struggle to determine the side of the diety. Yet another variation was trial by wager of law, which engaged the services of the neighbors as oath helpers. By their willingness in numbers to risk salvation to stand up for a disputant, the oath helpers were perceived to express a divine will. In some sense witnesses and in some sense decision makers, these laymen can be viewed as early jurors. The nature, origin, and extent of the use of such institutions in the several shires of Saxon England doubtless varied and are the subject of some uncertainty.

The royal judges appointed by Norman kings embraced Saxon traditions, including trial by ordeal, oath helping, wager of law, and the use of laymen to share responsibility for official decisions. A papal decree in 1215, which withdrew the clergy from participation in trials by ordeal, had the effect of withdrawing the imprimatur of the deity from the decisions of the royal courts. This apparently stimulated interest in alternative methods of trial that might deflect some of the odium of decision from the royal surrogate. Thus, the PETIT JURY (to be distinguished from the GRAND JURY) emerged in more nearly contemporary form in the thirteenth century as a feature of the Norman royal courts.

Thirteenth-century jury trial emerged chiefly in proceedings of TRESPASS, a form of action in which the lash of royal power was applied to maintain the peace of the realm. As trespass and its derivative forms of action came to dominate the COMMON LAW, so trial by jury became the dominant method of trial in civil matters coming before the royal law courts. Thus, jury trial was associated with the various forms of trespass on the case (from which the modern law of torts emerged), of assumpsit (from which the modern law of contracts emerged), and of replevin, an action important to the development of personal property rights. Indeed, one reason for the demise of some of the earlier royal writs, such as the writ of right, or even the writ of debt, was dissatisfaction with the mode of trial that accompanied the use of such writs.

A concurrent evolution led to the emergence of the jury as an important element of criminal justice in the royal courts. The royal inquest was a feature of early Norman royal governance; it was an important device for centralizing power in the royal government and was a proceeding for calling local institutions and affairs to account. The grand jury was a group of local subjects of the crown who were called upon to investigate, or answer from their own knowledge, regarding the observance by their neighbors of the obligations imposed upon them by royal command. By stages, the inquest came to be followed by a further proceeding to impose royal punishment on apparent wrongdoers. In the latter half of the twelfth century, the royal government was initiating such enforcement proceedings, thus supplementing the trespass proceedings which had earlier provided protection for the peace of the realm, but only on the initiative of a victim of wrongdoing. By 1164, there was a clear beginning of the use of petit juries in crown proceedings. By 1275, it was established that the petit jury of twelve neighbors would try the guilt of an accused, provided the accused consented to such a means of trial, which he was coerced to do.

One major theme in the evolution of the right to jury trial in royal courts was the development of a system of accountability to constrain lawlessness by juries. For some time, the only method available to royal courts to deal with such behavior was to prosecute (or, more precisely, to attaint) the jurors for rendering a false verdict. If a second jury so decided, a jury could be punished for this offense. The harshness of this remedy led to its demise, for the attaint jurors were reluctant to expose an earlier jury to disgrace and punishment. In the seventeenth century the writ of attaint was gradually replaced by the practice of granting a new trial when the first verdict was against the weight of the evidence. This practice came to be equally applicable to criminal as well as civil proceedings, except insofar as an accused could not twice be placed in jeopardy of conviction. (See DOUBLE JEOPARDY.)

A second major theme in the evolution of the right to jury trial in civil cases was its confinement to the common law courts when the Chancery emerged as an alternative system of adjudicating the use of the royal power. English chancellors were exercising a form of judicial power as early as the fifteenth century. An important feature of the Chancery (or proceedings in EQUITY as they came to be known) was the absence of the jury. Another important feature was the use by the chancellor of a broader range of judicial remedies, most prominently including the INJUNCTION, which were personal commands of the judge under threat of punishment for contumacy.

Nineteenth-century English law reform ultimately brought about the demise not only of equity as a separate judicial system, but also of the right to jury trial in civil cases. In a search for greater efficiency and dispatch, the jury system in the law courts was modified and limited, so that the jury trial is now seldom used in the United Kingdom, or in other parts of the Commonwealth, except in criminal cases.

The right to jury trial took quite a different turn in the United States. At the time of the Revolution, that right came to be celebrated as a means of nullifying the power of a mistrusted sovereign; hence the several constitutional provisions guaranteeing the continued exercise of the right. Moreover, there was a special mistrust of equity (where the English recognized no right to jury trial) in eighteenth-century America, based in large part on its close connection to the royal power. Accordingly, some of the states abolished it, others conferred its powers on their legislatures, while only some retained its colonial forms or created state chanceries to continue the English tradition.

In many parts of the early United States, there was a widely shared mistrust of professional lawyers and of judges drawn from that profession. Mistrust of officials in general and professional judges in particular was a feature of the Jacksonian politics of the first half of the nineteenth century, which was reflected in provisions for the election of judges and the reaffirmation of the importance of jury trial as a means of deprofessionalizing the exercise of judicial power. These political impulses were magnified in the populism of the late nineteenth century.

Indeed, the American legal profession came to be shaped in important degree around the institution of the jury; jury advocacy became in the popular mind the central activity of the American lawyer. During much of the nineteenth century, the most powerful intellectual force in American law was the work of WILLIAM BLACKSTONE, an English scholar of the previous century. Blackstone's *Commentaries* (1776) was the one book read by almost all American lawyers, and perhaps the only law book read by some. By no coincidence Blackstone was a staunch advocate of the right to jury trial in civil cases, an institution already in decline in his own country; his belief in the institution of the lay jury was one of his strongest links to the frontier society which he so significantly influenced.

Beginning as early as 1848 in New York, most American states adopted "merged" systems of procedure in civil cases. Merger united law and equity in a single judicial system; reformers were careful to retain the right to jury trial in actions "at law" and in some states even extended it to some matters properly described under the former system as "suits in equity." Through most of the nineteenth century, the federal courts played a secondary role in the American legal system, and Congress required their procedures to conform "as near as may be" to the procedural legislation of the states in which they sat. For the most part, this conformity seemed to apply to the forms of jury practice as well as to other details of procedure. It was not until 1938 that the FEDERAL RULES OF CIVIL PROCEDURE were promulgated for the federal courts, for the first time formally merging law and equity in federal courts in accordance with national standards. The FEDERAL RULES OF CRIMINAL PROCEDURE soon followed. A national system or method of conducting jury trials in federal courts for defining the scope of the jury's power and the judge's responsibility and for prescribing the limits of the right to jury trial at last emerged.

For a period of several decades following the reform era of the 1930s, the Supreme Court made the protection of the right to jury trial in civil cases a major item on its agenda. A number of its decisions enlarged on previous expectations about the scope of the right and increased the authority of the jury, for example, *Beacon Theaters, Inc. v. Westover* (1959) and *Rogers v. Missouri Pacific Railroad Co.* (Justice FELIX FRANKFURTER's dissent, 1957). Interest in the right to jury trial became very intense in the mid-1960s as a result of widespread CIVIL RIGHTS litigation, preoccupation with EQUAL PROTECTION, and the possible NULLIFICATION or impairment of federal law by locally selected juries.

In the last decade, there may have been some growth in consciousness of the disadvantages of jury trial in civil cases. Increasing attention has focused on trial efficiency, the effectiveness of the law, and alternative methods of dispute resolution. But it is too early to say that we have entered a period in which the distinctly American institution of jury trial will be seriously reexamined.

As much as for any procedural right, the beauty of the right to jury trial is in the eye of the beholder. For as long as there have been lay decision makers, there have been strong-minded critics and devoted defenders who have disputed the wisdom of the system with equal vehemence. The practice rests on values so basic and so unsuitable to proof or disproof that the debate seems unlikely to terminate. It is at least in part for this reason that so many reforms, from the Seventh Amendment to the Rules Enabling Act, sought to evade debate on the fundamental issues by ostensibly preserving the status quo in regard to the right to jury trial, leaving the issues of the scope of jury trial to other times and other forums. Rarely has Congress or any state legislature been able to address the merit of the right to jury trial without having its deliberative processes impaled on the sharp point of the debate. For the same reason, decisions to expand or contract, preserve or alter, existing practices have been and will continue to be greatly influenced by the predominance of one view or the other of the merits of the institution.

Supporters of the right to jury trial regard it as a keystone of democratic government. It is, indeed, a method of sharing power with those who are governed. It deflects the hostility toward public institutions otherwise engendered by the lash of public power. It is a remedy for judicial megalomania, the occupational hazard of judging.

Particularly in regard to criminal legislation, the right to jury trial provides a limit on the power of legislatures who eventually must countenance the nonenforceability of laws which citizens are unwilling to enforce. It is also a means of education: jurors learn about the law and share their learning with families and neighbors. In all these respects, it engenders trust. In general, supporters and critics alike agree that those benefits are more substantial in criminal than in civil litigation.

Critics observe, however, that juries are inefficient and may well be quite inaccurate in their perceptions and decisions. Involving many people in the making of a decision is inherently inefficient. It is necessary to invest time and expense in the selection of jurors. Trials proceed much more slowly because of the shorter attention span of lay persons in courtroom contexts and because additional participants entail additional interruptions and delays for personal reasons. Because of the inexperience of jurors, there has developed a substantial body of rules governing the admission of EVIDENCE which have as their purpose the protection of the jury from confusion and inflammation of prejudice. These strictures operate at times to increase the complexity of trials and to enlarge the possibility of mistrial or new trial, which is the result of error in the application of such rules of evidence. For these reasons, jury trials take substantially longer than nonjury trials and are substantially more expensive for the participants.

Moreover, as other critics emphasize, the deliberations of juries are undisciplined. Although jurors tend to be conscientious in the application of the governing law, the controlling rules are often dimly understood and not infrequently sacrificed in order to secure the requisite consensus. Whatever guidance or control the trial judge may supply, the chance of erratic decision is greater in jury than in nonjury trials.

Other adverse factors are less frequently mentioned. Jury service is in many cases a substantial burden to jurors; although they receive token payment, they are coerced to perform a duty that can sometimes be onerous. Particularly in communities characterized by disorder and social disintegration, jurors may even be frequent objects of intimidation and bribery; they are, in general, more difficult to protect from these vices than are judges, and they are perhaps also more vulnerable to such pernicious influences.

To a substantial degree, the perceived merits or demerits of the system will depend on particular features of the system which are designed to respond to the problems the system presents. Unfortunately, techniques for diminishing the demerits of jury trial often tend also to diminish its merits: the more control exercised over juries, the less advantage there is in assembling them. In the final analysis, almost every issue regarding the right to jury trial turns on the degree to which power is to be confided in professional officers of the law. Consensus on that basic issue being so distant a prospect, the contours of the institution as described below must be regarded as an unstable compromise, quite subject to change.

Instability is nowhere more clearly exemplified than in regard to JURY SIZE. Perhaps as early as the thirteenth century, Englishmen understood that a jury is a group composed of twelve persons. The method of selecting the jury might have varied, the duties assigned to the group may have been altered, but the one element of stability was their number, twelve. Some states experimented with the use of smaller juries, particularly in the trial of lesser crimes, and the Supreme Court in WILLIAMS V. FLORIDA (1970) held that the use of such groups as six is not itself a deprivation of due process of law. It was, however, long presumed that a common law jury is twelve and that such a number was required in federal courts by the Sixth and Seventh Amendments, unless a smaller number be agreed to by the parties. This presumption is reflected in the language of Federal Rule of Civil Procedure 48, which authorizes parties to agree to smaller juries.

Nevertheless, most federal district courts have in the last decade adopted local rules of court designating civil juries to consist of six persons. The validity of these local rules was sustained by the Supreme Court in *Colegrove v. Battin* (1973). The Court rested its decision on the absence of any straightforward legislative prohibition on juries of less than twelve and on the dubious assumption that there were no solid data demonstrating that twelve-person juries reach substantially different verdicts from six-person juries. The Court also manifested a conviction that six-person juries are more efficient than those composed of larger numbers, a conviction which is itself not amenable to solid empirical proof. However, in BALLEW V. GEORGIA (1978) the Court held that a five-member group was too small to be properly deliberative, representative, and free from intimidation and therefore did not afford due process. The Court's decisions have stimulated increased interest in the scientific examination of judicial institutions; the decisions have also called into question other traditional presumptions about juries, none of which carries more historical weight than did the tradition of twelve.

A second traditional feature of the common law jury has been the requirement of JURY UNANIMITY in reaching a verdict. Some states have experimented with the acceptance of verdicts supported by juries that are less than unanimous. In general, such provisions have called for super-majorities, such as a vote of ten or twelve jurors. The Supreme Court held in *Minneapolis and St. Louis Railway Co. v. Bombolis* (1916) that such provisions were not denials of due process for state court proceedings in-

volving issues of federal law, but later, in BURCH V. LOUISIANA (1979), it invalidated a Louisiana law that authorized verdicts of conviction on the basis of a five-to-one vote of a six-person jury. Despite these variations at the state level, however, the unanimity requirement remains a standard feature of federal jury practice, unless, as the Federal Rules authorize in civil cases, the parties agree on a lesser majority.

One effect of the unanimity requirement is to assure that the jury will deliberate on its decision rather than settle for a mere nose count. A secondary effect is to increase the likelihood that no decision will be reached, with the result that a new trial before a new jury will be required, unless the controversy is privately resolved without further litigation. A third effect is to enhance the role and responsibility of each individual juror, making each an important actor with power to control the ultimate outcome of the process. To the extent that the jury is intended to be a representative body, the unanimity requirement tends to protect litigants and interests that are associated with minority groups.

A third important feature of traditional common law jury practice was the mode of selecting the jury. Using the Norman nomenclature, the court administrative arm assembles a venire of citizens from whom the jury will be selected. Veniremen may be excused or disqualified by the judge and those remaining are then subject to a further process of selection by the parties. The latter process, known as VOIR DIRE examination, proceeds from a questioning of the jurors to their challenge by the parties on grounds of cause, or peremptorily if the parties would simply prefer other members of the venire. Peremptory challenges have perhaps always been limited in number, a somewhat larger number being allowed in criminal than in civil cases.

In recent decades, this traditional process has been subject to substantial criticism and pressure. Criticism proceeds from the premise that the jury should be in some degree representative of the community it helps to govern. Most of the criticism has been directed at the process of selecting veniremen, the usual earlier practice in this country having been to authorize a court administrator to select prospective jurors by methods that were usually elitist in premise and effect. In many communities, the usual method was the "key man" system, which invoked the assistance of community leaders to identify citizens of stature who would be deserving of the trust reposed in jurors. Such systems were common in federal courts. Indeed, it was not uncommon for a federal court to maintain a BLUE RIBBON list of veniremen of more than ordinary intelligence and experience who might be summoned to decide cases requiring more than ordinary skill on the part of the decision maker. Such methods produced juries that were anything but representative, in the proportional sense, of the communities from which they were selected.

In a legal environment favoring egalitarianism, such practices were doomed. As early as 1945, in *Thiel v. Southern Pacific Co.*, the Supreme Court upheld a challenge by a federal litigant to a venire selection method that seemed likely to result in underrepresentation of the working class in local jurors. In *Carter v. Jury Commission of Greene County* (1970), the Supreme Court refused to declare a state key-man system invalid on its face absent a showing that the scheme was purposefully adopted as a means of preventing some group (usually blacks) from being represented. Nevertheless, when such a scheme underrepresents a group consistently, a prima facie case of JURY DISCRIMINATION is established and the scheme may then be found unconstitutional as applied, as in *Turner v. Fouche* (1970). Congress anticipated these holdings by enacting federal jury selection legislation in 1968. Current legislation does repose some authority in local federal courts to administer jury selection, on condition that their methods produce juries that bear proximate resemblances to randomness. Of course, individual litigants are not entitled under the statute or the Constitution to have a jury that actually reflects the demography of the community; all that is assured is that the method of selection be one that is reasonably likely to produce such a panel.

In recent years, mounting attention has been given to the process of peremptory challenge and the practice of some local prosecutors to use these challenges to prevent minority representation on particular juries, especially those called to try minority members on serious criminal charges. The Supreme Court has held that a prosecutor's use of peremptory challenges in any single case is immune from attack; the Court held in SWAIN V. ALABAMA (1965) that the very concept of peremptory challenges entailed the right to act without explanation. Still, the Court did leave open the possibility that systematic use of peremptories to exclude members of some group might be found to violate the equal protection guarantee of the Fourteenth Amendment. In subsequent cases, however, proving to the Court's satisfaction that systematic discrimination did exist has been virtually impossible. Some state courts have gone beyond the federal standards and ruled that peremptory challenge of veniremen on the basis of membership in any group violates provisions of their state constitutions, for example, California in *People v. Wheeler* (1978).

Partly as a result of the practice of making juries more representative, a new issue has arisen regarding the competence of juries to deal with intricate technical disputes beyond the ken of ordinary citizens. The Third Circuit Court of Appeals held in *Matsushita Electric Industrial Company v. Zenith Radio Corporation* (1980) that the Seventh Amendment is subject to the Fifth Amendment,

that the use of juries in very complex civil cases may be a denial of due process of law. This question, also, has not reached the Supreme Court.

Litigants having a right to jury trial are entitled to a jury decision only on questions of fact, not on matters of law. The distinction between questions of fact and law can be stated clearly enough: the former pertain to the specific events in dispute; the latter to the legal principles to be applied. But the application of the distinction is often problematic. For this reason, juries often have to deal with issues containing substantial elements of legal interpretation. The classic example, which arises in both civil and criminal contexts, is a decision applying a general standard of negligence to the conduct of the accused or the defendant; the general standard takes more specific shape in the minds of jurors as they apply it to the events at hand.

Since the seventeenth century, it has been the responsibility of the trial judge to assure that the controlling law is obeyed by the jury; the trial judge is accountable to the appellate court for the effective performance of this duty. There are several steps in the usual common law jury trial at which the trial judge is obliged to perform this function.

A major function of the judge at a jury trial is to instruct the jury on the controlling law. This instruction is usually the last event before the jury retires to deliberate. If either party makes a timely objection to the judge's statement of law in his charge to the jury, any error in the instructions will be a solid ground for reversal.

In a civil trial, the judge should not instruct the jury at all unless there is a dispute in the evidence presented which might raise some doubt in a reasonable mind or about which jurors might reasonably differ. If the judge finds that there is no such dispute, he should direct the jury to find a verdict for the part entitled under the law to JUDGMENT. In cases of doubt about the application of this standard, the judge may prefer to reserve his ruling on a motion for directed verdict until after the jury has rendered a verdict. If the verdict is rendered contrary to the law, the judge may then enter a judgment notwithstanding the verdict in favor of the verdict loser. The Supreme Court has held in *Baltimore and Carolina Line v. Redman* (1935) that the judge may not take this latter step unless the motion for directed verdict was timely and the question properly reserved; otherwise, there is a violation of the Seventh Amendment because the judgment notwithstanding the verdict was unknown to English practice at the time of adoption of the Amendment.

In a criminal case the judge should direct a verdict for the accused when the prosecution has failed to offer proof of one or more elements of the offense charged. But the trial judge may not direct a verdict of guilty in a criminal case; to this extent, the Sixth Amendment assures the role of the jury as a bulwark against punishment deemed oppressive by the community, even if the punishment is required by the positive law. An element of natural justice is thereby introduced to the legal system.

In addition to his role as law officer, the trial judge also has some responsibility for the quality of fact-finding done by the jury. In either civil or criminal cases, he may set aside a verdict as contrary to the weight of the evidence. When exercising this prerogative, the trial judge is obliged to order a new trial before a second jury. In a criminal case, the power to order the new trial is confined by the constitutional constraint against double jeopardy. In a civil case, the power to grant a new trial may be exercised conditionally, but this power is subject to constitutional limitations. A conditional order of new trial is likely to occur where the trial judge regards a jury verdict as correct on the matter of liability but excessive in regard to the award of damages.

Some factual issues arising in jury-tried cases may be reserved for the judge. For example, in civil cases, issues of fact arising in a determination of the jurisdiction of the court must be decided by the judge. In criminal cases, sentencing is a function of the judge, not the jury, although the wisdom and propriety of the sentence often require factual determination.

With the exceptions noted, the division of function between judge and jury in federal courts has not been deemed a matter for constitutional adjudication. A fortiori, state practice in respect to these issues has not generally been regarded as presenting any constitutional problems of due process of law. The Supreme Court, however, has on occasion intervened to reverse state court judgments in actions arising under federal law on the ground that the federal law posed an issue for a jury which under the state practice was incorrectly left to the decision of a judge. Particularly in cases arising under the federal EMPLOYERS LIABILITY ACT, the Court was strict in limiting the role of the trial judge. Its decisions, based upon statutory grounds, may indicate that state jury practice must meet federal standards when state courts are called upon to enforce federal law. It is even possible that the Seventh Amendment will be found to be applicable to litigation of federal claims in state courts, not by reason of the Fourteenth Amendment, but by an inference of congressional intent.

The Sixth Amendment applies only to criminal proceedings that could have been tried by a jury at the time of its adoption in 1791. Even at that time, it was well understood that "petty" offenses might be tried without a jury. Federal legislation gives specific meaning to such offenses as those involving a punishment of imprisonment for six months or less and fines of $500 or less. In BALDWIN v. NEW YORK (1970) the Supreme Court held that due process requires jury trial in state court prosecutions for offenses involving imprisonment for more than six months. In *Bloom v. Illinois* (1968) the Court applied a similar standard to punishments imposed for contempt of court, although it conceded that there was some historical basis for treating contempt as a matter between litigant and judge, particularly where the contumacious act is committed in the presence of the court. In MCKEIVER V. PENNSYLVANIA (1971), however, the Court held that the right to jury trial is not applicable to a proceeding to determine the delinquency of a juvenile, even though a decision adverse to the juvenile might result in imprisonment for a period significantly in excess of six months; such proceedings, the Court said, are not strictly criminal because they involve less moral judgment about the conduct of the juvenile.

The Seventh Amendment has proved much more complex and troublesome. One major question has been the applicability of the amendment to claims brought under federal legislation enacted after the adoption of the amendment. A narrowly historical view would preclude the application of the right to such legislation-based claims, since they are not strictly actions "at common law." The Court has, however, generally extended the right to jury trial to statutory actions where the remedy pursued in the judicial proceeding was one that resembled a common law remedy. Thus, in *Pernell v. Southall Realty Co.* (1974) the Court held that there was a right to jury trial in a statutory action of eviction that was closely analogous to a common law action for ejectment. And in *Curtis v. Loether* (1974) the Court held that there was a right to jury trial in an action brought under the fair housing provisions of the CIVIL RIGHTS ACT OF 1964 because the remedy sought was compensatory damages of the sort that might have been recoverable in a common law action of trespass on the case.

In other cases, however, the Court has approved legislation creating administrative procedures and remedies that displace common law rights and thus eliminate jury-triable actions. In *National Labor Relations Board v. Jones & Laughlin Steel Corp.* (1937), the Court upheld the award of back pay in proceedings before the board, despite the close analogy to common law contract actions. This decision was extended in *Atlas Roofing Co. v. Occupational Safety and Health Administration* (1977), in which the Court upheld legislation providing for the recovery by a government agency of a civil penalty in a court proceeding where there was no right to jury trial. The Court emphasized that the case involved a "public right," to be distinguished from common law rights of private parties. In *Lorillard v. Pons* (1978) the Court interpreted the legislature to intend a statutory right to jury trial in proceedings brought under the AGE DISCRIMINATION ACT. In that case, as in *Curtis*, the Court avoided any indication of the applicability of the Seventh Amendment to the employment discrimination provisions of the Civil Rights Act, which, like the Age Discrimination Act, provides for back pay awards to be made by courts, not administrative agencies.

The most complex issues of the scope of the right to jury trial arise in complex litigation where matters that are within the compass of the Seventh Amendment coincide with other matters outside that compass. In general, the Supreme Court has tended to insist upon protection of the right to jury trial in such situations, even at the risk of submitting to a jury matters that would not be jury-triable if litigated alone. Illustrative is DAIRY QUEEN, INC. V. WOOD (1962) in which the plaintiff sought both an injunction and compensatory damages. Injunctive relief, unlike compensatory damages, is an equitable rather than a legal remedy and so is not subject to the right of trial by jury. The trial court deemed the injunction to be the primary relief sought and undertook to try the case without a jury, albeit with the intention of seating a jury to decide the measure of damages should it appear that a wrong had been committed. The Supreme Court reversed, holding that the jury-triable claim for damages must be tried first in order to protect the constitutional right to jury trial, leaving it for the judge later to decide on the availability of injunctive relief if the jury should determine that a wrong had been committed. Similarly, in BEACON THEATERS, INC. V. WESTOVER (1959) the Court held that a jury-triable counterclaim would have to be tried first, before a determination could be made on a related claim by the plaintiff that was not jury-triable.

These cases illustrate that the constitutional right to jury trial now tends to depend on the specific substantive right and remedy involved in the litigation, not on the general (common law or equity) context in which that right is disputed. This approach was illustrated in *Ross v. Bernhard* (1970), in which the Court held that a claim brought by a shareholder on behalf of the CORPORATION was jury-triable when the claim would have been triable by a jury had it been brought by the corporation itself; this decision would seem to be applicable as well to claims for damages brought by class representatives. This is so even though the procedures of STOCKHOLDER SUITS and CLASS ACTIONS are derived from the equity tradition, not from the practices of law courts. Thus, the increasingly widespread use of complex procedural devices that unite equitable and legal matters may in fact operate to enlarge the practical scope of the right to jury trial. This seems true despite the disclaimers set forth in such law reforms as the Federal Declaratory Judgment Act and the Federal Rules Enabling Act, which express the intent not to alter the existing scope of the right. That intent was not practicably attainable consistent with achieving the other aims of the procedural reforms, which include efficiency and dispatch.

On the other hand, a rule that the Seventh Amendment right to jury trial depends on the substantive right and remedy involved in the litigation is not always applied. Illustrative is *Katchen v. Landy* (1966), which upholds the power of the court to determine without a jury claims brought against a bankrupt estate, whether or not the claims might have been jury-triable if asserted directly against the bankrupt. The Court emphasized the practical needs of the bankruptcy system for dispatch in making such decisions; it was said that these considerations justified Congress in directing that they be made without juries. Thus, the scope of the constitutional right to jury trial in civil cases is a complex question, drawing heavily on historical analogues but also influenced by considerations of contemporary practicality. It is not a static right, but it is likely to take on new dimensions in the hands of future courts.

It may be concluded that the right of accused persons to a trial by jury has become a deeply entrenched feature of criminal litigation in the United States, broadly protected by the Sixth and Fourteenth Amendments, with the selection and role of the jury being aspects of the right that are themselves subject to constitutional control. The right to jury trial in civil cases, on the other hand, rests upon a different constitutional provision, which is inapplicable in state courts and may be somewhat less rigidly maintained even in federal courts, for the reason that it is less assuredly beneficial to the citizens to be protected.

PAUL D. CARRINGTON
(1986)

Bibliography

DAWSON, JOHN P.   1962   *A History of Lay Judges.* Cambridge, Mass.: Harvard University Press.

HELLER, FRANCIS H.   1951   *The Sixth Amendment to the Constitution of the United States.* Lawrence: University of Kansas Press.

JAMES, FLEMING   1963   Right to Jury Trial in Civil Cases. *Yale Law Journal* 72:655–693.

KALVEN, HARRY and ZEISEL, HANS   1966   *The American Jury.* Boston: Little, Brown.

McCART, SAMUEL N.   1964   *Trial by Jury.* Philadelphia: Chilton Books.

SCHULTZ, MARJORIE S., ed.   1980   The American Jury. *Law and Contemporary Problems.* Durham, N.C.: Duke University.

SPOONER, LYSANDER   1852   *An Essay on the Trial by Jury.* Boston: John P. Jewett Co.

VAN DYKE, JON M.   1977   *Jury Selection Procedures.* Cambridge, Mass.: Ballinger.

WOLFRAM, CHARLES   1973   The Constitutional History of the Seventh Amendment. *Minnesota Law Review* 57:639–747.

# TRIBAL ECONOMIC DEVELOPMENT AND THE CONSTITUTION

Contact between non-Indians and Native American tribal nations largely destroyed the traditional economies of tribal nations, which included agriculture, hunting and fishing, and associated trade networks. Fish and game were slaughtered or depleted, tribal land bases and water resources were lost or placed under federal control, populations declined, and traditional sociopolitical organizations that structured economic activity were disrupted and replaced with an oppressive federal bureaucracy. Today, despite the presence of significant mineral, water, timber, and other assets on some reservations, most of the 554 Indian nations recognized by the United States experience severe poverty and related social consequences. Unemployment rates as high as 50 percent are common, with some tribes suffering 90 percent unemployment or higher.

The Constitution played a supporting role in the devastation of traditional tribal economies and the impoverishment of reservations. Although the Constitution makes few and cryptic references to tribes, the constitutional plan of federal supremacy over Indian affairs has emboldened the Supreme Court to develop a body of constitutional COMMON LAW in this area. The grant of federal power over "commerce . . . with the Indian Tribes" in Article I, section 8, for example, has been embellished with notions of a federal guardianship over tribes to allow Congress nearly unlimited authority over internal tribal matters. Since the last decades of the nineteenth century, Congress has invoked this authority, also known as "plenary power," to support LEGISLATION abrogating TREATY promises that set aside lands for the "perpetual" use of the tribes. For example, Congress constructed dams that flooded tribal lands, divided or allotted tribal lands for individual tribal members, and opened tribal lands for homesteading by non-Indians. Congress also used its broad power to impose bureaucratic restraints on tribal resource use, to open tribal timber and mineral resources for exploitation by non-Indians without market-rate compensation, and to dictate tribal constitutions that organize tribal governing institutions as well as the ordinances that tribal governments enact. Experts on tribal economic development, such as Joseph Kalt of Harvard's Kennedy School of Government, have shown that without tribal control over the management of tribal affairs and the use of tribal resources, sustained economic development does not occur on reservations.

Constitutional constraints on congressional action, such as the DUE PROCESS and JUST COMPENSATION clauses of the Fifth Amendment, have not provided substantial protection for tribal resources and rights of self-government against federal interference. A partial explanation for this failure is the fact that tribes do not fit comfortably into the philosophy of individual rights reflected in the Constitution. Tribes' important rights and resources are held communally, and social groups such as clans or religious societies, rather than individuals, are viewed as the constituent social and political units. In constitutional decisions of the Supreme Court, these differences have meant, for example, that aboriginal tribal lands are not viewed as "PROPERTY" subject to just compensation in the event of expropriation unless Congress has "recognized" the tribal property claims by treaty or statute. Furthermore, federal conversion of tribal lands into allotted, individually owned lands has not been treated as a TAKING of those lands or a deprivation of due process or EQUAL PROTECTION. Federal laws that single out tribes for restrictions on economic activities or that regulate tribal members directly do not fall under the weight of federal constitutional protections for racial or ethnic minorities because tribes are treated as political entities rather than racial or ethnic groups. At most, the Court has provided theoretical protection for tribes by fashioning a federal trust responsibility that is supposed to ground and color federal plenary power, and by insisting that Congress be explicit when it curtails tribal property and self-government rights.

Since the 1970s, the federal government has proclaimed policies encouraging tribal self-determination and economic development. Two DOCTRINES within the constitutional common law of Indian affairs have helped advance this policy agenda. Both of these doctrines affirm and support tribal SOVEREIGNTY. First, federal constitutional supremacy has precluded states from imposing many of their taxes and regulations within tribal territories unless Congress consents. The lucrative gaming enterprises found on some reservations stem from this limitation on state regulation. However, tribes are not wholly protected against state restrictions. Responding to states' concerns, Congress has chosen to exercise its plenary power with respect to gaming, and has afforded states authority to preclude or negotiate over certain forms of tribal gaming. Furthermore, the Court has said that states may tax reservation-based retail sales to nonmembers where products are merely imported onto the reservation to take advantage of tax exemptions. Second, tribes are recognized as governments that enjoy SOVEREIGN IMMUNITY, subject to congressional or tribal waiver. According to the chair of the Mississippi Choctaw Tribe, which has one of the most thriving economies of any Indian nation in the United States, tribal sovereign immunity has been essential in fostering economic development because it nourishes institutions of self-government and protects the tribe against costly litigation and potential BANKRUPTCY. Thus contemporary tribal economic development is partly a legal artifact, born of constitutionally based doctrines reflecting the special status of tribes as governments engaged in business enterprises. These doctrines have created economic opportunities for tribes by conferring monopoly status in states where certain activities, such as WASTE disposal or gaming, are outlawed or heavily regulated. The new economic possibilities must be understood, however, in relation to a long history of economic devastation.

CAROLE GOLDBERG
(2000)

(SEE ALSO: *American Indians and the Constitution.*)

Bibliography

CLINTON, ROBERT N.   1993   Redressing the Legacy of Conquest: A Vision Quest for A Decolonized Federal Indian Law. *Arkansas Law Review* 46:77–159.

CORNELL, STEPHEN and KALT, JOSEPH, eds.   1992   *What Can Tribes Do? Strategies and Institutions in American Indian Economic Development.* Los Angeles: UCLA American Indian Studies Center.

DELORIA, VINE, JR.   1974   *Behind the Trail of Broken Treaties: An Indian Declaration of Independence.* Austin: University of Texas Press.

GOULD, SCOTT L.   1996   The Consent Paradigm: Tribal Sovereignty at the Millenium. *Columbia Law Review* 97:809–902.

MOHAWK, JOHN C.   1991   Indian Economic Development: An Evolving Concept of Sovereignty. *Buffalo Law Review* 39:495–503.

WORTHEN, KEVIN J. and FARNSWORTH, WAYNE R.   1996   Who Will Control the Future of Indian Gaming? "A Few Pages of History Are Worth a Volume of Logic." *Brigham Young University Law Review* 1996:407–448.

# TRIMBLE, ROBERT
(1776–1828)

Robert Trimble, appointed to the Supreme Court by JOHN QUINCY ADAMS on April 11, 1826, was born in Virginia and raised in Kentucky. He studied law, began practice in Paris, Kentucky, and became one of the leading lawyers of the state with a specialty in land litigation. To the Supreme Court he brought an independence of character, a respect for legality, and considerable judicial experience. From 1807 to 1808 he served on the Kentucky Court of Appeals and from 1817 to 1826 on the federal district court. His years on the district bench corresponded to a period of political-economic upheaval during which Kentucky openly resisted federal ADMIRALTY JURISDICTION and federal judicial interference with state relief measures. Both as district judge and as circuit partner with his friend Justice THOMAS TODD, Trimble held the line for federal ju-

dicial authority and objective legality as he saw it—so firmly in fact that he was threatened with IMPEACHMENT.

His integrity, ability, and nationalism won him an appointment to the Court on Todd's death. He served only twenty-seven months before his own death but long enough to have won the respect of JOHN MARSHALL and JOSEPH STORY; Story eulogized him as belonging "to that school, of which Mr. Chief Justice Marshall (himself a host) is the acknowledged head and expositor." Trimble spoke for the Court only fifteen times; ironically his lone constitutional opinion in OGDEN V. SAUNDERS (1827) called forth Marshall's only dissent in a constitutional case. The question was whether a state bankruptcy law applying to contracts made after the passage of the law was a violation of the CONTRACT CLAUSE. Trimble's clear-headed, practical opinion upholding state power remained controlling for most of the nineteenth century despite the dissents of Marshall and Story.

R. KENT NEWMYER
(1986)

Bibliography

STORY, JOSEPH   1829   Memoir of Judge Trimble. *American Jurist and Law Magazine* 1:149–157.

# *TRIMBLE v. GORDON*
430 U.S. 762 (1977)

A year before this decision, the Supreme Court had refused, in *Mathews v. Lucas* (1976), to hold that ILLEGITIMACY was a SUSPECT CLASSIFICATION requiring strict judicial scrutiny. In *Trimble*, a 5–4 majority invalidated an Illinois law that prevented illegitimate children from inheriting from their fathers who had not made wills. Discriminations based on illegitimacy, said Justice LEWIS F. POWELL for the majority, must be "carefully attuned to alternative considerations." Although paternity might be hard to prove in some cases, wholesale disinheritance of illegitimate children was unjustified. In this case a judicial paternity proceeding had determined the decedent to be the father.

Justice WILLIAM H. REHNQUIST dissented at length, criticizing the development of modern EQUAL PROTECTION doctrine. Except for classifications based on race or national origin, he would abandon all forms of STRICT SCRUTINY, requiring no more than a RATIONAL BASIS for legislative discrimination. Laws classifying according to legitimacy of parentage deserved no more heightened judicial scrutiny than did "other laws regulating economic and social conditions."

Only a year later, in LALLI V. LALLI (1978), a fragmented Court made *Trimble*'s precedential status uncertain.

KENNETH L. KARST
(1986)

## *TROP v. DULLES*
356 U.S. 86 (1958)

## *PEREZ v. BROWNELL*
356 U.S. 44 (1958)

In two cases decided the same day the Supreme Court ruled on the constitutionality of the EXPATRIATION provisions of the Nationality Act of 1940. In *Perez* the Court held (5–4) that revocation of CITIZENSHIP for voting in a foreign election was a valid exercise of governmental control over FOREIGN AFFAIRS.

In *Trop*, however, the Court held unconstitutional (5–4) the involuntary expatriation of a wartime deserter. Chief Justice EARL WARREN, for a plurality, contended that expatriation is CRUEL AND UNUSUAL PUNISHMENT; but WILLIAM J. BRENNAN, the one justice who changed sides, argued only that Congress's power over citizenship is less extensive when foreign affairs are not involved.

DENNIS J. MAHONEY
(1986)

## *TRUAX v. CORRIGAN*
257 U.S. 312 (1921)

A 1913 Arizona law, similar to the labor provisions of the CLAYTON ANTITRUST ACT, prohibited state court INJUNCTIONS against peaceful PICKETING. Following a dispute with restaurant proprietor William Truax, a local union peacefully picketed and distributed handbills calling for a BOYCOTT. Truax's business receipts dropped dramatically, and after the Arizona courts denied him relief, he appealed to the Supreme Court, contending that the state law deprived him of his property without DUE PROCESS OF LAW and violated the EQUAL PROTECTION clause of the FOURTEENTH AMENDMENT.

Chief Justice WILLIAM HOWARD TAFT, speaking for a 5–4 majority, held the state statute unconstitutional. He reasoned that Truax held a property right in his business; free access to it by employees and customers was incidental to that right. Concerted action that intentionally injured that right was a conspiracy and a tort. In this case, the union's activities constituted an "unlawful annoyance and hurtful nuisance." Such wrongs, Taft concluded, could not be remediless, and he declared that the anti-injunction law deprived Truax of due process. He also ruled that the law

violated equal protection by limiting the application of an injunction to a particular class.

Justice LOUIS D. BRANDEIS, dissenting, maintained that even if the employer had a constitutional right to be free from boycotting and picketing, the state was not compelled to protect that right with an injunction, as states were free to expand or control their EQUITY jurisdiction. In a separate dissent, Justice OLIVER WENDELL HOLMES argued that the state law was a valid "social experiment," however "futile or even noxious." Beyond that, he challenged the assumption equating "business" with a property right. Business, he asserted, was "a course of conduct," and like any other was subject to modification regarding what would justify doing it a harm.

STANLEY I. KUTLER
(1986)

## TRUMAN, HARRY S.
(1884–1972)

The thirty-third President began his career in local Democratic politics in Missouri. Truman served in various capacities, including county judge and planning official, and helped coordinate employment and relief programs during the early 1930s. After his election to the United States SENATE in 1934, he supported the NEW DEAL programs and specialized in transportation policy. Declining President FRANKLIN D. ROOSEVELT's offer of an appointment to the Interstate Commerce Commission, he was reelected to the Senate in 1940. During the war years he attracted notice as the effective chairman of a Senate investigating committee established to oversee the efficiency and fairness of defense contracting. Elected vice-president in 1944, he succeeded to the presidency the next year when Roosevelt died. He returned to the White House in 1949 for a second term, following an unexpected election victory.

Truman believed in a strong and active presidency, operating within a Constitution sufficiently flexible to accommodate executive initiatives for the public good. The Framers of the Constitution, Truman said, had deliberately left vague the details of presidential power, allowing the "experience of the nation to fill in the outlines." He disagreed with scholars who claimed that history makes the man: "I think that it is the man who makes history." His roster of favorite Presidents included GEORGE WASHINGTON, THOMAS JEFFERSON, ANDREW JACKSON, ABRAHAM LINCOLN, GROVER CLEVELAND, THEODORE ROOSEVELT, WOODROW WILSON, and Franklin Roosevelt.

Although criticized at times by liberals for providing inadequate leadership and action on CIVIL RIGHTS, Truman's record is impressive. In 1946 he created the President's Committee on Civil Rights. A year later it issued an important document, *To Secure These Rights*, that took a firm stand against various forms of RACIAL DISCRIMINATION. In 1948 Truman issued EXECUTIVE ORDER 9981, ending discrimination in the armed services, and in that same year delivered a powerful civil rights message to Congress and supported the inclusion of a civil rights plank in the Democrats' platform.

Truman's commitment to the BILL OF RIGHTS was tested by the issue of subversion that overshadowed his administration. As a student of history he was keenly aware of the hysteria that had fanned repressive episodes, from the Salem witch trials to the Red Scare of 1919. He felt prepared to handle the new cycle that took the form of anticommunism and indiscriminate labeling of "subversives." (See SUBVERSIVE ACTIVITIES AND THE CONSTITUTION.)

EXECUTIVE ORDER 9835, issued by Truman in 1947, established procedures to control subversive infiltration of the federal government. The effect was to deprive agency employees of fundamental elements of DUE PROCESS, including the right to receive specific charges against them and to confront their accusers. Even when an accused received clearance from a loyalty board, the data remained in the files, forcing the employee to answer the same charges with each move to a new job. Truman later admitted that the program, which thrived on secret evidence and secret informers, was filled with defects and injustices.

Truman began to give closer attention to CIVIL LIBERTIES. In a message to Congress on August 8, 1950, he warned that pending legislation on internal security would forbid dissent. When the internal security bill reached his desk in the fall of 1950, he delivered a ringing denunciation, protesting in his veto message that the bill would put government in the "thought control business." Especially objectionable to him was a provision requiring "Communist-front" and "Communist-action" groups to register with the attorney general. This placed on the government the responsibility for probing the "attitudes and states of mind" of organization leaders. Groups could be linked to the Communist party whenever their positions failed to "deviate" from those of the Communist movement. Thus, any organization dedicated to low-cost housing or other humanitarian goals espoused by the party could be branded a communist front. Truman called this feature "the greatest danger to FREEDOM OF SPEECH, press and assembly, since the ALIEN AND SEDITION LAWS of 1798." The veto message, delivered in the midst of an election campaign that featured charges from some Republicans about Democrats being soft on communism, was courageous and principled. Within a day both Houses of Congress easily overrode the veto. (See INTERNAL SECURITY ACT.)

Following North Korea's invasion of the south in June 1950, Truman dispatched American soldiers to Korea without seeking congressional support or approval. A month later the State Department issued a belated memorandum defending the President's legal authority to repel the attack. The memo claimed that Truman's action was justified by international law, the UNITED NATIONS CHARTER, "and the resolution pursuant thereto." However, the United Nations issued *two* resolutions on Korea, one of June 25 calling for the cessation of hostilities and the withdrawal of North Korean forces to the 38th parallel, and a second resolution (adopted two days later) recommending armed force to repel the attack. Truman intervened militarily before passage of the second resolution. (See KOREAN WAR.)

Truman placed General Douglas MacArthur in command of American forces in Korea. MacArthur wanted to widen the military front, probing deeply into North Korea. He objected repeatedly, in public, to the limited war policy adopted by the administration. Eventually he alienated Truman, top cabinet officials, the Joint Chiefs of Staff, and the National Security Council. Over the course of almost a year, Truman became convinced that MacArthur was untrustworthy and insubordinate, but his abrupt dismissal of the general on April 11, 1951, triggered a storm of protest across the nation. In explaining his decision, Truman said it was fundamental that "military commanders must be governed by the policies and directives issued to them in the manner provided by our laws and Constitution."

Only a few members of Congress questioned Truman's authority to send troops to Korea, but as part of a "Great Debate" in 1951, legislators challenged his constitutional power to send ground forces to Europe. Resolutions were introduced in each house to require congressional authorization before military forces could be sent abroad. Although these measures were not enacted, uneasiness about the scope of presidential war-making power persisted. After President LYNDON B. JOHNSON's commitment of American troops to Southeast Asia and subsequent military actions there by President RICHARD M. NIXON, Congress passed the WAR POWERS RESOLUTION of 1973 to restrict the President's military powers. (See EMERGENCY POWER.)

Truman's attitude about presidential power and constitutional constraints is illuminated by his 1952 seizure of steel mills. He believed that a pending strike would prevent production of materials needed for the war in Korea. (See EXECUTIVE ORDER 10340; STEEL SEIZURE CONTROVERSY.) At a news conference on April 17 he was asked whether his INHERENT POWERS permitted seizure of newspapers and radio stations. To the consternation of the press he replied that the President could act "for whatever is for the best of the country." A week later, complaining that speculation about him seizing the press and the radio was "hooey," he stated that he had "difficulty imagining the Government taking over and running those industries." Continuing to respond to concerns about his views of emergency power, on April 27 he wrote in a letter that presidential powers are "derived from the Constitution, and they are limited, of course, by the provisions of the Constitution, particularly those that protect the rights of individuals."

Meanwhile, the Justice Department was developing a different scenario for District Judge David Pine. Assistant Attorney General Homer Baldridge told Pine on April 24 that "there is not power in the Courts to restrain the President. . . ." After Pine had declared the seizure invalid, Truman claimed at a news conference on May 22 that "nobody" (including Congress and the Court) could take from the President his power to seize private property and to protect the welfare of the people. However, he said that he would abide by the Supreme Court's verdict, and when the decision fell on June 2 (see YOUNGSTOWN SHEET & TUBE CO. V. SAWYER), declaring the seizure invalid, he immediately ordered the government to relinquish possession of the mills.

Often careless with his remarks at press conference, for which he paid dearly, Truman came to the White House with a solid understanding of history and governmental institutions and processes. He maintained a deep respect for individual rights and civilian government. Through his personal integrity and honesty he helped moderate many of the repressive forces that operated during his years in office.

LOUIS FISHER
(1986)

Bibliography

HAMBY, ALONZO L. 1973 *Beyond the New Deal: Harry S. Truman and American Liberalism.* New York: Columbia University Press.

TRUMAN, HARRY S. 1955 *Year of Decisions.* Garden City, N.Y.: Doubleday.

——— 1956 *Years of Trial and Hope.* Garden City, N.Y.: Doubleday.

——— 1960 *Mr. Citizen.* New York: Bernard Geis.

# TRUMBULL, LYMAN
## (1813–1896)

An Illinois state supreme court judge (1848–1853) and United States senator (1855–1873), Lyman Trumbull opposed all SLAVERY expansion before 1861, and during the SECESSION crisis he argued that the Constitution already adequately protected slavery and no amendments, concessions, or compromises were necessary. A strong supporter of the Union war effort, Trumbull nevertheless believed that the war should be fought within the frame-

work of the Constitution. Thus, he opposed President ABRAHAM LINCOLN's unilateral suspension of HABEAS CORPUS, arbitrary arrests, and the closing of northern newspapers. Nonetheless, he supported legislation authorizing such actions. Trumbull gave mild support to the EMANCIPATION PROCLAMATION but doubted its constitutionality, and thus he introduced the resolution which led to the THIRTEENTH AMENDMENT. As chairman of the Senate Judiciary Committee during the war and Reconstruction, Trumbull initiated the first and second CONFISCATION ACTS, the CIVIL RIGHTS ACT OF 1866, the FREEDMEN'S BUREAU Extension Act (1866), and the first civil service reform legislation (1870). Despite his opposition to slavery and support of CIVIL RIGHTS, Trumbull was at heart a white supremacist and only reluctantly voted for the FIFTEENTH AMENDMENT. He opposed both punitive legislation for southern states that discriminated against blacks and the 1871 Ku Klux Klan Act, because of his lack of sympathy for blacks and his refusal to accept the fact that the CIVIL WAR had radically altered the nature of STATES' RIGHTS. He gave unenthusiastic support for ANDREW JOHNSON in 1865–1866, and, although disgusted with Johnson's vetos of his Civil Rights and Freedman's Bureau Bills, Trumbull voted against conviction of Johnson in the trial following IMPEACHMENT because he doubted Johnson had committed an impeachable act under the Constitution. A successful corporate lawyer, Trumbull argued EX PARTE MCCARDLE (1867) at the express request of General ULYSSES S. GRANT and was paid $10,000 for his services, even though he was a senator at the time. In 1876 Trumbull unsuccessfully argued the cause of Samuel Tilden before the Election Commission that considered the disputes over the Tilden-Hayes presidential election. (See COMPROMISE OF 1877.) Late in life he supported populism and the rights of workers, and in his last Supreme Court case he defended the labor organizer Eugene V. Debs in IN RE DEBS (1895).

PAUL FINKELMAN
(1986)

Bibliography

KRUG, MARK M. 1965 *Lyman Trumbull: Conservative Radical.* New York: A. S. Barnes & Co.

# *TRUPIANO v. UNITED STATES*

See: Search and Seizure; Search Incident to Arrest

# TRUTH, SOJOURNER
## (c. 1799–1883)

Sojourner Truth (née Isabella Baumfree), nineteenth-century ABOLITIONIST and FEMINIST, was born a slave, was not literate, and lived in poverty much of her life. Yet, in an age before mass media, she was a nationally renowned figure, known for her advocacy before, during, and after the CIVIL WAR.

Born in the Hudson River Valley in New York around 1799, she performed hard labor for a series of masters and was so renowned for her physical strength—she was nearly six feet tall—that her owner reneged on a promise to reward her exceptional hard work with her freedom. Refusing to rely anymore on a "slaveholders' promise," she freed herself by walking away from his farm in 1826, a year before the state's gradual manumission law freed her. Her five-year-old son was illegally sold in violation of the manumission law, and after a desperate search, she successfully sued to recover him.

In 1829, she left for New York City after experiencing a profound religious awakening. Her new life as preacher and advocate began on Pentecost, June 1, 1843, when she discarded her slave name and became Sojourner Truth. Leaving New York and joining the Northampton Association, an abolitionist community in Massachusetts, she became associated with important figures in the movement, such as WILLIAM LLOYD GARRISON and Frederick Douglass. In 1850, she authored her autobiography—an "as told to" account of her life story. By "selling the shadow to support the substance," as she often said, the book's sales proceeds became her primary and meager source of support.

Her lifelong work as a public speaker also began in earnest. By many accounts, she was a spellbinding speaker, often drawing on events from her difficult life to expose the evils of SLAVERY and reveal the interconnectedness between the abolitionist and feminist struggles. In 1851, Sojourner delivered a speech to an abolitionist convention in Akron, Ohio, where she made this linkage preeminent in what has become a piece of legendary oratory. As a formerly enslaved woman, Truth recalled that she had been worked "like a man," yet she was still a woman and like all women and black people was entitled to the rights due all human beings. This speech became well-known when, in 1863, Frances Gage, a prominent feminist, published a colorful rendition, using the phrase "And ar'n't I a woman?" Despite the fact that many historians consider it unlikely that this account is literally accurate, as other contemporaneous reports of the speech do not include the phrase, and Sojourner, whose first language was Dutch, did not speak in this dialect, "Ar'n't I a woman?" became her emblem, embodying her unrelenting focus on the relationship between the abolitionist and feminist causes.

Her insistence on this connection carried over into the RECONSTRUCTION era, where she strenuously argued that in the struggle for the FIFTEENTH AMENDMENT, suffrage for women should not be sacrificed in order to secure the vote for black men. Her refusal to compromise, as some promi-

nent male abolitionists had, was grounded in her concern that the failure to secure women's suffrage in conjunction with black male suffrage would mean that the vote for women would be indefinitely deferred and the interests and voices of black women marginalized—a concern that proved prophetic. In the period following the Civil War, between 1864 and 1870, she devoted herself to addressing the often horrendous living conditions facing the formerly enslaved black population. Without jobs or land, freedom was severely undermined and it was Sojourner's view, expressed in a petition to President ULYSSES S. GRANT in 1870, that freed people should be resettled in the West on public lands. In 1875, she returned to Battle Creek, Michigan, following the death of a beloved grandson who had been her constant companion. She did not have many active public appearances from that time until her death in 1883. She remained a commanding presence however, and a living symbol that repudiated racialized conceptions of womanhood and affirmed the importance of resisting all forms of subordination.

CHERYL I. HARRIS
(2000)

Bibliography

HARRIS, CHERYL I. 1993 Whiteness as Property. *Harvard Law Review* 106:1707–1791.
——— 1996 Finding Sojourner's Truth: Race, Gender and the Institution of Property. *Cardozo Law Journal* 18:309–409.
PAINTER, NELL IRVIN 1996 *Sojourner Truth: A Life, a Symbol.* New York: W. W. Norton.
WASHINGTON, MARGARET, ed. 1993 *Narrative of Sojourner Truth.* New York: Vintage Books.

# TUCKER, HENRY ST. GEORGE
## (1780–1848)

A political leader, scholar, and jurist, Henry St. George Tucker studied law under his father, ST. GEORGE TUCKER. He was a congressman (1815–1819), state judge (1824–1841), and professor of law at the University of Virginia (1841–1848). In his classroom lectures and in his textbook entitled *Lectures on Constitutional Law* (1843), he took a moderate STATES' RIGHTS position, steering, as he said, "a middle course between [the] dangerous extremes" of NULLIFICATION and centralization. His book is intended as a refutation of the nationalist position of JOSEPH STORY, but, although he regarded the Constitution as a compact among the states, he rejected nullification and SECESSION as remedies for violations by the federal government.

DENNIS J. MAHONEY
(1986)

Bibliography

BAUER, ELIZABETH KELLEY 1952 *Commentaries on the Constitution, 1790–1860.* New York: Columbia University Press.

# TUCKER, JOHN RANDOLPH
## (1823–1897)

A political leader, scholar, and attorney, John Randolph Tucker was the son of HENRY ST. GEORGE TUCKER and the grandson of ST. GEORGE TUCKER. He was attorney general of Virginia (1857–1865), congressman (1875–1887), professor of law at Washington and Lee University (1870–1875, 1888–1897), and president of the American Bar Association (1894). From his retirement from Congress until his death he worked on his two-volume commentary, *The Constitution of the United States*, which was published posthumously in 1899. Tucker continued the family's tradition of STATES' RIGHTS constitutionalism, proposing that the TENTH AMENDMENT was the key to understanding the Constitution. He was strikingly influenced by European political theorists, including J. K. Bluntschli, and rejected the ideas of NATURAL RIGHTS, human equality, and SOCIAL COMPACT in favor of the concept of an organic state.

DENNIS J. MAHONEY
(1986)

# TUCKER, N. BEVERLEY
## (1784–1851)

Jurist, scholar, and novelist Nathaniel Beverley Tucker developed his political views under the influence of his half-brother, JOHN RANDOLPH. As a judge and politician in Missouri (1815–1830) he fiercely resisted the MISSOURI COMPROMISE. Later, as a professor of law at William and Mary College (1834–1851) he was one of the most extreme advocates of a STATES' RIGHTS interpretation of the Constitution. He argued that SOVEREIGNTY resided in the several states and that the people of Virginia were obliged to obey federal law only because Virginia commanded them to do so. He defended SLAVERY and supported NULLIFICATION. His novel, *The Partisan Leader* (1836), advocated SECESSION and predicted a civil war.

DENNIS J. MAHONEY
(1986)

Bibliography

BAUER, ELIZABETH KELLEY 1952 *Commentaries on the Constitution, 1790–1860.* New York: Columbia University Press.

# TUCKER, ST. GEORGE
## (1751–1827)

St. George Tucker, who became known as the "American Blackstone," wrote the first commentary on the Constitution since THE FEDERALIST, a book that he recommended as a "masterly discussion." After a dozen years as a judge in Virginia, Tucker succeeded GEORGE WYTHE, with whom he had studied law, as professor of law at the College of William and Mary. Using WILLIAM BLACKSTONE's *Commentaries on the Laws of England* as his text, Tucker updated and domesticated Blackstone in his lectures, showing how the English law had changed in the United States and in Virginia. His lectures led in 1803 to the publication in five volumes of an annotated edition of Blackstone. Notwithstanding Tucker's 1,400 notes, the most creative parts of his work are to be found in his appendices, which run to 425 pages in the first volume, mostly an analysis of the United States Constitution. Although Tucker preferred a "federal" to a "consolidated" Union, he was a moderate who defended the American constitutional system, championed democracy, opposed SLAVERY, and made constructive criticisms. The appendix argued against a FEDERAL COMMON LAW OF CRIMES. Volume two's appendices included an extended proposal for the gradual abolition of slavery and a libertarian essay on FIRST AMENDMENT freedoms, in which Tucker discoursed on the reasons that religion, speech, and press should be "absolute" and "unrestricted," except for laws against personal defamation. Tucker's edition of Blackstone led to his appointment to the highest court of Virginia, where he served with distinction, followed in 1813 by an appointment as a United States district judge. Tucker held that position until shortly before his death. He ranks with the best of Jeffersonian jurists and theorists.

LEONARD W. LEVY
(1986)

# TUCKER ACT
## 24 Stat. 505 (1887)

Thirty-two years after establishing the Court of Claims, Congress enacted the Tucker Act, expanding that court's JURISDICTION to decide claims against the United States. Henceforth, the court might decide not only contract claims but also claims against the government founded on the Constitution and other damage claims not based on tort. Today the act confers jurisdiction over such cases on the United States CLAIMS COURT, along with jurisdiction over claims founded on various federal statutes and regulations. If the amount in controversy in such a case is less than $10,000, the UNITED STATES DISTRICT COURT exercises

CONCURRENT JURISDICTION—thus allowing persons with small claims to bring suit in their home districts rather than in Washington, D.C. The act creates no substantive rights but merely provides jurisdiction in cases in which the government's liability is founded on other principles of law. In effect, however, the act amounts to a waiver of the federal government's SOVEREIGN IMMUNITY, in recognition of the vital principle that government should not be above the law.

KENNETH L. KARST
(1986)

(SEE ALSO: *Federal Tort Claims Act.*)

Bibliography

WRIGHT, CHARLES A.; MILLER, ARTHUR R.; and COOPER, EDWARD H. 1985 *Federal Practice and Procedure*, 2nd ed. Vol. 14:270–294. St. Paul, Minn.: West Publishing Co.

# TUGWELL, REXFORD G.
## (1891–1979)

Economist Rexford Guy Tugwell was a member of President FRANKLIN D. ROOSEVELT's "brain trust" and an advocate of centralized economic planning by the federal government. After serving as undersecretary of agriculture and governor of Puerto Rico, he began a second career as a historian and constitutional theorist. His books on the Roosevelt years include *The Democratic Roosevelt* (1957, 1969) and *The Brains Trust* (1968). Tugwell's years as a government official convinced him that only a rewriting of the Constitution, emphasizing provisions for centralization, economic planning, and emergency powers, would produce an effective form of government. He denounced as undemocratic the accepted principles of FEDERALISM, and SEPARATION OF POWERS, and he stressed the need for total revision of the Constitution rather than gradual evolution through judicial interpretation. Tugwell frequently published his own proposals for a rewritten constitution. In *The Emerging Constitution* (1975) his proposals included: reduction of the states to administrative districts of a unitary national government; expansion of executive power, including EXECUTIVE PRIVILEGE; curtailment of the judiciary's power to pass judgment on actions of the national government to supervise the economy; and periodic revision of the Constitution through a simplified AMENDING PROCESS.

RICHARD B. BERNSTEIN
(1986)

# TUITION GRANTS

While parents have a constitutional right to send their children to private rather than public schools (see PIERCE V. SOCIETY OF SISTERS, 1925), the exercise of that right costs money. Such parents not only bear their share of the taxes that support public schools but also pay tuition to their children's schools. Not surprisingly, a regular item of business in Congress and the state legislatures is a proposal to relieve this "double burden" through some form of governmental relief. Two types of constitutional problems beset such proposals. Governmental aid to private schools may be attacked as STATE ACTION that promotes racial SEGREGATION or as an unconstitutional ESTABLISHMENT OF RELIGION.

Soon after the decision in BROWN V. BOARD OF EDUCATION (1954–1955), a number of southern states adopted a series of devices aimed at evading DESEGREGATION. One such device was the payment of state grants to private schools or to parents of private school children. The assumption was that when public schools were ordered to desegregate, white children would be withdrawn and placed in private schools. Some states went so far as to give local school boards the option of closing public schools and even selling those schools' physical plants to the operators of private schools which would be supported by tuition subsidized by the state. These private schools, it was expected, would be limited to white students. (More recently, federal CIVIL RIGHTS legislation has been applied to forbid that type of "segregation academy" to refuse black applicants. See RUNYON V. MCCRARY.) The Supreme Court held these tuition grant programs unconstitutional as evasions of *Brown* in cases such as GRIFFIN V. COUNTY SCHOOL BOARD (1964) and *Poindexter v. Louisiana Financial Assistance Commission* (PER CURIAM, 1968).

More recently, private schools in the North and West have acquired new white students following orders desegregating urban school systems. "White flight" means not only the departure of white families for the suburbs but also the transfer of white students from public to private schools. Estimates in the late 1970s suggested that as many as one-fifth of all enrollments in the nation's private schools were the result of "white flight." Proposals for governmental aid to private school children and their parents must therefore face a challenge based on the likely racially discriminatory impacts of various proposed forms of aid. Such impacts would not, of themselves, establish a constitutional violation; they would, however, be some evidence of an improper governmental purpose. (See LEGISLATION.)

Tuition grants limited to low-income parents of children enrolled in religious schools were held to violate the establishment clause in COMMITTEE FOR PUBLIC EDUCATION

v. NYQUIST (1973). That decision did not settle the question of the constitutionality of a hypothetical program in which the state gave *all* parents education vouchers, to be used to support schools of their choosing, public or private, religious or secular. (See GOVERNMENT AID TO RELIGIOUS INSTITUTIONS; MUELLER V. ALLEN.)

Proponents of voucher plans designed to aid private schools and their clienteles have gone to some lengths in an effort to tailor their proposals to meet these two types of constitutional objection. One proposal provides elaborate incentives for racial integration, such as bonuses for integrated schools. In the absence of strong incentives of some kind, it seems obvious that significant aid to private elementary and secondary education will have the effect of increasing racial segregation by increasing the educational mobility of middle class whites.

KENNETH L. KARST

(1986)

Bibliography

SUGARMAN, STEPHEN D.　1974　Family Choice: The Next Step in the Quest for Equal Educational Opportunity? *Law and Contemporary Problems* 38:513–565.

## *TURNER BROADCASTING SYSTEM, INC. v. FCC*
### 512 U.S. 622 (1994)

The development of the cable television industry has revolutionized the way most Americans watch television. Until the 1960s, television signals were broadcast through the air into people's homes and picked up by receivers in their television sets. Such signals used the electromagnetic spectrum, which has limited frequencies, and could only travel relatively short distances. Because of these technological limitations, Congress, through the Federal Communications Commission, claimed the power to regulate BROADCASTING in order to license and control the use of the limited number of frequencies or "channels" and to impose certain content restrictions and public interest obligations on the broadcasters given those licenses. In a 1969 case, RED LION BROADCASTING CO. V. FCC, the Supreme Court rejected a FIRST AMENDMENT challenge to those restrictions. The Court reasoned that the law was designed to expand, not restrict, the diversity of programming and was thus consistent with FREEDOM OF SPEECH principles.

Because of the short range of broadcast signals, however, viewers could only receive programs transmitted by local broadcasting "stations," and people in remote areas often received very poor signal reception. Cable television revolutionized this system. First, cable transmits video signals through fiberoptic cables, not electromagnetic frequencies, and thus has the capacity to carry or "broadcast" dozens, if not hundreds, of different channels at one time. Second, cable facilities can easily send their programs to distant places because they transmit their signals through cable wires, rather than through the air.

Initially, cable was primarily used to improve reception of broadcast stations in crowded urban or remote rural areas. But because of the large number of channels a cable system could transmit, the cable industry developed many new sources of programming. Because of better reception and broader programming, cable soon became the source of transmission of programming to approximately 60 percent of the households in America, although, unlike broadcasting, subscribers had to pay a monthly fee for the cable service.

Broadcasters felt threatened by this new source of programming and, more importantly, by the control that cable operators had over the broadcasters' ability to reach their audience. The broadcasters were dependent on cable operators to carry their programs, yet, they were in competition with the cable industry over channels and programming. Cable operators had a "chokehold" over broadcasters and television programming, threatening the future of "free T.V."

At the urging of the broadcast industry and others, Congress sought to address such concerns in the Cable Television Consumer Protection and Competition Act of 1992. That law mandated that all cable operators had to carry a reasonable number or percentage of "local commercial television stations" and local "noncommercial educational television stations" among the channels on their cable systems. The larger the number of channels, the more broadcast stations the system had to carry. Overall, the result was that approximately one-third of the channels on any cable system had to be made available for use by local commercial or noncommercial broadcast stations.

This "MUST CARRY" LAW was promptly challenged by cable system operators and cable channel programmers as violating their free speech rights. The cable operators claimed they were being forced by government to carry programming against their will. The programmers claimed that, as a consequence, there would be fewer cable channels available for their programming. In *Turner Broadcasting System v. FCC*, the Supreme Court held that those "must carry" rules passed constitutional muster. The Solomon-like decision contained something for both sides of the debate.

First, the Court gave the cable industry an important victory by clearly holding that the First Amendment broadly protects cable operators and programmers and affords them powerful rights of speech and press. In doing so, the Court rejected the government's contention that the permissible regulation of cable should be measured by the same deferential approach that marked the *Red Lion* framework for assessing the rights of broadcasters. The Court reasoned that greater deference to governmental regulation is premised on the spectrum scarcity that uniquely affects broadcasting and which does not obtain in cable technology. Accordingly, normal First Amendment standards apply in deciding whether the restrictions and requirements of the "must carry" law are constitutional.

Nevertheless, under those standards, the strictest judicial scrutiny is reserved for those rules that are content-based, rather than content-neutral. Here, the regulation was premised on the medium, not the message. Congress required cable operators to carry commercial and noncommercial broadcast stations not because of any favored content communicated by those media, but to insure that those media remain healthy and diverse in order to serve the 40 percent of American households that, by necessity or choice, prefer to rely on free television as their source of programming. Nor did the Court find any persuasive evidence that Congress was trying to discriminate against the viewpoints allegedly associated with cable programming or in favor of the viewpoints purportedly associated with broadcasting. Rather, Congress was validly concerned with the "chokehold" capacity of cable operators to shut out broadcasters. (The dissenters, however, contended that Congress did see content differences between the two separate media and was impermissibly preferring one set of viewpoints over another.)

As a result, said the Court, the content-neutral, "must carry" rules would be judged by an intermediate standard of First Amendment review, with the critical question being whether those requirements were important to protecting broadcasting strength and diversity. On this point, the Justices concluded that more evidence was necessary on how vulnerable the broadcast industry really was and whether the special protections afforded it were justified. Accordingly, the Court sent the matter back to the lower courts for the development of a more complete record on those issues. In 1997, the case returned to the Court. The majority ruled that the justifications for the law were valid and survived the standard of intermediate scrutiny; the four dissenters, however, insisted that STRICT SCRUTINY was warranted by the law's content-based purposes and that, even under intermediate scrutiny, the government had failed to demonstrate threats to the broadcast industry that would be cured by the "must carry" rules.

JOEL M. GORA
(2000)

Bibliography

MASETH, MICHAEL W. 1995 Comment: The Erosion of First Amendment Protections of Speech and Press: The "Must Carry" Provisions of the 1992 Cable Act. *Capital University Law Review* 24:423–456.

MEYERSON, MICHAEL I. 1995 Authors, Editors, and Uncommon Carriers: Identifying the "Speaker" Within the New Media. *Notre Dame Law Review* 71:79–125.

SYMPOSIUM 1997 Telecommunications Law: Unscrambling the Signals, Unbundling the Laws. *Columbia Law Review* 97:819–1201.

# TWELFTH AMENDMENT

The ELECTORAL COLLEGE, as contemplated in Article II of the Constitution, was to be a kind of "search committee," nominating outstanding men of various regions from among whom Congress would elect the President and Vice-President. The Framers expected each elector to cast his first vote for a candidate from his home state and his second for a national figure from another state. The delegates to the CONSTITUTIONAL CONVENTION assumed that the primary electoral divisions in the country were, and would remain, sectional.

The rise of POLITICAL PARTIES, which began almost immediately after the Constitution went into effect, belied that assumption. The parties nominated candidates, and the Electoral College had only to choose between the party slates; sectional loyalties were subordinated to ideological ones. In 1796, when party discipline was still developing, the Electoral College chose a Federalist President and a Republican Vice-President. In 1800 straight party voting produced a tie between THOMAS JEFFERSON and AARON BURR, the Republican nominees for President and Vice-President, respectively. The disgraceful performance of the HOUSE OF REPRESENTATIVES, which required thirty-five ballots to ratify the voters' choice, led directly to adoption of the Twelfth Amendment.

The amendment provided that the electors would vote for President and Vice-President in separate ballots; if no candidate obtained a majority of electoral votes, the House of Representatives (voting by states) would elect the President and the SENATE the Vice-President. Introduced by Senator DeWitt Clinton of New York, the amendment faced congressional opposition from Federalists and representatives of small states, each group fearing that its influence on presidential selection would be diminished. Once Congress proposed the Twelfth Amendment in 1804, the necessary thirteen states ratified it in less than six months—only the TWENTY-SIXTH AMENDMENT (1971) was ratified more quickly.

DENNIS J. MAHONEY
(1986)

# TWENTIETH AMENDMENT

Congress proposed the Twentieth Amendment, sponsored by Senator GEORGE W. NORRIS of Nebraska, on March 2,

1932; ratification was completed on January 23, 1933. The amendment provided that the President, Vice-President, and Congress begin their terms in the January following their election. Under the old scheme of Article I, section 4, congressmen had not taken their seats until thirteen months after their election, and a short "lame duck" session in election years included members who had already been defeated. The amendment also made provisions for PRESIDENTIAL SUCCESSION and authorized Congress to provide for a situation in which a President-elect or Vice-President-elect does not qualify by inauguration day.

DENNIS J. MAHONEY
(1986)

## TWENTY-FIFTH AMENDMENT

Congress proposed the Twenty-Fifth Amendment in July 1965, and ratification by the state legislatures was completed in February 1967. The amendment revised the constitutional provisions dealing with PRESIDENTIAL SUCCESSION, specifically providing that when a vacancy occurs in the office of President the Vice-President becomes (rather than "acts as") President. The amendment also provides for the orderly transfer of executive power in the event of a temporary presidential disability and for filling a vacancy in the office of Vice-President.

DENNIS J. MAHONEY
(1986)

Bibliography

FEERICK, JOHN D. 1976 *The Twenty-Fifth Amendment.* New York: Fordham University Press.

## TWENTY-FIRST AMENDMENT

The Twenty-First Amendment repealed the EIGHTEENTH AMENDMENT and rescinded the constitutional mandate for national PROHIBITION of alcoholic beverages. Congress proposed the amendment in February 1933; RATIFICATION was complete in December 1933. To the extent that the VOLSTEAD ACT depended upon the constitutional authority of the Eighteenth Amendment, that statute became inoperative upon the passage of the Twenty-First Amendment.

The second clause of the Twenty-First Amendment prohibits transportation or importation of intoxicating liquors into states or territories in contravention of local law. The clause apparently gives the states power to regulate interstate commerce in alcoholic beverages, including the authority to discriminate against out-of-state producers and distributors, thus freeing the states, as far as liquor is concerned, from COMMERCE CLAUSE restrictions. The Supreme Court has upheld that interpretation in several cases, notably *State Board v. Young's Market* (1936). The

Court suggested an even broader scope for state regulatory power under the amendment in *California v. LaRue* (1972), when it upheld a regulation banning sexually explicit entertainment in licensed taverns, and in *Elks' Lodge v. Ingraham* (1973), when it upheld a statute denying liquor licenses to private clubs that practiced RACIAL DISCRIMINATION.

The Twenty-First Amendment is the only constitutional amendment to have been ratified by state conventions rather than by the state legislatures. Congress chose this variant of the AMENDING PROCESS because proponents of repeal feared that antiliquor sentiment was dominant in many state legislatures, because of the overrepresentation of rural areas.

DENNIS J. MAHONEY
(1986)

## TWENTY-FOURTH AMENDMENT

The Twenty-Fourth Amendment, written by Senator Spessard Holland of Florida, was proposed by Congress on August 27, 1962, and became part of the Constitution on February 4, 1964. The amendment provides that the right of United States citizens to vote for federal officers shall not be denied or abridged for nonpayment of a POLL TAX or other tax.

A poll tax is simply a per capita tax and has no necessary relationship to election polling. However, several southern states made payment of the poll tax an electoral qualification in order to diminish the VOTING RIGHTS of black citizens. Bills to abolish the practice were introduced every year from 1939 on, and Holland, who believed statutory abolition to be beyond Congress's power, introduced his amendment every year from 1949 on.

By 1964, only five states retained payment of the poll tax as a qualification for voting. Because the Twenty-Fourth Amendment governed only federal elections, four states divided their elections, continuing to require poll tax payment for voting in state elections; but the Supreme Court held, in HARPER V. VIRGINIA BOARD OF ELECTIONS (1966), that this practice violated the Constitution by denying EQUAL PROTECTION OF THE LAWS.

DENNIS J. MAHONEY
(1986)

## TWENTY-SECOND AMENDMENT

Although, as ALEXANDER HAMILTON explained in THE FEDERALIST #69, the President was "to be re-eligible as often as the people of the United States shall think him worthy of their confidence," a constitutional custom dating back to the administration of GEORGE WASHINGTON limited the President of the United States to two terms in office. In

1940, however, with the Great Depression finally coming to an end and with most of the world already engaged in WORLD WAR II, FRANKLIN D. ROOSEVELT sought and won election to a third term. He was subsequently elected to a fourth term, although he died sixty days after that term began.

The Twenty-Second Amendment makes the two-term limit a part of the formal Constitution. Congress proposed the amendment in March 1947 and RATIFICATION was complete four years later.

The effect of the amendment on the balance of power between the executive and the legislature is not clear. Hamilton, who personally had advocated a life term for the President, speculated in *The Federalist* #71 that Presidents would become more submissive to Congress as elections approached; and DWIGHT D. EISENHOWER argued during his second term that his ineligibility for reelection was a guarantee that he was more disinterestedly public-spirited than congressmen who opposed him. In the 1980s, on the other hand, journalists and political scientists who had come to see elections as retroactively legitimating, rather than prospectively legitimating, began referring to President RONALD REAGAN as a "lame duck" even before his second inauguration.

The two-term limit is no longer controversial. Ever since the Constitutional Convention of 1789 there have been proposals for limiting the President to a single term, generally longer than four years, but none of these has ever been seriously considered as a constitutional amendment.

DENNIS J. MAHONEY
(1986)

# TWENTY-SEVENTH AMENDMENT

The Twenty-Seventh Amendment provides: "No law, varying the compensation for the services of the Senators and Representatives, shall take effect, until an election of Representatives shall have intervened." It is rooted in a recurring issue in Anglo-American legislative design: Who should pay representatives? In England, at first, constituents paid members of the House of Commons; throughout the eighteenth century members and candidates promised to take ever-lower wages or no wages at all, and, to win voters' support, competed to assume costs for municipal improvements such as new public buildings or repaved streets. Guarding against real and perceived corruption, American colonial and (after 1776) state governments paid legislators' salaries. Similarly, colonial and state governments paid delegates to the confederation and CONTINENTAL CONGRESSES.

The CONSTITUTIONAL CONVENTION OF 1787 had to decide what compensation senators and representatives should receive and from whom. The delegates concluded that having each state pay its own senators and representatives would create inequities among states and might preclude the ablest candidates from seeking office. Therefore, they framed the Constitution's compensation clause of Article I to have the general government pay senators and representatives and to empower Congress to set its own rate of compensation. ANTI-FEDERALISTS criticized the provision for assigning Congress that power and for insulating senators and representatives from state control. The ratifying conventions of Virginia, New York, and North Carolina recommended amendments barring laws changing legislative compensation from taking effect until after an election of representatives.

Responding to the nationwide demands for amendments, Representative JAMES MADISON of Virginia sorted through the over two hundred proposals to devise those he offered to the HOUSE OF REPRESENTATIVES on June 8, 1789. He chose rights-protecting amendments and "structural amendments" that did not invade the general government's just powers, with the compensation amendment in the latter group. It was the second of twelve amendments proposed by Congress to the states on September 26, 1789. Amendments three through twelve were ratified, becoming known as the BILL OF RIGHTS.

From 1791 through 1982, the compensation amendment languished in limbo, with two exceptions. On May 6, 1873, protesting the Forty-Second Congress's "salary grab" (by which Congress retroactively increased its pay by half), Ohio's legislature ratified the compensation amendment. On March 3, 1978, Wyoming's legislature ratified the amendment, protesting congressional compensation.

In 1982, Gregory D. Watson, then a sophomore at the University of Texas, wrote a paper arguing that the compensation amendment could still be ratified by the states. He then launched a one-man campaign to persuade state legislatures to ratify the amendment.

Most constitutional scholars argued that an implied time-limit on unratified proposed amendments invalidated the 1789 REAPPORTIONMENT and compensation amendments, the 1810 TITLES OF NOBILITY amendment, the 1861 Corwin Amendment, and the 1924 child-labor amendment. Yet, from 1983 to 1992, a parade of states ratified the compensation amendment. By May 7, 1992, it had amassed thirty-eight ratifications (counting those in 1789–1791, 1873, and 1978), enough to meet the three-fourths requirement of the Article V AMENDING PROCESS.

Should all the state ratifications or only those from 1983 through 1992 be deemed valid? Who decides whether an amendment is validly ratified? This latter task was a ministerial one left (1789 to 1951) to the Secretary of State, then (1951 to 1984) to the Administrator of General Services, and finally (since 1984) to the archivist of the United States. When, on May 18, 1992, Archivist Don W. Wilson accepted all the states' ratifications and certified the Amendment, House and SENATE leaders invoked the precedent of the FOURTEENTH AMENDMENT to establish Congress's final authority to confirm an amendment's ratification. On May 20, 1992, the House (414–3) and the Senate (99–0) confirmed the Twenty-Seventh Amendment.

Would the Twenty-Seventh Amendment invalidate the 1989 Ethics in Government Act, which established cost-of-living adjustments automatically keying congressional compensation to the cost-of-living index? In *Boehner v. Anderson* (1992), the U.S. District Court for the District of Columbia refused to decide the amendment's status but, assuming its validity, upheld the statute. On appeal, the U.S. Court of Appeals for the D.C. Circuit upheld the district court but also held the amendment a valid part of the Constitution.

The Twenty-Seventh Amendment's strange history continues to preoccupy constitutional scholars concerned with the theory and practice of constitutional change, but its uniqueness, the modest change it worked in the fabric of the constitutional system, and its pedigree as an amendment proposed by Madison will limit its significance to the abstract realm of CONSTITUTIONAL THEORY.

RICHARD B. BERNSTEIN
(2000)

Bibliography

ANASTAPLO, GEORGE   1995   *The Amendments to the Constitution: A Commentary.* Baltimore, Md.: Johns Hopkins University Press.

BERNSTEIN, RICHARD B.   1992   The Sleeper Wakes: The History and Legacy of the Twenty-Seventh Amendment. *Fordham Law Review* 61:497–557.

BERNSTEIN, RICHARD B. and AGEL, JEROME   1993   *Amending America: If We Love the Constitution So Much, Why Do We Keep Trying to Change It?* New York: Times Books/Random House.

KYVIG, DAVID E.   1996   *Explicit and Authentic Acts: Amending the U.S. Constitution, 1776–1995.* Lawrence: University of Kansas Press.

PORRITT, EDWARD and PORRITT, ANNIE G.   1909   *The Unreformed House of Commons: Parliamentary Representation Before 1832.* Cambridge, England: Cambridge University Press.

VILE, JOHN R.   1993   *Contemporary Questions Surrounding the Constitutional Amending Process.* Westport, Conn.: Praeger.

———   1994   *Constitutional Change in the United States: A Comparative Study of the Role of Constitutional Amendments, Judicial Interpretations, and Legislative and Executive Actions.* Westport, Conn.: Praeger.

———   1996   *Encyclopedia of Constitutional Amendments, Proposed Amendments, and Amending Issues, 1789–1995.* Santa Barbara, Calif.: ABC-CLIO.

# TWENTY-SIXTH AMENDMENT

Congress proposed the Twenty-Sixth Amendment on March 23, 1971. Ratification was completed in 107 days, the shortest time ever required to complete the AMENDING PROCESS. The amendment standardized the voting age in all federal, state, and local elections at eighteen.

Under the Constitution the power to establish qualifications for voting in all elections was left to the states, except that the qualifications to vote for representatives in Congress (and, after the SEVENTEENTH AMENDMENT, for senators) had to be the same as those to vote for members of the most numerous branch of the state legislature. Under various amendments, VOTING RIGHTS could not constitutionally be denied or abridged on account of race, color, previous servitude, sex, or failure to pay taxes; the FOURTEENTH AMENDMENT set twenty-one as the highest minimum age a state could require for voters. Before 1970 only four states had enacted a minimum voting age lower than twenty-one.

In the VOTING RIGHTS AMENDMENTS of 1970, Congress purported to lower the voting age to eighteen for all elections. The Supreme Court, in OREGON V. MITCHELL (1970), upheld the statute, insofar as it pertained to federal elections, under Article I, section 4, which authorizes Congress to regulate the time and manner of elections of its members; but the Court held the act unconstitutional insofar as it pertained to state elections. The decision threatened to throw the 1972 elections into chaos, because in most states the voting age for balloting for federal officials would have been different from the voting age for state races. The rapidity with which the amendment was ratified is attributable to a general desire to avoid such chaos.

Although Congress, in proposing the amendment, expressed confidence in the "idealism and concern and energy" the new voters would bring to the political system, the actual effect of the amendment has been less than revolutionary. Empirical studies have shown that eighteen-to-twenty-one-year-olds have the lowest voter turnout rate of any age group; and those who do vote do not differ markedly from the rest of the population concerning political parties or issues.

DENNIS J. MAHONEY
(1986)

# TWENTY-THIRD AMENDMENT

Proposed by Congress on June 17, 1960, the Twenty-Third Amendment became effective on March 29, 1961. The amendment includes residents of the DISTRICT OF COLUMBIA in the process of electing the President and Vice-President by allowing them to choose members of the ELECTORAL COLLEGE. The influence of the district is limited by the proviso permitting it no more electoral votes than the least populous state—in practice fixing the district's electoral votes at three.

As the amendment was introduced by Senator Kenneth Keating, of New York, it would have allocated the District of Columbia as many electoral votes as a state with the same population and would have permitted the district to elect representatives to Congress on the same basis. Representative Emmanuel Celler, of New York, chairman of the House Judiciary Committee, reduced it to its final form in order to insure passage. Celler's committee also separated the District of Columbia suffrage amendment from two other amendments (on Congressional vacancies and POLL TAXES) to which the SENATE had linked it.

There was some opposition from Republicans, who predicted the district would inevitably support Democratic candidates, and Southerners, who feared the amendment would increase the political power of blacks.

DENNIS J. MAHONEY
(1986)

## TWINING v. NEW JERSEY
### 211 U.S. 78 (1908)

*Twining* formed part of the line of decisions, from HURTADO V. CALIFORNIA (1884) and MAXWELL V. DOW (1900) to PALKO V. CONNECTICUT (1937), in which the Supreme Court denied that the traditional Fifth and SIXTH AMENDMENT rights of accused persons were FUNDAMENTAL RIGHTS protected against state infringement by the FOURTEENTH AMENDMENT. In *Twining*, an eight-man majority, speaking through Justice WILLIAM H. MOODY, held that neither the PRIVILEGES AND IMMUNITIES clause nor the DUE PROCESS clause incorporated the RIGHT AGAINST SELF-INCRIMINATION. The Court also considered whether some of the personal rights safeguarded by the BILL OF RIGHTS might be safeguarded against the states because to deny those rights would be to deny due process of law. That is, apart from the question whether the Fourteenth Amendment's protection of immunities and liberty had the effect of incorporating the Fifth Amendment right, the Court also decided the question whether the concept of due process itself was of such a nature as to include the right against self-incrimination. Was a denial of that right a denial of due process?

Although Moody admitted that the Court would not allow history to "strait-jacket" constitutional law, he resorted to "every historical test" to determine how history "rated" the right in question. Moody was a pathetically poor historian; his mangling of the little evidence he knew led him wrongly to conclude that the right against self-incrimination was neither a fundamental right nor part of due process of law. On that reading of history he decided that the state had not violated the Constitution by permitting a trial court to instruct the jury that they might draw adverse inferences against a defendant because of his reliance on the right against self-incrimination or his failure to testify.

Justice JOHN MARSHALL HARLAN delivered another lone dissenting opinion, arguing that immunity against self-incrimination, like the right to INDICTMENT by GRAND JURY and the right to TRIAL BY JURY, should be deemed fundamental and applicable to the states. Whether he believed that the privileges and immunities clause or the due process clause, or both, incorporated the right is not clear; but he certainly believed it to be essential to due process.

At the time the Court held a narrower view of PROCEDURAL DUE PROCESS, it used an expanded SUBSTANTIVE DUE PROCESS to protect CORPORATIONS and prevent Congress from protecting trade unions (see *Adair v. United States*, 1908). *Adamson v. California* (1947) reaffirmed *Twining*, but the Court overruled both cases in MALLOY V. HOGAN (1964).

LEONARD W. LEVY
(1986)

(SEE ALSO: *Incorporation Doctrine*.)

## TWO GUYS FROM HARRISON-ALLENTOWN v. MCGINLEY

See: Sunday Closing Laws

## TWO-LEVEL THEORY

In an important 1960 article, Harry Kalven, Jr., coined the phrase "two-level theory." As he described it, FIRST AMENDMENT methodology classified speech at two levels. Some speech was so unworthy as to be beneath First Amendment protection: no First Amendment review was necessary. Thus the Court in CHAPLINSKY V. NEW HAMPSHIRE (1942) had referred to "certain well-defined and narrowly limited classes of speech, the prevention and punishment of which has never been thought to raise any constitutional problem. These include the lewd and obscene, the profane, the libelous, and the insulting or fighting words." At the second level, speech of constitutional value was protected unless it presented a CLEAR AND PRESENT DANGER of a substantive evil.

In a subsequent article Kalven observed that in NEW YORK TIMES V. SULLIVAN (1964) neither the two-level approach nor the clear and present danger test was an organizing strategy or guiding methodology. He expressed the hope that the *Sullivan* Court's unwillingness to employ the two-level theory presaged the theory's demise along with the clear and present danger test. Kalven's hopes have been only partially realized. Perhaps partly as a result of his persuasive efforts, the Court has been willing to scrutinize state justifications for regulating some types of speech previously thought to raise no constitutional problem. *Chaplinsky's* off-hand assumption that each class of speech in its litany raises no constitutional problem is no longer credible. Nonetheless, the Court continues to be impressed by *Chaplinsky's* famous OBITER DICTUM that speech beneath the protection of the First Amendment occupies that status because its slight contribution to truth is outweighed by the state interests in order and morality.

Kalven's hope for the complete repudiation of the clear and present danger doctrine also remains unfulfilled. A variation of the doctrine occupies a secure doctrinal place in the context of INCITEMENT TO UNLAWFUL CONDUCT, and the DENNIS V. UNITED STATES (1951) version of the test has been employed by the Court in other contexts, as in *Landmark Communications, Inc. v. Virginia* (1978) and NEBRASKA PRESS ASSOCIATION V. STUART (1976).

If doctrine were described today in terms of levels, many levels would be necessary. At one level, there is the question whether a First Amendment problem is presented: an effort to communicate a message by assassination presumably raises no First Amendment problem. If cognizable First Amendment values are present, there remains the question whether any legal protection is appropriate: advocacy of illegal action often is unprotected despite the existence of cognizable First Amendment interests. If some protection is appropriate, further questions remain: what protection in what contexts, at what times, in what places, and concerning what modes of expression? A multitude of doctrinal tests now govern a multitude of contexts. Harry Kalven would appreciate the Court's sensitivity to the vicissitudes of human conduct, but likely would regret the absence of an overall vision.

STEVEN SHIFFRIN
(1986)

Bibliography

KALVEN, HARRY, JR. 1960 The Metaphysics of the Law of Obscenity. *Supreme Court Review* 1960:1–45.
——— 1964 The New York Times Case: A Note on "The Central Meaning of the First Amendment." *Supreme Court Review* 1964:191–221.

# TWO SOVEREIGNTIES RULE

This rule, which the Supreme Court repudiated in *Murphy v. Waterfront Commission* (1964), was a limitation on the RIGHT AGAINST SELF-INCRIMINATION. Based on the federal principle that one sovereignty has no interest in the law enforcement activities of another, the rule was that a person could not refuse to testify on the grounds that his disclosure would subject him to prosecution by another sovereignty or JURISDICTION. Thus he could be convicted of a federal crime on the basis of testimony compelled in a state proceeding or of a state crime on the basis of testimony compelled in a federal proceeding. In matters involving national supremacy, Congress can grant immunity against state prosecutions, but a state cannot immunize against a federal prosecution and one state cannot immunize against prosecution in another.

The rule entered American constitutional law in 1906 in *Hale v. Henkel* as a result of the Court's factual mistakes. In that case the appellant, who had received a grant of immunity against federal prosecution, sought reversal of his conviction for contempt by a federal court for refusing to answer questions that exposed him to state prosecution. The Court needlessly declared that English COMMON LAW had settled the question by a rule that "the only danger to be considered is one arising within the same jurisdiction and under that same sovereignty." The Court cited two English cases, one not in point and the other soon discredited by a decision unknown to the Court. In *United States v. Murdock* (1933), a unanimous Court "definitely settled that one under examination in a federal tribunal could not refuse to answer on account of probable incrimination under state law," a proposition resting on *Hale* and the two English precedents. By 1944 the Court made the two sovereignties rule reciprocal, so that a suspect could be whipsawed into incriminating himself in one jurisdiction by receiving a grant of immunity from another. State and federal authorities sometimes assisted each other, one compelling disclosure, the other prosecuting. So matters stood until the *Murphy* case.

Although granted immunity by New York and New Jersey, Murphy remained silent because his answers might incriminate him under federal law. He won a reversal of his conviction when the Supreme Court, in an opinion by Justice ARTHUR J. GOLDBERG, exposed the erroneous basis of the precedents and concluded that the two sovereignties rule had no support in history or in the policies underlying the Fifth Amendment right. On the same day, in

MALLOY V. HOGAN (1964), the Court extended that right to the states. Given that extension and a broad view of the right, the Court held that a state witness is protected against incrimination under both federal and state law and a federal witness is similarly protected. Justices BYRON R. WHITE and POTTER STEWART concurred separately. *Murphy* also stands for the proposition that use immunity rather than TRANSACTIONAL IMMUNITY satisfies the demand of the Fifth Amendment at least in a two sovereignties case.

A two sovereignties rule still operates with respect to DOUBLE JEOPARDY: a person may be prosecuted for both state and federal crimes committed by the same act.

LEONARD W. LEVY
(1986)

# TYLER, JOHN
## (1790–1862)

A Virginia lawyer, governor, and United States senator, John Tyler, a Democrat elected Vice-President as a Whig in 1840 became America's first accidental President upon the death of William Henry Harrison in 1841. This peaceful transition of leaders underscored the strength of the Constitution even though it frustrated the Whig politicians who had nominated Harrison. As President, Tyler was usually a constitutional strict constructionist, and many of his policies resembled those of ANDREW JACKSON. Tyler refused to interfere with the SOVEREIGNTY of Rhode Island during Dorr's Rebellion, but he was an early advocate of Texas annexation which was accomplished in the last months of his administration. In 1861 Tyler chaired the Washington Peace Conference, but after its failure he advocated SECESSION. The only former President to serve the Confederacy, Tyler was elected to the provisional Congress and the Confederate House of Representatives.

PAUL FINKELMAN
(1986)

Bibliography

MORGAN, ROBERT J.   1954   *A Whig Embattled: The Presidency of John Tyler.* Lincoln: University of Nebraska Press.

# *TYSON & BROTHER v. BANTON*
## 273 U.S. 418 (1927)

Citing Chief Justice WILLIAM HOWARD TAFT's opinion in WOLFF PACKING COMPANY V. COURT OF INDUSTRIAL RELATIONS (1923), Justice GEORGE SUTHERLAND found unconstitutional a New York statute regulating ticket "scalpers." The state based the law on a declaration that theater prices were AFFECTED WITH A PUBLIC INTEREST, but because the theater business did not fit Taft's categories, the law fell as a violation of FREEDOM OF CONTRACT and a denial of DUE PROCESS OF LAW.

Justice OLIVER WENDELL HOLMES dissented: "a state legislature may do whatever it sees fit to do unless it is restrained by some express prohibition in the [federal or state] constitution." Justice LOUIS D. BRANDEIS joined him and Justice HARLAN FISKE STONE wrote a separate dissent. All three urged rejection of the public interest concept—"a fiction intended to beautify what is disagreeable to the sufferers"—in favor of state regulation wherever the public welfare demanded it.

DAVID GORDON
(1986)

(SEE ALSO: *New State Ice Company v. Liebmann; Ribnik v. McBride.*)

# U

## ULLMANN v. UNITED STATES
### 350 U.S. 422 (1956)

Ullmann, relying on his right not to be a witness against himself, refused to testify before a federal GRAND JURY concerning his alleged communist activities. Though he received immunity against prosecution for any criminal transaction concerning which he was compelled to testify, he continued pertinacious. Ullmann argued against the constitutionality of the congressional Immunity Act of 1954 on the grounds that it did not immunize him from such disabilities as loss of job, expulsion from labor unions, compulsory registration as a subversive, passport ineligibility, and general public opprobrium. Thus he distinguished his case from BROWN V. WALKER (1896) on the theory that he had not received full transactional immunity. The Court rejected Ullmann's argument, 7–2. Justice FELIX FRANKFURTER for the majority reasoned that the Fifth Amendment's right to silence operated only to prevent the compulsion of testimony that might expose one to a criminal charge. The disabilities to which Ullmann claimed exposure were not criminal penalties. Justices WILLIAM O. DOUGLAS and HUGO L. BLACK, dissenting, would have held the immunity act unconstitutional on the ground that the right of silence created by the Fifth Amendment is beyond the reach of Congress. Douglas contended that the amendment was designed to protect against INFAMY, as well as prosecution, and against forfeitures—those disabilities of which Ullmann spoke—as well as criminal fines and imprisonment.

LEONARD W. LEVY
(1986)

## ULTRA VIRES

(Latin: "Beyond powers.") This term applies either to acts taken by a CORPORATION beyond the limits of its chartered (legally authorized) powers or to acts of a public official beyond his or her delegated authority.

DAVID GORDON
(1986)

## "ULYSSES," ONE BOOK ENTITLED, UNITED STATES v.
### 5F. Supp. 182 (1933)
### 72 F.2d 705 (1934)

Although it was not a decision of the Supreme Court, *Ulysses* was not merely a case involving a famous book and prominent judges but also a harbinger of modern decisions on OBSCENITY. Its standards for construing the COMMON LAW terms embodied in federal customs regulations were transmuted in UNITED STATES V. ROTH (1957) into constitutional principles for testing both federal and state legislation on the subject.

The handful of early obscenity cases that reached the Supreme Court mainly presented claims of technical error in the trials below. *Ulysses* presented clear questions of substantive standards for adjudging obscenity and lewdness. The established reputation of the book insured careful attention; Judge John M. Woolsey's lower court opinion was unmistakably written for the anthologies it ultimately graced. Judge AUGUSTUS N. HAND's appellate majority opinion was straightforward, but Judge Martin T. Manton's dissent was somewhat verbose.

Woolsey declared that the book successfully showed "how the screen [sic] of consciousness with its ever-shifting kaleidoscopic impression carries, as it were on a plastic palimpsest, . . . a penumbral zone residual of past impressions . . . not unlike the result of a double or, if that is possible, a multiple exposure on a cinema film. . . ."

The relevant statute on importation of books prohibited not pandering but obscenity. Woolsey announced without discussion that the test for obscenity required examination of the whole work. The standard was the effect on "what the French would call *l'homme moyen sensuel*—who plays, in this branch of legal inquiry . . . the same role . . . as does the "reasonable man in the law of torts. . . ." With this standard he found the book "somewhat emetic, nowhere . . . an aphrodisiac." He also found Joyce to have been sincere and lacking pornographic intent or the "leer of the sensualist."

At the appellate level Augustus Hand for himself and LEARNED HAND managed to come to grips with the central legal issue—whether isolated passages could render a work of art obscene. This was the test derived from *Regina v. Hicklin* (1868), the classic British case, and, they conceded, followed in *United States v. Bennett* (1879), a CIRCUIT COURT decision by Justice SAMUEL BLATCHFORD. They discounted other alleged precedents and argued that the isolated passages concept was not followed for works of science or medicine and should not be followed for literature either. They cited state decisions embracing the "dominant effect" notion, and read that test (together with their definition of the relevant audience) into the statute, concluding that other readings would be impractical and overrestrictive.

Manton, dissenting, insisted that federal decisions in the past had accepted the "isolated passages" test. As literature was for amusement only, the community could reasonably demand that it meet moral standards—those of average, not exceptional, individuals.

SAMUEL KRISLOV
(1986)

Bibliography

LOCKHART, WILLIAM B. and MCCLURE, ROBERT C. 1954 Literature, the Law of Obscenity, and the Constitution. *Minnesota Law Review* 38:295–395.

# UNCONSTITUTIONAL CONDITIONS

Although government may not be obligated to provide its citizens with a certain benefit or privilege, it is not free to condition granting the benefit or privilege on the recipient's relinquishing a constitutional right. Likewise, the government may not withhold or cancel the benefit by way of penalizing the assertion of a constitutional right. For example, in SHERBERT V. VERNER (1963) the Supreme Court held South Carolina's unemployment compensation act unconstitutional as applied to exclude a Seventh Day Adventist from benefits when she would not find a job releasing her from work on Saturdays. Withholding the benefits effectively penalized exercise of the claimant's RELIGIOUS LIBERTY.

It has sometimes been argued that a legislature's greater power of withholding a benefit must necessarily include the lesser power of granting the benefit with restrictions. On this theory, the recipient of the benefit is deprived of no right, for the right can be retained simply by rejecting the proffered benefit. This logic leads to drastic consequences as government becomes increasingly involved in supplying such vital needs as jobs, housing, welfare, and EDUCATION.

As early as *Frost & Frost Trucking Company v. Railroad Commission* (1926) the Court recognized the potential for excess conditions on the exercise of constitutional rights: "If the state may compel the surrender of one constitutional right as a condition of its favor, it may, in like manner, compel a surrender of all. It is inconceivable that guarantees embedded in the Constitution of the United States may thus be manipulated out of existence."

Subsequent courts have rarely been persuaded by arguments claiming an absolute power of government to condition and limit the grant of general benefits. Rather, they have generally recognized that the revocation of benefits amounts to regulatory activity by government, for which sufficient justification must be established if constitutional rights are restricted. This doctrine of unconstitutional conditions has been successfully applied to restrain assertions of unlimited governmental power in four major substantial areas: the privilege of out-of-state corporations to engage in local business; the use of public property and facilities; the receipt of entitlements and social service benefits; and government employment.

As early as 1839, the Supreme Court announced that a state might exclude out-of-state corporations from conducting business within its borders. In early cases, this power to exclude was held sufficient to justify highly unreasonable conditions on entry and even the arbitrary revocation of a corporation's license. Subsequent Court decisions, however, have subjected such regulations to DUE PROCESS standards. Given the Court's increasing sensitivity to national interests in economic growth and the smooth functioning of the federal system, it is not surprising that the Court invoked the doctrine of unconstitutional conditions to check a power previously thought to be virtually absolute.

In 1897 the Court upheld an ordinance that prohibited public speaking in a municipal park without a permit from the mayor. The Court reasoned that ownership of the land gave the city the right to withhold access completely; the city therefore could grant access on any conditions, including those restricting FIRST AMENDMENT freedoms. This logic has been invalidated by later decisions which have viewed the manipulation of access to streets and parks as regulatory activity subject to constitutional attack. (See PUBLIC FORUM.)

Given the large number of benefits now provided by government, the imposition of conditions on the recipients of such benefits raises a significant possibility of undermining individual liberties. The Supreme Court has used unconstitutional condition analysis to prevent such a result in cases involving unemployment compensation, WELFARE BENEFITS, public housing, tax exemptions, public education, and the mail services. One leading doctrinal basis for these decisions has been the guarantee of PROCEDURAL DUE PROCESS.

In *McAuliffe v. Mayor of New England* (1892) the Massachusetts Supreme Judicial Court denied the petition of a policeman who had been fined for violating a regulation restricting his political activity. Justice OLIVER WENDELL HOLMES, speaking for the state court, stated: "The petitioner may have a constitutional right to talk politics, but he has no constitutional right to be a policeman. . . . There are few employments for hire in which the servant does not agree to suspend his constitutional right of free speech, as well as of idleness, by the implied terms of his contract. The servant cannot complain, as he takes his employment on the terms which are offered him." More recently, however, courts have found conditions on employees unconstitutional irrespective of any abstract right to public employment. The courts have asked whether the condition restricts employment in a "patently arbitrary and discriminatory manner" in violation of due process, as set forth in WIEMAN V. UPDEGRAFF (1952), and whether, in withholding or revoking employment under conditions capable of improper application, the state is penalizing specific constitutional freedoms.

Although claims of unconstitutional conditions in these four areas have become less common in recent years, the doctrine has recently emerged in the sphere of CRIMINAL PROCEDURE, particularly in cases involving the guilty plea. PLEA BARGAINING effectively penalizes the exercise of the right to trial by rewarding those who plead guilty. In addition, it denies the individual the RIGHT AGAINST SELF-INCRIMINATION and the right to confront and cross-examine witnesses against him. The Court, however, has endorsed the use of plea bargaining. Rather than address the challenges raised by the unconstitutional conditions doctrine, the Court has insisted only that guilty pleas be "voluntary and intelligent" and that the plea bargaining process conform to certain standards of fairness. The tension between the principle of unconstitutional conditions and the Court's endorsement of plea bargaining seems likely to produce future controversy.

ARTHUR ROSETT
(1986)

Bibliography

VAN ALSTYNE, WILLIAM W. 1968 The Demise of the Right-Privilege Distinction in Constitutional Law. *Harvard Law Review* 81:1439–1464.

# UNCONSTITUTIONAL CONDITIONS
## (Update)

Unconstitutional conditions problems arise when government conditions allocation of a benefit such as public PROPERTY, jobs, or funds upon surrender of a constitutional right. Government's coercive deprivation of a right through the imposition of criminal or civil liability normally triggers a demand for strong justification. Government's mere exercise of budgetary discretion, however, normally triggers only deferential JUDICIAL REVIEW. The DOCTRINE of unconstitutional conditions holds that some selective allocations of benefits are equivalent to coercive deprivations of rights. The difficulty is in determining when this is so.

The Supreme Court has tended to steer between two polar positions. On the one hand, it has declined to hold that government has absolute allocative discretion when it acts in its capacity as property owner, employer, or patron. This view is epitomized by the famous epigram of Justice OLIVER WENDELL HOLMES, JR., in *McAuliffe v. Mayor of New England* (1892) that a policeman "may have a constitutional right to talk politics, but he has no constitutional right to be a policeman." On the other hand, the Court has also declined to hold that constitutional limits extend to government in these proprietary capacities as completely as they do to government in its sovereign capacity. Instead, the Court has tended to draw a series of public/private distinctions among conditions on benefits, categorizing some as akin to the exercise of sovereign power subject to strong constitutional constraints and others as the mere exercise of managerial prerogative.

FREEDOM OF SPEECH claims provide the most abundant recent examples of such categorization, which may be considered separately with respect to conditions upon speech on public property, speech by PUBLIC EMPLOYEES, and speech by recipients of public funds. Under a long line of decisions recognizing certain public property as PUBLIC FORUMS, government may not condition speakers' access to public streets or parks on submission to government content control or excessive time, place, or manner regulation. But a more recent line of decisions exempts a wide range of government property other than streets and parks from such constitutional limitations. For example, government may pick and choose which speakers may place circulars in public school teachers' mailboxes, solicit funds in charitable fund drives in public workplaces, demonstrate or petition on sidewalks abutting post offices, solicit donations in airport terminals, or participate in a candidate debate broadcast on public television—even though such discrimination would not be allowed among speakers in streets and parks. Each of these locations within the vast realm of government property has been deemed a "nonpublic forum," in which government may condition access as selectively as it likes so long as it acts reasonably and avoids discrimination on the basis of viewpoint.

The Court has divided claims against speech-restrictive conditions on public employment along similar lines. On the one hand, public employees do not shed their First Amendment rights at the workplace gate, and government may not without strong justification condition retention of their jobs on silence in their public capacities as citizens. A public school teacher may criticize a school board for spending too much on athletics, a clerical worker in a sheriff's office may express bantering disappointment that an attempted assassination of the President was unsuccessful, and civil servants may receive honoraria for their off-duty speeches or articles—all without job sanction unless the government can make a particularized showing that such speech will disrupt the workplace or impair government efficiency. On the other hand, public employees may be freely discharged or demoted for expressing mere LABOR grievances internal to their workplace, such as soliciting coworker expression of hostility toward the boss. Similarly, a government job or contract may not be conditioned upon PATRONAGE or the recipient's association with the incumbent POLITICAL PARTY, except in a narrow set of confidential or policymaking positions.

In challenges to the selective allocation of public funds to some speakers and not others, the Court has distinguished between the mere refusal to subsidize speech of particular content, which is constitutional unless aimed at the suppression of a particular viewpoint, and the impermissible use of the leverage of the government funding to alter what the speaker would otherwise say with private resources. For example, government may not condition a public BROADCASTING subsidy on a station's foregoing all editorializing even if funded with private contributions. But government may withhold a subsidy in the form of tax benefits from the lobbying efforts of a nonprofit organization when this nonsubsidy does not affect the nonlobbying speech or advocacy of the organization, and may limit family planning funds to those health care entities that agree not to advocate or counsel women about ABORTION. As the MAJORITY OPINION in RUST V. SULLIVAN (1991) stated, "when the government appropriates public funds to establish a program it is entitled to define the limits of that program."

The doctrine of unconstitutional conditions in the First Amendment area was largely the handiwork of the late Justice WILLIAM J. BRENNAN, JR., who wrote in SPEISER V. RANDALL (1958) and in SHERBERT V. VERNER (1963) that in an expanded WELFARE STATE, the deprivation of a government benefit might penalize or deter the exercise of constitutional rights to the same extent as a criminal fine. His assumption seemed to be that if government had enough market power, it could distort the interplay of ideas in society by wielding carrots as well as sticks. At the extreme, this is certainly true; if government were the sole provider of an opportunity, then a condition on government allocation of that opportunity would have the same effects as a coercive regulation, for there would be no escape from government monopoly. Brennan may also have assumed that, even if the public sector were more limited, rights-pressuring conditions on government benefits would create a caste system in which those who are dependent on government aid enjoy more constricted opportunity to exercise constitutional rights than those with private means.

The REHNQUIST COURT might well have been expected to be less receptive to the doctrine of unconstitutional conditions. Chief Justice WILLIAM H. REHNQUIST himself has been an ardent critic of the doctrine. For example, he criticized the majority's decision to give First Amendment scrutiny to public school library book removals in *Pico v. Board of Education* (1982), arguing that "the role of government as sovereign is subject to more stringent limitations than is the role of government as employer, property owner, or educator." He likewise criticized the majority in *Federal Communications Commission v. League of Women Voters* (1984), which invalidated anti-editorializing conditions on public broadcasting subsidies, for treating the government as "the 'Big Bad Wolf'" to the public broadcaster's "'Little Red Riding Hood'" when in fact "some of the food in the basket was given to Little Red Riding Hood by the Big Bad Wolf himself."

This view, as opposed to Brennan's, appears to assume that for most purposes government is not a monopolist but rather just one speaker among many, and therefore is not able to repress dissent as effectively through conditions on benefits as it can through regulation. One who loses public funds may seek private patrons, and there are private substitutes for public space or jobs. On this view, a condition on the allocation of public space, salary, or subsidy is not a coercive exercise of power so much as a contractual offer and acceptance. For example, Justice ANTONIN SCALIA, concurring in the Court's decision in *National Endowment for the Arts v. Finley* (1998), which upheld a condition that public arts grants meet general standards of "decency" and "respect" for public values, wrote that there is a fundamental difference "between 'abridging' speech and funding it," and that the First Amendment is simply inapplicable to the selective allocation of funds.

Nonetheless, the Holmesean views expressed in these examples by Rehnquist and Scalia have failed to garner a majority on the Court, leaving the doctrine of unconstitutional conditions intact if somewhat curtailed. The Court has continued to hold, moreover, that even when acting in its proprietary capacities, government, unlike a purely private landlord, employer, or patron, may not engage in viewpoint discrimination unless it is enlisting the sponsored person to express a message on the polity's behalf. For example, in ROSENBERGER V. RECTOR & VISITORS OF THE UNIVERSITY OF VIRGINIA (1995), a majority of the Court (joined among others by Rehnquist and Scalia) held that a public university that funds a range of student publications from a mandatory student activities fee may not decline to subsidize an avowedly Christian student magazine for reason of its religious perspective.

Nor are recent applications of the unconstitutional conditions principle limited to the First Amendment. In *South Dakota v. Dole* (1987), which upheld a requirement that states receiving federal highway funds raise their minimum drinking age, the Court suggested that there is some outer limit to how far the federal government may go in using regulatory conditions on federal funding to induce state adherence to federal policy. And in *Nollan v. California Coastal Commission* (1987) and DOLAN V. TIGARD (1994), the Court held that government may not use its power to withhold a ZONING variance as leverage to take access to property for reasons not closely related to the zoning law's purpose. In both the FEDERALISM and the TAKING OF PROPERTY areas, as in the free speech area, unconstitutional conditions doctrine helps limit the use of government economic leverage to influence the exercise of constitutional rights.

KATHLEEN M. SULLIVAN
(2000)

(SEE ALSO: *Government as Proprietor.*)

Bibliography

COLE, DAVID 1992 Beyond Unconstitutional Conditions: Charting Spheres of Neutrality in Government-Funded Speech. *New York University Law Review* 67:675–749.

EPSTEIN, RICHARD 1994 *Bargaining with the State.* Cambridge, Mass.: Harvard University Press.

POST, ROBERT C. 1996 Subsidized Speech. *Yale Law Journal* 106:151–195.

SULLIVAN, KATHLEEN M. 1989 Unconstitutional Conditions. *Harvard Law Review* 102:1413–1506.

# UNCONSTITUTIONALITY

The American concept of unconstitutionality was born before the Constitution was adopted. The STAMP ACT CONGRESS of 1765, for example, declared that acts of Parliament imposing TAXATION WITHOUT REPRESENTATION were unconstitutional and need not be obeyed. Then as now, of course, the British constitution was an unwritten collection of customs and usages, only partly reflected in statutes and COMMON LAW principles. Since the adoption of the earliest state constitutions, however, the statement that a governmental action is unconstitutional has been taken as an assertion that the action violates a written constitution. In common speech, "unconstitutional" normally refers to an action's invalidity under the United States Constitution, but in law the term also refers to invalidity under a state constitution. Legislation is not the only form of governmental action that may be unconstitutional. When police officers conduct unreasonable SEARCHES AND SEIZURES, for example, they act unconstitutionally. Similarly, a state court acts unconstitutionally when it enforces a racially RESTRICTIVE COVENANT.

An assertion of unconstitutionality can be made by anyone: a citizen making a complaint, a newspaper editorial writer, a lawyer arguing a case. The assertion may take on a more authoritative character when it is made by a public officer acting in a governmental capacity. Thus, the President might veto a bill passed by Congress on the ground that it is unconstitutional. (See CIVIL RIGHTS ACT OF 1866; JACKSON'S VETO OF THE BANK BILL.) Or, the President might refuse to enforce an act of Congress on similar grounds. Such a presidential refusal led the House of Representatives to adopt ARTICLES OF IMPEACHMENT against ANDREW JOHNSON, thus registering its view that Johnson's conduct was itself unconstitutional. An executive officer may decline to enforce a law for the purpose of allowing others to frame a TEST CASE, thus allowing the courts to rule on the law's validity. BOARD OF EDUCATION V. ALLEN (1968) resulted from one such refusal.

The official in *Allen* thought it important to get a judicial ruling on the constitutionality of the law in question. In fact, Americans have become accustomed to identifying the idea of unconstitutionality with a judicial declaration of unconstitutionality—and, in particular, with such a declaration by the Supreme Court. A lawyer, asked by a client whether a law is or is not constitutional, ordinarily will respond with a prediction of what the courts will hold.

From MARBURY V. MADISON (1803) forward, American courts have assumed that they have the power to disregard a statute that violates a constitutional norm. When a court holds a statute unconstitutional it refuses to give effect to the law in the case before it. Indeed, the *Marbury* opinion grounded the principle of JUDICIAL REVIEW in the need for a court to decide the case before it according to law, including the Constitution as the supreme law. Federal courts are not permitted to give ADVISORY OPINIONS on the law but make their constitutional rulings only in the context of concrete CASES AND CONTROVERSIES. Yet there is a sense in which any opinion is, in part, advisory. The statement of a reason for decision requires a court to move from the particulars of the case before it to the more abstract level of a rule or principle which can be applied later as a precedent in deciding another appropriate case. Occasionally, particularly in the area of the FREEDOMS OF SPEECH and of the PRESS, a court may hold a law INVALID ON ITS FACE. But even if the court merely says it is holding the law "invalid as applied," the ruling becomes a precedent for other applications to similar facts.

In a statement now famous for its inaccuracy, the Supreme Court said in *Norton v. Shelby County* (1886) that an unconstitutional law "is not a law; it confers no rights; it imposes no duties; it affords no protection; it creates no office; it is, in legal contemplation, as inoperative as though it had never been passed." The statement is misleading in two respects. First, courts are no better than anyone else at undoing the past. A great many actions may be taken on the basis of a statute in the time between its enactment and its judicial invalidation. Justice often requires that those actions be given effect: a corporation organized under an invalid statute will be bound under its contracts; an official who enforces a law in good faith before the law is held invalid will not be liable in damages for the action. In *Lemon v. Kurtzman II* (1973), the Supreme Court allowed Pennsylvania to reimburse church schools for educational services performed under a statute before the Court had held the law invalid in LEMON V. KURTZMAN I (1971).

Second, the *Norton* statement is misleading in the context of an OVERRULING of a previous decision that has held a statute invalid. In ADKINS V. CHILDREN'S HOSPITAL (1923) the Supreme Court had held the DISTRICT OF COLUMBIA MINIMUM WAGE LAW unconstitutional, but in WEST COAST HOTEL CO. V. PARRISH (1937), the Court overruled *Adkins*. Was it then necessary for Congress to reenact the law for it to be effective? The attorney general issued an opinion answering this question negatively, and no one now challenges that opinion's soundness.

Determining whether a court has actually held a law unconstitutional may prove more difficult than identifying the court's HOLDING on the underlying constitutional law. In dealing with a federal statute, for example, the Supreme Court may make clear its view of the Constitution's command, but it may not make clear whether it has held the statute invalid or construed the statute narrowly to avoid holding it unconstitutional. Such an ambiguity still bemuses collectors of antique trivia when they contemplate HODGSON V. BOWERBANK (1809).

Ultimately, the notion of unconstitutionality refers not so much to a fact—or even an opinion, judicial or otherwise—as to a decisional process. In that process courts play the most prominent role, but now and then they yield the center of the stage to other actors. (See ABRAHAM LINCOLN; THOMAS JEFFERSON; WATERGATE AND THE CONSTITUTION.)

KENNETH L. KARST
(1986)

Bibliography

BICKEL, ALEXANDER M. 1962 *The Least Dangerous Branch: The Supreme Court at the Bar of Politics.* Indianapolis: Bobbs-Merrill.

FIELD, OLIVER P. 1935 *The Effect of an Unconstitutional Statute.* Minneapolis: University of Minnesota Press.

# UNENUMERATED RIGHTS

The starting point for interpreting the NINTH AMENDMENT is its text: "The enumeration in the Constitution of certain rights shall not be construed to deny or disparage others retained by the people." The text and the rule of construction that requires plain meaning to be followed clearly establishes the existence of unenumerated rights. Why would the Framers have included an amendment that protects such rights in the midst of the BILL OF RIGHTS, which specifies rights in the first eight amendments?

The Framers scarcely had an alternative after they botched an explanation for their failure to have included a bill of rights as part of the original Constitution. They protected a few rights in it, but ignored most; and they subsequently made several frail and foolish explanations instead of confessing misjudgment and promising subsequent amendments. As a result they placed RATIFICATION in serious jeopardy. The Constitution was finally ratified only because crucial states, where ratification had been in doubt, accepted a pledge that a bill of rights would be added to the Constitution in the form of amendments.

THE FEDERALIST #84 presented a commonplace ratificationist argument that boomeranged and made necessary a provision safeguarding unspecified rights. According to ALEXANDER HAMILTON, a bill of rights was unnecessary and even dangerous, because by containing exceptions to powers not granted, it would provide a basis for repressive LEGISLATION. For example, to say that liberty of the press ought not be restricted furnished "a plausible pretense" for the very power feared, a power to legislate on the press, because a provision "against restraining the liberty of the press afforded a clear implication that a power to prescribe proper regulations concerning it was intended to be vested in the national government." Equally dangerous, the omission of some right in a catalogue of rights allowed the assumption that it was meant to be unguarded. JAMES MADISON, OLIVER ELLSWORTH, and JAMES WILSON, among other leading Framers, made the same damaging argument.

Their logic, which nearly undid their cause, surely merited public rejection. They proved that the particular rights that the unamended Constitution protected—no RELIGIOUS TESTS, bans on BILLS OF ATTAINDER and EX POST FACTO LAWS, and TRIALS BY JURY in criminal cases, among other rights—stood in grave jeopardy because to specify a right implied a power to violate it. Moreover, the inclusion of some rights in the Constitution implied, contradictorily, that all unenumerated ones were relinquished. The unsatisfactory arguments by ratificationists imperiled their cause and obliged them to reconsider.

Madison switched to the cause of amending the Constitution with a bill of rights in order to appease the fears of the people. When he rose in Congress to propose constitutional amendments, he asserted that the Constitution must "expressly declare the great rights of mankind." He acknowledged that a major objection to a bill of rights consisted of the argument that "by enumerating particular exceptions to the grant of power, it would disparage those rights which were not placed in that enumeration; and it might follow, by implication, that those rights which were not singled out, were intended to be assigned into the hands of the General Government, and were consequently insecure." This claim had become a ratificationist cliché that self-destructed because the Constitution explicitly protected several rights exposing all those omitted, including "the great rights of mankind" to governmental violation. Madison's solution was the simple proposal that became the Ninth Amendment. It was, he said, meant to guard against the possibility that unenumerated rights might be at risk as a result of the enumeration of some. By excepting enumerated rights from the grant of powers, no implication was intended and no inference should be drawn that rights not excepted from the grant of powers were at risk. As Madison phrased his proposal, it read as follows: "The exceptions [to power] here or elsewhere in the constitution made in favor of particular rights, shall not be so construed as to diminish the just importance of other rights retained by the people. . . ."

What were the unenumerated rights retained by the people? They had to be either "natural rights" or "positive rights," to use Madison's own terms. He distinguished "the preexistent rights of nature" from those "resulting from a SOCIAL COMPACT." He mentioned freedom of "speach" (sic) as a natural right, but failed to include it in his recommendations. (A committee rectified this oversight.) His omission illustrates his acknowledgment of an important right that briefly fell within the unenumerated category. In Madison's thinking, this category also included the natural right of the people to govern themselves and to alter their government when it was inadequate to its purposes. Those purposes embodied another unenumerated natural right: governments are instituted to secure the people "in the enjoyment of life and liberty, with the right of acquiring and using property and generally of pursuing and obtaining happiness and safety." Madison had borrowed from the preamble of the DECLARATION OF INDEPENDENCE, which expressed opinions on natural rights that were shared by virtually all Americans and were central to the meaning of the Ninth Amendment.

Its text meant what it said; its context consists of the widespread endorsement of natural rights at the time of the framing of the Bill of Rights. STATE CONSTITUTIONS referred to natural rights. Virginia's 1788 recommendations for amendments to the Constitution did so also, as had New York's and North Carolina's. At the Pennsylvania ratifying convention, James Wilson, second only to Madison as an architect of the Constitution, quoted the preamble of the Declaration of Independence and added, "This is the broad basis on which our independence was placed; on the same certain and solid foundation this system [the Constitution] is erected."

The Framers also believed that all people had a right to equal justice and to equality of rights before the law. That slaveholders subscribed to such opinions proves the inconsistency of some of the Framers and their inability to transform their societies. But ABRAHAM LINCOLN understood when he described the creation of a new nation "conceived in liberty and dedicated to the proposition that all men are created equal." The Ninth Amendment embodied the principle of equality as well as that of liberty. Madison himself, when presenting his recommended amendments, spoke of "the perfect equality of mankind." Other natural rights that were unenumerated included the right, then important, to hunt and fish; the RIGHT TO TRAVEL; the right to associate freely with others; and the right to intimate association or privacy in matters concerning family and sex, at least within the bounds of marriage. Such rights were fundamental to the pursuit of happiness.

In addition to natural rights, the unenumerated rights included some that were positive, deriving not from "Nature's God," but from social compacts that created governments. What positive rights were familiar when the Ninth Amendment became part of the Constitution, yet were not enumerated in the original text or the first eight amendments? The right to vote and hold office, the right of free elections, the right not to be taxed except by consent through representatives of one's choice, the right to be free from monopolies, the right to be free from standing armies in time of peace, the right to refuse military service on grounds of religious conscience, the right to choose a profession, and the right of an accused person to an initial presumption of innocence and to have the prosecution shoulder the responsibility of proving guilt beyond a REASONABLE DOUBT—all these were among existing positive rights protected by various state laws, state constitutions, and the COMMON LAW; and all were unenumerated. Any of these rights, among others, could legitimately be regarded as rights of the people before which the powers of government must be exercised in subordination.

In addition to rights then known, the Ninth Amendment probably had the purpose of providing the basis for unknown rights that time alone might disclose. Nothing in the thinking of the Framers foreclosed the possibility that new rights might claim the loyalties of succeeding generations. As EDMUND PENDLETON, Virginia's chief justice and a leading ratificationist, mused when the Bill of Rights was being framed, "May we not in the progress of things, discover some great and important [right], which we don't now think of?"

Without doubt, to read the Ninth Amendment as a cornucopia of unenumerated rights is an invitation to JUDICIAL ACTIVISM. As Professor John Hart Ely has written, if natural rights in particular are read into the amendment, it does not lend itself "to principled judicial enforcement." But neither do enumerated rights—natural or positive. FREEDOM OF SPEECH and DUE PROCESS OF LAW, to mention one of each kind of right, have resulted in some of the most subjective result-oriented constitutional JURISPRUDENCE in our history. The fact that judicial decisions can be unprincipled or biased does not detract from the principle expressed in a right, whether or not it is enumerated.

If the Ninth Amendment instructs us to look beyond its four corners for unenumerated rights of the people, as it does, it must have some content. To read it as if it is merely the converse side of the TENTH AMENDMENT is to confuse the two amendments, as did Professor Raoul Berger. He spoke of "the ninth's retention of rights by the states or the people." It is the Tenth Amendment that reserves powers, not rights, to the states or to the people. The Ninth Amendment, according to Berger, "was merely declaratory of a basic presupposition: all powers not "positively' granted are reserved to the people. It added no unspecified rights to the Bill of Rights." In fact, however,

an explicit declaration of the existence of unenumerated rights is an addition of unspecified rights to the Bill of Rights. Confusion between the Ninth and Tenth amendments originated with proposals for amendments by Virginia in 1788. Moreover, Madison himself argued that the line between a power granted and a right retained by the people amounted to the same thing if a right were named. Unenumerated rights, however, are not named, and no affirmative power has been delegated to regulate or abridge them.

Without doubt, the Ninth Amendment and its problem of identifying unenumerated rights continue to bedevil interpreters, on and off the bench. Courts do continue to discover rights that have no textual existence and might be considered unenumerated, but for the judicial propensity to ignore the Ninth Amendment and make believe that some unspecified right under discussion derives from a right that is enumerated. Opponents of such rights howl their denunciation of judicial activism. Court-invented rights exceed in number the rights enumerated. Judges have composed rights great and small, including the MIRANDA RULES, the right to engage in nude dancing with pasties and G-string, the right to engage in FLAG DESECRATION, the right to secure an ABORTION, or the right against the invasion of an expectation of privacy.

So long as we continue to believe that government is instituted for the sake of securing the rights of the people and must exercise its powers in subordination to those rights, the Ninth Amendment should have the vitality intended for it. The problem is not so much whether the rights it guarantees are as worthy of enforcement as are the enumerated rights; the problem, rather, is whether our courts should read out of the amendment rights worthy of our respect, which the Framers might conceivably have meant to safeguard, at least in principle.

LEONARD W. LEVY
(1992)

(SEE ALSO: *Freedom of Assembly and Association; Freedom of Intimate Association; Right of Privacy.*)

Bibliography

BARNETT, RANDY E., ed.   1988   Symposium on Interpreting the Ninth Amendment. *Chicago-Kent Law Review* 64:37–268.

BERGER, RAOUL   1980   The Ninth Amendment. *Cornell Law Review* 61:1–26.

CAPLAN, RUSSELL L.   1983   The History and Meaning of the Ninth Amendment. *Virginia Law Review* 69:223–268.

REDLICH, NORMAN   1989   The Ninth Amendment as a Constitutional Prism. *Harvard Journal of Law and Public Policy* 12: 23–28.

# UNIFORM CODE OF MILITARY JUSTICE ACT

See: Military Justice

# UNION PACIFIC RAILROAD CO. v. UNITED STATES

See: Sinking Fund Cases

# UNITARY EXECUTIVE

The idea of a unitary executive is neither new nor radical. The Framers rejected several proposals to split the executive, and there have been adherents of a strong centralized executive ever since, from GEORGE WASHINGTON to WILLIAM HOWARD TAFT to RONALD REAGAN. The language of Article II of the Constitution seemingly embraces some form of unitary executive by vesting "the EXECUTIVE POWER" in a President; assigning the President the responsibility to "take Care that the Laws be faithfully executed"; and directing the President to appoint all principal officers of the United States. Arguments today for greater centralized control based on the unitary executive ideal coalesce around two virtues: accountability and effective leadership.

The constitutional structure stresses accountability in order to secure individual liberty. Articles I, II, and III delineate powers that the branches are to exercise, the better to clarify the lines of constitutional authority. The President stands responsible for all discharge of policy, and is judged by his or her performance on election day. To be sure, voters cannot always call the President to account with respect to one particular issue given that they vote for a candidate based on that candidate's entire record. Nonetheless, the political process remains open to air misgivings about presidential leadership, and as those concerns mount in importance, they may become determinative at election time.

This is not to suggest that the President must personally craft all foreign and domestic policy initiatives. Congress can create new offices pursuant to the NECESSARY AND PROPER CLAUSE and delegate responsibility to government officials. But the President must be able to superintend that policy in order not to fragment and dissipate accountability. As ALEXANDER HAMILTON noted in *Federalist* No. 70:

> [It] often becomes impossible, amidst mutual accusations, to determine on whom the blame or the punishment of a pernicious measure ... ought really to fall. ... [The] circumstances which may have led to any national miscarriage or misfortune are sometimes so complicated that where there are a number of actors who may have had different degrees and kind of agency ... it may be impracticable to pronounce to whose account the evil which may have been incurred is truly chargeable.

Liberty is gained to the extent that one electorally accountable official stands responsible for such law implementation efforts. With a plural executive, responsibility may be shrouded, and the costs of determining who was responsible for what will increase.

Given the pervasive delegations by Congress, the President can maintain control for law administration principally through the APPOINTING AND REMOVAL POWER exercised over executive officials. Although there may be disagreement about the level of officer subject to the President's appointment power, those adhering to the unitary executive regard restrictions on the President's appointment authority with great suspicion. Congress's decision to reserve for its own officers implementation authority, as in the FEDERAL ELECTION CAMPAIGN ACT, or Congress's decision to vest appointment authority in the judiciary, as with the INDEPENDENT COUNSEL, undermine the accountability imperative.

Similarly, the power to remove officers represents the only formal means by which the President can control subordinates' ongoing exercise of power and ensure unified execution of the law. The power to remove an official is emblematic of a continuing relationship between the President and subordinate officials and, in the public eye, links those officials' conduct to the presidency itself. When Congress prevents the President from removing executive officers, as with the TENURE OF OFFICE ACT during RECONSTRUCTION, accountability is diminished.

Disagreement remains over the type of removal authority that must be wielded to ensure the rudiments of centralized control. The Supreme Court delphically stated in *Morrison v. Olson* (1988) that Presidents must retain control sufficient to discharge their "constitutionally appointed functions." *Morrison* apparently authorizes Congress to prevent the President from discharging most officials except upon a showing of "good cause," such as misconduct in office. Some would argue instead that the President must be able to discharge at will any senior executive official to preserve the close connection between the President and the exercise of administrative authority. A middle position is that the President should be able to remove any senior official for refusing to abide by lawful presidential policy. But, whatever the line drawn, those believing in the unitary executive insist that Congress not have the power to establish shadow executive departments.

At the same time, the idea of a unitary executive accords a single executive the responsibility to manifest "energy" in execution of the laws passed by Congress. Consolidating power in an energetic executive provides the best hope for protecting the public from external threats to the nation's SOVEREIGNTY as well as from internal threats of violence or anarchy. JAMES MADISON wrote in *Federalist* No. 37 that "[e]nergy in government is essential to . . . security against external and internal danger, and to prompt and salutary execution of the laws." A single executive can implement the laws with greater dispatch and efficiency.

The risks attendant upon conduct of FOREIGN AFFAIRS by a plural entity are perhaps most clear. A deliberative body cannot easily take the decisive measures, in diplomacy or in war, upon which our NATIONAL SECURITY depends. Disagreement may paralyze the governing body, preventing it from acting vigorously in response to foreign threats. These reasons presumably explain why Article II mandates that the President serve as COMMANDER-IN-CHIEF of the ARMED FORCES.

Similar arguments are valid on the domestic policy front. Congress sets the policy, but enormous influence can be wielded by those carrying out the legislative directives. Whether the issue be implementing health care reform initiatives or administering the grazing fee system, a unitary executive permits greater vigor in law administration. Consolidating control in the executive also permits flexibility in enforcement efforts as conditions change. In short, a unitary executive not only safeguards individual liberty by ensuring an avenue of political redress for all law administration but facilitates effective governance as well.

HAROLD J. KRENT
(2000)

Bibliography

CALABRESI, STEPHEN G. 1995 Some Normative Arguments for the Unitary Executive. *Arkansas Law Review* 48:23–104.

CALABRESI, STEPHEN G. and PRAKASH, SAIKRISHNA 1994 The President's Power to Execute the Laws. *Yale Law Journal* 104: 541–665.

CAMINKER, EVAN 1997 The Unitary Executive and State Administration of Federal Law. *Kansas Law Review* 45:1075–1112.

KRENT, HAROLD J. 1990 Fragmenting the Unitary Executive: Congressional Delegations of Administrative Authority Outside the Federal Government. *Northwestern University Law Review* 85:62–112.

LESSIG, LAWRENCE and SUNSTEIN, CASS R. 1994 The President and the Administration. *Columbia Law Review* 94:1–119.

STRAUSS, PETER L. 1984 The Place of Agencies in Government: Separation of Powers and the Fourth Branch. *Columbia Law Review* 84:573–669.

## UNITED BUILDING & CONSTRUCTION TRADES COUNCIL v. MAYOR AND COUNCIL OF CAMDEN

See: Privileges and Immunities

## UNITED JEWISH ORGANIZATIONS v. CAREY
### 430 U.S. 144 (1977)

Under the VOTING RIGHTS ACT OF 1965 New York sought approval of the United States attorney general for its REAPPORTIONMENT of voters in state legislative districts in Greater New York City. To increase the nonwhite majorities in certain districts, and thus secure approval, the legislature divided a Hasidic Jewish community into two districts, each with a nonwhite majority. Petitioners claimed that assignment of voters solely on the basis of race violated the FOURTEENTH and FIFTEENTH AMENDMENTS.

By a 7–1 vote, the Supreme Court upheld the race-conscious reapportionment. There was no majority opinion but a series of overlapping alignments. Four Justices, noting that the percentage of nonwhite-majority districts was less than the percentage of nonwhites in the county in question, said that the use of racial criteria to comply with the act was not limited to compensating for past discrimination. Other Justices emphasized the lack of stigma or legislative purpose to disadvantage the Hasidim. Justice WILLIAM J. BRENNAN, in a comprehensive opinion on race-conscious remedies, appeared to look ahead to REGENTS OF UNIVERSITY OF CALIFORNIA V. BAKKE (1978). Chief Justice WARREN E. BURGER dissented.

KENNETH L. KARST
(1986)

## UNITED MINE WORKERS v. CORONADO COAL COMPANY
### 259 U.S. 344 (1922)

## CORONADO COAL COMPANY v. UNITED MINE WORKERS
### 268 U.S. 295 (1925)

In two nearly identical cases, the Supreme Court provided opposite answers to the same question: does the SHERMAN ANTITRUST ACT apply to local strikes that indirectly restrain commerce? The United Mine Workers (UMW) struck to prevent an employer from closing its mines despite valid union contracts; violence and property damage resulted. The company sued the union claiming a Sherman Act conspiracy to restrain INTERSTATE COMMERCE. In its defense, the UMW claimed that it was exempt from suit because it was unincorporated and, because mining was local, that there had been no Sherman Act violation. On APPEAL to the Supreme Court, Chief Justice WILLIAM HOWARD TAFT declared for a unanimous bench that, although unions (even though unincorporated) could clearly be sued, the union had not violated the Sherman Act here. Mining was merely local; any interference concerned the PRODUCTION rather than the distribution of goods. Taft said no restraint of trade existed, absent an explicit showing of intent to restrain trade, unless the obstruction had "such a direct, material and substantial effect to restrain [commerce] that intent reasonably may be inferred." Taft thus introduced new tests of reasonableness (see RULE OF REASON) and intent.

The company soon appealed with new EVIDENCE. Again unanimous, the Supreme Court now said that when intent to restrain trade attended a decrease in production, a previously "indirect and remote obstruction" became a direct interference in violation of the law. The Court asserted that the evidence at the second trial demonstrated such intent. The Court's near reversal, a finding of intent where none had previously existed, probably resulted from a fear of the implications of the first decision. The effect of the later opinion was to hamper union organizing efforts and cast doubt on the legality of strikes generally; certainly intent could be found by Justices who were looking for it.

DAVID GORDON
(1986)

(SEE ALSO: *Labor and the Antitrust Laws.*)

# UNITED MINE WORKERS v. UNITED STATES
## 330 U.S. 258 (1947)

When John L. Lewis and the United Mine Workers went on strike in the spring of 1946 against coal operators throughout the country, President HARRY S. TRUMAN, acting as COMMANDER-IN-CHIEF, seized the mines by EXECUTIVE ORDER to protect the national interest during the emergency. The failure of subsequent negotiations prompted a call that autumn for a second strike, which the government forestalled by obtaining an INJUNCTION in federal district court. Lewis defied the injunction, incurring contempt citations, a personal fine of $10,000, and a fine against his union of $3,500,000.

Lewis appealed to the Supreme Court. Chief Justice

FRED M. VINSON, for a 7–2 majority, held that neither the NORRIS-LAGUARDIA nor the CLAYTON ACT deprived the district court of JURISDICTION to issue the injunction pending judicial interpretation of the contract between the government and the miners. The majority denied the assertion that the "employer" referred to in the acts included the government; neither legislative history nor subsequent policy demonstrated any intent to make those acts applicable to government-employee disputes. Moreover, even if the Norris-LaGuardia Act applied, the Court could legitimately issue an injunction to maintain existing conditions pending the court's decision on its jurisdiction. The Court upheld the contempt findings—asserting that the same conduct might constitute both civil and criminal contempt for which both coercive and punitive measures might be imposed—and the fine against Lewis, but remanded the case for redetermination of the union fine.

DAVID GORDON
(1986)

# UNITED NATIONS CHARTER
## 59 Stat. 1031 (1945)

The United Nations Charter, a multilateral treaty which serves as the "constitution" of the United Nations Organization, was drafted in San Francisco at the United Nations Conference on International Organization in 1945 and ratified by fifty-one original member states. Like the Constitution of the United States, the charter has proved to be a flexible instrument subject to broad interpretation.

The charter was ratified by the United States Senate, 89–2, and it became law, binding both internally and externally, when it entered into force on October 24, 1945. Treaties, properly executed and ratified, are international law, at least formally, and in the United States they also are domestic law by virtue of the SUPREMACY CLAUSE of Article IV of the Constitution.

Despite the charter's nearly unanimous endorsement by the Senate, it was eagerly suggested that, in removing the right of the United States to go to war at will and in authorizing the Security Council to commit the member states to war in certain circumstances, the charter improperly delegated to the United Nations powers and functions belonging to the federal government, including the power to declare war, vested in Congress, and the power to conduct war, vested primarily in the President as commander-in-chief.

Congress and the President are not, however, deprived by the charter of the powers to declare and conduct war, only of the right to exercise these powers in contravention of international law (including the charter). All treaties, the charter included, limit only the international legal right—not the constitutional authority—of states to do freely that which is within their power to do freely in the absence of a treaty. Moreover, as a sovereign nation, the United States has the final authority to decide how it will comply with the particular terms and requirements of a treaty; and as a permanent member of the Security Council, the United States retains, in any event, an absolute veto over any action that would commit the United States to unwelcome policy. When Congress and the President act to comply with their charter obligations, in accordance with the United Nations Participation Act of 1945, they do so pursuant to the TREATY POWER and to their more general FOREIGN AFFAIRS powers.

Another, more recent, matter of constitutional concern is the question of whether United States courts, state and federal, are bound by the human rights clauses of the charter and related instruments, such as the Universal Declaration of Human Rights. The United States Supreme Court has never addressed the question of whether the charter's human rights provisions are self-executing in the United States; lower courts have answered that question in the negative.

BURNS H. WESTON
(1986)

Bibliography

CAHILL, J. 1952 "The United Nations Charter as Law of the Land." *Albany Law Review* 15–16:51–57.

Charter of the United Nations and Statute of the International Court of Justice. Office of Public Information, United Nations, New York.

GOODRICH, M. and HAMBRO, E. 1949 *Charter of the United Nations: Commentary and Documents.* Boston: World Peace Foundation.

HENKIN, LOUIS 1972 *Foreign Affairs and the Constitution.* Mineola, N.Y.: Foundation Press.

## UNITED RAILWAYS & ELECTRIC CO. OF BALTIMORE v. WEST
### 280 U.S. 234 (1930)

This obscure case has no significance except to illustrate how the Supreme Court manipulated the FAIR RETURN rule of SMYTH V. AMES (1898) to prevent rate regulation, which the Court disapproved. A public service commission fixed rates that permitted the company to earn a profit of 6.26 percent. The company sought rates returning 7.44 percent. The Court used SUBSTANTIVE DUE PROCESS to void the commission's rates and decided that rates returning "7 percent, or even 8 percent, on the value of the property"

might be "necessary to avoid confiscation." Justices LOUIS D. BRANDEIS, OLIVER W. HOLMES, and HARLAN FISKE STONE dissented.

LEONARD W. LEVY
(1986)

## UNITED STATES v. . . .

See entry under name of other party

## UNITED STATES COIN & CURRENCY, UNITED STATES v.

See: *Marchetti v. United States*

## UNITED STATES COURT OF APPEALS FOR THE FEDERAL CIRCUIT

This court was created by the FEDERAL COURTS IMPROVEMENT ACT (1982), to take over the JURISDICTION of the COURT OF CUSTOMS AND PATENT APPEALS and the COURT OF CLAIMS. Its first judges were the judges of the superseded courts. It is a CONSTITUTIONAL COURT, whose twelve judges serve for life during good behavior.

The Federal Circuit, like the other UNITED STATES COURTS OF APPEALS, is an intermediate appellate court; its jurisdiction, however, is defined not by region but by subject matter. It has nationwide jurisdiction to hear APPEALS in cases chiefly of the types previously heard by the superseded courts: customs and patent matters, and claims against the United States. In the future, however, other types of cases may be added to the Federal Circuit's jurisdiction—tax appeals, for example. Such developments might relieve some of the pressure on the Supreme Court's docket, effectively removing certain technical and specialized areas from the Court's workload. Many proponents of the 1982 act regard the creation of this opportunity as the act's most important achievement.

KENNETH L. KARST
(1986)

## UNITED STATES COURTS OF APPEALS

The United States Courts of Appeals form the intermediate component of the three-tiered federal judiciary, lying between the UNITED STATES DISTRICT COURTS and the SUPREME COURT of the United States. As such, they normally serve as the first courts of review in the federal JU-DICIAL SYSTEM. But because of the natural limitations upon the Supreme Court's capacity, the Courts of Appeals are often also the final courts of review.

Article III, section 1, of the Constitution provides: "The JUDICIAL POWER OF THE UNITED STATES, shall be vested in one supreme Court, and in such inferior Courts as the Congress may from time to time ordain and establish." Thus, in contrast to the Supreme Court, inferior federal courts were not required by the Constitution; rather, their creation was left to the discretion of Congress. Such treatment reflected a compromise between two views, one favoring the mandatory creation of inferior courts, and the other completely opposed to the existence of any such courts.

The Courts of Appeals are relative newcomers to the federal judicial system, having been born with the CIRCUIT COURTS OF APPEALS ACT (Evarts Act) of 1891. The Courts of Appeals were created to solve an acute crisis in the federal judiciary stemming from the limited capacity of the existing system, which had remained largely unchanged since the JUDICIARY ACT OF 1789. That act had established a bilevel system of inferior federal courts. There were, first of all, single-judge "district courts," generally one per state. The Union was also divided into several "circuits." CIRCUIT COURT was to be held twice a year in each of the districts encompassed by a given circuit. At these sittings, cases would be heard by a three-judge panel consisting of two Supreme Court Justices and the district judge for the district in which the circuit court was being held.

Having determined to avail itself of its constitutional prerogative to establish inferior federal courts, Congress faced the further issue of those courts' appropriate function and JURISDICTION. In the debates over Article III, there had been substantial support for giving Congress the power to create only admiralty courts, rather than inferior courts of general jurisdiction. No such limitation was adopted, however. It has therefore been generally assumed that Congress is constitutionally free to define the role of the inferior federal courts however it chooses.

The manner that Congress selected in the 1789 act is of some interest. The district courts were, and remain today, trial courts or courts of first instance. The circuit courts, in distinct contrast to today's middle-tier courts, also functioned primarily as trial courts. In the area of private civil law, the circuit courts' jurisdiction was largely concurrent with that of the district courts: it encompassed cases within the DIVERSITY JURISDICTION, but not FEDERAL QUESTION cases. (Original federal jurisdiction was not extended to federal question cases until 1875.) Similarly, with respect to civil suits by the United States, both circuit and district courts were given ORIGINAL JURISDICTION, the only difference being that the requisite amount in controversy was higher for circuit court jurisdiction.

The circuit courts even had certain original jurisdiction that the district courts lacked. The first removal jurisdiction was vested in the circuit courts alone. And the circuit courts had exclusive jurisdiction over most federal crimes.

Nonetheless, the seeds of the modern federal courts of appeals were planted by the first Judiciary Act. The early circuit courts had appellate jurisdiction in civil cases involving disputes over amounts exceeding $50, and in admiralty cases exceeding $300. (A district judge sitting as a circuit judge was not, however, permitted to vote on appeals from his own decisions.) Unlike the modern courts of appeals, however, the circuit courts were the final federal forum for many of these cases. In civil suits, circuit court judgments were reviewable only when the amount in dispute exceeded $2,000. Judgments in criminal cases were categorically unreviewable.

The early circuit courts proved problematic, in the main because of the burden that circuit riding placed on the Supreme Court Justices. Congress attempted to alleviate that hardship by reducing from two to one the number of Justices required to sit on a circuit court, but the benefit of the reduction was more than outweighed by several important augmentations of the High Court's jurisdiction that were enacted by Congress during the century following the 1789 Judiciary Act. Most notable of such legislation was the JUDICIARY ACT OF 1875, which granted the lower courts, as well as the Supreme Court, nearly the full scope of Article III jurisdiction, including original federal question jurisdiction in the district and circuit courts. The federal courts, already vastly overloaded with cases, were virtually submerged after this act. Reform was inevitable.

Indeed, attempts to improve the judicial system had more than once been made. In 1801 Congress had enacted the JUDICIARY ACT OF 1801 (the "Law of the Midnight Judges"), which among other things had established permanent circuit judgeships, three to a circuit. When political tides shifted the following year, however, the act was repealed, and the system reverted essentially to its original condition, except that Congress permitted circuit court to be held by a single judge, rather than three. Much later, in 1869, Congress partially restored the plan of 1801 by creating a single permanent circuit judgeship for each of the nine circuits then in existence. And in 1887 and 1888 Congress passed a series of measures aimed at pruning the expanded jurisdiction of the lower federal courts.

But it was not until the Evarts Act that Congress provided structural reforms adequate to the crisis of judicial overload. The act established three-judge courts of appeals for each of the nine circuits, and increased the number of permanent circuit judgeships to two per circuit. The third appeals judge would in most instances be a district judge (though Supreme Court Justices remained eligible), but the act, following the rule set down by the Act of 1789, barred district judges from reviewing their own decisions.

Curiously, the Evarts Act left the old circuit courts standing, although it did remove their APPELLATE JURISDICTION. Until these courts were abolished in 1911, there thus functioned two sets of federal trial courts.

The Evarts Act provided for direct review by the Supreme Court of the decisions of the district courts and the old circuit courts, in some important cases. The new circuit courts of appeals would review the remainder. Under the act, a circuit court's decision in an admiralty or diversity case would be final, unless that court certified a question to the Supreme Court or the Supreme Court granted a WRIT OF CERTIORARI in order to review the circuit court's decision. In most other cases, circuit court decisions were appealable as of right.

Since the Evarts Act, only a few significant alterations have been made to the federal judicial system in general, and the courts of appeals in particular. The rules governing Supreme Court review are perhaps the most important arena of change. In 1925, Congress replaced appeal as of right with discretionary review for all circuit court judgments except those holding a state statute unconstitutional. In 1937, Congress passed a law permitting appeal to the Supreme Court from any judgment by a federal court holding an act of Congress unconstitutional in any civil case to which the United States is a party.

In 1948 the circuit courts established by the Evarts Act were renamed; each court is now known as the United States Court of Appeals for theCircuit. The number of circuits has also been increased; and there is now a "Federal Circuit" court to hear appeals from the CLAIMS COURT and from district courts in patent cases or in cases arising under the TUCKER ACT. Finally, procedures in the various courts of appeals were standardized in 1968 in the Federal Rules of Appellate Procedure. Each circuit, however, retains its own rule-making power for matters not covered by the Federal Rules.

The chief work of the courts of appeals is the review of final judgments of the United States district courts. The courts, however, are also empowered to review certain orders that are not strictly final, essentially when the benefit of such review clearly outweighs any attendant disruption and delay of district court proceedings. In addition, Congress has enabled the appeals courts to issue the extraordinary WRIT OF MANDAMUS and WRIT OF PROHIBITION in cases in which district courts may abuse their constitutional powers. Finally, the statutes governing many of the various federal administrative agencies provide for direct review

of agency adjudication and rule-making in the court of appeals for the circuit in which the party seeking review resides, or in the Court of Appeals for the District of Columbia Circuit. The latter circuit court has been a frequent forum for challenges, constitutional and otherwise, to federal agency action.

To understand the role of the courts of appeals in the development of constitutional law, it is necessary to understand the relationship between the appeals courts and the Supreme Court. As was noted above, since the JUDICIARY ACT OF 1925, the "Judges Bill," the Supreme Court has had a discretionary power of review of most circuit court decisions. Again, however, appeal as of right lies in cases in which the appeals court has held a state statute to be repugnant to the Constitution, laws, or treaties of the United States, and in civil cases in which either a court of appeals or a district court has held an act of Congress unconstitutional and the United States is a party. Nonetheless, neither type of case in which appeal is of right bulks very large in the overall volume of appeals from circuit courts, and of those, many are denied Supreme Court review for want of a substantial federal question.

Accordingly, the Supreme Court has the discretion to review or not to review the vast majority of decisions by the courts of appeals. Not surprisingly, because of the limited capacity of the High Court, its discretion is much more often exercised to deny review than to grant it. As a general rule, in fact, the Supreme Court tends not to review appeals court decisions unless the issues involved either have an urgent importance or have received conflicting treatment by different circuits, or both.

One might conclude that, because the Supreme Court does review important cases, the appeals courts have no significant role in the development of constitutional law. Constitutional law, however, is not the product solely of the Supreme Court.

To begin, the Supreme Court can only review a decision that a party seeks to have reviewed; not every losing party in the court of appeals may do so. For example, in *Kennedy v. Sampson* (1974) the District of Columbia Circuit construed the POCKET VETO clause of the Constitution (Article 1, section 7, clause 2) to bar the President from exercising the pocket veto power during brief, intrasession adjournments of Congress. The President then declined to seek review in the Supreme Court; he chose instead to acquiesce in the rule laid down by the appeals court. The court's decision thus became a cornerstone of the law respecting the presentation of laws for presidential approval.

Of course, as a glance at any constitutional law textbook or casebook reveals, the vast majority of important constitutional PRECEDENTS are produced not by the courts of appeals but by the Supreme Court. Decisions like *Ken-*

*nedy* are thus the exception, not the rule. Nonetheless, in several ways the appeals courts contribute significantly to the development of constitutional law.

Before a constitutional issue is decided by the Supreme Court, it will often have received a thorough ventilation by one or more circuit courts. The Supreme Court thus has the benefit of the circuit judges' consideration of difficult constitutional matters, and may sometimes explicitly adopt the reasoning of the court of appeals. For example, in *United States v. Dennis* (1950) the Second Circuit faced the difficult issue of whether, and if so, how, the CLEAR AND PRESENT DANGER test applied to a conspiracy to advocate the overthrow of the government by force and violence and to organize a political party for the purpose of such advocacy. The Court of Appeals, in an opinion by Judge LEARNED HAND, held that such advocacy was unprotected by the FIRST AMENDMENT even though the actual forceful overthrow of the government was not imminent. The Supreme Court affirmed the decision in DENNIS V. UNITED STATES (1951), and its opinion adopted much of Judge Hand's analysis, including Judge Hand's "clear and present danger" formula, namely, "whether the gravity of the 'evil,' discounted by its improbability, justifies such invasion of free speech as is necessary to avoid the danger."

The role of the courts of appeals in resolving novel issues of constitutional law, however, is only half of the picture. Equally important is the appeals courts' adjudication of cases raising issues on which the Supreme Court has already spoken. Because the High Court can only sketch the broad outlines of constitutional DOCTRINE, it remains for the lower courts to apply precedent, elaborate or clarify it, and extrapolate from it. Because appeal from the district courts to the appeals court is of right, and because most litigation never reaches the Supreme Court, it is in the courts of appeals that the Supreme Court's sketch is worked into a fully drawn landscape.

When the Supreme Court decides not to give plenary review to a case arising from an appeals court, what implication should be drawn concerning the value of the appeals court's opinion as a precedent? By denying a petition for certiorari or dismissing an appeal as of right for want of jurisdiction, the Court formally indicates no view of the merits or demerits of the appeals court's decision. Nonetheless, it is commonly thought that the Supreme Court generally does not decline to review an appeals court decision that it finds clearly incorrect. Similarly, when the Supreme Court summarily affirms an appeals court's decision, it is formally signaling its agreement with the result only, and not necessarily the reasoning of the lower court. Yet, such affirmances are popularly thought to indicate at least the Court's tentative agreement with the substance of the lower court's opinion.

Since the early 1960s, the federal courts at all three levels have experienced a dramatic and continuing increase in their workload. At the district and circuit levels, Congress has responded by adding judges to existing courts. When the number of judges in a circuit has become sufficiently great, Congress has divided the circuit into two. That course is not entirely satisfactory, however, because it tends to push the appeals courts in the direction of being regional, rather than national courts, and increases the likelihood of intercircuit conflict.

At the Supreme Court level, Congress has made no significant changes. Various proposals for reducing the Court's workload would also affect adjudication at the appeals court level. A frequent suggestion has been to establish a national court of appeals. In one version, the national court would sit only to resolve conflicts among the circuits, thereby eliminating a significant share of the Supreme Court's annual docket. In another version, the national court would screen cases to determine those worthy of Supreme Court review. Another proposal would reduce the Supreme Court's workload by eliminating appeal as of right. One effect of such a measure, of course, would be to increase the number of appeals court decisions that are effectively final.

CARL McGOWAN
(1986)

Bibliography

BATOR, PAUL M. et al. 1973 *Hart and Wechsler's The Federal Courts and the Federal System*, 2nd ed. Mineola, N.Y.: Foundation Press.

WRIGHT, CHARLES A. 1983 *Handbook of the Law of Federal Courts.* St. Paul, Minn.: West Publishing Co.

## UNITED STATES DISTRICT COURT FOR THE EASTERN DISTRICT OF MICHIGAN, UNITED STATES v.
### 407 U.S. 297 (1972)

Most Presidents have claimed inherent executive authority to use electronic surveillance for national security purposes without complying with conventional FOURTH AMENDMENT requirements such as prior court approval. In several earlier decisions, such as KATZ V. UNITED STATES (1967), and in the 1968 statute authorizing federal and state officials to use ELECTRONIC EAVESDROPPING, the issue had been left open.

During the VIETNAM WAR, Attorney General John N. Mitchell approved a wiretap "to gather intelligence information deemed necessary to protect the nation from attempts of domestic organizations to attack and subvert the existing structure of the government." The Supreme Court unanimously ruled that where threats by *domestic* organizations were concerned, neither section 2511(3) of the 1968 act nor the Constitution gave the President authority to use electronic surveillance without first obtaining a warrant from a magistrate. The Court thus rejected the President's claim of INHERENT POWER. The Court did not decide whether the Fourth Amendment's warrant requirement applied to activities of foreign powers or their agents; a 1978 statute now governs this. The Court also suggested that Congress could authorize standards for intelligence gathering for domestic security purposes that are less stringent than for law enforcement; Congress has not done so.

HERMAN SCHWARTZ
(1986)

# UNITED STATES DISTRICT COURTS

In enacting Article III, the Framers of the Constitution authorized the establishment of a federal judicial system consisting of a SUPREME COURT and such inferior courts as Congress might decide to establish. In the JUDICIARY ACT OF 1789 Congress created a Supreme Court, divided the country into three circuits, authorized a CIRCUIT COURT to sit in each circuit, and established a federal district court in each of the states. The Supreme Court was the only truly appellate court in the system. Unlike the modern courts of appeal, the old circuit courts, while exercising some appellate jurisdiction, were intended to be the chief federal trial courts. A Supreme Court Justice riding the circuit and judges of the district courts in the circuit manned each of these circuit courts.

The federal district courts were empowered to sit at various times in specified locations within the states where they were located. They were tribunals of very limited JURISDICTION and originally had as their main function the adjudication of admiralty and maritime matters. It was anticipated that the state trial courts or federal circuit courts would handle, as trial courts, the most important legal issues facing the new nation. The federal district courts were empowered to try minor criminal cases. In addition, they had CONCURRENT JURISDICTION with the circuit courts over suits by ALIENS for tort violations of a treaty or the law of nations, suits against consuls, and disputes in which the federal government initiated the proceeding and the matter in controversy was $100 or less. However, district court jurisdiction was exclusive in admiralty, over seizures of land for violation of federal statutes, and over seizures under import, navigation, and trade statutes.

This limited and specialized jurisdiction has steadily expanded. Today the district court is the only federal nonspecialized court, handling both criminal and civil matters. Among the latter are admiralty cases, federal question cases, and cases within the DIVERSITY JURISDICTION (cases between different states). In a diversity case the matter in controversy must exceed $10,000. No jurisdictional amount is normally required for the other exercises of the district court's civil jurisdiction. Appeals from a district court go to the UNITED STATES COURT OF APPEALS.

The first district court to be organized was the district court of New York. That court began functioning on November 3, 1789, and was the predecessor to the current district court for the Southern District of New York. Even today judges of the Southern District refer to theirs as the "Mother Court."

As the system was originally conceived, each state was to contain at least one federal district and one federal court. There has been no deviation from this pattern as the country has expanded from thirteen to fifty states. In addition, the DISTRICT OF COLUMBIA and the federal TERRITORIES (the Virgin Islands, PUERTO RICO, and Guam) are each organized as a federal district with a district court. In over half the states, although there may be a number of federal district judges who sit in separate locations throughout the state, there is only one federal district. Twelve states are divided into two federal districts; some states have three federal districts; and California, New York, and Texas are subdivided into four federal districts.

As the country has expanded, the number of federal district judges has increased. Since 1954 the roster of federal judges has grown through enactment of legislation authorizing additional judgeships for federal district courts nationwide. The Omnibus Judgeship Act of 1978 raised the number of authorized district judges from 399 to 516. The Southern District of New York has twenty-seven authorized judgeships, the largest number of any district in the country.

Federal district judges are nominated by the President and appointed with the ADVICE AND CONSENT of the Senate. The prevailing practice is for the selection of the nominee to come to the President from the Department of Justice. If one or both of the senators from the state in question belong to the President's party, the candidate for nomination is proposed by one or both senators and submitted to the Department of Justice for approval and recommendation to the President for nomination. Today few candidates are nominated and sent to the Senate for confirmation without first being found qualified by the American Bar Association. When the President decides to nominate a candidate, the FEDERAL BUREAU OF INVESTIGATION undertakes a security check. If the candidate is cleared, the President announces the nomination and sends the name to the Senate. The SENATE JUDICIARY COMMITTEE holds hearings, which are usually one-day affairs for candidates for federal district courts. If the Senate Judiciary Committee approves, the nomination is voted on by the full Senate.

An Article III judge has life tenure during GOOD BEHAVIOR, and his salary cannot be diminished while he is in office. The only way to remove a federal district judge from office is by IMPEACHMENT. Of course, a federal judge, like any other person, may be prosecuted for criminal law violations. Bribery has been the most frequent charge, but criminal prosecutions of federal judges are rare and attempts to remove them by impeachment have been infrequent.

When the first change of political power occurred in the United States at the national level, from the Federalist party to the Republican party of THOMAS JEFFERSON, the Jeffersonians commenced impeachment proceedings against two judges appointed by the Federalists and disliked by the Republicans: JOHN PICKERING, a judge of the district court in New Hampshire, and SAMUEL CHASE, an Associate Justice of the Supreme Court. Pickering was convicted by the Senate in 1803, but the requisite two-thirds Senate majority could not be mustered to convict Chase. Since that time impeachment to unseat a federal judge has not been a successful political weapon. Partisan politics has from time to time generated unsuccessful calls for impeachment of various judges.

A federal district court judgeship carries considerable prestige. It is a presidential appointment; it is a national rather than a local office; and federal district court judgeships are limited in number. District judges in the main have had prior careers as prominent or distinguished lawyers before going on the bench. They are drawn for the most part from the middle and upper strata of our society. They are generally alumni of the best known law schools of the nation or of the state in which they will serve. They have generally had successful careers in private practice, often with backgrounds as federal, state, or local prosecutors. A few are former academics, and some come to court from public service careers outside government.

Until the twentieth century, all federal district judges were white males. The first woman to be confirmed as a federal judge was Florence Allen, who was appointed to the Court of Appeals for the Sixth Circuit in 1934. The first woman appointed to the district court was Burneta Matthews, who was given an interim appointment to the District of Columbia bench in 1949. She was confirmed by the Senate in 1950 for a permanent appointment. Constance Baker Motley was the first black woman to be appointed to the federal bench. She was appointed to the District Court for the Southern District of New York in 1966, and in 1982 became chief judge of that court. WILLIAM HASTIE was the first black to be made a federal

judge. He was appointed to the District Court of the Virgin Islands in 1937 and in 1949 was named to the Court of Appeals for the Third Circuit. James Parsons, appointed judge of the Northern District of Illinois in 1961, was the first black named a district judge in the continental United States. Since these initial appointments the number of blacks, women, and members of other ethnic minorities has grown steadily.

The first Judiciary Act authorized each court to make rules for conducting its own business, and in 1842 the Supreme Court was empowered to regulate process, pleading, proof and DISCOVERY in EQUITY, admiralty, and law cases in the district and circuit courts. In 1938 uniform rules for conducting civil cases, entitled the FEDERAL RULES OF CIVIL PROCEDURE, were adopted for the federal system. In 1946 the FEDERAL RULES OF CRIMINAL PROCEDURE were enacted. These rules have achieved uniformity of procedure and practice in the federal district courts throughout the nation.

The typical calendar of civil cases in a federal district court contains a plethora of complex cases involving PATENT, trademark, and COPYRIGHT infringement claims; federal securities law violations; CIVIL RIGHTS infractions; private antitrust claims; shareholders' derivative suits; IMMIGRATION and NATURALIZATION cases; employment, age, and housing discrimination claims; and claims under a variety of other federal statutes, such as the FREEDOM OF INFORMATION ACT, Investment Advisers Act, Commodities Exchange Act, FAIR LABOR STANDARDS ACT, and Federal Employers' Liability Act. In addition, there are seamen's injury and cargo damage claims, HABEAS CORPUS petitions by both state and federal prisoners, and litigation based on diversity jurisdiction. The criminal case load involves a variety of infractions defined in the United States criminal code.

Among the primary functions of the federal district courts are the vindication of federal rights secured by the Constitution and laws of the United States. The federal district court is often called upon to hold a state law or act unconstitutional because it violates federal constitutional guarantees or has been preempted by federal legislation. Obviously, the exercise of this power by federal district courts has the potential for creating friction and disharmony between state and federal courts. A lower federal court's power to strike down a state law on federal constitutional grounds, in the face of a contrary ruling by the highest court of the state, is not an easy pill for state judges to swallow. Federal courts have devised doctrines of COMITY and ABSTENTION to ease the friction. A growing number of federal judges, recognizing that state judges, too, have a duty to protect and enforce federal rights, have been inclined to give increasing deference to state court determinations of federal constitutional questions.

A burgeoning federal caseload undoubtedly promotes this inclination toward accommodation and also promotes a tightening of limitations on federal habeas corpus review of state court criminal convictions. A habeas corpus petition enables a state prisoner, after unsuccessfully appealing his conviction through the state court system, to have the matter reviewed by the federal district court to determine whether the trial and conviction violated the defendant's federal constitutional rights. Not surprisingly, habeas corpus petitions have inundated the federal courts. While most are without merit, the few petitions of substance that succeed are another cause of federal-state court friction. Rules of limitations have been imposed requiring exhaustion of state remedies and forbidding review if the state court's denial of the appeal of the criminal conviction rests on the defendant's failure to conform to state governing procedure absent a showing of cause and prejudice. (See WAINWRIGHT V. SYKES.)

Diversity jurisdiction brings to the federal courts issues of state law that would ordinarily be tried in the state courts. The initial justification for giving federal courts jurisdiction over such cases was concern that parochialism would put the out-of-state complainant at a disadvantage in seeking redress in state court against a resident of the forum state.

Exercise of federal diversity jurisdiction was at one time a cause of federal-state confusion if not friction. The district courts in diversity cases have been required to follow applicable state statutes, but until 1938 they were free to disregard state decisional law and decide on the basis of their own notions of what the COMMON LAW was or should be. With the Supreme Court's decision in ERIE RAILROAD V. TOMPKINS (1938) federal courts were no longer free to disregard state court decisions. Federal courts may apply their own rules as to pleading and practice but on substantive issues must function as adjuncts of the state judiciary.

ERIE V. TOMPKINS has made clear that the diversity jurisdiction is a wasteful use of federal judicial resources. State court parochialism is no longer a justifiable basis for federal diversity jurisdiction. Because the federal court must apply state law, apart from federal procedural rules, the litigant is seldom better off in federal court than he would be if relegated to state courts, where increasing numbers of federal judges feel such cases belong. Congress, however, has shown little interest in divesting federal district courts of the diversity jurisdiction.

The federal district court is the place where litigation usually commences to test the constitutional validity of state or federal governmental action with national implication. These TEST CASES usually seek injunctive relief or DECLARATORY JUDGMENTS. These are suits in EQUITY; thus no jury is empaneled, and the district judge must determine both the facts and the law. The judge will articulate his or her findings of the facts and legal conclusions as to the constitutional validity of the governmental action being tested. The trial record and the district court's analysis are thus extremely important for appellate courts, particularly in cases of first impression.

It is the district court that decides in the first instance whether the government is violating a newspaper's FIRST AMENDMENT rights, an accused's RIGHT AGAINST SELF-INCRIMINATION, or a minority citizen's right to the equal protection of the laws. Organizations such as the AMERICAN CIVIL LIBERTIES UNION, the National Association for the Advancement of Colored People, Jehovah's Witnesses, environmental groups, corporations, and individuals initiate litigation in the district court to test the constitutionality of some federal, state, or local legislation or practice. (See TEST CASES.)

Such a case was *McLean v. Arkansas Board of Education* (D. Ark., 1982). The American Civil Liberties Union sought to challenge an Arkansas law requiring that creationism—a biblical story of man's and the world's creation, as opposed to Darwin's evolutionary theory for explaining the genesis of mankind—be taught in the public schools. The issue was tried first in the federal district court, which framed the issue in these terms: is creationism a religious doctrine or a valid scientific theory? The court heard and weighed testimony, chiefly from experts on both sides, and held that the Arkansas statute was an unconstitutional ESTABLISHMENT OF RELIGION.

Sometimes prior DOCTRINE has forecast the outcome. For instance, although the SEPARATE BUT EQUAL DOCTRINE on which school SEGREGATION had been founded was not overruled until BROWN V. BOARD OF EDUCATION (1954), earlier decisions such as SWEATT V. PAINTER (1950) and *McLaurin v. Oklahoma State Regents* (1950) pointed to that overruling. Nonetheless, the record amassed by several district courts, showing the psychological and education deprivation inflicted by segregation on black children, was crucial in enabling the Supreme Court to take the final step of overruling PLESSY V. FERGUSON (1896) and holding that segregated schools violated the right of minority school children to equal protection of the law.

Similarly, a federal district court facing a constitutional challenge to the HYDE AMENDMENT, a congressional provision largely denying Medicaid funds for the cost of abortions, held hearings for about a year. The trial record contained some 400 exhibits and 5,000 pages of testimony. The judge was required to digest this mountain of testimonial and documentary evidence and prepare cohesive findings of facts and conclusions of law. (See HARRIS V. MCRAE.)

The need for so long a trial and the condensation of so voluminous a record into a coherent decision is not commonplace. However, it is not unusual for a district judge to be required to master the facts in a complex trial lasting many months, and to set forth the facts found and legal conclusions in a comprehensive fashion.

In some cases the district court, as a supplement to its own adjudicative fact-finding, must make findings as to LEGISLATIVE FACTS as well. For instance, in FULLILOVE V. KLUTZNICK (1980) Congress had required at least ten percent of federal funds granted for local public works projects to be set aside for minority businesses. This legislation was attacked as unconstitutional racial discrimination. The district court framed the issue as the power of Congress to remedy past discrimination. The district judge relied on congressional findings that minorities had been denied access to entrepreneurial opportunities provided in building construction works financed by public funds. Based on this legislative finding and Congress's purpose to take remedial action, the district court found the set-aside to be a legitimate remedial act. The Supreme Court adopted this rationale, and upheld the quota.

At times, in a constitutional controversy, the district court, although adhering to judicial precedent requiring it to dismiss the constitutional challenge, may help to bring about a reversal of precedent by recognizing that a wrong exists which should be remedied. BAKER V. CARR (1962) was a challenge to Tennessee's malapportioned legislature. The district court, in its opinion, carefully and sympathetically tracked the contentions of the plaintiffs that the legislators had condoned gross inequality in legislative REPRESENTATION and debased the VOTING RIGHTS of a large number of citizens. The court, however, relied on COLEGROVE V. GREEN (1946) and dismissed the action. On review of this order, the Supreme Court ruled that the plaintiffs' allegations had stated a case within the district court's jurisdiction. Subsequently, REYNOLDS V. SIMS (1964) embodied the Supreme Court's famous ONE PERSON, ONE VOTE principle, requiring legislative districts to be constructed as nearly as possible of an equal number of voters. (See REAPPORTIONMENT.)

Issues of such magnitude are highly charged; it is not unusual, in these controversial circumstances, for the judge who decides a case contrary to the majority's view to face public criticism and in some cases even social ostracism.

Judge Waties Waring's unpopular decision in favor of blacks in voting and school cases led to his social ostracism in Charleston, South Carolina; Judge Skelly Wright became anathema to many whites in New Orleans for the same reason, and escaped that environment through appointment to the Court of Appeals of the District of Columbia Circuit. Similarly, Judge William Ray Overton, who decided the creationism case adversely to local sentiments, and Judge James B. MacMillan, who ordered a complex program of SCHOOL BUSING in Charlotte, North Carolina, were subjected to severe community criticism.

Although not so dramatic as the examples given, public criticism meets almost every district judge at one time or another for rendering an unpopular decision. Because most public controversies have a way of ending up in the federal courts, district judges must decide whether seniority systems must be modified to prevent the employment gains of minorities and women from being wiped out; whether regulations requiring physicians to report to parents abortions performed on teenagers are valid; whether the overcrowding and the rundown conditions of a prison require it to be closed; or whether permitting school authorities to provide for prayer or meditation violates the SEPARATION OF CHURCH AND STATE. The district judge normally sits alone, and does not share decision with others, as do federal appellate judges—and therefore is singularly exposed to abuse and pressure.

Life tenure helps secure the independence of the district judge in facing such issues. This independence is crucial, not only for the judge but also for a constitutional system that seeks to secure the rights of the unpopular and despised.

ROBERT L. CARTER
(1986)

Bibliography

ADMINISTRATIVE OFFICE OF THE UNITED STATES COURT. *Annual Report of the Director.* Washington, D.C.: Government Printing Office.

CLARK, D. S. 1981 Adjudication to Administration: A Statistical Analysis of Federal District Courts in the 20th Century. *Southern California Law Review* 55:65–152.

HALL, KERMIT 1976 The Antebellum Lower Federal Judiciary, 1829–1861. *Vanderbilt Law Review* 29:1089–1129.

—— 1981 California's Lower Federal First Judicial Appointments. *Hastings Law Journal* 32:819–837.

HENDERSON, DWIGHT F. 1971 *Courts for a New Nation.* Washington, D.C.: Public Affairs Press.

HOUGH, CHARLES M. 1934 *The U.S. District Court for the Southern District of New York.* New York: Maritime Law Association.

*Management Statistic for United States Courts.* 1981.

STECKLER, WILLIAM E. 1978 Future of the Federal District Courts. *Indiana Law Review* 11:601–620.

SURRENCY, ERWIN C. 1963 History of Federal Courts. *Missouri Law Review* 28:214–244.

THOMPSON, FRANK, JR. 1970 Impeachment of Federal Judges: A Historical Overview. *North Carolina Law Review* 49:87–121.

# UNITED STATES RAILROAD RETIREMENT BOARD v. FRITZ

See: Rational Basis; Substantive Due Process

## *UNITED STATES TRUST CO. v. NEW JERSEY*
### 431 U.S. 1 (1977)

This decision marked the beginning of the modern revitalization of the CONTRACT CLAUSE as a limitation on state legislative power. New York and New Jersey had promised, on issuing bonds to support their Port Authority, to limit severely their use of Authority revenues to subsidize rail passenger transportation. Twelve years later the states sought to divert commuters from automobiles to railroads; they raised bridge and tunnel tolls and, repealing their earlier promise, authorized use of the increased revenues to subsidize commuter railroads. The Supreme Court, 4–3, held the repeal unconstitutional as an impairment of the OBLIGATION OF CONTRACT.

The dissenters, led by Justice WILLIAM J. BRENNAN, accurately described the decision as the first in nearly forty years to invalidate economic legislation under the contract clause and argued vigorously for maintaining judicial deference to legislative power. For the majority, Justice HARRY A. BLACKMUN commented that the outright repeal had deprived bondholders of an important security interest and could be justified only if it were both "reasonable and necessary to serve an important public purpose." The repeal failed this heightened STANDARD OF REVIEW, because alternative means of diverting commuters to railroads were available: taxing parking or gasoline, for example.

KENNETH L. KARST
(1986)

(SEE ALSO: *Allied Structural Steel Company v. Spannaus.*)

## *UNITED STEELWORKERS OF AMERICA v. WEBER*
### 443 U.S. 193 (1979)

This was one of an important series of decisions upholding the legality of AFFIRMATIVE ACTION. In *Weber*, the Court held, 5–2, in an opinion by Justice WILLIAM J. BRENNAN, that a private affirmative action plan reserving for blacks fifty percent of the openings in a training program leading to plant employment did not violate Title VII of the CIVIL RIGHTS ACT OF 1964. *Weber* left open important questions about the permissible scope of affirmative action, including whether governments might resort to affirmative action without violating the Fifth or FOURTEENTH AMENDMENT, and the extent to which private affirmative action programs may "trammel the interests" of white employees.

THEODORE EISENBERG
(1986)

## UNIVERSAL MILITARY TRAINING AND SERVICE ACT

See: Selective Service Acts

## UNREASONABLE SEARCH

"Unreasonable" is the controlling word in the FOURTH AMENDMENT. In its first clause the amendment guarantees the right of the people to be free from unreasonable SEARCHES AND SEIZURES; its second clause stipulates the terms for issuance of a judicial warrant: probable cause, oath or affirmation, particularity of description. What is an unreasonable and therefore forbidden search? Conversely, what is a reasonable and permitted one? The amendment does not say. The answer, in large measure, depends on one's understanding of the relationship of the two clauses.

Two polar positions have dominated debate in the Supreme Court on this matter. The view that was in the ascendancy before 1946 and that has generally prevailed again since CHIMEL V. CALIFORNIA (1969), treats the two clauses in conjunction so that the unreasonable searches forbidden by the first clause are defined by the warrant requirements in the second clause: a reasonable search is one conducted subject to a proper warrant, an unreasonable search is one that is not. A second view, generally dominant between HARRIS V. UNITED STATES (1946) and 1969, holds that reasonableness is an autonomous principle, to be measured by all the circumstances rather than by the securing of a warrant (although this is one factor to be considered).

The conflict between the two readings of "unreasonable" essentially has centered on SEARCH INCIDENT TO ARREST, a recognized "emergency" exception to the warrant requirement since WEEKS V. UNITED STATES (1914). According to the second interpretation, once the privacy of the dwelling has legitimately been invaded to make a lawful arrest, it is reasonable to allow the search (for the purpose of disarming the arrestee and seizing EVIDENCE which he may seek to destroy) to blanket the entire premises in which the arrest was made. This is a matter of the greatest consequence, for the vast majority of searches are carried out incident to arrest. If, however, the warrant requirement is considered to be the core of the amendment, the search must be circumscribed to the extent required by the emergency and therefore confined to the person arrested and the area within his immediate reach.

To treat reasonableness as an independent standard is contrary to both history and logic. On logical grounds there seems little value to stringent warrant requirements that can be readily negated by "reasonable" WARRANTLESS

SEARCHES. History, too, sets its face against the notion. The Fourth Amendment's proscription of unreasonable searches, alone among the provisions of the BILL OF RIGHTS to set fair standards for the apprehension and trial of accused persons, has a rich historical background in American, as well as English, experience. The amendment is rooted in the restrictions which seventeenth- and eighteenth-century COMMON LAW judges in England placed on the search power (for example, WILKES CASES, 1763–1770). This power had been abused through the government's relentless hunt for political and religious dissidents during a phase of English history well understood in the colonies. The amendment stems more directly from the public outcry against indiscriminate searches for smuggled goods (authorized by GENERAL WARRANTS known as WRITS OF ASSISTANCE) during the last years of the colonial period in America, notably in Massachusetts. The main object of the Fourth Amendment, to prevent the recurrence of the detested general warrant, was to be accomplished by placing strict limits on the issuance of a warrant. The reasonableness clause, as seems clear from the historical record of the amendment's drafting in the first Congress, was meant to reemphasize, and perhaps strengthen, the warrant requirements in the second clause. To detach the reasonableness clause from the warrant clause by infusing it with independent potency serves to dilute the amendment's protection, exactly the opposite of the result its framers intended. It is insufficient to leave the initial determination of reasonableness to the police, with JUDICIAL REVIEW taking place retrospectively when the prosecutor seeks to introduce the fruits of the search in evidence. Many searches will produce no evidence, and even when evidence is found, the pressure on judges to rule against obviously guilty defendants will be great despite the illegality of the searches.

Consonant with the amendment's history, the Court at one time assigned an even broader meaning to "unreasonable" than is taken by the first view. In BOYD V. UNITED STATES (1886) the Court held that private papers are immune to seizure even under warrant—on the theory that one test of the reasonableness of a search is whether or not its purpose is to seize evidence that will force the person to incriminate himself. In contrast, contraband goods and fruits and instrumentalities of crime are deemed seizable because their possessor has no legal property right in them. In *Gouled v. United States* (1921) the Court logically extended the immunity granted private papers to all kinds of evidentiary materials (for example; clothing). However, this MERE EVIDENCE RULE, as it came to be known, was overturned as "wholly irrational" in WARDEN V. HAYDEN (1967), and probably little remains of the immunity granted to private papers (*Fisher v. United States*, 1976).

Other EXIGENT CIRCUMSTANCES, in addition to search incidental to arrest, which, in either view, permit the police to bypass the warrant requirement, include the rule of CARROLL V. UNITED STATES (1925), which permits the search of a moving vehicle on PROBABLE CAUSE to believe that it is transporting contraband; the ruling in *Schmerber v. California* (1966), which permits the compulsory taking of a blood sample from a driver to measure its alcoholic content where there is probable cause to believe he was intoxicated while driving; and the rule of *Warden v. Hayden* (1967), which permits the "hot pursuit" of a felon into a dwelling. Even in the absence of evidence that a crime has been committed, where the suspicious conduct of an individual leads an officer to believe that he or others are in danger and imminent action is imperative, he may stop the suspect and "frisk" the individual's outer clothing in order to disarm him of weapons he may be carrying. (See TERRY V. OHIO.)

In the case of search incidental to arrest, hot pursuit, or STOP AND FRISK, the emergency is self-evident, but it is no less genuine in the case of a moving vehicle or a blood test, for the delay involved in the obtaining of a warrant will usually defeat the object of the search. The automobile might by that time be far away, perhaps in another jurisdiction, and the percentage of alcohol in the blood gradually diminishes once intake ceases. These are only examples. Clearly any real emergency, as the sound of a shot or a cry for help coming from behind closed doors, would justify a warrantless search by the police.

The only kinds of searches known to the framers, and to which the Fourth Amendment was originally addressed, contained two elements: (1) entry into the dwelling (2) for the purpose of seizing evidence of crime. At first the Court considered the definition of search to be governed by this experience and maintained that warrants were not required for more modern types of searches that lacked one or the other of these elements. Thus searches for oral utterances conducted by WIRETAPPING which do not involve entry onto premises, as in OLMSTEAD V. UNITED STATES (1928), or inspection of dwellings to uncover nuisances to public health or safety, as in *Frank v. Maryland* (1959), were held not to be covered by the amendment. Subsequently, however, ELECTRONIC EAVESDROPPING (including wiretapping) and ADMINISTRATIVE SEARCHES were both brought under the amendment's protective umbrella in KATZ V. UNITED STATES (1967) and CAMARA V. MUNICIPAL COURT (1967), respectively. But a visit to the home by a caseworker for the purpose of determining whether a public assistance grant is being properly used does not amount to an unreasonable search and requires no warrant, as the Court held in WYMAN V. JAMES (1971).

A court order for the surgical removal of a bullet from the body of a suspect was ruled unreasonable in *Winston v. Lee* (1985)—at least when the need for the evidence is not "compelling"—because of the serious intrusion on privacy and the medical risks entailed.

In order to prevent the Fourth Amendment from being reduced to a mere parchment guarantee, evidence obtained through unreasonable search has since 1914 been excluded from trials in the federal courts (*Weeks v. United States*), and in the state courts as well since MAPP V. OHIO (1961). (See EXCLUSIONARY RULE.) Although the amendment contains no express command of exclusion, it has been construed to authorize the judiciary to apply such sanctions as are necessary to ensure compliance with the standard of reasonableness.

Like the rest of the Bill of Rights, the ban on unreasonable searches was originally intended to place restrictions only on the federal government. That ban became applicable to the states, as an element of FOURTEENTH AMENDMENT due process, in 1961 (*Mapp v. Ohio*), and the same standard of reasonableness now governs searches made by federal and state authorities (KER V. CALIFORNIA, 1963). (See INCORPORATION DOCTRINE.)

JACOB W. LANDYNSKI
(1986)

Bibliography

FELLMAN, DAVID   1976   *The Defendant's Rights Today.* Pages 277–284. Madison: University of Wisconsin Press.

LAFAVE, WAYNE R.   1978   *Search and Seizure: A Treatise on the Fourth Amendment.* Vol. 2:406–476, 498–609; vol. 3:2–140. St. Paul, Minn.: West Publishing Co.

LANDYNSKI, JACOB W.   1966   *Search and Seizure and the Supreme Court.* Pp. 30–44, 387–417. Baltimore: Johns Hopkins University Press.

———   1971   "The Supreme Court's Search for Fourth Amendment Standards: The Warrantless Search." *Connecticut Bar Journal* 45:2–39.

LEVY, LEONARD W.   1974   *Against the Law.* Pages 75–117. New York: Harper & Row.

# UNREASONABLE SEARCH
## (Update)

"Unreasonable search and seizure" is a technical phrase that refers to any governmental SEARCH AND SEIZURE deemed to violate the FOURTH AMENDMENT of the Constitution. In general, searches and seizures are unreasonable if the government undertakes them without properly authorizing SEARCH WARRANTS or, in exceptional circumstances not requiring warrants, in violation of the rules laid down for those exceptions. The Fourth Amendment provides, "The right of the people to be secure in their persons, houses, papers, and effects, against unreasonable searches and seizures, shall not be violated, and no Warrants shall issue, but upon probable cause, supported by Oath or affirmation, and particularly describing the place to be searched, and the persons or things to be seized." The amendment defines neither "unreasonable" nor "searches and seizures," and the judiciary has taken on the task of definition. The Supreme Court has concluded that particularized searches and seizures with a warrant, as called for by the amendment's warrant clause, establish the norm for reasonableness. It is the neutral, detached, judicial determination of good reason or "probable cause" to search foror seize particular persons or things in particular places that makes such acts presumptively "reasonable." Unauthorized searches and seizures, unless specially justified, are generally thought unreasonable.

Although searches and seizures based on proper warrants are the accepted constitutional norm, not all WARRANTLESS SEARCHES and seizures violate the Fourth Amendment. They do not if they are directed at objects or interests the amendment does not protect, if they do not constitute "searches" or "seizures" in the legal sense, or if they fall within one of the recognized exceptions to the warrant or probable cause requirements.

In KATZ V. UNITED STATES (1967), the Supreme Court stated that the Fourth Amendment, among other things, protected certain individual interests in privacy from unreasonable government search and seizure. Subsequent opinions have said the amendment protects an individual's REASONABLE EXPECTATION OF PRIVACY, a test involving both a subjective expectation of privacy and one that society is prepared to recognize as "reasonable." Where an individual has no reasonable expectation of privacy, the government may search and seize without a warrant and even without probable cause. Consequently, the government may search and seize things or matters that an individual of necessity or willingly exposes to the public. For example, the government may photograph one's features, lift one's fingerprints, tape public lectures, or place tracking devices on cars.

The second part of the *Katz* test requires that the expectation of privacy be one that society—here represented by the Supreme Court—is prepared to recognize as reasonable. One consequence of the Court's "reasonable expectation" definitions has been that police may freely examine some places where people might actually expect some privacy, at least in the sense of not contemplating that the government would seek evidence against them there. For example, the Court has held that persons have no reasonable expectation of privacy in trash placed out for collection. The Court has also held, in effect, that persons have no expectation that items hidden from ordinary view on real property will be free from aerial surveillance. Finally, it has held that an occupant of real property has an expectation of privacy only with regard to his or her home and its "curtilage," or the area immediately surrounding it and associated with intimate home uses. Consequently, even were one to hide something in dense, secluded woods on one's private property, the government could legitimately search the woods without a warrant or probable cause.

There are a number of recognized exceptions to the warrant requirement and even some to the probable cause requirement. These exceptions are made in situations in which, while the police have probable cause to search for and seize particular evidence or persons in particular places, some other circumstance—usually referred to as an "exigent" or emergency circumstance—makes it impossible, impracticable, self-defeating, or unwise to obtain a warrant. In situations in which the government demonstrates a special and important need for a limited search, the reasonableness of the search depends upon a balancing of the need to search against the intrusion the search entails. For such reasons, the Court has held several kinds of warrantless searches reasonable: SEARCHES INCIDENT TO ARREST; investigative STOPS-AND-FRISKS; AUTOMOBILE SEARCHES and searches of other mobile vehicles; inspection and regulatory searches, including BORDER SEARCHES; some employer drug-testing searches; and CONSENT SEARCHES.

An ARREST is a seizure of a person. Under COMMON LAW and constitutional rule, when police see a crime being committed or have probable cause to think that a specific person has committed a FELONY and may escape unless arrested, they may arrest without a warrant. Arrest may place police officers at risk if the person arrested has a weapon, and one arrested may wish to dispose of incriminating evidence. To protect themselves and others and to prevent destruction of evidence, officers arresting on probable cause may conduct a full BODY SEARCH of the arrestee and the area within his or her ready reach.

In contrast, warrantless searches and seizures within a home are presumptively unreasonable. Consequently, when police have probable cause to arrest someone who is at home and unlikely to flee while a warrant is sought, they must obtain an ARREST WARRANT.

There are police-civilian encounters short of arrest, usually called "investigative detentions" or "stops-and-frisks." Police rightly investigate suspicious circumstances or characters, and good police work may entail stopping and questioning persons on some reasonable suspicion. If police do stop someone to investigate, however, they may place themselves at risk if the person carries a weapon. On the other hand, a general police authority to stop and question anyone for any reason opens possibilities of police harassment. The Court has held therefore that although the procedure entails a seizure and a search, it is reasonable for officers to stop persons they reasonably suspect of criminal activity and of being armed and dangerous, for the purpose of questioning them and searching for weapons. Under this authority, when police have reasonable suspicion to think that luggage, parcels, or other containers contain contraband or EVIDENCE of a crime, they may detain them for a limited, unintrusive inspection, such as sniffing by a trained narcotics-detection dog.

Mobile vehicles present a special problem. Were police to seek a warrant for a vehicle they have probable cause to suspect contains evidence of a crime, the vehicle might leave the JURISDICTION in the interim. In addition, as the Court has held, because of extensive regulation of vehicles and the character of their public uses, there is a lesser expectation of privacy in vehicles than there is in homes or offices. Consequently, the Court has laid down the rule that when police have probable cause regarding a mobile vehicle, they may undertake a warrantless search of it. The authority remains even if the vehicle is unlikely to be moved or the police have immobilized it.

Governments undertake inspection or regulatory searches for a variety of purposes. Fire inspection codes often require home and building safety inspection. Airline safety dictates some inspection of luggage and persons flying. Entry into an agricultural pest quarantine zone calls for inspection for designated pests. Crossing an international border calls for inspection to ensure right of entry and search to ensure against smuggling of contraband or dutiable goods. In these situations, the need to inspect or search is great, any inconvenience is small, and the scope and the extent of associated interrogation and search is limited. Similarly, public safety or security may require mandatory drug testing for railway or airline employees where their inattention or dereliction of duty would involve an immediate risk of serious harm. In general, the combination of an overriding public interest and the relatively limited character of the search are thought to make such searches reasonable.

Consent searches constitute the final major exception to the warrant and probable cause requirements. Individuals may voluntarily waive their constitutional rights. One can therefore give up the search and seizure protections the Fourth Amendment accords by agreeing to a search. The major questions in such a case are whether there was voluntary consent to the search and whether the party consenting had authority to do so. Whether consent was voluntary or coerced is a factual question, but the state need not show that the person who allegedly gave consent knew that he or she had a right to refuse to give consent. The Court has also indicated that anyone who has common authority over premises or effects can consent to a search of them and that such consent holds against an absent nonconsenting person who shares the authority. In other words, third parties, who are not the targets of a search, can sometimes consent to searches aimed at securing evidence against a target.

GARY GOODPASTER
(1992)

(SEE ALSO: *Exigent Circumstances Search; Open Fields Doctrine; Plain View Doctrine.*)

Bibliography

AMSTERDAM, ANTHONY    1974    Perspectives on the Fourth Amendment. *Minnesota Law Review* 58:349–477.

LAFAVE, WAYNE    1987    *Search and Seizure: A Treatise on the Fourth Amendment,* 3 vols. St. Paul, Minn.: West Publishing Co.

LANDYNSKI, J.    1966    Search and Seizure and the Supreme Court. *Johns Hopkins University Studies in Historical and Political Science,* ser. 84, No. 1.

TAYLOR, TELFORD    1969    *Two Studies in Constitutional Interpretation.* Columbus: Ohio State University Press.

# UNWRITTEN CONSTITUTION

When the American colonists charged that some British colonial policies and practices were unconstitutional, they appealed to what was generally conceived as an unwritten constitutional tradition that combined the practical good sense of English experience with standards of conduct that were simply, or naturally, equitable and right. Though the principles of this constitutional tradition were scattered among state documents, reported cases of the COMMON LAW, treatises, and other writings, their status derived not from having been written or enacted but from their perceived origin in sources like custom, divine will, reason, and nature. These principles were thought superior to acts of Parliament, whose status did depend on their enactment.

While invoking unwritten HIGHER LAW, however, the colonists were implicitly challenging its efficacy. To the charge of TAXATION WITHOUT REPRESENTATION, Parliament responded with the theory of virtual representation. The colonists rejected this DOCTRINE and insisted that as a practical matter responsible government depended on the ballot, not on government's respect for natural justice. Belief in a higher law thus coexisted with a pessimistic view of human nature and a corresponding distrust of government.

Unlike Britain's constitution, the American Constitution was established through RATIFICATION, a form of enactment. As the supreme law of the land this enacted Constitution consigns appeals from its authority to the category of extralegal considerations. But foreclosing the constitutionality of appeals from the highest written law did not depreciate unwritten law as such, for the written or enacted law could still reflect unwritten standards of natural justice and reason whose status did not depend on enactment. This was the claim of those who campaigned for ratification, as was to be expected from the rhetoric typical of public attempts to persuade.

This is not to say that anyone saw the proposed constitution as entirely consistent with the dictates of reason and justice. SLAVERY and the equal REPRESENTATION in the SENATE of small and large states are examples of acknowledged compromises with contingencies that would not bend to principle. Nevertheless, the argument for ratification was full of references to higher norms as standards for evaluating constitutions, as principles behind its rules and institutions, and as objectives of the system as a whole. In THE FEDERALIST #9 and #10, ALEXANDER HAMILTON and JAMES MADISON not only presented the Constitution as an attempt to reconcile democracy with minority rights and the common good, but they also stated that the fate of democracy justly depended on that reconciliation. In *The Federalist* #78 Hamilton defended JUDICIAL REVIEW and recognized the role of judges in "mitigating the severity and confining the operations" of "unjust and partial" enactments. In *The Federalist* #51 Madison said, "Justice is the end of government" and that it "ever will be pursued until it is obtained, or until liberty be lost in the pursuit." And in the same number he described CHECKS AND BALANCES as a "policy of supplying, by opposite and rival interests, the defects of better motives." Taking this statement at face value would require as a prerequisite to a full understanding of the Constitution knowledge of the "better motives" that constituted part of the model for what the Framers wrote.

It is a matter of central importance that appeals to ideas like justice were not expressed as appeals to this or that particular version but to the general idea itself. Aware of the difference, Hamilton urged readers of *The Federalist* #1 to rise above "local prejudices little favorable to the discovery of truth." He recalled the frequent claim that Americans would decide the possibility of rational government for the whole of mankind, a claim that might redouble efforts to rise above parochialism by adding "the inducements of philanthropy to those of patriotism." Equally important, however, was his acknowledgment of the great number and power of "causes which . . . give a false bias to . . . judgement." And he urged "moderation" on those "ever so thoroughly persuaded of their being in the right." This appeal suggests the value of self-critical striving for truth, an attitude more of confidence in progress toward truth than in claims to possess it.

Further indication of the Constitution's dependence on

commitments that some theorists believe written constitutions can displace is the fact that properties of the Constitution as a whole influence the interpretation of its parts. In addition to the rhetoric of its PREAMBLE and of its draftsmen, the document reflects a concern for simple justice by virtue of its written character. As written communication to an audience of indefinite composition, size, and duration, the document presupposes that virtually anyone can come to understand what it means. Presupposing a large and lasting community of meaning, it anticipates a community of interests embracing all to whom it would potentially apply or who would accept it as a model.

Because of their content, provisions like the TENTH AMENDMENT and the old fugitive slave clause are at odds with the community of interests presupposed by the Constitution as a whole. They are at odds with themselves by virtue of their enunciation as parts of the whole. This tension justified JOHN MARSHALL's nationalist construction of the Tenth Amendment, ABRAHAM LINCOLN's view that the Constitution had put slavery on the path of ultimate extinction, and the Supreme Court's application of the BILL OF RIGHTS to the states through the INCORPORATION DOCTRINE. Observers have interpreted the acceptance of this kind of construction as a sign that the nation has an unwritten constitution. But therapeutic constructions might as easily indicate the power of a written constitution to undermine the parochial and particularistic aspects of its content, separable as the written word is from the physical presence of its authors and their particular needs and conceptions.

The implications of the Constitution's written character bear on a protracted debate among constitutional theorists over the possibility of limiting the discretion of judges in difficult constitutional cases involving human rights, especially rights to SUBSTANTIVE DUE PROCESS and EQUAL PROTECTION. Many participants in the debate share an academic moral skepticism that finds no meaning in general normative concepts beyond the particular conceptions of historical individuals or communities. They diminish simple justice with quotation marks, and they hold particular conceptions of justice interesting primarily as facts that influence other facts, not as beliefs that can be morally better or worse than other beliefs. Rejecting the object of its quest, they also reject traditional moral philosophy as a method of acquiring knowledge. They treat the beliefs of persons and communities as matters essentially of historical fact, to be established by empirical methods, with some room for conceptual analysis, but not for judgments of right and wrong.

To these commentators, talk of reason and justice is essentially rationalization of personal preference, class interest, community morality, and the like. And because they tend to believe that elected officials have a stronger claim to represent the community, they argue that judicial review often involves the imposition of minority preferences on the majority. In an effort to reconcile judicial review with majoritarianism these theorists have tried to link the meaning of general constitutional norms with the intentions of the Framers, tradition, existing and projected community morality, the institutional prerequisites of democratic decision, and other sources whose content they perceive essentially as matters of fact or uncontroversial inference. The effort has failed largely because each source yields conflicting options, not simple, consistent answers. And when the skeptics make their selections, they inevitably (if covertly and therefore irresponsibly) make normative judgments whose rationality their position would force them to deny.

The failure of these skeptical theorists to extirpate normative judgments from decisions about the meaning of constitutional provisions has strengthened the case for moral philosophy in constitutional inquiry, which, in turn, has exacerbated apprehension of unrestrained judicial power. But renewed concern for natural justice need not threaten hopes for limiting judicial discretion. Those who take seriously the idea of justice as something higher than their particular conceptions will value the self-critical striving for moral and political truth recommended in *The Federalist* #1. This attitude is itself a limitation on discretion of the most objectionable variety because it is the antithesis of willful assertiveness.

Arguments for taking natural justice seriously might begin by reflecting on the apparent power of ordinary political debate to change minds about justice and related ideas. This familiar fact shows that, as ordinary citizens understand it, political life presupposes simple justice. Moral skeptics err in supposing that continuing disagreement about justice proves that debate is pointless or that there is nothing to debate about. If there are moral truths to be known, as is ordinarily presupposed, agreement is not the test of what is right. Holding that agreement is the test may signal that one abandons ordinary presuppositions, but it is not an argument for doing so. Academic inquiry begins with ordinary presuppositions. And though constitutional theorists have not reached agreement (a good thing, for universal consensus would remove the impetus for reflection and improvement), they have been unable to avoid ordinary presuppositions about justice and the value of reasoning in deciding what the Constitution means. Perhaps this is a reason to value self-critical striving for the best constructions to which constitutional language, tradition, and opinion are open.

SOTIRIOS A BARBER
(1986)

(SEE ALSO: *Higher Law; Limited Government; Natural Rights and the Constitution*.)

Bibliography

BREST, PAUL   1981   The Fundamental Rights Controversy: The Essential Contradictions of Normative Constitutional Scholarship. *Yale Law Journal* 90:1063–1109.

GREY, THOMAS C.   1978   Origins of the Unwritten Constitution: Fundamental Law in American Revolutionary Thought. *Stanford Law Review* 30:843–893.

HARRIS, WILLIAM F., II   1982   Bonding Word and Polity: The Logic of American Constitutionalism. *American Political Science Review* 76:34–45.

MOORE, MICHAEL S.   1982   Moral Reality. *Wisconsin Law Review* 1982:1061–1156.

———   1985   A Natural Law Theory of Interpretation. *Southern California Law Review* 58:277–398.

## UPHAUS v. WYMAN
### 360 U.S. 72 (1959)

In PENNSYLVANIA V. NELSON (1956) the Court appeared to hold that the Smith Act preempted state antisubversion laws. Here the Court held that state JURISDICTION over sedition against the state, as opposed to sedition against the federal government, was not preempted. In *Sweezy v. New Hampshire* (1956) the Court had invalidated a subversion investigation by the New Hampshire attorney general. Here, using the interest-balancing techniques of BARENBLATT V. UNITED STATES (1959), decided the same day, the Court upheld a similar investigation by him in his capacity as a one-man legislative investigating committee.

MARTIN SHAPIRO
(1986)

## URSEY, UNITED STATES v.

See: Civil Forfeiture

## USE IMMUNITY

See: Immunity Grant

## UTILITY REGULATION

See: Economic Regulation

# VACCINATION

Vaccination is the introduction into the body of a vaccine to prevent disease. In the late nineteenth and early twentieth centuries a number of states made smallpox vaccination compulsory. The Supreme Court upheld the constitutionality of such a law in JACOBSON V. MASSACHUSETTS (1905), and *Jacobson's* continuing vitality as a precedent is routinely assumed.

The *Jacobson* opinion was written by Justice OLIVER WENDELL HOLMES, who regarded the case as he regarded LOCHNER V. NEW YORK (1905), decided later the same year over his dissent. For Holmes, the question in both cases was whether the legislative judgment had passed the bounds of reason. For the majority who found a violation of SUBSTANTIVE DUE PROCESS in *Lochner's* sixty-hour limit on bakers' weekly work but validated compulsory vaccination, the difference surely was that they saw vaccination as a soundly based health requirement. Yet the subsequent collapse of substantive due process as a constitutional limit on ECONOMIC REGULATION should not be taken as a return to the Holmes view equating invasions of the body with the general run of restrictions on liberty. Undoubtedly the standard of judicial review in such cases today is far more demanding than it was for Holmes in *Jacobson*.

A patient who refuses medical treatment, for example, surely has a constitutional right to do so, founded on the liberty protected by the due process clauses, absent the most compelling justification for state-ordered intrusion into his or her body. The right may come to be described in the privacy language used to explain the abortion decisions, which really rest not so much on privacy in its ordinary sense as on a woman's control over her own body and her own life. Similarly, the decisions involving invasion of the body to extract blood or other EVIDENCE for use in detecting crime make clear that such invasions must pass the test of strict judicial scrutiny of their justifications. Claims of RELIGIOUS LIBERTY may be added to the constitutional mix, as when a Jehovah's Witness refuses a blood transfusion, but with or without that ingredient the constitutional claim to autonomy over the body is strong.

The strength of the countervailing governmental interest in compelling vaccination would, of course, depend on the degree of danger to the public posed by unvaccinated persons. Now that smallpox is approaching worldwide eradication, the constitutional claim of a latter-day Jacobson would be far more substantial. Many doctors now recommend against smallpox vaccination, because—as Jacobson himself argued—the procedure involves a risk of contracting the disease. Given the vastly reduced public health justification for the inoculation, it is by no means clear that a compulsory smallpox vaccination law would survive constitutional challenge today. Undoubtedly, however, a state could constitutionally require vaccination for other diseases that significantly endanger public health.

KENNETH L. KARST
(1986)

Bibliography

TRIBE, LAURENCE H. 1978 *American Constitutional Law.* Pages 913–921. Mineola, N.Y.: Foundation Press.

# *VACCO v. QUILL*

See: Right to Die

# VAGRANCY LAWS

Historically, society has used vagrancy laws to punish undesirable or immoral persons considered to be dangerous because of their potential for engaging in criminal conduct. Such laws differed significantly from traditional criminal statutes in that they made it a crime to be a person of a specified status or condition. In the United States, the types of persons punished as "vagrants" have included rogues, vagabonds, habitual loafers, and others considered to be of immoral character.

The first vagrancy laws, which originated in England, required workers to live in specified locations and proscribed giving assistance to able-bodied beggars who refused to work. Late-fifteenth-century vagrancy laws provided that beggars and idle persons, after punishment, were to be banished.

Vagrancy legislation in the United States began in colonial times and closely followed the English model. In the nineteenth century, the Supreme Court in MAYOR OF NEW YORK V. MILN (1837) implicitly recognized both the objectives and necessity of such laws, stating in OBITER DICTUM: "We think it as competent and as necessary for a state to provide precautionary measures against this moral pestilence of paupers, vagabonds, and possible convicts; as it is to guard against the physical pestilence. . . ." More recently, the Court in EDWARDS V. CALIFORNIA (1941) expressly rejected this notion, observing that "[w]hatever may have been the notion then prevailing, we do not think that it will now be seriously contended that because a person is without employment and without funds he constitutes a 'moral pestilence.' Poverty and immorality are not synonymous."

*Edwards*, however, was a narrow decision, which struck down under the COMMERCE CLAUSE a California statute making it a misdemeanor to bring an indigent, nonresident alien into the state. Thus, notwithstanding *Edwards*, vagrancy laws continued broadly to proscribe various types of status crimes until the Supreme Court's decision in *Papachristou v. City of Jacksonville* (1972).

In *Papachristou* the Court held under the VAGUENESS DOCTRINE that a vagrancy statute was unconstitutional on its face. The ordinance, a typical example of a traditional vagrancy law, subjected the following persons to criminal penalty because the city deemed them to be "vagrants":

> Rogues and vagabonds . . . dissolute persons who go about begging, common gamblers, persons who use juggling or unlawful games or plays, common drunkards, common night walkers, thieves, pilferers or pickpockets, traders in stolen property, lewd, wanton and lascivious persons, keepers of gambling places, common railers and brawlers, persons wandering or strolling around from place to place without any lawful purpose or object, habitual loafers, dis-

orderly persons, persons neglecting all lawful business and habitually spending their time by frequenting houses of ill fame, gaming houses, or places where alcoholic beverages are sold or served, [and] persons able to work but habitually living upon the earnings of their wives or minor children.

Two fundamental constitutional defects arise from the vagueness inherent in traditional vagrancy laws. Initially, the definition of "vagrant" fails to give adequate notice of what criminal conduct is proscribed. As recognized in *Connally v. General Construction Co.* (1926), when a criminal statute "either forbids or requires the doing of an act in terms so vague that men of common intelligence must necessarily guess at its meaning and differ as to its application," the DUE PROCESS CLAUSE requires its invalidation under the vagueness doctrine. This doctrine was first applied to a vagrancy-type statute in *Lanzetta v. New Jersey* (1939), which held unconstitutional for vagueness a New Jersey "gangster" statute punishing any "person not engaged in any lawful occupation, known to be a member of a gang consisting of two or more persons, who has been convicted [of a crime or at least three disorderly person offenses]." *Papachristou* applied this doctrine to traditional vagrancy laws, in which the generalized and all-inclusive definitions may encompass many types of innocent behavior.

The second aspect of the vagueness doctrine, even more important than the requirement of fair notice, is that a criminal statute must set forth minimal guidelines to govern law enforcement. Absent such guidelines, a criminal statute is subject to substantial abuse by police officers, prosecutors, and jurors on the basis of their own personal predilections. Imprecise definitions, like those contained in traditional vagrancy statutes, give law enforcement officers virtually unbridled discretion to make arrests on mere suspicion rather than on PROBABLE CAUSE, and to use such arrests as a law enforcement tool to gather information and to interview persons about unrelated crimes. Moreover, as suggested in Justice HUGO L. BLACK's dissenting opinion in *Edelman v. California* (1953), they are also easily susceptible of being used against persons expressing unpopular views, as well as against the poor and minorities.

Traditional vagrancy statutes may also suffer from other constitutional defects. For example, *Robinson v. California* (1962) struck down a provision of a California vagrancy statute that made it a crime to be a "narcotics addict," on the ground that the statute violated the CRUEL AND UNUSUAL PUNISHMENT clause of the Eighth Amendment. In *Powell v. Texas* (1968), by contrast, the Court upheld a state statute that proscribed public drunkenness, even though the person so charged might suffer from chronic alcoholism. The Court noted in *Powell* that such a proscription differs from convicting someone for being an addict, a chronic alcoholic, mentally ill, or a leper. Rather than punishing mere status, the proscription focuses on the specific act of appearing drunk in public on a particular occasion—conduct that the state has an interest in prohibiting.

To the extent that vagrancy laws have been used to exclude undesirables from a state or otherwise to confine them geographically, *Edwards* recognizes that they may unreasonably burden INTERSTATE COMMERCE. Moreover, such restrictions also may unconstitutionally impair the RIGHT TO TRAVEL. And provisions of vagrancy laws that prohibit association with known thieves and other undesirables not only suffer from vagueness but also may violate an individual's right of association.

In view of the Supreme Court's decisions in the area of vagrancy laws, most of the antiquated provisions of such laws—which focus on controlling undesirables by proscribing various types of status or condition—no longer can withstand constitutional scrutiny.

JAMES R. ASPERGER<br>(1986)

(SEE ALSO: *Kolender v. Lawson.*)

Bibliography

AMSTERDAM, ANTHONY G.   1967   Federal Constitutional Restrictions on the Punishment of Crimes of Status, Crimes of General Obnoxiousness, Crimes of Displeasing Police Officers, and the Like. *Criminal Law Bulletin* 3:205–241.
FOOTE, CALEB   1956   Vagrancy-Type Law and Its Administration. *University of Pennsylvania Law Review* 104:603–650.
LACEY, FORREST W.   1953   Vagrancy and Other Crimes of Personal Condition. *Harvard Law Review* 66:1203–1226.

# VAGUENESS

The Fifth Amendment and FOURTEENTH AMENDMENT respectively prohibit the federal and state governments from taking life, liberty, or property without DUE PROCESS OF LAW. These provisions forbid the enforcement of any law that, in the classic words of *Connally v. General Construction Co.* (1926), "either forbids or requires the doing of an act in terms so vague that men of common intelligence must necessarily guess at its meaning and differ as to its application." Vagueness imperils the fair administration of legal sanctions in several ways. First, it threatens punishment of people who had no fair warning of what conduct to avoid. Second, by creating interpretive latitude for those who apply the law—police, prosecutors, judges, juries, and others—vagueness permits punishment to be inflicted selectively for arbitrary or improper reasons. Third, a law's vagueness hinders the efforts of reviewing courts

to control such abuses in the law's enforcement; the less clear the law is, the less visible—and correspondingly more difficult to detect and correct—are irregular instances of its administration.

To minimize these dangers, the due process requirement of reasonable clarity forbids enforcement even if the legislature constitutionally could have prohibited, through a clearer law than it did enact, all the behavior its vague law might have been intended to reach. When the uncertain coverage of a vague law might extend into areas of behavior that are constitutionally protected from regulation, however, the ordinary dangers of arbitrary enforcement are heightened, and two additional concerns emerge: the risk that a vague law, which inevitably poses an uncertain risk of prosecution, will inhibit people from exercising precious liberties that the government has no right to outlaw, and the possibility that the legislature did not explicitly focus on the liberty interest and thus did not actually decide that there was compelling reason to regulate it.

The deterrence of constitutionally guaranteed activity that vagueness may produce is akin to the deterrence produced by overbroad laws that encompass both behavior that legitimately may be regulated and behavior that is constitutionally protected. Vagueness differs from overbreadth in that the source of potential inhibition is the law's lack of clarity, not its excessive reach. Yet in both cases the ultimate threat is that those who wish to exercise constitutional rights will refrain from doing so for fear of being penalized. That vagueness may have the practical effect of overbroad regulation explains the common doctrinal confusion between the two concepts. Vagueness also differs from OVERBREADTH in another way: an uncertain law that addresses, even in its most expansive interpretation, only behavior that constitutionally may be regulated may still be void for vagueness, but, by definition, cannot be void for overbreadth.

Two questions dominate the law of vagueness: how much vagueness is tolerable before the law violates due process, and who may raise the vagueness objection. The Supreme Court appears to give different answers to each question, depending on whether or not the vagueness implicates constitutionally protected activity. Still, the constitutional issue of vagueness is always a question of degree, of how much interpretive uncertainty is tolerable before the legitimate regulatory interests of government must yield to the perils of vagueness. If the constitutional definition of vagueness is itself uncertain, the reason is that language is inherently imprecise. The public interest in regulating antisocial behavior would be sacrificed if due process mandated impossible standards of clarity before laws validly could be enforced.

The starting point for vagueness analysis is to ascertain

the nature of the standard that the law sets. This inquiry requires judges to consider not only the statutory language but also all interpretive aids that may add to the law's precision, such as accepted meanings in the relevant community (or in other areas of law) for terms contained in the statute, implementing regulations, past judicial interpretations that have clarified uncertain terms, and even judicial clarification in the very case raising the vagueness objection—if this after-the-fact clarification does not disregard the legislature's intent and if the challenger reasonably could have anticipated that the law could be construed to cover his conduct. The interpretive option often allows the Supreme Court and lower federal courts to avoid invalidating vague federal laws. When federal courts confront state laws, however, they are limited to determining whether state court clarification has cured any constitutional problems of vagueness. This difference largely explains why state laws are stricken for vagueness more often than are federal laws.

Once a law has received the benefit of all available clarification, a wide range of factors affects a court's judgment whether the law's remaining vagueness renders it unconstitutional. In a case in which the vagueness does not bear on constitutionally shielded behavior, only two vagueness objections are permitted: that the law is vague as applied to the particular behavior of the individual challenger, or that the law is INVALID ON ITS FACE for being unduly vague as applied to anyone, including the challenger, because no one who consulted it could derive fair warning of what conduct was prohibited or could determine whether the legislature meant one thing rather than another. In *Hoffman Estates v. Flipside* (1982) the Supreme Court confirmed that in deciding cases in which the latter objection is raised, greater uncertainty is constitutionally permissible when the law regulates a relatively narrow subject matter; when the law regulates economic behavior (because businesses more reasonably can be expected to consult laws in advance of acting than can individuals); when the law imposes civil rather than criminal penalties (because the consequences of noncompliance are less severe); and when the law applies only to those who intentionally or knowingly violate it (because there is less risk of unfair surprise). Historically, once the Supreme Court determined that ECONOMIC REGULATION posed no significant threat to constitutional freedoms, it became more tolerant of the imprecision in laws banning "unreasonable," "unjust," or "unfair" prices or business practices, as *United States v. National Dairy Products Corp.* (1963) illustrates. Moreover, the Court permits more uncertainty when it perceives the government's regulatory objective to be especially important—as SCREWS V. UNITED STATES (1945) demonstrated in upholding a rather vague CIVIL RIGHTS law protecting individuals—and also when it would be difficult for the legislature to delineate more precisely the penalized behavior.

The Court is especially receptive to a challenge based on vagueness when a law's uncertain coverage risks inhibiting constitutionally safeguarded freedoms. In the last half-century this receptivity has been manifested primarily in FIRST AMENDMENT cases. One indicator of the Court's increased sensitivity is the wide range of people who may now raise the vagueness objection. In cases implicating constitutionally protected activity, the Court not only entertains complaints that a law is vague as applied to the individual litigant or vague in all applications, but it sometimes permits those to whom a law clearly applies to object that it is facially invalid because it is unduly vague as to others. Despite Supreme Court rulings to the contrary both in earlier periods and in cases as recent as PARKER V. LEVY (1974) and BROADRICK V. OKLAHOMA (1973), and despite continuing voices of dissent that this practice allows one as to whom enforcement is fair to assert the hypothetical rights of others and confuses vagueness and overbreadth, the Court currently maintains, in such cases as YOUNG V. AMERICAN MINI THEATRES (1976) and KOLENDER V. LAWSON (1983), that such a person may have the whole law invalidated if the deterrent effect of its vagueness on others is real and substantial.

All of the factors that bear on the acceptable degree of vagueness in laws encompassing only unprotected conduct still apply, some more heavily, to laws that potentially reach constitutionally protected conduct. In addition, the Supreme Court seems to be concerned with other factors: how much protected freedom the vagueness might deter; how important the asserted freedom is; the judges' capacity to preserve the freedom through case-by-case application; the legislature's ability to reformulate the law in less inhibiting fashion; and the extent and importance of legitimate regulation that must be foregone if the law is voided for vagueness.

Although the Court does not always articulate these considerations, they appear to underlie many decisions. In *Baggett v. Bullitt* (1964) and *Cramp v. Board of Public Instruction* (1961), for example, the invalidation of LOYALTY OATH requirements for undue vagueness arrayed important freedoms of association against dubious government needs for assurance. More generally, when the enactment's vagueness risks suppression of unpopular expression or criticism of government, the Court's tolerance level is low. Thus in *Coates v. Cincinnati* (1971) an ordinance barring assembly of three or more persons "annoying" passers-by was held void, as was a law prohibiting "contemptuous treatment" of the American flag in *Smith v. Goguen* (1974).

On the other hand, even vagueness that inhibits valued expression is sometimes indulged if regulatory interests are perceived as powerful. Good examples are the extreme vagueness *Parker v. Levy* permitted the military in punishing "conduct unbecoming an officer and a gentleman" and the lesser, yet undoubted, uncertainty of laws prohibiting partisan political activity by PUBLIC EMPLOYEES that the Court upheld in *Broadrick v. Oklahoma.*

Similarly divergent assessments of the acceptable level of indefiniteness in statutes defining and proscribing OBSCENITY reflect conflict within the Court over the value of sexually explicit, but constitutionally protected, materials. The judgment that deterrence of some sexually explicit adult movies was no cause for alarm led a plurality in *Young v. American Mini Theatres* to uphold a ZONING ordinance restricting the concentration of adult theaters and bookstores in downtown Detroit. A similar judgment underlies the Court's willingness to permit inevitably vague definitions of obscenity to serve as the basis for criminal punishment. By contrast, Justice WILLIAM J. BRENNAN, who is more concerned about the potentially protected sexual expression that might be lost, declared in his important dissent in *Paris Adult Theatre I v. Slaton* (1973) his firm, if belated, conviction that vagueness in defining obscenity is virtually an insuperable problem. Even he, however, did not conclude that the distribution of obscene materials must consequently remain unregulated; rather, he suggested that the protection of juveniles and the privacy of unconsenting adults might render vagueness tolerable, though protection of consenting adults and community mores and aesthetics would not.

The complexity of the vagueness doctrine stems, then, from the dual nature of the constitutional protection that it offers. Individuals are protected in any case from arbitrary enforcement without a fair opportunity to conform their conduct to legitimate law, and the social interest in maximizing constitutional freedoms is central to judgments about vagueness when the law's indefiniteness threatens to inhibit those freedoms.

JONATHAN D. VARAT
(1986)

Bibliography

AMSTERDAM, ANTHONY B.    1960    The Void-for-Vagueness Doctrine in the Supreme Court. *University of Pennsylvania Law Review* 109:67–116.

BOGEN, DAVID S.    1978    First Amendment Ancillary Doctrines. *Maryland Law Review* 37:679, 714–726.

SCHAUER, FREDERICK    1978    Fear, Risk and the First Amendment: Unravelling the "Chilling Effect." *Boston University Law Review* 58:685.

## VALENTINE v. CHRESTENSEN

See: Commercial Speech

## VALLANDIGHAM, EX PARTE
1 Wallace 243 (1864)

In 1863, soldiers arrested, tried, and found guilty Negrophobic Democratic congressman Clement L. Vallandigham (Ohio) for violating Army orders against public expressions of Confederate sympathies. After returning to this country from banishment in rebel lines, which ABRAHAM LINCOLN had ordered, Vallandigham applied to the Supreme Court for a WRIT OF CERTIORARI to annul the military proceedings. The Court, accepting JURISDICTION, decided, without dissent, that it had no jurisdiction over appeals from military courts. The likelihood of direct clashes between the Court and the COMMANDER-IN-CHIEF thus receded to revive in EX PARTE MILLIGAN (1867).

HAROLD M. HYMAN
(1986)

## VALLEY FORGE CHRISTIAN COLLEGE v. AMERICANS UNITED FOR SEPARATION OF CHURCH AND STATE
454 U.S. 464 (1982)

Severely limiting the precedent of FLAST V. COHEN (1968), the Supreme Court here tightened the requirements for STANDING in a TAXPAYER'S SUIT against the federal government.

Under a general power from Congress to dispose of surplus federal property, the Department of Health, Education and Welfare (HEW) transferred land and buildings worth over $500,000 to a religious college that trained students for the ministry. Because HEW calculated that the government benefited from the transfer at a rate of 100 percent, the college paid nothing.

Federal taxpayers sued to set aside the transfer, contending that it amounted to an ESTABLISHMENT OF RELIGION. The Supreme Court held, 5–4, that the taxpayers lacked standing. The majority distinguished *Flast,* which had upheld taxpayer standing to challenge federal subsidies to church schools: *Flast* challenged an act of Congress; here plaintiffs challenged a decision by HEW. Furthermore, *Flast* involved injury to the plaintiffs as taxpayers: tax money was to be spent unconstitutionally. Here the Court dealt not with Congress's spending power but with the power to dispose of property.

The dissenters emphasized what everyone knew: absent taxpayer standing, no one has standing to challenge government donations of property to churches. In such cases the establishment clause is enforceable in the consciences of government officials, but not in court.

KENNETH L. KARST
(1986)

# VALUE PLURALISM AND THE CONSTITUTION

Value pluralism is the idea that legitimate human values and goals are many, often incompatible, and not reducible to any single overarching principle or conception of the good. Individuals, and certainly societies, have aspirations that conflict and therefore cannot all be fully realized. A society cannot have perfect human equality and perfect liberty, for example, because people will often exercise freedom to differentiate themselves, and hence to make themselves unequal to their fellows. Equality or freedom may be at odds with other values as well, like tradition, or the desire for social unity, or for social tolerance; good government may be at odds with self-government; secularism with the desire for shared faith; and so forth. Value pluralism implies the need for compromise and conciliation, and an open MARKETPLACE OF IDEAS—many of which may be good, although conflicting. Value pluralism is a theme closely identified with the thought of Sir Isaiah Berlin, the English philosopher and historian of ideas. As Berlin pointed out, pluralism itself is at odds with the dream of philosophical harmony: the quest for a unified system of true values, and for consistent right answers about how we should live. Many systems of belief in human history have held out this hope of ultimate unity—Platonist, religious, rationalist, or Marxist. Such "monism" can smack of tyranny, however. The idea that any one ideal or system of values represents all that is good may imply enforcing the ideal "by whatever means necessary."

Value pluralism, on the other hand, is associated with LIBERALISM, for a defining element of liberalism is respect for human autonomy—freedom for people to make their own choices about what is good and worthy in life. (Free people inevitably make various and conflicting choices. This does not trouble the pluralist who sees the possibility of good in many of these choices. It is the believer in a single ideal who may be more troubled by people making "wrong" choices.) As an outlook, therefore, value pluralism is congenial to the U.S. Constitution, since the Constitution is a liberal charter.

FREEDOM OF SPEECH, for example, has obvious overtones of value pluralism: among conflicting ideas, many may be good. So likewise for RELIGIOUS LIBERTY. The detailed plan for elective office-holding, which occupies a large chunk of the Constitution, also implies value pluralism. Free elections mean that officials and parties with conflicting ideals will tend to alternate with each other. This might seem perverse to a believer in a single ideal or in a unified system of values who would question why falsehood and wrong should be allowed to alternate with truth and goodness. But popular elections make more sense if there might be good in many of the conflicting ideals, from Federalist to Whig, and Democratic to Republican.

Value pluralism has equivocal implications for JUDICIAL REVIEW, one of the most distinctive features of American constitutionalism. The courts' power to strike down the acts of other branches of government can sometimes promote plurality of values in American life. Judicial review of censorship, or of restrictions on religious freedom, for example, can protect pluralism of thought or of religion at times when there might be strong majority pressures for uniformity. By striking down acts of Congress as going beyond federal power under the Constitution's FEDERALISM provisions, judicial review can also be a counterweight against the tendency of the national government to impose national uniformity. The courts can ensure that state or local governments are free to adopt various values and policies, instead of a single policy or ideal that is enforced nationwide.

But on the whole, the implications of value pluralism are in the direction of judicial restraint. Judicial review tends to impose a single standard, and to preempt the coexistence of competing interpretations of the Constitution in different parts of the country and at different times. This is because courts are hierarchical. Appellate review, supervised ultimately by the Supreme Court, means that only one judicial interpretation can prevail, at least in principle, at any given time. Deference to PRECEDENT and STARE DECISIS tends to preserve such sole, exclusive interpretations even over time. Nonjudicial branches of government, by contrast, are more pluralist. There are more of them—federal and state—and they are more independent of one another. A policy decision (or an interpretation of the Constitution) by any of them is more easily changed or OVERRULED than are the constitutional doctrines of the courts.

The perennial debate in America about the courts and the Constitution is not whether there should be judicial review, but how aggressive it should be and how broadly public issues should be treated as questions of constitutional law. To what extent (if at all) should ABORTION be a constitutional question? What about routine police procedure and public aid to private (including parochial) schools or their students? What about CAMPAIGN FINANCE or laws that treat the sexes differently? Value pluralism weighs against JUDICIAL ACTIVISM, at least during times when there is little realistic threat that social pressures would impose their own uniformity across the country in the absence of judicial intervention. With somewhat less constitutional law, there would be more scope for a plurality of policies, ideals, and values—many of which might conflict, but nonetheless (at least some of them) be good.

MAIMON SCHWARZSCHILD
(2000)

(SEE ALSO: *Nonjudicial Interpretation of the Constitution*.)

Bibliography

BERLIN, ISAIAH   1997   *The Proper Study of Mankind: An Anthology of Essays*. Henry Hardy and Roger Hausheer, eds. London: Chatto & Windus.

GRAY, JOHN   1996   Isaiah Berlin. Princeton, N.J.: Princeton University Press.

IGNATIEFF, MICHAEL   1998   Isaiah Berlin: A Life. New York: Metropolitan Books.

SCHWARZSCHILD, MAIMON   1988   Value Pluralism and the Constitution: In Defense of the State Action Doctrine. *Supreme Court Review* 1988:129–161.

———   1996   Pluralist Interpretation: From Religion to the First Amendment. *Journal of Contemporary Legal Issues* 7: 447–472.

# VAN BUREN, MARTIN
## (1782–1862)

Martin Van Buren of Kinderhook, New York, was admitted to the bar in 1803 and quickly established himself as a successful lawyer and politician. While serving in the New York legislature, Van Buren and a group of close associates known as the Albany Regency constituted the first political machine with a modern cast in the nation. As such the Regency gave a new direction to American politics.

But Van Buren did not consider the political process an end in itself; he saw in it a mode for achieving his notion of a Jeffersonian republic, in which a judicious division of power and responsibility between the central government and the states turned on a STRICT CONSTRUCTION of the Constitution. Opposition was expressed in BROAD CONSTRUCTION, along Hamiltonian lines. Between these two positions, the one emphasizing state power, the other national, the very essence of SOVEREIGNTY would be in constant conflict over public questions, a conflict he thought essential to the democratic governance of the states and the nation. He carried his ideas of an adversarial party system to Washington when elected a United States senator in 1821, and over the two terms he served, developed, and promoted them. Van Buren bound together into a cohesive program the personal factions that constituted his party. As he had planned, his partisan coalition gave im-

petus to a specific political opposition. Thus, he played a significant role in the formation of the current two-party system.

Van Buren articulated a historical view of strict construction. He was a frequent critic of the centralizing doctrines of the MARSHALL COURT and supported measures to curb JUDICIAL REVIEW. He drafted ANDREW JACKSON's veto of the MAYSVILLE ROAD BILL, the first comprehensive treatment of the responsibility of the central government to fund INTERNAL IMPROVEMENTS in the various states. Van Buren distinguished projects that were clearly intrastate from those that were interstate in character. In withholding the support of the national government for the economic development of the individual states, he relied partly on JAMES MONROE's veto of the Cumberland Road Bill, but he took care to assert that many projects purely local in character and initiated by a state might deserve support under constitutional provisions that provided for the common defense and the GENERAL WELFARE. His distinction depended upon many variables which could change with time and with circumstance.

Van Buren's second expression of what might be properly called the New Jeffersonianism was in the financial policy he pursued as President (1837–1841): the subtreasury system, which looked to the separation of the federal government from the state deposit banks. The federal government held most of the nation's specie currency, the basis of the paper money supply; thus it would act as a restraint on state banks, curbing their tendencies to speculation and ensuring a more equitable distribution of credit. His means may have been orthodox and deflationary, but they acted as a restriction upon state power, contrary to THOMAS JEFFERSON's ideas on government.

Van Buren's stand on the powers of Congress over the TERRITORIES, however, was a restatement of Jeffersonian views expressed in the NORTHWEST ORDINANCE of 1787. Van Buren added his own interpretation of Article IV, section 3, of the Constitution, which delegates to the Congress the power "to make needful rules and regulations respecting the territory or other property of the United States." In doing so he went further than JOHN MARSHALL and agreed with JOSEPH STORY who asserted that the power was exclusive and that "rules and regulations" covered all possible contingencies. Van Buren had supported the MISSOURI COMPROMISE as a proper exercise of congressional power even though, as a matter of precedent, he thought the Ordinance of 1787 excluded slavery from all territories. In the United States SENATE he voted against the bill organizing a territorial government for Florida because it sustained slavery. The most complete exposition of his stand on the territorial question of the late 1840s and 1850s is expressed in an address he prepared for the New

York Democratic legislative caucus. It was the basis for the platform of the Free Soil party in the campaign of 1848 and the spirit and the substance of the Republican party platform in the campaigns of 1856 and 1860.

W. JOHN NIVEN
(1986)

Bibliography

NIVEN, W. JOHN 1983 *Martin Van Buren and the Romantic Age of American Politics.* New York: Oxford University Press.

# VAN DEVANTER, WILLIS
## (1859–1941)

Colleagues and contemporary observers agreed that Willis Van Devanter was enormously influential during his twenty-six years on the Supreme Court. Chief Justice WILLIAM HOWARD TAFT, who as President appointed him in 1911, described his Wyoming associate as "my mainstay," "the most valuable man in our court," and the Justice who had "more influence" than any other. Justice LOUIS D. BRANDEIS, Van Devanter's ideological antipode, praised him as a "master of formulas that decided cases without creating precedents." Harvard's Professor FELIX FRANKFURTER aptly dubbed him Taft's "Lord Chancellor."

Van Devanter's backstage prominence contrasted vividly with his well-known "pen paralysis." He rarely spoke for the Court in major constitutional cases. During his tenure, Van Devanter averaged only fourteen written opinions each year; during the 1930s he averaged only three a year.

Van Devanter came to the Court after a career in Wyoming law and politics, followed by five years in the Interior Department. President THEODORE ROOSEVELT appointed him to the Eighth Circuit Court of Appeals in 1903; eight years later, President Taft elevated him to the Supreme Court. Taft, himself a former circuit judge, prized judicial experience as a criterion for appointment to the Supreme Court.

Although Van Devanter was one of the conservative "Four Horsemen" of the NEW DEAL era, two of his earlier opinions aligned him with the "liberal nationalistic" wing of the Court. In the second of the EMPLOYERS' LIABILITY CASES (1913) he upheld a federal statute holding railroads liable for injuries suffered by workers engaged in INTERSTATE COMMERCE. He boldly generalized about the sweep of the COMMERCE CLAUSE, describing the commerce power as "complete in itself," but he added that it did not extend to matters that had no "real or substantial relation to some part of such commerce." The previous year, in *Southern Railway Co. v. United States* (1911), he had written for the Court to sustain federal railroad safety legislation in a case involving an intrastate railroad which carried goods that had passed through interstate commerce. Again, Van Devanter found the commerce power plenary and operative if an intrastate matter affected interstate commerce. The decision anticipated Justice CHARLES EVANS HUGHES's consideration of intrastate effects on the commerce power in the *Shreveport Case* (*Houston, East and West Texas Railroad Company v. United States*, 1914), an opinion Van Devanter supported; yet, in the 1930s he consistently rejected similar arguments to expand the scope of federal ECONOMIC REGULATION.

Van Devanter's most important and enduring contribution to constitutional law came with his opinion broadly approving Congress's investigative powers. In *McGrain v. Daugherty* (1927) the plaintiffs had challenged a Senate committee's investigation of Harding administration scandals. Van Devanter recognized that historically "the power of inquiry—with process to enforce it—is an essential and appropriate auxiliary to the legislative function"; that the power might be abused, he added, was no argument against its existence.

Van Devanter usually supported governmental repression of political dissent in the WORLD WAR I era. In the early 1930s, however, he deviated from his ideological allies as he joined the majority in invalidating a section of California's criminal anarchy law in STROMBERG V. CALIFORNIA (1931). He also supported Justice GEORGE H. SUTHERLAND's pathbreaking opinion on Sixth Amendment rights in POWELL V. ALABAMA (1932). But a few years later, when the Court reverted to the CLEAR AND PRESENT DANGER doctrine for FIRST AMENDMENT cases, Van Devanter led the "Four Horsemen" in dissent. In HERNDON V. LOWRY (1937), which involved a black communist who had been convicted under Georgia state law, Van Devanter thought that Herndon's appeal to blacks was especially dangerous; Van Devanter's dissent reflected the suppressive BAD TENDENCY TEST and racist rhetoric, as well.

During the constitutional struggles over the New Deal, Van Devanter opposed the administration in every case except ASHWANDER V. TENNESSEE VALLEY AUTHORITY (1936). Even when his conservative colleagues resurrected the restrictive doctrines of UNITED STATES V. E. C. KNIGHT COMPANY (1895), a decision which he had circumvented in some of his early opinions, Van Devanter steadfastly opposed the expansion of national regulatory power. But he never spoke for that viewpoint, either in the majority or in dissent. Fittingly, however, he played a key role in what may have been FRANKLIN D. ROOSEVELT's most significant political defeat. During the consideration of Roosevelt's court-packing proposal in April 1937, Van Devanter announced his intention to take advantage of a new law allowing Justices to retire at full pay. The impending vacancy offered promise of a shift in the Court's ideological stance, and made the President's plan unnecessary for many administrative supporters. After his retirement from the Supreme Court, Van Devanter apparently was the first retired Justice who served regularly as a reserve judge.

STANLEY I. KUTLER
(1986)

Bibliography

PASCHAL, JOEL F. 1951 *Mr. Justice Sutherland: A Man Against the State.* Princeton, N.J.: Princeton University Press.
PRINGLE, HENRY F. 1939 *The Life and Times of William Howard Taft.* New York: Farrar & Rinehart.

## VAN HORNE'S LESSEE v. DORRANCE
### 2 Dallas 304 (1795)

*Van Horne's Lessee,* a circuit court case in the District of Pennsylvania, is memorable because of Justice WILLIAM PATERSON's charge to the jury, instructing them that a state act unconstitutionally violated property rights. His opinion can be read as a roadmap of the direction that constitutional law would take as a law of judicially implied limitations on legislation adversely affecting property rights. In lucid nonlegal language, Paterson spelled out judicial presuppositions and constitutional principles that were to become orthodox for well over a century. In discussing "What is a Constitution?" and analyzing the legislature's authority to pass its act divesting land titles, Paterson joined together the doctrines of JUDICIAL REVIEW and VESTED RIGHTS. Prefiguring FLETCHER V. PECK (1810) as well as the basic principle of MARBURY V. MADISON (1803), Paterson invoked the HIGHER LAW concept and the CONTRACT CLAUSE against the statute.

Having declared that "it will be the duty of the Court to adhere to the constitution, and to declare the act null and void" if it exceeds the legislature's authority, Paterson discoursed on the relationship between FUNDAMENTAL LAW and the rights of property. He found such rights inalienable, their preservation a primary object of "the social compact." Property, when vested, must be secure. For the government to take property without providing a recompense in value would be "an outrage," a "dangerous" display of unlimited authority, "a monster in legislation" that would "shock all mankind." To divest a citizen of his freehold even with compensation was a necessary "despotic" power to be exercised only in "cases of the first necessity." The reason was that the Constitution "encircles, and renders [a vested right] an holy thing. . . . It is a right not *ex gratia* from the legislature, but *ex debito* from the constitution. It is sacred. . . ."

Paterson informed the jury that courts must hold unconstitutional legislative encroachments on sacred property rights even in the absence of a written constitutional limitation on legislative powers. He relied on "reason, justice, and moral rectitude," "the principles of social alliance in every free government," and the "letter and spirit of the constitution." The letter, in this instance, turned out to be the clause in Article I, section 10, of the Constitution, prohibiting a state law impairing the OBLIGATION OF A CONTRACT. Paterson assumed that the contract clause extended to contracts to which the state was a party; that a previous state act recognizing a property interest of the original claimant was a contract within the protection of the contract clause; and that the divestiture of the titles, even with compensation, violated the clause. Paterson's charge was a textbook exposition of CONSTITUTIONALISM, higher law limitations, judicial review, courts as bulwarks of property rights, and the contract clause.

LEONARD W. LEVY
(1986)

## VATTEL, EMERICH DE
### (1714–1767)

Emerich de Vattel, the Swiss-born statesman and theorist of LIMITED GOVERNMENT, wrote his *Law of Nations* (1758) as an attempt to explain international law on the basis of NATURAL RIGHTS. He argued that men compacted to form sovereign states, and the state ordained a CONSTITUTION superior to any prince or legislature. Vattel reasoned that because the "legislature derives its power from the constitution, it cannot overleap the bounds of it without destroying its own foundation"—and this maxim was frequently cited by American revolutionary leaders including JAMES OTIS and SAMUEL ADAMS. Even more important for American constitutional thought was his assertion, often quoted by JAMES MADISON, that states joining a federal union retained their SOVEREIGNTY but were nevertheless bound by the terms of the union.

DENNIS J. MAHONEY
(1986)

## VEAZIE BANK v. FENNO
### 8 Wallace 533 (1869)

During the CIVIL WAR, Congress introduced national bank notes, secured by United States bonds, as one form of currency. Congress then decided to make its money supreme by driving out of circulation bank notes issued by state banks, and to that end it imposed a prohibitory ten percent tax on those notes. Veazie Bank objected on the grounds that the tax was not levied for revenue purposes but to drive state notes out of existence by the device of a DIRECT TAX, which must be apportioned among the states on the basis of population. Chief Justice SALMON P. CHASE, for a seven-member majority, upheld the constitutionality of the congressional tax statute. Chase declared that only taxes on land and CAPITATION TAXES were direct taxes. He found the constitutional authority for the statute in Congress's power to control the currency of the nation and for that purpose to restrain "the circulation as money of any notes not issued under its own authority." Without such a restraining power the attempt by Congress to secure a "sound and uniform currency for the country must be futile."

LEONARD W. LEVY
(1986)

# VENUE

"Venue" refers to the location of a trial. Article III of the Constitution specifies that federal crimes be tried "in the State where the said Crimes shall have been committed." This provision is reinforced by the SIXTH AMENDMENT's guarantee of TRIAL BY JURY "of the State and district wherein the crime shall have been committed." Although the INCORPORATION DOCTRINE has made the Sixth Amendment's jury trial guarantee applicable to the states, the Supreme Court has not yet had occasion to decide whether that amendment's venue provision also limits the states. However, state law itself usually provides for trial in the locality where the crime is alleged to have been committed.

Both the FEDERAL RULES OF CRIMINAL PROCEDURE and a number of state laws contemplate a change of venue when trial in the district otherwise appropriate risks prejudicing the fairness of a criminal trial. The availability of a change of venue has been offered by the Supreme Court as one argument against GAG ORDERS forbidding the press to publish information about pending prosecutions. (See FREE PRESS/FAIR TRIAL.)

Some crimes are committed in more than one place: interstate transportation of a stolen automobile, for example, or certain criminal conspiracies. The Supreme Court has upheld congressional legislation allowing prosecution in any of the districts in which such a crime is committed.

Venue in civil actions is not limited by the Constitution. By statute, Congress has established an elaborate set of rules governing venue in federal civil cases. Because these rules are designed for the parties' convenience, the right to assert them can be waived. Thus a defendant in a federal court civil action must raise the objection of improper venue before trial, at the pleadings stage of the case.

KENNETH L. KARST
(1986)

Bibliography

WRIGHT, CHARLES ALAN  1983  *The Law of Federal Courts*, 4th ed. Chap. 7. St. Paul, Minn.: West Publishing Co.

# VERMONT CONSTITUTION OF 1777
## (July 8, 1777)

In significant respects Vermont's early constitutional history was unique. It was never a colony, had no charter, and was not recognized as a separate government or state by the original thirteen, although it fully supported the American cause during the Revolution. Vermonters declared their independence not only from Great Britain but also from New York. A "convention" adopted a CONSTITUTION, prefaced by a declaration of rights, that was modeled after the extremely democratic PENNSYLVANIA CONSTITUTION OF 1776, but Vermont added three notable provisions. Its constitution was the first to outlaw slavery, the first to allow all male residents over twenty-one to vote even if they owned no property and paid no taxes, and the first to include a provision for JUST COMPENSATION in cases of EMINENT DOMAIN. Vermont joined the union as the fourteenth state in 1791.

LEONARD W. LEVY
(1986)

# VESTED RIGHTS

"Vested rights" are claims enforceable under law. Early in the history of the Republic, an assertive concept of vested rights became the core of a highly refined legal and constitutional doctrine that was invoked as a shield for private property against regulation by government. In EDWARD S. CORWIN's phrase, this became "the basic doctrine of American constitutional law."

An early expression of the doctrine was Justice WILLIAM PATERSON's opinion in VAN HORNE'S LESSEE V. DORRANCE (1795), stating that preservation of private property is "a primary object of the SOCIAL COMPACT," so that any law taking one person's freehold and vesting it in another without compensation must be seen as "inconsistent with the principles of reason, justice and moral rectitude . . . [and] contrary to the principle of social alliance in every free government." In expounding this doctrine, judges and treatise writers cited general principles of justice from natural law, civil law, and COMMON LAW. In pre-1860 contract and property law, the doctrine served in tandem with the CONTRACT CLAUSE and was regularly invoked by those opposing the expansion of state interventions under the taxation, EMINENT DOMAIN, and POLICE POWERS.

There is a difference between "vested interests" and "vested rights." The former are claims and expectations based on private contractual relationships and upon a property owner's understanding of the privileges, immunities, and responsibilities associated by law with the property in question. Interests become "rights" when courts agree to enforce such contractual relationships and understandings concerning property. This difference was recognized by Justice ROBERT H. JACKSON, in his opinion in *United States v. Willow Run Power Company* (1945), declaring: "Not all economic interests are "property rights'; only those economic advantages are "rights' which have the law back of them. . . ." A claim to a right (or "advantage"), Jackson stated, "is really a question to be answered" in judicial proceedings and decisions; it is not something to be taken a priori, even when ancient maxims and rules can be adduced in favor of the claim.

Justice Jackson's robust LEGAL REALISM was not the view that prevailed in legal and constitutional discourse during the nineteenth century. On occasion, individual judges or courts did defend legislative prerogatives against claims of vested rights in terms that foreshadowed Jackson's formulation. For example, a New York judge in 1835 denounced vested rights as an "indefinite" term that was "resorted to when no better argument exists." Any governmental action, he contended, imposed "burthens and duties" that redefined rights. Much more commonly found, however, were views founded on the notion that it was "manifest injustice by positive law" when legislation took away what Justice SAMUEL CHASE described in CALDER V. BULL (1798) as "that security for personal liberty, or private property, for the protection whereof the government was established."

State judges regularly invoked the vested rights doctrine, often explicitly merged with DUE PROCESS declarations, to review and sometimes invalidate legislation. Many judges applied natural-law principles associated with the Fifth Amendment, contending that they were a check upon the abuse of legislative power no less important than explicit state constitutional provisions or than the contract clause. Much relied upon, in such decisions, was Justice JOSEPH STORY's opinion in *Wilkinson v. Leland* (1829), contending that "the fundamental maxims of a free government seem to require that the rights of personal liberty and private property should be held sacred."

During JOHN MARSHALL's tenure as Chief Justice, the court introduced "vested rights" doctrine into contract clause rulings, as in Marshall's opinions in FLETCHER V. PECK (1810) and DARTMOUTH COLLEGE V. WOODWARD (1819). When conservative, property-minded state and federal judges applied Marshall's doctrines in broad terms in the 1830s and 1840s, the debate over vested rights began to center on whether or not corporate privileges, broadly construed, should be given the same protection as property held by individuals and quasi-public institutions. To conservatives such as DANIEL WEBSTER and Justice Story, a corporation's privileges and property rights under a franchise were merely a variant of an individual's rights in fee simple to a house or a tract of farmland. Webster, for example, viewed the action of Massachusetts in CHARLES RIVER BRIDGE COMPANY V. WARREN BRIDGE COMPANY (1837) as part of a "revolution against the foundations on which property rests." He raised the alarm again in his argument in WEST RIVER BRIDGE V. DIX (1848), denouncing broad use of the power of eminent domain as a dangerous kind of agrarian radicalism. There was a pragmatic side, as well, to the arguments of conservatives; both Story and Webster warned on many occasions that to allow legislatures unrestrained use of the police power or eminent domain, in derogation of vested property rights whether personal or corporate, would risk bringing all new investment (and material progress) to a halt.

Beginning with the decision in the *Charles River Bridge* case, the antebellum Supreme Court softened its stand on vested rights; state judges, however, kept the doctrine before the bar and the public. The high-sounding rhetoric of vested rights doctrine can easily obscure one of the important facts of the pre-Civil War period—the irony that in practice the antebellum state courts, as James Willard Hurst has shown, "tended to uphold vested rights only so long as they were felt to yield substantial or present returns in social function." Seldom did the courts support claims of vested rights that were invoked to protect "static" economic interests, attempting to block technological innovation or new forms of investment. Judges favored instead claims of "dynamic" rights that could be seen as forces for change and growth.

The adoption of the FOURTEENTH AMENDMENT opened the way to revival of vested rights doctrine in federal constitutional law. If anything, "vested rights" were now championed in enlarged forms. Leading conservative lawyers such as WILLIAM M. EVARTS, former Justice JOHN A. CAMPBELL, and John N. Jewett seized on the Fourteenth Amendment to forge the new, broader doctrine. Citing the concept of property as an "established expectation," they denied that government could deprive property owners of any expectation unless it paid compensation. They expanded the notion of property to include the right to engage in occupations; and they contended broadly that the rights of ownership included the right to compete freely in the quest for profits. Taking up arguments presented earlier by Campbell, Justice STEPHEN J. FIELD even attempted in his dissenting opinion in the SLAUGHTERHOUSE CASES (1873) to fuse the Fourteenth Amendment with the DECLARATION OF INDEPENDENCE—and thereby to throw the mantle of vested rights over economic interests and activities that he viewed as embraced by the phrase "pursuit of happiness." As he believed, such rights were beyond the legitimate reach of state regulation. Some conservative jurists and lawyers also found in the amendment's PRIVILEGES AND IMMUNITIES clause another prop for vested rights doctrine.

The newly expanded version of vested rights soon found its way into constitutional law, as Justice Field's views came to prevail with those of his colleagues. The traditional rhetoric of vested rights was harnessed to the FREEDOM OF CONTRACT doctrine, which became standard fare in the Court's decisions concerning the validity of laws regulating labor and business practices. In giving content to the doctrine of SUBSTANTIVE DUE PROCESS in the field of economic and social regulation, the Supreme Court marked out a meandering, uncertain, often absurd boundary between what it found to be legitimate police power and the "sacred" rights of property. The view, as Laurence Tribe has phrased it, "that certain settled expectations of a focused and crystallized sort should be secure against governmental disruption, at least without appropriate compensation" became a powerful weapon in the hands of the new industrial corporate interests— and at the same time became the center of political storms in the Populist and Progressive eras. Only with abandonment of economic due process in the late 1930s, together with the ascendancy of views such as Justice Jackson's harshly realist version of vested rights, did the concept recede in importance in constitutional law and in political strife.

In HOME BUILDING & LOAN ASSOCIATION V. BLAISDELL (1934), the Court gave notice that it was ready to uphold even so dramatic a state abridgment of private rights as a mortgage moratorium law. The Court would not, the majority declared, "throttle the capacity of the States to protect their fundamental interests." The common good, or the public interest, must also be honored in any system allocating constitutional powers and immunities. Thus the career of vested rights in the Webster-Story-Field tradition clearly had run its course. Nor for more than thirty years did debates in legislatures and courts return to the concerns of the conservative era; and even then the notion of "settled expectations" and related vested rights ideas were exhumed for application only in a fairly narrow context, relating to land use regulation and INVERSE CONDEMNATION. To that degree, at least, echoes of a doc-

trine rooted in natural law do continue to be heard in our own day.

HARRY N. SCHEIBER
(1986)

Bibliography

CORWIN, EDWARD S. 1914 The Basic Doctrine of American Constitutional Law. *Michigan Law Review* 12:247–276.

HURST, JAMES WILLARD 1956 *Law and the Conditions of Freedom in the Nineteenth Century United States.* Madison: University of Wisconsin Press.

McCLELLAN, JAMES 1971 *Joseph Story and the American Constitution.* Norman: University of Oklahoma Press.

McCURDY, CHARLES W. 1975 Justice Field and the Jurisprudence of Government-Business Relations. *Journal of American History* 61:970–1005.

TWISS, BENJAMIN R. 1942 *Lawyers and the Constitution: How Laissez Faire Came to the Supreme Court.* Princeton, N.J.: Princeton University Press.

# VETO POWER

After rejecting an absolute veto for the President, the delegates at the CONSTITUTIONAL CONVENTION OF 1787 granted the President a qualified power to veto congressional legislation, subject to an override by a two-thirds majority of each house of Congress. Some anti-Federalists objected to the veto as an encroachment upon the legislative power in violation of the SEPARATION OF POWERS doctrine, but ALEXANDER HAMILTON answered in THE FEDERALIST #73 that the President needed a veto to protect the executive branch from "depredations" by the legislature. The veto was also designed to be used against bills that were constitutionally defective, poorly drafted, or injurious to the community.

The Constitution provides that any bill not returned by the President "within ten Days (Sundays excepted)" shall become law "unless the Congress by their Adjournment prevent its Return, in which Case it shall not be a Law." The latter procedure, known as the POCKET VETO, was first used by President JAMES MADISON in 1812. In the POCKET VETO CASE of 1929, the Supreme Court decided that "adjournment" did not refer merely to final adjournment at the end of a Congress. The pocket veto could be used during any adjournment, final or interim, that "prevented" a bill's return to Congress. However, in *Wright v. United States* (1938) the Court considered a three-day recess by the Senate too short a period to constitute adjournment.

Further clarification of the pocket veto resulted from an action by President RICHARD M. NIXON. In 1970, during an adjournment of Congress for less than a week, he pocket-vetoed the Family Practice of Medicine Bill. An appellate court, in *Kennedy v. Sampson* (1974), held that an *intra*session adjournment of Congress does not prevent the President from returning a bill so long as Congress makes appropriate arrangements to receive presidential messages. The GERALD R. FORD and JIMMY CARTER administrations renounced pocket vetoes during *inter*session adjournments as well. This political accommodation restricted the pocket veto to the final adjournment at the end of the second session. President RONALD W. REAGAN, however, has used the pocket veto between the first and second sessions, provoking renewed litigation.

Other court decisions have clarified the boundaries of the veto power. In 1919, in *Missouri Pacific Railway Co. v. Kansas,* the Supreme Court announced that the Constitution required only two-thirds of a quorum in each House to override a veto, not two-thirds of the total membership. In 1899 the Court decided, in *La Abra Silver Mining Co. v. United States,* that the President could sign a bill after Congress recessed, and in *Edwards v. United States* (1932) the Court ruled that he could sign a bill after a final adjournment of Congress.

Statistics underscore the effectiveness of the President's veto. Of the 1,380 regular (return) vetoes from GEORGE WASHINGTON through Jimmy Carter, Congress overrode only ninety-four. There have also been 1,011 pocket vetoes, more than half of them directed by GROVER CLEVELAND and FRANKLIN D. ROOSEVELT against private relief bills.

Most of the governors of the states have been granted authority to veto individual items of a bill (the "item veto"). Congress has thus far resisted giving this power to the President, despite popular belief that such a power would increase "economy and efficiency" by combating "logrolling" and "pork-barrel" politics in Congress. Prominent among the arguments against the item veto is the danger that Presidents could use the authority to control the votes of individual members of Congress. A project in a member's district or state could be held hostage until he or she agreed to support a nominee or legislative proposal backed by the White House.

An informal type of item veto has evolved because Presidents selectively enforce the law. In signing a bill, Presidents have announced that they would refuse to carry out certain provisions which they considered unconstitutional or undesirable. The IMPOUNDMENT of funds has been a common example, but Presidents have also severed from authorization bills a number of sections they considered a "nullity," without binding force or effect.

LOUIS FISHER
(1986)

Bibliography

FISHER, LOUIS 1985 *Constitutional Conflicts between Congress and the President.* Princeton, N.J.: Princeton University Press.

JACKSON, CARLTON 1967 *Presidential Vetoes, 1792–1945.* Athens: University of Georgia Press.
MASON, EDWARD CAMPBELL 1890 *The Veto Power.* New York: Russell & Russell.

# VICE-PRESIDENCY

The American vice-presidency has historically occupied an ambiguous position. Although protocol ranks it the nation's second office, the duties assigned it have not been commensurate with that status. Pundits have frequently ridiculed the office and reformers have generously proposed modifying it. Yet for an institution that has engendered so much criticism the vice-presidency has undergone remarkably little constitutional change.

The office was conceived in the final days of the CONSTITUTIONAL CONVENTION OF 1787 for reasons that remain obscure. Some delegates suggested the need for an officer to preside over the SENATE and resolve tie votes. Others viewed the vice-presidency as a way to handle unexpected presidential vacancies. Finally, some saw the office as an expedient to ensure the election of a national President. They feared that presidential electors would invariably support their own state's favorite son, thereby frustrating efforts to select a chief executive. By creating a second office and by giving electors a second vote subject to the proviso that one of the votes must go to a person from a state other than the elector's these constitutional architects believed they would overcome provincial tendencies and provide the new nation with a consensus leader. The candidate with the most votes (provided that they constituted a majority) would be President, the runner-up Vice-President.

The system provided not only a national President but also vice-presidents of rare ability—JOHN ADAMS, THOMAS JEFFERSON, and AARON BURR. In 1800, however, the electoral votes for Jefferson and Burr deadlocked, although the Republican party had clearly intended Jefferson to be President. The constitutional crisis required thirty-six ballots of the House of Representatives before Jefferson prevailed. The initial system accordingly fell into disfavor, and in 1804 the states ratified the TWELFTH AMENDMENT which provided for separate election of President and Vice-President. Many legislators feared that the vice-presidency would attract only inferior candidates and accordingly proposed its abolition.

Although the office survived, the high caliber of its occupants did not. Most Vice-Presidents during the remainder of the nineteenth century were nonentities who brought few credentials to the office, did little while in it, and disappeared from public attention once their term ended. Presidents had little influence on the selection of their running mates. Party leaders typically chose the second candidate from a different wing of the party in order to balance the ticket. Presidents and Vice-Presidents frequently feuded over policy and personal differences. The Vice-President presided over the Senate, but did little else. As WOODROW WILSON wrote, "The chief embarrassment in discussing his office is, that in explaining how little there is to be said about it one has evidently said all there is to say."

The nineteenth century did, however, provide four occasions for Vice-Presidents to succeed to the presidency on the death of the incumbent. JOHN TYLER, MILLARD FILLMORE, ANDREW JOHNSON, and CHESTER A. ARTHUR all became President when their predecessors died in office. None, however, won a term of his own.

The ambiguous constitutional status of the office was one source of its problem. The office was a hybrid between the legislative and executive branches; its occupant was selected with the President, and yet his only constitutional duty resided in the legislative branch. Neither the Senate not the President was disposed to give great power to an officer which neither had selected and neither could remove. Some Presidents have viewed the vice-presidency as a legislative office and argued that the principle of SEPARATION OF POWERS precludes delegation of duties. Some Vice-Presidents have advanced this reasoning (or rationalization) to resist executive assignments. Moreover, since the presidency itself was relatively inactive for much of the nineteenth century, the President typically had little need to delegate duties to a Vice-President, especially one not politically or personally compatible.

During the twentieth century, the vice-presidency achieved greater importance. The rise in status of the office occurred primarily because of political change rather than constitutional reform. The presidency became the main beneficiary of increased activity of the federal government, especially from the New Deal onward. The President became the distributor of increased patronage, and therefore other political actors responded more willingly to his influence. Accordingly, presidential candidates, rather than party leaders, began to assume a larger role in selecting the running mate. Presidents thus had a chance to select compatible Vice-Presidents and an incentive to provide them with some assignments. Moreover, increased demands on the presidency provided opportunities for vice-presidential activity. Presidents have tended to use their Vice-Presidents as foreign envoys, commission chairmen, party leaders, public spokesmen, legislative liaison, and advisers. Ratification in 1967 of the TWENTY-FIFTH AMENDMENT, which in part provided a means for filling unexpected vice-presidential vacancies, recognized the new significance of the office. With a few notable exceptions, twentieth-century Vice-Presidents have been men of some accomplishment. Many have been presiden-

tial candidates prior to accepting the second position: virtually all subsequently were considered for their party's presidential nomination or received it. Since 1900, five Vice-Presidents—THEODORE ROOSEVELT, CALVIN COOLIDGE, HARRY S. TRUMAN, LYNDON B. JOHNSON, and GERALD FORD—have succeeded to the presidency upon death or resignation of the incumbent. Each one except Ford subsequently won his own term—and Ford lost but narrowly. Presidents JIMMY CARTER and RONALD REAGAN have done much to enhance the office by granting Vice-Presidents Walter F. Mondale and GEORGE BUSH, respectively, broad access to, and influence in, decision making.

The vice-presidency's enlarged significance this century has not silenced its critics. Some prominent students of American government recommend abolishing the office: they would generally handle an unexpected presidential vacancy by designating an interim President and holding special elections. Others would retain the vice-presidency but would attempt to augment its powers either by requiring that the Vice-President hold a leading cabinet position or have a vote or significant powers in the Senate. Finally, a third group of reformers seeks to change the process of nominating or electing Vice-Presidents. Proposals range from having presidential and vice-presidential candidates run together during primaries to holding separate elections for President and Vice-President. Although these proposals stimulate interesting debates, the prospects of significant formal changes in the vice-presidency are slim. Constitutional change rarely, if ever, comes easily. Proposed reforms of the vice-presidency would tend to create as many problems as they would solve. Growth in the office will probably depend largely on further changes in American politics and on the relation between future Presidents and Vice-Presidents.

JOEL K. GOLDSMITH
(1986)

Bibliography

FEERICK, JOHN 1965 *From Failing Hands.* New York: Fordham University Press.
GOLDSTEIN, JOEL K. 1982 *The Modern American Vice Presidency: Transformation of a Political Institution.* Princeton, N.J.: Princeton University Press.
WILLIAMS, IRVING G. 1956 *The Rise of the Vice Presidency.* Washington, D.C.: Public Affairs Press.

# VICINAGE

Of all the features constituting a citizen's right to a TRIAL BY JURY, none is so outdated or less of service than the Sixth Amendment provision guaranteeing "an impartial jury of the State and district wherein the crime [charged] shall have been committed." This specification of the geographic area from which jurors must be drawn should not be confused, however, with VENUE, which fixes the location of the trial itself.

The clause providing for a jury of the vicinage or neighborhood enjoys a time-worn heritage. In the thirteenth century jurors were usually witnesses or had personal knowledge of the event at issue. Although jurors eventually lost their character as witnesses, both EDWARD COKE and WILLIAM BLACKSTONE discussed the precise number of jurors who must come from the immediate locality. Vicinage became an issue in the colonial debate with England, and the Virginia Assembly, in 1769, asserted the colonists' right to "the inestimable Privilege of being tried by a Jury from the vicinage," a position echoed by the Continental Congress and listed as a grievance against the king in the DECLARATION OF INDEPENDENCE. The Sixth Amendment, framed shortly after the JUDICIARY ACT OF 1789, probably refers to the judicial districts established by that act.

Nevertheless, a federal defendant today "does not have a right under the Sixth Amendment to have jurors drawn from the entire district" (*Zicarelli v. Dietz*, 1980), and the Supreme Court has denied that trial juries "must mirror the community and reflect the various distinctive groups in the population" (*Taylor v. Louisiana*, 1975). State courts have generally been willing to narrow the vicinage requirement to a unit as small as an individual county, although federal courts have asserted that the Sixth Amendment clause applies "only to federal criminal trials, not to state criminal trials" (*Zicarelli*).

DAVID GORDON
(1986)

# VIETNAM WAR

Throughout American history, Presidents have dispatched armed forces abroad to protect the lives and property of United States citizens as well as American security interests. However, these military operations usually were limited in scope and duration, were conducted against relatively defenseless nations, and did not involve major powers. Thus, there was little opportunity to test the President's constitutional authority to send armed forces abroad without prior congressional authorization or a DECLARATION OF WAR. For various reasons, the KOREAN WAR did not furnish the occasion to test President HARRY S. TRUMAN's constitutional powers. The Vietnam War (1965–1973) was the first modern undeclared war that provided the opportunity to test the President's authority as COMMANDER-IN-CHIEF.

During the Vietnam War numerous litigants challenged the President's authority to initiate and conduct military hostilities without a congressional declaration of war or other explicit prior authorization. Such litigants denied that the GULF OF TONKIN RESOLUTION constituted authorization. Despite these challenges, the federal courts exhibited extreme caution in entering this twilight zone of concurrent power. The federal judiciary's reluctance to decide WAR POWERS controversies reveals a respect for the constitutional SEPARATION OF POWERS, an appreciation for the respective constitutional functions of Congress and the President in FOREIGN AFFAIRS, and a sense of judicial self-restraint. Nevertheless, toward the end of the Vietnam War, several lower federal courts entered the political thicket to restore the constitutional balance between Congress and the President.

Despite factual variations, the Vietnam War cases can be classified into four broad categories. One federal district court asserted categorically that the complaint raised a POLITICAL QUESTION beyond the court's JURISDICTION. A second agreed that the President's authority to conduct military activities without a declaration of war posed a nonjusticiable political question, but proceeded to determine whether the President had acted on his own authority, pursuant to, or in conflict with either the expressed or implied will of Congress. Courts in the third category concluded that the political question doctrine did not foreclose them from inquiring into the existence and constitutional sufficiency of joint congressional-presidential participation in prosecuting the war. Finally, some district courts decided cases on the substantive merits. Yet the Vietnam War ended without an authoritative Supreme Court decision.

At the war's end Congress enacted the War Powers Resolution (1973), which attempted to resolve the constitutional ambiguities posed by the separation of the congressional war powers from the President's office of commander-in-chief. Under the resolution, Congress can alternatively authorize continuation of military hostilities that the President has initiated or require him to disengage armed forces from foreign combat within sixty to ninety days. Practical problems aside, the resolution seems constitutionally flawed. The Supreme Court's decision in IMMIGRATION AND NATURALIZATION SERVICE V. CHADHA (1983) cast doubt on the constitutionality of the resolution's LEGISLATIVE VETO provision, which states that Congress can direct the disengagement of troops by CONCURRENT RESOLUTION. Moreover, if the Constitution vests the authority to initiate military hostilities exclusively in the Congress, can Congress constitutionally delegate this authority to the President, even for a limited period? Is the War Powers Resolution an undated declaration of war that allows the President to choose the time, the place, and the enemy?

The Framers of the Constitution conferred only a limited set of defensive war powers on the President. As commander-in-chief he superintends the armed forces in war and peace, defending the nation, its armed forces, and its citizens and their property against attack, and directing military operations in wartime. The Framers did not authorize the President to initiate military hostilities, to transform defensive actions into aggressive wars, or to defend allies against attack.

In the Framers' view, only Congress could change the nation's condition from peace to war. Yet neither the constitutional text nor the records of the CONSTITUTIONAL CONVENTION conclusively draw the boundary between congressional power to initiate war and presidential power to defend against attack. In the twentieth century, international terrorism, the Vietnam War, guerrilla and insurgency warfare, wars of "national liberation," and the global conflict between the United States and the Soviet Union have virtually erased the Framers' distinction between defensive and offensive war.

A long history of undeclared war and military hostilities demonstrates that the constitutional questions raised during the Vietnam War are inherent in the American constitutional system. Presidents will be confronted with demands and opportunities to intervene militarily to protect American national security interests and the security interests of the nation's allies. Before yielding to this temptation, future Presidents should recall one of the Vietnam War's most important lessons: the nation should not wage a protracted undeclared war without a continuing agreement between Congress and the President that reflects broad, sustained public support.

EDWARD KEYNES
(1986)

Bibliography

KEYNES, EDWARD   1982   *Undeclared War.* University Park: Pennsylvania State University Press.
REVELY, W. TAYLOR, III   1981   *War Powers of the President and Congress: Who Holds the Arrows and Olive Branch?* Charlottesville: University Press of Virginia.
SOFAER, ABRAHAM D.   1976   *War, Foreign Affairs, and Constitutional Power.* Cambridge, Mass.: Ballinger Publishing Co.

# VIETNAM WAR
## (Update)

The Vietnam War, more accurately labeled America's Indochina War, claimed 46,400 American lives. During its most active phase, from 1964 to 1973, it cost over $107 billion. American troop strength in the conflict reached a peak of 536,100 in March 1969. Yet the war was never formally declared.

Direct American involvement in Indochina began in 1949–1950 when Congress provided for financial and material assistance in "the general area of China" and for the use of noncombatant military advisers. Using this authority, President HARRY S. TRUMAN began sending aid to the associated states comprising French Indochina. When the KOREAN WAR heightened America's commitment in the Far East, Congress anticipated the pattern of coming years by approving additional aid. Following the end of France's military involvement in Indochina in 1954, the United States took the initiative in negotiating the Southeast Asia Collective Defense Treaty, which committed each of its adherents to meet "armed attack in the treaty area . . . in accordance with its constitutional processes." Prior to the treaty's approval by the Senate in 1955, Secretary of State John Foster Dulles interpreted this provision as meaning the President would seek congressional support before launching major military moves, but others hedged on whether such action was constitutionally required. Between 1954 and 1964, the United States provided more than $1 billion in military aid to South Vietnam and by late 1963 the American Military Assistance Advisory Group there had grown to 16,300.

In 1964 the war took on a new constitutional cast. South Vietnam's position having deteriorated, President LYNDON B. JOHNSON sought to continue a policy of measured firmness. In May and June he directed the State Department to begin drafting possible congressional resolutions to affirm the American commitment in Vietnam. This approach drew partly on the experience of the 1950s and early 1960s, when the United States response to crises involving the Formosa Straits, the Middle East, Berlin, and Cuba included congressional resolutions of support in 1955, 1957, 1961, and 1962. Although temporarily shelved, the project soon became urgent. On August 2, perhaps provoked by American-supported commando raids along the North Vietnamese coast, North Vietnam torpedo boats attacked an American destroyer on an intelligence mission in the Gulf of Tonkin. Two days later, another attack may have occurred. Johnson reported the attacks to the American people, but refrained from mentioning either the intelligence mission or doubts about whether the second attack had actually occurred. Congressional leaders received a fuller briefing but not a complete account. Giving them a draft resolution, Johnson asked for its prompt passage even as he ordered retaliatory air strikes against North Vietnam.

Following a perfunctory hearing and almost no floor debate, the House of Representatives passed the GULF OF TONKIN RESOLUTION by a vote of 416–0. In the Senate, owing especially to questions raised by Wayne Morse about the events in the Tonkin Gulf and about the problem of unconstitutionally delegating Congress's WAR POWERS, the hearing process and floor debate took slightly longer, but the measure won approval by 88 to 2, and Johnson signed it into law on August 10. After stating Congress's support for the President's determination "to take all necessary measures to repel any armed attack against the armed forces of the United States and to prevent further aggression," the resolution declared that peace in Asia was a vital American interest and that "the United States is, therefore, prepared, as the President determines, to take all necessary steps, including use of armed force, to assist any member or protocol state of the Southeast Asia Collective Defense Treaty requesting assistance in defense of its freedom."

In February 1965 the United States escalated its air war in Vietnam and soon began sending ground combat troops (as opposed to "advisers"). When voting in 1964, most congressmen had not contemplated this turn of events, yet Senator J. William Fulbright, chairman of the Foreign Relations Committee, had admitted during debate that the resolution could undergird major military action. In 1967, Under Secretary of State (and former Attorney General) Nicholas Katzenbach explained that the Tonkin Gulf Resolution was "as broad an authorization for the use of armed forces . . . as any declaration of war so-called could be in terms of our internal constitutional process." Significantly, however, its State Department drafters had carefully avoided any language conceding that congressional authorization was a requirement for escalating the American presence in Vietnam. This allowed continuing reliance on the President's own authority, as illustrated in February 1966 when a State Department legal memorandum argued that the President's direct powers under Article II covered the commitment in Vietnam. That being the case, the Southeast Asia Collective Defense Treaty's provision for action in accordance with American "constitutional processes" further authorized the war in Vietnam. But, explained the memorandum, the existence of the Tonkin Gulf Resolution and congressional appropriations for the conflict obviated the need to delineate precise constitutional boundaries.

Despite growing public and congressional criticism of the war, Congress enacted at least twenty-four laws supporting it between 1964 and 1969. Senator Morse's 1966 call for repeal of the Tonkin Gulf Resolution met defeat, as, for example, did antibombing amendments to appropriations bills in 1968. In 1967 the Senate Foreign Relations Committee began to consider a "National Commitments Resolution," after Fulbright, its chairman, switched to an antiwar stance. But the resulting measure, as adopted in June 1969, merely expressed "the sense of the Senate" that the commitment of troops abroad should result only from affirmative and explicit joint action by the President and Congress. Finally, in December 1970, Congress included repeal of the Tonkin Gulf Resolution as a

rider to the Foreign Military Sales Act, which President RICHARD M. NIXON signed in January 1971.

By this time, Nixon and his backers had accepted the argument of the Johnson administration that the resolution was constitutionally unnecessary—but with a twist. Whatever the constitutional basis for the war under Johnson, as Assistant Attorney General WILLIAM H. REHNQUIST explained after the Cambodian "incursion" in April 1970, Nixon inherited a conflict in progress and had "an obligation as commander-in-chief to take what steps he deems necessary to assure the safety of American forces in the field."

Such claims did not prevent senators of both parties and growing numbers of House Democrats from proposing limits on the war. Between late 1969 and mid-1973, ten restrictive measures became law. One barred use of combat troops in Thailand and Laos; another forbade further expenditures for ground operations in Cambodia. Still another, an amendment to a defense procurement act, stated that United States policy was to cease all military operations "at a date certain," but when Nixon signed the act, he denied that the policy declaration had "binding effect." In actuality, prior to the Vietnam cease-fire in January 1973, congressional "doves" were unable to pass ironclad restrictions.

Finally, after the Vietnam cease-fire, but while air attacks on Cambodia continued, Congress voted that no funds "may be expended to support directly or indirectly combat activities in, over, or from off the shores of Cambodia, or in or over Laos by United States forces." When Nixon vetoed the appropriations bill containing the cutoff and its supporters threatened to add similar language to all appropriations measures, a compromise emerged, signed by Nixon on July 1. The Second Supplemental Appropriations Act for 1973 forbade use of any funds in the act itself for military operations in Indochina and added that "after August 15, 1973, no other funds heretofore appropriated under any other Act may be expended for such purpose."

Doubtful of congressional action, opponents of the war had already turned to the judiciary in efforts to enjoin Johnson's warmaking and then Nixon's. Here the need for STANDING proved an initial barrier. At one time or another, federal district courts and courts of appeal held that taxpayers, citizens qua citizens, reservists, draft registrants, inductees, members of Congress, and probably states lacked the required immediate and concrete stake in the controversy. In some later cases, however, the barrier was relaxed, particularly for servicemen under orders to go to Vietnam, and in a few instances, courts finessed the problem of standing by first examining other issues.

Ultimately the POLITICAL QUESTION doctrine proved insuperable. In *Orlando v. Laird* (1971), for example, lower federal courts held that once a conflict reached the magnitude and duration of the war in Vietnam, the Constitution imposed the duty of some joint action by the President and Congress. This requirement established a manageable test that allowed judicial determination without running up against the political questions doctrine. The courts found, however, that the Tonkin Gulf Resolution, wartime extension of the SELECTIVE SERVICE ACT, and continuing appropriations satisfied the joint-action requirement. The issue raised by the decision of Congress and the President to use these means for collaboration rather than a DECLARATION OF WAR *was* a nonjusticiable political question. In *Mitchell v. Laird* (1973), which arose after repeal of the Gulf of Tonkin Resolution, a court of appeals went further, declaring that it could "not be unmindful of what every schoolboy knows"—that appropriations and draft extensions did not necessarily indicate congressional approval of the war. Yet the court would not substitute its judgment for the President's regarding the appropriate military means for concluding the conflict.

The closest the federal judiciary came to blocking American involvement in Indochina occurred after the Vietnam cease-fire itself. In *Holtzman v. Schlesinger* (1973) a member of Congress and three Air Force officers sought to enjoin further bombing of Cambodia. Federal District Judge Orin Judd in New York found that all existing legislative authorization for operations anywhere in Indochina had ceased with the end of the war in Vietnam. Moreover, as Judd interpreted it, the compromise specifying a funding cutoff on August 15 conferred no new authority. Accordingly, on July 25, 1973, he ordered the secretary of defense to stop the bombing, but the United States Court of Appeals for the Second Circuit promptly stayed his order. Lawyers for the plaintiffs next asked THURGOOD MARSHALL, the circuit's Justice on the Supreme Court, to vacate the stay, and when he declined, they tracked down Justice WILLIAM O. DOUGLAS, then vacationing in Washington State. Douglas issued the necessary order, but at the request of the government, Marshall polled the full Court by telephone and proceeded to reinstitute the stay.

On August 8 the court of appeals reversed Judd, holding that the relation of the continued bombing to implementation of the peace agreement did constitute a political question. In OBITER DICTA, it opined further that Judd had incorrectly interpreted the compromise on the funding cutoff and had erred in granting standing to Congresswoman Elizabeth Holtzman and the Air Force officers. The court's reliance in *Holtzman* on the political questions doctrine was consistent with the sweeping recognition of the doctrine in *Atlee v. Laird* (1972), the only lower court decision involving the constitutionality of the

war that the Supreme Court affirmed (although without opinion) rather than sidestep by denying CERTIORARI.

Three years earlier, Congress had begun to consider general war-powers legislation. By 1973 the House had passed a version imposing strict consulting and reporting requirements on the President, whereas the Senate's bill sought to define precisely the circumstances in which the President could use force without congressional authorization. In October 1973 both houses accepted a compromise measure. Its detailed mandatory sections stressed requirements for consultation and reporting and provided that if the President did not receive congressional approval within sixty days of committing forces to hostilities or situations of imminent hostilities, he had to withdraw them. (The President had another thirty days for withdrawal if he certified that the safety of the troops required the additional period.) Claiming the War Powers Resolution infringed on the constitutional authority of the President, Nixon vetoed it, but Congress overrode the veto. A clear legacy of the Indochina War, the law triggered ongoing debate in subsequent years regarding its constitutionality, wisdom, and effectiveness.

Throughout the war CIVIL LIBERTIES issues arose. Beginning in 1965–1966 growing numbers of opponents publicly demonstrated against American participation and its escalation and mounted focused protests against recruiting, the draft, and even military training. Ensuing criminal prosecutions (which war resisters often invited) included well-publicized and sometimes chaotic conspiracy trials that swept in prominent antiwar figures like pediatrician Benjamin Spock (of the "Boston Five") and social activist Tom Hayden (of the "Chicago Eight"). In addition, federal and some local agencies responded with domestic intelligence operations involving both surveillance and use of agents provocateurs. In part, the prosecutions and intelligence activities reflected the firm belief of both Johnson and Nixon that the domestic protest movement had connections to communism abroad.

In contrast to its largely hands-off approach to issues of external warmaking, the judiciary supported the antiwar position in key cases. Where juries convicted war resisters, appellate courts often proved receptive to FIRST AMENDMENT arguments and procedural challenges. In COHEN V. CALIFORNIA (1971), for example, the United States Supreme Court held that the words "Fuck the Draft" sewn on a jacket fell within the limits of protected expression. In UNITED STATES V. SEEGER (1965) and *Welsh v. United States* (1970) the Court in effect rewrote the Selective Service Act in order to broaden permissible grounds for conscientious objection. *Oestereich v. Selective Service Board* (1968) and *Breen v. Selective Service Board* (1970) disallowed use of selective service reclassification as a means of punishing opposition to the draft. But UNITED STATES V. O'BRIEN (1968) upheld legislation outlawing draft card destruction. In NEW YORK TIMES V. UNITED STATES (1971), although the Court allowed publication of the so-called Pentagon Papers, a majority of Justices eschewed an absolutist position, revealing instead an openness to some forms of censorship. And in LAIRD V. TATUM (1972) an attempt to stop the United States Army's domestic surveillance program failed when the Court found that the plaintiffs had suffered no personal injury.

Overall, the Vietnam War significantly broadened the range of constitutional debate in America. Although hardly an unambiguous example of executive warmaking, the war helped stigmatize further accretions to an "imperial presidency." Although not blocked by the judiciary, it drew judges partway into defining the external warmaking authority. And although far from the only source of domestic unrest and reaction in the 1960s and early 1970s, the conflict triggered a wide enough spectrum of opposition to give renewed respectability to dissent.

CHARLES A. LOFGREN
(1992)

(SEE ALSO: *Congress and Foreign Policy; Congressional War Powers; Executive Power; Executive Prerogative; Foreign Affairs; Presidential War Powers; Senate and Foreign Policy; War, Foreign Affairs, and the Constitution.*)

Bibliography
BANNAN, JOHN F. and BANNAN, ROSEMARY S.   1974   *Law, Morality and Vietnam: The Peace Militants and the Courts.* Bloomington: Indiana University Press.
GIBBONS, WILLIAM C.   1986–1989   *The U.S. Government and the Vietnam War: Executive and Legislative Roles and Relationships*, 3 vols., series in progress. Princeton: Princeton University Press.
KEYNES, EDWARD   1982   *Undeclared War: The Twilight Zone of Constitutional Power.* Chaps. 5–7. University Park: Pennsylvania State University Press.
STRUM, PHILIPPA   1976   The Supreme Court and the Vietnamese War. In Richard A. Falk, ed., *The Vietnam War and International Law: The Concluding Phase.* Vol. 4, pages 535–572. Princeton, N.J.: Princeton University Press.

# VILLAGE OF . . .

See entry under name of village

# VINSON, FRED M.
## (1890–1953)

Fred M. Vinson was appointed thirteenth CHIEF JUSTICE of the United States by President HARRY S. TRUMAN in 1946 and served in that office until his death. His appointment followed a distinguished career in all three branches of the federal government. That career profoundly influenced his performance as Chief Justice.

Born and raised in the jail of Louisa, Kentucky—his father was the town jailer—he devoted almost his entire professional career to the public sector. Shortly after his admission to the bar, he served as city attorney and as Commonwealth attorney. Elected to Congress in 1928, he was an influential member of that legislative body during the NEW DEAL years. His judicial experience commenced with appointment as judge of the United States Court of Appeals for the District of Columbia in 1937, and was broadened in 1942 when Chief Justice HARLAN FISKE STONE named him Chief Judge of the EMERGENCY COURT OF APPEALS. His executive branch experience began with his 1943 appointment as director of Economic Stabilization, followed in 1945 by three posts in rapid succession: Federal Loan administrator, director of War Mobilization and Reconversion, and secretary of the Treasury.

He was appointed Chief Justice in 1946 to a Court widely regarded as ridden not only with the usual ideological disagreements but also with severe personal animosities. One successful aspect of his tenure as Chief Justice was the substantial reduction of public exposure of these conflicts.

In 1949, the deaths of Justices FRANK MURPHY and WILEY B. RUTLEDGE were followed by the appointments of TOM C. CLARK and SHERMAN MINTON. These changes, which occurred just short of the midpoint of his tenure, shifted the balance of the Court to a more conservative position, one more consonant with his own judicial and political philosophy.

That philosophy must be ascertained more by inference than through direct revelation. During his seven years as Chief Justice, the number of cases heard by the Court declined; as Chief Justice he assigned comparatively few opinions to himself. The evidence makes clear, however, that his philosophy reflected his public and political experience, acquired during the New Deal and WORLD WAR II years, when a strong national government was deemed a *sine qua non* and loyalty to one's party and political confreres was a necessary condition of the success of the political process.

For him, the governmental institutions were democratically based, sound, and trustworthy; they were entitled to the loyalty of those whom they served and to protection from those who would destroy them. The judgments of the President and Congress that communism threatened both from without and from within were entitled to respect. The nation and its people fared better with a stable regime than with one of disruption; government was entitled at least to have time to respond to conflicts. The lowest person could rise to the highest office. Concomitantly—although the enactments of legislatures were normally to be respected—legal restrictions based upon race, disabling handicaps to the realization of the American dream, were disfavored. Even as his extensive federal governmental experience made him sympathetic to a strong central government, so his executive branch experience rendered him unafraid of strong executive power.

His tenure as Chief Justice spanned the Cold War era in which pro-Soviet attitudes that had developed during World War II became suspect. The rise of McCarthyism, the trial of Alger Hiss, the KOREAN WAR, the theft of atomic secrets, and like events dominated public discussion and government reaction.

These events pervaded the atmosphere in which major constitutional issues were presented. Thus, his views about loyalty are perhaps best represented in those cases that sustained noncriminal deprivations addressed to communists and those considered disloyal, for example, his opinion for the Court in AMERICAN COMMUNICATIONS ASSOCIATION V. DOUDS (1950); denial of TAFT-HARTLEY COLLECTIVE BARGAINING benefits); and his votes in *Bailey v. Richardson* (1951; denial of federal employment) and JOINT ANTI-FASCIST REFUGEE COMMITTEE V. MCGRATH (1951; blacklisting of suspected organizations).

His lack of sympathy for those whose purpose he viewed as destructive of the governmental institutions is evidenced in his PLURALITY OPINION in DENNIS V. UNITED STATES (1951), which sustained against a FIRST AMENDMENT claim the criminal convictions of communist leaders under the Smith Act, and his majority opinion in FEINER V. NEW YORK (1951), affirming the conviction of an antigovernment speaker who refused to stop speaking when ordered to do so by a police officer after members of the audience threatened to assault him.

His concern for institutional stability is reflected in his opinion in UNITED STATES V. UNITED MINE WORKERS (1947), sustaining the judiciary's use of the CONTEMPT POWER to halt a disruptive strike, and his dissenting opinion in YOUNGSTOWN SHEET & TUBE CO. V. SAWYER (1951), where he would have sustained the power of the President to seize steel mills to maintain steel production interrupted by a strike.

Overtaken by later cases, several of Vinson's most significant opinions advanced the elimination of RACIAL DISCRIMINATION and in theoretical terms expanded the interpretation of the EQUAL PROTECTION clause. Although the unanimous opinions he authored in SWEATT V. PAINTER (1950) and MCLAURIN V. BOARD OF REGENTS (1950) did not in terms overrule the SEPARATE BUT EQUAL DOCTRINE of PLESSY V. FERGUSON (1896), the rejection of the separate

Texas law school in *Sweatt* and of the special treatment of *McLaurin* made the demise of that doctrine inevitable. His most interesting and venturesome equal protection opinion was SHELLEY V. KRAEMER (1948), the RESTRICTIVE COVENANT case, whose doctrinal implications have yet to be satisfactorily delineated.

Vinson accorded the federal government expansive legislative power under the COMMERCE CLAUSE. Perceived conflicts between the federal government and the states were resolved in favor of a strong central government. Where the federal government had not spoken, his concern focused on discrimination against INTERSTATE COMMERCE and the out-of-stater, a position most clearly seen in the STATE TAXATION OF COMMERCE cases and TOOMER V. WITSELL (1948), the path-breaking interpretation of the PRIVILEGES AND IMMUNITIES clause of Article IV, which in effect extended his commerce clause philosophy to areas he thought the clause did not reach.

His general judicial approach inclined Vinson to focus on the particular facts of the case and to eschew promulgation of sweeping legal principles. He was slow to overrule earlier opinions and DOCTRINES. The power of the Court to invalidate federal executive and legislative actions on constitutional grounds was to be used sparingly; he never voted to invalidate an act of Congress or a presidential action. He was as apt as any member of his Court, save perhaps Justice FELIX FRANKFURTER, to avoid constitutional questions and, when those issues were faced, to take an intermediate rather than ultimate constitutional position. Clearly, Fred M. Vinson belonged to the "judicial restraint" school of Supreme Court Justices.

MURRAY L. SCHWARTZ
(1986)

Bibliography

KIRKENDALL, K.   1969   Fred M. Vinson. In Leon Friedman and Fred L. Israel, *The Justices of the United States Supreme Court*. Vol. 4:2639–2649. New York: Chelsea House.
PRITCHETT, C. HERMAN   1954   *Civil Liberties and the Vinson Court*. Chicago: University of Chicago Press.
SYMPOSIUM   1954   *Northwestern University Law Review* 49:1–76.

# VINSON COURT
## (1946–1953)

FRED M. VINSON was Chief Justice of the United States from June 24, 1946, until his death on September 8, 1953. During his seven-year period of service the Supreme Court was considerably less interesting, colorful, or originative of significant constitutional DOCTRINE than its predecessor, the STONE COURT, or its successor, the WARREN COURT. However, the Vinson Court did deal with serious and important issues, particularly Cold War challenges to CIVIL LIBERTIES and awakening concerns about RACIAL DISCRIMINATION.

Vinson was a close friend of President HARRY S. TRUMAN and an active Democrat who had had the unique experience of serving in all three branches of the federal government. Immediately preceding his appointment to the Court he had been secretary of the treasury. President Truman had made one previous appointment, naming HAROLD BURTON, a Republican and former SENATE colleague of Truman, to replace OWEN ROBERTS in 1945. The other seven justices were of course all holdovers from the Stone Court, which guaranteed a continuation of the judicial dialogue that had pitted the liberal activism of HUGO L. BLACK, WILLIAM O. DOUGLAS, FRANK MURPHY, and WILEY B. RUTLEDGE against the brilliant critiques of FELIX FRANKFURTER and ROBERT H. JACKSON, with the moderate STANLEY F. REED somewhere in the center.

The four-judge liberal bloc had within itself the votes required to grant CERTIORARI petitions, which ensured that civil liberties issues would continue to appear on the Court's agenda. When the liberals agreed, they needed only one additional vote to constitute a majority. But in the summer of 1949 Justices Murphy and Rutledge died, cutting the liberal bloc in half. President Truman filled these two vacancies by the appointment of TOM C. CLARK, his attorney general, and SHERMAN MINTON, who had been a New Deal senator from Indiana. The two new justices joined with Vinson, Reed, and Burton in a moderately conservative bloc which dominated the remaining four terms of the Vinson Court. An indication of the balance of power on the Court is provided by the number of dissents registered by each of the Justices during this four-year period: Clark 15, Vinson 40, Burton 44, Minton 47, Reed 59, Jackson 80, Frankfurter 101, Douglas 130, Black 148.

The most famous decision of the Vinson Court in terms of public reaction, and probably the most noteworthy as a contribution to constitutional theory, was YOUNGSTOWN SHEET TUBE CO. V. SAWYER (1952), generally known as the Steel Seizure Case. Here the Court by a vote of 6–3 held unconstitutional President Truman's seizure of the nation's steel mills in 1952, an action he justified as necessary to avert a nationwide strike that might have affected the flow of munitions to American troops in Korea. The President had no statutory authority for the seizure, which consequently had to be justified on a theory of inherent presidential power to meet emergencies.

Justice Black, supported by Douglas, flatly denied the existence of any inherent presidential powers. Justices Jackson and Frankfurter were less dogmatic, and the doctrine of the case is generally drawn from their opinions. As they saw it, the controlling factor was that Congress had considered granting the President seizure power to

deal with nationwide strikes when adopting the TAFT-HARTLEY ACT in 1947 but had decided against it. In addition, Jackson contributed a situational scale for ruling on claims of executive emergency power. Vinson, in his most famous dissent, upheld the President as having moved in an emergency to maintain the status quo until Congress could act, and he rejected the majority's "messenger boy" concept of the presidential office.

The fact that the Court could have avoided the constitutional issue in the Steel Seizure Case by various alternatives suggested that most of the justices believed it important to announce a check on presidential power. The decision was enormously popular with the press and public and has subsequently been accepted as an authoritative statement on the SEPARATION OF POWERS, establishing that actions of the president are subject to JUDICIAL REVIEW. There had been some doubt on this point since the failure of the post-CIVIL WAR suit against the president in MISSISSIPPI V. JOHNSON (1867). It established also that executive claims of power for which statutory authority is lacking, and which must consequently rely on the President's general Article II authority, are subject to strict judicial scrutiny.

Less significant in its doctrine than the Steel Seizure Case but almost as controversial was the Court's contempt ruling against John L. Lewis, leader of the coal miners, in 1947 (UNITED STATES V. UNITED MINE WORKERS). The government had seized the nation's bituminous coal mines in 1946 to end a crippling strike and had entered into a contract with Lewis on wages and working conditions. When Lewis subsequently terminated the contract unilaterally and resumed the strike, the government secured a contempt JUDGMENT and heavy fine against Lewis and the union. In his first major opinion Vinson upheld the conviction for contempt, ruling that the NORRIS-LAGUARDIA ACT limiting the issuance of labor INJUNCTIONS was not binding on the government as an employer.

A significant difference between the Stone and Vinson Courts was that WORLD WAR II had ended and the Cold War against communism had begun. The hunt for subversives in which the nation was caught up soon after the shooting war was over tainted the entire period of the Vinson Court and created difficult civil liberties issues. The government's principal weapon against suspected subversion was the Smith Act of 1940, which made it unlawful to teach and advocate the overthrow of the United States government by force and violence, or to organize a group for such a purpose.

Convictions of eleven leaders of the American Communist party under the Smith Act were upheld by the Supreme Court in DENNIS V. UNITED STATES (1951). In the most memorable event of his judicial career, Chief Justice Vinson wrote the Court's majority opinion defending the

Smith Act against contentions that it violated the FIRST AMENDMENT. The defendants admittedly had taken no action with the immediate intention of initiating a revolution. But Vinson held that the CLEAR AND PRESENT DANGER TEST, developed by Justice OLIVER WENDELL HOLMES and LOUIS D. BRANDEIS, did not require the government to wait until a "putsch" was about to be executed before acting against a conspiracy. Vinson accepted the reformulation of the test developed by Judge LEARNED HAND: "Whether the gravity of the "evil,' discounted by its improbability, justifies such invasion of free speech as is necessary to avoid the danger." He considered the communist "evil" to be that grave. Justices Black and Douglas dissented; Douglas pointed out that the prosecution had introduced no evidence of Communist party action aimed at overthrow of the government.

Vinson also wrote the Court's opinion in AMERICAN COMMUNICATIONS ASSOCIATION V. DOUDS (1950), upholding the Taft-Hartley Act noncommunist oath. This statute denied the protections and services of the WAGNER (NATIONAL LABOR RELATIONS) ACT to any labor organization whose officers failed to file affidavits that they were not members of the Communist party. The Chief Justice held that Congress in adopting this statute was acting to prevent the obstruction of commerce by "political strikes." The law was not aimed at speech but rather at harmful conduct carried on by persons who could be identified by their political affiliations and beliefs.

The Vinson Court was caught up in the final moments of the Cold War's most spectacular event, the execution of Julius and Ethel Rosenberg, who were charged with passing atomic "secrets" to the Russians. Review of the lower court conviction and subsequent APPEALS was routinely denied by the Supreme Court in 1952 and early 1953, as were also the initial petitions for STAY OF EXECUTION. But Justice Douglas thought that one final petition filed the day before execution was scheduled raised a new legal issue deserving consideration. He consequently granted a stay which the full Court set aside the next day, and the executions were then carried out. Douglas's action caused a brief furor and a congressman demanded his IMPEACHMENT. In the last opinion before his death Vinson defended Douglas's action as a proper response to protect the Court's JURISDICTION over the case pending a consideration of the legal issue raised. Black and Frankfurter joined Douglas in asserting that the stay should have been granted.

During the era of the Vinson Court, congressional committee investigations of communism developed into major political and media events. Senator Joseph McCarthy's pursuit of "Fifth Amendment Communists" got under way in 1950, too late to create issues for the Vinson Court. But the HOUSE COMMITTEE ON UN-AMERICAN ACTIVITIES had be-

gun operations in 1938, and by 1947 petitions for review of contempt citations against witnesses who had refused to reply to committee interrogation began to reach the Supreme Court. However, it declined review of all the cases that would have required a ruling on the constitutionality of the use of investigatory power, and it dealt only with certain less controversial issues of committee procedure and use of the Fifth Amendment privilege by witnesses.

A prominent feature of the Cold War period was concern about the loyalty of government employees. A LOYALTY OATH fad developed in nearly every state, which the Vinson Court legitimated in GERENDE V. BOARD OF SUPERVISORS OF ELECTIONS (1951) by upholding a Maryland law that required candidates for public office to file affidavits that they were not "subversive persons."

A loyalty program covering federal employees was set up by President Truman in 1947 and was continued by President DWIGHT D. EISENHOWER. It required checking the loyalty of all incumbent employees and all applicants for federal employment. A complex administrative organization of loyalty review boards was created, and to assist the boards the attorney general issued a list of organizations he found to be "totalitarian, fascist, communist, or subversive." Consideration of the constitutionality of this program split the Court 4–4 in *Bailey v. Richardson* (1951). But in JOINT ANTI-FASCIST REFUGEE COMMITTEE V. MCGRATH (1951), decided the same day, the Court by a vote of 5–3 challenged the attorney general's list as having been drawn up without appropriate investigation or DUE PROCESS. The dissenters were Reed, Vinson, and Minton. In spite of this opinion the list continued to be used for a number of years in government hiring and investigation.

At the state level a New York law providing for the removal of public school teachers on grounds of membership in listed subversive organizations was upheld in ADLER V. BOARD OF EDUCATION OF CITY OF NEW YORK (1952), Justice Minton reasoning that the purpose was constitutional and that procedural protections provided by the statute were adequate. Justices Black and Douglas dissented, and Frankfurter would have denied the appeal on technical grounds of STANDING and RIPENESS.

Apart from Cold War cases, FREEDOM OF SPEECH and FREEDOM OF THE PRESS did not suffer seriously at the hands of the Vinson Court. BURSTYN V. WILSON (1952) was in fact an advance in its holding that a motion picture could not be censored on the ground that it was "sacrilegious." A law censoring magazines featuring bloodshed and lust was struck down in *Winters v. New York* (1948) as void for vagueness. *Poulos v. New Hampshire* (1953) upheld licensing of meetings in public parks and streets, but only if the licenses were granted without discrimination, and the use of licensing ordinances to prevent unpopular religious groups or preachers from holding meetings in public parks was rebuffed in NIEMOTKO V. MARYLAND (1951) and KUNZ V. NEW YORK (1951).

In TERMINIELLO V. CHICAGO (1949) a divided Court reversed on rather technical grounds the conviction of a rabble-rouser for BREACH OF THE PEACE resulting from an incendiary speech. But FEINER V. NEW YORK (1951) upheld the conviction of a soap-box orator even though the situation was much less inflammatory than in *Terminiello*. Moreover, BEAUHARNAIS V. ILLINOIS (1952) approved a state law treating critical comments about racial groups as criminal and subjecting their authors to prosecution for GROUP LIBEL.

The Vinson Court dealt with a number of conflicts between freedom of expression and privacy but without producing any theories justifying or limiting privacy claims such as those subsequently developed in GRISWOLD V. CONNECTICUT (1965) by the Warren Court. Use of sound trucks in streets and parks was initially upheld in *Saia v. New York* (1948) against contentions of infringement on privacy, but in the following year the Court conceded that "loud and raucous" sound trucks could be forbidden (KOVACS V. COOPER). Radio broadcasts including commercial messages in DISTRICT OF COLUMBIA streetcars were permitted to continue by *Public Utilities Commission v. Pollak* (1952), even though CAPTIVE AUDIENCES might suffer, but *Breard v. City of Alexandria* (1951) protected householders by approving an ordinance forbidding door-to-door selling of magazine subscriptions. Justice Black charged that the latter decision violated the "preferred position" for First Amendment freedoms originated by the Roosevelt Court. The severest blow to that philosophy was *United Public Workers v. Mitchell* (1947) which upheld by a vote of 4–3 the HATCH ACT limits on political activity by public employees.

In a 1940 case, THORNHILL V. ALABAMA, the Court had strongly asserted that PICKETING in labor disputes was protected by the First Amendment. Almost immediately, however, the Court found it necessary to announce limits on this holding, a process the Vinson Court continued. The most significant case was GIBONEY V. EMPIRE STORAGE ICE CO. (1949), where the Court ruled unanimously against a union that was picketing to force an employer to enter into an illegal restrictive contract.

The issue of public financial aid to religious schools required the Vinson Court to make the first significant effort to interpret and apply the First Amendment ban on ESTABLISHMENT OF RELIGION. EVERSON V. BOARD OF EDUCATION (1947) involved a state arrangement under which parents could be reimbursed from public moneys for their children's bus fare to parochial schools. An unusual five-judge majority composed of three liberals (Black, Douglas, and Murphy) and two conservatives (Vinson and Reed)

held that the subsidy was simply a social welfare measure and that the First Amendment did not require exclusion of persons of any faith from the benefits of "public welfare legislation." Rutledge's vigorous dissent regarded payment for transportation to church schools as a direct aid to religious education and so unconstitutional.

The following year MCCOLLUM V. BOARD OF EDUCATION presented another church-state issue. The case involved a RELEASED TIME program of religious education under which public school children attended classes in Protestant, Roman Catholic, or Jewish religious instruction during school hours and in the school building. The Court's almost unanimous verdict of UNCONSTITUTIONALITY aroused a storm of criticism in church circles, and within four years the Court substantially reversed this ruling, upholding a New York City released time program that differed from *McCollum* only in that the classes were held off the school grounds (ZORACH V. CLAUSEN, 1952.) A similar reluctance to disturb the religious community was seen as the Court avoided on technical grounds of standing a ruling on the constitutionality of Bible-reading in the public schools (DOREMUS V. BOARD OF EDUCATION, 1952).

The Vinson Court's civil liberties record was distinctly better than that of its predecessors in one area, protection of minorities from discrimination. The prevailing constitutional rule was that established by PLESSY V. FERGUSON in 1896—that SEGREGATION of the races was constitutional provided treatment or facilities were equal. In practice, they were never equal, but over the years the Court had consistently avoided the difficult task of enforcing the *Plessy* rule. In the field of education, none of the few efforts to challenge unequal facilities had been successful. But in 1938 the HUGHES COURT made a small beginning, ruling in MISSOURI EX REL. GAINES V. CANADA that Missouri, which denied blacks admission to state law schools, must do so or set up a separate law school for blacks. MORGAN V. VIRGINIA (1946) invalidated a state Jim Crow law requiring racial segregation of passengers on public motor carriers, but the constitutional ground given was burden on INTERSTATE COMMERCE rather than denial of EQUAL PROTECTION.

The Vinson Court undertook cautiously to build on these beginnings. The COMMERCE CLAUSE justification used in the Virginia bus case was likewise employed in BOB-LO EXCURSION CO. V. MICHIGAN (1948). But the Vinson Court's boldest action against segregation came shortly thereafter in SHELLEY V. KRAEMER (1948). With Vinson writing the opinion, the Court declared that RESTRICTIVE COVENANTS binding property owners not to sell to minorities, although within the legal rights of property owners, were unenforceable. For a court to give effect to such a discriminatory contract, Vinson held, would amount to STATE ACTION in violation of the FOURTEENTH AMENDMENT.

The separate law school for blacks that Texas had established was declared unequal in SWEATT V. PAINTER (1950). The University of Oklahoma, forced to admit a black graduate student, required him to sit in a separate row in class, at a separate desk in the library, and at a separate table in the cafeteria. MCLAURIN V. OKLAHOMA STATE REGENTS (1950), with Vinson again writing the opinion, held these practices to be an unconstitutional impairment of the student's ability to learn his profession.

Vinson's opinion, however, rejected the opportunity to consider the broader issue of the *Plessy* SEPARATE BUT EQUAL rule. So attacks on the segregation principle continued, and the TEST CASES moved from the universities and graduate schools to the primary and secondary schools. In December 1952 BROWN V. BOARD OF EDUCATION and four other school segregation cases were argued for three days before the Court. But instead of a decision in June, the Court set the cases for reargument in October. The Chief Justice died in September, and so the Vinson Court's most momentous issue was passed on to the Warren Court.

Although the Stone Court had broken some new ground in CRIMINAL PROCEDURE, its record was mixed, particularly in guaranteeing the RIGHT TO COUNSEL and protection against UNREASONABLE SEARCHES and seizures. This latter issue surfaced in the Vinson Court's first term. One of the oldest problems in American constitutional law is whether the due process clause of the Fourteenth Amendment "incorporated" and made effective in state criminal proceedings the protections of the Fourth through the Eighth Amendments. As recently as 1937 in PALKO V. CONNECTICUT the Court had reiterated the principle that all state procedures consistent with ORDERED LIBERTY are acceptable.

In *Adamson v. California* (1947) the *Palko* doctrine survived on the Vinson Court, but by only a 5–4 vote. Justice Black led the minority. He relied on legislative history to establish his version of the intention of the framers of the Fourteenth Amendment and attacked the ORDERED LIBERTY test as substituting natural law and the notions of individual Justices for the precise and protective language of the BILL OF RIGHTS.

Although Black lost in *Adamson*, "ordered liberty" was a standard powerful enough to bring state criminal processes within the ambit of the FOURTH AMENDMENT in WOLF V. COLORADO (1949). However, Justice Frankfurter for the six-judge majority held only that SEARCHES AND SEIZURES by state law officers are bound by the standard of reasonableness; he declined to go further and impose on state prosecutions the EXCLUSIONARY RULE which prevents EVIDENCE secured by unconstitutional means from being offered in federal prosecutions. Justices Murphy, Douglas, and Rutledge, dissenting, contended that the exclusionary rule provided the only effective protection against police violation of the Fourth Amendment, and their view was finally adopted on the Warren Court in MAPP V. OHIO (1961).

With respect to right to counsel, the Vinson Court accepted the rule announced by the Stone Court in BETTS V. BRADY (1942) that the necessity for counsel depended upon the circumstances, such as the seriousness of the crime, the age and mental capacity of the defendant, and the ability of the judge. Applying the "special circumstances" rule in twelve cases, the Vinson Court concluded that in six the absence of counsel had resulted in denial of a FAIR TRIAL. In only one of the twelve was the Court unanimous. This experience was a factor in the Warren Court's decision in GIDEON V. WAINWRIGHT (1963) to abolish the confusing special circumstances rule and make counsel mandatory in all state felony prosecutions.

What was potentially one of the Vinson Court's most significant decisions for the federal system was nullified by Congress. In 1947 the Court ruled that subsurface land and mineral rights in California's three-mile coastal area belonged to the federal government (*United States v. California*), and in 1950 the Court applied the same rule to Texas. Congress retaliated in 1953 by ceding to the states ownership of land and resources under adjoining seas up to a distance of three miles from shore or to the states' historic boundaries.

In summary, the tendency of the Vinson Court was to follow a policy of judicial restraint, rejecting innovation or activism. The number of cases decided by full opinion fell below one hundred during three of the last four years, far less than the number typically decided by earlier Courts. The five justices who dominated the Court in its latter period were capable but lacking in style or originality. The four Justices of intellectual distinction—Black, Douglas, Frankfurter, and Jackson—generally paired off and pulled in opposite directions.

The pall of the Cold War hung over the Court. Confronted with the scandal of MCCARTHYISM, it was quiescent. Facing Smith Act prosecutions, the loyalty inquisition of federal employees, lists of subversive organizations, scrutiny of school teachers' associates, loyalty oaths, and deportation of ex-communists, the Court's response was usually to legitimate the government's action.

But in one field, significantly, there was a different kind of response. The Vinson Court did not evade the issue of racial discrimination. Although moving cautiously, as was appropriate considering the enormity of the problem, the Court nevertheless proceeded to bring denial of equal protection out of the limbo of neglect and unconcern into the focus of national consciousness and thereby prepared the way for its successor's historic decision on May 17, 1954.

C. HERMAN PRITCHETT
(1986)

Bibliography

FRANK, JOHN P. 1954 Fred Vinson and the Chief Justiceship. *University of Chicago Law Review* 21:212–246.

MURPHY, PAUL L. 1972 *The Constitution in Crisis Times, 1919–1969.* New York: Harper & Row.

PRITCHETT, C. HERMAN (1954) 1966 *Civil Liberties and the Vinson Court.* Chicago: University of Chicago Press.

SWINDLER, WILLIAM F. 1970 *Court and Constitution in the Twentieth Century: The New Legality, 1932–1968.* Indianapolis: Bobbs-Merrill.

# VIOLENCE AGAINST WOMEN ACT
## 108 Stat. 1903 (1994)

The Violence Against Women Act (VAWA) is a federal law passed by Congress in 1994 that allows people who have been subjected to acts of violence because of their sex to sue their victimizers in federal court for SEX DISCRIMINATION. It provides that "a person (including a person who acts under color of any statute, ordinance, regulation, custom, or usage of any State) who commits a crime of violence motivated by gender and thus deprives another of the right [to be free from crimes of violence motivated by gender] shall be liable to the party injured [in a civil action for relief]."

The basic idea is to place the power to sue and hold perpetrators accountable for sex-discriminatory acts of violence, such as rape and battery, in the hands of the survivors. This CIVIL RIGHTS remedy, in addition to empowering survivors of these abuses concretely to act on their own behalf, exposes the commonness and pervasiveness of these acts, puts them in context by connecting them with discrimination across society, dignifies the survivors of violent sex discrimination as bearers of civil rights, and states authoritatively that perpetrators are bigots as well as criminals.

The VAWA raises some old constitutional debates that, once resolved, open new constitutional possibilities.

The VAWA was passed because states, which enforce most criminal laws, were documented to have failed in protecting women from sexual and other physical violence on a large scale. By declaring a policy of zero tolerance for such abuse, and by conceiving gender-based violence to be a civil rights violation, Congress raised a new constitutional question: Is freedom from sexual assault a sex equality right? If so, should it be guaranteed under the Constitution's FOURTEENTH AMENDMENT as well as by a statute? Have state instrumentalities that failed to give women equal protection of the criminal laws been violating the Constitution all this time in a way that needs new legal scrutiny? Cases permitting suit against officials for sexual harassment, of men by men as well as of women by men, provide supportive PRECEDENTS.

Congress predicated its power to pass the VAWA both on the COMMERCE CLAUSE and on the FOURTEENTH AMENDMENT, SECTION 5, rekindling the old legal debates about the proper constitutional foundation and reach of federal civil rights laws. Early legal challenges to the VAWA have argued that men's violence against women is private, not public; reserved for states, not the federal government; criminal, not civil; and that it does not implicate INTERSTATE COMMERCE. Responses to these arguments have documented the substantial impact of violence against women on women's participation in economic life. Advocates for the law have argued that sex-based violence is a form of sex discrimination against which Congress is permitted to legislate. The states' abdication of, and bias in, enforcing laws against violence against women is hardly a private act. It is hardly private in the sense of being unique, personal, protectable, or exclusively individual. Nothing in the Constitution says it cannot be addressed civilly as well as criminally. They have also argued that the remedy supplements, rather than supplants, state criminal laws.

Assuming the law is found constitutional, concerns for its effectiveness arising from its language, passed as a compromise to restrict the number of cases brought, may arise. For example, the definition of "gender-motivated" is "because of gender or on the basis of gender, and due, at least in part, to an animus based on the victim's gender." One benefit of this language is that it clearly permits combined race-and-sex-based claims. One potential problem is that "animus," which requires some proof of perpetrator mental state, is often inaccessible to the victim other than through the act itself. Perpetrator mental state may also be beside the point of the injury to the victim. Future legislation and litigation under the VAWA will have to confront this and other barriers to effective recovery, and to the social change—equality of the sexes—that the VAWA was passed to promote.

CATHARINE A. MACKINNON
(2000)

Bibliography

FRAZEE, DAVID; NOEL, ANN M.; and BRENNEKE, ANDREA 1997 *Violence Against Women: Law and Litigation.* Deerfield, Ill.: Clark, Boardman, Callaghan.

NOURSE, VICTORIA F. 1996 Where Violence Relationship and Equality Meet: The Violence Against Women Act's Rights Remedy. *Wisconsin Women's Law Journal* 11:1–36.

SENATE JUDICIARY COMMITTEE 1992 *Violence Against Women: A Week in the Life of America: A Majority Staff Report.* Washington, D.C.: United States Government Printing Office.

# *VIRGINIA, EX PARTE*

See: *Strauder v. West Virginia*

## VIRGINIA, UNITED STATES v.
### 518 U.S. 515 (1996)

Virginia Military Institute (VMI) is a military-style school of higher education founded in 1839 with an all-male admissions policy. By the 1970s, VMI was the only single-sex public college in Virginia and had a record of producing leaders in government and business. At the request of a potential woman applicant, the United States brought suit in 1990 claiming that VMI's admissions policy violated the EQUAL PROTECTION guarantee of the FOURTEENTH AMENDMENT. After trial the district court rejected the claim, finding that VMI offered diversity to Virginia's higher educational system and that admission of women would alter VMI's distinctive adversative method, which involved barracks without privacy, strenuous exercise, and bonding through torment by upperclassmen.

The United States Court of Appeals for the Fourth Circuit reversed, holding that Virginia's provision of diversity for men only was unconstitutional. On remand the district court approved a "substantively comparable" program at a private women's college in Virginia. The Fourth Circuit affirmed.

The Supreme Court reversed, concluding that Virginia had relied on stereotypes about women and had not proved that the admission of women would destroy the adversative method. Justice RUTH BADER GINSBURG wrote the majority opinion for six Justices. Chief Justice WILLIAM H. REHNQUIST concurred, while Justice ANTONIN SCALIA dissented and Justice CLARENCE THOMAS did not participate. After applying "skeptical scrutiny" of official discrimination, detailing many inadequacies of the "comparable" program, and noting that there was no equivalent school for women, the Court held that Virginia had violated the equal protection clause; that women should be admitted to VMI; and that VMI should alter housing and skills requirements to accommodate "celebrated differences" of the female cadets. After the Supreme Court's decision, VMI considered abandoning state support and remaining all-male, but decided instead to admit women.

The VMI case footnoted, without comment, the argument that women's schools "dissipate" gender stereotypes. The constitutionality of all-women's schools or separate-but-equal SINGLE-SEX SCHOOLS was not before the court and, therefore, not decided.

CANDACE SAARI KOVACIC-FLEISCHER
(2000)

Bibliography

EPSTEIN, CYNTHIA FUCHS 1997 The Myths and Justifications of Sex Segregation in Higher Education: VMI and the Citadel. *Duke Journal of Gender Law & Policy* 4:101–118.
KOVACIC-FLEISCHER, CANDACE SAARI 1997 *United States v. Vir-*ginia's New Gender Equal Protection Analysis with Ramifications for Pregnancy, Parenting, and Title VII. *Vanderbilt Law Review* 50:845–915.
NEMKO, AMY 1998 Single-Sex Public Education after VMI: The Case for Women's Schools. *Harvard Women's Law Journal* 21:19–77.

## VIRGINIA v. RIVES

See: *Strauder v. West Virginia*

## VIRGINIA v. TENNESSEE

See: Interstate Compact

## VIRGINIA AND KENTUCKY RESOLUTIONS
### (1798–1799)

These resolutions declared the ALIEN AND SEDITION ACTS unconstitutional and sought to arouse political opposition by appealing to the legislatures of the several states. The strategy was devised by THOMAS JEFFERSON, the Vice-President, who secretly drafted the resolutions that were adopted by the Kentucky legislature. A similar but milder series was drafted by JAMES MADISON for the Virginia assembly. Both set forth the compact theory of the Constitution, holding that the general government was one of strictly delegated powers; that acts beyond its powers were void; and that, there being no ultimate arbiter of the Constitution, each state had "an equal right to judge for itself, as well of infractions as of the mode and measure of redress." (See THEORIES OF THE UNION.) Jefferson baptized the theory "NULLIFICATION," though the name was omitted by Kentucky; and Virginia spoke instead of the right of each state to "interpose" to arrest the evil.

Five of the nine Kentucky Resolutions were devoted to proving the unconstitutionality of the Alien and Sedition Laws. The Alien Law was attacked for want of power, for violation of a specific constitutional provision (Article I, section 9), and for denial of TRIAL BY JURY and other fair procedures. The Sedition Act was asserted to be outside the scope of the Constitution as well as a direct violation of the FIRST AMENDMENT. The resolutions offered no broadly philosophical plea for FREEDOM OF SPEECH and PRESS but met the threat of the Sedition Law at its most vulnerable point, as an invasion of rights reserved to the states. It belonged to each state, not the general government, to determine "how far the licentiousness of speech and of the press may be abridged without lessening their useful freedom." Kentucky urged the other state legislatures to concur in declaring the acts unconstitutional and void.

Replies to the resolutions, mostly from Northern legislatures under Federalist control, were uniformly unfavorable. Prodded by Jefferson, Kentucky adopted a second set of resolutions in November 1799, reaffirming the principles of the first and, incidentally, introducing the word "nullification." In January 1800 the Virginia assembly adopted Madison's Report, a masterly exposition of the dual sovereignty theory of the federal union and a powerful defense of CIVIL LIBERTIES.

The principal object of the resolutions was to secure the freedom of opposition, of debate, and of change through the political process. This object was secured by the Republican victory in the election of 1800. But in pursuing "a political resistance for political effect," in Jefferson's words, he and his associates were somewhat careless on points of constitutional theory. Whether the resolutions were meant as a declaration of opinion or as a "nullification" of federal law, whether the right claimed for the state was limited to "usurpations" of the compact or extended to "abuses" as well, whether the ultimate recourse was the natural right of revolution or a constitutional right of SECESSION, these points were left unclear. It mattered little in 1800, after the resolutions had done their work and then were forgotten; but it mattered a great deal a generation later when the "Resolutions of '98" were revived and tortured by JOHN C. CALHOUN into a defense, not of liberty, but of slavery.

MERRILL D. PETERSON
(1986)

Bibliography

KOCH, ADRIENNE and AMMON, HARRY   1948   The Virginia and Kentucky Resolutions: An Episode in Jefferson's and Madison's Defense of Civil Liberties. *William and Mary Quarterly* (3rd. ser.) 5:145–176.

MALONE, DUMAS   1962   *Jefferson and the Ordeal of Liberty.* Boston: Little, Brown.

# VIRGINIA CHARTER OF 1606
## (April 10, 1606)

This was the first royal charter issued for the planting of a colony in America. Charters were usually issued to private trading companies, as in this case, or to proprietary lords. The charter laid out boundaries, defined the relationship of the colony to the crown, and provided for a government. In this first charter, the government consisted only of a council. Subsequent charters for Virginia in 1609 and 1612 established the office of the governor; by 1619, in accord with a document called the "Great Charter" of 1618, elections were held and the first representative legislature in American history met at Jamestown. The enduring significance of Virginia's first charter lies in its provision that the colonists and their descendants "shall have and enjoy all Liberties, Franchises, and Immunities . . . as if they had been abiding and born, within this our Realm of England. . . ." Later charters for Virginia contained similar clauses. Their meaning was doubtless restricted at the time to legal rights of land tenure and inheritance, trial by jury, and little else; but the vague language (repeated in numerous other charters for colonies from New England to the South) allowed American colonists to believe that they were entitled to all the rights of Englishmen—their constitutional system and common law. Charters could be revoked and some were, but the American experience eventually led to written constitutions of fundamental law that contained bills of rights.

LEONARD W. LEVY
(1986)

# VIRGINIA DECLARATION OF RIGHTS AND CONSTITUTION OF 1776
## (June 12 and 29, 1776)

Virginia, the oldest, largest, and most prestigious of the original states, adopted a Declaration of Rights on June 12, 1776, and two weeks later its "Constitution or Form of Government." Each document was the first of its kind and considerably influenced constitution-making in the other states. The primary draftsman of both documents was GEORGE MASON, although the self-styled "convention" that adopted them included many luminaries, among them JAMES MADISON. The convention was actually an extralegal or provisional legislature similar in membership to the last House of Burgesses under the royal charter before the Revolution. The same convention enacted ordinary legislation and elected a governor under the new CONSTITUTION.

THOMAS JEFFERSON in his *Notes on Virginia*, written in 1781, observed that "capital defects" marred the work of the constitution-makers of 1776 who were acting without precedent. Property qualifications on the right to vote disfranchised about half the men of the state who served in the militia or paid taxes, and gross malapportionment, which benefited the old tidewater counties, diminished the representative character of the new government. The governor was little more than a ceremonial figurehead. The assembly elected him and his councillors as well as the state judges, and the governor had no veto power. Jefferson believed that concentrating the powers of government in the legislature, notwithstanding recognition of the principle of separation of powers, "is precisely the definition of despotic government. . . . An elective despotism was not the government we fought for." In fact, however, legislative supremacy characterized all the new state governments, excepting those of Massachusetts and New York.

The gravest deficiency of the Virginia system, according to Jefferson, was that the legislature, having framed the constitution and declaration of rights without having provided that they be perpetual and unalterable, could change them by ordinary legislation. That was true in theory, although the constitution lasted over half a century and rarely did the legislature enact measures inconsistent with it. In practice it was regarded a FUNDAMENTAL LAW, especially the declaration of rights.

That declaration was the most significant achievement of the convention. As the first such American document, it contained many constitutional "firsts," such as the statements that "all men" are equally free and have inherent rights which cannot be divested even by compact; that among these rights are the enjoyment of life, liberty, property, and the pursuit of happiness; and that all power derives from the people who retain a right to change the government if it fails to secure the people's objectives. The declaration recognized "the free exercise of religion and FREEDOM OF THE PRESS, and included clauses that were precursors, sometimes in rudimentary form, of the FOURTH through the Eighth AMENDMENTS of the Constitution of the United States. Inexplicably the convention voted down a ban on BILLS OF ATTAINDER and on EX POST FACTO LAWS and omitted the FREEDOMS OF SPEECH, assembly, and petition, the right to the writ of HABEAS CORPUS, GRAND JURY, proceedings, the right to compulsory process to secure EVIDENCE in one's own behalf, the RIGHT TO COUNSEL, and freedom from DOUBLE JEOPARDY. Although RELIGIOUS LIBERTY was guaranteed, the ban on an ESTABLISHMENT OF RELIGION awaited enactment of the VIRGINIA STATUTE OF RELIGIOUS FREEDOM in 1786. Madison's familiarity with his own state's bill of rights strongly influenced his draft of the amendments that became the BILL OF RIGHTS of the Constitution.

LEONARD W. LEVY
(1986)

Bibliography

LINGLEY, CHARLES R. 1910 *The Transition of Virginia from Colony to Commonwealth.* New York: Columbia University Press.

## VIRGINIA PLAN

At the CONSTITUTIONAL CONVENTION OF 1787, EDMUND RANDOLPH, arguing that the government of the union under the ARTICLES OF CONFEDERATION could not defend itself against state encroachments, introduced the alternative of a "national plan," probably the work of JAMES MADISON. In effect Virginia proposed to supersede the Articles by providing for a strong, central government of three branches, each with broad, undefined powers. The plan included a congress of two houses, the first elected by the people and the second by the first, both to be apportioned on the basis of a state's population of free inhabitants or its contributions to the national treasury. The most significant provision empowered congress to legislate in all cases of state incompetency or whenever state legislation might disrupt national harmony. Congress was also empowered to veto state laws. The sole check on congress was a qualified veto power vested in a council consisting of the executive and some judges. One provision required state officers to swear support of the new constitution, and another authorized the use of force against recalcitrant states. The Virginia Plan structured the deliberations of the Constitutional Convention and became the nucleus of the Constitution of the United States.

LEONARD W. LEVY
(1986)

Bibliography

BRANT, IRVING 1950 *James Madison: Father of the Constitution, 1787–1800.* Pages 23–54. Indianapolis: Bobbs-Merrill.

## VIRGINIA PRIVATE SCHOOL CASES

See: *Runyon v. McCrary*

## VIRGINIA STATE BOARD OF PHARMACY v. VIRGINIA CITIZENS CONSUMER COUNCIL
### 425 U.S. 748 (1976)

Traditionally COMMERCIAL SPEECH was assumed to lie outside the FIRST AMENDMENT's protection. This decision made clear that this assumption was obsolete. Virginia's rules governing professional pharmacists forbade the advertising of prices of prescription drugs. The Supreme Court, 7–1, held this rule invalid at the behest of a consumers' group, thus promoting the notion of a "right to receive" in the FREEDOM OF SPEECH. (See LISTENERS' RIGHTS.) The Court's opinion indicated that false or misleading commercial advertising might be regulated—a rule the Court would never apply to political speech. For a few years, this decision stood as the Court's principal commercial speech precedent, only to be assimilated in the comprehensive opinion in CENTRAL HUDSON GAS V. PUBLIC SERVICE COMMISSION (1980).

MARTIN SHAPIRO
(1986)

## VIRGINIA STATUTE OF RELIGIOUS FREEDOM
### (1786)

This historic statute, one of the preeminent documents in the history of RELIGIOUS LIBERTY, climaxed a ten-year struggle for the SEPARATION OF CHURCH AND STATE in Virginia. On the eve of the Revolution Baptists were jailed for unlicensed preaching, and JAMES MADISON exclaimed that the "diabolical Hell conceived principle of persecution rages." The Church of England (Episcopal) was the established church of Virginia, supported by public taxes imposed on all. The state CONSTITUTION of 1776 guaranteed that everyone was "equally entitled to the free exercise of religion," but the convention defeated a proposal by Madison that would have ended any form of an ESTABLISHMENT OF RELIGION. By the close of 1776 the legislature, responding to dissenter petitions, repealed all laws punishing any religious opinions or modes of worship, exempted dissenters from compulsory support of the established church, and suspended state taxation on its behalf. But the legislature reserved for future decision the question whether religion ought to be supported by voluntary contributions or by a new establishment of all Christian churches.

In 1779 an indecisive legislature confronted two diametrically opposed bills. One was a general assessment bill, providing that the Christian religion should be "the established religion" supported by public taxation and allowing every taxpayer to designate the church that would receive his money. The other was THOMAS JEFFERSON's Bill for Religious Freedom, which later provided the philosophical basis for the religion clauses of the FIRST AMENDMENT. The preamble, a classic expression of the American creed on intellectual as well as religious liberty, stressed that everyone had a "natural right" to his opinions and that religion was a private, voluntary matter of individual conscience beyond the scope of the civil power to support or restrain. Jefferson rejected the BAD TENDENCY TEST for suppressing opinions and proposed "that it is time enough for the rightful purposes of the civil government for its officers to interfere when principles break out into overt acts against peace and good order. . . ." The bill, which protected even freedom of irreligion, provided that no one should be compelled to frequent or support any worship. Neither Jefferson's bill nor the other could muster a majority, and for several years the legislature deadlocked.

Each year, however, support for an establishment grew.

When a liberalized general assessment bill was introduced in 1784, omitting subscription to articles of faith and giving secular reasons for the support of religion, the Presbyterian clergy backed it. Madison angrily declared that they were "as ready to set up an establishment which is to take them in as they were to pull down that which shut them out." Only Madison's shrewd politicking delayed passage of the general assessment bill until the legislature had time to evaluate the state of public opinion. MADISON'S MEMORIAL AND REMONSTRANCE turned public opinion against the assessment; even the Presbyterian clergy now endorsed Jefferson's bill. Madison reintroduced it in late 1785, and it became law in early 1786, completing the separation of church and state in Virginia and providing a model for a nation.

LEONARD W. LEVY
(1986)

Bibliography

STOKES, ANSON PHELPS   1950   *Church and State in the United States.* Vol. 1:366–394. New York: Harper & Row.

## VIRTUAL REPRESENTATION

See: Representation; Taxation without Representation

## VISAS

Although the Constitution does not directly mention the power to control and regulate IMMIGRATION, the Supreme Court, in CHAE CHAN PING V. UNITED STATES (1889), held that immigration control was an implied power inherent in national sovereignty. The Court has subsequently held that Congress has virtual plenary power to regulate or condition immigration and NATURALIZATION, and can admit noncitizens to the United States, regulate their presence within the country, and expel, deport, or exclude them. Congress may also accord resident ALIENS and citizens different treatment, but because aliens are persons within the meaning of the Fifth Amendment protection of persons, they are entitled to some PROCEDURAL DUE PROCESS rights. With that exception, the regulation of immigration and other admission of aliens to the United States is a matter of statutory law.

Congress, through various immigration and naturalization statutes, has created an elaborate system and set of rules and procedures governing the admission of foreigners to the United States and regulating their stay within the country. American law, like the law in other countries, requires most persons seeking to enter the United States to obtain visas from United States consular offices abroad. A visa is an official document indicating that the party to whom it was issued appears to qualify for legal entry into the United States in accordance with the immigration laws. As aliens enter the United States for many varied reasons (e.g., to transit, to visit, to study, to work, to conduct business, to join a relative, to become a resident), the visa also designates the purpose or type of entry. The latter factor governs the length of stay and the alien's lawful activities while in the United States. A visa is consequently a preliminary determination of admissibility, a designation of entry category, and a permission to apply for admission at the border. The issuance of a visa, while necessary, does not guarantee admission into the United States, for immigration officers, disagreeing with a consul's determination, may refuse to admit persons with valid visas. Such refusals occur infrequently, however, and in most cases a visa is tantamount to a permission to enter.

There are two broad classes of visas: immigrant visas, issued to those seeking permanent admission into the United States, and nonimmigrant visas, issued to those seeking only temporary admission for business or pleasure. The United States limits the number of those who may seek permanent admission, with the exception of immediate relatives of citizens—defined as spouses, children under twenty-one, and parents of American citizens over twenty-one. A complicated system of seven preferences sets priorities among immigration seekers according to statutory criteria of desirability. For example, this scheme assigns the first preference among immigration applicants to adult unmarried sons and daughters of American citizens. The statute assigns twenty percent of the total number of available immigrant visas to this category. Consequently, in passing on immigrant visa applications, consular officers must prefer unmarried sons and daughters over other applicants for up to twenty percent of immigrant visas.

There are thirty-two statutory grounds for denying immigrant visa applications, including ill health, homosexuality, poverty, criminal convictions, insanity, narcotic addiction, entry for purposes of prostitution, subversive affiliations, and participation in Nazi persecution.

Many classes of persons are eligible for nonimmigrant visas, including visitors for business or pleasure, foreign officials and international representatives, intracompany transferees, exchange visitors, students, temporary workers and trainees, transit aliens, treaty traders and investors, foreign media representatives, fiancés or fiancées of U.S. citizens, and spouses and children of persons in some of these categories. Each class has its own type of visa, and entry periods and other restrictions depend on the type of visa issued.

As the consular decision whether to issue a visa depends on factual determinations and judgments, consuls exercise considerable discretion. Because the immigration statutes do not provide for JUDICIAL REVIEW of visa denials, the issue arises whether the Constitution, at least in some cases, requires such review. In *Kleindienst v. Mandel* (1972) the American government excluded a Belgian Marxist seeking to enter the United States to attend lectures. Asserting a FIRST AMENDMENT right to receive information and ideas, persons who wished to hear, speak, and debate with Mandel claimed that the Constitution required the government to waive his excludability—in effect to issue him a nonimmigrant visa. Relying on Congress's plenary power over the admission of aliens, the Supreme Court held that the First Amendment did not override the ostensibly legitimate exclusion. Lower courts have read *Mandel* to preclude judicial review of consular visa denials. Consequently, short of administrative relief or statutory change, applicants denied visas have no remedy and cannot gain admission to the United States.

GARY GOODPASTER
(1992)

Bibliography

GORDON, CHARLES and ROSENFIELD, HARRY 1959 *Immigration Law and Procedure*. Albany N.Y.: Banks Publishing Co.

## VLANDIS v. KLINE
### 412 U.S. 441 (1973)

A Connecticut statute gave resident students at a state university certain tuition preferences. A student who had entered the university as a nonresident was relegated to that status for his or her full student career. The Supreme Court, 6–3, held the latter provision unconstitutional. A majority of five Justices, speaking through Justice POTTER STEWART, held that the provision created "a permanent and IRREBUTTABLE PRESUMPTION of non-residence." Because this presumption was "not necessarily or universally true in fact," it denied a student PROCEDURAL DUE PROCESS by denying a hearing on the issue of residence. Justice BYRON R. WHITE concurred on EQUAL PROTECTION GROUNDS. The dissenters suggested that the Court had, in fact, drifted into an area of SUBSTANTIVE DUE PROCESS that the Court had abandoned in the 1930s. The irrebuttable presumptions DOCTRINE had a brief vogue, but *Weinberger v. Salfi* (1975) placed it in mothballs.

KENNETH L. KARST
(1986)

## VOICE SAMPLES

See: Testimonial and Nontestimonial Compulsion

# VOID FOR VAGUENESS

See: Vagueness

# VOIR DIRE

Voir dire (Old French: "to speak the truth") refers to the questioning by the court or counsel of prospective jurors to determine their qualification for jury service.

Two types of objections may be raised to disqualify prospective jurors: peremptory challenges and challenges for cause. A peremptory challenge allows dismissal of a juror without cause. Most states provide each side with twenty such challenges for a capital offense, and a lesser number for other felonies and misdemeanors.

A challenge for cause requires the challenging party to prove potential prejudice to the case if the challenged juror should be accepted. There is generally no limit to such challenges. The typical statute permits such an objection if the juror is of unsound mind, lacks the qualifications required by law, is related to a party in the litigation, has served in a related case or GRAND JURY investigation, or has a "state of mind" that will prevent him from acting with impartiality.

In *Wainwright v. Witt* (1985) the Supreme Court stated that the standard to determine when a prospective juror should be excluded for cause is whether the juror's views would prevent or substantially impair the juror's duties in accordance with hisher instructions and oath.

Commonly, a prosecutor calls and examines twelve veniremen, exercises his challenges for cause and peremptory challenges, replaces those excused with others, and then tenders a group of twelve to the defense. The defendant follows a similar procedure. This process continues until the parties have exhausted their challenges or expressed their satisfaction with the jury.

Voir dire proceedings are usually open to the public. In *Press-Enterprise v. Superior Court* (1984) the trial judge had ordered that all but three days of a six-week voir dire for a rape-murder trial of a teenage girl be closed to the public and press and had refused to grant the defendant's pretrial motion for release of the voir dire transcript. The Supreme Court unanimously reversed, holding that voir dire proceedings in criminal trials should be presumptively open to the public, unless fair trial interests would be better served by closure.

Voir dire vests broad authority in the trial judge. A judge may refuse to allow questions deemed irrelevant or inappropriate. The Constitution, however, requires certain inquiries. In *Ham v. South Carolina* (1973) the Supreme Court held that where racial issues permeate or are inextricably bound up in a trial, the defendant is entitled to questioning specifically directed at racial prejudice. In *Ristano v. Ross* (1976), however, the Court held that this right does not extend to all cases in which the victim and the defendant are of different races. Questioning about general bias or prejudice will normally suffice. The Court held in *Rosales-Lopez v. United States* (1981) that judges may decide on a case-by-case basis whether racial overtones justify such questioning.

Finally, voir dire violates DUE PROCESS if its exclusion of a particular group seriously detracts from the jury's impartiality and ability to reflect dominant community values. In *Witherspoon v. Illinois* (1968) the Supreme Court invalidated a statute that had the effect of screening out jurors not enthusiastic about CAPITAL PUNISHMENT, but accepting those who were. Jurors may constitutionally be disqualified, however, by expressing an absolute refusal to impose the death penalty.

CHARLES H. WHITEBREAD
(1986)

Bibliography

KALVEN, HARRY and ZEISEL, HANS   1966   *The American Jury.* Boston: Little, Brown.

# VOLSTEAD ACT
## 41 Stat. 305 (1919)

Congress passed the Volstead National Prohibition Act, sponsored by Representative Andrew J. Volstead (Republican, Minnesota), on October 28, 1919. The act provided both for the continuation of wartime PROHIBITION and for enforcement of the EIGHTEENTH AMENDMENT. It was enacted over the veto of President WOODROW WILSON, who objected to the linking of those "two distinct phases of prohibition legislation."

To enforce the Eighteenth Amendment against private conduct the Volstead Act defined "intoxicating beverages" as any beverages containing at least 0.5% alcohol by volume, and provided stringent penalties for their manufacture, importation, transportation, sale, possession, or use. The constitutionality of the act was upheld in the National Prohibition Cases (*Rhode Island v. Palmer*, 1920), in which the Supreme Court, speaking through Justice WILLIS VAN DEVANTER, held that Congress's power under the amendment was complete and extended to intrastate as well as interstate transactions.

The Beer-Wine Revenue Act of March 1933 amended the Volstead Act by permitting the manufacture and sale of beer and wine with an alcohol content of up to 3.2%.

Passage of the TWENTY-FIRST AMENDMENT later the same year rendered the Volstead Act void.

DENNIS J. MAHONEY
(1986)

# VOLUNTARINESS

See: Police Interrogation and Confessions

# VON HOLST, HERMANN EDUARD
## (1841–1904)

A German immigrant who became chairman of the department of history at the University of Chicago, Hermann E. von Holst published a seven-volume *Constitutional and Political History of the United States* (1876–1892). The work is malproportioned; the last four volumes cover 1850–1861. Intent on condemning the "slavocracy," the author blamed the ANNEXATION OF TEXAS, the Mexican War, the KANSAS-NEBRASKA ACT, and the CIVIL WAR on a slaveholders' conspiracy. The decision in DRED SCOTT V. SANDFORD (1857), wrote von Holst, was "an unparalleled prostitution of the judicial ermine." Von Holst believed that centralized SOVEREIGNTY and a free society stood for morality and national salvation. Despite his valuable use of newspapers and public documents, his style is so turgid and his judgments are so biased that he is no longer read.

LEONARD W. LEVY
(1986)

# VOTING RIGHTS

"The right to vote freely for the candidate of one's choice is of the essence of a democratic society, and any restrictions on that right strike at the heart of representative government." So spoke Chief Justice EARL WARREN, on behalf of the Supreme Court, in REYNOLDS V. SIMS (1964).

The Chief Justice's words were in direct philosophic succession to principles of the primacy of representative political institutions announced by the FIRST CONTINENTAL CONGRESS 190 years before, in the Declaration and Resolves of October 14, 1774:

> [T]he foundation of English liberty, and of all free government, is a right in the people to participate in their legislative council: and as the English colonists are not represented, and from their local and other circumstances, cannot properly be represented in the British parliament, they are entitled to a free and exclusive power of legislation in their several provincial legislatures, where their right of representation can alone be preserved, in all cases

of taxation and internal policy, subject only to the negative of their sovereign, in such manner as has been heretofore used and accustomed.

The failure of King George III, through his ministers, to recognize the urgency of the colonists' demand for true representative institutions was one of the chief causes of revolution set forth in the DECLARATION OF INDEPENDENCE: "He has dissolved Representative Houses repeatedly, for opposing with manly firmness his invasions in the rights of the people. He has refused for a long time, after such dissolutions, to cause others to be elected; whereby the Legislative Powers, incapable of Annihilation, have returned to the People at large for their exercise."

The severing of the ties with Britain required the establishment, at the state level and at the national level, of new and more representative institutions of government. American constitutional history is characterized in part by the continuing enlargement of the right to vote, the mechanism which, in the American political tradition, has become the *sine qua non* of a valid system of REPRESENTATION. An anomaly presents itself: The Constitution, as amended, addresses aspects of the right to vote with far greater frequency than any other topic. Nonetheless, it has never been the function of the Constitution affirmatively to define the universe of voters. The Constitution's function has been narrower—progressively to limit the permissible grounds of disenfranchisement.

Prior to the AMERICAN REVOLUTION, eligibility to vote was not uniform among the colonies, but the variations were relatively minor. Broadly speaking, voting for colonial (as distinct from township or borough) officials was reserved to adult (generally meaning twenty-one or older) "freeholders." In equating property ownership and suffrage, the colonies were following a familiar English model. But landowning was far more widely dispersed in the colonies than in the mother country, so the proportion of colonists eligible to vote was larger.

There were not more than a few black or women freeholders in any of the colonies, and pursuant either to convention or to formal legal specification those few did not vote. Religious restrictions were also commonplace but varied somewhat among the colonies and at different times. In general, the franchise was the prerogative of the propertied, Protestant, white male.

With the coming of independence, all of the newly sovereign states except Connecticut and Rhode Island adopted new charters of government—"constitutions." Impelled by the rhetoric of revolution and the eagerness of thousands of militiamen to participate in the processes of governance, the drafters of the new state constitutions relaxed but did not abandon the property and religious qualifications for voting for state officials (and the correlative, and generally more stringent, qualifications for holding state office). As Max Farrand observed, Americans

> might declare that "all men are created equal," and bills of rights might assert that government rested upon the consent of the governed; but these constitutions carefully provided that such consent should come from property owners, and, in many of the States, from religious believers and even followers of the Christian faith. "The man of small means might vote, but none save well-to-do Christians could legislate, and in many states none but a rich Christian could be a governor." In South Carolina, for example, a freehold of 10,000 currency was required of the Governor, Lieutenant Governor, and members of the council; 2,000 of the members of the Senate; and, while every elector was eligible to the House of Representatives, he had to acknowledge the being of a God and to believe in a future state of rewards and punishments, as well as to hold "a freehold at least of fifty acres of land, or a town lot."

Under the ARTICLES OF CONFEDERATION, the state delegates in Congress constituted the nation's government. The Articles limited the numbers of delegates (no fewer than two and no more than seven per state) but left each state legislature free to determine the qualifications of those selected and the mode of their annual selection. The Articles did not preclude popular election of delegates, but the word "appointed," in the phrase "appointed in such manner as the legislature of each State shall direct," suggests that it was not anticipated that legislatures would remit to their constituents the power to choose those who would speak and vote for the states in Congress.

At the CONSTITUTIONAL CONVENTION OF 1787, the Framers divided on how the lower house was to be selected. JAMES MADISON told his fellow delegates that he "considered an election of one branch at least of the legislature by the people immediately, as a clear principle of true government." Madison's view carried the day. But then the Convention faced the question whether the Constitution should set the qualifications of those who were to elect representatives. GOUVERNEUR MORRIS of Pennsylvania proposed that only freeholders should vote. Colonel GEORGE MASON of Virginia found this proposal regressive: "Eight of nine States have extended the right of suffrage beyond the freeholders. What will the people there say, if they should be disfranchised." OLIVER ELLSWORTH of Connecticut also challenged Morris's proposal: "How shall the freehold be defined? Ought not every man who pays a tax to vote for the representative who is to levy and dispose of his money?" Morris was unpersuaded: "He had long learned not to be the dupe of words. . . . Give the votes to people who have no property, and they will sell them to

the rich who will be able to buy them." But BENJAMIN FRANKLIN took decisive issue with his fellow Pennsylvanian: "It is of great consequence that we should not depress the virtue and public spirit of our common people; of which they displayed a great deal during the war, and which contributed principally to the favorable issue of it." Morris's proposal was decisively defeated. The Convention instead approved the provision that has endured ever since, under which eligibility to vote for representatives is keyed, in each state, to that state's rules of eligibility to vote for members of the most numerous house of the state legislature.

When it came to designing the method of selecting the President and vice-president, the Convention devised the indirect election system of the ELECTORAL COLLEGE. The expectation was that the electors—themselves chosen from among the leading citizens of their respective states—would, through disinterested deliberation, select as the nation's chief executive officials the two persons of highest civic virtue, wholly without regard for the vulgar demands of "politics." According to ALEXANDER HAMILTON in THE FEDERALIST #68, "[t]he mode of appointment of the Chief Magistrate of the United States is almost the only part of the system, of any consequence, which has escaped without severe censure, or which has received the slightest mark of approbation from its opponents." But, measured against its intended purpose, no other structural aspect of the Constitution has wound up wider of the mark. The Framers of the Constitution wholly failed to anticipate the development of national political parties whose chief political goal would be the election of the party leader as President. That development has meant that since the fourth presidential election—that of 1800, in which THOMAS JEFFERSON defeated JOHN ADAMS—the electors in each state have themselves been selected as adherents of the political party prevailing in that state and thus have, with the rarest of exceptions, cast their electoral votes for the party's presidential and vice-presidential candidates. The system of electors remains to this day, but it has been entirely drained of its intended function.

Those who drafted the Constitution in 1787, and who saw it through ratification to the launching of the new ship of state in 1789, were America's aristocracy. The transformation of American politics from 1789 to the Civil War can be measured in the marked shift in class status of those who occupied the Presidency. The Presidents from GEORGE WASHINGTON to JOHN QUINCY ADAMS were all patricians. Most of the Presidents from ANDREW JACKSON to ABRAHAM LINCOLN were not. The growth of national parties, beginning with Jefferson and accelerating with Jackson, democratized politics by putting politicians in the business of seeking to enlarge their voting constituencies. Property qualifications gave way, for the most part, to taxpayer qualifications. And, in many states, these in turn were soon largely abandoned.

The erosion of property tests for voting did not mean that anything approximating universal suffrage was at hand. As one political scientist has summarized the situation:

> Apart from a few midwestern states, hungry for settlers, no one was very warm to the prospect of aliens and immigrants at the polls; all the states but Maine, Massachusetts, Vermont, New Hampshire, Rhode Island, and New York explicitly barred free blacks from voting, and New York imposed special property requirements on blacks which, while repeatedly challenged, were repeatedly upheld in popular referenda. Even in the tiny handful of northern states that did not exclude blacks by law, social pressures tended to accomplish the same end. New Hampshire and Vermont in 1857 and 1858 had to pass special laws against excluding blacks from voting. Chancellor James Kent concluded that only in Maine could the black man participate equally with the white man in civil and political rights. Women were universally denied the vote [Elliott 1974, p. 40].

In 1848, a year of revolution in Europe, 300 people gathered in a church in the little upstate New York town of Seneca Falls to consider the status of women. The most revolutionary item on the agenda was voting. Half a century before there had been a small outcropping of female voting in New Jersey, whose 1776 constitution had, perhaps inadvertently, used the word "inhabitants" to describe those who, if they met the property qualifications, could vote. It appears that by 1807, respectable New Jersey opinion had reached the consensus that laxity was slipping into license (at a local election in Trenton even slaves and Philadelphians were said to have cast ballots). At this point, "reform" was clearly called for: the legislature promptly altered the electoral code to bring New Jersey's voting qualifications back into conformity with the white maleness that characterized the electorate in the rest of the country and remained the accepted order of things until Seneca Falls.

The chief driving energies behind the SENECA FALLS CONVENTION were ELIZABETH CADY STANTON and Lucretia Mott. Stanton drafted the "Declaration of Principles" and the several resolutions which the convention was asked to adopt. The only resolution to receive less-than-unanimous endorsement was the ninth: "Resolved, that it is the duty of the women of this country to secure to themselves their sacred right to the elective franchise." That the franchise was a far more chimerical goal than other concerns (for example, property rights for married women) was recognized by Mott. She had asked Stanton not to submit the ninth resolution for the reason that "Thou will make us

ridiculous." The factor that may have tipped the balance in Stanton's decision not to subordinate her principle to Mott's pragmatism was the strong encouragement of Frederick Douglass. The great black leader supported the ninth resolution. He joined the cause of equal rights for women to the cause of abolition.

The women's movement maintained its close association with abolitionism through the CIVIL WAR. After the freeing of the slaves, the country's attention focused on the terms on which American blacks were to be brought into the mainstream of American life. The leaders of the women's movement hoped that the drive for women's suffrage would complement and be reinforced by the drive for black suffrage. But that was not to be. As the war neared its end, a number of Republican leaders began to recognize a strong partisan interest in creating black voters to counter the feared resurgence of the Democratic party; there were no comparable reasons for creating women voters. Many of the women leaders, recognizing the political realities, accepted—albeit with no enthusiasm—the priority given to the rights of blacks. But not Elizabeth Cady Stanton and SUSAN B. ANTHONY. Said Anthony: "I will cut off this right arm before I will ever work for or demand the ballot for the Negro and not the woman." (Anthony and Stanton then formed the National Woman Suffrage Association, while the other leaders worked through the American Woman Suffrage Association; the split was not to be healed for twenty-five years.)

In 1864 Abraham Lincoln appointed SALMON P. CHASE—Lincoln's former secretary of the treasure and one of his chief rivals for the Republican presidential nomination in 1860—to succeed ROGER B. TANEY as CHIEF JUSTICE of the United States. Chase's elevation to the Court did not abate his presidential ambitions and his attendant interest in promoting a favorable political environment. The new Chief Justice wrote to Lincoln, as he subsequently wrote to President ANDREW JOHNSON, urging that black suffrage be made a condition of the reconstruction of the rebel states. And by 1867 Chase had taken the position that Congress had constitutional authority to enfranchise blacks as a mode of enforcing the THIRTEENTH AMENDMENT: "Can anything be clearer than that the National Legislature charged with the duty of "enforcing by appropriate legislation' the condition of universal freedom, is authorized and bound to provide for universal suffrage? Is not *suffrage* the best security against *slavery* and *involuntary servitude*? Is not the legislation which provides the *best* security the most *appropriate*?" Chase lost interest in active promotion of black voting when it became apparent that his modest chances of being nominated for the presidency were more likely to be realized in the Democratic party than in the Republican party. In any event, the question whether the Thirteenth Amendment could have been a platform for enlarging the franchise became moot upon the adoption of the two other post-Civil War amendments, both of which expressly addressed the franchise—for blacks, not for women.

The FOURTEENTH AMENDMENT, ratified in 1868, dealt with black voting by indirection. By declaring that "[a]ll persons born or naturalized in the United States, and subject to the jurisdiction thereof, are citizens of the United States and of the State wherein they reside," the first sentence of the first section of the amendment overruled Roger B. Taney's pronouncement in DRED SCOTT V. SANDFORD (1857), that blacks, whether slave or free, could not be citizens within the contemplation of the Constitution. The second sentence of the first section sought to protect the CIVIL RIGHTS of blacks: First, it guaranteed "the privileges and immunities of citizens of the United States" against state abridgment and, second, it prohibited state denial to any person, whether citizen or not, of "life, liberty or property without DUE PROCESS OF LAW," or deprivation of the "EQUAL PROTECTION OF THE LAWS." The second section of the amendment spoke to the political rights of blacks. It provided that any state that denied participation in federal or state elections to "any of the male inhabitants of such State, being twenty-one years of age, and citizens of the United States . . . except for participation in rebellion, or other crime," should have its allocation of representatives and of presidential electors proportionately reduced. The framers of the amendment thus preserved the states' entitlement to discriminate but proposed a substantial penalty as the price of discrimination.

By 1869, after General ULYSSES S. GRANT's narrow victory in the 1868 presidential election, the Republican party recognized that black votes were essential to its survival. So the Republican leadership in Congress fashioned the FIFTEENTH AMENDMENT. That amendment, ratified in 1870, addressed the question of black voting directly. A citizen's entitlement to vote could not be "abridged by the United States or by any State on account of race, color, or previous condition of servitude."

Notwithstanding that the express language of the Fourteenth Amendment addressed male voting, and that the express language of the Fifteenth Amendment addressed discriminations rooted in "race, color or previous condition of servitude," some leaders of the women's movement contended that women were constitutionally entitled to vote. Arguing that the right to vote in a federal election was a privilege of national citizenship protected by section 1 of the Fourteenth Amendment, Susan B. Anthony actually persuaded election officials in Rochester, New York, to let her vote in 1872 notwithstanding that the New York constitution limited the franchise to men. Anthony was promptly charged with the crime of casting a ballot in a federal election in which she was not an eligible voter. The

presiding judge was Justice WARD HUNT of the Supreme Court. Justice Hunt rejected Anthony's constitutional claim in the following words:

> The right of voting, or the privilege of voting, is a right or privilege arising under the constitution of the state, and not under the Constitution of the United States. The qualifications are different in the different states. Citizenship, age, sex, residence, are variously required in the different states, or may be so. If the right belongs to any particular person, it is because such person is entitled to it by the laws of the state where he offers to exercise it, and not because of citizenship of the United States. If the state of New York should provide that no person should vote until he had reached the age of thirty years, or after he had reached the age of thirty years, or after he had reached the age of fifty, or that no person having grey hair, or who had not the use of all his limbs, should be entitled to vote, I do not see how it could be held to be a violation of any right derived or held under the Constitution of the United States. We might say that such regulations were unjust, tyrannical, unfit for the regulation of an intelligent state; but, if rights of a citizen are thereby violated they are of that fundamental class, derived from his position as a citizen of the state, and not those limited rights belonging to him as a citizen of the United States.

Read through the prism of a century of doctrinal hindsight, Justice Hunt's words seem—at least at first blush—somewhat surprising. The surprise is not occasioned by the fact that the Justice gave such short shrift to arguments based on the Fourteenth Amendment's PRIVILEGES AND IMMUNITIES CLAUSE, for we are accustomed to the fact that, ever since the SLAUGHTERHOUSE CASES (1873), the Supreme Court has read the grant of privileges and immunities flowing from national citizenship very restrictively. The surprise stems from Hunt's failure—which may also have been counsel's failure—to approach sex-based denial of the franchise (not to mention the assertedly analogous hypothetical denials based on age, physical handicap, or color of hair) in equal protection terms. The likely explanation is that in *Slaughterhouse* the Court doubted that "any action of a State not directed by way of discrimination against the negroes as a class, or on account of their race, will ever be held to come within the" equal protection clause.

Justice Hunt directed the jury to return a verdict of guilty and imposed a fine of $100.

Justice Hunt's rejection of Anthony's privileges and immunities claim was vindicated two years later by Chief Justice MORRISON R. WAITE's opinion for the unanimous Court in MINOR V. HAPPERSETT (1875). This was a civil suit brought in a Missouri state court by Virginia L. Minor, and her lawyer husband Francis Minor, to challenge the refusal of a Missouri election official to register her as a voter. The Minors contended that the provision of the Missouri constitution limiting the electorate to male citizens transgressed the privileges and immunities clause. In rejecting the Minors' contention, Chief Justice Waite demonstrated that limitation of the franchise to males had been the norm, despite the fact that women were citizens. Voting had not been a privilege of national citizenship prior to the Fourteenth Amendment. As the amendment "did not add to the privileges and immunities of a citizen," but merely "furnished an additional guaranty for the protection of such as he already had," Missouri's refusal to let Minor vote was not unconstitutional. *Minor v. Happersett* ended attempts to win the campaign for woman's suffrage by litigation. The road to the ballot box was to be political—persuading male legislators to pass laws giving women the vote.

It was to be a long road. In 1870 Wyoming's territorial legislature enacted a law entitling women to vote. Utah followed suit, but the victory there was temporary. An 1887 congressional statute forbidding Utah's Mormons from practicing polygamy also overrode the territorial legislature's grant of the franchise to women. Three years later Wyoming's first state constitution called for women's suffrage. Thereafter progress was slow. Many state campaigns were fought and most were lost. In the South, votes for women were seen as a harbinger of votes for blacks, and the states resisted accordingly; in the East, many industrialists mistrusted the links between some women's suffragists and trade union and other reform groups; in the Midwest, the women's suffrage movement was seen by the brewing interests as the advance guard of prohibition. By 1913 women could vote in only nine states; in that year Illinois admitted women to participation in presidential elections.

In 1912, THEODORE ROOSEVELT's Progressive party endorsed women's suffrage. This endorsement served as a reminder that Susan B. Anthony and her associates had sought to achieve women's suffrage not state-by-state but by amending the Constitution. Pressure for a women's suffrage amendment mounted during World War I when women entered the work force in record numbers. In 1918 WOODROW WILSON announced support for the proposed amendment, notwithstanding that women's suffrage was anathema to the white Democratic South. In 1919, with Democrats divided and Republicans strongly in favor, Congress submitted to the states a proposed amendment barring denial or abridgment of the right to vote in any election on grounds of sex. In 1920, the NINETEENTH AMENDMENT was ratified. In the 1920 elections one of the voters was Charlotte Woodward Pierce who, as a nineteen-year-old farm girl, had attended the Seneca Falls Convention in 1848.

Following the Civil War, the military occupation of the South ushered in a period in which blacks not only voted but were elected to office. With the adoption of the Fifteenth Amendment, there appeared to be some ground for supposing that black voting had achieved a legal infrastructure which might suffice even after the army departed. However, although the amendment bars race, color, and previous condition of servitude as criteria of eligibility to vote, it does not proscribe other criteria—such as literacy or taxpayer status—susceptible of adaptation as surrogates for racism. The lesson was that most blacks might be prevented from voting by educational or property qualifications.

Following the COMPROMISE OF 1877, which led to the withdrawal from the South of the last military units, the twilight of black participation in the southern political process began. Through the 1880s, some black voting continued—frequently in Populist alliance with poor whites. But in the 1890s, as a corollary of the spreading gospel of Jim Crow, the southern white political leadership forged a consensus to exclude blacks from the ballot box. Some of this was achieved by force, and some by skulduggery, but in large measure the forms of law were utilized. LITERACY TESTS and POLL TAXES were common exclusionary devices, as was closing Democratic primaries—the only real elections in most of the South—to blacks. The underlying rationale was that offered by Senator James Vardaman of Mississippi: "I am just as much opposed to Booker Washington as a voter, with all his Anglo-Saxon reinforcements, as I am to the cocoanut-headed, chocolate-covered, typical little coon, Andy Dottson, who blacks my shoes every morning. Neither is fit to perform the supreme function of citizenship."

By and large, the legal stratagems employed by the southern states to disenfranchise blacks succeeded. Poll taxes and literacy tests which did not on their face show a discriminatory purpose easily passed constitutional muster from BREEDLOVE V. SUTTLES (1937) to *Lassiter v. Northampton Election Board* (1959). To be sure, the Supreme Court did intervene in those rare instances in which the purpose to discriminate was evident on the face of the challenged restraint. A flagrant example was the so-called GRANDFATHER CLAUSE in Oklahoma's 1910 constitution, which exempted from the literacy requirement any would-be voter "who was, on January 1, 1866, or at any time prior thereto, entitled to vote under any form of government, or who at that time resided in some foreign nation, and [any] lineal descendant thereof." In GUINN V. UNITED STATES (1915) the Supreme Court held this literacy test invalid.

Because during the first half of the twentieth century the decisive voting in the South took place in Democratic primaries, not in the general elections, the cases of greatest practical as well as doctrinal consequence were those that challenged devices to maintain the whiteness of the "white primary."

In NIXON V. HERNDON (1927) a unanimous Court, speaking through Justice OLIVER WENDELL HOLMES, sustained the complaint of L. A. Nixon, who contended that he had been unconstitutionally barred from voting in a Texas Democratic primary through enforcement of a Texas statute that recited that "in no event shall a negro be eligible to participate in a Democratic party primary election held in the state of Texas." The Court held that this statutory racial exclusion contravened the Fourteenth Amendment.

The consequence of this ruling was described by Justice BENJAMIN N. CARDOZO in his opinion in NIXON V. CONDON (1932): "Promptly after the announcement of [the Herndon] decision, the legislature of Texas enacted a new statute . . . repealing the article condemned by this court; declaring that the effect of the decision was to create an emergency with a need for immediate action; and substituting for the article so repealed another bearing the same number. By the article thus substituted, "every political party in this State through its State Executive Committee shall have the power to prescribe the qualifications of its own members and shall in its own way determine who shall be qualified to vote or otherwise participate in such political party. . . ." Thereupon the executive committee of the Texas Democratic party voted to limit party membership and participation to whites, and L. A. Nixon was once again barred from voting in the Democratic primary. Once again Nixon brought a lawsuit, and once again he prevailed in the Supreme Court. Justice Cardozo, speaking for a majority of five, concluded that the new Texas statute delegated exercise of the state's power over primaries to party executive committees, with the result that the racial exclusion decided on by the executive committee was in effect the racially discriminatory act of the State of Texas and hence prohibited by the Fourteenth Amendment. Justice JAMES C. MCREYNOLDS, joined by three other Justices, dissented.

Three years later, in GROVEY V. TOWNSEND (1935), the Court considered the next refinement in the Texas Democratic primary—exclusion of blacks by vote of the party convention. Speaking through Justice OWEN J. ROBERTS, the Court this time unanimously concluded that the action taken by the Texas Democratic party was an entirely private decision for which the State of Texas was not accountable; accordingly, neither the Fourteenth nor the Fifteenth Amendment was transgressed.

Nine years later, toward the end of World War II, the Court, in SMITH V. ALLWRIGHT (1944), again considered the *Grovey v. Townsend* question. In the interval, seven of the Justices who had participated in *Grovey v. Townsend* had died or retired. Approaching the matter in a common sense way, the Court, with Justice Roberts dissenting, concluded that the role of the primary as a formal and vital predicate of the election made it an integral part of the state's voting processes and hence subject to the requirement of the Fifteenth Amendment. Accordingly, the Court in *Smith v. Allwright* overruled *Grovey v. Townsend*.

The resumption, after three-quarters of a century, of significant black participation in the southern political process dates from the decision in *Smith v. Allwright*. But the elimination of the most egregious legal barriers did not mean that all blacks were automatically free to vote. Hundreds of thousands of would-be black voters were still kept from the polls by fraud or force or both. In 1957, three years after the Court, in BROWN V. BOARD OF EDUCATION (1954), held that legally mandated racial SEGREGATION contravened the Fourteenth Amendment, Congress passed the first federal civil rights law enacted since the 1870s: a voting rights law which authorized modest federal supervision of the southern voting process. And the year 1964 witnessed ratification of the TWENTY-FOURTH AMENDMENT, barring exclusion of American citizens from voting in any federal election on grounds of failure to pay any poll tax or other tax. But as black demands for equal treatment multiplied, responsive abuses escalated.

In the spring of 1965, a Boston minister, one of scores of clergymen who had gone to Selma, Alabama, to help MARTIN LUTHER KING, JR., launch a voter registration drive, was murdered. A few days later, on March 15, 1965, President LYNDON B. JOHNSON addressed Congress:

> Many of the issues of civil rights are very complex and most difficult. But about this there can and should be no argument. Every American citizen must have an equal right to vote. There is no reason which can excuse the denial of that right. There is no duty which weighs more heavily on us than the duty we have to ensure that right.

> Yet the harsh fact is that in many places in this country men and women are kept from voting simply because they are Negroes.

> Every device of which human ingenuity is capable has been used to deny this right. The Negro citizen may go to register only to be told that the day is wrong, or the hour is late, or the official in charge is absent. And if he persists and if he manages to present himself to the registrar, he may be disqualified because he did not spell out his middle name or because he abbreviated a word on the application. And if he manages to fill out an application, he is given a test. The registrar is the sole judge of whether he passes this test. He may be asked to recite the entire constitution, or explain the most complex provisions of state laws. And even a college degree cannot be used to prove that he can read and write.

> For the fact is that the only way to pass these barriers is to show a white skin.

> Experience has clearly shown that the existing process of law cannot overcome systematic and ingenious discrimination. No law that we now have on the books—and I

have helped to put three of them there—can ensure the right to vote when local officials are determined to deny it. . . .

This time, on this issue, there must be no delay, or no hesitation or no compromise with our purpose.

We cannot, we must not refuse to protect the right of every American to vote in every election that he may desire to participate in. And we ought not, we must not wait another eight months before we get a bill. We have already waited a hundred years and more and the time for waiting is gone. . . .

But even if we pass this bill, the battle will not be over. What happened in Selma is part of a far larger movement which reaches into every section and state of America. It is the effort of American Negroes to secure for themselves the full blessings of American life.

Their cause must be our cause too. Because it is not just Negroes, but really it is all of us, who must overcome the crippling legacy of bigotry and injustice. And we shall overcome.

As a man whose roots go deeply into Southern soil I know how agonizing racial feelings are. I know how difficult it is to reshape the attitudes and the structure of our society.

But a century has passed, more than a hundred years, since the Negro was freed. And he is not fully free tonight.

It was more than a hundred years ago that Abraham Lincoln, the great President of the Northern party, signed the Emancipation Proclamation, but emancipation is a proclamation and not a fact.

A century has passed, more than a hundred years since equality was promised. And yet the Negro is not equal.

A century has passed since the day of promise. And the promise is unkept.

The time of justice has now come. I tell you that I believe sincerely that no force can hold it back. It is right in the eyes of man and God that it should come. And when it does, I think that day will brighten the lives of every American.

Congress enacted the VOTING RIGHTS ACT OF 1965. The act provided, among other things, for the suspension of literacy tests for five years in states or political subdivisions thereof in which fewer than "50 per cent of its voting-age residents were registered on November 1, 1964, or voted in the presidential election of November, 1964." This and other major provisions of the 1965 act were thereafter sustained in SOUTH CAROLINA V. KATZENBACH (1966), *Rome v. United States* (1980), and KATZENBACH V. MORGAN (1966), as appropriate ways of enforcing the Fifteenth and Fourteenth Amendments. Subsequent amendments to the 1965 act have broadened its coverage.

The 1944 decision in *Smith v. Allwright* was more than a new and hospitable judicial approach to the right of blacks to participate in the American political process. It was a major advance (as, four years later, was SHELLEY V. KRAEMER, 1948) toward the day—May 17, 1954—when a unanimous Court, speaking through Chief Justice Warren, was to hold, in *Brown v. Board of Education,* that the equal protection clause barred the legally mandated racial segregation of school children. Subsequent decisions, building on *Brown v. Board of Education,* soon made it plain that the equal protection clause barred all the legal trappings of Jim Crow. *Brown v. Board of Education* worked a fundamental change in the Court's and the nation's perception of the scope of judicial responsibility to vindicate those values.

In 1962, eight years after *Brown v. Board of Education,* the Court, in *Baker v. Carr,* held that allegations that a state legislature suffered from systematic malapportionment, under which districts of widely different populations were each represented by one legislator, stated a claim cognizable under the equal protection clause. The importance of *Baker v. Carr* cannot be overestimated. Chief Justice Warren thought it the most significant decision handed down by the Court during his sixteen years in the center chair. Even those who rank *Brown v. Board of Education* ahead of *Baker v. Carr* must nonetheless acknowledge that the latter decision set in motion a process that resulted in the redesign of numerous state legislatures and a myriad of local governing bodies, and, indeed, of the House of Representatives. That redesign has been required to meet the Court's pronouncement, in GRAY V. SANDERS (1963), that "[t]he conception of political equality from the Declaration of Independence, to Lincoln's Gettysburg Address, to the Fifteenth, Seventeenth, and Nineteenth Amendments can mean only one thing—one person, one vote." Long-standing patterns of malapportionment in which rural districts with relatively few inhabitants were represented on equal terms with heavily populated urban districts have become a thing of the past. (See REAPPORTIONMENT.)

Guaranteeing the voting rights of women and blacks and overcoming rampant malapportionment have cured the major inexcusable deficiencies of the American political process. In recent decades, certain lesser inequalities have also begun to be addressed.

From the beginning of the republic, Americans residing in the continental United States but not within any state—for example, those who lived in federal territories—had no way of voting in national elections. In the most egregious of anomalies, residents of the nation's capital were voiceless in the selection of the President who dwelt and governed in their own home town. So matters stood until 1964, when the TWENTY-THIRD AMENDMENT was added to the Constitution, giving the DISTRICT OF COLUMBIA a minimum of three electoral votes in presidential elections.

In the late 1960s, profound divisions in American opinion about America's military involvement in the VIETNAM WAR forced recognition of another anomaly—that tens of thousands of young men were being drafted to fight in an unpopular foreign war although they were not old enough to vote in national elections choosing the officials responsible for making decisions for war or for peace. In 1970, Congress, in amending the Voting Rights Act, included a provision forbidding abridgment of the right of any citizen to vote "on account of age if such citizen is eighteen years or older." The statute was promptly challenged in OREGON V. MITCHELL (1970). Four Justices concluded that Congress had the power to lower the voting age to eighteen. Four Justices concluded that Congress had no such power. The casting vote was that of Justice Hugo L. Black, who held that Congress could regulate the voting age in national elections but not in state elections. Because Americans vote every two years for state and national officials at the same time, *Oregon v. Mitchell* was an invitation to chaos. Within six months, Congress proposed and the requisite three-fourths of the states ratified, the TWENTY-SIXTH AMENDMENT which accomplished by constitutional mandate what Congress had been unable to achieve by statute.

In the course of two centuries law and conscience have combined to make the American suffrage almost truly universal. One massive obstacle remains: apathy. In recent national elections in the European democracies, seventy-two percent of the eligible electorate voted in Great Britain, seventy-nine percent in Spain, eighty-five percent in France, and eighty-nine percent in Italy and West Germany. By contrast, in the American presidential election of 1980, only fifty-three percent of those eligible voted. In America's 1984 presidential election, after both major parties had made massive efforts to register new voters, not more than fifty-five percent of those who could have voted made their way to the ballot box. A fateful question confronting American democracy is whether tens of millions of self-disenfranchised Americans will in the years to come find the energy and good sense to exercise the precious right won at such great labor at the Constitutional Convention, in Congress and state legislatures and the Supreme Court, and at Selma and Seneca Falls.

LOUIS H. POLLAK
(1986)

(SEE ALSO: *Rogers v. Lodge.*)

Bibliography

CHUTE, MARCHETTE G. 1969 *First Liberty: A History of the Right to Vote in America, 1619–1850.* New York: Dutton.

DUBOIS, ELLEN CAROL, ed. 1981 *Elizabeth Cady Stanton, Susan B. Anthony: Correspondence, Writings, Speeches.* New York: Shocken.

ELLIOTT, WARD E. Y. 1974 *The Rise of Guardian Democracy: The Supreme Court's Role in Voting Rights Disputes, 1845–1969.* Cambridge, Mass.: Harvard University Press.

FAIRMAN, CHARLES 1971 *Reconstruction and Reunion, 1864–1888.* New York: Macmillan.

FARRAND, MAX, ed. 1911 *The Records of the Federal Convention of 1787.* New Haven, Conn.: Yale University Press.

———, ed. 1921 *The Fathers of the Constitution.* New Haven, Conn.: Yale University Press.

FLEXNER, ELEANOR 1975 *Century of Struggle: The Woman's Right to Vote Movement in the United States.* Rev. ed. Cambridge, Mass.: Harvard University Press.

HIGGINBOTHAM, A. L., JR. 1984 "States' 'Rights' and States' 'Wrongs': Apartheid, Virginia and South African Style." Dubois Lecture, Harvard University.

MCKAY, ROBERT B. 1965 *Reapportionment: The Law and Politics of Equal Representation.* New York: Twentieth Century Fund.

WILLIAMSON, CHILTON 1960 *American Suffrage from Property to Democracy, 1760–1860.* Princeton, N.J.: Princeton University Press.

WOODWARD, C. VANN 1951 *Origins of the New South, 1877–1913.* Baton Rouge: Louisiana State University Press.

——— 1957 *The Strange Career of Jim Crow.* New York: Oxford University Press.

# VOTING RIGHTS
## (Update)

The 1980s began inauspiciously for supporters of minority voting rights when a plurality of the Supreme Court ruled in MOBILE V. BOLDEN (1980) that the VOTING RIGHTS ACT prohibited only intentional RACIAL DISCRIMINATION. Yet two years later, CIVIL RIGHTS forces, over the objections of the administration of President RONALD REAGAN, amended the Act to make clear that it was meant to prohibit laws or practices that had either the intent or the effect of discriminating against people on the basis of race. The bipartisan consensus in favor of a strengthened Voting Rights Act, the explicit standards in the authoritative U.S. SENATE report on the act, and the attention and élan that the 1981–1982 struggle restored to voting rights carried the movement to successes through the rest of the 1980s. At-large elections like those at issue in *Bolden*, which tend to minimize minority voting power, were declared illegal in many areas of the South and some outside it.

Even though the Court sustained attacks on at-large elections in its most important interpretation of the 1982 amendments in *Thornburg v. Gingles* (1986), critics such as political scientist Abigail Thernstrom and Justice CLARENCE THOMAS harshly denounced the trend. Electoral structures, Thernstrom thought, should be overturned only in the most egregious cases of discrimination against African Americans. Latinos, she claimed, did not suffer from enough discrimination to deserve protection. The Voting Rights Act, she announced, should never have deviated from what she asserted was its sole original intent, to protect the right to cast a ballot. In a lengthy concurrence to *Holder v. Hall* (1994), Thomas not only agreed with Thernstrom, but also went on to argue that the amended Voting Rights Act was never intended to apply to such electoral structures as at-large elections and redistricting, but only to guard an individual's right to register and vote, which he believed to be of merely symbolic importance anyway. Not only were Thernstrom's and Thomas's empirical assertions of racial electoral equality factually incorrect, but they also failed to apply their value judgments consistently when the Court vetoed pro-minority redistricting in SHAW V. RENO (1993) and its progeny, decisions that threatened to reverse many of the voting rights victories of the 1980s.

In the other major voting rights development of the 1990s, the Clinton Administration passed the National Voter Registration Act (NVRA), popularly known as "motor voter," which facilitated voter registration by requiring states to register voters for federal elections in offices that served the public, such as departments of motor vehicles and welfare and unemployment bureaus. Fearing a surge of new lower-class, pro-Democratic voters, several Republican governors refused to effectuate the law and unsuccessfully took it to court. By the time that the Court rejected the challenge, it had become clear that the large number of new registrants did not affiliate disproportionately with either major party. Estimates of additional registration produced by the NVRA ranged from 3.5 million to 9 million people in 1995–1996.

J. MORGAN KOUSSER
(2000)

(SEE ALSO: *Electoral Districting; Reapportionment.*)

Bibliography

CASPER, LYNNE M. and BASS, LORETTA E. 1998 Voting and Registration in the Election of November 1996. U.S. Bureau of the Census, *Current Population Reports: Population Characteristics.* Washington, D.C.: Government Printing Office.

DAVIDSON, CHANDLER and GROFMAN, BERNARD, eds. 1994 *Quiet Revolution in the South: The Impact of the Voting Rights Act, 1965–1990.* Princeton, N.J.: Princeton University Press.

GROFMAN, BERNARD and DAVIDSON, CHANDLER, eds. 1992 *Controversies in Minority Voting: The Voting Rights Act in Perspective.* Washington, D.C.: The Brookings Institution.

THERNSTROM, ABIGAIL M. 1987 *Whose Votes Count? Affirmative Action and Minority Voting Rights.* Cambridge, Mass.: Harvard University Press.

# VOTING RIGHTS ACT OF 1965 AND ITS AMENDMENTS
## 79 Stat. 437 (1965)

Despite Congress's efforts in the CIVIL RIGHTS ACTS OF 1957, 1960, and 1964 to protect the right to vote, the case-by-case approach of these laws proved ineffective in dealing with denials of VOTING RIGHTS to millions of blacks. By 1965, only seventy-one voting rights cases had been filed by the Department of Justice. And in 1964 only 19.4, 6.4, and 31.8 percent of eligible blacks were registered to vote in Alabama, Mississippi, and Louisiana, respectively. In Louisiana, comparable white registration stood at 80.2 percent.

The Voting Rights Act of 1965, amended in 1970, 1975, and 1982, provided additional protection of the right to vote. The 1965 act's most extraordinary features, its preclearance requirements, applied only to states or political subdivisions with low voter registration or participation. In such jurisdictions, most of which were in the South, the act suspended literacy, educational, and character tests of voter qualifications used to deny the right to vote in any elections. In addition, with a view to New York's Puerto Rican population, the act prohibited conditioning the right to vote on any English comprehension requirement for anyone who had completed sixth grade in a school in which the predominant classroom language was other than English. States and political subdivisions subject to the suspension of voting tests were barred from implementing other voting practices that had the effect of denying or abridging the right to vote without obtaining preclearance from a federal court or the ATTORNEY GENERAL.

The Voting Rights Act Amendments of 1970 and 1975 enhanced the preclearance provisions. The 1965 act's coverage had been triggered by low electoral participation in the 1964 election. The 1970 amendments extended the preclearance requirement through 1975 and suspended voting qualification tests or devices until 1975 in all jurisdictions, not just in jurisdictions covered by other provisions of the original 1965 act. The 1975 amendments extended the preclearance requirement through 1982 and suspended tests or devices indefinitely. The 1970 and 1975 amendments also added 1968 and 1972 to 1964 as years in which low electoral participation would trigger the act's coverage. The 1982 amendments imposed new preclearance standards to be effective until 2007.

The Supreme Court has taken an expansive view of the procedures covered by the act's preclearance requirement. In *Allen v. State Board of Elections* (1969), *Dougherty County Board of Education v. White* (1978), and other cases, the Court applied the act to voting practices that might affect minority voter effectiveness, as well as to practices directly limiting voter registration. Under these rulings, the act's preclearance requirements would govern changes in voting districts, or a county board of education's requirement that employees seeking elective office take an unpaid leave of absence.

A change in voting procedure raises the question whether the change triggers the act's preclearance requirement by having the effect of denying or abridging the right to vote. In deciding whether the requisite effect exists, the Supreme Court has held that the act covers effects even if they are not discriminatorily motivated. This standard, which is more stringent than the purposeful discrimination requirement the Court applies under the FOURTEENTH AMENDMENT and FIFTEENTH AMENDMENT, was upheld against constitutional attack in *Rome v. United States* (1980).

In addition to the preclearance requirements, the 1965 act included a nationwide prohibition upon voting qualifications or standards that deny or abridge voting rights on account of race. This prohibition applies whether the governmental unit is subject to the act's preclearance requirements or not. And, unlike the preclearance requirements, which apply only to changes in voting procedures, it applies to procedures that have long been in effect. A plurality opinion in MOBILE V. BOLDEN (1980) suggested that this provision only proscribed purposeful discrimination prohibited by the Constitution. In the 1982 amendments, however, Congress rejected a purposeful discrimination requirement and set forth standards governing findings of discriminatory effect.

In one of its remedies, the 1965 act continued and expanded a method of guaranteeing voting rights initiated in the FORCE ACT OF 1871. On a showing of widespread denials of voting rights, the act authorized a federal court to appoint federal voting examiners who themselves would examine and register voters for all elections, thereby superseding state election officials.

Addressing problems not covered by the 1965 act, the 1970 amendments lowered from twenty-one to eighteen the minimum voting age for all elections, prohibited states from imposing RESIDENCY REQUIREMENTS in presidential elections, and provided for uniform national rules for absentee voting in presidential elections. The 1975 amendments also sought to overcome linguistic barriers to political participation by requiring bilingual elections in certain political subdivisions. These language provisions brought Texas and Florida under the act's coverage. The 1982 amendments changed the expiration date of these provisions from 1985 to 1992, and added voter assistance provisions for the handicapped.

In general, the 1965 act and amendments have fared well in the Supreme Court. In SOUTH CAROLINA V. KATZENBACH (1966) and KATZENBACH V. MORGAN (1966) the Court upheld the constitutionality of the act. Following the Court's decision in NATIONAL LEAGUE OF CITIES V. USERY (1976) that certain integral state operations are beyond Congress's power to regulate under the COMMERCE CLAUSE, the constitutional attack was renewed. In *Rome v. United States* (1980) the Court held this argument inapplicable to cases involving Congress's power to enforce the Civil War amendments. In *United Jewish Organizations of Wil-liamsburgh, Inc. v. Carey*, (1977) the Court held that use of racial criteria to favor minority voters in an effort to comply with the Voting Rights Act did not violate the Fourteenth or Fifteenth Amendments. In OREGON V. MITCHELL (1970) the Supreme Court sustained most of the 1970 amendments but invalidated lowering the voting age in state and local elections. The latter ruling in *Mitchell*, however, soon was overturned by the TWENTY-SIXTH AMENDMENT.

The Voting Rights Act has been the most measurably successful CIVIL RIGHTS statute. In most southern states the gap between black and white voter registration shrank dramatically, and the number of elected black officials tripled between 1970 and 1975. Overt racial appeals no longer are a routinely successful part of southern political campaigns. The 1975 amendments confirmed a shift in attitude on civil rights matters. For the first time in the twentieth century, a majority of southern congressmen voted in favor of a federal civil rights statute.

THEODORE EISENBERG
(1986)

Bibliography

BELL, DERRICK A., JR. 1980 *Race, Racism and American Law*, 2nd ed. Boston: Little, Brown.

DORSEN, NORMAN et al. 1979 Emerson, Haber, and Dorsen's *Political and Civil Rights in the United States*, 4th ed. Vol. 2: 609–685. Boston: Little, Brown.

UNITED STATES SENATE, COMMITTEE ON THE JUDICIARY 1982 Senate Report No. 97–417, 97th Congress, 2d Session.

# VOTING RIGHTS ACT OF 1965 AND ITS AMENDMENTS
## 79 Stat. 437 (1965)
### (Update)

The Voting Rights Act (VRA) has been used primarily for two purposes: to guarantee African American voters in the South equal access to the ballot; and to enable racial minorities—especially blacks and Hispanics—to achieve political REPRESENTATION through electing their preferred candidates. Because the first purpose was more quickly achieved, BALLOT ACCESS is called the act's first-generation effect, and representation, the second-generation effect.

First-generation results were most dramatic in Mississippi, where the percentage of blacks registered increased from 6.7 in 1964 to 59.4 in 1968. In seven Southern states covered entirely by the act's preclearance provision, the black/white registration gap decreased from 44.1 percentage points in 1965 to 5 points in 1988. Second-generation results are reflected in the increases in black officeholding in the eleven-state South, where approximately 20 percent of the population is African American. In this region, between 1970 and 1985, the percentage of blacks in Congress increased from 0 to 1.7; in state senates, from 1.3 to 7.2; in state houses, from 1.9 to 10.8; and on city councils, from 1.2 to 5.6.

Increases in black and Hispanic officeholding in the South and Southwest, respectively, resulted largely from drawing majority–minority election districts. These were often created through legal challenges to racial GERRYMANDERING or to multimember or "at-large" election schemes, where plaintiffs invoked the FOURTEENTH AMENDMENT or sections 2 (as amended in 1982) and 5 of the VRA. Essential to this assault on the exclusion of minority-group members from government office was the concept of minority vote dilution which the Supreme Court endorsed in *White v. Regester* (1973) and later refined in *Thornburg v. Gingles* (1986).

The 1990s ELECTORAL DISTRICTING resulted in a sharp increase in Southern black members of Congress— from four in 1990 to seventeen in 1994. The U.S. Department of Justice under both Presidents GEORGE H.W. BUSH and WILLIAM J. CLINTON had required the creation of more "safe" black districts in the region to comply with the act. Several bizarrely shaped majority-black districts were crafted, and white voters challenged one in North Carolina. Consequently, the Court, most notably in SHAW V. RENO (1993) and its progeny, developed a theory under which the creation of districts whose predominant purpose is racial is unconstitutional. This controversial new cause of action threw into question the extent to which race-based redistricting, even as a remedy for minority vote dilution, is permissible. Courts have subsequently required that several majority–minority districts be redrawn.

The *Shaw* cases appear to respond to a growing chorus of criticism of the act's second-generation phase—criticism holding that federal intervention in redistricting to prevent minority vote dilution is either no longer needed or inevitably leads to proportional representation of minority groups, the right to which is expressly denied under section 2 of the VRA. Critics of *Shaw* fear that because of extensive racially polarized voting in the South and Southwest, the number of black and Hispanic officeholders there will decline.

CHANDLER DAVIDSON<br>(2000)

Bibliography

DAVIDSON, CHANDLER, and GROFMAN BERNARD, eds. 1994 *Quiet Revolution in the South: The Impact of the Voting Rights Act 1965–1990.* Princeton, N.J.: Princeton University Press.

GUINIER, LANI 1994 *The Tyranny of the Majority: Fundamental Fairness in Representative Democracy.* New York: Free Press.

ISSACHAROFF, SAMUEL; KARLAN, PAMELA S., and PILDES, RICHARD H. 1998 *The Law of Democracy: Legal Structure of the Political Process.* Westbury, N.Y.: Foundation Press.

KOUSSER, J. MORGAN 1999 *Colorblind Injustice: Minority Voting Rights and the Undoing of the Second Reconstruction.* Chapel Hill: University of North Carolina Press.

LUBLIN, DAVID 1997 *The Paradox of Representation: Racial Gerrymandering and Minority Interests in Congress.* Princeton, N.J.: Princeton University Press.

PILDES, RICHARD H. 1995 The Politics of Race. *Harvard Law Review* 108:1359–1392.

THERNSTROM, ABIGAIL 1987 *Whose Votes Count? Affirmative Action and Minority Voting Rights.* Cambridge, Mass.: Harvard University Press.

# VOUCHERS

Widespread discontent with public schools has precipitated demands that parents be given some choice about which school their children will attend. Several states have adopted laws affording parents some choice among public schools in their area. These laws have attracted few constitutional attacks. Many people argue that choice plans should be broadened to offer parents government vouchers redeemable at any accredited school, public or private, including religious, or parochial, schools. Supporters of this approach cite as a model the GI Bill, under which the federal government pays certain expenses of military veterans to attend any accredited college.

Proponents contend that vouchers will produce better education, especially for poor and minority students who often fare poorly in public schools. They cite the superior performance of private-school students. They also believe that public schools would be shaken out of the complacency induced by their monopoly on state funding and prodded to do better by competition from private schools. Further, proponents want parents to be able to choose for their children an education consistent with their values, whether religiously based or not. Opponents of vouchers deny that private schools generally provide a better education; they ascribe any superior performance to private schools' "skimming the cream" by taking better students. They also question whether public schools would benefit from increased competition. They feel that vouchers would lead to further skimming of the cream, leaving public schools to handle the most difficult students.

Critics further assert that voucher plans would be unconstitutional. They fear that vouchers would exacerbate racial segregation in violation of EQUAL PROTECTION as interpreted in BROWN V. BOARD OF EDUCATION (1954, 1955). They also argue that vouchers redeemed at parochial schools would constitute GOVERNMENT AID TO RELIGIOUS IN-

STITUTIONS and an unconstitutional ESTABLISHMENT OF RELIGION.

Defenders respond that vouchers would not worsen school segregation, which is already widespread, but that if they did, this effect would result from individual choices, not from STATE ACTION, which is necessary to invoke the FOURTEENTH AMENDMENT. Moreover, segregative effects could be avoided by requiring participating schools to meet certain standards of racial composition in admissions procedures. Defenders also deny that vouchers would establish religion. Pointing again to the GI Bill, they see vouchers merely giving parents a choice in obtaining a service that the government subsidizes for secular reasons; any benefit to religious institutions is incidental and thus of no constitutional concern. Critics reply that even an indirect benefit is an unlawful establishment.

No state has yet adopted a true voucher program, although a few have proposed limited programs for low-income children. Confused and conflicting Supreme Court pronouncements on aid to religious schools preclude any prediction of how the Court would handle the issue. Quite possibly, vouchers could be upheld for the same reasons that the GI Bill is considered constitutional, especially if steps were taken to avoid racial segregation. Some kind of voucher program might even be necessary to accommodate children with religious objections to what is taught in public schools.

GEORGE W. DENT
(1992)

(SEE ALSO: *Establishment Clause; Religion in Public Schools; Religious Fundamentalism; School Choice.*)

Bibliography

NOWAK, JOHN E. 1976 The Supreme Court, the Religion Clauses, and the Nationalization of Education. *Northwestern University Law Review* 70:883–909.

# W

## WABASH, ST. LOUIS & PACIFIC RAILWAY v. ILLINOIS
### 118 U.S. 557 (1886)

Tremendous growth in a national railroad network after the CIVIL WAR led to increasingly scandalous and harmful abuses. State efforts to control the problems were generally ineffective until *Munn v. Illinois* (1877). In that case, Chief Justice MORRISON R. WAITE allowed state regulation of railroads where Congress had not yet acted, "even though it may indirectly affect" those outside the state. Illinois had attempted to curb one area of abuse by forbidding LONG HAUL-SHORT HAUL DISCRIMINATION. So pervasive was this evil that it would be outlawed later in the INTERSTATE COMMERCE and MANN-ELKINS ACTS. The state sued the Wabash company to prevent it from charging more for shorter hauls; because significant portions of most long hauls lay outside Illinois, the issue lay in the constitutionality of a state regulation of INTERSTATE COMMERCE.

A 6–3 Supreme Court struck down the Illinois statute, undercutting the decisions in the GRANGER CASES (1877) without impairing the DOCTRINE of AFFECTATION WITH A PUBLIC INTEREST. Justice SAMUEL F. MILLER looked to the COMMERCE CLAUSE as securing a "freedom of commerce" across the country. The imposition, by individual states, of varying patterns of rates and regulations on interstate commerce was "oppressive" and rendered the commerce clause a "very feeble and almost useless provision." Miller then relied on the decision in COOLEY V. BOARD OF WARDENS OF PHILADELPHIA (1851) to declare that such regulation was clearly national, not local, in character even though Congress had not yet acted. In so doing, he altered the thrust of the *Cooley* test by examining the impact of state regulation on the nation instead of on the subjects involved. Miller concluded that "it is not, and never has been, the deliberate opinion of a majority of this court that a statute of a state which attempts to regulate the fare and charges by railroad companies [affecting interstate commerce] is a valid law."

Justices Horace Gray, Joseph P. Bradley, and Chief Justice Waite dissented, contending that the *Granger Cases* should have ruled the decision here. Citing WILLSON V. BLACK BIRD CREEK MARSH COMPANY (1829), Gray and his colleagues argued that "in the absence of congressional legislation to the contrary, [the railroads] are not only susceptible of state regulation, but properly amenable to it." They recited the litany of rights and powers granted the railroads by the state: "its being, its franchises, its powers, its road, its right to charge" all confirmed the state's right to regulate the road. The dissenters asserted that the Illinois statute affected interstate commerce only "incidentally" and not adversely. Subject to future congressional action, they would have affirmed the state action.

This decision effectively created a vacuum—Congress had not acted and the states were forbidden to act or even to control intrastate abuses. Together with an increasingly powerful reform movement, *Wabash* helped contribute to the passage of the Interstate Commerce Act in 1887, creating the first national regulatory body.

DAVID GORDON
(1986)

2817

## *WADE, UNITED STATES v.*
### 388 U.S. 218 (1967)

Wade's conviction of bank robbery depended heavily on the identification of him as the robber by two bank employees. After he was indicted and counsel appointed for him, the FEDERAL BUREAU OF INVESTIGATION arranged a LINEUP, which included Wade and five or six other people. Wade's counsel was not notified of the procedure; neither he nor anyone else representing Wade's interests was present.

The Supreme Court held that the lineup was a "critical stage" of the proceedings; thus, the Sixth Amendment guarantees a right to the presence of counsel at the pretrial identification if evidence of the lineup were to be used at the trial. The Court reasoned that counsel was necessary at this early stage in order to assure the fairness of the trial itself. The two premises were that eyewitness identification is treacherously subject to mistake, and that police methods in obtaining identifications are often and easily unduly suggestive. If a lawyer has been present at the lineup, later, at the trial, by his questioning of the eyewitnesses he will be able to show how any irregularities have tainted the in-court identification of the defendant.

*Wade* established a per se rule: if counsel is absent at the pretrial confrontation, the government may not use EVIDENCE that such an event happened. Whether the witness can nevertheless make an in-court identification depends on whether the unfair procedure tainted his present ability to identify: if he had not seen the uncounseled lineup, would he still be able to pick out the defendant?

Finally, the Court suggested that the pretrial confrontation might not be a "critical stage" if other methods were developed to assure against the risk of irreparable mistaken identification. In KIRBY v. ILLINOIS (1972) the Court restricted the holding in *Wade* to lineups held after defendants have been formally charged with crime.

BARBARA ALLEN BABCOCK
(1986)

## WADE-DAVIS BILL
### (July 2, 1864)

Republicans worried that under LINCOLN'S PLAN OF RECONSTRUCTION (December 8, 1863), the old state leadership might reverse emancipation. On July 2, 1864, Ohio's Senator Benjamin Wade and Maryland's Representative Henry Winter Davis passed a state-restoration bill that emphasized emancipation's permanence and equalized freedmen's CIVIL RIGHTS.

Their bill, implementing the Constitution's guarantee to each state of a REPUBLICAN FORM OF GOVERNMENT (Article IV, section 4), authorized the President to appoint a provisional governor for each conquered state. When a majority of white male citizens swore future loyalty to the Union, the governor was to initiate a CONSTITUTIONAL CONVENTION. Each new CONSTITUTION must incorporate emancipation, disfranchise high Confederates, and repudiate Confederate debts; then a majority of state voters, the President, and Congress must approve each constitution, and elections could proceed. State laws were to prevail excepting those on slavery. Criminal laws were to apply equally to whites and blacks.

ABRAHAM LINCOLN, unwilling to upset Arkansas's and Louisiana's progress under his 1863 policy, pocket-vetoed the bill. Advocating an abolition constitutional amendment to insure the legitimacy of emancipation, Lincoln suggested that Wade-Davis procedures, though vetoed, were satisfactory.

An election impended. If reelected, Lincoln would serve until 1869. His educability on race was outstanding. Almost all Republicans, including Wade and Davis, supported him. Had Lincoln signed their bill, it would have committed his successor to equal state justice for all residents.

HAROLD M. HYMAN
(1986)

Bibliography

HYMAN, HAROLD M.   1963   *A More Perfect Union: The Impact of the Civil War and Reconstruction on the Constitution.* Chap. 16. New York: Knopf.

## WAGNER ACT
### 49 Stat. 449 (1935)

Named after the New York senator who introduced and fought for it, the National Labor Relations Act (NLRA) extended the protection of the United States to organized labor. Robert Wagner framed the act to provide a constitutional basis for the protections given to labor by section 7(a) of the NATIONAL INDUSTRIAL RECOVERY ACT (NIRA) and by a National Labor Relations Board, which had been established and was operating under the sole authority of Public Resolution 44 and an EXECUTIVE ORDER. The Supreme Court confirmed the need for new legislation when, eleven days after the NLRA's enactment, it voided the NIRA in SCHECHTER POULTRY CORP. V. UNITED STATES (1935).

Congress based the Wagner Act on the COMMERCE CLAUSE: the denial by employers of employees' rights to organize and bargain collectively caused "strikes and other forms of industrial strife or unrest, which have the intent or necessary effect of burdening or obstructing [interstate] commerce." Congress added that unequal bargaining positions had exacerbated national economic instability. One section of the act guaranteed employees the right to organize, "to bargain collectively through representatives of their own choosing," and to act together to further these ends. Another section reinforced these rights by delineating employers' obligations; it defined and prohibited "unfair labor practices," including interference with the exercise of the above-mentioned rights, or discrimination to encourage or discourage union formation, administration, or membership. This section also outlawed discrimination against an employee for filing a complaint against his employer under the act and made it illegal to refuse to bargain collectively with a union's legal representative.

The act also provided for a National Labor Relations Board with broad supervisory powers to administer its provisions. The Board could issue complaints, hear and determine charges, and issue CEASE-AND-DESIST ORDERS which were enforceable upon application to federal circuit courts. Congress further empowered the board to hold representation elections and to certify the winner.

Wagner drafted the act carefully so that it would withstand scrutiny by the Supreme Court. Section 1—outlining the NLRA's policy—was rewritten after the decision in *Schechter* to specify the burdens placed upon INTERSTATE COMMERCE by labor unrest. The act's policy statement attributed that discord to the denial of workers' rights which this act would secure. Wagner's diligence paid off. A 5–4 majority of the Court upheld the NLRA in *NLRB v. Jones & Laughlin Steel Corporation* (1937). (See WAGNER ACT CASES.) The Wagner Act provided for strong independent unions in an effort to promote COLLECTIVE BARGAINING. By thus indirectly stimulating higher wages and increased consumer demand, the act helped guarantee a stable national economy and social justice for American labor. The TAFT-HARTLEY LABOR MANAGEMENT RELATIONS ACT, passed in 1947 partly to plug loopholes in the NLRA, governed union conduct much as employers' actions had earlier been regulated.

DAVID GORDON
(1986)

Bibliography

MILLIS, HARRY A. and BROWN, EMILY C.   1950   *From the Wagner Act to Taft-Hartley: A Study of National Labor Policy.* Chicago: University of Chicago Press.

TAYLOR, BENJAMIN J. and WITNEY, FRED   (1970) 1975   *Labor Relations Law,* 2nd ed. Pages 134–199. Englewood Cliffs, N.J.: Prentice-Hall.

# WAGNER ACT CASES

*NLRB v. Jones & Laughlin Steel Corp.*
301 U.S. 1 (1937)
*NLRB v. Fruehauf Trailer Co.*
301 U.S. 49 (1937)
*NLRB v. Friedman-Harry Marks Clothing Co.*
301 U.S. 58 (1937)
*Associated Press Co. v. NLRB*
301 U.S. 103 (1937)

The reinvigoration of the COMMERCE CLAUSE as a source of congressional power began with the first cases to reach the Supreme Court under the WAGNER (NATIONAL LABOR RELATIONS) ACT. That statute had been passed in 1935 in an effort to preserve the rights of employees in interstate industries to choose their own representatives and to bargain collectively with their employers. In 1930 the Supreme Court had held that the Railway Labor Act gave such rights to railroad employees. The NATIONAL INDUSTRIAL RECOVERY ACT (NIRA) of 1933 sought to extend such rights to other employees by requiring all codes of fair competition for other industries to contain similar provisions. The code system collapsed when the NIRA was invalidated in SCHECHTER POULTRY CORP. V. UNITED STATES in May 1935. The President and Congress believed that the denial of COLLECTIVE BARGAINING rights would lead to industrial unrest and strikes, which would necessarily obstruct INTERSTATE COMMERCE, and would also aggravate the Great Depression by depressing wage rates and the purchasing power of wage earners. As a result the National Labor Relations Act became law less than six weeks after the *Schechter* decision.

The act authorized the newly created National Labor Relations Board (NLRB), which succeeded similar boards created under the NIRA, to prevent employers from engaging in unfair labor practices "affecting [interstate] commerce," which was defined to mean "in commerce, or burdening or obstructing commerce," or which had led or might lead to a labor dispute burdening or obstructing commerce. These definitions were designed to embody the decisional law upholding the authority of Congress to regulate acts that "directly" obstructed interstate commerce. Congress assumed, correctly as it turned out, that the courts would construe the statute as "contemplating the exercise of control within constitutional bounds."

The NLRB's first cases were brought against employers engaged in interstate transportation and communication (bus lines and the Associated Press) and manufacturers who purchased their supplies and sold their products across state lines. Before these cases were decided, the

Supreme Court, in CARTER V. CARTER COAL CO. (1936), held that the substantially identical provisions of the Guffey-Snyder (Bituminous Coal Conservation) Act, enacted shortly after the Labor Relations Act, did not fall within the commerce power of Congress. In the *Carter* case the government had proved that coal strikes would burden not merely the interstate commerce of the immediate employers but also the interstate rail system and many other industries dependent upon coal. No stronger showing could be made under the Wagner Act for employers engaged in mining or manufacturing. As was to be expected, the courts of appeals, though sustaining the act as to companies engaged in interstate transportation and communication, deemed themselves bound by *Carter*, as well as *Schechter* and UNITED STATES V. BUTLER (1936) to hold that the act did not extend to manufacturers.

The first five NLRB cases to reach the Supreme Court involved a bus line, the Associated Press, and three manufacturers. The cases were argued together, beginning on February 8, 1937. Three days before, President FRANKLIN D. ROOSEVELT had announced his plan to appoint up to six new Supreme Court Justices, one for each justice over 70 years of age. On April 12, the Court affirmed the NLRB's rulings in all five cases. The opinions on the commerce clause issue in the bus and press cases were unanimous, although in the press case, four Justices dissented on FIRST AMENDMENT grounds. The cases against manufacturers—the Jones & Laughlin Steel Corporation, the Fruehauf Trailer Co., and a medium-size men's clothing manufacturer—were decided by a 5–4 vote. The membership of the Court had not changed since *Schechter* and *Carter*. But Chief Justice CHARLES EVANS HUGHES and Justice OWEN ROBERTS, who had been part of the majority of six who had rejected the labor relations provisions of the Guffey Act in *Carter*, now joined with Justices LOUIS D. BRANDEIS, HARLAN FISKE STONE, and BENJAMIN N. CARDOZO. The Chief Justice wrote the opinions in the manufacturers' cases.

In the *Carter* case, the majority opinion of Justice GEORGE SUTHERLAND had not denied the magnitude of the effect of coal strikes upon interstate commerce. The question, he held, was whether the effect was "direct," and that did not turn upon the "extent of the effect" or its "magnitude," but "entirely upon the manner in which the effect has been brought about"; "it connotes the absence of an efficient intervening agency or condition." The effect must "operate proximately—not mediately, remotely, or collaterally." Why "direct" should be so defined was not otherwise explained, except by the need for preserving the power of the states over PRODUCTION, even in interstate industries in which interstate competition would preclude state regulation. (See EFFECTS ON COMMERCE.)

The opinion of Chief Justice Hughes in the *Jones & Laughlin* case flatly rejected the *Butler* approach:

Giving full weight to respondent's contention with respect to a break in the complete continuity of the "STREAM OF COMMERCE" by reason of respondent's manufacturing operations, the fact remains that the stoppage of those operations by industrial strife would have a most serious effect upon interstate commerce. In view of respondent's far-flung activities, it is idle to say that the effect would be indirect or remote. It is obvious that it would be immediate and might be catastrophic. We are asked to shut our eyes to the plainest facts of our national life and to deal with the question of direct and indirect effects in an intellectual vacuum. . . . When industries organize themselves on a national scale, making their relation to interstate commerce the dominant factor in their activities, how can it be maintained that their industrial labor relations constitute a forbidden field into which Congress may not enter when it is necessary to protect interstate commerce from the paralyzing consequences of industrial war? We have often said that interstate commerce itself is a practical conception. It is equally true that interferences with that commerce must be appraised by a judgment that does not ignore actual experience.

The Chief Justice also met head on the argument that the federal power did not extend to activities in the course of production or manufacturing. Citing many antitrust cases, he declared: "The close and intimate effect which brings the subject within the reach of Federal power may be due to activities in relation to productive industry although the industry when separately viewed is local. . . . It is thus apparent that the fact that the employees here concerned were engaged in production is not determinative."

"The fundamental principle," Hughes stated, "is that the power to regulate commerce is the power to enact "all appropriate legislation' for "its protection and advancement'; to adopt measures "to promote its growth and insure its safety'; "to foster, protect, control and restrain.' That power is plenary and may be exerted to protect interstate commerce "no matter what the source of the dangers which threatened it." Hughes also invoked the SHREVEPORT DOCTRINE he had announced in HOUSTON EAST AND WEST TEXAS RAILWAY V. UNITED STATES (1914): "Although activities may be intrastate in character when separately considered, if they have such a close and substantial relation to interstate commerce that their control is essential or appropriate to protect that commerce from burdens and obstructions, Congress cannot be denied the power to exercise that control."

In deference to his own opinion in *Schechter*, the Chief Justice declared that "undoubtedly the scope of this power must be considered in the light of our dual system of government" so as not to "obliterate the distinction between what is national and what is local." In *Schechter* the effect upon commerce had been too "remote"; "to find "immediacy or directness' there was to find it "almost everywhere', a result inconsistent with the maintenance of our Federal system." With little explanation Hughes added that *Carter* was "not controlling."

Within a few weeks the Court sustained the constitutionality of the SOCIAL SECURITY ACT. Soon after Justices WILLIS VAN DEVANTER and Sutherland retired. And President Roosevelt's court-packing plan, not very surprisingly, got nowhere.

Subsequent Labor Board cases extended the application of the Labor Act far beyond the three manufacturers in the center of the interstate movement; it was sufficient that a strike would interfere with interstate movement of products (for example, *Santa Cruz Fruit Packing Co. v. NLRB*, 1938; *NLRB v. Fainblatt*, 1939; *Consolidated Edison Co. v. NLRB*, 1938). The unanimous opinion of the Court speaking through Justice Stone, with Hughes and Roberts still on the bench, in UNITED STATES V. DARBY (1941) explicitly rejected the concept that the Tenth Amendment limited the powers granted Congress by the Constitution. And other cases by now have extended the commerce power "almost everywhere." Nevertheless, the opinion in *Jones & Laughlin* remains a landmark in the interpretation of the commerce clause, as the definitive acceptance of the modern theories which recognize the power of Congress to control all aspects of the nation's integrated economic system.

ROBERT L. STERN
(1986)

Bibliography

CORTNER, RICHARD C. 1964 *The Wagner Act Cases*. Knoxville: University of Tennessee Press.
—— 1970 *The Jones & Laughlin Case*. New York: Knopf.
DODD, E. MERRICK 1945 The Supreme Court and Organized Labor, 1941–1945. *Harvard Law Review* 58:1018–1071.
GROSS, JAMES A. 1974 *The Making of the National Labor Relations Board: A Study in Economics, Politics, and the Law*, Vol. 1 (1933–1937). Albany: State University of New York Press.
STERN, ROBERT L. 1946 The Commerce Clause and the National Economy, 1933–1946. *Harvard Law Review* 59:645–693, 888–947.

## *WAINWRIGHT v. SYKES*
### 433 U.S. 72 (1977)

In *Sykes* the ADEQUATE STATE GROUND bar to federal HABEAS CORPUS, buried in FAY V. NOIA (1963), was unearthed and returned to service with little more than a coat of paint for disguise. *Noia* had held that a state prisoner was not barred from seeking federal habeas corpus relief merely because the applicant had failed to raise his or her federal

constitutional claim in the earlier state proceeding as required by state law. *Noia* was attacked within the Supreme Court and by some scholars for sacrificing finality of decision. State judges trumpeted their resentment at giving federal district courts the last word in the state criminal process.

*Sykes* was the culmination of the attack on *Noia* from within the Court. A state prisoner sought federal habeas corpus, arguing that his rights to a warning under MIRANDA V. ARIZONA (1966) had been violated when his statement was admitted into EVIDENCE at his state trial. He had not objected when the evidence was offered, as state law required. The Supreme Court held, 7–2, that federal habeas corpus was barred.

Justice WILLIAM H. REHNQUIST, for the majority, announced that failure to raise a federal constitutional claim in the manner required by state law bars resort to federal habeas corpus unless the applicant shows "cause" for the procedural default and "prejudice" from the forfeiture of the federal claim. Defendant had asserted no cause for the absence of timely objection, and prejudice was negated by other evidence of his guilt, independent of his statement.

KENNETH L. KARST
(1986)

## WAITE, MORRISON R.
### (1816–1888)

Morrison Remick Waite, sixth CHIEF JUSTICE of the United States, successfully led the Supreme Court in dealing with major constitutional problems concerning RECONSTRUCTION and business-government relations between 1874 and 1888.

Son of Henry Matson Waite, Chief Justice of the Connecticut Supreme Court of Errors, Morrison Waite read law after graduating from Yale College in 1837. In 1838 he removed to Ohio, where he built a flourishing legal practice specializing in commercial law, acquired substantial property interests, and joined the Whig party. Although prominent in the legal profession, Waite was virtually unknown in national affairs prior to his appointment as Chief Justice. He served one term in the Ohio legislature and a term on the Toledo city council, was appointed counsel to the Geneva Tribunal to negotiate the *Alabama* claims in 1872, and was elected president of the Ohio CONSTITUTIONAL CONVENTION of 1873.

The circumstances of Waite's appointment to the Court were remarkable, not so much because he lacked national political recognition as because he was the fifth person whom President ULYSSES S. GRANT nominated or asked to serve as Chief Justice. Yet Waite had early been touted for the position by leading Ohio politicians, and Grant had considered him a possibility from the beginning. His effective service at the Geneva Arbitration, professional reputation, and unwavering Republican party loyalty recommended him, and in January 1874 the Senate confirmed him by a 63–0 vote.

Waite's significance in American constitutional history is threefold. He wrote the first Supreme Court opinions interpreting the FOURTEENTH and FIFTEENTH AMENDMENTS in cases involving Negroes' CIVIL RIGHTS. Second, his 1877 opinions in *Munn v. Illinois* and the other GRANGER CASES established the basic principles of constitutional law governing state governments as they attempted to deal with economic changes caused by the industrial revolution. Third, Waite expressed a conception of JUDICIAL REVIEW that summarized dominant nineteenth-century ideas about constitutional adjudication and provided a model for twentieth-century theorists of judicial restraint.

The northern retreat from RECONSTRUCTION was well underway when Waite became Chief Justice, and the WAITE COURT did not attempt to reverse this political development. Under the circumstances, and given the circumscribed role of the judiciary in nineteenth-century constitutional politics, it had little choice but to acquiesce. In determining the meaning of the Fourteenth and Fifteenth Amendments and in applying federal civil rights laws, however, the Court could choose among several possible conceptions of national legislative power and federal-state relations. Waite guided the Court toward a moderate position of STATES' RIGHTS nationalism which upheld national power to protect civil rights within the framework of traditional FEDERALISM.

To understand this development it is necessary to advert to the SLAUGHTERHOUSE CASES (1873) and to Justice JOSEPH P. BRADLEY's circuit court opinion in UNITED STATES V. CRUIKSHANK (1874). In the former, the Supreme Court confirmed the theory of dual American CITIZENSHIP, stated that the Fourteenth Amendment did not add to the rights of national citizenship, and concluded that ordinary civil rights were attributes of state citizenship, regulation of which was beyond the authority of the United States. In the *Cruikshank* case, involving prosecution of whites in Colfax, Louisiana, for violating the civil rights of Negro citizens, Justice Bradley held that although the Fourteenth Amendment prohibited state rather than private denial of civil rights, under certain conditions the federal government was authorized to guarantee civil rights against interference by private individuals. The relevant circumstance, according to Bradley, was state failure to fulfill its affirmative duty to protect citizens' rights.

Chief Justice Waite wrote the majority opinion when *United States v. Cruikshank* (1876) was decided in the Supreme Court. Defendants were indicted under a sec-tion of the Force Act of 1870 that declared it a federal crime for two or more persons to deprive any citizen of rights secured by the Constitution or laws of the United States. Like Bradley in the CIRCUIT COURT, Waite found numerous flaws in the INDICTMENTS and on that ground ordered the defendants to be discharged, thus frustrating the federal civil rights enforcement effort. Nevertheless, Waite asserted national authority to enforce civil rights.

The Chief Justice followed the *Slaughterhouse* opinion in positing separate federal and state citizenships and in stating that the federal government could protect only those rights placed within its JURISDICTION. He held further that the FREEDOM OF ASSEMBLY, which the defendants were charged with violating, was a right of state rather than federal citizenship. The indictment, however, had incorrectly stated that denial of freedom of assembly by private persons was a federal crime within the meaning of the Force Act; therefore the indictment was invalid. Yet federal authority was not nugatory in civil rights matters. Waite pointed out that if the indictment had charged a violation of the right to assemble in order to petition the national government, it would have been proper under the act. Thus in protecting a federal right national authority was putatively effective against private individuals as well as states. Waite furthermore asserted an indirect federal power to protect rights of state citizenship against both state and private interference. The ordinary right of assembly was a state right, said Waite, over which "no direct power" was granted to Congress. This appeared to mean that if states failed to uphold civil rights within their jurisdiction, the federal government could provide the needed protection. Finally Waite noted that the indictments did not allege that the full and equal benefit of laws for the protection of whites was denied to blacks on account of race; accordingly the CIVIL RIGHTS ACT OF 1866 was not in point. The implication was that if a racially discriminatory purpose had been alleged, federal authority under the 1866 law could have been employed against private as well as against state denial of rights.

Waite also gave the opinion in UNITED STATES V. REESE (1876), the first Supreme Court case involving Fifteenth Amendment VOTING RIGHTS. State officials in Kentucky were indicted for refusing to accept the vote of a Negro citizen. Again the Court ruled against the federal government. Waite declared two provisions of the Force Act of 1870 unconstitutional because they did not in express terms limit the offense of state officials to denial of the right to vote on account of color. Insisting on the need for STRICT CONSTRUCTION of criminal statutes, he interpreted the act in a strained and technical manner as preventing any wrongful interference with voting rights, rather than simply interferences that were racially motivated. The Fifteenth Amendment authorized the federal government to deal only with the latter. It did not, said Waite, secure the right to vote, but only the right not to be discriminated against in voting on racial grounds. Observing that "Congress has not as yet provided by "appropriate legislation' for the punishment of the offense charged in the indictment," Waite in effect invited Republican lawmakers to enact a more tightly drawn enforcement act.

Waite's personal sympathies were enlisted in efforts to assist Negroes. As a trustee of the Peabody Fund in 1874 he signed a report endorsing a constitutional argument for federal aid to education, thus breaking the rule against extra-Court political involvement to which he scrupulously adhered throughout his judicial career. Although Waite accepted the abandonment of Reconstruction and held that Congress had no power "to do mere police duty in the States," his opinions nevertheless authorized federal interference against state and in some circumstances private denial of rights when racially motivated. In subsequent cases, most notably UNITED STATES V. HARRIS (1883), the CIVIL RIGHTS CASES (1883), and EX PARTE YARBROUGH (1884), the Waite Court amplified the principles set forth in the *Cruikshank* and *Reese* cases.

In the sphere of government-business relations, Waite was sympathetic to regulatory legislation within a political and legal framework that encouraged industrial expansion and a national free trade area. In the early 1870s, in response to farmers' and merchants' demands for relief from high shipping costs, several midwestern states adopted legislation setting maximum railroad rates. These laws appeared to discourage further railroad construction, and within a few years most of them were repealed or modified. Nevertheless, in the landmark *Granger Cases* the Supreme Court ruled on the constitutionality of these regulatory measures.

*Munn v. Illinois* (1877), Waite's most famous opinion, sustained an 1871 Illinois law that established maximum rates for grain elevators. Waite based his approval of the legislation on a broad conception of the STATE POLICE POWER, which he said authorized states to regulate the use of private property "when such regulation becomes necessary for the public good." He rejected the contention that state regulation of the rates charged by ferries, common carriers, or bakers was a deprivation of property without DUE PROCESS OF LAW in violation of the Fourteenth Amendment. Support for Waite's conclusion lay in numerous state COMMON LAW precedents asserting a public interest in certain kinds of property, such as lands bordering on watercourses, which were subject to government regulation. Like other judges in similar cases, and influenced by a memorandum prepared by Justice Bradley dealing with the instant case, Waite relied on a treatise of the seventeenth-century English judge Lord Chief Justice Sir Matthew Hale in asserting: "When property is "AF-

FECTED WITH A PUBLIC INTEREST, it ceases to be juris privati only." The grain elevator companies, Waite explained, exercised a virtual monopoly in the regional market structure; thus, they were affected with a public interest and subject to regulation by the state legislature. In the other *Granger Cases* Waite employed this principle to uphold state regulation of railroad rates.

Waite also approved state regulation of CORPORATIONS in a series of decisions that carried to a logical conclusion the principle by which the CONTRACT CLAUSE of the Constitution did not prevent state legislatures from reserving the power to alter charter grants. These cases included STONE V. MISSISSIPPI (1880), *Ruggles v. Illinois* (1883), and *Spring Valley Water Works v. Schotteler* (1883). This trend culminated in STONE V. FARMERS LOAN AND TRUST CO. (1886), known as the *Railroad Commission Cases*, in which Waite held that a state charter authorizing railroads to set reasonable rates did not divest a state of the power ultimately to determine what was a reasonable rate.

While generally approving regulatory legislation, Waite placed limitations on the POLICE POWER with a view toward protecting private property. In the *Railroad Commission Cases* he admonished: "This power to regulate is not a power to destroy; and limitation is not the equivalent of confiscation. Under pretence of regulating fares and freights the state cannot require a railroad corporation to carry persons or property without reward; neither can it do that which in law amounts to a TAKING of private property without due process of law." Rather than suggesting an irresistible tendency to accept the argument for SUBSTANTIVE DUE PROCESS that was later adopted by the Supreme Court, these and similar dicta indicate that Waite, like Justice STEPHEN J. FIELD who dissented in *Munn* and the other *Granger* cases, believed the essential constitutional problem in cases involving government-business relations was to determine the extent of the police power. Shortly after the *Munn* decision Waite wrote: "The great difficulty in the future will be to establish the boundary between that which is private, and that in which the public has an interest."

Waite epitomized nineteenth-century thinking about the nature of the judicial function and the power of judicial review. He believed the judiciary should play a subordinate role in public-policy making, and should especially defer to the political branches in questions concerning the reasonableness of legislation. His clearest and most forceful expression of this view appeared in *Munn v. Illinois* when he stated: "For us the question is one of power, not of expediency. If no state of circumstances could justify such a statute, then we may declare this one void, because in excess of the legislative power of the States. But if it could we must presume it did. Of the propriety of legislative interference within the scope of legislative power, the legislature is the exclusive judge." Waite acknowledged that legislative power might be abused. But "[f]or protection against abuses by legislatures," he observed, "the people must resort to the polls, not to the courts."

Waite effectively balanced the competing demands of state and federal authority as constitutional equilibrium was restored after the end of Reconstruction. In addition to the decisions already noted, he wrote the opinions in *Louisiana v. Jumel* (1882) and *New Hampshire v. Louisiana* (1882), both of which held that the ELEVENTH AMENDMENT prevented suits by bondholders attempting to force a state government to redeem its bonds. These decisions expressed the political logic of the COMPROMISE OF 1877 and marked a significant broadening of states' SOVEREIGN IMMUNITY under the Eleventh Amendment. In another notable case involving state power and women's rights, MINOR V. HAPPERSETT (1875), Waite adhered to a narrow interpretation of the Fourteenth Amendment in deciding that the right to vote was not an attribute of federal citizenship and that states could regulate the suffrage as they saw fit.

On the other hand, Waite upheld federal authority in the controversial SINKING FUND CASES (1879) and in PENSACOLA TELEGRAPH CO. V. WESTERN UNION TELEGRAPH CO. (1878). In the former, the Court confirmed the constitutionality of an act of Congress requiring the Union Pacific and Central Pacific railroads to set aside money from current income for the subsequent payment of its mortgage debts. In the latter case the Court upheld the rights of an interstate telegraph company operating under authority of an act of Congress against the rights of a company acting under a state charter. Waite also voted to strike down state tax legislation when it interfered with INTERSTATE COMMERCE, although he was less inclined than his colleagues to regard STATE TAXATION OF COMMERCE in this light.

Overcoming the resentment of several Justices who had aspired to the Chief Justiceship, Waite performed the administrative and other tasks of his position with great skill. In a larger political sense he was also a successful judicial statesman. During his tenure, as at few times in American constitutional history, the Supreme Court was remarkably free of congressional criticism. Waite achieved this success by confining JUDICIAL POLICYMAKING within limits approved by the nation's representative political institutions and public opinion.

HERMAN BELZ
(1986)

Bibliography

BENEDICT, MICHAEL LES 1979 Preserving Federalism: Reconstruction and the Waite Court. *Supreme Court Review* 1978: 39–79.

FRANTZ, LAUREN B. 1964 Congressional Power to Enforce the Fourteenth Amendment Against Private Acts. *Yale Law Journal* 73:1352–1384.

MAGRATH, PETER C. 1963 *Morrison R. Waite: The Triumph of Character.* New York: Macmillan.

SCHEIBER, HARRY N. 1971 The Road to *Munn:* Eminent Domain and the Concept of Public Purpose in the State Courts. *Perspectives in American History* 5:329–402.

TRIMBLE, BRUCE R. 1938 *Chief Justice Waite: Defender of the Public Interest.* Princeton, N.J.: Princeton University Press.

# WAITE COURT
## (1874–1888)

A new age of American constitutional law was at hand when MORRISON R. WAITE became CHIEF JUSTICE of the United States in 1874. Not only had the CIVIL WAR discredited many antebellum glosses on the "old" Constitution, consisting of the venerable document framed in 1787 and the twelve amendments adopted during the early republic, but it had also generated a "new" Constitution consisting of the THIRTEENTH AMENDMENT, the FOURTEENTH AMENDMENT, and the FIFTEENTH AMENDMENT. The range of choices at the Court's disposal was virtually unlimited as it reconstituted the old organic law and integrated the new. CHARLES SUMNER said it best just four years before Waite took the Court's helm. The tumultuous events of 1861–1869, he exclaimed, had transformed the Constitution into "molten wax" ready for new impression. An extraordinarily homogeneous group of men made this impression. Of the fourteen associate Justices who sat with Waite between 1874 and his death in 1888, only NATHAN CLIFFORD had been appointed by a Democrat and all but two—SAMUEL F. MILLER and JOHN MARSHALL HARLAN, both of Kentucky—had been born in the free states. All of them were Protestants. Thus the Republican party, which had subdued the South and created the "new" Constitution, had also reconstructed the federal judiciary. As the Waite Court proceeded to refashion the structure of American constitutional law, its work ineluctably reflected the values, aspirations, and fears that had animated the Republican party's northern Protestant constituency since the 1850s.

Fierce opposition to state SOVEREIGNTY concepts was a core element of Republican belief from the party's very inception. Republicans associated state sovereignty with proslavery constitutionalism in the 1850s, with SECESSION in 1861, and ultimately with the tragic war both engendered. Waite and his colleagues shared this aversion to state sovereignty dogma and repeatedly expressed it in controversies involving the IMPLIED POWERS of Congress under the "old" Constitution. In case after case the Court resisted limitations on federal power derived from state sovereignty premises and held, in effect, that Congress's authority to enact statutes deemed NECESSARY AND PROPER for the ENUMERATED POWERS had the same scope under the Constitution as it would if the states did not exist. On several occasions the Court even revived the idea that Congress might exercise any power inherent in national sovereignty as long as it was not specifically prohibited by the Constitution. This doctrine, first expounded by Federalist congressmen during debate on the Sedition Act of 1798, had been regarded as "exploded" by most antebellum statesmen. But its revival after the Civil War did have a certain logic. If there was one impulse that every member of the Waite Court had in common, it was the urge to extirpate every corollary of "southern rights" theory from American constitutional law and to confirm the national government's authority to exercise every power necessary to maintain its existence.

The revival of the implied powers doctrine began in the often overlooked case of *Kohl v. United States* (1876). There counsel challenged Congress's authority to take private property in Cincinnati as a site for public buildings on the ground that the Constitution sanctioned federal exercise of the EMINENT DOMAIN power only in the DISTRICT OF COLUMBIA. Article I, section 8, vested Congress with authority to acquire land elsewhere "for the erection of forts . . . and other needful buildings" only "by the consent of the legislature of the State in which the same shall be." This was by no means a novel argument. JAMES MADISON and JAMES MONROE had pointed to the national government's lack of a general eminent domain power when vetoing INTERNAL IMPROVEMENT bills, and proslavery theorists had invoked the same principle as a bar to compensated emancipation and colonization schemes. In *Pollard's Lessee v. Hagan* (1845), moreover, the TANEY COURT had said that "the United States have no constitutional capacity to exercise municipal jurisdiction, sovereignty, or eminent domain within the limits of a State or elsewhere, except in the cases in which it is expressly granted." But WILLIAM STRONG, speaking for the Court in *Kohl*, refused to take this doctrine "seriously." Congress's war, commerce, and postal powers necessarily included the right to acquire property for forts, lighthouses, and the like. "If the right to acquire property for such uses be made a barren right by the unwillingness of property holders to sell, or by the action of a State prohibiting a sale to the Federal Government," Strong explained, "the constitutional grants of power may be rendered nugatory. . . . This cannot be." Congress's eminent domain power must be implied, Strong concluded, for commentators on the law of nations had always regarded it as "the offspring of political necessity, and . . . inseparable from sovereignty."

HORACE GRAY sounded the same theme in the Legal Tender Cases (*Juilliard v. Greenman*, 1884), where the Court sustained Congress's authority to emit legal tender notes even in peacetime. With only STEPHEN J. FIELD dissenting, Gray asserted that because the power to make government paper a legal tender was "one of the powers belonging to sovereignty in other civilized nations, and not expressly withheld from Congress by the Constitution," it was unquestionably "an appropriate means, conducive and plainly adapted" to the execution of Congress's power to borrow money. In EX PARTE YARBROUGH (1884), decided the same day, the Court spoke the language of national sovereignty in an especially significant case. At issue there was the criminal liability of a Georgia man who had savagely beaten a black voter en route to cast his ballot in a federal election. The Court unanimously sustained the petitioner's conviction under the 1870 CIVIL RIGHTS ACT, which made it a federal crime to "injure, oppress, threaten, or intimidate any citizen in the free exercise or enjoyment of any right or privilege secured to him by the Constitution or laws of the United States." It did so on the ground that Congress's duty "to provide in an ELECTION held under its authority, for security of life and limb to the voter" arose not from its interest in the victim's rights so much as "from the necessity of the government itself." Samuel F. Miller explained that Congress's power to regulate the time, place, and manner of holding federal elections, conferred in Article I, section 4, implied a "power to pass laws for the free, pure, and safe exercise" of the suffrage. "But it is a waste of time," he added, "to seek for specific sources to pass these laws. . . . If this government is anything more than a mere aggregation of delegated agents of other States and governments, each of which is superior to the general government, it must have the power to protect the elections on which its existence depends from violence and corruption."

The Court's decisions in *Kohl, Juilliard,* and *Yarbrough* merely jettisoned antebellum canons of STRICT CONSTRUCTION. They did not impair the autonomy of state governments. The eminent domain power of the several states was not threatened by *Kohl*, the Constitution expressly prohibited the states from making anything but gold and silver a legal tender, and *Yarbrough* did not jeopardize Georgia's power to prosecute political assassins for assault or murder. Yet the Waite Court was as quick to defend exercises of Congress's powers in situations where counsel claimed that the states' autonomy was in jeopardy as in cases where their reserved powers remained unimpaired. *Ex parte Siebold* (1880) was the leading case in point. There the Court sustained a conviction for ballot stuffing under the 1871 ENFORCEMENT ACT, which made it a federal crime for any state official at a congressional election to neglect duties required of him by either state or federal law. Counsel for the petitioner argued that in PRIGG V. PENNSYLVANIA (1842) and *Kentucky v. Dennison* (1861) the Taney Court had held that the principle of divided sovereignty precluded acts of Congress compelling the co-operation of state officials in the execution of national law. "We cannot yield to such a transcendental view of State sovereignty," JOSEPH BRADLEY proclaimed for the Court in *Siebold*. "As a general rule," he said, "it is no doubt expedient and wise that the operations of the State and National Governments should, as far as practicable, be conducted separately, in order to avoid undue jealousies and jars." But the Constitution neither mandated an immutable boundary between spheres of federal and state power nor restricted Congress's choice of means in implementing its enumerated authority to regulate federal elections.

The Court's constitutional nationalism did have limits. Like most Republicans of the age, Waite and his colleagues resisted the idea of centralization with as much ardor as the concept of state sovereignty. They regarded the national government's competence as deriving from the powers specified in the Constitution or fairly implied from it; the residual powers of government, usually called "internal police," belonged exclusively to the several states. Thus decisions like *Kohl* and *Siebold*, as Waite and his associates understood them, did not contract the ambit of state JURISDICTION. Rather the court simply refused to recognize implied limitations on the powers of Congress derived from state sovereignty premises. The *Trade-Mark Cases* (1879) underscored the Waite Court's allegiance to this view of the federal system. There a unanimous Court, speaking through Miller, held that Congress had no authority to enact a "universal system of trade-mark registration." Miller's method of analysis was more revealing than the result. His first impulse was to determine which sphere of government ordinarily had responsibility for such matters in the constitutional scheme. "As the property in trade-marks and the right to their exclusive use rest on the laws of the States, and like the great body of the rights of persons and of property, depend on them for security and protection," he explained, "the power of Congress to legislate on the subject . . . must be found in the Constitution of the United States, which is the source of all the powers the Congress can lawfully exercise." This two-tier method not only reified DUAL FEDERALISM but also put the burden of demonstrating Congress's authority to act on the government. In the *Trade-Mark Cases* it could not do so. Trade-marks lacked "the essential characteristics" of creative work in the arts and sciences, consequently the statute could not be sustained under the COPYRIGHT or PATENT powers. And the commerce power, though admittedly "broad," could not be construed as to permit federal regulation of commercial relations between persons residing in the same state.

When the Waite Court turned to cases involving the "new" Constitution, the instinct to conceptualize rights

and powers in terms of dual federalism had fateful consequences. Beginning in UNITED STATES V. CRUIKSHANK (1876), the Court emasculated Congress's power "to enforce, by appropriate legislation," the rights guaranteed by the Fourteenth and Fifteenth Amendments. At issue was the validity of conspiracy convictions under the 1870 Civil Rights Act against a band of whites who had attacked a conclave of blacks in Grants Parish, Louisiana, killing from sixty to one hundred of them. The government claimed that the defendants had deprived the black citizens of their constitutional rights to hold a peaceful assembly, to bear arms, to vote, and to EQUAL PROTECTION OF THE LAWS safeguarding persons and property. The Court unanimously overturned the convictions. The CONSPIRACY law was not voided; indeed, the Court sustained a conviction under that very statute in *Yarbrough*. But Waite and his associates were determined to confine Congress's power to enact "appropriate legislation" in such a way to preserve what Miller called "the main features of the federal system." The Court had no choice in the matter, Joseph Bradley remarked on circuit in 1874, unless it was prepared "to clothe Congress with power to pass laws for the general preservation of social order in every State," or, in short, with a plenary power of "internal police."

Waite's opinion for the Court in *Cruikshank* contained two separate lines of argument. He began the first foray by pointing out that every American citizen "owes allegiance to two sovereigns, and claims protection from both." Because the two levels of government could protect the rights of citizens only "within their respective spheres," federal authorities could assert jurisdiction over perpetrators of violence only if the rights denied to victims were derived from the Constitution and laws of the United States. But in the SLAUGHTERHOUSE CASES (1873), decided ten months before Waite came to the Court, a majority of five had concluded that there were very few PRIVILEGES OR IMMUNITIES of national CITIZENSHIP and that the Fourteenth Amendment had not created any new ones. Fundamental rights of life, liberty, and property still rested upon the laws of the states, and citizens had to rely upon the states for the protection of those rights. Among the privileges of state citizenship, Waite explained in *Cruikshank*, were the rights to assemble, to bear arms, and to vote. Although guaranteed against infringement by Congress in the BILL OF RIGHTS, the rights to assemble and bear arms were not "granted by the Constitution" or "in any manner dependent upon that instrument for existence." The right to vote in state and local elections stood on the same footing because "the right to vote in the States comes from the States." The Fifteenth Amendment did give citizens a new right under the Constitution—exemption from RACIAL DISCRIMINATION when attempting to vote. Because the Grants Parish indictments did not aver that the defendants had prevented their victims "from exercising the right to vote on account of race," however, that count was as defective as the rest.

Waite's second line of argument in *Cruikshank* was designed to hold the votes of Joseph Bradley, Stephen J. Field, and NOAH SWAYNE. They had dissented in the *Slaughterhouse Cases*, claiming that the Fourteenth Amendment had been designed to reconstruct the federal system by creating a third sphere in the constitutional scheme—that of the individual whose FUNDAMENTAL RIGHTS were now protected against unequal and discriminatory state laws. Waite satisfied them by stating what came to be known as the STATE ACTION doctrine. He not only conceded that "[t]he equality of the rights of citizens is a principle of republicanism" but strongly implied that the Fourteenth Amendment had nationalized this principle under the equal protection clause, if not the privileges or immunities clause. But the amendment, he added, "does not . . . add any thing to the rights which one citizen had under the Constitution against another." The very language of the amendment's first section—"No state shall . . ."—suggested that it must be read not as a grant of power to Congress but as a limitation on the states. It followed that the exercise of fundamental rights did not come under the Constitution's protection until jeopardized by the enactment or enforcement of a state law. "This the amendment guarantees, but no more," Waite declared. "The power of the national government is limited to the enforcement of this guaranty."

The principles announced in *Cruikshank* doomed the rest of Congress's CIVIL RIGHTS program, all of which had been based on the assumption that the "new" Constitution might be employed as a sword to protect any interference with fundamental rights. A voting rights statute went down in UNITED STATES V. REESE (1876) because Congress had failed to limit federal jurisdiction over state elections to the prevention of racially motivated fraud or dereliction; the antilynching provisions of the 1871 Civil Rights Act were invalidated for want of state action in UNITED STATES V. HARRIS (1883). One latent function of *Cruikshank*, however, was to draw renewed attention to the equal protection clause as a shield for blacks and other racial minorities whose civil rights were imperiled by discriminatory state laws. Soon the docket was crowded with such cases, and the Court was compelled to wrestle with longstanding ambiguities in the Republican party's commitment to racial equality.

Republicans had always been quick to defend equal rights in the market, for it was the rights to make contracts and own property that distinguished free people from slaves. But many Republicans regarded the idea of equality before the law as wholly compatible with legalized race prejudice in the social realm. Words like "nation" and "race" were not merely descriptive terms in the nineteenth century; they were widely understood as objective manifestations of natural communities, the integrity of which government had a duty to maintain. Thus most Republicans never accepted the proposition that blacks ought to be free to marry whites and many denied the right of blacks to associate with whites even in public places. The framers of the "new" Constitution had neither abjured this qualified view of equality not incorporated it into the Fourteenth Amendment. The discretion of Waite and his colleagues was virtually unfettered. They could weave prevailing prejudices into equal protection jurisprudence or they could interpret the equality concept broadly, declare that the "new" Constitution was colorblind, and put the Court's enormous prestige squarely behind the struggle for racial justice.

Exponents of racial equality were greatly encouraged by STRAUDER V. WEST VIRGINIA (1880), the case of first impression. There a divided Court reversed the murder conviction of a black defendant who had been tried under a statute that limited jury service to "white male persons." The Fourteenth Amendment, William Strong explained for the majority, "was designed to secure the colored race the enjoyment of all the civil rights that under the law are enjoyed by white persons." This formulation was acceptable even to the two dissenters. According to Stephen J. Field and Nathan Clifford, however, jury service was not a "civil right." It was a "political right." The only rights Congress intended to protect with the Fourteenth Amendment, they contended, were those enumerated in the Civil Rights Act of 1866—to own property, to make and enforce contracts, to sue and give evidence. The equal protection clause, Field said, "secures to all persons their civil rights upon the same terms; but it leaves political rights . . . and social rights . . . as they stood previous to its adoption." But the *Strauder* majority was unimpressed by Field's version of the "original understanding" and it set a face of flint against his typology of rights. "The Fourteenth Amendment makes no attempt to enumerate the rights it designed to protect," Strong declared. "It speaks in general terms, and those are as comprehensive as possible." The very term equal protection, he added, implied "that no discrimination shall be made against [blacks] by the law because of their color."

*Strauder* seemed to open the door for judicial proscription of all racial classifications in state laws. John R. Tompkins, counsel for an interracial couple that had been sentenced to two years in prison for violating Alabama's antimiscegenation law, certainly read the case that way. But the idea of distinct spheres of rights—"civil" and "social" if no longer "political"—furtively reentered the Waite Court's jurisprudence in PACE V. ALABAMA (1883). Field, speaking for a unanimous Court, held that antimiscegenation laws were not barred by the Fourteenth Amendment as long as both parties received the same punishment for the crime. Equal protection mandated equal treatment, not freedom of choice; antimiscegenation laws restricted the liberty of blacks and whites alike. Underlying this disingenuous view was an unarticulated premise of enormous importance. In settings involving the exercise of "social rights" the equal protection clause did not prohibit state legislatures from enacting statutes that used race as a basis for regulating the rights of persons. The legal category "Negro" was not suspect per se. (See SUSPECT CLASSIFICATION.)

The concept of "social rights" also figured prominently in the CIVIL RIGHTS CASES (1883), decided ten months after *Pace*. There the Court struck down the CIVIL RIGHTS ACT OF 1875, which forbade the owners of theaters, inns, and public conveyances to deny any citizen "the full and equal benefit" of their facilities. Joseph Bradley, speaking for the majority, rejected the claim that the businesses covered by the act were quasi-public agencies; consequently the state action doctrine barred federal intervention under the Fourteenth Amendment. But Bradley conceded that the state action doctrine was not applicable in Thirteenth Amendment contexts. It not only "nullif[ies] all state laws which establish or uphold slavery," he said, but also "clothes Congress with power to pass all laws necessary and proper for abolishing all badges and incidents of slavery in the United States." With the exception of John Marshall Harlan, however, every member of the Waite Court equated the "badges and incidents of slavery" with the denial of "civil rights" and concluded that Congress had nearly exhausted its authority to enact appropriate legislation under the Thirteenth Amendment with the CIVIL RIGHTS ACT OF 1866. "[A]t that time," Bradley explained, "Congress did not assume, under the authority given by the Thirteenth Amendment, to adjust what may be called the social rights of man and races in the community; but only to declare and vindicate those fundamental rights which appertain to the essence of citizenship, and the enjoyment or deprivation of which constitutes the essential distinction between freedom and slavery." Bradley's opinion was circumspect in only one respect. Whether denial of equal accommodation "might be a denial of a right which, if sanctioned by the state law, would be obnoxious to the [equal protection] prohibitions of the Fourteenth Amendment," he said, "is another question." But that was true only in the most formal sense. Once the Court had identified two distinct spheres of rights under the Thirteenth Amendment, one "civil" and another "social," it was difficult to resist the impulse to link that standard with the doctrine expounded in *Pace* when deciding equal protection cases. Stephen J. Field and Horace Gray, the only members of the *Civil Rights Cases* majority still alive when

PLESSY V. FERGUSON (1896) was decided, had no qualms about state laws that required SEPARATE BUT EQUAL accommodations for blacks on public conveyances. Harlan was the sole dissenter on both occasions.

Equal opportunity in the market was one civil right that every member of the Waite Court assumed was guaranteed by the equal protection clause. Thus in YICK WO V. HOPKINS (1886) the Court invalidated the racially discriminatory application of a San Francisco ordinance that required all laundries, except those specifically exempted by the board of supervisors, to be built of brick or stone with walls one foot thick and metal roofs. No existing San Francisco laundry could meet such stringent building regulations, but the ordinance had the desired effect. The authorities promptly exempted the city's white operators and denied the petitions of their 240 Chinese competitors. "[T]he conclusion cannot be resisted," STANLEY MATTHEWS asserted for a unanimous Court, "that no reason for [this discrimination] exists except hostility to the race and nationality to which the petitioners belong, and which in the eye of the law is not justified." Yet the type of right divested was at least as important in *Yick Wo* as the fact of discrimination. The Court described laws that arbitrarily impaired entrepreneurial freedom as "the essence of slavery" while laws that denied racial minorities free choice in the selection of marriage partners and theater seats were not. But that was not all. The court invoked the absence of standards for administering the laundry ordinance as an independent ground for its unconstitutionality. The boundless discretion, or, as Matthews put it, "the naked and arbitrary power" delegated to the authorities was as decisive for the Court as the fact that the ordinance had been applied with "an evil eye and an unequal hand." In the Waite Court's view, however, the same kind of concern about official discretion was neither possible nor desirable in jury-service cases. In *Strauder* Strong conceded that jury selection officials might constitutionally employ facially neutral yet impossibly vague tests of good character, sound judgment, and the like. The Court had no choice but to presume that the jury commissioners had acted properly, Harlan explained in *Bush v. Kentucky* (1883), in the absence of state laws expressly restricting participation to whites. As blacks began to disappear from jury boxes throughout the South, it became clear that although *Strauder* put jury service in the "civil rights" category, in practical application it stood on a far lower plane than the rights enumerated in the Civil Rights Act of 1866. When Booker T. Washington counseled blacks to place economic opportunities ahead of all others in 1895, he expressed priorities that the Waite Court had long since embroidered into equal protection jurisprudence.

The path of DUE PROCESS was at once more tortuous and less decisive than the development of equal protection doctrine. In *Dent v. West Virginia* (1888), decided at the close of the Waite era, the Court conceded, as it had in the beginning, that "it may be difficult, if not impossible, to give to the terms "due process of law' a definition which will embrace every permissible exertion of power affecting private rights and exclude such as are forbidden." Yet two generalizations about the Waite Court's understanding of due process can be advanced with confidence. First, the modern distinction between PROCEDURAL and SUBSTANTIVE DUE PROCESS had no meaning for Waite and his colleagues. In their view, the Fifth and Fourteenth Amendments furnished protection for fundamental rights against arbitrary action, regardless of the legal form in which the arbitrary act had been clothed. In HURTADO V. CALIFORNIA (1884), where the majority rejected counsel's claim that the Fourteenth Amendment INCORPORATED the Bill of Rights, Stanley Matthews explained that because the due process concept embraced "broad and general maxims of liberty and justice," it "must be held to guaranty not particular forms of procedure, but the very substance of individual rights to life, liberty, and property." Even Miller, the most circumspect member of the Court, agreed in 1878 that a law declaring the property of A to be vested in B, "without more," would "deprive A of his property without due process of law." It is equally clear that the Court assumed that CORPORATIONS were PERSONS within the meaning of the Fifth and Fourteenth Amendments long before Waite acknowledged as much during oral argument in *Santa Clara County v. Southern Pacific Railroad Co.* (1886). As early as the GRANGER CASES (1877) the Court decided controversies in which railroad corporations challenged state regulation on due process grounds, and neither the defendant states nor the Justices breathed a doubt about the Court's jurisdiction. In the SINKING FUND CASES (1879), moreover, Waite stated emphatically in obiter dictum that the Fifth Amendment had always barred Congress "from depriving persons or corporations of property without due process of law."

Although every member of the Court accepted the essential premises of substantive due process, no statute was voided on due process grounds during the Waite era. Conventional assumptions about the boundary between the legislative and judicial spheres were largely responsible for the Court's reticence. In due process cases, at least, most of the period's Justices meant it when they stated, as Waite did in the *Sinking Fund Cases*, that "[e]very possible presumption is in favor of the validity of a statute, and this continues until the contrary is shown beyond a reasonable doubt." The most disarming demonstration of that Court's adherence to this principle came in *Powell v. Pennsylvania* (1888). At issue was an act that prohibited the manufacture and sale of oleomargarine. The legislature had labeled the statute as a public health measure, but it was no

secret that the law really had been designed to protect the dairy industry against a new competitor. Harlan, speaking for everyone but Field, conceded that counsel for the oleomargarine manufacturer had stated "a sound principle of constitutional law" when he argued that the Fourteenth Amendment guaranteed every person's right to pursue "an ordinary calling or trade" and to acquire and possess property. Indeed, the Court had furnished protection for those very rights in *Yick Wo*. "But we cannot adjudge that the defendant's rights of liberty and property, as thus defined, have been infringed," Harlan added, "without holding that, although it may have been enacted in good faith for the objects expressed in its title . . . it has, in fact, no real or substantial relation to those objects." And this the Court was not prepared to do. Defendant's offer of proof as to the wholesomeness of his product was insufficient, for it was the legislature's duty, not the judiciary's, "to conduct investigations of facts entering into questions of public policy." Nor could the Court consider the reasonableness of the means selected by the legislature: "Whether the manufacture of oleomargarine . . . is, or may be, conducted in such a way . . . as to baffle ordinary inspection, or whether it involves such danger to the public health as to require . . . the entire suppression of the business, rather than its regulation . . . are questions of fact and of public policy which belong to the legislative department to determine." Field, dissenting, claimed that the majority had not simply deferred to the legislature but had recognized it as "practically omnipotent."

Field overstated the predisposition of his colleagues, and he knew it. The Court seldom spoke with a luminous, confident voice in due process cases; majority opinions almost invariably revealed lingering second thoughts. Each time the Court said yes to legislatures, it reminded them that someday the Court might use the due process clause to say no. In *Powell*, for example, Harlan warned lawmakers that the Court was ready to intercede "if the state legislatures, under the pretence of guarding the public health, the public morals, or the public safety, should invade the rights of life, liberty, and property." Harlan did not explain how the Court might identify an act that had been passed "under the pretence" of exercising the police power, but he seemed to be confident that the Justices would be able to identify a tainted statute once they saw one. Waite's opinion in *Munn v. Illinois* (1877) was equally ambiguous. In one series of paragraphs he stated that the power to regulate prices was inherent in the police power; in another he suggested that price fixing was legitimate only if the regulated concern was a "business AFFECTED WITH A PUBLIC INTEREST." It followed from the latter proposition, though not from the former, that "under some circumstances" the Court might disallow regulation of prices charged by firms that were "purely and exclusively private." In *Munn* Waite was more certain about the reasonableness of rates lawfully fixed. "We know that it is a power which may be abused," he said; "but . . . [f]or protection against abuses by the legislatures the people must resort to the polls, not the courts." By 1886, however, Waite and some of his colleagues were not so sure. "[U]nder the pretense of regulating fares and freights," Waite declared in the *Railroad Commission Cases* (1886), "the State cannot require a railroad corporation to carry persons or property without reward; neither can it do that which in law amounts to a taking of private property for public use without JUST COMPENSATION, or without due process of law." This statement, like Harlan's similar remark in *Powell,* warranted many conflicting inferences. At the close of the Waite era, then, the scope of the JUDICIAL POWER under the due process clause was as unsettled as the clause's meaning.

When Waite died in 1888, a St. Louis law journal observed that he had been "modest, conscientious, careful, conservative, and safe." It was a shrewd appraisal not only of the man but of his Court's work in constitutional law. The Court's unwillingness to use judicial power as an instrument of moral leadership evoked scattered protests from racial egalitarians, who accused Waite and his colleagues of energizing bigotry, and from exponents of laissez-faire who complained that the Court had failed to curb overweening regulatory impulses in the state legislatures. But no criticism was heard from the Republican party's moderate center, where the Court had looked for bearings as it reconstructed the "old" Constitution and integrated the "new." In retrospect, it was THOMAS M. COOLEY, not Charles Sumner, who supplied the Waite Court with an agenda and suggested an appropriate style for its jurisprudence. The Republican party had resorted to "desperate remedies" and had treated the Constitution as if it were "wax" during the Civil War, he said in 1867. Now it was time for the bench and bar to ensure that postwar institutions were "not mere heaps of materials from which to build something new, but the same good old ship of state, with some progress toward justice and freedom."

CHARLES W. MCCURDY
(1986)

Bibliography

BENEDICT, MICHAEL LES 1979 Preserving Federalism: Reconstruction and the Waite Court. *Supreme Court Review* 1978: 39–79.

CORWIN, EDWARD S. 1913 *National Supremacy: Treaty Power versus State Power.* New York: Henry Holt.

——— 1948 *Liberty against Government.* Baton Rouge: Louisiana State University Press.

MAGRATH, PETER C. 1963 *Morrison R. Waite: The Triumph of Character.* New York: Macmillan.

MCCURDY, CHARLES W. 1975 Justice Field and the Jurisprudence of Government-Business Relations. *Journal of American History* 61:970–1005.

SCHMIDT, BENNO C. 1983 Juries, Jurisdiction, and Race Discrimination: The Lost Promise of Strauder v. West Virginia. *Texas Law Review* 61:1401–1499.

# WAIVER OF CONSTITUTIONAL RIGHTS

A potential beneficiary may waive almost any constitutional claim. Rights not of constitutional dimension also may be waived. The Supreme Court has struggled with the questions whether any special DOCTRINE governs waivers of constitutional rights and, if so, whether the special doctrine applies to all constitutional rights. These waiver issues, like much of the rest of constitutional law, took on massive new proportions with the rapid expansion of constitutional rights in the 1960s and 1970s. Prior to that era, there were relatively few rights eligible for waiver.

Distinctions between waivers of constitutional rights and waivers of other rights do not appear in very early cases. The most frequent waiver issue probably was whether a civil litigant had waived the SEVENTH AMENDMENT right to TRIAL BY JURY. *Hodges v. Easton* (1882), a case raising this issue, was the setting for one of the Supreme Court's important statements concerning waiver. In *Hodges* the Court acknowledged that litigants may waive the right but cautioned, in an oft-quoted statemt that seemed to contemplate special treatment for waivers of constitutional rights, that "every reasonable presumption shold be indulged against . . . waiver."

Then, as later would be true, there seemed to be a gap between the Court's statement of the waiver standard and its application of the standard in deciding cases. The Court's casual attitude toward waiver emerged in *Pierce v. Somerset Railway* (1898) and *Eustis v. Bolles* (1893), in which the Court found waivers of claims that state laws unconstitutionally impaired the OBLIGATION OF CONTRACT. In each case not only was "every reasonable presumption" against waiver not indulged; the Court went so far as to indicate that a state court's finding of waiver of constitutional rights did not even raise a federal issue reviewable by the Supreme Court. It may be, however, that the Court was insufficiently attentive to differences between the waiver issue and the existence of an independent and ADEQUATE STATE GROUND for decision, which would preclude Supreme Court review of the state court's judgment.

Although the Court had not become deeply involved in waiver issues, the legal community knew that waiver doctrine might have to be attuned to differences among constitutional rights. Through eight editions from 1868 to 1927, THOMAS M. COOLEY's treatise on constitutional law acknowledged that litigants may waive constitutional rights but it stated that in criminal cases this "must be true to a very limited extent only." Subsequent Supreme Court waiver doctrine at first would adhere to, and later partially undermine, Cooley's suggested distinction. But in his time, Cooley, himself a state supreme court justice, was on safe ground. As long as there were few constitutional rights regulating CRIMINAL PROCEDURE, one easily could limit their waivability.

The Court became more involved with waivers of constitutional rights in the 1930s. In *Aetna Insurance Co. v. Kennedy* (1937) and JOHNSON V. ZERBST (1938), cases raising civil and criminal procedure waiver issues, the Court seemed to indulge presumptions against waiver. And *Johnson v. Zerbst* supplied a new guiding rhetoric. Waiver required "an intentional relinquishment or abandonment of a known right or privilege." Again, though, the Court's articulated waiver standard sometimes was difficult to reconcile with the standard it applied. In *Rogers v. United States* (1951) a GRAND JURY witness who answered many questions was held to have waived her Fifth Amendment RIGHT AGAINST SELF-INCRIMINATION with respect to additional information.

The 1930s doctrinal seeds restricting waiver flowered in the 1960s. The most significant waiver developments concerned the question of a state criminal defendant's waiver of the right to assert a federal constitutional claim in a federal HABEAS CORPUS proceeding. A habeas corpus case, FAY V. NOIA (1963), became the touchstone for analysis of waiver of constitutional rights. *Fay* reaffirmed *Johnson v. Zerbst*'s waiver standard and required a conscious decision to forgo the privilege of seeking to vindicate federal rights. On the language of *Fay*, accidental waivers seemed impossible. The Court's reluctance to allow waivers of constitutional rights reached a high point in MIRANDA V. ARIZONA (1966), when the Court required that police inform suspects of their constitutional rights to assure that any waiver would be knowing.

The late WARREN COURT's reluctance to allow waivers of constitutional rights contrasts with the BURGER COURT's attitude. In one respect, a retreat from the 1960s standard seemed inevitable. For *Fay* and *Johnson* soon collided with the realities of the American criminal justice system. Through the PLEA BARGAINING process, the entire system depends upon widespread waivers of constitutional rights. In the trilogy of *McMann v. Richardson* (1970), *Parker v. North Carolina* (1970), and *Brady v. United States* (1970), holdings difficult to reconcile with the *Fay-Johnson* standard, this reality took hold. The trilogy effectively made a plea of guilty a waiver of nearly all constitutional procedure rights, known or unknown.

Another waiver issue, one with perhaps less of a foregone conclusion, further signaled the Court's shift in attitude. The FOURTH AMENDMENT guarantees the right to be free of UNREASONABLE SEARCHES and seizures and often requires police to obtain a warrant before conducting a search. For many years there was doubt about the relationship between searches conducted with consent, which need not comply with the Fourth Amendment's warrant requirement, and the concept of waiver. If consent were equated with a waiver of Fourth Amendment rights, then the *Johnson* standard seemed applicable. But since few who consent to searches are informed of their Fourth Amendment rights, it was difficult to characterize any waiver as knowing. The widespread practice of CONSENT SEARCHES seemed to hang in the balance.

A Court reluctant to allow waivers of constitutional rights might have adopted the *Miranda*-like solution of generally requiring the police to inform suspects of their Fourth Amendment rights before obtaining consent to a search. In SCHNECKLOTH V. BUSTAMONTE (1973) the Court, opting for a different extreme, preempted most Fourth Amendment waiver problems. It found that the *Johnson* standard had, almost without exception, "been applied only to those rights which the Constitution guarantees to a criminal defendant in order to preserve a FAIR TRIAL." Fourth Amendment claims were held not to be subject to the knowing and intelligent waiver requirement.

*Schneckloth*'s reasoning may have implications for other constitutional rights. It suggests that rights other than those relating to a fair trial are subject to a waiver standard more lenient than the *Johnson* test. But it did not signal a wholesale retreat from *Johnson*. After *Schneckloth*, in cases such as EDWARDS V. ARIZONA (1981), the Court reaffirmed that the *Johnson* standard governs waivers of the RIGHT TO COUNSEL.

In WAINWRIGHT V. SYKES (1977), where the Court squarely confronted *Fay*, it further limited 1960s waiver doctrine. Under *Wainwright*, failure to comply with state procedural rules effectively waives the right to raise a constitutional claim on federal habeas corpus. A habeas applicant must both explain his failure to comply with state procedures and show that his case was prejudiced by the constitutional flaw. The Court rejected *Fay*'s requirement of a knowing and deliberate waiver. In effect, the burden of proving nonwaiver had been placed on the defendant.

The waiver question also continued to arise in contexts not involving criminal procedure. In *D. H. Overmyer Co. v. Frick Company* (1972) and *Swarb v. Lennox* (1972) the Court reconfirmed earlier holdings that at least some civil litigants may contractually waive due process rights to NOTICE and hearing prior to a JUDGMENT and thereby effectively waive the opportunity to contest the validity of a debt. In *Parden v. Terminal Railway* (1964) states may have been surprised to learn that certain activities effectively waived their constitutional immunity from suit in federal court. For many years prior to *Parden*, it appeared that only an express waiver by states would be effective. But the Court found that by operating a railroad in INTERSTATE COMMERCE, a state effectively waived its immunity from employees' suits in federal court under the federal EMPLOYERS LIABILITY ACT. *Parden*'s reach was limited by *Employees v. Department of Public Health and Welfare* (1973), which refused to rely on the FAIR LABOR STANDARDS ACT to subject states to federal damage suits by employees. More important, EDELMAN V. JORDAN (1974) held that state participation in a federal program did not amount to consent to suit in federal court on claims relating to the program.

THEODORE EISENBERG
(1986)

Bibliography

COVER, ROBERT M. and ALEINIKOFF, T. ALEXANDER 1977 Dialectical Federalism: Habeas Corpus and the Court. *Yale Law Journal* 86:1035–1102.

LAFAVE, WAYNE R. 1978 *Search and Seizure: A Treatise on the Fourth Amendment* 8.1, 8.2, 11.1, 11.7 (f). St. Paul, Minn.: West Publishing Co.

TIGAR, MICHAEL E. 1970 Foreword: Waiver of Constitutional Rights: A Disquiet in the Citadel. *Harvard Law Review* 84: 1–28.

TRIBE, LAURENCE H. 1978 *American Constitutional Law.* Pages 133–138. Mineola, N.Y.: Foundation Press.

## WALKER, TIMOTHY
### (1802–1856)

Born in Massachusetts, Timothy Walker attended Harvard College and Harvard Law School where he studied with Justice JOSEPH STORY. He settled in Cincinnati in 1830 and opened a private law school, which eventually became part of the University of Cincinnati. He wrote on various legal subjects, but his primary contribution was his compilation of his lectures, *An Introduction to American Law* (1837), which he dedicated to Story, whose teachings and viewpoint he spread. A third of the work is on constitutional law, strongly nationalist in its orientation. By 1905 the book had gone through eleven editions.

LEONARD W. LEVY
(1986)

## WALKER v. BIRMINGHAM
### 388 U.S. 307 (1967)

The Supreme Court, 5–4, upheld criminal contempt convictions of eight black ministers, including MARTIN LUTHER KING, JR., for holding a CIVIL RIGHTS protest parade in violation of an INJUNCTION issued by an Alabama state court. The injunction, which forbade them from engaging in street parades without a permit, was issued EX PARTE, two days before the intended march. The order was based on a city ordinance that the Court later held unconstitutional for VAGUENESS in *Shuttlesworth v. Birmingham* (1969), a case arising out of the same events.

For the majority, Justice POTTER STEWART concluded that the ministers, once enjoined by a court order, were not entitled to disregard the injunction even if it had been granted unconstitutionally. Rather, they were obliged to ask the court to modify the order, or to seek relief from the injunction in another court.

Justice WILLIAM J. BRENNAN, for the four dissenters, pointed out that, in the absence of a court order, the FIRST AMENDMENT would have entitled the marchers to disregard the ordinance, which was INVALID ON ITS FACE. It was incongruous, he argued, to let the state alter this result simply by obtaining "the ex parte stamp of a judicial officer on a copy of the invalid ordinance." These views were echoed in separate dissents by Chief Justice EARL WARREN and Justice WILLIAM O. DOUGLAS. The *Walker* principle, though much criticized, remains the DOCTRINE of the Court.

KENNETH L. KARST
(1986)

(SEE ALSO: *Demonstration.*)

## WALKER v. SAUVINET
### 92 U.S. 90 (1876)

Walker lost a civil judgment in a trial decided by a judge, in conformance with state law, after the jury deadlocked and after Walker had demanded TRIAL BY JURY. The Court held, 7–2, that the SEVENTH AMENDMENT to the Constitution, guaranteeing trial by jury in civil actions at law, applied only in federal courts, and that the right to a jury trial in similar state cases was not a privilege of United States citizenship guaranteed by the PRIVILEGES AND IMMUNITIES clause of the FOURTEENTH AMENDMENT. This was the earliest rejection of the INCORPORATION DOCTRINE. Its result is still good law, long after the latter doctrine's triumph.

LEONARD W. LEVY
(1986)

## WALLACE v. JAFFREE
### 472 U.S. 38 (1985)

A 6–3 Supreme Court, in an opinion by Justice JOHN PAUL STEVENS, held UNCONSTITUTIONAL an Alabama statute that required public school children to observe a period of silence "for meditation or voluntary prayer." No member of the Court contested the constitutionality of the period of silence for meditation. As Justice SANDRA DAY O'CONNOR said in her CONCURRING OPINION, no threat to RELIGIOUS LIBERTY could be discerned from a room of "silent, thoughtful school children." Chief Justice WARREN E. BURGER added that there was no threat "even if they chose to pray." Burger willfully misunderstood or missed the point. Any student in any public school may pray voluntarily and silently at almost any time of the school day, if so moved. The state, in this case, sought to orchestrate group prayer by capitalizing on the impressionability of youngsters. Compulsory attendance laws and the coercive setting of the school provided a CAPTIVE AUDIENCE for the state to promote religion. Justice JOHN PAUL STEVENS emphasized the fact that the state act was "entirely motivated by a purpose to advance religion" and had "*no* secular purpose." The evidence irrefutably showed that. Accordingly, the Alabama act failed to pass the test of LEMON V. KURTZMAN (1971) used by the Court to determine whether a state violated the FIRST AMENDMENT's prohibition against an ESTABLISHMENT OF RELIGION.

Justice O'Connor, observing that Alabama already had a moment of silence law on its books, noted that during the silence, no one need be religious, no one's religious beliefs could be compromised, and no state encouragement of religion existed. "The crucial question," she wrote, "is whether the State has conveyed or attempted to convey the message that children should use the moment of silence for prayer." The only possible answer was that the state, by endorsing the decision to pray during the moment of silence, sponsored a religious exercise, thereby breaching the First Amendment's principle of SEPARATION OF CHURCH AND STATE.

LEONARD W. LEVY
(1986)

## WALZ v. TAX COMMISSION
### 397 U.S. 664 (1970)

In this 8–1 decision, the Supreme Court added a new element to the test for the constitutionality of financial aid to religious institutions. Chief Justice WARREN E. BURGER rejected Walz's claim that a state's grant of tax exemption to property used only for religious purposes violated the ESTABLISHMENT OF RELIGION clause of the FIRST AMENDMENT. Adding to tests already elaborated in ABINGTON SCHOOL DISTRICT V. SCHEMPP (1963), Burger required assurance that "the end result—the effect—[of a grant of tax exemption] is not an excessive government entanglement with religion. The test is inescapably one of degree."

Commenting that "the course of constitutional neutrality in this area cannot be an absolutely straight line," he said that taxing a church would have involved even more "entanglement" than exempting them. Justice WILLIAM O. DOUGLAS, dissenting, believed that TORCASO V. WATKINS (1961) governed. He concluded that "a tax exemption is a subsidy."

DAVID GORDON
(1986)

(SEE ALSO: *Government Aid to Religious Institutions.*)

## WAR, DECLARATION OF

See: Declaration of War

## WAR, STATE OF

See: State of War

## WARD v. ILLINOIS
### 431 U.S. 767 (1977)

The Supreme Court upheld, 5–4, a conviction for selling "sado-masochistic" materials. (See MISHKIN V. NEW YORK.) Justice BYRON R. WHITE, for the majority, said that a state law could pass the "patent offensiveness" part of the test of MILLER V. CALIFORNIA (1973) although it did not specifically define the proscribed materials; state court interpretations had followed *Miller*'s guidelines. The dissenters, led by Justice JOHN PAUL STEVENS, argued that the absence of the statutory definition specified by *Miller* left the law unconstitutionally vague.

KENNETH L. KARST
(1986)

## WARDEN v. HAYDEN
### 387 U.S. 294 (1976)

In *Gouled v. United States* (1921) the Court announced a rule that rings strange to the modern ear; when conducting an otherwise lawful search, police are authorized to search for contraband, fruits of crime, means and instrumentalities of crime, or weapons of escape, but they are not authorized to search for "mere evidence." The rationale for the MERE EVIDENCE RULE was never clear, but its main theme was that police could not take objects from an accused without asserting a superior property interest in the object seized. This requirement spurred judicial creativity in recognizing property interests and in broadly defining their scope.

In *Warden v. Hayden* the Supreme Court rejected this property-centered conception of FOURTH AMENDMENT jurisprudence. Police could seize evidence after all. Questions remained concerning the scope of searches for items previously regarded as mere evidence (such as diaries) and concerning the applicable standards for SEARCHES AND SEIZURES of "mere evidence" belonging to innocent parties.

STEVEN SHIFFRIN
(1986)

## WARE v. HYLTON
### 3 Dallas 199 (1796)

*Ware* established the fundamental principle of constitutional law that a state act may not violate a national treaty. An act of Virginia during the Revolution sequestered sterling debts owed by Virginians to British subjects and provided that such debts be discharged on payment (in depreciated currency) to the state. The Treaty of Paris of 1783 provided that creditors should meet with no lawful impediments to the recovery of full value in sterling, and Article VI of the Constitution made treaties of the United States the supreme law of the land. Ware, a British subject, brought an action in a federal court seeking such a recovery from Hylton, a Virginian. The prewar debts of Virginians to British creditors exceeded $2,000,000. Justice JAMES IREDELL, on circuit, ruled that the treaty did not revive any debt that had been discharged, and on the WRIT OF ERROR from the circuit court, JOHN MARSHALL, for Hylton, argued that a United States treaty could not annul a statute passed when the state was sovereign. He also denied the authority of the Supreme Court to question the validity of a state law, arguing that the Constitution had not expressly granted such an authority.

Iredell persisted in his opinion expressed below, but Justice SAMUEL CHASE, supported by the concurring opinions of the remainder of the Justices, declared that the SUPREMACY CLAUSE (Article VI), operating retroactively, nullified the state act, thereby reviving the sterling debt. Chase cloaked his opinion in sweeping nationalist doctrine that twisted history: "There can be no limitations on the power of the people to change or abolish the state constitutions, or to make them yield to the general government, and to treaties made by their authority." A treaty, he ruled, could not be supreme law if any state act could stand in its way; state laws contrary to the treaty were prostrated before it and the Constitution, which was the "creator" of the states. The *Ware* decision intensified Jeffersonian hostility to the consolidating and procreditor opinions of the federal courts. The decision's imperishable principle of

the supremacy of national treaties survived its origins—no doubt in part because JAY'S TREATY of 1794 had provided that the United States should assume the payment of the controversial debts.

LEONARD W. LEVY
(1986)

## WAR, FOREIGN AFFAIRS, AND THE CONSTITUTION

The United States became a nation among nations on July 4, 1776, fully endowed with SOVEREIGNTY, that is, the capacity to do whatever nations do in world politics. International law acknowledges that nations have the power to breach their international legal obligations and take the consequences so far as other nations are concerned. Constitutionally, breaches of international law by Congress or the President are binding on courts and citizens alike as official acts within the discretion of the political branches of the government. Thus the FOREIGN AFFAIRS powers, including the WAR POWERS, draw their substance from the matrix of public international law. In the language of PEREZ V. BROWNELL (1958), the Constitution recognizes in the national government "the powers indispensable to its functioning effectively in the company of sovereign nations."

In the CONSTITUTIONAL CONVENTION, a majority led by JAMES WILSON insisted that an "energetic" and independent President was needed to maintain the unity of a country that was already large and destined to become larger, and above all to help assure its safety in a turbulent and dangerous world. As EDWARD S. CORWIN wrote:

> [T]he fact is that what the Framers had in mind was not the cabinet system, as yet nonexistent even in Great Britain, but the "balanced constitution" of [JOHN] LOCKE, MONTESQUIEU, and [WILLIAM] BLACKSTONE, which carried with it the idea of a *divided initiative in the matter of legislation and a broad range of autonomous executive power or "prerogative."* Sir Henry Maine's dictum that "the American constitution is the British constitution with the monarchy left out," is, from the point of view of 1789, almost the exact reverse of the truth, for the presidency was designed in great measure to reproduce the monarchy of George III with the corruption left out, and also of course the hereditary feature [1957, pp. 14–15].

Actually, all comparisons of the British and American constitutions break down. The President is effectively both king and prime minister, but Congress is not Parliament, and its relation to the President is necessarily at arm's length.

The entire authority of the United States to act as a sovereign nation in world politics is confined by the Constitution to the national government and denied to the states. It is divided by the Constitution between the President and Congress.

The President is head of state as well as head of government, and therefore the ultimate embodiment of the nation's sovereignty, especially in times of crisis. ABRAHAM LINCOLN turned to his prerogative and residual powers as the source of much of his authority during the CIVIL WAR. In addition, the Constitution endows the President with "the" executive power of the United States, including without limitation the power to conduct diplomacy; to make treaties, with the ADVICE AND CONSENT of the Senate; and to serve as COMMANDER-IN-CHIEF of the armed forces; moreover, he is enjoined to see to it that the laws are faithfully executed.

The constitutional definition of the role of Congress in foreign affairs is comparably broad. Article I provides that "all LEGISLATIVE POWERS herein granted shall be vested in a Congress of the United States." Among the powers expressly granted to Congress are the powers to lay and collect taxes and provide for the common defense; regulate foreign commerce; establish an uniform rule of NATURALIZATION; define and punish piracies and FELONIES committed on the high seas and offenses against the law of nations; declare war, grant LETTERS OF MARQUE AND REPRISAL, and make rules concerning captures on land and water; and raise and support the armed forces, make rules for their government and regulation, and provide for organizing, arming, and disciplining the militia and calling forth the armed forces and the militia to execute the laws of the Union, suppress insurrections, and repel invasions. The problems of CITIZENSHIP and of foreign affairs in their more general aspects are not mentioned, but Congress's authority to legislate on such issues has been readily inferred by the Supreme Court as inherent in national sovereignty.

In short, the Constitution prescribes that the foreign affairs powers of the nation—including the war power—be shared between Congress and the President in accordance with the overriding principle of functional necessity. All the powers the nation requires in the international environment exist. Those which are executive in character are to be exercised by the President. Those which are legislative in nature are reserved for Congress. When in recess, however, Congress can meet only at the President's call, and can act in all cases only subject to the President's VETO POWER. As Corwin concluded, the Constitution invites the President and Congress "to struggle for the privilege of directing American foreign policy."

Sooner or later, most aspects of the conduct of foreign affairs involve both legislative and executive decisions; they are therefore the proper business of both Congress and the President, in a pattern that reflects subtle political judgments about how their cooperation can best be or-

ganized under the circumstances. A few functions are unique to each branch. Only the President can command the armed forces, call a special session of Congress, or conduct the diplomacy of the nation; and only Congress can declare war, appropriate money, or make certain conduct criminal. On the other hand, the President sometimes asks members of Congress to serve on diplomatic delegations. And Congress sometimes attempts to restrict the President's power to deploy or use the armed forces, although many constitutional authorities have regarded such restrictions as invasions of the President's executive power.

The flexibility of the constitutional arrangements for making and carrying out foreign policy is not peculiar to the field of foreign affairs. As JAMES MADISON saw from the beginning, the principle of the SEPARATION OF POWERS does not mean that the three branches of the government are really separate. Most of their powers are commingled. The branches are not independent but interdependent, and the preservation of the functional boundaries between the legislative and the executive depends as much on the reflexes of the political system as on rulings of the Supreme Court.

It was realized from the beginning that rigid rules about how Congress and the President should work together in the field of foreign affairs would be undesirable and indeed dangerous. As ALEXANDER HAMILTON wrote in THE FEDERALIST #23, "the authorities essential to the common defense . . . ought to exist without limitation, *because it is impossible to foresee or define the extent and variety of national exigencies or the correspondent extent and variety of the means which may be necessary to satisfy them.* The circumstances that endanger the safety of nations are infinite, and for this reason no constitutional shackles can wisely be imposed on the power to which the care of it is committed."

Diplomacy without force behind it has been and will remain a nullity. The use or the threat of armed force has been a normal instrument of American diplomacy, from secret warnings, "showing the flag," and conducting maneuvers, at one end of the spectrum, to programs of rearmament, partial mobilization, and the actual use of armed force—in times of "war" and of "peace," as international law defines those words—at the other. In the early days of the Republic, raids across the borders were commonplace. The problems of piracy and the slave trade required the frequent use of force, pursuant to treaty, statute, or the decisions of the President acting alone. Then and now, international law recognized the right of all states to use limited force in peacetime to cure forceful breaches of international law when no peaceful remedy was available. The United States has taken advantage of its rights in this regard to protect its borders, its ships, its citizens in peril abroad, and indeed, the rights of citizens whose monetary claims had not been paid by foreign governments. Moreover, the United States and other Western nations have sometimes intervened abroad on humanitarian grounds where organized government has broken down. Such exercises by the United States of its "inherent" right of self-defense have been carried out mainly, but not exclusively, on the authority of the President.

The threat to use force and even the use of force have been familiar features of diplomacy from the opening of Japan to President RICHARD M. NIXON's secret nuclear warnings that induced the Soviet Union not to attack Chinese nuclear installations. At the end of the Civil War, we deployed 50,000 troops along the Mexican border. France heeded our suggestion, withdrew its troops from Mexico, and left Maximilian to his fate. Similarly, in 1962, President JOHN F. KENNEDY assembled some 250,000 troops in Florida, and halted a Soviet vessel carrying military supplies to Cuba; the Soviet Union withdrew its nuclear missiles from Cuba. A few years earlier, at a moment of severe Soviet pressure against Turkey, President HARRY S. TRUMAN ordered the battleship *Missouri* to carry the body of a deceased Turkish ambassador to Istanbul for burial—manifestly a journey intended to be more than a courteous gesture to the people of Turkey. Such threats of force have been almost entirely within the province of the President.

The list of such incidents is long enough to demonstrate that throughout its history the United States government has called upon its armed forces to perform a wide variety of functions in support of its foreign policy. There have been five DECLARATIONS OF WAR in our national experience, and more than 200 episodes in which the President ordered the armed forces into combat, sometimes with the support of a treaty or of legislation passed before or after the event, more often on his own authority. The number of occasions on which the President secretly threatened to use force in aid of his diplomacy cannot be counted accurately, but is surely considerable.

The pattern of cooperation between the President and Congress with respect to war and foreign affairs has been the same since the first administration of President GEORGE WASHINGTON. This continuity of practice arises from the nature of things. Congress could and did admonish the President to protect frontier settlements from Indian raids but could not meet and vote every time the risk arose. In any event, it was the President's duty to protect the settlements with or without the support of a statute. The circumstances which may require the use of or the threat to use armed force are too protean, and pervade the conduct of foreign affairs too completely, to be compressed within a single procedure.

From the beginning of our government under the Constitution, a great deal of energy has been absorbed by attempts to define the respective roles of the President and of Congress in carrying out these functions. The participants in the debate are divided into two camps.

Hamilton's view of the Presidency dominates the judicial opinions, the pattern of practice, the writings of scholars, and the pronouncements of senators and representatives. To Hamiltonians, all national powers not granted to Congress or the courts are "executive" and therefore presidential, especially if they concern relations with foreign powers or the duties of the nation under international law.

But a dissenting opinion has persisted, based on the fear of executive power as dictatorship in disguise. Corwin calls it the "ultra-Whig" view. It opposes almost all claims to presidential independence, and regards the executive as no more than an obstreperous but indispensable servant of a "sovereign" Congress. This conception of the Presidency has been a mainstay of political attacks on Presidents for unpopular wars.

The Hamiltonian position crystallized during the neutrality controversy of 1793, an episode of immense importance to the formation of the Constitution. France had declared war against Great Britain. The United States was bound to France by the 1778 treaties of perpetual alliance which seemed to require the infant Republic, in the event of war between France and Britain, to give various forms of belligerent aid to France. Any such assistance would have been an act of war against Great Britain, which could easily have snuffed out the new nation. Washington and his cabinet were determined to preserve neutrality despite the treaties with France and the strongly pro-French bias of public opinion. After the Supreme Court refused Washington's request for an ADVISORY OPINION determining whether the President could issue a proclamation of neutrality on his own authority, Washington did so, and took special precautions to assure Great Britain of America's pacific intentions.

The concurrent nature of the foreign relations power was soon demonstrated. Juries would not convict American seamen for violating the President's neutrality proclamation. Congress then grudgingly passed a Neutrality Act, supporting the President's interpretation of the treaties with France. In due course, the Neutrality Act was enforced. Congress had the last word, but acted under circumstances carefully arranged by the President, acting independently.

Hamilton's *Pacificus* papers, defending the President's right to issue the Proclamation of neutrality, are among the most cogent of all our state papers on the conduct of foreign affairs. The President, said Hamilton, has the foreign affairs and war powers of the British monarch minus the limitations on those powers mentioned in the Constitution. Those limitations, being exceptions to the President's executive powers, should be strictly construed.

The President is the sole officer of the government empowered to communicate with foreign nations. This is an executive power. It was therefore the President's role to inform the nations about the position of the United States with respect to the European war. Next, Hamilton argued, it is the President's duty to preserve peace until Congress declares war. In this case, the President's duty required him faithfully to execute the international law of neutrality, and thus avoid giving offense to foreign powers. To carry out that duty, the President had to determine for himself whether a status of neutrality conformed to our national interests and was compatible with our obligations under the French treaties, and then to announce his position diplomatically. Hamilton said that the President has the authority and the duty to determine the operation of treaties in the first instance, an important example of his right as President to decide upon the obligations of the country to foreign nations until Congress does so within its own sphere.

Hamilton's analysis would lead to the conclusion that while only Congress can move the nation into a state of general war, the President can authorize more limited uses of force in peacetime for purposes of self-defense, the protection of citizens abroad, the fulfillment of treaty obligations, and the support of diplomacy.

The Ultra-Whig dissenting view draws an altogether different boundary between the respective war powers of the President and Congress. For the dissenters, Congress's power to "declare" war gives Congress entire control over every aspect of the war power, including neutrality. It means, they contend, that the President can never employ the armed forces, save to repel a sudden attack, unless Congress has first passed a "declaration of war." Some dissenters agree that Congress may authorize limited war in the international law sense, but insist that the declaration of war clause requires congressional action before the President uses force at all, except in cases of sudden attack. A few concede that circumstances may justify congressional approval after the event—after Pearl Harbor, for example, or the firing on Fort Sumter. And some even accept the decision of the Supreme Court in THE PRIZE CASES (1863), which upheld acts of Congress ratifying President Lincoln's blockade of the Confederacy, enacted some months after the President had instituted the blockade. But all the dissenters are dubious about statutes, treaties, or joint resolutions—and many have been put on the books since 1792—that may be invoked to support presidential uses of force years later. The Ultra-Whigs admit that the United States may, like other nations, sign treaties that have military provisions, but they are uneasy about the propriety of such commitments unless they are reiterated by Congress when they become the basis for military action.

There is no reason for such confusion to persist. The "declaration of war" authorized in the Constitution is bracketed in Article I, section 8, with "letters of marque and reprisal" and "captures on land and sea." All are terms of specific meaning in international law. A declaration of war has far-reaching consequences, including: the authorization of unlimited hostilities, the possible internment of enemy ALIENS, the sequestration of enemy property, and the imposition of regulations, such as censorship, that would be unthinkable in peacetime. But many kinds of hostilities recognized as legitimate under international law do not constitute "general war," and can therefore be initiated by official action less sweeping than a declaration of war. Most familiar are exercises of the right of self-defense against certain breaches of international law. Many are short, quick responses to a sudden threat; others become more prolonged conflicts. International law limits all such defensive campaigns to the use of as much force as is reasonably necessary to eliminate the original breach.

Hamilton's theory of presidential power is clearly the operative model of American constitutional law with respect to the international use of force. But the practice has not been nearly so symmetrical as Hamilton's logic. Every American President who has felt obliged to use the armed forces has vividly remembered the political attacks on "JOHN ADAMS' Undeclared War," and therefore sought to obtain congressional support for his policies as soon as it was politically feasible to do so. But such prudence has never helped a President saddled with an unpopular war. John Adams was supported by four successive statutes; they had no effect on the political outcry against him, or the fate of the Federalist party. Presidents Truman and LYNDON B. JOHNSON endured similar trials. As Johnson commented: "I said early in my Presidency that if I wanted Congress with me on the landing of Vietnam, I'd have to have them on the take off. And I did just that. . . . But I failed to reckon with one thing: the parachute. I got them on the take off, but a lot of them bailed out before the end of the flight."

Between the Congress of Vienna and the turn of the twentieth century, the United States was not a major actor in world politics; the central features of American foreign policy were Manifest Destiny and the MONROE DOCTRINE. Nonetheless, there were periods of tension between Congress and the President with respect to the conduct of foreign relations. The most acute of these episodes concerned the expansion of the nation to the Pacific and controversies about problems in Latin America and Canada. Some of the controversies reflected deep divisions between the parties and among the people, others no more than normal rivalry between the political branches of the government.

But the collapse of the old state system in 1914 imposed

new burdens on the United States, which in turn gave rise to profound disquiet in American opinion, exacerbating the traditional tension between Congress and the President with respect to the war power, and reaching a climax during the early 1970s. The VIETNAM WAR dragged on, accompanied by antiwar rioting of a kind the nation had not experienced since the Civil War. At the same time, the controversy over President Nixon's behavior with respect to Watergate poisoned the political atmosphere, and produced so strong a movement for the President's impeachment that he resigned.

In this atmosphere of extreme political excitement, Congress passed the War Powers Resolution of 1973. Its political purpose was to assure the people that Congress could and would protect the nation against future Vietnams. For the first time in nearly two hundred years, the Hamiltonian view of the Presidency and the war power suffered at least a nominal defeat.

The Resolution asserts congressional supremacy with regard to the war power, but it does not adopt an extreme form of the Ultra-Whig view. It does not say, for example, that the President can use force only if Congress has first declared war. Not does it seek to confine the President's use of force without prior congressional approval to cases of "sudden attack."

The Resolution purports to fulfill the intent of the Framers of the Constitution, as summarized in three propositions. First, the armed forces should not be involved in hostilities without the collective judgment of Congress and the President. Second, Congress has the power to pass all laws NECESSARY AND PROPER for carrying into execution the powers of the President. Third, the constitutional powers of the President as Commander-in-Chief can be exercised by him to introduce the forces into hostile situations only pursuant to a declaration of war or a "specific" statute, or in a national emergency created by an attack upon the United States. Clearly, this attempt at restatement omits the nation's obligations under treaties.

The Resolution requires the President to consult with Congress "in every possible instance" before introducing the armed forces into situations where hostilities are an imminent risk, and also to "consult" regularly with Congress after hostilities have begun until they are terminated. The resolution makes no attempt to define the term "consult," which is a word of political but not of constitutional meaning.

The War Powers Resolution requires the President to report to Congress within forty-eight hours and regularly thereafter whenever he has introduced armed forces into situations risking hostilities without a declaration of war. It further requires the President to terminate such a use of the armed forces within sixty days unless Congress has declared war, authorized hostilities in another "specific" form, or extended the sixty-day period to not more than ninety days. Where hostilities are being conducted abroad without a declaration of war or "specific" authorization in another form, the resolution authorizes Congress, by CONCURRENT RESOLUTION, to require the President to terminate hostilities and remove the armed forces.

If the War Powers Resolution were carried out literally, it would constitute the most revolutionary change in the Constitution ever accomplished—far more drastic in its effects than the shift of authority from the states to the national government which began after Civil War. It would subject the President to the orders of an omnipotent Congress. No future President could do what Lincoln did during the Civil War, or rely on the behavior of every strong President between Washington and Lyndon Johnson as precedents. The deterrent influence of American military power and of American treaties, already weakened after Vietnam, would decline even further. The United States would be the only country in the world that lacked the capacity to enter into treaties or conduct secret negotiations contemplating the use of force, and it would be hampered in many other ways in the conduct of its foreign relations. Enforcing the resolution would produce paradoxes. Although no future President could do what President Kennedy did during the Cuban Missile Crisis in 1962, the highly "specific" legal arrangements for the Vietnam War would have satisfied the Resolution's requirements. That war was authorized not only by the United Nations Charter and the Southeast Asia Collective Defense Treaty of 1954, but by the GULF OF TONKIN RESOLUTION of 1963 and other explicit acts of Congress as well. On the other hand, the sponsors of the Resolution have said that it does not affect the President's unique responsibilities with regard to the nuclear weapon. Above all, as has been evident in the decade since it was passed, the Resolution would convert almost every serious foreign policy problem into a debate between Congress and the President about constitutional power, making the conduct of foreign relations even more cumbersome and contentious than is the case already.

The War Powers Resolution is in profound conflict with the necessities of governance in a turbulent world and with the concept of the Presidency that has evolved from the experience of the nation under the Constitution. We can therefore predict that the Hamiltonian conception of the war powers will prevail as the constitutional norm, and that the War Powers Resolution will become a footnote to history, either through repudiation or desuetude.

Institutional pride may keep Congress from repealing the resolution, although repeal disguised as revision is not unthinkable. The courts will almost surely declare the Resolution unconstitutional if an appropriate case should arise. The ruling of the Supreme Court in IMMIGRATION AND NATURALIZATION SERVICE V. CHADHA (1983) is applicable to the chief operative parts of the War Powers Resolution. *Chadha* ruled that congressional action can have legislative effect only through acts or joint resolutions fully subject to the President's veto. If Congress cannot constitutionally terminate a war by passing a concurrent resolution, it can hardly do so by failing to pass such a resolution within sixty or ninety days.

In holding the War Powers Resolution unconstitutional, the Supreme Court may well go beyond *Chadha* to deal with more fundamental aspects of the separation of powers principle: the resolution's effect, for example, on the President's hitherto unquestioned power to conduct secret negotiations, receive surrenders, or negotiate cease-fire agreements; and its attempt, recalling the proposed BRICKER AMENDMENT, to require legislation before treaties can become the supreme law of the land.

Even if the resolution is neither repealed nor declared unconstitutional by the courts, it is unlikely to be an important influence on Presidents. The resolution does not correspond to the nature of the problems of foreign policy and national security with which the government has to deal, and therefore cannot function as effective law. At least eleven episodes involving the use of force or the imminent risk of using force occurred during the first decade after the War Powers Resolution was passed. In each case the President, while protesting that the resolution was unconstitutional, consulted with congressional leaders and kept Congress informed about events. In no case did the procedure mandated by the resolution prove convenient or appropriate, and in no case was it followed. In each case there were some congressional protests that the War Powers Resolution was being violated, and even suggestions that the President be impeached.

The President and Congress, separately and together, have been entrusted by history with sovereign prerogatives in exercising the foreign affairs and war powers of the nation. Those prerogatives have been in uneasy balance for two hundred years, an instance of the friction between the branches of government on which the Founding Fathers relied to preserve the liberties of the people. Over a wide range, the President and Congress can exercise their joint and several political discretion in dealing quickly with complex and swiftly moving events, often on the basis of fragmentary information. Within that zone, the only constitutional restraints on which the people can rely to secure them from the abuse of such political discretion is the electoral process itself, as Chief Justice Marshall remarked in GIBBONS V. OGDEN (1824).

But the choices committed by the Constitution to the care of Congress and the President are not unlimited, even when one gives full weight to the view that the war power is the power to wage war successfully. The foreign affairs and war powers are aspects of a government organized under a written Constitution dominated by the principle of democratic responsibility. Although the Supreme

Court has hesitated to pass on many conflicts between the President and Congress, it has intervened where exercises of the war power impinged upon CIVIL RIGHTS, or attempted radically to alter the equilibrium of the constitutional order.

Thus, certain constitutional limits on the President's war power emerged in its first major test—the neutrality crisis of 1793. President Washington could have used the armed forces or called up the militia to keep French privateers at the docks of Philadelphia or Charleston; in the event, he prudently refrained from such action. But he could not get American juries to convict American citizens indicted for violating a presidential proclamation. Similarly, YOUNGSTOWN SHEET & TUBE CO. V. SAWYER (1952) decided that the President had no INHERENT POWERS to seize steel mills as a step toward settling a strike during the Korean War when Congress had rejected such a procedure.

There are comparable constitutional limits on what Congress and the President acting together can do in the name of the war power. Congress can make it an offense to recruit soldiers within the United States for wars in which the United States is neutral, but it is doubtful whether it would be constitutional for Congress to forbid American citizens from going abroad to fight. In *Ex parte Merryman* (1861) and *Ex parte Milligan* (1867) the courts held that even in the midst of the Civil War, courts-martial could not try civilians while the ordinary courts were available. And in REID V. COVERT (1957) and *Kinsella v. United States* (1960) the Supreme Court struck down convictions imposed by courts-martial on the wives of military personnel living on American bases abroad.

The only exceptions to this line of cases are the JAPANESE AMERICAN CASES, decided during WORLD WAR II. These cases upheld the constitutionality of a statute authorizing the President to exclude citizens of Japanese descent from California, Oregon, and Washington, and requiring their internment in camps until they could be resettled in other parts of the country. These decisions have been severely criticized, and the Court's opinion in DUNCAN V. KAHANAMOKU (1946) can be interpreted as overruling them *sub silentio*. Until they are more decisively repudiated, however, they remain, as Justice Jackson said in KOREMATSU V. UNITED STATES (1944), "a loaded weapon ready for the hand of any authority that can bring forward a plausible claim of an urgent need."

EUGENE V. ROSTOW
(1986)

Bibliography

CORWIN, EDWARD S. (1940) 1957 *The President: Office and Powers, 1787–1957.* New York: New York University Press.
HENKIN, LOUIS 1972 *Foreign Affairs and the Constitution.* Mineola, N.Y.: Foundation Press.

RANDALL, JAMES G. (1926) 1951 *Constitutional Problems under Lincoln.* Urbana: University of Illinois Press.

REVELY, W. TAYLOR, III 1981 *The War Powers of the President and Congress.* Charlottesville: University Press of Virginia.

ROSTOW, EUGENE V. 1945 The Japanese American Cases: A Disaster. *Yale Law Journal* 54:489–533, reprinted in *The Sovereign Prerogative* (1962). New Haven: Yale University Press.

—— 1973 Statement, in Appendix to *War Powers*, Hearings before Subcommittee on National Security Policy and Scientific Developments, Committee on Foreign Affairs, House of Representatives, 93rd Congress, 1st Session, March 7–20, 1973, pp. 395–502; also in Rostow, Eugene v. 1972 Great Cases Make Bad Law: The War Powers Act. *Texas Law Review* 50:833–900.

SOFAER, ABRAHAM D. 1976 *War, Foreign Affairs, and Constitutional Power: The Origins.* Cambridge, Mass.: Ballinger Publishing Co.

TURNER, ROBERT F. 1983 *The War Powers Resolution: Its Implementation in Theory and Practice.* Philadelphia: Foreign Policy Research Institute.

# WAR POWERS

Not appearing in the Constitution, the phrase "war powers" nonetheless describes a cluster of powers exercised by the President or Congress, together or separately, to combat both domestic insurgency and foreign military enemies. They comprise those activities necessary "to wage war successfully," including the raising of troops, the provision of equipment and supplies, the mobilization of opinion, and the maintenance of security in loyal areas (during civil war or insurgency) or on the home front (during foreign war).

As with all governmental activity, the legitimacy of the war powers depends ultimately on explicit or implicit sources in the Constitution. Among these are the grants to Congress of authority "to declare War," to raise, maintain, and make rules for federal military forces, and "to provide for calling forth the Militia to execute the Laws of the Union, suppress Insurrections and repel Invasions." Other sources include the Article I authorization to suspend the privilege of the writ of HABEAS CORPUS "when in Cases of Rebellion or Invasion the public Safety may require it," the Article II clauses making the President COMMANDER-IN-CHIEF, giving him power to make treaties subject to Senate consent, and charging him to "take Care that the Laws be faithfully executed," and the Article IV commitments guaranteeing "to every State . . . a REPUBLICAN FORM OF GOVERNMENT" and pledging protection against invasion and domestic violence. Magnifying all these grants is the NECESSARY AND PROPER CLAUSE.

Contrariwise, only in exceptional circumstances have officials instituted TREASON prosecutions, for in Article III the Framers laid out strict evidentiary requirements, ow-ing to the crime's draconian connotations. But such seemingly plausible restrictions as the FIRST AMENDMENT and Fifth Amendment, the principle of SEPARATION OF POWERS, and the rule against delegation of power have seldom proved real barriers to effective wartime government; and generally JUDICIAL REVIEW has had little impact on the power to make war.

As early as 1792, Congress empowered the President to call forth state militias when "combinations too powerful to be suppressed by the ordinary course of judicial proceedings" prevented the execution of federal law. Used during the WHISKEY REBELLION (1794), and subsequently modified to include regular military forces and to clarify the President's authority to determine the existence of emergency, this provision later helped undergird President ABRAHAM LINCOLN's response to the siege of Fort Sumter. The ALIEN AND SEDITION ACTS of 1798 provide another early illustration of legislative-executive collaboration; adopted during the Quasi-War with France, they posed the enduring issue of reconciling CIVIL LIBERTIES with the perceived requirements of internal security.

Although Presidents THOMAS JEFFERSON and ANDREW JACKSON confronted serious opposition to enforcement of federal law during the Embargo and NULLIFICATION crises, the CIVIL WAR produced the first comprehensive test of the war powers' true potential. With only a slender statutory base—or none at all—for much of his action, Lincoln called out the militia, requested federal volunteer troops, increased the size of the regular army and navy, spent money from the treasury, established a naval blockade of the Confederacy, and suspended the privilege of the writ of habeas corpus. When Congress finally met at Lincoln's call, on July 4, 1861, it confronted not only a program already in place but also the President's explanation that his actions, "whether strictly legal or not, were ventured upon under what appeared to be a popular demand and a public necessity, trusting . . . that Congress would readily ratify them."

Besides retroactively endorsing much of the Lincoln program, Congress voted appropriations and passed confiscation, legal tender, and draft legislation to support the defeat of the rebellion. It also authorized Lincoln's seizure of the Union's telegraphs and railways in January 1862. The general rule of the Civil War, however, was executive initiative under the theory that the Constitution had been intended to provide government adequate to all contingencies. This view built on THE FEDERALIST #23 and LUTHER V. BORDEN (1849) and gained important wartime endorsement in the PRIZE CASES (1863). Its fullest elaboration appeared in *War Powers under the Constitution of the United States*, a massive exposition and compilation by William Whiting, the War Department's solicitor.

Even Lincoln's internal security program, which emphasized military arrest without warrant, detention without trial, and release once danger had passed, escaped serious censure during the war itself, despite the short-term imprisonment of some 13,000 to 25,000 northern civilians. Typical of Court review of war powers disputes, Chief Justice ROGER B. TANEY's attack on the suspension of habeas corpus, in *Ex parte Merryman* (1861), was feeble and futile, while the more serious blow in EX PARTE MILLIGAN came in 1866, after the war had ended.

In WORLD WAR I, WOODROW WILSON by no means ignored the Lincoln model; such key agencies as the War Industries Board and the Committee on Public Information rested solely on executive authority. But the bulk of the internal effort during 1917–1918 relied on congressional delegation of power. Wilson in turn delegated authority to a host of administrative agencies that exercised direct control of the sinews of war.

The resulting intervention contrasted markedly with the Civil War experience. Bolstering prewar statutes that had given the President power to place mandatory defense contracts with private firms, the Lever Act (1917) constituted the war's largest delegation of power. It allowed sweeping regulation of priorities, production, and prices throughout the economy; yet in only a minor detail did the Supreme Court eventually rule the act unconstitutional, in *United States v. Cohen Grocery Company* (1921). The Trading with the Enemy Act (1917) permitted control of foreign commodity and currency transactions, encountered no significant judicial challenge, and later provided a statutory base for President FRANKLIN D. ROOSEVELT's "Bank Holiday" during the economic emergency of the Great Depression. (Not until 1977 did Congress limit the law's availability to periods of declared war—and then provided a slightly narrower set of financial powers for use in other crises.) The SELECTIVE SERVICE ACT (1917) gave free rein to Wilson in establishing draft machinery and received strong endorsement in the SELECTIVE DRAFT LAW CASES (1918), a decision supplying precedent for upholding selective service legislation in World War II and the Cold War. The ESPIONAGE ACT (1917) and SEDITION ACT (1918) enlisted the judicial system and were upheld in SCHENCK V. UNITED STATES (1919), ABRAMS V. UNITED STATES (1919), and *Pierce v. United States* (1920). Over 1,900 prosecutions took place under these two measures, with 930 convictions.

In WORLD WAR II, President Roosevelt effectively combined the Lincoln and Wilson approaches. He based many actions and agencies on his INHERENT POWERS as commander-in-chief, even when tackling problems of domestic mobilization. The National War Labor Board is an example. Created in January 1942 to insure against labor strife and work stoppages in war industries, its orders were in theory only "informatory," "at most advisory"; yet companies violating the orders were denied federal contracts and needed materials. Recalcitrant workers risked revocation of their draft exemptions and denial of other jobs within the jurisdiction of the United States Employment Service. Although avowedly established under authority vested in Roosevelt "by the Constitution and the statutes of the United States" (a commonly used formula for World War II agencies), until June 1943 the Board actually had no statutory base but rather fell under the Office of Emergency Management, itself a creation within the Executive Office of the President.

Other action rested on legislation. In September 1939, well before American entry into the war, Roosevelt's declaration of a national emergency activated laws, some dating to before World War I, that empowered him to increase the size of the army and navy, regulate banking and currency dealing, take over factories and power plants, reallocate appropriations among executive departments and agencies, and censor wire and radio communications. The Lend-Lease Act (1941) delegated the broadest procurement powers ever given to a President, yet it was never challenged judicially. The Office of Price Administration, established under the Emergency Price Control Act (1942), provided the major wartime inflation fighting program; like the nonstatutory agencies, it often employed indirect sanction that proved impossible to challenge judicially. Decisions validating the act included YAKUS V. UNITED STATES (1944), *Bowles v. Willingham* (1944), and *Steuart and Brothers v. Bowles* (1944). Not surprisingly, the war's proliferation of alphabetical agencies dwarfed the New Deal's.

In addition, the government had a sedition law available (the Smith Act of 1940), but widespread support for the war meant relatively few prosecutions. The Japanese American relocation program—the single most blatant obstruction of CIVIL LIBERTIES in the nation's history—instead had its own flimsy legislative base and for practical purposes received judicial sanction in the Japanese American Cases—*Hirabayashi v. United States* (1943) and *Korematsu v. United States* (1944).

The lesson of the two world wars, as Clinton Rossiter accurately summarized, is "that in time of war Congress can pass just about any law it wants as a "necessary and proper' accessory to the delegated war powers; that the President can make just about any use of such law he sees fit; and that the people with their overt or silent resistance, not the Court with its power of judicial review, will set the only practical limits to arrogance of abuse." Indeed, even popular resistance, real or imagined, generally has proved more of a challenge to be subdued than a restrictive hurdle.

Punctuated by limited wars in Korea and Vietnam, the period of Cold War since 1945 conveys a similar lesson: if

Congress and the President act together, little likelihood exists of judicial challenge. In this respect President HARRY S. TRUMAN erred during the KOREAN WAR, when a plant seizure triggered *Youngstown Sheet and Tube Co. v. Sawyer* (1952). As for the VIETNAM WAR, Presidents LYNDON B. JOHNSON and RICHARD M. NIXON found that despite flagging public support, Congress kept voting supplies until the main fighting was over. For its part, the judiciary moved only gingerly when limiting use of war-related powers, as in NEW YORK TIMES V. UNITED STATES (1971) (government secrecy), and UNITED STATES V. UNITED STATES DISTRICT COURT (1972) (national security electronic surveillance). Moreover, the Supreme Court in LAIRD V. TATUM (1972) held that the courts lacked jurisdiction over a challenge to the use of military personnel to gather domestic intelligence pertaining to potential public disorder; and other courts managed to discover executive-legislative *agreement* in Congress's decision finally to cut appropriations for operations in or over Cambodia.

Future Presidents may not benefit so readily from legislative acquiescence. Soon after enacting the War Powers Resolution (1973) to control external warmaking by the President, Congress passed the NATIONAL EMERGENCIES ACT (1976). Recent studies had disclosed that four declarations of national emergency were still in effect, one dating to 1933 and another to 1950; these proclamations activated 470 provisions of federal law, many of which lingered from the two world wars and Korea. The 1976 law ended these existing emergencies two years after its passage, mandated periodic six-month review of any future emergency declarations, and made them terminable by CONCURRENT RESOLUTION—a procedure of doubtful constitutionality under IMMIGRATION AND NATURALIZATION SERVICE V. CHADHA (1983). The act also required Presidents to inform Congress fully of the legislative basis for emergency actions. But subsequent response to President JIMMY CARTER's declaration of national emergency over the Iranian hostage crisis (1979) indicated little congressional desire to adhere rigorously to the new requirements.

Whenever a crisis plausibly justifies their exercise, the war powers seem likely to continue to generate government centered in the executive branch, emphasizing energetic administration that transcends normal restrictions, and on occasion sufficiently vigorous to warrant the label "constitutional dictatorship."

CHARLES A. LOFGREN
(1986)

(SEE ALSO: *Congressional War Powers; Presidential War Powers*.)

Bibliography

CORWIN, EDWARD S. (1957) 1984 *The President: Office and Powers, 1787–1984*, 5th ed., revised by Randall W. Bland, Theodore T. Hindson, and Jack W. Peltason. New York: New York University Press.

FISHER, LOUIS 1985 *Constitutional Conflicts between Congress and the President*. Princeton, N.J.: Princeton University Press.

ROSSITER, CLINTON (1948) 1963 *Constitutional Dictatorship: Crisis Government in the Modern Democracies*. New York: Harcourt, Brace.

———— (1951) 1976 *The Supreme Court and the Commander in Chief*. Expanded edition by Richard P. Longaker. Ithaca, N.Y.: Cornell University Press.

# WAR POWERS
## (Update 1)

The phrase "war powers" does not appear in the Constitution. By the mid-1980s a complex of specific grants in the document nonetheless provided the federal government broad authority to protect national security through military action abroad and domestic mobilization. Court decisions and practice had established that when Congress and the President acted in concert, hardly any barriers existed, except on those rare occasions involving violations of the BILL OF RIGHTS. Executive action lacking congressional endorsement had proved more debatable, although less litigated. Courts had not effectively challenged presidential ventures abroad, nor had Congress itself institutionally challenged the President, save when the VIETNAM WAR was nearly over.

In the late 1980s little changed. Because of the absence of foreign conflicts sufficient to require domestic mobilization and controls, existing case law pertaining to the home front in wartime remained undisturbed, encapsulated in an earlier era. Indeed, this situation seemed likely to continue, because by the end of the decade shifts within the former "Communist bloc" significantly lessened the chance that the nation would again see massive domestic build-ups like those of WORLD WAR I and WORLD WAR II. (Reserve call-ups during the American confrontation and war with Iraq in 1990–1991 proved, however, that lesser mobilizations could still occur.)

Even the JAPANESE AMERICAN CASES sat untouched. To be sure, Congress offered its tardy amends for the World War II relocation program, providing modest compensation for surviving internees; and with an assist from academic researchers who uncovered evidentiary deficiencies and procedural irregularities in the wartime prosecutions, the original federal trial courts used the old writ of error *coram nobis* to vacate the convictions of Gordon Hirabayashi, Fred Korematsu, and Minoru Yasui. But the major Supreme Court decisions from 1943 and 1944 now served amazingly as authority for viewing race as a SUSPECT CLASSIFICATION.

Abroad, presidential war making continued. Following his popular intervention in Grenada in 1983 and his more controversial use of marines in Lebanon during the same period (which Congress finally authorized), President RONALD REAGAN sent naval forces to the Persian Gulf in 1987–1988 to protect oil shipments during the Iran-Iraq War. In December 1989 his successor, GEORGE BUSH, committed troops to combat in Panama, after failing to dislodge Panamanian dictator Manuel Noriega by other means. Then, beginning in August 1990, Iraq's invasion and occupation of Kuwait triggered an escalating response by Bush that recalled memories of both the KOREAN WAR and the VIETNAM WAR. Both Presidents skirted the reporting requirements of the 1973 War Powers Resolution. By late 1990 some twenty-one instances of presidential war making had arguably fallen under the coverage of the law since its passage, but in only one (during GERALD R. FORD's tenure) had a President explicitly reported to Congress that he had sent forces into hostilities or situations of imminent hostility.

The Panamanian episode typified the practice. Bush informed Congress, but stated that his report was "consistent with" the War Powers Resolution, not pursuant to it. In particular, he carefully avoided mention of section 4(a)(1), the provision defining the commitment of forces that triggers the law's requirement for troop withdrawal after sixty days unless Congress authorizes continuation. The military operations, Bush said, "were ordered pursuant to my constitutional authority with respect to the conduct of foreign relations and as Commander in Chief."

Such actions did not go entirely unchallenged. After Reagan ordered naval forces to the Persian Gulf, just as in 1982 after he sent military advisers into El Salvador, individual members of Congress asked the federal District Court for the District of Columbia to enjoin the President to file the report required to start the War Powers Resolution's sixty-day "clock." In Lowry v. Reagan (D.D.C. 1987) the court declined, invoking the D.C. Circuit's doctrine of "remedial discretion" by finding that the members' dispute was not with the President, but with their legislative colleagues who refused to pass legislation starting the clock. The court added that the POLITICAL QUESTIONS doctrine also barred the suit in its present form, because a court injunction could endanger diplomatic initiatives through multiple pronouncements on a sensitive matter.

The demonstrated ineffectiveness of the War Powers Resolution in turn led to proposals to amend it. This step became more urgent because most authorities viewed IMMIGRATION AND NATURALIZATION SERVICE V. CHADHA (1983) as invalidating the law's provision for use of a CONCURRENT RESOLUTION to terminate a military action prior to the sixty-day deadline. Suggested changes included tightening key definitions within the law, substituting joint resolutions for concurrent resolutions as the disallowance mechanism, specifying which members of Congress the President was to consult under the act's consultation requirement, eliminating the sixty-day limit on the use of force without congressional approval, and granting individual members of Congress standing in court challenges under the War Powers Resolution. By mid-1991, none of the proposals had passed.

These disputes, along with covert arms-for-hostages deals in the Middle East and support for the Contra rebels in Nicaragua, produced renewed debate over the constitutional locus of the external war-making power. Defenders of presidential initiatives predictably trotted out arguments for inherent EXECUTIVE POWER that dated back to ALEXANDER HAMILTON's "Pacificus" essays in 1793 and had received apparent endorsement in UNITED STATES V. CURTISS-WRIGHT EXPORT CORP. (1936). Critics again quickly pointed out the egregious historical errors in such defenses. Talk of an "imperial Congress" also missed the point, they argued, because the constitutional framework contemplated congressional control of foreign commitments and policy decisions relating to military force. In December 1990, while the Iraqi crisis heightened, U.S. District Judge Harold H. Greene agreed in Dellums v. Bush (D.D.C. 1990) that the Constitution gives Congress authority over offensive warfare. At the same time, relying on the doctrine of RIPENESS, he declined to enjoin President Bush from acting without congressional authorization. Although denying he needed it before ordering an attack on Iraq, Bush requested congressional approval anyway in January 1991, and received it with votes of 52–47 in the Senate and 250–183 in the House of Representatives.

Overall, neither side clearly prevailed in the recurring constitutional disputes over warmaking. The subject remained largely within the "zone of twilight" identified during the Korean War by Justice ROBERT H. JACKSON in YOUNGSTOWN SHEET & TUBE CO. V. SAWYER (1952).

CHARLES A. LOFGREN
(1992)

(SEE ALSO: *Congress and Foreign Policy; Congressional War Powers; Foreign Affairs and the Constitution; Presidential War Powers; Senate and Foreign Policy; War, Foreign Affairs, and the Constitution.*)

Bibliography

ELY, JOHN HART 1988 Suppose Congress Wanted a War Powers Act That Worked. *Columbia Law Review* 88:1379–1431.

HENKIN, LOUIS et al. 1989 The Constitution in Its Third Century: Foreign Affairs. *American Journal of International Law* 83:713–900. Symposium Issue.

WORMUTH, FRANCIS D. and FIRMAGE, EDWIN B. 1989 *To Chain the Dog of War: The War Power of Congress in History and Law,* 2nd ed. Urbana: University of Illinois Press.

# WAR POWERS
## (Update 2)

The war powers have generated two principal constitutional issues. The first concerns the locus of power to initiate hostilities. The Constitution gives Congress the power to decide whether the nation should go to war while leaving the President authority to "repel sudden attacks." Since the 1950s, however, Presidents have repeatedly claimed that their FOREIGN AFFAIRS and COMMANDER-IN-CHIEF powers now permit them to initiate hostilities of any type, without Congress's approval.

This claimed presidential war power is defended on several grounds, none of which squares with ORGINAL INTENT. First, it is said that, given their "limited objectives," today's military conflicts are not "wars"; instead, they are labeled "peacekeeping" operations, "police actions," "humanitarian interventions," "offensive military attacks," or "nation building," for which congressional approval is allegedly unnecessary. Second, it is asserted that the power to "repel sudden attacks" permits the executive to initiate so-called "defensive wars" to protect U.S. interests throughout the world. Third, it is argued that because Presidents have previously used military force without Congress's approval, the power to declare war now belongs to the executive; this ignores YOUNGSTOWN SHEET AND TUBE CO. V. SAWYER (1952), IMMIGRATION AND NATURALIZATION SERVICE V. CHADHA (1983), and NEW YORK V. UNITED STATES (1992), which held that even long-standing practice cannot justify one branch's usurping the power of another. Finally, Presidents assert that they may use military force to implement the UNITED NATIONS CHARTER and mutual defense pacts such as the North Atlantic Treaty Organization (NATO) and the South East Asia Treaty Organization (SEATO) even though these treaties commit the U.S. to respond only in accord with its "constitutional processes."

President WILLIAM J. CLINTON has relied on these arguments in using military force without congressional approval. He unilaterally ordered missile strikes against Baghdad, Iraq, claiming this was an act of "self-defense" against an earlier attempt on the life of President GEORGE H. W. BUSH. Clinton used combat troops for "nation building" in Somalia without congressional sanction. He threatened to invade Haiti "to carry out the will of the United Nations," denying that Congress's permission was needed. He ordered air strikes in Bosnia and Kosovo as part of joint UN–NATO operations, without prior consent from Congress.

Lawsuits challenging presidential war-making have uniformly failed on JUSTICIABILITY grounds. *Raines v. Byrd* (1997) will make future challenges by members of Congress even more difficult. *Raines* suggested that as a matter of SEPARATION OF POWERS, Congress lacks STANDING to challenge actions of the President because the role of Article III courts is to protect the "rights and liberties of individual citizens," not redress "injury to official authority or power."

The second major question involving the war powers is the extent to which they may support domestic LEGISLATION. This became a critical issue after WORLD WAR I when Congress invoked its war powers to enact liquor PROHIBITION, operate the nation's rail and communications systems, outlaw profiteering, prosecute strikers, suppress radicals, and censor the leftist press. The Supreme Court, though upholding most of these laws, agreed that war powers legislation is subject to JUDICIAL REVIEW. Since the expansion of the COMMERCE CLAUSE in the late-1930s, Congress has had little need to use its war powers for domestic purposes. Yet to the extent UNITED STATES V. LÓPEZ (1995) signals a narrowing of the commerce power, Congress may again be tempted to invoke its war powers in the domestic sphere. Should this occur, questions concerning the scope of these powers may return to center stage.

CHRISTOPHER N. MAY
(2000)

(SEE ALSO: *Congress and Foreign Policy; Congressional Standing; Congressional War Powers; Presidential Powers; Senate and Foreign Policy; War, Foreign Affairs, and the Constitution.*)

Bibliography
ELY, JOHN HART 1993 *War and Responsibility: Constitutional Lessons of Vietnam and its Aftermath.* Princeton, N.J.: Princeton University Press.
FISHER, LOUIS 1995 *Presidential War Power.* Lawrence: University Press of Kansas.
MAY, CHRISTOPHER N. 1989 *In the Name of War: Judicial Review and the War Powers since 1918.* Cambridge, Mass.: Harvard University Press.
U.S. SENATE, COMMITTEE ON FOREIGN RELATIONS 1967 *National Commitments.* Senate Report No. 797, 90th Congress, 1st Session. Washington, D.C.: Government Printing Office.

# WAR POWERS ACTS
First War Powers Act
55 Stat. 838 (1941)
Second War Powers Act
56 Stat. 176 (1942)

Enacted less than two weeks after the bombing of Pearl Harbor (see WORLD WAR II), the First War Powers Act was similar to the WORLD WAR I Overman Act (1917). It delegated to the President virtually complete authority to reorganize the executive branch, the independent government agencies, and government corporations in any manner he deemed appropriate to expedite prosecution of the war. That power, and reorganizations accomplished under it, were to remain in force until six months after the end of the war. The act also authorized the President to censor mail and other forms of communication between the United States and foreign countries.

The Second War Powers Act, passed three months after the first, further strengthened the executive branch for conduct of the war. It authorized acquisition of land for military or naval purposes, by condemnation if necessary. It also suspended some provisions of the HATCH ACT (1939), relaxed NATURALIZATION standards for ALIENS serving in the armed forces, established procedures for war production contracting, and authorized several other adjustments of governmental affairs.

The War Powers Acts, like their predecessors, represented an attempt to accommodate the concentration of power necessary for the prosecution of the war to the accustomed forms of constitutional government.

DENNIS J. MAHONEY
(1986)

# WARRANT

See: Arrest Warrant; General Warrant; Search Warrant

# WARRANTLESS SEARCH

The FOURTH AMENDMENT makes no explicit provision for warrantless searches. The first clause of the amendment provides simply that "the right of the people to be secure in their persons, houses, papers, and effects, against unreasonable SEARCHES AND SEIZURES, shall not be violated." This general prohibition is followed by another clause that provides more particularly for the issuance of SEARCH WARRANTS. The amendment itself does not indicate what connection there is between the two clauses (which are separated only by a comma and the word "and"). Accordingly, its application to various kinds of warrantless searches has depended heavily on which clause the Supreme Court favors. On the one hand, the first clause might be regarded as the main provision, searches pursuant to a warrant being only one type of reasonable search that is authorized. Or, if the second clause be emphasized, the absence of a search warrant might be regarded ordinarily as itself making a search unreasonable, the requirement of a warrant being disregarded only in

exceptional circumstances including particularly lack of an opportunity to obtain one.

Some kinds of warrantless search are obviously necessary to the performance of other official duties. A police officer who unexpectedly makes an ARREST of someone committing a violent crime may necessarily search him for weapons. If the Fourth Amendment were deemed to prohibit every search without a warrant, one would be driven to the conclusion that the arresting officer's conduct was not a search at all within its contemplation. Current interpretation of the Fourth Amendment has avoided such an all-or-nothing approach. The amendment is applicable to a very wide range of official conduct interfering with expectations of privacy; within that context, the prevailing rules have established a number of situations in which a warrant to search is unnecessary.

The first such situation is the SEARCH INCIDENT TO AN ARREST. The need for an arresting officer to ensure that the person whom he arrests does not have in his possession a weapon or means of escape is the basis for the most frequently applied exception to the requirement of a warrant. Because police actively engaged in crime prevention often come on circumstances calling for an arrest without advance notice, a search incident to the arrest must be made without a warrant. Although not strictly necessary to effectuate the arrest, another reason for allowing a search is to prevent the arrestee from destroying EVIDENCE in his possession. The Supreme Court said in CHIMEL V. CALIFORNIA (1969) that all three justifications are sufficient to authorize a search of the arrestee's person and the area "within his immediate control" from which he might grab something. That general rule defines an area that may be searched without a warrant following an arrest, whether or not there is particular reason to believe that anything subject to seizure is there to be grabbed and, indeed, whether or not there is reason to believe that the arrestee is likely to grab anything. In effect, the rule authorizes a not-too-intensive search of the arrestee, including small containers on his person like a wallet or purse, and a small area around the place of the arrest. If a person were arrested in his home, the rule would authorize a limited search of the table or desk at which he sat, but not all the contents of the room or the contents of other rooms.

The scope of this rule illustrates a general feature of the exceptions to the warrant requirement. Although from time to time the Court has intimated that such exceptions depend on an emergency that demands a search before a warrant could practicably be obtained, the rule does not depend on a particularized finding of that kind. In some cases, the rule has been applied to uphold a search even though the arresting officers could easily have (or even had) removed the person from the area searched or immobilized him. (One might note also that the rule applies fully to arrests that are not unanticipated, even though in that case a warrant could presumably have been obtained.) The evident rationale is that a warrantless search incident to an arrest is so often necessary that it is impractical to require particular justification in each case.

Warrants are not required for AUTOMOBILE SEARCHES in various circumstances. Although automobiles (and other motor vehicles) as private places enjoy the protection of the Fourth Amendment, two distinct lines of analysis have markedly limited the application to them of the requirement of a search warrant. Automobiles, the Supreme Court has said, are subject to much greater regulation and inspection than dwellings; the expectation of privacy in them is much less. Having reached that judgment, the Court has not modified it to differentiate between areas like the back seat that are generally open to view and closed or concealed areas like the trunk or glove compartment that are not.

If police officers obtain lawful custody of an automobile which they have PROBABLE CAUSE to search for evidence of a crime, a warrantless search is allowed for some period, a few hours at least, after custody is obtained. This rule is based not only on the lesser expectation of privacy attached to an automobile but also on its mobility and the unpredictability with which custody often is obtained. The Supreme Court has not been persuaded that the immobilization of the car while it is in custody ordinarily makes it unnecessary to allow a search until a warrant has been obtained. Second, if officers have lawful custody of an automobile and routinely follow a regular custodial procedure, like an inventory of its contents, a search performed as part of the procedure is permitted. The routine nature of such practices, which are followed by many police departments, has persuaded the Supreme Court that they are reasonable. (Also, the arrest-incident exception authorizes a thorough search of the passenger compartment of an automobile, including all containers within it, as an incident of the arrest of an occupant.)

A search at the time and place of an arrest is likely to be limited by the circumstances to weapons or means of escape and only the most obvious evidentiary items. Later, when the person is about to be placed in detention or while he is in detention, there is opportunity for a more thorough search; sometimes, the evidentiary significance of an item is not plain at the time of the arrest and is revealed as the investigation proceeds. The police have authority to make a very thorough search without a warrant of items removed from the arrested person and held by them while he is lawfully detained temporarily in a jail or similar facility. The arrest, it has been said, being the more significant interference with liberty, includes the lesser intrusion on privacy occasioned by the search. Furthermore, a search is authorized at the time and place of the arrest and it is routine administrative procedure to impound and perhaps inventory a person's effects before he is placed in a cell; therefore, it is reasoned, the fact that some time elapses between the arrest and the search has no constitutional significance.

The most general exception to the requirement of a search warrant allows the police and other public officials to search without a warrant in EXIGENT CIRCUMSTANCES: an emergency furnishing adequate grounds for a search that has to be carried out before a warrant can be obtained. A search incident to the unanticipated arrest of a potentially dangerous person is an example of this more general category, although justified by a special rule. Another example is an entry and search of private premises while in "hot pursuit" of someone who has just committed a crime; police officers are not required to interrupt the chase until they have obtained a warrant. Similarly, officers responding to a cry for help or acting to avert a danger inside private premises need not wait to obtain a warrant. It has usually been held also that if officers have particular, reliable information that specific evidence of crime is about to be destroyed and there is not time to obtain a warrant, they can enter to prevent its destruction.

In such cases, authority to search without a warrant is tailored to the emergency. The officers claiming the authority must not themselves be responsible for the existence of the emergency; if, for example, they unreasonably delayed applying for a warrant until it was too late, they could not then assert their inability to obtain a warrant. Also, the authority extends only as far as the emergency requires. Entering in hot pursuit, officers could also search for weapons that the person whom they are pursuing might use against them; but once having him in custody, they could not continue to search solely for evidence.

The regulation of persons and goods entering or leaving the country has always been understood to provide a special basis for warrantless searches. Public officials who supervise traffic across the border are authorized to inspect goods and to require a person crossing the border to submit to a thorough search. (See BORDER SEARCHES.) Some comprehensive statutory programs for the regulation of industry and commerce have authorized warrantless entries and inspections. Such procedures have been upheld if a requirement of a warrant might be expected to frustrate the regulatory program and the business in question is generally subject to close governmental supervision: for example, gun and liquor dealerships, and mines. Similarly, the Supreme Court has held that inspection visits to the home by a welfare official can be made a condition of receipt of public welfare. In other cases, the Court has concluded that the regulatory purpose of a statute did not require that warrantless (unannounced) searches be allowed.

In some circumstances, a brief invasion of personal privacy less intrusive than a full search is allowed without a warrant. Most common is the protective "frisk" or pat-down of a person whose conduct a police officer has reason to investigate and who he reasonably suspects may be armed. There being no opportunity to obtain a warrant, the safe performance of the officer's investigative duty justifies a limited search for weapons. Likewise, traffic officers are allowed to make routine checks for driver's licenses and automobile registrations, so long as the checks follow an established pattern or there are specific grounds for a departure from the pattern. Routine inspection of passengers and carry-on luggage has been upheld as a regulatory measure to prevent airplane hijacking. In these cases, not only is the procedure in question thought to be less objectionable than a full search; there is no way to accomplish the legitimate objective of the procedure consistently with a requirement of a warrant.

The Fourth Amendment does not insist that persons protect a privacy that they are willing to forego. Accordingly, a warrant to search is not required if a person having authority to do so voluntarily admits public officials and permits them to search. A consensual search that is successful often is challenged later on the grounds that consent was not given fully voluntarily or did not extend to the actual search; or, if the premises are shared by others, it may be claimed that the person who consented did not have the independent authority to do so. While a resolution of such issues may depend on difficult matters of fact, the basic principle that a search with consent does not require a warrant is unquestioned.

Those who believe that the requirement of a search warrant is a significant protection against UNREASONABLE SEARCHES may conclude that the Supreme Court has drawn the categories of lawful warrantless searches too broadly. Categories like the search incident to arrest, automobile search, and jail search appear to depend only on the premises that such searches often are fruitful and sometimes have to be made before a warrant can be obtained. But the categories are general and require neither premise to be fulfilled in the particular case; each of them encourages the police to make a large number of searches routinely, without particular justification. This approach, it can be argued, is inconsistent with the plain purpose of the Fourth Amendment to prohibit *general* searches: unfocused, unlimited rummaging in the privacy of individuals.

Critics of the Court have observed also that its analysis of warrantless searches is to a considerable degree incoherent. Why, for example, should an arrest justify the search of any area surrounding the arrestee, if he can be and often is removed from that place before the search is made? Why should automobiles, which often are used for the same private purposes as dwellings, be treated categorically as less private? Why should an arrest automatically defeat the person's separate interest in the privacy of items in his possession? The Court's failure to provide convincing answers to such questions has rendered this part of Fourth Amendment DOCTRINE only a set of rules without supporting rationale.

A defense of the rules for warrantless searches begins with the premise that warrants are peculiarly appropriate for planned investigative searches and have much less utility in the ordinary unplanned encounters between police or other public officials and private persons. If legitimate police duties justify an encounter, then a search related in purpose is also legitimate. This approach places a great deal of emphasis on the requirement that a search be "reasonable" and construes that term with attention to common police practices as well as the individual interest in privacy. To limit warrantless searches to cases of manifest necessity would blink the natural—and therefore reasonable—impulse of police officers to search whatever is legitimately in their custody and may furnish evidence of crime. Some explanation for the breadth of the exceptions to the requirement of a warrant may lie also in the fact that the issue is almost always tested in the context of a criminal prosecution, when the defendant seeks the protection of the EXCLUSIONARY RULE to avoid the admission of incriminating evidence that a search has uncovered.

LLOYD L. WEINREB
(1986)

Bibliography

AMERICAN LAW INSTITUTE   1975   *A Model Code of Pre-Arraignment Procedure.* Philadelphia: American Law Institute.
AMSTERDAM, ANTHONY G.   1974   Perspectives on the Fourth Amendment. *Minnesota Law Review* 58:349–477.
LAFAVE, WAYNE R.   1978   *Search and Seizure.* St. Paul, Minn.: West Publishing Co.
LANDYNSKI, JACOB W.   1966   *Search and Seizure and the Supreme Court.* Baltimore: Johns Hopkins University Press.
WEINREB, LLOYD L.   1974   Generalities of the Fourth Amendment. *University of Chicago Law Review* 42:47–85.

# WARREN, CHARLES
## (1868–1954)

Charles Warren was a Boston lawyer who, as assistant attorney general of the United States, drafted the ESPIONAGE ACT and argued many cases before the Supreme Court. He became an expert on constitutional and legal history. He wrote excellent books in the tradition of the old school of high-minded conservative nationalists who rejected CHARLES BEARD's economic interpretation. Among his leading books are *A History of the American Bar, A History of Harvard Law School, The Supreme Court in United States History*, which won the Pulitzer Prize, *Congress, the Constitution, and the Supreme Court*, and *The Making of the Constitution.* His works still merit reading and remain influential. His article on the JUDICIARY ACT OF 1789 helped lead the Supreme Court in ERIE RAILROAD V. TOMKINS (1938) to overrule almost a century of decisions based on SWIFT V. TYSON (1842).

LEONARD W. LEVY
(1986)

# WARREN, EARL
## (1891–1974)

The fourteenth CHIEF JUSTICE of the United States, Earl Warren presided over the most sweeping judicial reinterpretation of the Constitution in generations. He served from October 1953 to June 1969. In that time the SUPREME COURT, overruling the doctrine that SEPARATE BUT EQUAL facilities for black persons satisfied the requirement of EQUAL PROTECTION, outlawed official racial SEGREGATION in every area of life. The Court ended the long-established rural bias of legislative representation by opening the question to judicial scrutiny and then ruling that citizens must be represented equally in state legislatures and the national House of Representatives. It imposed constitutional restraints for the first time on the law of LIBEL, hitherto a matter entirely of state concern. It applied to the states the standards set by the BILL OF RIGHTS for federal CRIMINAL PROCEDURE: the right of all poor defendants to free counsel, for example, and the prohibition of unreasonable SEARCHES AND SEIZURES, enforced by the EXCLUSIONARY RULE. It limited government power to punish unorthodox beliefs and enlarged the individual's freedom to express herself or himself in unconventional, even shocking ways.

The WARREN COURT, as it was generally called, had as profound an impact on American life as any Supreme Court since the time of JOHN MARSHALL. It was extraordinary not only in the scale but in the direction of its exercise of power. From Marshall's day to the Court's clash with President FRANKLIN D. ROOSEVELT in the 1930s judges had exercised a conservative influence in the American system. Shortly before his appointment to the Court in 1941 ROBERT H. JACKSON wrote that "never in its entire history can the Supreme Court be said to have for a single hour been representative of anything except the relatively conservative forces of its day." But the Warren Court in its time was perhaps *the* principal engine of American liberal reform.

Earl Warren seemed an unlikely figure to lead such a judicial revolution. He was a Republican politician, the elected attorney general of California and for three terms its phenomenally popular governor. In 1948 he was the Republican candidate for vice-president, on the ticket headed by Thomas E. Dewey. On naming him Chief Justice, President DWIGHT D. EISENHOWER emphasized his "middle-of-the-road philosophy." Yet within a few years billboards in the South demanded Warren's IMPEACHMENT, and the paranoid right charged that he was doing the work of communism. Putting aside the rantings of extremists, there was no doubt that as Chief Justice Warren consistently favored liberal values and unembarrassedly translated them into constitutional doctrine. Where did that commitment come from in a man whose appearance was that of a bland, hearty political figure?

There were in fact clues in his life and earlier career. He was born in Los Angeles in 1891, the son of a Norwegian immigrant who worked for the Southern Pacific Railroad. He knew poverty and personal tragedy. As a young man he was a railroad callboy, waking up the gangs, and he saw men with their legs cut off in accidents carried in on planks. His father was murdered, the murderer never found: a traumatic event that must have helped to point Warren in the direction of justice, legal and social. He put himself through college and law school at the University of California. After a brief try at private practice he spent all his life in public office, as a local prosecutor and crusading district attorney before winning statewide office.

In California politics he at first had the support of conservatives. As attorney general he blocked the nomination of Max Radin, a law professor known as a legal realist, to the state supreme court because Radin was a "radical." As attorney general and governor Warren was a leading proponent of the WORLD WAR II federal order removing all persons of Japanese ancestry from the West Coast and putting them in desolate camps; opposing their return in 1943, he said, "If the Japs are released, no one will be able to tell a saboteur from any other Jap." (In a memoir published after his death, Warren wrote: "I have since deeply regretted the removal order and my own testimony advocating it, because it was not in keeping with our American concept of freedom and the rights of citizens. . . .")

But in 1945 Warren astounded political California by proposing a state program of prepaid medical insurance. Characteristically, he did so not for ideological but for human, practical reasons: he had fallen ill and realized how catastrophic serious illness would be for a person without resources. Then, in his last two terms as governor, he became an apostle of liberal Republicanism. A later Democratic governor, Edmund G. Brown, said Warren "was the best governor California ever had. . . . He felt the people of California were in his care, and he cared for them."

Many Americans and other people around the world saw that same paternal image in Earl Warren the Chief Justice, for he became an international symbol. He represented the hope of authority bringing justice to the downtrodden, an American vision of change by law rather than by rebellion. A single case gave Warren that status: BROWN V. BOARD OF EDUCATION, the 1954 school segregation decision. In recent years the Supreme Court had chipped away at PLESSY V. FERGUSON, the 1896 decision allowing what were termed "separate but equal" facilities but what were almost always in fact grossly inferior schools and other public institutions for blacks. Yet in 1953 seventeen southern and border states, with forty percent of the national enrollment, still confined black children to separate public schools; moreover, there was involved here, unlike higher education, the compulsory daily association of children. The emotional content of the legal question was high. The Court had given the most gingerly handling to the question, restoring the issue to the calendar for reargument.

Warren became Chief Justice before the second argument. The following May he delivered the opinion for a unanimous Court holding public school segregation unconstitutional. The unanimity was itself a striking feature of the result, and a surprising one. Expected southern resistance made unanimity politically essential, but the known attitudes of some members of the Court had suggested the likelihood of dissents. Richard Kluger's exhaustive study has demonstrated that the new Chief Justice played a crucial part in his management of the process inside the Court. After argument he delayed formal discussion of the cases in conference to avoid the development of rigid positions among the nine Justices. Then he stated as his view that the separate-but-equal doctrine could not be maintained unless one thought blacks inherently inferior: an approach likely to induce shame in any judge prepared to argue for that outcome. He persuaded his colleagues even then to avoid a formal vote but to continue discussing the cases, in tight secrecy, among themselves. He wrote an opinion in simple terms. Finally, he persuaded reluctant members of the Court to join for the sake of unanimity. A law clerk present at a late meeting between the Chief Justice and the most reluctant, STANLEY F. REED, remembers him saying, "Stan, you're all by yourself in this now. You've got to decide whether it's really the best thing for the country."

What is known about the process of decision in the school cases throws lights on one question asked during his lifetime: did Chief Justice Warren exercise leadership or have influence in the Court beyond his own vote in conference? He shared that bench with men of strong personality and conviction: in particular HUGO L. BLACK, who said the judicial duty was to follow the literal language of the Constitution and found in it absolutes, and FELIX FRANKFURTER, who scorned absolutes and said the Court should defer to the political branches of government in applying the uncertain commands of the Constitution. Warren came to the Court utterly inexperienced in its work; how could he have effective influence? The school cases show that he did.

No Chief Justice can command his associates' beliefs. If Warren had served with different, more conservative colleagues, many of the views that made history might have been expressed by him in dissent. Changes while he was on the Court greatly affected the trend of doctrine, in particular the retirement of Justice Frankfurter in 1962 and his replacement by ARTHUR J. GOLDBERG, who was much readier to join Warren in intervening on behalf of liberal values. But the identification of that Court with its Chief Justice, for all its logical imperfection, has substantial basis in reality.

Warren wrote the opinions of the Court not only in *Brown* but in later cases that dramatically overturned expectations. The most important of these—Warren himself thought them the weightiest decisions of his years on the Court—were the REAPPORTIONMENT cases. A divided Supreme Court in COLEGROVE V. GREEN (1946) had refused to entertain an attack on numerical inequality in political districts, an opinion by Justice Frankfurter saying that courts must stay out of the "political thicket." In 1962 the Warren Court, in an opinion by Justice WILLIAM J. BRENNAN, overthrew that doctrine of reluctance and said that federal courts could consider issues of fairness in districting. The decision in BAKER V. CARR left open the substantive questions: must the population be the test of equality, or may states weigh geography or other factors in districting? Does the same standard apply to both houses of legislatures? The answers were given by Chief Justice Warren in 1964, in terms so firm that some who listened in the courtroom felt as if they were at a second American constitutional convention. In REYNOLDS V. SIMS Warren said for a 6–3 majority that every house of every state legislature must be apportioned on the basis of population alone, with the districts as nearly equal as practicable. Few cases in any court ever had so direct and immediate an impact on a nation's politics; reapportionment was required in most of the fifty states, ancient legislative expectations were upset, new suburban power vindicated. Justice JOHN MARSHALL HARLAN predicted in dissent, as had Justice Frankfurter in *Baker v. Carr*, that the courts would not be able to manage the apportionment litigation—or to enforce their decisions against political resistance. But the gloomy prediction was wrong. Resistance from political incumbents quickly collapsed; nothing like the emotional public opposition to the school segregation cases developed in any region.

Emotions were aroused by Warren's opinion in MIRANDA V. ARIZONA (1966), holding that before questioning an arrested person the police must warn him that he has a right to remain silent and a right to see a lawyer first—one provided by the state if he cannot afford one—and that a confession obtained in violation of that rule is inadmissible at trial. The decision touched a nerve among police, prosecutors, and others convinced that judges were impeding the fight against crime. *Miranda* climaxed a series of cases holding local police to the standards of the Bill of Rights: for example, MAPP V. OHIO (1961), exclusion of illegally obtained evidence; GIDEON V. WAINWRIGHT (1963), right to counsel; *Griffin v. California* (1965), right against self-incrimination;, each overruling an earlier decision. In *Spano v. New York* (1959) Warren commented: "The abhorrence of society to the use of involuntary confessions does not turn alone on their inherent untrustworthiness. It also turns on the deep-rooted feeling that the police must obey the law while enforcing the law; that in the end life and liberty can be as much endangered from illegal methods used to convict those thought to be criminals as from the actual criminals themselves." Impatient with reviewing the facts in case after case of claimed coercion, the Court under Warren sought a general prophylactic rule—and wrote it in *Miranda*.

Objection to the *Miranda* decision came not only from the law enforcement community. More dispassionate critics saw it as an example of overreaching by the Warren Court. The opinion seemed more legislative in character than judicial, laying out what amounted to a code of police procedure with little basis in precedent. Moreover, the Court did not confront a situation in which reform by other means was blocked, as it had with school segregation and malapportioned legislatures; various reformers were working on the confession problem.

Freedom of expression was another subject of fundamental constitutional development during the Warren years. The most important single decision was probably NEW YORK TIMES V. SULLIVAN (1964), holding that a public official may not recover libel damages unless the statement was published with knowledge of its falsity or in reckless disregard of truth or falsity. That opinion was by Justice Brennan. Justice WILLIAM O. DOUGLAS wrote for the Court in LAMONT V. POSTMASTER GENERAL (1965), holding that a statute requiring the post office to detain "Communist political propaganda" from abroad unless the addressee requested its delivery violated the FIRST AMENDMENT—the first federal statute that the Supreme Court ever held invalid under that amendment. Warren joined in these and other expansive decisions. He wrote for a 5–4 majority in UNITED STATES V. ROBEL (1967), striking down a law that forbade the employment in defense plants of

any member of an organization required to register under the Subversive Activities Control Act. Warren's opinion for a unanimous Court in *Bond v. Floyd* (1966) held that the Georgia legislature could not exclude a duly elected member because he had expressed admiration for draft resisters.

The one area of expression in which Warren departed from the majority of his colleagues was OBSCENITY. He thought that local and national authorities should have a relatively free hand to combat what he evidently regarded as a social evil. Thus, while in *Miranda* imposing a national standard for fair pretrial procedures in criminal cases, he argued in dissent in JACOBELLIS V. OHIO (1964) that each local community should be allowed to fix its own standard of obscenity, a view that became the law under Chief Justice WARREN E. BURGER in MILLER V. CALIFORNIA (1973). Another example of a departure from Warren's usual approach came when gambling was involved. He generally favored broad application of the right against self-incrimination; but when the rule was applied for the benefit of a gambler in MARCHETTI V. UNITED STATES (1968), he alone dissented. Once again he saw a social evil.

Scholarly critics of Chief Justice Warren saw the obscenity and gambling cases as illustrating a fundamental shortcoming in a judge: a concern to reach particular results rather than to work out principles applicable whoever the parties in a case might be. In Warren's view, it seemed, justice consisted not in providing a philosophically satisfactory process and basis of decision but in seeing that the right side, the good side, won in each case. Many of the commentators regretted the lack of a consistent doctrinal thread in his opinions. There was nothing like Justice Black's exaltation of the constitutional text, or Justice Frankfurter's institutional concern for self-restraint.

G. Edward White, in a full-length study of Warren's work, rejected the general scholarly view that Warren had no rudder as a judge and lacked craftsmanship. He was an ethicist, White concluded, who saw his craft as "discovering ethical imperatives in a maze of confusion"—and in the Constitution. Thus the prosecutor so hard on corruption that he was called a boy scout, the Californian politician who stood aloof from party machines lest he be sullied, became a judicial enforcer of ethical imperatives. In general his sympathy lay with the little person, with victims, with people excluded from the benefits of our democracy. But he also was in the tradition of the American Progressives, who thought that government could be made to work for the people. Those two themes came together in the reapportionment cases, decisions designed to make democracy work better by making the electoral process fairer. John Hart Ely, in an analysis of judicial review as practiced in the Warren years, suggested that many of the pathbreaking decisions had a democratic structural purpose: to assure access for the powerless and thus make the system work.

There was a directness, a simplicity in Warren's opinions on the largest issues. "Legislators represent people," he wrote in the reapportionment cases, "not acres or trees. Legislators are elected by voters, not farms or cities or economic interests. . . . The weight of a citizen's vote cannot be made to depend on where he lives." When the Court held unconstitutional a statute depriving a native-born American of his citizenship for deserting the armed forces in time of war, TROP V. DULLES (1958), Warren for a plurality argued that EXPATRIATION was a CRUEL AND UNUSUAL PUNISHMENT in violation of the Eighth Amendment. The death penalty would not have been "cruel," he conceded, but the deprivation of citizenship was, for it caused "the total destruction of the individual's status in organized society" and cost him "the right to have rights."

Warren's whole career suggests that he was a person born not to muse but to act—and to govern. That view provides a connecting thread through all the offices he held. In each he exerted his powerful abilities in the ways open to him. As a prosecutor he fought crime. As wartime attorney general and governor he was a patriot, worrying about spies. In the postwar years, he turned to the social problems of an expanding California. As Chief Justice, too, he was committed to action, to using the opportunities available to make an impression on American life: to break the pattern of malapportionment, to attack local police abuses, to condemn racial discrimination. The instinct to govern did not leave Earl Warren when he put on a robe.

Many regarded him as a heroic figure because he put aside philosophical concerns and technical legal issues and dealt squarely with what he considered outrageous situations. And there were outrages in American life: official racism, political discrimination, abuse of police authority, suppression of free expression. Warren as Chief Justice had the conviction, the humanity, and the capacity for growth to deal effectively with those issues inside that prickly institution, the Supreme Court. But there were those who shared Justice LEARNED HAND's doubts about rule by judges, however beneficent. "For myself," Hand wrote in 1958, with the contemporary Supreme Court in mind, "it would be most irksome to be ruled by a bevy of Platonic Guardians, even if I knew how to choose them, which I assuredly do not." Earl Warren may have been the closest thing the United States has had to a constitutional Platonic Guardian, dispensing law without any sensed limit of authority except what he saw as the good of society. He was a decent, kindly law-giver. But the exercise of such power by other judges—before and after Warren—has not always had kindly or rational results. The questions about judicial power remain after its extraordinary uses in the Warren years.

ANTHONY LEWIS
(1986)

Bibliography

ELY, JOHN HART 1980 *Democracy and Distrust: A Theory of Judicial Review.* Cambridge, Mass.: Harvard University Press.
KLUGER, RICHARD 1975 *Simple Justice: The History of Brown v. Board of Education and Black America's Struggle for Equality.* New York: Knopf.
SCHWARTZ, BERNARD 1983 *Superchief.* Garden City, N.Y.: Doubleday.
WHITE, G. EDWARD 1982 *Earl Warren: A Public Life.* New York: Oxford University Press.

# WARREN COURT

It was surely the best known Supreme Court in history, and probably the most controversial. Its grand themes—racial equality, REAPPORTIONMENT, the separation of religion and education, DUE PROCESS—became matters of public consciousness. Its leading judges—HUGO L. BLACK, WILLIAM O. DOUGLAS, FELIX FRANKFURTER, JOHN MARSHALL HARLAN, and EARL WARREN—became personages in whom the general public took an interest. When the Warren Court came into being in October 1953, the Supreme Court was the least known and least active of the major branches of government; by the retirement of Chief Justice Warren in June 1969, nearly everyone in American life had been affected by a Warren Court decision, and a great many Americans had firm opinions about the Supreme Court. When Warren was appointed Chief Justice, few commentators took note of the fact that he had had no previous judicial experience and had spent the last twelve years as a state politician. By the time WARREN E. BURGER succeeded Warren as Chief Justice the process of nominating a Justice to the Supreme Court had become an elaborate search for the "experienced," uncontroversial, and predictable nominee, and the Court was to lower its profile again.

The Warren Court years, then, were years in which the Supreme Court of the United States made itself a vital force in American culture. A striking pattern of interchange between the Court and the general public emerged in these years. As public issues, such as CIVIL RIGHTS or legislative malapportionment surfaced, these issues became translated into constitutional law cases. The Court, expanding the conventional ambit of its JURISDICTION, reached out to decide those cases, thereby making an authoritative contribution to the public debate. As the Court continued to reach out, the public came to rely on its presence, and the American JUDICIAL SYSTEM came to be perceived as a forum for the resolution of contemporary social problems. The use of the Supreme Court as an institution for redressing grievances ignored by Congress or state legislatures became common with the Warren Court.

The origins of the Warren Court can officially be traced to September 8, 1953, when Chief Justice FRED M. VINSON died of a heart attack. By September 30, President DWIGHT D. EISENHOWER had named Warren, the governor of California who had been a rival candidate for the Republican presidential nomination in 1952, as Vinson's successor. This nominal creation of the Warren Court did not, however, hint at its character. Indeed that character was not immediately apparent. Even the Court's first momentous decision, BROWN V. BOARD OF EDUCATION (1954), announced in May of its first term, was in some respects a holdover from the Vinson Court. *Brown* had been argued before the Vinson Court, was based in part on Vinson Court precedents chipping away at RACIAL DISCRIMINATION in education, and was decided by a Court whose only new member was its Chief Justice. It was a cautious decision, apparently assuming that DESEGREGATION would be a long and slow process.

But *Brown* was also the Warren Court's baptism of fire. All the elements that were to mark subsequent major Warren Court decisions were present in *Brown*. *Brown* involved a major social problem, racial discrimination, translated into a legal question, the constitutionality of SEPARATE BUT EQUAL public schools. It posed an issue that no other branch of government was anxious to address. It raised questions that had distinctively moral implications: in invalidating racial SEGREGATION the Court was condemning the idea of racial supremacy. And it affected the lives of ordinary citizens, not merely in the South, not merely in public education, for the Court's series of PER CURIAM decisions after *Brown* revealed that it did not consider racial segregation any more valid in other public facilities than it had in schools. The Warren Court had significantly altered race relations in America.

The context of the Warren Court's first momentous decision was decisive in shaping the Court's character as a branch of government that was not disinclined to resolve difficult social issues, not hesitant to foster social change, not reluctant to involve itself in controversy. By contrast, the legislative and executive branches appeared as equivocators and fainthearts. The Warren Court was deluged with criticism for its decision in *Brown*, both from persons who resisted having to change habits of prejudice and from scholars who faulted the reasoning of the Court's opinion. This response only seemed to make the Court more resolute.

The deliberations of *Brown* also served to identify some of the Justices whose presence was to help shape the character of the Warren Court. Earl Warren transformed a closely divided Court, which had postponed a decision on *Brown* because it was uncertain and fragmented on the case's resolution, into a unanimous voice. That transformation was a testament to Warren's remarkable ability to relate to other people and to convince them of the rightness of his views. In *Brown* he had argued that those who would support the separate but equal doctrine should recognize that it was based on claims of racial superiority. That argument struck home to at least two Justices, TOM C. CLARK and STANLEY F. REED, who had grown up in the South. When Warren had finished his round of office visits and discussions, he had secured nine votes for his majority opinion and had suppressed the writing of separate concurrences. ROBERT H. JACKSON, a long holdout in *Brown* who was dubious about the possibility of finding a doctrinal rationale to invalidate the separate but equal principle, joined Warren's opinion and left a hospital bed to appear in court the day the decision was announced.

A silent partner in the *Brown* decision had been Felix Frankfurter. By the late 1950s Frankfurter's jurisprudence, which stressed a limited role for judges in reviewing the constitutionality of legislative decisions, had rigidified, isolating Frankfurter from many other justices and identifying him as one of the guardians of a theory of judicial self-restraint. Judicial self-restraint in *Brown* would have supported the separate but equal doctrine, since that doctrine itself signified a judicial reluctance to disturb legislative enactments forcibly separating persons on the basis of race. Frankfurter, however, could not abide the consequences of continued deference to the separate but equal doctrine, but he did not want to expose the lack of "restraint" that his position assumed. He accordingly confided his views on *Brown* only to Warren and worked toward fashioning a decree—containing the controversial phrase ALL DELIBERATE SPEED as a guideline for implementing desegregation—that would temper the shock of the *Brown* mandate. At the appropriate moment he joined Warren's opinion.

The partnership of Warren and Frankfurter in the segregation cases contrasted with the usual posture of both Justices on the Warren Court. Warren's approach to judging, with its relative indifference to doctrinal reasoning and to institutional considerations, its emphasis on the morally or ethically appropriate result, and its expansive interpretation of the Court's review powers, was the antithesis of Frankfurter's. For the most part the two men sharply disagreed over the results or the reasoning of major Warren Court decisions, with Frankfurter enlisting a stable of academic supporters in his behalf and Warren seeking to bypass doctrinal or institutional objections to make broad ethical appeals to the public at large.

The presence of two other significant Warren Court Justices, HUGO BLACK and WILLIAM O. DOUGLAS, was also felt in *Brown*. Black, a native of Clay County, Alabama, and fleetingly a member of the Ku Klux Klan, had been an opponent of racial discrimination since being elected to the Senate in 1926. He had supported the Vinson Court precedents crippling "separate but equal," for which he had received outspoken criticism in his home state. His position in *Brown* was well known early on: an uncompromising opposition to discriminatory practices. Such positions were characteristic of Black on the Warren Court. He staked out positions decisively, held them with tenacity, and constantly sought to convert others to his views. His theory of constitutional adjudication, which placed great emphasis on a "literal" but "liberal" construction of BILL OF RIGHTS protections, was a major contribution to Warren Court jurisprudence.

Equally outspoken and tenacious, and even more activist than Black, was William O. Douglas, whose academic experience, which paralleled Frankfurter's, had generated a strikingly different conception of judicial behavior. Douglas did not agonize over issues of institutional deference and doctrinal principle; he took his power to make law as a given and sought to use it to promote values in which he believed. The values were principally those associated with twentieth-century libertarianism and egalitarianism. Douglas spoke out for small business, organized labor, disadvantaged minorities, consumers, the poor, dissidents, and those who valued their privacy and their freedom from governmental restraint. Douglas's role on the Warren Court was that of an ideologue, anxious to secure results and confident that he could find doctrinal justifications. Together, Black and Douglas prodded the Court to vindicate even the most unpopular forms of free expression and minority rights.

While the Warren Court was generally regarded as an activist Court and a liberal Court, it was not exclusively so, and not all its members could be characterized as either activists or liberals. Until his retirement in 1962, at the midway point of Warren's tenure, Frankfurter had vociferously protested against an excessively broad interpretation of the Court's review powers, a position that resulted in his supporting the constitutionality of a number of "conservative" legislative policies. Other Justices on the Warren Court were either disinclined to exercise sweeping review powers or less enthusiastic than Warren, Black, or Douglas about the policies of twentieth-century liberalism. Most influential among those Justices was John Harlan, an Eisenhower appointee who joined the Court in 1955 and remained until 1971.

Harlan frequently and adroitly rejected the assumptions of Warren Court majorities that "every major social ill in this country can find its cure in some constitutional "principle" and that the Court could be "a general haven for reform movements." Moreover, in a group of Justices who were often impatient to reach results and not inclined to linger over the niceties of doctrinal analysis, Harlan distinguished himself by producing painstakingly crafted opinions. Often Harlan's quarrels with a majority would be over the method by which results were reached; his concurrences and dissents regularly demonstrated the complexities of constitutional adjudication.

The Warren Court will be best known for its identification with three themes: egalitarianism, liberalism, and activism. From *Brown* through POWELL V. MCCORMACK (1969), Earl Warren's last major opinion, the Court demonstrated a dedication to the principle of equality, a principle that, in Archibald Cox's felicitous phrase, "once loosed . . . is not easily cabined." Race relations were the initial context in which the Court attempted to refine the meaning of equal justice in America. Once the ordeal of *Brown* was concluded, that meaning seemed comparatively straightforward. In a series of *per curiam* opinions, the Court extended *Brown* to public beaches, parks, recreational facilities, housing developments, public buildings, eating facilities, and hospitals. The conception of equality embodied by these decisions was that of equality of opportunity: blacks could not be denied the opportunity of access to public places.

*Brown* had been rationalized by the Court on similar grounds: the gravamen of the injustice in a segregated school system was a denial of equal educational opportunities to blacks. But equality of opportunity became difficult to distinguish, in the race cases, from the conception of equality of condition. The Court presumed that classifications based on race were constitutionally suspect and seemed to suggest that equal justice in the race relations area required something like color-blindness. Classifications based on race or skin color not only denied black Americans equal opportunities, they also were not based on any rational judgment, since the human condition transcended superficial differences of race. After the *per curiams*, the massive resistance to *Brown*, and the civil rights movement of the 1960s, the Court gradually perceived that equality in race relations necessitated the eradication of stigmas based on skin color. This momentum of egalitarianism culminated in *Loving v. Virginia* (1967), in which the Court invalidated state prohibitions of miscegenous marriages, thereby affirming the absence of fundamental differences between blacks and whites.

Between the *per curiams* and *Loving* had come skirmishes between the Court and groups resisting its mandates for change in race relations. COOPER V. AARON (1963) involved a challenge by the governor of Arkansas to compulsory integration in the Little Rock school system. The Court, in an unprecedented opinion signed individually by all nine Justices, reaffirmed the obligations of Southern schools to integrate. *Goss v. Board of Education* (1963) invalidated minority-to-majority transfer plans whose purpose was to allow students to attend schools outside their districts in which their race was in the majority. HEART OF ATLANTA MOTEL V. UNITED STATES (1964) and *Katzenbach v. McClung* (1964) used the Constitution's COMMERCE CLAUSE and the CIVIL RIGHTS ACT OF 1964 to prevent hotels and restaurants from refusing service to blacks. BURTON V. WILMINGTON PARKING AUTHORITY (1961) and *Evans v. Newton* (1966) showed the Court's willingness to use the DOCTRINE of "STATE ACTION" to compel ostensibly private establishments (restaurants and parks) to admit blacks.

After *Loving* the Court grew impatient with resistance to the implementation of its decrees in *Brown*. In GREEN V. NEW KENT COUNTY SCHOOL BOARD (1968) the Court scrutinized the actual effect of "freedom of choice" plans, where students attended schools of their own choice. The Court found that the system perpetuated segregation when eighty-five percent of the black children in a school district had remained in a previously all-black school and no white child had chosen to attend that school, and advised that "delays are no longer tolerable." Finally, in ALEXANDER V. HOLMES COUNTY BOARD OF EDUCATION (1969) the Court declared that the time for racial integration of previously segregated school systems was "at once." *Green* and *Alexander* compelled integration of schools and other public facilities. Equality of condition had become the dominant means to achieve the goal of equality.

One can see a similar trend in the area of reapportionment. For the first half of the twentieth century, including the early years of the Warren Court, state legislatures were not apportioned solely on the basis of population. Upper houses of legislatures had a variety of means for electing their members, some deliberately unresponsive to demographic concerns, and few states apportioned legislative seats on the basis of ONE PERSON, ONE VOTE. In *Baker v. Carr* (1962), however, the Court announced that it would scrutinize Tennessee's system of electing state legislators to see if it conformed to the population of districts in the state. Justice WILLIAM J. BRENNAN, a former student of Frankfurter's, rejected the POLITICAL QUESTION doctrine Frankfurter had consistently imposed as a barrier to Court determination of reapportionment cases. Frankfurter wrote an impassioned dissent in *Baker*, but the way was clear for constitutional challenges to malapportioned legislatures. By 1964 suits challenging legislative apportionment schemes had been filed in more than thirty states.

Chief Justice Warren's opinion for the Court in REYNOLDS V. SIMS (1964), a case testing Alabama's reapportionment system, demonstrated how the idea of equality had infused the reapportionment cases. "We are cautioned," he wrote, "about the dangers of entering into political thickets and mathematical quagmires. Our answer to this: a denial of constitutionally protected rights demands judicial protection; our oath and our office require no less of us. . . . To the extent that a citizen's right to vote is debased, he is that much less a citizen." Equality did not mean merely an equal opportunity to have representatives from one's district in a state legislature, but that all votes of all citizens were to be treated equally: voting, like race relations, was to be an area in which equality of condition was to prevail.

The Court provided for such equality even where the state's citizens had indicated a preference for another scheme. In LUCAS V. FORTY-FOURTH GENERAL ASSEMBLY (1964), the Court invalidated Colorado's districting plan apportioning only one house of the legislature on a population basis. This plan had been adopted after a statewide referendum in which a majority rejected population-based apportionment for both houses. Warren found that the scheme did not satisfy the equal protection clause because it was not harmonious with the principle of one person, one vote. Voting was a condition of CITIZENSHIP, not just an opportunity to participate in government.

In free speech cases, the Warren Court struggled to move beyond a "marketplace" approach, in which majorities could perhaps suppress speech with distasteful content, to an approach where all speakers were presumed to have an equal right to express their thoughts. The approach was first developed in "communist sympathizer" cases, where a minority of the Court objected to laws making it a crime to be a member of the Communist party or to advocate Communist party doctrine. Eventually, in BRANDENBURG V. OHIO (1969), a unanimous Court distinguished between "mere advocacy" of views and "incitement to imminent lawless action." That case involved statements made by a member of the Ku Klux Klan at a rally that were derogatory of blacks and Jews. The fact that the speaker was known to belong to an organization historically linked to racism and violence was not enough to hinder expression of his views.

*Brandenburg* united, without entirely clarifying, a number of strands of Warren Court FIRST AMENDMENT doctrine. In the OVERBREADTH cases, such as *NAACP v. Alabama ex rel. Flowers* (1964), APTHEKER V. SECRETARY OF STATE (1964), KEYISHIAN V. BOARD OF REGENTS (1967), and UNITED STATES V. ROBEL (1967), the Court found that legitimate governmental prohibitions on speech that employed "means which sweep unnecessarily broadly" violated the First Amendment, because they might deter the behavior of others who could not legitimately be prohibited from speaking. In the SYMBOLIC SPEECH cases, the Court considered the permissibility of wearing black arm bands (TINKER V. DES MOINES COMMUNITY SCHOOL DISTRICT, 1969) or burning draft cards (UNITED STATES V. O'BRIEN, 1968) or mutilating flags (*Street v. New York*, 1969) as a means of protesting the Vietnam War. Finally, in the "sit-in" and "picketing" cases, such as COX V. LOUISIANA (1964), *Brown v. Louisiana* (1966), and ADDERLEY V. FLORIDA (1966), the Court sought to distinguish protected "expression" from unprotected but related "conduct." In none of these areas was the Court's doctrinal position clear—draft card burners and picketers were denied constitutional protection, although flag mutilators and "sit-in" demonstrators were granted it—but the decisions revealed the Warren Court's interest in carving out an area of First Amendment protection that was not dependent on public support for the speaker or his actions.

The Warren Court also attempted to extend the First Amendment's reach into other doctrinal areas, notably defamation and OBSCENITY. In NEW YORK TIMES V. SULLIVAN (1964) the Court concluded that common law libel actions could raise First Amendment issues. The Court's opinion, which found that the First Amendment gave rise to a constitutional privilege to make false and defamatory statements about public officials if the statements were not made with recklessness or malice, expressed concern that libel law could be used as a means of punishing "unpopular" speech. Justice Brennan's majority opinion referred to "a profound national commitment to the principle that debate on public issues should be uninhibited, robust, and wide-open," and spoke of the "inhibiting" effects of civil damages on "those who would give voice to public criticism."

Once the First Amendment was seen as relevant to defamation cases, the future of common law principles in the area of libel and slander seemed precarious. *New York Times v. Sullivan* had established a constitutional privilege to publish information about "public officials." *Rosenblatt v. Baer* (1966) widened the meaning of "public official" to include a supervisor of a county-owned ski resort; *Curtis Publishing Co. v. Butts* (1967) and *Associated Press v. Walker* (1967) included "public figures" as well as public officials in the category of those in whose affairs the general public had a special interest; *Time, Inc. v. Hill* (1967) found a privilege to disclose "private" but newsworthy information.

The defamation cases showed the tendency of the equality principle to expand once set in motion: it seemed hard to distinguish different rules for public officials, public figures, and matters of public interest. Such was also true in the area of obscenity. Once the Court recognized, as it did in ROTH V. UNITED STATES (1957), that First Amendment concerns were relevant in obscenity cases, and yet a core of unprotected expression remained, it was forced to define obscenity. Thirteen obscenity cases between 1957 and 1968 produced fifty-five separate opinions from the Justices, but the meaning of "obscene" for constitutional

purposes was not made much clearer. Some Justices, such as Black and Douglas, decided that obscene speech was entitled to as much constitutional protection as any other speech, but a shifting majority of the Court continued to deny protection for expressions that, by one standard or another, could be deemed "obscene." Among the criteria announced by Court majorities for labeling a work "obscene" was that it appeal to a "prurient interest," and that it be "patently offensive" and "utterly without redeeming social value." Justice Stewart, in JACOBELLIS V. OHIO (1964), announced a different criterion: "I know [obscenity] when I see it." Eventually, after *Redrup v. New York* (1967), the Court began to reverse summarily all obscenity convictions whenever five Justices, for whatever reason, adjudged a work not to be obscene.

A final area of unprotected expression involved the FIGHTING WORDS doctrine of CHAPLINSKY V. NEW HAMPSHIRE (1942). A series of Warren Court cases, including *Edwards v. South Carolina* (1963), *Gregory v. Chicago* (1969) and even *New York Times v. Sullivan*, with its language about "vehement, caustic, and sometimes unpleasantly sharp attacks on government and public officials," may have reduced *Chaplinsky* to insignificance.

The pattern of First Amendment decisions, taken with its opinions on race relations and reapportionment, not only demonstrated the Warren Court's shifting conceptions of equality but stamped it in the popular mind as a "liberal" Court. Liberalism has been identified, in the years after World War II, with support for affirmative government and protection of civil rights; the Warren Court was notable for its efforts to insure that interventionist government and civil libertarianism could coexist. But in so doing the Warren Court redefined the locus of interventionist government in America. *Brown v. Board of Education* was a classic example. Congress and the state legislatures were not taking sufficient action to preserve the rights of blacks, so the Court intervened to scrutinize their conduct and, where necessary, to compel them to act. This role for the Court was a major change from that performed by its predecessors. "Liberal" judging in the early twentieth century, according to such defenders of interventionist government as Felix Frankfurter and LOUIS D. BRANDEIS, meant judicial self-restraint: the Supreme Court was to *avoid* scrutiny of state and federal legislation whose purpose was to aid disadvantaged persons. The Warren Court eschewed that role to become the principal interventionist branch of government in the 1950s and 1960s.

In addition to its decisions in race relations and reapportionment, two other areas of Warren Court activity helped augment its public reputation as a "liberal" Court. The first area was CRIMINAL PROCEDURE: here the Court virtually rewrote the laws of the states to conform them to its understanding of the Constitution's requirements. The most important series of its criminal procedure decisions, from a doctrinal perspective, were the INCORPORATION DOCTRINE cases, where the Court struggled with the question of whether, and to what extent, the due process clause of the FOURTEENTH AMENDMENT incorporates procedural protections in the Bill of Rights, making those protections applicable against the states. The Warren Court began a process of "selective incorporation" of Bill of Rights safeguards, applying particular protections in given cases but refusing to endorse the incorporation doctrine in its entirety. This process produced some landmark decisions, notably MAPP V. OHIO (1961), which applied FOURTH AMENDMENT protections against illegal SEARCHES AND SEIZURES to state trials, and BENTON V. MARYLAND (1969), which held that the Fifth Amendment's DOUBLE JEOPARDY guarantee applied to the states. Other important "incorporation" cases were GRIFFIN V. CALIFORNIA (1965), maintaining a RIGHT AGAINST SELF-INCRIMINATION; MALLOY V. HOGAN (1964), applying the Fifth Amendment's self-incrimination privilege to state proceedings; and DUNCAN V. LOUISIANA (1968), incorporating the Sixth Amendment's right to TRIAL BY JURY in criminal cases.

A major consequence of selective incorporation was that fewer criminal convictions were obtained in state trials. Particularly damaging to state prosecutors were the decisions in *Mapp* and *Mallory*, which eliminated from state court trials illegally secured evidence and coerced statements of incrimination. The Court also tightened the requirements for police conduct during the incarceration of criminal suspects. *Malloy v. United States* (1957) insisted that criminal defendants be brought before a magistrate prior to being interrogated. MIRANDA V. ARIZONA (1966) announced a series of constitutional "warnings" that the police were required to give persons whom they had taken into custody. *Miranda* had been preceded by another significant case, ESCOBEDO V. ILLINOIS (1964), which had required that a lawyer be present during police investigations if a suspect requested one. Further, the landmark case of GIDEON V. WAINWRIGHT (1963) had insured that all persons suspected of crimes could secure the services of a lawyer if they desired such, whether they could afford them or not.

The result of this activity by the Warren Court in the area of criminal procedure was that nearly every stage of a POLICE INTERROGATION was fraught with constitutional complexities. The decisions, taken as a whole, seemed to be an effort to buttress the position of persons suspected of crimes by checking the power of the police: some opinions, such as *Miranda*, were explicit in stating that goal. By intervening in law enforcement proceedings to protect the rights of allegedly disadvantaged persons—a high percentage of criminals in the 1960s were poor and

black—the Warren Court Justices were acting as liberal policymakers.

Church and state cases were another area in which the Court demonstrated its liberal sensibility, to the concern of many observers. Affirmative state action to promote religious values in the public schools—heretofore an aspect of America's educational heritage—was likely to be struck down as a violation of the establishment clause. In ENGEL V. VITALE (1962) the Court struck down nondenominational prayer readings in New York public schools. A year after *Engel* the Court also invalidated a Pennsylvania law that required reading from the Bible in ABINGTON TOWNSHIP SCHOOL DISTRICT V. SCHEMPP (1963) and a Maryland law that required recitation of the Lord's Prayer in *Murrary v. Curlett* (1963). (See RELIGION IN PUBLIC SCHOOLS.) In *McGowan v. Maryland* (1961), however, the Court permitted the state to impose SUNDAY CLOSING LAWS. Chief Justice Warren, for the Court, distinguished between laws with a religious purpose and laws "whose present purpose and effect" was secular, even though they were originally "motivated by religious forces." The Court invoked *McGowan* in a subsequent case, BOARD OF EDUCATION V. ALLEN (1968), which sustained a New York law providing for the loaning of textbooks from public to parochial schools.

Liberalism, as practiced by the Warren Court, produced a different institutional posture from earlier "reformist" judicial perspectives. As noted, liberalism required that the Court be both an activist governmental institution and a defender of minority rights. This meant that unlike previously "activist" Courts, such as the Courts of the late nineteenth and early twentieth century, its beneficiaries would be nonelites, and unlike previously "reformist" Courts, such as the Court of the late 1930s and 1940s, it would assume a scrutinizing rather than a passive stance toward the actions of other branches of government. Had the Warren Court retained either of these former roles, *Brown, Baker v. Carr*, and *Miranda* would likely not have been decided as they were. These decisions all offended entrenched elites and required modifications of existing governmental practices. In so deciding these cases the Warren Court was assuming that activism by the judiciary was required in order to produce liberal results. With this assumption came a mid-twentieth-century fusion of affirmative governmental action and protection for CIVIL LIBERTIES.

Maintaining a commitment to liberal theory while at the same time modifying its precepts required some analytical refinements in order to reconcile the protection of civil liberties with claims based on affirmative governmental action. In *Brown* the desires of some whites and some blacks to have a racially integrated educational experience conflicted with the desires of some whites and some blacks to limit their educational experiences to persons of their own race. The Court chose to prefer the former desire, basing its judgment on a theory of the educational process that minimized the relevance of race. That theory then became a guiding assumption for the Court's subsequent decisions in the race relations area.

Similar sets of intermediate distinctions between goals of liberal theory were made in other major cases. In the REAPPORTIONMENT cases the distinction was between REPRESENTATION based on population, a claim put forth by a disadvantaged minority, and other forms of proportional representation that had been endorsed by legislative majorities. The Court decided to prefer the former claim as more democratic and then made the one-person, one-vote principle the basis of its subsequent decisions. In the school prayer cases the distinction was between the choice of a majority to ritualize the recognition of a public deity in the public school and the choice of a minority to deny that recognition as out of place. The Court decided to prefer the latter choice as more libertarian. In the criminal procedure cases the distinction was between a majoritarian decision to protect the public against crime by advantaging law enforcement personnel in their encounters with persons suspected of committing crimes, and the claims of such persons that they were being unfairly disadvantaged. The Court chose to prefer the latter claims as being more consistent with principles of equal justice.

When the Warren Court reached the end of its tenure, liberalism clearly did not merely mean deference toward the decisions of democratic and representative bodies of government. It meant deference toward these decisions only if they promoted the goals of liberal policy: equality, fairness, protection of civil rights, support for disadvantaged persons. Under this model of liberal policymaking, the Supreme Court was more concerned with achieving enlightened results than it was with the constitutional process by which these results were reached. Liberalism and judicial activism went hand in hand.

As it became clear that the Court's activism was designed to promote a modified version of liberalism, the Court became vulnerable to public dissatisfaction with liberal policies. Such dissatisfaction emerged in the 1970s. The internal contradictions of liberalism became exposed in such areas as AFFIRMATIVE ACTION in higher education and forced busing in primary education, and the saving distinctions made by the Court in earlier cases appeared as naked policy choices whose legitimacy was debatable. If affirmative preference, based on race, for one class of applicants to an institution of higher learning results in disadvantage to other classes, equality of condition has not been achieved and equality of educational opportunity has been undermined. If some families are compelled to send their children to schools where they are racial minorities

in order to achieve "racial balance" throughout the school system, the resulting "balance" may well disadvantage more people than it advantages. Equality and social justice have turned out to be more complicated concepts than mid-twentieth-century liberalism assumed.

The egalitarianism and the liberalism of the Warren Court paled in significance when compared to its activism. If contemporary America has become a "litigious society," as it is commonly portrayed, the Warren Court helped set in motion such trends. Social issues have habitually been transformed into legal questions in America, but the Warren Court seemed to welcome such a transformation, finding constitutional issues raised in contexts as diverse as reapportionment and prayers in the public schools. As the Court created new sources of constitutional protection, numerous persons sought to make themselves the beneficiaries. Sometimes the Court went out of its way to help the organizations litigating a case, as in the civil rights area. The result was that the lower courts and the Supreme Court became "activist" institutions—repositories of grievances, scrutinizers of the conduct of other branches of government, havens for the disadvantaged.

In the academic community, Warren Court activism was from the first regarded as more controversial than Warren Court egalitarianism. The reason was the prominence in academic circles of a two-pronged theory of JUDICIAL REVIEW, one prong of which stressed the necessity of grounding judicial decisions, in the area of constitutional law, in textually supportable principles of general applicability, and the other prong of which resurrected Frankfurter's conception of a limited, deferential role for the Court as a lawmaking institution. The Warren Court, according to academic critics, repeatedly violated the theory's dual standards. Decisions like *Brown v. Board, Baker v. Carr*, GRISWOLD V. CONNECTICUT (1965), a case discovering a RIGHT OF PRIVACY in the Constitution that was violated by statutes forbidding the use of BIRTH CONTROL pills, and HARPER V. VIRGINIA BOARD OF ELECTIONS (1966), a case invalidating POLL TAX requirements on voting as violating the EQUAL PROTECTION clause because such requirements conditioned VOTING RIGHTS on wealth, had not been sufficiently grounded in constitutional doctrine. There was no evidence that the Fourteenth Amendment was intended to reach segregated schools and there were no judicial decisions supporting that position. The Constitution did not single out for protection a right to vote, let alone a right to have one's vote weighed equally with the votes of others. "Privacy" was nowhere mentioned in the constitutional text. The framers of the Constitution had assumed a variety of suffrage restrictions, including ones based on wealth. In short, leading Warren Court decisions were not based on "neutral principles" of constitutional law.

Nor had the Court been mindful, critics felt, of its

proper lawmaking posture in a democratic society where it was a conspicuously nondemocratic institution. In *Brown* it had ostensibly substituted its wisdom for that of Congress and several Southern states. In *Baker* it had forced legislatures to reapportion themselves even when a majority of a state's voters had signified their intention to staff one house of the legislature on grounds other than one person, one vote. In *Engel v. Vitale* it had told the public schools that they could not have government-formulated compulsory prayers, even though the vast majority of school officials and parents desired them. It had fashioned codes of criminal procedure for the police, ignoring Congress's abortive efforts in that direction. It had decided, after more than 200 years of defamation law, that the entire area needed to be reconsidered in light of the First Amendment.

A role for the Court as a deferential, principled decision maker was, however, not sacrosanct. Few Supreme Courts had assumed such a role in the past. All of the "great cases" in American constitutional history could be said to have produced activist decisions: MARBURY V. MADISON (1803), establishing the power of judicial review; MCCULLOCH V. MARYLAND (1819) and GIBBONS V. OGDEN (1824), delineating the scope of the federal commerce power; DRED SCOTT V. SANDFORD (1857), legitimizing SLAVERY IN THE TERRITORIES; the LEGAL TENDER CASES, deciding the constitutionality of legal tender notes; POLLOCK V. FARMERS LOAN AND TRUST (1895), declaring an income tax unconstitutional; LOCHNER V. NEW YORK (1905), scuttling state hours and wages legislation; UNITED STATES V. BUTLER (1936), invalidating a major portion of the New Deal's administrative structure. Activism was an ancient judicial art.

The Warren Court's activism differed from other Courts' versions principally not because its reasoning was more specious or its grasp of power more presumptuous but because its beneficiaries were different. Previous activist decisions had largely benefited entrenched elites, whether slaveowners, entrepreneurs, "combinations of capital," or businesses that sought to avoid government regulation. The activist decisions of the Warren Court benefited blacks, disadvantaged suburban voters, atheists, criminals, pornographers, and the poor. The Warren Court's activism facilitated social change rather than preserving the status quo. The critics of the Court had forgotten that the role they espoused for the judiciary had been created in order to facilitate change and promote the interests of the disadvantaged. In the 1950s and 1960s the "democratic" institutions charged with that responsibility had become unresponsive, so the Warren Court had acted in their stead. It was ironic that the same critics who were shocked at the Court of the 1930s' resistance to the New Deal should protest against a Court that was reaching the results they had then sought.

Activism was the principal basis of the Court's controversiality; egalitarianism its dominant instinctual reaction; liberalism its guiding political philosophy. The combination of these ingredients, plus the presence of some judicial giants, gave the Warren Court a prominence and a visibility that are not likely to be surpassed for some time. But even though countless persons in the American legal profession today were shaped by Warren Court decisions, one can see the Warren Court receding into history. That Court seemed to have been led, in the final analysis, by a conception of American life that appeared vindicated by the first fifty years of twentieth-century experience. That conception held that American society was continually progressing toward a nobler and brighter and more enlightened future. As Earl Warren wrote in a passage that appears on his tombstone:

> Where there is injustice, we should correct it;
> where there is poverty, we should eliminate it;
> where there is corruption, we should stamp it out;
> where there is violence, we should punish it;
> where there is neglect, we should provide care;
> where there is war, we should restore peace;
> and wherever corrections are achieved we should add them permanently to our storehouse of treasures.

In that passage appears the Warren Court sensibility: a sensibility dedicated to the active pursuit of ideals that have seemed less tangible and achievable with the years.

G. EDWARD WHITE
(1986)

Bibliography

BICKEL, ALEXANDER  1970  *The Supreme Court and the Idea of Progress.* New York: Harper & Row.
BLACK, CHARLES  1970  The Unfinished Business of the Warren Court. *University of Washington Law Review* 46:3–45.
COX, ARCHIBALD  1968  *The Warren Court.* Cambridge, Mass.: Harvard University Press.
KURLAND, PHILLIP  1970  *Politics, the Constitution, and the Warren Court.* Chicago: University of Chicago Press.
LEVY, LEONARD W., ed.  1972  *The Supreme Court under Earl Warren.* New York: Quadrangle Books.
MCCLOSKEY, ROBERT  1960  *The American Supreme Court.* Chicago: University of Chicago Press.
WECHSLER, HERBERT  1959  Toward Neutral Principles of Constitutional Law. *Harvard Law Review* 73:1–23.
WHITE, G. ROBERT  1976  *The American Judicial Tradition.* New York: Oxford University Press.
——— 1982  *Earl Warren: A Public Life.* New York: Oxford University Press.

# WARTH v. SELDIN

See: *Simon v. Eastern Kentucky Welfare Rights Organization*

# WASHINGTON, BUSHROD
## (1762–1829)

Bushrod Washington served on the United States Supreme Court for thirty-one years, but he did not hand down many important DECISIONS. Lacking the analytical sweep of JOHN MARSHALL and the erudition and energy of JOSEPH STORY, he invariably supported their opinions which strengthened the power of the central government and encouraged the development of the economy. In fact, he was so closely allied with Chief Justice Marshall that another Justice on that Court, WILLIAM JOHNSON of South Carolina, observed that the two "are commonly estimated as a single judge."

Washington was well connected by birth. His mother came from a prominent Virginia family and his father, John, was a particularly close brother of GEORGE WASHINGTON. He graduated from the College of William and Mary in 1778 and served in the Continental Army. After the war he studied law in Philadelphia under JAMES WILSON. Returning to Virginia in 1787, he was admitted to the bar and elected to the Virginia state ratifying convention, where he supported the adoption of the United States Constitution. Following this he practiced law in Richmond, where he developed a reputation for being diligent and extremely knowledgeable. Many young men, including HENRY CLAY, came to read law under his direction. During the 1790s he joined the Federalist Party, and in 1798 JOHN ADAMS appointed him to the Supreme Court. A short time later, as the "favorite nephew" of the former President, he became executor of Washington's will and inherited Mount Vernon and his uncle's public and private papers, which he made available to Marshall for his *Life of George Washington*.

Bushrod Washington was particularly effective and conscientious in the performance of his circuit-riding duties, especially when he presided over jury trials. His tact and sense of fair play allowed him to enforce the Sedition Act of 1798 in a number of cases without engaging in the partisan politics that made SAMUEL CHASE and WILLIAM PATERSON so controversial. His most famous circuit court decision came in the case *United States v. Bright* (1809). This was the TREASON trial of a general of the Pennsylvania state militia who had been formally authorized to resist the United States Supreme Court's decision in *United States v. Peters* (1809). Following a confrontation with a federal marshal, and after President JAMES MADISON threatened to use force, the state eventually backed down, whereupon Bright and several other officers were arrested, tried, and convicted. (Madison eventually pardoned them on humanitarian grounds.) Bushrod Washington handled the trial, which took place in Philadelphia amid a highly charged atmosphere, with great skill, maintaining both decorum and the authority of the federal government. Sentencing Bright, he declared, "A State has no constitutional power . . . to employ force to resist the execution of a decree of a federal court, though such decree is deemed to have been beyond the JURISDICTION of the Court to make. . . ."

Several other decisions rendered by Bushrod Washington are of interest. In a concurring opinion in DARTMOUTH COLLEGE V. WOODWARD (1819) he tried to reign in some of the implications of Marshall's more sweeping decision. In GREEN V. BIDDLE (1823) he handed down what proved to be an unenforceable decision invalidating various Kentucky statutes adopted to protect settlers from absentee landlords. Finally, in OGDEN V. SAUNDERS (1827), he openly broke with Marshall, abandoned his own earlier circuit court decision in *Golden v. Prince* (1814), and declared that a state BANKRUPTCY ACT that had a prospective application did not violate the CONTRACT CLAUSE.

Bushrod Washington died in Philadelphia on November 26, 1829.

RICHARD E. ELLIS
(1986)

Bibliography

BLAUSTEIN, ALBERT P. and MERSKY, ROY M. 1969 Bushrod Washington. Pages 243–257 in Leon Friedman and Fred L. Israel, eds., *Justices of the Supreme Court, 1789–1969*. New York: Chelsea House.

# WASHINGTON, GEORGE
## (1732–1799)

The people of the United States are indebted to no man so much as they are to George Washington. And the debt extends to his role in the creation of the American Constitution. As the general who led the revolutionary armies to victory and so vindicated American independence, as one of the few men who had traveled in virtually every part of the United States, including the vast Western wilderness, and as a leading citizen of northern Virginia, Washington was actively involved in the movement of affairs that culminated in the CONSTITUTIONAL CONVENTION OF 1787. When the Convention met, he became its presiding officer. During the controversy over the RATIFICATION OF THE CONSTITUTION, the opposition to a strong executive was overcome by the universal assumption that Washington would be the first man to hold the office. When the Constitution was ratified and Washington did become President, he self-consciously seized the opportunity to set precedents for the conduct of governmental affairs. And when, after two terms in that office he handed over the reins of executive authority, he did so in perfect constitutional order and retired to his country seat.

The third son of a prosperous planter, Washington learned the surveying trade in his teens, and as a surveyor he traveled widely in the area west of the Appalachian Mountains. At twenty-one he was appointed to major in the Virginia militia, and when the French and Indian War broke out in 1754 he was promoted to lieutenant colonel and placed second in command of a regiment dispatched to the Ohio Valley. On his colonel's death, Washington took command and managed, without supplies, funds, competent subordinates, or trained noncommissioned officers and troops, to achieve initial military success. He was subsequently made an aide to the British commanding general, and in 1755, at the age of twenty-three, was promoted to colonel and made commander-in-chief of all Virginia forces, the highest ranking American military officer.

In 1759, Washington married Martha Custis, the wealthiest widow in Virginia, and, adding her holdings to his own, achieved a financial independence that would subsequently permit him to engage in a career of uncompensated public service. For a decade and a half he lived the life of a gentleman planter, with the attendant civic duties of serving as a justice of the peace and as a member of the House of Burgesses.

In 1769 Washington introduced in the House of Burgesses a series of resolutions (drafted by his friend and neighbor GEORGE MASON) denying the right of the British Parliament to tax the colonies and initiating the first ASSOCIATION. After passage of the Intolerable Acts in 1774, Washington introduced in the house the Fairfax County Resolves closing Virginia's trade with Britain. He was also elected a delegate to the FIRST CONTINENTAL CONGRESS, which he attended in military uniform.

The Revolutionary War began in Spring 1775 when the Massachusetts militia forcibly resisted the attempt of British troops to seize its weapons and supplies. In June, on the motion of JOHN ADAMS, the CONTINENTAL CONGRESS adopted the Massachusetts militia as the Continental Army and appointed Washington commander-in-chief. The war lasted eight and one-half years, and Washington was the American commander for the whole period. The war was not an unrelieved military success on the American side, but the commander did learn to deal with Congress and with foreign allies, and he became, in his own person, the symbol of American national unity. Just before resigning his commission in 1783, he resisted the suggestion that the army, which had been shamefully left unpaid, should overthrow the Congress and establish its own government.

After his return to private life in 1784, Washington devoted his time to management of his property in Virginia and in the Ohio Valley. He became president of the Potomac Company, which had as its object the development of the Potomac River as a navigable waterway. And he engaged in a wide correspondence, always urging, in letters dealing with politics, the strengthening of the Union and an increase in the powers of Congress under the ARTICLES OF CONFEDERATION. In March 1785 he was host to a conference of commissioners from Maryland and Virginia that was supposed to discuss the navigation of the Potomac River but that, in the event, called for a broader conference—the Annapolis Convention—that ultimately led to the Constitutional Convention of 1787.

Pleading pressures of financial reverses and ill health, Washington was reluctant to accept election as a delegate to the Convention, but he did so at the repeated urging of JAMES MADISON and EDMUND RANDOLPH. At Philadelphia he was unanimously elected president of the Convention, although, as most of the debates were conducted in a committee of the whole house, he did not actually have to preside on most occasions. Although Washington did not take an active part in the recorded debates of the Convention, his attendance and his signature on the document as president of the Convention were offered as a guarantee of the result.

The first ELECTORAL COLLEGE under the new Constitution was elected in January 1789, and every member cast one of his two votes for George Washington. Washington learned of the result on April 14. His journey from Virginia to New York took a week, and involved parades and ceremonies in every town he passed through along the way; the affection and gratitude of the population were genuine, and Washington's task was to retain them while directing the executive affairs of the government.

Following his inauguration on April 30, Washington immediately began the business of running the executive branch of government. Everything he did set a precedent, not only for America but for the world, because his position as a republican chief executive was unique. Attention had to be given to such matters as the form of address and the conduct of social events so as to insure both the dignity of the federal executive and the republicanism of the country.

Every act in the process of governing had to be done a first time: the performance of each executive task, however routine, set the pattern for the permanent conduct of the presidency. The first bill to pass the new Congress was presented for Washington's signature on June 1: he affixed his signature, and the first statute under the Constitution became law. The first occasion for negotiating a treaty arose in August; in strict compliance with Article II, section 2, Washington appeared in person before the Senate to ask for ADVICE AND CONSENT and, when the Senate referred the matter to committee he stalked out. Since that day, Presidents have submitted treaties to the Senate after they are negotiated, but no President has asked for the Senate's advice before negotiations begin.

Statutes creating the three executive departments of state, war, and treasury were enacted during the summer of 1789. Washington appointed his fellow Virginian THOMAS JEFFERSON to be the first secretary of state, his wartime chief of artillery, General Henry Knox, to be secretary of war, and his former aide, Colonel ALEXANDER HAMILTON, to be secretary of the treasury. Although the Constitution provides only that the President may require written opinions from the principal executive officers, and that only as to their peculiar duties, Washington began the practice of meeting regularly with the three secretaries and the attorney general, Edmund Randolph, to discuss affairs of state generally. From this practice has come the notion of the American CABINET, as well as the accepted opinion that the heads of the executive departments are responsible primarily to the President, and not to Congress, for their official conduct.

But Washington had to appoint not only his cabinet officers but also every official in the executive branch down to customs inspectors and lighthouse keepers. Although the Constitution permitted Congress to vest inferior appointments in the chiefs of the departments, Congress did not immediately do so. Washington was besieged with applications from would-be federal bureaucrats. Indeed, had Congress desired to hamstring the President it might have been enough just to leave all federal appointments in his hands.

Besides the cabinet officers, the most important appointees were the Justices of the Supreme Court. The JUDICIARY ACT OF 1789 provided for six Justices. Washington nominated his friend JOHN JAY, who had been secretary of foreign affairs in the old government, to be Chief Justice. The other five nominees were drawn from different states, both to facilitate their performance of circuit duty and to make the Court representative of the whole country. Among them were three men who had been Washington's fellow delegates to the Constitutional Convention, JAMES WILSON, JOHN RUTLEDGE, and JOHN BLAIR. (See SUPREME COURT, 1789–1801.)

Once the machinery was in place, the issue became what policy the new government would follow. Washington, who had relied on Congressman James Madison for the machinery, turned to Secretary of the Treasury Hamilton for the policy. Hamilton's program was set forth in a series of reports submitted over the next two years. The program called for an alliance between the federal government and the wealthier citizens to promote the unity and prosperity of the nation. The Hamiltonian program provoked a controversy over the proper interpretation of constitutional provisions conferring power on the national government. Hamilton argued for BROAD CONSTRUCTION; Jefferson, for STRICT CONSTRUCTION. The arguments were reduced to writing at Washington's request to help him to decide whether to sign or to veto the BANK OF THE UNITED STATES ACT (1790). Washington, convinced by Hamilton's doctrine of IMPLIED POWERS, signed the act.

The French Revolution of 1789 provoked a further division between Washington's chief advisers. Most Americans initially sympathized with the French overthrow of the monarchy and the attempt to establish a republican form of government. But as the French Revolution became more extreme and expansionary, and as the conservative states of Europe mobilized to resist it, opinion became divided. Jefferson and his supporters continued to sympathize with the revolution, while Hamilton and his allies were inclined to side with the embattled British.

By 1793, the Wars of the French Revolution had become global, and American interests, particularly American shipping, were suffering the effects. Washington, with the assent of his whole cabinet, issued a PROCLAMATION OF NEUTRALITY in April 1793, warning American citizens to refrain from becoming involved on either side. Hamilton published a series of newspaper articles asserting, among other things, that the proclamation had been necessary because of the active support of France on the part of the Jeffersonians. Madison, replying in his own newspaper essays, claimed that Washington, by his unilateral issuance of the proclamation, had usurped the power of Congress to declare war and of the Senate to share in treaty making.

The first party lines in American politics under the Constitution had been drawn, and drawn on constitutional grounds. Jefferson resigned from the cabinet at the end of 1793. Thereafter, Washington's was a "Federalist" administration, with Jefferson, Madison, and the "Republicans" in opposition.

The WHISKEY REBELLION of 1794 presented the first organized resistance to the national government. Western Pennsylvania farmers, upset by an excise on whiskey that seemed unduly to burden their section of the country, threatened to use force to impede collection of the tax. Washington called 15,000 militiamen into federal service and himself set out to command the expedition. The rebellion was ultimately put down without bloodshed, and when two rebel leaders were subsequently convicted of TREASON, Washington pardoned them.

The administration's foreign policy also led to controversy at about the same time. Chief Justice Jay had been sent to Britain to negotiate a settlement of certain continuing difficulties in relations between the two countries. JAY'S TREATY contained many provisions favorable to British interests, and apparently detrimental to the economic interests of some regions of the United States, especially the South and West. The treaty also provoked constitutional controversy about the operation of the TREATY POWER. For example, would the Senate be required to advise and consent to the treaty as it was presented, or could the Senate amend a treaty? And could the President and the Senate enter into treaty commitments that would involve the expenditure of funds without the concurrence of the House of Representatives whose agreement was required for the appropriation of the funds? The treaty was approved in a partisan vote, but with a reservation suspending operation of certain objectionable provisions.

Washington chose not to seek a third term as President in the election of 1796. He was dismayed and distressed by the bitterness of the partisan rivalries that had grown up among men who had once been close colleagues, and he himself attempted always to remain above the partisan fray. WASHINGTON'S FAREWELL ADDRESS to his countrymen contained his strictures against the spirit of party, as well as his advice on foreign affairs and on public morality.

Even after his retirement to his estate at Mount Vernon, Washington could not escape either public service or partisan intrigue. When war with France seemed inevitable in 1798, President JOHN ADAMS nominated and the Senate unanimously confirmed Washington as COMMANDER-IN-CHIEF. There immediately followed a scramble among Federalist military men for the subordinate general officer positions. Washington supported Hamilton, who ultimately became second in command. Under the circumstances it is not surprising that Washington thought of the Republicans, who had been pro-French, as dangerous men and that he supported the ALIEN AND SEDITION ACTS.

Nevertheless, when Washington died in 1799 he was eulogized by Federalists and Republicans alike. More than any other individual, Washington was responsible for America's being independent, adopting the Constitution, and having a functioning republican government.

DENNIS J. MAHONEY
(1986)

Bibliography

COOKE, JACOB E. 1987 Organizing the National Government. In Levy, Leonard W., and Mahoney, Dennis J., eds., *The Constitution: A History of Its Framing and Ratification.* New York: Macmillan.

FLEXNER, JAMES THOMAS 1965–1972 *George Washington.* 4 Vols. Boston: Little, Brown.

FREEMAN, DOUGLAS SOUTHALL 1948–1957 *George Washington.* 7 Vols. New York: Scribner's.

MARSHALL, JOHN (1804–1807) 1925 *The Life of George Washington.* 5 Vols. New York: Wm. H. Wise & Co.

MATTESON, DAVID M. 1970 *The Organization of the Government under the Constitution.* New York: Da Capo Press.

# WASHINGTON v. DAVIS
## 426 U.S. 229 (1976)

This landmark decision concerns the relevance of a decision maker's motives in EQUAL PROTECTION cases. Black candidates for the Washington, D.C., police force alleged that the District's selection criteria had an adverse discriminatory effect upon the employment prospects of minorities and that the effect violated the FOURTEENTH AMENDMENT's equal protection clause and ANTIDISCRIMINATION LEGISLATION. In an opinion by Justice BYRON R. WHITE, the Supreme Court held that discriminatory effects, standing alone, are insufficient to establish an equal protection violation. Proof of purposeful discrimination is necessary. The Court also rejected the candidates' statutory claim. In an opinion that did not address the constitutional question, Justice WILLIAM J. BRENNAN, joined by Justice THURGOOD MARSHALL, dissented from the Court's disposition of the statutory issue. In a concurring opinion, Justice JOHN PAUL STEVENS discussed the relationship between discriminatory effects and proof of discriminatory intent and articulated his reasons for rejecting the statutory claim.

In settling a long-standing controversy over whether a decision maker's motives may constitute the basis for an equal protection claim, the Court climbed two interesting doctrinal hills. Prior to *Davis*, cases such as *Whitcomb v. Chavis* (1971) and *White v. Regester* (1973) expressly had suggested that unintentional disproportionate effects on a minority may constitute the basis for an equal protection claim. Justice White's opinion ignores these precedents but warns against the broad consequences of such a HOLDING. Such a rule "would raise serious questions about, and perhaps invalidate, a whole range of tax, welfare, public service, regulatory, and licensing statutes that may be more burdensome to the poor and to the average black than to the more affluent white."

In addition, contrary to *Davis*'s holding, a line of opinions dating back to FLETCHER V. PECK (1810) and reaffirmed in UNITED STATES V. O'BRIEN (1968) and PALMER V. THOMPSON (1971), clearly had stated that legislators' motives may not form the basis of constitutional attacks on statutes. Without alluding to all of the relevant precedents, the Court reinterpreted *Palmer* and suggested that some of its language had constituted mere OBITER DICTA.

As a practical matter, *Davis*, when combined with subsequent similar cases such as ARLINGTON HEIGHTS V. METROPOLITAN HOUSING DEVELOPMENT CORP. (1977) and MOBILE V. BOLDEN (1980), curtailed litigants' ability to bring successful equal protection claims. Proof of intentional discrimination is difficult to obtain and judges are reluctant to deem officials intentional wrongdoers. Indeed, it was six years after *Davis* before the Court, in *Rogers v. Lodge* (1982), sustained a finding of intentional discrimination in a racial equal protection case.

THEODORE EISENBERG
(1986)

## WASHINGTON v. GLUCKSBERG

See: Right to Die

## WASHINGTON v. HARPER
### 494 U.S. 1028 (1990)

A Washington state prison policy authorized the treatment of a prisoner with antipsychotic drugs against his or her will, provided that the prisoner be (1) mentally ill, and (2) either gravely disabled or likely to do serious harm to others. These two findings were to be made by a committee consisting of a psychiatrist, a psychologist, and an official of the institution in which mentally ill prisoners were held. The state supreme court held that this procedure, which lacked fully adversarial procedural guarantees such as those available in a court proceeding, denied a mentally ill prisoner PROCEDURAL DUE PROCESS OF LAW. The Supreme Court reversed, 6–3.

Justice ANTHONY M. KENNEDY wrote for the Court. The prisoner had a "liberty interest" in being free from arbitrary administration of a psychotropic drug; however, the procedure provided by the state was sufficient to satisfy the demands of due process. A court in a single proceeding cannot adequately evaluate the intentions or likely behavior of a medically ill person; such an evaluation requires ongoing observation of the kind available to the members of the committee given responsibility for the decisions here. The risks of an antipsychotic drug are mainly medical risks, which can best be evaluated by professionals. Although the state's policy does not allow representation by counsel, it does provide for a lay adviser who understands the psychiatric issues; this assistance is sufficient to satisfy due process.

Justice JOHN PAUL STEVENS wrote for the dissenters. In his view, the state policy violated both SUBSTANTIVE DUE PROCESS and procedural due process. In support of the first objection, he argued that the policy authorized invasion of the prisoner's liberty not only for his own medical interests but also to maintain order in the institution. The second objection was that, considering the seriousness of the invasion of the prisoner's liberty interest, the committee was insufficiently independent of the institution's administration to satisfy the requirements of a fair hearing.

KENNETH L. KARST
(1992)

## WASHINGTON v. SEATTLE SCHOOL DISTRICT NO. 1

See: *Crawford v. Board of Education*

## WASHINGTON v. TEXAS

See: Compulsory Process, Right to; Evidence

## WASHINGTON'S FAREWELL ADDRESS
### (September 17, 1796)

When President GEORGE WASHINGTON decided, in the summer of 1796, not to seek a third term, he published an address to the American people embodying his advice on how to insure the survival of the new constitutional order. The first draft was prepared by Washington himself; the final version was drafted under Washington's direction by ALEXANDER HAMILTON, incorporating suggestions from JAMES MADISON and JOHN JAY.

The first, and longest, section of the address comprises an encomium of the federal union and a warning against the dangers of factionalism, and especially of sectionalism. Washington urged that Americans regard the Union as "the support of your tranquility at home, your peace abroad, of your safety, of your prosperity, of that very liberty which you so highly prize." The central section of the address commends religion as a support for free government. Anything that weakened religious belief, he argued, would corrupt public morals, undermine the efficacy of oaths, and threaten the national capacity for self-government. The final section of the address contains Washington's advice on FOREIGN AFFAIRS and defense. Washington opposed permanent alliances and standing armies as incompatible with constitutional democracy.

Advice in the address concerning specific constitutional questions includes Washington's deprecation of the "spirit of encroachment" that would subvert the SEPARATION OF POWERS and his admonition against hasty adoption of constitutional amendments.

DENNIS J. MAHONEY
(1986)

Bibliography
EIDELBERG, PAUL 1974 *A Discourse on Statesmanship: The Design and Transformation of the American Polity.* Chicago: University of Illinois Press.

# WASTE, POLLUTION, AND THE CONSTITUTION

The rise of environmental consciousness since the early 1970s has made solid waste disposal through recycling an important issue of public policy. The disposal of solid wastes raises interstate issues as some states find it difficult to use local landfills for their locally generated wastes. Air and water pollution also have important interstate effects, as pollution generated in one state flows into another.

Most regulation of air and water pollution occurs through federal statutes, the Clean Air and Clean Water Acts. These statutes prescribe federal standards and are largely administered by the federal Environmental Protection Agency. State environmental agencies play a role in enforcing them, but only if the state agencies comply with rather detailed federal requirements. Solid waste disposal is regulated under the Resource Recovery and Conservation Act, which prescribes relatively strict federal standards for disposing of hazardous wastes, and less strict ones for disposing of other solid wastes. States receive federal funds to administer plans that comply with the federal requirements.

States have done relatively little to regulate the interstate effects of air and water pollution. Solid wastes are different. Many local landfills are full or nearly so, and local residents frequently do not wish to expand environmentally unattractive landfills. States and cities have therefore adopted regulations to conserve local landfill space. The Supreme Court has considered the constitutionality of such regulations in five cases.

The leading case is PHILADELPHIA V. NEW JERSEY (1978), invalidating a statute prohibiting the importation of waste generated outside the state. The Court held that the statute expressly discriminated against out-of-state commerce, and was therefore subject to a "virtually per se rule" of invalidity. The state's reason for imposing the ban was simply to conserve a local resource, landfill space. But conservation could be achieved by restricting intakes, no matter what their source. The COMMERCE CLAUSE, the Court said, was designed to prohibit states from addressing their problems by insulating themselves from other states. The Court followed this holding in *Fort Gratiot Sanitary Landfill, Inc. v. Michigan Department of Natural Resources* (1992), invalidating a Michigan statute barring local landfills from accepting waste generated outside the county in which the landfill was located.

The Court also invoked the *Philadelphia* principle to invalidate Alabama and Oregon statutes that taxed the deposit in local landfills of waste generated elsewhere at a higher rate than locally generated waste, *Chemical Waste Management, Inc. v. Hunt* (1992); *Oregon Waste Systems v. Department of Environmental Quality* (1994). The higher fee would discourage out-of-state waste producers from using local landfills, but this was simply another version of the pure conservation goal found insufficient in *Philadelphia*. Nor did the extra fee compensate the state for any special costs it incurred in accepting out-of-state waste for disposal.

Flow-control ordinances are the most important techniques for dealing with solid wastes. They direct all waste generated in a town to a single recycling facility, and are thought to encourage recycling because expensive recycling facilities require a guaranteed flow of waste to be financially viable, while waste producers prefer to dispose of waste at cheaper, nonrecycling landfills. The Court struck down a flow-control ordinance in *C & A Carbone, Inc. v. Clarkstown* (1994), finding that it denied out-of-state waste haulers access to locally generated waste. In the wake of *Carbone*, lower courts have divided over the constitutionality of other flow-control ordinances.

Congress can authorize states to enforce even discriminatory regulations. None of the Court's decisions deals with the question of congressional authorization, but the Court has generally required a rather specific statement by Congress before it will find authorization for discriminatory regulation.

MARK TUSHNET
(2000)

Bibliography

HEINZERLING, LISA 1995 The Commercial Constitution. *Supreme Court Review* 1995:217–276.
VERCHICK, ROBERT R. M. 1997 The Commerce Clause, Environmental Justice, and the Interstate Garbage Wars. *Southern California Law Review* 70:1239–1310.

# WATERGATE AND THE CONSTITUTION

The Watergate scandal, starting with an illegal break-in at Democratic National Committee headquarters in June 1972 and ending with President GERALD R. FORD pardoning RICHARD M. NIXON in September 1974, produced one of the most significant constitutional crises in modern times. It raised a number of unsettling issues central to the constitutional structure of SEPARATION OF POWERS.

The two major constitutional issues Watergate brought into focus were EXECUTIVE PRIVILEGE and the scope of the IMPEACHMENT power. In September 1972 a GRAND JURY indicted the Watergate burglars but the Justice Department closed the investigation despite evidence of a wider conspiracy. Following the November election, the Watergate burglary trial began. In it defendants claimed they had been pressured to remain silent and plead guilty; that perjury was committed; and that "others" were involved. Such allegations led to the creation of a Senate Watergate Committee, headed by SAM ERVIN, which began taking testimony, revealing a White House program of political espionage that included Watergate. Witnesses suggested that the President was participating in a coverup and that the President had made tape recordings of conversations in his office. The Ervin Committee attempted to subpoena such tapes, but the President refused to surrender them, claiming executive privilege. The committee then went to the courts, which in two cases (*Nixon v. Sirica*, 1973, and *Senate Select Committee on Presidential Campaign Activities v. Nixon*, 1974) attempted to define the line between a committee's power to compel testimony in order to perform its functions and the need for privacy in presidential communications. A third case, UNITED STATES V. NIXON (1974), arose out of a criminal prosecution of the President's aides. Both the prosecutor and the defense sought to subpoena the tapes, and the President again resisted. Chief Justice WARREN E. BURGER, for a unanimous Supreme Court, conceded a "presumptive privilege" for executive communications, but ruled that respect of the integrity of the judicial process required the courts to weigh any such claim against the importance of assuring the production in court of relevant evidence and ultimately of protecting the system of criminal justice. The Court thus ordered certain tapes produced. Their disclosures, which came at the height of the House of Representatives' impeachment process, demonstrated the President's active complicity in the coverup conspiracy from the first moment. This led Nixon to resign to avoid impeachment for "high crimes and misdemeanors."

The impeachment process was fraught with constitutional difficulties. Nixon's firing of a Senate-approved special prosecutor, given sweeping powers to investigate the Watergate scandal, had produced the initial demands for his impeachment. In October the House Judiciary Committee launched an impeachment inquiry. Questions promptly arose as to what constituted an impeachable offense, and what "other high crimes and misdemeanors" might include. Must these be criminal in nature and intent, or might they be quasi-political, involving gross breach of public trust? Was maladministration impeachable, or must a statutory offense or a serious crime be demonstrated? The President's attorneys argued the latter. The committee staff indicated a President might be removed for "substantial misconduct," not necessarily of specific criminal nature. This controversy was mooted by the revelations of the disputed tapes and by the resignation, but not before the House committee recommended three ARTICLES OF IMPEACHMENT to the House at large. Rejecting two articles dealing with income tax violations and

the secret bombing of Cambodia, which raised the question of the extent of presidential emergency power in FOREIGN AFFAIRS, the Committee contended that "Richard M. Nixon warrants impeachment and trial and removal from office" for other charges. These were: that he prevented, obstructed, and impeded the administration of justice; that he repeatedly engaged in conduct violating the constitutional rights of citizens, impairing the due and proper administration of justice and the conduct of lawful inquiries, or contravening the laws governing agencies of the executive branch and the purposes of these agencies; and that he failed without lawful cause or excuse to produce papers and things as directed by duly authorized subpoenas issued by the Committee on the Judiciary of the House of Representatives. Included as substantiating detail were fourteen examples of interfering or endeavoring to interfere with conduct of investigations by the Department of Justice of the United States, the Federal Bureau of Investigation, the Watergate special prosecutor, and congressional committees; endeavoring to misuse the Central Intelligence Agency; the electronic surveillance of private citizens; the break-in of a psychiatrist's office; and the unlawful campaign financing practices of the Committee to Re-elect the President.

An unresolved constitutional issue arose in September 1974: whether a subsequent President can issue a pardon in the absence of either a conviction or an INDICTMENT. A final question will trouble historians for years: did the Constitution work in Watergate, or did the crisis demonstrate fundamental failures in the governmental system?

PAUL L. MURPHY
(1986)

Bibliography

KURLAND, PHILLIP 1978 *Watergate and the Constitution*. Chicago: University of Chicago Press.
MILLER, ARTHUR S. 1979 *Social Change and Fundamental Law*. Westport, Conn.: Greenwood Press.
MURPHY, PAUL L. 1979 Misgovernment by Judiciary? Watergate and the Constitution. *Harvard Civil RightsCivil Liberties Law Review* 14:783–799.

# WATER POLLUTION CONTROL ACT

See: Environmental Regulation and the Constitution

# WATER POWER ACT
41 Stat. 1063 (1920)

The failure to capitalize on the vast water power resources of the country led increasingly, in the early twentieth century, to efforts to develop and regulate unused power on public lands and navigable rivers. After a number of failed attempts at national legislation, Congress finally passed the Water Power Act in 1920.

The act established a Federal Power Commission (FPC), to be composed of the secretaries of war, agriculture, and interior, with authority to approve water power projects "for the development and improvement of navigation, and for the development, transmission, and utilization of power" on any navigable river or public lands. The act empowered the FPC to license projects for up to fifty years; it also directed preferential treatment for state or municipal projects. The rates charged for the use of water were to include only FPC expenses; moreover, the act required licensees to charge "reasonable, nondiscriminatory and just" rates and prohibited combinations or other agreements to limit output or fix prices. The act stipulated that rate-fixing and regulation be administered according to the procedures outlined in the INTERSTATE COMMERCE ACT.

The Supreme Court approved extensive federal controls in UNITED STATES V. APPALACHIAN ELECTRIC POWER COMPANY (1940).

DAVID GORDON
(1986)

# WATER QUALITY IMPROVEMENT ACT

See: Environmental Regulation and the Constitution

# WATERS v. CHURCHILL
511 U.S. 661 (1994)

Cheryl Churchill disliked her supervisor, Cynthia Waters, and the new cross-training program for nurses established at the public hospital that employed her. When Churchill aired some of these complaints in the hospital cafeteria, her conversation was overheard by another nurse. After a short investigation in which that nurse and the other party to the conversation claimed that Churchill had made "unkind" remarks about Waters, Waters fired Churchill. A lower federal court ruled that the firing violated Churchill's FIRST AMENDMENT right to FREEDOM OF SPEECH because she had not, in fact, criticized her boss.

The Supreme Court reversed. The majority held that PUBLIC EMPLOYEES may be discharged on the basis of remarks their supervisors, after a reasonable investigation, thought they said, even when the actual remarks were constitutionally protected speech. The government interest in "efficient employment decisionmaking," Justice SANDRA

DAY O'CONNOR'S declared in her PLURALITY OPINION, justified abandoning "the evidentiary rules used by courts" when evaluating the speech rights of public employees. The Justices could not tell from the record whether Churchill was constitutionally fired for expressing distaste for her employer or unconstitutionally fired for criticizing the cross-training program. Hence, the case was remanded to the lower court.

*Waters v. Churchill* highlights the tendency of the REHNQUIST COURT to make case-specific decisions, particularly when O'Connor is the swing vote. Her MAJORITY OPINION gives little indication of what constitutes a reasonable investigation, except to indicate that one was conducted in this case. Nor is the constitutional difference between criticizing a public employer and criticizing a program instituted by a public employer spelled out. The main lesson may be that public employees should not criticize their supervisors in places where others may overhear their conversations.

MARK A. GRABER
(2000)

(SEE ALSO: *National Treasury Employees Union, United States v.; Public Employees and Free Speech.*)

# WATKINS v. UNITED STATES
354 U.S. 178 (1957)

# SWEEZY v. NEW HAMPSHIRE
354 U.S. 234 (1957)

Watkins, a labor leader called to testify before the House Committee on Un-American Activities, had been told by the union president that he would lose his position if he claimed his RIGHT AGAINST SELF-INCRIMINATION. He thus claimed a FIRST AMENDMENT privilege when he declined to answer the committee's questions about the membership of other people in the Communist party. He also objected that these questions were beyond the scope of the committee's activities. For his refusal to answer, Watkins was convicted of contempt of Congress. The Supreme Court reversed his conviction, 8–1.

Writing for the Court, Chief Justice EARL WARREN rested decision on a narrow point: Watkins had been denied PROCEDURAL DUE PROCESS, for he had not been given a sufficient explanation of the subject of inquiry, and thus could not know whether the committee's questions were "pertinent to the questions under inquiry," as the contempt statute specified. Warren's opinion, however, strongly suggested that the Court would be prepared to confront the whole issue of LEGISLATIVE INVESTIGATIONS into political association. He remarked on the use of such investigations to subject people to public stigma, and the absence in such proceedings of effective protection of procedural fairness. "We have no doubt that there is no congressional power to expose for the sake of exposure," Warren wrote. "Who can define the meaning of "un-American'?" Justice TOM C. CLARK, the sole dissenter, appeared to object as much to these broad OBITER DICTA as to the actual decision. He complained of the Court's "mischievous curbing of the informing function of Congress."

In *Sweezy*, a COMPANION CASE to *Watkins*, the Court held, 6–2, that a state legislative investigation could not constitutionally compel Sweezy to answer questions about the Progressive party and about a lecture he had given at the University of New Hampshire. Chief Justice Warren wrote a PLURALITY OPINION for four Justices, concluding that Sweezy's contempt conviction violated procedural due process because the state legislature had not clearly authorized the attorney general, who conducted the investigation, to inquire into those subjects. Justice FELIX FRANKFURTER, joined by Justice JOHN MARSHALL HARLAN, concurred, arguing that the state had unconstitutionally invaded Sweezy's FOURTEENTH AMENDMENT liberty—here, his "political autonomy," a plain reference to the First Amendment. Justice Frankfurter used a (for him) familiar BALANCING TEST, but articulated a COMPELLING STATE INTEREST standard for cases of invasions of political privacy. The Frankfurter opinion is notable for its early articulation of the constitutional dimension of ACADEMIC FREEDOM. It also led, the following year, to the Court's explicit recognition of the FREEDOM OF ASSOCIATION in NAACP V. ALABAMA (1958). Justice Clark again dissented, now joined by Justice HAROLD H. BURTON.

A number of members of Congress reacted angrily to these opinions and others decided the same year, such as YATES V. UNITED STATES (1957) and *Jencks v. United States* (1957). (See JENCKS ACT.) Bills were proposed in Congress to limit the Supreme Court's jurisdiction over cases involving controls of subversive activities. In the event, not much "curbing" was done, and in retrospect *Watkins* and *Sweezy* appeared to be no more than trial balloons. Two years later, in BARENBLATT V. UNITED STATES (1959), a majority of the Court backed away from the expected confrontation with Congress.

KENNETH L. KARST
(1986)

# WAYNE, JAMES M.
## (1790?–1867)

After service as an elected official and judge in Georgia and as a Jacksonian Democrat in Congress, James Moore Wayne served thirty-two years as an Associate Justice of the United States Supreme Court. Despite this lengthy tenure he produced no significant opinions, though he consistently strove to protect national authority, CORPORATIONS, and SLAVERY. During the CIVIL WAR, his nationalist outlook induced him to remain on the Court as a Unionist.

Wayne, son of a well-to-do Savannah factor and rice planter, was educated at the College of New Jersey (Princeton), read law in New Haven and in his native Savannah, and was admitted to the Georgia bar in 1811. He was a member of the Georgia House of Representatives from 1815 to 1817, mayor of Savannah from 1817 to 1819, and successively judge of a court of common pleas and of the Superior Court. He later served in two state CONSTITUTIONAL CONVENTIONS, the second time as president. In 1829, Wayne was elected to the United States House of Representatives, where he prominently supported ANDREW JACKSON. He promoted Indian removal from his native state, backed Jackson's Bank policies, and stood by the President during the Nullification Crisis in South Carolina. He was the only member of the Georgia delegation to support the FORCE BILL. In his last term, he became chairman of the Foreign Relations Committee.

Jackson nominated Wayne to take the seat of Justice WILLIAM JOHNSON of South Carolina, and he was confirmed in 1835. Justice BENJAMIN R. CURTIS later called Wayne one of the "most high-toned Federalists on the bench," referring to Wayne's tenacious nationalism. This outlook was most apparent in COMMERCE CLAUSE cases. In the PASSENGER CASES (1849), Wayne was one of a majority that held unconstitutional state statutes regulating the ingress of ship passengers on the ground that insofar as such laws "practically operated as regulations of commerce, or as restraints upon navigation," they were unconstitutional. The power to regulate foreign and INTERSTATE COMMERCE was "exclusively vested in congress." Unlike his fellow Southerner, Chief Justice ROGER B. TANEY, he was not troubled by the implications of this position for the states' control of slavery. Wayne joined in Justice JOHN MCLEAN's nationalist dissent in COOLEY V. BOARD OF WARDENS (1851), arguing that Congress's control of interstate and FOREIGN COMMERCE was exclusive of state power.

The same nationalist spirit produced other opinions upholding federal authority. In *Dobbins v. Erie County* (1842) Wayne struck down a local tax on a federal officer. He was an enthusiastic proponent of federal admiralty jurisdiction, and in *Waring v. Clarke* (1847) he extended that jurisdiction to tidal waters of the Mississippi River well above New Orleans. In *Louisville, Cincinnati, and Charleston Railroad Co. v. Letson* (1844) Wayne rejected a rule, origi nally fashioned by Chief Justice JOHN MARSHALL, that restricted the access of corporations to federal courts by requiring that for purposes of DIVERSITY JURISDICTION, all their shareholders be citizens of a state different from all parties on the other side. Wayne instead adopted the rule that a corporation's CITIZENSHIP for diversity purposes is derived from the state where it was chartered and where its officers conducted business.

Wayne was sympathetic to corporate investors, as his CONTRACT CLAUSE opinions reveal. He dissented without opinion in WEST RIVER BRIDGE V. DIX (1848), in which the Court permitted a state to use its EMINENT DOMAIN powers to destroy a corporate charter. In the Ohio Bank Tax cases, Wayne consistently voted to strike down state attempts to modify tax exemptions claimed by banks. One of these cases, DODGE V. WOOLSEY (1856), produced what was probably Wayne's most memorable opinion. Condemning the effort of Ohio Democrats to destroy a tax exemption by an amendment to the state constitution, Wayne sermonized: "moral obligations never die. If broken by states and nations, though the terms of reproach are not the same with which we are accustomed to designate the faithlessness of individuals, the violation of justice is not the less."

Wayne was himself a slaveholder and no less dedicated to his section than other southern jurists such as Taney and PETER DANIEL. He considered slavery a vital component of southern society, beyond control of the federal government except for purposes of protection. But, unlike Taney, Wayne remained coolly assured about the constitutional security of slavery, and he was not blinded by the state-sovereignty dogmatism that warped his Chief's opinions in slavery cases. The Constitution itself, Wayne believed, incorporated express protections for slavery's security. In his concurrence in PRIGG V. PENNSYLVANIA (1842) Wayne went along with JOSEPH STORY's assertion that states need not support enforcement of the federal Fugitive Slave Act, but only on the ground that to admit any state role at all would be to invite Northern states to interfere with the capture and rendition of fugitives.

Wayne played a mischievous role in DRED SCOTT V. SANDFORD (1857) though his brief concurring opinion merely endorsed entirely Taney's opinion. Wayne first urged that the Chief Justice write the opinion for the Court's majority rather than Justice SAMUEL NELSON, whose opinion would evade the larger issues in the case by a narrow jurisdictional ruling, and he formally moved that the Court address itself to all issues, not just the jurisdictional ones. Scholars have suggested that Taney's opinion incorporated portions of a draft opinion that Wayne did not submit. Yet Wayne was no fanatic on the subject of slavery. On circuit, he delivered a vigorous jury charge in the trial of officers of the notorious slave ship *Wanderer,* upholding the power of the federal government to hang slavers.

The Civil War forced a severe test of Wayne's conflicting loyalties. After SECESSION, he supported his son's decision to resign his commission in the United States Army and accept appointment as Georgia's adjutant general, but

Wayne elected to remain on the federal bench. Georgia retaliated by confiscating his property and declaring him an enemy alien. In 1861, Wayne denied a HABEAS CORPUS petition from a soldier who claimed that ABRAHAM LINCOLN's call for troops was illegal. In conformity with that position, Wayne joined the five-member majority in the PRIZE CASES (1863), upholding the legality of Lincoln's action in imposing a blockade around the seceding states. He wrote for the Court in EX PARTE VALLANDIGHAM (1864), refusing to review the conviction of an Ohio Copperhead congressman by a military commission. In EX PARTE MILLIGAN (1866), where the majority held that Congress could not authorize military commissions for areas outside the theater of war, Wayne joined the four-man minority who argued for congressional discretion in using military commissions. But there are indications that Wayne's Unionist views would not be extrapolated to accept all aspects of Republican RECONSTRUCTION. He joined the majority in the TEST OATH CASES (1867), holding state and federal proscriptive oaths unconstitutional. He refused to hold CIRCUIT COURTS in his circuit in areas under military occupation. His death on July 5, 1867, ended his grief at the devastation that secession, war, and Reconstruction had brought to his beloved state.

WILLIAM M. WIECEK
(1986)

Bibliography

GATELL, FRANK O. 1969 James M. Wayne. In Leon Friedman and Fred L. Israel eds., *The Justices of the United States Supreme Court 1789–1969: Their Lives and Major Opinions.* New York: Chelsea House Publishers.

LAWRENCE, ALEXANDER A. 1943 *James Moore Wayne: Southern Unionist.* Chapel Hill: University of North Carolina Press.

# *WAYTE v. UNITED STATES*
## 470 U.S. 598 (1985)

After a presidential proclamation directing young men to register for a possible draft, David Wayte did not register, but wrote letters to government officials stating that he did not intend to do so. These letters went into a SELECTIVE SERVICE file of men who had given similar notices or who had been reported by others for failing to register. The government adopted a policy of "passive enforcement" of registration: it would prosecute only men named in this file. Government officials wrote letters warning the men to register or face prosecution, and FEDERAL BUREAU OF INVESTIGATION agents urged Wayte in person to register during a grace period. He refused and was indicted for failure to register. The federal district court dismissed Wayte's indictment, holding that the government had not rebutted his preliminary showing of selective prosecution. The court of appeals reversed, holding that Wayte had not shown that the government had prosecuted him because of his protest. The Supreme Court affirmed, 7–2.

Justice LEWIS F. POWELL wrote the OPINION OF THE COURT. Claims of selective prosecution, he said, must be judged under ordinary EQUAL PROTECTION standards, which, as the Court held in WASHINGTON V. DAVIS (1976), require a showing of intentional discrimination. Here, the government's awareness that "passive enforcement" would fall disproportionately on protesters was an insufficient showing of intent to punish protest. Given the government's policy of urging compliance after receiving notice of failure to register, Wayte was not prosecuted for protesting, but for persisting in refusing registration.

Wayte's FIRST AMENDMENT challenge also focused on the enforcement system's disparate impact on protesters. Applying the formula of UNITED STATES V. O'BRIEN (1968), Justice Powell concluded that "passive enforcement" passed the test. The government interest in national security was important, and unrelated to the suppression of expression; and the enforcement system burdened speech no more than was necessary to secure registration.

Justice THURGOOD MARSHALL dissented, joined by Justice WILLIAM J. BRENNAN, arguing that Wayte had been denied effective opportunity for DISCOVERY of information concerning the motivations of high government officials for prosecuting him. Thus, he could not fully support his claim that the prosecution was designed to punish his protest. The majority dismissed this argument, saying—contrary to the dissenters' view—that Wayte had not presented the issue to the Supreme Court.

KENNETH L. KARST
(1986)

# WEALTH DISCRIMINATION

Wealth discrimination—the state's allocation of resources on the basis of ability to pay—has received the attention of the courts only recently. Sensitivity to the plight of the poor was an outgrowth of the CIVIL RIGHTS movement of the 1960s. Thus, the first constitutional issue raised by EQUAL PROTECTION claims of the poor was whether poverty-based discrimination is analogous to RACIAL DISCRIMINATION for purposes of the applicable STANDARD OF REVIEW.

Advocates of this analogy stress the poor's lack of political power and the public's antipathy to the poor and to programs, such as welfare, enacted to ameliorate poverty. They argue that the Supreme Court should give less deference to legislative judgments when reviewing poverty discrimination claims than it does when reviewing ECONOMIC REGULATIONS challenged by those able to pursue

nonjudicial means of redress. However, at no time during the more than quarter of a century since the Court's first decision in this area, GRIFFIN V. ILLINOIS (1956), has a majority of the Court ever embraced the analogy to race for purposes of equal protection review.

The *Griffin* decision held unconstitutional a state's refusal to provide an INDIGENT convicted criminal defendant with a free transcript necessary to obtain meaningful appellate review. In so holding, *Griffin* enunciated a potentially expansive principle of "equal justice": "[A] state can no more discriminate on account of poverty than on account of religion, race, or color. . . . There can be no equal justice when the kind of trial [or APPEAL ] a man gets depends on the amount of money he has."

Since *Griffin,* the Supreme Court has struck down poverty-based discrimination in only a few other cases, most notably DOUGLAS V. CALIFORNIA (1963) and BODDIE V. CONNECTICUT (1971). *Douglas* held unconstitutional a state's refusal to appoint counsel for an indigent seeking appellate review of a criminal conviction; and *Boddie* held unconstitutional a state's refusal to waive court access fees which deprived an indigent plaintiff of access to the only available forum for obtaining a divorce.

In the vast majority of poverty-based discrimination cases, however, the Supreme Court has treated the poor's claims, whether they involve access to the judicial process itself, equal educational opportunity, or the very means of survival, the same as any other challenged "social and economic" regulation. Thus, the Court has applied the RATIONAL BASIS standard of review to uphold a $50 bankruptcy filing fee against a debtor too poor to pay it; a state financing system that allocated educational resources according to the tax bases of school districts; and an allocation of WELFARE BENEFITS that discriminated on the basis of family size. (See *United States v. Kras,* 1973; SAN ANTONIO INDEPENDENT SCHOOL DISTRICT V. RODRIGUEZ, 1973; DANDRIDGE V. WILLIAMS, 1971.)

Several reasons may underlie the Court's refusal actively to scrutinize legislation adversely affecting the poor. If the Court holds a payment requirement unconstitutional as applied to the poor, someone must decide who is poor enough to qualify for this affirmative relief. Moreover, such a holding may require the legislative branch to reallocate its budget to provide the funds necessary to pay for what the poor cannot afford, something which the courts are always reluctant to do, especially in times of economic recession.

Another reason for judicial restraint lies in the need for line-drawing. If not all poverty-based inequalities or deprivations are unconstitutional—as surely they are not in a market economy—then the Court must delineate those interests that are sufficiently "vital" or "fundamental" to justify stricter judicial scrutiny when the state allocates such interests through a pricing system that deprives poor people from access to them. Obvious candidates include basic necessities such as food, housing, and other means of subsistence. Beginning with its 1971 decision in *Dandridge*, however, the Supreme Court consistently has refused to treat any such interests as entitled to a heightened equal protection standard of review. Moreover, in MAHER V. ROE (1977) the Court carried this refusal to apply a meaningful equal protection standard to any discriminatory "social and economic" legislation to the extreme of validating a provision prohibiting Medicaid funding of abortion although other, including pregnancy-related medical care costs, were funded and the choice to seek an abortion rather than bear a child had been held to be constitutionally protected. Moreover, *Maher* upheld this discrimination even though, unlike the discrimination upheld in all similar prior cases, it cost rather than saved taxpayer dollars. (See HARRIS V. MCRAE, 1980.)

The Court's refusal since 1971 to treat "vital interests" of the poor as comparable to constitutionally guaranteed rights is one matter. In *Maher*, however, the Court validated discrimination only among the poor and solely on the basis of the poor's attempt to exercise a constitutionally guaranteed right of choice otherwise available to everyone. The recent jurisprudence of wealth discrimination legitimates and reinforces a dual system of constitutional rights, leaving the poor—who disproportionately are composed of women, children, the aged, and racial minorities—with paper rights beyond their financial reach.

BARBARA BRUDNO
(1986)

Bibliography

BINION, GAYLE   1982   The Disadvantaged Before the Burger Court: The Newest Unequal Protection. *Law & Policy Quarterly* 4:37–69.

BRUDNO, BARBARA   1976   *Poverty, Inequality, and the Law.* St. Paul, Minn.: West Publishing Co.

——   1980   Wealth Discrimination in the Supreme Court: Equal Protection for the Poor from *Griffin* to *Maher*. Pages 229–246 in Ron Collins, ed., *Constitutional Government in America.* Durham, N.C.: Carolina Academic Press.

# WEBB-KENYON ACT
## 37 Stat. 699 (1913)

Although the Supreme Court had generally refused to uphold laws that it characterized as STATE REGULATION OF COMMERCE, a series of decisions in the late nineteenth and early twentieth centuries deferred to such action. Reacting to a clear invitation in the Court's opinion in LEISY V. HARDIN (1890), holding that absent congressional authorization a state could not prevent the importation and first sale of liquor in the original package, Congress passed the Wilson Act. The law subjected intoxicating liquor "to the operation and effect of the laws of [a] State or territory enacted in the exercise of its [STATE] POLICE POWERS" despite the liquor's journey in INTERSTATE COMMERCE and the ORIGINAL PACKAGE DOCTRINE. The Court sustained that act in *In re Rahrer* (1891).

The Webb-Kenyon Act, passed over the veto of President WILLIAM HOWARD TAFT, divested liquor of its interstate character when introduced in violation of state law. Congress thus effectively allowed state prohibition laws to regulate national commerce in liquor. The Court upheld this act in CLARK DISTILLING COMPANY V. WESTERN MARYLAND RAILWAY CO. (1917).

DAVID GORDON
(1986)

Bibliography

SEMONCHE, JOHN E.   1978   *Charting the Future: The Supreme Court Responds to a Changing Society, 1890–1920.* Westport, Conn.: Greenwood Press.

# WEBSTER, DANIEL
## (1782–1852)

As a leading lawyer and politician for forty years, Daniel Webster influenced constitutional development as few others have. When the young New Hampshire representative arrived in Washington in 1813, he immediately became a spokesman for New England interests and remained so until the mid-1820s despite an interruption of congressional service (1817–1823) upon moving to Boston. For most of the time from 1827 to his death in 1852, he was an eloquent nationalist in the SENATE. Except for two periods as secretary of state under Tyler and Fillmore, he spent the last quarter-century of his life in that body, expounding the principles of a perpetual Union and a flexible Constitution. In either role, sectionalist or nationalist, he applied constitutional ideas to political issues with uncommon ability.

During the early years his FEDERALIST partisanship and loyalty to a commercial constituency led him to oppose Republican policies of embargo and war. Using economic coercion to maintain maritime rights, he believed, intolerably stretched the power to regulate commerce, indeed, it destroyed commerce. And prosecuting an offensive war against Britain caused other constitutional errors: misuse of militia, proposals for federal conscription, encroachment on STATES' RIGHTS. Though not a delegate to the HARTFORD CONVENTION, Webster approved its resolutions. Later he sought, unconvincingly, to dissociate himself from it. His sectionalism persisted when he opposed the postwar trend toward a protective tariff (1816–1824). Again he voiced a strict constructionist interpretation of the COMMERCE CLAUSE to promote low rates desired by merchants and a system of laissez-faire in the first phase of industrialization.

In the late 1820s, he shifted to a nationalist position concurrently with JOHN C. CALHOUN's shift in the opposite direction. In behalf of rising manufacturers, he joined HENRY CLAY in advocating governmental policies to achieve economic growth and American self-sufficiency. No longer did he oppose use of the commerce power for broad goals. When South Carolina nullified the tariff of 1832, his oratorical duel with Calhoun provided an opportunity to reiterate more comprehensively his constitutional thought, dramatically set forth in his earlier debate with ROBERT HAYNE. Beyond the tariff question, he countered the doctrines of state sovereignty and NULLIFICATION with the concept of a perpetual Union, created by the people, not the states, and composed of two spheres of authority, national and state, both responsible to the people. In event of conflict, Article VI of the Constitution required national supremacy; and the Supreme Court had long performed its proper duty of upholding that rule.

Soon slavery became the focus of politics. Ever since writing a memorial on the Missouri question in 1820, Webster had advocated a national power to prevent western extension of slavery; but he conceded Congress could not touch it in existing states and he soft-pedaled the moral question. Subsequently he opposed ANNEXATION OF TEXAS and further territorial acquisitions from Mexico, fearing they would disrupt the Union. When, in the great congressional debate of 1850, controversy reached a climax, he preferred compromise to save the Union instead of legislation against extension of slavery, constitutionally possible though it was. Antislavery forces attacked him furiously—the more so when the fugitive slave law, a part of the compromise, appeared to violate CIVIL LIBERTIES. As senator, he had inclined toward TRIAL BY JURY for suspected runaways; as secretary of state he insisted upon strict observance of the statute prescribing summary process.

He was very active in the Supreme Court as well as in Congress. Altogether, he argued 168 cases, of which twenty-five involved constitutional questions. He won about half and influenced doctrinal development even in some he lost. Regularly, he set forth nationalistic arguments to limit state power in a day when most congressional powers were dormant. More successful when JOHN MARSHALL was Chief Justice (to 1835) than when ROGER B. TANEY presided, he made a deep impression on the governmental structure. Of the cases strengthening nationalism, MCCULLOCH V. MARYLAND (1819) stands out. Here, though overshadowed by WILLIAM PINKNEY, Webster con-

tributed to a definition of the Union identical to that in his Senate speeches against nullification. And he introduced the aphorism that the power to tax involves the power to destroy. OSBORN V. BANK OF THE UNITED STATES (1824) provided opportunities to advocate expansion of federal court JURISDICTION in the whole field of corporate rights.

The first commerce case the Court heard involved steamboat monopoly (GIBBONS V. OGDEN, 1824). Contending for an exclusive congressional power over INTERSTATE COMMERCE, Webster would have been satisfied with a rule of partially concurrent power. Marshall sympathized with the first option but did not rest his decision on either formula, therefore postponing a judicial guideline. Over the next twenty-five years, Webster participated in several other cases, such as the LICENSE CASES (1847) and the PASSENGER CASES (1849), in an unavailing effort to obtain an exclusive-power decision. At last, in COOLEY V. BOARD OF WARDENS (1851), his protege, Justice BENJAMIN CURTIS, spoke for a majority in laying down a partially concurrent-power standard which preserved about as much exclusive national authority as Webster wished. *Cooley* remains good constitutional law.

Webster's nationalism was not an abstract idea. He connected it with the sanctity of property rights as the very foundation of a dynamic economy. Best illustrating this belief are the CONTRACT CLAUSE cases in which he appeared. DARTMOUTH COLLEGE V. WOODWARD (1819) is a classic in the long history of VESTED RIGHTS shielded from state interference. He relied upon the contract clause of the Constitution as if it were an early version of SUBSTANTIVE DUE PROCESS of law. Though the contract clause, even the concept of vested rights of property, has declined, the notion of active judicial defense of individual constitutional rights flourishes in the area of civil liberties. The *Dartmouth* case was only Webster's first of several dealing with the contract clause.

Webster's career reflected the junction of personal capacity with a favorable setting to establish nationhood and to invigorate a capitalist economy. Still, he may have been flawed by moral oversights and may have encouraged an inequitable distribution of wealth and privilege. Perhaps his contemporaries sensed weaknesses such as these as they passed over him in electing their presidents.

MAURICE G. BAXTER
(1986)

(SEE ALSO: *Constitutional History, 1801–1829; Constitutional History, 1829–1848.*)

Bibliography

BARTLETT, IRVING H. 1978 *Daniel Webster.* New York: W. W. Norton.

BAXTER, MAURICE G. 1966 *Daniel Webster and the Supreme Court.* Amherst: University of Massachusetts Press.

—— 1984 *One and Inseparable: Daniel Webster and the Union.* Cambridge, Mass.: Harvard University Press.

FUESS, CLAUDE M. 1930 *Daniel Webster*, 2 vols. Boston: Little, Brown.

# WEBSTER v. REPRODUCTIVE HEALTH SERVICES
## 492 U.S. 490 (1989)

The *Webster* case had been advertised as the one in which the Supreme Court might overrule ROE V. WADE (1973), but in the event the decision offered only minor adjustments at the margins of the constitutional doctrine governing a woman's right to have an ABORTION. The decision's political consequences, however, were anything but minor.

From the time of the *Roe* decision, Missouri has produced a steady stream of legislation designed to restrict women who seek abortions and the doctors who attend them. In this case the Court considered several provisions of a 1986 Missouri law: (1) the preamble, containing the legislature's "findings" that human life begins at conception and that "unborn children have protectable interests in life, health, and well-being"; (2) a prohibition on the use of public facilities or employees to perform abortions; (3) a prohibition against public funding of abortion counseling; and (4) a requirement that a doctor conduct a fetal viability test before performing an abortion. Chief Justice WILLIAM H. REHNQUIST wrote for the Court.

The Court refused to pass on the preamble, saying that, for all the Justices knew, the "findings" had no effect beyond the expression of the legislature's value judgment. The Court upheld the prohibition on using public facilities or public employees in performing abortions, reaffirming the holdings of MAHER V. ROE (1977) and HARRIS V. MCRAE (1980) that the state has no constitutional duty to provide assistance to women who cannot afford abortions. The controversy over the prohibition on using public money for abortion counseling was dismissed for MOOTNESS because the plaintiffs agreed that this part of law did not affect them.

On the validity of the viability-testing provision there was no OPINION OF THE COURT. Chief Justice Rehnquist, for three Justices, interpreted this requirement to conflict with the analysis in *Roe v. Wade* and concluded that, to the extent of the conflict, *Roe* must give way. The testing requirement might make abortions more costly, but it "permissibly further[ed] the State's interest in protecting potential human life" and was constitutional. Justice SANDRA DAY O'CONNOR agreed that the testing requirement was valid, but thought it was consistent with the Court's prior decisions. She thus resisted the invitation to address the question of *Roe*'s continuing force and reaffirmed her earlier position that a law should not be invalidated unless it "unduly burdens" the right to seek an abortion. Justice ANTONIN SCALIA, concurring in upholding the testing requirement, agreed with the dissenters that the Chief Justice's opinion on this issue would effectively overrule *Roe*. He thought, however, that the Court should perform its overruling of *Roe* more explicitly and criticized the majority for failing to do so. In an especially scornful footnote, he rejected Justice O'Connnor's position and lectured her on the vocabulary of "viability."

Justice HARRY A. BLACKMUN, for three Justices, dissented, strongly reaffirming the correctness of *Roe v. Wade* and its successor decisions. He saw the Chief Justice's opinion on Missouri's requirement of viability testing as, in effect, calling for *Roe* to be overruled and added his gloomy prediction of a piecemeal process of overruling "until sometime, a new regime of old dissenters and new appointees will declare what the plurality intends: that *Roe* is no longer good law."

The most important result of *Webster* was political: the mobilization of nationwide support for reproductive freedom. In the year following *Webster*, forty-four legislatures met, and about two-thirds of them considered proposals to restrict abortions; only four adopted restrictions. If *Roe* was a catalyst for the "prolife" movement, *Webster* was a catalyst for the "prochoice" movement. Governors, legislators, and even the President seemed to recognize that two strong views now demanded a hearing.

KENNETH L. KARST
(1992)

# WEEKS v. UNITED STATES
## 232 U.S. 383 (1914)

*Weeks v. United States* was the Court's single most creative decision under the FOURTH AMENDMENT. To save the amendment as a living constitutional guarantee, the Court endowed it with an enforcement feature, ordering the exclusion from federal trials of EVIDENCE obtained through unlawful seizure. Without this EXCLUSIONARY RULE, seized evidence, regardless of its origin, would always be admissible. The rule thus has provided the occasion for judicial articulation of Fourth Amendment reasonableness in later cases.

Under COMMON LAW, and for the first century of the Constitution's existence, evidence unlawfully seized by government officers was nonetheless admissible in evidence. In BOYD V. UNITED STATES (1886) the Court implicitly discarded this common law principle, but the exclusionary rule, as it has come to be called, was not explicitly enthroned until the *Weeks* decision. The reason for admitting unlawfully seized evidence, a standard still followed in nearly all other countries, is readily understood. Unlike coerced confessions, which are excluded from trial in all civilized countries because of their untrustworthiness, the fruit of an illegal search is just as reliable when taken without a shadow of authority as when taken under warrant. To exclude the evidence allows a criminal to go free. Absent the exclusionary rule, however, the Fourth Amendment might become a mere paper guarantee of freedom from UNREASONABLE SEARCHES without an effective enforcement process. Unlike other guarantees in the BILL OF RIGHTS (for example, RIGHT TO COUNSEL), the Fourth Amendment affects the pretrial stage of the case and is—apart from the exclusionary rule—not within the power of the trial court to enforce. The secrecy in which searches are planned and executed makes it impossible to seek the advance protection of an INJUNCTION, a regular practice when FIRST AMENDMENT freedoms are threatened.

The unanimous *Weeks* opinion said that if unconstitutionally seized evidence were admitted, the Fourth Amendment "might as well be stricken from the Constitution." Furthermore, if the evidence were admitted, courts become parties to the misdeeds of the police, thus compromising the integrity of the judicial process.

The opinion did not, however, make clear whether the exclusionary rule was required by the Constitution or merely was the product of the Court's supervisory power over the lower federal courts and thus subject to negation by Congress. Even if the rule is rooted in the Fourth Amendment, the question remains whether it is a personal right of the defendant or just a deterrent against unlawful searches, discardable if other deterrents can be found. The *Weeks* opinion appeared to endorse the first position; use of the evidence, said the Court, would constitute "a denial of the constitutional rights of the accused." More recent decisions, however, favor the deterrent theory. Nonetheless, one who is not himself the victim of an unlawful search but is implicated in crime by the seizure does not have STANDING to challenge admission of the evidence.

JACOB W. LANDYNSKI
(1986)

## WEEMS v. UNITED STATES
### 217 U.S. 349 (1910)

In *Weems*, the Court held that punishment is cruel and unusual if it is grossly excessive for the crime. Paul Weems, a government official in the Philippines, was convicted of falsifying pay records. Under a territorial law inherited from the Spanish penal code, Weems was sentenced to *cadeña temporal*, a punishment involving fifteen years of hard labor in chains, permanent deprivation of political rights, and surveillance by the authorities for life. Since the Philippine Bill of Rights was Congress's extension to the Philippines of rights guaranteed by the Constitution, the meaning of CRUEL AND UNUSUAL PUNISHMENT was the same in both documents.

DENNIS J. MAHONEY
(1986)

## WELFARE BENEFITS

Nothing in the Constitution requires the United States or any state to provide public relief to those unable to earn adequate subsistence. Throughout most of history that relief has been the responsibility of private charity or local government. But several provisions of the Constitution impose an obligation on government officials, where such relief is provided, to refrain from imposing arbitrary standards or procedures. That obligation is generally recognized by legislative bodies and, since the late 1960s, has become a special concern of the federal courts.

The courts have treated questions concerning the extension or withdrawal of public welfare benefits under the PRIVILEGES AND IMMUNITIES, EQUAL PROTECTION, and DUE PROCESS clauses of the Constitution. In SHAPIRO V. THOMPSON (1969) the Supreme Court held that a one-year RESIDENCE REQUIREMENT for welfare eligibility infringed the right of interstate migration, a privilege protected by Article IV and the FOURTEENTH AMENDMENT, and also denied equal protection of the laws to indigent interstate travelers. In GRAHAM V. RICHARDSON (1971) the Court held that denial of benefits to resident ALIENS was a denial of equal protection. However, in DANDRIDGE V. WILLIAMS (1970) the Court decisively rejected argument that WEALTH DISCRIMINATION was a SUSPECT CLASSIFICATION or that welfare subsistence was a FUNDAMENTAL INTEREST. And in *Jefferson v. Hackney* (1972), the Court declined to hold that the equal protection clause required a state to compute the need for public assistance according to the same standard for each of the various welfare programs. Nonetheless in GOLDBERG V. KELLY (1970) the Court held that once benefits were granted they could not be discontinued without PROCEDURAL DUE PROCESS, including NOTICE and FAIR HEARING.

DENNIS J. MAHONEY
(1986)

## WELFARE PROGRAMS

See: Entitlement

# WELFARE RIGHTS

Is there a constitutional right of indigent people to basic survival assistance from the state? The current Supreme Court says no, but there is a strong argument that a future Supreme Court should recognize a positive constitutional right to basic subsistence.

The current Court's view was essentially settled in DANDRIDGE V. WILLIAMS (1971), when the Court ruled that a state law setting a maximum grant of WELFARE BENEFITS to any one family, regardless of family size, was to be categorized as ECONOMIC REGULATION. On this assumption the law should be upheld if it were supported by a RATIONAL BASIS, which the Court found to be present.

For a decade and a half prior to that time, the Court had tantalized scholars and advocates with a series of holdings requiring provision of transcripts to indigent criminal defendants in GRIFFIN V. ILLINOIS (1956), outlawing the POLL TAX because of its impact in barring indigent people from voting in HARPER V. VIRGINIA STATE BOARD OF ELECTIONS (1966), mandating a face-to-face hearing before welfare benefits could be terminated in GOLDBERG V. KELLY (1970), and invalidating durational RESIDENCE REQUIREMENTS for welfare in SHAPIRO V. THOMPSON (1969).

These opinions suggested there was something particularly unacceptable or vulnerable about indigence that required special treatment of indigent people by the state. Some welfare advocates thought the Court might strike down America's patchwork income-maintenance system, in which there was no statutory obligation to help two-parent families and states could set payment levels as they chose.

*Dandridge* was the Court's response, followed as the decade wore on by declarations, in *Lindsey v. Normet* (1972), that there is no constitutional right to any minimum level of housing and, in MAHER V. ROE (1977), that there is no right to any minimum level of health care.

Yet a kernel of DOCTRINE remains to support the notion of a right to subsistence help. Indigence does require the state to take steps it would not otherwise have to take, at least when some other liberty or property interest is also at stake. The state, for example, has no obligation to provide a transcript to the rich, and it can impose durational residential requirements or differential fees for nonresidents applicable to a number of state benefits. But when indigence is involved, the liberty or property interests concerned become vital enough to require a different response from the state.

The Court's handling of public education provides a particularly important clue. In SAN ANTONIO INDEPENDENT SCHOOL DISTRICT V. RODRIQUEZ (1973), the Court, while upholding Texas's system of school finance, noted that a refusal to provide public education altogether would present a different case, a point it reiterated in *Papasan v. Allain* (1986). Considering that the wealthy can purchase education for their children, these references imply some obligation to provide education for those who cannot afford it. One argument supporting such a claim is that it is difficult to exercise one's political rights effectively without education. The same commonsense argument applies more generally to the status of indigence. Lack of food and shelter impedes political participation, among other things. Insofar as families with children are involved, indigence interferes gravely with the liberty interest in family relations recognized in MEYER V. NEBRASKA (1923). The door left open in *Rodriguez* has important implications.

If the state has a special obligation to protect some liberty and property interests when indigence is also present, it is arguable that there is an analogous liberty interest in not being indigent. Because indigence in an extreme form represents a threat to life itself, it is arguable that the state has an obligation to provide basic subsistence.

The Supreme Court has been reluctant throughout American history to declare any positive constitutional rights—rights creating affirmative obligations for the state to act, even though it has committed no legal wrong. Nonetheless, an alternative stream of doctrine, more muted and episodic, has permitted the Court to impose on the states affirmative obligations to act. For example, the Court's strained efforts to find state action in SHELLEY V. KRAEMER (1948) and MARSH V. ALABAMA (1946) might be characterized as imposing constitutional obligations on states to intervene to nullify unacceptable private arrangements or outcomes of private activities. The claim of a right to a subsistence, or "survival," income can well be said to rest on a similar state obligation to intervene to alter unacceptable market outcomes and vindicate individual liberty interests.

The argument for a right to subsistence does not need to rest solely on the idea of a positive right. For the nonelderly the current welfare system, in terms of cash and cash-equivalent assistance, consists primarily of Aid to Families with Dependent Children (AFDC) and food stamps. Because the states set payment levels for AFDC benefits, combined payment levels under the two programs vary from less than half the poverty level up to a point near the poverty level ($9,435 for a family of three in 1988). The states do not seek to justify this variation by reference to any regional difference in the cost of living—or, indeed, by reference to any other factor. The median state's benefits approximate two-thirds of the poverty-level income. In other words, in half the states welfare assistance brings a family with children up to less than two-thirds of what the government itself says is required to achieve a bare minimum standard of living. No substantial cash or cash-equivalent federal assistance other than food stamps is available to nondisabled nonelderly individuals or to couples without children.

It is not excessive to argue that this system lacks a rational basis. If any degree of heightened scrutiny were attached to legislation affecting the indigent, it is hard to see how the current welfare system could be justified in the face of an EQUAL PROTECTION challenge. Surely the current Supreme Court would not respond positively to these arguments. Yet similar arguments might be taken seriously by Justices of the future.

PETER B. EDELMAN
(1992)

(SEE ALSO: *Economic Equal Protection; Welfare State.*)

Bibliography

BLACK, CHARLES L., JR. 1985 Further Reflections on the Consitutional Justice of Livelihood. *Columbia Law Review* 86: 1103–1117.

EDELMAN, PETER B. 1987 The Next Century of Our Constitution: Rethinking Our Duty to the Poor. *Hastings Law Journal* 39:1–61.

# WELFARE RIGHTS
## (Update)

The twentieth century has witnessed the continuing evolution of a variety of governmental programs aimed at providing aid, in cash or in kind, to the poor. Once a supplement to private and religious charitable programs, governmental aid to the poor has become the single most important source of poverty relief in contemporary America. Some of these programs are denominated insurance programs, providing benefits to people who make, or have made for them, contributions to a fund upon the occurrence of certain events. The most important examples of these types of programs are Social Security and unemployment insurance. The former provides payments to certain categories of the aged, the infirm, and their dependents, and the latter provides for a finite number of periodic payments in the event of certain kinds of job loss. In each case, such payments can significantly exceed and usually bear very little relationship to an individual's contributions to the "fund" from which payments are made. What we have come to know as "welfare" does not include programs such as these. Instead, welfare, or public assistance, has come to mean public programs, financed from federal, state, or local funds, that furnish financial assistance or assistance in kind to families or individuals who meet specific conditions. The most important program of in-kind aid is administered through the Food Stamp Act of 1964, which subsidizes the purchase of food by per-

mitting a recipient to pay for food with program vouchers (or "food stamps"). For able-bodied unemployed men, for women without minor children, or for two-parent families, the most likely sources of public assistance are state or local programs of general assistance. These are the oldest programs of American public assistance and trace their origins directly to the Elizabethan Poor Laws. These programs serve as the last resort of governmental aid for people who are ineligible for unemployment compensation or Social Security related programs, and who are unable to qualify for any other program of governmental assistance.

For roughly sixty years prior to 1996, however, the largest and most significant form of welfare was the elaborate system of federal supplemental payments to states for payments to certain categories of the poor, primarily poor women with minor children. This federal grant program was known as Aid to Families with Dependant Children (AFDC). AFDC was originally conceived as a program to provide supplemental federal assistance to state welfare programs targeted to destitute children where the family breadwinner was dead, disabled, or absent. Most of the beneficiaries were white widows. By the 1990s, it had evolved into a primary source of benefits for poor women who headed their households alone and had minor children. Disproportionate numbers of beneficiaries were Latina or African American. While the federal government provided most of the funds for the program, and imposed significant regulations for the administration and availability of the program, participating states retained great latitude in the construction of their programs. Under AFDC rules, no eligible person could be denied benefits, but states had wide latitude in setting benefit levels and in implementing the minimal program requirements imposed by federal rules. The AFDC program proved highly controversial during the last forty or so years of its existence. Political liberals tended to believe that the program was too restrictive, its benefit levels too low, and its reliance on state administration archaic. Political conservatives insisted that the AFDC program benefits were too high, subsidized out-of-wedlock births and single-parent homes (which they considered an undesirable substitute for MARRIAGE), and created a "culture of dependency" passed down from mothers to children.

By 1995, political conservatives had won the day. Their solution to the problem posed by AFDC was the enactment of the Personal Responsibility and Work Opportunity Reconciliation Act of 1996 (PRWORA). The act eliminated the entitlement status of payments, replacing AFDC with Temporary Assistance for Needy Families (TANF). Federal assistance continues to be delivered to the states as a targeted supplement to state assistance programs, but now such payments are bundled as block grants to the states. TANF grants remain contingent upon compliance with a number of minimum federal requirements, but the quantity and scope of such requirements have decreased substantially from those under the old AFDC program. PRWORA tightens the rules for the receipt of food stamps, permits states the power to deny cash assistance to children born to women while they are receiving benefits, and tightens rules of eligibility for Medicare and Supplemental Social Security Income payments. Under PRWORA, state aid programs must impose significant work requirements on recipients and must meet certain minimum state funding requirements based on the level of state contributions to their AFDC programs. In addition, PRWORA gives a state broad authority to limit the amount of aid recipients may receive over their lifetime and to restrict aid to young mothers and documented and undocumented noncitizen immigrants. PRWORA also creates a comprehensive system for collecting child support payments from absent fathers.

Beyond these minimal federal requirements, PRWORA devolved substantial authority over the scope and means of the provision of benefits to the individual states. Subject to minimal standards set forth in PRWORA or in related regulations, states have authority to set benefit levels, eligibility criteria, and time limits for welfare benefits. Indeed, a state now appears to have power to determine the form of benefit as well as its level. In-kind benefits may be substituted for cash benefits, though few states have chosen to shift significantly to programs of in-kind benefits. States have leeway to define work requirements and the punishments for individual failure to comply, and to set the terms for income and asset acquisition for recipients making the transition from welfare benefits to self-sufficiency. As a result, much of the political conflict over welfare policy has shifted from the federal level to the state level, and the possibility of uniform standards of poverty relief is remote.

The Supreme Court has given great deference to legislative judgments, both state and federal, concerning WELFARE BENEFITS. As the Court wrote in DANDRIDGE V. WILLIAMS (1970), "here we deal with state regulation in the social and economic field, not affecting freedoms guaranteed by the Bill of Rights." "Congress is not, by virtue of having instituted a social welfare program, bound to continue it at all, much less at the same benefit level," the Court explained in *Bowen v. Gilliard* (1987). Where the Justices are persuaded that the issue is "economic" or "social," they have declined to extend federal constitutional protection to the substantive right to benefits. Thus, the Court held that the federal Constitution does not create a right to subsistence nor does it compel states to raise benefit levels to some minimally acceptable level. Nor is the federal government constitutionally compelled to maintain programs at any particular funding level. In contrast, several state courts have interpreted their state constitutions as requiring the provision of benefits.

The Supreme Court's deference has extended beyond the realm of welfare benefit programs. In a perversely ironic example of this reasoning, the Court held in *United States v. Kras* (1973) that the poor have no constitutional right to seek the protection of the federal bankruptcy laws without paying filing fees. The Court reasoned that there existed no constitutional right to bankruptcy protection and that the fees did not deny the indigent plaintiff the EQUAL PROTECTION OF THE LAWS. Rather than being a fundamental right, "bankruptcy legislation is in the area of economics and social welfare. This being so, the applicable standard, in measuring the propriety of Congress' classification, is that of the rational justification." A similar result was reached in *Ortwein v. Schwab* (1973), in which the Court held that the Constitution does not prohibit the imposition of a fee for appellate review of state administrative determination of welfare benefits.

On the other hand, the Court has applied federal constitutional principles of procedural fairness to deprivations of property in both the commercial and welfare context. In a celebrated decision, GOLDBERG V. KELLY (1970), the Court held that constitutional DUE PROCESS principles required the state to afford recipients meaningful notice and a meaningful opportunity to be heard before terminating welfare benefits. But the rights accorded under *Goldberg* left the basic structure of welfare untouched. It increased the cost to the state of individual deprivations but did not prohibit the state from limiting or eliminating welfare entirely.

Litigation over programs in aid of the poor has generated a significant body of case law treating issues of FEDERALISM, but not really touching on the fundamental constitutional condition of the poor themselves. In each of these cases, all decided under the AFDC rules, the Court shifted to the federal government the locus of the authority to interpret and control state welfare programs largely dependent on federal support. In these cases, the Court has consistently reasoned that because federal money was being used to subsidize and largely finance state welfare programs, and because the transfer of such money was conditioned by compliance with a host of complicated and far-reaching rules, the proper interpretation and implementation of such programs at the state level became the province of the federal government, subject to limitations, if any, of the federal Constitution.

This reasoning was sharpened in three cases in which the Court chose to concentrate on issues of federalism in the interpretation of the welfare statutes themselves. In *King v. Smith* (1968), the Court interpreted federal welfare rules to preclude Alabama from denying welfare benefits to otherwise eligible families because the mother might have an intimate relationship with a man who was not her husband. In *Townsend v. Swank* (1971), the Court determined that states had no power to vary the terms of optional programs under federal welfare legislation. In *Carlson v. Remillard* (1972), state rules that denied benefits to the family of a soldier serving in the VIETNAM WAR were voided for conflicting with federal welfare eligibility rules. In each of these cases, the Court focused on a determination of the appropriate level of governmental authority to make and alter the challenged welfare rules, rather than on the substance of the welfare rules themselves. In each of the cases, the Court favored the federal over the state power to regulate welfare. The Court, however, carefully avoided constitutionalizing its placement of power or limiting the power of government to change the substance of the rules at issue. The federal government was constitutionally free to devolve power to the states, or to legislate a different substantive result—just as Congress did when it overhauled the federal government's involvement in welfare in the form of PRWORA.

The poor fare better when deprivations related to their socioeconomic position also directly affect another constitutionally protected right or interest. The most important "fundamental interests" protected by the courts are the RIGHT TO TRAVEL, the right to family life, and the right to liberty. The most significant case in this vein was SHAPIRO V. THOMPSON (1969), which held that special waiting period requirements for eligibility for federal categorical relief programs unreasonably burdened the constitutionally protected right to travel. State residency rules were not at issue in this case; instead, the Court was concerned only with the power of states to create, through waiting period rules, unacceptable local deviations in a federally subsidized program, which might hinder the ability of beneficiaries to take advantage of the program's terms nationally. In a sense, the case held no more than that the right of the poor to travel was no less worthy of protection than the right to interstate commerce in goods.

In SAENZ V. ROE (1999), the Court again visited the issue of state residency rules for the receipt of state government assistance. In striking down a California provision limiting new residents, for the first year they lived in California, to the amount of benefits they would have received in the state of their former residence, the Court reaffirmed the constitutional protection of the right to travel and, more importantly, expanded on the meaning of the PRIVILEGES AND IMMUNITIES clause of the Fourteenth Amendment. The Court held that the privileges and immunities clause guarantees the right of newly arrived citizens of a state to be treated the same as all other citizens. Though the Constitution does not restrict a state's right to limit benefits, a state cannot create different levels of benefits based on the duration of residence of its citizens.

The Court has also been solicitous of a poor person's right to family life. A poor person has a constitutionally protected right to access to a divorce court under BODDIE V. CONNECTICUT (1971). Preservation of the right of indigents to control their family lives has also been protected based on the Court's interpretation of the due process and equal protection clauses of the Fourteenth Amendment. In *Lassiter v. Department of Social Services* (1981), the Court held that under certain circumstances the state is constitutionally required to appoint counsel for an indigent person seeking to defend against state proceedings to terminate parental rights. The poor also have, under M.L.B. V. S.L.J. (1996), the right to access to appeals from decisions terminating their parental rights without having to pay court fees.

In criminal cases, the poor have been conceded the RIGHT TO COUNSEL and access to the courts, without charge, under some circumstances. These include, under GIDEON V. WAINRIGHT (1963), when the indigent defendant is charged with a felony or, under DOUGLAS V. CALIFORNIA (1963), when the indigent defendant is accorded an appeal as of right. Indigents must also, under GRIFFIN V. ILLINOIS (1956), be provided with the record required for a criminal appeal.

LARRY CATÁ BACKER
(2000)

Bibliography

ABRAMOVITZ, MIMI 1988 *Regulating the Lives of Women: Social Welfare Policy From Colonial Times to the Present.* Boston: South End Press.

BACKER, LARRY CATÁ 1995 Medieval Poor Law in Twentieth Century America: Looking Back Towards a General Theory of Modern American Poor Relief. *Case Western Reserve Law Review* 1995:871–1041.

—— 1996 Poor Relief, Welfare Paralysis, and Assimilation. *Utah Law Review* 1996:1–49.

HANDLER, JOEL F. and HASENFELD, YEHESKEL 1991 *The Moral Construction of Poverty: Welfare Reform in America.* Newbury Park, Calif.: Sage Publication.

KATZ, MICHAEL 1989 *The Undeserving Poor: From the War on Poverty to the War on Welfare.* New York: Pantheon Books.

MARMOR, THEODORE 1990 *America's Misunderstood Welfare State: Persistent Myths, Enduring Realities.* New York: Basic Books.

MURRAY, CHARLES 1984 *Losing Ground: American Social Policy, 1950–1980.* New York: Basic Books.

# WELFARE STATE

The United States Constitution, unlike many constitutions in the world, does not mandate WELFARE RIGHTS. For example, the Soviet Constitution of 1977 provided for "guaranteed work, health protection, [and] education." In contrast, our Constitution guarantees FREEDOM OF SPEECH, FREEDOM OF THE PRESS, and VOTING RIGHTS that cannot be denied because of race or sex. The people can then use the right to vote and the right of free speech and other such rights to persuade legislators to enact laws providing for welfare rights such as WORKERS' COMPENSATION, public education, aid to dependent children, Social Security benefits, medicare, and so forth. The United States Constitution, in short, guarantees democracy, and with democracy the people can choose to have as much or as little of a welfare state as they wish.

Such is the modern view of the American Constitution, but it was not always so. To understand the modern view we must first look briefly at the historical background. Toward the end of the last century and during the first part of this century until President FRANKLIN D. ROOSEVELT's 1937 COURT-PACKING plan, the Supreme Court was antagonistic toward the early efforts of the state and federal governments leading to the modern welfare state. The Court, often over biting dissents, invalidated efforts to enact a progressive federal income tax, minimum-wage legislation, maximum-hour laws, child labor laws, and so forth.

Justice OLIVER WENDELL HOLMES, JR., was one who dissented from the Court's efforts (through the use of the DUE PROCESS clause, a belief in "liberty of contract," and a narrow interpretation of federal commerce powers) to limit the power of the government to engage in social welfare legislation. Holmes's dissent in LOCHNER V. NEW YORK (1905) objected to the majority's decision invalidating a state law setting sixty hours as the maximum workweek for bakers. "The liberty of the citizen to do as he likes so long as he does not interfere with the liberty of others to do the same, which has been a shibboleth for some well-known writers, is interfered with by school laws, by the Post Office, by every state or municipal institution which takes his money for purposes thought desirable, whether he likes it or not. The Fourteenth Amendment does not enact Mr. Herbert Spencer's Social Statics." Later, in ADKINS V. CHILDREN'S HOSPITAL (1923), when the Court invalidated a federal law setting minimum wages for women and children in the DISTRICT OF COLUMBIA, Holmes said in dissent, "Pretty much all law consists in forbidding men to do some things that they want to do, and contract is no more exempt from law than other acts."

Within five years of Holmes's leaving the Court (after FDR's Court-packing plan of 1937 failed), the Court effectively overruled more than a quarter-century of opinions and recognized the power of the state and federal governments to engage in a wide range of activities that promoted various aspects of a modern welfare state. Although the constitutional power of government to provide welfare benefits does not constitutionally obligate it to do so, the Constitution does place important limits on the government's discretion.

The Constitution assures that once the state grants welfare rights, those benefits are not distributed in a way that violates substantive guarantees. For example, there is no constitutional requirement that a state enact legislation providing public housing for poor people. However, the Fourteenth Amendment forbids the state, once it has provided for public housing, to pass out such benefits in a way that violates the EQUAL PROTECTION OF THE LAW. Thus, if a state builds public housing, it cannot then exclude poor people who are black, for to do so would constitute RACIAL DISCRIMINATION in violation of the equal protection clause. Similarly, if the state provides for medical services as part of its welfare program, the state cannot deny those medical services to Democrats or Socialists, because that would unconstitutionally deprive someone of a governmental benefit because of that person's beliefs, in violation of the FIRST AMENDMENT as applied to the states through the INCORPORATION DOCTRINE.

Implied constitutional rights, like explicit ones, limit the states when they distribute welfare benefits. For example, the Constitution does not explicitly grant a RIGHT TO TRAVEL within the United States, and yet the right certainly exists. As Justice POTTER J. STEWART noted in UNITED STATES V. GUEST (1966), although the right to travel "finds no explicit mention in the Constitution," the explanation may be that "a right so elementary was conceived from the beginning to be a necessary concomitant of the stronger Union the Constitution created. In any event, freedom to travel throughout the United States has long been recognized as a basic right under the Constitution."

Thus, in EDWARDS V. CALIFORNIA (1941) the Court invalidated, under the commerce clause, a California statute that made it a misdemeanor to assist in bringing into that state any indigent person who was not already a resident of California and was known to be an indigent. The Court rejected the state's argument that the migration of poor persons brought severe health and financial problems to the state. The concurring opinion of Justice ROBERT H. JACKSON noted that "indigence' itself is neither a source of rights nor a basis for denying them." Otherwise, the heritage of our constitutional privileges and immunities "is only a promise to the ear to be broken to the hope, a teasing illusion like a munificent bequest in a pauper's will."

Later, in SHAPIRO V. THOMPSON (1969), the Court invalidated several state statutes and a District of Columbia statute that denied welfare benefits to persons who had not resided within the jurisdiction for at least one year. The Court struck these durational RESIDENCE REQUIREMENTS because the state laws violated the equal protection clause of the Fourteenth Amendment and because the law of the District of Columbia (which is not governed by the Fourteenth Amendment because it is not a state) violated the equal protection component that has been found within the due process clause of the Fifth Amendment (which restricts the federal government).

The Court argued that the effect of the residence requirements was to deter the entry of indigents into jurisdictions with durational residence requirements, thus burdening the indigents' right to interstate travel. Because this right to travel is "fundamental," the Court would invalidate the statutory classification unless the state could show that it was "necessary to promote a *compelling* governmental interest" (emphasis in original). The majority rejected the argument that the durational residence requirement was necessary to deter indigents who migrated solely to obtain another jurisdiction's more favorable welfare benefits, holding that no state has the right to exclude poor persons from its borders. Nor may a state distinguish between new and old residents when that distinction burdens the fundamental right to travel. The states (and the District of Columbia), said the Court, may not create subclasses of citizens based on the length of time that persons have been residents. The states, in short, may require that indigents be residents of the state at the time they apply for welfare benefits, but the states may not impose durational residence requirements.

Similarly, in *Memorial Hospital v. Maricopa County* (1974) the Court invalidated an Arizona statute requiring a one-year durational residence in a county as a condition for receiving nonemergency medical care at the county's expense. The Court said that medical care, like welfare assistance, is "a basic necessity of life"; hence, the case was governed by *Shapiro v. Thompson*.

However, in *Starns v. Malkerson* (1971) the Court upheld a University of Minnesota regulation providing that no student could qualify as a resident for purposes of lower in-state tuition unless the student had been a resident of Minnesota for a year. College tuition, unlike food, clothing, or shelter, is not one of the basic necessities of life.

In HARPER V. VIRGINIA STATE BOARD OF ELECTIONS (1966) the Court invalidated a Virginia law conditioning voting on payment of an annual POLL TAX of $1.50. Voting, said the Court, is a FUNDAMENTAL RIGHT preservative of our other rights, and hence, a state violates the equal protection clause whenever it makes the affluence of the voter or payment of any fee a requirement for voting. The state has the power to fix qualifications for voting, such as requiring residence and voting registration. But "wealth, like race, creed, or color, is not germane to one's ability to participate intelligently in the electoral process."

The Court has also held that indigents must be granted equal access to various aspects of the criminal process that are basic to the fair determination of their guilt or innocence. Once the state has fulfilled this duty by giving indigents the opportunity for a FAIR TRIAL and access to the initial appellate process, there is no requirement that the state go further and level all economic distinctions by continuing to provide free counsel throughout successive appeals and collateral attacks.

These cases illustrate an important aspect of Supreme Court jurisprudence involving welfare rights and the Constitution. When the Court reviews certain classifications under the equal protection clause—for example, a classification based on race or color—the Court treats the classification as "suspect" and unlikely to be approved unless the state can demonstrate that the SUSPECT CLASSIFICATION is necessary to promote a COMPELLING STATE INTEREST. Thus, in cases like BROWN V. BOARD OF EDUCATION (1954), the Court invalidated state laws requiring school SEGREGATION according to race. Similarly, the Court engages in active review under the equal protection clause of state laws that classify "fundamental" rights (like the right to travel or the right to vote) on the basis of poverty.

Modern Supreme Court Justices have concluded that where suspect classes or fundamental rights are not at issue there is nothing in the Constitution that authorizes judges to decide economic policy regarding the allocation of income and wealth through the review of legislative classifications. Poverty, unlike race, is not a suspect classification. And there is no fundamental constitutional right to be free of poverty. As a general matter, the state constitutionally may engage in legislative classifications that pass out benefits or burdens in ways that disadvantage poorer people so long as the law has a RATIONAL BASIS. Thus, a state may enact a progressive income tax, even though such a law requires richer persons to pay a greater percentage of their income to the states than poorer persons. Or a state may enact a sales tax on food, although such a regressive tax requires poorer persons to pay a greater percentage of their income to the states than do richer persons.

For example, the Court rejected the challenge to the welfare law involved in DANDRIDGE V. WILLIAMS (1970). In that case, the Court upheld state legislation that set a maximum amount for welfare aid to any one family; the law, in effect, offered lessened benefits for children born to families over a certain size. The appellees in that case argued that the law violated the equal protection clause by discriminating against them because of their larger families. The majority rejected the claim: "In the area of economics and social welfare, a State does not violate the Equal Protection Clause merely because the classifications made by its laws are imperfect. If the classification has some "reasonable basis,' it does not offend the Constitution simply because the classification "is not made with mathematical nicety or because in practice it results in some inequality."' There is a fundamental right to travel; there is no fundamental right to welfare.

Similarly, although a woman may have a constitutional right to an ABORTION under certain circumstances, it is constitutional for the state to deny state funding for medically necessary abortions, even when it is providing funds for childbirth. The state need not provide affirmative assistance to a poor woman to procure an abortion any more than the state must provide subsidized airfare to protect an indigent's right to travel.

SAN ANTONIO INDEPENDENT SCHOOL DISTRICT V. RODRIGUEZ (1973) upheld the constitutionality of a state property tax system that financed primary and secondary education in such a way as to create different districts with large variations in the amount of money spent on the education of children, depending on where the children lived. Some districts were much richer than others, with the poorer districts having much less taxable wealth subject to the property tax. The majority found nothing in the allocation of education opportunities based on district wealth that furnished a constitutional justification for active and close judicial supervision of the legislative policy. The Court emphasized that it had never adopted an active standard of review solely because the law burdened poor persons in the allocation of benefits, unless those benefits were deemed to be fundamental constitutional rights.

However, in a footnote to the majority opinion in *Rodriguez,* Justice LEWIS F. POWELL suggested that if a state set up an educational system that absolutely deprived poor children of the opportunity for any education, legislative choice might raise problems under the equal protection clause: "If elementary and secondary education were made available by the State only to those able to pay a tuition assessed against each pupil, there would be a clearly defined class of "poor' people—definable in terms of their inability to pay the prescribed sum—who would be absolutely precluded from receiving an education. That case would present a far more compelling set of circumstances for judicial assistance than the case before us today."

In short, the issue in fundamental rights cases is whether the statute in question limits the fundamental right in a way that violates the Constitution, and not whether the statute is fair or unfair to poor people. In fact, the law in question may be unconstitutional, even though it seeks to level wealth distinctions in the exercise of the fundamental right rather than to create wealth distinctions. In BUCKLEY V. VALEO. (1976), for example, the Court invalidated limits on campaign spending by candidates for public office as an unconstitutional burden on the fundamental right to free speech, guaranteed by the First Amendment. Although Congress designed the legislation in part to equalize the ability to run for office between persons of differing wealth, the Court found no interest of a sufficiently compelling magnitude to justify the limitation on free speech rights.

In addition to these substantive guarantees, the Constitution also provides procedural protections for persons entitled to welfare benefits under state or federal law. The due process clause of the Fourteenth Amendment forbids a state to deprive any person of life, liberty, or property without due process of law. The Fifth Amendment similarly restricts the federal government. Since 1970, the Supreme Court has recognized that government welfare benefits may constitute statutory ENTITLEMENTS , a new type of "property" that the government may not take away without offering basic procedural protections.

In GOLDBERG V. KELLY (1970) the Court held that a state could not constitutionally terminate public assistance payments for a recipient without affording her the opportunity for an evidentiary hearing prior to the termination. As the Court later explained in BOARD OF REGENTS V. ROTH (1972):

> To have a property interest in a benefit, a person clearly must have more than an abstract need or desire for it. . . . He must have a legitimate claim of entitlement to it. It is a purpose of the ancient institution of property to protect those claims upon which people rely in their daily lives, reliance that must not be arbitrarily undermined. It is a purpose of the constitutional right to a hearing to provide an opportunity for a person to vindicate those claims.
>
> Property interests, of course, are not created by the Constitution. Rather, they are created and their dimensions are defined by existing rules or understandings that secure certain benefits and that support claims of entitlements to those benefits. Thus, the welfare recipients in *Goldberg v. Kelly* had a claim of entitlement to welfare benefits that was grounded in the statute defining eligibility for them.

Government need not offer welfare or other such benefits to its citizens. But once government decides to offer such benefits and establishes standards that define when a person is eligible, the government has created an entitlement and cannot arbitrarily deny those benefits. It must provide PROCEDURAL DUE PROCESS. The government may provide benefits in cash, such as social security benefits or farm subsidies; it may offer benefits in kind, such as free housing in a publicly-owned building; it may offer benefits in hybrid forms, such as food stamps, which can only be redeemed for particular items. In all cases, once the government establishes such benefits as entitlements, the government can withdraw them from particular individuals only after it offers procedural protections such as fair notice and an opportunity to be heard.

The U.S. Constitution does not demand a welfare state. Yet the Constitution is flexible and adaptable enough to allow it. The Constitution guarantees that if the state does provide for welfare protection, the state's largess will be subject to various substantive and procedural limitations.

RONALD D. ROTUNDA
(1992)

(SEE ALSO: *Campaign Finance; Economic Due Process; Economic Equal Protection; Economic Regulation; Poverty Law and the Constitution; Substantive Due Process.*)

Bibliography

NOWAK, JOHN E. and ROTUNDA, RONALD D. 1991 *Constitutional Law,* 4th ed. St. Paul, Minn.: West Publishing Co.

REICH, CHARLES 1964 The New Property. *Yale Law Journal* 73:733–787.

ROTUNDA, RONALD D. et al. 1986 *Treatise on Constitutional Law: Substance and Procedure.* 3 vols. St. Paul, Minn.: West Publishing Co.

VAN ALYSTYNE, WILLIAM 1968 The Demise of the Right-Privilege Distinction in Constitutional Law. *Harvard Law Review* 81:1439–1464.

WINTER, RALPH 1972 Poverty, Economic Equality, and the Equal Protection Clause. *Supreme Court Review* 1972:41–102.

## WELSH v. WISCONSIN
### 466 U.S. 740 (1984)

In *Welsh* the Supreme Court considered and rejected an exception to its rule of PAYTON V. NEW YORK (1984) that the FOURTH AMENDMENT prohibits a warrantless arrest in one's home in the absence of EXIGENT CIRCUMSTANCES. Police made a warrantless night entry of a private home to arrest a man for committing the nonjailable offense of driving while drunk. Justice WILLIAM J. BRENNAN for a 6–2 Court rejected the state's reliance on the hot pursuit doctrine because the police had not in fact engaged in a pursuit. In view of the state's classification of a first-offense drunk-driving offense as a minor crime meriting merely a fine, the Court also rejected the argument that the need to get a blood-alcohol test without delay provided an exigent circumstance.

LEONARD W. LEVY
(1986)

## WENGLER v. DRUGGISTS MUTUAL INSURANCE COMPANY
### 446 U.S. 142 (1980)

Missouri's workers' compensation law provided death benefits to all widows but only to widowers who proved actual dependence on their wives or incapacity to earn a living. The Supreme Court, 8–1, held this SEX DISCRIMINATION invalid, following CRAIG V. BOREN (1976) and CALIFANO V. GOLDFARB (1977).

KENNETH L. KARST
(1986)

## WESBERRY v. SANDERS
### 376 U.S. 1 (1964)

After BAKER V. CARR (1962) held that legislative districting presented a justiciable controversy, the Supreme Court held in *Wesberry,* 8–1, that a state's congressional districts are required by Article I, section 2, of the Constitution to be as equal in population as is practicable. That section provides that representatives are to be chosen "by the People of the several States." Justice JOHN MARSHALL HARLAN dissented on both textual and historical grounds.

Later decisions make clear that no justifications can excuse substantial deviation from population equality in congressional districting.

KENNETH L. KARST
(1986)

## WEST COAST HOTEL COMPANY v. PARRISH
### 300 U.S. 379 (1937)

This decision sustaining a Washington state minimum wage statute in March 1937 signaled a seismic shift in judicial philosophy toward acceptance of the validity of social and economic legislation. Together with the WAGNER ACT CASES, the decision reflected a new, favorable judicial attitude toward the NEW DEAL, thus defusing FRANKLIN D. ROOSEVELT's COURT-PACKING proposal.

The constitutionality of minimum wage legislation had a peculiar history. In MULLER V. OREGON (1908) and BUNTING V. OREGON (1917) the Justices had approved state laws regulating maximum working hours, including provisions for overtime wages. In 1917, the Court divided evenly on an Oregon minimum wage law. WILLIAM HOWARD TAFT, among others, confidently presumed that LOCHNER V. NEW YORK's (1905) rigorous FREEDOM OF CONTRACT doctrines no longer applied. Yet in 1923, a 5–3 majority of the Court reaffirmed the *Lochner* ruling, and in ADKINS V. CHILDREN'S HOSPITAL (1923) the Court invalidated a DISTRICT OF COLUMBIA minimum wage statute. New Chief Justice Taft sharply attacked the majority's reasoning. He found no distinction between MAXIMUM HOUR AND MINIMUM WAGE LAWS: one was the "multiplier and the other the multiplicand." Although Taft reiterated his belief that *Lochner* had been tacitly overruled, *Lochner* nevertheless persisted until the *Parrish* decision in 1937.

After *Adkins*, the Court invalidated other state minimum wage laws. The Great Depression, however, stimulated new state laws, perhaps encouraged by Justice GEORGE SUTHERLAND'S OBITER DICTUM that "exceptional circumstances" might justify such legislation. But in MOREHEAD V. NEW YORK EX REL. TIPALDO (1936), a 5–4 majority held to the *Adkins* precedent and invalidated a recent New York law. The Court's opinion masked Justice OWEN J. ROBERTS's uneasiness. Roberts had supported PIERCE & BUTLER, JAMES C. MCREYNOLDS, George Sutherland, and WILLIS VAN DEVANTER in *Tipaldo*, but he later revealed that the state counsel's argument that *Adkins* merely be distinguished, and not overthrown, had obliged him to follow the precedent. Six months later, Roberts provided the key vote to consider the Washington law. On the surface, the procedure was justified on the ground that the state court had upheld the statute, but the combination of the *Tipaldo* dissenters' strongly held views on constitutionality and Roberts's skepticism toward *Adkins* dictated a full-scale review of the issue.

Roberts later stated that he had decided in favor of the statutes after arguments in December 1936 and that he had successfully urged delaying the decision pending HARLAN FISKE STONE's recovery from illness in order to mass a majority. Stone returned shortly after Roosevelt submitted his court-packing proposal in early February. Chief Justice CHARLES EVANS HUGHES then withheld the announcement until March 29, perhaps to avoid appearances of political submission.

Hughes's majority opinion decisively repudiated *Lochner* and *Adkins*. He argued that the Constitution nowhere enshrined freedom of contract and that "regulation which is reasonable in relation to its subject and is adopted in the interests of the community is DUE PROCESS." Seeking to deflect the outraged protests of his more conservative brethren, Hughes invoked Taft's *Adkins* dissent: "That challenge persists and is without any satisfactory answer."

Invoking the public interest doctrine of NEBBIA V. NEW YORK (1934), Hughes asked what could be "closer to the public interest than the health of women and their protection from unscrupulous and overreaching employers?" Accordingly, Hughes held that the minimum wage statute

was reasonable and not "arbitrary or capricious." That, he concluded, "is all we have to decide."

Sutherland, speaking for the dissenters, passionately reiterated his *Adkins* doctrine. More broadly, Sutherland also implicitly addressed Stone's scathing dissent in UNITED STATES V. BUTLER (1936), which had pleaded for judicial self-restraint and an end to judges' imposition of their own social and economic predilections. The notion of self-restraint, Sutherland retorted, was "ill considered and mischievous"; it belonged "in the domain of will and not of judgment." Judges were bound to enforce the Constitution, he said, according to their own "conscientious and informed convictions." Sutherland concluded that freedom of contract remained the rule. The intervening economic conditions altered nothing, for "the meaning of the Constitution," he said, "does not change with the ebb and flow of economic events." Sutherland's dissent was both an apologia and an obituary for a judicial philosophy eclipsed by new realities.

STANLEY I. KUTLER
(1986)

Bibliography

MASON, ALPHEUS T.  1956  *Harlan Fiske Stone*. New York: Viking Press.

# WESTON v. CITY COUNCIL OF CHARLESTON
## 2 Peters 449 (1829)

The Supreme Court, in an opinion by Chief Justice JOHN MARSHALL, held unconstitutional a city ordinance taxing interest-bearing stock of the United States, on the grounds that the tax burdened the ENUMERATED POWER of the United States to borrow money on its credit. The principle of the opinion, that an instrumentality of the United States is immune from taxation by state and local governments, derived from MCCULLOCH V. MARYLAND (1819).

LEONARD W. LEVY
(1986)

(SEE ALSO: *Intergovernmental Immunity*.)

# WEST RIVER BRIDGE COMPANY v. DIX
## 6 Howard 529 (1848)

The *West River Bridge* case challenged a Vermont law of 1839 authorizing county officials to expropriate the rights of way, real estate, or entire franchises of chartered companies in order to provide their communities with free public roads. County officials condemned the entire franchise and property of the West River Bridge Company, which had been given a hundred-year franchise under a charter of 1795 for a bridge near Brattleboro, an important market town. The stockholders were awarded $4,000 in damages. The company's appeal was rejected by the Vermont Supreme Court, and the case was then carried to the United States Supreme Court.

DANIEL WEBSTER, as counsel for the company, sought in his arguments to reopen virtually all the issues of CHARLES RIVER BRIDGE V. WARREN BRIDGE COMPANY (1837). He contended that rising popular disregard for franchised rights of corporations would legitimate the worst "levelling ultraisms or Antirentism or Agrarianism or Abolitionism." Eminent domain was a power inappropriate to republican government, he contended, and the bridge taking was in blatant violation of the CONTRACT CLAUSE. Nonetheless, the Court, with Justice JAMES M. WAYNE dissenting, upheld Vermont's action. Each of the three opinions filed declared that eminent domain was a power fundamental to the states, had long been exercised by them, was not restrained by the contract clause, and extended as much to franchises as to any other type of property. As the first Supreme Court ruling that dealt directly with the states' power of eminent domain and related procedural matters, *West River Bridge* complemented the *Charles River Bridge* decision; both supported the states' authority to accommodate technological change and social and entrepreneurial needs.

HARRY N. SCHEIBER
(1986)

## WEST VIRGINIA BOARD OF EDUCATION v. BARNETTE

See: Flag Salute Cases

## WHALEN v. ROE
### 429 U.S. 589 (1977)

Rejecting a claim based on the constitutional RIGHT OF PRIVACY, a unanimous Supreme Court upheld a New York law requiring storage in a computer file of the names and addresses of persons who obtain, by doctors' prescriptions, such drugs as opium, methadone, cocaine, and amphetamines. Justice JOHN PAUL STEVENS, writing for the Court, noted that previous decisions recognizing a right of privacy had involved two different kinds of interests: (1) "avoiding disclosure of personal matters"; and (2) "in-

dependence in making certain kinds of important decisions." Both interests were arguably implicated here; there was some risk of disclosure of a drug user's name, and that risk could have deterred the prescription or use of such drugs even when they were medically advisable. Nonetheless, and despite a district court finding that the state had not proved the necessity of storing this personal information, the Court concluded that the law was valid. The state's interest in DRUG REGULATION was vital; the legislature was entitled to experiment with reasonable means for achieving that end. Balanced against this objective, the invasions of privacy were too slight to constitute invasions of either patients' or doctors' constitutional liberties.

KENNETH L. KARST
(1986)

## WHEATON, HENRY
### (1785–1848)

Henry Wheaton read law in his native Providence, Rhode Island, and studied civil law in France in 1805–1806. While in France he translated the new *Code Napoléon* into English. He became the first official reporter for the United States Supreme Court under an 1816 statute creating that position. From 1816 to 1827 Wheaton edited twelve volumes of United States Reports. While official reporter he argued a number of cases, including GIBBONS V. OGDEN (1824). In *Wheaton v. Peters* (1834) he unsuccessfully sued his successor, Richard Peters. The Supreme Court ruled that no individual could hold a COPYRIGHT on Supreme Court opinions. From 1827 to 1846 Wheaton held various diplomatic positions and wrote extensively on international law. His works included *Elements of International Law, History of the Law of Nations* (1842) and an essay on the African slave trade (1842). He was the foremost American expert on international law during his lifetime.

PAUL FINKELMAN
(1986)

Bibliography

BAKER, ELIZABETH F. 1937 *Henry Wheaton, 1785–1848.* Philadelphia: University of Pennsylvania Press.

## WHEELER, BURTON K.
### (1882–1975)

A Montana Democrat, Burton K. Wheeler ranked with GEORGE NORRIS of Nebraska and William Borah of Idaho as one of the major liberal leaders of the United States

SENATE, where Wheeler served from 1923 to 1946. In the 1924 presidential campaign, ROBERT M. LA FOLLETTE of Wisconsin headed the Progressive party ticket, with Wheeler as his running mate. They attracted more votes than any previous third party, and their platform provided an agenda for the NEW DEAL. One plank urged an amendment to the Constitution providing that a two-thirds majority in both houses of Congress might override any judicial decision holding a congressional enactment unconstitutional. Although Wheeler was a critic of the Supreme Court and of JUDICIAL REVIEW, he insisted that a constitutional amendment was the only proper means of reform; accordingly, he broke with FRANKLIN D. ROOSEVELT in 1937 by opposing his COURT-PACKING plan. It was Wheeler, an ally of Justice LOUIS D. BRANDEIS, who produced the letter by Chief Justice CHARLES EVANS HUGHES that contributed to the 10–8 vote against the bill by the Senate Judiciary Committee. Wheeler remained a liberal, though he was an isolationist in foreign affairs.

LEONARD W. LEVY
(1986)

Bibliography

WHEELER, BURTON K. with HEALY, PAUL F. 1962 *Yankee from the West.* New York: Doubleday.

# WHIG PARTY

The Whig party emerged as a coalition of politicians opposed to ANDREW JACKSON and Jacksonian Democracy. Some prominent Whigs, like DANIEL WEBSTER, traced their political roots to the old FEDERALIST party, while others, like HENRY CLAY, had been Jeffersonian Democrats. Most had also been National Republicans and, as such, supported the presidencies of JAMES MONROE and JOHN QUINCY ADAMS. When the Anti-Masonic party collapsed, most of its members became Whigs. Some extreme STATES' RIGHTS southerners briefly affiliated with the Whigs in reaction to Jackson's heavy-handed response to South Carolina in the NULLIFICATION controversy. A few Democrats joined the Whigs because they disagreed with Jackson over the BANK OF THE UNITED STATES or because they were disillusioned with Old Hickory's successor, MARTIN VAN BUREN. In the 1850s the Whig party collapsed. Most northern Whigs joined the REPUBLICAN PARTY, while southern Whigs became Know-Nothings or Democrats.

Whigs favored high tariffs, federally funded INTERNAL IMPROVEMENTS, a national banking system, a relatively weak presidency, and deference to Supreme Court rulings on constitutional questions. In 1832 the Young Men's National Republican Convention, which nominated Henry Clay for President, resolved "that the Supreme Court of the United States is the only tribunal recognized by the constitution for deciding, in the last resort, all questions arising under the constitution and laws of the United States, and that, upon the preservation of the authority and jurisdiction of that court inviolate, depends the existence of the Union."

The Whig party avoided taking any position on SLAVERY, seeking northern compromise on the issue in return for southern support for northern economic interests. Northern Whigs, like Daniel Webster, ABRAHAM LINCOLN, and WILLIAM H. SEWARD, opposed slavery with differing degrees of passion. In the 1830s some Whig congressmen, led by John Quincy Adams and Joshua Giddings, fought for the right to petition Congress on slavery. Adams viewed this as a constitutional right guaranteed by the petition clause of the FIRST AMENDMENT. However, when Whigs controlled Congress and the White House in the early 1840s, they, too, adopted gag rules to prevent the reading of abolitionist petitions. Southern Whigs supported slavery, but they never supported southern extremists. Indeed, southern Whigs opposed states' rights, southern nationalism, and SECESSION; however, in 1861 southern ex-Whigs, like ALEXANDER STEPHENS, ROBERT TOOMBS, and Judah P. Benjamin, became confederate leaders.

Whigs from both sections opposed the ANNEXATION OF TEXAS, the Mexican War, and other aggressions of Manifest Destiny. During the Mexican War they argued that President JAMES K. POLK had exceeded his constitutional authority by sending troops into southern Texas and Mexico to provoke war.

The Whigs won only two presidential elections. General William Henry Harrison, elected in 1840, died a month after taking office and was succeeded by JOHN TYLER, a former states' rights Democrat who had little sympathy for many Whig positions. Under Tyler the Whigs passed a major but short-lived BANKRUPTCY law and a higher tariff. President Tyler vetoed two Whig-sponsored bills to reestablish a national banking system.

In 1848 the Whigs captured the White House with another war hero, General ZACHARY TAYLOR, by avoiding taking a stand on any major issues. Whigs generally supported the COMPROMISE OF 1850, which was passed as individual pieces of legislation and signed into law by the deceased Taylor's vice-president, MILLARD FILLMORE, a moderate Whig from New York. By 1852, however, the party was deeply divided over the compromise and slavery in general. After 1850 the Whig party collapsed in the South, as southerners abandoned the party that appeared to be dominated by staunch antislavery men such as Senator William Seward of New York. After 1854 most northern Whigs also abandoned the party, either for the nativist American (Know-Nothing) party or the Republican party.

Constitutionally the Whigs stood for a strong Union and

federal intervention in the economy. Whigs argued for a broad reading of federal power under the COMMERCE CLAUSE and an expansive JUDICIAL POWER. Although neither was appointed by a Whig President, Justices JOSEPH STORY and JOHN MCLEAN came to symbolize Whig views of the Constitution. The greatest symbol of the party's constitutional position was not, however, a judge, but the attorney and politician Daniel Webster.

Even before the Whig party was formed, Webster presented "Whig-like" arguments in the DARTMOUTH COLLEGE V. WOODWARD (1819) and GIBBONS V. OGDEN (1824), in which he argued for a strict interpretation of the CONTRACT CLAUSE and a reading of the Constitution that gave Congress exclusive jurisdiction over INTERSTATE COMMERCE. He made similar arguments in GROVES V. SLAUGHTER (1841), the LICENSE CASES (1847), and the PASSENGER CASES (1849). The bedrock of Whig constitutional nationalism was best stated by Webster's 1830 reply to Senator ROBERT YOUNG HAYNE's argument in favor of nullification and Webster's speech supporting the Compromise of 1850. In answering Hayne, Webster declared, "I go for the Constitution as it is, and for the Union as it is." Webster argued, "It is, sir, the people's Constitution, the people's government, made for the people, made by the people, and answerable to the people." He concluded with the ringing plea for "Liberty *and* Union, now and for ever, one and inseparable." In his March 7, 1850, speech Webster supported the compromise measures, declaring, "I wish to speak today, not as a Massachusetts man, nor as a Northern man, but as an American, and a member of the Senate of the United States." He told his colleagues, "I speak today for the preservation of the Union." These measures, introduced by the Whig Clay and supported by Webster, symbolize the constitutional principles of the Whigs—support for the Union and compromise above all else—and the reason for their collapse. By the mid-1850s, compromise based on blind fidelity to the Union was no longer possible in a nation torn by sectional strife and about to go to war over slavery. Significantly, perhaps, the last Whig President, Millard Fillmore, opposed secession but also opposed all of Lincoln's policies to stop secession. By this time, however, the supporters of Whig nationalism and CONSTITUTIONALISM had followed such Whigs as Seward and Lincoln into the Republican party.

PAUL FINKELMAN
(1992)

Bibliography

BARTLETT, IRVING H. 1978 *Daniel Webster.* New York: Norton.
MCCORMICK, RICHARD P. 1966 *The Second American Party System.* Chapel Hill: University of North Carolina Press.
VAN DEUSEN, GLYNDON G. 1973 The Whig Party. In Arthur M. Schlesinger, Jr., ed., *History of U.S. Political Parties.* Vol. 1, pages 332–493. New York: Chelsea House.

# WHISKEY REBELLION
## (1794)

The "rebellion" in western Pennsylvania provided the first test of the power of the federal government to suppress insurrections and enforce obedience to its laws. Frontier farmers, who were also small distillers, resisted the whiskey excise from its passage in 1791. When the resistance erupted in violence in July 1794, President GEORGE WASHINGTON issued a proclamation ordering the rebels to submit to the law or face military coercion under an act authorizing employment of the militia in such cases. After a peace mission failed, he called up 15,000 militia from Pennsylvania and neighboring states. The army marched, and the rebellion quickly collapsed without bloodshed; two ringleaders, tried and convicted of TREASON, were subsequently pardoned by the President. FEDERALIST leaders exulted in this crushing of rebellion, which they viewed as part of a plot against the government, while their Republican counterparts denounced the force as excessive and intended to overawe opposition to the administration.

MERRILL D. PETERSON
(1986)

Bibliography

BALDWIN, LELAND D. 1939 *Whiskey Rebels: The Story of a Frontier Uprising.* Pittsburgh: University of Pittsburgh Press.

# WHITE, BYRON R.
## (1917– )

In 1962 President JOHN F. KENNEDY appointed Byron R. White to replace CHARLES E. WHITTAKER and become the ninety-third Justice to serve on the Supreme Court. White was forty-four years old and had no previous judicial experience. He had been a CLERK for Chief Justice FRED N. VINSON in 1946–1947, however, and was the first former law clerk subsequently appointed to that tribunal. His only other significant government experience had come during the preceding year, after President Kennedy had appointed him deputy attorney general. White had managed the Justice Department, recruited lawyers, and evaluated candidates for federal judgeships. His CIVIL RIGHTS enforcement experience included a stint in Montgomery, Alabama, where local authorities had failed to prevent mob violence against the freedom riders, an interracial group protesting racial SEGREGATION in public transportation. White restored order with the help of 400 federal marshals, providing Kennedy with a significant national victory over recalcitrant state officials.

Whatever White lacked in government experience, he made up in personal capacities. Born in rural Colorado, White came of age there during the Depression. He worked in the beet fields as a boy and later won a scholarship to the University of Colorado, where he was first in his class and an all American football player. He played professional football, and for several months, until the European outbreak of World War II, he studied as a Rhodes scholar in England, where he first met John Kennedy. He began studying law at Yale in 1939 and again topped his class. The war interrupted his studies, and he served as a naval intelligence officer in the South Pacific, where he again encountered Kennedy. He was graduated in 1946, and after his clerkship, returned to Colorado to practice law. In 1959 he organized support for Kennedy as the Democratic nominee for President. Following Kennedy's nomination, he chaired Citizens for Kennedy, a nationwide volunteer group. His public service followed.

When White joined the WARREN COURT, its most vigorous efforts to nationalize CIVIL LIBERTIES and limit government power in favor of individual rights and egalitarian values lay just ahead. White voted regularly with the majority to invalidate discrimination against racial minorities and the politically powerless in areas such as school DESEGREGATION and REAPPORTIONMENT, and to sustain the constitutionality of federal civil rights legislation. Nonetheless, he acquired a reputation as a moderate-to-conservative Justice for his frequent dissents in major decisions, such as MIRANDA V. ARIZONA (1966), which imposed new constitutional limits on police discretion; for his willingness to uphold laws excluding communists from government positions; and for his general inclination toward judicial self-restraint.

With President RICHARD M. NIXON's four Court appointments from 1969–1971, the deferential positions White previously had articulated in dissent increasingly became majority views in the BURGER COURT. But White also dissented from decisions undermining egalitarian opinions he had joined in the Warren era. The Court had changed around him—not an uncommon occurrence for Justices serving for long periods.

The Court's shift, together with White's failure to articulate a comprehensive personal vision of an ideal balance of individual liberty and government power, has led some observers to conclude that White lacks a coherent judicial philosophy. The votes and written opinions of this independent, tough-minded jurist, however, do reveal a distinctive vision of the Supreme Court's role in constitutional law, a vision compatible with White's personal history.

One pervasive attitude in White's approach is skepticism and humility about the authority and capacity of the Court to second-guess the efforts of other government officials in dealing with difficult societal problems. White's opinions reflect deference to the good faith assessments and pragmatic judgments of police, administrative officials, and state and federal judges—particularly when he is convinced that they have readier access to relevant information than the Court does, or that government flexibility is needed. He reserves the highest deference for legislative judgments, out of respect for LEGISLATIVE POWER, especially that of the national Congress, as the most legitimate source of law in a democratic society. This second tenet emphasizes the primacy of legislative decisions in allocating the benefits and burdens of government programs, balancing individual rights and community needs, and structuring government operations.

The corollary is that White's deference disappears if good faith and pragmatism are absent. When prejudice infects government decision making, when the interests of the disadvantaged systematically are excluded from consideration in government processes, or when individual liberty is sacrificed for minimal public gain, White readily and consistently supports constitutional prohibitions. He embraces a strongly individualistic ideology that demands fair government treatment of citizens as individuals and holds ordinary citizens and government officials accountable for their individual conduct.

White's individualism produces a powerful egalitarian ethic that takes two different forms. One is constitutional invalidation of government action that treats people stereotypically, with insufficient regard for their individual worth, merits, and capacities. The other is constitutional approval of government efforts to equalize opportunities for the disadvantaged.

These general themes explain much of Justice White's participation in the Court's work. His opposition to stringent constitutional limits on law enforcement practices, absent significant abuse of a particular defendant's liberty, reflects deference to the difficulties of enforcement and the flexibility it requires, as well as to the judgment that guilty individuals have no great claim to benefit from police misconduct that has not harmed them. Deference, pragmatism, and rugged individualism underlie White's position in *Miranda* and his majority opinion in *United States v. Leon* (1984), establishing a GOOD FAITH EXCEPTION to the EXCLUSIONARY RULE. His Court opinions holding that the states must provide TRIAL BY JURY if substantial imprisonment is possible, but that the states may convict with less than unanimous verdicts and with juries of only six members, illustrate a compromise between a belief in the importance of the jury in protecting individual liberty and tolerance for pragmatic modifications of its traditional features when the modifications do not seriously undermine its basic value. The heavy weight he has placed behind sanctioning guilty individuals gives way, however, when government interferes with a fair presentation of the defendant's side, as by denying the RIGHT TO COUNSEL. In civil cases, too, in contexts as diverse as PROCEDURAL DUE PROCESS and the CONTRACT CLAUSE, he has tolerated pragmatic (and unbiased) responses to perceived governmental needs.

White's deference to national LEGISLATIVE POWER has led him to reject both FEDERALISM objections that Congress has usurped reserved state power, as in OREGON V. MITCHELL (1970) and NATIONAL LEAGUE OF CITIES V. USERY (1976), and SEPARATION OF POWERS objections that Congress has invaded the Court's or the President's power, as in his provocative dissents in NORTHERN PIPELINE CONSTRUCTION CO. V. MARATHON PIPELINE CO. (1982), dealing with the powers of LEGISLATIVE COURTS in BANKRUPTCY cases, and IMMIGRATION AND NATURALIZATION SERVICE V. CHADHA (1983), in which the majority struck down the LEGISLATIVE VETO. He also opposed individual rights challenges to legislative efforts that promote equality, such as the affirmative action program upheld in FULLILOVE V. KLUTZNICK (1980), and Congress's attempt to equalize campaign spending, partially invalidated over White's dissent in BUCKLEY V. VALEO (1976). In these cases, deference and attachment to egalitarian values worked together; when they are in conflict, however, White tends to put aside deference and vote to strike down federal laws that discriminate on such invidious bases as race or sex.

White is as vigorous in opposing biased or arbitrary government judgments as he is in supporting justifiable, pragmatic ones. He will not invoke the Constitution to impose affirmative obligations on government, but will do so to prevent the government from imposing unfair burdens. He is reluctant to recognize constitutional immunities for even the highest level officials, preferring to hold that no one is above the law. That frequent theme appears most prominently in his dissent in NIXON V. FITZGERALD (1982), arguing that the President is legally accountable for abuse of government power, and in his opinions interpreting the SPEECH AND DEBATE CLAUSE as fully immunizing members of Congress from inquiry into legislative conduct, but providing no immunity for nonlegislative acts.

More broadly, White has voted to invalidate government policies founded on prejudice or bad motive without more, but usually would not invalidate laws adopted with proper motives, whatever their impact. Thus, in WASHINGTON V. DAVIS (1976) White led the Court in making proof of intentional discrimination a necessary condition for finding a violation of the equal protection clause. He also

would have made intent a sufficient condition, however, as he articulated in dissent in PALMER V. THOMPSON (1971). He has been both generous in finding proof of illicit intent and forceful in insisting that, once wrongdoing is shown, the harm be remedied fully, especially in cases of RACIAL DISCRIMINATION. And when the impact of governmental action significantly impairs the democratic process, as in reapportionment cases, White also has supported judicial intervention.

In FIRST AMENDMENT cases, too, White is strict about disallowing government discrimination against disfavored viewpoints, but tolerant of significant limitations on individual expression that are inevitable byproducts of legitimate government aims, a theme illustrated by his opinion in BROADRICK V. OKLAHOMA (1973). That opinion also represents White's consistent belief that the OVERBREADTH and VAGUENESS doctrines should be used only sparingly to strike statutes with a neutral and uncertain inhibiting effect on the general populace—a position readily held by a believer in hardy individualism. He is likewise unreceptive to arguments that the press needs wide immunity from libel and other actions lest fear of liability deter them from vigorous and important expression. Thus, although this Justice with considerable personal experience as the object of media attention strongly supported First Amendment limits on press liability for reporting about public officials, he vigorously dissented in GERTZ V. ROBERT WELCH, INC. (1974) from the Court's granting the powerful media constitutional immunity from liability to helpless individuals who seek redress for the ravaging of their reputations. Indeed, he generally opposes affording the press any special privileges, except in cases of prior restraint or when the press serves as the public's monitor of government. Finally, White has been relatively deferential to regulations of OBSCENITY and SUBVERSIVE ADVOCACY, the former an example of deference to strong community views which invade little important freedom and the latter an example of deference to the community's right to protect its democratic character.

White's concern for the constitutional obligation to purge arbitrariness from government decision making extends naturally to questions of procedural fairness. Although White would allow government considerable flexibility in defining procedures, he has insisted that appropriate procedures be provided if government deprives a person of a government-created liberty or property entitlement, even if the government was under no initial obligation to create it. So conceived, procedural due process promotes individualized application of law on the basis of personal responsibility and guards against arbitrary decisions.

White's emphasis on equality and fair, if flexible, process generally stops short of imposing substantive limits on government policy. His normal disinclination to go beyond constitutional text or history and recognize new fundamental liberties tends to yield, however, when a state restricts personal autonomy by a law that deviates from most other states' laws or is of minimal efficacy in achieving proper objectives. Thus, White dissented in ROE V. WADE (1973), where the Court used SUBSTANTIVE DUE PROCESS analysis to invalidate laws regulating abortion, but he concurred in GRISWOLD V. CONNECTICUT (1965), arguing that the state's atypical law against marital use of contraceptives violated substantive due process because of its "marginal utility to the declared objective" of deterring illicit sexual relationships. Similarly, he initially voted against the death penalty in *Furman v. Georgia* (1972), not because it constituted CRUEL AND UNUSUAL PUNISHMENT but because it was administered arbitrarily and too infrequently to achieve its deterrent aims. Later, he voted to uphold mandatory death penalty laws applied broadly and consistently. Still, he wrote the major opinion in COKER V. GEORGIA (1977), holding the death penalty for rape cruel and unusual, largely because most states had refrained from imposing it for crimes not producing death.

Normally, White's limited belief in NATURAL RIGHTS jurisprudence surfaces as increased scrutiny of legislative means when government policy implicates broadly accepted liberties and the threat of inequality or arbitrariness is high. Perhaps not surprisingly, given his personal experience, he not only finds family choice fundamental, but educational opportunity, too. Thus, he has been especially adamant to invalidate school SEGREGATION, inequality of expenditures among a state's school districts, and school discipline that involves corporal punishment or lacks procedural safeguards. He is equally adamant that public aid to the secular functions of parochial schools, a policy that supports educational choice and quality, does not constitute a prohibited ESTABLISHMENT OF RELIGION— a distinct minority view on the Court.

JONATHAN D. VARAT
(1986)

Bibliography

ISRAEL, FRED   1969   Byron R. White. In Leon Friedman and Fred Israel, eds., *The Justices of the Supreme Court: Their Lives and Major Opinions.* Vol. 4:2951–2961. New York: Chelsea House.

LIEBAMAN, LANCE   1972   Swing Man on the Supreme Court. *New York Times Magazine*, October 8, 1972.

SERNARD, SCHWARTZ   1983   *Super Chief: Earl Warren and His Supreme Court: A Judicial Biography.* New York: New York University Press.

WOODWARD, BOB and ARMSTRONG, SCOTT   1979   *The Brethren: Inside the Supreme Court.* New York: Simon & Schuster.

# WHITE, BYRON R.
## (1917–   )
## (Update 1)

When he was appointed to the Supreme Court in 1962, Byron White, at the age of forty-four, was a symbol of the vigor, youth, and intellectual power of the JOHN F. KENNEDY administration. From a poor rural background, he had ranked first in the class of 1938 at the University of Colorado, becoming a football All American and winning a Rhodes Scholarship. By the time he graduated from Yale Law School in 1946, he had briefly studied at Oxford, played two seasons of professional football, served as a naval intelligence officer in the Pacific, and twice encountered John Kennedy (once at Oxford, once in the Pacific). After clerking for Chief Justice FRED M. VINSON, White joined a law practice in Denver where he remained for fourteen years. When Kennedy won the Democratic nomination for President in 1960, White chaired the nationwide volunteer group Citizens for Kennedy. His service as deputy attorney general under ROBERT KENNEDY included screening candidates for judicial appointments and supervising federal marshals protecting workers in the CIVIL RIGHTS MOVEMENT in the South. He had been at the job only fourteen months when the President nominated him to fill the vacancy created by the resignation of CHARLES WHITTAKER.

During his nearly thirty years on the Court, White has generally reflected the commitments of the President who appointed him: to equal opportunity, to effective law enforcement, and to enablement of government as it responds to new challenges—with less concern for individual rights, group rights, and STATES' RIGHTS. To the distress of those who would prefer greater elaboration of a philosophical vision, he has approached the judicial task in a lawyerly and pragmatic fashion, although sometimes in excessively cryptic opinions. His independence and analytic bent of mind have often isolated him from more ideological colleagues. As he has served with twenty other Justices during times of great ferment on the Court, his role has changed considerably. He was in the majority in fewer than half of the 5–4 decisions during the 1960s, in more than sixty percent of the 5–4 decisions during the 1970s, and in nearly three-fourths of the 5–4 decisions during the 1980s—more frequently than any other Justice during that decade. Although profound changes in American society (often shaped by the Court itself) have significantly affected the issues before him and, to a lesser extent, his resolution of particular issues, a review of his work on the Court reveals significant consistency in perspective, method, and conviction.

White knows that judges make law. His time at Yale Law School was the heyday of that school's celebration of LEGAL REALISM. As he explained in dissent in MIRANDA V. ARIZONA (1966), "[T]he Court has not discovered or found the law in making today's decision; what it has done is to make new law and new public policy in much the same way that it has in the course of interpreting other great clauses of the Constitution. . . . [I]t is wholly legitimate . . . to inquire into the advisability of its end product in terms of the long-range interest of the country."

White also understands that the triumph of the administrative state, marked especially by an affirmative and vigorous federal government, has forever altered the shape of American political institutions, including the Court. For White, however, neither legal realism nor expanding concepts of national political authority and responsibility justify the exercise of "raw judicial power." A recurring theme of his opinions is that the judiciary undermines its own legitimacy when it seeks to achieve political objectives not sanctioned by the other branches of government or when it promotes social transformation resisted by the democratic institutions of society.

White's confidence in the good faith and capabilities of democratic institutions—Congress especially, but also the executive, state legislatures, and juries—exceeds that of other justices of the "left" or of the "right." For White, the powers of government are limited neither by abstract conceptions of individual autonomy, nor by any extrademocratic mandate for perfection in human affairs. Rather, government power is limited by the very forces that legitimate it: the people acting through fair and free elections and a Constitution that both authorizes and specifically checks government actors.

In the spirit of the NEW DEAL and of President Kennedy, White gives great weight to securing and preserving federal authority, especially Congress's authority. Where Congress has legislated (or federal agencies have acted pursuant to delegated power), he is disposed to find federal PREEMPTION of state law. Where Congress has not legislated, he gives wide berth to the DORMANT COMMERCE CLAUSE. Where states seek to regulate federal entities, he is disposed to place limits on state power. He does not view the TENTH AMENDMENT as a limitation on Congress's regulatory power; he would permit Congress to abrogate state SOVEREIGN IMMUNITY under the ELEVENTH AMENDMENT; and he recognizes significant legislative power to implement the FOURTEENTH AMENDMENT. Where Congress has delegated interpretative authority to ADMINISTRATIVE AGENCIES, he is strongly disposed to defer to agency interpretations of statutes. In many ways, he has been the preeminent nationalist on the Court in the modern era. For instance, White was the only dissenter to the Court's 1978 decision upholding the multistate tax compact, which had not been approved by Congress, because of its "*potential* encroachment on federal supremacy."

White's understanding of the SEPARATION OF POWERS in our national government, as set forth in a series of powerful dissents, is similarly rooted in his recognition that Congress needs latitude to solve economic problems and to reallocate governance authorities in response to the growing demands on national institutions in the post-New Deal era. Thus, he urged in BUCKLEY V. VALEO (1976) that "Congress was entitled to determine that personal wealth ought to play a less important role in political campaigns than it has in the past." He lamented in NORTHERN PIPELINE CO. V. MARATHON PIPE LINE CO. (1982) that "at this point in the history of constitutional law" the Court should not have "looked[ed] only to the constitutional text" to determine Congress's power "to create adjudicatory institutions designed to carry out federal policy." He explained in IMMIGRATION NATURALIZATION SERVICE V. CHADHA (1983) that the LEGISLATIVE VETO "is an indispensable political invention that . . . assures the accountability of independent regulatory agencies and preserves Congress' control on lawmaking." And the budget-balancing legislation of BOWSHER V. SYNAR (1986) was "one of the most novel and far reaching legislative responses to a national crisis since the New Deal."

White conceives of a more limited role for the federal courts, not to supplement or second-guess Congress's policies, but to ensure their implementation by state and federal actors. His concurrence in *Chapman v. Houston Welfare Rights Organization* (1979)—urging that in the CIVIL RIGHTS legislation of the RECONSTRUCTION Congress had provided a remedy for denial not only of constitutional rights but also of rights created by federal statutes—was subsequently adopted by a majority of the Court. White would also more narrowly construe EXECUTIVE IMMUNITY than would a majority of his colleagues. He is less willing than many others on the Court, however, to infer a private cause of action to enforce federal rights where Congress has lodged responsibility for enforcement with a federal agency or has provided for administrative remedies. Nor is he uniformly activist on issues of POLITICAL QUESTION, STANDING, and other prudential limitations on JUDICIAL REVIEW. Although he has sometimes resisted efforts to restrict HABEAS CORPUS jurisdiction, he has joined in limiting the bases on which habeas review may upset a criminal conviction.

To achieve consistency in CONSTITUTIONAL INTERPRETATION, White has taken an expansive view of the Supreme Court's JURISDICTION over state court decisions. Moreover, often dissenting from denial of CERTIORARI, he has regularly urged the Court to use its discretionary jurisdiction to review apparent inconsistencies in the lower courts. His longstanding extrajudicial campaign for creation of a national court of appeals or similar structure to ensure uniformity in federal law may finally have run its course in view of the reduction in the Supreme Court's workload in recent terms.

White's clear sense of the primacy of democratic institutions is reflected in his commitment to the protection of rights to participate in the electoral process. From AVERY V. MIDLAND COUNTY (1968) to *Board of Estimate of the City of New York v. Morris* (1989), he has led the Court in expansively interpreting the principle of ONE PERSON, ONE VOTE to subject varieties of political apportionment and GERRYMANDERING to judicial review, even as he has taken a relatively permissive and pragmatic approach to apportionment disparities. His dissent in MOBILE V. BOLDEN (1980) effectively became the majority position two terms later in ROGERS V. LODGE (1982), which eased the burden of minority challenges to electoral districting schemes that perpetuate purposeful RACIAL DISCRIMINATION. As indicated in *Buckley* and subsequent cases, White would go further than other Justices in permitting Congress to regulate the electoral processes to root out potential corruption and inequality, even at the cost of some inhibition of free speech.

More generally, his FIRST AMENDMENT jurisprudence permits significant intrusions on the media, whether in the form of the FAIRNESS DOCTRINE as in RED LION BROADCASTING CO. V. FCC (1969); SEARCH WARRANTS, as in ZURCHER V. STANFORD DAILY (1978); SUBPOENAS, as in BRANZBURG V. HAYES (1972); or LIBEL law, as in HERBERT V. LANDO (1979) and his dissent in GERTZ V. ROBERT WELCH, INC. (1974). White is likewise deferential toward regulation and prosecution of OBSCENITY, CHILD PORNOGRAPHY, and SUBVERSIVE ADVOCACY. He has been a leading opponent of a strict, separatist conception of the ESTABLISHMENT OF RELIGION and would, for instance, permit state aid for secular activities in parochial schools.

Although White gives broad scope to LEGISLATIVE POWER, he has usually subjected the legislative product to close scrutiny for invidious purpose or for insufficient relationship to a legitimate purpose. For a time, White's purpose analysis produced a more activist Fourteenth Amendment jurisprudence than the majority of the Court was willing to embrace; for example, he argued in dissent in PALMER V. THOMPSON (1971) that a Mississippi town should not be permitted to close its swimming pool where its purpose was to prevent implementation of a DESEGREGATION order. White's scrutiny of purpose is decidedly nonactivist, however, in the face of minority challenges to government programs that have disparate racial impact without discriminatory intent. In the seminal case of WASHINGTON V. DAVIS (1976), he held for a 7–2 majority that

disparate impact alone does not constitute the kind of racial discrimination that presumptively violates the constitutional principle of EQUAL PROTECTION OF THE LAWS. White has not adopted the view that the Constitution prohibits all "reverse discrimination" to counteract diffuse societal discrimination. His joint opinion in REGENTS OF UNIVERSITY OF CALIFORNIA V. BAKKE (1978), permitting government to take race into account in university admissions, reflects his oft-demonstrated concern for equal educational opportunity. His votes, in FULLILOVE V. KLUTZNICK (1980) and METRO BROADCASTING, INC. V. FEDERAL COMMUNICATIONS COMMISSION (1990), to uphold federal minority "set-aside" and race-preference requirements underscore his deference to Congress even as he voted, in RICHMOND (CITY OF) V. J. A. CROSON CO. (1989), to strike down a LOCAL GOVERNMENT's "set-aside" scheme.

For a decade after he joined the majority opinion in GRIGGS V. DUKE POWER CO. (1971), White appeared content with permitting disparate impact alone to be sufficient for broad RACE-CONSCIOUS remedies in EMPLOYMENT DISCRIMINATION cases brought under Title VII of the CIVIL RIGHTS ACT OF 1964. In 1979, he even joined in endorsing a private employer's use of RACIAL QUOTAS intended to eliminate the effects of societal discrimination. White began to express significant dissatisfaction with aspects of the prevailing Title VII jurisprudence in a series of opinions, mostly dissenting, in the mid-1980s. By the end of the decade, amid indications that the disparate-impact test invited use of racial quotas, White commanded a majority in *Wards Cove Packing Co. v. Antonio* (1989) to shift the BURDEN OF PROOF in disparate-impact cases.

In school desegregation cases, however, White has been as ready as any member of the Court to find evidence of past purposeful discrimination and to approve broad remedies. His majority opinion in COLUMBUS BOARD OF EDUCATION V. PENICK (1979) permitted inference of purposeful discrimination from evidence of long-past misconduct and a continued discriminatory effect, and placed the burden on the defendant school system to prove that it had not caused any current racial SEGREGATION in its schools. In addition, he would hold the state, not the defendant school district, ultimately responsible for removing the effects of purposeful discrimination; in this view, neither the happenstance of school-district boundaries nor state laws impeding school funding may stand in the way of remedial decrees. Thus he was in a minority in MILLIKEN V. BRADLEY (1974) in arguing and a remedy of interdistrict SCHOOL BUSING, and he wrote the 5–4 decision in *Jenkins v. Missouri* (1990) upholding the power of the federal district court to order a defendant school board to impose tax increases in violation of fiscally restrictive state law.

One may infer several reasons for White's different stances in school desegregation cases and employment discrimination cases. Even outside the race-discrimination context, White has adopted an ethic of group equality in EDUCATION, as demonstrated in his dissent in SAN ANTONIO INDEPENDENT SCHOOL DISTRICT V. RODRIGUEZ (1973), where he would have struck down school-financing schemes that leave the poorest school districts with the most impoverished schools. Moreover, the proof of purposeful racial discrimination by school districts is often palpable, but it is difficult to trace disparate racial impact in the job market to purposeful discrimination by a defendant employer. In addition, although busing does not deny schooling to any child, White has expressed particular unhappiness with quota systems that take jobs away from nondiscriminating white workers. Finally, judicial imposition of systems of RACIAL PREFERENCE in employment would cause upheavals in collective bargaining, seniority systems, and other underpinnings of industrial society.

White's belief in the legitimacy of the law in ordering our social life, along with his confidence in the institutions of government, have made him reluctant to impose "decriminalization," either directly (by limiting legislative power to punish) or indirectly (by insisting on perfection from police, prosecutors, and others charged with achieving criminal justice). Even as he joined the holding in *Furman v. Georgia* (1972), striking down a scheme of CAPITAL PUNISHMENT that provided no guidance for the sentencing authority, White noted the good faith of Georgia in granting discretion to sentencing juries out of a "desire to mitigate the harshness" of capital punishment laws. Subsequently, he has voted to uphold carefully structured death penalty laws, rejecting the arguments that juries "disobey or nullify their instructions" and that others who retain discretion, such as prosecutors, inevitably wield it arbitrarily. Invoking the Court's ill-famed journey earlier in this century into the realm of SUBSTANTIVE DUE PROCESS, he has refused to make the judgment that the death penalty cannot comport with the Constitution. White has, however, recognized substantive limitations on the types of crimes for which this penalty may be imposed; he wrote the Court's opinion in COKER V. GEORGIA (1977), holding the death penalty disproportionate for the rape of an adult, and the Court's opinion in ENMUND V. FLORIDA (1982), holding capital punishment improper where a murder conviction was based solely on a theory of felony murder.

The criteria of "reasonableness" and "good faith," at the core of much of White's JURISPRUDENCE, are especially prominent in his approach to the FOURTH AMENDMENT— which has largely become the law of the land. He has been the leading proponent of clear and simple rules governing police SEARCH AND SEIZURE. He understands the Constitution's requirement that searches and seizures be "reasonable" to have broad applicability, if shallow in depth;

he wrote the opinion in CAMARA V. MUNICIPAL COURT (1967), which spawned a new jurisprudence upholding an array of regulatory searches on less than PROBABLE CAUSE, but he also wrote TENNESSEE V. GARNER (1985), which prohibited use of deadly force against fleeing felons, and he has recognized the Fourth Amendment's applicability to subpoenas issued by GRAND JURIES. His oft-stated antipathy to the EXCLUSIONARY RULE as a remedy for Fourth Amendment violations finally led to adoption of the GOOD FAITH EXCEPTION to this rule in *United States v. Leon* (1984). White has likewise taken a functional and pragmatic approach to the Sixth Amendment's right to TRIAL BY JURY. He has resisted efforts to limit criminal investigations and forfeitures through broad application of the RIGHT TO COUNSEL; he has dissented from interpretations of the Fifth Amendment RIGHT AGAINST SELF-INCRIMINATION that depart from historical practice and impede reliable administration of justice; and he has been at the forefront of the Court in permitting great leeway in PLEA BARGAINING, as in *Brady v. United States* (1970).

White's opinions on CRIMINAL PROCEDURE reveal not only his perspective on issues of criminal justice but also his unusual commitment to the rule of STARE DECISIS in constitutional adjudication, which has sometimes led to the perception that he is "unpredictable." Like many Justices, White is ready to overrule previous decisions that prove unworkable or ill-advised. For instance, he joined BATSON V. KENTUCKY (1986), which, overruling his own SWAIN V. ALABAMA (1965), subjected preemptory jury challenges to judicial review for racial discrimination; *Batson* acknowledged that *Swain's* confidence in state prosecutors had not been vindicated. Yet White, more than other Justices and regardless of ideological inclination, has on most issues sought to adhere to constitutional PRECEDENT not yet overruled. Thus, although he dissented forcefully in *Miranda*, he has clearly accepted the major contours of that decision. Indeed, he wrote EDWARDS V. ARIZONA (1981), which went beyond the core of *Miranda* in prohibiting all questioning once the suspect in custody has requested an attorney. Similarly, despite his long, carefully composed dissent in PAYTON V. NEW YORK (1980), which required an ARREST WARRANT to arrest persons in their homes, White ten years later wrote the majority opinion applying *Payton* to the arrest of someone hiding out overnight in a friend's home. Even where he would vote to overrule a precedent, White has sometimes exasperated observers by refusing to cast the fifth vote for simply narrowing the reach of the precedent, insisting he is bound until it is expressly overruled.

The most controversial decision by White upholding government power to invoke the criminal process is BOWERS V. HARDWICK (1986), which refused to strike down a Georgia law forbidding consensual sodomy between men.

White conceived the issue much as he had the issue in the death penalty cases: whether the Supreme Court should bypass political institutions to establish a new social order. White had long objected to the Court's discovery of new constitutional rights deriving from the concept of "privacy." His concurrence in GRISWOLD V. CONNECTICUT (1965) declined to find a general RIGHT OF PRIVACY, emphasizing instead the lack of a rational relationship between the statute's ban on distributing BIRTH CONTROL information to married persons and the purported purpose of the statute. ROE V. WADE (1973), the decision establishing a broad right to ABORTION throughout pregnancy, evoked a response reminiscent of his *Miranda* dissent: "The Court simply fashions and announces a new constitutional right . . . with scarcely any reason or authority." In dissents in subsequent privacy rights cases during the 1970s and early 1980s, including MOORE V. CITY OF EAST CLEVELAND (1977), which struck down a ZONING ordinance that narrowly defined "single family," White even more explicitly compared the Court's "new" substantive due process with the efforts of the Court in LOCHNER V. NEW YORK (1905) to impose its will on a divided polity. By 1986, in THORNBURGH V. AMERICAN COLLEGE OF OBSTETRICIANS AND GYNECOLOGISTS, he advocated overruling *Roe*, urging that the right it recognized was neither "implicit in the concept of ordered liberty," nor "deeply rooted in the nation's history and traditions." For White, *Bowers* was a replay of *Thornburgh*, with the important difference that he was writing the majority opinion. As White must have anticipated, once the majority had adopted his approach to enunciation of a FUNDAMENTAL RIGHT, it was only a matter of time before *Roe* itself would begin to collapse, as indeed it did in WEBSTER V. REPRODUCTIVE HEALTH SERVICES (1989).

Yet White himself had recognized certain fundamental liberty interests that may be subsumed under the label substantive due process—including, in *Griswold*, "the right to be free of regulation of the intimacies of the marriage relationship" and, in a long series of cases (continuing even after *Bowers*) dealing with ILLEGITIMACY, the rights of natural parents "in the companionship . . . of their children." White's purpose-based jurisprudence might have considered proscriptions of sodomy as different from anti-abortion laws. In the latter, the organized community may have the purpose of protecting human life, whereas in the former, its motiviation may simply be antipathy towards homosexuals—a purpose that could be recognized (but that White in 1986 declined to recognize) as invidious. Here as elsewhere, White's jurisprudence seldom puts the Court ahead of the country. For him, the Court's primary role in constitutional lawmaking is not to pioneer or even to lead, but rather to secure for the whole nation the democratic consensus that has already been reached.

KATE SMITH

(1992)

Bibliography

HUTTON, MARY CHRISTINE    1986    The Unique Perspective of Justice White: Separation of Powers, Standing and Section 1983 Cases. *Administrative Law Review* 40:377–414.

LIEBMAN, LANCE    1987    Justice White and Affirmative Action. *University of Colorado Law Review* 58:471–496.

NELSON, WILLIAM E.    1987    Deference and the Limits to Deference in the Constitutional Jurisprudence of Justice Byron R. White. *University of Colorado Law Review* 58:347–364.

O'DONNELL, PIERCE    1987    Common Sense and the Constitution: Justice White and the Egalitarian Ideal. *University of Colorado Law Review* 58:433–470.

STUDENT NOTE    1987    The Intercircuit Tribunal and Perceived Conflicts: An Analysis of Justice White's Dissents from Denial of Certiorari During the 1985 Term. *New York University Law Review* 62:610–650.

# WHITE, BYRON R.
## (1917–  )
## (Update 2)

When Byron R. White retired from the Supreme Court in 1993, the vacancy he created received more attention than his legacy. For the first time since 1967 (with the appointment of THURGOOD MARSHALL), and only the second time since his own appointment in 1962, a President from the Democratic Party would have the power to nominate a member to the Court. *The New York Times* editorially dismissed White's career: acknowledging that he was "one of the more remarkable people to serve on the Court," the *Times* nonetheless found him to be "more a witness than a moving force." White indirectly demurred and was later quoted as saying, "I don't have a doctrinal legacy; I shouldn't"—implying, as he often said, that the role of Justices is to decide particular cases, not to build theoretical structures.

Notwithstanding his own modesty and the judgments of the press, White had a substantial impact on the work of the Court during his lengthy tenure. He played a major role in the development of FIRST AMENDMENT doctrine, especially in the areas of press shield laws, BRANZBURG V. HAYES (1972); LIBEL, HERBERT V. LANDO (1979); CHILD PORNOGRAPHY; and the PUBLIC FORUM doctrine. He wrote major opinions for the Court in LABOR, ANTITRUST, and FEDERAL JURISDICTION. He was one of the leading exponents, and protectors, of a broad reading of congressional power, particularly vis-à-vis claimed STATES' RIGHTS. From AVERY V. MIDLAND COUNTY (1968) to ROGERS V. LODGE (1982), he was one of the Court's resident experts on VOTING RIGHTS law. He also played a central role in the development of doctrinal exceptions to the EXCLUSIONARY RULE.

White will probably be remembered not for his opinions for the Court but for a number of DISSENTING OPIN-

IONS, in which he took the majority to task—often in fierce terms—for its reasoning and for the practical consequences of its decision. From MIRANDA V. ARIZONA (1966) to ROE V. WADE (1973) to GERTZ V. WELCH (1974) to IMMIGRATION AND NATURALIZATION SERVICE V. CHADHA (1983), White never hesitated to express his misgivings over the Court's craft or what he viewed as its audacity. "Judges have an exaggerated view of their role in our polity," he told a friend privately after a decade on the Court, and his sharply worded separate opinions drove home the point.

The credo manifested indelibly in two areas, SEPARATION OF POWERS and SUBSTANTIVE DUE PROCESS. His first major statement on separation of powers was a separate opinion in BUCKLEY V. VALEO (1976), in which he was prepared to defer to Congress's judgment that limitations on both raising and spending money in federal elections were necessary notwithstanding concerns, embraced by the majority, that FREEDOM OF SPEECH protected spending decisions. He again voted to sustain Congress's device for handling the flood tide of federal litigation in NORTHERN PIPELINE CO. V. MARATHON PIPELINE CO. (1982). In *Chadha*, he dissented heatedly when the Court invalidated the LEGISLATIVE VETO in what he saw as both a wooden and unnecessary reading of the Constitution.

His written record on substantive due process was not fully developed or so widely respected. His dissent in *Roe v. Wade* was more a declaration of conviction than a sustained theoretical statement, and it was not until his dissent in MOORE V. CITY OF EAST CLEVELAND (1977) that he produced a fully expressed critique of the Court's revival of the old doctrine associated with LOCHNER V. NEW YORK (1905). His complaint was that the Court was using vague language in the Constitution to impose its own will on a divided polity—an exercise both illegitimate and, he eventually suggested, dangerous to the Court's own political capital. The issue was fundamental to White's view of his role, and so it is ironic that his final major opinion in the area is among his most widely and severely criticized. In BOWERS V. HARDWICK (1986), he wrote for a five-Justice majority rejecting a claim that consensual homosexual conduct in private between adults was protected by the DUE PROCESS clause of the FOURTEENTH AMENDMENT. To argue that the "claimed right" was "deeply rooted in this nation's history and tradition" or "implicit in the concept of ordered liberty"—the traditional formula used by the Court for upholding such a right—was, White wrote, "at best, facetious." The opinion seemed not to take the claim seriously and was condemned by many as an intellectual "hit-and-run incident." White was not uniformly hostile to claims labeled substantive due process: he joined the majority in GRISWOLD V. CONNECTICUT (1965), where he acknowledged constitutional protection for the "intimacies of the marriage relationship," and was committed—both before and after *Bowers*—to supporting the constitutional claims of natural parents to the "companionship . . . of their children." For White, well-established social norms enjoyed constitutional protection, but novel or controversial claims were beyond the constitutional pale.

Assessment of White's career which focused only on his views or his often difficult opinions tended to obscure the fact that he was one of the hardest working Justices on the Court during the period in which he served. He wrote 1,275 opinions—495 opinions for the Court, 249 concurring opinions, and 572 dissents. He sat during a period in which the Court grew more fractionated and participated in more 5–4 decisions than any other Justice in the Court's history except WILLIAM J. BRENNAN, JR. His tenure was also one of the longest in the institution's history: only nine others sat longer. In retirement, he continued to sit actively on federal courts of appeals and he also chaired a special commission charged with advising Congress on the structure of the federal Court of Appeals for the Ninth Circuit.

DENNIS J. HUTCHINSON
(2000)

Bibliography

HUTCHINSON, DENNIS J. 1998 *The Man Who Once Was Whizzer White.* New York: Free Press.

IDES, ALLAN 1993 The Jurisprudence of Byron White. *Yale Law Journal* 103:419–461.

LEE, REX and WILKINS, RICHARD G. 1994 On Greatness and Constitutional Vision: Justice Byron R. White. *Brigham Young Law Review* 1994:291–312.

# WHITE, EDWARD D.
## (1845–1921)

Born and raised in Louisiana, the son of a slaveholding sugar planter and a Confederate veteran, Edward Douglass White was an archetype of the "New South" political leader. The masters of the region's economic and social development from the 1880s until WORLD WAR I combined the interests of antebellum planters with those of northern and local capitalists eager to build railroads and tap the area's coal, iron, and timber. The South's new ruling class "redeemed" Dixie from the egalitarian schemes of Radical Republicans and carpetbaggers by supporting RUTHERFORD B. HAYES for President and accepting the national hegemony of the GOP's conservative wing. In return, these leaders of the "New South" received from the Republicans a promise to remove federal troops from the region, a free hand with respect to the Negro, and a junior partnership in the management of the nation's economic affairs. (See COMPROMISE OF 1877.)

While tending his family's plantation and building a prosperous legal practice in New Orleans, White became a chief political confidant and ally of Governor Francis Nicholls, the leader of the state's conservative Democrats, who rewarded him with an appointment to the Louisiana Supreme Court and then a seat in the United States SENATE in 1891. While in Washington, the portly, florid, long-haired junior senator from Louisiana adopted a rigid STATES' RIGHTS and laissez-faire posture on most issues. However, he fervently supported high duties on foreign sugar and lavish federal bounties to the planters in his home state. White led the Senate's successful revolt against President GROVER CLEVELAND's efforts to lower the protective tariff in 1893. Nevertheless, the beleaguered head of the Democratic party nominated him to the Supreme Court a year later, following the death of SAMUEL BLATCHFORD and the Senate's rejection of two earlier nominees.

White took his seat as the junior member of the FULLER COURT at one of the important turning points in the history of the federal judiciary. The country seethed with unrest generated by the worst depression of the nineteenth century. Violent confrontations between workers and employers erupted on the nation's major railroads as well as in coal mines, steel mills, and other factories. Debt-ridden farmers formed the radical Populist Party, which demanded government control of the money supply and banking system and nationalization of the major trunk rail lines. Insurgent Democrats nominated the youthful William Jennings Bryan, who ran on a platform promising inflation of the money supply, higher taxes on the wealthy, and a curb on trusts and other monopolies. In this atmosphere of class strife and regional polarization, men of property and standing looked to the Supreme Court to defend the constitutional ark against dangerous innovations. Fuller and most of his colleagues were equal to the task of repelling the radical hordes.

Even before the economic collapse, a majority of the Justices had served warning that they would not tolerate legislative attacks on corporate property and profits. Legislative power to fix railroad rates, they warned, was not without limits; corporations were PERSONS, entitled to the judicial protection of the FOURTEENTH AMENDMENT'S DUE PROCESS clause; and no rate imposed by legislative fiat could be deemed "reasonable" without final judicial review. Then, in a series of cases that reached the Court together during the depths of the depression in 1895, the Justices quashed federal efforts to prosecute the sugar trust under the SHERMAN ANTITRUST ACT in UNITED STATES V. E. C. KNIGHT CO. (1895); upheld the contempt conviction of the labor leader Eugene V. Debs for his role in the Pullman boycott in IN RE DEBS (1895); and declared unconstitutional the first federal income tax levied since the Civil War in POLLACK V. FARMER'S LOAN AND TRUST CO. (1895). These three decisions displayed the FULLER COURT's conservative colors and represented a major victory for big business, the wealthy, and the enemies of organized labor.

Like the majority of his brethren, Justice White showed no sympathy for Debs and the militant working class movement he represented. White also endorsed Fuller's reasoning in the sugar trust case, which limited the scope of the Sherman Act to monopolies of interstate trade or commerce and left to the individual states all authority to curb monopolies over production. But he joined Justice JOHN MARSHALL HARLAN, the outspoken champion of nationalism and federal power, in denouncing the majority's assault on the income tax statute. White had been a member of the Senate that passed the income tax measure as part of the tariff package in 1892, and, although he did not endorse the levy, neither did he doubt the constitutional power of Congress to adopt it. In order to invalidate the law, the majority had to ignore two weighty precedents, one dating from 1796. This was too much for White, who argued eloquently that "the conservation and orderly development of our institutions rests on our acceptance of the results of the past, and their use as lights to guide our steps in the future. Teach the lesson that settled principles may be overthrown at any time, and confusion and turmoil must ultimately result."

The income tax dissent revealed an important aspect of White's jurisprudence which remained constant during his years as an associate Justice and later as Chief Justice after 1911. Although deeply conservative and devoted to the judicial protection of private property, White was also a pragmatist capable of endorsing moderate reforms that had clear constitutional sanction and that served to cap the pressures for more radical change. Though not adverse to overturning a few precedents himself, White usually did so in the pursuit of policies that strengthened rather than weakened the dominant economic forces of corporate capitalism.

In this spirit, he endorsed the judicial imperialism inherent in Justice Harlan's opinion in SMYTH V. AMES (1898), which made the federal judiciary the final arbiter of utility rates, but he also enforced the progressive reforms of the Theodore Roosevelt-William Howard Taft era which revitalized the regulatory authority of the Interstate Commerce Commission (ICC) over the nation's major railroads. In a series of decisions, culminating in White's opinion in INTERSTATE COMMERCE COMMISSION V. ILLINOIS CENTRAL RAILROAD CO. (1910), the majority sustained the ICC's fact-finding and rate-fixing powers as mandated by Congress. White's views were compatible with the interests of the railroads, which looked to the ICC to prevent financially ruinous rate wars, and with those of reformers like Roosevelt, who believed that such regulation would curb the appetite for government ownership of the carriers.

White rendered his greatest service to the conservative

cause in the area of antitrust law by promoting the view that the Sherman Act prohibited only "unreasonable" restraints of trade, a perspective pregnant with possibilities for enlarged judicial control over the country's economic structure, yet wholly compatible with the desires of big business. But it took White over a decade to defeat the contrary views of other Justices, who remained more wedded to the old Jacksonian belief in competition and the dangers of monopoly.

In the wake of the *E. C. Knight* decision restricting federal antitrust efforts to INTERSTATE COMMERCE, the Department of Justice began a campaign to stamp out railroad cartels and pools designed to divide up traffic and fix rates. A majority of the Justices, led by Harlan and RUFUS W. PECKHAM, a passionate spokesman for laissez-faire economics, sustained the government's efforts in this area on the theory that the Sherman Act outlawed *all* restraints of trade, even those that might be deemed "reasonable" in view of particular business conditions such as rate wars and destructive competition. In the first of these cases, UNITED STATES V. TRANS-MISSOURI FREIGHT ASSOCIATION (1897), White wrote a long, rambling dissent which accused the majority of misreading the antitrust law, defying the traditions of the COMMON LAW with respect to restraints of trade, and jeopardizing the economic progress brought to the nation by business combinations and consolidations.

White continued to dissent in the *Joint Traffic Association Case* (1898) and in NORTHERN SECURITIES CO. V. UNITED STATES (1904), where a five-Justice majority upheld the government's suit against the Morgan-Harriman rail monopoly between Chicago and the Pacific Northwest. In each case, White argued that the antitrust law, incorporating the ancient doctrines of the common law, prohibiting only "unreasonable" restraints of trade. Technically, White was correct, but all of the methods condemned in *Trans-Missouri, Joint Traffic Association,* and *Northern Securities* would have been indictable at common law as well, because their fundamental objective had been to fix prices contrary to the public interest. This fact seems to have eluded White, who believed that the Harlan-Peckham approach threatened the demise of valuable business enterprises by virtue of judicial abdication to the prosecutorial zeal of misguided reformers in the executive branch. In this perception, he enjoyed the support of three other justices, including OLIVER WENDELL HOLMES, who also looked upon the Rockefellers, Morgans, and Harrimans as agents of social and economic progress.

Four changes in the personnel of the Court between 1909 and 1911 gave White a new majority for his doctrine a year later when the government's suits against Standard Oil and American Tobacco finally reached the Justices after years of litigation. Speaking now as Chief Justice of the United States, having been appointed to the center chair by President Taft, White sustained the government's case against the monopolists but cast aside the Harlan-Peckham interpretation of the Sherman Act. Henceforth, the majority decreed, only "unreasonable" trade restraints would be indictable under the Sherman Act and the Justices on the Supreme Court would determine where the line should be drawn between legal and illegal competitive behavior. Harlan wrote a melancholy dissent against this sharp reversal of doctrine, which seemed to teach that "settled principles may be overthrown at any time, and confusion and turmoil must ultimately result."

White's RULE OF REASON doctrine provoked a storm of protest from progressives in the Congress, who denounced the Justices for mutilating the antitrust law, arrogating to themselves too much power over the economic system, and giving big business a hunting license to continue its predatory ways. Although Congress added the CLAYTON ACT amendments to the antitrust law in 1914, specifically outlawing a substantial list of business practices, White's rule of reason carried the day. The Court quashed the government's efforts to break up the shoe machinery monopoly in 1913 and also threw out the case against United States Steel in 1920, a year before White died. There was extraordinary historical irony in the fact that it was a Southerner and a veteran of the Rebel army who advanced antitrust doctrines that sealed the triumph of industrial capitalism and big business in American life.

For a Southerner, a Democrat, and a spokesman for states' rights in the Senate, White displayed considerable toleration for the expansion of federal economic controls by means of the COMMERCE CLAUSE and the TAXING AND SPENDING POWER. In the Senate he had taken an active role in fighting a federal law to regulate the trade in agricultural "futures," noting that it would invade the JURISDICTION of the states and create "the most unlimited and arbitrary government on the face of God's earth." As a Justice, however, he joined Harlan's path-breaking opinion in the Lottery Case, CHAMPION V. AMES (1903), which greatly expanded the NATIONAL POLICE POWER via the interstate commerce clause. A year later he wrote the Court's opinion in MCCRAY V. UNITED STATES (1904), which affirmed the power of Congress to impose a prohibitive levy upon oleomargarine and thus employ its tax powers for regulatory purposes.

White drew back, however, from the logical implications of the national police power when Congress sought to apply it to other areas of social and economic life. He was willing to permit the extension of the commerce power to federal regulation of adulterated foods and interstate traffic in prostitution, but he joined Justice WILLIAM R. DAY's opinion in HAMMER V. DAGENHART (1918), which declared unconstitutional Congress's attempt to eradicate child labor. He also rejected federal efforts to tax and regulate narcotics traffic in UNITED STATES V. DOREMUS (1919), although the majority found this use of the federal taxing power compatible with White's own views in *McCray*. He sanctioned Congress's adoption of an eight-hour day for interstate train crews which brought an end to the disastrous nationwide rail strike, but he joined three other dissenters in *Block v. Hirsh* (1921) when Holmes and the majority upheld the national legislature's power to impose rent controls upon property in the DISTRICT OF COLUMBIA during the emergency of World War I.

White displayed equal inconsistency in cases where state ECONOMIC REGULATIONS came under DUE PROCESS challenge. The one thread of coherence seemed to be his growing conservatism and abiding dislike for organized labor. He dissented in LOCHNER V. NEW YORK (1905) along with Harlan and Day, noting that "no evils arising from such legislation could be more far-reaching than those that might come to our system of government if the judiciary ... should enter the domain of legislation, and upon grounds merely of justice or reason or wisdom, annul statutes that had received the sanction of the people's representatives." He also voted to sustain the Oregon and California maximum hours laws for women in MULLER V. OREGON (1908) and *Miller v. Wilson* (1915). But he balked at the overtime pay provisions and general maximum hours limitation in BUNTING V. OREGON (1917) and sided with the majority in the three leading cases of the period which protected employers' use of YELLOW DOG CONTRACTS against both state and federal efforts to eliminate this notorious antiunion device: *Adair v. United States* (1908), COPPAGE V. KANSAS (1915), and HITCHMAN V. HITCHMAN COAL & COKE CO. (1917).

In 1919, White joined JOSEPH MCKENNA, WILLIS VAN DEVANTER, and JAMES C. MCREYNOLDS in dissent against the Court's opinion in the *Arizona Employers' Liability Cases* (1919), which upheld that state's law shifting the cost of industrial accidents to employers. And during his final term on the Court, he joined the majority in scuttling the anti-INJUNCTION provisions of the Clayton Antitrust Act and affirming the illegality of secondary boycotts. If not the most reactionary member of the Supreme Court with respect to organized labor, White certainly ran a close race for that honor with Justices Day, MAHLON PITNEY, and McReynolds.

White had been elevated to the chief justiceship by William Howard Taft, who coveted the position for himself and feared that a younger nominee might forever prevent that happy development. Taft realized his lifelong ambition in 1921, when White died. Predictably, White's eulogizers compared his career to that of John Marshall and other immortals of the bench, but a more accurate assessment is that constitutional law showed his imprint until 1937.

MICHAEL E. PARRISH
(1986)

Bibliography

DISHMAN, ROBERT 1951 Mr. Justice White and the Rule of Reason. *The Review of Politics* 13:229–248.

HIGHSAW, ROBERT B. 1981 *Edward Douglass White: Defender of the Conservative Faith.* Baton Rouge: Louisiana State University Press.

KLINKHAMER, MARIE CAROLYN 1943 *Edward Douglass White, Chief Justice of the United States.* Washington, D.C.: Catholic University Press.

SEMONCHE, JOHN E. 1978 *Charting the Future: The Supreme Court Responds to a Changing Society, 1890–1920.* Westport, Conn.: Greenwood Press.

# WHITE, UNITED STATES v.
## 401 U.S. 745 (1971)

During the reign of OLMSTEAD V. UNITED STATES (1927) the Supreme Court consistently ruled, in cases including ON LEE V. UNITED STATES (1952) and LOPEZ V. UNITED STATES (1963), that government informers who deceptively interrogated criminal suspects and either secretly transmitted the conversations to eavesdropping government agents with concealed recorders or secretly recorded the conversations, had committed no TRESPASS, and therefore the FOURTH AMENDMENT was inapplicable. The use of spies without complying with Fourth Amendment controls was reaffirmed in HOFFA V. UNITED STATES (1966). KATZ V. UNITED STATES (1967), however, abolished the trespass requirement for Fourth Amendment protection and focused on the personal PRIVACY interests that were entitled to protection. Some therefore thought *On Lee* was no longer good law. In *United States v. White*, however, the Court held otherwise. Though there was no clear majority for either approving or disapproving *On Lee*, four Justices voted to reaffirm that decision, and Justice HUGO L. BLACK concurred to make a majority on the ground that *Olmstead*'s trespass requirement should be retained. The *On Lee* doctrine was thus reaffirmed.

Justice BYRON R. WHITE, for the plurality, ruled that a person is not protected by the Fourth Amendment against a faithless friend, regardless of whether a trespass is involved. An expectation of such protection is not "justifiable" under the *Katz* standard. Police have always been allowed to use the evidence of faithless associates who turn to the police or are informers: "one contemplating illegal activities must realize and risk that his companions may be reporting to the police." The fact that the faithless friend was wired, transmitting the conversation to others or recording it for later replaying, makes no constitutional difference.

The dissents focused on the latter point. Justice JOHN MARSHALL HARLAN rejected the "assumption of risk" rationale of the majority, stressing that the real question was which risks the law *should* force people to assume. Whereas the use of unwired spies or contemporaneous recording to ensure reliability are both justifiable, simultaneous overhearing by third parties is different; free discourse would be seriously jeopardized if people were forced to assume the risk that their words were being simultaneously transmitted to third parties and transcribed. "Were third-party bugging a prevalent practice, it might well smother that spontaneity—reflected in frivolous, impetuous, sacrilegious, and defiant discourse—that liberates daily life." Justice Harlan emphasized that the dissenters' views would not prohibit the use of wired informers but would only bring the practice under Fourth Amendment warrant and other procedures.

Even though the principal *White* opinion did not command a majority, it kept *On Lee* in effect and freed the government from Fourth Amendment restrictions on the use of spies and informers, wired or otherwise.

HERMAN SCHWARTZ
(1986)

(SEE ALSO: *Electronic Eavesdropping.*)

# WHITE COURT
## (1910–1921)

"The condition of the Supreme Court is pitiable, and yet those old fools hold on with a tenacity that is most discouraging," President WILLIAM HOWARD TAFT wrote in May 1909 to his old friend HORACE H. LURTON. Taft would have his day. One year later, Chief Justice MELVILLE W. FULLER spoke at the Court's memorial service for Justice DAVID J. BREWER: "As our brother Brewer joins the great procession, there pass before me the forms of Mathews and Miller, of Field and Bradley and Lamar and Blatchford, of Jackson and Gray and of Peckham, whose works follow them now that they rest from their labors." These were virtually Fuller's last words from the bench, for he died on Independence Day, 1910, in his native Maine. RUFUS W. PECKHAM had died less than a year earlier. WILLIAM H. MOODY, tragically and prematurely ill, would within a few months have to cut short by retirement one of the few notable short tenures on the Court. JOHN MARSHALL HARLAN had but one year left in his remarkable thirty-four-year tenure. By 1912, five new Justices had come to the Court who were not there in 1909: a new majority under a new Chief Justice.

The year 1910 was a significant divide in the history of the country as well. The population was nearly half urban, and immigration was large and growing. The country stood on the verge of enacting humane and extensive labor regulation. A year of Republican unrest in Congress and THEO-DORE ROOSEVELT's decisive turn to progressive agitation, 1910 was the first time in eight elections that the Democrats took control of the House. In the same year, the National Association for the Advancement of Colored People was founded. It was a year of progressive tremors that would eventually shake the Supreme Court to its foundations with the appointment of LOUIS D. BRANDEIS in 1916. But the five appointments with which President Taft rehabilitated his beloved Court between 1909 and 1912 had no such dramatic impact. There was a significant strengthening of a mild progressive tendency earlier evident within the Court, but the new appointments brought neither a hardening nor a decisive break with the DOCTRINES of laissez-faire constitutionalism and luxuriant individualism embodied in such decisions as LOCHNER V. NEW YORK (1905) and *Adair v. United States* (1908). Taft's aim was to strengthen the Court with active men of sound, if somewhat progressive, conservative principles. Neither Taft nor the nation saw the Court, as both increasingly would a decade later, as the storm center of pressures for fundamental constitutional change.

Taft's first choice when Peckham died in 1909 was his friend Lurton, then on the Sixth Circuit, and a former member of the Tennessee Supreme Court. Lurton, a Democrat, had been a fiery secessionist in his youth, and in his short and uneventful four-year tenure he combined conservationism on economic regulation, race, and labor relations. Taft's second choice was not so modest. When Taft went to Governor CHARLES EVANS HUGHES of New York to replace Brewer, he brought to the Court for the first of his two tenures a Justice who would emerge as one of the greatest figures in the history of American law, and a principal architect of modern CIVIL LIBERTIES and CIVIL RIGHTS jurisprudence. As governor of New York, Hughes was already one of the formidable reform figures of the Progressive era, and his later career as a presidential candidate who came within a whisper of success in 1916, secretary of state during the 1920s, and Chief Justice during the tumultuous years of the New Deal, mark him as one of the most versatile and important public figures to sit on the Court since JOHN MARSHALL.

Taft's choice of the Chief Justice to fill the center seat left vacant by Fuller was something of a surprise, although reasons are obvious in retrospect. EDWARD D. WHITE was a Confederate veteran from Louisiana, who had played a central role in the Democratic reaction against Reconstruction in that state and had emerged as a Democratic senator in 1891. He had been appointed Associate Justice in 1894 by President GROVER CLEVELAND and had compiled a respectable but unobtrusive record in sixteen years in the side seat. He had dissented with able force from the self-inflicted wound of POLLOCK V. FARMERS' LOAN & TRUST CO. (1895), holding unconstitutional the federal income tax, and his antitrust dissents in TRANS-MISSOURI FREIGHT ASSOCIATION (1897) and UNITED STATES V. NORTHERN SECURITIES COMPANY (1904) embodied sound good sense. He had done "pioneer work," as Taft later called it, in ADMINISTRATIVE LAW. White had a genius for friendship and, despite a habit of constant worrying, extraordinary personal warmth. OLIVER WENDELL HOLMES summed him up in these words in 1910: "His writing leaves much to be desired, but his thinking is profound, especially in the legislative direction which we don't recognize as a judicial requirement but which is so, especially in our Court, nevertheless." White was sixty-five, a Democrat, a Confederate veteran, and a Roman Catholic, and his selection by Taft was seen as adventurous. But given Taft's desire to bind up sectional wounds, to spread his political advantage, to put someone in the center seat who might not occupy Taft's own ultimate ambition for too long, to exemplify bipartisanship in the choice of Chief Justice, and on its own sturdy merits, the selection of White seems easy to understand.

Along with White's nomination, Taft sent to the Senate nominations of WILLIS VAN DEVANTER of Wyoming and JOSEPH R. LAMAR of Georgia. Van Devanter would sit for twenty-seven years, and would become one of the Court's most able, if increasingly conservative, legal craftsmen. Lamar would last only five years, and his death in 1915, along with Lurton's death in 1914 and Hughes's resignation to run for President, opened up the second important cycle of appointments to the White Court.

The Taft appointees joined two of the most remarkable characters ever to sit on the Supreme Court. John Marshall Harlan, then seventy-eight, had been on the Court since his appointment by President RUTHERFORD B. HAYES in 1877. He was a Justice of passionate strength and certitude, a man who, in the fond words of Justice Brewer, "goes to bed every night with one hand on the Constitution and the other on the Bible, and so sleeps the sleep of justice and righteousness." He had issued an apocalyptic dissent in *Pollock*, the income tax case, and his dissent in PLESSY V. FERGUSON (1986), the notorious decision upholding racial SEGREGATION on railroads, was an appeal to the conscience of the Constitution without equal in our history. The other, even more awesome, giant on the Court in 1910 was Holmes, then seventy, but still not quite recognized as the jurist whom BENJAMIN N. CARDOZO would later call "probably the greatest legal intellect in the history of the English-speaking judiciary." The other two members of the Court were JOSEPH MCKENNA, appointed by President WILLIAM MCKINLEY in 1898, and WILLIAM R. DAY, appointed by President Theodore Roosevelt in 1903.

The Supreme Court in 1910 remained in "truly republican simplicity," as Dean Acheson would recall, in the old Senate chamber, where the Justices operated in the midst of popular government, and in the sight of visitors to the Capitol. No office space was available, and the Justices worked in their homes. Their staff allowance provided for a messenger and one clerk, and their salaries were raised in 1911 to $14,500 for the Associate Justices and $15,000 for the Chief Justice. The Court was badly overworked and the docket was falling further and further behind, not to be rescued until the JUDICIARY ACT OF 1925 gave the Court discretion to choose the cases it would review.

In the public's contemporaneous view, if not in retrospect, the most important cases before the White Court between 1910 and 1921 did not involve the Constitution at all, but rather the impact of the SHERMAN ANTITRUST ACT on the great trusts. UNITED STATES V. STANDARD OIL COMPANY (1911) and *American Tobacco Company v. United States* (1911) had been initiated by the Roosevelt administration to seek dissolution of the huge combinations, and when the cases were argued together before the Supreme Court in 1911, the *Harvard Law Review* thought public attention was concentrated on the Supreme Court "to a greater extent than ever before in its history."

The problem for the Court was to determine the meaning of restraint of trade amounting to monopoly. The answer offered by Chief Justice White for the Court was the famous RULE OF REASON, under which not all restraints of trade restrictive of competition were deemed to violate the Sherman Act, but rather only those "undue restraints" which suggested an "intent to do wrong to the general public . . . thus restraining the free flow of commerce and tending to bring about the evils, such as enhancement of riches, which were considered to be against public policy." Under this test, the Court deemed Standard Oil to have engaged in practices designed to dominate the oil industry, exclude others from trade, and create a monopoly. It was ordered to divest itself of its subsidiaries, and to make no agreements with them that would unreasonably restrain trade. The court ruled that the American Tobacco Company was also an illegal combination and forced it into dissolution.

Antitrust was perhaps the dominant political issue of the 1912 presidential campaign, and the rule of reason helped to fuel a heated political debate that produced the great CLAYTON ACT and FEDERAL TRADE COMMISSION ACT of 1914. Further great antitrust cases came to the White Court, notably *United States v. United States Steel Company*, begun in 1911, postponed during the crisis of WORLD WAR I, and eventually decided in 1920. A divided Court held that United States Steel had not violated the Sherman Act, mere size alone not constituting an offense.

The tremendous public interest generated by the antitrust cases before the White Court was a sign of the temper of the political times, in which the regulation of business and labor relations was the chief focus of progressive attention. In this arena of constitutional litigation, the White Court's record was mixed, with perhaps a slight progressive tinge. On the great questions of legislative power to regulate business practices and working arrangements, the White Court maintained two parallel but opposing lines of doctrines, the one protective of laissez-faire constitutionalism and freedom from national regulation, the other receptive to the progressive reforms of the day.

In the first four years after its reconstitution by Taft, the Supreme Court handed down a number of important decisions upholding national power to regulate commerce for a variety of ends. The most expansive involved federal power to regulate railroads—and to override competing state regulation when necessary. *Atlantic Coast Line Railroad v. Riverside Mills* (1911) upheld Congress's amendment of the HEPBURN ACT imposing on the initial carrier of goods liability for any loss occasioned by a connecting carrier, notwithstanding anything to the contrary in the bill of lading. FREEDOM OF CONTRACT gave way to the needs of shippers for easy and prompt recovery. More significantly, in the second of the EMPLOYERS' LIABILITY CASES (1912), the Court upheld congressional legislation imposing liability for any injury negligently caused to any employee of a carrier engaged in INTERSTATE COMMERCE. This legislation did away with the fellow-servant rule and the defense of contributory negligence, again notwithstanding contracts to the contrary. In 1914, in the famous *Shreveport Case* (*Houston, East & West Texas Railway Company v. United States*), the Court upheld the power of the Interstate Commerce Commission to set the rates of railroad hauls entirely within Texas, because those rates competed against traffic between Texas and Louisiana. The Court overrode the rates set by the Texas Railroad Commission in the process. And in the most important COMMERCE CLAUSE decision of the early years of the White Court, the MINNESOTA RATE CASES (1913), the Court upheld the power of the states to regulate railroad rates for intrastate hauls, even when that regulation would force down interstate rates, so long as there had been no federal regulation of those rates. Thus, state power over rates was not invalidated because of the possibility of prospective federal regulation, and a large loophole between state and federal power was closed.

Outside the area of carrier regulation, the White Court was also friendly to national regulation by expanding the NATIONAL POLICE POWER doctrine. HIPOLITE EGG CO. V. UNITED STATES (1911) upheld the PURE FOOD AND DRUG ACT of 1906 in regulating adulterated food and drugs shipped in interstate commerce, whether or not the material had come to rest in the states. "Illicit articles" that traveled in interstate commerce were subject to federal control, the Court said, although with a doctrinal vagueness and confusion that would come back to haunt the Court in HAMMER V. DAGENHART (1918). In HOKE V. UNITED STATES (1913)

the Court upheld the MANN ACT, which punished the transportation in interstate commerce of women "for the purpose of prostitution or debauchery, or for any other immoral purpose."

Taft got his opportunity for a sixth appointment—more appointments in one term than any President in our history since GEORGE WASHINGTON—when Harlan died in 1911. He filled the vacancy with MAHLON PITNEY, chancellor of New Jersey. The reasons for this appointment are obscure, but like other Taft appointments Pitney was a sound, middle-of-the-road, good lawyer with little flair or imagination. As if to prepare for the coming flap over Brandeis, the Pitney appointment ran into trouble because of the nominee's alleged antilabor positions. But Pitney prevailed, and he would serve on the Court until 1922.

If ever in the history of the Supreme Court successive appointments by one President have seemed to embrace dialectical opposites, WOODROW WILSON's appointments of JAMES C. MCREYNOLDS in 1914 and Louis D. Brandeis in 1916 are the ones. McReynolds would become an embittered and crude anti-Semite; Brandeis was the first Jew to sit on the Supreme Court. McReynolds would become the most rigid and doctrinaire apostle of laissez-faire conservatism in constitutional history, the most recalcitrant of the "Four Horsemen of Reaction" who helped to scuttle New Deal legislation in the early 1930s. Brandeis was the greatest progressive of his day, on or off the Court. McReynolds was an almost invariable foe of CIVIL LIBERTIES and CIVIL RIGHTS for black people; Brandeis was perhaps the driving force of his time for the development of civil liberties, especially freedom of expression and rights of personal privacy. What brought these opposites together in Wilson's esteem, although he came to regret the McReynolds appointment, was antitrust fervor. McReynolds's aggressive individualism and Brandeis's progressive concern for personal dignity and industrial democracy coalesced around antitrust law, and this was the litmus test of the day for Wilson. Thus, possibly the most difficult and divisive person ever to sit on the Supreme Court and possibly the most intellectually gifted and broadly influential Justice in the Court's history took their seats in spurious, rather Wilsonian, juxtaposition.

Wilson's third appointment was handed him by the resignation of his rival in the presidential election of 1916. As it became plain that Hughes was the only person who could unite the Republican party, he came under increasing pressure from Taft and others to make himself available. He did. Wilson nominated JOHN H. CLARK of Ohio to replace Hughes. One of the most pregnant speculations about the history of the Supreme Court is what might have happened had Hughes remained on the bench. He might well have become a Chief Justice in 1921 instead of Taft, and under his statesmanlike influence, the hardening of doctrine that led to the confrontation over the New Deal and the Court-packing plan might not have happened.

Although two of Wilson's three appointments were staunch progressives, the Supreme Court seemed to adopt a somewhat conservative stance as it moved toward the decade of erratic resistance to reform that would follow in the 1920s. Federal reform legislation generally continued to pass muster, but there was the staggering exception of the *Child Labor Case* in 1918. And the Court seemed to strike out at labor unions, in both constitutional and antitrust decisions.

In *Hammer v. Dagenhart* (1918) the Supreme Court stunned Congress and most of the country when it invalidated the first federal CHILD LABOR ACT. The extent of child labor in the United States during the Progressive era was an affront to humanitarian sensibilities. One child out of six between the ages of ten and fifteen was a wage earner. Prohibition and regulation of child labor became the central reform initiatives of the progressive impulse. In 1916, overcoming constitutional doubts, Wilson signed the KEATING-OWEN ACT, which forbade the shipment in interstate or foreign commerce of the products of mines where children sixteen and under had been employed, or of factories where children younger than fourteen worked, or where children fourteen to sixteen had worked more than eight hours a day, six days a week. Child labor was not directly forbidden, but was severely discouraged by closing the channels of interstate commerce.

A narrow majority of the Court, in an opinion by Justice Day, held that this law exceeded the federal commerce power. Day reasoned that the goods produced by child labor were in themselves harmless, and that the interstate transportation did not in itself accomplish any harm. This reasoning was entirely question-begging, because it was the possibility of interstate commerce that imposed a competitive disadvantage in states that outlawed child labor in comparison with less humanitarian states. Moreover, the reasoning was flatly inconsistent with the opinion in *Hipolite Egg* and *Hoke*. But the majority plainly regarded the federal child labor legislation as an invasion of the domestic preserves of the states. Holmes, joined by McKenna, Brandeis, and Clarke, issued a classic dissent.

With the preparations for an advent of American involvement in World War I, the Supreme Court recognized broad federal power to put the economy on a wartime footing. The burden of constitutional resistance to reform legislation shifted to cases involving state laws. Here the main hardening in doctrinal terms came in cases involving labor unions. Otherwise, a reasonable progressivism prevailed. Thus, in BUNTING V. OREGON (1917) the Court upheld the maximum ten-hour day for all workers in mills and factories, whether men or women. However, two minimum wage cases from Oregon were upheld only by the fortuity of an equally divided Supreme Court, Brandeis having recused himself.

The most chilling warning to progressives that laissez-faire constitutionalism was not dead came in COPPAGE V. KANSAS (1915). The issue was the power of a state to prohibit by legislation the so-called YELLOW DOG CONTRACT, under which workers had to promise their employers not to join a union. The Court in *Coppage* held such laws unconstitutional: to limit an employer's freedom to offer employment on its own terms was a violation of freedom of contract.

The Supreme Court's race relations decisions between 1910 and 1921 constitute one of the Progressive era's most notable, and in some ways surprising, constitutional developments. Each of the Civil War amendments was given unprecedented application. For the first time, in the *Grandfather Clause Cases* (1915), the Supreme Court applied the FIFTEENTH AMENDMENT and what was left of the federal civil rights statutes to strike down state laws calculated to deny blacks the right to vote. For the first time, in BAILEY V. ALABAMA (1911) and UNITED STATES V. REYNOLDS (1914), the Court used the THIRTEENTH AMENDMENT to strike down state laws that supported PEONAGE by treating breach of labor contracts as criminal fraud and by encouraging indigent defendants to avoid the chain gang by having employers pay their fines in return for commitments to involuntary servitude. For the first time, in BUCHANAN V. WARLEY (1917), it found in the FOURTEENTH AMENDMENT constitutional limits on the spread of laws requiring racial separation in residential areas of cities and towns, and also for the first time, in *McCabe v. Atchison, Topeka & Santa Fe Railway* (1914), it put some teeth in the equality side of the SEPARATE BUT EQUAL DOCTRINE by striking down an Oklahoma law that said that railroads need not provide luxury car accommodations for blacks on account of low demand.

To be sure, only with respect to peonage could the White Court be said to have dismantled the legal structure of racism in any fundamental way. After the White Court passed into history in 1921, blacks in the South remained segregated and stigmatized by Jim Crow laws, disfranchised by invidiously administered LITERACY TESTS, white PRIMARY ELECTIONS, and POLL TAXES; and victimized by a criminal process from whose juries and other positions of power they were wholly excluded. But if the White Court did not stem the newly aggressive and self-confident ideology of racism inundating America in the Progressive era, neither did it put its power and prestige behind the flood, as had the WAITE COURT and FULLER COURT that preceded it—and, at critical points, it resisted. The White Court's principled countercurrents were more symbols of hope than effective bulwarks against the racial prejudice that permeated American law. But the decisions taken together mark the first time in American history that the Supreme Court opened itself in more than a passing way to the promises of the Civil War amendments.

World War I generated the first set of cases that provoked the Supreme Court for the first time since the FIRST AMENDMENT was ratified in 1791 to consider the meaning of freedom of expression. The cases, not surprisingly, involved dissent and agitation against the war policies of the United States. The war set off a major period of political repression against critics of American policy.

In the first three cases, SCHENCK V. UNITED STATES, FROHWERK V. UNITED STATES, and IN RE DEBS (1919), following the lead of Justice Holmes, the Supreme Court looked not to the law of SEDITIOUS LIBEL for justification in punishing speech but rather to traditional principles of legal responsibility for attempted crimes. In English and American COMMON LAW, an unsuccessful attempt to commit a crime could be punished if the attempt came dangerously close to success, while preparations for crime—in themselves harmless—could not be punished. With his gift of great utterance, Holmes distilled these doctrinal nuances into the rule that expression could be punished only if it created a CLEAR AND PRESENT DANGER of bringing about illegal action, such as draft resistance or curtailment of weapons production. Given his corrosive skepticism and his Darwinian sense of flux, the clear and present danger rule later became in Holmes's hands a fair protection for expression. But in the hands of judges and juries more passionate or anxious, measuring protection for expression by the likelihood of illegal action proved evanescent and unpredictable.

There were other problems with the clear and present danger rule. It took no account of the value of a particular expression, but considered only its tendency to cause harmful acts. Because the test was circumstantial, legislative declarations that certain types of speech were dangerous put the courts in the awkward position of having to second-guess the legislature's factual assessments of risk in order to protect the expression. This problem became clear to Holmes in ABRAMS V. UNITED STATES (1919), in which a statute punishing speech that urged curtailment of war production was used to impose draconian sanctions on a group of radical Russian immigrants who had inveighed against manufacture of war material that was to be used in Russia. In this case, Holmes and Brandeis joined in one of the greatest statements of political tolerance ever uttered.

In 1921, the year Edward Douglass White died and Taft became Chief Justice, Benjamin Cardozo delivered his immortal lectures, "The Nature of the Judicial Process." Cardozo pleaded for judges to "search for light among the social elements of every kind that are the living forces behind the facts they deal with." The judge must be "the interpreter for the community of its sense of law and order . . . and harmonize results with justice through a method of free decision." Turning to the Supreme Court, Cardozo stated: "Above all in the field of constitutional law, the method of free decision has become, I think, the dominant one today."

In this view, we can see that Cardozo was too hopeful, although his statement may have been offered more as an admonition than a description. The method of "free decision," exemplified for Cardozo by the opinions of Holmes and Brandeis, remained in doubt notwithstanding the inconsistent progressivism of the White Court, and would become increasingly embattled in the decades to come.

BENNO C. SCMIDT, JR.
(1986)

Bibliography

BICKEL, ALEXANDER M. and SCHMIDT, BENNO C., JR. 1984 *The Judiciary and Responsible Government 1910–1921.* Vol. IX of the Holmes Devise History of the Supreme Court. New York: Macmillan.

CARDOZO, BENJAMIN N. 1921 *The Nature of the Judicial Process.* New Haven, Conn.: Yale University Press.

CHAFEE, ZECHARIA 1949 *Free Speech in the United States.* Cambridge, Mass.: Harvard University Press.

HIGHSAW, ROBERT B. 1981 *Edward Douglass White.* Baton Rouge: Louisiana State University Press.

SEMONCHE, JOHN E. 1978 *Charting the Future: The Supreme Court Responds to a Changing Society 1890–1920.* Westport, Conn.: Greenwood Press.

SWINDLER, WILLIAM F. 1969 *Court and Constitution in the 20th Century: The Old Legality 1889–1932.* Indianapolis: Bobbs-Merrill.

# WHITE PRIMARIES

See: *Grovey v. Townsend; Nixon v. Condon; Nixon v. Herndon;* Primary Election; *Smith v. Allwright; Terry v. Adams*

# WHITING, WILLIAM

See: Commentators on the Constitution

# *WHITNEY v. CALIFORNIA*
## 274 U.S. 357 (1927)

SCHENCK V. UNITED STATES (1919), ABRAMS V. UNITED STATES (1919), GITLOW V. NEW YORK (1925), and *Whitney* are the four leading FREEDOM OF SPEECH cases of the 1920s in which the CLEAR AND PRESENT DANGER rule was announced but then rejected by the majority in favor of the BAD TEN-DENCY test announced in *Gitlow*. In *Whitney*, Justice ED-WARD SANFORD repeated his *Gitlow* argument that a state law does not violate FIRST AMENDMENT rights by employing the "bad tendency" test as the standard of reasonableness in speech cases. The state may reasonably proscribe "utterances . . . tending to . . . endanger the foundations of organized government." Here Justice Sanford added that "united and joint action involves even greater danger to the public peace and security than the isolated utterances . . . of individuals." Miss Whitney had been convicted of organizing and becoming a member of an organization that advocated and taught CRIMINAL SYNDICALISM in violation of the California Criminal Syndicalism Act of 1919. The Court upheld the act's constitutionality.

After *Schenck*, the clear and present danger position had been reiterated in dissenting opinions by OLIVER WEN-DELL HOLMES and LOUIS D. BRANDEIS in *Abrams* and *Gitlow*. Brandeis, joined by Holmes, concurred in *Whitney*. Brandeis's reason for concurring rather than dissenting was that Whitney had not properly argued to the California courts that their failure to invoke the danger test was error, and that the Supreme Court might not correct errors by state courts unless those errors were properly raised below.

Brandeis's concurrence was a forceful reiteration of the value to a democracy of freedom of speech for even the most dissident speakers. The framers knew that "fear breeds repression; that repression breeds hate; that hate menaces stable government; that the path of safety lies in the opportunity to discuss freely supposed grievances . . . and that the fitting remedy for evil counsels is good ones." Brandeis reemphasized the imminence requirement of the danger rule. "To courageous, self-reliant men, with confidence in the power of free and fearless reasoning applied through the processes of popular government, no danger flowing from speech can be deemed clear and present, unless the incidence of the evil apprehended is so imminent that it may befall before there is opportunity for full discussion. If there be time . . . to avert the evil by the process of education, the remedy to be applied is more speech, not enforced silence."

*Whitney* is often cited for an addition by Brandeis to the original clear and present danger formula. The evil anticipated must be not only substantive but also serious. "The fact that speech is likely to result in some violence or in destruction of property is not enough to justify its suppression. There must be the probability of serious injury to the state. . . ."

The Court overruled *Whitney* in BRANDENBURG V. OHIO (1969).

MARTIN SHAPIRO
(1986)

# WHITTAKER, CHARLES
## (1901–1973)

A considerable number of Justices who served on the United States Supreme Court resembled T. S. Eliot's famous Mr. Prufrock: "an attendant lord, one that will do [to swell a progress, start a scene or two. . . .] Deferential, glad to be of use, [Politic, cautious, and meticulous;] Full of high sentence, but a bit obtuse. . . ." Charles Whittaker, a self-made man from Kansas, appointed to the Court by President DWIGHT D. EISENHOWER, was one of these.

Whittaker joined the WARREN COURT in 1957, after earlier service on the Eighth Circuit Court of Appeals. His tenure was distinguished only by its brevity and by his own inability to develop a coherent judicial philosophy apart from the orthodox political and social conservatism of the Republican Middle West. His retirement and that of Justice FELIX FRANKFURTER in 1962 marked the beginning of the Warren Court's most liberal and activist phase.

Several DEPORTATION and coerced confession cases best exemplified Whittaker's ad hoc approach to constitutional issues and the confusion that often plagued his opinions. Writing for a majority of six Justices in *Bonetti v. Roger* (1958), he overturned the federal government's attempt to deport an ALIEN who had entered the country in 1923, joined the Communist party for a brief period during the 1930s, left the country to fight in the Spanish Civil War, and finally returned to the United States without rejoining the party. Earlier, Whittaker had voted to sustain the deportation of another alien who had resided continuously in the United States for forty years and whose only offense did not constitute a crime when he committed it (*Lehmann v. Carson*). Two years after *Bonetti*, he voted to uphold the termination of Social Security benefits to aliens deported for their membership in the Communist party during the Great Depression in *Fleming v. Nestor* (1960).

Whittaker displayed little more consistency in the coerced confession cases. In *Moore v. Michigan* (1957), he voted to reverse the murder conviction of a black teenager with a seventh-grade education and a history of head injuries, who had confessed to the crime without the benefit of a lawyer. During the next term, however, he voted, in *Thomas v. Arizona* (1958), to sustain the murder conviction of a black man in Arizona, who had confessed after a twenty-hour interrogation which included the placing of a rope around his neck by a member of the sheriff's posse.

Sometimes, Whittaker joined the Warren Court's liberal bloc, as in TROP V. DULLES (1958), where five Justices declared unconstitutional a provision of the Nationality Act of 1940 depriving wartime deserters of their CITIZEN-SHIP. He also joined the liberals in *Perez v. Brownell* (1958) when they dissented against the EXPATRIATION of American citizens who voted in foreign elections. (See TROP V. DULLES, 1958.) Whittaker also wrote the opinion in *Staub v. Baxley* (1958), invalidating a city ordinance that required union organizers to secure a permit before soliciting new members.

More frequently, however, Whittaker cast his vote with the Court's conservative bloc led by Justices John Marshall Harlan, Tom C. Clark, and FELIX FRANKFURTER. In *Beilan v. Board of Education* (1958) he helped to sanction the firing of public school teachers who refused to answer questions about their possible affiliation with the Communist party. He approved the contempt conviction of a college professor who refused to cooperate with a state legislative committee investigating subversive groups in UPHAUS V. WYMAN (1959). He likewise voted to compel the registration of the Communist party under the Subversive Activities Control Act and to allow bar examiners in California to deny admission to a candidate who refused to answer their inquiries about his past membership in the party. (See COMMUNIST PARTY V. SUBVERSIVE ACTIVITIES CONTROL BOARD, 1961; KONIGSBERG V. STATE BAR OF CALIFORNIA, 1961.)

During his final term on the Court, Whittaker continued to affirm his conservative leanings by dissenting in MAPP V. OHIO (1961). He also joined in the Court's dismissal on jurisdictional grounds of an attack on Connecticut's anti-birth control statute in *Poe v. Ullman* (1961). After retiring from the bench, he became a legal adviser to the General Motors Corporation as well as a shrill critic of the CIVIL RIGHTS and anti-VIETNAM WAR protest movements.

MICHAEL E. PARRISH
(1986)

Bibliography

BERMAN, D. M. 1959 Mr. Justice Whittaker: A Preliminary Appraisal. *Missouri Law Review* 24:1–28.

FRIEDMAN, LEON 1969 Charles Whittaker. Pages 2893–2904 in Leon Friedman and Fred L. Israel, eds., *The Justices of the United States Supreme Court, 1789–1969: Their Lives and Major Opinions.* New York: Chelsea House.

# *WICKARD v. FILBURN*
## 317 U.S. 111 (1942)

In 1941, by an amendment to the AGRICULTURAL ADJUSTMENT ACT of 1938, Congress brought the national power to regulate the economy to a new extreme, yet the Supreme Court unanimously sustained the regulation in a far-reaching expansion of the commerce power. The price of wheat, despite marketing controls, had fallen. A bushel on the world market in 1941 sold for only forty cents as a result of a worldwide glut, and the wheat in American storage bins had reached record levels. To enable American growers to benefit from government fixed prices of $1.16 per bushel, Congress authorized the secretary of agriculture to fix production quotas for all wheat, even that consumed by individual growers. Filburn sowed twenty-three acres of wheat, despite his quota of only eleven, and produced an excess of 239 bushels for which the government imposed a penalty of forty-nine cents a bushel. Filburn challenged the constitutionality of the statute, arguing that it regulated production and consumption, both local in character; their effects upon INTERSTATE COMMERCE, he maintained, were "indirect."

Justice ROBERT H. JACKSON for the Court wrote that the question would scarcely merit consideration, given UNITED STATES V. DARBY (1941), "except for the fact that this Act extends federal regulation to production not intended in any part for commerce but wholly for consumption on the farm." The Court had never before decided whether such activities could be regulated "where no part of the product is intended for interstate commerce intermingled with the subjects thereof." Taking its law on the scope of the commerce power from GIBBONS V. OGDEN (1824) and the SHREVEPORT DOCTRINE, the Court repudiated the use of mechanical legal formulas that ignored the reality of a national economic market; no longer would the reach of the COMMERCE CLAUSE be limited by a finding that the regulated activity was "production" or its economic effects were "indirect." The rule laid down by Jackson, which still controls, is that even if an activity is local and not regarded as commerce, "it may still, whatever its nature, be reached by Congress if it exerts a substantial economic effect on interstate commerce, and this irrespective of whether such effect is what might at some earlier time have been defined as 'direct' or 'indirect.'" (See EFFECTS ON COMMERCE.)

How could the wheat grown by Filburn, which he fed to his own animals, used for his own food, and kept for next year's seed, be regarded as having a "substantial economic effect" on interstate commerce? Wheat consumed on the farm by its growers, the government had proved, amounted to over twenty percent of national production. Filburn consumed a "trivial" amount, but if he had not produced what he needed for his own use in excess of his allotted quota, he would have had to buy it. By not buying wheat, such producer-consumers depressed the price by cutting the demand. His own contribution to the demand for wheat was trivial, but "when taken with that of others similarly situated," it was significant. Congress had authorized quotas to increase the price of the commodity; wheat consumed on the farm where grown could burden a legitimate congressional purpose to stimulate demand and force up the price. Thus, even if a single bushel of Filburn's infinitesimal production never left his farm, Congress could reach and regulate his activity, because all the Filburns, taken collectively, substantially affected commerce.

LEONARD W. LEVY
(1986)

Bibliography

STERN, ROBERT L. 1946 The Commerce Clause and the National Economy, 1933–1946. *Harvard Law Review* 59:901–909.

# WICKERSHAM, GEORGE
## (1858–1936)

Appointed attorney general in 1909 by WILLIAM HOWARD TAFT, George Wickersham argued and won STANDARD OIL COMPANY V. UNITED STATES (1911) and *American Tobacco Company v. United States* (1911). He initiated more prosecutions under the SHERMAN ANTITRUST ACT in four years than his predecessor had in seven, prompting business leaders to call for his resignation. As chairman of the Wickersham Committee from 1929 to 1931, he directed an investigation of the entire system of federal jurisprudence. The commission reported on problems raised by political penetrations of courts, lax criminal law enforcement, abuses of constitutional rights, and various sociological influences contributing to crime.

DAVID GORDON
(1986)

# WIDMAR v. VINCENT
## 454 U.S. 263 (1981)

In order to avoid activity that might constitute an ESTABLISHMENT OF RELIGION, the University of Missouri at Kansas City barred a student religious group from meeting on the campus for religious teaching or worship. The Supreme Court, 8–1, held that the University, having "created a forum generally open for use by student groups," was forbidden by the FIRST AMENDMENT's guarantee of the FREEDOM OF SPEECH to exclude the religious group. Because the exclusion was based on the content of the group's speech, it was unconstitutional unless necessary to serve a COMPELLING STATE INTEREST. The exclusion was not necessary to avoid establishment clause problems, for no state sponsorship of religion was implied when the university provided a forum generally open to all student groups.

Justice JOHN PAUL STEVENS, concurring, said that any university necessarily makes many distinctions based on speech content. Here, however, the university discriminated on the basis of the viewpoint of particular speakers, and that was forbidden by the First Amendment.

Justice BYRON R. WHITE dissented, arguing that the state could constitutionally "attempt to disentangle itself from religious worship."

KENNETH L. KARST
(1986)

(SEE ALSO: *Public Forum.*)

# WIEMAN v. UPDEGRAFF
## 344 U.S. 183 (1952)

In an OPINION written by Justice TOM C. CLARK, the Supreme Court struck down an Oklahoma LOYALTY OATH for state employees that required signers to affirm that they were not and had not been for five years members of organizations designated by the attorney general of the United States as "communist front" or "subversive." Clark, who as attorney general had initiated the federal list in 1947, held that the statute violated the DUE PROCESS clause because it did not distinguish innocent membership from knowing membership in the proscribed organizations.

MICHAEL E. PARRISH
(1986)

# WIGMORE, JOHN HENRY
## (1863–1943)

John Henry Wigmore was perhaps the foremost American legal scholar and educator of the twentieth century. A professor of law at Northwestern University Law School for fifty years (1893–1943), nearly thirty of them as its dean (1901–1929), Wigmore played the leading role in developing it into one of the nation's leading law schools. Wigmore also helped to found numerous professional and academic organizations, among them the American Institute of Law and Criminology (1909) and the American Bar Association's Sections on Criminal Law (1920) and on International and Comparative Law (1934).

Wigmore wrote an extraordinary number of books and articles on almost every field of the law, but his most significant works focused on evidence, criminal law and criminology, and international and comparative law. His great *Treatise on Evidence* (1904; third ed., 1940; subsequently revised by others) established itself as the dominant work in its field and was acclaimed as the greatest treatise on any single subject of the law. Although some critics objected to the *Treatise*'s introduction of new terms, its length and elaborate organization, and its occasional divergence from the current state of the law, most scholars welcomed it as the most systematic overview of its subject, and it had great influence on many states' revisions of their rules of EVIDENCE and on the Federal Rules of Evidence (1969–1975). Wigmore's other major works on evidence were his *Pocket Code of Evidence* (1910; third ed., 1942) and his *Principles of Judicial Proof* (1913, third ed., 1937). His other books include *A Panorama of the World's Legal Systems* (1928; second ed., 1936), *A Kaleidoscope of Justice* (1941), *Problems of Law: Its Past, Present and Future* (1920), and casebooks on evidence (1906; third ed., 1932) and on torts (1910–1912).

RICHARD B. BERNSTEIN
(1986)

Bibliography

ROALFE, WILLIAM R. 1977 *John Henry Wigmore: Scholar and Reformer.* Evanston, Ill.: Northwestern University Press.

## WILKES CASES
### 19 Howell's State Trials (1763–1768)

Counting derivative trials, the Wilkes Cases embraced at least forty cases from 1763 to 1769; all emanated ultimately from a single GENERAL WARRANT issued by the British secretaries of state on April 26, 1763, against *The North Briton*, No. 45, a periodical trenchantly critical of the Grenville administration. Numerous categories of the general warrant, which allowed its bearer to arrest, search, and seize at his discretion, had operated in England for centuries. The warrant of April 26, however, was of an atypical variety, based on custom rather than statute, which the government used against dissident publications; it resulted in the search of at least five houses, the arrest of forty-nine persons, and the seizure of thousands of manuscripts and books.

Although hundreds of such warrants had issued since the Restoration, the latest crop of victims included John Wilkes, a powerful member of Parliament and principal author of *The North Briton*. When Wilkes sued every official connected with the warrant, many of the others arrested promptly did the same.

The trials unfolded in distinct series. In *Huckle v. Money*, the first trial on July 6, 1763, CHARLES PRATT, the Chief Justice of the Court of Common Pleas, criticized the *North Briton* warrant because it specified no person, had been issued without a formal complaint under oath, and thus lacked PROBABLE CAUSE. When this case reached the full Common Pleas, Pratt extended his attack to the

general search feature of the warrant, holding that it, as well as its companion power of general arrest, violated MAGNA CARTA.

The outcome of the *North Briton* trials incited suits by earlier victims of secretarial warrants. In the most famous of these trials, *Entick v. Carrington* (1765), which accrued from a general warrant against *The Monitor*, the emphasis shifted to the powers of general, confiscatory seizure in such warrants. Pratt, now ennobled as Lord Camden, condemned the use of seized personal papers against their owner as self-incriminatory. Moreover, Camden continued, because private property was inherently sacred, any invasion of it without express legal authority was a trespass even if it merely involved touching the soil or grass. He conceded that the inspection of private papers was not itself a legal trespass, but he insisted that the disclosure of the personal secrets they contained greatly magnified the harm from the physical trespass of their seizure.

Although Pratt in *Wilkes v. Wood* (1763) had condemned even general warrants authorized by statute, WILLIAM MURRAY (Lord Mansfield), in a final appeal of *Huckle v. Money*, upheld statutory warrants and denounced only those not based on parliamentary enactment. When Pratt shifted to the same grounds in *Entick*, the effect was to confine the assault on general warrants to the variant based on custom, and to preserve a greater number that derived from statute. In 1766 a resolution against general warrants did emerge from the House of Commons, but an effort to transform it into binding, comprehensive legislation failed.

WILLIAM J. CUDDIHY
(1986)

Bibliography

HOLDSWORTH, SIR WILLIAM 1938 *A History of English Law.* 7th ed. 15 vols. Vol. 10:99–100, 658–672. London: Methuen.
NOBBE, GEORGE 1939 *The North Briton.* New York: Columbia University Press.

## WILLIAMS, ROGER
### (1603–1683)

Arriving in New England in 1631, Roger Williams preached in Plymouth and Salem, but almost immediately clashed with the Massachusetts authorities over issues involving both church and state. He attacked Massachusetts's right to its land on the grounds that the land had not been purchased from the Indians—only granted by the king. He claimed that the colonial churches had not broken sharply enough with the Church of England, and he denied that magistrates had power to punish in religious matters. Under sentence of banishment from Massachusetts, Williams fled to Providence in 1636 and formed a settlement there. By 1644 he had secured a patent from the English government combining his own and neighboring towns into the colony of Rhode Island and Providence Plantations.

Although always a Calvinist, Williams adhered to no church after his departure from Massachusetts except for a brief period as a Baptist; rather, he lived as a Seeker. RELIGIOUS LIBERTY was his abiding passion, and he defended it primarily for its benefits to religion. Drawing the analogy of church as garden and world as wilderness, he insisted that only a wall between the two could preserve the integrity of the church.

Williams believed that allowing the state any power in church affairs made the state the arbiter of religious truth, an area in which its lack of competence only perverted religion. To demonstrate the absurdity of state attempts to proclaim the true church, he cited history, especially the recent multiple changes in religious allegiance on the part of the English government, and he expressed the psychological insights that rulers tended to advance their own religious preferences as truth and that persecutors always justified their actions in religion's name.

Williams's political views flowed from his religious theories. For him the Israel of the Old Testament was a figurative entity and not, as Massachusetts Puritans claimed, a model for government. He saw government as a SOCIAL COMPACT drawn up between citizens for secular purposes only. Just as civil interference ruined religion, so religious interference disrupted government—by accusations of heresy against civil leaders and demands for their removal from office. He believed that governing was an art, for which Christianity did not necessarily constitute a gift.

Carrying his arguments in favor of religious liberty to their logical and remarkably radical conclusions, Williams contended that liberty should be extended to all law-abiding citizens, including Roman Catholics (whom he abhorred), non-Christians, and even those he considered blasphemers. By opposing monopolization of Rhode Island's land by its original settlers, he strove to keep the colony open to newcomers of all religions and to enable them to settle there on an equal social and economic basis with already-established inhabitants.

Beyond Rhode Island's fidelity to his ideals of religious freedom, Williams exerted hardly any influence. His views shocked his contemporaries, and throughout his life he bore the stigma of radicalism. During the colonial years, his writings almost disappeared. Succeeding centuries, however, have restored his reputation by correctly perceiving him as a prophet and forerunner of modern religious liberty.

THOMAS CURRY
(1986)

Bibliography

MILLER, PERRY 1953 *Roger Williams: His Contribution to the American Tradition.* Indianapolis: Bobbs-Merrill.
MORGAN, EDMUND S. 1967 *Roger Williams: The Church and the State.* New York: Harcourt, Brace & World.

## WILLIAMS v. FLORIDA
### 399 U.S. 78 (1970)

The rule of *Williams* is that trial by a jury of six in a noncapital FELONY case does not violate the constitutional right to TRIAL BY JURY in a state prosecution. Trial by jury had historically meant trial by a jury of twelve, neither more nor less. Justice BYRON R. WHITE for the Supreme Court found no rationale for the figure of twelve, which he called "accidental" and "superstitious." If Congress enacted a statute providing for juries of less than twelve in federal prosecutions, the Sixth Amendment would be no bar, according to this case. A jury of six is practical: it can be selected in half the time, costs only half as much, and may reach its verdict more quickly. According to White, "there is no discernible difference between the results reached by the two different-sized juries," but in fact a jury of six hangs less frequently, significantly changes the probability of conviction, and convicts different persons. White claimed that the size of the jury should be large enough to promote group deliberation and allow for a representative cross-section of the community, and he claimed that a jury of six serves those functions as well as a jury of twelve. In fact the Court was wrong. Only Justice THURGOOD MARSHALL dissented on the question of jury size, in an opinion that rested strictly on precedent. Williams also contended that Florida violated his RIGHT AGAINST SELF-INCRIMINATION by its notice-of-alibi rule, but he convinced only Justices HUGO L. BLACK and WILLIAM O. DOUGLAS.

LEONARD W. LEVY
(1986)

(SEE ALSO: *Jury Size.*)

## WILLIAMS v. MISSISSIPPI
### 170 U.S. 213 (1898)

*Williams* is a realistic snapshot of our constitutional law on race at the turn of the century. A black man was tried in Mississippi for the murder of a white, convicted by an all-white jury, and sentenced to death. He alleged that he had been denied the EQUAL PROTECTION OF THE LAWS guaranteed by the FOURTEENTH AMENDMENT, because the laws of the state were rigged in such a way as to exclude members of his race from jury service. In Mississippi, to be eligible for jury service one must be qualified to vote. To be a voter one must have paid his POLL TAX and have satisfied registration officials that he could not only pass a LITERACY TEST but also could understand or reasonably interpret any clause of the state constitution; registration officials had sole discretion to decide whether an applicant had the requisite understanding. In Mississippi at that time, a black graduate of Harvard Law School could not satisfy white officials. The state convention of 1890 clearly adopted new qualifications on the right to vote in order to insure white supremacy by disfranchising black voters. Under prior laws there were 190,000 black voters; by 1892 only 8,600 remained, and these were soon eliminated. Blacks disappeared from jury lists after 1892.

A unanimous Supreme Court, speaking through Justice JOSEPH MCKENNA, held that the state constitution and laws passed under it, prescribing the qualifications of voters and jurors, did not on their face discriminate racially. McKenna also declared that the discretion vested in state and local officials who managed elections and selected juries, while affording the opportunity for unconstitutional RACIAL DISCRIMINATION, was not constitutionally excessive. Yet McKenna said, "We gather . . . that this discretion can be and has been exercised against the colored race, and from these lists jurors are selected." The Court recognized that a law on its face might be impartial and be administered "with an evil eye and an unequal hand," but it held that "it has not been shown that their actual administration was evil; only that evil was possible under them."

LEONARD W. LEVY
(1986)

## WILLIAMS v. VERMONT
472 U.S. 14 (1985)

Vermont levied a use tax on automobiles, collected upon each car's registration. No tax was imposed if the car was bought in Vermont, and a Vermont sales tax was paid. If the car was purchased outside Vermont, the use tax was reduced by the amount of any sales tax paid to the other state—but only if the registrant was then a Vermont resident. Persons who had bought cars outside Vermont before becoming Vermont residents sued in state court, challenging the constitutionality of this scheme. The Vermont courts denied relief, but the Supreme Court, 6–3, held that the discrimination against newcomers violated the EQUAL PROTECTION clause. Justice BYRON R. WHITE wrote the OPINION OF THE COURT.

As it had done for half a century, the Court avoided the much-discussed question whether a state must give a credit for payment of another state's sales tax in such cir-

cumstances. Instead, the Court followed ZOBEL V. WILLIAMS (1982) and held that the discrimination against newcomers to Vermont served no legitimate statutory purpose. As in *Zobel*, Justice WILLIAM J. BRENNAN, concurring, wrote that the discrimination threatened the "federal interest in free interstate migration." (See RIGHT TO TRAVEL.) Justice HARRY A. BLACKMUN, for the dissenters, favored a REMAND to the state courts for clarification whether the law in fact so discriminated. Even if it did, he argued, Vermont could legitimately tax in rough proportion to automobiles' use on Vermont roads.

KENNETH L. KARST
(1986)

## WILLIAMSON, HUGH
(1735–1819)

Hugh Williamson, mathemetician, physician, and Presbyterian minister, signed the Constitution as a North Carolina delegate to the CONSTITUTIONAL CONVENTION OF 1787. A frequent but not very influential speaker, he was the first to propose the six-year term for senators. He supported RATIFICATION in the North Carolina convention and served in the first two Congresses.

DENNIS J. MAHONEY
(1986)

## WILLIAMSON v. LEE OPTICAL CO.
348 U.S. 483 (1955)

Justice WILLIAM O. DOUGLAS, for an 8–0 Supreme Court, announced that "the day is gone when this Court uses the DUE PROCESS CLAUSE to strike down state business regulation. Without any inquiry into actual legislative history, Douglas upheld an Oklahoma law regulating eyeglass sales, suggesting various hypothetical reasons why the legislature might have thought it necessary.

DENNIS J. MAHONEY
(1986)

## WILLOUGHBY, WESTEL W.
(1867–1945)

Westel Woodbury Willoughby taught political science at Johns Hopkins University (1894–1933) and was a founder of the American Political Science Association. He wrote nearly two dozen books, including *The Supreme Court of the United States* (1890), *The Nature of the State* (1896), *The American Constitutional System* (1904), and *The Con-*

*stitutional Law of the United States* (1910; second edition, 1922).

Willoughby rejected the notion that FEDERALISM implied division of SOVEREIGNTY between the central government and the states. He described the Constitution in terms of LIMITED GOVERNMENT, but regarded the central government as possessing the ultimate authority in the country and believed that in crisis situations (such as civil war) the rights of both states and citizens must yield to the INHERENT POWER of national self-preservation. Because he thought the government must at other times be limited to constitutionally DELEGATED POWERS he was especially critical of the decisions in the INSULAR CASES.

DENNIS J. MAHONEY
(1986)

# WILLSON v. BLACK BIRD CREEK MARSH CO.
## 2 Peters 245 (1829)

Chief Justice JOHN MARSHALL's opinion for a unanimous Supreme Court cannot be reconciled with his opinions in GIBBONS V. OGDEN (1824) and BROWN V. MARYLAND (1827), neither of which he mentioned in Willson. Delaware had authorized the company to dam a navigable tidewater creek, obstructing the navigation of Willson's sloop, licensed under the same Federal Coastal Licensing Act that had proved decisive in *Gibbons*. The Court sustained the constitutionality of the state statute as a measure calculated to improve marshland property and the health of its inhabitants. The Coastal Licensing Act notwithstanding, the Court found that Congress had chosen not to govern the many small navigable creeks of the eastern coast. In effect, the Court sustained the POLICE POWER in a case involving local circumstances affecting the COMMERCE CLAUSE "in its dormant state," that is, unexercised by Congress.

Marshall's *Willson* opinion is so laconic, almost unreasoned, and uncharacteristic of the great Chief Justice that it has never been satisfactorily explained. FELIX FRANKFURTER, in his book *The Commerce Clause*, surmised that Marshall understood that a completely exclusive commerce power might overdiminish STATES' RIGHTS and that Marshall realized the need for effective state regulation of local problems. Taking into consideration "the circumstances of the case," Marshall acknowledged the state interest in enhancing property values and improving the public health. Accordingly he opened the door to the police power because the state's objectives, unlike the situations in *Gibbons* and *Brown*, were not the regulation of commerce per se. *Willson*, however, left a confused legacy

for the TANEY COURT, which divided in MAYOR OF NEW YORK V. MILN (1837) and produced doctrinal chaos in the LICENSE CASES (1847) and the PASSENGER CASES (1849). Not until COOLEY V. BOARD OF WARDENS (1851) did the Taney Court find a formula that purported to reconcile Marshall's doctrines in *Gibbons* and *Willson*.

LEONARD W. LEVY
(1986)

# WILMOT PROVISO
## (1846)

The proviso was introduced by Congressman David Wilmot (Democrat, Pennsylvania) as an amendment to a $2,000,000 appropriations bill requested by President JAMES K. POLK to finance the Mexican War. The proviso prohibited SLAVERY in any territory acquired from Mexico, thus enabling northern Democrats, like Wilmot, to support the war without supporting slave expansion and more slave states. The proviso passed the HOUSE, but the SENATE adjourned without acting on the appropriations bill. In 1847 the proviso was added to a new $3,000,000 war appropriations bill. The Senate refused to accept the proviso, and in a bitterly debated compromise, the House agreed to the appropriation without the proviso. Despite its failure in Congress, the proviso raised serious constitutional and political issues. Southerners argued that they had contributed to the war effort and ought to be allowed to settle in the conquered territories without any special disabilities. Northerners condemned the war, especially after the defeat of the proviso, as aggression by an expansionist "slave power." The proviso led to the formation of the Free Soil Party, which was committed to prohibiting SLAVERY IN THE TERRITORIES. Free Soilers ran particularly well in some northern Democratic districts.

PAUL FINKELMAN
(1986)

Bibliography

MORRISON, CHAPLAIN W. 1967 *Democratic Politics and Sectionalism: The Wilmot Proviso Controversy.* Chapel Hill: University of North Carolina Press.

# WILSON, JAMES
## (1742–1798)

James Wilson was one of the most influential members of the founding generation. He was born in Scotland and educated as a classical scholar at the University of St. Andrews. He immigrated to America in 1765, whereupon he served as a tutor at the College of Philadelphia while he studied law with the celebrated JOHN DICKINSON. His keen and perceptive mind, superb classical education, and excellent legal training prepared him to play a major role in the creation of the new American republic. He was a frequent delegate from Pennsylvania to the Second CONTINENTAL CONGRESS, one of six men who signed both the DECLARATION OF INDEPENDENCE and the Constitution, and second only to JAMES MADISON in his contribution to the deliberations of the CONSTITUTIONAL CONVENTION. He produced what was probably the most widely distributed and discussed defense of the new Constitution in his Statehouse Speech of October 6, 1787. He was the principal figure in the efforts to secure RATIFICATION OF THE CONSTITUTION by Pennsylvania, whose approval was indispensable to the success of the whole constitutional movement. He was a major architect of the significant Pennsylvania Constitution of 1790. He was one of the six original Justices of the United States Supreme Court. He was the first professor of law appointed after the founding of the new republic, and he was the only Framer to formulate a general theory of government and law—this in his lectures on law, delivered in 1791–1792 at what would later become the University of Pennsylvania.

Wilson was and remains influential, however, not so much because of the roles he played as for the ideas he articulated, the arguments he made, and the institutional arrangements he favored. Among the principal Framers, Wilson was the most committed to, and trusting of, unmitigated majoritarian democracy. He favored the simplicity of immediate consent and self-restraint to the complexity of procedural protections and constitutional contrivances. Relying heavily on the Scottish moralists (especially Thomas Reid), Wilson argued that men are naturally social; imbued with a sense of goodness, veracity, and benevolence; and possessed of a progressive intuitive sense that can be improved with practice so as to carry society "above any limits which we can now assign." As a consequence, he trusted them to elect leaders who would govern soberly and well, especially over a large and "comprehensive Federal Republic" such as the United States. He saw no need to protect the people from themselves. Madison's "republican remed[ies] for the diseases most incident to republican government" were, he believed, unnecessary. The government would be good to the extent that its branches were prompted, through their competition with one another, to serve the people and to reflect faithfully their wishes. Wilson brought this view of government and his commitment to majoritarianism to the Federal Convention, where his influence was clearly felt. He contributed significantly to the Convention's understanding of SEPARATION OF POWERS, figured prominently in

determining the institutional arrangements and powers of the legislative, executive, and judicial branches, and helped to make FEDERALISM possible with his arguments concerning the dual SOVEREIGNTY of the people.

Wilson contributed to the Convention's understanding of separation of powers by arguing that it properly consists not of functionally separated branches but of coordinate and equal branches that perform a blend of functions in order to balance, not separate, powers. As he declared, "The separation of the departments does not require that they should have separate objects but that they should act separately tho' on the same objects." Wilson was aware that the various governmental branches, even though popularly elected, would occasionally be activated by "an official sentiment opposed to that of the General Government and perhaps to that of the people themselves." On those occasions, separation of powers would be necessary to insure the fidelity of these popular agents. Wilson also contributed to the Convention's understanding by stressing that separation of powers not only prevents governmental tyranny but also contributes to governmental efficiency. Aware that the democratic process of mutual deliberation and consent can paralyze government when swift and decisive action is necessary, he argued that government would be more efficient if its different functions were performed by separate and distinct agencies.

Wilson's influence on the legislative branch was felt primarily in the HOUSE OF REPRESENTATIVES and in his promotion of reflective, as opposed to refining, representation. He argued in the Convention that "the Government ought to possess not only first, the force but secondly, the mind or sense of the people at large. The Legislature ought to be the most exact transcript of the whole Society." Wilson regarded representation as a "chain of communication" between the people and those to whom they have delegated the powers of government. Its purpose is not to "refine" the people's sentiments; rather, it is to communicate through links "sound and strong" the exact feelings of the people. Strong as this chain might be, however, Wilson was unwilling to trust it completely. So long as the legislature was perfectly reflective of the people, no problem was presented; however, there was no way to ensure this. On occasion, the legislature might come to possess and perceive an interest distinct from, and perhaps contrary to, the public at large. On that occasion, a single legislature would be dangerous, and thus Wilson argued for a divided legislature with a numerous House of Representatives, so close in political style and feelings to those it represented that it would constitute their "exact transcript," and a popularly elected Senate organized around the principle of proportional representation, thereby providing a "double representation" for the people. Wilson was one of the first to argue that it is possible for the people, simply through the electoral process, to have two different agents or representatives speaking for them at the same time. He did not fear that this common election would erode the material distinctions, and consequently the benefits that resulted from these material distinctions, between the two branches of the legislature. He trusted in the development of a "point of honor" between the two branches: they would "be rivals in duty, rivals in fame, rivals for the good graces of their common constituents." His views on the Senate, though unsuccessful at the Convention, were largely vindicated with the passage of the SEVENTEENTH AMENDMENT.

Wilson's contributions to the shape and powers of the executive branch were perhaps most significant of all. He was the first delegate to propose "that the Executive consist of a single person." He argued that the executive, no less than the legislature, needed to be restrained and controlled. But, "in order to control the legislative authority, you must divide it. In order to control the Executive, you must unite it." The advantage of clear-cut responsibility would reinforce and assure those other "very important advantages" that are also obtained from a single executive, including energy, vigor, dispatch, firmness, consistency, and stability. Wilson was also the first delegate at the Convention to suggest that the President should be elected directly by the people. When this proposal failed to gain general support, he was then the first to propose an ELECTORAL COLLEGE scheme, a modification of which ultimately found its way into the Constitution. He also favored a relatively brief presidential tenure of three years and reeligibility. These features would insure that the President would become and remain "the Man of the People."

Wilson's "Man of the People" was to be more than simply derived from their midst; he was also to be capable of acting vigorously on their behalf. As Wilson stressed in the Pennsylvania ratifying convention, the President was to be captain of the ship of state, holding firmly to the helm and allowing the vessel to "proceed neither in one direction or another without his concurrence." He was to be powerful and independent enough to protect the people from the excesses, instabilities, and injustices of legislative dominance. Wilson's captain was to take his bearings from the people and set his course according to their dictates. Because the people would not be easily misled, Wilson, unlike THE FEDERALIST, would not have the President provide the people with direction or resist them when they were wrong.

Wilson also labored at the Convention for the establishment of a powerful judiciary. Because the judges would be appointed by the President and confirmed by the SENATE, he understood the judiciary to be "drawn from the same source, animated by the same principles, and directed to the same ends" and therefore "as much the friend of the people" as the other branches. As a consequence, it could be entrusted with the power of JUDICIAL REVIEW. So entrusted, it could serve as a "noble guard" defending the fundamental principles and will of the people as expressed in the Constitution from governmental sentiments—especially legislative sentiments—which from time to time might come to oppose them.

Wilson also helped to make federalism possible by arguing in the Convention that the people could create and assign power to more than "one set of immediate representatives." The delegates could preserve the states and at the same time establish a new national government because of the dual sovereignty of the people. He argued that both the states and the national government receive their authority directly from the people and owe their responsibility directly to them. The people are the sovereign foundation of all governments. As such, they can construct two levels of government and assign different powers to them. They can take powers from the state governments and place them in the national government. Wilson employed this same argument in the Pennsylvania ratifying convention to taunt those Anti-Federalists who contended that the people could not give to the national government whatever powers and for whatever purposes they pleased. He also operated from these premises in CHISHOLM V. GEORGIA (1793), his only truly important Supreme Court decision, in which he declared that the people of the United States had formed themselves into "a nation for national purposes" and that, consequently, states as well as individual persons were subject to the JUDICIAL POWER of the United States.

Wilson embraced and defended the "comprehensive Federal Republic" created by the Constitution not only because the people had chosen to construct such a level of government over them but also because he believed that a reciprocating relationship existed between the structure of government and the character of the people. A petty state would produce, he believed, petty men. The only lessons they would learn would be those of "low Vice" and "illiberal Cunning." Only a large republic would sustain and nourish the good qualities of the people. Only a large republic would produce noble citizens, worthy of the great political trust Wilson would place in them.

Central to Wilson's constitutional thought was his confidence in the good qualities of the people. In this regard, he differed from his fellow Framers, in that he relied upon what The Federalist considered "the weaker springs of human character." This difference was critical then and remains so now: Wilson's commitment to unrestrained majoritarian democracy stands in sharp contrast to the Constitution's more complex mitigated democracy that relies not so much on men as on institutions for our political salvation.

RALPH A. ROSSUM
(1986)

Bibliography

ADAMS, RANDOLPH GREENFIELD, ed. 1930 *Selected Political Essays of James Wilson.* New York: Knopf.
McCLOSKEY, ROBERT GREEN, ed. 1967 *The Works of James Wilson.* 2 Vols. Cambridge, Mass.: Harvard University Press.
ROSSUM, RALPHY A. 1976 James Wilson and the "Pyramid of Government": The Federal Republic. *Political Science Reviewer* 6:113–142.
SMITH, CHARLES PAGE 1956 *James Wilson: Founding Father.* Chapel Hill: University of North Carolina Press.

# WILSON, WOODROW
## (1856–1924)

Dr. Thomas Woodrow Wilson was both a scholar and an active participant in American constitutional development. Trained in history and law, Wilson became one of the first practitioners of the new academic political science that was born in America toward the close of the nineteenth century. He taught at Bryn Mawr College and Wesleyan University, and became a professor at, and later president of, Princeton University.

As a political scientist, Wilson urged fundamental reforms in the American system of government. In his first book, *Congressional Government* (1885), he argued that instead of the balance of powers envisaged by the Founders, American government was dominated by the legislative branch and, in particular, by a few powerful congressional committees. Wilson advocated cabinet government as he supposed it to exist in Great Britain, dominated by a strong executive. In *Constitutional Government in the United States* (1908), Wilson argued that under the Constitution the President had authority to exercise vigorous leadership of the whole American political system. In other works, Wilson advocated the scientific study of techniques of public administration and the training of a new class of civil servants who would be independent of political influence or control. Professional administrators, Wilson believed, should be left free to devise the most efficient means of carrying into effect the general policy decisions of the political branches of the government. (See PROGRESSIVE CONSTITUTIONAL THOUGHT.)

A progressive Democrat, Wilson was elected governor of New Jersey in 1910, and President of the United States two years later, when THEODORE ROOSEVELT broke with President WILLIAM HOWARD TAFT and split the Republican party. Wilson's platform called for a "New Freedom," characterized by a vigorous ANTITRUST policy, reduced tariffs, legislation to benefit organized labor, and creation of the federal reserve banking system.

During Wilson's terms of office, the Seventeenth, Eighteenth, and NINETEENTH AMENDMENTS were added to the Constitution. But ordinary legislation did as much to change the distribution and use of governmental power as did formal constitutional amendments. The FEDERAL RESERVE ACT (1913) placed control of the nation's money and credit in the hands of an independent, semi-private banking system. The FEDERAL TRADE COMMISSION ACT (1914), brainchild of Boston attorney LOUIS D. BRANDEIS, created an independent REGULATORY AGENCY with specific authority to make regulations having the force of law.

Among the least creditable achievements of the Wilson administration was the introduction of official racial SEGREGATION in executive departments of the federal government for the first time since the CIVIL WAR. Wilson himself approved the change of policy, arguing that segregation was in the best interests of black federal employees, but he did not regard it as a matter of major concern.

Wilson asserted a broad conception of executive power in military and FOREIGN AFFAIRS. In 1913 the United States assumed control of the foreign policy of Nicaragua and American marines put down an insurgent movement in that country. Wilson also deployed marines twice, in 1914 and 1916, to suppress insurrections in the Dominican Republic. Between 1913 and 1917 the United States intervened continuously, and ultimately unsuccessfully, in the internal politics of Mexico. For none of these military adventures did Wilson have specific congressional authorization; he relied instead on his power as COMMANDER-IN-CHIEF of the armed forces.

Although Wilson campaigned for reelection in 1916 on the slogan, "He kept us out of war," the United States entered WORLD WAR I just one month after his second inauguration. The war emergency provided the rationale for a vast expansion of federal power. The Overman Act (1917) created a virtual presidential dictatorship over the machinery of the government; the RAILROAD CONTROL ACT commandeered the private rail network and consolidated it under government auspices; the SELECTIVE SERVICE ACT authorized the drafting of millions of young men into the military; and the ESPIONAGE ACT and the SEDITION ACT provided a basis for controlling civilian dissent. In a sense, the war provided the essential basis—a strongly held vision of the public good—for many of the reforms the Progressives had long advocated. For at least two decades afterward, political activists and reformers would hark back to the sense of unity that World War I provided.

American intervention enabled Britain and France to defeat the Germans and their allies, and so the American government was entitled to a leading voice in dictating the peace terms. Wilson was unable, however, to secure ratification of the Treaty of Versailles and the League of Nations Covenant by the United States Senate. Republicans, led by Senator HENRY CABOT LODGE, opposed these measures, which seemingly would have subordinated American SOVEREIGNTY to an international body and permanently involved the United States in European quarrels.

In 1919, exhausted by a national campaign to win support for the Versailles Treaty, Wilson suffered a debilitating stroke. For the last year of his presidency the erstwhile advocate of strong presidential leadership tried, and failed, to govern the country from his sickbed. The constitutional problem of presidential disability would not be resolved until passage of the TWENTY-FIFTH AMENDMENT.

DENNIS J. MAHONEY
(1986)

Bibliography

BETH, LOREN P. 1971 *The Development of the American Constitution: 1877–1917.* New York: Harper & Row.
BRAGDON, HENRY W. 1967 *Woodrow Wilson: The Academic Years.* Cambridge, Mass.: Belknap Press.
LINK, ARTHUR S. 1947–1974 *Woodrow Wilson,* 6 vols. Princeton, N.J.: Princeton University Press.

## WILSON v. NEW
### 243 U.S. 332 (1917)

Congress passed the ADAMSON EIGHT-HOUR ACT in 1916 to avert a threatened nationwide railroad strike and to prevent disruption of INTERSTATE COMMERCE. The act prescribed an eight-hour day for railway workers and prohibited any reduction in pay for the shorter hours. Congress thereby regulated wages (pending the report of a commission established by the act) as well as hours. A United States District Court enjoined enforcement of the act, and that decision was appealed to the Supreme Court.

Chief Justice EDWARD D. WHITE, for a 5–4 Supreme Court, sustained the act as a legitimate exercise of congressional power. Asserting that Congress's power to establish working hours was "so clearly sustained as to render the subject not disputable," White faced the issue: did the COMMERCE CLAUSE give Congress the power to set wages? Despite reservations about government interference with FREEDOM OF CONTRACT, the majority held that the Adamson Act only supplemented contracting parties' rights. Moreover, Congress might set a temporary wage standard to protect interstate commerce when private parties failed to exercise their contract rights. Although the strike threatened an emergency, the emergency created no new powers, but it might provide an occasion for exercise of the commerce power.

The dissenters contended either that the act violated the Fifth Amendment as a TAKING OF PROPERTY or that the act lay outside the scope of Congress's commerce power because wages and hours were only remotely connected with interstate commerce.

DAVID GORDON
(1986)

## WINONA AND ST. PETER RAILROD CO. v. BLAKE

See: Granger Cases

## WINSHIP, IN RE
### 397 U.S. 358 (1970)

A 6–3 Supreme Court, speaking through Justice WILLIAM J. BRENNAN, held here that among the constitutional rights available in juvenile proceedings is the standard of proof beyond a REASONABLE DOUBT. A twelve-year-old was charged with a crime which, if done by an adult, would be larceny. The applicable New York statute required only a preponderance of evidence for conviction, and three successive New York courts rejected the contention that the FOURTEENTH AMENDMENT required a higher standard of proof. Tracing the requirement back to early United States history, Brennan found "virtually unanimous adherence" to the reasonable doubt standard in COMMON LAW jurisdictions. He extolled its protective value and spoke of the "vital role" of this "indispensable" standard. "We explicitly hold that the DUE PROCESS Clause protects the accused against conviction except upon proof beyond a reasonable doubt of every fact necessary to constitute the crime with which he is charged." Moreover, Brennan could find no obstacle to extending this right to juveniles. Justice HUGO L. BLACK, dissenting, charged the majority with amending the BILL OF RIGHTS. "Nowhere in that document is there any statement that conviction of crime requires proof of guilt beyond a reasonable doubt."

DAVID GORDON
(1986)

## WIRETAPPING

Telephone tapping is probably the best known form of electronic surveillance. The Supreme Court originally ruled in OLMSTEAD V. UNITED STATES (1928) that neither the Fifth nor the FOURTH AMENDMENT could be used to control wiretapping. In KATZ V. UNITED STATES (1967), however, the Supreme Court declared that what people reasonably expect to keep private is entitled to constitutional protection under the Fourth Amendment.

Both before and after the *Katz* decision, wiretapping was regulated by statute. Between 1934 and 1968, Section 605 of the COMMUNICATIONS ACT prohibited virtually all wiretapping except for NATIONAL SECURITY purposes. The Justice Department construed the statute so narrowly, however, that it had little effect: federal and state officials tapped extensively, as did private parties, and there were few prosecutions.

In 1968, Congress enacted Title III of the OMNIBUS CRIME CONTROL AND SAFE STREETS ACT, which prohibits telephone tapping except by federal and state officials who obtain prior judicial approval. Before issuing such approval, the court must have PROBABLE CAUSE to believe that EVIDENCE of a specific crime listed in the statute, and relating to a particular person, will be found by tapping a specific phone. Interceptions must be minimized, and notice of the interception must ultimately be given to the target of the surveillance.

Critics claim that the minimization and judicial supervision requirements are ineffective, that wiretapping is inherently indiscriminate, and that it is of little value for major crimes. Proponents assert that the technique is useful, and that the procedural protections are effective.

Wiretapping within the United States to obtain foreign national security intelligence is governed by the Foreign Intelligence Surveillance Act (1978), which creates a special warrant procedure for judicial issuance of permission to wiretap. Both wiretap statutes have been held constitutional.

HERMAN SCHWARTZ
(1986)

(SEE ALSO: *Criminal Justice and Technology; Electronic Eavesdropping*.)

Bibliography

SCHWARTZ, HERMAN 1977 *Taps, Bugs, and Fooling the People.* New York: Field Foundation.

# WIRT, WILLIAM
## (1772–1834)

A Virginian lawyer, William Wirt helped defend James Callender in his SEDITION trial (1800) and helped prosecute AARON BURR for TREASON (1806). As United States attorney general under JAMES MONROE and JOHN QUINCY ADAMS (1817–1829), Wirt initiated the system of preserving the "opinions of the Attorneys General" for future use. While attorney general, Wirt followed the common practice of arguing private cases. In association with DANIEL WEBSTER he helped successfully to argue DARTMOUTH COLLEGE V. WOODWARD (1819), MCCULLOCH V. MARYLAND (1819), and GIBBONS V. OGDEN (1824). Wirt's national perspective in these cases was similar to his official policy as attorney general.

PAUL FINKELMAN
(1986)

Bibliography

KENNEDY, JOHN P. 1850 *Memoirs of the Life of William Wirt.* Philadelphia: Lea & Blanchard.

# WISCONSIN v. MITCHELL
## 508 U.S. 476 (1993)

On October 7, 1989, in Kenosha, Wisconsin, Todd Mitchell, a nineteen-year-old black man, directed and encouraged a number of young black men and boys to attack a fourteen-year-old white boy, Gregory Riddick. Mitchell selected Riddick solely on the basis of his race. Mitchell was convicted of aggravated battery for his role in the severe beating—a crime that carries a maximum sentence of two years under Wisconsin law. His crime also implicated the Wisconsin HATE CRIME statute that provides for the enhanced penalty of bias motivated crimes. Under this statute, the potential penalty for an aggravated battery is increased by five years if the perpetrator of the assault selected his victim on the basis of a set of enumerated group characteristics, including race, ethnicity, and religion.

Mitchell challenged his conviction under the hate crime statute, claiming that the enhancement of his prison term was a violation of his right to FREEDOM OF SPEECH under the FIRST AMENDMENT. The Wisconsin Supreme Court reversed the conviction in an opinion announced the day after R. A. V. V. CITY OF ST. PAUL (1992) was decided by the U.S. Supreme Court, and adopted much the same approach as did Justice ANTONIN SCALIA for the majority of the Court in *R. A. V.* The Wisconsin court held that the penalty enhancement law "punishes the defendant's biased . . . thought and thus encroaches upon First Amendment rights."

The U.S. Supreme Court reversed the Wisconsin court and upheld Mitchell's sentence, including the enhanced portion. In defending its bias crime statute from constitutional attack, Wisconsin emphasized the precise form and content of that statute, particularly stressing that the statute punished discriminatory selection of a victim. Wisconsin contended that *R. A. V.* had been concerned with the regulation of expression while the Wisconsin bias crime statute proscribed not expression but conduct—the intentional discriminatory selection of a victim.

The U.S. Supreme Court largely based its decision on this speech-conduct distinction. Indeed, this was precisely the basis of the Court's distinction between the St. Paul ordinance that was struck down in *R. A. V.* and the Wisconsin statute. Writing for a unanimous Court, Chief Justice WILLIAM H. REHNQUIST wrote that "whereas the ordinance struck down in *R. A. V.* was explicitly directed at expression (i.e., 'speech' or 'messages' . . .), the statute in this case is aimed at conduct unprotected by the First Amendment."

Although the speech-conduct distinction has been criticized by scholars as deeply flawed, since *Mitchell*, states have defended the constitutionality of their bias crime laws by arguing that their statutes do not interfere with the expression of prejudicial ideas but are addressed solely to the implementation of those views in conduct.

FREDERICK M. LAWRENCE
(2000)

Bibliography

JACOBS, JAMES B. and POTTER, KIMBERLY 1998 *Hate Crimes: Criminal Law and Identity Politics.* New York: Oxford University Press.

LAWRENCE, FREDERICK M. 1999 *Punishing Hate: Bias Crimes Under American Law.* Cambridge, Mass.: Harvard University Press.

## *WISCONSIN v. YODER*
### 406 U.S. 205 (1972)

Wisconsin's school-leaving age was sixteen. Members of the Old Order Amish religion declined, on religious grounds, to send their children to school beyond the eighth grade. Wisconsin chose to force the issue, and counsel for the Amish defendants replied that while the requirement might be valid as to others, the free exercise clause of the FIRST AMENDMENT required exemption in the case of the Amish.

Chief Justice WARREN E. BURGER, speaking for the Supreme Court, was much impressed by the Amish way of life. He rejected Wisconsin's argument that belief but not action was protected by the free exercise clause, and cited SHERBERT V. VERNER (1963). Nor was the Chief Justice convinced by the state's assertion of a COMPELLING STATE INTEREST. Nothing indicated that Amish children would suffer from the lack of high school education. Burger stressed that the Amish would have lost had they based their claim on "subjective evaluations and rejections of the contemporary social values accepted by the majority."

Justice BYRON R. WHITE filed a concurring opinion in which Justices WILLIAM J. BRENNAN and POTTER STEWART joined. White found the issue in *Yoder* much closer than Burger. White pointed out that many Amish children left the religious fold upon attaining their majority and had to make their way in the larger world like everyone else.

Justice WILLIAM O. DOUGLAS dissented in part. He saw the issue as one of CHILDREN'S RIGHTS in which Frieda Yoder's personal feelings and desires should be determinative. Justice Stewart, joined by Justice Brennan, filed a brief concurrence which took issue with Douglas on this point, and noted that there was nothing in the record which indicated that the religious beliefs of the children in the case differed in any way from those of the parents.

RICHARD E. MORGAN
(1986)

## WISDOM, JOHN MINOR
### (1905–1999)

John Minor Wisdom, a patrician son of the Old South who became one of the prime architects of the progressive New South, is, along with LEARNED HAND, HENRY J. FRIENDLY, and Irving Kaufman, one of a select group of judges who never sat on the Supreme Court but is regarded as producing the most long-lasting and profound impact on American jurisprudence in the twentieth century. Although universally known for his learned, literate, and path-breaking opinions in the field of CIVIL RIGHTS, among the more than 1,500 opinions Wisdom authored over the course of his forty-two years as an active and senior judge on the U.S. Court of Appeals for the Fifth Circuit, are numerous seminal opinions in a diverse area of subjects, including trust, railroad reorganization, criminal, tax, and maritime law.

Wisdom's roots run deep in Southern soil. His mother was a descendant of the Minors of Virginia, a wealthy and socially prominent member of the landed gentry whose ancestors arrived in the state from Holland in the 1650s. The Wisdoms emigrated from England to America in 1730 and eventually settled in New Orleans in the 1840s where John Wisdom's grandfather built a successful cotton and tobacco commission business. John Wisdom's maternal grandfather, David Cohen Labatt, a leading Jewish lawyer in New Orleans and distant cousin of Judah P. Benjamin, received the first law degree conferred by the forerunner of what became Tulane Law School. Eighty-one years later, John Wisdom also received a law degree from Tulane.

A legal career, however, was not preordained for young John Wisdom. Following in his father's footsteps, John Wisdom received his undergraduate degree at Washington & Lee University. (Throughout his career, John Wisdom proudly displayed his father's certificate of scholarly achievement containing the faded signature of the college's president, Robert E. Lee.) Anticipating a career as a literary critic, John Wisdom enrolled at Harvard University in 1925, where he intended to obtain a Master of Arts, and possibly, thereafter, a doctoral degree in English. But after arriving, he learned that his lack of training in Latin or Greek precluded his participation in the program, so he stayed for only one year, choosing to audit courses at the Law School. The experience convinced him that he wanted to become a lawyer, and so he returned home to attend Tulane Law School, where he was graduated at the top of his class in 1929.

While building a highly successful law firm with a law school classmate, Wisdom turned some of his boundless energy to the field of politics. Committed to the notion that a strong two-party system was an essential element of a vibrant democracy, Wisdom committed himself to resuscitating Louisiana's long dormant REPUBLICAN PARTY. With the help of his wife, the former Bonnie Mathews, and a small band of devoted followers, Wisdom built up a political machine in the state and was instrumental in securing the Republican Party presidential nomination for DWIGHT D. EISENHOWER in 1952. Five years later, Eisenhower turned to Wisdom to fill a vacant spot on the Fifth Circuit, the appellate court with JURISDICTION over the entire Deep South—Florida, Georgia, Alabama, Mississippi, Texas, and Louisiana. Wisdom served on that court until his death in 1999, two days shy of his ninety-fourth birthday.

Wisdom's opinions are noted for their unpretentious eloquence, comprehensive and scholarly reliance on history, philosophy, and literature, their vision, and their bedrock commitment to fairness. As the intellectual leader of a group of progressive Fifth Circuit judges derisively called "The Four," Wisdom was the author of opinions that ordered the enrollment of James Meredith into the then-segregated University of Alabama, overturned the racially discriminatory jury selection system in Orleans Parish, mandated the DESEGREGATION of all public parks and playgrounds in New Orleans, struck down Louisiana's racist voter registration law, upheld the use of voluntary, racially based AFFIRMATIVE ACTION by a private employer, and held that involuntarily committed psychiatric patients had a constitutional right to adequate treatment in state mental institutions. In *United States v. Jefferson County Board of Education* (1966), the case Wisdom viewed as his most important opinion, he rejected the widely held view in the South that while the Constitution prohibited discrimination, it did not affirmatively require integration. He held that school boards had an affirmative duty to develop desegregation plans and advised them "the only school de-

segregation plan that meets constitutional standards is one that works."

JOEL WM. FRIEDMAN
(2000)

Bibliography

BASS, JACK 1981 *Unlikely Heroes*. New York: Simon & Schuster.

READ, FRANK T. and MCGOUGH, LUCY S. 1978 *Let Them Be Judged*. Metuchen, N.J.: Scarecrow Press.

FRIEDMAN, JOEL WM. 1995 John Minor Wisdom's Battle Against the Political Bosses. *Tulane Law Review* 69:1439–1511.

—— 1996 Judge Wisdom and the 1952 Republican National Convention. *Washington and Lee Law Review* 53:33–97.

# WITNESSES, JURORS, AND THE FREEDOM OF SPEECH

The 1990s witnessed a dramatic increase in "checkbook journalism," in which individuals are paid for providing information to the print or electronic media. Although numerous aspects of this practice may be troubling, the greatest concern has been expressed over the prospect of payment to actors in the judicial system who sell their stories to the news. Specifically, the specter of witnesses at trial and jurors realizing financial gain from their service in high-profile trials has caused many to argue for legal restrictions on the ability of certain trial participants to cash in on their fifteen minutes of fame. In turn, such a prospect has raised the fear that critical FIRST AMENDMENT rights to FREEDOM OF SPEECH will be sacrificed.

Obviously, most criminal trials proceed without anyone being compensated by the media for telling his or her story. In the vast majority of crimes, public interest would not sustain the payment of money for the "exclusive" scoop. In high-profile trials, however, the lure of the dollar may very well prevail. Although the frenzy of tabloid journalism surrounding the O. J. Simpson murder trial comes most readily to mind, the practice of checkbook journalism long preceded that case. For example, the woman who assisted the alleged rape victim of William Kennedy Smith—and who later became a pivotal witness at trial—received $40,000 from the media for her story. Two witnesses in the child-molestation charges against pop star Michael Jackson sold their stories to television.

Yet the Simpson trial set new records both for press coverage and for prices paid for stories concerning the double-murder of Nicole Brown Simpson and Ron Goldman. Witness Jill Shively sold her story of seeing O. J. Simpson driving near the murder scene; two other witnesses who worked in a knife store and who testified at a preliminary hearing that Simpson had purchased a knife were paid $12,500 for their story by the tabloid *National Enquirer*.

Witnesses (or potential witnesses) are not the only ones to cash in on their involvement in the judicial system; jurors have also discovered that jury duty can be profitable. Perhaps the best-known example of juror journalism arose out of the trial of Bernard Goetz, who was accused of shooting several youths after they had attempted to mug him on the New York subway. Two jurors ultimately sold their views about the case to the news media. During another high-profile trial, the boyfriend of the jury forewoman tried to negotiate with several newspapers for the sale of the foreperson's account of the trial. One juror during the Rodney King trial stated that although she had no current plans to sell her story, the idea appealed to her capitalistic instincts.

What, if anything, is wrong about such financial endeavors, either by witnesses or jurors? Simply, the concern is that money corrupts. Permitting witnesses to profit from selling their stories may threaten the integrity of a criminal trial in several ways. It may lead the jury to discredit the testimony of a truthful witness, or even cause an attorney to decide not to call a witness out of fear that the jury will react negatively. Alternatively, a witness may testify falsely on the stand, because the lure of money has prompted the witness to lie or embellish the truth to the media, and that false story has become the version frozen in place.

The integrity of the judicial system is also threatened when a juror sells—or anticipates selling—the story of his or her JURY SERVICE. The lure of the dollar may encourage a potential juror to lie during VOIR DIRE in order to obtain a seat on a high-profile jury. The juror's perception of the testimony may be altered by her conflicting roles of juror and journalist. A juror seeing dollar signs may seek the "truth" that most effectively sells a story. Finally, there is the concern that a juror will manipulate a verdict to ensure the most dramatic—and salable—outcome.

These are legitimate concerns, and they have led several states to adopt laws restricting the ability of witnesses or jurors—or both—to profit from their service. These laws, however, constitute a restriction on speech and hence raise potential First Amendment problems. Information concerning criminal acts—be it about the victim, the alleged perpetrator, the behavior of the police, or others—provides useful information on matters of public concern. Financial remuneration, moreover, may cause a critical witness to come forward who otherwise might not. Suppose this nation faced a scandal on the magnitude of WATERGATE, and the only person with information refused to divulge it without monetary gain.

Similarly, juror speech is valuable. A juror's report may explore or criticize the workings of the judiciary and ex-

pose flaws and potential abuses. Explanations of how the deliberations progressed could reinforce notions that the jury system does work, and thus increase public confidence in the justice system.

Ultimately, whether laws restricting juror or witness speech violate the freedom of speech will turn on information that today remains merely a matter of speculation. How real is the risk that the payment of money will subvert a witness's oath to tell the truth or the juror's promise to be impartial? The evidence remains theoretical. Until such time—if ever—that the alleged harm of checkbook journalism becomes more substantiated, it is unlikely that the courts will—or should—sanction a law that decreases expression on critical social and political issues.

MARCY STRAUSS
(2000)

Bibliography

STRAUSS, MARCY   1994   Juror Journalism. *Yale Law and Policy Review* 12:389–423.
——   1996   From Witness to Riches: The Constitutionality of Restricting Witness Speech. *Arizona Law Review* 38:291–329.

# WITTERS v. WASHINGTON DEPARTMENT OF SERVICES FOR THE BLIND
## 474 U.S. 481 (1986)

Suffering from a progressive eye condition, Witters sought state financial assistance to attend a Bible college to prepare himself for a career as a minister. Washington State generally provided aid to visually handicapped persons seeking education or training for careers so they could be self-supporting. Nevertheless, the state denied Witters aid, citing the Washington State constitution's prohibition of public aid to religion. The state supreme court upheld the denial, but on ESTABLISHMENT CLAUSE grounds, holding that aid to Witters would advance religion as its primary effect and thus violate the second prong of the LEMON TEST. The U.S. Supreme Court unanimously reversed.

Writing the opinion of the Court, Justice THURGOOD MARSHALL said it would be inappropriate to view the funds ultimately flowing to the Bible college in this case as the result of state action to aid religion. Marshall noted that the financial assistance "is paid directly to the student, who transmits it to the educational institution of his or her choice. Any aid provided under Washington's program that ultimately flows to religious institutions does so only as a result of the genuinely independent and private choices of aid recipients." Marshall further emphasized that the program "is in no way skewed toward religion" and "creates no financial incentive for students to undertake sectarian education." Finally, Marshall stressed that nothing indicated any significant proportion of state money provided under the program would flow to religious institutions if Witters's claim was granted.

That last reason was not dispositive for a majority of Justices, five of whom joined concurring opinions that noted the applicability of MUELLER V. ALLEN (1983) to *Witters*. In *Mueller* the Court had upheld general tax deductions for certain school expenses, despite the fact that over ninety percent of these tax benefits went to those who sent their children to religious schools.

JOHN G. WEST, JR.
(1992)

## WOLF v. COLORADO
### 338 U.S. 25 (1949)

In *Wolf* the Supreme Court held that "the core" of the FOURTH AMENDMENT's freedom from UNREASONABLE SEARCHES was "basic" and thus incorporated in the FOURTEENTH AMENDMENT as a restriction on searches by state officers, but that its enforcement feature, the EXCLUSIONARY RULE (in effect for federal trials since 1914), was not. The refusal to require the exclusionary rule for state trials was largely based on considerations of FEDERALISM. The Court reasoned, first, that the exclusionary rule could scarcely be considered "basic" when the COMMON LAW rule of admissibility was still followed both in the English-speaking world outside the United States and in most of the American states, and second, that suits in tort against offending officers could be "equally effective" in deterring unlawful searches. The experience of the following twelve years proved the suit in tort to be a paper remedy rather than an effective sanction, leading the Court to overrule *Wolf* and impose the exclusionary rule on the states in MAPP V. OHIO (1961).

JACOB W. LANDYNSKI
(1986)

## WOLFF PACKING COMPANY v. COURT OF INDUSTRIAL RELATIONS
### 262 U.S. 522 (1923)

Reversing a trend of broad definitions of public utilities, the Supreme Court voided a Kansas law declaring certain businesses to be AFFECTED WITH A PUBLIC INTEREST, and thus subject to regulation. A unanimous Court could find no justification for the statute and held that affectation derived from the nature of a business, not from the declaration of a state legislature. The Court thus returned to

a concept implicit in *Munn v. Illinois* (1877): that a public interest inhered in monopolistic enterprises. (See GRANGER CASES.) Chief Justice WILLIAM HOWARD TAFT defined three categories of businesses clothed with a public interest: public utilities, occupations traditionally regulated (such as innkeepers), and those "businesses which, though not public at their inception, may be fairly said to have risen to be such, and have become subject in consequence to some government regulation."

DAVID GORDON
(1986)

(SEE ALSO: *Economic Regulation; Public Use.*)

## WOLMAN v. WALTER
### 433 U.S. 229 (1977)

Ohio's aid plan for independent schools had six components: (1) the loan of textbooks; (2) the supply of standardized testing and scoring material; (3) the provision of diagnostic services aimed at identifying speech, hearing, and psychological problems; (4) the provision, off non-public school premises, of therapeutic, guidance, and remedial services; (5) the loan to pupils of instructional materials such as slide projectors, tape recorders, maps, and scientific gear; and (6) the provision of transportation for field trips similar to the transportation provided public school students.

Justice HARRY BLACKMUN delivered what was in part an opinion of the Supreme Court and in part a PLURALITY OPINION in which only Chief Justice WARREN E. BURGER, Justice POTTER STEWART, and Justice LEWIS F. POWELL joined.

The Court upheld the loan of textbooks, the supply of testing materials, the therapeutic services, and the provision of diagnostic services on non-public school premises. The Court found unconstitutional the provisions for lending secular instructional materials and for field trip transportation.

This case indicated the extent to which the "wall between church and state" was in fact a blurred, indistinct, and variable barrier.

RICHARD E. MORGAN
(1986)

## WOMAN SUFFRAGE

When American women voted in the election of 1920, they did so for the first time as a constitutional right protected by the NINETEENTH AMENDMENT. The amendment's ratification marked the end of a long struggle that was bound up with both the shifting status of the ballot and the political development of a women's movement.

The struggle, which began formally at the women's rights convention at SENECA FALLS, New York, in 1848, emerged when most states had already dropped their property qualifications for white male voters. "Resolved," averred ELIZABETH CADY STANTON, "that it is the duty of the women of this country to secure to themselves the sacred right to elective franchise." Yet in the context of the mid-nineteenth century the right to elective franchise still was not a national, constitutional issue. Moreover, voting embodied so powerful a symbol of personal autonomy that granting it to women was profoundly controversial. In fact, woman suffrage, as contemporaries called it, barely won the support of the delegates at Seneca Falls.

RECONSTRUCTION transformed woman suffrage into a compelling constitutional issue. The second clause of the FOURTEENTH AMENDMENT introduced the word "male" into the Constitution, and the FIFTEENTH AMENDMENT, which prohibited abridging the VOTING RIGHTS of black males, was silent on the disfranchisement of females. Inasmuch as the two amendments seemed at once essential to the rights of freedmen and inimical to the cause of woman suffrage, the women's movement divided over their ratification.

The spacious terms of the first clause of the Fourteenth Amendment, however, sparked numerous challenges to women's disfranchisement. SUSAN B. ANTHONY created a dramatic test in the election of 1872 by registering and voting with fifteen other New York women, thereby violating a federal election statute, but her case did not reach the Supreme Court. The case that did was launched by Virginia Minor, who with her attorney-husband, Francis, sued the state of Missouri for restricting suffrage to males. The plaintiff's brief in MINOR V. HAPPERSETT (1875) argued that women had been empowered to vote in federal elections from the inception of the Constitution, had actually voted for a time in New Jersey, and were simply reaffirmed in their right to vote by the terms of the Fourteenth Amendment. The disfranchisement of women, the brief asserted, was a BILL OF ATTAINDER, an infringement on FREEDOM OF SPEECH, a form of involuntary servitude, and a violation not only of DUE PROCESS but of the constitutional guarantee that every state shall have a REPUBLICAN FORM OF GOVERNMENT. In a unanimous decision drafted by Chief Justice MORRISON R. WAITE, the Court ruled that suffrage was neither protected in the original text of the Constitution nor incorporated in the PRIVILEGES AND IMMUNITIES of CITIZENSHIP guaranteed by the Fourteenth Amendment.

By the 1890s, the drive for suffrage had stalled, despite the unification of the two wings of the women's movement. State-by-state campaigns yielded disappointing results, and after *Minor* a constitutional amendment was needed to ensure suffrage nationwide. Headway came with the bold campaigns of the Congressional Union (later called the Woman's party), an organization founded in 1913 by Alice Paul and Lucy Burns to replicate the militant tactics of English feminists. Picketing, arrests, and hunger strikes generated attention at a time when resistance to women voting was ebbing. Giving women the vote was regarded increasingly as a way of bringing their domestic concerns into the political arena and therefore as a potential instrument of Progressive reform. The final strategy for victory came from the lobbying efforts of Carrie Chapman Catt, president of the National American Woman Suffrage Association, who not only pulled a recalcitrant WOODROW WILSON into the suffrage camp but also capitalized on the temporary gratitude of the nation for the wartime service of its women.

NORMA BASCH
(1992)

(SEE ALSO: *Feminist Theory and Constitutional Law; Gender Rights; Progressive Constitutional Thought; Progressivism; Woman Suffrage Movement; Women in Constitutional History.*)

Bibliography

DuBois, ELLEN CAROL 1987 Outgrowing the Compact of the Fathers: Equal Rights, Woman Suffrage, and the United States Constitution, 1820–1878. *Journal of American History* 74:836–862.

FLEXNOR, ELEANOR (1959) 1968 *Century of Struggle: The Woman's Rights Movement in the United States.* Cambridge, Mass.: Harvard University Press.

# WOMAN SUFFRAGE MOVEMENT

The first formal demand for equal political rights for women was made by ELIZABETH CADY STANTON at the 1848 SENECA FALLS CONVENTION. Among the radical pioneers of the early women's rights movement, woman suffrage was at first controversial, because electoral politics was considered disreputable and partisanship fundamentally male. However, after the CIVIL WAR and the abolition of SLAVERY, questions of CITIZENSHIP and enfranchisement had moved to the top of the national political agenda, and woman suffrage was widely accepted by women's rights activists as their foremost demand. At this point we can properly begin to speak about an American woman suffrage movement.

At war's end, woman suffrage leaders expected that white women would win the franchise along with freedmen and freedwomen via the establishment of universal suffrage. However, the Republican authors of the FIFTEENTH AMENDMENT refused to include "sex" alongside "race, color and previous condition of servitude" as federally prohibited disfranchisements. The woman suffrage forces disagreed over how to deal with this setback, as a result of which two rival organizations were formed. In one last effort to secure woman suffrage as part of RECONSTRUCTION, one of these societies, the National Woman Suffrage Association, developed an innovative constitutional argument. They contended that women as well as men had been made national citizens by the first clause of the FOURTEENTH AMENDMENT; inasmuch as the franchise must be regarded as the defining right of citizenship, women thus already possessed the ballot and had merely to exercise it. In 1875, in MINOR V. HAPPERSETT the Supreme Court ruled against this construction and held that while women were indeed citizens, voting was not a right but a privilege, which could be constitutionally denied to women.

Over the next decades, the woman suffrage movement gained adherents. Of greatest importance was the endorsement of woman suffrage, as the best means to control liquor and protect the home, by the Woman's Christian Temperance Union under the leadership of Frances Willard. By 1890, woman suffrage, which had begun as a radical demand among a handful of antebellum ultraist reformers, was gaining ground among respectable, politically mainstream middle-class American women. That year, the two suffrage societies buried their differences and combined to form the National American Woman Suffrage Association. As woman suffrage became more acceptable, the movement, which had been forged in the fires of abolition and emancipation, became increasingly racist in its arguments and organizations. Nonetheless, in these same years African American women, who well knew the power of the vote, actively pursued votes for women through their own pro-suffrage societies, such as the National Association of Colored Women.

The constitutional upheavals of the Reconstruction era had left unresolved the question of where SOVEREIGNTY over the electorate lay, with the several states or with the federal government. Through the late nineteenth and early twentieth centuries, while the progress to federal woman suffrage was stalled, advocates of votes for women concentrated on securing their goal by amending the constitutions of particular states. In 1869 and 1870, respectively, the territorial legislatures of Wyoming and Utah enacted woman suffrage provisions, which were retained when they became states in the 1890s. In 1893, Colorado became the first state in which the male electorate voted to amend the state constitution so as to grant women full VOTING RIGHTS. Idaho (1896), Washington (1910), and California (1911) followed. By 1912, there were ten "woman suffrage states," all west of the Mississippi. In the East, however, the "state method" could not prevail. In 1915,

voters in four major eastern states—New Jersey, New York, Pennsylvania, and Massachusetts—decisively defeated woman suffrage referenda. At this point, woman suffragists turned their attention back to winning a federal amendment.

By the first decade of the twentieth century, the suffrage movement itself was also changing. Steady growth in the female labor force and massive immigration altered both the composition and approaches of suffragism. New suffrage organizations oriented toward wage-earning women were founded in New York, Boston, and San Francisco. Female college graduates, whose numbers were growing, also flooded into the movement. The suffragist tactical arsenal was reinvented as well, as advocates moved their demands into public spaces, organized mass parades, conducted automobile caravans, and became adept at street-corner speaking.

As an expression of these changes, a second national organization, the Congressional Union (subsequently known as the Woman's Party) was formed in 1913. Its goal was to pursue more aggressively a woman suffrage amendment to the federal Constitution. Known as the "militants," this new wing turned to the voting women of the ten "suffrage states," urging women to vote against the reelection of President WOODROW WILSON in 1916 to punish the Democrats for refusing to support a federal suffrage amendment. Once the United States entered WORLD WAR I, however, the militants switched from electoral methods to civil disobedience, picketing the White House, for which many were arrested and jailed. Meanwhile, the majority of American suffragists, who were associated with the moderate National American Woman Suffrage Association, continued to rely on congressional lobbying.

By 1920, the combination of these approaches, plus the political transformations following the war, finally led to the passage and ratification of the NINETEENTH AMENDMENT to the Constitution, which prohibited the states from disfranchising its citizens on the grounds of sex.

ELLEN CAROL DuBOIS
(2000)

Bibliography

DuBois, ELLEN CAROL 1978 *Feminism and Suffrage.* Ithaca, N.Y.: Cornell University Press.
——— 1998 *Woman Suffrage and Women's Rights.* New York: New York University Press.
FLEXNER, ELEANOR and FITZPATRICK, ELLEN 1996 *Century of Struggle: The Woman's Rights Movement in the United States.* Cambridge, Mass.: Harvard University Press.
KRADITOR, AILEEN 1965 *Ideas of the Woman Suffrage Movement, 1890–1920.* New York: Columbia University Press.
WHEELER, MARJORIE SPRUILL, ed. 1995 *One Woman, One Vote:*

*Rediscovering the Suffrage Movement.* Troutdale, Oregon: New Sage Press.

# WOMEN IN CONSTITUTIONAL HISTORY

At first glance, women seem missing from much of the historical landscape of the Constitution, and in the few instances where they do appear, they suffer negative consequences for their legal status. Before the CIVIL WAR sex did not even figure as a contested constitutional classification, and for a century after the war virtually every effort to eradicate its discriminatory aspects met with defeat at the hands of the Supreme Court. Indeed, until the 1970s, when the Court began to apply closer scrutiny to sex as a discriminatory category, the Constitution seems to have treated women as women with either casual indifference or zealous paternalism. Yet, on closer inspection, the role of gender in the life of the Constitution has been longer, larger, and more subtle than this first impression suggests. The constitutional status of gender, moreover, has been shaped by shifting conceptions of legal equality, the evolving relationship between the states and the federal government, and the changing circumstances in women's day-to-day lives.

FEDERALISM goes a long way toward illuminating the constitutional role of gender in the first stage of its development. Given the sharp delineation between the appropriate rights and duties of men and women in both the life and the law of the early Republic, the original text of the Constitution, which employs terms such as "persons," is remarkably gender-neutral. The Framers could afford to be gender-neutral in their language precisely because state laws were gender-specific. The Framers were hardly indifferent, then, to gender as a legal classification; rather, federalism obviated the need to frame it in national constitutional terms.

State statutes and constitutions spelled out the exclusion of women from the political process, while COMMON LAW assumptions and precedents informed their legal disabilities. The principles of coverture, which placed a married woman under the tutelage of her husband, influenced legal attitudes toward women in general. Of course, single women, unlike their married counterparts, could enter into contracts, sue, and be sued. However, the tendency of the law to define all women as wives and mothers rather than as citizens, property owners, or wage earners, or as dependent and relative rather than as independent and autonomous, was pervasive in constitutional approaches to gender. But reform efforts to define the role of women more broadly were also pervasive. They began officially in the 1840s when women's rights advocates organized to demand both legal and political equality at the state level, and these efforts have animated new conceptions of constitutional equality from the antebellum era to the present day.

After the Civil War, gender entered into formal constitutional discourse largely as a corollary of race. Although the second section of the FOURTEENTH AMENDMENT incorporated the word "male" into the Constitution, the DUE PROCESS and EQUAL PROTECTION clauses of the first section held the potential to apply to gender as well as to race. The consequences for women were ambiguous. On the one hand, SEX DISCRIMINATION acquired a new legitimacy as a result of constitutional tests of the RECONSTRUCTION amendments; on the other hand, it became a legal issue that was suffused with constitutional import.

Nonetheless, postbellum efforts to enhance the constitutional status of women via judicial decision failed miserably. In BRADWELL V. ILLINOIS (1873), the Supreme Court denied Myra Bradwell's claim that her right to practice law was among the PRIVILEGES AND IMMUNITIES of citizenship protected under the Fourteenth Amendment. In MINOR V. HAPPERSETT (1875), the Court denied that Missouri's restriction of suffrage to males violated the privileges and immunities of Virginia Minor's citizenship. And despite admitting Belva Lockwood to practice before its bar, the Court in *In re Lockwood* (1894) held that states could apply the word "person" in the Fourteenth Amendment to men only.

However, legal equality between women and men was not a consistent goal of the women's movement, and by the turn of the century, female reformers were clearly selective in their support of it. They backed special protective labor legislation for women workers not only in the hope that such legislation would be extended to all workers but also in the belief that long hours and hazardous working conditions were particularly injurious to women as potential mothers. If in hindsight their arguments seem oblivious to the constitutional risks of protecting women exclusively and to the disadvantages created for women in the labor market, in their own day they evoked a powerful appeal.

That appeal was perhaps best encapsulated in the voluminous BRANDEIS BRIEF, written for MULLER V. OREGON (1908), a case in which the Court upheld maximum-hour laws for women and thereby exempted them from a laissez-faire commitment to the principle of FREEDOM OF CONTRACT. The rationale in the brief remained popular among progressive reformers long after *Muller*. Indeed, by the 1920s the vast majority of women who had worked for women's political equality by supporting the NINETEENTH AMENDMENT were against the proposed EQUAL RIGHTS AMENDMENT largely because they feared its effects on special health and labor legislation for women. The

Supreme Court, however, was now prepared to view women as the complete equals of men, at least with regard to their capacity to contract for wages. In ADKINS V. CHILDREN'S HOSPITAL (1923), the Court undermined statutory attempts to put a floor under women's wages by invalidating a DISTRICT OF COLUMBIA MINIMUM WAGE LAW. Underscoring the equality women enjoyed as a result of the Nineteenth Amendment, the *Adkins* opinion applied the principle of freedom of contract to women workers without overtly overturning *Muller,* and *Adkins* itself was not overruled until WEST COAST HOTEL CO. V. PARRISH (1938).

Efforts to apply the equal protection clause to sex as a discriminatory classification met with further defeats in the post-WORLD WAR II era. In GOESAERT V. CLEARY (1948), for example, adjudicated at a time when men were returning to jobs that had been filled temporarily by women, the Court upheld a Michigan statute prohibiting a woman from selling or serving liquor unless she was the wife or daughter of the tavernkeeper. Equal protection, the decision averred, did not require perfect symmetry, and in *Hoyt v. Florida* (1961) the Court relied on similar reasoning to reject an effort to block sex discrimination in the jury selection process.

Yet as women entered the work force in unprecedented numbers after World War II and as the divorce rate soared, it became even harder to sustain the old legal prototype of protection and dependence. As a result of a burgeoning CIVIL RIGHTS MOVEMENT and a revitalized women's movement, the analogies between sex and race as discriminatory categories came to the forefront of constitutional discourse in the 1960s, and they were applied in turn to a host of new federal CIVIL RIGHTS statutes. Significant breakthroughs in the constitutional status of women came in the 1970s not only with the heightened judicial scrutiny of sex discrimination but also with the growing legitimation of REPRODUCTIVE AUTONOMY. No less important symbolically was the 1981 appointment of SANDRA DAY O'CONNOR, the first woman to serve as a Justice of the Supreme Court.

The change in constitutional attitudes toward gender was heralded by *Reed v. Reed* (1971), a decision that invalidated a statutory preference for males in appointing the administrators of intestate estates on the ground of the law's inherent irrationality. Inasmuch as the state's purposes were "as well served by a gender-neutral classification as one that gender-classifies and therefore carries with it the baggage of sexual stereotypes," the Court determined that the state "cannot be permitted to classify on the basis of sex." FRONTIERO V. RICHARDSON (1973), the closest the Court came to regarding sex as a suspect classification, struck down a rule that disadvantaged the dependents of servicewomen, relative to the dependents of servicemen, in calculating dependency benefits. A series

of subsequent cases equalized Social Security payments, welfare benefits, and workers' compensation. *Stanton v. Stanton* (1975) ruled that girls were entitled to child support up to the same age as boys; *Orr v. Orr* (1979) held that a state law could not exempt women of means from paying alimony on the same basis as men; and CRAIG V. BOREN (1976) invalidated a law that differentiated between the sexes in setting the statutory age for buying 3.2 percent beer.

Clearly the decision that most dramatically altered both the lives and the status of women in this blizzard of judicial reinterpretation was ROE V. WADE (1973), which followed the rationale the Court had used in GRISWOLD V. CONNECTICUT (1965) to prohibit a state ban on BIRTH CONTROL. The *Roe* decision, which struck down a Texas statute defining ABORTION as a criminal offense, did so not on the equality-based theory that it was a violation of women's rights but rather on the ground that it violated an implied constitutional RIGHT OF PRIVACY. Nonetheless, except for the last trimester of pregnancy, the *Roe* opinion significantly subordinated the power of the state to that of a woman and her doctor.

However, ambivalence toward scrutinizing sex discrimination strictly was evident in many quarters. Even as the Court moved toward upholding equal rights for women through its reinterpretations of the equal protection clause, it never subjected its scrutiny of sex to the same rigorous standards that it applied to race, and there were some indications in the 1980s of a retreat from the stance it had taken in the 1970s. Because the issues were by no means simple, to cite rules on pregnancy leave as one example, there were radical feminists as well as conservative women who continued to support preferential or differential treatment for women. Furthermore, the right of reproductive autonomy, a hotly contested issue that right-to-life adherents elevated into a political litmus test for candidates at all levels of government, became especially vulnerable to inroads by the end of the 1980s. Finally, the political campaign for women's constitutional rights stalled on a distinct note of defeat. The failure of the EQUAL RIGHTS AMENDMENT to be ratified by three-quarters of the states after it had passed Congress meant that the Constitution still stood without a discrete provision on which to ground the eradication of the remaining sex inequalities in state law, much less to prevent new ones from emerging.

NORMA BASCH
(1992)

(SEE ALSO: *Anthony, Susan Brownell; Feminist Theory; Gender Rights; Labor and the Constitution; Labor Movement; Racial Discrimination; Stanton, Elizabeth Cady; Woman Suffrage; Women Suffrage Movement.*)

Bibliography

BAER, JUDITH 1986 *The Chains of Protection: The Judicial Response to Women's Labor Legislation.* Westport, Conn.: Greenwood Press.

BERRY, MARY FRANCES 1986 *Why Era Failed: Politics, Women's Rights, and the Amending Process of the Constitution.* Bloomington: Indiana University Press.

## WONG KIM ARK, UNITED STATES v.
### 169 U.S. 649 (1898)

This case, decided at a time when prejudice against people of Chinese ancestry was widespread, maintained the integrity of the CITIZENSHIP clause of section one of the FOURTEENTH AMENDMENT. Congressional legislation, known as the CHINESE EXCLUSION ACTS, denied citizenship to Chinese immigrants, and a treaty with China provided that no subject of China in the United States could be naturalized. Neither the exclusion acts nor the treaty applied in this case, however, because Wong Kim Ark had been born in San Francisco. When he was about twenty-one he visited his parents who had returned to China after living in the United States approximately twenty years. On his return to San Francisco, he was denied entry to the United States on the grounds that he was not a citizen. The Supreme Court held, 6–2, that the government's policy in refusing NATURALIZATION to persons of Chinese ancestry could not constitutionally be applied to anyone born in the United States whose parents, regardless of ancestry, were domiciled in this country and did not have diplomatic status.

LEONARD W. LEVY
(1986)

## WONG SUN v. UNITED STATES
### 371 U.S. 471 (1963)

In *Wong Sun* the Supreme Court held that an incriminating oral statement made by a suspect that derives immediately from his unlawful arrest is inadmissible in evidence as a FRUIT OF THE POISONOUS TREE, no less than the derivative EVIDENCE obtained from an unlawful search, as in SILVERTHORNE V. UNITED STATES (1920), or from unlawful wiretapping, as in NARDONE V. UNITED STATES (1939). However, when the taint of the earlier illegality is dissipated (as it was in this case, by a suspect voluntarily returning to make a statement several days after his arraignment and release on his own recognizance), the evidence is admissible.

In addition, *Wong Sun* contributed to the elaboration of PROBABLE CAUSE standards by holding that flight from an officer is not in itself such a strong inference of guilt as to establish probable cause for an arrest.

JACOB W. LANDYNSKI
(1986)

## WOOD v. STRICKLAND
### 420 U.S. 308 (1975)

This was an early case in the development of EXECUTIVE IMMUNITY from DAMAGES in CIVIL RIGHTS actions alleging constitutional violations. The case involved the liability of school board members for alleged violations of students' DUE PROCESS rights. The Supreme Court, in an opinion by Justice BYRON R. WHITE, clarified its holding in SCHEUER V. RHODES (1974) by expressly stating that the good faith defense of executive officials contained both subjective and objective elements. An official must subjectively believe he is doing right and must not act in "ignorance or disregard of settled, indisputable law." *Harlow v. Fitzgerald* (1982) later undermined the subjective component of *Wood's* test. (See NIXON V. FITZGERALD.)

THEODORE EISENBERG
(1986)

## WOODBURY, LEVI
### (1789–1851)

Levi Woodbury was a New Hampshire lawyer, state supreme court justice (1817–1823), governor (1823–1824), United States senator (1825–1831; 1841–1842), secretary of the navy (1831–1834), secretary of the treasury (1834–1841), and United States Supreme Court Justice (1845–1851). A staunch Jacksonian Democrat, Woodbury supported territorial expansion, STRICT CONSTRUCTION, and STATES' RIGHTS, while opposing the BANK OF THE UNITED STATES, abolitionists, and high tariffs. Although a conservative, Woodbury advocated public schools, female education, and prison reform. He personally disliked slavery but believed it was constitutionally protected and that all agitation over it should cease.

On the New Hampshire bench Woodbury supported the state in DARTMOUTH COLLEGE V. WOODWARD (1819). As treasury secretary, Woodbury continued President ANDREW JACKSON's Bank War and advocated an independent treasury. He believed that Congress lacked constitutional power to recharter the Bank, and as late as 1841 he asserted that MCCULLOCH V. MARYLAND (1819) neither set a valid precedent nor determined the constitutionality of any future bank charter.

In 1830, as a senator, Woodbury criticized the Supreme Court for its "manifest and sleepless opposition . . . to the strict construction of the Constitution" which had created "a diseased enlargement of the powers of the General Government and throwing chains over States-Rights. . . ." Woodbury attempted to stop these tendencies in his brief tenure on the Supreme Court. In the LICENSE CASES (1847), Woodbury joined the majority in upholding state PROHIBITION statues. In the PASSENGER CASES (1849), he asserted, in dissent, that states could constitutionally regulate immigrants without violating the Constitution's COMMERCE CLAUSE. In LUTHER V. BORDEN (1848), he agreed with the majority that the case involved a POLITICAL QUESTION beyond the court's JURISDICTION, but he nevertheless modified his states' rights position to condemn the use of martial law in Rhode Island. In *Warning v. Clarke* (1847), he again dissented, this time to assert state jurisdiction over navigable rivers. In a rare deviation from his states' rights philosophy, Woodbury wrote the majority opinion in *Planters' Bank v. Sharpe* (1848), overturning a Mississippi statute and court decision because both impaired the OBLIGATION OF CONTRACTS in violation of the Constitution.

Woodbury's most important majority opinion was written in *Jones v. Van Zandt* (1847), where he upheld a particularly harsh interpretation of the Fugitive Slave Law of 1793. Van Zandt, an Ohio Quaker, had given a ride to a group of blacks walking on a road in Ohio. Woodbury held Van Zandt financially liable for the escape of these fugitive slaves, even though at the time Van Zandt had no notice they were fugitives. Woodbury asserted that the Constitution had "flung its shield" over slavery, giving masters a COMMON LAW right to recapture their property. Woodbury held that the Fugitive Slave Law was a constitutionally proper enforcement of this right. Somewhat inconsistently, he then asserted that slavery itself was "a political question, settled by each State for itself." In 1848 Woodbury sought the presidential nomination. He was considered a likely candidate in 1852, because his *Van Zandt* opinion gave him southern support, while as a Northerner he might get grudging support from Free Soil Democrats. He campaigned for the nomination from the bench until his death in 1851.

PAUL FINKELMAN
(1986)

Bibliography

GATELL, FRANK O. 1968 Levi Woodbury. Pages 843–872 in Leon Friedman and Fred L. Israel, eds., *The Justices of the United States Supreme Court, 1789–1969: Their Lives and Major Opinions.* New York: Chelsea House.

## WOODRUFF v. PARHAM
### 8 Wallace 123 (1869)

*Woodruff* produced a retreat from the broad enunciation of the ORIGINAL PACKAGE DOCTRINE in BROWN V. MARYLAND (1827). In that case Chief Justice JOHN MARSHALL had said in an OBITER DICTUM that the DOCTRINE applied "equally to importations from a sister State. . . ." In this case the city of Mobile, Alabama, had taxed various commodities and transactions including goods imported from other states and sold in their original and unbroken packages. Woodruff alleged that this tax violated the constitutional clause forbidding state IMPOSTS or duties on imports. The Court ruled unanimously that the clause applied only to goods imported from foreign countries. Because the tax did not discriminate against the products of other states, it did not burden INTERSTATE COMMERCE.) In effect, the Court limited the original package doctrine to FOREIGN COMMERCE.

LEONARD W. LEVY
(1986)

## WOODS, WILLIAM B.
### (1824–1887)

William Burnham Woods of Ohio was appointed to the Supreme Court in 1880 after eleven years of service as United States circuit judge for the Fifth Circuit. His tenure on the Supreme Court was brief (1881–1887); virtually all of his OPINIONS for the Court dealt with private law questions that came up under DIVERSITY JURISDICTION. He is remembered primarily for his collaboration with Justice JOSEPH P. BRADLEY, first on circuit, then on the Supreme Court, in the formulation of a jurisprudence for the FOURTEENTH AMENDMENT. Although initially disposed to give the amendment a BROAD CONSTRUCTION, Woods ultimately retreated in the face of a more circumspect majority on the Supreme Court.

Woods's first meeting with Bradley, who had been assigned to the circuit upon his appointment to the Supreme Court, occurred at New Orleans in 1870. There they advanced a broad interpretation of the Fourteenth Amendment's PRIVILEGES AND IMMUNITIES clause in *Live Stock Dealers & Butchers Assn. v. Crescent City Co. & Board of Metropolitan Police* (1870), the first case, Woods noted in the report, in which the amendment was fully considered by a federal tribunal. The privileges and immunities of United States citizens, they contended, embraced all "fundamental rights," including that of pursuing any lawful employment in a lawful manner. "It is possible," Bradley admitted, "that those who framed the article were not themselves aware of the far reaching character of its terms," but its language clearly applied "as well to white as colored persons" and protected the rights of both against arbitrary state laws. Working from memoranda prepared by Bradley, Woods indicated in *United States v. Hall* (1871) that FREEDOM OF SPEECH and FREEDOM OF ASSEMBLY were among the FUNDAMENTAL RIGHTS guaranteed by the Fourteenth Amendment, opening the door for IN-

CORPORATION of the BILL OF RIGHTS through the privileges and immunities clause. Over the dissents of Bradley and three others, however, the Supreme Court rejected each of these pioneering doctrinal formulations in the landmark SLAUGHTERHOUSE CASES (1873). Eleven years later, in BUTCHERS UNION SLAUGHTERHOUSE CO V. CRESCENT CITY LIVE STOCK CO. (1884), Woods joined with Bradley and Justices STEPHEN J. FIELD and JOHN MARSHALL HARLAN in one last trenchant protest against the majority's emasculation of the privileges and immunities clause. Woods surrendered altogether in *Presser v. Illinois* (1886), where he spoke for a unanimous Court in holding that the Bill of Rights was a limitation only on the power of the federal government and in no way restricted the states.

Woods's initial construction of Congress's affirmative powers under the Fourteenth Amendment was especially spacious. In *Hall*, the case of first impression, Woods overruled defendants' demurrer to a conspiracy INDICTMENT under the Civil Rights Act of 1870. A federal statute punishing private action such as assault, he asserted, was certainly an "appropriate" exercise of national power, for "denying the EQUAL PROTECTION OF THE LAWS included the omission to protect, as well as the omission to pass laws for protection." (See STATE ACTION.) In UNITED STATES V. CRUIKSHANK (1874), however, Bradley led a retreat from this position. There counsel for the defendants again attacked the constitutionality of the conspiracy measure, insisting that it usurped the state's exclusive JURISDICTION over crimes such as murder. Woods disagreed and stood on the DOCTRINE advanced in his *Hall* opinion. But Bradley conceded that protection of rights against private action was primarily the duty of the states, and his views prevailed in the Supreme Court. Woods then abandoned the *Hall* formulation. Seven years later in UNITED STATES V. HARRIS (1883), his most important Supreme Court opinion, Woods prominently displayed his penchant for following the lead of others. The results were tragic. In *Harris* he not only embraced Bradley's *Cruikshank* position but also invalidated the Ku Klux Klan Act (FORCE ACT OF 1871) on the grounds that it failed to restrict criminal liability to persons who conspired to divest rights because of the victim's race. As drafted, Woods explained for the Court, the statute covered instances even where whites assaulted whites; consequently it was "broader than is warranted" by the Thirteenth Amendment.

CHARLES W. McCURDY
(1986)

Bibliography

FILLER, LOUIS 1969 William B. Woods. In Leon Friedman and Fred L. Israel (eds.), *The Justices of the United States Supreme Court 1789–1969: Their Lives and Major Opinions*. Pp. 1327–1336. New York: Chelsea House.

FRANTZ, LAURENT B. 1964 Congressional Power to Enforce the Fourteenth Amendment against Private Acts. *Yale Law Journal* 73:1353–1384.

## WOODS v. CLOYD W. MILLER COMPANY
### 333 U.S. 138 (1948)

A unanimous Supreme Court here upheld the Housing and Rent Act of 1947 which had extended wartime price controls into peacetime. Writing for the Court, Justice WILLIAM O. DOUGLAS declared that legislation adopted under the WAR POWERS could constitutionally be continued in effect in economically essential areas of public policy even after the cessation of hostilities.

DAVID GORDON
(1986)

## WOODSON v. NORTH CAROLINA

See: Capital Punishment Cases of 1976

## WORCESTER v. GEORGIA

See: Cherokee Indian Cases

## WORKERS' COMPENSATION LEGISLATION

Workers' compensation legislation provides workers compensation for losses resulting from injury, disablement, or death when the losses result from work-related accidents, casualties, or disease. The legislation replaces TORT liability with a schedule of benefits based upon the loss or impairment of the wage-earning capacity of the worker. All fifty states in the Union have workers' compensation statutes.

Under the COMMON LAW, employers often were able to defeat employees' tort actions by invoking the doctrines of contributory negligence, negligence of fellow servants, or assumption of risk. Frequently the employer did not even need these defenses, for the employee first had to prove the employer's negligence in order to recover. Accordingly, many victims of work-related injuries went uncompensated.

In order to extend the protection afforded workers and to contain costly and time-consuming litigation of industrial accidents, states enacted workers' compensation legislation with no requirement of negligence or fault as a prerequisite to liability. Employers were simultaneously protected against what were perceived to be excessively large JUDGMENTS through a limited and determinant payout. The statutes essentially substitute a system of insurance for liability based on fault.

In *Ives v. South Buffalo Railway Company* (1911) New York's highest court struck down the state's first compulsory compensation requirements as unconstitutional, on the ground that they violated the state and federal DUE PROCESS clauses. However, the Supreme Court held in NEW YORK CENTRAL RAILROAD COMPANY V. WHITE (1917) that a compulsory compensation system does not violate the United States Constitution, at least for "hazardous employment." In the case of the New York statute, New York promptly amended its constitution to authorize compulsory plans.

The general rule in this area of law is that if an injury is fully or partly covered by the statute, the statutory remedy is exclusive. Many jurisdictions do not allow compensation for injuries caused by a worker's willful misconduct or unreasonable failure to observe safety rules or use safety devices.

WILLIAM B. GOULD<br>(1986)

Bibliography

MALONE, WEX S. et al. 1980 *Cases and Materials on Workers' Compensation and Employment Rights*, 2nd ed. St. Paul, Minn: West Publishing Co.

# WORKPLACE HARASSMENT AND THE FIRST AMENDMENT, I

Workplace harassment law punishes speech that is "severe or pervasive" enough to create a "hostile, abusive, or offensive work environment" based on race, religion, sex, national origin, age, disability, or veteran status and, in some jurisdictions, sexual orientation, marital status, or political affiliation.

This is a broad standard, and courts have applied it broadly. Courts have imposed liability based on religious proselytizing, sexually themed jokes, offensive political statements, and other speech that is generally entitled to full FIRST AMENDMENT protection. They have even gone so far as to enjoin private employees from, for instance, any "remarks or slurs contrary to their fellow employees' religious beliefs," and "any and all offensive . . . speech implicating considerations of race."

The breadth of harassment law is exacerbated by its VAGUENESS, and by the fact that it must be enforced by employers. To prevent liability, a cautious employer must suppress any statement that, when aggregated with other statements, may be found by a jury to create an "offensive work environment." This risk causes many employment experts to urge employers to, for instance, take down even legitimate sexually suggestive art, suppress all sexually themed jokes, and "proscribe all speech . . . that may constitute [religious] harassment."

Does harassment law infringe the FREEDOM OF SPEECH? It is a content- and viewpoint-based restriction on speech. It is imposed by the government acting as sovereign, not as employer or proprietor. It does not fit within the traditional exceptions to free speech protections, such as FIGHTING WORDS or OBSCENITY. It cannot be salvaged through a CAPTIVE AUDIENCE argument, because courts have long recognized that, outside the home, people must often be captive to offensive speech (for instance, picket lines that call them "scab," and that they must see twice a day for many weeks). And it cannot fit into a workplace speech exception, because the cases have (correctly) recognized no such exception: The lunchroom or office water cooler is where many Americans talk about social and political questions; and virtually every place, including a street, a university, or a library is, after all, someone's workplace.

Of course, private employers may restrict their employees' speech without First Amendment problems; the First Amendment applies only to government action. But harassment law involves the *government's* pressuring employers to restrict their employees' speech, on pain of multimillion-dollar liability. Private colleges, private newspaper owners, private commercial landlords, and private employers certainly can restrict speech on their own property; but this right does not empower the government to require that these property owners impose such restrictions.

A useful thought experiment is to imagine a law that says: "Any employer who tolerates speech critical of soldiers shall be liable to lawsuits by veterans and relatives of soldiers killed in action who find that such speech creates an offensive work environment for them." (This is actually not far from what veteran-status harassment law does.) Surely this law would be condemned as unconstitutional; and in most respects, harassment law is structurally similar to this proposal.

Lower courts are all over the map on this question; in coming years, the Supreme Court probably will have to resolve it and decide under what conditions harassment law, when applied to otherwise protected speech, is constitutional. (To the extent that harassment law also punishes sexual extortion, unwanted physical conduct, and speech that is otherwise proscribable, such as threats, it poses no First Amendment difficulty.)

EUGENE VOLOKH<br>(2000)

(SEE ALSO: *Employee Speech Rights (Private)*.)

Bibliography

BROWNE, KINGSLEY R. 1991 Title VII as Censorship: Hostile-Environment Harassment and the First Amendment. *Ohio State Law Journal* 52:481–550.

EPSTEIN, DEBORAH 1996 Can a "Dumb Ass Woman" Achieve Equality in the Workplace? Running the Gauntlet of Hostile Environment Harassing Speech. *Georgetown Law Journal* 84:399–451.

ESTLUND, CYNTHIA 1997 Freedom of Expression in the Workplace and the Problem of Discriminatory Harassment. *Texas Law Review* 75:687–777.

VOLOKH, EUGENE 1992 Freedom of Speech and Workplace Harassment Law. *UCLA Law Review* 39:1791–1872.

——— 1997 What Speech Does "Hostile Work Environment" Harassment Law Restrict? *Georgetown Law Journal* 85:627–648.

# WORKPLACE HARASSMENT AND THE FIRST AMENDMENT, II

Claims of sexual and racial harassment have been routinely adjudicated by courts on statutory and constitutional grounds as discrimination for twenty-five years in cases in which many or most of the acts being litigated have been words, pictures, and expressive conduct. Although most sexual and racial harassment plaintiffs seek relief for verbal and other arguably expressive conduct, including threats and rape, in only a very few instances have defendants even attempted to claim that such activity, while actionable as discrimination, is nonetheless protected from judicial redress by the FREEDOM OF SPEECH guarantee of the FIRST AMENDMENT. Defendants have not claimed that saying "have sex with me or you're fired" or "sleep with me and I'll give you an A" or hanging a noose over an African American's desk and posting Ku Klux Klan literature is First Amendment protected expression at work and at school, where—unlike in the rest of society—equality is legally guaranteed. Sexual and racial harassment have been treated as acts rather than as speech.

Those cases that have frontally addressed the potential legal conflict between equality and speech at work have centered on the presence and use of PORNOGRAPHY. In the two such cases to date, *Robinson v. Jacksonville Shipyards* (1991) and *Johnson v. Los Angeles* (1994), one court held that the pornography displays were actionable as discrimination; the other held that they were protected speech, so long as the materials were used privately.

In schools, the question of a possible conflict between equality rights and speech rights in the harassment setting has been adjudicated principally in the context of free expression challenges to antidiscrimination procedures in public universities. In two leading actions in which this challenge has been made, *Doe v. University of Michigan* (1989) and *UMW Post, Inc. v. Board of Regents* (1991), both focusing on the schools' prohibitions on racist and homophobic HATE SPEECH, the procedures lost. The equality interest that might have supported the procedures was barely raised, however.

Legal academics have produced a substantial theoretical literature arguing both sides of this question that the world of practice has treated as a virtual nonissue.

The ultimate resolution of any tension in this unsettled area remains in doubt. The Supreme Court's major PRECEDENT in the area, R. A. V. V. CITY OF ST. PAUL (1992), invalidated a local bias-crime ordinance under the First Amendment in its application to an incident of cross-burning as an impermissible restraint on free speech on the basis of content. Yet the ruling appeared to permit the prohibition of sexually derogatory words under Title VII. Although St. Paul's statute was found to reach too broadly into protected expression, the question remains open whether acts legally actionable as sexual harassment, including those found to create discriminatorily hostile environments when sexually abusive conduct is severe or pervasive, will be found to be protected by the free speech guarantee.

Given the fact that, where STATE ACTION exists, sexual harassment claims are also recognized under the FOURTEENTH AMENDMENT EQUAL PROTECTION clause, a potential for conflict between two clauses of the Constitution arises. The First Amendment may thereby be challenged to adapt to equality rights that were not part of the original Constitution.

CATHARINE A. MACKINNON
(2000)

(SEE ALSO: *Employee Speech Rights (Private); Racial Discrimination; Sex Discrimination.*)

Bibliography

BECKER, MARY 1996 How Free is Speech at Work? *UC Davis Law Review* 29:815–873.

BROWNE, KINGSLEY R. 1991 Title VII As Censorship: Hostile Environment Harassment and the First Amendment. *Ohio State Law Journal* 52:481–550.

FALLON, RICHARD H., JR. 1994 Sexual Harassment, Content Neutrality, and the First Amendment Dog That Didn't Bark. *Supreme Court Review* 1994:1–56.

MACKINNON, CATHARINE A. 1993 *Only Words.* Cambridge, Mass.: Harvard University Press.

VOLOKH, EUGENE 1997 What Speech Does "Hostile Work Environment" Harassment Law Restrict? *Georgetown Law Journal* 85:627–648.

# WORLD WAR I

The United States entered World War I on a note of Wilsonian idealism, but the shattering experience of wartime mobilization ended the era of PROGRESSIVISM. Broad federal powers, previously used to further domestic reforms, were expanded to meet the demands of international conflict. These changes accelerated the trends toward national centralization and executive authority. Thus, ironically, WOODROW WILSON, who had been elected on a platform of firm but limited government control, brought Leviathan to the nation.

With little in the way of precedents, Congress and the President were pressed to extend national government control to a vast new range of complex subjects. The result was multitudinous delegations of power to President Wilson, designed to allow the executive branch to develop programs to meet the changing requirements of a fluid war situation. The breadth of this legislation was startling. Acts to achieve wartime economic mobilization and efficient use of natural resources were augmented by a SELECTIVE SERVICE ACT vesting the President with authority to raise an army by conscription. Espionage and sedition legislation afforded power to punish dissenting expression that might impede the war effort. The Trading with the Enemy Act gave the government power to control trade with enemy nations and to become an alien-property custodian for the duration of the war. The same measure authorized censorship of all communications by mail, cable, radio, or otherwise with foreign countries, and gave the postmaster general almost absolute censorship powers over the American foreign-language press. More sweepingly, the act empowered the chief executive to take over and operate the rail and water transportation systems of the country, along with the telegraph and telephone systems. In creating a modified executive dictatorship for the war period, these actions also raised complex constitutional questions, the answers to which reflected crisis pressures.

The LEVER FOOD AND DRUG CONTROL ACT of 1917 is a case in point. One of the most important war measures, it authorized broad federal control of the domestic economy, a sphere of regulation traditionally reserved to the states. The law gave the President virtually unlimited discretionary power to license the manufacture and distribution of food and related commodities, to take over and operate mines and factories, to regulate exchanges, and to fix commodity prices. The measures precipitated a bitter debate in Congress. Critics called it a violation of the TENTH AMENDMENT and thus of STATES' RIGHTS, but Congress enacted it on a theory of the WAR POWERS and on the argument that the industries controlled were affected with a public interest. During the war, the act was not challenged in court. In *United States v. L. Cohen Grocery Co.* (1921) the Supreme Court voided the price-fixing provision, which failed to specify what constituted unjust process. By concentrating on the detailed phrasing of only one section,

the Court implicitly accepted the broad grant of power. Indeed, it did not reach the issue of the government's authority to regulate prices under the war power. The Court thus recognized that the requirements of modern war left little FEDERALISM in wartime.

Another example of expanding federal power and increased executive authority was presidential seizure and governmental operation of the nation's rail networks. As early as 1916, the Army Appropriations Act had authorized the President "'in time of war . . . to take possession and assume control of any system of transportation." After Wilson took over the railroads in 1917, Congress passed the Railway Administration Act of 1918, providing for government operation of the rails and compensation of their owners. The Court upheld this executive seizure in *Northern Pacific Railway Co. v. North Dakota* (1919), Chief Justice EDWARD D. WHITE invoking Congress's war powers, which, he argued, reach as far as necessary to meet the emergency. The Court also approved the government's takeover of telephone and telegraph lines in a series of cases argued with the railroad suit, notably *Dakota Central Telephone Co. v. South Dakota* (1919).

The wartime period also brought the long crusade for PROHIBITION to a successful conclusion. The Lever Act, under the mandate of preserving scarce food resources, authorized the President to limit or forbid the use of foodstuffs for production of alcoholic beverages. Beginning in December 1917, Wilson issued a series of war proclamations that in effect established near total prohibition. Congress joined in, passing the Wartime Prohibition Act in November 1918, prohibiting the manufacture or distribution of alcoholic beverages until the war came to a formal end and demobilization had been completed.

In the meantime, Congress had approved the EIGHTEENTH AMENDMENT, which the states ratified in January 1919, although not without an attack on the constitutionality of the amendment, the first time such action had taken place. Subsequently, a case reached the Supreme Court, *Rhode Island v. Palmer* (1920), where a large number of "wet" attorneys submitted briefs against the measure. The Constitution, they contended, had not created an unlimited amendment power, and ordinary legislation should not be made part of it. Thus, the Eighteenth Amendment had exceeded legitimate amending limits. Second, they argued that Section 2 altered traditional lines of authority by giving both Congress and the states concurrent enforcement powers, thereby undermining the federal system. The Court brushed aside these and other arguments, seeing no radical invasion of the original POLICE POWER of the states.

The Overman bill came before Congress in early 1918 and provoked substantial resistance to further expansion of presidential authority. The measure was inspired by a desire to introduce some order and flexibility into the chaotic welter of wartime bureaus, commissions, and other special agencies, and to straighten out overlapping jurisdictions that were creating administrative confusion. The measure gave the President a blank check to reorganize the executive agencies "as he may deem necessary, including any functions, duties, and powers hitherto by law conferred on any executive department." The act was to remain in force until a year after the close of the war. By its terms the President could reassign any function, no matter where it had been lodged previously, even if Congress had specifically given that responsibility to a particular agency. The bill imposed no checks on presidential discretion and provided no standards for evaluating the executive's conduct.

The constitutionality of the measure elicited vigorous debate. Supporting senators argued that the bill was a necessity and that it was limited, for the President could create no new functions but merely transfer those already in existence. But critics argued that the bill could not be justified by the war power, for many departments and functions unrelated to the war might be affected by its terms. Republican Senator Frank Brandagee of Connecticut denounced the bill as an attempt to force Congress to "abdicate completely its legislative power and confer it upon the executive branch of the government." The measure passed in the SENATE in late April, with the majority senators overlooking constitutional doubts. A bitter Brandagee then offered an ironic amendment, providing that "if any power, constitutional or not, has been inadvertently omitted from this bill, it is hereby granted in full." The Overman Act, like the Lever Act, demonstrated that ordinary restraints upon delegation of legislative power to the President had been shelved for the duration of the war. The Supreme Court was not afforded an opportunity to pass on the act's constitutionality.

President Wilson wisely did not exercise the tremendous authority delegated to him by this measure and previous ones. Instead, he used ordinance-making powers to establish a series of commissions, boards, bureaus, and government-owned corporations to carry on wartime functions. These agencies included the Office of Food Administration; the Office of Fuel Administration; the National War Labor Board, for handling labor disputes during the war; and other agencies to deal solely with aspects of wartime transportation. The War Industries Board had complete authority over all war purchases and eventually came to exercise almost total control over all industry.

Wilson also created, by EXECUTIVE ORDER, the Committee on Public Information, whose principal responsibility was to "manufacture" public sentiment favorable to measures necessary to the conduct of the war. Run by a flamboyant journalist, George Creel, the committee operated as a loosely knit, ever-changing, but always powerful organization spreading information and propagating beliefs for the American people. With no authority beyond the executive order that created it, the committee worked alongside the Food Administration, the Fuel Administration, and many other agencies, pouring out publicity and propaganda to promote the war effort. It also worked with the Post Office Department to restrict circulation of news and propaganda, in the process imposing a type of informal censorship.

The CIVIL LIBERTIES implications of the Committee on Public Information were troubling to a number of liberal Americans, yet it faced no court challenge to its actions. Other governmental restrictions on individual freedoms, however, did elicit legal challenges. The Selective Service Act was the first. As opponents of the war questioned its constitutionality, lower courts expedited various draft cases, permitting an early test case in the Supreme Court. In the SELECTIVE DRAFT LAW CASES of January 1918, a unanimous Court found the constitutional authority to impose compulsory military service in Congress's powers to declare war and to "raise and support armies." Pushing aside states' rights challenges and a charge that conscription was "involuntary servitude," forbidden by the THIRTEENTH AMENDMENT, the Court also shrugged off a challenge that the measure's conscientious-objection exception violated the FIRST AMENDMENT because it amounted to an ESTABLISHMENT OF RELIGION. Thus sustained, the act was administered at the local level through "neighborhood" civilian draft boards, the government hoping thereby to create the illusion that the process was democratic and free of national control.

While conscription curtailed the freedom of those drafted, the freedom of critics of the war was constrained through other legislation. Although Congress adopted no general censorship law, it did enact two statutes limiting press and speech freedoms. The ESPIONAGE ACT of 1917 drafted to "outlaw spies and subversiveon expression that might disrupt the war effort by causing disobedience in the armed forces or by obstructing recruitment and enlistment. The Justice Department prosecuted more than 2,000 cases under the 1917 act, and a comparable number of prosecutions were brought under similar state laws. Congress's SEDITION ACT amendment (1918) broadened the scope of punishable criticism, providing criminal penalties for eight offenses, coming generally under the concept of SEDITIOUS LIBEL, or unjustifiably criticizing the government, its officials, and its policies. Again the act was enforced broadly to silence public criticism.

Test cases on the two measures had to await the postwar period. In SCHENCK V. UNITED STATES (1919), OLIVER WENDELL HOLMES, JR., spoke for the Court in sustaining the Espionage Act, finding the expression of a Socialist party leader presented a CLEAR AND PRESENT DANGER to recruitment. However, in ABRAMS V. UNITED STATES (1919), when the Court sustained the amended Sedition Act, Holmes dissented, contending that the defendant's expression had not met that standard. The Court sustained all federal and state curtailment of unpopular expression, leaving a restrictive set of precedents to govern interpretation of the First Amendment. But criticism of this behavior and of the Palmer raids spawned a civil liberties movement, which in subsequent years became a central feature of American constitutional development.

PAUL L. MURPHY
(1992)

(SEE ALSO: *Executive Power; Executive Prerogative; Presidential Ordinance-Making Power; Presidential Powers; War, Foreign Affairs, and the Constitution.*)

Bibliography

CUFF, ROBERT D. 1973 *The War Industries Board: Business-Government Relations During World War I.* Baltimore, Md.: Johns Hopkins University Press.

KENNEDY, DAVID M. 1980 *Over Here: The First World War and American Society.* New York: Oxford University Press.

MURPHY, PAUL L. 1979 *World War I and the Origin of Civil Liberties in the United States.* New York: Norton.

# WORLD WAR II

The inherent conflict between the organizational needs of a nation at war and individual rights raised several constitutional questions during World War II. Although the Roosevelt administration showed far greater sensitivity to the protection of CIVIL LIBERTIES than did the administration of WOODROW WILSON, restrictions on individual rights did take place, most notably the incarceration of thousands of Japanese American citizens.

As the nation prepared for war even before Pearl Harbor, FRANKLIN D. ROOSEVELT adopted the view that the Constitution allowed the President great flexibility in meeting his obligations as COMMANDER-IN-CHIEF. With Congress reluctant to act, Roosevelt expanded his foreign policy prerogatives by negotiating secret EXECUTIVE AGREEMENTS. In October 1939 the United States and nineteen Latin American states established a "neutrality belt" through the Declaration of Panama. In August 1941, Roosevelt and Winston Churchill defined the war aims of the free world in the Atlantic Charter. The most famous executive agreement involved a swap of fifty overage American destroyers in exchange for British naval bases in the Caribbean. Although conservatives attacked the President's alleged dictatorial behavior, a majority in Congress and of the American people supported the agreements.

In May 1941 the President proclaimed an "unlimited" emergency to justify various defensive measures for the western hemisphere. What this meant, and on what constitutional authority it relied, remained uncertain. Attorney General FRANK MURPHY declared that "the constitutional duties of the Executive carry with them the constitutional powers necessary for their proper performance." Like ABRAHAM LINCOLN and Woodrow Wilson before him, Roosevelt believed in "the adequacy of the Constitution"—that whether or not specific powers were spelled out, the Constitution granted the President and Congress sufficient authority to meet any crisis.

Roosevelt's use of executive agreements and EXECUTIVE ORDERS, revolutionary in themselves, masked the fact that more often than not he sought—and received—legislative authorization. The Neutrality Act of 1939, the Draft Act of 1940, the Lend-Lease Act of 1941 all gave the President broad discretion; following Pearl Harbor, Congress passed a series of measures giving the chief executive extensive powers over the economy and the government. Roosevelt not only fully utilized these powers but told the nation that he would exercise whatever authority he thought necessary for the successful prosecution of the war. At one point, Roosevelt warned that if Congress failed to repeal a portion of the 1942 Price Control Act, "I shall accept the responsibility and I will act. . . . The President has the power, under the Constitution, and under Congressional acts, to take measures necessary to avert a disaster." But, he assured the people, he would always act with due regard to the Constitution, and "when the war is won, the powers under which I act automatically revert to the people—where they belong."

Although wartime measures are often challenged in the courts, unless there is an egregious violation of a specific constitutional prohibition the courts will affirm the law or delay a decision until the end of hostilities. The Supreme Court heard several challenges to the sweeping price-fixing provisions in the Emergency Price Control Act of 1942. Although Congress had set few limitations on presidential discretion and although these delegations of authority far exceeded the scope of those struck down in SCHECHTER POULTRY CORPORATION V. UNITED STATES (1935), the Court rejected all challenges to the law; the judiciary would not second-guess the executive and legislative branches on what had to be done to win the war.

The seizure of property to avert labor disputes, the freezing of wages and prices, and even executive agreements with the force of law are less troubling in wartime than restrictions placed on individual liberties. In World War I the Justice Department and the postal authorities had shown little regard for constitutional protection of dissident speech and publication. Because no pro-German or antiwar sentiment existed between 1941 and 1945 comparable to that of the earlier war, the Roosevelt adminis-tration expressed—and, for the most part, maintained—a firmer commitment to civil liberties. The wartime Justice Department, headed successively by Frank Mur-phy, ROBERT H. JACKSON, and FRANCIS BIDDLE, showed itself unwilling to stifle expression in the name of national unity.

Many of the worst abuses during World War I had re-sulted from prosecutions under state criminal laws, but the Roosevelt administration avoided a repetition of those abuses. It asserted sole federal control over internal se-curity through the ALIEN REGISTRATION ACT of 1940, and a few months later the Supreme Court affirmed federal su-premacy. In HINES V. DAVIDOWITZ (1941) the Court over-turned a Pennsylvania alien registration statute on the ground that the federal law had preempted the field.

The administration did, however, seek to revoke the citizenship of allegedly disloyal naturalized citizens of German and Italian origin, on the supposition that current disloyal or even dissident behavior proved they had earlier secured citizenship under false pretenses. The case testing this policy happened to involve neither a Nazi nor a Fascist sympathizer but a communist. The government based its case on the claim that membership in the Communist party proved the defendant did not have the "true faith and allegiance to the United States" that citizenship de-manded. The Court, by a 6–3 majority, rejected the gov-ernment's claim in *Schneiderman v. United States* (1943). Although citizenship constituted a privilege granted by Congress, Justice Frank Murphy explained, once a person became a citizen he or she enjoyed all the rights guaran-teed by the Constitution, especially freedom of thought and expression. This and other cases reversing denatural-ization orders indicated how far the nation had moved from its anti-alien hysteria of World War I, at least in terms of freedom to express unpopular ideas.

The country did, however, deprive one group of basic constitutional rights in what has remained the greatest civil liberties stain on the Roosevelt administration's record—the incarceration of more than 110,000 men, women, and children of Japanese origin, two-thirds of them native-born American citizens, solely on the basis of race. Anti-Japanese sentiment, especially on the West Coast, long predated the war, but the attack on Pearl Har-bor whipped it up to hysterical proportions. Fears of fifth-column attacks and sabotage, reinforced by Japanese military victories, led to demands that both Japanese ali-ens (Issei) and American citizens of Japanese ancestry (Ni-sei) be removed from the coastal areas and relocated inland.

On February 19, 1942, President Roosevelt signed EX-ECUTIVE ORDER 9066 authorizing military officials to des-ignate parts of the country as "military areas" from which any and all persons might be excluded. Roosevelt issued the order on his authority as commander-in-chief, but army lawyers feared that so slender a constitutional reed might not support evacuating large numbers of citizens solely on the basis of their race. So they asked for, and received, congressional affirmation of 9066 on March 21.

Three days later, the army declared a curfew along the coastal plain for German and Italian nationals and for all persons of Japanese ancestry. Three days after that, both Issei and Nisei were prohibited from leaving the military areas, and then on May 9, they were excluded from West Coast military zones. Japanese Americans could comply with these contradictory orders only by reporting to cen-tral depots, from which they would be transferred to re-location centers in the interior. Although families could stay together, they had to leave homes and jobs and dis-pose of their property within a matter of days, often sus-taining severe losses in the process. Amazingly, the Japanese and Japanese Americans responded coopera-tively, and a number of younger Nisei volunteered to serve in the army, where their units turned out to be among the most highly decorated in the European theater of opera-tions.

A race-based policy of such striking dimensions could hardly avoid constitutional challenge, and within a short time the nation's High Court had placed its imprimatur on relocation. In *Hirabayashi v. United States* (1943), a native-born citizen had been arrested for failing to report to a control center and for violating the curfew. The Court, speaking through Chief Justice HARLAN F. STONE, unani-mously affirmed the curfew as lying within the presidential WAR POWERS as well as congressional authority. Although any RACIAL DISCRIMINATION was "odious to a free people," the Court would not challenge the discretion of the mili-tary in its interpretation of the war powers.

Justices Murphy, WILLIAM O. DOUGLAS, and WILEY B. RU-TLEDGE entered concurring opinions that practically amounted to dissents; Murphy in particular noted the "melancholy resemblance" between American treatment of the Japanese and the incarceration of Jews in Nazi-dominated Europe. But the three reluctantly consented to what they perceived as an unconstitutional program be-cause of the supposedly critical military situation.

The Justices heard two other relocation cases in 1944, and in both they shied away from the central question of constitutional authority for the detention of peaceful American citizens. In *Korematsu v. United States*, an American citizen, turned down for voluntary army service because of ulcers, had refused to leave the military zone. Justice HUGO L. BLACK's majority opinion tried to separate the issue of exclusion from that of detention and found the war powers of Congress and the President sufficient to sustain an order excluding certain persons, for whatever reason, from designated military zones. Black rather ingenuously said that race had nothing to do with the case; Fred Korematsu had been ordered to leave the area not merely because he was Japanese, but because of military necessity. This time Justices Murphy, Jackson, and OWEN J. ROBERTS entered strenuous dissents, with Roberts bluntly declaring that Korematsu had been convicted "for not submitting to imprisonment in a concentration camp."

The same day, in *Ex parte Endo,* the Court unanimously authorized a writ of HABEAS CORPUS to free Mitsuye Endo, a citizen whose loyalty had been clearly established. Although the AMERICAN CIVIL LIBERTIES UNION had hoped to make this case a challenge to the entire relocation program, Justice Douglas carefully skirted that issue. He confined his ruling to the narrow question of whether the government could detain persons whose loyalty had been confirmed. There is evidence that Douglas wanted to go further, but that even this late in the war, other members of the Court still did not feel free to challenge the relocation program.

There has been general condemnation of the relocation program and of the Court's decisions affirming it from that day forward, and the judgment of history has clearly been that the Roosevelt administration and the Court erred badly. In later years, Congress took several steps to apologize to the Japanese Americans and, at least partially, to indemnify them for their suffering and losses. Gordon Hirabayashi, Fred Korematsu, and others also succeeded in overturning their convictions on the basis of the misconduct of government attorneys in misleading the Supreme Court.

The Court also considered constitutional issues involving treason and espionage. Ever since Aaron Burr's trial (1807), the Court had held to a restricted definition of treason, from which it did not depart during World War II. It drew a sharp distinction between civilian trials for treason and military trials for espionage, in which different criteria for evidence and guilt prevailed.

The first case arose from the arrest of eight Germans put ashore from submarines with orders to sabotage American defense plants. Quickly arrested and tried by military tribunals, which sentenced six of them to death, they appealed to the Supreme Court. In *Ex parte Quirin* (1942) a unanimous Court affirmed the powers of the President to establish military commissions with appropriate jurisdiction to try such cases. Chief Justice Stone's elaborate opinion, however, also implied that even spies and prisoners of war had some rights under the Constitution; that implication had no basis in either American or English law, and the Court soon backed down. In *Ex parte Yamashita* (1946) Stone conceded that a Japanese general tried for war crimes had no constitutional rights and could appeal his conviction only to military authorities.

In two treason cases involving American citizens arising from the German saboteur incident, the Court adhered to a strict interpretation of treason, "levying War against [the United States], or in adhering to their Enemies, giving them Aid and Comfort." In CRAMER V. UNITED STATES (1945), Justice Jackson held for a 5–4 Court that the overt act had to be traitorous in intent by itself, and not merely appear so because of surrounding circumstances. In HAUPT V. UNITED STATES (1947), however, the Court moved away from this rigorous intent standard to sustain the conviction of the father of one of the Germans, whose activities were "'steps essential to his design for treason."

The government then prosecuted other Americans who had aided the enemy during the war, such as Douglas Chandler, who had broadcast English-language programs from Berlin during the war. The Chandler case raised the issue of whether treason could take place only within the territorial limits of the United States. In *Kawakita v. United States* (1952) the Court ruled that treason encompassed activities by American citizens anywhere.

MELVIN I. UROFSKY
(1992)

(SEE ALSO: *Executive Power; Executive Prerogative; Japanese American Cases; Naturalization; Stone Court; War, Foreign Affairs, and the Constitution.*)

Bibliography

HURST, J. WILLARD 1971 *The Law of Treason in the United States.* Westport, Conn.: Greenwood Press.

IRONS, PETER 1983 *Justice at War.* New York: Oxford University Press.

ROSSITER, CLINTON L. 1976 *The Supreme Court and the Commander-in-Chief.* Ithaca, N.Y.:Cornell University Press.

# WORTMAN, TUNIS
## (?–1822)

A New York lawyer prominent in Tammany politics, Tunis Wortman contributed significantly to the emergence of a libertarian theory of the FIRST AMENDMENT following the Sedition Act of 1798. His philosophic book, *An Enquiry, Concerning the Liberty, and Licentiousness of the Press* (1800), whose publication ALBERT GALLATIN and other Jeffersonian congressmen helped underwrite, was the era's most systematic presentation of the case for an absolutist interpretation of freedom of publication (excluding personal libels). Wortman regarded prosecutions for SEDITIOUS LIBEL as incompatible with republican government.

LEONARD W. LEVY
(1986)

# WRIGHT, J. SKELLY
## (1911–1988)

J. Skelly Wright was serving as the U.S. attorney for New Orleans when he was appointed to the Federal District Court bench by President HARRY S. TRUMAN in 1948. At the time of his appointment, Wright, at thirty-seven, was the youngest judge on the federal bench. From 1956 to 1962, he presided over the DESEGREGATION of the New Orleans school district, becoming in the process "the most hated man in New Orleans." Displaying real boldness, he ruled unconstitutional various state statutes adopted with the apparent goal of thwarting desegregation. In 1962, President JOHN F. KENNEDY wanted to appoint Wright to the Fifth Circuit Court of Appeals (whose jurisdiction then covered much of the South). This appointment, however, was blocked by Senator Russell Long, for reasons of Louisiana politics. Instead, the President ended up appointing Wright to the District of Columbia Circuit. Wright sat on this court for twenty-five years, eventually becoming its Chief Judge.

On the D.C. Circuit, Wright proved to be a liberal activist; indeed, his career is one of the purest examples of this genre of judging. A genuinely humble man, he was distinctly gratified by a judicial position that enabled him, in his words, to "make a contribution." He was the author of a large number of noteworthy opinions, dealing with such issues as the unconscionability defense in contract law, the implied warranty of habitability in residential leases, the broad rule-making powers of the Federal Trade Commission, the impermissibility of ex parte contracts in the course of informal rule making, and the proper scope of the National Environmental Protection Act. Designated in one instance to sit as a district court judge, Wright issued an opinion that required the D.C. school system to equalize spending between schools that were de facto white and those that were black, to cure problems of teacher segregation, and to end a rigid system of student ability grouping. In its time, the Wright opinion was a leader in the development of what was then called the "new equal protection."

Judge Wright's interests in public law were also reflected in his authorship of a significant number of major law review articles, including one advocating the revival of the antidelegation doctrine. In his articles and his opinions as well, Wright was a remarkable stylist, writing with a directness and sense of purpose that gave his work a distinctive voice.

Having retired from the court a year before, Wright died in 1988.

GARY T. SCHWARTZ
(1992)

Bibliography

MILLER, ARTHUR SELWYNE 1984 *A "Capacity for Outrage": The Judicial Odyssey of J. Skelly Wright.* Westport, Conn.: Greenwood Press.

SYMPOSIUM 1980 Judge J. Skelly Wright. *Hastings Constitutional Quarterly*:857–999.

# WRIGHT v. VINTON BRANCH OF MOUNTAIN TRUST BANK OF ROANOKE
## 300 U.S. 440 (1937)

Despite the decision in LOUISVILLE JOINT STOCK LAND BANK V. RADFORD (1935), Congress had to act on behalf of farmers losing their farms through foreclosures. A revised FRAZIER-LEMKE ACT fixed a three-year stay of proceedings with the proviso that a federal bankruptcy court might shorten that period if the economic emergency ended. The new act also provided that the mortgagee retained a lien on the property. But except for a few other minor changes the act remained the same, allowing the bankrupt mortgagor to retain possession of the property and to purchase it at its newly appraised value. Justice LOUIS D. BRANDEIS, for a unanimous Supreme Court, found that the new act was free of the objectionable features of the original and did not violate the Fifth Amendment's DUE PROCESS clause. President FRANKLIN D. ROOSEVELT'S COURT-PACKING plan may have influenced the Court to temper its views.

LEONARD W. LEVY
(1986)

# WRIGHTWOOD DAIRY CO., UNITED STATES v.
## 315 U.S. 110 (1942)

# ROCK ROYAL CO-OP, INC., UNITED STATES v.
## 307 U.S. 533 (1939)

These decisions are among the more significant results of the post-1936 interpretation of the COMMERCE CLAUSE as a source of federal power extending to virtually the entire national economy. The AGRICULTURAL MARKETING AGREEMENT ACT of 1937 authorized the secretary of agriculture to fix minimum prices for all milk in INTERSTATE COMMERCE, or burdening or affecting commerce. In *Rock Royal* the price-fixing provisions governed sales by local dairy farmers to dealers who processed the milk and transported it. Those opposing federal authority contended that the regulated transactions included INTRASTATE COMMERCE whose sales were fully completed *before* any interstate commerce began. Holding the statute constitutional, the Court declared that the national power to fix production quotas and prices applied to local milk because its marketing was "inextricably intermingled with and directly affected the marketing of milk which moved across state lines." In *Wrightwood*, the milk subject to regulation under the same statute was entirely intrastate and none of it was intermingled with milk that crossed state lines. Nevertheless the Court unanimously held that it was the EFFECT ON INTERSTATE COMMERCE, not the source of the injury to it, that was "the sole criterion of Congressional power." Accordingly, the commerce power extended to intrastate transactions whose regulation made the regulation of interstate commerce effective, including intrastate transactions whose competitive price affected interstate ones. Both cases were decided on a thoroughgoing application of the SHREVEPORT DOCTRINE.

LEONARD W. LEVY
(1986)

# WRIT OF ASSISTANCE

See: Assistance, Writ of

# WRIT OF CERTIORARI

See: Certiorari, Writ of

# WRIT OF ERROR

See: Error, Writ of

# WRIT OF HABEAS CORPUS

See: Habeas Corpus

# WRIT OF MANDAMUS

See: Mandamus, Writ of

# WRIT OF PROHIBITION

See: Prohibition, Writ of

# WRITS OF ASSISTANCE CASE

See: Paxton's Case

# WYGANT v. JACKSON BOARD OF EDUCATION
## 476 U.S. 267 (1986)

Although the *Wygant* decision did not produce a majority opinion, it advanced the growth of constitutional doctrine governing AFFIRMATIVE ACTION. A school board and a teachers' union had approved an affirmative action plan as a response to complaints of past RACIAL DISCRIMINATION in the hiring of teachers. To maintain minority-hiring gains in the event of a contraction in teacher employment, the plan protected some minority teachers against layoffs. When some minority teachers were retained while some nonminority teachers with greater seniority were laid off, the laid-off teachers challenged the layoff provision in federal court. By a 5–4 vote, the Supreme Court held the provision a violation of the EQUAL PROTECTION OF THE LAWS.

Justice LEWIS F. POWELL, for four Justices, concluded that the appropriate STANDARD OF REVIEW was STRICT SCRUTINY. Using this standard, he rejected the lower courts' two justifications for the layoff provision: as a means of keeping minority teachers to serve as role models for students and as a remedy for past societal discrimination. He agreed that past discrimination by the school board itself was a COMPELLING STATE INTEREST that would justify some RACE-CONSCIOUS remedies, assuming that the board had evidentiary support for determining that remedial action was warranted. Here no such determination had been made, but Justice Powell was unwilling to remand the case for exploration of this issue. Even if the purpose were remedial, he concluded, the layoff provision was an impermissible remedy because it was too burdensome on innocent nonminority teachers. Preferential hiring, he intimated, would be acceptable; layoffs, however, placed the whole burden on particular individuals.

Justice SANDRA DAY O'CONNOR concurred separately to emphasize that a public employer that wished to adopt an affirmative action plan need not make a contemporaneous finding of past wrongdoing. Such a requirement would undermine the employer's incentive to meet its civil rights obligations. Rather, the employer could show "a disparity between the percentage of qualified blacks on a school's teaching staff and the percentage of qualified minorities in the relevant labor pool" that would support a prima facie case of EMPLOYMENT DISCRIMINATION under Title VII of the CIVIL RIGHTS ACT OF 1964. Justice BYRON R. WHITE added a brief concurrence emphasizing the difference between a hiring preference and a preference in avoiding layoffs.

Justice THURGOOD MARSHALL dissented, joined by Justices WILLIAM J. BRENNAN, JR., and HARRY A. BLACKMUN. Marshall argued that the case should be remanded to the trial court for further findings about the board's past discrimination, but also disagreed with the majority Justices' disposition on the merits. The board's interest in preserving a valid policy for affirmative action in hiring, he argued, was a sufficient state purpose, and the layoff provision was sufficiently narrowly tailored to pass the test of constitutionality. Justice JOHN PAUL STEVENS also dissented, arguing that the board's interest in educating children justified measures to assure a racially integrated faculty, irrespective of any showing of past discrimination.

*Wygant* was a way station on the road to RICHMOND V. J. A. CROSON CO. (1989), in which a majority of the Supreme Court explicitly adopted the rhetoric of strict scrutiny for reviewing state-sponsored affirmative action programs. Justice Powell's and Justice O'Connor's opinions, taken together, also provided a "how to do it" manual for public employers that want to adopt affirmative-action plans for achieving integrated work forces.

KENNETH L. KARST
(1992)

Bibliography

KARST, KENNETH L. 1989 *Belonging to America: Equal Citizenship and the Constitution*, pages 158–167. New Haven, Conn.: Yale University Press.
SULLIVAN, KATHLEEN 1986 Sins of Discrimination: Last Term's Affirmative Action Cases. *Harvard Law Review* 100:78–98.

# *WYMAN v. JAMES*
## 400 U.S. 309 (1971)

In *Wyman* the Supreme Court held that a recipient of Aid to Families with Dependent Children must permit a home visit by a caseworker, when the law requires it, or forfeit her right to public assistance. The Supreme Court did not consider it to be a search in FOURTH AMENDMENT terms. Even if the visit were a search, the Court said it was reasonable: it was made for the benefit of the child; it was "a gentle means" of assuring that tax funds are properly spent; the caseworker was not a "uniformed authority"; and the recipient had the choice of invoking her right to refuse or forfeiting the benefits. Three dissenting Justices (WILLIAM O. DOUGLAS, WILLIAM J. BRENNAN, THURGOOD MARSHALL), protested that the Court had granted more pro-

tection to a commercial warehouse than to a "poor woman's home."

JACOB W. LANDYNSKI
(1986)

# *WYNEHAMER v. PEOPLE OF NEW YORK*
## 13 N.Y. 378 (1856)

Although out of joint with its times, *Wynehamer* became a classic case of pre-1937 American constitutional history, exemplifying our constitutional law as a law of judicially implied limitations on legislative powers, drawn from the DUE PROCESS clause for the benefit of VESTED RIGHTS. The case involved the constitutionality of a state prohibition act. More than a dozen states had such legislation before the Civil War. The New York law involved in *Wynehamer* prohibited the sale of intoxicating liquor and the possession of liquors for sale, and it ordered the forfeiture and destruction of existing supplies as public nuicances. The fundamental issue raised by such legislation was whether property which had not been taken for a public use could be destroyed in the name of the public health and morals, without any compensation to the owner. Everywhere, except in New York, the state courts held that a mere license to sell liquor was not a contract in the meaning of the CONTRACT CLAUSE, and that a charter to make and sell liquor was subject to the RESERVED POLICE POWER to alter, amend, or repeal it. Moreover, liquor, like explosives or narcotics, was a peculiar kind of property, dangerous to the public safety, morals, and health. Legislatures could never relinquish their control over such matters, not even by a contract in the form of a charter. As Chief Justice ROGER B. TANEY had said in the 1847 LICENSE CASES, nothing in the United States Constitution prevented a state from regulating the liquor traffic "or from prohibiting it altogether."

The New York Court of Appeals, however, held the state prohibition statute unconstitutional on the grounds that it violated the due process clause of the state constitution. The various opinions of the state judges used the novel concept of SUBSTANTIVE DUE PROCESS about half a century before the Supreme Court of the United States accepted that concept. The conventional and previously sole understanding of due process had been that it referred to regularized and settled procedures insuring mainly a fair accusation, hearing, and conviction. And, the doctrine of vested rights notwithstanding, the orthodox view of the POLICE POWER authorized the legislature, as Chief Justice LEMUEL SHAW of Massachusetts had said, "to declare the possession of certain articles of property ...

unlawful because they would be injurious, dangerous, and noxious; and by due process of law, by proceeding IN REM, to provide both for the abatement of the nuisance and for the punishment of the offender, by the seizure and confiscation of the property, by the removal, sale or destruction of the noxious article" (*Fisher v. McGirr*, 1854). Accordingly the opinion of the New York court was startling when it said, "All property is alike in the characteristic of inviolability. If the legislature has no power to confiscate and destroy property in general, it has no such power over any particular species." The court showed that the prohibition statute simply annihilated existing property right in liquors. The crucial lines of the opinion declared that the right not to be deprived of life, liberty, or property without due process of law "necessarily imports that the legislature cannot make the mere existence of the rights secured the occasion of depriving a person of any of them, even by the forms which belong to "due process of law.' For if it does not necessarily import this, then the legislative power is absolute."

Thus even if the legislature provided all the forms of due process by laying down proper procedures for prosecuting violators of the statute, as in this case, due process had still been denied. The court, in effect, looked at the substance of the statute, found it denied persons of their property, and then held it unconstitutional for denying "due process," even if it did not deny due process. One can make sense out of this by realizing that the court had rewritten the due process clause to mean that property cannot be deprived with or without due process. The Court in effect redpenciled the due process clause out of the constitution, or as EDWARD S. CORWIN said, *Wynehamer* stands for "nothing less than the elimination of the very phrase under construction from the constitutional clause in which it occurs." The difficulty, however, is that the court had to its own mind kept and relied on the due process clause. It added a new meaning to supplement the old one. It constitutionally changed process into substance by holding that the statute's infirmity lay in what it did, not how it did it. Due process as a substantive limitation on legislative powers was then an absurd concept. Substantive process was oxymoronic, like thunderous silence.

Another way of understanding *Wynehamer*'s substantive due process is to realize that the court believed that due process had substance. The court in effect accused the legislature of retaining the forms of due process without its substance, that is, of providing mere empty formalities and labeling them due process, because the effective deprivation of property was not by judicial process but by legislative fiat.

*Wynehamer*, an aberration at the time, was everywhere repudiated yet destined for ultimate acceptance by the highest court of the land and destined, too, to become the source of a major doctrine in American constitutional history.

LEONARD W. LEVY
(1986)

Bibliography

CORWIN, EDWARD S.  1948  *Liberty against Government*. Chap. 3. Baton Rouge: Louisiana State University Press.
MOTT, RODNEY L.  1926  *Due Process of Law*. Pages 311–326. Indianapolis: Bobbs-Merrill.

# WYTHE, GEORGE
## (1726–1806)

George Wythe served almost uninterruptedly in Virginia's House of Burgesses from 1754 to 1775 and was a delegate to the FIRST CONTINENTAL CONGRESS in 1774, later signing the DECLARATION OF INDEPENDENCE. With his pupil Thomas Jefferson (John Marshall and HENRY CLAY were also his students) and EDMUND PENDLETON, Wythe revised Virginia's laws. He was appointed to the Virginia Court of Chancery in 1778; one year later he became the first professor of law in the United States, enabling him to influence the course of American jurisprudence. His opinion in COMMONWEALTH V. CATON (1782) approved, in theory, a court's right to restrain a legislative act violative of the constitution. Wythe was a delegate to the CONSTITUTIONAL CONVENTION OF 1787 and chairman of its rules committee, but judicial duties obliged him to leave the convention early. At the Virginia convention he worked for RATIFICATION OF THE CONSTITUTION. Wythe opposed slavery and freed the slaves he inherited.

DAVID GORDON
(1986)

Bibliography

CLARKIN, WILLIAM  1970  *Serene Patriot: A Life of George Wythe*. Albany, N.Y.: Alan Publications.

# WYZANSKI, CHARLES E., JR.
## (1906–1986)

Charles E. Wyzanski, Jr., contributed to constitutional law both as a barrister and as a federal judge. He was the son of a Boston real estate developer and graduated with distinction from Phillips Exeter Academy, Harvard College, and Harvard Law School. He had been attracted to law by a reading of *Freedom of Speech*, by ZECHARIAH CHAFEE, JR. On the recommendation of Professor FELIX FRANKFURTER, he served successively as law clerk to Judges AUGUSTUS N. HAND and LEARNED HAND, whose broad cultivation, legal acumen, and largeness of spirit became the greatest influence on his professional life.

After a brief association with the Boston law firm of Ropes and Gray, and not yet thirty years old, he was called to Washington to be solicitor of the Labor Department under Secretary Frances Perkins. There he drafted the public works provisions of the Industrial Recovery Act and the Charter of the International Labor Organization. For the Immigration and Naturalization Service, then within the Labor Department, he drew up a plan for collective private guarantees of the welfare of immigrants, which unblocked entry into the United States; this remained his proudest achievement.

He was brought to the Office of the SOLICITOR GENERAL in 1935 to strengthen the presentation of crucial New Deal cases in the Supreme Court. He had a central role in the government's victories in the National Labor Relations Act and the Social Security cases in 1937, although when congratulated on his success he would reply that the cases were won "not by Mr. Wyzanski but by Mr. Zeitgeist." He had been on the point of resigning because of his opposition to the Court-packing plan, but was persuaded by Judge A. N. Hand to remain until he could present the government's arguments in these cases.

After returning to Ropes and Gray, he was appointed by President FRANKLIN D. ROOSEVELT in 1941 to the UNITED STATES DISTRICT COURT in Massachusetts, where he served for forty-five years. As a judge he was morally demanding, bold, and courageous, sometimes testing the limits of judicial power, whether on the side of severity, as in municipal corruption cases, or of leniency, as in cases of draft resistance. Notable among the latter was *United States v. Sisson* (1969), where he rejected the defendant's argument that the VIETNAM WAR was an undeclared war and therefore unconstitutional, holding that this claim presented a POLITICAL QUESTION. Wyzanski then set aside the guilty verdict on the ground, barely advanced by counsel, that the defendant's CONSCIENTIOUS OBJECTION to the conflict, though not strictly satisfying the statutory religious standard for an exemption, nevertheless warranted acquittal under American moral traditions. In his judicial opinions, as in his probing essays and speeches, Wyzanski's search was for enduring, historically attested values.

PAUL A. FREUND
(1992)

(SEE ALSO: *Immigration and Alienage.*)

Bibliography

IN MEMORIAM 1987 In Memoriam: Charles E. Wyzanski, Jr. *Harvard Law Review* 100:705–727.
WYZANSKI, C. E., JR. 1965 *Whereas: A Judge's Premises.* Boston: Little, Brown.

# YAKUS v. UNITED STATES
## 321 U.S. 414 (1944)

The EMERGENCY PRICE CONTROL ACT of 1942 delegated power to fix prices and rents to the Office of Price Administration (OPA). Under the act, challenges to the legality of OPA regulations could not be made in federal district court enforcement proceedings, even those aimed at imposing criminal penalties, but must be made in separate proceedings in the EMERGENCY COURT OF APPEALS. The Supreme Court sustained this limitation on the district courts in civil enforcement proceedings in *Lockerty v. Phillips* (1944). In *Yakus*, the Court upheld the limitation in the context of a criminal prosecution. The Court also rejected attacks on the act as an unconstitutional DELEGATION OF POWER for failing to provide sufficient guidelines. Chief Justice HARLAN FISKE STONE, for the Court, said that the act contained specific objectives: "to stabilize prices and to prevent speculative, unwarranted and abnormal increases in prices and rents." It also mentioned standards for price-setting: administrators should consult industry and consider current prices. Because the act accorded with earlier decisions and because its standards were "sufficiently definite and precise," Stone could find no unauthorized delegation of power. Justice OWEN ROBERTS, dissenting, believed that the case presented substantially the same issue as SCHECHTER POULTRY CORPORATION V. UNITED STATES (1935) which the majority, he said, had clearly overruled. Justice WILEY RUTLEDGE also dissented, joined by Justice FRANK MURPHY. Rutledge argued that Congress could not constitutionally command the federal courts to enforce administrative orders, disregarding their possible unconstitutionality. The Rutledge view seems likely to prevail in the absence of a wartime emergency.

DAVID GORDON
(1986)

# YAMASHITA, IN RE
## 327 U.S. 1 (1947)

A 6–2 Supreme Court here refused to consider the claim of an enemy officer, charged with war crimes before an American military tribunal in the Philippines, that he had been denied the DUE PROCESS OF LAW guaranteed by the Fifth Amendment. The Court held that it had JURISDICTION only to consider whether the military tribunal had authority to try the accused.

When General Tomoyuki Yamashita surrendered in 1945, an American military commission tried him on charges that he permitted atrocities against both civilians and prisoners of war, in violation of the law of war. Yamashita's military counsel applied to the Supreme Court for leave to file petitions for writs of HABEAS CORPUS and prohibition, challenging the jurisdiction and legal authority of the commission. Chief Justice HARLAN FISKE STONE, for the majority, denied leave to file but wrote an opinion on the jurisdictional issues. He found that Congress had legally authorized the commission's establishment under the WAR POWERS, and that the charge was adequate to state a violation of the law of war. Stone also denied that the American Articles of War (which incorporated the law of war) forbade the admission of hearsay and opinion EVIDENCE.

Justices FRANK MURPHY and WILEY RUTLEDGE, dissenting, argued eloquently for the extension of the due process clause.

DAVID GORDON
(1986)

## *YARBROUGH, EX PARTE*
### 110 U.S. 651 (1884)

This is the only nineteenth-century case in which the Supreme Court sustained the power of the United States to punish private persons for interfering with VOTING RIGHTS. Yarbrough and other members of the Ku Klux Klan assaulted a black citizen who voted in a congressional election. The United States convicted the Klansmen under a federal statute making it a crime to conspire to injure or intimidate any citizen in the free exercise of any right secured to him by the laws of the United States. The Court, in a unanimous opinion by Justice SAMUEL F. MILLER, held that the United States "must have the power to protect the elections on which its existence depends, from violence and corruption." Miller's reasoning is confused. Congress had passed the statute in contemplation of its power to enforce the FOURTEENTH AMENDMENT. In UNITED STATES V. CRUIKSHANK (1876) the Court had ruled that the same statute could not reach private, rather than state, actions. Miller thought the situation different when Congress sought to protect rights constitutionally conferred, and he stressed Article I, section 4, which empowered Congress to alter state regulations for the election of members of Congress. But that provision did not apply here. In UNITED STATES V. REESE (1876) the Court had ruled that the FIFTEENTH AMENDMENT did not confer the right to vote on anyone, but only a right to be free from RACIAL DISCRIMINATION in voting. Here, however, Miller ruled that "under some circumstances," the Fifteenth Amendment, which was not the basis of the statute, may operate as the source of a right to vote. In the end Miller declared, "But it is a waste of time to seek for specific sources of the power to pass these laws." In JAMES V. BOWMAN (1903), involving the right to vote in a federal election, the Court held unconstitutional an act of Congress without reference to *Yarbrough*.

LEONARD W. LEVY
(1986)

## YATES, ROBERT
### (1738–1801)

Judge Robert Yates, who in 1777 had served on the committee that drafted the state constitution, was a delegate from New York to the CONSTITUTIONAL CONVENTION OF 1787. A trusted, if undistinguished, follower of Governor George Clinton, Yates represented the antinationalist viewpoint then dominant in New York politics. He and JOHN LANSING consistently outvoted ALEXANDER HAMILTON and kept New York in the STATES' RIGHTS camp. But on July 10 Yates and Lansing walked out, charging that the Convention was exceeding its authority.

In the contest over RATIFICATION OF THE CONSTITUTION Yates was an active ANTI-FEDERALIST. His "Brutus" letters were an able and articulate presentation of the dangers opponents feared would result from adoption of the Constitution, including annihilation of the states and usurpation by the federal courts. Yates was a delegate to the New York ratifying convention where he voted against ratification.

Yates kept notes of the debates of the federal convention from its first meeting through July 5. He did not publish the notes himself, but they were published in 1821 and are, after JAMES MADISON's, the best record of the early proceedings.

DENNIS J. MAHONEY
(1986)

Bibliography

ROSSITER, CLINTON   1966   *1787: The Grand Convention.* New York: Macmillan.

## *YATES v. UNITED STATES*
### 354 U.S. 298 (1957)

Following DENNIS V. UNITED STATES (1951), Smith Act conspiracy prosecutions were brought against all second-rank United States Communist party officials, and convictions were secured in every case brought to trial between 1951 and 1956. In June 1957, however, the Supreme Court, in *Yates*, reversed the convictions of fourteen West Coast party leaders charged with Smith Act violations. The Court, speaking through Justice JOHN MARSHALL HARLAN, declared that the *Dennis* decision had been misunderstood. The Smith Act did not outlaw advocacy of the abstract doctrine of violent overthrow, because such advocacy was too remote from concrete action to be regarded as the kind of indoctrination preparatory to action condemned in *Dennis*. The essential distinction, Harlan argued, was that those to whom the advocacy was addressed had to be urged to *do* something, now or in the future, rather than merely *believe* in something. Without formally repudiating the "sliding scale" reformulation of CLEAR AND PRESENT DANGER set forth in the *Dennis* opinion, the Court erected a stern new standard for evaluating convictions under the Smith Act, making conviction under the measure difficult. As to INDICTMENTS for involvement in organizing the Communist party in the United States, the Court also took a narrow view. Organizing, Harlan maintained, was only the original act of creating such a group, not any continuing process of proselytizing and recruiting. Since the indictments had been made some years following the postwar organizing of their party, the federal three-year statute of limitations had run out. The Court cleared five of the defendants, remanding the case of nine others for retrial. The ruling brought an abrupt end to the main body of Smith Act prosecutions then under way.

PAUL L. MURPHY
(1986)

## *YBARRA v. ILLINOIS*
### 444 U.S. 85 (1979)

Although three dissenting Justices complained that the Supreme Court majority had narrowed the STOP-AND-FRISK RULE of TERRY V. OHIO (1968), Justice POTTER STEWART for the Court did not doubt that an officer may pat down a suspect for a concealed weapon. Stewart regarded *Terry* as an exception to the requirement of PROBABLE CAUSE. Here no such cause existed to search a person suspected neither of criminal activity nor of having a weapon. A police officer, having a warrant to search a tavern and its bartender, patted down a bystander, felt no weapon, but removed from his pocket a cigarette pack containing heroin. The Court reversed the man's conviction, because the warrant did not include him, and probable cause to search him was absent.

LEONARD W. LEVY
(1986)

## YELLOW DOG CONTRACT

The yellow dog contract was a device used by employers prior to the NEW DEAL era to prevent collective bargaining by employees. By a yellow dog contract a worker agreed not to join or remain a member of a labor organization and to quit his job if he joined one. At a time in our history when the courts shaped the law so that its major beneficiary was industrial capitalism, yellow dog contracts were enforceable, even though workers had little choice in accepting their terms. Workers either signed such contracts or forfeited the opportunity of working. In effect, a yellow dog contract blackmailed an employee into promising not to join a union; his supposed free choice to accept a job or look elsewhere for work turned out to be a choice between being blackmailed or blacklisted. In one perspective, yellow dog contracts robbed workers of their

FREEDOM OF CONTRACT. The courts thought otherwise, however.

In the 1890s fifteen states enacted laws that promoted COLLECTIVE BARGAINING by outlawing yellow dog contracts, and in 1898 section 10 of the ERDMAN ACT, passed by Congress, also outlawed their use by interstate railroads. In *Adair v. United States* (1908) the Supreme Court held the Erdman Act unconstitutional. SUBSTANTIVE DUE PROCESS of law provided one ground of decision. The Court reasoned that section 10 abridged freedom of contract, a liberty the Court found in the Fifth Amendment's DUE PROCESS CLAUSE, because Congress had violated the right of workers to make contracts for the sale of their labor. In COPPAGE V. KANSAS (1915) the Court applied this reasoning to state statutes that had banned yellow dog contracts.

Having disabled both the national commerce power and the STATE POLICE POWER from forbidding yellow dog contracts, the Court then sustained the legality of such contracts. In HITCHMAN COAL AND COKE CO. V. MITCHELL (1917) the Court reversed a federal circuit court's determination that a yellow dog contract was not an enforceable contract. Justice MAHLON PITNEY for a six-member majority declared, "The employer is as free to make non-membership a condition of employment as the worker is free to join the union." The Court added that the right to make such a contract was "part of the constitutional rights of personal liberty and private property, not to be taken away even by legislation," which the Court had already voided. The extent to which these decisions thwarted unionization cannot be gauged.

Congress revived the Erdman Act's provision when it passed the Railway Labor Act of 1926, and in the NORRIS-LAGUARDIA ACT of 1932 declared yellow dog contracts to be contrary to American public policy and unenforceable "in any court of the United States." The major industrial states passed "little Norris-LaGuardia acts." By the time these statutes came before the Supreme Court, it found ways to sustain them.

LEONARD W. LEVY
(1986)

## *YICK WO v. HOPKINS*
### 118 U.S. 356 (1886)

This is one of the basic decisions interpreting the EQUAL PROTECTION OF THE LAWS clause of the FOURTEENTH AMENDMENT. A San Francisco ordinance made criminal the conduct of a laundry business in any building not made of stone or brick, with such exceptions for wooden structures as administrative officials might make. Officials used their discretion in a grossly discriminatory manner, licensing about eighty wooden laundries run by Caucasians and denying licenses to about two hundred applicants of Chinese extraction. The Supreme Court unanimously held, in an opinion by Justice STANLEY MATTHEWS, that the ordinance, though racially neutral on its face, was applied so unequally and oppressively by public authorities as to deny equal protection. Thus the Court looked beyond the law's terms to its racially discriminatory administration and applied the benefits of the Fourteenth Amendment to Oriental ALIENS, that is, "to all persons . . . without regard to any difference of race, of color, or of nationality."

LEONARD W. LEVY
(1986)

## *YOUNG, EX PARTE*
### 209 U.S. 123 (1908)

The question in this case—one of the most important of the present century—was whether a citizen might resort to a federal court to vindicate a constitutional right against state infringement and, pending a final JUDGMENT, obtain freedom from civil or criminal suits by a temporary INJUNCTION directed to an officer of the state. The Supreme Court held that, the ELEVENTH AMENDMENT notwithstanding, a federal court might issue such an injunction.

A Minnesota statute fixed railroad rates and (to deter institution of a TEST CASE) made the officers and employees of the railroads personally liable to heavy fines and imprisonment if those rates were exceeded. A STOCKHOLDER'S SUIT in EQUITY was filed in federal Circuit Court to prevent enforcement of or compliance with the statute, on the ground that it violated the FOURTEENTH AMENDMENT by depriving the railroads of property without DUE PROCESS OF LAW. The federal court issued a temporary injunction restraining the state attorney general, Edward T. Young, from taking steps to enforce the statute. When Young defied the injunction the court found him in contempt and committed him to the custody of the United States marshal.

Young petitioned the Supreme Court for a writ of HABEAS CORPUS, contending that the suit for injunction was really against the state and that, under the Eleventh Amendment, the state could not be sued in federal court without its consent. The Court denied Young's petition, Justice JOHN MARSHALL HARLAN alone dissenting.

Justice RUFUS PECKHAM, for the Court, argued that if the Minnesota law was unconstitutional, then Young, attempting to enforce it, was stripped of his official character and became merely a private individual using the state's name to further his own illegitimate end. Incongruously, the end Young was furthering was unconstitutional only because it involved STATE ACTION. The "private wrong" was a fiction

adopted by the Court to circumvent the Eleventh Amendment.

Congress reacted to the *Young* decision by passing a law (substantially repealed in 1976) requiring that federal court injunctions against enforcement of state laws alleged to be unconstitutional issue only from special THREE-JUDGE COURTS and providing, in such cases, for direct APPEAL to the Supreme Court.

The doctrine of *Young* remains valid law today. Although it originally arose in connection with due process protection of economic liberty, the doctrine provides a remedy for state action infringing CIVIL RIGHTS or CIVIL LIBERTIES. But the doctrine of *Young* applies only to equitable relief, and the Eleventh Amendment remains bar to actions for monetary damages that will be paid out of the state treasury.

DENNIS J. MAHONEY
(1986)

(SEE ALSO: *Edelman v. Jordan; Osborn v. Bank of the United States.*)

## *YOUNG v. AMERICAN MINI THEATRES, INC.*
### 427 U.S. 50 (1976)

In *Young v. American Mini Theatres, Inc.* the Supreme Court upheld a Detroit ZONING ordinance requiring adult theaters to be located certain distances from residential areas and specified businesses. Four Justices led by Justice JOHN PAUL STEVENS argued that adult movies ranked low in the hierarchy of FIRST AMENDMENT values. Four dissenting Justices led by Justice POTTER STEWART argued that the First Amendment recognized no hierarchy for types of protected speech. Justice LEWIS F. POWELL agreed with the dissent, but voted to uphold the ordinance, arguing that the theater owners had asserted no First Amendment interest of their own and that the First Amendment interests of others, including moviemakers and potential audiences, were not endangered.

STEVEN SHIFFRIN
(1986)

## *YOUNGER v. HARRIS*
### 401 U.S. 37 (1971)

Harris, indicted under California's CRIMINAL SYNDICALISM LAW, sought a federal court INJUNCTION to compel the district attorney to cease prosecution in the state court. The district court held the law unconstitutional and issued the injunction. The Supreme Court reversed, 8–1, severely limiting DOMBROWSKI V. PFISTER (1965).

Justice HUGO L. BLACK, for the Court, rested decision on two interlocking grounds. First, a state prosecution was pending; because any claim that the underlying state law was unconstitutional could be made in the state proceeding, there was no "irreparable injury" to justify an injunction. Second, the national government should avoid intruding into "the legitimate activities of the state." Although a federal court might enjoin a state prosecution commenced in bad faith to harass the exercise of FIRST AMENDMENT rights, the claim that the law was unconstitutional on its face did not satisfy this bad-faith harassment requirement. (See ABSTENTION DOCTRINES.)

After *Younger,* the California courts held the syndicalism law invalid.

KENNETH L. KARST
(1986)

# *YOUNGSTOWN SHEET & TUBE CO. v. SAWYER*
### 343 U.S. 579 (1952)

In a landmark restriction on presidential power, the Supreme Court in 1952 held invalid President HARRY S. TRUMAN's seizure of the steel mills. Justice HUGO L. BLACK, joined by five other Justices, delivered the opinion of the Court. Chief Justice FRED M. VINSON, dissenting with Justices STANLEY F. REED and SHERMAN MINTON, believed that military and economic emergencies justified Truman's action.

Each of the five concurring Justices wrote separate opinions, advancing different views of the President's emergency power. Only Justices Black and WILLIAM O. DOUGLAS insisted on specific constitutional or statutory authority to support presidential seizure of private property. Assigning the lawmaking function exclusively to Congress, they allowed the President a role only in recommending or vetoing laws. On existing precedent, this concept of the SEPARATION OF POWERS doctrine was far too rigid. Previous Presidents had engaged directly in the lawmaking function without express constitutional or statutory authority, often with the acquiescence and even blessing of Congress and the courts.

The other four concurring Justices (FELIX FRANKFURTER, ROBERT H. JACKSON, HAROLD BURTON, and TOM C. CLARK) did not draw such a strict line between the executive and legislative branches, nor did they try to delimit the President's authority to act in future emergencies. Frankfurter thought it inadvisable to attempt a comprehensive defi-

nition of presidential power, based on abstract principles, without admitting powers that had evolved by custom: a "systematic, unbroken, executive practice, long pursued to the knowledge of the Congress and never before questioned . . . may be treated as a gloss on "executive Power." Burton withheld opinion on the President's constitutional power when facing an "imminent invasion or threatened attack," while Clark agreed that the Constitution gave the President extensive authority in time of grave and imperative national emergency.

Jackson identified three categories of presidential power, ranging from actions based on express or implied congressional authorization (putting executive authority at its maximum) to executive measures that were incompatible with congressional policy (reducing presidential power to its lowest ebb). In between lay a "zone of twilight" in which President and Congress shared authority. Jackson said that congressional inertia, indifference, or acquiescence might enable, if not invite, independent presidential action. He further argued that the ENUMERATED POWERS of the President required "scope and elasticity" and said he would "indulge the widest latitude of interpretation" when presidential powers were turned against the outside world for the security of the United States.

Considering the four concurrences and three dissents, the Steel Seizure Case was far from a repudiation of the inherent power doctrine. Nevertheless, a majority of the Court did reach agreement on important principles: presidential actions, including those of an "emergency" nature, are subject to JUDICIAL REVIEW; the courts may enjoin executive officers from carrying out presidential orders that conflict with statutory policy or the Constitution; and independent presidential powers in domestic affairs are especially vulnerable to judicial scrutiny when Congress has adopted a contrary statutory policy. The Steel Seizure Case has supplied the Supreme Court with an important precedent for curbing subsequent exercises of presidential power in areas such as the Pentagon Papers case (NEW YORK TIMES V. UNITED STATES, 1971), electronic surveillance, IMPOUNDMENT, and EXECUTIVE PRIVILEGE.

LOUIS FISHER
(1986)

(SEE ALSO: *Executive Order 10340; Steel Seizure Controversy.*)

Bibliography

MARCUS, MAEVA 1977 *Truman and the Steel Seizure Case: The Limits of Presidential Power.* New York: Columbia University Press.

WESTIN, ALAN F. 1958 *The Anatomy of a Constitutional Law Case.* New York: Macmillan.

# ZABLOCKI v. REDHAIL
## 434 U.S. 374 (1978)

In LOVING V. VIRGINIA (1967) the Supreme Court had struck down a MISCEGENATION statute flatly forbidding interracial marriage, resting decision on both EQUAL PROTECTION and SUBSTANTIVE DUE PROCESS grounds. In *Zablocki* the Court protected the "right to marry" in a setting where race was irrelevant. Wisconsin required a court's permission for the marriage of a resident parent who had been ordered to support a child not in his or her custody. Permission would be granted only when the candidate proved compliance with the support obligation and showed that the children were not likely to become public charges. Because he could not comply with the law, Redhail was denied a marriage license. The Supreme Court held, 8–1, that this denial was unconstitutional.

The case produced six opinions. Justice THURGOOD MARSHALL, for the majority, rested on equal protection grounds. Marriage was a FUNDAMENTAL INTEREST, protected by the constitutional RIGHT OF PRIVACY. The Wisconsin law interfered "directly and substantially" with the right to marry and was not necessary to effectuate important state interests. Justice POTTER STEWART concurred on due process grounds. Justice LEWIS F. POWELL, also concurring, objected to the Court's STRICT SCRUTINY test; such an inquiry would cast doubt on such limits on marriage as "bans on incest, bigamy, and homosexuality, as well as various preconditions to marriage, such as blood tests." Using a more relaxed STANDARD OF REVIEW, he nonetheless found the statute wanting on both due process and equal protection grounds. Justice JOHN PAUL STEVENS concurred, calling the law a "clumsy and deliberate legislative discrimination between the rich and poor" whose irrationality violated equal protection. Justice WILLIAM H. REHNQUIST, in lone dissent, rejected the notion that marriage was a "fundamental" right and argued for the strict judicial nonscrutiny that had become his trademark.

For all the diversity of the Justices' views, little turns on the choice between equal protection and due process grounds, or on conclusory assertions about the proper standard of review. *Zablocki* makes clear that significant state interference with the freedom to marry demands correspondingly weighty justification.

KENNETH L. KARST
(1986)


# ZEMEL v. RUSK
## 381 U.S. 1 (1965)

In *Zemel* the Supreme Court sustained (6–3) the constitutionality of the secretary of state's refusal to validate passports for travel to Cuba. Chief Justice EARL WARREN, for the majority, rejected two arguments for the petitioner: that he had a RIGHT TO TRAVEL under the DUE PROCESS clause of the Fifth Amendment; and that he had a FIRST AMENDMENT right to travel to Cuba to gather information.

DENNIS J. MAHONEY
(1986)

(SEE ALSO: *Richmond Newspapers, Inc. v. Virginia.*)

## ZENGER'S CASE
### (1735)

Had John Peter Zenger, the printer of the *New-York Weekly Journal*, attacked the provincial assembly of New York instead of its hated royal governor, he would have been summarily convicted at the bar of the house, jailed, and forgotten by posterity. But he was tried by a jury, brilliantly defended by a great lawyer, and saved for posterity by James Alexander's report of *A brief Narrative of the Case and Tryal of John Peter Zenger* (1736). Alexander, the editor of the paper which Zenger printed, probably wrote the articles that led to the prosecution and, as a lawyer, prepared the case for Andrew Hamilton.

Scalded by the paper's weekly articles against his administration, Governor William Cosby ordered an information against its printer for SEDITIOUS LIBEL; a GRAND JURY had refused to indict, the assembly had refused to cooperate, and the local government, defending "liberty of the press," protested. Zenger, in other words, symbolized the popular party against a detested administration. Not surprisingly the jury acquitted him after brief deliberation, against the instructions of Chief Justice James DeLancey, who presided at the trial before the Supreme Court of Judicature.

The law was against Zenger. Both the prosecutor and the judge accurately informed the jury that seditious libel consisted of scandalizing the government by adversely reflecting on those entrusted with its administration, by publishing material tending to breed popular contempt for the administration, or by alienating the affections of the people for government in any way. Moreover, the truth of a libel magnified its criminality. But Hamilton's reply had greater appeal. If the people could not remonstrate against the oppressions and villainies of their governors, confining themselves always to truthful accusations, they would in no time lose their liberty and property. Hamilton did not repudiate the law of seditious libel; he argued, rather, that Zenger's statements being true were not libels. When the court rejected the proposition that truth should be a defense to a charge of seditious libel, Hamilton appealed to the jury over the court. He argued that the jury, like the press, was a bastion of popular liberty. It should ignore the court's instruction to return a special verdict on the question whether Zenger had, in fact, published the statements charged; a special verdict would leave to the court a ruling on the question of law whether those statements were criminal. Hamilton urged the jury, instead, to return a general verdict of "not guilty," thus deciding the law as well as the fact. The jury returned a general verdict of "not guilty."

The jury's general verdict was a safe way of striking at the unpopular governor and endorsing the right of the people, through the press, to criticize their government. The jury's verdict did not, however, alter the settled law. Not until the Sedition Act of 1798 (see ALIEN AND SEDITION ACTS) did truth as a defense and the power of the jury to render a general verdict in cases of seditious libel become part of American law; and, as the enforcement of that infamous statute showed, embattled libertarians came to discover that they should have repudiated the doctrine of seditious libel rather than grasp at Zengerian principles.

LEONARD W. LEVY
(1986)

(SEE ALSO: *New York Times v. Sullivan; People v. Croswell.*)

Bibliography

KATZ, STANLEY NIDER  1972  *A Brief Narrative of the Case and Trial of John Peter Zenger ... by James Alexander.* Cambridge, Mass.: Harvard University Press.
LEVY, LEONARD W.  1960  Did the Zenger Case Really Matter? Freedom of the Press in Colonial New York. *William and Mary Quarterly,* 3d ser., 17:35–50.

## ZOBEL v. WILLIAMS

See: Privileges and Immunities; Right to Travel

## ZONING

When a local government decides how to allocate land uses it acts under the POLICE POWER exercised by the states and their governmental subdivisions to regulate for the public health, safety, and welfare. The first zoning ordinances appeared early in the twentieth century as a result of urbanization and the encroachment of factories and noxious uses in residential neighborhoods. In EUCLID V. AMBLER REALTY (1926) the Supreme Court upheld a comprehensive local zoning ordinance, rejecting a SUBSTANTIVE DUE PROCESS attack. Although today's zoning ordinances are more sophisticated than the simple division of land uses upheld in *Euclid*, the basic constitutional issues raised by zoning decisions remain an unusually stable area of constitutional law.

Because a zoning ordinance is adopted by a legislative body, and because zoning amendments are legislative decisions in most states, the constitutional scrutiny applied to zoning is no different from that applied to LEGISLATION at any governmental level. The courts use the due process analysis of *Euclid* to uphold zoning if they find a reasonable relationship between the zoning and the city's police power objectives. Like other social and economic legislation, zoning comes to court clothed with a presumption of validity. A court will not question the wisdom or the motives of legislators. If a court finds any RATIONAL BASIS to support zoning as an implementation of the public health, safety, and welfare, the ordinance will be held valid. A court considers factors such as increased traffic and congestion, compatibility with adjacent uses, and impact on land values of neighboring properties. Courts often apply a fairly debatable rule: if reasonable minds can differ on the reasonableness of an ordinance, the municipal decision must be upheld. Some state courts are more willing than the federal courts to use theories of STATE CONSTITUTIONAL LAW to strike down zoning regulations.

Although a court may be reluctant to question the police power objectives of zoning, it may be more inclined to examine the effects of a zoning restriction on the value of property. Even when a zoning ordinance achieves public objectives, it may be held to be a TAKING OF PROPERTY if it denies a property owner all economic use of his land. The leading case is *Pennsylvania Coal Co. v. Mahon* (1972).

Other guarantees may also serve as bases for constitutional challenges to zoning ordinances. The FIRST AMENDMENT repeatedly forms the basis of attacks on local sign ordinances and ordinances regulating adult businesses. In the 1960s and 1970s, a series of "exclusionary zoning" cases challenged a municipal refusal to rezone to allow mobile homes, apartments, or anything other than single family homes on large lots. Arguing that such practices violated the EQUAL PROTECTION clause, landowners and hopeful future residents had varying success. The Supreme Court was originally not interested in fashioning a federal constitutional remedy. In ARLINGTON HEIGHTS V. METROPOLITAN HOUSING DEVELOPMENT CORP. (1977) it severely restricted the authority of the federal courts to find RACIAL DISCRIMINATION in exclusionary zoning. Some state courts have been more aggressive. In *Southern Burlington County NAACP v. Mount Laurel* (1975), for example, the New Jersey Supreme Court held, on both substantive due process and equal protection grounds, that a municipality cannot close its doors to the housing needs of the region, including low-cost housing. Then, in *Cleburne v. Cleburne Living Center, Inc.*, (1985) the Supreme Court gave some indication that it would examine more rigorously the exclusionary classifications in zoning ordinances.

Zoning ordinances also require landowners to obtain development permission under a host of administrative procedures that vary from one JURISDICTION to another. Whether it be subdivision or site plan approval, variances, special or conditional uses, or environmental permits, the process is rife with constitutional pitfalls for local administrative bodies. The standards for approving or denying permits must be made specific in the ordinance; otherwise, a state court may hold that the ordinance unconstitutionally delegates legislative authority to an administrative body. Applicants must be given PROCEDURAL DUE PROCESS, including NOTICE and an opportunity to be heard, and, in some states, even quasi-judicial procedures. The agency's decision must be based on evidence sufficient to support it.

Perhaps the most serious danger to the constitutional status of zoning is the threat of a radical departure in the judicial relief afforded a victorious landowner. Under the SEPARATION OF POWERS doctrine, the traditional judicial relief for invalid zoning has been to grant an INJUNCTION prohibiting its enforcement and allow the municipality to rezone. A few courts in the 1970s held that confiscatory zoning amounted to taking of property for public purposes and required cities to compensate landowners. The Supreme Court has not yet decided the availability of this remedy under the federal Constitution.

Damages for a taking may be available under SECTION 1983, TITLE 42, UNITED STATES CODE. In MONELL V. DEPARTMENT OF SOCIAL SERVICES (1978) the Supreme Court held that municipalities can be sued under Section 1983, and the specter of money damages for any denial of constitutional rights in the zoning process became a reality. The damage to a landowner whose economic return is restricted by zoning and who must proceed through a time-consuming local zoning process perhaps including litigation can be substantial. The traditional constitutional deference afforded local government under its police power remains, but the possible consequences of stepping outside constitutional bounds have become severe.

Zoning ordinances now include sophisticated techniques, such as computer-based point systems for approving new development, incentive and bonus programs, and the transfer of development rights. These new techniques have not yet been extensively tested in the courts, but they raise constitutional problems similar to those raised by conventional zoning. Judicial attention in the years to come will focus on the constitutionality of these techniques and on the suitability of a damage remedy in zoning cases.

DANIEL R. MANDELKER
BARBARA ROSS
(1986)

Bibliography

MANDELKER, DANIEL R. 1982 *Land Use Law*. Charlottesville, Va.: Michie Co.

WILLIAMS, NORMAN, JR. 1974 *American Land Planning Law*. Chicago: Callaghan Co.

# ZONING
## (Update)

Zoning—the public allocation into use categories of privately held land and the subsequent regulation of land development—is by and large a legislative act undertaken by thousands of local governments. As a legislative exercise of the POLICE POWER, zoning determinations have long been presumed to be constitutionally and statutorily valid by the courts. This acceptance has not prevented the leveling of strong criticism at the zoning process. The criticism occurs on two levels: first, there is the belief that expanded social welfare conceptions of the police power are uneasily reconciled with private PROPERTY and the constitutional protection thereof, and second, even if a particular zoning measure is constitutional, its effects may be economically inefficient or socially exclusionary.

The constitutional concern over modern zoning practice is often raised in terms of the Fifth Amendment's prohibition against the TAKING OF PROPERTY for public use without the payment of JUST COMPENSATION. This constraint against the federal government has been judicially incorporated into the Fourteenth Amendment's due process limitations upon state power. Influenced by WILLIAM BLACKSTONE and JOHN LOCKE, the founding generation understood the taking clause as protecting the liberty engendered by private property. The most significant—perhaps only—qualifications of this liberty was that property not be used to injure one's neighbor. The principal drafter of the Fifth Amendment, JAMES MADISON, affirmed this conception by excluding from the idea of private property uses that harmed others by not "leav[ing] to everyone else the like advantage."

Had modern applications of zoning been similarly confined to the prevention of harms or nuisances, such public control would have triggered little controversy. It is scarcely surprising, though now often overlooked, that the initial case favoring zoning's general constitutionality, EUCLID V. AMBLER REALTY (1926), stressed a nuisanceprevention rationale for public land use control. The highly influential AMICUS CURIAE brief filed in favor of the ordinance for the National Conference of City Planning stated that "the Police Power endeavors to prevent evil by checking the tendency toward it and seeks to place a margin of safety between that which is permitted and that which is sure to lend to injury or loss." Fifty years later, however, conceptions of the police power had grown dramatically, and as a consequence, governmental control of land use had become far more intrusive. The opinion of the Supreme Court in PENN CENTRAL TRANSPORTATION CO. V. NEW YORK CITY (1978) boldly asserted that valid exercises of the police power do not depend upon the "noxious' quality of the prohibited uses but rather on the ground that the restrictions were reasonably related to the implementation of a policy . . . expected to produce a widespread public benefit."

Recent Supreme Court decisions may curb somewhat this accelerated growth of the police power. Rejecting as constitutionally infirm prior state doctrines that had limited relief for overzealous zoning exercises to invalidation, the Court has now clearly held that the compensation clause of the Fifth Amendment is self-executing; moreover, the Court held in *First English Evangelical Lutheran Church v. County of Los Angeles* (1987) that just compensation is required for either temporary or permanent regulatory takings—that is, substantial deprivations of economic value by regulation. In actual fact, the Court seldom finds a taking based on a single factor of economic loss; generally, the Court also considers the investment expectations of the landowner and the relations between the zoning objective and both the regulatory means chosen to advance it and the landowner's contribution to the land use "problem" to be solved. One closely divided opinion of the Court, *Nollan v. California Coastal Commission* (1987), held that zoning regulations are to be judged by a higher level of judicial scrutiny than that applied in the review of other economic legislation.

Other cases such as LORETTO V. TELEPROMPTER, INC. (1982) make clear that any regulation accompanied by physical invasion or use by the public merits compensation. The total destruction of a "core" PROPERTY RIGHT, such as the ability to transfer property interests at death, is also constitutionally improper, as the Court stated in *Hodel v. Irving* (1987). Overall, the Court's recent decisions in the zoning area have established a constitutional outer limit premised upon the distinction between regulatory burdens that can be fairly placed on an individual property owner and those that more properly should be borne by the community at large through a general tax system. This principle may mean that exotic uses of the zoning power—say, withholding permits until an office developer makes a substantial contribution to the community housing or cultural fund—will be increasingly suspect.

While the Supreme Court has recently addressed the more egregious abuses of zoning, there remains substantial dissatisfaction with zoning in practice. Zoning measures continue to be presumed valid in state and federal courts, notwithstanding the Supreme Court's suggestion of heightened scrutiny, with the frequent result that physically and locationally indistinguishable property may be arbitrarily classed in very different use categories. Because the resulting value differences are profound, zoning measures are under the constant pressure of amendment or variance without meaningful standards. Regrettably, in some communities the wide-ranging discretion exercised by zoning authorities has invited serious corruption.

Zoning is also heavily reliant upon "specification standards" to accomplish land use objectives indirectly. For example, a typical zoning ordinance employs height, minimum lot, and setback limits to encourage open space and reduce or disperse density. Meeting these limits produces a monotony of design and often is not the most efficient method for accomplishing the open space objective. The advance specification of use requirements also introduces a highly static impediment to change, not to mention the consequent administrative cost and delay. These costs are most often borne by the housing consumer, and recent studies suggest that the regulatory cost burden can be as high as twenty-five percent of the finished price of a home.

The costly administrative burdens of zoning are most strongly felt by the least-affluent. To the extent that the lower economic stratum of society in a given locality is predominantly composed of members of racial or ethnic minorities, this cost obviously worsens racial SEGREGATION in housing. Absent a racially discriminatory intent, this effect does not constitute a denial of federal EQUAL PROTECTION, as the Court held in ARLINGTON HEIGHTS V. METROPOLITAN HOUSING DEVELOPMENT CORPORATION (1977). However, zoning practices that exclude low-income, multifamily structures and have a discriminatory impact may constitute a violation of the federal Fair Housing Act, as was the case in *Huntington Branch, NAACP v. Town of Huntington* (2nd Cir. 1988).

A variety of alternatives have been proposed to overcome these undesirable zoning effects. To supply greater procedural and distributional fairness, some JURISDICTIONS have more closely tied zoning decisions to comprehensive land use planning and have recharacterized zoning as an administrative or quasi-judicial decision. Such reforms not only supply more specific standards but also supply greater judicial supervision of abuse. To enhance the efficiency of zoning, other communities are experimenting with performance zoning systems, which articulate overall community objectives but leave the actual accomplishment of land use goals to plans submitted by individual landowners. Finally, as a general matter, modern subdivisions with detailed private covenants restricting use are less affected by zoning than are land areas within older central cities. Arguably, private controls are more sensitive to market demand and less apt to be applied uniformly over an entire community, and are therefore less exclusionary.

DOUGLAS W. KMIEC
(1992)

Bibliography

BLAESSER, BRIEN et al., eds. 1989 *Land Use and the Constitution*. Chicago: Planners Press, American Planning Association.
ELLICKSON, ROBERT C. and TARLOCK, A. DAN, eds. 1981 *Land Use-Controls.* Boston: Little, Brown.
HAAR, CHARLES M. and KAYDEN, JERROLD S., eds. 1989 *Zoning and the American Dream.* Chicago: Planners Press, American Planning Association.
KMIEC, DOUGLAS W. 1986 *Zoning and Planning Deskbook* (with 1991 Supplement). New York: Clark Boardman.
SYMPOSIUM 1988 The Jurisprudence of Takings. *Columbia Law Review* 88:1581–1794.

# ZORACH v. CLAUSEN
## 343 U.S. 306 (1952)

This was the Supreme Court's second encounter with a RELEASED TIME program. In MCCOLLUM V. BOARD OF EDUCATION (1948), the Court had invalidated an arrangement by which teachers entered public schools to provide religious instruction. *Zorach* involved New York City's released time program in which instruction was offered off school premises. According to the requests of their parents, public school children were allowed to leave school for specific periods of time to go to church facilities. Nonparticipating students remained in their regular classrooms.

Justice WILLIAM O. DOUGLAS delivered the OPINION OF THE COURT sustaining the constitutionality of New York's program. Douglas emphasized that, as opposed to *McCollum*, no public facilities were used. The schools, Douglas said, were merely rearranging their schedules to accommodate the needs of religious people.

Justices HUGO L. BLACK, ROBERT H. JACKSON, and FELIX FRANKFURTER dissented. Black and Jackson argued that children were compelled by law to attend public schools and that to release them for religious instruction used governmental compulsion to promote religion. In a slap at Douglas's presumed presidential ambitions, Jackson said, "Today's judgment will be more interesting to students of psychology and of the judicial process than to students of constitutional law."

RICHARD E. MORGAN
(1986)

# ZURCHER v. STANFORD DAILY
## 436 U.S. 547 (1978)

In *Zurcher v. Stanford Daily* the police chief of Palo Alto, California, appealed from a federal district court decision declaring that a search of a college newspaper's office conducted pursuant to a duly authorized search warrant had infringed upon FOURTH AMENDMENT and FIRST AMENDMENT rights. There was no contention that the newspaper or any of its staff was reasonably suspected of the commission of a crime, nor was it contended that weapons, contraband, or fruits of a crime were likely to be found on the premises. Rather, the police secured a warrant on a showing of PROBABLE CAUSE for the conclusion that photographic evidence of a crime was to be found somewhere on the premises. The Supreme Court thus addressed the general question of the standards that should govern the issuance of warrants to search the premises of persons not themselves suspected of criminal activity and the specific question whether any different standards should apply to press searches.

The Court ruled that the innocence of the party to be searched was of no constitutional importance. So long as there was probable cause to believe that evidence of a crime was to be found on premises particularly described, no further showing was needed. Specifically, the Court declined to "reconstrue the Fourth Amendment" to require a showing that it would be impracticable to secure a subpoena *duces tecum* before a warrant could be issued.

That the party to be searched was a newspaper the Court regarded as of some moment but not enough to prefer subpoenas over warrants. Instead, the Court observed that warrant requirements should be applied with "particular exactitude when First Amendment interests would be endangered by the search."

The Court expressed confidence that magistrates would safeguard the interests of the press. Magistrates could guard against the type of intrusions that might interfere with the timely publication of a newspaper or otherwise deter normal editorial and publication decisions. Nor, said the Court, "will there be any occasion or opportunity for officers to rummage at large in newspaper files." The Court asserted that "the warrant in this case authorized nothing of this sort." Yet, as the *Zurcher* opinion discloses, the police searched "the Daily's photographic laboratories, filing cabinets, desks, and wastepaper baskets." The Court's application of the particular exactitude standard seems neither particular nor exact.

*Zurcher* is the first case squarely to authorize the search and seizure of mere evidence from an innocent party; it has raised difficult questions of Fourth Amendment reasonableness as applied to searches of other innocent third parties such as lawyers and judges. By suggesting that press values be considered in an assessment of reasonableness, it opens the door for further distinctions between searches of media and nonmedia persons. By suggesting that the reasonableness of a search is a requirement that may go beyond probable cause and specificity, it reopens discussion about the relationship between the two clauses of the Fourth Amendment.

STEVEN SHIFFRIN
(1986)

# Appendix 1

# The Call for the Federal Constitutional Convention

RESOLUTION OF CONGRESS

*1787, February 21*

WHEREAS there is provision in the Articles of Confederation & perpetual Union for making alterations therein by the Assent of a Congress of the United States and of the legislatures of the several States; And whereas experience hath evinced that there are defects in the present Confederation, as a means to remedy which several of the States and particularly the State of New York by express instruction to their delegates in Congress have suggested a convention for the purposes expressed in the following resolution and such Convention appearing to be the most probable means of establishing in these states a firm national government

Resolved that in the opinion of Congress it is expedient that on the second Monday in May next a Convention of delegates who shall have been appointed by the several states be held at Philadelphia for the sole and express purpose of revising the Articles of Confederation and reporting to Congress and the several legislatures such alterations and provisions therein as shall when agreed to in Congress and confirmed by the states render the federal constitution adequate to the exigencies of Government & the preservation of the Union.

# Appendix 2

# *Articles of Confederation*

*Articles of Confederation and perpetual Union between the States of New Hampshire, Massachusetts Bay, Rhode Island and Providence Plantations, Connecticut, New York, New Jersey, Pennsylvania, Delaware, Maryland, Virginia, North Carolina, South Carolina, and Georgia.*

ARTICLE I. The style of this Confederacy shall be "The United States of America."

ART. II. Each State retains its sovereignty, freedom, and independence, and every power, jurisdiction, and right, which is not by this Confederation expressly delegated to the United States in Congress assembled.

ART. III. The said States hereby severally enter into a firm league of friendship with each other, for their common defence, the security of their liberties, and their mutual and general welfare, binding themselves to assist each other against all force offered to, or attacks made upon them, or any of them, on account of religion, sovereignty, trade, or any other pretence whatever.

ART. IV. The better to secure and perpetuate mutual friendship and intercourse among the people of the different States in this Union, the free inhabitants of each of these States, paupers, vagabonds and fugitives from justice excepted, shall be entitled to all the privileges and immunities of free citizens in the several States; and the people of each State shall have free ingress and regress to and from any other State, and shall enjoy therein all the privileges of trade and commerce, subject to the same duties, impositions, and restrictions as the inhabitants thereof respectively, provided that such restrictions shall not extend so far as to prevent the removal of property imported into any State, to any other State of which the owner is an inhabitant; provided also, that no imposition, duties, or restriction shall be laid by any State, on the property of the United States, or either of them.

If any Person guilty of or charged with treason, felony, or other high misdemeanor in any State, shall flee from justice, and be found in any of the United States, he shall, upon demand of the governor or executive power of the State from which he fled, be delivered up and removed to the State having jurisdiction of his offence.

Full faith and credit shall be given in each of these States to the records, acts, and judicial proceedings of the courts and magistrates of every other State.

ART. V. For the more convenient management of the general interests of the United States, delegates shall be annually appointed in such manner as the legislature of each State shall direct, to meet in Congress on the first Monday in November, in every year, with a power reserved to each State to recall its delegates, or any of them, at any time within the year, and to send others in their stead, for the remainder of the year.

No State shall be represented in Congress by less than two, nor by more than seven members; and no person shall be capable of being a delegate for more than three years in any term of six years; nor shall any person, being a delegate, be capable of holding any office under the United States for which he or another for his benefit receives any salary, fees, or emolument of any kind.

Each State shall maintain its own delegates in a meeting of the States, and while they act as members of the committee of the States.

In determining questions in the United States, in Congress assembled, each State shall have one vote.

Freedom of speech and debate in Congress shall not be impeached or questioned in any court or place out of Congress, and the members of Congress shall be protected in their persons from arrests and imprisonments, during the time of their going to and from, and attendance on, Congress, except for treason, felony, or breach of the peace.

ART. VI. No State, without the consent of the United States in Congress assembled, shall send any embassy to, or receive any embassy from, or enter into any conference, agreement, alliance, or treaty with any king, prince, or state; nor shall any person holding any office of profit or trust under the United States, or any of them accept of any present, emolument, office, or title of any kind whatever from any king, prince, or foreign state; nor shall the United States in Congress assembled, or any of them, grant any title of nobility.

No two or more States shall enter into any treaty, confederation, or alliance whatever between them, without the consent of the United States in Congress assembled, specifying accurately the purposes for which the same is to be entered into, and how long it shall continue.

No State shall lay any imposts or duties, which may interfere with any stipulations in treaties entered into by the United States in Congress assembled, with any king, prince, or state, in pursuance of any treaties already proposed by Congress, to the courts of France and Spain.

No vessels of war shall be kept up in time of peace by any State, except such number only as shall be deemed necessary by the United States in Congress assembled, for the defence of such State or its trade; nor shall any body of forces be kept up by any State, in time of peace, except such number only as in the judgment of the United States in Congress assembled shall be deemed requisite to garrison the forts necessary for the defence of such State; but every State shall always keep up a well regulated and disciplined militia, sufficiently armed and accoutred, and shall provide and constantly have ready for use, in public stores, a due number of field-pieces and tents, and a proper quantity of arms, ammunition, and camp equipage.

No State shall engage in any war without the consent of the United States in Congress assembled, unless such State be actually invaded by enemies, or shall have received certain advice of a resolution being formed by some nation of Indians to invade such State, and the danger is so imminent as not to admit of a delay till the United States in Congress assembled can be consulted; nor shall any State grant commissions to any ships or vessels of war, nor letters of marque or reprisal, except it be after a declaration of war by the United States in Congress assembled, and then only against the kingdom or state, and the subjects thereof, against which war has been so declared, and under such regulations as shall be established by the United States in Congress assembled, unless such State be infested by pirates, in which case vessels of war may be fitted out for that occasion, and kept so long as the danger shall continue, or until the United States in Congress assembled shall determine otherwise.

ART. VII. When land forces are raised by any State for the common defence, all officers of or under the rank of colonel shall be appointed by the legislature of each State respectively, by whom such forces shall be raised, or in such manner as such State shall direct; and all vacancies shall be filled up by the State which first made the appointment.

ART. VIII. All charges of war and all other expenses that shall be incurred for the common defence or general welfare, and allowed by the United States in Congress assembled, shall be defrayed out of a common treasury, which shall be supplied by the several States, in proportion to the value of all land within each State, granted to or surveyed for any person, as such land and the buildings and improvements thereon shall be estimated according to such mode as the United States in Congress assembled, shall from time to time direct and appoint.

The taxes for paying that proportion shall be laid and levied by the authority and direction of the Legislatures of the several States within the time agreed upon by the United States in Congress assembled.

ART. IX. The United States in Congress assembled shall have the sole and exclusive right and power of determining on peace and war, except in the cases mentioned in the sixth article—of sending and receiving ambassadors—entering into treaties and alliances, provided that no treaty of commerce shall be made whereby the legislative power of the respective States shall be restrained from imposing such imposts and duties on foreigners as their own people are subjected to, or from prohibiting the exportation or importation of any species of goods or commodities whatsoever—of establishing rules for deciding, in all cases, what captures on land or water shall be legal, and in what manner prizes taken by land or naval forces in the service of the United States shall be divided or appropriated—of granting letters of marque and reprisal in times of peace—appointing courts for the trial of piracies and felonies committed on the high seas, and establishing courts for receiving and determining finally appeals in all cases of captures, provided that no member of Congress shall be appointed a judge of any of the said courts.

The United States in Congress assembled shall also be the last resort on appeal in all disputes and differences now subsisting or that hereafter may arise between two or more States concerning boundary, jurisdiction, or any other cause whatever; which authority shall always be exercised in the manner following:—Whenever the legislative or executive authority or lawful agent of any State in controversy with another shall present a petition to Congress stating the matter in question and praying for a hearing, notice thereof shall be given by order of Congress to the legislative or executive authority of the other State in controversy, and a day assigned for the appearance of the parties by their lawful agents, who shall then be directed to appoint, by joint consent, commissioners or judges to constitute a court for hearing and determining the matter in question; but if they cannot agree, Congress shall name three persons out of each of the United States, and from the list of such persons each party shall alternately strike out one, the petitioners beginning, until the number shall be reduced to thirteen; and from that number not less than seven, nor more than nine names, as Congress shall direct, shall, in the presence of Congress, be drawn out by lot, and the persons whose names shall be so drawn, or any five of them, shall be commissioners or judges, to hear and finally determine the controversy, so always as a major part of the judges who shall hear the cause shall agree in the determination; and if either party shall neglect to attend at the day appointed, without showing reasons, which Congress shall judge sufficient, or, being present, shall refuse to strike, the Congress shall proceed to nominate three persons out of each State, and the Secretary of Congress shall strike in behalf of such party absent or refusing; and the judgment and sentence of the court to be appointed, in the manner before prescribed, shall be final and conclusive; and if any of the parties shall refuse to submit to the authority of such court, or to appear or defend their claim or cause, the court shall nevertheless proceed to pronounce sentence or judgment, which shall in like manner be final and decisive, the judgment or sentence and other proceedings being in either case transmitted to Congress, and lodged among the acts of Congress for the security of the parties concerned: provided that every commissioner, before he sits in judgment, shall take an oath, to be administered by one of the judges of the Supreme or Superior court of the State where the cause shall be tried, *well and truly to hear and determine the matter in question according to the best of his judgment, without favor, affection, or hope of reward,* provided also that no State shall be deprived of territory for the benefit of the United States.

All controversies concerning the private right of soil, claimed under different grants of two or more States, whose jurisdictions as they may respect such lands and the States which passed such grants are adjusted, the said grants or either of them being at the same time claimed to have originated antecedent to such settlement of jurisdiction, shall, on the petition of either party to the Congress of the United States, be finally determined as near as may be in the same manner as is before prescribed for deciding disputes respecting territorial jurisdiction between different States.

The United States in Congress assembled shall also have the sole and exclusive right and power of regulating the alloy and value of coin struck by their own authority, or by that of the respective States—fixing the standard of weights and measures throughout the United States—regulating the trade and managing all affairs with the Indians, not members of any of the States, provided that the legislative right of any State within its own limits be not infringed or violated—establishing and regulating post-offices from one State to another, throughout all the United States, and exacting such postage on the papers passing through the same as may be requisite to defray the expenses of the said office—appointing all officers of the land forces in the service of the United States, excepting regimental officers—appointing all the officers of the naval forces, and commissioning all officers whatever in the service of the United States—making rules for the government and regulation of the said land and naval forces, and directing their operations.

The United States in Congress assembled shall have authority to appoint a committee, to sit in the recess of Congress, to be denominated "A Committee of the States," and to consist of one delegate from each State; to appoint such other committees and civil officers as may be necessary for managing the general affairs of the United States under their direction; and to appoint one of their number to preside, provided that no person be allowed to serve in the office of president more than one year in any term of three years—to ascertain the necessary sums of money to be raised for the service of the United States, and to appropriate and apply the same for defraying the public expenses—to borrow money, or emit bills on the credit of the United States, transmitting every half-year to the respective States an account of the sums of money so borrowed or emitted—to build and equip a navy—to agree upon the number of land forces, and to make requisitions from each State for its quota, in proportion to the number of white inhabitants in such State; which requisition shall be binding, and thereupon the legislature of each State shall appoint the regimental officers, raise the men, and cloathe, arm and equip them in a soldier-like manner, at the expense of the United States, and the officers and men so cloathed, armed, and equipped shall march to the place appointed, and within the time agreed on by the United States in Congress assembled; but if the United States in Congress assembled shall, on consideration of circumstances, judge proper that any State should not raise men, or should raise a smaller number than its quota, and that any other State should raise a greater number of men than the quota thereof, such extra number shall be raised, officered, cloathed, armed, and equipped in the same as the quota of such State, unless the legislature of such State shall judge that such extra number cannot be safely spared outside of the same, in which case they shall raise, officer, cloath, arm, and equip as many of such extra number as they judge can be safely spared: and the officers and men, so cloathed, armed and equipped shall march to the place appointed, and within the time agreed on, by the United States in Congress assembled.

The United States in Congress assembled shall never engage in a war, nor grant letters of marque and reprisal in time of peace, nor enter into any treaties or alliances, nor coin money, nor regulate the value thereof, nor ascertain the sums and expenses necessary for the defence and welfare of the United States, or any of them, nor emit bills, nor borrow money on the credit of the United States, nor appropriate money, nor agree upon the number of vessels of war to be built or purchased, or the number of land or sea forces to be raised, nor appoint a commander-in-chief of the army or navy, unless nine States assent to the same; nor shall a question on any other point, except for adjourning from day to day, be determined, unless by the votes of a majority of the United States in Congress assembled.

The Congress of the United States shall have power to adjourn to any time within the year, and to any place within the United States, so that no period of adjournment be for a longer duration than the space of six months, and shall publish the journal of their proceedings monthly, except such parts thereof relating to treaties, alliances, or military operations, as in their judgment require secrecy; and the yeas and nays of the delegates of each State on any question shall be entered on the journal, when it is desired by any delegate; and the delegates of a State, or any of them, at his or their request, shall be furnished with a transcript of the said journal, except such parts as are above excepted, to lay before the legislatures of the several States.

ART. X. The Committee of the States, or any nine of them, shall be authorized to execute, in the recess of Congress, such of the powers of Congress as the United States in Congress assembled, by the consent of nine States, shall from time to time think expedient to vest them with: provided that no power be delegated to the said Committee, for the exercise of which, by the Articles of Confederation, the voice of nine States in the Congress of the United States assembled is requisite.

ART. XI. Canada acceding to this Confederation, and joining in the measures of the United States, shall be admitted into and entitled to all the advantages of this Union; but no other colony shall be admitted into the same, unless such admission be agreed to by nine States.

ART. XII. All bills of credit emitted, monies borrowed, and debts contracted by or under the authority of Congress, before the assembling of the United States in pursuance of the present Confederation, shall be deemed and considered as a charge against the United States, for payment and satisfaction whereof the said United States and the public faith are hereby solemnly pledged.

ART. XIII. Every State shall abide by the determinations of the United States in Congress assembled, on all questions which by this Confederation are submitted to them. And the Articles of this Confederation shall be inviolably observed by every State, and the Union shall be perpetual; nor shall any alteration at any time hereafter be made in any of them, unless such alteration be agreed to in a Congress of the United States, and be afterwards confirmed by the legislatures of every State.

AND WHEREAS it hath pleased the Great Governor of the world to incline the hearts of the legislatures we respectively represent in Congress to approve of and to authorize us to ratify the said Articles of Confederation and perpetual Union. KNOW YE, that we, the undersigned delegates, by virtue of the power and authority to us given for that purpose, do by these presents, in the name and in behalf of our respective constituents, fully and entirely ratify and confirm each and every of the said Articles of Confederation and perpetual Union, and all and singular the matters and things therein contained: and we do further solemnly plight and engage the faith of our respective constituents that they shall abide by the determinations of the United States in Congress assembled, on all questions which by the said Confederation are submitted to them. And that the Articles thereof shall be inviolably observed by the States we respectively represent, and that the Union shall be perpetual.

# Appendix 3

# *The Constitution of the United States*

*In the following printed copy of the Constitution, spelling, capitalization, and punctuation conform to the text of the engrossed parchment.*

We the People of the United States, in Order to form a more perfect Union, establish Justice, insure domestic Tranquility, provide for the common defence, promote the general Welfare, and secure the Blessings of Liberty to ourselves and our Posterity, do ordain and establish this Constitution for the United States of America.

## ARTICLE I.

SECTION. 1. All legislative Powers herein granted shall be vested in a Congress of the United States, which shall consist of a Senate and House of Representatives.

SECTION. 2. The House of Representatives shall be composed of Members chosen every second Year by the People of the several States, and the Electors in each State shall have the Qualifications requisite for Electors of the most numerous Branch of the State Legislature.

No Person shall be a Representative who shall not have attained to the Age of twenty five Years, and been seven Years a Citizen of the United States, and who shall not, when elected, be an Inhabitant of that State in which he shall be chosen.

Representatives and direct Taxes shall be apportioned among the several States which may be included within this Union, according to their respective Numbers, which shall be determined by adding to the whole Number of free Persons, including those bound to Service for a Term of Years, and excluding Indians not taxed, three fifths of all other Persons. The actual Enumeration shall be made within three Years after the first Meeting of the Congress of the United States, and within every subsequent Term of ten Years, in such Manner as they shall by Law direct. The Number of Representatives shall not exceed one for every thirty Thousand, but each State shall have at Least one Representative; and until such enumeration shall be made, the State of New Hampshire shall be entitled to chuse three, Massachusetts eight, Rhode-Island and Providence Plantations one, Connecticut five, New-York six, New Jersey four, Pennsylvania eight, Delaware one, Maryland six, Virginia ten, North Carolina five, South Carolina five, and Georgia three.

When vacancies happen in the Representation from any State, the Executive Authority thereof shall issue Writs of Election to fill such Vacancies.

The House of Representatives shall chuse their speaker and other Officers; and shall have the sole Power of Impeachment.

SECTION. 3. The Senate of the United States shall be composed of two Senators from each State, chosen by the Legislature thereof, for six Years; and each Senator shall have one Vote.

Immediately after they shall be assembled in Consequence of the first Election, they shall be divided as equally as may be into three Classes. The Seats of the Senators of the first Class shall be vacated at the Expiration of the second Year, of the second Class at the Expiration of the fourth Year, and of the third Class at the Expiration of the sixth Year, so that one third may be chosen every second Year; and if Vacancies happen by Resignation, or otherwise, during the Recess of the Legislature of any State, the Executive thereof may make temporary Appointments until the next Meeting of the Legislature, which shall then fill such Vacancies.

No Person shall be a Senator who shall not have attained to the Age of thirty Years, and been nine Years a Citizen of the United States, and who shall not, when elected, be an Inhabitant of that State for which he shall be chosen.

The Vice President of the United States shall be President of the Senate, but shall have no Vote, unless they be equally divided.

The Senate shall chuse their other Officers, and also a President pro tempore, in the Absence of the Vice President, or when he shall exercise the Office of President of the United States.

The Senate shall have the sole Power to try all Impeachments. When sitting for that Purpose, they shall be on Oath or Affirmation. When the President of the United States is tried, the Chief Justice shall preside: And no Person shall be convicted without the concurrence of two thirds of the Members present.

Judgment in Cases of Impeachment shall not extend further than to removal from Office, and disqualification to hold and enjoy any Office of honor, Trust or Profit under the United States: but the Party convicted shall nevertheless be liable and subject to Indictment, Trial, Judgment and Punishment, according to law.

SECTION. 4. The Times, Places and Manner of holding Elections for Senators and Representatives, shall be prescribed in each State by the Legislature thereof; but the Congress may at any time by Law make or alter such Regulations, except as to the Places of chusing Senators.

The Congress shall assemble at least once in every Year, and such Meeting shall be on the first Monday in December, unless they shall by Law appoint a different Day.

SECTION. 5. Each House shall be the Judge of the Elections, Returns and Qualifications of its own Members, and a Majority of each shall constitute a Quorum to do business; but a smaller Number may adjourn from day to day, and may be authorized to compel the Attendance of absent Members, in such Manner, and under such Penalties as each House may provide.

Each House may determine the Rules of its Proceedings, punish its Members for disorderly Behaviour, and, with the Concurrence of two thirds, expel a Member.

Each House shall keep a Journal of its Proceedings, and from time to time publish the same, excepting such Parts as may in their Judgment require Secrecy; and the Yeas and Nays of the Members of either House on any question shall, at the Desire of one fifth of those Present, be entered on the Journal.

Neither House, during the Session of Congress, shall, without the Consent of the other, adjourn for more than three days, nor to any other Place than that in which the two Houses shall be sitting.

SECTION. 6. The Senators and Representatives shall receive a Compensation for their Services, to be ascertained by Law, and paid out of the Treasury of the United States. They shall in all Cases, except Treason, Felony and Breach of the Peace, be privileged from Arrest during their Attendance at the Session of their respective Houses, and in going to and returning from the same; and for any Speech or Debate in either House, they shall not be questioned in any other Place.

No Senator or Representative shall, during the Time for which he was elected, be appointed to any civil Office under the Authority of the United States, which shall have been created, or the Emoluments whereof shall have been encreased during such time; and no Person holding any Office under the United States, shall be a Member of either House during his Continuance in Office.

SECTION. 7. All Bills for raising Revenue shall originate in the House of Representatives; but the Senate may propose or concur with Amendments as on other Bills.

Every Bill which shall have passed the House of Representatives and the Senate, shall, before it become a Law, be presented to the President of the United States; If he approve he shall sign it, but if not he shall return it, with his Objections to that House in which it shall have originated, who shall enter the Objections at large on their Journal, and proceed to reconsider it. If after such Reconsideration two thirds of that House shall agree to pass the Bill, it shall be sent, together with the Objections, to the other House, by which it shall likewise be reconsidered, and if approved by two thirds of that House, it shall become a Law. But in all such Cases the Votes of both Houses shall be determined by yeas and Nays, and the Names of the Persons voting for and against the Bill shall be entered on the Journal of each House respectively. If any Bill shall not be returned by the President within ten Days (Sundays excepted) after it shall have been presented to him, the Same shall be a Law, in like Manner as if he had signed it, unless the Congress by their Adjournment prevent its Return, in which Case it shall not be a Law.

Every Order, Resolution, or Vote to which the Concurrence of the Senate and House of Representatives may be necessary (except on a question of Adjournment) shall be presented to the President of the United States; and before the Same shall take Effect, shall be approved by him, or being disapproved by him, shall be repassed by two thirds of the Senate and House of Representatives, according to the Rules and Limitations prescribed in the Case of a Bill.

SECTION. 8. The Congress shall have Power To lay and collect Taxes, Duties, Imposts and Excises, to pay the Debts and provide for the common Defence and general Welfare of the United States; but all Duties, Imposts and Excises shall be uniform throughout the United States;

To borrow Money on the credit of the United States;

To regulate Commerce with foreign Nations, and among the several States, and with the Indian Tribes;

To establish an uniform Rule of Naturalization, and uniform Laws on the subject of Bankruptcies throughout the United States;

To coin Money, regulate the Value thereof, and of foreign Coin, and fix the Standard of Weights and Measures;

To provide for the Punishment of counterfeiting the Securities and current Coin of the United States;

To establish Post Offices and post Roads;

To promote the Progress of Science and useful Arts, by securing for limited Times to Authors and Inventors the exclusive Right to their respective Writings and Discoveries;

To constitute Tribunals inferior to the supreme Court;

To define and punish Piracies and Felonies committed on the high Seas, and Offences against the Law of Nations;

To declare War, grant Letters of Marque and Reprisal, and make rules concerning Captures on Land and Water;

To raise and support Armies, but no Appropriation of Money to that Use shall be for a longer Term than two Years;

To provide and maintain a Navy;

To make Rules for the Government and Regulation of the land and naval Forces;

To provide for calling forth the Militia to execute the Laws of the Union, suppress Insurrections and repel Invasions;

To provide for organizing, arming, and disciplining, the Militia, and for governing such Part of them as may be employed in the Service of the United States, reserving to the States respectively, the Appointment of the Officers, and the Authority of training the Militia according to the discipline prescribed by Congress;

To exercise exclusive Legislation in all Cases whatsoever, over such District (not exceeding ten Miles square), as may, by Cession of particular States, and the Acceptance of Congress, become the Seat of the Government of the United States, and to exercise like Authority over all Places purchased by the Consent of the Legislature of the State in which the Same shall be for the Erection of Forts, Magazines, Arsenals, dock-Yards, and other needful Buildings;—And

To make all Laws which shall be necessary and proper for carrying into Execution the foregoing Powers, and all other Powers vested by this Constitution in the Government of the United States, or in any Department or Officer thereof.

SECTION. 9. The Migration or Importation of such Persons as any of the States now existing shall think proper to admit, shall not be prohibited by the Congress prior to the Year one thousand eight hundred and eight, but a Tax or duty may be imposed on such Importation, not exceeding ten dollars for each Person.

The Privilege of the Writ of Habeas Corpus shall not be suspended, unless when in Cases of Rebellion or Invasion the public Safety may require it.

No Bill of Attainder or ex post facto Law shall be passed.

No Capitation, or other direct, Tax shall be laid, unless in Proportion to the Census or Enumeration herein before directed to be taken.

No Tax or Duty shall be laid on Articles exported from any State.

No Preference shall be given by any Regulation of Commerce or Revenue to the Ports of one State over those of another; nor shall Vessels bound to, or from, one State, be obliged to enter, clear or pay Duties in another.

No money shall be drawn from the Treasury, but in Consequence of Appropriations made by Law; and a regular Statement and Account of the Receipts and Expenditures of all public Money shall be published from time to time.

No Title of Nobility shall be granted by the United States: And no Person holding any Office of Profit or Trust under them, shall, without the Consent of the Congress, accept of any present, Emolument, Office, or Title, of any kind whatever, from any King, Prince, or foreign State.

SECTION. 10. No State shall enter into any Treaty, Alliance, or Confederation; grant Letters of Marque and Reprisal; coin Money; emit Bills of Credit; make any Thing but gold and silver Coin a Tender in Payment of Debts; pass any Bill of Attainder, ex post facto Law, or Law impairing the Obligation of Contracts, or grant any Title of Nobility.

No State shall, without the Consent of the Congress, lay any Imposts or Duties on Imports or Exports, except what may be absolutely necessary for executing it's inspection Laws: and the net Produce of all Duties and Imposts, laid by any State on Imports or Exports, shall be for the Use of the Treasury of the United States; and all such Laws shall be subject to the Revision and Controul of the Congress.

No State shall, without the Consent of Congress, lay any Duty of Tonnage, keep Troops, or Ships of War in time of Peace, enter into any Agreement or Compact with another State, or with a foreign Power, or engage in War, unless actually invaded, or in such imminent Danger as will not admit of delay.

## ARTICLE II.

SECTION. 1. The executive Power shall be vested in a President of the United States of America. He shall hold his Office during the Term of four Years, and, together with the Vice President, chosen for the same Term, be elected, as follows

Each State shall appoint, in such Manner as the Legislature thereof may direct, a Number of Electors, equal to the whole Number of Senators and Representatives to which the State may be entitled in the Congress: but no Senator or Representative, or Person holding an Office of Trust or Profit under the United States, shall be appointed an Elector.

The Electors shall meet in their respective States, and vote by Ballot for two Persons, of whom one at least shall not be an inhabitant of the same State with themselves. And they shall make a List of all the Persons voted for, and of the Number of Votes for each; which List they shall sign and certify, and transmit sealed to the Seat of the Government of the United States, directed to the President of the Senate. The President of the Senate shall, in the Presence of the Senate and House of Representatives, open all the Certificates, and the Votes shall then be counted. The Person having the greatest Number of Votes shall be the President, if such Number be a Majority of the whole Number of Electors appointed; and if there be more than one who have such Majority, and have an equal Number of Votes, then the House of Representatives shall immediately chuse by Ballot one of them for President: and if no Person have a Majority, then from the five highest on the List the said House shall in like Manner chuse the President. But in chusing the President, the Votes shall be taken by States, the Representation from each State having one Vote; A quorum for this Purpose shall consist of a Member or Members from two thirds of the States, and a Majority of all the States shall be necessary to a Choice. In every Case, after the Choice of the President, the Person having the greatest Number of Votes of the Electors shall be the Vice President. But if there should remain two or more who have equal Votes, the Senate shall chuse from them by Ballot the Vice President.

The Congress may determine the Time of chusing the Electors, and the Day on which they shall give their Votes; which Day shall be the same throughout the United States.

No Person except a natural born Citizen, or a Citizen of the United States, at the time of the Adoption of this Constitution, shall be eligible to the Office of President; neither shall any Person be eligible to that Office who shall not have attained to the Age of thirty five Years, and been fourteen Years a Resident within the United States.

In Case of the Removal of the President from Office, or of his Death, Resignation, or Inability to discharge the Powers and Duties of the said Office, the Same shall devolve on the Vice President, and the Congress may by Law provide for the Case of Removal, Death, Resignation or Inability, both of the President and Vice President, declaring what Officer shall then act as President, and such Officer shall act accordingly, until the Disability be removed, or a President shall be elected.

The President shall, at stated Times, receive for his Services, a Compensation, which shall neither be encreased nor diminished during the Period for which he shall have been elected, and he shall not receive within that Period any other Emolument from the United States, or any of them.

Before he enter on the Execution of his Office, he shall take the following Oath or Affirmation:—"I do solemnly swear (or affirm) that I will faithfully execute the Office of President of the United States, and will to the best of my Ability, preserve, protect and defend the Constitution of the United States."

SECTION. 2. The President shall be Commander in Chief of the Army and Navy of the United States, and of the Militia of the several States, when called into the actual Service of the United States; he may require the Opinion, in writing, of the principal Officer in each of the executive Departments, upon any Subject relating to the Duties of their respective Offices, and he shall have Power to grant Reprieves and Pardons for Offences against the United States, except in Cases of Impeachment.

He shall have Power, by and with the Advice and Consent of the Senate, to make Treaties, provided two thirds of the Senators present concur; and he shall nominate, and by and with the Advice and Consent of the Senate, shall appoint Ambassadors, other public Ministers and Consuls, Judges of the supreme Court, and all other Officers of the United States, whose Appointments are not herein otherwise provided for, and which shall be established by Law: but the Congress may by Law vest the Appointment of such inferior Officers, as they think proper, in the President alone, in the Courts of Law, or in the Heads of Departments.

The President shall have Power to fill up all Vacancies that may happen during the Recess of the Senate, by granting Commissions which shall expire at the End of their next Session.

SECTION. 3. He shall from time to time give to the Congress Information of the State of the Union, and recommend to their Consideration such Measures as he shall judge necessary and expedient; he may, on extraordinary Occasions, convene both Houses, or either of them, and in Case of Disagreement between them, with Respect to the Time of Adjournment, he may adjourn them to such Time as he shall think proper; he shall receive Ambassadors and other public Ministers; he shall take Care that the Laws be faithfully executed, and shall Commission all the Officers of the United States.

SECTION. 4. The President, Vice President and all civil Officers of the United States, shall be removed from Office on Impeachment for, and Conviction of, Treason, Bribery, or other high Crimes and Misdemeanors.

## ARTICLE III.

SECTION. 1. The judicial Power of the United States, shall be vested in one supreme Court, and in such inferior Courts as the Congress may from time to time ordain and establish. The Judges, both of the supreme and inferior Courts, shall hold their Offices during good Behaviour, and shall, at stated Times, receive for their Services, a Compensation, which shall not be diminished during their Continuance in Office.

SECTION. 2. The judicial Power shall extend to all Cases, in Law and Equity, arising under this Constitution, the Laws of the United States, and Treaties made, or which shall be made, under their Authority;—to all Cases affecting Ambassadors, other public Ministers and Consuls;—to all Cases of admiralty and maritime jurisdiction;—to Controversies to which the United States shall be a Party;—to Controversies between two or more States;—between a State and Citizens of another State;—between Citizens of different States;—between Citizens of the same State claiming Lands under Grants of different States, and between a State, or the Citizens thereof, and foreign States, Citizens or Subjects.

In all Cases affecting Ambassadors, other public Ministers and Consuls, and those in which a State shall be Party, the supreme Court shall have original Jurisdiction. In all the other Cases before mentioned, the supreme Court shall have appellate Jurisdiction, both as to Law and Fact, with such Exceptions, and under such Regulations as the Congress shall make.

The Trial of all Crimes, except in Cases of Impeachment, shall be by Jury; and such Trial shall be held in the State where the said Crimes shall have been committed; but when not committed within any State, the Trial shall be at such Place or Places as the Congress may by Law have directed.

SECTION. 3. Treason against the United States, shall consist only in levying War against them, or in adhering to their Enemies, giving them Aid and Comfort. No Person shall be convicted of Treason unless on the Testimony of two Witnesses to the same overt Act, or on Confession in open Court.

The Congress shall have Power to declare the Punishment of Treason, but no Attainder of Treason shall work Corruption of Blood, or Forfeiture except during the Life of the Person attainted.

## ARTICLE IV.

SECTION. 1. Full Faith and Credit shall be given in each State to the public Acts, Records, and judicial Proceedings of every other State. And the Congress may by general Laws prescribe the Manner in which such Acts, Records and Proceedings shall be proved, and the Effect thereof.

SECTION. 2. The Citizens of each State shall be entitled to all Privileges and Immunities of Citizens in the several States.

A person charged in any State with Treason, Felony, or other Crime, who shall flee from Justice, and be found in another State, shall on Demand of the executive Authority of the State from which he fled, be delivered up, to be removed to the State having Jurisdiction of the Crime.

No Person held to Service or Labour in one State, under the Laws thereof, escaping into another, shall, in Consequence of any Law or Regulation therein, be discharged from such Service or Labour, but shall be delivered upon on Claim of the Party to whom such Service or Labour may be due.

SECTION. 3. New States may be admitted by the Congress into this Union; but no new State shall be formed or erected within the Jurisdiction of any other State; nor any State be formed by the Junction of two or more States, or Parts of States, without the Consent of the Legislatures of the States concerned as well as of the Congress.

The Congress shall have Power to dispose of and make all needful Rules and Regulations respecting the Territory or other Property belonging to the United States; and nothing in this Constitution shall be so construed as to Prejudice any Claims of the United States, or of any particular State.

SECTION. 4. The United States shall guarantee to every State in this Union a Republican Form of Government, and shall protect each of them against Invasion; and on Application of the Legislature, or of the Executive (when the Legislature cannot be convened) against domestic Violence.

## ARTICLE V.

The Congress, whenever two thirds of both Houses shall deem it necessary, shall propose Amendments to this Constitution, or, on the Application of the Legislatures of two thirds of the several States, shall call a Convention for proposing Amendments, which, in either Case, shall be valid to all Intents and Purposes, as Part of this Constitution, when ratified by the Legislatures of three fourths of the several States, or by Conventions in three fourths thereof, as the one or the other Mode of Ratification may be proposed by the Congress; Provided that no Amendment which may be made prior to the Year One thousand eight hundred and eight shall in any Manner affect the first and fourth Clauses in the Ninth Section of the first Article; and that no State, without its Consent, shall be deprived of its equal Suffrage in the Senate.

## ARTICLE VI.

All Debts contracted and Engagements entered into, before the Adoption of this Constitution, shall be as valid against the United States under this Constitution, as under the Confederation.

This Constitution, and the Laws of the United States which shall be made in Pursuance thereof; and all Treaties made, or which shall be made, under the Authority of the United States, shall be the supreme Law of the Land; and the Judges in every State shall be bound thereby, any Thing in the Constitution or Laws of any State to the Contrary notwithstanding.

The Senators and Representatives before mentioned, and the Members of the several State Legislatures, and all executive and judicial Officers, both of the United States and of the several States, shall be bound by Oath or Affirmation, to support this Constitution; but no religious Test shall ever be required as a Qualification to any Office or public Trust under the United States.

## ARTICLE VII.

The Ratification of the Conventions of nine States, shall be sufficient for the Establishment of this Constitution between the States so ratifying the Same.

The Word "the", being interlined between the seventh and eighth Lines of the first Page, the Word "Thirty" being partly written on an Erazure in the fiftienth Line of the first Page, The Words "is tried" being interlined between the thirty second and thirty third Lines of the first Page and the Word "the" being interlined between the forty third and forty fourth Lines of the second Page.
Attest William Jackson
Secretary

DONE in Convention by the Unanimous Consent of the States present the Seventeenth Day of September in the Year of our Lord one thousand seven hundred and Eighty seven and of the Independence of the United States of America the Twelfth. IN WITNESS whereof We have hereunto subscribed our Names:

G° WASHINGTON

Presid^t and deputy from Virginia

| DELAWARE | GEO: READ<br>GUNNING BEDFORD jun<br>JOHN DICKINSON<br>RICHARD BASSETT<br>JACO: BROOM | NEW HAMPSHIRE | JOHN LANGDON<br>NICHOLAS GILMAN |
|---|---|---|---|
| MARYLAND | JAMES MCHENRY<br>DAN OF ST. THOS. JENIFER<br>DANL. CARROLL | MASSACHUSETTS | NATHANIEL GORHAM<br>RUFUS KING |
| VIRGINIA | JOHN BLAIR—<br>JAMES MADISON JR. | CONNECTICUT | WM. SAML. JOHNSON<br>ROGER SHERMAN |
| | | NEW YORK | ALEXANDER HAMILTON |
| NORTH CAROLINA | WM. BLOUNT<br>RICHD. DOBBS SPAIGHT<br>HU WILLIAMSON | NEW JERSEY | WIL: LIVINGSTON<br>DAVID BREARLEY<br>WM. PATTERSON<br>JONA: DAYTON |
| SOUTH CAROLINA | J. RUTLEDGE<br>CHARLES COTESWORTH PINCKNEY<br>CHARLES PINCKNEY<br>PIERCE BUTLER | PENNSYLVANIA | B. FRANKLIN<br>THOMAS MIFFLIN<br>ROBT. MORRIS<br>GEO. CLYMER<br>THOS. FITZSIMONS<br>JARED INGERSOLL<br>JAMES WILSON<br>GOUV MORRIS |
| GEORGIA | WILLIAM FEW<br>ABR BALDWIN | | |

## AMENDMENT I

Congress shall make no law respecting an establishment of religion, or prohibiting the free exercise thereof; or abridging the freedom of speech, or of the press; or the right of the people peaceably to assemble, and to petition the Government for a redress of grievances.

## AMENDMENT II

A well regulated Militia, being necessary to the security of a free State, the right of the people to keep and bear Arms, shall not be infringed.

## AMENDMENT III

No Soldier shall, in time of peace be quartered in any house, without the consent of the Owner, nor in time of war, but in a manner to be prescribed by law.

## AMENDMENT IV

The right of the People to be secure in their persons, houses, papers, and effects, against unreasonable searches and seizures, shall not be violated, and no Warrants shall issue, but upon probable cause, supported by Oath or affirmation, and particularity describing the place to be searched, and the persons or things to be seized.

## AMENDMENT V

No person shall be held to answer for a capital, or otherwise infamous crime, unless on a presentment or indictment of a Grand Jury, except in cases arising in the land or naval forces, or in the Militia, when in actual service in time of War or public danger; nor shall any person be subject for the same offence to be twice put in jeopardy of life or limb; nor shall be compelled in any criminal case to be a witness against himself, nor be deprived of life, liberty, or property, without due process of law; nor shall private property be taken for public use, without just compensation.

## AMENDMENT VI

In all criminal prosecutions, the accused shall enjoy the right to a speedy and public trial, by an impartial jury of the State and district wherein the crime shall have been committed, which district shall have been previously ascertained by law, and to be informed of the nature and cause of the accusation; to be confronted with the witnesses against him; to have compulsory process for obtaining witnesses in his favor, and to have the assistance of counsel for his defence.

## AMENDMENT VII

In Suits at common law, where the value in controversy shall exceed twenty dollars, the right of trial by jury shall be preserved, and no fact tried by a jury, shall be otherwise re-examined in any Court of the United States, than according to the rules of the common law.

## AMENDMENT VIII

Excessive bail shall not be required, nor excessive fines imposed, nor cruel and unusual punishments inflicted.

## AMENDMENT IX

The enumeration in the Constitution, of certain rights, shall not be construed to deny or disparage others retained by the people.

## AMENDMENT X

The powers not delegated to the United States by the Constitution, nor prohibited by it to the States, are reserved to the States respectively, or to the people.

## AMENDMENT XI

The Judicial power of the United States shall not be construed to extend to any suit in law or equity, commenced or prosecuted against one of the United States by Citizens of another State, or by Citizens or Subjects of any Foreign State.

## AMENDMENT XII

The Electors shall meet in their respective states, and vote by ballot for President and Vice-President, one of whom, at least, shall not be an inhabitant of the same state with themselves; they shall name in their ballots the person voted for as President, and in distinct ballots the person voted for as Vice-President, and they shall make distinct lists of all persons voted for as President, and of all persons voted for as Vice-President, and of the number of votes for each, which lists they shall sign and certify, and transmit sealed to the seat of the government of the United States, directed to the President of the Senate;—The President of the Senate shall, in the presence of the Senate and House of Representatives, open all the certificates and the votes shall then be counted;—The person having the greatest number of votes for President, shall be the President, if such number be a majority of the whole number of Electors appointed; and if no person have such majority, then from the persons having the highest numbers not exceeding three on the list of those voted for as President, the House of Representatives shall choose immediately, by ballot, the President. But in choosing the President, the votes shall be taken by states, the representation from each state having one vote; a quorum for this purpose shall consist of a member or members from two-thirds of the states, and a majority of all the states shall be necessary to a choice. And if the House of Representatives shall not choose a President whenever the right of choice shall devolve upon them, before the fourth day of March next following, then the Vice-President shall act as President, as in the case of the death or other constitutional disability of the President.—The person having the greatest number of votes as Vice-President, shall be the Vice-President, if such number be a majority of the whole number of Electors appointed, and if no person have a majority, then from the two highest numbers on the list, the Senate shall choose the Vice-President; a quorum for the purpose shall consist of two-thirds of the whole number of Senators, and a majority of the whole number shall be necessary to a choice. But no person constitutionally ineligible to the office of President shall be eligible to that of Vice-President of the United States.

### AMENDMENT XIII

SECTION 1. Neither slavery nor involuntary servitude, except as a punishment for crime whereof the party shall have been duly convicted, shall exist within the United States, or any place subject to their jurisdiction.

SECTION 2. Congress shall have power to enforce this article by appropriate legislation.

### AMENDMENT XIV

SECTION 1. All persons born or naturalized in the United States, and subject to the jurisdiction thereof, are citizens of the United States and of the State wherein they reside. No State shall make or enforce any law which shall abridge the privileges or immunities of citizens of the United States; nor shall any State deprive any person of life, liberty, or property, without due process of law; nor deny to any person within its jurisdiction the equal protection of the laws.

SECTION 2. Representatives shall be apportioned among the several States according to their respective numbers, counting the whole number of persons in each State, excluding Indians not taxed. But when the right to vote at any election for the choice of electors for President and Vice President of the United States, Representatives in Congress, the Executive and Judicial officers of a State, or the members of the Legislature thereof, is denied to any of the male inhabitants of such State, being twenty-one years of age, and citizens of the United States, or in any way abridged, except for participation in rebellion, or other crime, the basis of representation therein shall be reduced in the proportion which the number of such male citizens shall bear to the whole number of male citizens twenty-one years of age in such State.

SECTION 3. No person shall be a Senator or Representative in Congress, or elector of President and Vice President, or hold any office, civil or military, under the United States, or under any State, who, having previously taken an oath, as a member of Congress, or as an officer of the United States, or as a member of any State legislature, or as an executive or judicial officer of any State, to support the Constitution of the United States, shall have engaged in insurrection or rebellion against the same, or given aid or comfort to the enemies thereof. But Congress may by a vote of two-thirds of each House, remove such disability.

SECTION 4. The validity of the public debt of the United States, authorized by law, including debts incurred for payment of pensions and bounties for services in suppressing insurrection or rebellion, shall not be questioned. But neither the United States nor any State shall assume or pay any debt or obligation incurred in aid of insurrection or rebellion against the United States, or any claim for the loss or emancipation of any slave; but all such debts, obligations and claims shall be held illegal and void.

SECTION 5. The Congress shall have power to enforce, by appropriate legislation, the provisions of this article.

## AMENDMENT XV

SECTION 1. The right of citizens of the United States to vote shall not be denied or abridged by the United States or by any State on account of race, color, or previous condition of servitude.

SECTION 2. The Congress shall have power to enforce this article by appropriate legislation.

## AMENDMENT XVI

The Congress shall have power to lay and collect taxes on incomes, from whatever source derived, without apportionment among the several States, and without regard to any census or enumeration.

## AMENDMENT XVII

The Senate of the United States shall be composed of two Senators from each State, elected by the people thereof, for six years; and each Senator shall have one vote. The electors in each State shall have the qualifications requisite for electors of the most numerous branch of the State legislatures.

When vacancies happen in the representation of any State in the Senate, the executive authority of such State shall issue writs of election to fill such vacancies: *Provided*, That the legislature of any State may empower the executive thereof to make temporary appointments until the people fill the vacancies by election as the legislature may direct.

This amendment shall not be so construed as to affect the election or term of any Senator chosen before it becomes valid as part of the Constitution.

## AMENDMENT XVIII

SECTION 1. After one year from the ratification of this article the manufacture, sale, or transportation of intoxicating liquors within, the importation thereof into, or the exportation thereof from the United States and all territory subject to the jurisdiction thereof for beverage purposes is hereby prohibited.

SECTION 2. The Congress and the several States shall have concurrent power to enforce this article by appropriate legislation.

SECTION 3. This article shall be inoperative unless it shall have been ratified as an amendment to the Constitution by the legislatures of the several States as provided in the Constitution, within seven years from the date of the submission hereof to the States by the Congress.

## AMENDMENT XIX

The right of citizens of the United States to vote shall not be denied or abridged by the United States or by any State on account of sex.

Congress shall have power to enforce this article by appropriate legislation.

## AMENDMENT XX

SECTION 1. The terms of the President and Vice President shall end at noon on the 20th day of January, and the terms of Senators and Representatives at noon on the 3d day of January, of the years in which such terms would have ended if this article had not been ratified; and the terms of their successors shall then begin.

SECTION 2. The Congress shall assemble at least once in every year, and such meeting shall begin at noon on the 3d day of January, unless they shall by law appoint a different day.

SECTION 3. If, at the time fixed for the beginning of the term of the President, the

President elect shall have died, the Vice President elect shall become President. If a President shall not have been chosen before the time fixed for the beginning of his term, or if the President elect shall have failed to qualify, then the Vice President elect shall act as President until a President shall have qualified; and the Congress may by law provide for the case wherein neither a President elect nor a Vice President elect shall have qualified, declaring who shall then act as President, or the manner in which one who is to act shall be selected, and such person shall act accordingly until a President or Vice President shall have qualified.

SECTION 4. The Congress may by law provide for the case of the death of any of the persons from whom the House of Representatives may choose a President whenever the right of choice shall have devolved upon them, and for the case of the death of any of the persons from whom the Senate may choose a Vice President whenever the right of choice shall have devolved upon them.

SECTION 5. Sections 1 and 2 shall take effect on the 15th day of October following the ratification of this article.

SECTION 6. This article shall be inoperative unless it shall have been ratified as an amendment to the Constitution by the legislatures of three-fourths of the several States within seven years from the date of its submission.

## AMENDMENT XXI

SECTION 1. The eighteenth article of amendment to the Constitution of the United States is hereby repealed.

SECTION 2. The transportation or importation into any State, Territory, or possession of the United States for delivery or use therein of intoxicating liquors, in violation of the laws thereof, is hereby prohibited.

SECTION 3. This article shall be inoperative unless it shall have been ratified as an amendment to the Constitution by conventions in the several States, as provided in the Constitution, within seven years from the date of the submission hereof to the States by the Congress.

## AMENDMENT XXII

SECTION 1. No person shall be elected to the office of the President more than twice, and no person who has held the office of President, or acted as President, for more than two years of a term to which some other person was elected President shall be elected to the office of the President more than once. But this Article shall not apply to any person holding the office of President when this Article was proposed by the Congress, and shall not prevent any person who may be holding the office of President, or acting as President, during the term within which this Article becomes operative from holding the office of President or acting as President during the remainder of such term.

SECTION 2. This Article shall be inoperative unless it shall have been ratified as an amendment to the Constitution by the legislatures of three-fourths of the several States within seven years from the date of its submission to the States by the Congress.

## AMENDMENT XXIII

SECTION 1. The District constituting the seat of Government of the United States shall appoint in such manner as the Congress may direct:

A number of electors of President and Vice President equal to the whole number of Senators and Representatives in Congress to which the District would be entitled if it were a State, but in no event more than the least populous State; they shall be in addition to those appointed by the States, but they shall be considered, for the purposes of the election of President and Vice President, to be electors appointed by a State; and they shall meet in the District and perform such duties as provided by the twelfth article of amendment.

SECTION 2. The Congress shall have power to enforce this article by appropriate legislation.

## AMENDMENT XXIV

SECTION 1. The right of citizens of the United States to vote in any primary or other election for President or Vice President, for electors for President or Vice President, or for Senator or Representative in Congress, shall not be denied or abridged by the United States or any State by reason of failure to pay any poll tax or other tax.

SECTION 2. The Congress shall have power to enforce this article by appropriate legislation.

## AMENDMENT XXV

SECTION 1. In case of the removal of the President from office or of his death or resignation, the Vice President shall become President.

SECTION 2. Whenever there is a vacancy in the office of the Vice President, the President shall nominate a Vice President who shall take office upon confirmation by a majority vote of both Houses of Congress.

SECTION 3. Whenever the President transmits to the President pro tempore of the Senate and the Speaker of the House of Representatives his written declaration that he is unable to discharge the powers and duties of his office, and until he transmits to them a written declaration to the contrary, such powers and duties shall be discharged by the Vice President as Acting President.

SECTION 4. Whenever the Vice president and a majority of either the principal officers of the executive departments or of such other body as Congress may by law provide, transmit to the President pro tempore of the Senate and the Speaker of the House of Representatives their written declaration that the President is unable to discharge the powers and duties of his office, the Vice President shall immediately assume the powers and duties of the office as Acting President.

Thereafter, when the President transmits to the President pro tempore of the Senate and the Speaker of the House of Representatives his written declaration that no inability exists, he shall resume the powers and duties of his office unless the Vice President and a majority of either the principal officers of the executive department or of such other body as Congress may by law provide, transmit within four days to the President pro tempore of the Senate and the Speaker of the House of Representatives their written declaration that the President is unable to discharge the powers and duties of his office. Thereupon Congress shall decide the issue, assembling within forty-eight hours for that purpose if not in session. If the Congress, within twenty-one days after receipt of the latter written declaration, or, if Congress is not in session, within twenty-one days after Congress is required to assemble, determines by two-thirds vote of both Houses that the President is unable to discharge the powers and duties of his office, the Vice President shall continue to discharge the same as Acting President; otherwise, the President shall resume the powers and duties of his office.

## AMENDMENT XXVI

SECTION 1. The right of citizens of the United States, who are eighteen years of age or older, to vote shall not be denied or abridged by the United States or by any State on account of age.

SECTION 2. The Congress shall have power to enforce this article by appropriate legislation.

## AMENDMENT XXVII

No law, varying the compensation for the services of the Senators and Representatives, shall take effect, until an election of Representatives shall have intervened.

# Appendix 4

# *Resolution Transmitting the Constitution to Congress*

IN CONVENTION

*Monday, September 17, 1787*

PRESENT, *The States of New-Hampshire, Massachusetts, Connecticut, Mr. Hamilton from New-York, New Jersey, Pennsylvania, Delaware, Maryland, Virginia, North Carolina, South Carolina, and Georgia.*

*Resolved,* That the [following] Constitution be laid before the United States in Congress assembled, and that it is the opinion of this convention, that it should afterwards be submitted to a convention of delegates, chosen in each State by the people thereof, under the recommendation of its legislature, for their assent and ratification; and that each convention assenting to, and ratifying the same should give notice thereof to the United States in Congress assembled.

*Resolved,* That it is the opinion of this convention, that as soon as the conventions of nine States shall have ratified this Constitution, the United States in Congress assembled should fix a day on which electors should be appointed by the States which shall have ratified the same, and a day on which the electors should assemble to vote for the President, and the time and place for commencing proceedings under this Constitution; that after such publication the electors should be appointed, and the senators and representatives elected; that the electors should meet on the day fixed for the election of the President, and should transmit their votes certified, signed, sealed, and directed, as the Constitution requires, to the secretary of the United States in Congress assembled; that the senators and representatives should convene at the time and place assigned; that the senators should appoint a president of the Senate, for the sole purpose of receiving, opening, and counting the votes for President; and that after he shall be chosen, the Congress, together with the President, should without delay proceed to execute this Constitution.

*By the unanimous order of the convention.*

GEORGE WASHINGTON, *President.*

WILLIAM JACKSON, *Secretary.*

# Appendix 5

# *Washington's Letter of Transmittal*

IN CONVENTION

*September 17, 1787*

SIR,

WE HAVE now the honor to submit to the consideration of the United States in Congress assembled, that Constitution which has appeared to us the most advisable.

The friends of our country have long seen and desired, that the power of making war, peace, and treaties, of levying money and regulating commerce, and the correspondent executive and judicial authorities should be fully and effectually vested in the general government of the Union: but the impropriety of delegating such extensive trust to one body of men is evident—Hence results the necessity of a different organization.

It is obviously impracticable in the federal government of these States, to secure all rights of independent sovereignty to each, and yet provide for the interest and safety of all—Individuals entering into society, must give up a share of liberty to preserve the rest. The magnitude of the sacrifice must depend as well on situation and circumstances as on the object to be obtained. It is at all times difficult to draw with precision the line between those rights which must be surrendered, and those which may be reserved; and on the present occasion this difficulty was increased by a difference among the several States as to their situation, extent, habits, and particular interests.

In all our deliberations on this subject we kept steadily in our view, that which appears to us the greatest interest of every true American, the consolidation of our Union, in which is involved our prosperity, felicity, safety, perhaps our national existence. This important consideration, seriously and deeply impressed on our minds, led each State in the Convention to be less rigid on points of inferior magnitude, than might have been otherwise expected; and thus the Constitution, which we now present, is the result of a spirit of amity, and of that mutual deference and concession which the peculiarity of our political situation rendered indispensable.

That it will meet the full and entire approbation of every State is not perhaps to be expected; but each will doubtless consider, that had her interest alone been consulted, the consequences might have been particularly disagreeable or injurious to others; that it is liable to as few exceptions as could reasonably have been expected, we hope and believe; that it may promote the lasting welfare of that country so dear to us all, and secure her freedom and happiness, is our most ardent wish.

With great respect,

We have the honor to be

SIR,

Your Excellency's most

Obedient and Humble Servants,

GEORGE WASHINGTON, President

By Unanimous Order of the Convention

HIS EXCELLENCY

THE PRESIDENT OF CONGRESS

# Appendix 6

# *The Birth of the Constitution: A Chronology*

## 1786

| | |
|---|---|
| September 11–14 | Annapolis Convention. |
| September 20 | Report of Annapolis Convention, calling for a Constitutional Convention, submitted to Congress. |
| October 11 | Congress sends Annapolis Convention report to committee. |
| November 23 | New Jersey elects delegates. |
| December 4 | Virginia elects delegates. |
| December 30 | Pennsylvania elects delegates. |

## 1787

| | |
|---|---|
| January 6 | North Carolina elects delegates. |
| January 17 | New Hampshire elects delegates. |
| February 3 | Delaware elects delegates. |
| February 10 | Georgia elects delegates. |
| February 21 | Congress calls Constitutional Convention. |
| March 3 | Massachusetts elects delegates. |
| March 6 | New York elects delegates. |
| March 8 | South Carolina elects delegates. |
| March 14 | Rhode Island refuses to elect delegates. |
| April 23–May 6 | Maryland elects delegates. |
| May 14 | Day appointed for beginning of Convention; quorum not present. |
| May 14–17 | Connecticut elects delegates. |
| May 25 | Quorum is present (seven states represented); Convention begins. |
| May 29 | Governor Edmund Randolph introduces the Virginia Plan. |
| June 15 | William Paterson introduces the New Jersey Plan. |
| July 16 | Great Compromise approved: voting power in first house of Congress to be apportioned by population; states to have equal voting power in the second house. |
| August 6 | Committee on Detail submits draft to Convention. |
| September 12 | Committee on Style submits draft to Convention. |
| September 15 | Draft Constitution approved by unanimous vote of the states represented in the Convention. |
| September 17 | Constitution is signed; Convention adjourns. |
| September 26–28 | Proposed Constitution debated in Congress. |

| | |
|---|---|
| September 28 | Congress transmits Constitution to the states for ratification action. |
| September 29 | Pennsylvania calls state convention. |
| October 17 | Connecticut calls state convention. |
| October 25 | Massachusetts calls state convention. |
| October 26 | Georgia calls state convention. |
| October 31 | Virginia calls state convention. |
| November 1 | New Jersey calls state convention. |
| November 6 | Delegates to Pennsylvania convention elected. |
| November 10 | Delaware calls state convention. |
| November 12 | Delegates to Connecticut convention elected. |
| November 19–January 7, 1788 | Delegates to Massachusetts convention elected. |
| November 20 | Pennsylvania convention begins. |
| November 26 | Delegates to Delaware convention elected. |
| November 27–December 1 | Delegates to New Jersey convention elected. |
| December 1 | Maryland calls state convention. |
| December 3 | Delaware convention begins. |
| December 4–5 | Delegates to Georgia convention elected. |
| December 6 | North Carolina calls state convention. |
| December 7 | Delaware convention ratifies Constitution (30–0). |
| December 11 | New Jersey convention begins. |
| December 12 | Pennsylvania convention ratifies Constitution (46–23). |
| December 14 | New Hampshire calls state convention. |
| December 18 | New Jersey convention ratifies constitution (38–0). |
| December 25 | Georgia convention begins. |
| December 31–February 12, 1788 | Delegates to New Hampshire convention elected. |

## 1788

| | |
|---|---|
| January 3 | Connecticut convention begins. |
| January 9 | Connecticut convention ratifies Constitution (128–40). |
| January 9 | Massachusetts convention begins. |
| January 19 | South Carolina calls state convention. |
| February 1 | New York calls state convention. |
| February 6 | Massachusetts convention ratifies Constitution (187–168) and proposes amendments. |
| February 13–22 | New Hampshire convention holds first session. |
| March 1 | Rhode Island calls state referendum on Constitution. |
| March 3–31 | Delegates to Virginia convention elected. |
| March 24 | Rhode Island voters reject Constitution in referendum (2711–239). |
| March 28–29 | Delegates to North Carolina convention elected. |
| April 7 | Delegates to Maryland convention elected. |
| April 11–12 | Delegates to South Carolina convention elected. |
| April 21 | Maryland convention begins. |
| April 26 | Maryland convention ratifies Constitution (63–11). |
| April 29–May 3 | Delegates to New York convention elected. |
| May 12 | South Carolina convention begins. |
| May 23 | South Carolina convention ratifies Constitution (149–73) and proposes amendments. |
| June 2 | Virginia convention begins. |
| June 17 | New York convention begins. |
| June 18 | New Hampshire convention begins second session. |
| June 21 | New Hampshire convention ratifies Constitution (57–47) and proposes amendments. |
| June 25 | Virginia convention ratifies Constitution (89–79) and proposes amendments. |

| | |
|---|---|
| July 2 | New Hampshire's ratification received by Congress; as this is the ninth state ratification, a committee is appointed to effect the transition from government under the Articles of Confederation to government under the Constitution. |
| July 21 | North Carolina convention begins. |
| July 26 | New York convention ratifies Constitution (30–27) and proposes amendments. |
| August 2 | North Carolina convention proposes amendments, but does not ratify the Constitution. |
| September 13 | Congress sets dates for presidential election and for first meeting of Congress under the Constitution. |
| November 20 | Virginia legislature requests Congress to call a second constitutional convention. |
| November 30 | North Carolina calls second state convention. |

### 1789

| | |
|---|---|
| May 4 | Representative James Madison announces, during congressional debate, his intention to introduce constitutional amendments. |
| May 5–6 | Petitions to Congress from legislatures of Virginia and New York, asking Congress to call a second constitutional convention, are reported and filed. |
| June 8 | Madison, in a speech in the House of Representatives, introduces amendments that will become the Bill of Rights. |
| July 21 | Madison's proposed amendments referred to select committee of the House of Representatives. |
| July 28 | Select committee reports back the proposed amendments; its report is tabled. |
| August 14–18 | Congress debates proposed amendments in Committee of the Whole. |
| August 21–22 | Delegates to second North Carolina convention elected. |
| August 24 | House of Representatives approves and sends to the Senate seventeen proposed amendments, including the provisions of the Bill of Rights. |
| September 2 | Senate begins debate on the Bill of Rights. |
| September 9 | Senate approves a version of the Bill of Rights. |
| September 21 | The Senate and House versions of the Bill of Rights are referred to a conference committee. |
| September 24 | House of Representatives approves (37–14) conference committee version of the Bill of Rights. |
| September 25 | Senate approves conference committee version of the Bill of Rights. Twelve amendments to the Constitution, including the ten now known as the Bill of Rights, are proposed by Congress to the states. |
| November 16 | Second North Carolina convention begins. |
| November 20 | New Jersey legislature ratifies the Bill of Rights. |
| November 21 | North Carolina convention ratifies Constitution (194–77) and proposes amendments. |
| December 19 | Maryland legislature ratifies the Bill of Rights. |
| December 22 | North Carolina legislature ratifies Bill of Rights. |

### 1790

| | |
|---|---|
| January 17 | Rhode Island calls state convention. |
| January 18 | South Carolina legislature ratifies the Bill of Rights. |
| January 25 | New Hampshire legislature ratifies the Bill of Rights. |
| January 28 | Delaware legislature ratifies the Bill of Rights. |
| February 8 | Delegates to Rhode Island convention elected. |
| February 24 | New York legislature ratifies the Bill of Rights. |

| | |
|---|---|
| March 1 | Rhode Island convention begins. |
| March 10 | Pennsylvania legislature ratifies the Bill of Rights. |
| May 29 | Rhode Island convention ratifies Constitution (34–32) and proposes amendments. |
| June | Rhode Island legislature ratifies the Bill of Rights. (N.B.: exact date in June of Rhode Island's ratification is unknown.) |

### 1791

| | |
|---|---|
| March 4 | Vermont admitted to the Union. |
| November 3 | Vermont legislature ratifies Bill of Rights. |
| December 15 | Virginia legislature ratifies the Bill of Rights. |

# Appendix 7

# *Important Events in the Development of American Constitutional Law*

| | |
|---|---|
| 1215 | Magna Carta. |
| 1225 | Magna Carta reissued in the modified form that became the English statute. |
| 1295 | Parliament of three estates established, the model for all future English parliaments. |
| 1297 | Confirmatio Cartarum. |
| 1322 | That no statute could be made except by consent of both lords and commons was established and declared. |
| 1354 | The phrase "due process of law" was first used in a statute. |
| 1387 | By statute the king was forbidden to levy imposts, duties, or surcharges without consent of Parliament; the king could no longer legally raise revenue by his own authority alone. |
| 1407 | The king agreed that all revenue measures must originate in the House of Commons; this practice was followed in Article I, section 7, of the Constitution. |
| 1606 | Edward Coke was appointed Chief Justice of Common Pleas. He was made Chief Justice of the King's Bench ("Lord Chief Justice of England") in 1613. |
| | First Virginia Charter. |
| 1608 | *Calvin's Case.* |
| 1610 | *Bonham's Case.* |
| 1619 | The General Assembly of Virginia met, the first representative assembly in the New World. |
| 1620 | Mayflower Compact. |
| 1628 | Petition of Right. |
| 1629 | Charter of Massachusetts Bay Company. |
| 1635 | Massachusetts General Court established a committee to write fundamental laws to limit magistrate, "in resemblance to a Magna Carta." |
| | Roger Williams banished by the General Court of Massachusetts. He founded Providence Plantation in 1636. |
| | In instructions to Governor Wyatt, the Virginia Assembly was officially recognized as a permanent institution, to meet at least annually. |
| 1639 | Fundamental Orders of Connecticut. |
| 1641 | Courts of High Commission and Star Chamber abolished; oath *ex officio* abolished. |
| | Massachusetts Body of Liberties. |
| | The Grand Remonstrance charged King Charles I with various unlawful acts and demanded that executive power be exercised by ministers in whom Parliament had confidence. |
| 1643 | Roger Williams's *The Bloudy Tenent of Persecution.* |
| 1644 | John Milton's *Areopagitica*, a plea against prior restraint and censorship, published. |
| 1644 | Massachusetts General Court became bicameral, as Assistants met separately from Assembly. |
| 1647 | Massachusetts General Laws and Liberties. |

| | |
|---|---|
| 1649 | Maryland Toleration Act. |
| 1652 | Roger Williams's pamphlet *The Bloudy Tenent Yet More Bloudy* published. |
| 1653 | The Instrument of Government, the short-lived written constitution of the English commonwealth, promulgated by Oliver Cromwell. |
| 1660–1696 | Navigation Acts. |
| 1662 | Royal Charter for Connecticut (constitution until 1818). |
| 1663 | Royal Charter of Rhode Island (constitution until 1842). |
| 1664 | New York granted to Duke of York as proprietary colony; the proprietor to have complete power to make laws. |
| 1670 | *Bushell's Case.* |
| 1679 | Habeas Corpus Act. |
| 1682 | Pennsylvania Frame of Government. |
| 1687 | William Penn's *The Excellent Priviledge of Liberty and Property* published; it included the first text of and commentary on Magna Carta published in America. |
| 1689 | Act of Toleration. |
| | English Bill of Rights. |
| | John Locke's *Letter Concerning Toleration.* |
| 1690 | John Locke's *Two Treatises of Government.* |
| 1695 | The last English licensing act, restricting freedom of the press, expired. |
| 1698 | Algernon Sidney's *Discourses Concerning Government.* |
| 1701 | Pennsylvania Charter of Liberties. |
| 1720–1721 | Trenchard and Gordon's essays, *Cato's Letters* and *The Independent Whig,* first published. |
| 1733 | Molasses Act. |
| 1735 | *Zenger's Case.* |
| 1748 | Montesquieu's *Spirit of the Laws.* |
| 1754 | Albany Plan of Union proposed by the Albany Congress. |
| 1758 | Emerich de Vattel's *Law of Nations and of Nature.* |
| 1762 | Massachusetts General Court voted a ban on general warrants; it was disallowed by the Governor. |
| 1763 | *Paxton's Case* (Writs of Assistance Case). |
| 1764 | James Otis, in *The Rights of the British Colonies Asserted and Proved,* denied the right of Parliament to tax the Americans and maintained that a court could judge an act of Parliament void if it was contrary to natural justice. |
| | The Sugar Act (American Revenue Act) was the first attempt by the British Parliament to tax the colonists for revenue purposes. |
| 1765 | *Entick v. Carrington.* |
| | Stamp Act. |
| | Stamp Act Congress. |
| 1765–1769 | William Blackstone's *Commentaries on the Laws of England* published. |
| 1766 | A county court in Northhampton County, Virginia, in an advisory opinion, declared the Stamp Act unconstitutional and therefore void. |
| | Declaratory Act. |
| 1767–1768 | John Dickinson's *Letters from a Farmer in Pennsylvania* published. |
| 1768 | Massachusetts Circular Letter. |
| 1772 | *Somerset's Case.* |
| 1773 | Constitutional debate in Massachusetts; Governor James Hutchinson, in a message to the General Court, asserted that supreme power must rest somewhere; the alternatives were parliamentary rule or independence. The General Court replied that sovereignty could be, and, in fact, already was, divided. |
| 1774 | Coercive Acts (Intolerable Acts), including Administration of Justice Act. |
| | First Continental Congress. |
| | The Association. |
| | Joseph Galloway proposes his Plan of Union. |
| | Thomas Jefferson's *Summary View of the Rights of British America.* |
| 1775 | Second Continental Congress convened. |
| | Declaration of the Causes and Necessity of Taking Up Arms. |

| | |
|---|---|
| 1776 | Thomas Paine's *Common Sense.* |
| | Declaration of Independence. |
| | Dickinson's draft of Articles of Confederation submitted to Congress. |
| 1776–1780 | First state constitutions written. |
| 1777 | Articles of Confederation approved by Congress and submitted to states. |
| 1779 | Congressional resolution asked states to cede their western lands to the United States. |
| 1780 | *Holmes v. Walton* (New Jersey). |
| 1781 | Articles of Confederation ratified and in force. |
| 1783 | *Quock Walker's Case* (Massachusetts). |
| 1784 | *Rutgers v. Waddington* (New York). |
| | James Madison's "Memorial and Remonstrance" against religious assessments. |
| 1786 | Virginia Statute for Religious Freedom. |
| | Ten Pound Act Cases (New Hampshire). |
| | *Trevett v. Weeden* (Rhode Island). |
| | Annapolis Convention. |
| 1787 | *Bayard v. Singleton.* |
| | Congress adopted resolution calling federal Constitutional Convention. |
| | John Adams's *Defense of the Constitutions of Government of the United States.* |
| | Constitutional Convention met in Philadelphia and drafted Constitution of the United States. |
| | Northwest Ordinance. |
| | Congress transmitted Constitution to the states for ratification. |
| 1787–1788 | *The Federalist.* |
| 1788 | Constitution ratified by required nine states. |
| | Congress adopted ordinance to put Constitution into effect. |
| 1789 | George Washington chosen President. |
| | Departments of State, War, and Treasury created. |
| | Judiciary Act of 1789. |
| | Habeas Corpus Act. |
| | Bill of Rights proposed. |
| | President Washington appeared in person to ask the Senate's advice and consent relative to an Indian treaty; failure to act cost the Senate a role as the President's council of advice. |
| 1790 | Alexander Hamilton's Report on the Public Credit. |
| | Treason Act. |
| 1791 | *Champion and Dickason v. Casey.* |
| | Bank of the United States Act. |
| | Bill of Rights ratified and in effect. |
| | Hamilton's Report on Manufactures. |
| 1792 | *Hayburn's Case.* |
| | President Washington used the presidential veto power for the first time, vetoing a reapportionment bill he thought unconstitutional. |
| 1793 | *Chisholm v. Georgia.* |
| | First Fugitive Slave Act. |
| | The Supreme Court, presented with a list of questions from the President and the cabinet concerning relations with France, refused to give an advisory opinion. |
| | Washington's Proclamation of Neutrality in the Wars of the French Revolution. |
| 1794 | Jay's Treaty. |
| | Whiskey Rebellion in Pennsylvania against federal alcohol tax. Suppressed by militia of four states under federal control. |
| 1795 | *Van Horne's Lessee v. Dorrance.* |
| | Post Office Department created. |
| | *Ware v. Hylton.* |
| 1796 | *Hylton v. United States.* |
| | Washington's Farewell Address. |
| | XYZ Affair began three-year undeclared war with France. |
| 1798 | Alien and Sedition Acts. |
| | *Calder v. Bull.* |

|  | Department of the Navy created. |
|  | Eleventh Amendment ratified and in effect. |
|  | Virginia and Kentucky Resolutions. |
| 1799 | Second set of Kentucky Resolutions claimed states could nullify unconstitutional acts of Congress. |
| 1801 | Electoral College tie between Thomas Jefferson and Aaron Burr resolved in House of Representatives; this led to the Twelfth Amendment. |
|  | John Marshall became Chief Justice. |
|  | Judiciary Act of 1801. |
| 1802 | Judiciary Act of 1801 repealed; Judiciary Act of 1802 enacted. |
| 1803 | *Marbury v. Madison.* |
|  | *Stuart v. Laird.* |
|  | Louisiana Purchase Treaty. |
| 1804 | John Pickering, United States District Court judge for New Hampshire, having been impeached by the House of Representatives of malfeasance and intemperance, was convicted by the Senate and removed from office. |
|  | Twelfth Amendment ratified and in effect. |
| 1805 | Samuel Chase, Associate Justice of the Supreme Court, having been impeached by the House of Representatives of oppressive and partisan conduct, was acquitted by the Senate. |
| 1807 | *Ex Parte Bollman and Swartwout.* |
|  | Abolition of the Slave Trade Act. |
|  | Embargo Act. |
|  | Trial of Aaron Burr (*United States v. Burr*). |
| 1809 | Massachusetts Resolutions declared the Embargo unconstitutional and not legally binding. |
|  | *United States v. Judge Peters* (Olmstead Case). |
| 1810 | *Fletcher v. Peck.* |
| 1812 | *New Jersey v. Wilson.* |
|  | *United States v. Hudson and Goodwin.* |
| 1814 | Hartford Convention. |
| 1815 | *Terrett v. Taylor.* |
|  | Second Bank of the United States Act. |
| 1816 | *Martin v. Hunter's Lessee.* |
| 1817 | Madison's veto of Bonus Bill (on constitutional grounds). |
| 1819 | Secretary of War Calhoun recommended a program of internal improvements as a defense measure. |
|  | *Dartmouth College v. Woodward.* |
|  | *McCulloch v. Maryland.* |
|  | *Sturges v. Crowninshield.* |
| 1820 | John Taylor of Caroline's *Construction Construed* published, arguing that the Supreme Court was destroying the independence of the states and of the other branches of the federal government. |
|  | Missouri Compromise. |
| 1821 | *Cohens v. Virginia.* |
| 1822 | Cumberland Road Bill vetoed by President James Monroe, who also recommended a constitutional amendment authorizing the United States to build and operate internal improvements. |
| 1823 | Monroe Doctrine. |
|  | *Corfield v. Coryell.* |
| 1824 | *Gibbons v. Ogden.* |
|  | *Osborn v. Bank of the United States.* |
| 1825 | John Quincy Adams (who had finished second in the Electoral College vote) elected president by the House of Representatives. |
|  | *Eakin v. Raub.* |
| 1826–1830 | James Kent's *Commentaries on American Law.* |
| 1827 | *Brown v. Maryland.* |
|  | *Martin v. Mott.* |
|  | *Ogden v. Saunders.* |

| 1828 | South Carolina Exposition and Protest. |
|---|---|
| | *American Insurance Company v. Canter.* |
| 1829 | *Willson v. Black Bird Creek Marsh Company.* |
| 1830 | Maysville Road Bill vetoed by President Andrew Jackson. |
| | Daniel Webster and Robert Young Hayne participated in a great debate in the Senate on the nature of the Constitution. |
| | *Craig v. Missouri.* |
| | *Providence Bank v. Billings.* |
| 1831 | William Lloyd Garrison founded *The Liberator.* |
| | *Cherokee Nation v. Georgia* (first of the Cherokee Indian Cases). |
| 1832 | Jackson's Veto of the Bank Bill. |
| | Vice-President John C. Calhoun, in his Fort Hill Address, explained his theory of nullification. |
| | South Carolina Ordinance of Nullification of the Tariff Act of 1828. |
| | Jackson's Proclamation to the People of South Carolina. |
| | *Worcester v. Georgia.* |
| 1833 | Force Act of 1833. |
| | Joseph Story's *Commentaries on the Constitution.* |
| | *Barron v. Baltimore.* |
| 1836 | First congressional "gag rule" on antislavery petitions imposed. |
| | Roger B. Taney became Chief Justice. |
| 1837 | Membership of Supreme Court increased from seven to nine. |
| | *New York v. Miln.* |
| | *Briscoe v. Bank of Kentucky.* |
| | *Charles River Bridge v. Warren Bridge Company.* |
| 1839 | *Bank of Augusta v. Earle.* |
| 1841 | *Groves v. Slaughter.* |
| 1842 | Reapportionment Act required representatives to be elected by district. |
| | *Dobbins v. Erie Company.* |
| | *Swift v. Tyson.* |
| | *Prigg v. Pennsylvania.* |
| 1843 | *Bronson v. Kinzie.* |
| 1844 | Texas Annexation Treaty signed; rejected by Senate. |
| 1845 | Congress, by joint resolution, approved the annexation of Texas and provided for admission of Texas as a state. |
| | Congress provided for uniform presidential election day. |
| 1847 | License Cases. |
| 1848 | Oregon Act. |
| | Treaty of Guadalupe Hidalgo. |
| | *West River Bridge Company v. Dix.* |
| 1849 | Passenger Cases. |
| | *Luther v. Borden.* |
| 1850 | Compromise of 1850. |
| | Nashville Convention Resolutions asserted fight of secession. |
| | *Strader v. Graham.* |
| 1850–1858 | Personal Liberty Laws adopted by states: Vermont in 1850; Connecticut and Rhode Island in 1854; Maine, Massachusetts, and Michigan in 1855; Kansas in 1857; Wisconsin in 1858. |
| 1851 | *Cooley v. Board of Wardens.* |
| 1852 | *Pennsylvania v. Wheeling Bridge Company.* |
| | *The Genesee Chief v. Fitzhugh.* |
| 1854 | Kansas-Nebraska Act. |
| | *Ohio Life Insurance & Trust Company v. DeBolt.* |
| | *In re Booth* (Wisconsin Supreme Court held Fugitive Slave Act of 1850 unconstitutional). |
| 1855 | Connecticut adopted law requiring literacy test for voting. |
| | Court of Claims created. |
| 1856 | *Murray's Lessee v. Hoboken Land Improvement Company.* |
| | *Wynehamer v. New York.* |
| | *Dodge v. Woolsey.* |

| | |
|---|---|
| 1857 | *Dred Scott v. Sandford.* |
| 1858 | Lincoln-Douglas debates. |
| 1859 | *Ableman v. Booth.* |
| 1860 | Crittenden Compromise proposed. |
| | Senator Jefferson Davis introduced a proposal for a federal slave code. |
| | South Carolina Ordinance of Secession. |
| 1861 | First federal income tax imposed as a war measure. |
| | President Abraham Lincoln proclaimed insurrection, called for troops, suspended habeas corpus. |
| | Secession of ten other states; Confederate Constitution adopted. |
| | *Kentucky v. Dennison.* |
| 1862 | Abolition of slavery in the territories. |
| | Emancipation Proclamation. |
| | Homestead Act. |
| 1863 | Gettysburg Address. |
| | Lincoln's Proclamation of Amnesty and Reconstruction. |
| 1864 | Lincoln's pocket veto of the Wade-Davis Bill. |
| | Salmon P. Chase became Chief Justice. |
| 1865 | Freedmen's Bureau founded. |
| | Joint Committee on Reconstruction established. |
| | Thirteenth Amendment ratified and in effect. |
| | Writ of habeas corpus restored by presidential proclamation. |
| 1866 | Civil Rights Act of 1866. |
| | *Ex Parte Milligan.* |
| 1867 | First Reconstruction Act. |
| | Habeas Corpus Act. |
| | Tenure of Office Act. |
| 1868 | *Ex parte McCardle.* |
| | Fourteenth Amendment ratified and in effect. |
| | Impeachment of Andrew Johnson. |
| | Johnson's proclamation of general amnesty. |
| | *Texas v. White.* |
| 1869 | Wyoming adopts women's suffrage. |
| 1870 | Department of Justice established. |
| | Fifteenth Amendment ratified and in effect. |
| | *Hepburn v. Griswold.* |
| 1871 | Force Act of 1871. |
| | *Knox v. Lee.* |
| | Ku Klux Klan Act. |
| 1872 | Congress established uniform date for congressional elections. |
| 1873 | Slaughterhouse Cases. |
| 1874 | Morrison R. Waite became Chief Justice. |
| 1875 | Civil Rights Act of 1875. |
| 1876 | Disputed election: Tilden-Hayes. |
| | *Munn v. Illinois.* |
| | *United States v. Cruikshank.* |
| | *United States v. Reese.* |
| 1877 | Compromise of 1877 settled disputed election and ended Reconstruction. |
| 1880 | Chinese Exclusion Treaty. |
| | *Strauder v. West Virginia.* |
| 1881 | Kansas adopted prohibition of alcohol (first state prohibition statute). |
| | *Springer v. United States.* |
| | *Kilbourn v. Thompson.* |
| 1882 | Chinese Exclusion Act (enacted over presidential veto). |
| 1883 | Civil Rights Cases. |
| 1884 | *Juilliard v. Greenman.* |
| | *Ex parte Yarbrough.* |
| | *Hurtado v. California.* |

| | |
|---|---|
| 1886 | *Wabash, St. Louis & Pacific Railway v. Illinois.* |
| | *Boyd v. United States.* |
| | *Yick Wo v. Hopkins.* |
| 1887 | Interstate Commerce Act. |
| 1888 | Melville W. Fuller became Chief Justice. |
| 1890 | *Chicago, Milwaukee & St. Paul Railroad v. Minnesota.* |
| | *Leisy v. Hardin.* |
| | Sherman Antitrust Act. |
| 1892 | *Counselman v. Hitchcock.* |
| 1894 | Force Act of 1871 repealed. |
| | *Reagan v. Farmers' Loan and Trust Company.* |
| 1895 | *United States v. E. C. Knight Company.* |
| | *Pollock v. Farmers' Loan and Trust Company.* |
| | *In re Debs.* |
| 1896 | *Plessy v. Ferguson.* |
| | *Allgeyer v. Louisiana.* |
| 1897 | Trans-Missouri Freight Case. |
| | *Chicago, Burlington & Quincy Railroad v. Chicago.* |
| 1898 | *Holden v. Hardy.* |
| | *Smyth v. Ames.* |
| | *Williams v. Mississippi.* |
| 1899 | *United States v. Wong Kim Ark.* |
| 1901 | New Alabama constitution: literacy and property tests, plus grandfather clause, required for voting (effect was to disenfranchise blacks). |
| 1903 | *Champion v. Ames.* |
| | First direct primary elections (in Wisconsin). |
| | Panama Canal Treaty (Hay-Bunau Treaty). |
| 1904 | *Northern Securities Company v. United States.* |
| 1905 | *Swift & Company v. United States.* |
| | *Lochner v. New York.* |
| 1906 | Hepburn Act. |
| 1908 | *Muller v. Oregon.* |
| | *Adair v. United States.* |
| | *Loewe v. Lawlor.* |
| | *Ex parte Young.* |
| | *Twining v. New Jersey.* |
| 1910 | Edward D. White became Chief Justice. |
| | Mann-Elkins Act. |
| 1911 | *United States v. Grimaud.* |
| | *Standard Oil Company v. United States.* |
| 1913 | Federal Reserve Act (Owen-Glass Act). |
| | Sixteenth Amendment ratified and in effect. |
| 1914 | Federal Trade Commission Act. |
| | *Weeks v. United States.* |
| | Shreveport Rate Case. |
| 1916 | Child Labor Act (Keating-Owen Act). |
| 1917 | Selective Service Act. |
| 1918 | Selective Draft Law Cases. |
| | *Hammer v. Dagenhart.* |
| 1919 | Eighteenth Amendment ratified and in effect. |
| | *Schenck v. United States.* |
| | Senate rejects Treaty of Versailles. |
| | Volstead Act. |
| | *Abrams v. United States.* |
| 1920 | Esch-Cummings Transportation Act. |
| | *Missouri v. Holland.* |
| | *United States v. United States Steel Corporation.* |

Nineteenth Amendment ratified and in effect.
Palmer Raids.

1921   *Bailey v. Drexel Furniture Company.*
Budget and Accounting Act.
William Howard Taft became Chief Justice.

1923   *Adkins v. Children's Hospital.*
*Moore v. Dempsey.*
*Massachusetts v. Mellon.*

1924   Child Labor Amendment proposed by Congress.

1925   *State v. Scopes* (Tennessee).
*Pierce v. Society of Sisters.*
*Gitlow v. New York.*

1926   *Meyers v. United States.*

1927   *Nixon v. Herndon.*

1928   *Olmstead v. United States.*

1930   Charles Evans Hughes became Chief Justice.

1931   *Near v. Minnesota.*

1932   Norris-La Guardia Act.
*Powell v. Alabama.*

1933   National Industrial Recovery Act.
Securities Act of 1933.
Tennessee Valley Authority Act.
Twentieth Amendment ratified and in effect.
Twenty-First Amendment ratified and in effect.

1934   Communications Act.
*Nebbia v. New York.*
*Home Building and Loan Company v. Blaisdell.*
Securities Exchange Act of 1934.

1935   National Labor Relations Act (Wagner Act).
Social Security Act.
*Schechter Poultry Corporation v. United States.*
*Norris v. Alabama.*
*Humphrey's Executor v. United States.*

1936   *Brown v. Mississippi.*
*United States v. Butler.*
*Ashwander v. Tennessee.*
*Carter v. Carter Coal Company.*

1937   Franklin D. Roosevelt announced Court-packing scheme.
*West Coast Hotel Company v. Parrish.*
Wagner Act Cases.
Social Security Act Cases.
*United States v. Curtiss-Wright Export Corporation.*
*Palko v. Connecticut.*

1938   Fair Labor Standards Act.
Food, Drug and Cosmetics Act.
House of Representatives establishes committee to investigate un-American activities.
*Johnson v. Zerbst.*
*Missouri ex rel. Gaines v. Canada.*

1939   *Graves, New York ex rel., v. O'Keefe.*
Hatch Act.

1940   Alien Registration Act (Smith Act).
*Cantwell v. Connecticut.*

1941   Fair Employment Practices Commission established by executive order.
Harlan F. Stone became Chief Justice.
*United States v. Darby Lumber Company.*

1942   *Wickard v. Filburn.*
*Betts v. Brady.*

|      | President Roosevelt approved program of relocation of Japanese Americans. |
|------|-----|
|      | *Skinner v. Oklahoma.* |
| 1943 | *McNabb v. United States.* |
|      | *Hirabayashi v. United States.* |
|      | *West Virginia Board of Education v. Barnette* (Second Flag Salute Case). |
| 1944 | *Korematsu v. United States.* |
|      | *Smith v. Allwright.* |
| 1946 | Frederick M. Vinson became Chief Justice. |
| 1947 | *Everson v. Board of Education.* |
|      | First Hoover Commission established. |
|      | National Labor-Management Relations Act (Taft-Hartley Act) passed over President Harry S. Truman's veto. |
|      | National Security Act. |
| 1948 | Executive orders banned racial segregation in the armed forces and in civilian federal employment. |
|      | *Illinois ex rel. McCollum v. Board of Education.* |
|      | *Shelley v. Kraemer.* |
|      | Selective Service Act. |
|      | *Sipuel v. Board of Regents.* |
| 1949 | *Wolf v. Colorado.* |
| 1950 | *American Communications Association v. Douds.* |
|      | Internal Security Act (McCarran Act). |
|      | *Sweatt v. Painter.* |
|      | *McLaurin v. Oklahoma State Regents for Higher Education.* |
| 1951 | *Dennis v. United States.* |
|      | Twenty-Second Amendment ratified and in effect. |
| 1952 | Immigration and Nationality Act (McCarran-Walter Act) became law over Truman's veto. |
|      | President Truman ordered seizure of steel mills. |
|      | *Youngstown Sheet & Tube Company v. Sawyer* (Steel Seizure Case). |
| 1953 | Earl Warren became Chief Justice. |
| 1954 | *Brown v. Board of Education of Topeka.* |
|      | Censure of Joseph McCarthy by the United States Senate. |
|      | Communist Control Act. |
| 1955 | *Brown v. Board of Education II* ("all deliberate speed"). |
| 1956 | *Ullmann v. United States.* |
| 1957 | Civil Rights Act of 1957. |
|      | President Dwight D. Eisenhower ordered federal troops to enforce desegregation order in Little Rock, Arkansas. |
|      | *Watkins v. United States.* |
|      | *Yates v. United States.* |
|      | *Mallory v. United States.* |
|      | *Roth v. United States, Alberts v. California.* |
| 1958 | *Cooper v. Aaron.* |
| 1959 | *Barenblatt v. United States.* |
| 1960 | Civil Rights Act of 1960. |
| 1961 | *Communist Party v. Subversive Activities Control Board.* |
|      | *Mapp v. Ohio.* |
|      | Twenty-Third Amendment ratified and in effect. |
| 1962 | *Baker v. Carr.* |
|      | *Engel v. Vitale.* |
| 1963 | *Edwards v. South Carolina.* |
|      | *Gray v. Sanders.* |
|      | *Gideon v. Wainwright.* |
| 1964 | Civil Rights Act of 1964. |
|      | Gulf of Tonkin Resolution. |
|      | *Wesberry v. Sanders.* |
|      | *Reynolds v. Sims.* |

*New York Times Co. v. Sullivan.*
*Heart of Atlanta Motel v. United States.*
*Malloy v. Hogan.*
*Escobedo v. Illinois.*

1965     *Pointer v. Texas.*
*Albertson v. Subversive Activities Control Board.*
*Griswold v. Connecticut.*
Voting Rights Act of 1965.

1966     *Miranda v. Arizona.*
*South Carolina v. Katzenbach.*
*Harper v. Virginia State Board of Elections.*
*Miranda v. Arizona.*

1967     *Klopfer v. North Carolina.*
*In re Gault.*
*Warden v. Hayden.*
*Katz v. United States.*
Thurgood Marshall became the first African American Justice of the Supreme Court.

1968     *Duncan v. Louisiana.*
*Jones v. Alfred H. Mayer Co.*
*Terry v. Ohio.*

1969     *Benton v. Maryland.*
*Chimel v. California.*
Warren E. Burger became Chief Justice.

1970     *In re Winship.*
*Williams v. Florida.*

1971     *New York Times Company v. United States* (Pentagon Papers Case).
*Swann v. Charlotte-Mecklenburg County Board of Education.*
*McKeiver v. Pennsylvania, In re Burrus.*
*Lemon v. Kurtzman.*
*New York Times Co. v. United States, United States v. The Washington Post.*

1972     Equal Rights Amendment proposed by Congress.
*Furman v. Georgia* (Capital Punishment Cases of 1972).
*Kastigar v. United States.*
*Johnson v. Louisiana.*
*Apodaca v. Oregon.*
*Jackson v. Georgia.*
*Branch v. Texas.*
*Argersinger v. Hamlin.*
*Branzburg v. Hayes.*

1973     *Miller v. California.*
*Roe v. Wade.*

1974     Resignation of President Richard M. Nixon.
*United States v. Nixon.*

1976     *Buckley v. Valeo.*
*National League of Cities v. Usery.*
*Gregg v. Georgia, Proffitt v. Florida, Jurek v. Texas* (Capital Punishment Cases of 1976).

1977     Panama Canal Treaties.

1978     *Ballew v. Georgia.*
*First National Bank of Boston v. Bellotti.*
*Regents of University of California v. Bakke.*
District of Columbia Representation Amendment proposed by Congress.
Simple majority of Congress voted to extend ratification deadline for Equal Rights
    Amendment (original proposal had required a two-thirds vote).

1979     *United Steelworkers of America v. Weber.*

1981     Sandra Day O'Connor became the first woman Justice of the Supreme Court.

1982     Extended deadline for ratification of Equal Rights Amendment expired.
*Plyler v. Doe.*

| | |
|---|---|
| 1983 | *Immigration and Naturalization Service v. Chadha.* |
| 1985 | Deadline for ratification of District of Columbia Representation Amendment expired. |
| | Gramm-Rudman-Hollings Balanced Budget Act. |
| | *American Booksellers Association v. Hudnut* (7th Cir.; judgment affirmed by U.S. Supreme Court, 1986). |
| 1986 | *Batson v. Kentucky.* |
| | *Bowers v. Hardwick.* |
| | Iran-Contra Affair. |
| | *Pacific Gas & Electric Company v. Public Utilities Commission of California.* |
| | William H. Rehnquist became Chief Justice. |
| 1987 | *McCleskey v. Kemp.* |
| 1988 | *Hustler Magazine and Larry Flint v. Jerry Falwell.* |
| | *Morrison v. Olson.* |
| 1989 | *DeShaney v. Winnebago County Department of Social Service.* |
| | *Richmond (City of) v. J. A. Croson Co.* |
| | *Texas v. Johnson.* |
| 1990 | Americans with Disabilities Act of 1990. |
| | *Cruzan v. Director, Missouri Department of Health.* |
| | *Employment Division, Department of Human Resources of Oregon v. Smith.* |
| | *Missouri v. Jenkins.* |
| 1992 | *Lee v. Weisman.* |
| | *Lucas v. South Carolina Coastal Council.* |
| | *New York v. United States.* |
| | *Planned Parenthood v. Casey.* |
| | *R.A.V. v. City of St. Paul.* |
| | Twenty-Seventh Amendment ratified and in effect. |
| 1993 | *Nixon v. United States.* |
| | *Shaw v. Reno.* |
| 1994 | *Turner Broadcasting System v. FCC.* |
| | Violence Against Women Act. |
| 1995 | *Adarand Constructors, Inc. v. Peña.* |
| | *Hurley v. Irish-American Gay, Lesbian, and Bisexual Group of Boston.* |
| | *Rosenberger v. Rectors & Visitors of the University of Virginia.* |
| | *United States v. López.* |
| | *U.S. Term Limits v. Thornton.* |
| 1996 | Antiterrorism and Effective Death Penalty Act. |
| | *44 Liquormart, Inc. v. Rhode Island.* |
| | *Romer v. Evans.* |
| | *Seminole Tribe v. Florida.* |
| | *United States v. Virginia.* |
| 1997 | *Agostini v. Felton.* |
| | *Boerne v. Flores.* |
| | *Clinton v. Jones.* |
| | *Printz v. New York.* |
| | *Reno v. ACLU.* |
| | *Washington v. Glucksberg* and *Vacco v. Quill.* |
| 1998 | *Clinton v. New York.* |
| | Impeachment of President William J. Clinton. |
| 1999 | *Alden v. Maine.* |
| | *Saenz v. Roe.* |

# Glossary

**abstention*** Any of several doctrines by which federal courts delay or avoid decision, allowing issues of state law or entire cases to be decided by state courts.

**action** A court case. Before the unification of law and equity, an "action" at law was distinguished from a proceeding in equity.

**advisory opinion*** A judicial opinion on a question of law, rendered without deciding the rights of parties to an adversary proceeding. In the federal courts, advisory opinions are barred by the "case or controversy" requirement.

**amicus curiae*** [Latin: friend of the court] One who, although not a party to the case, submits a brief suggesting how the case, or certain issues in the case, should be decided.

**appeal*** Review of a court decision by a higher court to determine whether errors of law were made. Appeal is a particular type of review, but the word is sometimes used more generally, to refer to any review of a lower court decision.

**appellate jurisdiction*** The legitimate authority of a higher court to hear and decide appeals from lower courts.

**bail*** Money deposited with a court to guarantee the appearance of a defendant for trial, permitting his release from jail until trial.

**bill of attainder*** A legislative finding of guilt and imposition of punishment without a court trial.

**brief*** A document filed on behalf of a litigant, at trial or on appeal, stating the facts of the case and arguing the legal basis for a decision in the litigant's favor.

**case law** The body of law established in court decisions, as distinct from customary and statutory law. Case law is the most important component of the common law.

**certification*** A procedure by which a lower court requests from a higher court (or a federal court requests from a state court) guidance on questions of law relative to a case pending in the lower court.

**certiorari*** [Latin: to be made more certain] A form of writ directing a lower court to forward the record of a case to a higher court for review; it is the primary form of discretionary appellate review by the U.S. Supreme Court.

**civil law** (1) the body of law dealing with the private rights and duties of individuals, distinguished from criminal law; (2) a body of law derived from the Roman legal codes that is in force in continental Europe and elsewhere, distinguished from common law. Civil law, in the latter sense, is the basis of much of the private law of Louisiana, and it is the original source of some aspects of property law in Texas and in states formed from the Mexican Cession.

* Entries marked with an asterisk have a separate article in the *Encyclopedia*.

**class action\*** A legal action brought by one or more litigants in the name of a numerous class of whom the particular litigants claim to be representative, or an action against a numerous class of defendants.

**comity\*** The respect owed by one court or governmental agency to the official acts of a court or agency in another jurisdiction.

**common law\*** The body of legal custom and accumulated precedent inherited from England, sometimes inaccurately described as "judge-made law."

**concurrent powers\*** Governmental powers that may be exercised either by the national or by the state government.

**concurring opinion\*** A separate opinion filed by a judge of a multimember court indicating agreement with the decision of a case but setting forth alternative or additional reasons for reaching the result.

**consent decree\*** A court order that makes legally binding an agreement between the parties to a case to settle it without further litigation.

**declaratory judgment\*** A judicial order determining the legal rights of the parties in a particular case, anticipating future controversy rather than remedying past injury. Equitable in form, declaratory relief is available in federal court by virtue of an act of Congress.

**de facto\*** [Latin: in fact] Existing in fact, whether or not existing in law or by right.

**defendant** The party against whom an action is brought. At the appellate level the party moved against is called the appellee or respondent.

**de jure** [Latin: in law] Existing in law or by virtue of official acts; distinguished from de facto (q.v.).

**dictum (pl. dicta)** [Latin: something said] Formerly, an authoritative pronouncement. Now, commonly used as an abbreviation of "obiter dictum" (q.v.).

**dissenting opinion\*** An opinion by a judge of a multimember court who disagrees with the court's decision in a case.

**diversity jurisdiction\*** The legitimate authority of federal courts to hear cases in which the parties have "diversity of citizenship," that is, when they are citizens of different states or of a state and a foreign country.

**dual federalism\*** A doctrine of constitutional interpretation according to which the reserved powers of the states operate as limitations on the power of the national government.

**due process of law\*** The fair and regular procedures established by law. Under the Fifth and Fourteenth Amendments, the government may deprive a person of life, liberty, or property only after due process. The due process clauses of the Constitution protect both procedural and substantive rights.

**equity\*** A system of jurisprudence parallel to and corrective of the common law, based on principles of fairness rather than on the letter of the law. In most American jurisdictions, law and equity have been merged.

**error\*** A form of writ issued by a higher court directing a lower court to submit a case for appellate review. The writ of error is no longer used in the federal courts, having been superseded by appeal (q.v.).

**exclusionary rule\*** A rule excluding evidence obtained in violation of a defendant's rights from admission at the defendant's trial as proof of guilt.

**ex parte\*** [Latin: from one party; from the part (of)] (1) A hearing or other legal act at which only one side of a case is represented; (2) in the heading of a case, an identification of the party who is applying for judicial relief.

**ex post facto\*** [Latin: from after the fact] A law that makes criminal, or that increases the criminal penalty for, an act committed before the law was passed.

**ex relatione** [Latin: from what has been related (by)] Legal actions brought by the state upon information supplied by or at the instigation of a private party are said to be "ex relatione." In reports, it is abbreviated "ex rel."

**federal question jurisdiction\*** The legitimate authority of a federal court to hear and decide cases "arising under" the Constitution, laws, or treaties of the United States.

**grand jury\*** An investigatory body that is usually empowered to issue indictments or presentments charging persons with crimes.

**habeas corpus\*** [Latin: you shall have the body] A form of writ directing a custodial official to appear before a judge with the person of a prisoner and to give a satisfactory legal justification for having the person in custody. The writ of habeas corpus is frequently used by state prisoners to obtain federal court review of their convictions.

**immunity** In criminal cases, a grant of exemption from prosecution made in return for testimony; in intergovernmental relations, the exemption of government instrumentalities from taxation by other levels of government. In general, an exemption from a legally imposed duty or liability; along with privileges, immunities are protected by Article IV and by the Fourteenth Amendment.

**incorporation\*** (1) A doctrine according to which certain specific provisions of the Bill of Rights are made applicable against state authority by virtue of the "due process" clause of the Fourteenth Amendment; (2) a doctrine according to which certain territories are made so intimately a part of the United States that certain constitutional protections become applicable to the inhabitants.

**indictment\*** A formal statement by a grand jury charging a person with a criminal offense.

**in forma pauperis\*** [Latin: in the manner of a poor person] A proceeding in which the court waives requirements that a litigant pay certain fees and comply with certain formal requirements, granted because the litigant cannot afford to comply but ought not to be barred from access to the court.

**injunction\*** A form of writ prohibiting or .requiring the performance of a specific act by a particular person. An injunction is a form of remedy available under a court's equity power.

**in personam\*** [Latin: against the person] A manner of proceeding in a case so that the decision and remedy are directed against a particular person.

**in re\*** [Latin: in the matter (of)] A way of titling the report of a case in which there are no adversary parties.

**in rem\*** [Latin: against the thing] A manner of proceeding in a case so that the decision and remedy affect the status of property with reference to the whole world rather than to particular individuals.

**judgment\*** The official decision by a court of a case or controversy, including the remedy ordered, excluding the reasons for the ruling.

**judicial review\*** The power of a court to review legislation or other governmental acts, including the acts of administrative agencies. The term is used especially for court review to determine whether an act is in conformance with the Constitution.

**jurisdiction\*** Legitimate authority. The term is sometimes limited to the legitimate authority of courts to hear and decide cases.

**jury** A body of lay citizens exercising responsibility for hearing and deciding facts in the judicial system; a jury is either a grand jury (q.v.) or a petit jury (q.v.).

**justiciability\*** The status of a case or controversy indicating that it may appropriately be heard and decided by a court.

**litigant** A party to a legal action.

**magistrate** At the time the Constitution was written and in general, a government official, especially of the executive or judicial branch. In contemporary technical usage, a judicial officer authorized to conduct certain kinds of hearings, to issue certain kinds of orders, or to try minor offenses.

**mandamus\*** [Latin: we command] A form of writ directed to a government official or a lower court directing the performance of an act appropriate to that official's or court's duties.

**mootness\*** The status of a case or controversy indicating that it no longer involves a legal question appropriate to be heard and decided by a court.

**nolo contendere\*** [Latin: I do not wish to contest (it).] A plea entered by a criminal defendant equivalent in effect to a plea of guilty in the criminal case but not amounting to an admission of guilt that might be used in another case, either civil or criminal.

**obiter dictum\*** [Latin: said by the way] Any words in a court's opinion that are not required for the decision of the case, and that are therefore, in theory, not binding as precedent. The term is often misleadingly abbreviated to "dictum" or to its plural, "dicta."

**original jurisdiction\*** The legitimate authority of a court to hear and decide cases in the first instance. Original jurisdiction is distinguished from appellate jurisdiction (q.v.).

**ordinance** Any statute. In recent times, most commonly used for enactments by cities, counties, or other local governments.

**per curiam\*** [Latin: by the court] An unsigned opinion, attributable to the whole court and not to an individual judge as author.

**petit jury\*** The ordinary trial jury; a body of lay persons who hear evidence and decide questions of fact in a civil or criminal case.

**plaintiff**   The party who brings an action. At the appellate level, the moving party is called the appellant or the petitioner.

**police power***   The general authority of government to regulate the health, safety, morals, and welfare of the public.

**political question***   An issue reserved for decision by the legislative and executive branches of government, and so not appropriately decided by a court.

**precedent***   A past decision, resolving issues of law, which is relied on in the decision of later cases.

**preemption***   A doctrine according to which legislation by the national government explicitly displaces or conflicts with state legislation or has so pervaded a particular area or topic of regulation as to preclude state legislation on the same subject.

**presentment***   A formal report of a grand jury charging a person with a criminal offense; a presentment differs from an indictment in that the former is prepared on the grand jury's own initiative while the latter is initiated by the public prosecutor. Reports of the results of grand jury investigations are often referred to as "presentments" even when they do not contain criminal charges.

**ratio decidendi***   [Latin: reason for being decided]   The reasoning supporting the decision of a court in a particular case, establishing a precedent.

**remand***   The action of a higher court in returning a case to a lower court for decision or for further proceedings.

**ripeness***   The status of a case when circumstances have advanced to the point of sufficient specificity and concreteness to justify decision or review.

**seriatim***   [Latin: serially]   One at a time, in sequence; used to describe the opinions of judges on multi-member tribunals where custom does not permit a single "opinion of the court."

**special master***   A person appointed by a court to perform certain functions in a case, especially to hear evidence and to make findings of fact.

**standing***   The legal status of a litigant indicating that he is a proper party to litigate an issue or a case or controversy.

**stare decisis***   [Latin: to stand by what has been decided]   A doctrine requiring that courts, in deciding cases, should adhere to the principles of law established in prior cases, called precedents (q.v.).

**state action***   Official action by a state or under color of state law, an essential element of a claim of right raised under the "due process" or "equal protection" clause of the Fourteenth Amendment.

**statute**   A law enacted by a legislature; a part of the formal, written law. Also called an "act" of Congress or of the legislature, a statute is to be distinguished from a constitution and also from customary or common law and case law.

**subpoena***   [Latin: under penalty]   An order to appear and testify at a proceeding (*subpoena ad testificandum*) or to produce physical evidence at a proceeding (*subpoena duces tecum*).

**transactional immunity**   Immunity from prosecution for any offense mentioned in testimony given in exchange for the grant of immunity, regardless of other evidence that may be acquired independently.

**ultra vires**   [Latin: beyond (its) power]   An action by a person, corporation, or public agency that is beyond the actor's legitimate authority.

**use immunity**   Immunity from prosecution based upon or using evidence of an offense given by a witness in exchange for the grant of immunity. Prosecution may occur only if it is based on independently acquired evidence.

**venue***   The place where a case is to be heard.

**vested rights***   Legally recognized rights, especially property rights, of which a person may not be deprived without due process of law.

**writ**   A court order.

# Case Index

## HOW TO READ A CASE CITATION

A case citation tells the reader where the decision and opinion in a case have been reported. It gives, in shorthand form, all the information necessary to find a copy of the report.

The elements of a typical citation are the volume number, the name of the reporter or of the compilation, (the series number,) the page number of the first page of the report, (the court or jurisdiction,) and the year in which the case was decided. Any information that is unnecessary or inapplicable is omitted. Thus,

### 384 U.S. 346 (1966)

is the citation to the case reported in volume 384 of the United States Reports, beginning on page 346; the case (*Miranda v. Arizona*) was decided in 1966 by the Supreme Court of the United States. So far, there is only one series of volumes in the United States Reports, and all cases in the United States Reports are Supreme Court cases or matters disposed of by Supreme Court Justices. And

### 13 N.Y. 378 (1858)

is the citation to the case reported in volume 13 of the New York Reports beginning on page 378; the case (*Wynehamer v. People*) was decided in 1858 by the New York Court of Appeals (the highest court of New York).

Many volumes of reports, especially reports of older cases, bear the name of the reporter rather than of the jurisdiction. Some volumes of reports, especially specialized volumes, have names indicating neither the reporter nor the jurisdiction. The table that follows lists the reports in which cases cited in this *Encyclopedia* are to be found:

| | |
|---|---|
| U.S. | United States Reports |
| Dall. | Dallas (= United States Reports, vols. 1–4) |
| Cranch | Cranch (= U.S. Reports vols. 5–13) |
| Wheat. | Wheaton (= U.S. Reports vols. 14–25) |
| Pet. | Peters (= U.S. Reports vols. 26–41) |
| How. | Howard (= U.S. Reports vols. 42–65) |
| Black | Black (= U.S. Reports vols. 66–67) |
| Wall. | Wallace (= U.S. Reports vols. 68–90) |
| S.Ct. | West's Supreme Court Reporter (cited only when the citation to U.S. Reports was unavailable at the time of compilation) |

Vol. 1: 1–418; Vol. 2: 419–964; Vol. 3: 965–1524; Vol. 4: 1525–2084; Vol. 5: 2085–2632; Vol. 6: 2633–2994

| F. | Federal Reporter (F. 2d = Federal Reporter, 2d series) |
| F. Supp. | Federal Supplement |
| F. Cas. | Federal Cases |
| Ct. Cl. | U.S. Court of Claims Reports |
| Dane Abr. | Dane's Abridgment of American Law |
| Gill & J. | Gill & Johnson (Maryland) |
| Pick. | Pickering (= Massachusetts Reports vols. 18–41) |
| Metc. | Metcalf (= Massachusetts Reports vols. 42–54) |
| Cush. | Cushing (= Massachusetts Reports vols. 55–66) |
| Gray | Gray (= Massachusetts Reports vols. 67–82) |
| Quincy | Quincy's Reports (Massachusetts) |
| Hals. | Halsted's New Jersey Reports |
| N.J. Super. | New Jersey Superior Court Reports |
| Abb. Prac. | Abbott's New York Practice Reports |
| Hill | Hill's New York Reports |
| Johns. | Johnson's New York Reports |
| Johns. Cas. | Johnson's New York Cases |
| N.Y.S. | New York Supplement (N.Y.S. 2d = N.Y. Supplement, 2d series) |
| Martin | Martin's North Carolina Reports |
| Serg. & R. | Sergeant & Rawles's Pennsylvania Reports |
| Whart. | Wharton's Pennsylvania Reports |
| Bay | Bay's South Carolina Reports |
| P. | West's Pacific Reporter (P. 2d = Pacific Reporter, 2d series) |
| State Abbreviations | Reports of the state's highest court |
| A.C. | Appeal Cases (English) |
| E.R. | East's King's Bench Reports (English) |
| Eng. Rep. | English Reports |
| How. St. Tr. | Howell's State Trials (English) |
| Mod. | Modern English Cases |

*Numbers in **boldface** refer to the main entry on the subject.*

# A

Abbate v. United States [359 U.S. 187 (1959)], **164**

Abbott Laboratories v. Gardner [387 U.S. 136 (1967)], 2279

Abington School District v. Schempp [374 U.S. 203 (1963)], **1**, 167, 421, 855, 859, 1206, 1585, 1602, 2176–2177, 2322, 2370, 2372, 2541, 2833, 2856

Ableman v. Booth [21 How. 506 (1859)], **1–2**, 4, 341, 409, 430, 1160, 1248, 2432, 2650, 2654

Abood v. Detroit Board of Education [431 U.S. 209 (1977)], **4**, 1552, 1553

Abrams v. United States [250 U.S. 616 (1919)], **15–17**, 328, 422, 426, 1046, 1127, 1135, 1264, 1296, 1298, 1299, 1300, 1670–1671, 1983, 1990, 2077, 2318, 2319, 2352, 2353, 2580, 2841, 2901, 2902, 2929

Adair v. United States [208 U.S. 161 (1908)], **25–26**, 684, 838, 920, 1115, 1162, 1163, 1175, 1268, 1547, 1572, 1642, 1709, 1911, 2278, 2571, 2744, 2896, 2897, 2939

Adams v. New York [192 U.S. 585 (1904)], 2334

Adams v. Storey [1 F. Cas. 141, No. 66 (C.C.D. N.Y. 1817)], 1635

Adams v. Tanner [244 U.S. 590 (1917)], **32**

Adams v. Williams [407 U.S. 143 (1972)], 120, 2552

Adamson v. California [332 U.S. 46 (1947)], **33**, 186, 187, 814, 815, 816, 830, 1008, 1086, 1102, 1231, 1233, 1267, 1271, 1355, 1665, 1769, 1896, 2037, 2293, 2302, 2744, 2796

Adarand Constructors, Inc. v. Peña [505 U.S. 200 (1995)], **33–34**, 57, 58, 401, 432, 469, 623, 917, 1845, 2108, 2169, 2456, 2538

Adderley v. Florida [385 U.S. 39 (1966)], **34**, 816, 1082, 1213, 2855

Addington v. Texas [441 U.S. 418 (1979)], 1718, 1884, 2060

Addyston Pipe & Steel Co. v. United States [175 U.S. 211 (1899)], 106, 429, 1162, 1711

Adickes v. S. H. Kress & Co. [348 U.S. 144 (1970)], 444–445

Adkins v. Children's Hospital [261 U.S. 525 (1923)], 15, **35–36**, 263, 284, 743, 797, 838, 845, 1115, 1313, 1699, 1710, 1715, 1760, 1761, 1764, 1869, 2281, 2310, 2509, 2529, 2544, 2571, 2626, 2635, 2639, 2752, 2878, 2882, 2921

Adler v. Board of Education of City of New York [342 U.S. 485 (1952)], 22, **36**, 1536, 2794

Aetna Life Insurance Co. v. Haworth [300 U.S. 227 (1937)], 51, 2831

Aetna Life Insurance Co. v. Kennedy [301 U.S. 389 (1937)], 2831

Afroyim v. Rusk [387 U.S. 253 (1967)], **59**, 367, 957, 1077

Agins v. Tiburon [447 U.S. 255 (1980)], 889, 2510

Agnello v. United States [269 U.S. 20 (1925)], **61**, 355, 2343

Agostini v. Felton [521 U.S. 203 (1997)], 61, 202, 1209, 1604, 1846, 2179, 2426

Aguilar v. Felton [473 U.S. 402 (1985)], 61, **63**, 202, 1209, 1603, 1842, 2375, 2378

Aguilar v. Texas [378 U.S. 108 (1964)], **63–64**, 1327, 1368, 2024, 2330–2331, 2469

Agurs, United States v. [427 U.S. 97 (1976)], 793, 972, 2004

Ah Sin v. Wittman [198 U.S. 500 (1905)], 2088

Air Pollution Variance Board of Colorado v. Western Alfalfa Corp. [416 U.S. 861 (1974)], 902

Ake v. Oklahoma [470 U.S. 68 (1985)], **64**, 1680, 1719, 2045

Akron v. Akron Center for Reproductive Health [462 U.S. 416 (1983)], 10, 192, 1175, 1841, 1843, 1870, 2206, 2207, 2208

Alabama Public Service Commission v. Southern Railway [341 U.S. 341 (1951)], 19

Alabama v. King & Boozer [314 U.S. 1 (1941)], 1384

Alabama v. White [496 U.S. 325 (1990)], 1096

A.L.A. Schechter Poultry Corp v. United States. *See* Schechter Poultry Corp. v. United States

Alaska, United States v. [521 U.S. 1 (1997)], 1840

Alberts v. California [354 U.S. 476 (1957)], 1538, 1837, **2296**

Albertson v. Subversive Activities Control Board [382 U.S. 70 (1965)], **64**, 1335, 1385, 2578, 2581

Alden v. Maine [119 S.Ct. 2240 (1999)], 625, 777, 881, 904, 2169, 2459

Alderman v. United States [394 U.S. 165 (1969)], **64–65**, 1083, 1857, 2335

Alexander v. Holmes County Board of Education [396 U.S. 19 (1669)], **65**, 69, 773, 2854

Alexander v. United States [509 U.S. 544 (1993)], 985

Alfred Dunhill of London, Inc. v. Republic of Cuba [425 U.S. 682 (1976)], 25

A.L.I.V.E., State v. *See* State v. A.L.I.V.E.

Allegheny Pittsburgh Coal Co. v. County Commission of Webster County [488 U.S. 336 (1989)], 428–429, 840

Allen v. Alabama State Board of Education (1999) [164 F. 3d 1347 (11th Cir. 1999)], 57

Allen v. Illinois [478 U.S. 364 (1986)], 1720, 2373

Allen v. McCurry [449 U.S. 90 (1980)], 193

Allen v. State Board of Elections [393 U.S. 544 (1969)], 2812

Allen v. Wright [468 U.S. 737 (1984)], **70**, 122, 1844, 2473, 2532

Allenberg Cotton Co. v. Pittman [419 U.S. 20 (1974)], 2517

Allen-Bradley Company v. Local Union #3 [325 U.S. 797 (1945)], **70**, 107, 1545

Allgeyer v. Louisiana [165 U.S. 578 (1897)], 32, **70**, 241, 844–845, 1115, 1175, 1499, 1890, 2243, 2571

Allied Structural Steel Co. v. Spannaus [438 U.S. 234 (1978)], **70–71**, 677, 678, 1836

Allstate Insurance Co. v. Hague [450 U.S. 971 (1981)], 357, 358, 960

Almeida-Sanchez v. United States [413 U.S. 266 (1973)], **71**, 209

Alvarez-Machain, United States v. [504 U.S. 655 (1992)], **71–72**

Amalgamated Food Employees Union v. Logan Valley Plaza [391 U.S. 308 (1968)], 1676, 1677, 1907, 2414, 2415, 2487

Ambach v. Norwick [441 U.S. 68 (1979)], 66, **72**, 858, 2583

Amerada Hess Corp. v. Director, New Jersey Division of Taxation [490 U.S. 66 (1989)], **83**, 2516

American Banana Co. v. United Fruit Co. [213 U.S. 347 (1909)], 958, 959

American Booksellers Assn., Inc. v. Hudnut [475 U.S. 1001 (1986)], 1054, 1057, 1967–1968

American Civil Liberties Union v. Reno. *See* Reno v. ACLU

American Communications Association v. Douds [339 U.S. 382 (1950)], **79**, 187, 279, 1108, 1241, 2642, 2792, 2794

American Federation of Labor v. American Sash & Door Co. [335 U.S. 538 (1949)], 1458

American Insurance Company v. Canter [26 U.S. (I Pet.) 511 (1828)], 83, 563, 568, 569, 1019, 1589–1590, 1612, 1644, 1686, 2671, 2673

American Party of Texas v. White [415 U.S. 767 (1974)], 1942

American Power & Light Co. v. Securities and Exchange Commission [329 U.S. 90 (1947)], 1768, 1796, 2079–2080

American Publishing Company v. Fisher [166 U.S. 464 (1897)], 1517

American Steel Foundries v. Tri-City Labor Council [257 U.S. 184 (1921)], 2638

American Tobacco Co., United States v. [221 U.S. 106 (1911)], 455–456, 749, 1030, 1165, 2298, **2472**, 2898, 2904

Amistad, The [40 U.S. (15 Pet.) 518 (1841)], 2555, 2654

Anderson, United States v. [17 U.S.C.M.A. 588, 38 C.M.R. 386 (1968)], 2505

Anderson v. Celebrezze [460 U.S. 780 (1983)], 158, 1942

Anderson v. Dunn [19 U.S. 204 (1821)], 1433, 1589

Anderson v. Laird [446 F. 2d 283 (D.C. Cir. 1971)], 2186

Anderson v. Liberty Lobby [477 U.S. 242 (1986)], 1609

Anderson v. Mt. Clemens Pottery Co. [328 U.S. 680 (1946)], 967

Andrews v. Ballard [498 F. Supp. 1038 (S.D. Tex. 1980)], 2328

Antelope, The [23 U.S. (10 Wheat.) 66 (1825)], 334

Anthony, United States v. [24 F. Cas. 833 (C.C. N.Y. 1877) (No., 14, 460)], 360, 361

Anthony v. County of Sacramento [898 F. Supp. 1435 (E.D. Cal. 1995)], 2092

Apex Hosiery Company v. Leader [310 U.S. 469 (1940)], **107**

Apodaca v. Oregon [406 U.S. 404 (1972)], 264, 830, **1434–1435**, 1510, 1517, 1518

Appalachian Electric Power Co., United States v. [311 U.S. 377 (1940)], **107**, 2866

Aptheker v. Secretary of State [378 U.S. 500 (1959)], **116**, 187, 1200, 1400, 1868, 1950, 2276, 2574, 2854

Archibald Freeland v. Heron, Lenox and Company [11 U.S. 147 (1812)], 832

Argersinger v. Hamlin [407 U.S. 25 (1972)], 23, **116**, 971, 1745, 2262

Arguello v. United States [444 U.S. 860 (1855)], 2653

Arizona v. Evans [514 U.S. 1 (1995)], 2169

Arizona v. Fulminante [499 U.S. 279 (1991)], 1271, 2455

Arizona v. Hicks [480 U.S. 321 (1987)], 1913, 1914

Arizona v. Mauro [481 U.S. 520 (1987)], 1743, 2240

Arizona v. Robertson [486 U.S. 675 (1988)], 1743, 1744

Arizona v. Rumsey [467 U.S. 203 (1984)], 1869

Arizona v. Youngblood [488 U.S. 51 (1988)], 2032

Arizona Governing Committee v. Norris [463 U.S. 1073 (1983)], 2393

Arizonans for Official English v. Arizona [520 U.S. 43 (1997)], 20, 1197, 1759, 1848

Arkansas v. Sanders [442 U.S. 753 (1979)], 2332

Arkansas Educational Television Commission v. Forbes [523 U.S. 666 (1998)], 470

Arkansas Writers' Project, Inc. v. Ragland [481 U.S. 221 (1987)], 1055

Arlington Heights v. Metropolitan Housing Development Corporation [429 U.S. 252 (1977)], 96, **116**, 1586, 1593, 1875, 2107, 2220, 2862, 2945, 2947

Armour & Co. v. Wantock [323 U.S. 126 (1944)], 967

Armstrong, United States v. [517 U.S. 456 (1996)], 2058, 2059, 2088

Arnett v. Kennedy [416 U.S. 134 (1974)], **118–119**, 184, 898, 1205, 2025, 2027, 2033, 2158

Arnold, Schwinn & Co., United States v. [388 U.S. 365 (1967)], 2542

Arredondo, United States v. [31 U.S. (6 Pet.) 691 (1832)], 156

Ash, United States v. [413 U.S. 300 (1973)], **127**, 962, 2264

Ashcraft v. Tennessee [320 U.S. 728 (1944)], 1924

Ashton v. Cameron County Water Improvement District [298 U.S. 513 (1937)], **127–128**, 161, 1767

Ashwander v. Tennessee Valley Authority [297 U.S. 288 (1936)], **128**, 142, 220, 1444, 1714, 2543, 2667, 2780

Associated Press v. NLRB [301 U.S. 103 (1937)], 921, **2819–2821**

Associated Press v. Walker [388 U.S. 130 (1967)], 1805, 2709, 2855

Association of Data Processing Service Organizations v. Camp [397 U.S. 150 (1970)], 2474

Atascadero State Hospital v. Scanlon [473 U.S. 234 (1985)], **133**, 193

Atchison, Topeka & Santa Fe Railway Co., United States v. [233 U.S. 173 (1914)], 749, 1642, 1666

Atchison, Topeka & Santa Fe Railway Co. v. Robinson [219 U.S. 219 (1914)], 1642

Atlantic Coast Line Railroad v. Riverside Mills [219 U.S. 186 (1911)], 2899

Atlas Roofing Co. v. Occupational Safety and Health Administration [430 U.S. 442 (1976)], 902, 2729

Atlee v. Laird [347 F. Supp. 689 (E.D. Pa 1972)], 2790

Attorney General of New York v. Soto-Lopez [476 U.S. 898 (1986)], **137**, 914, 2277, 2305

Austin v. Michigan Chamber of Commerce [494 U.S. 652 (1990)], **139–140**, 296, 688, 691, 1237, 2535

Austin v. United States [509 U.S. 602 (1993)], 985

Avery v. Midland County [390 U.S. 474 (1968)], **142**, 2890, 2892

Ayers, In re [123 U.S. 443 (1887)], 877

# B

Babbitt v. United Farm Workers [442 U.S. 289 (1979)], 1867

Badham v. Eu [694 F. Supp. 664 (N.D. Cal. 1988)], 1189

Baehr v. Lewin [852 P. 2d 44 (Haw. 1993)], **147**, 2307, 2309

Baehr v. Miike [910 P. 2d 112 (Haw. 1996)], 2309

Baggett v. Bullitt [377 U.S. 360 (1964)], 1867, 2776

Bailey, United States v. [444 U.S. 394 (1980)], 193, 194

Bailey v. Alabama [219 U.S. 219 (1911)], **151**, 1310, 1897, 2900

Bailey v. Drexel Furniture Co. [259 U.S. 20 (1922)], **151–152**, 349, 350, 1261, 1585, 1704, 1779, 2452, 2635, 2660

Bailey v. Richardson [341 U.S. 918 (1951)], 279, 946, 2792, 2794

Bajakajian, United States v. [524 U.S. 321 (1998)], 985, 2056

Baker v. Carr [369 U.S. 186 (1962)], **152–153**, 229, 233, 237, 440, 500, 659, 869, 871, 1042, 1188, 1203, 1227, 1239, 1476, 1477, 1486, 1488, 1579, 1612, 1949, 1950, 1951–1952, 1953, 1987, 2131, 2132, 2133, 2138, 2202, 2210, 2227–2228, 2228, 2383, 2450, 2594, 2765, 2810, 2849, 2854, 2856, 2857, 2858, 2881

Bakery Drivers Local v. Wohl [315 U.S. 769 (1942)], 1550

Baldwin v. Fish & Game Commission [436 U.S. 371 (1978)], **157**, 2020

Baldwin v. Franks [120 U.S. 678 (1887)], 1024

Baldwin v. G.A.F. Seelig, Inc. [294 U.S. 511 (1935)], 314, 1864, 2514, 2523

Baldwin v. New York [399 U.S. 66 (1970)], **157**, 1516, 1745, 2729

Ball, State v. *See* State v. Ball

Ball v. United States [470 U.S. 856 (1985)], 2158

Ballard, United States v. [322 U.S. 78 (1944)], 734, 1047, 2172, 2190

Ballew v. Georgia [435 U.S. 223 (1978)], **157–158**, 264, 1516, 1517, 1518, 2441, 2727

Baltimore and Carolina Line v. Redman [295 U.S. 654 (1935)], 2728

Baltimore City Department of Social Services v. Bouknight [493 U.S. 549 (1990)], 2241

Balzac v. Porto Rico [258 U.S. 398 (1922)], 1376, 2080, 2672

Banco Nacional de Cuba v. Sabbatino [376 U.S. 398 (1964)], 25, 1077, 1390, 1468

Bancroft, United States v. [260 U.S. 706 (1922)], 2505

Bank of Augusta v. Earle [38 U.S. (13 Pet.) 519 (1839)], 156, 325, 1710, 2648, 2653

Bank of Nova Scotia v. United States [487 U.S. 250 (1988)], 1223

Bank of United States v. Deveaux [9 U.S. (5 Cranch) 61 (1809)], 1705, 2653

Bank of United States v. Planters' Bank of Georgia [22 U.S. (9 Wheat.) 904 (1824)], 25

Bantam Books, Inc. v. Sullivan [372 U.S. 58 (1963)], **161–162**

Barber v. Page [390 U.S. 719 (1968)], 933

Barbier v. Connolly [113 U.S. 27 (1885)], 2508

Barclay v. Florida [463 U.S. 939 (1983)], 303

Barefoot v. Estelle [463 U.S. 880 (1983)], **162**

Barenblatt v. United States [360 U.S. 109 (1959)], 155, **162–163**, 187, 188, 421, 1193, 1241, 1305, 1595, 1596, 2772, 2867

Barker v. Hardway [394 U.S. 905 (1969)], 1082

Barker v. Wingo [407 U.S. 514 (1972)], **163**, 2465–2467

Barnard v. Thorstenn [489 U.S. 546 (1989)], 1530

Barnes v. Glen Theatre, Inc. [501 U.S. 560 (1991)], 1830, 1832

Barr v. Matteo [360 U.S. 546 (1959)], 943

Barron v. Baltimore [32 U.S. (7 Pet.) 243 (1833)], 119, 178, 722, 888, 1086, 1090, 1353, 1354, 1356, 1462, 1809, 2217, 2426, 2497, 2508, 2570

Barron v. Burnside [121 U.S. 186 (1887)], 585

Barron v. City of Baltimore [32 U.S. (7 Pet.) 243 (1833)], **163**

Barrows v. Jackson [346 U.S. 249 (1953)], **163–164**, 2223

Barsky v. Board of Regents [347 U.S. 442 (1954)], 231, 234

Bartels v. Iowa [262 U.S. 404 (1923)], 315

Bartkus v. Illinois [359 U.S. 121 (1959)], **164**, 808

Bas v. Tingy [4 U.S. 322 (4 Dall. 37) (1800)], 549, 1756, 2505

Bassett v. Mayhew [137 U.S. 496 (1890)], 1889

Bates v. Little Rock [361 U.S. 516 (1960)], 1193, 1773

Bates v. State Bar of Arizona [433 U.S. 350 (1977)], **165**, 190, 193, 1109, 1868

Batson v. Kentucky [476 U.S. 79 (1986)], **165**, 195, 1510, 1511, 1514, 1680, 1898–1899, 2088, 2106, 2170, 2490, 2627, 2891

Bauman v. Ross [167 U.S. 348 (1897)], 1519

Bayard v. Singleton [1 Martin 42 (North Carolina, 1787)], **165–166**, 541, 1756, 2462

Beacon Theatres, Inc. v. Westover [359 U.S. 500 (1958)], **166**, 2388, 2726, 2730

Beal v. Doe [432 U.S. 438 (1977)], 194, 1665, 2205

Beauharnais v. Illinois [343 U.S. 250 (1952)], **167**, 187, 815, 1130, 1235–1236, 1411, 1837, 1966, 2145, 2795

Beazell v. Ohio [269 U.S. 167 (1925)], 958

Beck v. Ohio [479 U.S. 89 (1964)], 2023, 2330

Bedford Cut Stone Co. v. Journeymen Stonecutters Association [273 U.S. 37 (1927)], 107, **167–168**, 831, 2638

Behrens v. Pelletier [516 U.S. 299 (1996)], 1336

Beilan v. Board of Education [357 U.S. 599 (1958)], 2903

Bekins, United States v. [304 U.S. 37 (1938)], 128, 161, 1767

Bell v. Hood [327 U.S. 678 (1946)], 1344

Bell v. Maryland [378 U.S. 226 (1964)], **168**, 816, 2420, 2486

Bell v. Wolfish [441 U.S. 520 (1979)], 205, 729, 2005, 2244

Belle Terre (Village of) v. Boraas [416 U.S. 1 (1974)], 973, 1123–1124, 1757, 2574

Bellotti v. Baird [443 U.S. 622 (1979)], 6, 2208

Belmont, United States v. [301 U.S. 324 (1937)], **168**, 737, 942, 951, 1073, 1390, 1909–1910, 1997

Benanti v. United States [355 U.S. 96 (1955)], 873, 1774

Bender v. Williamsport [475 U.S. 534 (1986)], **168–169**, 906

Bendix Autolite Corp. v. Midwesco Enterprises, Inc. [486 U.S. 888 (1988)], 2517

Bennett, United States v. [24 F. Cas. 1093, No. 14, 571 (C.C.D. N.Y. 1879)], 2748

Bennis v. Michigan [517 U.S. 1163 (1996)], 2056

Benton v. Maryland [395 U.S. 784 (1969)], **169–170**, 722, 808, 1355, 1676, 1875, 2039, 2856

Berea College v. Kentucky [211 U.S. 45 (1908)], **170**, 1168, 1890

Berger v. New York [388 U.S. 41 (1967)], **170**, 187, 873, 874, 971, 1296, 1527

Berman v. Parker [348 U.S. 26 (1954)], 889, 2076, 2079, 2506

Bethel School District v. Fraser [478 U.S. 675 (1986)], **170**, 351, 381, 860, 1134, 1281, 2535

Betts v. Brady [316 U.S. 455 (1942)], **170**, 186, 280, 1102, 1193–1194, 1462, 1869, 2039, 2261, 2263, 2265, 2282, 2796

Bibb v. Navajo Freight Lines, Inc. [359 U.S. 520 (1959)], **171**, 2514

Bigelow v. Virginia [421 U.S. 809 (1975)], 190, 193

Bishop v. Wood [426 U.S. 341 (1976)], 119, **184**, 1888, 2026, 2029

Bishop Processing Company v. Gardner [275 F. Supp. 780 (1968)], 900

Biswell, United States v. [404 U.S. 983 (1972)], 44

Bivens v. Six Unknown Named Agents of Federal Bureau of Narcotics [403 U.S. 388 (1971)], **185**, 192, 238, 652, 653, 739, 740, 741, 748, 979, 1218, 1344, 2708

Blackburn v. Alabama [361 U.S. 199 (1960)], 1923

Blackmer v. United States [284 U.S. 421 (1932)], 1765

Blanchette v. Connecticut General Insurance Corps. [419 U.S. 102 (1974)], 420

Bland, United States v. [283 U.S. 636 (1931)], 1198

Block v. Community Nutrition Institute [464 U.S. 991 (1984)], 1218

Block v. Hirsh [256 U.S. 135 (1921)], 2896

Blockburger v. United States [284 U.S. 299 (1932)], 809, 811, 982, 983, 985

Bloom v. Illinois [391 U.S. 194 (1968)], 435, 2729

Blum v. Bacon [457 U.S. 132 (1982)], 2587–2588

Blum v. Yaretsky [454 U.S. 815 (1982)], **200**, 2492

Blyew v. United States [80 U.S. (13 Wall.) 581 (1872)], **200–201**, 403, 2424, 2564

BMW of North America v. Gore [517 U.S. 559 (1996)], 2055, 2056, 2083

Board of Curators v. Horowitz [435 U.S. 78 (1978)], **201**, 856

Board of Directors of Rotary International v. Rotary Club of Duarte [481 U.S. 537 (1987)], 1110, 1237, 2017, 2398

Board of Education v. Allen [392 U.S. 236 (1968)], **201–202**, 348, 349, 1206, 1601, 2373, 2468, 2751–2752, 2856

Board of Education v. Nyquist [413 U.S. 757 (1973)], 349

Board of Education v. Pico [457 U.S. 853(1982)], 21, **202**, 235, 351, 860, 1137, 1216

Board of Education v. Rowley [458 U.S. 176 (1982)], 860

Board of Education of Kiryas Joel Village School District v. Grumet [512 U.S. 687 (1994)], **202**, 927, 1604, 1783, 2179, 2195, 2456

Board of Education of Oklahoma City Public Schools v. Dowell [498 U.S. 237 (1991)], 859

Board of Education of the Westside Community Schools v. Mergens [496 U.S. 226 (1990)], **203**, 906, 1207, 1602, 2178, 2185, 2323

Board of Estimate of the City of New York v. Morris [489 U.S. 688 (1989)], 2890

Board of Public Utilities Commissioners v. Ynchausti [251 U.S. 401 (1920)], 1376

Board of Regents v. Roth [408 U.S. 564 (1972)], **203**, 897, 1678, 2026, 2053, 2054, 2880

Board of Regents v. Tomanio [444 U.S. 939 (1980)], 2227

Board of Trade v. Olsen [262 U.S. 1 (1922)], 2416

Board of Trustees of State University of New York v. Fox [492 U.S. (1989)], **203–204**, 462

Bob Jones University v. United States [461 U.S. 574 (1983)], 97, **204**, 1237, 2017

Bob-Lo Excursion Co. v. Michigan [333 U.S. 28 (1948)], **204**, 2795

Boddie v. Connecticut [401 U.S. 371 (1971)], 23, **204**, 799, 1121, 1269, 1362, 2869, 2877

Boehner v. Anderson [809 F. Supp. 138 (D.D.C. 1992)], 2743

Boerne (City of) v. Flores [521 U.S. 507 (1997)], 625, 991, 992, 1092, 1531, 1824, 1845, 2169, 2182, 2195, 2456, 2504

Bogan v. Scott-Harris [523 U.S. 44 (1998)], 1335

Bolger v. Youngs Drug Product Corporation [463 U.S. 60 (1983)], 2206

Bolling v. Sharpe [347 U.S. 497 (1954)], 53, 179, **206–207**, 253, 388, 912, 1172, 1265, 2015, 2099, 2408

Bollman, Ex parte, v. Swartwout [8 U.S. (4 Cranch) 75 (1807)], **207**, 278, 1246, 2716

Bollman et al., United States v. [5 U.S. (1 Cranch) 373 (1807)], 705, 2284

Bolton v. Harris [395 F. 2d 642 (1968)], 1718, 1719

Bonaparte v. Camden & A. R. Co. [3 F. Cas. 821, No. 1, 617 (C.C.D. N.J. 1830)], 360

Bond v. Floyd [385 U.S. 116 (1966)], 2582, 2850

Bonham's Case [8 Coke 113b (English) (1610)], **207–208**, 439, 512, 1286, 1473, 1865, 1866, 1888–1889

Bonitz v. Fair [804 F. 2d 164 (1st Cir. 1986)], 205

Booth v. Maryland [482 U.S. 496 (1987)], **208–209**, 1889, 2369

Borden Milk Co. v. Barella [325 U.S. 679 (1945)], 1539

Bose Corporation v. Consumers Union of the United States, Inc. [466 U.S. 485 (1984)], 1377, 1805, 2709–2710

Boston Beer Co. v. Massachusetts [97 U.S. 25 (1878)], **211–212**, 1350, 1829, 2507

Boston Firefighters Union, Local 718 v. Boston Chapter, NAACP [468 U.S. 1206 (1983)], 1760

Boston Stock Exchange v. State Tax Commission [429 U.S. 318 (1977)], 2521

Boston Water Power Co. v. Boston & Worcester Railroad [23 Pick. 360 (Mass. 1839)], 889

Bounds v. Smith [430 U.S. 817 (1977)], 23, **212**

Bourjaily v. United States [483 U.S. 171 (1987)], 492

Bouvia v. Superior Court [179 Cal. App. 3d 1127 (1986)], 2269

Bowen v. Gilliard [483 U.S. 587 (1987)], 2876

Bowen v. Kendrick [487 U.S. 589 (1988)], **212–213**, 924, 925, 1207, 1208, 1843, 2378–2379

Bowen v. Owens [476 U.S. 340 (1986)], 2397

Bowen v. Roy [486 U.S. 693 (1986)], 2380

Bowers v. Hardwick [478 U.S. 186 (1986)], 192, **213**, 381, 400, 700, 1813, 1831, 1979, 2162, 2247, 2287, 2308, 2401, 2403, 2404, 2405, 2575–2576, 2577, 2891–2892, 2893

Bowie v. City of Columbia [378 U.S. 374 (1964)], 2223

Bowles v. Willingham [321 U.S. 503 (1944)], 886, 887, 2841

Bowlin v. Commonwealth [2 Bush 5 (Ky.) (1867)], 403

Bowman v. Chicago & Northwestern Railway [125 U.S. 465 (1888)], **213–214**, 1266, 1698

Bowman v. Iowa [62 N.W. 729 (Iowa 1895)], 1168

Bowsher v. Synar [478 U.S. 714 (1986)], **214**, 269, 621, 762, 949, 1454, 2536, 2889

Boyd v. Nebraska ex rel. Thayer [143 U.S. 135 (1892)], 1785

Boyd v. United States [116 U.S. 616 (1886)], **215–216**, 218, 2141, 2236, 2334, 2339, 2340, 2767, 2872

Boynton v. Virginia [364 U.S. 454 (1960)], 136

Braden v. United States [365 U.S. 431 (1961)], 187, 1305

Bradfield v. Roberts [175 U.S. 291 (1899)], 348, 2371

Bradley v. Fisher [80 U.S. (13 Wall.) 335 (1872)], 1453

Bradwell v. Illinois [83 U.S. (16 Wall.) 130 (1873)], 218, **218**, 342, 1185, 1199, 2392, 2612, 2920

Brady v. Maryland [373 U.S. 83 (1963)], 720, 793, 2004

Brady v. United States [397 U.S. 742 (1970)], 2367, 2831, 2891

Bram v. United States [168 U.S. 532 (1897)], 1923, 2237

Branch v. Texas [408 U.S. 238 (1972)], **309–310**

Brandenburg v. Ohio [395 U.S. 444 (1969)], **225–226**, 238, 427, 709, 724, 769, 770, 815, 1056, 1109, 1127, 1129, 1135, 1154, 1264, 1353, 1871, 1966, 2353, 2454, 2582, 2854, 2902

Brandon v. Guilderland [635 F. 2d 971 (2d Cir. 1980)], 906

Branti v. Finkel [445 U.S. 507 (1980)], **226**, 892, 1886, 1939, 2535

Branzburg v. Hayes [408 U.S. 665 (1972)], **226–227**, 271, 1143, 1145, 1215, 1976, 2199–2200, 2413, 2890, 2892

Brass v. North Dakota ex rel. Stoeser [153 U.S. 391 (1894)], 2414

Braswell v. United States [487 U.S. 99 (1988)], **227**, 2241

Braunfeld v. Brown [366 U.S. 599 (1961)], 2191, 2412, 2584

Bray v. Alexandria Women's Health Clinic [506 U.S. 263 (1993)], **227**, 2399–2400

Bread v. Alexandria [341 U.S. 622 (1951)], 461, 2795

Breard v. Greene [523 U.S. 371 (1998)], 71, 1081, 1390

Breed v. Jones [421 U.S. 519 (1975)], 1184, 1523

Breedlove v. Suttles [302 U.S. 277 (1937)], **228**, 284, 1271, 1961, 2808

Breen v. Selective Service Local Board [396 U.S. 460 (1970)], 2790–2791

Breithaupt v. Abram [352 U.S. 432 (1957)], **229**

Brewer v. Hoxie School District [238 F. 2d 91 (1956)], 2488

Brewer v. Williams [430 U.S. 378 (1977)], **242**, 1922, 1929, 2238, 2264

Brewster v. United States [408 U.S. 501 (1972)], **242**, 501, 2464

Bridges v. California [309 U.S. 649 (1941)], 187, **244**, 426, 1102, 1149, 2076

Briggs v. Elliott [349 U.S. 294 (1954)], 748

Briggs v. McKellar [2 Abb. Prac. 30 (1855)], 1594

Bright, United States v. [24 F. Cas. 1232, No. 14642 (C.C.D. Pa. 1809)], 2859

Brignoni-Ponce, United States v. [422 U.S. 873 (1975)], 209

Brinegar v. United States [338 U.S. 160 (1949)], **244**, 721, 1410, 2330

Briscoe v. Bank of Commonwealth of Kentucky [36 U.S. (11 Pet.) 257 (1837)], 162, **244–245**, 1686, 1712, 2556–2557, 2648, 2651

Broadrick v. Oklahoma [413 U.S. 601 (1973)], **250–251**, 1275, 1802, 1868, 2776–2777, 2887

Brock v. Roadway Express, Inc. [481 U.S. 252 (1987)], 2033

Brockett v. Spokane Arcades, Inc. [472 U.S. 491 (1985)], **251**, 1867, 1968

Brolan v. United States [236 U.S. 216 (1915)], 1081

Bronson v. Kinzie [42 U.S. (1 How.) 311 (1843)], **251–252**, 677, 1301, 2648, 2653

Bronson v. Rodes [74 U.S. (7 Wall.) 229 (1869)], 1753

Brooks v. United States [267 U.S. 432 (1925)], 1262

Brotherhood of Railroad Trainmen v. Virginia [377 U.S. 1 (1964)], 1109

Broussard v. Patton [410 U.S. 942 (1972)], 2505

Brower v. County of Inyo [489 U.S. 543 (1989)], 2338

Brown, United States v. (1965), 174, 1561

Brown v. Allen [344 U.S. 443 (1953)], **253**, 1245, 1250, 1253, 1255

Brown v. Board of Education [347 U.S. 483 (1954); 349 U.S. 294 (1955)], 5, 6, 15, 53, 69, 83, 88, 136, 153, 155, 206, 207, 210, 225, 229, 232, 237, **253–256**, 273, 277, 280, 352, 375, 376, 380, 383, 388, 389, 390, 391, 394, 395, 396, 399, 411, 497, 510, 607, 630, 658, 664, 683, 700, 701, 725, 748, 771, 772, 774, 801, 818, 859, 863, 909–910, 991, 1002, 1008, 1025, 1042, 1086, 1229, 1265, 1267, 1373, 1393, 1449, 1458, 1485, 1488, 1528, 1579, 1615, 1631, 1645, 1676, 1678, 1740, 1744, 1748–1749, 1774, 1792, 1822, 1860, 1870, 1915, 1918, 1950, 1987, 2062, 2078, 2094, 2098, 2099, 2100, 2108, 2109, 2145, 2157, 2159, 2219, 2228, 2253, 2282, 2293, 2309–2310, 2320, 2321, 2355, 2369–2370, 2403, 2420, 2438, 2441, 2443, 2444, 2446, 2458, 2485–2486, 2594, 2608, 2610, 2615, 2677, 2696, 2713–2714, 2738, 2764, 2796, 2809–2810, 2814, 2849, 2852, 2853, 2855, 2857, 2858, 2879

Brown v. Glines [444 U.S. 348 (1980)], 117

Brown v. Louisiana [383 U.S. 131 (1966)], 1082, 2855

Brown v. Maryland [25 U.S. (12 Wheat.) 419 (1827)], **256**, 341, 832, 1348, 1612, 1686, 1864, 2521, 2523, 2697–2698, 2908, 2923

Brown v. Mississippi [297 U.S. 278 (1936)], **256**, 329, 1741, 1923, 1924, 2038, 2087, 2238, 2594

Brown v. Socialist Workers '74 Campaign Committee [459 U.S. 87 (1982)], **257**, 295, 2535

Brown v. Texas [443 U.S. 47 (1979)], 826, 1913, 2023

Brown v. United States [12 U.S. (8 Cranch) 100 (1814)], 2554

Brown v. United States [381 U.S. 437 (1965)], **257**, 1648, 2005

Brown v. Walker [161 U.S. 591 (1896)], 252, **257**, 1334, 2236, 2414, 2747

Browning-Ferris Industries of Vermont Inc. v. Kelco Disposal Inc. [492 U.S. 257 (1989)], 2081–2082, 2710

Bruton v. United States [391 U.S. 123 (1968)], 480–481, 492, 933

Bryant v. Zimmerman [278 U.S. 63 (1928)], 1109

Buchanan v. Angelone [522 U.S. 269 (1998)], 306

Buchanan v. Warley [245 U.S. 60 (1917)], **259**, 388, 909, 2219, 2222, 2354, 2484, 2900

Buck v. Bell [274 U.S. 200 (1927)], **259**, 284, 789, 791–792, 840, 909, 973, 1296, 1298, 1720–1721, 2528

Buckley v. American Constitutional Law Foundation [525 U.S. 182 (1999)], 788, 1372

Buckley v. Fitzsimmons [509 U.S. 259 (1993)], 654, 1335

Buckley v. Valeo [424 U.S. 1 (1976)], 76, 91, 139–140, 155, 238, 257, **260**, 274, 295, 296, 297, 298, 369, 872, 987, 1047, 1060, 1108, 1130, 1131–1132, 1216, 1275, 1827, 1932–1933, 1937, 1938, 1941, 1942, 2007, 2052, 2154, 2214, 2278, 2384, 2469, 2594, 2659, 2880, 2887, 2889, 2893

Buckley II. *See* Buckley v. American Constitutional Law Foundation

Budd v. New York [143 U.S. 517 (1892)], 199, 241, 1166, 1227

Budd v. State [117 N.Y. 621 (1889)], 1288

Bullington v. Missouri [451 U.S. 430 (1981)], 302, 810, 812

Bunting v. Oregon [243 U.S. 426 (1917)], 35, 36, **263**, 421, 838, 845, 1639, 1699, 1764, 2572, 2635, 2881, 2896, 2900

Burbank v. Lockheed Air Terminal [411 U.S. 624 (1973)], **263**, 901

Burch v. Louisiana [441 U.S. 130 (1979)], **264**, 1517, 1518, 2727

Burdick v. Takushi [504 U.S. 428 (1992)], **264–265**

Burford v. Sun Oil Company [319 U.S. 315 (1943)], 19, 20

Burlington (City of) v. Dague [505 U.S. 557 (1992)], 414

Burlington Industries, Inc. v. Ellerth [524 U.S. 742 (1998)], 2400

Burnet v. Coronado Oil & Gas Co. [285 U.S. 393 (1932)], 1869, 1987

Burnham v. Superior Court of California [495 U.S. 604 (1990)], 2162, 2163

Burns Baking Co. v. Bryan [264 U.S. 504 (1924)], **278**, 2445

Burns v. Fortson [410 U.S. 686 (1973)], 831, 2275

Burns v. Ohio [360 U.S. 252 (1950)], 2262

Burns v. Reed (1991), 654, 1335

Burr, United States v. [4 Cranch 469 (1807)], 433, 953, 1488, 1673

Burr v. Duryee [68 U.S. (1 Wall.) 578 (1864)], 1230

Burroughs v. United States [290 U.S. 534 (1934)], 1941, 2007

Burson v. Freeman [504 U.S. 191 (1992)], **278–279**

Burstyn, Inc., v. Wilson [343 U.S. 495 (1952)], 198, **279**, 1147, 2189, 2794

Burton v. Wilmington Parking Authority [365 U.S. 715 (1961)], 200, **280**, 420, 1411, 1758, 2486, 2492, 2854

Bush v. Kentucky [107 U.S. 110 (1883)], 1038, 2828

Bush v. Lucas [462 U.S. 367 (1983)], 653, 740, 1344

Bush v. Vera [517 U.S. 952 (1996)], 2137, 2159

Bushell's Case [6 How. St. Tr. 999 (English) (1670)], **282–283**, 1512, 1892, 1894

Busher, United States v. [817 F. 2d 1409 (9th Cir. 1987)], 983

Butcher's Union Slaughterhouse v. Crescent City Slaughterhouse [111 U.S. 746 (1884)], **283**, 2924

Bute v. Illinois [333 U.S. 640 (1948)], 280, 2261

Butler, United States v. [297 U.S. 1 (1936)], 62, 152, **284–285**, 457, 458, 486–487, 1186, 1284, 1313, 1715, 1780, 1797, 2281, 2288, 2468, 2540, 2544, 2545, 2561, 2659, 2681, 2820, 2858, 2882

Butler v. McKellar [494 U.S. 407 (1990)], 2156

Butler v. Michigan [352 U.S. 380 (1957)], **285**, 351

Butler v. Perry [240 U.S. 328 (1916)], 506

Butler v. United States [297 U.S. 1 (1936)], 697

Butterworth v. Smith [494 U.S. 624 (1990)], 1223

Butz v. Economou [438 U.S. 478 (1978)], 185, **285**, 944, 1335

Byars v. United States [273 U.S. 28 (1925)], 2416

Byers v. Edmondson [712 So.2d 681 (1998)], 1154

# C

C & A Carbone, Inc. v. Town of Clarkstown [511 U.S. 383 (1994)], 1010, 2518, 2864

Caban v. Mohammed [441 U.S. 380 (1979)], 973, 2395

Cabell v. Chávez-Salido [454 U.S. 432 (1982)], 66, 194, 368, 1331

Cadman, State v. See State v. Cadman

Calandra, United States v. [414 U.S. 338 (1974)], **290**, 938, 1362, 1667, 2044, 2335

Calder v. Bull [3 U.S. (3 Dall.) 386 (1798)], **290**, 337, 376, 561, 842, 844, 958, 1174, 1286–1287, 1404, 1883, 2209, 2225, 2424, 2570, 2603, 2649, 2783

Caldwell v. Jennison [Mass., unreported (1781)], 467, 1623

Calhoun v. Cook [332 F. Supp. 804 (1975)], 773–774

Califano v. Aznavorian [439 U.S. 170 (1978)], 2276

Califano v. Gautier Torres [435 U.S. 1 (1978)], 2080

Califano v. Goldfarb [430 U.S. 199 (1977)], **293**, 2392, 2393, 2399, 2445, 2881

Califano v. Jobst [429 U.S. 1089 (1977)], 1671–1672

Califano v. Webster [430 U.S. 313 (1977)], **293**, 2392, 2399

Califano v. Westcott [443 U.S. 76 (1979)], **293–294**, 2391

California, Legislature of the State of v. Eu [816 P. 2d 1309 (Cal. 1991)], 2671

California, United States v. [297 U.S. 175 (1936)], 1211

California, United States v. [332 U.S. 19 (1947)], 1840

California, United States v. [381 U.S. 139 (1965)], 1840

California v. Acevedo [500 U.S. 565 (1991)], 2169

California v. Ciraolo [476 U.S. 207 (1986)], 712, 1093, 2140, 2141, 2337, 2342

California v. Green [399 U.S. 149 (1970)], 933

California v. Greenwood [486 U.S. 35 (1988)], **294**, 1093, 2337

California v. Hodari [499 U.S. 621 (1991)], 2455

California v. LaRue [409 U.S. 109 (1972)], 1830, 2741

California v. Prysock [452 U.S. 355 (1981)], 2044

California v. Ramos [463 U.S. 992 (1983)], 303

California v. Thompson [312 U.S. 672 (1941)], 792

California v. Zook [336 U.S. 725 (1949)], 1988

California Federal Savings & Loan v. Guerra [479 U.S. 272 (1987)], 1844, 2397, 2399

California Medical Association v. FEC [453 U.S. 182 (1981)], 1933

Callins v. Collins [510 U.S. 1141 (1994)], 196, 306, 733

Calvin's Case [2 How. St. Tr. 559 (English) (1608)], **294**, 363, 1227

Camara v. Municipal Court [387 U.S. 523 (1967)], 42, 43, 44, **294**, 1095, 2331, 2333, 2336, 2341, 2767, 2891

Caminetti v. United States [242 U.S. 470 (1917)], **1294**, 1396, 1777

Camps Newfound/Owatonna, Inc. v. Town of Harrison, Maine [520 U.S. 564 (1997)], 806, 2494–2495, 2524

Cannon v. University of Chicago [441 U.S. 677(1979)], 853, 1975, 2706

Canton (City of) v. Harris [485 U.S. 933 (1989)], 2158

Cantwell v. Connecticut [310 U.S. 296 (1940)], 179, **299**, 734, 894, 1107, 1317, 2174, 2185, 2186, 2188, 2189, 2198

Canty v. Alabama [309 U.S. 629 (1940)], 1924

Capital Punishment Cases of 1972. See Furman v. Georgia; Jackson v. Georgia; Branch v. Texas

Capital Punishment Cases of 1976. See Green v. Oklahoma; Gregg v. Georgia; Jurek v. Texas; Proffitt v. Florida; Roberts v. Louisiana; Woodson v. North Carolina

Capitol Square Review and Advisory Board v. Pinette [515 U.S. 753 (1995)], **312–313**, 2173, 2194

Caplin & Drysdale, Chartered v. United States [491 U.S. 617 (1989)], 983, 2043, 2112

Carey v. Board of Education [598 F. 2d 535 (1979)], 860, 2206

Carey v. Piphus [435 U.S. 247 (1978)], 739, 2350

Carey v. Population Services International [431 U.S. 678 (1977)], 182, **316–317**, 1118, 1234, 1672, 2204, 2208, 2242, 2573

Carleson v. Remillard [406 U.S. 598 (1972)], 2877

Carlson v. Green [442 U.S. 940 (1980)], 185, 739, 740, 1344

Carlson v. Landon [342 U.S. 524 (1952)], 149, 150, 187, 2005

Carolene Products Company, United States v. [304 U.S. 144 (1938)], **317–318**, 382, 383, 793, 794, 838, 845, 910, 1050, 1101, 1116, 1177, 1237, 1263, 1288, 1311, 1381, 1447, 1810, 1814, 1957–1958, 1990, 2121–2122, 2293, 2302, 2471, 2545, 2549, 2572, 2575, 2576, 2624

Carpenters & Joiners Union, Local No. 213 et al. v. Ritter's Cafe et al. [314 U.S. 595 (1942)], 1550, 1555

Carrington v. Bash [380 U.S. 89 (1965)], 2542

Carroll v. President and Commissioners of Princess Anne [393 U.S. 175 (1968)], **319**

Carroll v. United States [267 U.S. 132 (1925)], 244, **319–320**, 956, 1714, 2332, 2340, 2767

Carter v. Carter Coal Co. [298 U.S. 238 (1936)], 184, 314, **321**, 457, 458, 459, 737, 743, 744, 1313, 1547, 1715, 1760, 1778, 2281, 2388–2389, 2415, 2543, 2560, 2820–2821

Carter v. Jury Commission of Greene County [396 U.S. 320 (1970)], 1510, 2728

Carter v. Texas [177 U.S. 442 (1900)], 1510

Carter v. West Feliciana Parish School Board [396 U.S. 290 (1970)], 773

Castanada v. Partida [430 U.S. 482 (1977)], 794, 2441

Causby v. United States [328 U.S. 256 (1946)], 2643

Central Greyhound Lines v. Mealey [334 U.S. 653 (1948)], 2494

Central Hudson Gas & Electric Corp. v. Public Service Commission of New York [447 U.S. 557 (1980)], 190, 203, 204, **327**, 461, 462, 463–464, 1969, 2351, 2801

Central Pacific Railroad Co. v. Gallatin [99 U.S. 727 (1879)], **2419–2420**

Central Transportation Co. v. New York City [438 U.S. 104 (1978)], 2646

Cervantes v. United States [57 U.S. (16 How.) 619 (1854)], 2653

Chadwick, United States v. [433 U.S. 1 (1977)], 2332, 2344

Chae Chan Ping v. United States [130 U.S. 581 (1889)], 128–129, 130, **328**, 356, 1071, 1163, 1328, 1329, 1330, 2801

Chamberlain v. Chandler [5 F. Cas. 413, No. 2, 575 (C.C.D. Ma. 1823)], 360

Chambers v. Florida [309 U.S. 227 (1940)], 185–186, **329**, 383, 1924, 2238

Chambers v. Maroney [399 U.S. 42 (1970)], **329–330**, 2332

Chambers v. Mississippi [405 U.S. 1205 (1973)], 480, 933–934, 1976

Champion v. Ames [188 U.S. 321 (1903)], 241, **330**, 350, 586, 804, 821, 1161, 1244, 1261, 1290, 1294, 1666, 1704, 1709, 1777, 1830, 1890, 2414, 2583, 2895

Champion and Dickason v. Casey [Cir.Ct., Rhode Island (1792)], **330**, 2602

Chandler v. Florida [449 U.S. 560 (1981)], **330**, 972, 1143, 1151, 1152

Chandler v. Miller [620 U.S. 305 (1997)], **330–331**, 824, 827

Chaplinsky v. New Hampshire [315 U.S. 568 (1942)], **331**, 1042, 1056, 1128, 1141, 1769, 1808, 1838, 2189, 2744–2745, 2855

Chapman, In re [166 U.S. 661 (1897)], 1594, 1981

Chapman v. California [386 U.S. 18 (1967)], 260, 1107, 1109, 1237, 1270, 2045

Chapman v. Houston Welfare Rights Organization [441 U.S. 600 (1979)], 2227, 2889

Chapman v. United States [365 U.S. 610 (1961)], 2344

Chappell v. Wallace [462 U.S. 296 (1983)], 653

Charles River Bridge Company v. Warren Bridge Company [36 U.S. (11 Pet.) 420 (1837)], 162, 325, **331–334**, 675, 1000, 1300, 1686, 2059, 2556, 2647–2648, 2648, 2650, 2653, 2698, 2783, 2883

Charlton v. Kelly [229 U.S. 447 (1913)], 1950

Chemical Waste Management, Inc. v. Hunt [504 U.S. 334 (1992)], 2864

Cherokee Indian Cases [5 Peters 1 (1831), 6 Peters 515 (1832)], 80, **343–345**

Cherokee Nation v. Georgia [5 Pet. 1 (1831)], 81, **343–345**, 1535, 2698

Chevron USA Inc. v. Natural Resources Defense Council [467 U.S. 837 (1984)], 269, 1599

Chicago v. Morales [527 U.S. 41 (1999)], **345**

Chicago and Alton Railroad v. Tranbarger [238 U.S. 67 (1915)], 1350

Chicago and Southern Air Lines v. Waterman S. S. Corp. [333 U.S. 103 (1948)], 951

Chicago Board of Trade v. Olsen [262 U.S. 1(1923)], 456

Chicago, Burlington & Quincy Railroad v. Chicago [166 U.S. 226 (1897)], 178, **345–346**, 1267, 2079

Chicago, Burlington & Quincy Railroad v. Illinois ex rel. Drainage Commissioners [200 U.S. 561 (1906)], 2508

Chicago, Burlington & Quincy Railroad Co. v. Iowa [94 U.S. 155 (1877)], **1224–1225**

Chicago, Milwaukee & St. Paul Railroad Co. v. Ackley [94 U.S. 179 (1877)], **1224–1225**

Chicago, Milwaukee & St. Paul Railway Co. v. Minnesota [134 U.S. 418 (1890)], 199, 217, 240–241, 322, **346**, 970, 1166, 1227, 1559, 1572, 1734

Chimel v. California [395 U.S. 752 (1969)], **355**, 2333, 2344, 2766, 2845

Chisholm v. Georgia [2 U.S. (2 Dall.) 419 (1793)], 198, **356**, 497, 673, 876, 877, 878, 879, 1217, 1404, 1418, 1467, 1673, 1863, 2440, 2459, 2603, 2609, 2910

Church of Jesus Christ of Latter Day Saints v. United States [136 U.S. 1 (1890)], 218, **358–359**, 734, 1961

Church of the Lukumi Babalu Aye, Inc. v. City of Hialeah [508 U.S. 520 (1993)], 359, 2181, 2194, 2456

Cicenia v. La Gay [357 U.S. 504 (1959)], 2263

Cipriano v. Houma [395 U.S. 701 (1966)], 1542

Citizens Against Rent Control v. Berkeley [454 U.S. 290 (1981)], 295, 1933

City Council of Los Angeles v. Taxpayers for Vincent [466 U.S. 789 (1984)], **369**

City of . . . See name inverted, e.g., Canton (City of) v. Harris

Civil Rights Cases [109 U.S. 3 (1883)], 201, 217, 375, 389, 401, 403, **408–410**, 479, 527, 709, 909, 1038, 1089, 1166, 1168, 1240, 1267, 1293, 1437, 1459, 1698, 1919, 2217, 2354, 2483, 2485, 2486, 2487, 2491, 2676, 2693, 2823, 2828

Civil Service Commission v. National Association of Letter Carriers. See United States Civil Service Commission v. National Association of Letter Carriers

Clark v. Barnard [108 U.S. 436 (1883)], 1468

Clark v. Jeter [486 U.S. 456 (1988)], 400, 915, 1824

Clark v. Nash [198 U.S. 361 (1905)], 1890, 2079

Clark Distilling Co. v. Western Maryland Railway Co. [242 U.S. 311 (1917)], **421**, 2870

Clarke v. Harwood [3 U.S. (3 Dall.) 342 (1797)], 2602

Classic, United States v. [313 U.S. 299 (1941)], 410, **423**, 1025, 1042, 1796, 1797, 1940, 1941, 2007, 2282, 2329, 2436, 2550

Cleburne (City of) v. Cleburne Living Center, Inc. [473 U.S. 432 (1985)], **428–429**, 790, 792, 857, 914, 1382, 1721, 2061, 2122, 2287, 2397, 2405, 2533, 2945

Clements v. Logan [455 U.S. 942 (1981)], 347

Cleveland v. United States [329 U.S. 14 (1946)], 1961

Cleveland Board of Education v. LaFleur [414 U.S. 632 (1974)], **430**, 1120, 1122, 1405, 1565, 2155, 2394

Cleveland Board of Education v. Loudermill [467 U.S. 1204 (1985)], 492, 898, 2033

Clinton v. City of New York [524 U.S. 417 (1998)], 243, 626, 1627, 2169, 2386

Clinton v. Jones [520 U.S. 681 (1997)], 243, 432, **433–434**, 625, 954, 1335, 1342, 1994, 2169, 2386, 2537

Clinton v. Virginia [377 U.S. 158 (1964)], 1850

Clyatt v. United States [197 U.S. 207 (1905)], 1897

Coates v. Cincinnati [402 U.S. 611 (1971)], 2776

Cochran v. Louisiana [281 U.S. 370 (1930)], 349, **434–435**

Codispoti v. Pennsylvania [418 U.S. 506 (1974)], **435**

Coffin v. Reichard [142 F. 2d 443 (6th Cir. 1944)], 2012

Cohen v. California [403 U.S. 15 (1971)], 192, 313, 331, **435–436**, 1042, 1269, 1808, 1846, 1966, 2631, 2790

Cohen v. Cowles Media Co. [501 U.S. 663 (1991)], **436**, 1377, 1438

Cohen Grocery Co., United States v. [255 U.S. 81 (1921)], 1605, 2841, 2927

Cohens v. Virginia [6 Wheat. 265 (1821)], 162, **436–439**, 556, 741, 878, 1191, 1250, 1469, 1477, 1496, 1674, 1683, 1690, 1910, 2280, 2554, 2555, 2590–2591, 2616, 2654

Coker v. Georgia [433 U.S. 584 (1977)], 302, **440**, 2368, 2888, 2891

Colautti v. Franklin [439 U.S. 379 (1979)], 1916, 2207

Cole v. Richardson [405 U.S. 676 (1972)], 1648

Cole v. Young [351 U.S. 536 (1956)], 946

Colegrove v. Battin [413 U.S. 149 (1973)], 1950, 1951, 2388, 2727

Colegrove v. Green [328 U.S. 549 (1946)], 152, 186, 233, 237, **440–441**, 500, 870, 1203, 1852–1853, 2132, 2133, 2202, 2765, 2849

Coleman v. Miller [307 U.S. 433 (1939)], 73, 74, 349, **441**, 2117

Colgate v. Harvey [296 U.S. 404 (1935)], **441**, 1655, 2626

Colgrove v. Battin [413 U.S. 149 (1973)], 1516, 1517

Collector v. Day [78 U.S. (11 Wall.) 113 (1871)], 218, 340, **442**, 580, 999, 1037, 1226, 1319, 1383, 1384, 2544

College Savings Bank v. Florida Prepaid Postsecondary Education Expense Board [527 U.S. 666 (1999)], 625, 880, 881

Colliflower v. Garland [342 F. 2d 369 (9th Cir. 1965)], 82

Collins v. City of Harker Heights [503 U.S. 115 (1992)], **442**

Collins v. Hardyman [341 U.S. 651 (1948)], 96, 1230, 1410, 2485

Colonnade Catering Corporation v. United States [396 U.S. 814 (1970)], 44

Colorado v. Barrett [479 U.S. 523 (1987)], 2240

Colorado v. Connelly [479 U.S. 157 (1986)], **444**, 1743, 1930, 2240

Colorado v. Spring [479 U.S. 564 (1987)], 1743, 1930–1931, 2240

Colorado Republican Federal Campaign Committee v. Federal Election Commission [518 U.S. 604 (1996)], 297, 1938

Colorado River Water Conservation District v. United States [424 U.S. 800 (1976)], 18

Columbia (City of) v. Omni Outdoor Advertising, Inc. [499 U.S. 365 (1991)], 2558

Columbia Broadcasting System, Inc. v. Davis [510 U.S. 1315 (1994)], 1378

Columbia Broadcasting System, Inc. v. Democratic National Committee [412 U.S. 94 (1973)], 271, **445**, 1628

Columbia Broadcasting System, Inc. v. Federal Communications Commission [453 U.S. 367 (1981)], 247, **445–446**

Columbus Board of Education v. Penick [443 U.S. 449 (1979)], **446–447**, 759, 2320, 2890

Commercial National Bank of Cleveland v. Iola [154 U.S. 617 (1873)], 783

Commissioner of Internal Revenue v. Glenshaw Glass Co. [348 U.S. 426 (1955)], 2421

Committee for Public Education and Religious Liberty v. Nyquist [413 U.S. 757 (1973)], **464**, 2187, 2321, 2375–2376, 2738–2739

Committee for Public Education and Religious Liberty v. Regan [444 U.S. 646 (1980)], **464–465**, 1207, 2371, 2375

Commodity Future Trading Commission v. Schor [478 U.S. 833 (1986)], 949, 1827

Common Cause v. Schmitt [512 F. Supp. 489 (1982)], 295

Commonwealth v. Alger [7 Cush. 53 (Mass. 1851)], 562, 2506, 2648

Commonwealth v. Aves [18 Pick. 193 (Mass. 1836)], **466–467**, 560, 819

Commonwealth v. Blackington [24 Pick. 352 (Mass. 1837)], 2507

Commonwealth v. Caton [4 Call. Reports (Va., 1782)], 198, **467**, 541, 1891–1892, 2500, 2935

Commonwealth v. Griffin [2 Pick. 11 (Mass. 1823)], 1159

Commonwealth v. Hunt [4 Metc. 111 (Mass. 1842)], 561, 708, 1546–1547

Commonwealth v. Jennison [Mass., unreported (1783)], **467**, 737

Commonwealth v. Kneeland [20 Pick. 206 (Mass. 1838)], 198

Commonwealth v. Moffett [383 Mass. 201 (1981)], 2263

Commonwealth v. Sacco and Vanzetti [255 Mass. 369 (1921)], **467–468**, 921, 1101

Commonwealth Edison Co. v. Montana [453 U.S. 927 (1981)], 455, 1565

Communist Party of Indiana v. Whitcomb [414 U.S. 441 (1974)], 871, 2582

Communist Party of the United States v. Subversive Activities Control Board [367 U.S. 1 (1961)], **472**, 2581

Community Communications Co. v. City of Boulder [456 U.S. 1001 (1982)], 363

Complete Auto Transit, Inc. v. Brady [430 U.S. 274 (1977)], 194, 806, 2494, 2522

Connally v. General Construction Co. [269 U.S. 385 (1926)], 2774, 2775

Connally v. Georgia [429 U.S. 245 (1977)], 2332

Connecticut v. Doehr [501 U.S. 1 (1991)], 2035

Connecticut v. Menillo [423 U.S. 245 (1975)], 2206

Connecticut Board of Pardons v. Dumschat [452 U.S. 458 (1981)], 2366

Connell Construction Co. v. Plumbers & Steam Fitters Local [100 421 U.S. 616 (1975)], 1545, 1546

Connick v. Myers [461 U.S. 138 (1983)], 892, 1677

Consolidated Edison Co. v. NLRB [305 U.S. 197 (1938)], 2821

Consolidated Edison Co. v. Public Service Commission [447 U.S. 530 (1980)], 1237

Constantine, United States v. [296 U.S. 287 (1935)], 2658, 2660

Continental Illinois National Bank and Trust Co. v. Chicago, Rock Island & Pacific Railway Co. [294 U.S. 648 (1935)], 161

Continental T.V., Inc. v. GTE Sylvania, Inc. [433 U.S. 36 (1977)], 2542

Cook v. United States [288 U.S. 102 (1933)], 2722

Cooley v. Board of Wardens of Philadelphia [53 U.S. (12 How.) 299 (1851)], 455, **681–682**, 735, 742, 807, 844, 1162, 1712, 1739, 1904, 2356, 2512–2513, 2566, 2593, 2649, 2652, 2654, 2817, 2867, 2871, 2908

Coolidge, United States v. [14 U.S. (I Wheat.) 415 (1816)], 981

Coolidge v. New Hampshire [403 U.S. 443 (1971)], 187, **682–683**, 1913, 1914, 2332, 2345, 2541, 2680

Cooper v. Aaron [358 U.S. 1 (1958)], 237, 607, 667, **683**, 772, 1458, 1475, 1488, 1583, 1822, 1824, 1915, 2078, 2298, 2853–2854

Coppage v. Kansas [236 U.S. 1 (1915)], **684–685**, 749, 838, 1115, 1309, 1547, 1699, 1911, 2278, 2571, 2896, 2900, 2939

Corbin's Case [S.Ct., New Hampshire (1891)], 802

Cordwainers Cases [Phila. Mayor's Ct. (1806); New York (1810)], 561, 1546

Corfield v. Coryell [6 F. Cas. 546 No. 3, 230 (1823)], 360, **686**, 842, 1172, 2019, 2021, 2274, 2424

Cornelius v. NAACP Legal Defense & Educational Fund [473 U.S. 788 (1985)], **686–687**, 1237, 1899

Cornell Steamboat Co. v. United States [321 U.S. 634 (1944)], 1103

Coronado Coal Company v. United Mine Workers [268 U.S. 295 (1925)], 107, **2756–2757**

Corporation of Presiding Bishop of Church of Jesus Christ of Latter Day Saints v. Amos [483 U.S. 327 (1987)], 924, 2175, 2193, 2195, 2380

Corrigan v. Buckley [271 U.S. 323 (1926)], 403, **693**, 2222, 2410, 2642

Cortez, United States v. [449 U.S. 411 (1981)], 2552

Costello v. United States [350 U.S. 359 (1956)], 1222, 1361, 1362

Costello v. Wainwright [397 F. Supp. 20 (M.D. Florida, 1975)], 2012

Cotting v. Kansas City Stockyards Co. [183 U.S. 79 (1901)], 52

Counselman v. Hitchcock [142 U.S. 547 (1892)], 64, 257, **694–695**, 1334, 1526, 2232, 2236

County of Allegheny v. American Civil Liberties Union [492 U.S. 573 (1989)], 203, **695**, 924, 925, 1054–1055, 1530, 1602, 1843, 1846, 2166, 2196, 2197, 2379

County of Sacramento v. Lewis [523 U.S. 833 (1998)], 711, 1932, 2456

County of Washington v. Gunther [452 U.S. 161 (1981)], 474

Cousins v. Wigoda [419 U.S. 477 (1975)], 1942–1943, 2007

Cox v. Louisiana [379 U.S. 536 (1965)], 188, 371, **702**, 1200, 1922, 2855

Cox v. New Hampshire [312 U.S. 569 (1941)], 373, **702**, 1082, 2189, 2198

Cox Broadcasting Co. v. Cohn [420 U.S. 469 (1975)], **702–703**, 2014

Coy v. Iowa [487 U.S. 1012 (1988)], 491, **703**, 1844

Coyle v. Smith [221 U.S. 559 (1911)], **703**

Craig v. Boren [429 U.S. 190 (1976)], 229, 233, 238, 293, 400, **704**, 857, 915, 917, 1157, 1196, 1746, 1902, 2392, 2399, 2530, 2533, 2538, 2881, 2921

Craig v. Harney [331 U.S. 367 (1947)], 1149, 1150

Craig v. Missouri [29 U.S. (4 Peters) 410 (1830)], 174, **704**, 1686, 1712, 2648, 2651

Cramer v. United States [325 U.S. 1 (1945)], **705**, 1279, 1282, 2551, 2716–2718, 2931

Cramp v. Board of Public Instruction [368 U.S. 278 (1961)], 2776

Crandall v. Nevada [73 U.S. (6 Wall.) 35 (1868)], 341, 630

Crane v. Kentucky [476 U.S. 683 (1986)], 2043

Crawford v. Los Angeles Board of Education [458 U.S. 527 (1982)], 122, **706**, 774, 786

Crawford-El v. Britton [523 U.S. 574 (1998)], 653

Crews, United States v. [445 U.S. 463 (1980)], 1158

Crist v. Bretz [137 U.S. 28 (1978)], 808

Crooker v. California [357 U.S. 433 (1958)], 2263

Crosby, United States v. [11 U.S. (7 Cranch) 115 (1871)], 361

Crowell v. Benson [285 U.S. 22 (1932)], 41, 1481

Crowley v. United States [187 U.S. 651 (1903)], 1376

Cruikshank, United States v. [92 U.S. 542 (1876)], 95, 217, 403, 430, 580, **733**, 1024, 1035, 1037–1038, 1041, 1070, 1106, 1125, 1240, 1272, 1319, 1432, 1733, 2485, 2822–2823, 2826–2827, 2924, 2938

Cruz v. Beto [405 U.S. 319 (1972)], 2190

Cruz v. New York [481 U.S. 186 (1987)], 492

Cruzan v. Director, Missouri Department of Health [497 U.S. 261 (1990)], 790, 1884–1885, 1915, 2163, 2246, 2267–2268, 2268–2269, 2269, 2314, 2532, 2577–2578

CTS Corp. v. Dynamics Corp. of America [481 U.S. 69 (1987)], 805, 2516–2517

Cummings v. Board of Education [175 U.S. 528 (1899)], 1168

Cummings v. Missouri [71 U.S. (4 How.) 277 (1867)], 257, 339, 1035

Curtis v. Loether [415 U.S. 189 (1974)], 2729–2730

Curtis Publishing Company v. Butts [388 U.S. 130 (1967)], 1607–1608, 2067, 2709, 2855

Curtiss-Wright Export Corporation, United States v. [299 U.S. 304 (1936)], 600, **736–737**, 761, 951, 959, 1071–1072, 1328, 1344, 1904, 1997, 2289, 2385, 2627, 2843

# D

Dairy Queen, Inc. v. Wood [369 U.S. 469 (1962)], **739**, 2388, 2730

Dakota Central Telephone Co. v. South Dakota [250 U.S. 163 (1919)], 2927

Dames & Moore v. Regan [453 U.S. 654 (1981)], 615, **741**, 887, 942, 951, 1076, 1992, 1998

Dandridge v. Williams [397 U.S. 471 (1970)], 377, **741–742**, 1120, 1677, 1973, 2310, 2870, 2873, 2874, 2876, 2879–2880

Daniel v. Waters [515 F. 2d 485 (6th Cir. 1975)], 2327

Daniel Ball, The [27 U.S. (10 Wall.) 557 (1871)], 340, 1467

Daniels v. Williams [474 U.S. 327 (1986)], 2032, 2035

Darby Lumber Co., United States v. [312 U.S. 100 (1941)], 349, 458, 460, 524, 598, 684, 693, **743–744**, 846, 966, 1011, 1012, 1262, 1548, 1700, 1778, 1796, 1822, 1830, 2046, 2293, 2566, 2668, 2821, 2903

Darnel's Case (Five Knights Case) [3 How. St. Tr. 1 (English) (1627)], 148, 1246, 1903

Dartmouth College v. Woodward [17 U.S. (4 Wheat.) 518 (1819)], 162, 362, 555, 673, 674–675, 681, 690, 692, **744–746**, 802, 832, 1673, 1686, 1910, 2218, 2556, 2611, 2653, 2704, 2783, 2859, 2871, 2885, 2913, 2922

Daubert v. Merrell Dow Pharmaceuticals, Inc. [509 U.S. 579 (1993)], 58, 243

Davidson v. New Orleans [96 U.S. 97 (1878)], 217, 1732, 1733, 1749

Davis v. Alaska [415 U.S. 308 (1974)], 480, 491

Davis v. Bandemer [478 U.S. 109 (1986)], 868, 871, 1188–1189, 1952, 2137, 2535

Davis v. Beason [133 U.S. 333 (1890)], 748, 1961, 2173, 2186

Davis v. Board of School Commissioners [402 U.S. 33 (1971)], 2627

Davis v. Massachusetts [167 U.S. 43 (1897)], 1212

Davis v. Michigan Department of Treasury [489 U.S. 803 (1989)], 1384, 2533

Davis v. Mississippi [394 U.S. 721 (1969)], 235

Davis v. Monroe County Board of Education [526 U.S. 629 (1999)], 2400

Davis v. North Carolina [384 U.S. 737 (1966)], 2438

Davis v. Passman [442 U.S. 228 (1979)], 185, 739, 740, **748**, 1344

Davis v. United States [512 U.S. 452 (1994)], 1931

Day-Brite Lighting, Inc. v. Missouri [342 U.S. 421 (1952)], 1700

Dayton Board of Education v. Brinkman [433 U.S. 406 (1977) and 443 U.S. 526 (1979)], **446–447**, 759

Dayton-Goose Creek Railroad Co. v. United States [263 U.S. 456 (1924)], **750**, 922, 2415

Dean Milk Company v. Madison [340 U.S. 349 (1951)], 420, **750**, 1228, 1573, 2514

DeBartolo Corp. v. Florida Gulf Coast Building Trades [485 U.S. 568 (1988)], 1553

Debs, In re [158 U.S. 564 (1895)], 241, 430, 448, 583, **750–751**, 751, 947, 1164, 1168, 1409, 1851, 2591, 2735, 2894, 2901

Debs v. United States [249 U.S. 211 (1919)], **751**, 923, 1299–1300, 2580

De Chastellux v. Fairchild [15 Penn. State 18 (1850)], 833, 1192

Decoster, United States v. [487 F. 2d 1197 (1979)], 2265

DeFunis v. Odegaard [416 U.S. 312 (1974)], 54, **759–760**, 1759, 1760, 2104, 2146

DeGeofroy v. Riggs [133 U.S. 258 (1890)], 2722

Degraffenreid v. General Motors Assembly Division [413 F. Supp. 142 (E.D. Mo. 1976)], 2089–2090, 2091

DeGregory v. New Hampshire Attorney General [383 U.S. 825 (1966)], 1596

De Jonge v. Oregon [299 U.S. 353 (1937)], 724, **760**, 1107, 1149, 1241, 1311, 2594

Delaware v. Fensterer [474 U.S. 15 (1985)], 492

Delaware v. New York [385 U.S. 895 (1966)], 867, 1765

Delaware v. Prouse [440 U.S. 648 (1979)], 120, 140, 2331

Delaware v. Van Arsdall [475 U.S. 673 (1986)], 491

Delaware, Lackawanna & Western Railroad Co. v. Yurkonis [238 U.S. 439 (1915)], 749

Delaware Tribal Business Committee v. Weeks [430 U.S. 73 (1977)], 80, 81, 2536

DeLima v. Bidwell [182 U.S. 1 (1901)], 1376

Dellinger, United States v. [472 F. 2d 340 (1972)], 709

Dellums v. Bush [752 F. Supp. 1141 (1990)], 2843

De Lovio v. Boit [7 F. Cas. 418, No. 3, 776 (C.C.D. Ma. 1815)], 360

Democratic Party v. LaFollette [448 U.S. 909 (1981)], 1942–1943, 2007

Dennis, United States v. [183 F. 2d 201 (1950)], 225, 226, 1264, 2761

Dennis v. United States [341 U.S. 494 (1951)], 68, 146, 155, 187, 279, 427, 428, 709, **769–770**, 1055, 1127, 1135, 1198, 1353, 1411, 1789, 1955, 2249, 2546, 2581, 2582, 2745, 2761, 2792, 2793, 2938

Dent v. West Virginia [129 U.S. 114 (1889)], 2829

Denver Area Education Telecommunications Consortium v. FCC [518 U.S. 727 (1996)], 243, 249

Department of Agriculture v. Moreno [413 U.S. 528 (1973)], **770**, 1123, 2287

Department of Agriculture v. Murry [413 U.S. 508 (1973)], **770**

Department of Commerce v. Montana [503 U.S. 442 (1992)], 326

Department of Commerce v. United States House of Representatives [525 U.S. 316 (1999)], 326

Department of Justice v. Reporters' Committee for Freedom of the Press [489 U.S. 749 (1989)], 482

Department of Revenue of Montana v. Kurth Ranch [511 U.S. 767 (1994)], 811, 2660

Department of Revenue of Washington v. Association of Washington Stevedoring Companies [434 U.S. 815 (1978)], 194, 1348, 2522

Derby v. Blake [2 Dane Abr. 649 (Mass. 1799)], 673

DeShaney v. Winnebago County Department of Social Services [489 U.S. 189 (1989)], 195, **774–775**, 1529, 2164, 2576

Desist v. United States [394 U.S. 244 (1969)], 1083

Desmond, United States v. [670 F. 2d 414 (3d Cir. 1982)], 1513

DeSylva v. Ballentine [351 U.S. 570 (1956)], 978

DeWitt, United States v. [76 U.S. (9 Wall.) 41 (1869)], 335, 340

Diamond v. Chakrabarty [447 U.S. 303 (1980)], 1881

Diamond v. Charles [476 U.S. 54 (1986)], 1450

DiFrancesco, United States v. [449 U.S. 117 (1980)], 783, 809

Dillon v. Gloss [256 U.S. 368 (1920)], 73, 2117

Dionisio, United States v. [410 U.S. 1 (1973)], **764**, 2333

Di Re, United States v. [332 U.S. 581 (1948)], 2023

DiSanto v. Pennsylvania [273 U.S. 34 (1927)], **792**, 1879

Dixon, United States v. [509 U.S. 688 (1993)], 811, 985

Dobbins v. Commissioners of Erie County [41 U.S. 435 (1842)], 442, 1384, 2867

Dodge v. Woolsey [59 U.S. (18 How.) 331 (1856)], 298, 325, **801**, 2648, 2868

Doe v. Bolton [410 U.S. 179 (1973)], 816, 2020, 2204, 2205, 2206, 2207, **2284–2286**, 2394. See Roe v. Wade

Doe v. Commonwealth's Attorney [403 F. Supp. 1199 (1976)], 973, 1124, 2407

Doe v. McMillan [412 U.S. 306 (1972)], 2464

Doe v. United States [487 U.S. 201 (1988)], 2240–2241

Doe v. University of Michigan [721 F. Supp. 852 (E.D. Mich. 1989)], 2926

D'Oench Duhme & Co. v. F.D.I.C. [314 U.S. 592 (1942)], 978

Doggett v. United States [505 U.S. 647 (1992)], 2467

Dolan v. City of Tigard [512 U.S. 374 (1994)], **802–803**, 905, 2055, 2151, 2646

Dombrowski v. Pfister [380 U.S. 479 (1965)], **803**, 1867, 1868, 2941

Donaldson v. O'Connor [422 U.S. 563 (1974)], 789

Donovan v. Dewey [452 U.S. 594 (1981)], 42, 44

Dooley v. United States [182 U.S. 222 (1901)], 1376

Doran v. Salem Inn, Inc. [422 U.S. 922 (1975)], 2156

Dorchy v. Kansas [272 U.S. 306 (1926)], 1553

Doremus, United States v. [249 U.S. 86 (1919)], 350, **804**, 1274, 1779, 1790, 2658

Doremus v. Board of Education [342 U.S. 429 (1952)], **804**, 1779, 2662, 2795, 2895–2896

Dorr v. United States [195 U.S. 138 (1904)], 1376

Dorsey v. Stuyvesant Town Corporation [299 N.Y. 512 (1949-1950)], 2484

Dothard v. Rawlinson [433 U.S. 321 (1977)], 406

Dougherty County Board of Education v. White [439 U.S. 32 (1978)], 2812

Douglas v. California [372 U.S. 353 (1963)], 23, 741, **817**, 935, 1232, 1362, 1415, 2262, 2295, 2310, 2869, 2877

Douglas v. Seacoast Products [431 U.S. 265 (1977)], 1677

Douglass v. Pike County [101 U.S. 677 (1880)], 676

Dow Chemical Company v. United States [476 U.S. 227 (1986)], 712

Dowd Box Co. v. Courtney [369 U.S. 502 (1962)], 1554

Dowdell v. United States [221 U.S. 325 (1911)], 1376

Dowling v. United States [493 U.S. 342 (1990)], 810

Downes v. Bidwell [182 U.S. 244 (1901)], 1376, 2080, 2672

Draper v. United States [358 U.S. 307 (1959)], **818**, 1368, 2330

Dred Scott v. Sandford [60 U.S. (I 9 How.) 393 (1857)], 4, 15, 146, 164, 169, 179, 183, 190, 258, 298, 314, 325, 335, 338, 364, 367, 374, 387, 402, 411, 485, 497, 566, 569, 582, 652, 658, 667, 735, 736, 743, 754, 795, 813, **818–820**, 829, 884, 908, 909, 1148, 1175, 1230, 1287, 1290, 1293, 1356, 1432, 1459, 1468, 1475, 1572, 1582, 1620, 1623, 1624, 1625, 1670, 1675, 1712, 1736, 1748, 1791, 1821, 1901, 1919, 1947, 1959, 2021, 2054, 2095, 2099, 2216, 2217, 2389, 2424, 2425, 2427, 2432, 2436, 2556–2557, 2561, 2584, 2591, 2598, 2609, 2612, 2630, 2647, 2649–2650, 2653, 2655–2656, 2673, 2804, 2807, 2858, 2868

Dronenburg v. Zech [741 F. 2d 1388 (D.C. Cir. 1984)], 210, 1196, 1197

Drummond, United States v. [350 F. 2d 983 (8th Cir. 1965)], 2719

Duchess of Hamilton's Case [88 Eng. Rep. 651 (1712)], 208

Duckworth v. Arkansas [314 U.S. 390 (1941)], 1103

Duckworth v. Eagan [492 U.S. 195 (1989)], 1253, 1743, 1744, 1931, 2240

Duke Power Co. v. Carolina Environmental Study Group [438 U.S. 51 (1978)], 2278–2279, 2473, 2532, 2706

Dun & Bradstreet, Inc. v. Greenmoss Builders, Inc. [472 U.S. 749 (1985)], **829–830**, 1608, 1609, 2709–2710

Dunaway v. New York [442 U.S. 200 (1979)], 120, 2331

Duncan, In re. See Duncan v. McCall

Duncan v. Kahanamoku [327 U.S. 304 (1946)], 385, **830**, 886, 1246, 1796, 1998, 2551, 2839

Duncan v. Louisiana [391 U.S. 145 (1968)], 157, 170, 435, 710, 720, 722, **830**, 1269, 1288, 1356, 1434, 1510, 1515, 1517, 1700, 1709, 2037, 2039, 2040, 2041, 2138, 2573, 2724, 2856

Duncan v. McCall [139 U.S. 449 (1891)], 2210

Dunn v. Blumstein [405 U.S. 330 (1972)], **830–831**, 2275, 2305

Duplex Printing Press Co. v. Deering [254 U.S. 443 (1921)], 422, **831**, 1825, 1911

Duren v. Missouri [439 U.S. 357 (1979)], 1510, 2391

Dyer, West Virginia ex rel., v. Sims [341 U.S. 22 (1951)], 901

# E

E. C. Knight Company, United States v. See Knight Company, E. C., United States v.

Eagle, The, v. Frazier [75 U.S. (8 Wall.) 15 (1869)], 1791

Eakin v. Raub [12 Sargeant & Rawle 330 (Pa., 1825)], **833**, 1192

Earley v. DiCenso [403 U.S. 602 (1971)], 1206, 1601

Eastern Enterprises v. Apfel [524 U.S. 498 (1998)], 905, 2055, 2056, 2226

Eastern States Retail Lumber Dealers' Association v. United States [234 U.S. 600 (1914)], 214

Eastlake (City of) v. Forest City Enterprises, Inc. [426 U.S. 668 (1976)], 2536

Edelman v. California [344 U.S. 357 (1953)], 2774

Edelman v. Jordan [415 U.S. 651 (1974)], **853**, 877, 878, 879, 1060, 1468, 1562, 1869, 2832

Edgar v. MITE Corp. [457 U.S. 604 (1982)], 2350, 2516, 2517

Edmond v. United States [520 U.S. 651 (1997)], 2386

Edmonson v. Leesville Concrete Co. [500 U.S. 614 (1991)], 1514, 1515, 1531, 1899, 2490

Edwards, United States v. [415 U.S. 800 (1974)], 2344

Edwards v. Aguillard [482 U.S. 578 (1987)], 707, 859, 924, 925, 1602, 1603, 2174, 2177, 2185, 2327, 2379

Edwards v. Arizona [451 U.S. 477 (1981)], **861**, 1742–1743, 1928, 2831, 2891

Edwards v. California [314 U.S. 160 (1941)], 286, **861**, 913, 1362, 1973, 2021, 2274, 2774–2775, 2878

Edwards v. Healy [412 U.S. 772 (1975)], 1196

Edwards v. South Carolina [372 U.S. 229 (1963)], 767, 1305, 2855

Edwards v. United States [286 U.S. 482 (1932)], 2785

Eichman, United States v. [496 U.S. 310 (1990)], 76, 179, 192, 238, 1063–1064, 1136, 2538

Eisenstadt v. Baird [405 U.S. 438 (1972)], 4, 182, **863**, 973, 1118, 1120, 1122, 1234, 1672, 1811, 2203–2204, 2242, 2246, 2247, 2248, 2285, 2394, 2573

Eisner v. Macomber [252 U.S. 189 (1920)], **863–864**, 2421

Electrical Workers Local No. 501 v. NLRB [341 U.S. 694 (1951)], 215

Electric Bond & Share Co. v. Securities and Exchange Commission [303 U.S. 419 (1938)], 2079, 2350

Elfbrandt v. Russell [384 U.S. 11 (1966)], **882**, 1536, 2066

Eliason, United States v. [41 U.S. (6 Pet.) 291 (1842)], 1994

Elk v. Wilkins [112 U.S. 94 (1884)], 82, 183, 587, 1227, 1698

Elkins v. United States [364 U.S. 206 (1960)], **882**, 936, 2335, 2416

Elk's Lodge #2043 v. Ingraham [422 U.S. 924 (1973)], 2741

Elledge v. Florida [525 U.S. 944 (1998)], 243

Elrod v. Burns [427 U.S. 347 (1976)], 226, 235, 268, 892, 1108, 1885, 1886, 1939, 1940, 2300

Employees v. Department of Public Health and Welfare [411 U.S. 279 (1973)], 853, 1060, 2832

Employers' Liability Cases (First) [207 U.S. 463 (1908)], 459, **893**, 1756, 2780, 2899

Employers' Liability Cases (Second) [223 U.S. 1 (1912)], **893**

Employment Division, Department of Human Resources of Oregon v. Smith [484 U.S. 872 (1990)], 24, 82, 195, 359, 624, 658, 679, 823, **894–895**, 1207, 1351, 1831, 1851, 2165–2166, 2169, 2175, 2176, 2178, 2181, 2182, 2184, 2192, 2194–2195, 2322

Emspak v. United States [349 U.S. 190 (1955)], 1305

Endo, Ex parte [323 U.S. 283 (1944)], 1247, **1415–1417**, 2931

Endo v. United States [323 U.S. 282 (1944)], 129

Engel v. Vitale [370 U.S. 421 (1962)], 1, 167, 188, 855, 859, **896**, 927, 2176, 2177, 2322, 2323, 2324, 2372, 2594, 2856, 2858

Engle v. Isaac [456 U.S. 107 (1982)], 1841

Enmund v. Florida [458 U.S. 782 (1982)], 302, **896**, 2368, 2369, 2891

Entick v. Carrington [19 How. St. Tr. 1029 (1765)], 216, 1099, 2236, 2905

Environmental Protection Agency v. State Water Reserve Control Board [426 U.S. 200 (1976)], 901

Epperson v. Arkansas [393 U.S. 97 (1968)], 706, 855–856, **905–906**, 1083, 1520, 1585, 2177, 2327, 2373

Equal Employment Opportunity Commission v. Arabian American Oil Company [499 U.S. 244 (1991)], 960

Equal Employment Opportunity Commission v. Wyoming [460 U.S. 226 (1983)], 59, 193, 881, **907**, 1181, 2520

Erie Railroad Co. v. Tompkins [304 U.S. 64 (1938)], 220, 317, 466, 513, 798, **921**, 977, 1103, 1390, 1439, 1468, 1493, 1496, 1869, 2556, 2593, 2629, 2648, 2764

Erznoznik v. Jacksonville [422 U.S. 205 (1975)], **922**, 1195

Escobedo v. Illinois [378 U.S. 478 (1964)], **922–923**, 1200, 1280, 1741, 1925, 1926, 1927–1928, 2263, 2264, 2856

Esposito, United States v. [1990 U.S. App. Lexis 12631 (3d. Cir. 1990)], 982

Estelle v. Gamble [429 U.S. 97 (1976)], 721, 730–731, 1885, 2350

Estelle v. Smith [451 U.S. 454 (1981)], 302, **929**, 1742

Estelle v. Williams [425 U.S. 501 (1976)], 971

Estes v. Texas [381 U.S. 532 (1965)], 330, **929**, 972, 1150, 2541

Eu v. San Francisco County Democratic Central Committee [489 U.S. 214 (1989)], 1938–1939, 2008

Euclid (Village of) v. Ambler Realty Company [272 U.S. 365 (1926)], 259, 284, 889, **929**, 2151, 2311, 2510, 2626, 2646, 2944, 2946

Eustis v. Bolles [150 U.S. 361 (1893)], 2830

Evans v. Abney [396 U.S. 435 (1970)], **930–931**, 2411, 2487

Evans v. Jeff D. [475 U.S. 717 (1986)], 413, 414

Evans v. Newton [382 U.S. 296 (1966)], 930, 2487, 2854

Everson v. Board of Education [330 U.S. 1 (1947)], 24, 179, 187–188, 197, 201, 349, 795, 924, 925, 927, 928, **931–932**, 1102, 1206, 1355, 1704, 2157, 2171, 2187, 2302, 2370, 2373, 2706, 2795

Evitts v. Lucey [469 U.S. 387 (1985)], **935**, 2045

Examining Board v. Flores de Otero [426 U.S. 572 (1976)], 66, 2081

Ex parte . . . *See* case name inverted, e.g., McCardle, Ex parte

Exxon Corporation v. Eagerton [462 U.S. 176 (1983)], 71

Exxon Corporation v. Governor of Maryland [437 U.S. 117 (1978)], 1381, 2515

Exxon Corporation v. Wisconsin Department of Revenue [447 U.S. 207 (1980)], 2523

# F

Fair Assessment of Real Estate Association v. McNary [454 U.S. 100 (1981)], 447

Fairfax Devisee v. Hunter's Lessee [11 U.S. (7 Cranch) 603 (1813)], 1689, 2555

Falbo v. United States [321 U.S. 802 (1944)], 1769

Fallbrook Irrigation District v. Bradley [164 U.S. 112 (1896)], 2075

Faragher v. City of Boca Raton [524 U.S. 775 (1998)], 2400

Fare v. Michael C. [442 U.S. 707 (1979)], 1743

Faretta v. California [422 U.S. 806 (1975)], **974**

Farmer v. Brennan [511 U.S. 825 (1994)], 654

Farrington v. Tokushige [273 U.S. 284 (1927)], 858

Farwell v. Boston and Worcester Railroad [4 Metc. 49 (Mass.) (1842)], 561

Fatico, United States v. [579 F. 2d 707 (. 2d Cir. 1978)], 2367

Fay v. New York [332 U.S. 261 (1947)], 35, 199, 1509, 2389

Fay v. Noia [372 U.S. 391 (1963)], 235, 238, **975**, 1253, 1269, 1758, 2156, 2821, 2831

Federal Communications Commission v. League of Women Voters of California [458 U.S. 364 (1984)], 247, 2469, 2530, 2534, 2568, 2750

Federal Communications Commission v. National Right to Work Committee [459 U.S. 197 (1982)], 1933

Federal Communications Commission v. Pacifica Foundation [438 U.S. 726 (1978)], 235, 247, 248, 351, **981**, 1043, 1057, 1147, 1236, 1392, 2530, 2534

Federal Election Commission v. Massachusetts Citizens for Life (MCFL) [479 U.S. 238 (1986)], 296, 691, 1237

Federal Election Commission v. National Conservative Political Action Committee [470 U.S. 480 (1985)], 296

Federal Energy Agency v. Algonquin SNG, Inc. [426 U.S. 548 (1976)], **987**

Federal Energy Regulatory Commission v. Mississippi [456 U.S. 742 (1982)], 193, 901, 1181

Federal Power Commission v. Hope Natural Gas Co. [320 U.S. 591 (1944)], 970, **1023**, 2437

Federal Power Commission v. Natural Gas Pipeline Company [315 U.S. 575 (1942)], 2437

Federal Radio Commission v. Nelson Brothers [289 U.S. 266 (1933)], 761, 1612

Federal Trade Commission v. Gratz [253 U.S. 421 (1920)], **1030**, 1714

Federal Trade Commission v. Ruberoid Co. [343 U.S. 470 (1952)], 2384

Feiner v. New York [340 U.S. 315 (1951)], 16–17, 188, 426, **1031**, 1055, 1304–1305, 2145, 2669, 2792, 2795

Feldman v. United States Oil Refining Co. [322 U.S. 487 (1944)], 719

Felker v. Turpin [518 U.S. 1051 (1996)], 1503

Ferber v. New York. *See* New York v. Ferber

FERC v. Mississippi [456 U.S. 742 (1982)], 1637

Ferguson v. Skrupa [372 U.S. 726 (1963)], 691, 838, 839, **1034**, 1050, 1175, 2510

Fernandez v. Wiener [326 U.S. 340 (1945)], 784

Ferreira, United States v. [54 U.S. (13 How.) 40 (1853)], 2384

Fiallo v. Bell [430 U.S. 787 (1977)], 1329, 1331

Fibreboard Paper Products v. NLRB [379 U.S. 203 (1964)], 1548

Field v. Clark [143 U.S. 649 (1892)], **1039**

Finley v. Lynn [10 U.S. (6 Cranch) 238 (1810)], 2704

Firefighters Local Union No. 1784 v. Stotts [467 U.S. 561 (1984)], 54, 397, **1044–1045**, 1760, 1842

First English Evangelical Lutheran Church v. County of Los Angeles [482 U.S. 304 (1987)], 890, 2535, 2946

First National Bank of Boston v. Bellotti [435 U.S. 765 (1978)], 295, 296, 687, 688, 690, 691, 692, **1060**, 1275, 1372, 2157, 2160, 2351

First National City Bank v. Banco Nacional de Cuba [406 U.S. 759 (1972)], 25

First National Maintenance Corp. v. NLRB [452 U.S. 666 (1981)], 1548

Fisher, United States v. [6 U.S. (2 Cranch) 358 (1804)], 1344, 1685

Fisher v. McGirr [1 Gray 1 (Mass. 1854)], 2935

Fisher v. United States [425 U.S. 391 (1976)], 2240, 2241, 2767

Fiske v. Kansas [274 U.S. 380 (1927)], 723–724, 2311

Fitzpatrick v. Bitzer [427 U.S. 445 (1976)], 877, 879, 880, 894, **1060**, 1468, 2153, 2504

Five Gambling Devices, United States v. [346 U.S. 441 (1953)], 1410

Five Knights Case (Darnel's Case) 3 How. St.Tr. 1 (English) (1628)], 1186

Flag Salute Cases [310 U.S. (1940); 319 U.S. 624 (1943)], 814, **1064–1066**, 2549–2550

Flagg Brothers, Inc. v. Brooks [436 U.S. 149 (1978)], 445, **1064**, 1411, 2030, 2489, 2492

Flast v. Cohen [392 U.S. 83 (1968)], 495, 876, **1066–1067**, 1465, 2475, 2659, 2662, 2777–2778

Flemming v. Nestor [363 U.S. 603 (1960)], 2445, 2902

Fletcher v. Peck [10 U.S. (6 Cranch) 87 (1810)], 30, 344, 667, 673, 674–675, 744, 745, 802, **1067–1068**, 1175, 1260, 1287, 1673, 1682, 1685, 1904, 2554, 2570, 2648, 2653, 2664, 2676, 2781, 2783, 2862

Fletcher v. Weir [455 U.S. 603 (1982)], 1927

Flint v. Stone Tracy Co. [220 U.S. 107 (1911)], 2421

Florida v. Bostick [501 U.S. 429 (1991)], 1097

Florida v. Riley [488 U.S. 445 (1989)], 712, 1093, 2141, 2337

Florida v. Royer [460 U.S. 491 (1983)], 2333, 2338

Florida Avocado Growers v. Paul [372 U.S. 132 (1963)], 2511

Florida Bar v. Went For It, Inc. [515 U.S. 618 (1995)], **1068**

Florida Prepaid Postsecondary Education Expense Board v. College Savings Bank, U.S. [527 U.S. 627 (1999)], 625, 880, 992, 1845

Florida Star v. B.J.F. [491 U.S. 524 (1989)], 1145

Foley v. Connelie [435 U.S. 291 (1978)], 66, 72, **1068**, 2583

Follett v. Town of McCormick [321 U.S. 573 (1944)], 1427, 2191

Fong Haw Tan v. Phelan [333 U.S. 6 (1948)], 1331

Fong Yue Ting v. United States [149 U.S. 698 (1893)], 128, 130, 771, 1167, 1227, 1330

Food Lion, Inc. v. American Broadcasting Co. (ABC) [194 F. 3d 505 (4th Cir. 1999)], **1069**, 1438

Ford v. Wainwright [477 U.S. 399 (1986)], **1070–1071**, 1720

Fordice, United States v. [505 U.S. 717 (1992)], 58

Ford Motor Company v. Equal Employment Opportunity Commission [454 U.S. 1030 (1981)], 194, 1842

Forsyth County, Georgia v. Nationalist Movement [505 U.S. 123 (1992)], 195, **1082**

Fort Gratiot Sanitary Landfill, Inc. v. Michigan Department of Natural Resources [504 U.S. 353 (1992)], 2864

Fortnightly Corp. v. United Artists Television, Inc. [392 U.S. 390 (1968)], 2449

Fort Wayne Books, Inc. v. Indiana [489 U.S. 46 (1989)], 1153

44 Liquormart, Inc v. Rhode Island [517 U.S. 484 (1996)], 464, 1135, 1830, 2170

Foster v. Illinois [332 U.S. 134 (1947)], 2261

Foster v. Nielson [27 U.S. (2 Pet.) 253 (1829)], 1612, 1950, 2722

Foster and Elam v. Neilson (1829), 1080

Foster-Fountain Packing Co. v. Haydel [278 U.S. 1 (1928)], 2514

$405,089.23, United States v. [518 U.S. 267 (1996)], 811

Fox v. Washington [236 U.S. 273 (1915)], 1299

Frady, United States v. [456 U.S. 152 (1982)], 1253

Frances and Eliza v. Coates [21 U.S. 398 (1823)], 832

Francis v. Resweber [331 U.S. 786 (1947)], 815

Frank v. Mangum [237 U.S. 309 (1915)], **1100–1101**, 1310, 1758, 1911, 2638

Frank v. Maryland [359 U.S. 360 (1959)], 42, 43, 2767

Franklin v. Massachusetts [505 U.S. 788 (1992)], 326

Franks v. Delaware [438 U.S. 154 (1978)], 2345

Frazee v. Illinois Department of Employment Security [489 U.S. 829 (1989)], **1105**, 2192, 2380

Frazier v. Cupp [94 U.S. 731 (1969)], 2690

Freedman v. Maryland [380 U.S. 51 (1965)], **1105–1106**

Freeman v. Hewitt [329 U.S. 249 (1949)], **1148**, 2522

Fremont v. United States [17 How. 542 (1855)], 2653

Freund v. United States [260 U.S. 60 (1938)], 1077

Freytag v. Commissioner of Internal Revenue [501 U.S. 868 (1991)], 2386

Friends of the Earth, Inc. v. Laidlaw Environmental Services [120 S.Ct. 693 (2000)], 905

Fries, John, United States v. [3 U.S. (3 Dall.) 515 (1800)], 1902

Frisbie v. United States [157 U.S. 160 (1895)], 241

Frisby v. Schultz [487 U.S. 474 (1988)], **1156**

Frohwerk v. United States [249 U.S. 204 (1919)], 709, 923, **1156**, 1299, 2580, 2901

Frontiero v. Richardson [411 U.S. 677 (1973)], 229, 232, 238, 508, 704, **1156–1157**, 1185, 1196, 2155, 2390, 2391, 2393, 2921

Frost & Frost Trucking Co. v. Railroad Commission [271 U.S. 583 (1926)], 2626, 2748

Frothingham v. Mellon [262 U.S. 447 (1923)], 1066, **1157**, 1464, 1795, 1797, 2468, 2481, 2626, 2659, 2661–2662

Fry v. United States [421 U.S. 542 (1975)], 1011, 1012, 1776, 2154, 2155

Fuentes v. Shevin [407 U.S. 67 (1972)], 2053

Fullilove v. Klutznick [449 U.S. 448 (1980)], 53, 54, 55, 56, 391, 397, 623, 794, **1172**, 1530, 1587, 1588, 2105, 2106, 2108, 2109, 2110, 2111, 2153, 2160, 2230, 2231, 2530, 2536, 2538, 2597, 2599, 2765, 2887, 2890

Furman v. Georgia [408 U.S. 238 (1972)], 236, 274, 300–301, 302, 303, 304, 305, 306, **309–310**, 310, 720, 721, 732, 1288, 2319, 2368, 2443, 2888, 2891

## G

Gaffney v. Cummings [412 U.S. 735 (1973)], 1188, 2134

Gagnon v. Scarpelli [411 U.S. 778 (1973)], 2263

Gallagher v. Crown Kosher Super Market [366 U.S. 617 (1961)], 2191, 2584

Gambino v. United States [275 U.S. 310 (1927)], 2416

Gannett Co., Inc. v. DePasquale [443 U.S. 368 (1979)], 1151, **1180–1181**, 1214, 1979, 2010, 2077, 2231, 2232

García v. San Antonio Metropolitan Transit Authority [469 U.S. 528 (1985)], 59, 190, 191, 193, 276, 362, 623–624, 684, 806, 903, 907, 967, 990, 991, 995, 1012, 1089, **1181–1182**, 1211, 1229, 1292, 1477, 1549, 1637, 1776–1777, 1803, 1822, 1841, 1844, 1845, 2155, 2169, 2481, 2503, 2520, 2587, 2668

Gardner v. Florida [430 U.S. 349 (1977)], 302

Garland, Ex parte [71 U.S. (4 Wall.) 333 (1867)], 257, 318, 339, 1030, 1182

Garner v. Florida [430 U.S. 349 (1977)], 2367

Garrett v. United States [471 U.S. 773 (1985)], 982–983

Garrison v. Louisiana [379 U.S. 64 (1964)], 1047, 1805, 2353

Garrity v. New Jersey [385 U.S. 493 (1967)], **1183**, 2238

Gaston County v. United States [395 U.S. 285 (1969)], 2102

Gault, In re [387 U.S. 1 (1967)], 352, 492, 1083, **1183–1184**, 1269, 1523, 1524, 1709, 1718, 2265

Gebser v. Lago Vista Independent School District [524 U.S. 274 (1998)], 2400

Geduldig v. Aiello [417 U.S. 484 (1974)], 1032, 2394, 2397, 2399

Geer v. Connecticut [161 U.S. 519 (1896)], 1212

Gelbard v. United States [408 U.S. 41 (1972)], **1184**

Gelpcke v. Dubuque [68 U.S. (1 Wall.) 175 (1864)], 341, 676, 1733, 2628

Gelston v. Hoyt [16 U.S. (3 Wheat.) 246 (1818)], 1685

General Building Constructors Association, Inc. v. Pennsylvania [16 U.S. 375 (1982)], 403, 2221

General Dynamics Corp., United States v. [410 U.S. 979 (1973)], 2542

General Electric Co. v. Gilbert [429 U.S. 125 (1976)], 406, 2394, 2395

Gentile v. State Bar of Nevada [501 U.S. 1030 (1991)], 1152

Georgia v. McCollum [505 U.S. 42 (1992)], 195, 1899, 2088, 2490

Georgia v. Rachel [384 U.S. 780 (1966)], 414, 2227

Georgia v. Stanton [73 U.S. (6 Wall.) 50 (1868)], 335, 339, **1745–1746**, 1950, 2471

Georgia Railroad & Banking Co. v. Smith [128 U.S. 174 (1889)], 1163

Gerende v. Board of Supervisors of Elections [341 U.S. 56 (1951)], **1187**, 2794

Gerstein v. Pugh [420 U.S. 103 (1975)], 121, 716, 1369, 2024, 2332

Gertz v. Robert Welch, Inc. [418 U.S. 323 (1974)], 271, 829, 830, **1189**, 1236, 1608, 1671, 1822, 1976, 1978, 1979, 2014, 2709, 2887, 2890, 2893

Gettysburg Electric Railway Co., United States v. [160 U.S. 668 (1896)], 889

Gibbons v. Ogden [22 U.S. (9 Wheat.) 1 (1824)], 454–455, 456, 459, 660, 675, 693, 743, 832, 835, 844, 845, 861, 1011, **1189–1192**, 1266, 1396, 1425, 1534, 1540, 1611–1612, 1636, 1674, 1683, 1686, 1690, 1707, 1768–1769, 1776, 1778, 1896, 1988, 2115, 2274, 2506, 2512, 2555, 2560–2561, 2565, 2586–2587, 2593, 2611, 2652–2653, 2697, 2839, 2858, 2871, 2883, 2885, 2903, 2908, 2913

Gibbs v. United Mine Workers of America [383 U.S. 715 (1966)], 1891

Giboney v. Empire Storage & Ice Co. [336 U.S. 490 (1949)], 188, **1192**, 1907, 2795

Gibson v. Florida Legislative Investigation Committee [372 U.S. 539 (1963)], 155, 187, **1192–1193**, 1200, 1595–1596, 2243

Gideon v. Wainwright [372 U.S. 335 (1963)], 23, 170, 186, 720, 817, 971, 1083, **1193–1194**, 1200, 1369, 1462, 1869, 1981, 2043, 2261–2262, 2263, 2609, 2796, 2856, 2877

Gilbert v. California [388 U.S. 263 (1967)], 1627

Gilbert v. Minnesota [254 U.S. 325 (1920)], 595

Gilchrist v. Collector [10 F. Cas. 355 (C.C.D. S.C. 1808) (No. 5, 420)], 885

Giles v. Teasley [193 U.S. 146 (1904)], 1041

Gillette v. United States [401 U.S. 437 (1971)], 506, 666, 1677, 2188

Gillock, United States v. [445 U.S. 360 (1979)], 2464

Ginsberg v. New York [390 U.S. 629 (1968)], 351, 353, 1083, **1194–1195**

Ginzburg v. United States [383 U.S. 463 (1966)], 1270

Girouard v. United States [328 U.S. 61 (1946)], **1198**, 2326

Gitlow v. New York [268 U.S. 652 (1925)], 146, 179, 284, 426, 1050, 1126, 1128, **1198–1199**, 1285, 1296, 1300, 1352, 1354, 1787, 1959, 2186, 2310, 2311, 2318, 2319, 2580, 2640, 2901–2902

Given, United States v. [25 F. Cas. 1324 (C.C.D.D. 1873) (No. 15, 210)], 360, 361

Gladstone Realtors v. Village of Bellwood [436 U.S. 956 (1979)], 1854

Glass v. The Sloop Betsy [3 U.S. (3 Dall.) 6 (1794)], 1418, 2603

Glickman v. Wileman Brothers and Elliott Inc. [521 U.S. 457 (1997)], 476

Glidden v. Zdanok [370 U.S. 530 (1962)], 419, 696, 1019, 1590

Globe Newspaper Company v. Superior Court [457 U.S. 596 (1982)], 1152, **1199**, 1214, 2529

Glona v. American Guarantee & Liability Insurance Co. [391 U.S. 73 (1968)], 1325–1326, **1605–1606**

Go Bart v. United States [282 U.S. 344 (1931)], 2344

Godcharles v. Wigeman [113 Pa.St. 431 (Penna. 1886)], 1735–1736

Godfrey v. Georgia [446 U.S. 420 (1980)], 302, **1199**

Goesaert v. Cleary [335 U.S. 464 (1948)], **1199**, 2392, 2398, 2921

Gold Clause Cases (1935), 211, 734, **1201–1202**, 1311, 1488

Goldberg v. Kelly [397 U.S. 254 (1970)], 119, 184, 231, 233–234, 237, 492, 816, 897, 966, **1200–1201**, 1362, 1678, 1697–1698, 1887–1888, 1973, 1974, 2026, 2033–2034, 2252, 2445, 2468, 2873, 2874, 2876, 2880

Golden v. Prince [10 F. Cas. 1542 (C.C.D. Pa. 1814) (No. 5, 509)], 2859

Goldfarb v. Virginia State Bar [421 U.S. 773 (1975)], **1202**

Goldman v. United States [316 U.S. 129 (1942)], 711, 873, 1850, 2416

Goldman v. Weinberger [475 U.S. 503 (1986)], 895, **1202**, 1822, 2192, 2380

Goldstein v. California [412 U.S. 546 (1973)], 685

Goldwater v. Carter [444 U.S. 996 (1979)], 320, 616, 1075, **1203**, 1993, 2360, 2533, 2722

Gomillion v. Lightfoot [364 U.S. 339 (1960)], 362, 1042, 1187, **1203**, 1585, 1586, 1637, 2202

Gompers v. Buck's Stove & Range Company [221 U.S. 418 (1911)], **1203–1204**, 1559

Gong Lum v. Rice [275 U.S. 78 (1927)], 129, 388, **1204**, 2282, 2642

Goodell v. Jackson [20 Johns. 693 (N.Y. 1823)], 1535

Gooding v. Wilson [405 U.S. 518 (1972)], 234, 1042

Goodman v. Lukens Steel Co. [482 U.S. 656 (1987)], 1844

Goss v. Board of Education [373 U.S. 683 (1963)], 2854

Goss v. Lopez [419 U.S. 565 (1975)], 201, 856, 966, **1205**, 1975, 2027

Gouled v. United States [255 U.S. 298 (1921)], 1722, 2339, 2340, 2345, 2767, 2833

Grace v. United States [461 U.S. 171 (1983)], **1218**

Grady v. Corbin [495 U.S. 508 (1990)], 809, 810, 811, 982, 983, 985, 2112

Graham v. Collins [506 U.S. 461 (1993)], 2696

Graham v. Commissioner of Internal Revenue [490 U.S. 680 (1989)], 2380, 2468

Graham v. John Deere Co. of Kansas City [383 U.S. 1 (1966)], 1881, 1882

Graham v. Richardson [403 U.S. 365 (1971)], 66, 190, 194, **1218–1219**, 1331, 1333, 2583, 2873

Grand Rapids School District v. Ball [473 U.S. 373 (1985)], **63**, 1603, 1604, 2375, 2378

Granger Cases (1877), 217, 240, 321, 931, 1037, 1164, **1224–1225**, 1397, 2817, 2822–2823, 2829

Gravel v. United States [408 U.S. 606 (1972)], **1226**, 1323, 2359, 2464

Graver Tank & Manufacturing Co. v. Linde Air Products Co. [340 U.S. 845 (1950)], 1882

Graves v. New York ex rel. O'Keefe [306 U.S. 466 (1939)], 340, 442, **1226**, 1384, 1869, 2544

Gray v. Davis [10 F. Cas. 1006 (C. C. W. D. Tx. 1871)], 360

Gray v. Sanders [372 U.S. 368 (1963)], **1227–1228**, 1533, 2132–2133, 2810

Gray v. United States [21 Ct.Cl. 340 (1884)], 2505

Great American Federal Savings & Loan Association v. Novotny [442 U.S. 366 (1979)], 894

Great Atlantic & Pacific Tea Co. v. Cottrell [424 U.S. 366 (1976)], **1228**, 2514

Great Northern Railway Co. v. Sunburst Oil & Refining Co. [287 U.S. 580 (1932)], 2224

Greater New Orleans Broadcasting Association v. United States [527 U.S. 173 (1999)], 464

Green v. Biddle [8 Wheaton 1 (1823)], 423, 438, **1228**, 1686, 2859

Green v. County School Board of New Kent [391 U.S. 430 (1968)], 229, 232, 237, 397, 772–773, 859, **1229**, 2854

Green v. Georgia [442 U.S. 95 (1979)], 302, 934

Green v. Oklahoma [428 U.S. 907 (1976)], **310–312**

Green v. United States [356 U.S. 165 (1957)], 720, 807

Greene v. McElroy [360 U.S. 474 (1959)], 421, 946, 1650

Greenholtz v. Inmates of Nebraska Penal and Correctional Complex [442 U.S. 1 (1979)], 897, 2367

Greenough v. Greenough [11 Penn. State 489 (1849)], 833

Greenwood v. Peacock [384 U.S. 808 (1966)], 414–415, 2227

Greer v. Spock [424 U.S. 828 (1976)], 117, 2069

Gregg v. Georgia [428 U.S. 153 (1976)], 239, 300, 301, 302, 303, 305, 306, 308, **310–312**, 732, 1703, 2368, 2443

Gregoire v. Biddle [339 U.S. 949 (1949)], 943

Gregory v. Ashcroft [501 U.S. 452 (1991)], 624, 991, **1229**, 2503

Gregory v. Chicago [394 U.S. 111 (1969)], 188, 2855

Griffin v. Breckenridge [403 U.S. 88 (1971)], 96, 227, 423, 709, **1230–1231**, 1241, 1293, 2274, 2487

Griffin v. California [380 U.S. 609 (1965)], 33, 815, **1231**, 1665, 2039, 2238, 2458, 2850, 2856

Griffin v. County School Board of Prince Edward County [377 U.S. 218 (1964)], 772, **1231**, 1374, 1375, 1585, 1757, 2738

Griffin v. Illinois [351 U.S. 12 (1956)], 23, 377, 741, 817, **1231–1232**, 1362, 1750–1751, 2262, 2310, 2869, 2874, 2877

Griffin v. Wisconsin [483 U.S. 868 (1987)], 2337

Griffiths, In re [413 U.S. 717 (1973)], 66, 1987, **2582–2583**

Griggs v. Duke Power Co. [401 U.S. 924 (1971)], 96, 99, 100, 396, 406, 408, **1232**, 2102, 2107, 2392, 2890

Grimaud, United States v. [220 U.S. 506 (1911)], **1232**, 1558

Griswold v. Connecticut [381 U.S. 479 (1965)], 4, 182, 187, 210, 211, 239, 274, 315, 316, 317, 381, 508, 667, 816, 839, 863, 973, 1108, 1118, 1120, 1122, 1175, **1233–1234**, 1269, 1289, 1393, 1461–1462, 1480, 1586, 1639, 1671, 1724, 1810, 1812, 1813, 1896, 2052, 2203, 2204, 2242, 2243, 2246, 2247, 2248, 2284, 2285, 2326, 2328, 2394, 2448, 2528, 2573, 2577, 2594, 2795, 2857, 2888, 2892, 2893, 2921

Grosjean v. American Press Co., Inc. [297 U.S. 233 (1936)], 315, 1138–1139, **1234**, 1317, 2626

Grossman, Ex parte [267 U.S. 87 (1925)], **1235**

Grosso v. United States [390 U.S. 62 (1968)], **1670**

Grove City College v. Bell [465 U.S. 555 (1984)], 98, 2568

Groves v. Slaughter [40 U.S. (15 Pet.) 449 (1841)], 156, **1238**, 1712, 2649, 2652, 2654, 2698, 2885

Grovey v. Townsend [295 U.S. 45 (1935)], **1238**, 1818, 2282, 2436, 2437, 2809

Guardians Association v. Civil Service Commission [463 U.S. 582 (1983)], 1563

Guest, United States v. [383 U.S. 745 (1966)], 423, 709, 733, 1089, **1239–1241**, 1679, 2275, 2491, 2694, 2878

Guinn v. United States [238 U.S. 347 (1915)], 909, 1041, 1219, **1242**, 1629, 2808

Gully v. First National Bank [299 U.S. 109 (1936)], 1027

Gutknecht v. United States [396 U.S. 295 (1970)], 2448

Guy W. Capps, Inc., United States v. (4th Circuit, 1953), 941

# H

Haggar Co. v. Helvering [308 U.S. 389 (1940)], 1860

Hague v. Congress of Industrial Organizations [307 U.S. 496 (1939)], 921, 1107, **1256**, 1317, 1549, 1796, 2021, 2067, 2349, 2594

Haig v. Agee [453 U.S. 280 (1981)], 959, 1077, 1141, **1256–1257**, 2146, 2574

Hale v. Henkel [201 U.S. 43 (1906)], 2139, 2745

Haley v. Ohio [332 U.S. 596 (1948)], 1522

Hall, United States v. [23 F. Cas. 79 (C.C. Ala. 1871) (No. 15, 282)], 360, 361, 2923

Hall v. DeCuir [95 U.S. 485 (1877)], 204, 217, 430, **1257**, 1645, 1761, 2282, 2564

Halper, United States v. [490 U.S. 435 (1989)], 810, 811, 985

Halter v. Nebraska [205 U.S. 34 (1907)], 1061

Ham v. McClaws [1 Bay 93 (S.C. 1789)], 1287

Ham v. South Carolina [409 U.S. 524 (1973)], 2803

Hamilton v. Alabama [368 U.S. 52 (1961)], 2263

Hamilton v. Board of Regents of the University of California [292 U.S. 245 (1934)], **1261**

Hamilton v. McClaughry [136 F. 445 (1905)], 2505

Hamm v. City of Rock Hill [379 U.S. 306 (1964)], 2420, 2486

Hammer v. Dagenhart [247 U.S. 251 (1918)], 151–152, 349, 421, 456, 458, 459, 743, 744, 749, 804, 827, 846, 861, 1001, 1011, **1261–1262**, 1290, 1528, 1547, 1585, 1709, 1777–1778, 1830, 2049, 2635, 2638, 2658, 2668, 2676–2677, 2895, 2899, 2900

Hampton v. Mow Sun Wong [426 U.S. 88 (1976)], **1262**, 1332, 1586–1587, 2529, 2530, 2536

Hampton v. United States [425 U.S. 484 (1976)], 899

Hampton, J. W., & Co. v. United States [276 U.S. 394 (1928)], 760, **1262**

Hancock v. Train [426 U.S. 167 (1976)], 901

Hanna v. Plummer [380 U.S. 460 (1963)], 1029

Hanover National Bank v. Moyses [186 U.S. 181 (1902)], 160–161

Hans v. Louisiana [134 U.S. 1 (1890)], 877, 878, 879, 995, 1217, 2504

Hansberry v. Lee [311 U.S. 32 (1940)], 422

Harisiades v. Shaughnessy [342 U.S. 580 (1952)], 771

Harlow v. Fitzgerald [457 U.S. 800 (1982)], 944, 1336, **1819**, 1977, 2708, 2922

Harmelin v. Michigan [501 U.S. 957 (1991)], 316, 732, 984

Harmon v. Taylor [273 U.S. 668 (1927)], 2219

Harmon v. Thornburgh [878 F. 2d 484 (D.C. Cir. 1989)], 822

Harper v. Virginia State Board of Elections [383 U.S. 663 (1966)], 312, 377, 608, 631, 815–816, 866, 1175, 1269, **1271–1272**, 1288, 1362, 1401, 1542, 1679, 1961, 2713–2714, 2741, 2857, 2874, 2879

Harper & Row, Publishers v. Nation Enterprises [471 U.S. 539 (1985)], 1377

Harriman v. Interstate Commerce Commission [211 U.S. 407 (1908)], 749

Harris, United States v. [106 U.S. 629 (1883)], 95–96, 403, 709, 1024, 1038, 1070, 1088, 1230, 1240, **1272**, 1698, 1733, 2331, 2823, 2827, 2924

Harris v. Alabama [513 U.S. 504 (1995)], 1254

Harris v. Forklift Systems, Inc. [510 U.S. 17 (1993)], 1136, 2400

Harris v. McRae [448 U.S. 297 (1980)], 6, 7, **1272–1273**, 1324, 1885, 2097, 2205–2206, 2394, 2542, 2764, 2872

Harris v. New York [401 U.S. 222 (1971)], 938, **1273**, 1743, 1744, 1927

Harris v. Rosario [446 U.S. 651 (1980)], 2080, 2081

Harris v. United States [331 U.S. 145 (1947)], 2344, 2766

Harrison v. United States [392 U.S. 219 (1968)], 1158

Harriss, United States v. [347 U.S. 612 (1954)], 1636

Harte-Hanks Communications v. Connaughton [491 U.S. 657 (1989)], 1609

Hartford Fire Insurance v. California [509 U.S. 764 (1993)], 960

Hartford Steam Boiler Inspection & Insurance Co. v. Harrison [301 U.S. 459 (1937)], 840

Hartzel v. United States [332 U.S. 680 (1944)], 923

Haupt v. United States [330 U.S. 631 (1947)], **1279**, 2718, 2931

Havens Realty Corporation v. Coleman [455 U.S. 363 (1982)], 2221, 2475

Haver v. Yaker [76 U.S. (9 Wall.) 32 (1869)], 2359

Hawaii v. Mankichi [190 U.S. 197 (1903)], 1376

Hawaii Housing Authority v. Midkiff [467 U.S. 229 (1984)], **1279**

Hawke v. Smith [253 U.S. 221 (1920)], 73, 862, 1950, 2118

Hayburn's Case [2 U.S. (2 Dall.) 409 (1792)], **1279–1280**, 1418, 1464, 1902, 2384, 2601

Haynes v. United States [390 U.S. 85 (1968)], **1670**

Haynes v. Washington [373 U.S. 503 (1963), **1280**

Hazelwood School District v. Kuhlmeier [484 U.S. 260 (1988)], 351, 381, 860, 1134, **1281**, 2069, 2167, 2441

Hazen Paper Co. v. Biggins [507 U.S. 604 (1993)], 60

Head v. Amoskeag Manufacturing Company [113 U.S. 9 (1884)], 1227

Head Money Cases [112 U.S. 580 (1884)], 1329

Healy v. James [408 U.S. 169 (1972)], 855, 1108

Healy v. The Beer Institute, Inc. [491 U.S. 324 (1989)], 2517

Heart of Atlanta Motel v. United States [379 U.S. 241 (1964)], 390, 405, 420, 459, 913, 1026, 1240, **1282–1283**, 2016, 2420, 2486, 2694, 2854

Heath v. Alabama [474 U.S. 82 (1985)], 810–811, **1283**

Heck v. Humphrey [512 U.S. 477 (1994)], 654

Heckler v. Chaney [470 U.S. 821 (1985)], 1218

Heffron v. International Society for Krishna Consciousness, Inc. [452 U.S. 640 (1981)], 235, **1283**, 2189–2190

Heller v. Doe [509 U.S. 312 (1993)], 428, 2170

Helling v. McKinney [509 U.S. 25 (1993)], 2695

Helstoski, United States v. [442 U.S. 477 (1979)], 2464

Helvering v. Bruun [309 U.S. 461 (1940)], 2421

Helvering v. Davis [301 U.S. 619 (1937)], 314, **1283–1284**, 2445, 2481, 2541, 2659, 2660–2661

Helvering v. Gerhardt [304 U.S. 405 (1938)], 2544

Helvering v. Griffiths [318 U.S. 371 (1943)], 2421

Henderson v. New York [92 U.S. 259 (1876)], 1328

Henderson v. United States [314 U.S. 625 (1950)], 280

Henneford v. Silas Mason Co. [300 U.S. 577 (1937)], 314

Hennington v. Georgia [163 U.S. 299 (1896)], 2584

Henry, United States v. [447 U.S. 264 (1980)], 2264

Henry v. United States [361 U.S. 98 (1959)], 1929, 2024

Hensley, United States v. [469 U.S. 221 (1985)], 2553

Hepburn v. Ellzey [6 U.S. (2 Cranch) 445 (1805)], 796

Hepburn v. Griswold [75 U.S. (8 Wall.) 603 (1870)], 335–336, 340, 430, 697, 736, 746, 1175, 1230, 1354, 1572, 1581, 1582, 1732, 1752–1753, 1791, 2563, **2913–2914**

Herb v. Pitcairn [321 U.S. 759 (1945)], 722

Herbert v. Lando [441 U.S. 153 (1979)], 1141, **1285**, 2200, 2890, 2892

Hernandez v. Commissioner of Internal Revenue [490 U.S. 680 (1989)], 2380

Hernandez v. Texas [347 U.S. 475 (1954)], 1509

Herndon v. Lowry [301 U.S. 242 (1937)], 284, 354, 426, **1285–1286**, 1296, 1353, 1955, 2281–2282, 2780

Hewitt v. Helms [459 U.S. 460 (1983)], 2013, 2532

Hicklin v. Orbeck [437 U.S. 518 (1978)], 157, 1212, **1286**, 2020

Hicks v. Miranda [422 U.S. 332 (1975)], 18

Hills v. Gautreaux [425 U.S. 284 (1976)], **1289**, 2221

Hinderlider v. La Plata River & Cherry Creek Ditch Co. [304 U.S. 92 (1938)], 977, 1398

Hines v. Davidowitz [312 U.S. 52 (1941)], 1077, **1289–1290**, 1593, 1989, 2930

Hipolite Egg Company v. United States [220 U.S. 45 (1911)], 330, **1290**, 1294, 2084, 2899, 2900

Hirabayashi v. United States [320 U.S. 81 (1943)], 129, 131–132, **1415–1417**, 2841, 2930

Hishon v. King & Spalding [467 U.S. 69 (1984)], 1844

Hitchcock v. Aicken [1 Caines 460; 3 Johns. Cas. 2d ed. 595 New York (1803)], 1635

Hitchman Coal & Coke Co. v. Mitchell [245 U.S. 229 (1917)], 219, 421, **1292**, 1547, 1825, 1911, 2896, 2939

H. J. Inc. v. Northwestern Bell Telephone Co. [492 U.S. 229 (1989)], 983, 2111

H. L. v. Matheson [450 U.S. 398 (1981)], 353, 1916

Ho Ah Kow v. Nunan [12 F. Cas. 252 (C.C. Ca. 1879) (No. 6, 546)], 130, 360, 1038

Hobbie v. Unemployment Appeals Commissioner of Florida [480 U.S. 136 (1987)], 2192, 2380

Hobson v. Hansen [265 F. Supp. 902 (D.C.D.C. 1967)], 790

Hodel v. Indiana [452 U.S. 314 (1981)], 1779

Hodel v. Irving [481 U.S. 704 (1987)], 2946

Hodel v. Virginia Surface Mining & Reclamation Association [452 U.S. 264 (1981)], 459, 901, 907, 1182, **1292**, 1345, 1779

Hodges v. Easton [106 U.S. 408 (1882)], 2830

Hodges v. United States [203 U.S. 1 (1906)], 1167, 1168, **1292–1293**, 1890, 2087, 2693

Hodgson and Thompson v. Bowerbank [9 U.S. (5 Cranch) 303 (1809)], 65, **1293–1294**, 1465, 2752

Hodgson v. Minnesota [497 U.S. 417 (1990)], 1845, 2122, 2248

Hoffa v. United States [385 U.S. 293 (1966)], 873, **1294**, 1850, 1914, 2896

Hoffman Estates v. Flipside [455 U.S. 489 (1982)], 2776

Hoke v. United States [227 U.S. 308 (1913)], 330, 749, 1290, **1294**, 1652, 1666, 1790, 2899, 2900

Holden v. Hardy [169 U.S. 366 (1898)], 26, 241, 252, 583, 845, 1115, 1162, **1294**, 1699, 1764, 2571–2572, 2572

Holder v. Hall [512 U.S. 874 (1994)], 2811

Holland v. Illinois. *See* Batson v. Kentucky

Hollingsworth v. Virginia [3 U.S. (3 Dall.) 378 (1798)], 73

Holmes v. Jennison [39 U.S. (14 Pet.) 540 (1840)], 156, 258, 1712

Holmes v. Walton [9 N.J. Law 444 (1780)], 541, **1298**

Holt v. Sarver [309 F. Supp. 362 (1969)], 1374

Holtzman v. Schlesinger [361 F. Supp. 553 (E. D. N.Y. 1973)], 2790

Home Building & Loan Association v. Blaisdell [290 U.S. 398 (1934)], 70, 252, 628, 631, 677, **1300–1301**, 1311, 1350, 1634, 1645, 1789, 1836, 2218, 2226, 2281, 2784

Honda Motor Company v. Oberg [512 U.S. 415 (1994)], 2082–2083

Hood & Sons, H. P., v. DuMond [336 U.S. 525 (1949)], 835, 1103, 1410, 2514

Hooper v. Bernalillo County Assessor [472 U.S. 612 (1985)], 2277

Hooven & Allison Co. v. Evatt [325 U.S. 892 (1945)], 1864

Hopwood v. Texas [78 F. 3d 932 (5th Cir. 1996)], 57, **1304**

Horton v. California [496 U.S. 128 (1990)], 1914

Hosmer v. United States [76 U.S. (9 Wall.) 432 (1872)], 2324

Houchins v. KQED, Inc. [438 U.S. 1 (1978)], 1144, 1215, 1979, 2271, 2328

Houston v. Moore [18 U.S. (5 Wheat.) 1 (1820)], 2555

Houston, East & West Texas Railway Co. v. United States [234 U.S. 342 (1914)], 862, **1308**, 1310, 1312, 1396, 1652, 1740, 1778, 1912, 2415, 2560, 2780, 2820, 2899

Hoxie, United States v. [26 F. Cas. 397 (C.C. Ver. 1808) (No. 15, 407)], 885

Hoyt v. Florida [368 U.S. 57 (1961)], 274, 1509, 2389–2390, 2663, 2921

Huckle v. Money [95 E.R. 768 (1763)], 1099, 2905

Hudgens v. National Labor Relations Board [424 U.S. 507 (1976)], 369, **1308**, 1672, 1677, 2060, 2415, 2487

Hudnut v. American Booksellers Association [475 U.S. 1001 (1986)], 2398

Hudson v. Palmer [468 U.S. 517 (1984)], 205, 1093, 2011

Hudson v. United States [522 U.S. 93 (1997)], 811, 985, 2401

Hudson and Goodwin, United States v. [11 U.S. (7 Cranch) 32 (1812)], 337, 980, 981, 1425, 1433

Hudson County Water Co. v. McCarter [209 U.S. 349 (1908)], 1565

Hughes v. Alexandria Scrap Corp. [426 U.S. 794 (1976)], 1212

Hughes v. Oklahoma [441 U.S. 322 (1979)], 1212, 2158, 2514

Hughes v. Superior Court [339 U.S. 460 (1950)], 1550

Humphrey's Executor v. United States [295 U.S. 602 (1935)], 111, 599–600, **1318–1319**, 1772, 1847, 2149, 2384, 2626, 2636

Hunt v. McNair [413 U.S. 734 (1973)], 2375

Hunt v. Washington State Apple Advertising Commission [432 U.S. 333 (1977)], 806, 1381, 2515

Hunter v. City of Pittsburgh [207 U.S. 161 (1907)], 362, 1637

Hunter v. Erickson [393 U.S. 385 (1969)], 785, 787, **1320**, 1415, 1503, 1637, 2220, 2487

Hunter v. Underwood [471 U.S. 222 (1985)], 915, 2106

Huntington Branch National Association for the Advancement of Colored People v. Town of Huntington [844 F. 2d 926 (. 2d Cir. 1988)], 2221, 2947

Hurd v. Hodge [334 U.S. 24 (1948)], 403, 1307, 2223, **2410–2411**

Hurley v. Irish-American Gay, Lesbian, and Bisexual Group of Boston [515 U.S. 557 (1995)], **1320**

Huron Portland Cement Company v. Detroit [362 U.S. 440 (1960)], **1320**

Hurtado v. California [110 U.S. 516 (1884)], 710, 1267, **1321–1322**, 1354, 1361, 1510–1511, 1698, 1700, 1874, 2036, 2569, 2744, 2829

Hustler Magazine and Larry Flynt v. Jerry Falwell [485 U.S. 46 (1988)], 436, 1133, 1146, **1322**, 2710

Hutcheson, United States v. [312 U.S. 219 (1941)], 107, 1545

Hutchinson v. Proxmire [443 U.S. 111 (1979)], 501, **1323–1324**, 2359, 2464

Hutto v. Davis [454 U.S. 370 (1982)], 729, 732, 822

Hutto v. Finney [437 U.S. 678 (1978)], 730, 731

Hylton v. United States [3 U.S. (3 Dall.) 171 (1796)], 337, 784, 1260, **1324**, 1404, 1883, 1959, 1960, 2602, 2603, 2611

# I

ICC. *See* Interstate Commerce Commission

Idaho v. Coeur d'Alene Tribe [521 U.S. 261 (1997)], 2504

Idaho v. Wright [497 U.S. 805 (1990)], 492

Illinois v. Gates [462 U.S. 213 (1983)], 64, **1327**, 1368, 2024, 2331, 2345, 2469

Illinois v. Krull [480 U.S. 340 (1987)], 2338

Illinois v. Lafayette [462 U.S. 640 (1983)], 2344

Illinois v. Perkins [496 U.S. 292 (1990)], **1327**

Illinois v. Rodriguez [497 U.S. 177 (1990)], **1327–1328**, 2690

Illinois Central Railroad Company v. Interstate Commerce Commission [206 U.S. 441 (1907)], 1398

Imbler v. Pachtman [424 U.S. 409 (1976)], **1328**, 1335, 1454

Immigration and Naturalization Service v. Cardoza Fonseca [480 U.S. 421 (1987)], 2314

Immigration and Naturalization Service v. Chadha [462 U.S. 919 (1983)], 172, 269, 274, 343, 380, 449, 495, 499, 612, 614, 616, 620, 654, 760, 762, 886, 887, 949, 1219, **1333**, 1386, 1460, 1488, 1529, 1599–1600, 2129, 2148, 2385, 2386, 2496, 2609–2610, 2787, 2838–2839, 2842, 2843, 2844, 2887, 2889, 2893

Immigration and Naturalization Service v. Delgado [466 U.S. 210 (1984)], 1330, 2338

Immigration and Naturalization Service v. Lopez-Mendoza [468 U.S. 1032 (1984)], 2044

Inadi, United States v. [475 U.S. 387 (1986)], 492

Indiana ex rel. Anderson v. Brand [302 U.S. 678 (1938)], 677

Indian Motorcycle Co. v. United States [283 U.S. 570 (1931)], 1384

Industrial Commission v. McCartin [330 U.S. 622 (1947)], 1769

Industrial Union Department, AFL-CIO v. American Petroleum Institute [448 U.S. 607 (1980)], 2536

Ingraham v. Wright [430 U.S. 651 (1977)], 729, 856, 974, **1369–1370**, 1975, 2027, 2030, 2350

In re . . . *See* case name inverted, e.g., Primus, In re

Insular Cases [182 U.S. 1 (1901)], 587, 1161, 1169, 1176, 1358, **1375–1376**, 2672

International Brotherhood of Teamsters v. United States [431 U.S. 324 (1977)], 406

International Harvester Company, United States v. [274 U.S. 693 (1927)], 2298

International Longshoremen's Association v. Allied International, Inc. [456 U.S. 212 (1982)], 1551

International Longshoremen's Union v. Boyd [347 U.S. 222 (1954)], 2278

International Society for Krishna Consciousness v. Lee [505 U.S. 672 (1992)], **1391**, 1531

International Union, UMWA v. Bagwell [512 U.S. 821 (1994)], 195

Interstate Commerce Commission v. Alabama Midland Railway Co. [168 U.S. 144 (1897)], 882, 1266, **1397–1398**, 1642

Interstate Commerce Commission v. Cincinnati, New Orleans & Texas Pacific Railway Co. [167 U.S. 479 (1897)], 882, **1397–1398**, 1666, 2048

Interstate Commerce Commission v. Illinois Central Railroad [215 U.S. 452 (1910)], 1397, **1398**, 2894

Iron Silver Mining Co. v. Campbell [135 U.S. 286 (1890)], 1732

Irvin v. Dowd [366 U.S. 717 (1961)], 1150, **1405**, 2077

Irvine v. California [347 U.S. 128 (1954)], 1102, **1405**, 1410, 1850

Isaac Williams, United States v. [148 U.S. 654 (1799)], 883

Ives v. South Buffalo Railway Company [127 U.S. 205 (1911)], 2925

# J

Jackson, Ex parte [6 U.S. 727 (1878)], 1970

Jackson v. Bishop [404 F. 2d. 571 (1968)], 730

Jackson v. Georgia [408 U.S. Z38 (1972)], **309–310**

Jackson v. Indiana [406 U.S. 715 (1972)], 1718

Jackson v. Metropolitan Edison Company [419 U.S. 345 (1974)], **1411**, 1677–1678, 2487, 2489, 2492

Jackson v. Steamboat Magnolia [61 U.S. (20 How.) 296 (1858)], 298

Jackson v. Virginia [443 U.S. 307 (1979)], 722–723, 1253

Jacobellis v. Ohio [378 U.S. 184 (1964)], **1414**, 1452, 1716, 1734, 1965, 2850, 2855

Jacobs, In re [98 N.Y. 98 (1885)], 931, **1414**

Jacobson v. Massachusetts [197 U.S. 11 (1905)], 259, 749, 1065, **1415**, 1884, 1986, 2190, 2328, 2773

Jaffree v. Board of School Commissioners [459 U.S. 1314 (1983)], 2177

James v. Bowman [190 U.S. 127 (1903)], 1024, 1041, **1415**, 2938

James v. Illinois [493 U.S. 307 (1990)], 1530, 2045

James v. Valtierra [402 U.S. 137 (1971)], **1415**, 2220

James Daniel Good Real Property, United States v. [510 U.S. 43 (1993)], 2035, 2056

Jamison v. Texas [318 U.S. 413 (1943)], 2189, 2198

Janis, United States v. [428 U.S. 433 (1976)], 2044, 2335, 2416–2417

January and Patterson, United States v. [11 U.S. 572 (1813)], 832

Japanese American Cases (1943-1944), 186, 206, 794, 909, 944, 945, 1241, **1415–1417**, 2290, 2293, 2302, 2505, 2550, 2842

Japan Line, Ltd. v. County of Los Angeles [441 U.S. 434 (1979)], 194, 1081, 1390, 2522

Jean v. Nelson [474 U.S. 846 (1985)], 1329, 1331

J. E. B. v. Alabama [511 U.S. 127 (1994)], 195, 1511, 1514, 1899, 2170, 2399

Jefferies v. Harris County Community Action Association [615 F. 2d 1025 (5th Cir. 1980)], 2090–2091

Jefferson v. Hackney [406 U.S. 535 (1972)], 2873

Jefferson County Board of Education, United States v. [372 F. 2d 836 (5th Cir. 1966)], 2915

Jelke Co., John F., v. Emery [193 Wis. 311 (1927)], 1114

Jencks v. United States [353 U.S. 667 (1957)], 607, 1426, 2867

Jenison, In re [375 U.S. 14 (1963)], 2190

Jenkins v. Anderson [447 U.S. 231 (1980)], **1426**, 1927

Jenkins v. Missouri [495 U.S. 33 (1990)], 2890

Jenness v. Fortson [403 U.S. 431 (1971)], 158, 1942

Jennison, In re [375 U.S. 14 (1963)], 2192

J. I. Case Co. v. Borak [377 U.S. 426 (1964)], 2706

Jimmy Swaggart Ministries v. Board of Equalization of California [493 U.S. 378 (1990)], **1427**, 2380

Jin Fuey Moy, United States v. [241 U.S. 394 (1916)], 821

John Doe, Inc. I, United States v. [481 U.S. 102 (1987)], 1223

Johns, United States v. [469 U.S. 478 (1985)], **1427**

Johnson, United States v. [383 U.S. 169 (1966)], 2464

Johnson v. Avery [393 U.S. 483 (1969)], **1434**

Johnson v. Los Angeles [865 F. Supp. 1430 (C.D. Cal. 1994)], 2926

Johnson v. Louisiana [406 U.S. 356 (1972)], 264, **1434–1435**, 1517, 1518

Johnson v. Mayor & City Council of Baltimore [515 F. Supp. 1287 (1985)], 59

Johnson v. McIntosh [8 Wheat. 543 (1823)], 81

Johnson v. Railway Express Agency, Inc. [421 U.S. 454 (1975)], 403, 893, 1437

Johnson v. Robinson [415 U.S. 361 (1974)], 1482

Johnson v. Texas [491 U.S. 397 (1989)], 2315

Johnson v. Texas [509 U.S. 350 (1993)], 306

Johnson v. Transportation Agency [480 U.S. 616 (1987)], 100, **1435**, 1844, 2397–2398

Johnson v. United States [333 U.S. 10 (1948)], 2023, 2330

Johnson v. Zerbst [304 U.S. 458 (1938)], 186, 1193, **1436**, 2260, 2261, 2831

Joint Anti-Fascist Refugee Committee v. McGrath [341 U.S. 123 (1951)], 187, 279, 946, **1436**, 2025, 2792, 2794

Joint Traffic Association, United States v. [171 U.S. 505 (1898)], 320, 2895

Jones, United States v. [109 U.S. 513 (1883)], 1227

Jones v. Alfred H. Mayer Co. [392 U.S. 409 (1968)], 96, 98, 146, 403, 405, 407, 911, 1026, 1088, 1241, 1277, 1283, 1293, **1437**, 1854, 1887, 2016, 2087, 2099, 2220, 2227, 2299, 2355, 2483, 2487, 2542, 2694

Jones v. North Carolina Prisoners' Union [433 U.S. 119 (1977)], 2012

Jones v. Opelika [319 U.S. 104 (1942)], 814, 1065–1066, 1768, 2302, 2546

Jones v. Rath Packing Co. [430 U.S. 519 (1977)], 1677, 2588

Jones v. Securities & Exchange Commission [298 U.S. 1 (1936)], **1437–1438**

Jones v. Thomas [491 U.S. 376 (1989)], 810, 1530

Jones v. United States [463 U.S. 354 (1983)], 1719, 1720

Jones v. Van Zandt [46 U.S. (5 How.) 215 (1847)], 2389, 2923

Jones v. Wolf [443 U.S. 595 (1979)], 2190

Jorn, United States v. [400 U.S. 470 (1971)], 808

Joyce v. City and County of San Francisco [846 F. Supp. 843 (N.D. Cal. 1994)], 1301

Judge Peters, United States v. *See* Peters, Judge, United States v.

Juilliard v. Greenman [110 U.S. 421 (1884)], 1227, 1582, 2825

Jurek v. Texas [428 U.S. 262 (1976)], 302, **310–312**

Just v. Marinette County [201 NW. 2d 761 (Wis. 1972)], 903

Ju Toy, United States v. [198 U.S. 253 (1905)], 1167

# K

Kadderly v. City of Portland (Oregon) [74 P. 710 (1903)], 1371–1372

Kadrmas v. Dickinson Public Schools [487 U.S. 450 (1988)], 914, 2397, 2538

Kagama, United States v. [118 U.S. 375 (1886)], 81

Kahn v. Anderson [255 U.S. 1 (1921)], 2505

Kahn v. Shevan [416 U.S. 351 (1974)], 2391

Kahriger, United States v. [345 U.S. 22 (1953)], 152, 996, 1670, 1779, 2658, 2660

Kaimowitz v. Department of Mental Health Civil No. 73-19434-AW [Wayne County, Michigan, Cir. Ct., July 10, 1973)], 2061

Kaiser Aetna v. United States [444 U.S. 164 (1979)], 1564, 2054

Kalina v. Fletcher [522 U.S. 118 (1997)], 654, 1335

Kansas v. Colorado [206 U.S. 46 (1907)], 1344

Kansas v. Hendricks [521 U.S. 346 (1997)], 243, 2406, 2695

Karcher v. Daggett [464 U.S. 725 (1983)], 871, 2134, 2535

Karo, United States v. [468 U.S. 705 (1984)], 875

Kassell v. Consolidated Freightways Corp. of Delaware [450 U.S. 662 (1981)], 1587, 2124, 2514

Kastigar v. United States [406 U.S. 441 (1972)], 64, 622, 694, 1335, **1526–1527**, 1857, 2237

Katchen v. Landy [382 U.S. 323 (1966)], 2730

Katz v. United States [389 U.S. 347 (1967)], 711, 873, 1093, 1296, **1527**, 1850, 2139–2140, 2169, 2247, 2333, 2336, 2337–2338, 2340, 2342, 2343, 2416, 2542, 2761, 2767, 2768, 2896, 2913

Katzenbach v. McClung [379 U.S. 294 (1964)], 390, 405, 459, 1026, 1089, 1241, **1282–1283**, 1778, 2016, 2486, 2694, 2854

Katzenbach v. Morgan [384 U.S. 641 (1966)], 96, 238, 1026, 1090, 1240, **1527**, 1629, 1856, 2810, 2813

Kawakita v. United States [342 U.S. 932 (1952)], 2931

Kelley v. Johnson [425 U.S. 238 (1976)], 1811, 2574

Kemmler, In re [136 U.S. 436 (1890)], **1529**

Kendall, United States ex rel. Stockes v. [37 U.S. (12 Pet.) 524 (1838)], 289, 705, 2698

Kennedy v. Mendoza-Martinez [372 U.S. 144 (1963)], 1200

Kennedy v. Sampson [511 F. 2d 430 (D.C. Cir. 1974)], 1816, 1921, 2760–2761, 2784

Kennerley, United States v. [209 F. Supp. 119 (1913)], 1264

Kent v. Dulles [357 U.S. 116 (1958)], 1077, **1535**, 1587, 1593, 1950

Kent v. United States [383 U.S. 541 (1966)], 1522

Kentucky v. Dennison [65 U.S. (24 How.) 66 (1861)], 1158, 2825–2826

Kentucky v. Stincer [482 U.S. 730 (1987)], 491

Kentucky Department of Corrections v. Thompson [490 U.S. 454 (1989)], 2033

Kepner v. United States [195 U.S. 100 (1903)], 1376

Ker v. California [374 U.S. 23 (1963)], **1535**, 2023, 2768

Kessler v. Strecker [305 U.S. 587 (1939)], 284

Keyes v. School District No. 1 of Denver [413 U.S. 189 (1973)], 229, 232, 237, 446, 447, 773, 859, **1535–1536**, 1975, 2320

Keyishian v. Board of Regents [385 U.S. 589 (1967)], 22, 36, 230, 234, 238, 855, **1536**, 1552, 1648, 2066, 2854

Keystone Bituminous Coal Association v. DeBenedictis [480 U.S. 470 (1987)], 890, 903, 2053, 2535, 2645

Kidd v. Pearson [128 U.S. 1 (1888)], **1536**, 1559, 2513

Kilbourn v. Thompson [103 U.S. 168 (1881)], **1536**, 1589, 1594, 1708, 2384

Kimbell Foods, Inc., United States v. [440 U.S. 715 (1979)], 978

Kimel v. Florida Board of Regents [120 S.Ct. 631 (2000)], 881

Kimmelman v. Morrison [477 U.S. 365 (1986)], 1253

King v. Smith [392 U.S. 309 (1968)], 2876–2877

King v. Warickshall [1 Leach 263 (1783)], 1922

Kingsley Books, Inc. v. Brown [354 U.S. 436 (1957)], **1538**

Kingsley International Pictures Corp. v. Regents [360 U.S. 684 (1959)], **1538**

Kinnerbrew, Ex parte [35 F. 52 Court (1888)], 1878

Kinsella v. Krueger [354 U.S. 1 (1957)], **2170**

Kinsella v. United States ex rel. Singleton [361 U.S. 234 (1960)], 421, 2839

Kirby v. Illinois [406 U.S. 682 (1972)], 923, 962, **1538–1539**, 1627, 2818

Kirchberg v. Feenstra [450 U.S. 455 (1981)], 2390, 2391, 2399

Kirkpatrick v. Preisler [394 U.S. 526 (1969)], 865, 2134

Kirschbaum v. Walling [316 U.S. 517 (1942)], 459, **1539**

Klein, In re [1 How. 277 (1843)], 160

Klein, United States v. [80 U.S. (13 Wall.) 128 (1872)], 495, 1469, 1501

Kleindienst v. Mandel [408 U.S. 753 (1972)], 1628, 2802

Kleppe v. New Mexico [426 U.S. 529 (1976)], 900

Klopfer v. North Carolina [386 U.S. 213 (1967)], 440, **1539**, 2039, 2465

Knight Company, E. C., United States v. [156 U.S. 1 (1895)], 106, 241, 321, 455, 459, 583, 585, 846, 861, 1037, 1162, 1165, 1266, 1409, 1528, **1539–1540**, 1641, 1715, 1778, 1828, 1850, 2046, 2048, 2413, 2414, 2415, 2560, 2591, 2630, 2780, 2894, 2895

Knotts, United States v. [460 U.S. 276 (1983)], 711, 712, 875, 2141

Knowlton v. Moore [178 U.S. 41 (1900)], 784

Knox v. Lee [78 U.S. (11 Wall.) 682 (1871)], 336, 430, 697, 1201, 1581, 1582, 1753, 2563

Knoxville Iron Co. v. Harbison [183 U.S. 13 (1901)], 2414

Kohl v. United States [91 U.S. 367 (1876)], 1970, 2825

Kokinda, United States v. [497 U.S. 720 (1990)], 1213, 2167

Kolender v. Lawson [461 U.S. 352 (1983)], **1540–1541**, 1841, 2776

Konigsberg v. State Bar of California [353 U.S. 252 (1957); 366 U.S. 36 (1961)], 606, 1109, **1541**

Korematsu v. United States [323 U.S. 214 (1944)], 129, 131–132, 909, 1237, 1247, **1415–1417**, 1646, 1769, 2095, 2282, 2624–2625, 2839, 2841, 2930–2931

Kotch v. Board of River Pilot Commissioners [330 U.S. 552 (1947)], 815

Kovacs v. Cooper [336 U.S. 77 (1949)], 461, 1351, 1391, **1542**, 1990–1991, 2145, 2453, 2546, 2795

Kramer v. Union Free School District No. 15 [395 U.S. 621 (1969)], 866, **1542**

Kras, United States v. [409 U.S. 434 (1973)], 23, 194, 204, 1678, 1680, 2029, 2876

Krofft v. McDonald's Corp. [562 F. 2d 1157 (1977)], 686

Krulewitch v. United States [336 U.S. 440 (1949)], 708, 1241

Kumho Tire Co. v. Carmichael [526 U.S. 127 (1999)], 243

Kungys v. United States [485 U.S. 759 (1988)], 366

Kunz v. New York [340 U.S. 290 (1950)], 1411, **1542**, 2189, 2198, 2795

Kusper v. Pontikes [414 U.S. 51 (1973)], 1942, 2007, 2008

# L

La Abra Silver Mining Co. v. United States [175 U.S. 423 (1899)], 2785

La Vengeance, United States v. [3 U.S. (3 Dall.) 297 (1796)], 883

Labine v. Vincent [401 U.S. 532 (1971)], 816

Ladue (City of) v. Gilleo [512 U.S. 43 (1994)], **1556–1557**

Laird v. Tatum [408 U.S. 1 (1972)], 481, **1557**, 2244, 2791, 2842

Lake v. Cameron [364 F. 2d 657 (1966)], 1718

Lake Country Estates v. Tahoe Regional Planning Agency [440 U.S. 391 (1979)], 1335, **1558**, 1591

Lakeside v. Oregon [435 U.S. 333 (1978)], 2530

Lalli v. Lalli [439 U.S. 259 (1978)], 1326, **1558**, 2395, 2733

Lam v. University of Hawaii [40 F. 3d 1551 (9th Cir.1994)], 2091, 2092

Lambert v. Yellowley [275 U.S. 581 (1926)], 2311

Lamb's Chapel v. Center Moriches Union Free School District [508 U.S. 384 (1993)], 1209, **1559–1560**, 2070, 2179, 2194

Lamont v. Postmaster General of the United States [381 U.S. 301 (1965)], 179, **1560**, 1628, 2850

Landgraf v. USI Film Products [511 U.S. 244 (1994)], 99, 2225

Landmark Communications, Inc. v. Virginia [435 U.S. 829 (1978)], 2745

Landon v. Plascencia [459 U.S. 21 (1982)], 1329, 1330

Lane v. Cotton [88 Eng. Rep. 1458 (1701)], 1217

Lane v. Wilson [307 U.S. 268 (1939)], 909, 1219, 1220, 1629, 2349

Lane County v. Oregon [74 U.S. (7 Wall.) 71 (1869)], 1011, 1037

Lanier, United States v. [520 U.S. 259 (1997)], 986, 2400

Lanier v. South Carolina [474 U.S. 25 (1986)], 1844

Lanza, United States v. [260 U.S. 377 (1922)], 164, **1562**

Lanzetta v. New Jersey [306 U.S. 451 (1939)], 345, 1109, 2774

Lapeyre v. United States [84 U.S. (17 Wall.) 191 (1873)], 1995

Larkin v. Grendel's Den, Inc. [459 U.S. 116 (1982)], **1562**, 1653

Larry P. v. Riles [495 F. Supp. 926 (N.D. Cal. 1979)], 790

Larson v. Domestic and Foreign Commerce Corp. [337 U.S. 682 (1949)], **1562**, 2460

Larson v. Valente [456 U.S. 228 (1982)], 734, **1562–1563**

Lassiter v. Department of Social Services [452 U.S. 18 (1981)], 23, 974, 1123, 1362, 1524, 1527, 2025, 2033, 2265, 2808, 2877

Lassiter v. Northhampton County Board of Elections [360 U.S. 45 (1959)], 1089, 1527, 1629

Lau v. Nichols [414 U.S. 563 (1974)], 406, 857, 859, **1563**

Lauf v. E. G. Shinner & Company [303 U.S. 323 (1938)], 1825–1826

Lawrence County v. Lead-Deadwood School District [469 U.S. 256 (1985)], 1637

Leach v. Carlile Postmaster [358 U.S. 228 (1921)], 1296

Lear v. Robertson [463 U.S. 248 (1983)], 2399

Leary v. United States [395 U.S. 6 (1969)], **1572–1573**

Lebron v. National Railroad Passenger Corp [513 U.S. 374 (1995)], **1573–1574**, 2018, 2490–2491

Lee, United States v. [455 U.S. 252 (1882)], 1227, **1575**, 2191, 2460

Lee v. Illinois [476 U.S. 530 (1986)], 492

Lee v. Madigan [358 U.S. 228 (1959)], 2505

Lee v. Oregon [107 F. 3d 1382 (9th Cir. (1997)], 2270

Lee v. Washington [390 U.S. 333 (1968)], 2011

Lee v. Weisman [505 U.S. 577 (1992)], 1531, **1575–1576**, 1603, 1846, 2179, 2324

Lefkowitz, United States v. [285 U.S. 452 (1932)], 284, 2344

Legal Tender Cases [12 Wall. 457 (1870-1884)], 334, 335–336, 340, 580, 2825

Lego v. Twomey [404 U.S. 477 (1972)], 1743

LeGrand v. Darnall [2 Peters 664 (1829)], 832

Lehigh Valley Railroad, United States v. [254 U.S. 255 (1920)], 421

Lehman v. Shaker Heights (City of) [418 U.S. 298 (1974)], 313, 1213

Lehmann v. Carson [352 U.S. 915 (1957)], 771, 2902

Leisy v. Hardin [135 U.S. 100 (1890)], 586, 1168, 1227, **1601**, 1864, 2513, 2870

Leland v. Oregon [343 U.S. 790 (1952)], 718

Lemon v. Kurtzman I [403 U.S. 602 (1971)], 61, 63, 464, 924, 925, 926, 1206, 1208, 1560, 1563, **1601–1602**, 1603–1604, 1672, 1763, 1842, 1845, 2110, 2196, 2321, 2371, 2374, 2699, 2752, 2833

Lemon v. Kurtzman II [411 U.S. 192 (1973)], **1601–1602**, 2752

Leon, United States v. [468 U.S. 897 (1984)], 1204, 2044, 2156, 2335, 2338, 2340, 2886, 2891

Leser v. Garnett [258 U.S. 130 (1922)], 73, 2118

Levitt v. Committee for Public Education [413 U.S. 472 (1973)], 465, 2375

Levy v. Louisiana [391 U.S. 68 (1968)], 816, 915, 1325–1326, 1401, **1605–1606**

Lewis v. Casey [516 U.S. 804 (1996)], 2013

Lewis v. New Orleans [415 U.S. 130 (1974)], 1868

Lewis v. United States [385 U.S. 206 (1955)], 1670

License Cases [46 U.S. (5 How.) (1847)], 325, 562, 742, 844, 1601, 1791, 2409, 2506, 2648, 2652, 2871, 2885, 2908, 2923, 2934

Liggett Company v. Baldridge [278 U.S. 105 (1928)], 2545, 2571

Liggett Company v. Lee [288 U.S. 517 (1933)], 220, 314

Lincoln County v. Luning [133 U.S. 529 (1890)], 877, 878, 879, 1767

Lincoln Electric Co. v. Commissioner of Internal Revenue [338 U.S. 949 (1951)], 1994

Lincoln Federal Labor Union v. Northwestern Iron & Metal Co. [335 U.S. 525 (1949)], 185, 1175, 2278

Linda R. S. v. Richard D. [410 U.S. 614 (1973)], 201, 2107, 2473

Lindh v. Murphy [521 U.S. 320 (1997)], 103

Lindsey v. Normet [405 U.S. 56 (1972)], 1301, 2874

Linkletter v. Walter [381 U.S. 618 (1965)], 2224

Linmark Associates v. Willingboro [431 U.S. 85 (1977)], **1628**

Little v. Barreme [6 U.S. (2 Cranch) 170 (1804)], 448, 1684

Live Stock Dealers & Butchers Association v. Crescent City Live Stock Landing & Slaughterhouse Co. and Board of Metropolitan Police [77 U.S. (10 Wall.) 273 (1870)], 360, 2923

Livingston v. Van Ingen [5 Johns. 507 (1812)], 1534, 2697

Lloyd Corp. v. Tanner [407 U.S. 551 (1972)], 1566, 2415, 2498

Loan Association v. Topeka [87 U.S. (20 Wall.) 455 (1875)], 376, 431, 584, 783, 1037, 1175, **1636**, 1733, 1734, 2075, 2570, 2571

Local 28, Sheet Metal Workers International Association v. EEOC [478 U.S. 421 (1986)], 55

Local 174 v. Lucas Flour [369 U.S. 95 (1962)], 1550

Lochner v. New York [198 U.S. 45 (1905)], 5, 11, 12, 33, 35, 36, 154, 224, 252, 263, 284, 314, 382, 667, 685, 692, 725, 749, 838, 839, 845, 1007, 1115, 1162, 1163, 1164, 1166, 1167, 1168, 1175, 1211, 1263, 1288, 1294, 1296, 1479, 1547, 1552, 1572, 1633, **1638–1639**, 1699, 1710, 1715, 1724, 1736, 1764, 1768, 1890, 1908, 1911, 1990, 2049, 2095, 2226, 2278, 2339, 2509, 2571, 2572, 2575, 2577, 2635, 2645, 2712–2713, 2714, 2773, 2858, 2878, 2881–2882, 2892, 2893, 2896, 2897

Lockerty v. Phillips [319 U.S. 182 (1943)], 886, 2937

Lockett v. Ohio [438 U.S. 586 (1978)], 303, 308, 2368

Lockwood, In re [154 U.S. 116 (1894)], 2920

Loewe v. Lawlor [208 U.S. 274 (1908)], 25, 1162, 1203, **1641–1642**, 1756, 1911

Logan v. Zimmerman Brush Company [455 U.S. 422 (1982)], 193, 2029

Loper v. New York City Police Department [999 F. 2d 699 (2d Cir. 1993)], 1301

López, United States v. [514 U.S. 549 (1995)], 242, 354, 624, 776, 823, 847, 904, 991, 1010, 1277, 1531, 1570–1571, **1642–1643**, 2169, 2660, 2696

Lopez v. United States [373 U.S. 427 (1963)], **1643**, 1845, 2456, 2844, 2896

Loretto v. Teleprompter Manhattan CATV Corporation [458 U.S. 419 (1982)], 890, **1643–1644**, 2646, 2946

Lorillard v. Pons [434 U.S. 575 (1978)], 2729

Los Angeles v. Lyons [461 U.S. 95 (1983)], 1218

Los Angeles v. Preferred Communications [476 U.S. 488 (1976)], 249

Los Angeles v. Taxpayers for Vincent [466 U.S. 789 (1984)], 2534

Los Angeles Department of Water and Power v. Manhart [435 U.S. 702 (1978)], 406, 2393

Lottery Case. *See* Champion v. Ames

Loud Hawk, United States v. [474 U.S. 302 (1986)], 2466

Louisiana v. Jumel [107 U.S. 711 (1882)], 2824

Louisiana et al., United States v. [394 U.S. 836 (1969)], 1840

Louisiana ex rel. Francis v. Resweber [330 U.S. 853 (1947)], 280, 1102

Louisiana Light and Power Company v. Thibodaux [360 U.S. 25 (1959)], 19

Louisville, Cincinnati, and Charleston Railroad v. Letson [43 U.S. (2 How.) 497 (1890)], 2653, 2867

Louisville, New Orleans & Texas Pacific Railway v. Mississippi [133 U.S. 587 (1890)], **1645**, 1918

Louisville Joint Stock Land Bank v. Radford [295 U.S. 555 (1935)], 161, 677, 1105, **1644–1645**, 2932

Louisville Railroad Co. v. Letson [43 U.S. (2 How.) 497 (1844)], 325

Lovasco, United States v. [431 U.S. 783 (1977)], 2466

Lovell v. City of Griffin [303 U.S. 444 (1938)], 1317, **1645**, 2186

Lovett, United States v. [328 U.S. 303 (1946)], 174, 257, 495, 629, **1645**, 2066

Loving v. Virginia [388 U.S. 1 (1967)], 147, 403, 799, 973, 1118, **1645–1646**, 1671, 1724, 1745, 2097, 2098, 2307, 2309, 2355, 2853, 2943

Low v. Austin [80 U.S. (13 Wall.) 29 (1872)], 1725, 1864

Lowe v. City of Monrovia [775 F. 2d 998 (9th Cir. 1985)], 2092

Lowe v. Securities and Exchange Commission [472 U.S. 181 (1985)], 2351

Lowry v. Reagan [676 F. Supp. 333 (D.D.C. 1987)], 2843

Lubin v. Panish [415 U.S. 709 (1974)], 158

Lucas v. Forty-Fourth General Assembly [377 U.S. 713 (1964)], 153, 2228, 2520, 2854

Lucas v. South Carolina Coastal Council [505 U.S. 1003 (1992)], 848, 905, **1650–1651**, 2055, 2149, 2150, 2646

Lugar v. Edmonson Oil Co. [457 U.S. 922 (1982)], 2489, 2492

Lujan v. Defenders of Wildlife [504 U.S. 555 (1992)], 905, **1651**, 2475

Lukumi Babalu Aye, Inc. v. City of Hialeah [508 U.S. 520 (1993)], 2456

Lustig v. United States [338 U.S. 74 (1949)], 2416

Luther v. Borden [48 U.S. (7 How.) 1 (1849)], 340, 430, 577, 785, 804, 1238, 1239, 1613, **1652–1653**, 1949, 2202, 2210, 2648, 2654, 2840, 2923

Lutheran Church-Missouri Synod v. Federal Communications Commission [141 F. 3d 344 (D.C. Cir. 1998)], 57

Lynch v. Donnelly [465 U.S. 668 (1984)], 924, 1055, 1602, 1603, **1653**, 1842, 1843, 1845, 2196, 2198, 2376–2377, 2379

Lynch v. Household Finance Corp. [405 U.S. 538 (1972)], 836, 1256, 2227, 2349

Lynch v. Torquato [343 E. 2d [370 (1965)], 1275

Lyng v. Automobile, Aerospace and Agricultural Implement Workers [485 U.S. 360 (1988)], 914

Lyng v. Castillo [477 U.S. 635 (1986)], 914, 2533

Lyng v. Northwest Indian Cemetery [485 U.S. 439 (1988)], 82, **1653**, 2192, 2380

# M

MacDonald, United States v. [456 U.S. 1 (1982)], **1655**, 2465–2466

Machinists v. Street [367 U.S. 740 (1961)], 1552, 1553

Machinists Lodge 76 v. Wisconsin Employment Relations Commission [427 U.S. 132 (1976)], 1554

MacIntosh, United States v. [283 U.S. 605 (1931)], 507, 1198

Mack v. United States [521 U.S. 98 (1997)], 2169

Madden v. Kentucky [309 U.S. 83 (1940)], 441, **1655**, 2021

Madsen v. Women's Health Center, Inc. [512 U.S. 753 (1994)], 94

Mahan v. Howell [410 U.S. 315 (1973)], **1664–1665**, 2134

Maher v. Roe [432 U.S. 464 (1977)], 6, 1272, **1665**, 1680, 1885, 2205, 2206, 2394, 2870, 2872, 2874

Maine v. Taylor [477 U.S. 131 (1986)], 806

Maine v. Thiboutot [448 U.S. 1 (1980)], 2350

Mallory v. United States [354 U.S. 449 (1957)], 1029, 1713, 1852, 2856

Malloy v. Hogan [378 U.S. 1 (1964)], 722, **1665–1666**, 1923, 2041, 2237, 2286, 2744, 2745–2746, 2856

Malone v. Bowdoin [369 U.S. 643 (1962)], 2460

Mann, State v. *See* State v. Mann

Manson v. Brathwaite [432 U.S. 98 (1977)], 481, 962

Maple Flooring Manufacturers Association v. United States [268 U.S. 563 (1925)], 2311

Mapp v. Ohio [367 U.S. 643 (1961)], 119, 186, 273, 277, 420, 722, 882, 936, 1092, 1102, 1355, 1462, 1535, **1666–1667**, 1869, 2039, 2043–2044, 2155, 2169, 2224, 2334, 2614, 2768, 2796, 2850, 2856, 2903, 2917

Marbury v. Madison [5 U.S. (1 Cranch) 137 (1803)], 109–110, 212, 266, 322, 339, 378, 433, 437–438, 466, 489, 497, 509, 513, 526, 541, 552, 627, 638, 652, 667, 683, 697, 740, 741, 833, 1192, 1287, 1293, 1367, 1393, 1422, 1424, 1443–1444, 1444–1445, 1465, 1468, 1469–1470, 1472, 1474, 1475, 1476, 1477, 1481, 1487, 1496, 1583, 1663, **1667–1670**, 1673, 1675, 1682, 1683–1684, 1739, 1821, 1859, 1863, 1883, 1949, 1951, 1953, 1955, 1963, 1986, 1987, 2202, 2236, 2297, 2384, 2460, 2529, 2561, 2589–2590, 2602, 2669, 2682, 2752, 2781, 2858

Marchetti v. United States [390 U.S. 39 (1968)], **1670**, 1779, 2452, 2658–2659, 2850

Marion, United States v. [404 U.S. 307 (1971)], 2465

Marks v. United States [430 U.S. 188 (1977)], 2534

Marron v. United States [275 U.S. 192 (1927)], 2339, 2344, 2345

Marsh v. Alabama [326 U.S. 501 (1946)], 389, 692, 1308, **1672**, 2015, 2414, 2485, 2487, 2492, 2874

Marsh v. Chambers [463 U.S. 783 (1983)], **1672**, 2178, 2376

Marshall v. Baltimore and Ohio Railroad [57 U.S. (16 How.) 314 (1853)], 298, 1230

Marshall v. Barlow's Inc. [436 U.S. 307 (1978)], 44, **1681**, 2334

Marshall v. United States [360 U.S. 310 (1959)], 981

Marshfield Family Skateland, Inc. v. Town of Marshfield [464 U.S. 987 (1983)], 482

Marston v. Lewis [410 U.S. 679 (1973)], 831, 2275

Martin v. City of Struthers [319 U.S. 157 (1943)], 1411, 1565, 2189

Martin v. Hunter's Lessee [14 U.S. (1 Wheat.) 304 (1816)], 109, 436, 438, 555, 832, 1250, 1465, 1466, 1496, 1503, 1682, 1685, **1688–1691**, 2280, 2554, 2555, 2590

Martin v. Mott [25 U.S. (12 Wheat.) 19 (1827)], 416, 574, 1686, **1691**, 2554

Martinez-Fuerte, United States v. [428 U.S. 543 (1976)], 209, 2088

Martino v. Michigan Window Cleaning Co. [327 U.S. 173 (1946)], 1539

Maryland v. Baltimore Radio Show [38 U.S. 912 (1950)], 2077

Maryland v. Buie [494 U.S. 325 (1990)], 1097, 2162

Maryland v. Craig [497 U.S. 836 (1990)], 491, 703, **1691**, 2316

Maryland v. Wilson [519 U.S. 408 (1997)], 1097, 2711

Maryland v. Wirtz [392 U.S. 183 (1968)], 967, 990, 1012, 1181, 1211, 1776

Maryland Committee for Fair Representation v. Tawes [377 U.S. 656 (1964)], 2228

Massachusetts v. Laird [400 U.S. 886 (1970)], 755, **1692**

Massachusetts v. Mellon [262 U.S. 447 (1923)], 684, **1157**, 2468, 2519, 2626, 2659

Massachusetts Board of Retirement v. Murgia [427 U.S. 307 (1976)], 59, 60, 61, **1693–1694**

Masses Publishing Co. v. Patten [244 Fed. 535 (1917)], 225–226, 1264, **1696**, 2318

Massiah v. United States [377 U.S. 201 (1964)], **1696**, 1925, 1929, 2264

Masson v. New Yorker Magazine, Inc. [501 U.S. 496 (1991)], 1609, **1696–1697**

Mastro Plastics v. NLRB [348 U.S. 910 (1956)], 1550

Mathews v. DeCastro [429 U.S. 181 (1976)], 2034, 2445

Mathews v. Diaz [426 U.S. 67 (1976)], 66, 368, 1332, 2468

Mathews v. Eldridge [424 U.S. 319 (1976)], 837, 965, 966, 1370, 1565, **1697–1698**, 1879, 1979, 2027, 2032–2033, 2445

Mathews v. Lucas [427 U.S. 495 (1976)], 1326, 2732

Matilda's Case (Birney v. Ohio) [80 Ohio 230 (1837)], 560

Matlock, United States v. [415 U.S. 164 (1974)], 2334, 2690

Matsushita Electric Industrial Co. v. Zenith Radio Corp. [631 F. 2d 1069 (1980)], 2728

Maxwell v. Dow [176 U.S. 581 (1900)], 1354, **1700**, 1874, 2038, 2744

Mayor of New York v. Miln [36 U.S. (11 Pet.) 102 (1837)], 162, 1328, 1686, **1700**, 1712, 2555, 2556, 2648, 2652, 2654, 2698, 2774, 2908

Maze, United States v. [414 U.S. 395 (1974)], 2158

Mazer v. Stein [347 U.S. 201 (1954)], 685

Mazurie, United States v. [419 U.S. 544 (1975)], 761

McAllister v. United States [141 U.S. 174 (1891)], 429

McAuliffe v. Mayor of New Bedford [155 Mass. 216 (1892)], 892, 2065, 2749

McCabe v. Atchison, Topeka & Santa Fe Railroad [235 U.S. 151 (1914)], 1310, 2900

McCardle, Ex parte [74 U.S. (7 Wall.) 506 (1869)], 318, 335, 339, 340, 497, 579, 746, 1256, 1456, 1469, 1494, 1501, **1701**, 1732, 2591, 2609, 2735

McCarthy v. Arndstein [262 U.S. 355 (1924)], 2236

McCleskey v. Kemp [481 U.S. 279 (1987)], 97, 239, 304, 306, 307, 308, 309, 396, 733, 915, **1702–1703**, 1980, 2088, 2106–2107, 2164, 2368, 2397, 2443

McClesky v. Zant [499 U.S. 467 (1991)], 2455

McCollum v. Board of Education [333 U.S. 203 (1948)], 188, 1102, **1703–1704**, 2145, 2171, 2172, 2176, 2198, 2371, 2377, 2795, 2947

McCormick v. Talbot [61 U.S. (20 How.) 402 (1858)], 1230

McCracken v. Hayward [43 U.S. (2 How.) 608 (1844)], 156

McCray v. Illinois [386 U.S. 300 (1967)], 1368, 2895

McCray v. United States [195 U.S. 27 (1904)], 151, 340, 818, **1704**, 2658

McCulloch v. Maryland [17 U.S. 316 (1819)], 75, 160, 250, 258, 317, 376, 410, 436, 438, 442, 458, 484, 497, 498, 555, 559, 627, 628, 630, 659, 667, 690, 692, 693, 744, 777, 900, 995, 999, 1011, 1013, 1015, 1214, 1226, 1259, 1290, 1345, 1346, 1347, 1367, 1383, 1414, 1425, 1446, 1461, 1474, 1487, 1582, 1583, 1585, 1587, 1611, 1633, 1674, 1682, 1685, 1686, 1690, **1705–1707**, 1751, 1752, 1753, 1790, 1821, 1855, 1865, 1869, 1910, 1970, 2078, 2280, 2493, 2544, 2554, 2560, 2586–2587, 2653, 2662, 2667–2668, 2687, 2712, 2858, 2871, 2882, 2913, 2922

McDaniel v. Paty [435 U.S. 887 (1978)], 2193, 2197

McDermott v. Wisconsin [228 U.S. 115 (1913)], 2583

McDonald v. Santa Fe Trail Transportation Co. [427 U.S. 273 (1976)], 2155, 2694

McDonald v. Smith [472 U.S. 479 (1985)], 2558

McDonnell Douglas Corp. v. Green [411 U.S. 792 (1973)], 406

McElvane v. Brush [142 U.S. 155 (1891)], **1529**

McGautha v. California [402 U.S. 183 (1971)], 299, 310, 311

McGill v. Brown [Federal, Supreme Court (1833)], 156

McGowan v. Maryland [366 U.S. 420 (1961)], 2122, 2191, 2373, 2584, 2585, 2856

McGrain v. Daugherty [273 U.S. 135 (1927)], 1536, 1594–1595, **1708**, 2360, 2780

McIntyre v. Ohio Elections Commission [514 U.S. 334 (1995)], 91

McKeiver v. Pennsylvania [403 U.S. 528 (1971)], 1184, 1523, 1524, **1709**, 2729

McLaughlin v. Florida [379 U.S. 184 (1964)], 1646, 1745

McLaughlin v. Tilendis [398 F. 2d 298 (7th Cir. 1968)], 1553

McLaurin v. Oklahoma State Regents [339 U.S. 637 (1950)], 388, 1745, **2628–2629**, 2764, 2792, 2796

McLean v. Arkansas Board of Education [211 U.S. 539 (1909)], 241, 749

McLean v. Arkansas Board of Education [529 F. Supp. 1255 (1982)], 2764

McLemore, United States v. [1714 45 U.S. (4 How.) 286 (1846)], 2459

McMann v. Richardson [397 U.S. 759 (1970)], 1158, 2831

McMillan v. Pennsylvania [477 U.S. 79 (1986)], 2367–2368

McNabb v. United States [318 U.S. 332 (1943)], 1029, 1102, 1713, 2145

McNally v. United States [483 U.S. 350 (1987)], 2535

McRay v. United States [195 U.S. 27 (1904)], 1790

Meachum v. Fano [427 U.S. 215 (1976)], 2532

Mechanik, United States v. [475 U.S. 66 (1986)], 1222–1223

Medina v. California [505 U.S. 437 (1992)], 710

Meech v. Hillhaven West, Inc. [776 F. 2d 488 (Mont. 1989)], 1554

Meek v. Pittenger [421 U.S. 349 (1975)], 349, 2375

Memoirs v. Massachusetts [383 U.S. 413 (1966)], 1194, 1414, **1716–1717**, 1734

Memorial Hospital v. Maricopa County [415 U.S. 250 (1974)], 1677, 2275, 2305, 2879

Mempa v. Rhay [389 U.S. 128 (1967)], 2263, 2367

Memphis v. Greene [451 U.S. 100 (1981)], 1679, **1717**, 2221, 2694

Memphis Fire Department v. Stotts. *See* Firefighters Local Union No. 1784 v. Stotts

Mendenhall, United States v. [446 U.S. 544 (1980)], 120

Meritor Savings Bank, FSB v. Vinson [477 U.S. 57 (1986)], **1722–1723**, 1844, 2397

Merryman, Ex parte [17 F. Cas 144 (C.C. Ma. 1861) (No. 9, 486)], 164, 886, 1432, 1736, 2839, 2841

Metro Broadcasting, Inc. v. Federal Communications Commission [497 U.S. 547 (1990)], 33, 56, 238, 239, 469, 623, 916, 917, 1147, 1304, **1723–1724**, 2108, 2109, 2165, 2169, 2456, 2537, 2890

Metromedia, Inc. v. San Diego [453 U.S. 490 (1981)], 461, 902, 2529

Metropolitan Board v. Barrie [34 NY 657 (1866)], 1572

Metropolitan Life Insurance Company v. Ward [470 U.S. 869 (1985)], 428, 840, **1724**

Metropolitan Washington Airports Authority v. Citizens for the Abatement of Aircraft Noise [501 U.S. 252 (1991)], 2386

Meyer v. Grant [486 U.S. 414 (1988)], 1372, 1939

Meyer v. Nebraska [262 U.S. 390 (1923)], 45, 315, 858, 973, 1118, 1122, 1523, 1671, 1714, **1724**, 2188, 2308, 2573, 2642, 2874

Miami Herald Publishing Company v. Tornillo [418 U.S. 241 (1974)], 248, 271, 968, 1047, 1142, 1144, 1147, 1391, 1671, **1725**, 2144

Michael H. v. Gerald D. [491 U.S. 110 (1989)], 2162, 2316, 2575

Michael M. v. Superior Court [450 U.S. 464 (1981)], **1725**, 2395, 2399, 2418, 2533

Michelin Tire Company v. Administrator of Wages [423 U.S. 276 (1976)], 256, 1348, **1725**, 1864, 2493

Michigan v. Chesternut [486 U.S. 567 (1988)], 2338

Michigan v. Long [463 U.S. 1032 (1983)], 34, 2529, 2552

Michigan v. Mosley [423 U.S. 96 (1975)], 1927, 1928

Michigan v. Summers [452 U.S. 692 (1981)], **1725**, 2332

Michigan v. Tucker [417 U.S. 433 (1974)], 1927

Michigan Department of State Police v. Sitz [496 U.S. 444 (1990)], 826, 1096, **1725–1726**, 2162

Middendorf v. Henry [425 U.S. 25 (1976)], **1726**, 1726–1727

Midland Asphalt Corp. v. United States [489 U.S. 794 (1989)], 1223

Milkovich v. Lorain Journal Co. [497 U.S. 1 (1990)], 1146, **1729–1730**

Milk Wagon Drivers Union v. Meadowmoor Dairies [312 U.S. 287 (1941)], 187

Miller, United States v. [425 U.S. 435 (1976)], 713, 1822, 2140

Miller v. Albright [523 U.S. 420 (1998)], 367, 2400, 2419, 2538

Miller v. Board of Public Works [195 Cal. 477 (1925)], 2510

Miller v. California [413 U.S. 15 (1973)], 251, 1130, **1734–1735**, 1839, 1965, 1967, 2833, 2850

Miller v. Horton [152 Mass. 540 (1891)], 943

Miller v. Johnson [515 U.S. 900 (1995)], 58, 868, **1735**, 2093, 2137, 2409

Miller v. Schoene [276 U.S. 272 (1928)], 2640

Miller v. United States [78 U.S. (11 Wall.) 268 (1871)], 340, 490, 746

Miller v. United States [307 U.S. 174 (1939)], 2113, 2348

Miller v. Wilson [236 U.S. 373 (1915)], 1309, 1312, 2896

Millett v. People of Illinois [117 Ill. 294 (1886)], **1735–1736**

Milligan, Ex parte [71 U.S. (4 Wall.) 2 (1867)], 335, 338–339, 340, 386, 402, 430, 448, 498, 579, 746, 747, 830, 886, 947, 949, 1035, 1246, 1247, 1428, 1463, 1701, 1727, 1732, **1736**, 1955, 2085, 2143, 2628, 2777, 2839, 2841, 2868

Milliken v. Bradley [418 U.S. 717 (1974)], 391, 773, 1289, 1638, **1736–1737**, 1747, 2221, 2321, 2399, 2890

Milliken v. Bradley [433 U.S. 267 (1977)], 774, 853, 1562, **1736–1737**

Mills v. Alabama [384 U.S. 214 (1966)], 872

Mills v. Board of Education [384 F. Supp. 866 (D.D.C. 1973)], 790

Mills v. Duryee [11 U.S. (7 Cranch) 481 (1813)], 1635

Mills v. Hableutzel [456 U.S. 91 (1982)], 1824

Mills v. Rogers [457 U.S. 291 (1982)], 2061

Milnot Co. v. Richardson [350 F. Supp. 221 (N.D. 111. 1972)], 839

Milwaukee Social Democratic Publishing Co. v. Burleson [255 U.S. 407 (1920)], 1296

Mina Queen and Child v. Hepburn [11 U.S. 290 (1813)], 832

Mincey v. Arizona [437 U.S. 385 (1978)], 956, 1743

Minersville School District v. Gobitis [310 U.S. 586 (1940)], 814, **1064–1066**, 2186, 2189, 2545

Minneapolis and St. Louis Railway Co. v. Bombolis [241 U.S. 211 (1916)], 2727

Minnesota v. Barber [136 U.S. 313 (1890)], 1266, **1739**

Minnesota v. Clover Leaf Creamery Co. [449 U.S. 456 (1981)], 2515

Minnesota v. Dickerson [508 U.S. 366 (1993)], 1912, 1913

Minnesota Mortgage Moratorium Case [290 U.S. 398 (1934)], 2713

Minnesota Rate Cases [230 U.S. 352 (1913)], 283, 1308, 1310, 1312

Minnesota State Board for Community Colleges v. Knight [465 U.S. 271 (1984)], 22

Minor v. Happersett [88 U.S. (21 Wall.) 162 (1875)], 68, 91, 370, **1740**, 1808, 2210, 2676, 2807–2808, 2824, 2918, 2919, 2920

Miranda v. Arizona [384 U.S. 436 (1966)], 186, 270, 273, 276, 277, 421, 507, 700, 716, 815, 923, 1200, 1269, 1273, 1280, 1579, 1679, **1741–1744**, 1802, 1852, 1856, 1922, 1923, 1925, 1926–1929, 1930–1931, 2044, 2087, 2155, 2169, 2229–2230, 2238, 2239–2240, 2255, 2256, 2263–2264, 2444, 2454, 2456, 2594, 2609, 2614, 2821, 2831, 2850, 2856, 2886, 2889, 2893

Mishkin v. New York [383 U.S. 502 (1966)], 2833

Mississippi, United States v. [380 U.S. 128 (1965)], 877

Mississippi v. Johnson [71 U.S. (4 Wall.) 475 (1867)], 335, 339, 579, **1745**, 1950, 2471, 2793

Mississippi v. Stanton [154 U.S. 554 (1868)], 746, 1745, 2628

Mississippi University for Women v. Hogan [458 U.S. 718 (1982)], 857, **1746**, 1842, 1844, 2390, 2392, 2399, 2418, 2538

Missouri v. Holland [252 U.S. 416 (1920)], 243, 631, 901, 940, 992, 1011, 1081, 1389, 1446, 1633, **1746**, 1983, 1992, 2722

Missouri v. Jenkins [495 U.S. 33 (1990)], 400, 652, 653, 1471, 1529, **1747**

Missouri v. Jenkins [515 U.S. 70 (1995)], **1747**

Missouri ex rel. Gaines v. Canada [305 U.S. 337 (1938)], 284, 1307, 1311, 1714, **1748–1749**, 1797, 2420, 2594, 2795

Missouri Pacific Railroad v. Humes [115 U.S. 512 (1885)], **1749**

Missouri Pacific Railway Co. v. Kansas [248 U.S. 276 (1919)], 2785

Mistretta v. United States [488 U.S. 361 (1989)], 195, 762, 984, **1749–1750**, 2386

Mitchell v. Forsyth [472 U.S. 511 (1985)], 1336

Mitchell v. Helms [119 S.Ct. 2336 (1999)], 1604

Mitchell v. Laird [488 F. 2d 611 (D.C. Cir. 1973)], 2790

Mitchum v. Foster [407 U.S. 225 (1972)], **1750**

M. L. B. v. S. L. J. [519 U.S. 102 (1996)], **1750–1751**, 2877

Mobile v. Bolden [446 U.S. 55 (1980)], 1677, 1679, **1751**, 1765, 2102, 2108, 2135, 2202, 2811, 2813, 2862, 2890

Monaco v. Mississippi [292 U.S. 313 (1965)], 877

Monell v. Department of Social Services of New York City [436 U.S. 658 (1978)], 363, 853, 1218, **1751**, 1754, 1767–1768, 1871, 2349–2350, 2945

Monge v. California [524 U.S. 721 (1998)], 812

Monitor Patriot Co. v. Roy [401 U.S. 265 (1971)], 1805

Monongahela Navigation Co. v. United States [148 U.S. 312 (1893)], 1519

Monroe v. Pape [365 U.S. 167 (1961)], 96, 423, 444, 445, 652, 739, 853, 955, 1025, 1104, 1217, 1373, 1751, **1754**, 1767–1768, 2329, 2349

Monsanto, United States v. [491 U.S. 600 (1989)], 983, 2112

Montana Department of Revenue v. Kurth Ranch [511 U.S. 767 (1994)], 811, 2660

Monterey (City of) v. Del Monte Dunes [526 U.S. 687 (1999)], 2151

Monterey Mechanical Co. v. Wilson [125 F. 3d 702 (9th Cir. 1998)], 57

Montgomery County Board of Education, United States v. [395 U.S. 225 (1969)], 169

Moody v. Daggett [429 U.S. 78 (1976)], 2013

Mooney, State v. See State v. Mooney

Mooney v. Holohan [294 U.S. 103 (1935)], 722

Moore v. City of East Cleveland, Ohio [431 U.S. 494 (1977)], 274, 973, 1123, 1289, **1756–1757**, 1976, 1987, 2052, 2247, 2534–2535, 2574, 2577, 2892, 2893

Moore v. Dempsey [261 U.S. 86 (1923)], 468, 722, 1100, 1321, **1757–1758**, 2038, 2638, 2641

Moore v. Illinois [55 U.S. (14 How.) 13 (1852)], 1230

Moore v. Illinois [434 U.S. 220 (1977)], 962

Moore v. Michigan [355 U.S. 155 (1957)], 2902

Moore v. Missouri [159 U.S. 673 (1895)], 316

Moore v. Ogilvie [394 U.S. 814 (1969)], 1464

Moorman Manufacturing Co. v. Blair [437 U.S. 267 (1978)], 2523

Moose Lodge No. 107 v. Irvis [407 U.S. 163 (1972)], 1411, **1758**

Mora v. Mejias [115 F. Supp. 610 (D.P.R. 1953)], 2080

Moran v. Burbine [475 U.S. 412 (1986)], 1743, 1931, 2043, 2240

More, United States v. [7 U.S. (3 Cranch) 159 (1805)], 1469

Morehead v. New York ex rel. Tipaldo [298 U.S. 587 (1936)], 284, 697, 838, 1116, 1313, 1699, **1760–1761**, 2156, 2281, 2288, 2289, 2544, 2882

Morey v. Doud [354 U.S. 457 (1957)], 840, 1800

Morgan v. Kerrigan [530 F. 2d 401 (1st Cir. 1976)], 2443

Morgan v. Virginia [328 U.S. 373 (1946)], 204, 280, 1257, 1275, **1761**, 2145, 2795

Morissette v. United States [341 U.S. 925 (1951)], 2511

Morris, United States v. [125 F. 322 (1903)], 403

Morris v. Mathews [475 U.S. 237 (1986)], 810

Morrison v. Olson [487 U.S. 654 (1988)], 115, 269, 621, 1342, 1359, 1360, 2129, 2157, 2169, 2314, 2386, 2462–2464

Morrissey v. Brewer [408 U.S. 472 (1972)], 2027

Morse v. Republican Party of Virginia [517 U.S. 186 (1996)], 1938, 2008

Morton v. Mancari [417 U.S. 535 (1974)], 83, 1784

Moses v. Railroad [21 111. 516 (1859)], 2507

Motor Vehicle Manufacturers Institute v. State Farm Mutual [463 U.S. 29 (1983)], 269

Mountain Timber Co. v. Washington [243 U.S. 219 (1917)], 1911

Mt. Healthy City Board of Education v. Doyle [429 U.S. 274 (1977)], 1586

Mt. Vernon-Woodberry Co. v. Alabama Interstate Power [240 U.S. 30 (1916)], 2075

Mozert v. Hawkins County Board of Education [827 F. 2d 1058 (6th Cir. 1987)], 859, 2380

Mueller v. Allen [459 U.S. 820 (1983)], 464, 924, **1763**, 2322, 2376, 2378, 2739, 2917

Mugler, State v. See State v. Mugler

Mugler v. Kansas [123 U.S. 623 (1887)], 240, 357, 889, 1168, **1764**, 2050, 2510

Mulford v. Smith [307 U.S. 38 (1939)], 62, 458

Mullane v. Central Hanover Bank & Trust [339 U.S. 306 (1950)], 1830

Muller v. Oregon [208 U.S. 412 (1908)], 36, 224–225, 241, 263, 845, 1115, 1166, 1547, 1591, 1699, 1710, 1756, **1764–1765**, 2389, 2399, 2440, 2443, 2446, 2529, 2572, 2713, 2881, 2896, 2920

Munn v. Illinois [94 U.S. 113 (1877)], 52, 53, 199, 217, 240–241, 346, 409, 431, 584, 844, 1166, 1205, **1224–1225**, 1698, 1734, 1789, 1890, 2048, 2281, 2509, 2510, 2547, 2563, 2817, 2822–2823, 2829–2830, 2917

Munoz-Flores, United States v. [495 U.S. 385 (1990)], 2533

Munro v. Socialist Workers Party [479 U.S. 189 (1986)], 158

Murchison, In re [349 U.S. 133 (1955)], 970

Murdock, United States v. [290 U.S. 389 (1933)], 2745

Murdock v. Memphis [87 U.S. (20 Wall.) 590 (1875)], 1466

Murdock v. Pennsylvania [319 U.S. 105 (1943)], 460, 814, 1427, **1768**, 1990, 2191, 2302

Murphy v. Florida [421 U.S. 794 (1975)], **1770**

Murphy v. Ford [390 F. Supp. 1372 (1975)], **1770**

Murphy v. Waterfront Commission of New York Harbor [378 U.S. 52(1964)], 1334, 2237, 2745–2746

Murray v. Carrier [477 U.S. 478 (1986)], 1253, 1844

Murray v. Corlett [374 U.S. 203 (1963)], 1, 2856

Murray v. Giarratano [492 U.S. 1 (1989)], 2043

Murray v. Hoboken Land Company [59 U.S. (18 How.) 272 (1856)], 829

Murray v. United States [487 U.S. 533 (1988)], 2338

Murray's Lessee v. Hoboken Land & Improvement Co. [59 U.S. (18 How.) 272 (1865)], 735, **1771**, 2036

Muskrat v. United States [219 U.S. 346 (1911)], 323, **1771**

Musser v. Utah [333 U.S. 95 (1948)], 511

Myers v. Anderson [238 U.S. 368 (1915)], 1041, 1242

Myers v. United States [272 U.S. 52 (1926)], 110–111, 289, 495, 948, 1318–1319, 1611, 1714, **1772**, 1847, 2000, 2149, 2384, 2626, 2636

# N

NAACP v. . . . *See* National Association for the Advancement of Colored People

Nabozny v. Podlesny [92 F. 3d 446 (7th Cir. 1996)], 2404

Nader v. Schaffer [429 U.S. 989 (1976)], 1942

Naim v. Naim [197 Va. 80 (1955-1956)], 1744

Napier v. Atlantic Coast Line R.R. [272 U.S. 605 (1926)], 1988

Nardone v. United States [308 U.S. 539 (1937)], 711, 873, 1774, **1774**, 1850, 2417, 2922

Nashville Gas Co. v. Satty [434 U.S. 136 (1977)], 2394

Nathanson v. United States [290 U.S. 41 (1933)], 63

National Association for the Advancement of Colored People v. Alabama ex rel. Flowers [377 U.S. 288 (1964)], 35, 2854

National Association for the Advancement of Colored People v. Alabama ex rel. Patterson [357 U.S. 449 (1958)], 260, 1107, 1109, 1237, 1270, 1549, **1773**, 1932, 2243, 2474, 2574, 2867

National Association for the Advancement of Colored People v. Button [371 U.S. 415 (1963)], 229, 230, 231, 234, 238, 1109, **1773**, 2071

National Association for the Advancement of Colored People v. Claiborne Hardware Co. et al. [458 U.S. 886 (1982)], 215, 1153, 1237, 1551, 1556, 2529

National Broadcasting Company v. United States [319 U.S. 190 (1943)], 247

National Cable Television Association v. United States [415 U.S. 336 (1974)], 762, 2148

National Collegiate Athletic Association v. Tarkanian [488 U.S. 179 (1988)], 2032, 2489

National Credit Union Administration v. First National Bank & Trust [522 U.S. 479 (1998)], 2474

National Dairy Products Corp., United States v. [372 U.S. 29 (1963)], 2776

National Endowment for the Arts v. Finley [524 U.S. 569 (1998)], 1057, 1137, 1531, 2070, 2751

National Labor Relations Board v. Fainblatt [306 U.S. 601 (1939)], 2821

National Labor Relations Board v. Fansteel Metallurgical Corp. [306 U.S. 240 (1939)], 1550

National Labor Relations Board v. Friedman-Marks Clothing [301 U.S. 58 (1937)], 1715, **2819–2921**

National Labor Relations Board v. Fruehauf Trailer Co. [301 U.S. 49 (1937)], **2819–2821**

National Labor Relations Board v. Fruit and Vegetable Packers [337 U.S. 58 (1964)], 1550

National Labor Relations Board v. Gissel Packing [395 U.S. 575 (1969)], 1551

National Labor Relations Board v. Jones & Laughlin Steel Corp. [301 U.S. 1 (1937)], 458, 692, 846, 862, 1012, 1035, 1312, 1314, 1547, 1548, 1554, 1639, 2289, 2560, 2677, 2729, **2819–2821**

National Labor Relations Board v. Retail Employees Local No. 1001 [447 U.S. 607 (1980)], 215, 1550, 1907

National Labor Relations Board v. Virginia Electric & Power Co. [314 U.S. 469 (1941)], 1551

National League of Cities v. Usery [426 U.S. 833 (1976)], 59, 190, 193, 276, 362, 623, 684, 827, 903, 907, 967, 988, 990, 991, 995, 1002, 1011, 1012, 1089, 1181, 1211, 1292, 1549, **1776–1777**, 1845, 2153, 2154, 2155, 2169, 2459, 2481, 2520, 2587, 2668, 2813, 2887

National Mutual Insurance Company v. Tidewater Transfer Company [337 U.S. 583 (1949)], 629, 796, 798

National Organizations For Women, Inc. v. Scheidler [510 U.S. 249 (1994)], 1153

National Prohibition Cases (1920), 73, 862

National Treasury Employees Union v. United States [513 U.S. 454 (1995)], 892, **1782**, 2328

National Treasury Employees Union v. Von Raab [489 U.S. 656 (1989)], 331, 822, 825, 826, 1096, 1529, **1782–1783**, 2337, 2423

Native American Church v. Navajo Tribal Council [272 F. 2d 131 (1959)], 81–82

Neagle, In re [135 U.S. 1 (1890)], 947, 2311

Neal v. Delaware [103 U.S. 370 (1880)], 1509

Near v. Minnesota [283 U.S. 697 (1931)], 179, 284, 1138, 1144, 1145, 1149, 1311, 1317, 1714, **1787–1788**, 1805, 1806, 2009, 2311, 2326, 2594

Nebbia v. New York [291 U.S. 502 (1934)], 53, 321, 838, 845, 1077, 1116, 1175, 1225, 1301, 1311, 1714, 1760, 1761, **1788–1789**, 1796, 2281, 2509, 2510, 2571, 2575, 2882

Nebraska Press Association v. Stuart [427 U.S. 539 (1976)], 271, 1142, 1150–1151, 1179, 1181, **1789**, 2010, 2077, 2745

Negre v. Larsen [401 U.S. 437 (1971)], 1049

Neil v. Biggers [409 U.S. 188 (1972)], 962

Nevada v. Hall [440 U.S. 410 (1979)], 447, 881

Newberry v. United States [256 U.S. 232 (1921)], 423

New Energy Company of Indiana v. Limbach [486 U.S. 269 (1988)], 2517

New England Divisions Case [261 U.S. 184 (1923)], 2639

New England Power Co. v. New Hampshire [455 U.S. 331 (1982)], 2514

New Hampshire v. Louisiana [108 U.S. 76 (1882)], 2824

New Hampshire Supreme Court v. Piper [470 U.S. 274 (1985)], **1798–1799**, 2020

New Jersey v. Portash [440 U.S. 450 (1979)], 1335

New Jersey v. T.L.0. [468 U.S. 1214 (1984)], 825, 856, 2337, 2532

New Jersey v. T.L.0. [469 U.S. 325 (1985)], **1799**

New Jersey v. Wilson [11 U.S. (7 Cranch) 164 (1812)], 1350, 1686, **1799**, 1910, 2059

New Jersey Steam Navigation Co. v. Merchant's Bank [47 U.S. (6 How.)], 1791

New Mexico, United States v. [456 U.S. 926 (1982)], 1384, 2587

New Negro Alliance v. Sanitary Grocery Company [303 U.S. 552 (1938)], 1826

New Orleans v. Dukes [427 U.S. 297 (1976)], 840, 1220, **1800**

New Orleans Water Works Co. v. St. Tammany Water-Works Co. [14 F. 194 (1882)], 1877–1878

Newport News Shipbuilding of Drydock Co. v. EEOC [462 U.S. 669(1983)], 2395

Newport (City of) v. Fact Concerts, Inc. [453 U.S. 247 (1981)], 1768

New State Ice Company v. Liebmann [285 U.S. 262 (1932)], 220, 838, 998, 1008, 1425, 1788, **1802**, 2746

New York, Ex parte No. 1 [256 U.S. 490 (1921)], 878

New York v. Belton [453 U.S. 454 (1981)], 2332

New York v. Burger [482 U.S. 691 (1987)], 43, 44, 2337

New York v. Ferber [458 U.S. 747 (1982)], 350, 351, **1802**, 1868, 2529–2530, 2531

New York v. Miln [36 U.S. (11 Pet.) 102 (1837)], 2687

New York v. Quarles [467 U.S. 649 (1984)], 1742, **1802–1803**, 1841, 1927–1928

New York v. United States [326 U.S. 572 (1946)], 1211, 1226, 1239, 1845

New York v. United States [505 U.S. 144 (1992)], 354, 624, 904, 991, 992, 1009, **1803–1804**, 2169, 2844

New York v. Uplinger [467 U.S. 246 (1984)], 2296

New York Central Railroad Company v. Lockwood [84 U.S. 357 (1873)], 217

New York Central Railroad Company v. White [243 U.S. 188 (1917)], 1554, **1804**, 2925

New York City Transit Authority v. Beazer [440 U.S. 568 (1979)], 406

New York ex rel. Bryant v. Zimmerman [278 U.S. 63 (1928)], 1237

New York State Club Association v. New York City [487 U.S. 1 (1988)], 1110, 2398

New York Telephone Co. v. New York State Department [440 U.S. 519 (1979)], 1988

New York Times Co. v. Sullivan [376 U.S. 254 (1964)], 16, 167, 179, 231, 234–235, 237, 354, 461, 482, 815, 1056, 1127, 1130, 1134, 1139, 1141, 1146, 1150, 1189, 1235, 1236, 1285, 1322, 1607, 1608, 1788, **1804–1805**, 1821, 1898, 1966, 1978, 2009, 2014, 2067, 2353, 2454, 2558, 2579, 2594, 2708–2709, 2745, 2850, 2855

New York Times Co. v. United States [403 U.S. 713 (1971) (per curiam)], 188, 377, 1129, 1139, 1140, 1145, 1232, 1438, **1805–1807**, 2326, 2448, 2464, 2542, 2842, 2941

Niemotko v. Maryland [340 U.S. 268 (1951)], **1807**, 2198, 2795

Nishimura Eiku v. United States [142 U.S. 651 (1892)], 129, 365, 1328, 1329

Nix v. Williams [467 U.S. 431 (1984)], 1157, **1815**, 2045, 2336, 2338

Nixon, United States v. [418 U.S. 683 (1974)], 328, 377, 433, 609, 952–953, 954, 955, 1044, 1118, 1215, 1342, 1359, 1488, 1816, **1817–1818**, 1822, 1955, 1994, 2384, 2448, 2529, 2865

Nixon v. Administrator of General Services [408 F. Supp. 321 (1976)], 1708

Nixon v. Administrator of General Services [433 U.S. 425 (1977)], 269, **1818**

Nixon v. Condon [286 U.S. 73 (1932)], 284, 1041, 1238, 1307, **1818**, 1941, 2007, 2809

Nixon v. Fitzgerald [457 U.S. 731 (1982)], 433, 944, 954, 1335, **1819**, 1994, 2887

Nixon v. Herndon [273 U.S. 536 (1927)], 1041, 1296, 1818, **1819**, 1941, 2007, 2349, 2492, 2641, 2675, 2809

Nixon v. Sirica [487 F. 2d 700 (1973)], 2865

Nixon v. United States [506 U.S. 224 (1993)], 1340, 1454, **1819–1820**, 1953

NLRB. *See* National Labor Relations Board

Noble State Bank v. Haskell [219 U.S. 104 (1911)], 2509

Nollan v. California Coastal Commission [483 U.S. 825 (1987)], 802, 890, 903, 905, 1381, 2053, 2054, 2055, 2576, 2645, 2646, 2751, 2946

Nordlinger v. Hahn [505 U.S. 1 (1992)], 787

Norman v. Baltimore & Ohio Railroad Co. [294 U.S. 240 (1935)], **1201–1202**

Norris v. Alabama [294 U.S. 587 (1935)], 1311, **1825**, 1959

Norris v. Clymer [2 Pa. 277 (1845)], 833

North American Co. v. Securities and Exchange Commission [327 U.S. 686 (1946)], 459, 1768, 2079

Northeastern Women's Center v. McMonagle (1989), 1153

Northern Pacific Railway Co. v. North Dakota [236 U.S. 585 (1919)], 2927

Northern Pacific Railway Co. v. United States [356 U.S. 1 (1958)], 104, 1540

Northern Pipeline Construction Co. v. Marathon Pipe Line Co. [458 U.S. 50 (1982)], 161, 274, 524, 621, 1019, 1464, 1590, **1827–1828**, 2154, 2697, 2887, 2889, 2893

Northern Securities Co. v. United States [193 U.S. 197 (1904)], 749, 1163, 1165, 1166–1167, 1168, **1828**, 2413, 2895, 2898

North Haven Board of Education v. Bell [456 U.S. 512 (1982)], 853

Northwest Airlines v. Minnesota [322 U.S. 292 (1944)], 1103

Northwest Central Pipeline Corp. v. State Corporation Commission of Kansas [489 U.S. 493 (1989)], 2517

Northwestern Fertilizer Co. v. Hyde Park [97 U.S. 659 (1878)], 675, 1350, **1828–1829**

Northwestern Laundry v. Des Moines [239 U.S. 486 (1916)], 901

Norton v. Shelby County [118 U.S. 425 (1886)], 2752

Nortz v. United States [294 U.S. 317 (1935)], **1201–1202**

Norwood v. Harrison [413 U.S. 455 (1973)], 2017

Nostrand v. Little [368 U.S. 436 (1960)], 1648

Noto v. United States [351 U.S. 902 (1961)], 68

Nye v. United States [320 U.S. 755 (1941)], 1102, 1103

Nyquist v. Mauclet [432 U.S. 1 (1977)], 66

# O

O'Bannon v. Town Court Nursing Center [447 U.S. 773 (1980)], 194, 2029

O'Brien, United States v. [391 U.S. 367 (1968)], 369, 818, 1232, 1584, 1585–1586, 1831, **1836**, 1837, 2631, 2632, 2791, 2854, 2862, 2869

O'Brien v. Brown [409 U.S. 1 (1972)], **1837**, 2669

O'Callahan v. Parker [395 U.S. 258 (1969)], 1727

O'Connor v. Donaldson [422 U.S. 563 (1975)], 789, 1718, **1846**, 1884, 2025, 2061

O'Connor v. Ortega [480 U.S. 709 (1987)], 2337

O'Donoghue v. United States [289 U.S. 516 (1933)], 1463

Oestereich v. Selective Service Board No. 11 [393 U.S. 233 (1968)], 2790

Ogden v. Saunders [12 Wheat. 213 (1827)], 677, 832, 842, 1433, 1662, 1682, 1686, 1752, 1836, **1848–1849**, 2653, 2698, 2732, 2859

O'Gorman & Young v. Hartford Insurance Co. [282 U.S. 251 (1931)], 220

O'Hare Truck Service v. City of Northlake [518 U.S. 712 (1996)], 1886

Ohio v. Akron Center for Reproductive Health [110 S.Ct. 2841 (1990)], 196, **1293**

Ohio v. Roberts [448 U.S. 56 (1980)], 481, 492, 933

Ohio v. Robinette [519 U.S. 33 (1996)], 2711

Ohio Life Insurance & Trust Co. v. Debolt [57 U.S. (16 How.) 416 (1854)], 2648

Ohralik v. Ohio State Bar Association [436 U.S. 447 (1978)], 1135

Okanogan Indian v. United States [279 U.S. 655 (1929)], **1921**, 2784

Oklahoma Tax Commission v. Jefferson Lines, Inc. [514 U.S. 175 (1995)], 806, 2494, 2495

Oklahoma v. Civil Service Commission [330 U.S. 127 (1947)], 684, 987, 1780

Olcott v. the Supervisors [83 U.S. (6 Wall.) 678 (1873)], 2075

Olden v. Kentucky [488 U.S. 227 (1988)], 491

Oliver, In re [333 U.S. 257 (1948)], **1849**

Oliver v. United States [466 U.S. 170 (1984)], **1849**, 2140, 2343

Ollman v. Evans [750 F. 2d 970, 996 (D.C. Cir. 1984)], 210, 1861

Olmstead v. United States [277 U.S. 438 (1928)], 221, 284, 711, 719, 721, 872, 873, 1296, 1527, 1633, 1774, **1849–1850**, 1853, 2061, 2139, 2241, 2247, 2290, 2340, 2342, 2542, 2573, 2636, 2767, 2896, 2913

Olney v. Arnold [3 U.S. (3 Dall.) 308 (1796)], 2602

O'Lone v. Estate of Shabazz [482 U.S. 342 (1987)], 895, 1201, **1851**, 2012, 2380

Olsen v. Nebraska ex rel Reference & Bond Association [313 U.S. 236 (1941)], **1851**, 2510

On Lee v. United States [343 U.S. 747 (1952)], 873, **1853**, 2896, 2897

Oncale v. Sundowner Offshore Services [523 U.S. 75 (1998)], 100, 2400

O'Neil v. Vermont [144 U.S. 155 (1892)], 1354, **1529**, 2037

One 6.5 mm. Mannlicher-Carcano Military Rifle, United States v. [250 F. Supp. 410 (N.D. Tex. 1966)], 372

Oregon v. Bradshaw [462 U.S. 1039 (1983)], **861**, 1928

Oregon v. Elstad [470 U.S. 298 (1985)], 1742, 1841, **1856**, 1927–1928, 2240

Oregon v. Hass [420 U.S. 714 (1975)], 1927

Oregon v. Mathiason [429 U.S. 492 (1977)], 1927

Oregon v. Mitchell [400 U.S. 122 (1970)], 274, 440, 608, 1089, 1090, 1629, **1856**, 1941, 2596, 2598, 2609, 2743, 2811, 2813, 2887

Oregon Waste Systems v. Department of Environmental Quality [511 U.S. 93 (1994)], 2864

Orlando v. Laird [317 F. Supp. 1013 (E.D.N.Y. 1970) (1971)], 2789

Orloff v. Willoughby [345 U.S. 83 (1953)], 117–118

Orozco v. Texas [394 U.S. 324 (1969)], 1742, **1864–1865**

Orr v. Orr [440 U.S. 268 (1979)], 973, 2392, 2393, 2921

Ortwein v. Schwab [410 U.S. 656 (1971)], 23, 204, 2876

Osborn v. Bank of the United States [22 U.S. (9 Wheat.) 738 (1824)], 423, 438, 555, 740, 877, 1228, 1463, 1466, 1467–1468, 1686, **1865**, 2871

Osborn v. Ozlin [310 U.S. 53 (1940)], 1548

Osborne v. Ohio [495 U.S. 103 (1990)], 350

Osgood v. Chicago, Danville, and Vincennes R. R. Co. [18 F. Cas. 876 (C.C. Ill. 1875) (No. 10, 604)], 360

O'Shea v. Littleton [414 U.S. 488 (1974)], 1375, 1454, **1865**

Otis v. Parker [187 U.S. 606 (1902)], 1296

Overmeyer, D. H., Co. v. Frick Co. [405 U.S. 174 (1972)], 2831

Owen v. City of Independence [445 U.S. 622 (1980)], 1768, **1871**, 2350

Owens, United States v. [484 U.S. 554 (1988)], 492

Ownbey v. Morgan [256 U.S. 94 (1921)], 2544

Oyama v. California [332 U.S. 633 (1948)], 66, 129, 131–132, **1871**

Ozawa v. United States [260 U.S. 178 (1922)], 129

# P

Pace v. Alabama [106 U.S. 583 (1883)], 1038, 1646, 1698, 1744, 1745, **1873**, 2827–2828

Pacific Gas and Electric Company v. California Public Utilities Commission [475 U.S. 1 (1986)], 688, 690

Pacific Gas and Electric Company v. Energy Resources Commission [461 U.S. 190 (1983)], 484

Pacific Mutual Life Insurance Co. v. Haslip [499 U.S. 1 (1991)], 195, 2314, 2315

Pacific Railroad Removal Cases [115 U.S. 1 (1885)], 1497

Pacific Railway v. Illinois [118 U.S. 557 (1886)], 217

Pacific States Telephone & Telegraph Co. v. Oregon [223 U.S. 118 (1912)], 785, 789, 1238–1239, 1372, 1950, 2210

Padula v. Webster [822 F. 2d 97 (D.C. Cir. 1987)], 2405

Palermo v. United States [360 U.S. 343 (1959)], 1426

Palko v. Connecticut [302 U.S. 319 (1937)], 33, 164, 170, 315, 830, 1176, 1355, 1855, **1874–1875**, 1990, 2038, 2238, 2293, 2572–2573, 2744, 2796

Palmer v. Thompson [403 U.S. 217 (1971)], 1585–1586, **1875**, 2487, 2862, 2887, 2890

Palmore v. Sidoti [466 U.S. 429 (1984)], 46, 800, 1123, **1875–1876**, 2308, 2402

Palmore v. United States [411 U.S. 389 (1973)], 1590

Panama Refining Company v. Ryan [293 U.S. 388 (1935)], 41, 314, 457, 504, 736, 761, 1316, 1776, **1876–1877**, 2317, 2385

Papachristou v. City of Jacksonville [405 U.S. 156 (1972)], 816, 2774

Papasan v. Allain [478 U.S. 265 (1986)], 2874

Paquete Habana [175 U.S. 677 (1900)], 1077, 1390

Paradise, United States v. [480 U.S. 149 (1987)], **1877**, 2106

Parden v. Terminal Railway [377 U.S. 184 (1964)], 853, 877, 879, 881, 1382, 1468, 2831–2832

Parham v. Hughes [441 U.S. 347 (1978)], 1326, 2395

Parham v. J. R. [442 U.S. 584 (1979)], 353, 974, **1878–1879**, 2031

Paris Adult Theater I v. Slaton [413 U.S. 49 (1973)], 235, 1236, **1734–1735**, 1831, 1838, 1839, 2443, 2777

Parker v. Brown [317 U.S. 341 (1943)], **1879**, 2461, 2511

Parker v. Davis [78 U.S. (12 Wall.) 457 (1871)], 697, 1581, 2563

Parker v. Levy [417 U.S. 733 (1974)], 117, 1727, **1879**, 2776–2777

Parker v. North Carolina [397 U.S. 790 (1970)], 2831

Parratt v. Taylor [451 U.S. 527 (1981)], 653, 2350

Passenger Cases [48 U.S. (7 How.) 283 (1849)], 325, 742, 1230, 1328, 1712, 1791, 1869, 2274, 2409, 2648, 2652, 2867, 2871, 2885, 2908, 2923

Patsy v. Board of Regents [457 U.S. 496 (1982)], 19, 955

Patterson v. Colorado [205 U.S. 454 (1907)], 1299, 1354, 2318

Patterson v. Illinois [487 U.S. 285 (1988)], 1743, 1930

Patterson v. McLean Credit Union [491 U.S. 164 (1989)], 98, 398, 407, 1530, **1887**

Patton v. Mississippi [332 U.S. 463 (1947)], 1678

Patton v. United States [281 U.S. 276 (1930)], 1515, **1887**

Paul v. Davis [424 U.S. 693 (1976)], 442, 482, 653, **1887–1888**, 1888, 2155, 2350

Paul v. Virginia [75 U.S. (8 Wall.) 168 (1869)], 341, 585, 736, 805, **1888**, 2458, 2513, 2549

Paxton's Case [51 Mass. Repts. 469 (1761)], 208, 1099, 1323, 1865, 1866, **1888–1889**

Payne v. Tennessee [501 U.S. 808 (1991)], **1889**

Payton v. New York [445 U.S. 573 (1980)], 121, 1820, **1889**, 2332, 2333, 2524, 2881, 2891

Peik v. Chicago & Northwestern Railway Co. [94 U.S. 164 (1877)], **1224–1225**

Pell v. Procunier [417 U.S. 817 (1974)], **1891**, 2011

Penhallow v. Doane's Administrators [3 U.S. (3 Dall.) 54 (1795)], 1404, 1883, 2603

Penn Central Transportation Co. v. New York City [438 U.S. 104 (1978)], 238, 902, 1564, **1892–1893**, 2150, 2535, 2644, 2946

Pennell v. City of San Jose [485 U.S. 285 (1988)], 2158

Pennhurst State School & Hospital v. Halderman [451 U.S. 1, 457 U.S. 1131 (1981, 1984)], 19, 775, 790, 1562, 1721, 1780, 1891, **1893–1894**, 2660–2661

Penn Mutual Indemnity Co. v. Commissioner of Internal Revenue [277 U.S. F. 2d 16 (1976)], 2421

Pennoyer v. Neff [95 U.S. 714 (1878)], 1500

Pennsylvania v. Finley [481 U.S. 551 (1987)], 2043

Pennsylvania v. Mimms [434 U.S. 106 (1977)], 2552, 2711

Pennsylvania v. Nelson [350 U.S. 497 (1956)], 279–280, 421, 606, **1894**, 2351, 2772

Pennsylvania v. Ritchie [480 U.S. 39 (1987)], 492

Pennsylvania v. Union Gas Co. [485 U.S. 958 (1989)], 878, 879, 880, 995, 1010, 1529, 2504

Pennsylvania v. Wheeling and Belmont Bridge Co. [59 U.S. (18 How.) 421 (1852, upheld 1856)], 742, 1712, 1791

Pennsylvania Association for Retarded Children v. Pennsylvania [334 F. Supp. 1257 (E.D. Pa. 1971)], 790

Pennsylvania Coal Company v. Mahon [260 U.S. 393 (1922)], 889, 890, 902, 1175, 1296, 1400–1401, 1651, 2054, 2509–2510, 2640, 2644, 2645, 2646, 2647, 2945

Penry v. Lynaugh [492 U.S. 302 (1989)], 306, 1843, **1895**, 2369

Pensacola Telegraph Co. v. Western Union Telegraph Co. [96 U.S. 1 (1878)], 1319, **1896**, 2824

Pentagon Papers case. See New York Times v. United States

Peonage Cases [320 U.S. 527 (1903)], 1897

People v. Bogdanoff [254 N.Y. 16 (1930)], 2258

People v. Croswell [3 Johnson's Cases 336 (NY 1804)], 1260, 1534, **1897–1898**

People v. Hobson [401 NY S. 2d 967 (1976)], 2264

People v. Jackson & Co. [9 Mich. 285 (1861)], 2507

People v. Lemmon [20 N.Y. 562 (1860)], 4

People v. Ruggles [8 Johns. 290 (1811)], 1534

People v. Wheeler [583 P. 2d 748 (1978)], 2728

Perez v. Brownell [356 U.S. 44 (1958)], 1950, **2733**, 2834, 2902–2903

Perez v. Ledesma [410 U.S. 82 (1971)], 756

Perez v. United States [402 U.S. 146 (1971)], 459, 1567, 1778–1779, **1899**, 2415–2416

Perkins v. Elg [307 U.S. 325 (1939)], 956

Permian Basin Area Rate Cases [390 U.S. 747 (1968)], 2385

Pernell v. Southall Realty Co. [416 U.S. 363 (1974)], 2729

Perry v. Sinderman [408 U.S. 593 (1972)], 203, 897

Perry v. United States [294 U.S. 330 (1935)], **1201–1202**, 2288

Perry Education Association v. Perry Local Educators' Association [460 U.S. 37 (1983)], 686, 1213, **1899–1900**, 2052, 2068

Personnel Administrator of Massachusetts v. Feeney [442 U.S. 256 (1979)], 474, 1679, **1902**, 2392–2393, 2533

Peters, Judge, United States v. [9 U.S. (5 Cranch) 115 (1809)], 883, **1441–1442**, 1685, 1902, 2859

Peters v. Hobby [349 U.S. 331 (1955)], 946, 2438, 2448

Peters v. Kiff [407 U.S. 493 (1972)], 1510

Peters v. New York [392 U.S. 40 (1968)], 2552–2553, 2553

Petersburg Judges of Elections, United States v. [27 F. Cas. 506 (C.C. D.C. 1874) (No. 16, 036)], 207

Peterson v. City of Greenville [373 U.S. 244 (1963)], 371

Petit v. Minnesota [177 U.S. 164 (1900)], 2584

Petition of R.M.G. [454 A. 2d 776 (D.C. Cir. 1982)], 46

Pettigrew v. United States [97 U.S. 385 (1878)], 1727, 1732, **1879**

Philadelphia v. New Jersey [437 U.S. 617 (1978)], 806, 1010, **1904**, 2514, 2566, 2864

Philadelphia & Reading Railroad v. Pennsylvania [82 U.S. (15 Wall.) 232 (1873)], 747, **1904**, 2521

Philadelphia and Trenton Railroad, In re [6 Whart. 25 (1840)], 1192

Philadelphia Newspapers, Inc. v. Hepps [475 U.S. 767 (1986)], 1609, 2534

Phillips v. Martin Marietta Corporation [400 U.S. 542 (1971)], 2091

Phillips v. Washington Legal Foundation [524 U.S. 156 (1998)], 2646

Phillips Petroleum Co. v. Shutts [472 U.S. 797 (1985)], 358

Pickering v. Board of Education [391 U.S. 563 (1968)], 856, 892, 1676, 1677, 1886, 2066

Pickett v. Brown [461 U.S. 1 (1983)], 1824

Pico v. Board of Education [457 U.S. 853 (1982)], 2750

Pierce v. Hill Military Academy [268 U.S. 510 (1925)], 2188

Pierce v. Society of Sisters [268 U.S. 510 (1925)], 315, 352, 353, 854, 858, 1118, 1122, 1372, 1714, **1908**, 2188, 2321, 2374, 2519, 2573, 2641–2642, 2738

Pierce v. Somerset Railway [171 U.S. 641 (1898)], 2830

Pierce v. United States [386 U.S. 547 (1920)], 1911, 2841

Pierson v. Ray [386 U.S. 547 (1967)], 944, 1335, 1453, **1908–1909**, 2319

Pike v. Bruce Church, Inc. [397 U.S. 137 (1970)], 806, 2514–2515, 2516

Pine Grove Township v. Talcott [86 U.S. (19 Wall.) 666 (1874)], 676

Pink, United States v. [315 U.S. 203 (1942)], 737, 942, 951, 1390, **1909–1910**, 1997

Pinkerton v. United States [328 U.S. 640 (1946)], 708

Pinkus v. United States [436 U.S. 293 (1978)], 351

Piqua Branch of the State Bank of Ohio v. Knoop [57 U.S. (16 How.) 369 (1854)], 298, 325, 676, 801, 1350, 1712, **1910–1911**

Pitts v. Black [608 F. Supp. 696 (S.D. N.Y. 1984)], 1302

Pittsburgh Melting Company v. Toten [248 U.S. 1 (1918)], 749

Place, United States v. [462 U.S. 696 (1983)], 713, 1914

Planned Parenthood v. Casey [505 U.S. 833 (1992)], 11, 12, 13, 14, 15, 196, 432, 625, 1531, 1813–1814, 1845, **1914–1916**, 2097, 2122–2123, 2159, 2168, 2316, 2456, 2714

Planned Parenthood Association v. Ashcroft [462 U.S. 476 (1983)], 353, 2207, 2208

Planned Parenthood of Central Missouri v. Danforth [428 U.S. 52 (1976)], 5–6, 192, 353, 974, **1916**, 2206, 2207, 2208, 2528

Plant v. Woods [176 Mass. 492 (1900)], 1547

Planters Bank v. Sharp [47 U.S. (6 How.) 301 (1848)], 742, 2923

Plessy v. Ferguson [163 U.S. 537 (1896)], 12, 15, 54, 129, 170, 253, 254, 259, 375, 388, 389, 399, 411, 527, 587, 771, 794, 909, 991, 1166, 1167, 1204, 1265, 1267, 1631, 1870, **1918–1920**, 1950, 1987, 2062, 2094, 2109, 2159, 2217, 2253, 2282, 2308, 2354, 2369, 2403, 2443, 2458, 2484, 2597, 2599, 2693, 2713–2714, 2764, 2792, 2795, 2796, 2828, 2849, 2898

Plurality Opinion in Board of Education v. Pico (1982), 855, 856

Plyler v. Doe [457 U.S. 202 (1982)], 66, 183, 233, 239, 275, 365, 428, 857, 914, 1077, 1330, 1331, **1920**, 1976, 1980

Pocket Veto Case (Okanogan Indians v. United States) [279 U.S. 655 (1929)], **1921**, 2784

Poe v. Ullman [367 U.S. 497 (1961)], 12, 1233, 1269, 1270, 1520, 2247, 2456, 2903

Poelker v. Doe [432 U.S. 519 (1977)], 6, 1665, 2205

Poindexter v. Greenhow [114 U.S. 269 (1885)], 1698

Poindexter v. Louisiana Financial Assistance Commission [389 U.S. 571 (1968)], 2738

Pointer v. Texas [380 U.S. 400 (1955)], 932, 1269, **1921**, 2039

Polaroid Corp. v. Eastman Kodak Co. [490 U.S. 1047 (1989)], 1882

Police Department of Chicago v. Mosley [408 U.S. 92 (1972)], 1215, 1677, 1907, **1921–1922**, 2070

Polk County v. Dodson [454 U.S. 312 (1981)], 2492

Pollard's Lessee v. Hagan [45 U.S. (3 How.) 212 (1845)], 2825

Pollock v. Farmers' Loan & Trust Company [158 U.S. 601 (1895)], 241, 252, 320, 357, 429, 583, 784, 836, 994, 1036, 1164–1165, 1167, 1168, 1227, 1244, 1268, 1409, 1869, **1959–1960**, 1964, 2048, 2421, 2543, 2591–2592, 2598, 2609, 2628, 2858, 2894, 2897

Pollock v. Williams [322 U.S. 4 (1944)], **1960–1961**

Pope v. Williams [193 U.S. 621 (1904)], 69

Porterfield v. Webb [263 U.S. 225 (1923)], 129, 131, 284

Posadas de Puerto Rico Associates v. Tourism Company of Puerto Rico [478 U.S. 328 (1986)], 462, 464, 1133, **1969**

Postal Clerks v. Blount [404 U.S. 802 (1971)], 1553

Pottinger v. Miami [810 F. Supp. 1551 (S.D. Fla.1992)], 1301

Poulos v. New Hampshire [345 U.S. 395 (1953)], 2794–2795

Powell v. Alabama [287 U.S. 45 (1932)], 284, 720, 1193, 1311, 1355, 1959, **1981**, 2036, 2038, 2087, 2260–2261, 2263, 2265, 2626, 2780

Powell v. McCormack [395 U.S. 486 (1969)], 501, 502, 1306, 1476, 1488, 1950, **1981**, 2670, 2853

Powell v. Pennsylvania [127 U.S. 678 (1888)], 586, 1114, 1115, 2829, 2830

Powell v. Texas [392 U.S. 514 (1968)], 730, 1484, 2774–2775

Powers v. Ohio [499 U.S. 400 (1991)], 165, 1514, 1515, 1899

Preiser v. Rodriguez [411 U.S. 475 (1973)], 955

Press-Enterprise Co. v. Superior Court [464 U.S. 501 (1984)], 1214, 2803

Press-Enterprise Co. v. Superior Court [478 U.S. 1 (1986)], 1152, 1214

Presser v. Illinois [116 U.S. 252 (1886)], 1729, 2113, 2924

Price, United States v. [383 U.S. 787 (1966)], 733, **2006**

Price Waterhouse v. Hopkins [490 U.S. 228 (1989)], 1844

Prigg v. Pennsylvania [41 U.S. (16 Pet.) 539 (1842)], 409, 562, 1159, 1230, 1712, 1901, **2006**, 2430, 2431, 2506, 2554–2555, 2649, 2654, 2698, 2825, 2868

Primus, In re [436 U.S. 412 (1978)], 2071

Prince v. Bartlett [8 Cranch 431 (1814)], 832

Prince v. Massachusetts [312 U.S. 158 (1944)], 353, **2008**, 2191

Principality of Monaco v. Mississippi [292 U.S. 313 (1934)], 878

Printz v. United States [521 U.S. 98 (1997)], 624, 904, 991, 1531, 1803, 1845, 2169, 2456, 2503

Prize Cases [2 Black (67 U.S.) 635 (1863)], 325, 340, 415, 430, 649, 746, 886, 949, 1230, 1736, 1791, 2628, 2837, 2840, 2868

Pro-Choice Network of Western New York v. Schenck [519 U.S. 357 (1997)], 94

Procunier v. Martinez [416 U.S. 396 (1974)], 2012, **2046**

Procunier v. Navarette [434 U.S. 555 (1978)], 2319

Proffitt v. Florida [428 U.S. 242 (1976)], 302, **310–312**

Progressive, The, United States v. [467 F. Supp. 990 (W.D. Wisc. 1979)], 2326–2327

Propeller Genesee Chief v. FitzHugh [53 U.S. (12 How.) 443 (1851)], 742, 1791, 1870, **2051**, 2648, 2650, 2654

Providence Bank v. Billings [29 U.S. (4 Pet.) 514 (1830)], 333, 675, 1686, **2059–2060**, 2653

Prudential Insurance Company v. Benjamin [328 U.S. 408 (1946)], 817, 1012, 1822, **2060**

Prudential Insurance Company v. Cheek [252 U.S. 567 (1922)], 1045–1046

PruneYard Shopping Center v. Robins [447 U.S. 74 (1980)], 1320, 2054, **2060**, 2154, 2157–2158, 2415

Ptasynski, United States v. [462 U.S. 74 (1983)], 784

Public Clearing House v. Coyne [194 U.S. 497 (1904)], 1970

Public Utilities Commission v. Pollack [343 U.S. 451 (1952)], 313, 2795

Pulley v. Harris [460 U.S. 1036 (1984)], 303

Pulliam v. Allen [466 U.S. 522 (1984)], 654, 1335, 1454

Pumpelly v. Green Bay Co. [80 U.S. (13 Wall.) 166 (1872)], 1037

# Q

Quackenbush v. Allstate Insurance Co. [517 U.S. 706 (1996)], 20

Quern v. Jordan [440 U.S. 332 (1979)], **2–85**, 853, 2350

Quick Bear v. Leupp [210 U.S. 50 (1908)], 82, 2371

Quilloin v. Walcott [434 U.S. 246 (1978)], 2395

Quinlan, In re [355 A. 2d 647 (N.J. Super. Ct. (1976)], 2268

Quinn v. United States [349 U.S. 155 (1955)], 1305, 1595, 2237

Quirin, Ex parte [317 U.S. 1 (1942)], 1247, **2085**, 2551, 2719, 2931

# R

Rabinowitz, United States v. [339 U.S. 56 (1950)], 1102, 1264, 1740, 2344

Rahrer, In re [140 U.S. 545 (1891)], 1168, 1601, 2513, 2870

Railroad Commission Cases [116 U.S. 352 (1886)], 199, 2823, 2830

Railroad Commission of Texas v. Pullman Company [312 U.S. 496 (1941)], 18–19, 1373

Railroad Company, United States v. [84 U.S. (17 Wall.) 322 (1873)], 1319

Railroad Company v. Maryland [88 U.S. (21 Wall.) 456 (1875)], 217

Railroad Company v. Peniston. *See* Union Pacific Railroad v. Peniston

Railroad Retirement Board v. Alton Railroad Co. [295 U.S. 496 (1935)], 457, 459, 1311, 2115, **2115**, 2226, 2281

Railway Employees' Department v. Hanson [351 U.S. 225 (1956)], 1552, 1553

Railway Express Agency v. New York [336 U.S. 106 (1949)], 840, 1588, 1592, **2115**

Railway Labor Executives' Association v. Gibbons [455 U.S. 457 (1982)], 161

Raines v. Byrd [521 U.S. 811 (1997)], 243, 502, 626, 1627, 2475, 2844

Rakas v. Illinois [439 U.S. 128 (1978)], 2044, 2156, 2335

Ramsey, United States v. [431 U.S. 606 (1977)], 209

Randall v. Brigham [74 (7 Wall.) 523 (1869)], 1335, 1453

Randall v. Meese [854 F. 2d 472 (D.C. Cir. 1988)], 1196

Rassmussen v. United States [197 U.S. 516 (1905)], 1169, 1376

R. A. V. v. City of St. Paul [505 U.S. 377 (1992)], 891, 1056–1057, 1136, 1154, 1276, 1278, **2123–2124**, 2538, 2913, 2926

Rawlings v. Kentucky [448 U.S. 98 (1980)], 2044

Ray v. Blair [343 U.S. 214 (1952)], 1942

Raymond Motor Transportation Company v. Rice [434 U.S. 429 (1978)], **2124**, 2514

Raynes v. Baird [521 U.S. 811 (1997)], 2387

Reagan v. Farmer's Loan & Trust Co. [154 U.S. 362 (1894)], 241, 346, 970, 1166, **2129–2130**, 2437

Real Estate Association v. McNary [454 U.S. 100 (1981)], 2156

Red Lion Broadcasting Co. v. Federal Communications Commission [395 U.S. 367 (1969)], 247, 248, 249, 446, 968, 969, 1147, 1391, 1671, 1723, 1725, 2144, **2144**, 2739–2740, 2890

Redrup v. New York [386 U.S. 767 (1967)], 2855

Reed v. Farley [512 U.S. 339 (1994)], 2467

Reed v. Reed [404 U.S. 71 (1971)], 270, 914, 1032, 1156, 1185, 1196, 2390, 2393, 2398–2399, 2921

Reese v. United States [92 U.S. 214 (1876)], 217, 430, 1024, 1041, 1070, 1319, 1415, **2145–2146**, 2822–2823, 2827, 2938

Reeves, Inc. v. Stake [447 U.S. 429 (1980)], 1212, 2052, 2515

Regan v. Taxation With Representation of Washington, Inc. [461 U.S. 540 (1983)], 1237

Regan v. Wald [468 U.S. 222 (1984)], **2146**

Regents of the University of California v. Bakke [438 U.S. 265 (1978)], 22, 35, 53, 54, 55, 57, 96, 122, 169, 194, 232, 238, 239, 277, 376, 391, 397, 406, 760, 794, 917, 1172, 1304, 1379, 1563, 1587, 1677, 1679, 1760, 1976, 1978, 1980, 2078, 2094, 2104, 2109, 2110, 2111, **2146–2147**, 2231, 2529, 2713, 2756, 2890

Regina v. Hicklin [16 W.R. 801 (1868)], 2748

Regional Rail Reorganization Act Cases [419 U.S. 102 (1974)], 161, 2278

Reid v. Covert [354 U.S. 1 (1957)], 386, 603, 959, 960, 1727, 1950, 1992, **2170**, 2672, 2719, 2722, 2839

Reidel, United States v. [402 U.S. 351 (1971)], 1677

Reitman v. Mulkey [387 U.S. 369 (1967)], 280, 785, 786, **2170–2171**, 2220, 2487, 2492

Remington, United States v. (2d Cir. 1953), 1221

Rendell-Baker v. Kohn [457 U.S. 830 (1982)], **200**, 2018, 2492

Rennie v. Klein [462 F. Supp. 1131 (D.N.J. 1978)], 790, 1720

Reno v. ACLU [521 U.S. 844 (1997)], 249, 471, 969, 1057, 1148, 1392

Reno v. Condon [120 S.Ct. 666 (2000)], 993

Renton (City of) v. Playtime Theatres [475 U.S. 41 (1986)], 381, 1054, 1057, 1133, 1832, **2199**

Respublica v. Chapman [1 Dall. 53 (Penna. 1781)], 364

Retail Clerks v. Schermerhorn [373 U.S. 746 (1963)], 2278

Reves v. Ernst & Young [494 U.S. 56 (1990)], 1860

Rewis v. United States [401 U.S. 808 (1971)], 1570

Reynolds, United States v. [235 U.S. 133 (1914)], 1897, 2008, 2900

Reynolds v. Sims [377 U.S. 533 (1964)], 152, 153, 172, 233, 237, 273, 274, 277, 326, 440, 866, 871, 1227, 1268, 1271, 1462, 1853, 2133, 2134, 2202, **2227–2229**, 2520, 2713–2714, 2765, 2804, 2849, 2854

Reynolds v. United States [98 U.S. 145 (1879)], 299, 748, 973, 1048, 1065, 1290, 1768, 1961, 2180, 2186, **2229**

Rhode Island v. Innes [446 U.S. 291 (1980)], 1742, 1922, 1928, **2229–2230**, 2238

Rhode Island v. Palmer [253 U.S. 350 (1920)], 2803, 2927

Rhodes v. Chapman [452 U.S. 337 (1981)], 730

Rhodes v. Iowa [170 U.S. 412 (1890)], 1168

Ribnik v. McBride [277 U.S. 350 (1928)], 1115, 1851, **2230**, 2746

Rice v. Cayetano [120 S.Ct. 1044 (2000)], 1784

Rice v. Paladin Enterprises, Inc. [128 F. 3d 233 (4th Cir. 1997)], 1154

Rice v. Sante Fe Elevator Corp. [331 U.S. 218 (1947)], 1988, 1989

Richards v. Wisconsin [520 U.S. 385 (1997)], 1097

Richardson, United States v. [418 U.S. 166 (1974)], 1215, 2662

Richardson v. Marsh [481 U.S. 200 (1987)], 492

Richardson v. McKnight [521 U.S. 399 (1997)], 243

Richmond (City of) v. Deans [281 U.S. 704 (1930)], 2219, 2468

Richmond (City of) v. J. A. Croson Co. [488 U.S. 469 (1989)], 33, 55, 56, 398, 400, 623, 848, 915, 1530, 1679–1680, 1843, 1845, 2106, 2108, 2165, 2169, **2230–2231**, 2313, 2398, 2537, 2538, 2890, 2934

Richmond Newspapers, Inc. v. Virginia [448 U.S. 555 (1980)], 271, 972, 1107, 1117, 1132, 1142, 1144, 1145–1146, 1151, 1181, 1214, 1215, 1811, 1812, 1979, 2010, 2077, **2231–2232**, 2271–2272

Rideau v. Louisiana [373 U.S. 723 (1963)], 1150

Riggs v. Taylor [22 U.S. (9 Wheat.) 485 (1824)], 2704

Ristano v. Ross [424 U.S. 589 (1976)], 2803

Rivera v. Marcus [696 F. 2d 1016 (2d Cir. 1982)], 1084

Rivera-Rodriguez v. Popular Democratic Party [452 U.S. 1 (1982)], 865, 1943

Rizzo v. Goode [423 U.S. 362 (1976)], 276, 1375, 2155, 2156, **2280**

Robbins v. California [453 U.S. 420 (1981)], 2295

Robbins v. Shelby County Taxing District [120 U.S. 489 (1887)], 217, 1162, 1227

Robel, United States v. [389 U.S. 258 (1967)], 1650, 1868, **2280–2281**, 2850, 2854

Roberts v. City of Boston [5 Cush. (Mass.) 198 (1850)], 735, 771, 1086, 1204, 1918, **2282–2283**, 2354, 2583

Roberts v. Louisiana [428 U.S. 325 (1976)], **310–312**

Roberts v. United States Jaycees [468 U.S. 609 (1984)], 1110, 1119, 1237, 2016–2017

Robertson v. Wegmann [436 U.S. 584 (1978)], 403, 2227

Robinson, United States v. [414 U.S. 218 (1973)], 2156, **2283**, 2331–2332, 2343

Robinson v. Cahill [118 NJ Super 223 (1973)], 2498

Robinson v. California [370 U.S. 660 (1962)], 729, 731, 1484, 2542, 2774

Robinson v. DiCenso [403 U.S. 602 (1971)], 1601

Robinson v. Jacksonville Shipyards [760 F. Supp. 1486 (M.D. Fla. 1991)], 2926

Rochin v. California [342 U.S. 165 (1952)], 186, 229, 485, 1102, 1405, 2037, 2039, 2041, **2283–2284**, 2561

Rock Royal Co-Op, Inc., United States v. [307 U.S. 533 (1939)], 63, 1316, **2932–2933**

Rodriguez v. McLoughlin [49 F. Supp. 2d 186 (S.D. N.Y. 1999)], 1084

Roe v. Wade [410 U.S. 113 (1973)], 5, 6, 7, 8, 9, 11–12, 13, 14, 92–93, 155, 182, 189, 190, 191, 192, 195, 196, 210, 211, 270, 274, 277, 315, 316, 381, 383, 473, 508, 625, 700, 725, 759, 792, 800, 816, 839, 1008, 1118, 1175, 1196–1197, 1233, 1272, 1291, 1293, 1324, 1393, 1449, 1461–1462, 1480, 1530, 1531, 1615, 1639, 1665, 1680, 1811, 1812, 1813, 1843, 1845, 1861, 1900, 1901, 1914–1916, 1979, 2020, 2052, 2056, 2057, 2078, 2126, 2156, 2158, 2159, 2163, 2168, 2203, 2204–2207, 2208, 2242, 2244, 2246, 2247, 2248, 2268, **2284–2286**, 2313, 2328, 2394, 2448, 2454–2455, 2456, 2528, 2574, 2575, 2576, 2577, 2578, 2594, 2699, 2714, 2872, 2888, 2892, 2893, 2921

Roemer v. Board of Public Works [426 U.S. 736 (1976)], 2375

Rogers v. Bellei [401 U.S. 815 (1971)], 366, 957

Rogers v. Lodge [458 U.S. 613 (1982)], 1765, **2286**, 2863, 2890, 2892

Rogers v. Missouri Pacific Railroad Co. [352 U.S. 521 (1957)], 2296, 2726

Rogers v. Okin [634 F. 2d 650 (1980)], 1719, 1720

Rogers v. Richmond [365 U.S. 534 (1961)], 1924, **2286**

Rogers v. United States [340 U.S. 367 (1951)], 2831

Rome (City of) v. United States [446 U.S. 156 (1980)], 879, 1089, 2810, 2812, 2813

Romer v. Evans [517 U.S. 620 (1996)], 383, 400, 429, 432, 787, 788, 917, 1197, 1531, 2122, 2123, 2170, **2286–2287**, 2404, 2405, 2456, 2538

Ronan, Sheriff, United States ex rel. Hover v. [3 F. 117 (1887)], 1878

Roosevelt v. Meyer [68 U.S. (1 Wall.) 512 (1863)], 2628

Rosales-Lopez v. United States [449 U.S. 819 (1981)], 2803

Rosario v. Rockefeller [410 U.S. 752 (1973)], 2007

Rose v. Lundy [455 U.S. 509 (1982)], 193, 2532

Rose v. Mitchell [443 U.S. 545 (1979)], 1253

Rosenberg v. United States [346 U.S. 273 (1953)], 1102, **2294**, 2719

Rosenberg v. United States [360 U.S. 367 (1959)], 1426

Rosenberger v. Rector & Visitors of the University of Virginia [515 U.S. 809 (1995)], 926, 1136, 1209, 2070, 2173, 2179, 2194, **2294**, 2322, 2456, 2568, 2751

Rosenblatt v. Baer [383 U.S. 75 (1966)], 1805, 2855

Rosenbloom v. Metromedia, Inc. [403 U.S. 29 (1971)], 1189, 1608

Rosenfeld v. New Jersey [408 U.S. 901 (1972)], 1042

Ross, In re [140 U.S. 453 (1891)], 958, 959

Ross, United States v. [456 U.S. 798 (1981)], **2294–2295**, 2332

Ross v. Bernhard [396 U.S. 531 (1970)], 2388, 2730

Ross v. Moffitt [417 U.S. 600 (1974)], 23, 817, 2262, **2295**

Rostker v. Goldberg [453 U.S. 57 (1981)], 117, 507, 1679, **2295–2296**, 2395–2396, 2399, 2418, 2472, 2533

Roth v. United States [354 U.S. 476 (1956)], 235, 1100, 1194, 1269, 1414, 1716, 1734, 1837, 1965, 1968, **2296**, 2747, 2855

Rothstein v. Wyman [462 F. 2d 226 (1972)], 1708

Rouse v. Cameron [373 F. 2d 451 (D.C. Cir. 1966)], 1718

Royall, Ex parte [117 U.S. 241 (1886)], 955, 1249

Royster, F. S. Guano, Company v. Virginia [253 U.S. 412 (1920)], 1588

Rubin v. Coors Brewing Co. [514 U.S. 476 (1995)], 1135

Ruggles v. Illinois [108 U.S. 526 (1883)], 2823

Rummel v. Estelle [445 U.S. 263 (1980)], 729, 731, **2299**

Rundle v. Delaware and Raritan Canal Co. [55 U.S. (14 How.) 80 (1852)], 742

Runyon v. McCrary [427 U.S. 160 (1976)], 96, 98, 403, 407, 1026, 1277, 1437, 1530, 1887, 2227, **2299–2300**, 2488, 2694, 2738

Russell, United States v. [411 U.S. 423 (1973)], 899

Russello v. United States [464 U.S. 16 (1983)], 2112

Rust v. Sullivan [500 U.S. 173 (1991)], 196, 1136, 1531, 2070, 2169, **2300**, 2455, 2567–2568, 2750

Rutan v. Republican Party of Illinois [497 U.S. 62 (1990)], 948, 1213, 1886, 1939, **2300–2301**

Rutgers v. Waddington [New York Mayor's Court (1784)], 541, 828, 1258, **2301**

## S

Sable Communications of California, Inc. v. FCC [492 U.S. 115 (1989)], 351, 778, 1148

Saenz v. Roe [526 U.S. 489 (1999)], 778, 2277, **2305–2306**, 2877

Safeco NLRB v. Retail Store Employees Union. See National Labor Relations Board v. Retail Employees Local No. 1001

Saffle v. Parks [494 U.S. 484 (1990)], 1530

Saia v. New York [334 U.S. 558 (1948)], 2453, 2795

St. Amant v. Thompson [390 U.S. 727 (1967)], 1805

St. Louis and O'Fallon Railroad v. United States [279 U.S. 461 (1929)], 1714

Sakol v. Commissioner of Internal Revenue [439 U.S. 859 (1978)], 2421

Sale v. Haitian Centers Council [509 U.S. 155 (1993)], 71

Salerno, United States v. [481 U.S. 739 (1987)], 150, 1915, 2043, 2162, **2306–2307**

San Antonio Independent School District v. Rodriguez [411 U.S. 1 (1973)], 275, 352, 857, 859, 1637–1638, 1677, 1920, 1974–1975, 1977–1978, 1980, **2309–2310**, 2387, 2408, 2498, 2874, 2880, 2891

Sanchez, United States v. [340 U.S. 42 (1950)], 2658

San Diego Building Trades v. Garmon [359 U.S. 236 (1959)], 1554

San Diego Gas and Electric Company v. City of San Diego [450 U.S. 621 (1981)], 890, 1401, 2149

Sandin v. Conner [515 U.S. 472 (1995)], 2013

San Francisco Arts & Athletics v. United States Olympic Committee [483 U.S. 522 (1987)], 1377, 2489

San Mateo County v. Southern Pacific Railroad [116 U.S. 138 (1882)], 1900

Santa Clara County v. Southern Pacific Railroad [118 U.S. 394 (1886)], 526, 687, 1900, 2829

Santa Cruz Fruit Packing Co. v. NLRB [303 U.S. 453 (1938)], 2821

Santobello v. New York [404 U.S. 257 (1971)], 2367

Santosky v. Kramer [455 U.S. 745 (1982)], 974, 1523, 2027

Sauer v. City of New York [206 U.S. 536 (1907)], 1890

Saxbe v. Washington Post Co. [417 U.S. 843 (1974)], 1979

Saylor, United States v. [322 U.S. 385 (1944)], 423

Scales v. United States [367 U.S. 203 (1961)], 68, 1108, **2311–2312**, 2581

Scarborough v. United States [431 U.S. 563 (1977)], 2416

Schad v. Mt. Ephraim [452 U.S. 61 (1981)], 1830, 1868, **2317**, 2530

Schaeffer v. United States [251 U.S. 466 (1920)], 221

Schall v. Martin [467 U.S. 253 (1984)], 149, 2005, 2307, **2317**

Schechter Poultry Corp. v. United States [295 U.S. 495 (1935)], 41, 267, 457, 459, 599, 698, 736, 743, 744, 761, 846, 1311, 1313, 1316, 1760, 1776, 1795, 2283, 2288, **2317–2318**, 2385, 2560, 2818–2821, 2929, 2937

Schenck v. Pro Choice Network [519 U.S. 357 (1997)], 243, 1050

Schenck v. United States [249 U.S. 47 (1919)], 146, 328, 426, 709, 923, 1135, 1154, 1198, 1264, 1298, 1352, 2186, 2198, **2318–2319**, 2580, 2841, 2901, 2902, 2928–2929

Scheuer v. Rhodes [416 U.S. 232 (1974)], 944, **2319**

Schick v. Reed [419 U.S. 256 (1974)], 1878, **2319**

Schilb v. Kuebel [404 U.S. 357 (1971)], 149

Schiro v. Farley [510 U.S. 222 (1994)], 812

Schlesinger v. Ballard [419 U.S. 498 (1975)], 2391, 2396

Schlesinger v. Reservist Committee to Stop the War [418 U.S. 208 (1974)], 1977, 2662

Schmerber v. California [384 U.S. 757 (1966)], 205, 711, 800, 824, 956, 1083, 2041, 2238, **2310**, 2340–2341, 2458, 2767

Schneckloth v. Bustamonte [412 U.S. 218 (1973)], 507, 1250, **2319–2320**, 2334, 2711, 2831

Schneider v. District of Columbia [348 U.S. 26 (1953)], 2076

Schneider v. Rusk [377 U.S. 163 (1964)], 1785

Schneider v. State [308 U.S. 147 (1939)], 1317

Schneider v. Town of Irvington [308 U.S. 147 (1939)], 2198

Schneiderman v. United States [320 U.S. 807 (1943)], 2281, 2551, 2930

Schnell v. Davis [336 U.S. 933 (1949)], 1629, **2320**

Scholey v. Rew [90 U.S. (23 Wall.) 331 (1875)], 784

School Board of Nassau County v. Arline [480 U.S. 273 (1987)], 791

Schulte, D. A., v. Gangi [326 U.S. 712 (1940)], 1539

Schwabe v. New Mexico Board of Bar Examiners [353 U.S. 232 (1957)], 606, **2325**

Schweiker v. Chilicky [487 U.S. 412 (1988)], 653, 740

Schweiker v. Wilson [450 U.S. 221 (1981)], 193

Schwimmer, United States v. [279 U.S. 644 (1929)], 284, 1198, 1296, 1300, **2325–2326**

Scopes v. State. See Tennessee v. Scopes

Scott v. Emerson [15 Mo. 682 (1852)], 819

Scott v. Illinois [436 U.S. 925 (1979)], 116, 1745, 2262

Scott v. United States [436 U.S. 128 (1978)], 874

Scottsboro Cases, 1281

SCRAP, United States v. See Students Challenging Regulatory Agency Procedures (SCRAP), United States v.

Screws v. United States [325 U.S. 91 (1945)], 410, 423, 444, 445, 709, 1025, 1103–1104, 1240, 1410, **2329**, 2776

Searight v. Stokes [44 U.S. (3 How.) 151 (1845)], 742

Sears, Roebuck & Co. v. San Diego Carpenters [436 U.S. 180 (1978)], 1554

Seattle Times v. Rhinehart [467 U.S. 20 (1984)], 1145, 1152

Sedima, S.P.R.L. v. Imrex Co. [473 U.S. 479 (1985)], 2112

See v. City of Seattle [387 U.S. 541 (1967)], 42, 43, 44, 294

Seeger, United States v. [380 U.S. 163 (1965)], 505, 1049, 2173, 2188, **2353–2354**, 2790

Selective Draft Law Cases [245 U.S. 366 (1918)], 506, 748

Semayne's Case (1602, 1604), 1098

Seminole Tribe of Florida v. Florida [517 U.S. 44 (1996)], 87, 776, 880, 881, 904, 992, 1010, 1531, 1845, 2169, 2456, 2504

Senate Select Committee on Presidential Campaign Activities v. Nixon [498 F. 2d 725 (D.C. Cir. 1974)], 2865

Senn v. Tile Layers Union [301 U.S. 468 (1937)], 220, 1548

Serrano v. Priest [5 Cal. 3d 584 (1971)], 1591, **2387**, 2498

Service v. Dulles [354 U.S. 363 (1957)], 946

Sewall v. Hancock (Super. Ct.) Quincy [457 (Mass. 1768)], 1866

Seymour v. McCormick [60 U.S. (19 How.) 96 (1854)], 1230, 1432

Shadwick v. City of Tampa [407 U.S. 345 (1972)], 2332

Shapiro v. Thompson [394 U.S. 618 (1969)], 231, 233, 238, 837, 1973, 1974, 2275, 2277, 2305, 2306, **2408**, 2574, 2873, 2874, 2877, 2878–2879

Sharpe, United States v. [470 U.S. 675 (1985)], 2553

Sharpless v. Philadelphia [21 Pa. 147 (1853)], 2074

Shaughnessy v. United States ex rel. Mezei [354 U.S. 206 (1953)], 719, 1410, **2408**

Shaw v. Hunt [517 U.S. 899 (1996)], 2409

Shaw v. Reno [509 U.S. 630 (1993)], 868, 870, 871, 917, 1511–1512, 1735, 1783, 2093, 2108, 2136, 2137, 2169, **2409–2410**, 2812, 2814

Sheldon v. Sill [49 U.S. (8 How.) 441 (1850)], 1502

Shelley v. Kraemer [334 U.S. 1 (1948)], 163, 210, 259, 375, 393, 403, 725, 909, 930, 1025, 1042, 1678, 2101–2102, 2219, 2222, 2223, **2410–2411**, 2485, 2486, 2487, 2492, 2792, 2795, 2810, 2874

Shelton v. Tucker [364 U.S. 479 (1960)], 1108, 1573, 1773, 2542

Sheppard v. Maxwell [384 U.S. 333 (1966)], 972, 1150–1151, 1179, 2077

Sherbert v. Verner [374 U.S. 398 (1963)], 231, 238, 487, 506, 821, 823, 1105, 2169, 2180–2181, 2181, 2191, 2192, 2194, 2377, **2412**, 2469, 2700, 2748, 2750, 2914

Shreveport Case. See Houston, East and West Texas Railway Co. v. United States

Shuttlesworth v. Birmingham [394 U.S. 147 (1969)], 2832

Sibron v. New York [392 U.S. 40 (1968)], 2023, 2552, **2675–2676**, 2676

Sicurella v. United States [348 U.S. 385 (1955)], 2186

Siebold, Ex parte [100 U.S. 371 (1880)], 2825–2826

Sierra Club v. Morton [405 U.S. 727 (1972)], **2416**, 2565, 2661

Silkwood v. Kerr-McGee Corp. [464 U.S. 238 (1984)], 2706

Silverman v. United States [365 U.S. 505 (1961)], 1850, 2139, **2416**

Silverthorne Lumber Co. v. United States [251 U.S. 385 (1920)], 2336, **2417**, 2922

Simmons v. United States [390 U.S. 377 (1968)], 962

Simon v. Eastern Kentucky Welfare Rights Organization [426 U.S. 26 (1976)], 275, **2417**, 2565

Simon & Schuster, Inc. v. Members of The New York State Crime Victims Board [502 U.S. 105 (1991)], 1351

Simopouloas v. Virginia [462 U.S. 506 (1983)], 2207

Sims' Case [7 Cush. 285 (Mass. 1851)], 2409

Sinclair v. United States [279 U.S. 263 (1929)], 2360

Sing Tuck, United States v. [194 U.S. 161 (1904)], 1167

Sinking Fund Cases [99 U.S. 700 (1879); 99 U.S. 727 (1879)], 52, 217, 583, 802, 1354, **2419–2420**, 2563, 2824, 2829

Sioux Nation of Indians, United States v. [448 U.S. 371 (1980)], 82

Sipuel v. Oklahoma State Hospital Board of Regents [332 U.S. 631 (1948)], **2420**

Sisson, United States v. [District Court of Mass. 297 F. Supp. 902 (1969)], 2936

Skinner v. Mid-America Pipeline Company [490 U.S. 212 (1989)], 762, 1401

Skinner v. Oklahoma [316 U.S. 535 (1942)], 182, 1118, 1122, 1289, 1404, 1646, 2097, 2098, 2203, 2244, **2421–2422**, 2528, 2550, 2562, 2573, 2577

Skinner v. Railway Labor Executives Association [489 U.S. 602 (1989)], 331, 825, 1529, 1782, 2328, 2337, **2422–2423**

Skipper v. South Carolina [476 U.S. 1 (1986)], 2368

Slaughterhouse Cases [83 U.S. (16 Wall.) 36 (1873)], 201, 217, 218, 283, 298, 313, 319, 336, 341, 342, 402, 430, 431, 527, 580, 581, 733, 746, 844, 909, 912, 1024, 1036, 1037, 1091, 1164, 1173, 1288, 1319, 1354, 1448, 1459, 1732, 1733, 1754, 1809, 1814, 2021, 2048–2049, 2217, 2305, 2349, **2423–2424**, 2426, 2509, 2564, 2570, 2571, 2628, 2693, 2784, 2807, 2822, 2826–2827, 2924

Sloan v. Lemon [413 U.S. 825 (1973)], **464**

Slochower v. Board of Education [350 U.S. 551 (1956)], 279, 1702, 2238

Smith v. Alabama [124 U.S. 465 (1888)], 977

Smith v. Allwright [321 U.S. 649 (1944)], 411, 423, 692, 1042, 1238, 1275, 1678, 1939, 1941, 2007, 2008, 2145, 2282, 2320, **2436–2437**, 2485, 2487, 2550–2551, 2675, 2809–2810

Smith v. Board of School Commissioners [827 F. 2d 684 (11th Cir. 1987)], 859

Smith v. Cahoon [283 U.S. 553 (1931)], 840

Smith v. Goguen [415 U.S. 566 (1974)], 192, 1061, 2776

Smith v. Hooley [393 U.S. 374 (1969)], 2465

Smith v. Illinois [469 U.S. 91 (1984)], 1743

Smith v. Maryland [442 U.S. 735 (1979)], 713, 875, 2140–2141, 2334

Smith v. Murray [477 U.S. 527 (1986)], 1253, 1844

Smith v. Organization of Foster Families [431 U.S. 816 (1977)], 1083, 1124

Smith v. Phillips [455 U.S. 209 (1982)], 793

Smith v. United States [507 U.S. 197 (1993)], 2315–2316

Smith v. Wade [456 U.S. 924 (1983)], 739

Smith, George Otis, United States v. [286 U.S. 6 (1932)], 2612

Smuck v. Hobson [408 F. 2d 175 (1969)], 790

Smyth v. Ames [169 U.S. 466 (1898)], 199, 346, 969, 970, 1023, 1166, 1267, 1285, 1666, 2129–2130, **2437**, 2640, 2758, 2894

Snepp v. United States [444 U.S. 507 (1980)], 1140, **2438**

Sniadach v. Family Finance Corp. [395 U.S. 337 (1969)], 1362

Snyder v. Massachusetts [290 U.S. 606 (1934)], 315, 1176, 2281, 2706

Société Internationale v. Rogers [357 U.S. 197 (1958)], 960

Sokolow, United States v. [490 U.S. 1 (1989)], 482, 2338

Solem v. Helm [463 U.S. 277 (1983)], 316, 729–730, 732, 983, 1976, 2367, **2446–2447**

Solesbee v. Balkcom [339 U.S. 9 (1950)], 1176

Somerset's Case [98 Eng. Rep. 499 (K.B., 1772)], 2, 334, 467, 560, 818, 1771, **2451–2452**, 2520, 2649

Sonzinsky v. United States [300 U.S. 506 (1937)], 152, 1186, **2452**, 2658

Sorrells v. United States [287 U.S. 435 (1932)], 899

Sosna v. Iowa [419 U.S. 393 (1975)], 799, 1121, 2275, 2277, **2452**

South Carolina v. Baker [485 U.S. 505 (1988)], 994, 1384

South Carolina v. Gathers [490 U.S. 805 (1989)], 2369

South Carolina v. Katzenbach [383 U.S. 301 (1966)], 96, 1026, 1240, 1629, **2456–2457**, 2810, 2813

South Carolina v. United States [199 U.S. 437 (1905)], 241, 1211

South Carolina State Highway Department v. Barnwell Bros., Inc. [303 U.S. 177 (1938)], 317, 2122, 2456, 2459, 2513, 2514

South Dakota v. Dole [483 U.S. 203 (1987)], 487, 994, 995, 1844, 2468, 2661, 2751

South Dakota v. Neville [459 U.S. 553 (1983)], 1841, **2458**

Southeastern Community College v. Davis [442 U.S. 397 (1979)], 2152

South-Eastern Underwriters Association v. United States [322 U.S. 533 (1944)], 106, 459, 1888, 2060, **2458**

Southern Burlington NAACP v. Mount Laurel [423 U.S. 808 (1975)], 2945

Southern Pacific Co. v. Arizona ex rel. Sullivan [325 U.S. 761 (1945)], 817, 835, 836, 1591, 2124, **2458–2459**, 2513–2514

Southern Pacific Co. v. Jensen [244 U.S. 205 (1917)], 1467

Southern Railway Co. v. United States [222 U.S. 20 (1911)], 2780

Southwestern Bell Tel. Co. v. Public Service Commission [262 U.S. 276 (1923)], 221

Spain, In re [47 F. 208 (1891)], 360

Spallone v. United States [493 U.S. 265 (1990)], 1471, 2221

Spano v. New York [360 U.S. 315 (1959)], 1923, 2039, 2850

Sparf & Hansen v. United States [56 U.S. 51 (1895)], 1513

Spaulding v. Vilas [161 U.S. 483 (1896)], 943

Spaziano v. Florida [468 U.S. 447 (1984)], 303, 2535

Speiser v. Randall [357 U.S. 513 (1958)], 230, 231, 234, **2467**, 2568, 2750

Spence v. Washington [418 U.S. 405 (1974)], 1061

Spencer v. Texas [385 U.S. 554 (1967)], 722

Spinelli v. United States [393 U.S. 410 (1969)], 120, 1327, 1368, 2024, 2330, **2469**

Spock, United States v. [416 F. 2d 165 (1969)], 709

Sporhase v. Nebraska [458 U.S. 941 (1982)], 2514, 2566

Sprague, United States v. [282 U.S. 716 (1931)], 73, 862, 2118

Springer v. Government of the Philippine Islands [277 U.S. 189 (1928)], 949, 2384

Springer v. United States [102 U.S. 586 (1881)], 784, 1959, **2470**, 2628

Spring Valley Water Works v. Schottler [110 U.S. 347 (1883)], 2823

Springville City v. Thomas [166 U.S. 707 (1897)], 1517

Stack v. Boyle [342 U.S. 1 (1951)], 148, 149, 150, 2005

Stafford v. Wallace [258 U.S. 495 (1922)], 593, **2470**, 2560, 2635

Standard Oil Company of Indiana v. United States [164 F. 376 (1908)], 1234, 1652, 2898, 2904

Standard Oil Company of New Jersey v. United States [221 U.S. 1 (1911)], 88, 106, 455, 688, 749, 1030, 1165, 1557, 2049, 2298, **2472**

Stanford v. Kentucky [492 U.S. 361 (1989)], 306, 1843, 2315, 2369, **2475–2476**

Stanley, United States v. [483 U.S. 669 (1987)], 653

Stanley v. Georgia [394 U.S. 557 (1969)], 350, 1676, 1734–1735, 1838, 2061, 2247, **2476**

Stanley v. Illinois [405 U.S. 645 (1969)], 2243

Stanley v. Illinois [405 U.S. 645 (1972)], 1123, 1404, 1524

Stanton v. Stanton [421 U.S. 7 (1975)], 2391, 2392, 2921

Starns v. Malkerson [401 U.S. 985 (1971)], 2275, 2879

Starret City Associates, United States v. [488 U.S. 946 (1988)], 2221

State v. A.L.I.V.E. [606 P. 2d 769 (1980)], 2496

State v. Ball [124 N.H. 226 (1983)], 2498

State v. Cadman [476 A.2d 1148 (Me. 1984)], 2498

State v. Mann [North Carolina S.Ct. (1829)], 558, 2425

State v. Mooney [588 A. 2d 145 (Conn. 1991)], 1302

State v. Mugler [123 U.S. 623 (1887)], 240

State v. United States & Canada Express Company [60 N.H. 219 (1880)], 802

State Board v. Young's Market [299 U.S. 59 (1936)], 2741

State Freight Tax Case [83 U.S. 232 (1873)], 747, 2563

State of . . . See specific state names

State Tax on Foreign-Held Bonds Case [82 U.S. 300 (1872)], 341

State Tax on Railway Gross Receipts Case [82 U.S. 284 (1872)], 341

Staub v. Baxley [355 U.S. 313 (1958)], 2903

Steagald v. United States [451 U.S. 204 (1981)], 121, 2333, **2526**

Steamboat New World v. King [57 U.S. (16. How.) 469 (1854)], 735

Steele v. Louisville & Nashville Railroad Co. [323 U.S. 192 (1944)], 1554

Steele v. United States [367 U.S. 505 (1925)], 2332

Steel Seizure Case. See Youngstown Sheet and Tube v. Sawyer

Steelworkers v. United States [361 U.S. 39 (1959)], 1553

Steffel v. Thompson [415 U.S. 452 (1974)], 2279

Stellwagen v. Clum [245 U.S. 605 (1981)], 161

Sterling v. Constantin [298 U.S. 378 (1932)], 2594

Sterling v. Cupp [625 P. 2d 123 (1981)], 2498

Stettler v. O'Hara [243 U.S. 629 (1917)], 35, 263, **2529**

Steuart and Brothers v. Bowels [322 U.S. 398 (1944)], 887, 2841

Steward Machine Company v. Davis [300 U.S. 652 (1937)], 314, 987, 1157, 1186, 1284, 1316, 1554, 1780, 2115, 2445, **2540–2541**, 2660–2661

Stewart Dry Goods Company v. Lewis [287 U.S. 9 (1935)], 314

Stone v. Farmer's Loan & Trust Company [116 U.S. 307 (1886)], 1037, 1350, 2049, **2547**, 2823

Stone v. Graham [449 U.S. 39 (1980)], 855, 1602, 1603, 2177, 2372

Stone v. Mississippi [101 U.S. 814 (1880)], 676, 1350, **2547**, 2665, 2823

Stone v. Powell [428 U.S. 465 (1976)], 18, 1251, 1253, 1758, 1975, 2044, 2225, 2319, 2456, **2547–2548**

Stone v. Wisconsin [94 U.S. 181 (1877)], **1224–1225**

Stoner v. California [376 U.S. 483 (1964)], 2690

Storer v. Brown [415 U.S. 724 (1974)], 158, 1942

Stovall v. Denno [388 U.S. 293 (1967)], 962, 1627

Strader v. Graham [51 U.S. (10 How.) 83 (1951)], 818, 1230, 2431–2432, **2557**, 2649, 2654, 2655

Strauder v. West Virginia [100 U.S. 303 (1879)], 95, 200, 388, 403, 408, 414, 1038, 1509, 1919, 2088, 2099, **2558–2559**, 2564, 2628, 2827, 2828

Street v. New York [394 U.S. 576 (1969)], 1083, 2855

Streetwatch v. National Railroad Passenger Corp. [875 F. Supp. 1055 (S.D. N.Y. 1995)], 1301

Strickland v. Washington [466 U.S. 668 (1984)], 2043

Strickley v. Highland Boy Gold Mining Co. [200 U.S. 527 (1906)], 2079

Stromberg v. California [283 U.S. 359 (1931)], 179, 284, 1311, 1714, 1788, 2311, **2563**, 2630, 2780

Strunk v. United States [412 U.S. 434 (1973)], 2465

Stuart v. Laird [5 U.S. (I Cranch) 299 (1803)], 1498, 1668, 1669, 1684, **2564**, 2589

Students Challenging Regulatory Agency Procedures (SCRAP), United States v. [412 U.S. 669 (1973)], 2473, 2475, **2564–2565**

Stump v. Sparkman [435 U.S. 349 (1978)], 1335, 1453, **2565**

Sturges v. Crowninshield [17 U.S. (4 Wheat.) 122 (1819)], 161, 555, 627, 677, 1635, 1673, 1685, 1835–1836, **2565**

Sugarman v. Dougall [413 U.S. 634 (1973)], 66, 72, 1068, 2160, **2582–2583**

Sullivan, United States v. [332 U.S. 689 (1948)], 1069, **2583**

Sullivan v. Little Hunting Park, Inc. [396 U.S. 229 (1969)], 403, 1854

Sumner v. Shuman [483 U.S. 66 (1987)], 2368

Sunshine Anthracite Coal Company v. Adkins [310 U.S. 381 (1940)], 184

Superintendent, Massachusetts Correctional Institution v. Hill [472 U.S. 445 (1985)], 2013, 2033

Superintendent of Belchertown State School v. Saikewicz [370 N.E.2d 417 Mass 728 (1977)], 2268

Supreme Court of Virginia v. Consumers Union of the United States [446 U.S. 714 (1980)], 1591

Sutherland v. Illinois [29 Ill. App. 3d 199 (1976)], 1061

Swain v. Alabama [380 U.S. 202 (1965)], 165, 971, 1509, 1510, 1680, 1898, 2088, **2627**, 2728, 2891

Swann v. Charlotte-Mecklenburg Board of Education [402 U.S. 1 (1971)], 273, 773, 859, 1232, 1459, 1535, 2102, 2111, 2146, 2320, **2627**

Swarb v. Lennox [405 U.S. 191 (1972)], 2831

Sweatt v. Painter [330 U.S. 629 (1950)], 253, 388, **2628–2629**, 2764, 2792, 2796

Sweezy v. New Hampshire [354 U.S. 234 (1957)], 22, 279, 477, 1595, 1702, 2772, **2866–2867**

Swift v. Tyson [41 U.S. 1 (1842)], 220, 360, 466, 921, 977, 1184, 1496, 1559, 1733, 1869, 2555–2556, 2593, **2629**, 2648, 2654

Swift & Co. v. United States [196 U.S. 375 (1905)], 252, 455, 861, 1162, 1234, 1540, 1733, 1756, 2413, 2470, 2559–2560, **2629–2630**, 2635

Swisher v. Brady [438 U.S. 204 (1978)], 1523

Sylvester, United States v. [C.C. Pa., unreported (1799)], 980

Syracuse Peace Council v. Federal Communications Commission [867 F. 2d 654 (D.C. Cir. 1989)], 969

# T

Takahashi v. Fish & Game Commission [334 U.S. 410 (1948)], 66, 129, 131–132, 1077, 1219, 1871, **2642–2643**

Talbot v. Janson [311 (3 Dal.) 133 (1795)], 364

Talley v. California [363 U.S. 60 (1960)], 2574

Talton v. Mayes [163 U.S. 376 (1896)], 81

Tarble's Case [80 U.S. (13 Wall.) 397 (1871)], 341, 1037, 1248

Tashjian v. Republican Party of Connecticut [479 U.S. 208 (1986)], 1938–1939, 2008

Taylor v. Alabama [457 U.S. 687 (1982)], 1841

Taylor v. Carry [61 U.S. (20 How.) 583 (1858)], 298

Taylor v. Georgia [315 U.S. 25 (1942)], 286

Taylor v. Louisiana [419 U.S. 522 (1975)], 1196, 1509, 1510, 2391, **2663**, 2787

Taylor v. Mississippi [319 U.S. 583 (1943)], 426, 2189

Taylor v. Porter [4 Hill 140 (1843)], 1287

Taylor & Marshall v. Beckham [178 U.S. 548 (1900)], 1950

Teague v. Lane [489 U.S. 288 (1989)], 239, 1253, 1895, 2044, 2156, 2162

Teamsters Local 695 v. Vogt, Inc. [354 U.S. 284 (1957)], 1907

Tennessee v. Davis [100 U.S. 257 (1880)], 445

Tennessee v. Garner [471 U.S. 1 (1985)], 1932, 2338, **2665–2666**, 2891

Tennessee v. Scopes [154 Tenn. 105 (1925)], 378, 2327, **2666**

Tennessee v. Street [471 U.S. 409 (1985)], 492

Tennessee Coal, Iron & Railroad v. Muscoda Local #123 [321 U.S. 590 (1944)], 967

Tennessee Valley Authority, United States ex rel., v. Welch [327 U.S. 546 (1946)], 889, 2075–2076

Tenney v. Brandhove [341 U.S. 367 (1951)], 1335, 1453, 1558, 1591, 2464, **2667**

Tennie v. City of New York Department of Social Services of the New York City Human Resources Administration [W.L. 6156 (S.D. N.Y. 1987)], 2092

Ten Pound Act Cases [New Hampshire, unreported (1786)], 165, 541

Terminiello v. Chicago [337 U.S. 1 (1949)], 426, 767–768, 1031, 2145, **2669**, 2795

Terrace v. Thompson [263 U.S. 197 (1923)], 129, 131, 1871

Terrett v. Taylor [13 U.S. (9 Cranch) 43 (1815)], 1175, 1287, 1636, 2280, 2556, 2570, 2649, **2671**

Terry v. Adams [345 U.S. 461 (1953)], 1042, 1941, 2007, 2008, 2485, 2492, **2675**

Terry v. Ohio [392 U.S. 1 (1968)], 119–120, 205, 937, 956, 1095, 1912, 1913, 2023, 2140, 2331, 2333, 2336, 2337, 2341, 2450, 2552, 2553, **2675–2676**, 2767, 2939

Test Oath Cases [4 Wallace 277 (1867); 4 Wallace 333 (1867)], 174, 335, 339, 340, 430, 579, 958

Texas, United States v. [162 U.S. 1 (1892)], 1469

Texas v. Brown [460 U.S. 730 (1983)], **2680**

Texas v. Johnson [491 U.S. 397 (1989)], 179, 192, 235, 238, 382, 1053–1054, 1062–1063, 1133, 1530, 2538

Texas v. White [74 U.S. (7 Wall.) 700 (1869)], 336, 339, 340, 580, 746, 999, 1007, 1238, 1424, 1732, 2142, 2143, 2628, 2680, **2680**, 2688

Texas & Pacific Railroad Company v. Interstate Commerce Commission [162 U.S. 197 (1896)], 1266

Texas Industries, Inc. v. Radcliff Materials, Inc. [451 U.S. 630 (1981)], 978

Texas Monthly, Inc. v. Bullock [489 U.S. 1 (1989)], 924, 927, 1208, 2193, 2195, 2380, **2680–2681**

Textile Workers Union v. Darlington Manufacturing Co. [380 U.S. 263 (1965)], 1548

Textile Workers Union v. Lincoln Mills [383 U.S. 448 (1957)], 1468, 1587

Thiel v. Southern Pacific Co. [316 U.S. 698 (1945)], 1515, 2728

Thind, United States v. [261 U.S. 204 (1923)], 129

Thomas v. Arizona [356 U.S. 390 (1958)], 2902

Thomas v. Collins [323 U.S. 516 (1945)], 1549, 1628, 1990, 2302

Thomas v. Review Board of Indiana [450 U.S. 707 (1981)], 2174, 2188, 2192, **2696**

Thomas v. Union Carbide Agricultural Products Co. [473 U.S. 568 (1985)], **2697**

Thompson v. Consolidated Gas Utilities Corp. [300 U.S. 55 (1937)], 1175

Thompson v. Louisville [362 U.S. 199 (1960)], 109

Thompson v. Oklahoma [487 U.S. 815 (1988)], 1843, 2369, **2698–2699**

Thornburg v. Gingles [478 U.S. 30 (1986)], 869, 1188, 2093, 2136, 2811, 2814

Thornburgh v. Abbott [490 U.S. 401 (1989)], 1134

Thornburgh v. American College of Obstetricians and Gynecologists [476 U.S. 747 (1986)], 192, 196, 2451, **2699**, 2892

Thornhill v. Alabama [310 U.S. 88 (1940)], 426, 1192, 1317, 1400, 1550, 1555, 1556, 1769, 1866, 1907, **2699**, 2795

Thornton v. Caldor, Inc. [472 U.S. 703 (1985)], 2193, 2195, 2377, 2585, **2699**

Thorpe v. Rutland Railroad [26 Verm. 140 (1854)], 2507

Tidal Oil Co. v. Flanagan [263 U.S. 444 (1924)], 676

Tileston v. Ullman [318 U.S. 44 (1943)], 1233

Tilton v. Richardson [403 U.S. 372 (1971)], 1207, 2374–2375

Time, Incorporated v. Firestone [424 U.S. (1976)], 2067

Time, Incorporated v. Hill [385 U.S. 374 (1967)], 260, 1107, 1109, 1237, 1270, 2014

Times-Mirror Company v. California [314 U.S. 252 (1941)], **244**

Timmons v. Twin Cities Area New Party [520 U.S. 351 (1997), 1886, 1938, **2701–2702**

Tinker v. Des Moines Independent Community School District [393 U.S. 503 (1969)], 351, 353, 854, 855, 860, 1082, 1281, 2630–2631, **2702–2703**, 2854

Tison v. Arizona [481 U.S. 137 (1987)], 306, 2368

Tollett v. Henderson [411 U.S. 258 (1953)], 2265

Tomanio v. Board of Regents [446 U.S. 478 (1980)], 403

Tony and Susan Alamo Foundation v. Secretary of Labor [471 U.S. 290 (1985)], 2192, 2380

Toomer v. Witsell [334 U.S. 385 (1948)], 157, 1212, 2020, **2705**, 2792

Torcaso v. Watkins [367 U.S. 488 (1961)], 2188, 2190, 2197, **2706**, 2833

Toscanino, United States v. [398 F. Supp. 916 (1974)], 959

Toth, United States ex rel., v. Quarles [350 U.S. 11 (1955)], 1018, 1247, 1727, **2710**

Town of . . . See name inverted, e.g., West Hartford (Town of) v. Operation Rescue

Townsend v. Sain [372 U.S. 293 (1963)], **2710–2711**

Townsend v. Swank [404 U.S. 282 (1971)], 2877

Trade-Mark Cases [100 U.S. 82 (1879)], 2826

Trafficante v. Metropolitan Life Insurance Company [409 U.S. 205 (1972)], 323, 2221

Trans-Missouri Freight Association, United States v. [166 U.S. 290 (1897)], 320, 429, 783, 1244, 1711, 1828, 2298, 2413, **2714–2715**, 2895, 2898

Trans-World Airlines, Inc. v. Hardison [432 U.S. 63 (1977)], 405

Treasury Employees Union v. Von Raab. See National Treasury Employees Union v. Von Raab

Trebilock v. Wilson [79 U.S. (12 Wall.) 687 (1872)], 1753

Tregor's Case [Y.B. Pasch., 8 Edw. III, pl. 26 (1334)], 208

Treigle v. Acme Homestead Association [297 U.S. 189 (1936)], 2510

Trenton (City of) v. New Jersey [262 U.S. 182 (1923)], 362, 1211

Trevett v. Weeden [Rhode Island (1786)], 541, 2602, **2723–2724**

Trial of the Seven Bishops [How. St. Tr. 12:183 (1688)], 2272

Trimble v. Gordon [430 U.S. 762 (1977)], 1326, 1558, 2153, 2155, 2160, **2732–2733**

Trono v. United States [199 U.S. 521 (1905)], 1376

Trop v. Dulles [356 U.S. 86 (1958)], 309, 721, 730, 731, 2041, **2733**, 2851, 2902

Truax v. Corrigan [257 U.S. 312 (1921)], 1547, 1548, 1911, 2029, 2635, 2636, 2638, 2640, **2733**

Truax v. Raich [239 U.S. 33 (1915)], 1310

Trupiano v. United States [334 U.S. 699 (1948)], 119, 1769, 2344

Tucker, United States v. [404 U.S. 443 (1972)], 2367

Tumey v. Ohio [273 U.S. 510 (1927)], 970, 2640–2641

Turkette, United States v. [452 U.S. 576 (1981)], 2111

Turner, In re [455 U.S. 1009 (1867)], 335, 336, 341, 2424

Turner v. Department of Employment Security [423 U.S. 44 (1975)], 2394

Turner v. Fouche [396 U.S. 346 (1970)], 2728

Turner v. Murray [476 U.S. 28 (1986)], 2106

Turner v. Safley [482 U.S. 78 (1987)], 1134, 2012

Turner Broadcasting System v. FCC [512 U.S. 622 (1994)], 249, 469, 691, 969, 1772, **2739–2740**

Turner Broadcasting System v. FCC [520 U.S. 180 (1997)], 249, 691, 1147, 1531

Turpin v. Mailet [2d Cir., en banc, 1978-1979], 514

Twining v. New Jersey [211 U.S. 78 (1908)], 33, 256, 1354, 1665, 1756, 1874, 2233, 2237, **2744**

Two Guys from Harrison-Allentown, Inc. v. McGinley [366 U.S. 852 (1961)], 2191, 2584

Tyler v. Defrees [78 U.S. (11 Wall.) 331 (1870)], 1732

Tyler Pipe Industries, Inc. v. Washington State Department of Revenue [483 U.S. 232 (1987)], 806

Tyson & Brother v. Banton [273 U.S. 418 (1927)], 52, 838, 1115, 1802, 2230, 2311, **2746**

# U

Ullmann v. United States [350 U.S. 422 (1956)], 989, 1334, 2233, 2236, **2747**

"Ulysses," One Book Entitled, United States v. [5 F. Supp. 182 (1933)], **2747–2748**

Umbehr v. Heiser [518 U.S. 668 (1996)], 1886

UMW Post, Inc. v. Board of Regents of Wisconsin [774 F. Supp. 1163 (E.D. Wisc. 1991)], 2926

Underhill v. Hernandez [168 U.S. 250 (1897)], 25

Union Pacific Railroad Co. v. Peniston [85 U.S. (18 Wall.) 5 (1873)], 217

Union Pacific Railroad Co. v. United States [99 U.S. 700 (1879)], **2419–2420**

United Building and Construction Trades Council of Camden County and Vicinity v. Mayor and Council of the City of Camden [465 U.S. 208 (1984)], 363, 1212, 1798, 2020, 2468

United Jewish Organization of Williamsburgh, Inc. v. Carey [430 U.S. 144 (1977)], 794, 1188, 2135, 2137, 2202, **2756**, 2813

United Mine Workers v. Coronado Coal Co. [359 U.S. 344 (1922)], 422, **2756–2757**

United Mine Workers v. Gibbs [383 U.S. 715 (1966)], 1466

United Mine Workers v. Pennington [381 U.S. 657 (1965)], 1545, 1546

United Mine Workers v. United States [330 U.S. 258 (1947)], **2757**, 2792, 2793

United Public Workers v. Mitchell [330 U.S. 75 (1947)], 1275, 2145, 2278, 2795

United Railways & Electric Co. of Baltimore v. West [280 U.S. 234 (1930)], 970, **2758**

United Shoe Machinery Co., United States v. [247 U.S. 32 (1918)], 421, 2298

United States v. . . . *See* case name inverted, e.g., Nixon, United States v.

United States & Canada Express Company, State v. *See* State v. United States & Canada Express Company

United States Civil Service Commission v. National Association of Letter Carriers [413 U.S. 548 (1973)], 251, 268, 1275

United States Coin & Currency, United States v. [401 U.S. 715 (1971)], **1670**

United States Department of Agriculture v. Moreno [413 U.S. 528 (1973)], 428

United States District Court for the Eastern District of Michigan, United States v. [407 U.S. 297 (1972)], 649, 873, 875, 1129, 1781, 1816, 2345, 2449, **2761–2762**, 2842

United States ex rel. Toth v. Quarles. *See* Toth, United States ex rel., v. Quarles

United States Glue Co. v. Town of Oak Creek [247 U.S. 321 (1918)], 2521–2522

United States Postal Service v. Greenburgh Civic Association [453 U.S. 114 (1981)], 1900

United States Railroad Retirement Board v. Fritz [449 U.S. 166 (1980)], 193, 2122, 2536, 2572

United States Steel Corporation, United States v. [251 U.S. 417 (1920)], 421, 749, 2298, 2898

United States Term Limits v. Thornton [514 U.S. 779 (1995)], 76, 624, 989, 1531, 2537, 2670

United States Trust Co. of New York v. New Jersey [431 U.S. 1 (1977)], 70, 676, 677, 1381, 1836, 2665, **2766**

United Steelworkers of America v. Weber [443 U.S. 193 (1979)], 53, 54, 55, 100, 397, 406, 945, 1172, 1435, 2153, 2155, **2766**

Uphaus v. Wyman [360 U.S. 72 (1959)], 187, 1595, **2772**, 2903

Ursery, United States v. [518 U.S. 267 (1996)], 811, 985

Usery v. Turner Elkhorn Mining Co. [428 U.S. 1(1976)], 2226

# V

Vale v. Louisiana [399 U.S. 30 (1970)], 1820, 2332

Valentine v. Chrestensen [316 U.S. 52 (1942)], 460

Vallandigham, Ex parte [68 (1 Wall.) 243 (1864)], 338, 416, 430, 746, 1736, 2628, **2777**, 2868

Valley Forge Christian College v. Americans United for Separation of Church and State [454 U.S. 464 (1982)], 1067, 1443, 2659, 2662, **2777–2778**

Vance v. Bradley [440 U.S. 93 (1979)], 59

Vance v. Terrazas [440 U.S. 970 (1980)], 957

Van Horne's Lessee v. Dorrance [2 U.S. (2 Dall.) 304 (1795)], **290**, 360, 673, 1067, 1883, 2603, **2781**, 2782

Van Huffel v. Harkelrode [283 U.S. 817 (1931)], 161

Vanzant v. Waddel [2 Yeng. (Tenn.) 260 (1829)], 2510

Vasquez v. Hillery [474 U.S. 254 (1986)], 1223

Veazie Bank v. Fenno [75 U.S. (8 Wall.) 533 (1869)], 151, 340, 784, 1753, 1790, 2658, **2781–2782**

Vegelahn v. Guntner [167 Mass. 92 (1869)], 1547

Ventresca, United States v. [380 U.S. 102 (1965)], 1368, 2330

Verdugo-Urquídez, United States v. [494 U.S. 259 (1990)], 960, 1332, 2338

Vermont Yankee Nuclear Power Corp. v. Natural Resources Defense Council [435 U.S. 519 (1978)], 2312

Vernonia School District 47J v. Acton [515 U.S. 646 (1995)], 331, 826–827, 2456

Village of . . . *See* name inverted, e.g., Euclid (Village of) v. Ambler Realty Company

Virginia, Ex parte [100 U.S. 339 (1880)], 2482, **2558–2559**, 2564

Virginia, United States v. [518 U.S. 515 (1996)], 400, 917, 1197, 1824, 2092, 2170, 2307, 2398, 2404, 2418, 2456, **2798**

Virginia v. Browner [80 F. 3d 869 (4th Cir. 1996)], 904

Virginia v. Rives [100 U.S. 313 (1880)], 403, 1787, **2558–2559**, 2564

Virginia v. Tennessee [148 U.S. 503 (1893)], 1072, 1399

Virginia v. West Virginia [78 U.S. (11 Wall.) 39 (1870)], 340, 746

Virginia v. West Virginia [206 U.S. 290 (1907)], 877

Virginia Coupon Cases (1885), 1227

Virginia State Board of Pharmacy v. Virginia Citizens' Consumer Council [425 U.S. 748 (1976)], 165, 190, 193, 194, 461, 462, 836, 1060, 1135, 1628, 2157, 2350–2351, **2800–2801**

Vitek v. Jones [445 U.S. 480 (1980)], 492

Vlandis v. Kline [412 U.S. 441 (1973)], 1405, 2277, 2802

Voinovich v. Quilter [507 U.S. 146 (1993)], 2137

Von Moltke v. Gillies [332 U.S. 708 (1948)], 1436

Von's Grocery Co., United States v. [384 U.S. 270 (1966)], 2542

# W

Wabash, St. Louis & Pacific Railway v. Illinois [118 U.S. 557 (1886)], 455, 846, 1227, 1397, 1698, **2817**

Wabol v. Villacrusis [958 F. 2d 1450 (9th Cir. 1992)], 2672

Wade, United States v. [388 U.S. 218 (1967)], 235, 492, 962, 1083, 1538, 1627, 1852, 2264, **2818**

Wagner Act Cases (1937), 349, 692, 743, 1266, 1311, 2677

Wainwright v. Sykes [433 U.S. 72 (1977)], 18, 35, 239, 975, 1101, 1758, 2156, 2764, **2821**, 2831

Wainwright v. Witt [469 U.S. 412 (1985)], 2803

Walder v. United States [347 U.S. 62 (1954)], 1273, 2045, 2335

Wales v. Stetson [2 Mass. 142 (1806)], 673

Waley v. Johnston [316 U.S. 101 (1942)], 1248

Walker v. Birmingham [388 U.S. 307 (1967)], **2832**

Walker v. Jennison [Mass., unreported (1781)], 467

Walker v. Sauvinet [92 U.S. 90 (1876)], 2724, **2832**

Wallace v. Jaffree [472 U.S. 38 (1985)], 859, 924, 1602, 1603, 1842, 1843, 2157, 2174, 2177, 2193, 2322–2323, 2323, 2373, **2832–2833**

Wallace v. Van Riswick [92 U.S. 202 (1872)], 134

Wallace & Tiernan Company, United States v. [336 U.S. 793 (1949)], 186

Waller v. Florida [397 U.S. 387 (1970)], 809

Waller v. Georgia [467 U.S. 39 (1984)], 1152

Walter v. United States [447 U.S. 649 (1980)], 2332

Walters v. National Association of Radiation Survivors [473 U.S. 305 (1985)], 2033

Walton v. Arizona [497 U.S. 639 (1990)], 2535

Walz v. Tax Commission [397 U.S. 664 (1970)], 464, 1206, 1207, 2191, 2373–2374, **2833**

Ward, United States v. [449 U.S. 851 (1980)], 902

Ward v. Illinois [431 U.S. 767 (1977)], **2833**

Ward v. Rock Against Racism [491 U.S. 781 (1989)], 2167–2168

Ward v. Texas [316 U.S. 547 (1942)], 1924

Warden v. Hayden [387 U.S. 294 (1967)], 956, 1722, 1913, 2339, 2344, 2345, 2767, **2833–2834**, 2834

Warder v. La Belle Creole [1 Pet. Adm. 31, 29 F. Cas. 215 (No. 17, 165) (1792)], 1902

Wardius v. Oregon [412 U.S. 470 (1973)], 971

Wards Cove Packing Co. v. Antonio [490 U.S. 642 (1989)], 99, 396, 407–408, 2107, 2164, 2890

Ware v. Hylton [3 U.S. (3 Dallas) 199 (1796)], 336, 1284, 1404, 1418, 1883, 2603, 2611, **2834**

Waring v. Clarke [46 U.S. (5 How.) 441 (1847)], 2867, 2923

Warth v. Seldin [422 U.S. 490 (1975)], 70, 275, 1464, 1975, 1977, 2220, 2417, 2474–2475, 2565

Washington v. Davis [426 U.S. 229 (1976)], 96, 116, 395, 400, 446, 911, 992, 1232, 1401, 1510, 1875, 1902, 2102, 2164, 2220–2221, 2392, **2862–2863**, 2869, 2887, 2890

Washington v. Glucksberg [521 U.S. 702 (1997)], 2057, 2269–2270, 2307, 2577–2578

Washington v. Harper [494 U.S. 210 (1990)], 790, 1530, 1720, 1884, 1885, 2061, **2863**

Washington v. Seattle School District No. 1 [458 U.S. 457 (1982)], 122, **706**, 785, 786, 1637

Washington v. Texas [388 U.S. 14 (1967)], 479–480, 933

Waters v. Churchill [511 U.S. 661 (1994)], 892, **2866**

Watkins v. United States [354 U.S. 178 (1957)], 163, 421, 1305, 1595, 1702, 2237, 2384, **2866–2867**

Watson, United States v. [423 U.S. 411 (1976)], 119, 121, 2332, 2333

Watson v. Jones [80 U.S. (13 Wall.) 679 (1872)], 2190

Watts, United States v. [519 U.S. 148 (1997)], 811

Watts v. United States [394 U.S. 705 (1969)], 1153

Waugh v. Board of Trustees of the University of Mississippi [237 U.S. 589 (1915)], 1109

Wayman v. Southard [23 U.S. (10 Wheat.) 1 (1825)], 760

Wayte v. United States [470 U.S. 598 (1985)], **2868–2869**

Weatherford v. Bursey [429 U.S. 545 (1977)], 793

Weaver v. Graham [450 U.S. 24 (1981)], 958

Weaver v. Palmer Bros. Co. [270 U.S. 402 (1924)], 284

Weber v. Aetna Casualty and Surety Company [406 U.S. 164 (1972)], 2155

Webster v. Reproductive Health Services [492 U.S. 490 (1989)], 6–7, 9, 11, 12, 93, 192, 196, 381, 625, 1530, 1843, 2078, 2158, 2313, 2454, 2576, **2872**, 2892

Weeks v. United States [232 U.S. 383 (1914)], 61, 355, 882, 936, 956, 1092, 1667, 2334, 2335, 2339, 2340, 2343, 2416, 2417, 2766, 2768, **2872–2873**

Weems v. United States [217 U.S. 349 (1910)], 730, 731, 1376, **2873**

Weinberger v. Salfi [422 U.S. 749 (1975)], 1405, 2445, 2802

Weinberger v. Wiesenfeld [420 U.S. 636 (1975)], 1196, 1587, 2391–2392, 2393, 2445

Weiner v. United States [357 U.S. 349 (1958)], 2149

Weiss v. United States [510 U.S. 163 (1994)], 2386

Welsh v. United States [398 U.S. 333 (1970)], 505, 2173, 2193, 2790

Welsh v. Wisconsin [466 U.S. 740 (1984)], **2881**

Welton v. Missouri [91 U.S. 275 (1876)], 2521

Wengler v. Druggists Mutual Insurance Co. [446 U.S. 142 (1980)], 2392, **2881**

Wesberry v. Sanders [376 U.S. 1 (1964)], 186, 440, 500, 865, 1227, 1306, 1462, 2133, **2881**

Wessman v. Gittens [160 F. 3d 790 (1st Cir. 1998)], 57

West v. Atkins [487 U.S. 42 (1988)], 2018

West Coast Hotel Company v. Parrish [300 U.S. 379 (1937)], 15, 317, 692, 698, 743, 797, 838, 845, 1034, 1116, 1296, 1311, 1313–1314, 1547, 1699, 1714–1715, 1869, 2281, 2289, 2572, 2575, 2752, **2881–2882**, 2921

Western Air Lines, Inc. v. Criswell [472 U.S. 400 (1985)], 59

Western Livestock v. Bureau of Revenue [303 U.S. 250 (1938)], 2522

West Hartford (Town of) v. Operation Rescue [915 F. 2d 92, 103 (. 2d Cir. 1990)], 2112

West Lynn Creamery, Inc. v. Healy [512 U.S. 186 (1994)], 806, 2494, 2495, 2518

Weston, United States v. [448 F. 2d 626 (9th Cir. 1971)], 2367

Weston v. City Council of Charleston [27 U.S. (2 Pet.) 449 (1829)], 1384, 1686, **2882**

West River Bridge Co. v. Dix [47 U.S. (6 How.) 507 (1848)], 675–676, 742, 887–888, 2074, 2653, 2783, 2868, **2882–2883**

Westside Community Schools v. Mergens. *See* Board of Education of the Westside Community Schools v. Mergens

West Virginia ex rel. Dyer v. Sims [341 U.S. 22 (1951)], 901

West Virginia State Board of Education v. Barnette [319 U.S. 624 (1943)], 313, 426, 814, 855, 858, **1064–1066**, 2186, 2188, 2302, 2545–2546, 2574

Whalen v. Roe [429 U.S. 589 (1977)], 482, 800, 2242, 2243, 2245, 2574, **2883**

Wheaton v. Peters [33 U.S. (8 Pet.) 591 (1834)], 685, 977, 1712, 2698, 2883

Wheeler, United States v. [4 U.S. 313 (1978)], 80

Wheeler v. Greene [280 U.S. 49 (1979)], 2498

Wheeler et al., United States v. [254 F. 611 (1912)], 1763

Whitcomb v. Chavis [403 U.S. 124 (1971)], 1765, 2862

White, United States v. [401 U.S. 745 (1971)], 711–712, 873, 875, 1853, 2140, 2236, 2333–2334, 2334, 2896, **2896–2897**

White v. Hart [80 U.S. (13 Wall.) 646 (1872)], 339, 340

White v. Massachusetts Council of Construction Employers [460 U.S. 204 (1983)], 363

White v. Regester [412 U.S. 755 (1973)], 1665, 1765, 2093, 2134, 2814, 2862

White v. Texas [310 U.S. 530 (1940)], 1924

White v. Weiser [412 U.S. 783 (1973)], 1665

Whiteley v. Warden [401 U.S. 560 (1971)], 2023

Whitney v. California [274 U.S. 357 (1927)], 221, 222, 226, 426, 427, 723, 724, 1050, 1107, 1959, 2311, 2319, 2580, 2582, **2901–2902**

Whren v. United States [517 U.S. 806 (1996)], 1097–1098, 2711

Wickard v. Filburn [317 U.S. 111 (1942)], 62, 459, 460, 524, 601, 744, 835, 846, 847, 861, 862, 1192, 1345, 1346, 1396, 1399, 1410, 1549, 1715, 1778, 2046, 2293, 2481, 2549, **2903–2904**

Widmar v. Vincent [454 U.S. 263 (1981)], 169, 203, 906, 926, 1560, 2173, 2177, 2193, 2198, 2323, 2372, **2904**

Wieman v. Updegraff [344 U.S. 183 (1952)], 187, 421, 892, 1648, 1649–1650, 2066, 2749, **2904**

Wiener v. United States [357 U.S. 249 (1958)], 1319

Wilkes v. Wood [19 St.Tr. 1153 (1763)], 1099, 2905

Wilkes Cases [19 How. St. Tr. (1763-1770)], 872, 1186, 1771, 1781, 1912, 2236, 2766, **2905**

Wilkinson v. Leland [27 U.S. (2 Pet.) 627 (1829)], 2649, 2783

Wilkinson v. United States [365 U.S. 399 (1961)], 1305

Will v. Michigan Department of State Police [491 U.S. 58 (1989)], 1529

William, The, United States v. [28 F. Cas. 614 (D. Mass. 1808)], 885

Williams v. Florida [399 U.S. 78 (1970)], 830, 1434, 1516, 1517, 1887, 2443, 2727, **2906**

Williams v. Georgia [349 U.S. 375 (1955)], 420

Williams v. Mississippi [170 U.S. 213 (1898)], 1629, **2906–2907**

Williams v. New York [337 U.S. 241 (1949)], 2367

Williams v. North Carolina [317 U.S. 287 (1942)], 799, 1269

Williams v. Rhodes [393 U.S. 23 (1968)], 158, 872, 1942, 2701

Williams v. United States [189 U.S. 516 (1933)], 419

Williams v. Vermont [472 U.S. 14 (1985)], 2277, **2907**

Williamson v. Lee Optical Company [348 U.S. 483 (1955)], 4, 835–836, 839, 840, 1381, 2542, **2907**

Willow River Power Co., United States v. [324 U.S. 499 (1945)], 2054, 2783

Willson v. Black Bird Creek Marsh Co. [27 U.S. (2 Pet.) 245 (1829)], 1686, 2817, **2908**

Wilson, Ex parte [114 U.S. 417 (1885)], 1031

Wilson v. Garcia [471 U.S. 261 (1985)], 1844

Wilson v. New [243 U.S. 332 (1917)], 33, 421, 748, 1699, **2912**

Wilson v. Seiter [501 U.S. 294 (1991)], 654

Wilton v. Seven Falls Co. [515 U.S. 277 (1995)], 20

Winona and St. Peter Railroad v. Blake [94 U.S. 180 (1877)], **1224–1225**

Winship, In re [397 U.S. 358 (1970)], 238, 264, 718, 816, 1184, 1355, 1523, 2041, 2139, 2255, **2912**

Winston v. Lee [470 U.S. 753 (1985)], 206, 1094–1095, 2338, 2767–2768

Winters v. New York [333 U.S. 507 (1948)], 2794

Winthrop v. Larkin [421 U.S. 35 (1975)], 2149

Wiscart v. D'Auchy [3 U.S. (3 Dall.) 321 (1796)], 882, 2617

Wisconsin v. Mitchell [508 U.S. 476 (1993)], 1276, 1278, 2124, **2913–2914**

Wisconsin v. New York [517 U.S. 1 (1996)], 326

Wisconsin v. Yoder [406 U.S. 205 (1972)], 270–271, 353, 506, 854, 858, 894, 895, 974, 1049, 2174, 2181–2182, 2187, 2192, 2194, 2377, **2914**

Witherspoon v. Illinois [391 U.S. 510 (1968)], 2442, 2803

Withrow v. Williams [507 U.S. 680 (1993)], 2456

Witte v. United States [515 U.S. 389 (1995)], 811

Witters v. Washington Department of Services for the Blind [474 U.S. 481 (1986)], 61, 924, 926, 1208, 1209, 1604, 2322, 2378, **2916–2917**

Wittmer v. Peters [87 F. 3d 916 (7th Cir. 1996)], 57

Wolf v. Colorado [338 U.S. 25 (1949)], 882, 936, 1405, 1462, 1666, 1870, 2038–2039, 2224, 2334, 2416, 2796, **2917**

Wolff v. McDonnell [418 U.S. 539 (1974)], 492, 897, 2011, 2012, 2013

Wolff Packing Co. v. Court of Industrial Relations [262 U.S. 522 (1923)], 52, 1115, 2281, 2635, 2639, 2746, **2917**

Wolman v. Walter [433 U.S. 229 (1977)], 349, 2375, **2917**

Women's Medical Professional Corporation v. Voinovich [130 F. 3d 187 (6th Cir. 1997)], 14

Wong Kim Ark, In re [71 F. 282 (1897)], 1763

Wong Kim Ark, United States v. [169 U.S. 649 (1898)], 129, 131, 367, 1167, 1227, 1763, **2922**

Wong Sun v. United States [371 U.S. 471 (1963)], 121, 1157, 2330, 2336, 2417, **2922**

Wong Wing v. United States [163 U.S. 228 (1896)], 1329, 1330, 2414

Wong Yang Sung v. McGrath [339 U.S. 33 (1950)], 266

Wood v. Lovett [313 U.S. 362 (1941)], 677

Wood v. Strickland [420 U.S. 308 (1975)], 944, 2319, **2922**

Woodruff v. Parham [75 U.S. (8 Wall.) 123 (1869)], 341, 1864, **2923**

Woods v. Cloyd W. Miller Company [333 U.S. 138 (1948)], **2924**

Woodson v. North Carolina [428 U.S. 280 (1976)], 301, **310–312**

Wooley v. Maynard [430 U.S. 705 (1977)], 2574

Woolmington v. D.P. [A.C.462 (English) (1935)], 718

Wooster v. Plymouth [51 N.H. 193 (1882)], 802

Worcester v. Georgia [31 U.S. (6 Pet.) 515 (1832)], 81, 325, **343–345**, 1408, 1535, 1612, 1685, 1712, 2698

Worrall, United States v. [2 U.S. (2 Dall.) 384 (1798)], 337, 980, 1902

Worthen Co. v. Kavanaugh [295 U.S. 56 (1935)], 677

Wright v. Deacon [5 Serg. & R. 62 (Penn., 1819)], 1159
Wright v. Rockefeller [376 U.S. 52 (1965)], 1188, 2202
Wright v. United States [302 U.S. 583 (1938)], 1921, 2784
Wright v. Vinton Branch of Mountain Trust Bank of Roanoke [300 U.S. 440 (1937)], 161, 1105, 1175, 1645, **2932**
Wrightwood Dairy Co., United States v. [315 U.S. 110 (1942)], 63, 2415, **2932–2933**
Wurts v. Hoagland [114 U.S. 606 (1885)], 1227
Wyatt v. Aderholt [503 F. 2d 1305 (5th Cir. 1974)], 789
Wyatt v. Stickney [344 F. Supp. 387 (1971)], 1374
Wygant v. Jackson Board of Education [476 U.S. 267 (1986)], 55, 57, 915, 1435, 1723, 1843, 1978, 2106, 2398, 2536–2537, 2538, **2933–2934**
Wyman v. James [400 U.S. 309 (1971)], 42, 192, 2468, 2767, **2934**
Wynehamer v. People of New York [13 N.Y. 378 (1856)], 562, 844, 1572, 2050, 2409, 2649, **2934–2935**

# Y

Yakus v. United States [321 U.S. 414 (1944)], 886, 887, 2841, **2937**
Yamashita, In re [327 U.S. 1 (1947)], 2302, 2931, **2937–2938**
Yamataya v. Fisher [189 U.S. 86 (1903)], 129
Yarbrough, Ex parte [110 U.S. 651 (1884)], 423, 1041, 1733, 1940, 2823, 2825, **2938**
Yasui v. United States [320 U.S. 115 (1943)], 129
Yates v. United States [354 U.S. 298 (1957)], 68, 187, 226, 427, 428, 511, 709, 769, 770, 815, 1109, 1198, 1296, 1870–1871, 2581, 2867, **2938–2939**
Ybarra v. Illinois [444 U.S. 85 (1979)], 2023–2024, **2939**
Yerger, Ex parte [75 U.S. (8 Wall.) 85 (1869)], 339, 340, 1256, 1701
Yick Wo v. Hopkins [118 U.S. 356 (1886)], 129, 130, 368, 388, 907, 1038, 1167, 1331, 1698, 2059, 2828, 2829, **2939–2940**
Yonkers Board of Education, United States v. [486 U.S. 1055 (1987)], 2221

Young, Ex parte [209 U.S. 123 (1908)], 652, 739, 853, 877, 878–879, 880, 904, 1166, 1167, 1217, 1343, 1373, 1504, 1739, 1893, 2349, 2504, **2940**
Young v. American Mini Theatres, Inc. [427 U.S. 50 (1976)], 1048, 1236, 1839, 2529, 2776–2777, **2940**
Young v. Miller [883 F. 2d 1276 (6th Cir. 1989)], 822
Young v. New York City Transit Authority [903 F. 2d 146 (2d Cir. 1990)], 1301
Youngberg v. Romeo [457 U.S. 307 (1982)], 729, 1718–1719, 1721, 1885, 2061
Younger v. Harris [401 U.S. 37 (1971)], 18, 275, 447, 803, 1008, 1373, 1375, 1750, 1865, 2280, 2284, **2940–2941**
Youngstown Sheet & Tube Company v. Sawyer [343 U.S. 579 (1952)], 185, 279, 377, 420, 433, 649, 748, 951, 1010, 1344, 1347, 1569, 1995, 1996, 2145, 2384, 2448, 2460, 2592, 2735, 2792, 2793, 2839, 2842, 2843, 2844, **2941**

# Z

Zablocki v. Redhail [434 U.S. 374 (1978)], 799, 1118, 1123, 1671–1672, 1724, 2307, 2573, **2943**
Zacchini v. Scripps-Howard Broadcasting Co. [433 U.S. 562 (1977)], 686, 1377, 2014
Zant v. Stephens [462 U.S. 862 (1983)], 303
Zemel v. Rusk [381 U.S. 1 (1965)], 1950, 2146, 2276, **2943**
Zenger's Case [New York (1735)], 180, 374, 1138, 1260, 1512, 1870, 1897, 2352–2353, **2944**
Zicarelli v. Dietz [406 U.S. 472 (1980)], 2787
Zinermon v. Burch [494 U.S. 113 (1990)], 2035
Zobel v. Williams [457 U.S. 55 (1982)], 428, 1812, 2020, 2275–2276, 2277, 2305, 2907
Zobrest v. Catalina Foothills School District [509 U.S. 1 (1993)], 61, 1209, 1604, 2456
Zorach v. Clausen [343 U.S. 306 (1952)], 24, 1704, 2145, 2171–2172, 2371, 2372, 2795
Zschernig v. Miller [389 U.S. 429 (1968)], 25, 1073, 1390
Zurcher v. Stanford Daily [436 U.S. 547 (1978)], 1143, 1722, 1822, 2200, 2890, **2947–2948**

# Name Index

*Numbers in **boldface** refer to the main entry on the subject.*

## A

Abraham, Kenneth, 627
Abrams, Jacob, 1710
Acheson, Dean, 1101
Ackerman, Bruce, 77, 524, 525, 659–660, 764, 1291, 1826, 2174
Acton, John, 376
Adair, Douglas, 1260
Adams, Charles Francis, 3
Adams, Henry, **26**, 665, 676
Adams, John, **26–30**, 30, 32, 65, 67, 125, 228, 337, 489, 515, 534, 549, 550, 551, 697, 705, 737, 752, 755, 836, 883, 954, 1016, 1034, 1058, 1156, 1174, 1257, 1418, 1419, 1420, 1423, 1424, 1497, 1610, 1667, 1673, 1681, 1695, 1756, 1866, 1883, 1934, 1963, 2297, 2499, 2579, 2590, 2600, 2601, 2609, 2662, 2785, 2805, 2837, 2860, 2862
Adams, John Quincy, 29, **30–31**, 162, 288, 289, 291, 385, 416, 424, 556, 557, 559, 560, 563, 564, 728, 866, 867, 1408, 1412, 1425, 1684, 1712, 1754, 1755, 2001, 2119, 2131, 2554, 2555, 2590, 2611, 2656, 2687, 2700, 2732, 2805, 2884, 2913

Adams, Samuel, 26, **31–32**, 85, 1284, 1323, 1664, 1694–1695, 2347, 2781
Addams, Jane, 78
Agee, Philip, 1256–1257
Agnew, Spiro T., 609
Agresto, John, 1459
Akerman, Ames T., 134, 1225
Alberdi, Juan Bautista, 1367
Albright, Madeleine, 2003
Alexander, James, 2944
Allen, Florence, 2612, 2763
Allen, William B., 93
Althusius, Johannes, 634
Alvarez-Machain, Humberto, 71
Amar, Akhil, 1503
Ambrose, Spenser, 1897–1898
Ames, Fisher, 32, **88**
Ames, James Barr, 1101
Amory, Rufus G., 2611
Amsterdam, Anthony, 1093
Andros, Sir Edmund, 2183
Annan, Kofi, 2003
Anne, Queen of England, 532
Anthony, Susan Brownell, **91–92**, 370, 1092, 1319, 2477, 2806–2808, 2918
Aquinas, Thomas, 369
Archer, Sir John, 1338
Arenella, Peter, 2240

Aristide, Jean-Bertrand, 2003
Aristotle, 185, 343, 634, 668, 1946, 1949, 2297, 2346
Armstrong, Scott, 508
Arnold, Richard S., 1440
Arnold, Thurman, **119**, 435, 453, 665
Arrow, Kenneth, 870
Arthur, Chester A., **121**, 198, 240, 504, 1164, 1182, 2001–2002, 2786
Ashley, James, 2540
Attucks, Crispus, 2431
Augustine, Saint, 374
Austin, John, 2462

## B

Bache, Benjamin, 980
Backus, Isaac, **145**
Bacon, Augustus O., 930
Bailey, Gamaliel, 3
Bailyn, Bernard, 1323
Baker, George F., 1594
Baker, Howard, 1402
Bakke, Allan, 54, 1978
Baldridge, Homer, 2735
Baldwin, Abraham, **155–156**, 1611, 2682

Baldwin, Henry, **157**, 344, 360, 1238, 1412, 1686, 2555, 2651
Baldwin, Roger N., 78, **157**, 921, 2324
Ballinger, Richard A., 219
Bancroft, George, **159**, 443
Barber, Benjamin, 1947
Barbour, Philip P., **162**, 557, 1412, 1700, 2652
Barker, Ernest, 1563
Barrett, Edward, 2516
Bassett, Richard, **164**
Bates, Edward, **164**, 886
Bator, Paul, 1502
Batson, James, 165
Bayard, James A., 2362
Beale, Robert, 1098
Beard, Charles A., 159, **166–167**, 452, 528, 545, 754, 834, 1380, 1660, 1711, 2047
Beauvoir, Simone de, 907
Beck, James M., 452
Becker, Frank J., 167
Beckley, John, 1058
Bedford, Gunning, Jr., 48, 544
Beer, Lawrence Ward, 1365
Begin, Menachem, 320
Belknap, William, 319
Bell, Derrick, 2222
Bell, Griffin B., 135, 1359
Bell, John, 747
Bellah, Robert, 665
Belz, Herman, 776
Benjamin, Judah P., 2884, 2914
Bennett, Robert, 127
Bentham, Jeremy, 526, 1387, 2053
Bentley, Arthur, 2047
Benton, Thomas Hart, **169**, 704, 1161, 1412
Berger, Raoul, 631, 952, 1086, 1860, 1861, 2754
Berkeley, John, 1799–1800
Berle, Adolph, 591
Berlin, Isaiah, 2778
Berns, Walter, 895
Bernstein, Richard, 1984
Beveridge, Albert J., **171**, 841, 1669, 1705, 1706, 1707
Bickel, Alexander M., 113, **173**, 365, 453, 632, 655, 658, 661, 767, 912, 1086, 1477, 1478, 1542, 1587, 1634, 1760, 1792, 2244, 2491, 2525, 2635, 2713–2714
Biddle, Francis, 65, **173**, 1416, 2290, 2930
Biddle, Nicholas, 160
Biden, Joseph, 209, 1813, 1814
Bingham, John A., 4, 178, **180–181**, 1085, 1088, 1091, 1357, 1528, 2425

Bin Laden, Osama, 2003
Binney, Horace, **181**, 2611
Birney, James G., 3, **181–182**, 334, 560
Bivens, Webster, 185
Black, Charles, 1502, 1792
Black, Charles L., Jr., 255, 630, 1792, 1861, 2108, 2490
Black, Hugo L., 1, 17, 33, 34, 59, 65, 70, 104, 112, 116, 118, 131–132, 157, 164, 166, 168, 179, 185, **185–188**, 201, 204, 226, 244, 253, 276, 279, 280, 317, 381, 383, 420, 427, 440, 441, 458, 603, 604, 667, 696, 699, 710, 720, 739, 769, 786, 787, 807, 814, 815, 816, 830, 838–839, 855–856, 861, 896, 906, 927, 929, 930, 931, 959, 960, 970, 1008, 1034, 1065, 1082, 1086, 1101, 1102, 1103, 1106, 1139, 1140, 1149, 1175, 1192, 1194, 1213, 1231, 1232, 1233, 1235, 1236, 1240, 1256, 1269, 1271, 1288, 1289, 1320, 1355, 1410, 1411, 1415, 1417, 1436, 1447, 1450, 1527, 1538, 1565, 1585–1586, 1591, 1645, 1672, 1702, 1704, 1709, 1716–1717, 1769, 1806, 1810, 1820, 1849, 1856, 1864–1865, 1870–1871, 1874, 1896, 1922, 1924, 1925, 1996, 2021, 2037, 2076, 2079, 2133, 2145, 2159, 2170, 2171, 2246, 2262, 2282, 2283, 2284, 2289, 2292–2293, 2294, 2296, 2302, 2323, 2370, 2408, 2414, 2458, 2510, 2541, 2545, 2546, 2548, 2549, 2562, 2572, 2581, 2582, 2583, 2593, 2604, 2624, 2703, 2706, 2714, 2747, 2793, 2794, 2795, 2796, 2811, 2849, 2851, 2853, 2855, 2896, 2906, 2912, 2930–2931, 2941, 2947
Black, Jeremiah S., **188–189**, 200, 1736
Blackmun, Harry A., 7, 8, 10, 12, 14, 15, 72, 157, 185, **189–196**, 212, 213, 242, 272, 274, 279, 293, 301, 304, 306, 307, 327, 359, 376, 436, 465, 687, 695, 706, 713, 733, 775, 783, 785, 790, 839, 895, 907, 1012, 1054, 1055, 1082, 1140, 1181, 1202, 1219, 1273, 1283, 1291, 1332, 1518, 1602, 1651, 1665, 1703, 1709, 1749, 1776, 1806, 1817, 1831, 1845, 1915, 1916, 2070, 2081, 2094, 2104, 2123, 2141, 2157, 2161, 2204, 2206, 2231, 2246, 2247, 2284–2285, 2313, 2314, 2379, 2391, 2441, 2537, 2561, 2574, 2583, 2607, 2681, 2699, 2766, 2872, 2907, 2917, 2934
Blackstone, William, 84, **196–197**, 208, 245, 361, 373, 440, 450, 501, 512, 593, 641, 661, 681, 753, 828, 836, 842, 1034, 1035, 1049, 1098, 1138, 1177,

1217, 1337, 1338, 1596, 1606, 1640, 1674, 1695, 1807, 1868, 2052, 2057, 2225, 2236, 2252, 2346, 2382, 2461, 2506, 2507, 2716, 2725, 2737, 2787, 2834, 2946
Blaine, James G., 197, 587, 1265
Blair, Francis Preston, 1412
Blair, Henry W., 587
Blair, John, **198**, 467, 1279, 2600, 2601, 2603, 2861
Blatchford, Samuel, **198–199**, 346, 694, 2748, 2894
Bloch, Charles J., 452
Blount, William, **199**, 2358
Blumberg, Abraham, 2444
Bluntschli, J. K., 2737
Blyew, John, 200
Bobitt, Philip, 657
Bodin, Jean, 2461
Boggs, Danny, 14
Bolingbroke, Lord, 84
Bollman, Erik, 705
Bonaparte, Charles J., 134–135, 976
Bond, Hugh Lennox, **207**
Bonham, Thomas, 208
Booth, John Wilkes, 2476
Booth, Sherman M., 1, 2432
Borah, William E., 595, 2883
Borden, Lizzie, 1756
Bork, Robert H., 50, 114–115, 209, 507–508, 658, 667, 699, 1291, 1394, 1543, 1612–1613, 1801, 1813, 1860, 1861, 1862, 2121, 2127, 2161, 2246, 2248, 2313, 2314, 2326, 2364, 2454, 2455
Boudin, Louis B., **212**, 453
Boudinot, Elias, 2611
Bourne, Randolph, 662
Bouvia, Elizabeth, 2269
Bowditch, William I., 3
Boyd, James Edmund, 2676–2677
Bracton, Henry, 2297
Bradley, Joseph P., 52, 199, 201, 211–212, 215–216, **216–218**, 218, 336, 338, 340, 341, 342, 346, 358–359, 360, 403, 408, 409, 479, 909, 1185, 1225, 1581, 1753, 2141, 2420, 2423, 2424, 2482, 2507, 2563, 2564, 2628, 2817, 2821, 2823, 2826–2827, 2828, 2923
Bradley, Stephen R., 2429
Bradwell, Myra, 218, 342, 2612, 2920
Brandagee, Frank, 2928
Brandeis, Louis D., 15, 32, 35, 49, 52, 112, 113, 128, 142, 146, 167, 173, 215, **219–222**, 222–225, 241, 278, 285, 314, 317, 321, 348, 375, 377, 388, 421, 426, 427, 441, 457, 458, 468, 495, 595, 709, 711, 719, 721, 723, 724, 792, 831, 864, 872, 873, 921, 970, 977, 998,

1018, 1030, 1050, 1103, 1107, 1129, 1155, 1175, 1198, 1263, 1269, 1274, 1292, 1299, 1314, 1319, 1321, 1352, 1425, 1438, 1444, 1456, 1606, 1633–1634, 1645, 1646, 1681, 1710, 1715, 1760, 1772, 1802, 1849–1850, 1851, 1869, 1874, 1911, 1955, 1987, 2047, 2060, 2115, 2156, 2230, 2241–2242, 2246, 2281, 2310, 2313, 2319, 2325, 2326, 2352, 2437, 2440, 2443, 2445, 2446, 2454, 2502, 2531, 2543, 2544, 2545, 2549, 2573, 2580, 2592, 2593, 2634–2635, 2636, 2637, 2640, 2641, 2642, 2646, 2713, 2733, 2746, 2758, 2780, 2794, 2820, 2855, 2884, 2897, 2899, 2900, 2901, 2902, 2911, 2932

Brandenburg, Clarence, 1136

Brandhove, William, 2667

Brant, Irving, **226**

Braxton, Carter, 246, 537, 2499

Brearly, David, **228**, 520, 521

Breckenridge, John, **228**, 747, 1668

Brennan, William J., Jr., 1, 7, 54, 56, 63, 64, 71, 119, 133, 137, 152, 164, 179, 184, 185, 190, 192, 200, 203, **229–240**, 242, 251, 272, 277, 281, 293, 296, 300, 301, 304, 309, 310, 311, 312, 316–317, 327, 350, 369, 380, 440, 444–445, 465, 482, 508–509, 666, 676, 677, 687, 695, 704, 707, 718, 720, 748, 773, 778, 790, 815, 830, 863, 878, 890, 895, 897, 899, 907, 916, 927, 929, 930, 935, 975, 982, 983, 987, 994, 1012, 1054, 1060, 1062, 1063, 1064, 1068, 1106, 1117–1118, 1120, 1125, 1127, 1140, 1157, 1181, 1189, 1194, 1197, 1199, 1202, 1203, 1214, 1229, 1239, 1240, 1273, 1281, 1283, 1285, 1286, 1293, 1327, 1332, 1367, 1401, 1411, 1414, 1426, 1427, 1435, 1450, 1458–1459, 1480, 1481, 1527, 1535, 1538, 1563, 1587, 1602, 1634, 1653, 1665, 1672, 1680, 1703, 1709, 1716, 1723, 1724, 1730, 1735, 1737, 1758, 1776, 1789, 1806, 1810, 1812, 1822, 1837–1838, 1844, 1845, 1851, 1856, 1859, 1877, 1879, 1885, 1888, 1893, 1900, 1902, 1920, 1969, 2033, 2082, 2106, 2127, 2136, 2141, 2149, 2155, 2161, 2168, 2196, 2199, 2200, 2204, 2210, 2214, 2247, 2266, 2267, 2276, 2277, 2295, 2296, 2300, 2306, 2313, 2317, 2319, 2325, 2335, 2338, 2364, 2370–2371, 2379, 2395, 2408, 2412, 2417, 2422, 2438, 2445, 2452, 2453, 2455, 2475, 2476, 2498, 2502, 2548, 2573, 2607, 2646, 2665, 2680–2681, 2697, 2712, 2733, 2750, 2756, 2766, 2777,

2832, 2849, 2854, 2862, 2869, 2881, 2893, 2907, 2912, 2914, 2934

Brest, Paul, 657, 658, 1395

Brewer, David J., 52, 112, **240–242**, 263, 330, 750–751, 893, 1164, 1168, 1169, 1267, 1273, 1344, 1415, 1764, 1828, 1897, 2129–2130, 2414, 2437, 2633, 2897

Breyer, Stephen G., **242–243**, 297, 307, 312, 431, 433, 1530–1531, 1627, 2083, 2168, 2270, 2387, 2419, 2455, 2456

Brezhnev, Leonid, 616

Bricker, John, 243, 603, 1389, 1921

Bridges, Harry, 244

Brill, Alida, 1577

Bristow, Benjamin, 200, 1265

Brooks, Preston, 2584

Broom, Jacob, **252**

Brown, Edmund, 2125, 2848

Brown, Henry B., **252–253**, 257, 1036, 1162, 1164, 1169, 1227, 1273, 1294, 1376, 1704, 1756, 1918, 1919, 1960

Brown, John, 1955, 2715, 2718

Brownell, Herbert, 135, 976

Brownmiller, Susan, 1838

Bryan, William Jennings, 1165, 1375, 2048, 2437, 2501, 2666, 2894

Bryce, James, **257–258**, 499, 1338, 2501

Buchanan, James, 189, **258–259**, 325, 338, 429, 430, 565, 566, 570, 1230, 1413, 1526, 1574, 1620, 1625, 1686, 1822, 1901, 1962, 2064, 2435–2436, 2476, 2480, 2539, 2655

Buck, Carrie, 791

Burdick, Alan, 265

Burger, Warren E., 64, 112, 137, 158, 165, 172, 185, 189, 190, 192, 204, 214, 242, **269–272**, 272, 273, 275, 277, 301, 317, 406, 440, 447, 699, 712, 794, 830, 831, 863, 906, 907, 935, 1049, 1068, 1140, 1151, 1172, 1189, 1199, 1202, 1214, 1215, 1273, 1333, 1394, 1453, 1459, 1536, 1557, 1562, 1575, 1599, 1601–1602, 1648, 1653, 1655, 1672, 1679, 1734, 1737, 1757, 1806, 1811, 1817, 1846, 1857, 1876, 1878, 1899, 1920, 1922, 1976, 2077, 2105, 2152, 2157, 2159, 2160, 2168, 2196, 2205, 2208, 2231, 2271, 2276, 2277, 2285, 2351, 2385, 2443, 2579, 2594, 2605, 2606, 2623, 2627, 2663, 2699, 2756, 2833, 2850, 2851, 2865, 2914, 2917

Burgess, John W., **278**, 452, 588

Burke, Aedanus, 177

Burke, Edmund, 29, 197, 377, 693, 1874

Burke, John, 980

Burke, Thomas, 538

Burlamacqui, Jean-Jacques, 752

Burns, Lucy, 2918

Burr, Aaron, 207, **278**, 550, 552, 866, 1674, 1688, 1934, 2346, 2561, 2740, 2785, 2913, 2931

Burton, Harold, 112, 114, **279–280**, 804, 815, 830, 931, 1436, 1704, 1761, 2294, 2793, 2867, 2941

Bush, George H. W., 12, 86, 92–93, 115, **280–282**, 407, 431, 432, 617, 623, 625, 776, 969, 1063, 1079, 1242, 1304, 1680, 1826, 1916, 1933, 2002, 2003, 2160, 2161, 2168, 2453, 2454, 2455, 2695, 2786, 2814, 2843, 2844

Butler, Andrew, 2583–2584

Butler, Benjamin F., **283**, 504, 884, 1339, 1736

Butler, Pierce (1744–1822), **283**, 502, 517, 1610, 2544, 2637

Butler, Pierce (1866–1939), 228, 259, 278, **283–284**, 317, 362, 441, 457, 458, 697, 921, 1101, 1261, 1264, 1284, 1311, 1314, 1760, 2326, 2636, 2637

Byrd, Harry F., 2458

Byrd, Robert C., 626, 1627, 2361

Byrnes, James F., **285–286**, 861, 2289, 2292–2293, 2302, 2548

# C

Cabell, Samuel J., 980

Cady, Margaret Livingston, 2476

Cahn, Edmond, 15, **290**, 1991

Cahn, Jean Camper, 1975

Calabresi, Steven, 990

Caldwell, John, 467

Caldwell, Seth, 467

Calhoun, John C., 31, 110, 156, 169, **290–293**, 384, 385, 451, 522, 556, 557, 558, 559, 560, 563, 565, 566, 567, 569, 747, 754, 957, 1392, 1412, 1425, 1612, 1706, 1755, 1832–1833, 2201, 2346, 2359, 2434, 2457, 2519, 2527, 2651, 2663, 2687, 2799, 2871

Callendar, John, 337

Callender, James T., 67, 1339, 2913

Calley, William, 1954

Calvert, Cecil, 1691

Calvert, George, 1647

Camden, Lord. *See* Pratt, Charles (Lord Camden)

Campbell, John A., **298–299**, 325, 801, 2423, 2424, 2783–2784

Cannon, Joseph G., 589, 1825

Cantwell, Jesse, 299

Cantwell, Newton, 299

Cantwell, Russell, 299

Cardozo, Benjamin N., 112–113, 128, 219, 221, 285, **313–316**, 317, 321, 376, 441, 457, 458, 601, 677, 1027, 1155, 1176, 1263, 1283, 1284, 1303, 1314, 1355, 1438, 1532, 1563, 1715, 1760, 1855, 1874, 1875, 1877, 1982, 1990, 2038, 2115, 2156, 2281, 2293, 2317–2318, 2445, 2446, 2523, 2540, 2541, 2572, 2589, 2592, 2634, 2713, 2809, 2820, 2898, 2901

Carloss, Helen, 2612

Carmichael, Stokely, 412

Carpenter, Matthew H., **318–319**, 2423

Carr, Robert K., **319**, 738

Carroll, Daniel, **319**

Carswell, G. Harrold, 49, 112, 114–115, 191, 699, 1817, 2364

Carter, James Coolidge, **320**, 357, 1876, 1921, 1959, 1960, 1993, 1994, 2003, 2127, 2160, 2357, 2362

Carter, Jimmy, 97, 112, 114, 289, **320**, 598, 614–615, 616, 617, 741, 942, 1002, 1003, 1019, 1196, 1359, 1704, 2785, 2786, 2842

Carter, Robert L., 772

Carteret, George, 1799–1800

Cartwright, Thomas, 2236

Cary, John W., **321–322**

Cass, Lewis, 3, 563, 566, 569, 1962, 2435

Castro, Fidel, 1532, 1534

Cato, 324

Catron, John, 258, **325**, 338, 1230, 2022, 2435

Catt, Carrie Chapman, 2918

Celler, Emmanuel, 167, 2744

Chafee, Zechariah, Jr., **328–329**, 592, 1255, 1299, 1606, 1607, 1716, 1736, 1959, 2935

Chambers, Julius L., 1774

Chambers, Whittaker, 604, 1305, 1595

Chandler, Douglas, 2931

Charles I, 444, 529, 1173, 1693, 1903, 2382

Charles II, 532, 1892, 2230, 2382

Chase, Salmon P., 3, 182, 218, **334–336**, 337, 339, 340, 342, 360, 560, 567, 746, 1238, 1581–1582, 1652, 1701, 1727, 1732, 1736, 1752–1753, 2142, 2216, 2389, 2591, 2612, 2628, 2680, 2782, 2806

Chase, Samuel, 111, 290, **336–337**, 376, 498, 552, 561, 667, 844, 958, 980, 1156, 1175, 1194, 1286–1287, 1339, 1340, 1456, 1478, 1668, 1673, 1682, 1684, 1688, 1821, 1883, 2116, 2209, 2284, 2424, 2570, 2591, 2601, 2602, 2649, 2763, 2783, 2834, 2859

Child, Lydia Maria, 4

Chipman, Nathaniel, **356**, 449

Choate, Joseph H., **356–357**, 1165, 1764, 1959, 1960

Choate, Rufus, 2611

Choper, Jesse, 1460

Churchill, Cheryl, 2866

Churchill, Winston, 374, 2929

Cicero, 634, 1286, 1731, 2297, 2346

Claiborne, Harry, 1341

Clark, Charles E., **420**

Clark, David, 2676–2677

Clark, Grenville, 2290

Clark, Homer, Jr., 46

Clark, Jonas, 2439–2440, 2899

Clark, Kenneth, 772, 2441, 2443

Clark, Ramsey, 420

Clark, Tom C., 1, 136, 152, 229, 279, 280, **410–421**, 696, 750, 855, 929, 1150, 1231, 1240, 1405, 1426, 1486, 1595, 1649–1650, 1666, 1667, 1676, 1717, 1741, 1991, 2228, 2262, 2344, 2607, 2791, 2793, 2852, 2867, 2903, 2904, 2941

Clarke, John H., 32, 151, 831, 864, 1030, 1292, 1715, 1911, 2230, 2635, 2637, 2900

Clay, Henry, 30, 88, 110, 169, 292, **423–425**, 477, 555, 556, 559, 565, 812, 845, 1228, 1385, 1408, 1409, 1557, 1701, 1706, 1710, 1732, 2359, 2431, 2662, 2859, 2871, 2884, 2885, 2935

Clayton, Henry, 425

Clayton, John M., 566, 2435

Cleland, John, 1716

Cleveland, Grover, 114, 241, **429–430**, 582, 681, 751, 755, 920, 1160, 1164, 1182, 1409, 1559, 1711, 1784, 1890, 2291, 2733, 2785, 2894, 2897

Clifford, Nathan, 338, **430–431**, 1581, 1582, 1636, 2022, 2559, 2564, 2824, 2827

Clinton, DeWitt, 2740

Clinton, George, 2938

Clinton, Hillary, 625–626

Clinton, Robert, 1503

Clinton, William J., 13, 34, 102, 127, 242, 249, 282, **431–433**, 433, 434, 623, 625, 776, 777, 954, 1078–1079, 1080, 1340, 1343, 1360, 1626–1627, 1784, 1826, 1840, 2002–2003, 2168, 2182, 2386, 2405, 2814, 2844

Clymer, George, **434**

Cobb, Howell, 2527

Coffin, William Sloane, 709

Cohen, Dan, 436

Cohen, Felix S., 2053

Cohen, Lloyd, 2058

Cohen, Morris R., **435**, 1192, 2053, 2572

Cohen, Willliam, 2276

Coke, Sir Edward, 208, 363, **439–440**, 512, 634, 638, 641, 828, 1098, 1286, 1321, 1352, 1473, 1571, 1664, 1866, 1888, 1903, 2234, 2236, 2356, 2569, 2716, 2718, 2787

Coker, Ehrlich, 440

Cole, David, 1196

Collins, larry, 442

Commager, Henry Steele, **447–448**, 1365

Commons, John R., 692

Condorcet, Marquis de (Marie-Jean Caritat), 870

Conkling, Roscoe, 4, **504**, 1182, 1900

Connally, Thomas T., **504**, 2362

Connor, Bull, 379

Convitz, Milton R., 738

Cooke, Jay, 1594

Cooley, Thomas M., 196, 197, 451, 583, 584, 593, 674, **680–681**, 1288, 1350, 1711, 1736, 2075, 2346, 2347, 2508, 2512, 2571, 2701, 2712–2713, 2830, 2831

Coolidge, Calvin, 590, 593, 594, 595, **682**, 1025, 1262, 1263, 1358, 1842, 2543, 2548, 2634, 2637, 2786

Cooper, Thomas, 67, **683**, 1832, 2346

Coplon, Judith, 946

Corcoran, Tom, 1101

Corwin, Edward S., 452, 453, **693–694**, 698, 827, 927, 946, 995, 1036, 1227, 1244, 1339, 1396, 1474, 1485, 1607, 1634, 1753, 1960, 1986, 2641, 2782, 2834, 2835, 2836, 2935

Corwin, Thomas, 694

Cosby, William, 2944

Cotton, John, 1694

Cover, Robert M., 527, **701–702**

Covington, Hayden, 1065, 2189

Cox, Archibald, 152, 153, 209, 1359, 1997, 2204–2205, 2228, 2449, 2450, 2853

Cox, James, 1264

Cramer, Anthony, 705, 1279

Cranch, William, **705**

Crandall, Prudence, 558

Crawford, William H., 30, 556, 2430

Creel, George, 2928

Crittenden, John J., 134, **728**, 1748, 2435

Croly, Herbert D., **728**, 2047

Cromwell, Oliver, 174, 530, 1618, 2212

Crosskey, William W., 453, 516, 517, **728–729**, 1396, 1643

Croswell, Harry, 1897

Cruzan, Nancy, 2266, 2267

Cummings, Homer S., 697, 698, **734–735**, 2288, 2592

Curry, Betty, 127

Curtis, Benjamin R., 184, 430, 451, 455, 681, **735–736**, 820, 1791, 1888, 2356, 2593, 2650, 2651, 2652, 2867, 2871

Curtis, George Ticknor, 450, **736**

Cushing, Caleb, 114, 1018

Cushing, William, 467, **737–738**, 2554, 2590, 2600, 2601, 2602

Cushman, Robert E., **738**

Custis, Martha, 2860

# D

Dagenhart, Reuben, 1262

Dahl, Robert, 1478

Dahrendorf, Ralf, 908

Dallas, Alexander, 156, 181, **739**, 2600

Dallas, George M., 563

Daly, Charles, Patrick, 1594

Dana, Richard Henry, 504, 1756

Dane, Nathan, 449, **742**, 1829, 2556

Daniel, Peter V., 162, 298, 682, **742–743**, 1617, 2555, 2649, 2651, 2868

Darby, Fred, 743

Darrow, Clarence, 1281, 2327, 2666

Darwin, Charles, 21, 706, 1633, 2712–2713

Daugherty, Harry M., 134, 1358, 1594–1595, 1708

Davie, William R., 166

Davis, Angela, 1955

Davis, David, 338, 339, 498, **746–747**, 1036, 1581, 1736, 1753

Davis, Garrett, 1087

Davis, Henry Winter, 2818

Davis, Jefferson, 451, 566, 567, **747–748**, 2436, 2527, 2705, 2718

Davis, John W., 553, 597, 660, **748**, 1295, 1685, 2611, 2612, 2637

Davis, Kenneth Culp, 2297

Davis, Wylie, 253

Dawes, Thomas, 516

Dawkins, Andy, 2702

Day, William R., 259, 685, **748–749**, 804, 864, 893, 1164, 1261, 1274, 1310, 1651, 2292, 2637, 2895, 2896, 2898, 2900

Dayton, Jonathan, **749–750**

Deane, Silas, 2237

Debs, Eugene V., 241, 750, 751, 923, 1710, 1955, 2580, 2894

DeConcini, Dennis, 1813

De Funis, Marco, 54

de la Croix, Jacques Vincent, 1365

Delancey, James, 2944

De Lolme, Jean-Louis, 245

Dennis, Eugene, 769, 770

Denton, Jeremiah, 2365

Derrida, Jacques, 757

DeShaney, Joshua, 774

Deutsch, Jan, 1792

Devanter, Willis Van, 421, 457, 458, 697, 698, 893, 1311, 1314, 1498

Devlin, Lord Patrick, 1801

Dewey, John, 448, 662, 1982–1983, 1984, 2047, 2848

Dewey, Thomas E., 1767

DeWitt, John, 118, 1416

Dexter, Samuel, 2611

Diamond, Martin, 1947

Dicey, Albert V., 633, 2297, 2298

Dickens, Charles, 2681

Dickinson, John, 124–125, 513, 517, 519, 537, 543, 545, **779–780**, 1099, 1866, 2225, 2438, 2909

Dies, Martin, **780**, 1305, 1595

Dillinger, John, 598

Dillon, John F., 451, 583, 584, **783–784**, 2075

Dirksen, Everett M., 2228

Doe, Charles, **802**

Dole, Robert, 431

Donaldson, Kenneth, 1846

Dorr, Thomas W., 561, 1652, 2210, 2715

Dottson, Andy, 2808

Douglas, Stephen A., 3, 258, 477, 565, 569, 667, 747, **812–813**, 820, 1148, 1149, 1161, 1356, 1475, 1525–1526, 1574, 1620, 1622–1623, 1625, 1962, 1963, 2201, 2217, 2435, 2436, 2452, 2527, 2583, 2655, 2673, 2705

Douglas, William O., 1, 17, 22, 24, 33, 43, 54, 112, 116, 119, 152, 157, 164, 168, 201, 204, 226, 229, 239, 242, 244, 251, 253, 263, 272, 273, 274, 301, 309, 313, 420, 427, 430, 445, 458, 631, 696, 709, 710, 719, 720, 721, 760, 769, 771, 804, **813–817**, 817, 818, 830, 839, 861, 882, 896, 929, 930, 1023, 1035, 1065, 1066, 1070, 1102, 1103, 1106, 1108, 1118, 1140, 1148, 1149, 1150, 1183, 1188, 1189, 1198, 1228, 1231, 1233, 1234, 1235, 1240, 1271, 1272, 1282, 1289, 1336, 1401, 1410, 1411, 1434, 1480, 1481, 1485–1486, 1522, 1536, 1538, 1568, 1581, 1588, 1602, 1605, 1702, 1709, 1716–1717, 1735, 1737, 1758, 1768, 1785, 1806, 1810, 1811, 1836, 1851, 1870, 1879, 1896, 1899, 1961, 1990, 2077, 2097, 2115,

2145, 2155, 2172, 2200, 2203, 2228, 2242, 2243, 2246, 2283, 2284, 2289, 2292–2293, 2294, 2296, 2302, 2412, 2421–2422, 2506, 2510, 2528, 2531, 2545, 2546, 2548, 2549, 2550, 2562, 2573, 2582, 2606, 2607, 2714, 2747, 2790, 2793, 2794, 2795, 2796, 2832, 2833, 2850, 2851, 2853, 2855, 2906, 2907, 2914, 2924, 2930, 2931, 2934, 2941, 2947

Douglass, Frederick, 3, 180, 504, 1091, 2366, 2736, 2806

Dowling, Noel T., **817**

Downs, Anthony, 764

Drayton, William, 2439

Duane, James, **828**, 2301

Duane, William, 1408

Duer, William Alexander, 449

Dukakis, Michael, 282

Dulany, Daniel, **829**

Dulles, John Foster, 2788

Dunne, Finley Peter, 589

Dunning, William A., 452

Du Ponceau, Peter S., **831**

Duvall, Gabriel, 162, 677, **831–832**, 1683

Duxbury, Neil, 1578

Dworkin, Andrea, 1054, 1134, 1965

Dworkin, Ronald, 508, 626, 629, 1394, 1579, 1634, 2576

# E

Earl, Robert, 1414

Easterbrook, Frank, 1054, 1967–1968, 2681

Eastland, James O., 2365

Edmunds, George, 2413

Edward III, 1663–1664

Edwards, Pierpont, 980

Ehrlich, Isaac, 311

Eichman, Shawn, 1063

Eisenhower, Dwight D., 112, 133, 136, 190, 191, 232, 236, 244, 254, 255, 270, 281, 288, 289, 603–604, 606, 607, 608, 614, 683, 909, 945, 1003, 1025, 1155, 1265, 1319, 1390, 1430, 1541, 1649, 1815, 1853, 1935–1936, 1969, 2002, 2319, 2438, 2541, 2633, 2742, 2794, 2848, 2852, 2902, 2915

Elhauge, Einer, 2670

Eliot, T. S., 2902

Ellesmere, Lord Chancellor, 294

Elliot, Jared, 512

Elliot, Jonathan, 2120

Ellison, Ralph, 1430, 2354

Ellsberg, Daniel, 126, 1806, 1816, 2010

Ellsworth, Oliver, 515, 517, 520, **882–884**, 979, 980, 1011, 1020, 1228, 1668, 1682, 1882, 1883, 2591, 2600, 2601, 2634, 2753, 2805
Ely, John Hart, 318, 383, 658, 767, 1481, 1503, 1860, 2204, 2754, 2850–2851
Emerson, John, 818
Emerson, Thomas I., 1236
Emmet, Thomas A., 2611
Emmett, Thomas, 1190
Endo, Mitsuye, 2931
Enmund, Earl, 896
Epstein, Richard, 2576
Ernst, Morris, **921**
Ervin, Samuel J., 135, **922**, 1543, 2365, 2865
Escobedo, Daniel, 922, 1925
Estes, Billie Sol, 929, 1143
Eule, Julian N., 787, **929–930**
Evarts, William M., 321, 361, 736, **931**, 1414, 1903, 2783

## F

Fairman, Charles, 1086
Fall, Albert B., 1358
Falwell, Jerry, 1133, 1146, 1322
Farrand, Max, **975**, 2805
Faubus, Orville, 607
Feeley, Malcolm, 990
Feeney, Helen, 2392–2393
Fehrenbacher, Don E., 2432
Fenno, Richard F., Jr., 288
Ferguson, Danny, 625
Fessenden, William Pitt, 4, **1034**, 1085, 1436
Few, William, **1035**
Field, David Dudley, **1035**, 1582, 1736
Field, Stephen J., 70, 96, 112, 130, 217, 218, 240, 328, 338, 341, 342, 359, 360, 361, 583, 748, 813, **1035–1039**, 1161, 1164, 1224, 1230, 1267, 1354, 1453, 1581, 1709, 1733, 1734, 1749, 1764, 1888, 1982, 2021, 2048, 2311, 2420, 2423, 2424, 2508, 2512, 2559, 2563, 2564, 2628, 2679, 2784, 2823, 2825, 2827, 2828, 2829, 2923
Fillmore, Millard, 49, 416, 565, 574, 728, 735, **1044**, 2001, 2431, 2786, 2884, 2885
Filmer, Robert, 1639
Fish, Stanley, 1984
Fishbourn, Benjamin, 2359
Fisher, Sidney George, 451
Fisk, Jim, 1035
Fiske, John, **1060**, 1711
FitzSimons, Thomas, 174, **1061**

Fleming, Macklin, 723
Foner, Eric, 1291
Ford, Gerald R., 89, 266, 273, 281, 608, 609, 611, 755, 1003, **1070**, 1262, 1336, 1339, 1529, 1574, 1770, 1817, 1878, 1994, 2002, 2014, 2125, 2161, 2312, 2529, 2531, 2785, 2786, 2843, 2864
Fortas, Abe, 50, 112, 114, 142, 190, 191, 201, 312, 490, 699, 905, **1082–1083**, 1183, 1194, 1240, 1429, 1434, 1523, 2006, 2364, 2703
Foster, Daniel, 370
Foucault, Michel, 724
Fraenkel, Osmond K., **1099**
France, Anatole, 395
Franck, Thomas M., 494, 495
Frank, Jerome N., 62, 435, **1099–1100**, 1580
Frank, Leo, 1100, 1310
Frankfurter, Felix, 22, 33, 35, 36, 53, 69, 78, 112, 113, 142, 152, 153, 155, 164, 167, 173, 179, 186, 196, 198, 220, 221, 233, 237, 238, 244, 253, 254, 274, 276, 279, 280, 285, 286, 322, 351, 354, 355, 427, 440, 444, 458, 468, 477, 587, 629, 658, 659, 718, 719, 769, 770, 777, 814, 815, 830, 870, 931, 970, 996, 1008, 1018, 1031, 1065, 1066, **1101–1104**, 1148, 1155, 1176, 1194, 1195, 1198, 1199, 1200, 1203, 1232, 1235, 1245, 1267, 1268, 1274, 1299, 1355, 1399, 1405, 1410, 1446, 1450, 1458, 1460, 1461, 1465, 1470, 1486, 1497, 1498, 1532, 1542, 1548, 1563, 1569–1570, 1587, 1594, 1595, 1634, 1645, 1704, 1713, 1734, 1768, 1779, 1812, 1825, 1869, 1924, 1949, 1950, 1990–1991, 2025, 2037, 2038, 2076, 2077, 2123, 2132, 2186, 2187, 2202, 2233, 2261, 2284, 2286, 2289, 2292–2293, 2294, 2302, 2313, 2324, 2329, 2344, 2416, 2417, 2445, 2446, 2458, 2522, 2541, 2545, 2546, 2548, 2550, 2561, 2569, 2576, 2581, 2604, 2641, 2650, 2660, 2667, 2675, 2684, 2713, 2726, 2747, 2780, 2792, 2793, 2794, 2796, 2849, 2851, 2852, 2867, 2902, 2903, 2908, 2935, 2941, 2947
Franklin, Benjamin, 29, 124–125, 287, 512, 521, 522, 537, 545, 752, 834, 997, **1104–1105**, 1418, 1420, 1647, 1874, 2235, 2644–2645, 2805
Frémont, John C., 884
Freud, Sigmund, 1696–1697, 2647
Freund, Ernst, **1154–1155**, 2511
Freund, Paul A., 377, **1155**, 2205, 2623
Friederich, Carl, 778
Friedman, Barry, 990

Friedrich, Carl J., 637
Friendly, Henry J., **1155–1156**, 1268, 2914
Fries, John, 337, 1156
Fulbright, J. William, 2360, 2362, 2789
Fuller, Alvan T., 468
Fuller, Lon, 525–526, 631, 1578–1579, 2297
Fuller, Melville W., 199, 241, 330, 359, 430, 846, 893, **1160–1163**, 1163–1170, 1376, 1601, 1641, 1704, 1959–1960, 2210, 2634, 2897
Fulton, Robert, 454–455, 1636
Furneaux, Philip, **1177**, 1870

## G

Gage, Frances, 2736
Gallatin, Albert, 26, 551, **1180**, 1419, 1998, 2931
Galloway, Joseph, 443, 1059, **1180**
Gandhi, Mohandas Karamchand, 369
Garfield, James A., 121, 504, **1182**, 1698, 1736, 1877, 1892, 2002
Garland, Augustus H., **1182**, 2679
Garraty, John, 1528
Garrison, William Lloyd, 2, 182, 558, 561, **1182–1183**, 2216, 2736
Gault, Gerald, 1183, 1523
Gelhorn, Walter, 738
Genêt, Edmond, 516, 548
George II, 532, 1888
George III, 27, 294, 385, 536, 636, 753, 2383, 2439, 2834
George, Walter F., 244
Gerry, Elbridge, 174, 175, 503, 522, 542, 544, 545, 755, 1187, **1187**, 1457, 2120, 2134
Gibson, John Bannister, 156, 560, 833, **1192**
Giddings, Joshua, 3, 385, 562, 1499, 2884
Gideon, Clarence Earl, 1193–1194
Gilbert, Geoffrey, 1922–1923, 2234, 2237
Gilbert, Joseph, 1710
Giles, William, **1194**, 1684
Gilligan, Carol, 1032
Gilman, Nicholas, **1194**
Gilmore, Gary, 302
Gilmore, Grant, 526
Gingrich, Newt, 775
Ginsburg, Douglas H., 114, 2127, 2364
Ginsburg, Ruth Bader, 307, 313, 330, 431, 473, **1195–1198**, 1439, 1530, 1735, 1750, 2168, 2270, 2398, 2418, 2419, 2455, 2456, 2702, 2798

Ginzberg, Eli, 2390
Gitlow, Benjamin, 146
Gladstone, William, 159
Glover, Joshua, 1
Gobitis, Lillian, 1065
Gobitis, William, 1065
Godkin, E. L., 584
Goetz, Bernard, 2916
Goldberg, Arthur J., 1, 116, 168, 238,
    242, 274, 277, 702, 929, 1101, 1193,
    **1200**, 1282, 1532, 1595–1596, 1810,
    1812, 1925, 2204, 2246, 2528, 2745,
    2849
Goldman, Emma, 2325
Goldman, Ron, 2915
Goldwater, Barry, 2126
Golove, David, 1826
Gompers, Samuel, 36, 425, 1203
Goodnow, Frank J., 452, 582, **1205**
Goodrich, Chauncey, 2611
Gordon, Thomas, 324
Gorham, Nathaniel, 48, **1205**, 1751–
    1752, 2700
Gortari, Carlos Salinas de, 1826
Goudy, William C., 322, **1205–1206**
Gould, Jay, 783, 1035
Graham, Howard Jay, 585
Gramm, Phil, 1219
Grant, Ulysses S., 82, 114, 121, 197, 201,
    207, 216, 318, 319, 334, 336, 339, 340,
    404, 478, 504, 579, 580, 581, 697, 783,
    1018, 1039, 1041, 1070, **1225**, 1265,
    1319, 1409, 1428, 1581, 1626, 1753,
    1816, 2311, 2476, 2563, 2609, 2735,
    2736, 2807, 2821
Grassley, Charles E., 2365
Gravel, Mike, 1226, 2359, 2464
Gray, Horace, 198, 429, 1036, 1164,
    **1226–1227**, 1582, 1731, 2604, 2620,
    2817, 2825, 2828
Gray, John Chipman, 1226
Grayson, William, 177, 541
Greeley, Horace, 2216
Greene, Harold H., 2843
Greenleaf, Simon, 333
Grey, Thomas, 632, 1984
Gridley, Josiah, 1888
Grier, Robert C., 216, 258, 325, 338,
    339, **1229–1230**, 1581, 2022, 2680
Griffin, Stephen M, 659, 660
Grimke, Sarah, 2391
Griswold, Erwin N., 1195, **1232–1233**
Griswold, Roger, 2611
Grodzin, Morton, 1006
Grosscup, Peter S., **1234–1235**, 2630
Grotius, Hugo, 634, 1866
Grow, Galusha A., 1302
Gunier, Lani, 432

Gunther, Gerald, 318, 676, 1502, 1586,
    2203, 2562
Gurfein, Murray, 1806
Guthrie, William D., 357, **1244**, 1704
Guthrie, Woody, 816

# H

Hague, Frank, 379
Haines, Charles G., **1257**
Halderman, Terri Lee, 1893
Hale, Sir Matthew, 52, 53, 1098, 1224,
    2716, 2823
Hale, Robert, 2053, 2572
Hall, Dominick, 1407
Hamilton, Alexander, 29, 44, 47, 90,
    110–111, 113, 123, 159, 174, 175, 214,
    250, 265, 268, 278, 287, 291, 336, 343,
    356, 377, 386, 449, 484, 489, 493,
    496–497, 497, 517, 519, 520, 523, 524,
    539, 541, 542, 546, 547–548, 549, 551,
    563, 673, 699, 728, 754, 755, 763,
    834–835, 841, 845, 864, 869, 877, 883,
    899, 949, 950, 957–958, 980, 995,
    1013–1015, 1016, 1058, 1059, 1061,
    1180, 1185, 1187, 1194, 1204, **1257–**
    **1260**, 1287, 1290, 1324, 1336, 1337,
    1338, 1340, 1346, 1390, 1394, 1404,
    1418, 1421, 1454, 1466, 1467, 1469,
    1473, 1475, 1487, 1501, 1503, 1534,
    1537, 1575, 1610, 1611, 1618–1619,
    1621, 1635, 1636, 1641, 1655, 1657,
    1658, 1660, 1668, 1674, 1692, 1705,
    1752, 1754, 1755, 1762, 1790, 1882,
    1883, 1897, 1934, 1947, 1948, 1962,
    1997, 2019, 2045, 2116, 2119, 2201,
    2209, 2249, 2301, 2324, 2360, 2439,
    2461, 2468, 2560, 2601, 2611, 2659,
    2660–2661, 2661, 2662, 2664, 2681,
    2741–2742, 2752–2753, 2755, 2770,
    2784, 2805, 2835, 2836, 2837, 2843,
    2861, 2863, 2938
Hamilton, Andrew, 1260, 2352–2353,
    2944
Hamilton, Walton H., 53, 119, 517, 633,
    639, **1260–1261**
Hammond, James Henry, 1833
Hancock, John, 752
Hand, Augustus N., **1262–1263**, 2748,
    2936
Hand, Learned, 17, 146, 155, 225, 313,
    328, 708, 769, 923, 943, 961, 1221,
    **1263–1264**, 1299, 1476, 1478, 1579,
    1696, 1792, 2562, 2684, 2748, 2761,
    2794, 2851, 2914, 2936
Hanway, Caster, 2539
Harbison, Winfred A., 1528

Harding, Warren G., 106, 112, 261, 283,
    288, 289, 590, 593, 595, 699, 751,
    1020, 1025, **1264**, 1303, 1358, 2002,
    2310, 2360, 2411, 2625, 2634, 2637,
    2780
Hardwick, Michael, 381, 2401
Harlan, John Marshall (1833–1911), 15,
    25, 26, 54, 112, 170, 199, 217, 218,
    240, 330, 408, 409, 410, 749, 794, 795,
    846, 909, 970, 1038, 1162, 1163, 1164,
    1168, 1169, 1227, 1261, **1265–1268**,
    1272, 1322, 1354, 1376, 1397, 1415,
    1540, 1558, 1638, 1700, 1709, 1764,
    1787, 1828, 1830, 1918, 1919, 1960,
    2037, 2094, 2253, 2298, 2437, 2456,
    2472, 2482, 2483, 2487, 2693–2694,
    2744, 2824, 2828, 2829–2830, 2894,
    2895, 2896, 2898, 2899, 2923, 2940
Harlan, John Marshall (1899–1971), 11,
    12, 25, 140, 142, 152, 163, 164, 168,
    170, 179, 185, 204, 280, 299, 300, 303,
    310, 311, 320, 407, 505, 631, 667, 696,
    709, 712, 817, 830, 863, 929, 959, 975,
    1034, 1066, 1093, 1107, 1140, 1219,
    1228, 1231, 1233, 1237, 1240, **1268–**
    **1270**, 1271, 1273, 1437, 1527, 1535,
    1595, 1605, 1666, 1667, 1670, 1681,
    1717, 1741–1742, 1750, 1773, 1806,
    1812, 1814, 1856, 1987, 2037, 2038,
    2132, 2140, 2159, 2171, 2193, 2247,
    2280, 2295, 2296, 2308, 2333–2334,
    2342, 2456, 2475, 2487, 2491, 2581,
    2604, 2606, 2849, 2851, 2853, 2867,
    2881, 2896–2897, 2903, 2938–2939
Harmon, Judson, 429
Harrington, James, 28, 521, 661, 2211,
    2215
Harrison, Benjamin, 112, 240, 867, 1164,
    **1273**, 1409, 1711, 1763, 1850, 2291,
    2412
Harrison, Robert H., 2600
Harrison, William Henry, 112, 114, 559,
    2001, 2434, 2746, 2884
Hart, Henry M., 1246, **1274**, 1466,
    1469, 1474, 1502, 1578, 1579, 1792,
    2313
Hartz, Louis, 1614
Hastie, William Henry, **1275**, 1761,
    2763
Haswell, Anthony, 1883
Hatch, Orin, 2182
Haupt, Hans Max, 1279
Haupt, Herbert, 1279
Hawthorne, Nathaniel, 892, 1782,
    2183
Hay, John, 1169
Hayden, Lewis, 370
Hayden, Tom, 2790

Hayek, F. A., 633, 2297
Hayes, Rutherford B., 207, 218, 387, 478, 504, 581, 582, 803, 867, 1164, 1182, 1265, **1280**, 1698, 2893, 2898
Hayne, Robert Y., 559, **1280**, 2686, 2885
Haynsworth, Clement F., Jr., 49, 112, 114, 191, 699, 1816, 2364
Hays, Arthur Garfield, 921, **1280–1281**
Haywood, William, 1955
Helm, Jerry, 2446–2447
Helms, Jesse, 1079
Helvidius. *See* Madison, James
Hendricks, Leroy, 2406
Henfield, Gideon, 980
Henkin, Louis, 1470, 1826
Hennings, Thomas, 2365
Henry II, 1220
Henry III, 1663
Henry IV, 1987
Henry VIII, 1647
Henry, Patrick, 176, 177, 180, 522, 523, 528, 1011, **1284**, 1575, 1610, 1673, 1689, 1785–1786, 1891, 1985, 2119, 2120, 2249, 2346–2347, 2601
Herbert, Anthony, 1141, 1285
Herblock, 1322
Herndon, Angelo, 2281–2282
Hildreth, Richard, 133, 450, **1289**
Hill, Anita, 2695
Hill, C. M., 674
Hill, James J., 1594
Hill, Joe, 1954
Hills, Roderick, Jr., 990
Hinckley, John, 1719
Hirabayashi, Gordon, 1417, 2107, 2842
Hiss, Alger, 604, 1305, 1595, 1815, 2792
Hitler, Adolf, 1047, 2545
Hoadley, Bishop, 2597
Hobbes, Thomas, 635, 753, 1052, 1610, 1611, 1639, 1786, 1787, 2461–2462, 2567
Hoffa, James, 1294
Hofstadter, Richard, 1947
Hogan, Joe, 1746, 2418
Hohfeld, Wesley N., 2053
Holdsworth, Sir William S., 175, 1338
Holland, Ray P., 1746
Holland, Spessard, 2741
Hollings, Ernest, 1219
Holmes, Oliver Wendell, Jr., 15, 16, 17, 32, 35, 36, 52, 53, 69, 111, 112, 146, 151, 154, 167, 173, 222, 226, 236, 252, 259, 278, 284, 313, 314, 328, 388, 421, 426, 427, 428, 429, 435, 468, 527, 585–586, 597, 627, 631, 659, 665, 685,

692, 709, 719, 744, 749, 751, 756, 789, 791, 792, 795, 805, 831, 833, 835, 838, 839, 840, 864, 873, 889, 890, 892, 901, 902, 903, 909, 943, 958, 961, 970, 1041, 1046, 1047, 1050, 1100, 1127, 1128, 1129, 1156, 1162, 1164, 1175, 1184, 1198, 1212, 1261, 1263, 1264, 1267, 1292, **1295–1298**, 1298, 1299, 1300, 1308, 1310, 1315, 1352, 1354, 1446, 1459, 1460, 1463, 1473, 1486, 1532, 1548, 1558, 1563, 1565, 1580, 1592, 1606, 1633, 1638, 1646, 1649, 1651, 1652, 1670–1671, 1681, 1682, 1710, 1715, 1716, 1721, 1724, 1746, 1757, 1758, 1761, 1772, 1778, 1802, 1828, 1849–1850, 1851, 1890, 1904, 1911, 1955, 1983, 1987, 1990, 2047, 2054, 2065, 2066, 2075, 2076–2077, 2230, 2251–2252, 2290, 2292, 2310, 2318, 2319, 2325, 2326, 2352, 2353, 2408, 2417, 2437, 2445, 2446, 2470, 2509–2510, 2544, 2545, 2549, 2560, 2571, 2580, 2589, 2593, 2594, 2604, 2607, 2629, 2631, 2634, 2636, 2637, 2640, 2641, 2643–2644, 2645, 2646, 2647, 2678, 2684, 2712, 2733, 2746, 2749, 2758, 2773, 2794, 2809, 2878, 2895, 2898, 2901, 2902, 2928–2929
Holst, Hermann von, 452
Holtzman, Elizabeth, 2790
Hooker, Thomas, 512, 1176, **1303**, 1364, 2439
Hoover, Herbert C., 49, 112, 114–115, 281, 313, 456, 590, 593, 595–596, 597, 601, 602, 1018, 1025, **1303**, 1310, 1599, 2143, 2281, 2546, 2548, 2589, 2592, 2612, 2636
Hoover, J. Edgar, 873, 976, **1303–1304**
Hopkinson, Joseph, 156, 744
Hornblower, William B., 114
Horowitz, Donald, 1947
Hotman, François, 634
House, Edward, 1714
Houston, Charles H., **1307**, 1676, 1678, 2411, 2612
Howard, Jacob M., 1085, 1087, **1308**, 1357, 2210
Howe, Mark DeWolfe, **1308**
Howell, David, 2723
Hruska, Roman, 2623
Hughes, Charles Evans, 15, 107, 112–113, 128, 151, 220, 221, 256, 317, 321, 348, 373, 421, 435, 441, 457, 458, 510, 595, 600, 631, 685, 697, 698, 702, 760, 795, 841, 846, 862, 899, 1018, 1065, 1100, 1107, 1201, 1241, 1256, 1300–1301, 1303, 1308, **1309–1312**, 1312, 1314, 1316, 1317, 1337, 1452, 1460,

1463, 1488, 1582, 1645, 1739, 1748, 1753, 1760, 1788, 1825, 1874, 1877, 1912, 1959, 2009, 2078, 2115, 2157, 2173, 2281, 2289, 2292, 2317, 2544, 2546, 2548, 2560, 2563, 2589, 2592, 2593, 2597, 2605, 2606, 2607, 2608, 2612, 2613, 2634, 2713, 2780, 2820–2821, 2882, 2884, 2897, 2899
Hull, William, 1727
Hulme, Obadiah, 515
Hume, David, 1613, 1640, 2053, 2212
Humphrey, Hubert H., 158, 472, **1318**, 1815
Humphrey, William, 1318
Hunt, Ward, 361, 1225, **1319**, 2564, 2807
Hunter, David, 1688
Hunter, George, 2666
Hurst, J. Willard, 2783, **1321**
Hussein, Saddam, 2002, 2003
Hutchinson, R., 674
Hutchinson, Thomas, 31, 512, 997, **1323**, 1889, 2461
Huxley, Aldous, 87
Hyde, Henry J., 1324

# I

Ingersoll, Jared, **1369**, 2611
Innes, Harry, 2704
Innocent III (Pope), 1663
Iredell, James, 166, 290, 356, 980, 1175, 1279, 1286–1287, 1290, 1336, **1403–1404**, 1664, 1682, 2462, 2600, 2601, 2602, 2834
Ireton, Henry, 2381
Irons, Peter, 1417, 2677

# J

Jackson, Andrew, 30, 90, 110, 112, 114, 157, 160, 162, 169, 288, 291, 292, 325, 344, 345, 384, 424, 425, 499, 525, 556, 557, 559, 560, 565, 566, 575, 667, 675, 742, 832, 866, 954, 1036, 1069, 1274, 1385, **1407–1409**, 1411, 1413, 1414, 1424, 1425, 1457, 1474, 1488, 1583–1584, 1614, 1675, 1685, 1700, 1701, 1710, 1711, 1712, 1821, 1833, 1935, 1998, 2457, 2591, 2609, 2628, 2647, 2651, 2656, 2687, 2733, 2746, 2779, 2805, 2840, 2867, 2884, 2922
Jackson, Howell E., 1164, 1165, 1227, 1273, **1409–1410**, 1959, 1960
Jackson, James, 1668
Jackson, Jesse, 432

Jackson, Robert H., 117, 204, 244, 254, 444, 452, 459, 461, 600, 705, 708, 719, 721, 804, 814, 835, 840, 858, 861, 913, 931, 942, 951, 978, 1010, 1065–1066, 1103, 1147, 1192, 1202, 1279, 1318, 1344, 1362, 1396, **1410–1411**, 1417, 1461, 1543, 1565, 1588, 1704, 1768, 1925, 1960–1961, 1973, 1995, 1996, 2008, 2021, 2054, 2078, 2115, 2152, 2154, 2159, 2172, 2190, 2282, 2283, 2289, 2292–2293, 2302, 2329, 2384, 2408, 2422, 2458, 2546, 2548, 2550, 2574, 2581, 2593, 2597, 2660, 2783, 2793, 2796, 2843, 2848, 2852, 2878, 2903, 2930, 2941, 2947

Jackson, Vicki, 990

Jackson, William, 516

Jacobs, Clyde, 2075

Jaffe, Erik, 2057

Jaffe, Louis, 41

James I (England) and VI (Scotland), 294, 439, 2297

James II, 532, 635, 752, 1173, 1693, 1804, 2183

James, William, 448, 1005, 1263, 1982, 1984

Jameson, J. Franklin, 1909

Jaworski, Leon, 1359, 1955

Jay, John, 126, 288, 330, 346, 356, 449, 518, 540, 549, 947, 1013–1015, 1016, 1020, 1279, 1417–1419, 1419, 1486, 1673, 1682, 1750, 1947, 2440, 2600, 2601, 2603, 2861, 2863

Jefferson, Thomas, 26, 29, 30, 67, 76, 83, 85, 89, 160, 171, 174, 176, 177, 180, 185, 188, 197, 228, 250, 271, 278, 287, 288, 337, 343, 373, 424, 438, 440, 489, 493, 495, 503, 509, 513, 519, 525, 534, 541, 546, 547, 548, 549, 550, 552, 553, 554, 556, 558, 559, 575, 590, 637, 648, 665, 683, 697, 705, 728, 742, 752, 754, 779, 831, 832, 864, 866, 885, 896, 899, 907, 931, 948, 953, 954, 980, 1013, 1015, 1016, 1045, 1046, 1049, 1174, 1177, 1180, 1194, 1257, 1259, 1268, 1290, 1343, 1365, 1385, 1392, 1412, **1419–1423**, 1423–1426, 1432, 1474, 1478, 1487, 1488, 1496, 1498, 1515, 1534, 1575, 1583, 1610, 1611, 1621, 1633, 1635, 1644, 1655, 1658, 1662, 1667, 1675, 1681, 1682–1683, 1684, 1685, 1686, 1689, 1692, 1705, 1707, 1744, 1748, 1752, 1754, 1787, 1790, 1821, 1832, 1855, 1856, 1870, 1874, 1881, 1884, 1891, 1897, 1934, 1947, 1963, 2000, 2045, 2050, 2051, 2052, 2116, 2121, 2125, 2126, 2185, 2193, 2201, 2209, 2249, 2280, 2284, 2290,

2324, 2353, 2370, 2371, 2383, 2387, 2427, 2429, 2434, 2439, 2479, 2499, 2500, 2501, 2519, 2554, 2560, 2561, 2564, 2591, 2593, 2600, 2662, 2671, 2681, 2684, 2686–2687, 2704, 2712, 2718–2719, 2733, 2740, 2763, 2779, 2785, 2798–2800, 2801, 2805, 2840, 2861, 2935

Jeffrey, William W., Jr., 728

Jencks, Clinton E., 1426

Jenifer, Daniel of St. Thomas, **1426**

Jenner, William E., 2592

Jennison, Nathaniel, 467

Jensen, Merrill, 518, **1426–1427**

Jessup, Philip, 1390

Jeter, Mildred, 2307

Jewett, John N., 2783

John, King, 1663, 2035, 2297, 2569

Johnson, Andrew, 89, 110, 112, 114, 126, 159, 180, 181, 188, 283, 288, 335, 338, 339, 402, 478, 499, 576, 577, 578, 582, 736, 908, 931, 948, 1034, 1084, 1086, 1225, 1307, 1339, 1340, 1343, 1349, 1357, 1413, **1427–1429**, 1436, 1625, 1728, 1732, 1736, 1745, 2001, 2142, 2143, 2360, 2389, 2453, 2471, 2476, 2527, 2540, 2584, 2591, 2609, 2669, 2692, 2693, 2735, 2751, 2786, 2806

Johnson, Frank, 276

Johnson, Gregory, 1062–1063

Johnson, John G., 2612

Johnson, Lyndon B., 50, 53, 59, 112, 113, 114, 266, 378, 386, 390, 405, 420, 598, 610, 613, 614, 699, 721, 777, 843, 1002, 1003, 1018, 1026, 1082, 1153, 1200, 1232, 1242, 1318, 1402, **1429–1432**, 1533, 1534, 1615, 1640, 1676, 1679, 1704, 1816, 1852, 1876, 1954, 1973, 2220, 2453, 2592, 2734, 2786, 2788–2789, 2790, 2809, 2837, 2838, 2842

Johnson, Paul, 1435

Johnson, Reverdy, **1432**

Johnson, Richard, 162, 1228

Johnson, Thomas, **1432**, 2601

Johnson, William, 438, 885, 980, 981, 1067, 1191, 1425, **1432–1433**, 1635, 1683, 1684, 1689, 2859, 2867

Johnson, William S., 1228, **1433–1434**, 1762

Johnston, Samuel, 1403

Jones, Joseph Lee, 2542

Jones, Laura, 2123

Jones, LeRoi, 1955

Jones, Paula Corbin, 433, 625, 2386

Jones, Thomas G., 1897

Jones, Walter, 2611

Joyce, James, 78, 921

Judd, Orin, 2790

Julian, George, **1499**

Justinian, 374

# K

Kahn, Paul, 1979

Kallen, Horace, 662

Kalt, Joseph, 2731

Kalven, Harry, Jr., 751, 1304, 1510, **1525**, 1837, 1900, 1965, 2068, 2744–2745

Kammen, Michael, 1577, 2712

Kanka, Megan, 2400

Kantrowitz, Arthur, 2328

Karst, Kenneth L., 1966, 2393

Katzenbach, Nicholas, 2789

Katzmann, Frederick, 468

Kaufman, Irving, 906, 2914

Kaus, Otto, 865

Keating, Kenneth, 2744

Keller, Helen, 78

Kelly, Alfred H., **1528**

Kendall, Amos, 384, 560, 705, 1412

Kennard, George, 200

Kennedy, Anthony M., 7, 9, 12, 14, 55, 56, 98, 139, 192, 202, 203, 265, 296, 298, 359, 380, 382, 624, 695, 732, 787, 848, 916, 918, 925, 926, 983, 989, 1055, 1062, 1068, 1133, 1208, 1293, 1327, 1332, 1391, 1396, 1471–1472, 1515, **1529–1532**, 1576, 1602, 1651, 1735, 1747, 1750, 1813, 1831, 1845, 1886, 1915, 1977, 2055, 2082, 2123, 2127, 2137, 2157, 2158, 2159, 2161, 2168, 2169, 2176, 2196, 2226, 2231, 2248, 2313, 2315, 2324, 2338, 2379, 2409, 2419, 2422, 2455, 2456, 2681, 2698, 2863

Kennedy, Duncan, 724

Kennedy, Edward M., 112, 242, 1813, 2157, 2182

Kennedy, John F., 134, 152, 288, 372, 390, 405, 433, 598, 608, 610, 613, 614, 867, 1020, 1025, 1155, 1179, 1200, 1402, **1532–1533**, 1676, 1679, 1704, 1781, 1815, 1853, 1854, 1921, 1951, 2002, 2610, 2836, 2838, 2885, 2886, 2888, 2932

Kennedy, Robert F., 134–135, 136, 873, 1532, **1533–1534**, 1852, 1951, 2888

Kent, James, 333, 450, 744, 842, 1190, 1191, 1365, **1534–1535**, 1617, 1635, 1898, 2075, 2507, 2556, 2697–2698

Key, Francis Scott, 2611

Keynes, John Maynard, 262

Khrushchev, Nikita, 1815

King, Martin Luther, Jr., 369, 370, 407, 411, 412, 873, 875, 1026, 1082, 1153, 1304, **1536–1537**, 1607, 1614, 1774, 1804–1805, 1854, 2220, 2486, 2709, 2809, 2832

King, Rodney, 812, 2916

King, Rufus, 517, 542, 647, 673, 1337, **1537–1538**, 1751, 1762, 1829

Kirchheimer, Otto, 1954

Kittay, Eva Feder, 1966

Kleindienst, Richard G., 134

Kluger, Richard, 1528, 2849

Knott, James, 1969

Knox, Henry, 288, 546, 2861

Knox, John Jay, 1752

Knox, Philander C., 135, **1540**, 1756, 2413, 2629

Korematsu, Fred, 1417, 2107, 2842, 2931

Kosciusko, Thaddeus, 1365

Kosmin, Barry A., 2180

Kramer, Larry, 990

Kristol, Irving, 1838

Krock, Arthur, 1439

Kurland, Philip B., 910, **1542–1543**, 1792, 2385, 2411

Kyd, Stuart, 361

## L

Labatt, David Cohen, 2914

Lachman, Seymour P., 2180

LaFave, Wayne, 713

La Follette, Robert, 597, 1479, **1557**, 2637–2638, 2641, 2884

Laird, Melvin, 1692

Lamar, Joseph R., 113, 1100, 1203, 1232, **1558–1559**, 2634, 2898

Lamar, L. Q. C., 359, 430, 1164, **1559**

Lambert, Jacques, 1365

Landis, James M., 852, 1101, 1399, **1560**, 2147

Lando, Barry, 1285

Langdell, Christopher Columbus, 1226, 1578, 1580

Langdon, John, 537, 1058, **1561**

Lansing, John, 519, 1258

Lansing, John, Jr., **1561**, 2938

Laski, Harold J., 219, 591, 1299, 1308, 1363, **1563**

Latrobe, Benjamin, 1681

Law, Sylvia, 2204

Lawrence, Philip K., 1710

Lawrence, William, 4

Leary, Timothy, 1572

Leavitt, Joshua, 3

Lebron, Michael, 1573

Lee, Charles, 134

Lee, Edmund J., 2611

Lee, Rex Edwin, **1574–1575**, 2451

Lee, Richard Henry, 32, 177, 536, 541, 752, **1575**, 1692, 2116, 2499

Lee, Robert E., 2915

Leflar, Robert, 253

Leigh, Benjamin W., 558

Leland, John, **1601**

Lempert, Richard, 1516

Lerner, Max, 665, 745

Levi, Edward H., 1461

Levinson, Sanford, 510

Levy, Howard, 1879

Levy, Leonard W., 373, 1474, 1606, 1607, 1922–1923, 2239, 2507

Lewinsky, Monica, 127, 433, 434, 625, 954, 955, 1360, 2386

Lewis, Anthony, 2325

Lewis, John L., 2757, 2793

Lewis, Morgan, 1897

Lewis, William Draper, 196, 1705

Lieber, Francis, 451, 2557, 2688

Lilburne, John, 512, 515, 828, **1617–1618**, 1664, 2234, 2237, 2238, 2381

Lilienthal, David, 1101

Lincoln, Abraham, 30, 89, 112, 126, 134, 164, 180, 181, 258, 288, 325, 334, 335, 339, 343, 373, 378, 386, 415, 416, 451, 491, 496, 499, 504, 536, 537, 563, 565, 567, 570, 571, 573, 574, 575, 577, 649, 667, 694, 736, 746, 747, 754, 813, 820, 884, 886, 949, 1035, 1148, 1149, 1230, 1256, 1265, 1356, 1409, 1432, 1475, 1583, 1612, 1614, **1619–1623**, 1624–1625, 1640, 1648, 1659, 1706, 1731, 1752, 1791, 1821–1822, 1908, 1955, 1959, 1963, 1994, 2001, 2022, 2096, 2125, 2142, 2201, 2216, 2249, 2290, 2291, 2346, 2389, 2427, 2432–2433, 2436, 2457, 2469–2470, 2476, 2480, 2519, 2527, 2539, 2556, 2580, 2584, 2591, 2609, 2628, 2650, 2651, 2673, 2688, 2691–2692, 2705, 2733, 2735, 2753, 2771, 2777, 2805, 2806, 2818, 2835, 2837, 2838, 2840, 2868, 2884, 2885, 2929

Lincoln, Levi, 134, 332, 467, **1623–1624**, 2236, 2554, 2590, 2611

Lindbergh, Charles, 1179

Linde, Hans, 2122, 2502

Lindsay, Vachel, 816

Lippman, Walter, 2047

Livingston, Brockholst, 885, 1898

Livingston, Edward, 559, 560, 2611

Livingston, Henry Brockholst, **1635–1636**, 1636, 1683, 1684–1685, 2697

Livingston, Robert, 455

Livingston, Robert R., Jr., 752, **1636**

Livingston, William, **1636**

Llewellyn, Karl N., 1578, 1580, 2443, 2681

Locke, John, 185, 324, 512, 521, 530, 593, 634–635, 649, 661, 673, 752, 760, 836, 886, 1052, 1114, 1117, 1387, 1614, **1639–1640**, 1786, 1787, 1946, 1962, 1963, 2051, 2052, 2130, 2193, 2211, 2248, 2290, 2297, 2346, 2382, 2439, 2499, 2593, 2834, 2946

Lockhart, William B., **1640–1641**

Lockwood, Belva A., 2612, 2920

Lodge, Henry Cabot, **1641**, 2360, 2912

Lofgren, Charles, 2121

Long, Huey, 1139, 1234

Long, Russell, 2932

Longworth, Nicholas, 598

Lovejoy, Owen, 3

Loving, Richard, 2307

Lowell, A. Lawrence, 328, 468, 590

Lowell, James Russell, 527

Luban, David, 224

Lurton, Horace H., 113, 1308, **1651–1652**, 2634, 2897, 2898

Luther, Martin, 2188

Lutz, Donald, 659

Lyell, Charles, 706

Lynch, Gerard, 2112

Lyon, Mathew, 67, 1883

## M

MacArthur, Douglas, 1367, 2734

Machiavelli, Niccolo, 649

MacKinnon, Catharine, 1054, 1134, 1278, 1965, 1967, 1968

MacMillan, James B., 2765

Macon, Nathaniel, 438, 1412, **1655**

Madison, Dolley, 1663

Madison, James, 3, 30, 48, 65, 74, 75, 85, 90, 101, 110–111, 114, 148, 159, 160, 163, 174, 176, 177, 178, 180, 226, 288, 291, 322, 326, 342, 343, 356, 375, 378, 386, 424, 437, 438, 449, 454, 467, 484, 495, 496, 503, 505, 508, 509, 510, 514–515, 516, 518, 519, 520, 521, 522, 523, 536, 540, 543, 546, 547, 548, 551, 552, 553, 554, 558, 559, 563, 635, 645, 661, 665, 673, 728, 739, 752, 755, 763, 785, 794, 795, 805, 806, 829, 832, 835, 841, 869, 877, 896, 927–928, 931, 947–948, 950, 995, 997, 998, 999, 1010–1011, 1013–1015, 1016, 1045, 1047, 1049, 1057, 1058, 1099, 1180, 1185, 1187, 1190, 1238, 1259, 1274, 1290, 1337, 1344, 1371, 1385, 1389,

1392, 1394, 1418, 1420, 1424, 1442,
1458, 1487, 1564, 1601, 1610, 1613,
**1655–1659**, 1659–1663, 1668, 1682,
1684, 1687, 1691, 1701, 1705–1706,
1727, 1751, 1752, 1754, 1755, 1762,
1790, 1809, 1812, 1857, 1858, 1880,
1882, 1910, 1933, 1937, 1947, 1951,
1956, 1957, 1962, 1963, 2045–2046,
2047, 2051, 2052, 2063, 2095, 2116,
2118, 2119, 2120, 2157, 2187, 2193,
2194, 2201, 2209, 2212, 2213, 2249,
2251, 2280, 2346, 2347, 2348, 2353,
2358, 2370, 2371, 2381, 2383, 2388,
2440, 2461, 2468, 2479, 2500, 2501,
2519, 2540, 2554, 2560, 2590, 2609,
2659, 2660, 2661, 2662, 2663–2664,
2682, 2686–2687, 2689, 2700, 2712,
2719, 2742–2743, 2753, 2754, 2756,
2770, 2781, 2784, 2798–2800, 2801,
2805, 2825, 2835, 2859, 2860, 2861,
2863, 2909, 2938, 2946
Maine, Sir Henry, 526, 562, 672, 2834
Malcolm, Janet, 1696
Malcolm, Joyce, 2348
Malcolm X, 412
Mann, Horace, 3, 2431
Mansfield, Lord. *See* Murray, William
  (Lord Mansfield)
Mapplethorpe, Robert, 1136
Marbury, William, 697, 1444, 1632,
  1667–1668, 2297, 2590
Marshall, George C., 118, 373, 1687
Marshall, John, 25, 29, 75, 109–111, 156,
  163, 171, 188, 197, 198, 207, 212, 241,
  256, 266, 277, 278, 325, 333, 337, 339,
  341, 344, 345, 348, 356, 376, 378, 436,
  437, 438, 439, 450, 452, 454, 455, 456,
  459, 460, 466, 493, 497, 498, 509, 526,
  552, 555, 556, 558, 559, 563, 568, 569,
  570, 571, 626, 627, 628, 629, 630, 638,
  659, 667, 673, 674, 675, 677, 692, 693,
  704, 741, 745, 832, 833, 841, 842, 845,
  861, 864, 877, 883, 899, 900, 947, 953,
  981, 995, 1011, 1013, 1015, 1019,
  1067–1068, 1080, 1163, 1175, 1189,
  1190, 1191, 1192, 1265, 1266, 1268,
  1284, 1287, 1290, 1294, 1338, 1344,
  1345, 1348, 1383, 1394, 1396, 1399,
  1422, 1424, 1433, 1441, 1443–1444,
  1445, 1446, 1460, 1461, 1463, 1465,
  1466, 1468, 1469, 1472, 1473, 1474,
  1487, 1496, 1498, 1534–1535, 1582,
  1583, 1585, 1587, 1589–1590, 1611–
  1612, 1617, 1633, 1635, 1652, 1662,
  1667, 1668–1670, **1672–1676**, 1688,
  1700, 1705, 1706, 1707, 1712, 1731,
  1739, 1752, 1768, 1778, 1790, 1799,
  1821, 1835–1836, 1849, 1854–1855,

1864, 1865, 1869, 1882, 1883, 1902,
  1904, 1910, 1953, 1963, 1970, 1986,
  2059, 2078, 2119, 2120, 2202, 2236,
  2280, 2288, 2297, 2384, 2387, 2408,
  2497, 2504, 2506, 2512, 2554, 2555,
  2556, 2557, 2560, 2561, 2562, 2564,
  2565, 2570, 2587, 2589, 2590, 2591,
  2600, 2601, 2602, 2604, 2611, 2616,
  2633–2634, 2636, 2647, 2651–2652,
  2653–2654, 2662, 2664–2665, 2667–
  2668, 2671, 2672, 2673, 2682, 2687,
  2688, 2698, 2712, 2713, 2716, 2732,
  2771, 2779, 2783, 2834, 2839, 2848,
  2859, 2867, 2871, 2882, 2896, 2897,
  2908, 2923, 2935
Marshall, T. H., 367
Marshall, Thurgood, 7, 23, 64, 112, 113,
  139–140, 158, 165, 170, 190, 200, 203,
  212, 214, 239, 251, 272, 296, 300, 301,
  304, 309, 310, 389, 440, 465, 490, 666,
  676, 695, 706, 721, 742, 772, 786, 790,
  831, 892, 895, 899, 914, 1012, 1018,
  1054, 1060, 1064, 1068, 1071, 1140,
  1172, 1181, 1197, 1203, 1214, 1233,
  1275, 1283, 1285, 1292, 1293, 1327,
  1411, 1415, 1426, 1427, 1429, 1450,
  1528, 1532, 1558, 1628, 1648, 1665,
  1672, **1676–1681**, 1681–1687, 1689,
  1690, 1694, 1709, 1717, 1723, 1724,
  1730, 1735, 1737, 1758, 1761, 1770,
  1774, 1789, 1806, 1831, 1844, 1845,
  1879, 1889, 1899, 1902, 1907, 1920,
  1922, 1939, 2033, 2082, 2141, 2155,
  2157, 2168, 2196, 2200, 2231, 2247,
  2275, 2295, 2306, 2307, 2310, 2313,
  2314, 2317, 2334, 2379, 2398, 2411,
  2414, 2417, 2422–2423, 2438, 2451,
  2452, 2453, 2548, 2612, 2677, 2695,
  2790, 2862, 2869, 2892, 2906, 2916–
  2917, 2934, 2943
Martin, Luther, 48, 517, 519, 523, 541,
  543, 661, 754, 1228, 1426, 1473,
  **1687–1688**, 1706, 1755, 2611
Marx, Gary, 713
Maslow, Will, 83
Mason, Alpheus, 665, 694
Mason, George, 49, 72, 123, 148, 175,
  287, 288, 522, 541, 542, 545, 677, 795,
  1337, **1692**, 1729, 1751, 2051, 2118,
  2119, 2499, 2500, 2503, 2799, 2805,
  2860
Mason, James, 2431
Mathews, Bonnie, 2915
Matthews, Burneta, 2763
Matthews, Stanley, 3, 199, 681, 1321–
  1322, **1698–1699**, 2828–2829, 2940
Mayhew, Jonathan, 512
Mayo, Henry B., 865

McAdoo, William, 1338–1339
McBain, Howard L., 453
McCaleb, Theodore H., 1710
McCardle, William, 339, 497, 1701
McCarren, Patrick A., 82–83, 605, 1595,
  1649
McCarthy, Joseph R., 605, 606, 780, 789,
  863, 976, 1233, 1318, 1595, 1649,
  1701–1702, 2358, 2794
McClellan, George B., 884, 1265, 2527
McClosky, Herbert, 1577
McClosky, Robert G., 1702, **1703**
McCloy, John J., 2290
McConnell, Michael, 895
McCormack, John, 1981
McCormick, Charles, 1923
McCormick, Cyrus, 1230
McCormick, Robert, 2064
McCree, Wade Hampton, Jr., **1704–
1705**
McDougal, Myres, 1826
McDougall, Alexander, 2235
McDuffie, George, 558
McFarland, Carl, 734
McFarlane, Robert, 622, 1403
McGowan, Carl, 1460, **1707–1708**
McGrath, J. Howard, 1358
McHenry, James, 517, **1708**
McIlwain, Charles, 1338, **1708–1709**
McKeldin, Theodore R., 2438
McKenna, Joseph, 26, 263, 1290, 1294,
  **1709–1710**, 1711, 2635, 2637, 2896,
  2898, 2900, 2907
McKinley, John, 159, 325, **1710–1711**,
  2651
McKinley, William, 589, 597, 749, 1164,
  1329, 1709, **1711**, 1763, 1784, 2002,
  2048, 2291, 2580, 2898
McKitrick, Eric, 1339
McLaughlin, Andrew C., 159, 1006,
  **1711**, 1909
McLean, John, 184, 245, 675, 681, 820,
  1238, 1412, 1617, 1686, **1711–1713**,
  1791, 2555, 2628, 2651, 2867, 2885
McMillan, James B., 2627
McReynolds, James C., 32, 107, 127,
  128, 259, 284, 317, 441, 457, 458, 697,
  698, 737, 743, 921, 1030, 1065, 1201–
  1202, 1284, 1311, 1314, **1714–1715**,
  1724, 1753, 1772, 1908, 2470, 2544,
  2563, 2573, 2636, 2637, 2809, 2882,
  2896, 2899
Mead, William, 1512
Meese, Edwin, 135, 616, 667, 1291,
  1394, 1715, 1801, 2127, 2451, 2714
Meiklejohn, Alexander, 17, 231, 426,
  427, 769, 1047, 1126, 1128, 1628,
  **1716**, 1922, 2214

Mellen, G. W. F., 3
Melville, Herman, 892, 1782
Merriam, Charles E., 717
Metzenbaum, Howard, 46
Michelman, Frank, 1588, 1973, 1974, 2033, 2576
Micke, William, 310
Mifflin, Thomas, **1726**
Mill, John Stuart, 15, 350, 1046, 1126, 1671, 1730–1731, 1838, 2534, 2593
Miller, Arthur Selwyn, 1792
Miller, George L., 1224
Miller, John, 355
Miller, Samuel F., 112, 216, 218, 283, 338, 339, 341, 342, 747, 1037, 1175, 1184, 1339, 1536, 1581, 1582, 1594, 1636, **1731–1734**, 1736, 1753, 2075, 2423–2424, 2570, 2679, 2680, 2817, 2824, 2825–2826, 2828, 2938
Milligan, Lambden, 1736
Milton, John, 1046, 1671, 1737–1739, 1807, 1949, 2172, 2211, 2381, 2593
Ming, William R., 1528
Minor, Francis, 2807–2808
Minor, Virginia, 2807–2080, 2920
Minton, Sherman, 279, **1740**, 1991, 2675, 2791, 2793, 2794, 2941
Miranda, Ernesto, 1741, 1925–1926
Mistretta, John, 1749
Mitchell, Billy, 1954
Mitchell, John N., 134–135, 2761–2762
Mitchell, Todd, 2913
Mitchell, William D., 596, 2612
Monaghan, Henry, 1860, 1862, 1867
Mondale, Walter F., 616, 2786
Monroe, James, 30, 288, 291, 424, 433, 454, 506, 554, 555, 556, 558, 941, 1075, 1190, 1385, 1407, 1425, 1636, 1689, 1712, **1754**, 1755, 1874, 2468, 2609, 2697, 2779, 2825, 2884, 2913
Montesquieu, Charles Louis de S., Baron de, 214, 245, 343, 376, 521, 635, 637, 641, 661, 1010, 1013, 1470, 1640, **1755–1756**, 2211, 2212, 2382, 2716, 2834
Moody, William H., 135, 893, 1164, **1756**, 2292, 2630, 2744, 2897
Moore, Alfred, **1756**, 2601
Moore, Inez, 1756
Morgan, J. P., 219, 224, 1594
Morgan, Thomas J., 587
Morison, Samuel Eliot, 1339
Morrill, Justin, 1087, 1761
Morris, Gouverneur, 49, 287, 521, 661, 947, 1487, 1751, 1752, 1753, **1761–1762**, 1985, 1986, 2358, 2479, 2805
Morris, Robert, 1761, 1762, **1762–1763**
Morrison, Alexia, 2463

Morrow, William W., **1763**
Morse, Wayne, 2788–2789
Mosley, Earl, 1922
Motley, Constance Baker, 2763
Mott, Lucretia, 370, 2366, 2477, 2806
Mounier, J. J., 2500
Muhlenberg, Frederick A., 1058
Mulroney, Brian, 1826
Mundt, Karl, 1766–1767
Munro, William B., 453
Murphy, Frank, 33, 129, 131, 136, 244, 331, 385, 458, 605, 815, 830, 861, 945, 1025, 1042, 1065, 1233, 1355, 1417, **1768–1769**, 1907, 2008, 2282, 2283, 2289, 2292–2293, 2302, 2329, 2545–2546, 2548, 2549, 2699, 2791, 2793, 2795, 2796, 2929, 2930, 2931, 2937, 2938
Murphy, Jack, 1770
Murphy, Paul L., **1769–1770**
Murray, William (Lord Mansfield), 2, 197, 1099, 1338, **1770–1771**, 2452, 2712, 2905
Myrdal, Gunnar, 2441

# N

Nast, Thomas, 1322
Nathanson, Nathaniel, 2529, 2531
Neagle, David, 2311
Neale, Thomas, 1970
Nearing, Scott, 78
Nedham, Marchamont, 2382
Nell, William C., 370
Nelson, Samuel, 113, 339, 340, 1230, 1581, 1582, 1745, **1791–1792**, 2022, 2557, 2698, 2868
Nelson, Steve, 1894
Neuborne, Burt, 378
Newman, Jon O., 1452
Newton, Isaac, 1633, 2712–2713
Nicholls, Francis, 2894
Nietzsche, Friedrich, 757
Nimmer, Melville B., **1807–1808**
Nixon, L. A., 2809
Nixon, Richard M., 48, 49, 65, 112, 113, 114–115, 126–127, 158, 190, 191, 209, 248, 250, 260, 262, 266, 270, 272, 281, 289, 377, 380, 433, 494, 495, 498, 609, 610, 614, 615, 617, 618, 679, 699, 715, 755, 773, 863, 875, 886, 949, 1003, 1026, 1070, 1075, 1232, 1242, 1307, 1339, 1341, 1349, 1359, 1360, 1402, 1595, 1615, 1650, 1676–1677, 1737, 1766–1767, 1770, 1781, 1793, **1815–1817**, 1817–1818, 1819, 1822, 1878, 1954, 1969, 1994, 1995, 2002, 2152,

2156, 2159, 2160, 2227, 2312, 2320, 2365, 2384, 2414–2415, 2448, 2481, 2487, 2541, 2561–2562, 2592–2593, 2609, 2614, 2627, 2664, 2734, 2784–2785, 2789, 2790, 2836, 2838, 2842, 2864, 2865, 2886
Nixon, Walter, 1340, 1341
Noia, Charles, 975
Noonan, John T., Jr., 92
Noriega, Manuel, 2002, 2843
Norris, Clarence, 1825
Norris, George W., 595, 596, 598, 1310–1311, **1825**, 2079, 2666, 2740–2741, 2883
North, Lord, 245
North, Oliver, 622, 1403
Nortz, E. C., 1201

# O

Oakely, Thomas, 1190
Oaks, Dallin H., 938
O'Brien, David, 817, 818
O'Brien, John Lord, 1606–1607
O'Connor, Sandra Day, 7, 8, 9, 10, 12, 14, 24, 55, 56, 58, 63, 70, 98, 112, 113, 137, 165, 203, 251, 273, 277, 312, 359, 508, 616, 686, 695, 703, 732, 827, 848, 892, 894–895, 915, 916, 924, 925, 983, 991, 1032, 1054, 1068, 1110, 1156, 1202, 1209, 1253, 1283, 1293, 1391, 1427, 1435, 1529, 1530, 1531, 1602, 1653, 1691, 1723, 1724, 1735, 1746, 1783, 1813, 1824, 1831, **1841–1846**, 1856, 1877, 1885, 1886, 1895, 1915, 1928, 2012, 2020, 2056, 2082, 2108, 2122, 2123, 2127, 2137, 2158, 2159, 2161, 2168, 2169, 2173, 2175, 2196, 2207, 2226, 2231, 2248, 2269, 2270, 2276, 2313, 2314, 2315, 2338, 2379, 2387, 2392, 2409, 2418, 2419, 2456, 2582, 2589, 2607, 2661, 2666, 2681, 2697, 2698, 2699, 2833, 2866, 2872, 2921, 2933, 2934
Ogden, David B., 436
Old, William, 451
Olmstead, Gideon, 1441, 1442
Olmstead, Roy, 1849
Olney, Richard, 429, **1850–1851**, 1959
Olson, Theodore, 2463
Ordronaux, John, 452
Ortega y Gassett, José, 378
Otis, James, Jr., 132, 208, 512, 533, 1097, 1099, 1174, **1865–1866**, 1888–1889, 2781
Otis, Samuel A., 1058
Overton, William Ray, 2765

# P

Pacificus. *See* Hamilton, Alexander

Paine, Thomas, 27, 84, 246, 513, 537, 1365, **1874**, 2297

Paley, William, 85

Palmer, A. Mitchell, 135, 1303, **1875**, 2352

Palmieri, Edmund, 1195

Palmore, Linda, 1875–1876

Pardee, Don Albert, **1877–1878**

Parker, Isaac, 332, 1159

Parker, Joel, 451

Parker, John J. H., 49, 114–115, 595, 1303, 2638

Parker, Theodore, 370, 2431

Parsons, James, 2763

Paschal, George Washington, 2680

Passman, Otto, 748

Paterson, William, 290, 360, 517, 519, 520, 542–543, 673, 980, 1067, 1324, 1432, 1682, 1800, **1882–1884**, 2051, 2564, 2601, 2602, 2781, 2782, 2859

Patman, Wright, 2283

Patterson, James, 1339

Paul, Alice, 2918

Payne, Daniel A., 2433

Peckham, Rufus W., 70, 241, 330, 430, 844, 1163, 1164, 1165, 1166, 1167, 1169, 1288, 1415, 1638, 1651, 1700, 1704, 1710, **1890–1891**, 2298, 2414, 2635, 2714–2715, 2895, 2897, 2940

Peckham, Wheeler H., 114

Peirce, Charles, 757, 1982

Pekelis, Alexander A., 83

Pendleton, Edmund, 467, 1692, **1891–1892**, 2662, 2754, 2935

Pendleton, George H., 1892

Penn, Lemuel A., 1240

Penn, William, 282, 489, 635, 1512, 1664, 1800, **1892**, 1894

Pepper, George Wharton, 2612

Perkins, Frances, 2936

Perot, Ross, 431

Perry, Michael, 1502, 2175

Perry, Twila, 46

Peters, Richard, 156, 980, 1156, 1441, **1902**, 2601, 2883

Pfeffer, Leo, 83

Phelps, Edward J., **1903**

Philips, Josiah, 174

Phillips, Wendell, 3, 2431, 2540

Pickering, John, 552, 1673, 1684, 1821, **1906**, 2763

Pierce, Charlotte Woodward, 2808

Pierce, Franklin, 258, 298, 416, 477, 565, 566, 574, 1413, 1625, **1908**

Pierce, William, 517, **1908**

Pinckney, Charles, 180, 287, 322, 385, 436, 502, 517, 520, 522, 661, 805, 1800, **1909**, 2601

Pinckney, Charles Cotesworth, 522, 1432, **1909**

Pine, David, 2527, 2735

Pinkney, William, 1706, **1910**, 2611, 2871

Pitney, Mahlon, 684, 864, 1100, 1308, 1309, 1350, 1804, **1911–1912**, 2571, 2634, 2637, 2896, 2899, 2939

Pitt, William, 533, **1912**, 2657

Pitt, William, the Younger, 245

Plato, 1364, 1946

Plessy, Homer A., 1918

Plutarch, 2211

Pocahontas, 1646

Poindexter, John M., 622, 1403

Polenberg, Richard, 2219

Polk, James K., 159, 416, 430, 563, 565, 574, 1229, 1413, 1620, **1958–1959**, 2469–2470, 2527, 2884, 2908

Pollak, Louis, 1792

Pollak, Walter H., **1959**

Pollock, Sir Frederick, 527, 751, 1296, 1308

Pollock, Stewart, 2502

Pomeroy, John N., 451, 1429

Posner, Richard, 657, 658, 660, 2444

Pound, Roscoe, 154, 328, 378, 674, 864, 1192, 1580, 1715, **1972**, 1982, 2442, 2444, 2445–2446

Powell, Adam Clayton, Jr., 501, 1306, 1981

Powell, Colin, 118

Powell, Lewis F., Jr., 22, 53, 56, 57, 72, 113, 114, 116, 133, 158, 165, 209, 226, 239, 272, 274, 277, 301, 305, 307, 310, 318, 327, 380, 396, 430, 440, 447, 464, 688, 706, 707, 710, 712, 794, 829, 830, 831, 915, 1060, 1071, 1135, 1143, 1157, 1181, 1189, 1203, 1205, 1237, 1250, 1285, 1304, 1326, 1328, 1370, 1394, 1396, 1416, 1426, 1434, 1459, 1526, 1529, 1530, 1535, 1558, 1586, 1587, 1588, 1599–1600, 1602, 1665, 1679, 1702, 1703, 1724, 1737, 1756, 1781, 1789, 1817, 1819, 1849, 1886, 1893, 1920, 1939, **1975–1980**, 2046, 2104, 2127, 2146, 2154, 2159, 2161, 2168, 2200, 2205, 2207, 2208, 2232, 2247, 2299, 2309, 2313, 2319–2320, 2385, 2390, 2401, 2415, 2417, 2418, 2450, 2517, 2582–2583, 2694, 2706, 2713, 2732, 2869,

2880, 2917, 2933, 2934, 2940, 2943

Powell, Thomas Reed, 817, 1000, 1007, **1980–1981**, 2641

Powys, Sir Thomas, 208

Pratt, Charles (Lord Camden), 216, 512, 1099, **1985**, 2236, 2657, 2905

Preston, Thomas, 26

Price, Richard, 512

Prigg, Edward, 2006, 2430

Pritchett, C. Herman, 1461

Prosser, William L., 2014

Proxmire, William, 1324, 2359, 2464

Publius, 1786

Pufendorf, Samuel, 752

# Q

Quackenbush, Charles, 20

Quincy, Edmund, 3–4

Quinlan, Karen Ann, 2268

# R

Radin, Max, 2848

Raleigh, Sir Walter, 439

Randolph, Edmund, 26, 114, 134, 160, 288, 322, 454, 520, 521, 522, 544, 546, 877, 980, 1015, 1158, 1259, 1882, 1909, **2115–2116**, 2119, 2358, 2601, 2611, 2684, 2703, 2800, 2860, 2861

Randolph, John, 337, 551, 558, 1339, **2117**, 2346, 2591, 2737

Rantoul, Robert, 560

Ratner, Leonard, 1502

Raulston, John T., 2666

Ravara, Joseph, 980

Rawle, William, 450, **2124**, 2346

Rawls, John, 2174, 2297

Read, George, **2124**

Reagan, Ronald, 9, 12, 48, 50, 92–93, 98, 112, 113, 114–115, 206, 209, 248, 262, 273, 280, 281, 282, 289, 432, 614, 615, 616, 617, 619, 620, 621–622, 625, 699, 715, 776, 824, 948, 969, 1003, 1008, 1018, 1062, 1079, 1219, 1291, 1304, 1394, 1402, 1529, 1574, 1576, 1626, 1680, 1719, 1744, 1813, 1840, 1841, 1842, 1844, 1857, 1887, 1916, 1993, 1994, **2124–2129**, 2154, 2157, 2159, 2160, 2168, 2312, 2313, 2315, 2361, 2451, 2453, 2481, 2501, 2589, 2610, 2695, 2742, 2755, 2785, 2786, 2811, 2843

Redfield, Isaac, 2507

Reed, Sally, 2390

Reed, Stanley F., 33, 107, 244, 253, 254, 317, 458, 804, 921, 1065, 1198, 1256, 1436, 1645, 1655, 1704, 1713, 1761, 1768, **2144–2145**, 2289, 2292–2293, 2437, 2548, 2793, 2794, 2795, 2849, 2852, 2941

Rehnquist, William H., 7, 8, 9, 10, 12, 15, 56, 64, 71, 98, 115, 117, 118–119, 150, 158, 165, 184, 192, 201, 204, 212, 226, 251, 263, 272, 276, 277, 293, 296, 301, 317, 327, 331, 345, 347, 359, 380, 381, 429, 430, 440, 446, 447, 464, 487, 508, 690, 695, 704, 707, 711, 732, 761, 762, 775, 788, 802, 831, 853, 898, 899, 935, 983, 993, 1012, 1054, 1055, 1060, 1062, 1063, 1064, 1071, 1082, 1157, 1172, 1199, 1202, 1203, 1205, 1214, 1292, 1322, 1327, 1332, 1345, 1391, 1396, 1411, 1443, 1471, 1529, 1530, 1562, 1570, 1587, 1600, 1602, 1634, 1643, 1679, 1722, 1724, 1725, 1726, 1729–1730, 1747, 1750, 1758, 1763, 1776, 1801, 1802, 1817, 1824, 1831, 1841, 1842, 1844, 1879, 1885, 1886, 1888, 1889, 1893, 1900, 1927, 1969, 2012, 2033, 2055, 2056, 2060, 2127, **2152–2160**, 2196, 2199, 2205, 2207, 2232, 2246, 2262, 2266, 2268–2269, 2270, 2275, 2287, 2295, 2299, 2300, 2306, 2313, 2314, 2315, 2317, 2351, 2379, 2395, 2409, 2418, 2452, 2455, 2456, 2463, 2472, 2487, 2492, 2502, 2535, 2537, 2572, 2576, 2589, 2605, 2606, 2620, 2646, 2663, 2680, 2681, 2695, 2696, 2699, 2700, 2702, 2732, 2750, 2751, 2789, 2798, 2821, 2872, 2914, 2943

Reich, Charles, 377
Reid, Thomas, 2909
Reno, Janet, 1360
Reston, James, 1104
Reynolds, William Bradford, 616, 2451
Rhett, Robert B., 1833
Rhodes, James, 2319
Richards, David, 1838
Richardson, Elliot, 209, 1359, 2449
Riddick, Gregory, 2913
Ritchie, Thomas, 1412
Roane, Spencer, 438, 555, 1424, 1668, 1686, 1689, 1705, 1706, 1707, **2280**, 2590–2591
Roberts, Owen D., 2612
Roberts, Owen J., 107, 284–285, 299, 317, 321, 444, 457, 458, 697, 1065, 1107, 1193, 1256, 1285, 1303, 1311, 1314, 1316, 1317, 1416, 1417, 1447, 1715, 1768, 1789, 2021, 2066, 2115, 2261, **2281–2282**, 2329, 2437, 2544,

2548, 2681, 2793, 2809, 2820, 2882, 2931, 2937
Robinson, Joseph T., 698, 2289
Rock, John S., 2611–2612
Rockefeller, John D., 2472
Rockefeller, Nelson, 679
Rodell, Fred, 453
Rodney, Caesar A., **2284**
Roe, Gilbert E., 2047
Roosevelt, Eleanor, 607
Roosevelt, Franklin D., 4, 62, 70, 75, 112, 113, 114, 119, 130, 131, 142, 168, 171, 173, 185, 226, 230, 260, 262, 266, 285, 343, 348, 373, 378, 379, 386, 420, 431, 452, 456, 458, 495, 496, 498, 504, 527, 590, 591, 594, 596–597, 597–600, 601–602, 609, 614, 697, 698, 699, 734, 736, 754, 813, 814, 875, 885, 886, 942, 944, 954, 976, 1002, 1101, 1202, 1288, 1301, 1311, 1312–1313, 1316, 1318, 1349, 1366, 1410, 1416, 1429, 1437, 1452, 1456, 1457, 1478, 1479, 1488, 1494, 1532, 1563, 1582, 1595, 1615, 1634, 1714, 1715, 1740, 1751, 1761, 1768, 1775, 1793, 1794, 1796, 1815, 1825, 1935, 1954, 1995, 1999, 2002, 2079, 2085, 2115, 2124, 2125, 2126, 2127, 2143, 2274, 2281, **2287–2291**, 2292, 2302, 2317, 2364, 2437, 2453, 2505, 2544, 2548, 2551, 2592, 2604, 2633, 2666, 2733, 2738, 2742, 2780, 2785, 2820, 2841, 2848, 2878, 2881, 2884, 2929, 2930, 2932, 2936
Roosevelt, Theodore, 112, 134, 433, 575, 588, 589–590, 597, 748, 941, 1024, 1025, 1161, 1164, 1167, 1234, 1263, 1284, 1540, 1557, 1641, 1709, 1714, 1756, 1828, 1995–1996, 2047, 2287, **2291–2292**, 2413, 2591, 2634, 2733, 2780, 2786, 2808, 2894, 2897, 2898, 2911
Root, Elihu, 1746
Rosenberg, Ethel and Julius, 280, 2294, 2794
Rosenberg, Gerald, 701
Rossiter, Clinton, 265, 324, 1402, 1996, **2295**
Rostow, Eugene, 1416, 1792
Roth, Samuel, 1838
Rousseau, Jean-Jacques, 448, 1052, 1904, 2346, 2461
Royce, Josiah, 1263
Rubin, Edward, 990
Ruckleshaus, William, 209, 2449
Rudman, Warren B., 1219
Ruffin, Edmund, 1833
Ruffin, Thomas, 558
Russell, Charles T., 2189

Russell, Francis, 468
Russo, Anthony, 2010
Rutherford, Joseph F., 1065
Rutledge, Edward, 538, 2601
Rutledge, John, 48, 49, 440, 1432, **2301**, 2359, 2364, 2600, 2601, 2861
Rutledge, Wiley B., 33, 112, 204, 440, 815, 931, 1199, 1355, 1704, 1740, 1990, 1991, 2008, 2060, 2289, 2292–2293, **2302–2303**, 2370, 2529, 2530, 2531, 2535, 2546, 2548, 2549, 2583, 2791, 2793, 2796, 2930, 2937, 2938

## S

Sacco, Nicola, 78, 467, 468, 1281
Sacks, Albert, 1274, 1578, 1579
Sadat, Anwar, 320
Sadler, John, 2381–2382
St. Clair, Arthur, Jr., 1594, 1711
St. John, Henry (Viscount Bolingbroke), 512
Sallust, 2211
Sanborn, John B., 191
Sandalow, Terrance, 632
Sanford, Edward, 35, 146, 1198, 1264, 1921, **2310–2311**, 2326, 2637, 2902
Sanford, John F. A., 818
Sanger, Margaret, 182, 1122, 2325
Santayana, George, 1263
Sawyer, Charles, 2526
Sawyer, Lorenzo, **2311**
Sax, Joseph, 2511
Scalia, Antonin, 7, 8, 9, 10, 11, 12, 15, 55, 56, 98, 115, 139, 192, 202, 203, 204, 209, 227, 239, 243, 296, 312, 345, 359, 380, 381, 508, 695, 703, 707, 732, 733, 778, 805, 894, 895, 903, 918, 982, 983, 990, 1012, 1055, 1062, 1208, 1253, 1291, 1293, 1327, 1435, 1460, 1529, 1530, 1573, 1576, 1602, 1627, 1651, 1691, 1750, 1766, 1782–1783, 1814, 1831, 1832, 1885, 1886, 1939, 2056, 2082, 2108, 2123–2124, 2127, 2150, 2151, 2157, 2158, 2159, 2160, 2161, 2163, 2168, 2173, 2196, 2231, 2248, 2287, 2300–2301, **2312–2316**, 2324, 2327, 2337, 2379, 2387, 2409, 2419, 2454, 2456, 2463, 2475, 2517, 2518, 2568, 2607, 2645, 2681, 2696, 2698–2699, 2711, 2751, 2798, 2913
Scalia, Catherine Louise Panaro, 2312
Scalia, S. Eugene, 2312
Scheiber, Harry N., 889, 890
Schenck, Charles, 1710
Schick, Maurice, 2319
Schlesinger, Arthur, Jr., 1349, 1402, 1996

Schofield, John M., 1429
Schouler, James, 452, **2324**
Schroeder, Theodore, **2324–2325**
Schuck, Peter, 183
Schumpeter, Joseph, 333
Schwartz, Bernard, **2325**
Schwellenbach, Lewis, 1794
Schwimmer, Rosiki, 2325–2326
Scopes, John, 78, 157, 2666
Scott, Dred, 736, 2432
Scott, Winfield, 2476
Seabrook, Whitemarsh, 1832
Seale, Bobby, 1955
Seidman, Louis Michael, 2123
Selden, John, 828, **2355–2356**
Sellin, Thorsten, 309
Serrano, Andres, 1136
Seward, William H., 3, 1085, 2117, 2216,
    **2389**, 2431, 2584, 2663, 2692, 2884,
    2885
Shakespeare, William, 491
Shapiro, David L., 2154
Shapiro, Martin, 1792
Shapiro, Michael, 2060
Sharfman, Isaiah, 1396
Sharpe, Granville, 512
Shaw, Lemuel, 198, 332, 467, 560, 561,
    562, 681, 708, 889, 1160, 1617, 1918,
    2282, 2283, **2408–2409**, 2417, 2506–
    2507, 2508, 2510, 2583, 2648, 2934–
    2935
Shays, Daniel, 2410
Shellabarger, Samuel, 339, 504–505
Sheppard, Sam, 1150, 1179
Sherman, John, 1339, 2412, 2413
Sherman, Roger, 48, 175, 538, 543, 752,
    1228, **2412**
Sherwood, Forest, 1257
Shiras, George, 112, 330, 1164, 1273,
    **2413–2414**
Shirley, J. M., 674
Shively, Jill, 2915
Sickles, Daniel, 2476
Sidney, Algernon, 2211
Sidoti, Anthony, 1875–1876
Sieyès, Emmanuel Joseph (Abbé),
    2500
Simon, Paul, 2365
Simpson, Nicole Brown, 2915
Simpson, O. J., 1152, 2915
Sims, Thomas, 2431
Singer, Joseph William, 1984
Sirica, John, 1817
Skinner, Quentin, 630
Smith, Abby, 370
Smith, Adam, 593, 834, 1946
Smith, Alfred E., 597
Smith, Gerrit, 3

Smith, J. Allen, 453, 754, 2046–2047,
    **2436**
Smith, James Everet, 1932
Smith, James Morton, 738, 1770
Smith, Joseph, 2715
Smith, Melancton, 763
Smith, Roger, 183
Smith, William French, 134–135
Smith, William Kennedy, 2915
Smith, William Loughton, 1058
Smolin, David, 2175
Snepp, Frank W., 2438
Sobeloff, Simon E., **2438**
Soper, Philip, 900–901
Sorauf, Frank, 1940
Souter, David H., 12, 14, 50, 103, 202,
    211, 238, 281, 282, 312, 359, 436, 732,
    803, 1291, 1320, 1530, 1531, 1651,
    1680, 1747, 1813, 1831–1832, 1845,
    1915, 2161, 2168, 2179, 2246, 2270,
    2419, **2453–2456**, 2518, 2702, 2714
Spaight, Richard Dobbs, 166, 1403,
    **2462**
Spencer, Herbert, 451, 593, 2878
Spinoza, Baruch, 1870
Spock, Benjamin, 709, 2441, 2790
Spooner, Lysander, 3
Stalin, Joseph, 1702
Stanbery, Henry S., 1429, 1736, **2471**
Stanford, Leland, 1709
Stanton, Edwin M., 126, 134, 288, 579,
    948, 1225, 1339, 1428, 1745, **2476**,
    2540, 2669
Stanton, Elizabeth Cady, 91, 370, 1092,
    2253, 2366, **2476–2477**, 2806, 2918
Stanton, Harriot, 2477
Stanton, Henry Brewster, 2476
Stanton, Theodore, 2477
Starr, Kenneth, 127, 433, 434, 625, 954,
    1360, 2386
Steinbeck, John, 861
Stephens, Alexander H., 451, 478, 1622,
    1623, **2527–2528**, 2705, 2884
Steuben, Friedrich Wilhelm von, 831
Stevens, John Paul, 7, 12, 15, 54, 56, 59,
    157, 170, 203, 214, 226, 273, 277, 279,
    293, 298, 301, 304, 310, 313, 327, 345,
    369, 429, 433, 442, 444, 465, 505, 626,
    687, 695, 704, 803, 871, 890, 914,
    1012, 1062, 1063, 1064, 1068, 1118,
    1144, 1214, 1237, 1254, 1272, 1293,
    1435, 1530, 1575, 1586–1587, 1627,
    1651, 1672, 1717, 1725, 1726, 1757,
    1782, 1783, 1831, 1843, 1877, 1889,
    1893, 1915, 1969, 2033, 2052, 2122,
    2123, 2137, 2161, 2168, 2182, 2196,
    2206, 2208, 2230, 2231, 2232, 2242–
    2243, 2244, 2245, 2247, 2266, 2267,

    2270, 2277, 2295, 2306, 2313, 2314,
    2317, 2379, 2392, 2395, 2419, 2438,
    2455, 2456, **2529–2539**, 2574, 2605,
    2620, 2698, 2699, 2702, 2832–2833,
    2862, 2863, 2883, 2904, 2940, 2943
Stevens, Thaddeus, 4, 181, 504, 1085,
    1339, 1528, 1728, 2216, 2520, **2539–
    2540**
Stevens, Wallace, 668
Stevenson, Adlai, 1200
Stewart, Alvan, 3, 561
Stewart, Potter J., 1, 70, 142, 152, 170,
    203, 226, 242, 273, 277, 280, 301, 310,
    311, 430, 446, 447, 741, 830, 896, 897,
    899, 906, 927, 929, 1018, 1123, 1139,
    1140, 1172, 1199, 1230, 1240, 1271,
    1272, 1273, 1285, 1320, 1414, 1452,
    1527, 1542, 1548, 1602, 1646, 1666,
    1716–1717, 1735, 1737, 1741, 1789,
    1806, 1812, 1846, 1879, 1899, 1902,
    1904, 1928, 1965, 1976, 2102, 2161,
    2200, 2228, 2230, 2242, 2271, 2275,
    2299, 2412, 2415, 2476, 2487, **2541–
    2543**, 2565, 2589, 2604, 2608, 2627,
    2746, 2802, 2832, 2855, 2878, 2914,
    2917, 2939, 2940, 2943
Stewart, Richard B., 902
Stimson, Henry L., 2290
Stone, Geoffrey R., 1646
Stone, Harlan Fiske, 52, 107, 112–113,
    114, 134, 152, 219, 221, 285, 286, 314,
    317, 321, 388, 441, 457, 458, 595, 693,
    697, 743, 792, 793, 795, 814, 817, 830,
    838, 910, 1011, 1018, 1050, 1065,
    1101, 1102, 1177, 1198, 1226, 1256,
    1262, 1263, 1290, 1311, 1314, 1381,
    1404, 1416, 1438, 1439, 1715, 1760–
    1761, 1802, 1874, 1879, 1990, 2085,
    2115, 2121–2122, 2156, 2172, 2227,
    2230, 2281, 2282, 2288, 2289, 2292–
    2293, 2302, 2310, 2318, 2349, 2422,
    2437, 2445, 2458, 2471, 2494, 2522,
    **2543–2547**, 2548, 2575, 2576, 2589,
    2592, 2593, 2604, 2605, 2606, 2624,
    2634, 2636, 2637, 2645, 2668, 2746,
    2758, 2791, 2820, 2882, 2931, 2937
Storing, Herbert J., 101, **2553**
Story, Joseph, 112, 156, 159, 162, 245,
    298, 333, 344, 360, 362, 423, 437, 438,
    450, 466, 555, 559, 560, 561, 562, 563,
    674, 675, 677, 681, 735, 742, 745, 746,
    813, 832, 842, 981, 1159, 1175, 1228,
    1230, 1265, 1336, 1337, 1365, 1465,
    1479, 1503, 1633, 1635, 1662, 1682,
    1683, 1685, 1689–1690, 1691, 1700,
    1710, 1712, 1901, 1986, 1994, 2006,
    2121, 2218, 2346, 2348, 2430, 2506,
    2512, **2553–2557**, 2590, 2629, 2648,

Story, Joseph (continued)
2649, 2651, 2654, 2670, 2671, 2681,
2684, 2698, 2732, 2736, 2779, 2783,
2832, 2859, 2868, 2885
Stourzh, Gerald, 635
Stowe, Harriet Beecher, 180, 1091
Strader, Jacob, 2431
Strong, William, 200, 216, 336, 338, 340,
1038, 1225, 1581, 1582, 1753, 1904,
2420, 2559, **2563–2564**, 2825, 2827
Sullivan, L. B., 1805
Sumner, Charles, 3, 4, 404, 504, 577,
735, 1086, 1339, 2217, 2282, 2360,
2431, 2433, 2520, 2521, 2540, 2557,
**2583–2584**, 2612, 2691, 2824, 2830
Sumner, William Graham, 451
Sustein, Cass, 2576
Sutherland, George, 35–36, 219, 284,
315, 321, 441, 457, 458, 628, 631, 697,
720, 736–737, 951, 1101, 1157, 1193,
1194, 1234, 1264, 1301, 1311, 1314,
1318, 1344, 1437, 1634, 1710, 1724,
1887, 1904, 2143, 2260, 2281, 2544,
2608, **2625–2627**, 2636, 2637, 2746,
2780, 2820, 2882
Swaggart, Jimmy, 1427
Swartwout, Samuel, 705
Swayne, Noah, 218, 338, 339, 341, 403,
1184, 1581, 1698, 1736, 1753, 1829,
2564, **2628**, 2680, 2827
Swindler, William, 1458
Swisher, Carl B., 453, **2630**
Synar, Michael, 1219

# T

Tacitus, 2211
Taft, Horace, 2635
Taft, Robert A., 289, 603, 1651, 1687,
1715, 1935, **2633**
Taft, William Howard, 15, 35, 36, 52,
110–111, 112, 113, 114, 151, 219, 221,
260, 261, 281, 283, 346, 348, 421, 448,
460, 588, 589–590, 593, 594, 607, 699,
748, 750, 1020, 1024, 1167, 1262,
1263, 1264, 1309, 1337, 1376, 1452,
1497–1498, 1540, 1558, 1709, 1714,
1764, 1772, 1850, 1911, 1996, 2210,
2281, 2291, 2292, 2298, 2310, 2311,
2314, 2421, 2470, 2501, 2544, 2545,
2546, 2560, 2595, 2604, 2605, 2606,
2626, **2633–2637**, 2637–2642, 2733,
2746, 2755, 2757, 2780, 2881, 2882,
2894, 2895, 2896, 2897, 2898, 2899,
2904, 2911, 2917
Talleyrand, Charles, 1673
Tallmadge, James, 1748

Taney, Roger B., 1, 2, 110, 112, 113, 114,
134, 145–146, 159, 164, 169, 183, 190,
244, 252, 256, 258, 325, 333, 335, 364,
367, 416, 455, 568, 569, 579, 667, 675,
735, 742, 754, 801, 819, 820, 829, 832,
844, 886, 908, 909, 1158, 1160, 1230,
1238, 1287, 1290, 1356, 1409, 1412,
1432, 1613, 1617, 1620, 1623, 1625,
1652–1653, 1710, 1712, 1736, 1748,
1791, 1869, 1901, 1910, 1947, 2006,
2022, 2202, 2210, 2216, 2217, 2274,
2408, 2424, 2425, 2432, 2436, 2506,
2512, 2555, 2556, 2557, 2561, 2587,
2591, 2604, 2630, **2647–2650**, 2651–
2656, 2664–2665, 2687, 2698, 2806–
2807, 2841, 2867, 2868, 2871, 2934
Tappan, Lewis, 3
Taylor, Harriet, 1730, 2346
Taylor, John, 438, 450, 556, 1424, 1705,
1707, **2662–2663**
Taylor, Zachary, 112, 114, 477, 564, 565,
1044, 1959, 2001, 2430, **2663**, 2884
Tazewell, Littleton W., 2611
Ten Broek, Jacobus, 907, **2665**
Tenney, Jack B., 2667
Thacher, Oxenbridge, 1888
Thatch, C. C., Jr., 947
Thayer, James Bradley, 1101, 1161, 1263,
1446, 1460, 1588, 1705, 2214, **2684–
2685**
Thayer, Webster Bradley, 468
Thernstrom, Abigail, 2811–2812
Thomas, Clarence, 12, 15, 58, 282, 298,
345, 407, 727, 733, 990, 1530, 1643,
1750, 1751, 2056, 2108, 2159, 2168,
2169, 2225, 2287, 2315, 2406, 2409,
2419, 2455, 2456, 2670, 2695, **2695–
2696**, 2798, 2811–2812
Thomas, Lorenzo, 2669
Thomas, Norman, 78
Thompson, Francis, 69
Thompson, Seymour D., 199
Thompson, Smith, 675, 1238, 1683,
1686, 1700, 1898, 2649, 2652, **2697–
2698**
Thoreau, Henry David, 369, 370, 816,
1049
Thornberry, Homer, 114
Thorpe, Francis Newton, 680, **2700**
Thorpe, Merle, 452
Thurmond, Strom, 112, 605, 1813, 2520
Tiedeman, Christopher G., 451, 528,
585, 1155, 2508, 2571, **2701**
Tiffany, Joel, 3
Tilden, Samuel J., 189, 319, 478, 581
Tilghman, William, 1159
Tillich, Paul, 2173
Tilson, John G., 589

Tocqueville, Alexis de, 137, 331, 498,
510, 526, 1236, 1365, 1476, 1681,
1837, 1955, 1982, 2073, 2461–2462,
2480, 2651, **2703–2704**
Todd, Thomas, 1683, **2704**, 2732
Tollison, Robert, 2064
Toombs, Robert A., 2527, **2705**, 2884
Tourgee, Albion, 1167
Tower, John, 115, 1402
Trenchard, John, 324
Tribe, Laurence H., 659–660, 1503,
1826, 2094, 2298, 2316
Trimble, Robert, **2732**
Truax, William, 2733
Truman, Harry S., 68, 112, 113, 114,
118, 137–138, 279, 289, 319, 389, 393,
420, 433, 503, 598, 603, 604, 605, 606,
607, 748, 886, 942, 944, 945, 946, 948,
976, 1025, 1075, 1358, 1385, 1402,
1430, 1436, 1532, 1541, 1649, 1687,
1702, 1740, 1921, 2081, 2384, 2411,
2448, 2453, 2526, 2614, 2633, 2642,
**2733–2735**, 2757, 2786, 2787, 2788,
2791, 2793, 2794, 2836, 2837, 2842,
2932, 2941
Trumbull, John, 1059
Trumbull, Lyman, 339, 842, 1087, 1088,
2691, **2735**
Truth, Sojourner, **2735–2736**
Tucker, Henry St. George, 197, 450,
1688, 1908, 2424, **2736–2737**, 2737
Tucker, John Randolph, 197, 451, **2737**
Tucker, Nathaniel Beverly, 197, **2737**
Tucker, St. George, 196, 450, 979, 1424,
2736, 2737, **2737**
Tugwell, Rexford G., 62, **2738**
Tullock, Gordon, 2064
Turgot, Robert Jacques, 28
Turnbull, Robert J., 1832
Turner, Nat, 558
Tussman, Joseph, 907
Twyn, William, 2352
Tyler, John, 49, 90, 113, 292, 425, 558,
559, 561, 563, 1425, 1652, 1791, 2001,
**2746**, 2786, 2884
Tyndale, William, 2236

# U

Unger, Roberto, 2297
Upshar, Abel Parker, 450, 558

# V

Vagts, Detlev, 1826
Vallandigham, Clement L., 416, 2777

Van Buren, Martin, 292, 557, 565, 742, 1163, 1190, 1413, 1710, 2430, 2656, **2779–2780**, 2884

Vandenberg, Arthur, 2362–2363

Van Devanter, Willis, 112, 284, 2289, 2544, 2592, 2634, 2635, 2636, 2637, **2780–2781**, 2803, 2821, 2882, 2896, 2898

Vane, Henry, 515

Vanzetti, Bartolomeo, 78, 467, 468, 1281

Vardaman, James, 2808

Varnum, James, 2723–2724

Vattel, Emerich de, 633, 941, 1694, **2781**

Vaughan, John, 282

Vesey, Denmark, 2

Viktora, Robert, 2123

Viner, Charles, 512

Vining, John, 177

Vinson, Fred M., 79, 163, 204, 254, 279, 420, 607, 769, 1031, 1264, 1996, 2144, 2145, 2294, 2411, 2581, 2604–2605, 2607, 2629, 2705, 2757, **2791–2792**, 2792–2797, 2852, 2885, 2888, 2941

Volstead, Andrew J., 2803

Voltaire, 245

Von Holst, Hermann Eduard, 26, **2804**

# W

Wade, Benjamin, 2818

Wagner, Robert, 2818–2819

Waite, Henry Matson, 53, 2229, 2821

Waite, Morrison R., 52, 199, 216, 217, 733, 747, 833, 844, 1168, 1224, 1225, 1257, 1290, 1740, 1789, 1896, 1900, 2145, 2210, 2420, 2547, 2807–2808, 2817, **2821–2824**, 2824–2830, 2918

Walker, Quock, 467

Walker, Robert J., 566

Walker, Timothy, 450, 2557, **2832**

Wallace, George C., 1815

Wallace, Henry, 62

Wallace, John, 1184, 1338

Walpole, Sir Robert, 245

Walter, Sir John, 1338

Walworth, Reuben, 560

Walwyn, William, 1870

Ward, Lester Frank, 448

Ward, Nathaniel, 1694

Wardle, Lynn, 92

Waring, Waties, 2765

Warner, Richard, 1984

Warren, Charles, 114, 159, 2453, **2847–2848**

Warren, Earl, 69, 112, 113, 152, 164, 168, 206, 229, 238, 254, 255, 257, 272, 280, 607, 630, 700, 721, 771–772, 815, 818, 863, 899, 909, 912, 929, 937, 946, 1020, 1066, 1082, 1161, 1240, 1394, 1416, 1451, 1461, 1485–1486, 1538, 1542, 1595, 1615, 1646, 1670, 1679, 1702, 1741, 1792, 1810, 1836, 1839, 1857, 1894, 1923, 1926, 1981, 1987, 2127, 2205, 2228, 2246, 2280, 2290, 2296, 2341, 2408, 2450, 2453, 2457, 2520, 2549, 2584–2585, 2593, 2594, 2605, 2606, 2607, 2608–2609, 2631, 2645, 2676, 2710, 2713, 2733, 2804, 2810, 2832, **2848–2851**, 2851–2858, 2858, 2866–2867, 2943

Warren, Robert Penn, 69

Warren, Samuel, 223

Washington, Booker T., 1024, 2808, 2828

Washington, Bushrod, 360, 686, 842, 979, 1172, 1228, 1442, 1682, 1683, 2019, 2424, 2601, **2859**

Washington, George, 29, 47, 49, 51, 113, 160, 198, 250, 287, 288, 323, 336, 346, 448, 454, 518, 520, 521, 546, 547, 548, 549, 551, 553, 737, 755, 796, 866, 883, 946, 949, 950, 953, 954, 980, 1013, 1015, 1058, 1074, 1161, 1238, 1257, 1279, 1284, 1290, 1404, 1418, 1419, 1421, 1432, 1464, 1594, 1596, 1610, 1641, 1657, 1692, 1751, 1752, 1762, 1790, 1883, 1897, 1902, 1909, 1934, 1947, 1949, 1991, 2000, 2045, 2115, 2116, 2119, 2124, 2292, 2301, 2359, 2364, 2428, 2468, 2600, 2601, 2634, 2688, 2733, 2741, 2755, 2785, 2805, 2836, 2839, 2859, **2859–2862**, 2863, 2885, 2899

Waters, Cynthia, 2866

Watson, Gregory D., 2742

Wayne, James M., 338, 681, 1412, 1712, 1736, 2555, **2867–2868**, 2883

Wayte, David, 2868

Weber, Max, 2031

Webster, Daniel, 110, 159, 162, 292, 332, 333, 556, 557, 559, 562, 563, 565, 566, 567, 735, 736, 744, 745, 887–888, 913, 1191, 1280, 1557, 1641, 1686, 1706, 1903, 2359, 2431, 2512, 2556, 2611, 2612, 2622, 2651, 2686, 2783, **2870–2872**, 2883, 2885, 2913

Wechsler, Herbert, 255, 990, 1466, 1474, 1475, 1476, 1477, 1502, 1578, 1583, 1744, 1792–1793, 2313, 2545

Weed, Thurlow, 2663

Weis, Joseph F., Jr., 2623

Weisbard, Edward, 494

Wellington, Harry, 1587

Wells, H. G., 588

Weyl, Walter, 2047

Whately, Thomas, 533

Wheare, K. C., 1364

Wheaton, Henry, **2883**

Wheeler, Burton K., 698, 2592, **2883–2884**

Wheelwright, John, 2235

Whitaker, Johnson, 1955

White, Byron R., 7, 12, 15, 25, 54, 56, 59, 137, 157, 158, 165, 168, 182, 192, 201, 208, 213, 214, 226, 242, 250, 251, 257, 265, 272, 294, 301, 307, 310, 329, 350, 368, 407, 428, 429, 435, 436, 440, 446, 465, 676, 677, 691, 695, 710, 712, 720, 762, 778, 830, 869, 882, 898, 929, 1012, 1044, 1054, 1055, 1060, 1064, 1110, 1140, 1181, 1188, 1189, 1204, 1205, 1206, 1214, 1216, 1226, 1233, 1273, 1281, 1283, 1320, 1322, 1331, 1333, 1370, 1434, 1471, 1529, 1532, 1533, 1536, 1538, 1558, 1574, 1600, 1602, 1666, 1717, 1737, 1741–1742, 1747, 1789, 1799, 1802, 1806, 1819, 1831, 1832, 1868, 1889, 1899, 1926, 1928, 1952, 1976, 2040, 2123, 2156, 2171, 2196, 2200, 2205, 2207, 2232, 2248, 2277, 2280, 2285, 2286, 2295, 2299, 2310, 2313, 2314, 2351, 2379, 2412, 2452, 2476, 2487, 2489, 2575–2576, 2604, 2606, 2620, 2627, 2663, 2665–2666, 2680, 2699, 2746, 2802, 2833, 2862, **2885–2893**, 2896, 2904, 2906, 2914, 2922, 2933

White, Edward D., 113, 421, 430, 688, 893, 1164, 1168, 1169, 1242, 1376, 1558, 1704, 1828, 1869, 1960, 2210, 2298, 2356, 2472, 2610, 2634–2635, 2714, **2893–2896**, 2897, 2901, 2912, 2927

White, G. Edward, 2850

White, James Boyd, 1514

Whitelock, James, 634

Whiting, William, 451

Whitman, Walt, 816, 999

Whitney, Anita, 222

Whittaker, Charles E., 280, 863, 1203, 2885, 2888, **2902–2903**

Wickersham, George, 594, **2904**

Wigmore, John H., 480, 1594, 1922, 2237, **2904–2905**

Wilkes, John, 2905

Willebrandt, Mabel Walker, 2612

William III, 530, 1693, 1970

Williams, G. Mennen, 1704

Williams, George H., 134

Williams, Roger, 374, 1045, 1870, 2125, 2185, 2197, 2230, 2370, **2905–2906**

Williams, Samuel, 2381
Williams, Wendy, 2204
Williamson, Hugh, **2907**
Willoughby, Westel W., 452, **2907–2908**
Wilmot, David, 568, 2435, 2908
Wilson, Don W., 2743
Wilson, Henry, 2216
Wilson, James, 48, 84, 125, 356, 517, 518, 521, 534, 538, 543, 661, 673, 754, 877, 947, 980, 995, 998, 1067, 1105, 1279, 1336, 1337, 1357, 1467, 1610, 1657, 1682, 1751, 1762, 1949, 2133, 2215, 2600, 2602, 2603, 2684, 2700, 2716, 2753, 2859, 2861, **2908–2911**
Wilson, Peter, 183
Wilson, Woodrow, 33, 49, 112, 219, 261, 274, 288, 289, 378, 425, 452, 460, 494, 499, 582, 588, 590, 591, 595, 596, 597, 665, 728, 748, 751, 1025, 1030, 1101, 1167, 1262, 1303, 1309, 1402, 1429, 1528, 1532, 1557, 1633, 1714, 1746, 1772, 1935, 2002, 2047, 2114, 2287, 2292, 2356, 2360, 2634, 2637, 2733,

2786, 2803, 2808, 2899, 2900, **2911–2912**, 2918, 2919, 2927, 2928, 2929
Wingate, Edmond, 2235
Winthrop, John, 531
Wirt, William, 334, 2611, **2913**
Wisdom, John Minor, 2313, **2914–2915**
Wise, Stephen S., 83
Witherspoon, Joseph, 92
Wolcott, Alexander, 2554
Wong Kim Ark, 2922
Wood, Gordon S., 1291
Wood, Stephen, 2676
Woodbury, Levi, 735, 1652, **2922–2923**
Woodhull, Victoria, 2477
Woods, William B., 1272, **2923–2924**
Woodward, Bob, 508
Woodward, C. Vann, 772
Woolsey, John M., 2747–2748
Worcester, Samuel, 344
Wortman, Tunis, **2931**
Wright, J. Skelly, 2765, **2932**
Wright, Silas, 1412
Wright, Susan Webber, 433, 434
Wyman, Bruce, 591

Wythe, George, 86, 228, 423, 467, 1419, 1610, 1692, 1891, 2500, 2737, **2935**
Wyzanski, Charles E., Jr., **2935–2936**

## Y

Yamashita, Tomoyuki, 2937
Yancey, William L., 1833
Yasui, Minoru, 1417, 2107, 2842
Yates, Robert, 516, 519, 520, 1258, 1662–1663, **2938**
Yñíguez, Maria-Kelly, 1759
Yoder, Frieda, 2914
Young, Arthur, 84
Young, Edward T., 2940

## Z

Zeisel, Hans, 1510, 1517, 1525
Zenger, John Peter, 178, 180, 1512, 2352–2353, 2944
Zubly, J. J., 513

# Subject Index

*Numbers in **boldface** refer to the main entry on the subject.*

## A

AAA. *See* Agricultural Adjustment Act
Abolitionist constitutional theory, **2–4**
  Birney cases, 182
  civil disobedience, 1183
  constitutional challenges, 558, 560
  Declaration of Independence, 754
  due process, 2
  fugitive slavery, 1159
  of Garrison, 1183
  guarantee clause, 1239
  incorporated into Fourteenth Amendment, 181
  natural law invocation, 2210
  personal liberty laws, 3, 4, 1159, 1901, 2006
  petition campaigns, 2, 31, 385, 2274, 2425, 2884
  privileges and immunities invocation, 1287–1288
  on slavery in the territories, 2425, 2434
  slave trade prohibition, 2050
  state suicide theory, 2520
  substantive due process, 2, 829
  Thirteenth Amendment and, 2691

  *See also* Slavery and the Constitution
Abolition of slavery. *See* Emancipation Proclamation; Thirteenth Amendment
Abortion and the Constitution, **4–5, 6–9** (update 1a), **9–11** (update 1b), **11–14** (update 2a), **14–15** (update 2b)
  balancing test, 155
  Blackmun opinion legalizing, 190, 191, 192, 196, 1291, 2204, 2284
  and Burger Court, 270, 274, 277, 2163
  civil liberty issue, 376, 380
  communitarians on, 473
  constitutional amendment proposal, 76, 92, 123, 2126, 2127, 2205
  counseling restraints, 2300
  and Court activism, 1393
  and courts as social change agents, 701
  *Doe v. Bolton*, 2284–2286
  equal protection clause argument, 1197
  fetal viability, 2207
  Fourteenth Amendment application, 5, 15, 2057
  fundamental interests, 1173, 1175, 2204

  *Griswold* precedent, 182, 1233–1234
  historical abortion practices, 1291
  Hyde Amendment, 6, 7, 1324, 2205–2206
  implied rights, 2163
  informed consent, 12
  invalidation of state laws, 2284
  and judicial policymaking, 1461–1462
  *Maher v. Roe*, 1665, 2286
  minors' rights, 6, 11, 192, 317, 352, 353, 1293, 2123, 2208
  parental and spousal consent invalidation, 192
  parental notification, 6, 11, 12, 192, 1123, 1293, 2122, 2208
  partial-birth bans, 13, 14–15
  permissible vs. impermissible restrictions, 13
  *Planned Parenthood of Central Missouri v. Danforth*, 1916
  *Planned Parenthood v. Casey*, 11–14, 625, 1914–1916, 2122–2123, 2168
  privacy basis, 5, 8, 10–11, 12, 92, 94, 274, 1118, 1233, 1615, 2052, 2242, 2284, 2285, 2921
  privileges and immunities clause application, 2020

Abortion and the Constitution (continued)
  property rights in human body argument, 2057
  public funding restrictions, 6, 7, 1272–1273, 1324, 1665, 1974, 2158, 2205–2206, 2286, 2872, 2880
  public understanding of *Roe* decision, 2078
  and race, 2097
  rational basis test, 2122–2123
  Reagan views, 2126
  and Rehnquist Court, 2164, 2168
  and reproductive autonomy, 2203–2209
  *Roe v. Wade*, 190, 191, 192, 196, 270, 274, 277, 381, 383, 625, 1461, 1680, 1811, 2163, 2203, 2204–2207, 2242, 2248, 2284–2286, 2921
  *Roe v. Wade* reaffirmation, 2699
  and sex discrimination, 2394
  spousal consent, 6, 2207
  subsidized speech and, 2568
  Thomas view, 2695
  *Thornburgh v. American College of Obstetricians and Gynecologists*, 2699, 2892
  undue burden test, 12, 13
  and unenumerated rights, 10–11
  wealth discrimination, 6, 7, 8–9, 1324, 1665, 1974, 2205, 2286, 2870
  *Webster v. Reproductive Health Services*, 6–9, 192, 196, 381, 625, 2158, 2872, 2892
  and well-being of women, 6–9, 12–13, 1615
  *See also* Anti-abortion movement; Reproductive autonomy
Absolutism (freedom of speech and press), **17**
  Black-Douglas full protection theory, 815
  First Amendment rights, 1047, 1051
  subject to balancing tests, 154–155
  Wortman's exposition, 2931
Abstention doctrine, **17–20, 20–21** (update)
  injunction, 1373
Academic freedom, **21–23**
  constitutional issues, 855–856
  as teaching of creationism argument, 2185
Access to the courts, **23**
  *Bounds v. Smith*, 212
  civil liberties and, 377
  as fundamental constitutional right, 212
  *Griffin v. Illinois*, 1231–1232

indigent rights, 204, 380, 799, 817, 1231–1232, 1974, 2877, 2879
  *in forma pauperis*, 1368–1369
  for parental rights, 1750
  as prisoner's right, 2013, 2046
  *See also* Fair trial
Accommodation of religion, **24**
  broad vs. narrow view, 2194–2195
  endorsement test vs., 2196
  establishment clause, 926–927
  and religion as "viewpoint" ruling, 1559–1560
  religious speech, 2172–2173
  specially created school district for disabled Hasidic children, 202
  *See also* Government aid to religious institutions; Religious liberty
Accusation. *See* Right to be informed of accusation
ACLU. *See* American Civil Liberties Union
Acquittal against the evidence. *See* Jury nullification
Act of state doctrine, **24–25**
  courts and foreign relations, 1077
  exercise of federal common law authority, 978, 1468
Act of Toleration. *See* Toleration Act
ADA. *See* Americans with Disabilities Act
Adamson Eight-Hour Act, **33**
  Erdman Act, 921
ADEA. *See* Age Discrimination in Employment Act
Adequate state grounds, **34–35**
  and appellate jurisdiction, 109, 1027
  and habeas corpus, 2821
Administrative agencies, **36–38, 38–40** (update)
  abstention, 19
  administrative law, 37, 40–42
  for American Indians, 81, 82
  damages claims against, 740
  delegation of power to, 761–762, 1935
  for District of Columbia, 797–798
  drug testing, 824, 825–826
  executive orders, 944
  freedom of contract, 1112
  and judicial legislation, 1460
  and judicial review, 1481–1482
  justification for, 38–40
  legislative court as, 1590
  legislative powers, 1597, 1598–1599, 1994–1995
  and presidential spending power, 2000–2001
  regulatory, 2147–2148

ripeness of challenge, 2279
  and separation of power, 37–38, 40, 41, 267, 269
  World War I, 2928
  World War II, 2290
  *See also* Bureaucracy
Administrative law, **40–42**
  administrative agencies, 37, 40–42
  cease and desist orders in, 325
  fair hearing, 465–466
  inauguration and extension of, 1001
  interest group litigation, 1378
  judicial review, 1481–1482
  regulatory agencies, 2148
Administrative Procedure Act (1946), 37, 39, 266, 267, 2312
*Administrative Process, The* (Landis), 1560
Administrative search, **42–43, 43–44** (update)
  probable cause, 43–44, 294, 1095
  reasonable grounds for, 2337
  Rehnquist Court expansion of, 1096
  unreasonable search, 2767
  warrantless, 294
Admiralty and maritime jurisdiction, **44–45**
  Eleventh Amendment, 879
  expansion beyond tide ebb and flow, 2051
  federal judicial power, 1466–1467, 1489, 1495
  Federal Rules of Civil Procedure, 1029
  ocean law, 1840–1841
  Peters and, 1902
  Story's contribution, 360, 2556
Adolescent Family Life Act (1981), 212
Adoption, race, and the Constitution, **45–47**
Adversary trial. *See* Rights of the criminally accused
Advertising. *See* Commercial speech
Advice and consent, **47**
  appointing and removal power, 109–111, 287, 1059
  and appointments clause, 114–116
  executive agreements, 939–941
  executive power, 947
  federal judicial appointments, 1018, 1456
  politically motivated withholding of, 776–777, 1079–1080
  regulatory agency appointments, 2147
  as Senate function, 47, 109, 114–116, 2358, 2359, 2363
  treaty power, 1073, 1079–1080, 1991, 1996

Advice and consent to Supreme Court nominations, **47–51**
  appointment of Justices, 111, 114, 1018–1019
  Bork controversial nomination, 209, 210–211, 1393
  confirmation process, 112, 489–490, 1018–1019
  Hughes controversial nomination as Chief Justice, 1310–1311
  judicial independence, 1456
  Thomas controversial nomination, 282, 2695
Advisory opinion, **51**
  adequate state grounds, 34
  and judicial independence, 1456
  and justiciability, 1520
  by legislative court, 1590
AEDPA. *See* Antiterrorism and Effective Death Penalty Act
Affectation doctrine. *See* Affected with a public interest
Affected with a public interest, **52–53**
  and economic regulation, 52, 844, 2829–2830, 2917
  and freedom of contract, 52, 53, 1115, 1166
  *Granger* cases, 52, 53, 1224, 1225, 2817
  and Oklahoma law licensing ice dealers, 1802
  and state interstate commerce control, 2817
  and state milk price-controls, 1788–1789
  and wartime federal regulation, 1605
Affirmative action, **53–55, 55–56** (update 1), **57–58** (update 2)
  *Bakke* challenge, 1976, 1978, 2146–2147
  in broadcast licensing, 469, 1723–1724, 2165
  California direct ballot vote to end, 787
  city ordinance invalidated, 2230–2231
  and civil liberties, 376
  and civil rights, 392, 395, 397–398, 400–401, 406
  Clinton administration support, 432, 623
  and "colorblind" constitution, 781
  Contract with America (1994) opposition, 776
  and critical race theory, 727
  decisions upholding, 2766
  for developmentally disabled people, 775

economics of, 848
  as equal protection issue, 54, 55–56, 912, 915–917
  executive orders, 945, 1026
  gender-based, 2397–2398, 2418
  in higher education, 759–760
  *Hopwood v. Texas*, 1304
  as past discrimination remedy, 1435
  race-consciousness, 2094–2095, 2230–2231
  and racial discrimination, 2103–2105
  racial discrimination distinction, 232
  and racial diversity ruling, 2146–2147
  Rehabilitation Act, 2152
  Rehnquist Court, 2169, 2170
  retrenchment cases, 55–56
  *Richmond (City of) v. J. A. Croson Co.*, 2230–2231
  Scalia's views, 2313
  and seniority, 1044–1045
  Stevens's views, 2536, 2538
  strict scrutiny, 33–34, 57, 58
  Thomas's views, 2695
  voluntary racial quota plan upheld, 1172
  as voting issue, 393
  *Wygant v. Jackson Board of Education*, 2933–2934
Affirmative action, economics of. *See* Economics of affirmative action
Afrocentric schools, **58**
Age discrimination, **59–60, 60** (update)
  antidiscrimination legislation, 95, 881
  *Equal Employment Opportunity Commission (EEOC) v. Wyoming*, 907
  federal civil rights protection, 1027
  Railroad Retirement Act, 2114
  and uniformed state police, 1693–1694
Age Discrimination Act (1975), **60–61**, 406, 1027
  as antidiscrimination legislation, 95
  *Gregory v. Ashcroft*, 1229
Age Discrimination in Employment Act (1967), 59–60, 88, 95
Agricultural Adjustment Act of 1933, **62**
  and commerce clause, 456–457
  unconstitutionality, 284–285, 599, 697, 2288
Agricultural Adjustment Act of 1938, **62**
  and commerce clause, 458
Agricultural bankruptcy. *See* Frazier-Lemke Acts
Agricultural Marketing Agreement Act (1937), **62–63**
  *Parker v. Brown*, 1879
Agriculture. *See* Subjects of commerce

Aid to Families with Dependent Children (AFDC), 2874, 2875–2876, 2934
Alban Plan (1754), 1104
Alcohol
  American Indian prohibitions, 82
  blood test from unconscious person, 229
  drunk-driving blood test, 205, 2458
  as exception to U.S. drug policy, 678
  interstate commerce in, 213–214
  license cases, 1229, 1230, 1617
  minimum drinking age, 994
  original package doctrine, 256, 1348, 1612, 1617
  Prohibition Amendment, 72, 73, 74–75, 862, 2050, 2927
  sobriety checkpoints, 1096, 1726
  and state regulation of commerce, 1601, 2870
  Volstead Act, 2803–2804
  World War I prohibitions, 2927
Alien, **65–67**
  authorized removal, 1325
  birthright citizenship, 65, 131, 183
  Blackmun antidiscrimination opinion, 190
  Chinese Exclusion Act, 328, 355
  citizenship, 364, 365, 366, 367, 368
  civil service appointments and, 2582–2583
  denaturalization, 768–769
  deportation restraints, 1333, 1503–1504
  deportation, 65, 67, 128–129, 768–769, 770–771, 1330, 1331
  as discrete and insular minority, 794
  due process rights, 1077, 1325, 1330, 1332
  eligibility for citizenship, 2642
  employer sanctions for unauthorized alien workers, 1333
  equal protection rights, 130, 131–132, 376, 1077, 1331, 1920
  fair hearing rights, 1077
  Illegal Immigration Reform and Immigrant Responsibility Act, 1325
  Internal Security Act, 1386
  and judicial activism, 1448
  land ownership, 1871, 2642
  migrant workers, 1329–1330
  Palmer raids, 65, 1875
  preemption doctrine, 1289–1290
  property ownership limitations, 129, 131
  right to pursue livelihood, 2642–2643
  state employment discrimination, 1068, 1262

Alien (continued)
　status of, 367
　suspect classification, 66, 72
　undocumented workers, 1330
　and unreasonable search, 71
　visa, 2802
　welfare benefits, 66, 1077, 1218–1219,
　　1331–1333
Alienage. *See* Immigration and alienage
Alien and Sedition Acts (1798), **67**
　amnesty, 89
　broad construction justifying, 250
　as Federalist measure, 1016
　First Amendment absolutism
　　argument, 17
　and First Amendment rights, 1049,
　　1126, 1608
　as First Amendment violation, 1139
　as legislative-executive war power
　　collaboration, 2840
　Paterson and, 1883
　presidential pardons, 1422
　and sedition, 2351
　and seditious libel law, 1126, 1138
　targets and wide enforcement of, 65,
　　67, 1016, 1138
　Virginia and Kentucky Resolutions
　　against, 65, 67, 228, 1016, 1049,
　　1421, 2798–2799
　and war hysteria, 29, 549, 1016
Alien Registration Act (1940), **67–68**
　and criminal syndicalism laws, 723
　*Dennis v. United States*, 769–770,
　　1353
　as federal control over internal
　　security, 2930
　incitement/abstract teaching distinc-
　　tion, 1109, 1353, 2938–2939
　preemption doctrine, 1289–1290
　*Scales v. United States*, 2311
　seditious membership, 2351
　subversive advocacy, 2581, 2582
　*Yates* conviction reversals, 2938–
　　2939
Alien suffrage, **68–69**
All deliberate speed, **69**
　*Alexander v. Holmes County*
　　immediate desegregation ruling, 65,
　　69
　*Brown II* ruling, 255
　Frankfurter and, 2852
　immediate desegregation vs., 65, 69,
　　772
　in school desegregation, 772
Amending process, **72–75, 75–76**
　　(update)
　anti-abortion proposals, 76, 92, 123,
　　2126, 2127, 2205

Article V Conventions Clause, 123–
　124
balanced-budget amendment, 153–
　154, 2129
Becker Amendment, 167
Blaine Amendment, 197–198
Bricker Amendment, 243–244
and constitutional reform, 650–651
and constitutional theory, 659
and democratic theory, 765
election regulation, 865, 866
Electoral College, 866
equal rights amendment, 918–919
and federalism principles, 999, 1007
initiatives, 1372
and interposition, 1393
Jacksonian vs. nullifactionist views,
　1413
Jeffersonian view, 1423
joint resolution, 1437
line-item veto, 76, 1627, 2129
need for, 2316
new amendment proposals, 76, 2129
prayer in schools proposals, 76, 123,
　2125–2126, 2127
Progressive reforms, 2047
Reagan proposals, 2125–2126, 2127,
　2129
*See also* Ratification of constitutional
　amendments; *specific amendments*
Amendment process (outside Article V),
　**76–78**
and Article V conventions clause, 123–
　124
and living Constitution, 1633
American Anti-Slavery Society, 2, 3
American Association of University
　Professors, 21
American Bar Association
　abortion law, 2285
　Bork nomination, 209
　Committee on the Federal Judiciary,
　　112
　federal judicial nominee scrutiny, 1019
　gag order, 1179
American Civil Liberties Union, **78–79**
　Bork nomination opposition, 209
　and Burger Court, 273
　as defender of civil liberties, 379
　and draft card burning, 817–818
　Fraenkel as counsel, 1099
　Hays as counsel and director, 1280–
　　1281
　history of, 157
　and loyalty oath, 157
　public interest law, 2071
　on Roosevelt's (Franklin D.) civil
　　liberties record, 2290–2291

*Tennessee v. Scopes*, 2666
work during the 1920s, 595
American Colonization Society, 181–182
*American Commonwealth, The* (Bryce),
　258
*American Constitution, The: Its Origins
　and Development* (Kelly and
　Harbison), 1528
American Convention of Abolition
　Societies, 1
American flag. *See* Flag desecration;
　Flag salute cases
American Indians and the Constitution,
　**79–81, 81–83** (update)
　birthright citizenship, 183
　Cherokee Indian Cases, 343–345,
　　1408, 1535, 2183
　citizenship status in late nineteenth
　　century, 587
　Civil Rights Act of 1968 protections,
　　407
　and commerce clause, 453–454
　Curtis Act granting full citizenship,
　　594
　*Employment Division, Department of
　　Human Resources of Oregon v.
　　Smith*, 624, 679
　granting of tax immunity, 1799
　peyote sacramental use, 82, 821–822,
　　823, 1653, 2165–2166, 2181, 2192,
　　2194–2195
　removal policy, 1408
　*Seminole Tribe v. Florida*, 880–881
　"terminated" tribes, 607
　tribal economic development, 2731–
　　2732
　tribal sovereignty, 82, 1535, 1612
　voting rights, 1306
American Jewish Congress, **83**
　public interest law, 2071
*American Jury, The* (Kalven and Zeisel),
　1525
American Law Institute, 1451
*American Presidency, The* (Rossiter),
　2295
American Revolution and constitutional
　theory, **83–86**
　abolitionist constitutional theory, 2
　Articles of Confederation, 124–126
　criticism of British constitution, 246
　Declaration of Independence, 752–
　　753, 754
　fundamental law, 1173
　Paine's writings, 27, 1874, 2297
　republicanism ideology, 2211, 2212
　revolutionaries as constitutionalists,
　　2249
　Rossiter work on, 2295

Washington as commander-in-chief, 2860
Americans with Disabilities Act (1990), **86–87, 87–88** (update)
  as antidiscrimination legislation, 791
  constitutional aspiration, 664
American System, **88**
  and internal improvements, 30, 1385, 1700–1701
  Jacksonian opposition, 1408, 1412
Amicus curiae, **89**
  abortion-rights briefs, 7, 9
  American Jewish Congress briefs, 83
  antisegregation briefs, 259
  Brandeis brief, 225
  interest group litigation, 1379
  Justice Department civil rights briefs, 136
  reapportionment brief, 152–153
  right to counsel, 2261
Amnesty, **89**
  for Confederate rebels, 1625
  for undocumented residential aliens, 1333
  Vietnam War, 89, 1070
  *See also* Pardoning power
Amplified speech. *See* Sound trucks and amplifiers
Ancillary jurisdiction, **89–90**
  Federal Rules of Civil Procedure, 1028–1029
Annapolis Convention (1785), **90**
  Dickinson presidency, 779–780
Annexation of Texas, **90**
  unconstitutionality arguments, 563
  Webster opposition, 2871
  Whig opposition, 2884
Anonymous political speech, **90–91**
Anti-abortion movement, **92–93, 93–94** (update)
  clinic demonstration enjoinment, 227
  clinic violence, 13
  constitutional amendment proposals, 76, 92, 123, 2126, 2127, 2205
  Contract with America (1994), 776
  no-abortion-counseling case, 2300
  public interest law, 2071
  Reagan support, 2126
  reproductive autonomy restrictions, 2205–2206
  RICO Act application to, 1153
  state abortion restrictions, 2, 5–15, 2205–2208
  strength of, 2286
  *See also* Hyde Amendment
Antidiscrimination legislation, **94–96, 97–98** (update 1), **99–100** (update 2a), **100–101** (update 2b)

age discrimination, 60, 60–61, 95
Civil Rights Act of 1964, 406
color of law, 2092
coverage expansion, 100
disabilities discrimination, 86–88, 790–791, 2152
disintegrating consensus over, 97–98
Education Amendments of 1972 (Title IX), 95, 406, 853, 1027
federal protection of civil rights, 1024, 1025–1027
Fourteenth Amendment, section 5 enforcement, 1089
freedom of association, 1110–1111, 2017
and majoritarian democracy, 766
open housing laws, 1853–1854
public accommodations, 1282–1283
race and sex discrimination, 2089–2093
religious exemptions, 2195
state initiative overturning of, 2170–2172
state vs. private discrimination, 1089, 2017
voting rights, 1042, 2145
Anti-Federalist constitutional thought, **101–102**
  and Bill of Rights, 176–177, 178, 1091, 1421
  constitutional amendments, 72
  executive defiance of "unconstitutional" laws, 943
  general welfare clause, 1186, 1187
  and Jacksonianism, 1412
  Martin (Luther) statement, 1688
  minoritarian bias concerns, 1957
  ratification opposition, 1561, 1575
  representation theory, 102, 763
  Yates's "Brutus" letters, 2938
Antipeonage Act (1867). *See* Peonage
Antislavery. *See* Abolitionist constitutional theory
Anti-Slavery Society (American), 384, 385
Antiterrorism and Effective Death Penalty Act (1996), **102–103**
  and capital punishment, 307
  as habeas corpus law revision, 103, 654, 1254–1255, 1503, 1504
  as limit on federal jurisdiction, 1503
  terrorist designations under, 2674
Antitrust law, **103–107**
  applied to labor unions, 70, 107, 166–167, 1545–1546, 1555, 1641–1642
  applied to legal profession, 1202
  Bork writings on, 209–210
  Cellar-Kefauver Act, 603

Clarke (John) support of, 421
Clayton Act, 425–426
consent decrees, 507
Federal Trade Commission Act, 1030–1031
and Fuller Court, 1165–1166
Justice Department prosecution, 1540
*Knight Company, E. C., United States v.*, 1539–1540, 1641, 1642, 2046, 2048
manufacturing monopoly exclusion, 1539–1540
McReynolds views, 1714
production exemptions, 2046
rule of reason, 2298, 2895, 2898
Sherman Antitrust Act, 1165–1166, 1641–1642, 2048, 2292, 2298–2299, 2412–2413
*Standard Oil Company, United States v.*, 2298
*United States Steel Corporation, United States v.*, 2298
and White Court, 2898–2899
White's (Edward) conservative views, 2895
APA. *See* Administrative Procedure Act
Appeal, **107–108**
  access to the courts, 23
  in capital punishment cases, 305, 311
  direct to Supreme Court, 1499
  and double jeopardy, 809
  Emergency Court of Appeals, 885–886
  harmless error limitations, 2045
  indigent rights, 817
  interest group litigation, 1378
  right to counsel, 2262
  rule of four, 2296
Appellate jurisdiction, **108–109**
  adequate state grounds, 34–35, 1027
  appeal, 108
  Article III provision, 1468, 1469
  certiorari writ, 328, 1490
  circuit courts, 360, 361, 1490, 1497
  congressional regulation of Court's, 497, 1494
  extension to state courts, 1688–1691
  federal judicial system, 1490
  federal question jurisdiction, 1027
  Federal Rules of Criminal Procedure, 1029
  final judgment rule, 1044
  habeas corpus review, 1249
  judicial collegiality, 1451–1452
  Judiciary Act of 1789, 1495
  Judiciary Act of 1927, 1498
  *Martin v. Hunter's Lessee*, 1688–1691
  *McCardle, Ex parte*, 1494

Appellate jurisdiction (continued)
  original jurisdiction vs., 1468
  rehearing, 2152
  remand, 2198
  of Supreme Court, 108–109, 402,
    436–437, 1502, 2588, 2592, 2596,
    2616, 2617, 2618
  Supreme Court limitation, 1503, 1504
  Supreme Court reorganization, 1498
Appointing and removal power, presi-
    dential, **109–111**
  Clay opposition to, 425
  and First Congress, 1059
  free use of, 1772
  and good behavior, 1338
  *Humphrey's Executor v. United States,*
    1318–1319, 2149
  and impeachment articles of Andrew
    Johnson, 126, 1428–1429
  and independent agency member
    removal, 2149
  and independent counsel, 115
  independent regulatory commission
    members, 600
  Jackson's exercise of, 1408–1409
  Madison endorsement of removal
    power, 546
  *Myers v. United States,* 1318, 1319,
    2000, 2149
  presidential will in, 2000
  Senate advice and consent, 47–51
  Senate blockage, 1079
  Tenure of Office Act, 1428, 2669
Appointment of Supreme Court justices,
    **111–113**
  appointment clause, 114
  confirmation process, 490
  increased number in Grant adminis-
    tration, 1581–1582
  and judicial independence, 1455–1456
  and judicial strategy, 1485–1486
  Senate advice and consent to, 47, 114,
    1018–1019
Appointments clause, **113–116**
  advice and consent, 48
  Constitutional Convention of 1787
    and, 48–49, 113–114
  federal judiciary, 1017–1020
  Senate confirmation process, 489
Apportionment. *See* Electoral districting;
    Reapportionment
*Areopagitica* (Milton), 1046, 1737–1739
Armed forces, **117–118**
  civil-military control, 385–387
  Civil War, 571
  conscientious objection, 505–506
  desegregation, 118, 605, 946
  as domestic law enforcers, 1568–1569

loyalty-security program, 1649
police action, 1921
Posse Comitatus Act, 448, 1969
President as commander-in-chief of,
    448
presidential deployment authority,
    1075
public forum doctrine, 2069–2070
quartering of troops prohibition,
    2689
segregation, 1024
sexual orientation and, 117, 118, 432,
    2401–2403
yalmulke prohibition, 1202, 2192
*See also* Military justice; Presidential
    war powers
Arrest, **119–120**
  automobile search, 141
  bail, 147–151
  felony, 119, 121, 1031
  informant's tip, 1368
  *Miranda* rules, 1926
  *Payton v. New York,* 1889
  privilege from, 2251
  probable cause, 2023–2024
  in public vs. private places, 121
  search incident to, 2283, 2343–2344,
    2845
  and warrantless search, 2845
  *See also* Police interrogation and
    confessions
Arrest warrant, **120–121**
  Fourth Amendment, 1092
  *Payton v. New York,* 1889
  probable cause and, 2330
  state action and, 2488–2489
  *See also* Warrantless search
Article I courts. *See* Legislative court
Article III. *See* Judicial independence;
    Judicial power; Judicial system,
    federal
Article III and public choice theory,
    **122–123**
  environmental regulation, 904–905
  government wrongs, 1217
  taxpayers' suit against public aid to
    religious schools, 1066
Article III courts. *See* Constitutional
    courts
Article IV. *See* Domestic violence clause;
    Full faith and credit; Privileges and
    immunities
Article V. *See* Amending process;
    Amendment process (outside
    Article V)
Article V conventions clause, **123–124**
  and amending process, 74, 75, 77,
    123–124

Articles of Confederation, **124–126**
  Adams (Samuel) and drafting of, 32
  and amending process, 75, 539–540
  and Annapolis Convention, 90
  and citizenship, 364
  congressional privileges and immuni-
    ties, 501
  and Constitutional Convention of
    1787, 517, 542, 2020
  and constitutionalism, 643
  Dickinson and drafting of, 779
  Duane and drafting of, 828
  and emergence of federalism, 989,
    997–998, 1010, 1013
  executive offices established by
    Congress, 287
  foreign titles prohibition, 2703
  Franklin proposal, 105
  full faith and credit, 1170
  history of, 537, 538, 539
  interstate extradition, 1158
  Jensen defense of, 1426–1427
  lack of taxing power, 2658
  McLaughlin on, 1711
  and Northwest Ordinance, 1829
  privilege from arrest, 2019
  privileges and immunities, 805, 2019
  and Shays' Rebellion, 803
  spending power, 2468
Articles of impeachment of Andrew
    Johnson, **126**
  Bingham as committee chairman,
    181
  and Chase Court, 338
  and presidential removal power, 110
  seen as precedent against impeach-
    ment, 1340
  Stanton firing as catalyst, 2476
  and Tenure of Office Act, 110, 126,
    1339, 1428–1429, 2476, 2669
Articles of impeachment of Richard M.
    Nixon, **126–127**
  and Nixon resignation, 1339, 1342
  offenses cited, 609, 1341
Articles of impeachment of William J.
    Clinton, **127**
  and independent counsel, 625, 1360
  offenses as private misconduct, 431,
    433, 1340, 1341–1342
Asian Americans and the Constitution,
    **128–130**
  Chinese immigrants, 586, 2939–2940
  education discrimination against non-
    English-speaking students, 1563
  Japanese American cases, 1415–1417,
    2930–2931
  naturalization rights upheld, 2922
  segregation ruling, 1204

*Wong Kim Ark, United States v.*, 367, 2922
*Yick Wo v. Hopkins*, 2939–2940
Asian immigrants and constitutional history, **130–132**
    Chinese Exclusion Act, 355–356, 1328
    citizenship, 1167, 1328, 2922
    discriminatory measures, 133–1331, 1328–1329, 2939–2940
    Fuller Court rulings, 1167
Assembly, freedom of. *See* Freedom of assembly and association
Assistance, writ of, **132**
    colonial attacks on, 1099, 1174, 2236
    Fourth Amendment, 1097
    general warrant and, 1098, 1186
    Paxton's case, 132, 1099, 1888
Assisted suicide. *See* Right to die
Association, freedom of. *See* Freedom of association
Association, The, **132–133**
    Adams (Samuel) and, 32
    adopted at First Continental Congress, 534, 672
    constitutional history before 1776, 534
Atomic Energy Act (1954), **133**, 2326
Attainder, bill of. *See* Bill of attainder
Attainder of treason, **133–134**
Attorney general and Department of Justice, **134–137**
    antitrust prosecution, 1540
    civil rights cases, 136, 404, 405
    Civil Rights Division, 404, 410–411, 1025
    civil rights enforcement, 1024, 1025, 1533
    crime enforcement, 1569
    Federal Bureau of Investigation, 975–977, 1304
    independent counsel, 115, 620–621, 1358, 1359, 1360, 1361
    interest group litigation, 1378
    Judiciary Act of 1789, 1495
    "opinions" preservation, 2913
    and public policy, 134
    qualifications for attorney general, 135–136
    special prosecutor, 2462
    Subversive Activities Control Board, 1385
    wiretapping, 2913
    *See also* Solicitor general
Attorney General's Commission on Pornography. *See* Meese Commission
Attorney General's List, **137–138**
    Executive Orders 9836 and 10450, 945

innocent vs. knowing membership, 2904
    loyalty-security program, 138, 604, 1649
    struck down, 1436, 1650
    voided, 1436, 1650
Attorney speech, **138–139**
    First Amendment protection, 165
    personal injury solicitation, 1065
Automobile pursuits. *See* Police pursuits and constitutional rights
Automobile search, **140–141, 141** (update)
    exigent circumstance and, 2332
    expectation of privacy and, 2332
    incident to arrest, 2283
    invalid search warrant, 683
    probable cause, 140, 244, 319, 329, 2169, 2846
    *Ross, United States v.*, 2294–2295
    search warrant for, 140, 141, 329–330
    sobriety checkpoints, 1096
    traffic stops, 209, 2711
    unreasonable, 2769
    warrantless, 140, 141, 244, 329, 1427, 2295, 2846, 2847
Avoidance doctrine, **142–143**

## B

Badges of servitude, **145–146**
    Civil Rights Cases, 409, 1437, 1919
    racial quotas, 2110
    restrictive covenant as, 2223
    segregation as, 201, 1918, 1919
    and Thirteenth Amendment, 1437, 1918, 2016
Bad tendency test, **146–147**
    and clear and present danger, 422, 426, 1299
    and freedom of speech, 146, 1129, 1646, 2311
    *Gitlow v. New York*, 2310, 2902
    *People v. Croswell*, 1898
    Pitney and, 1911
    and religious liberty, 1177
    and revolutionary speech, 1198–1199
Bail, **147–150, 150–151** (update)
    cost-benefit arguments, 150
    and preventive detention, 149, 150, 2005
    rights against excessive, 722, 729, 2257
    and wealth discrimination, 149, 716
Bail Reform Act (1966), 1984, 2306, 2365
Bail Reform Act (1984), 149, 150, 151

Balanced-budget amendment, **153–154**
    constitutional convention proposal, 76, 123, 153, 618
    Reagan's views, 2126, 2129
Balanced Budget and Emergency Deficit Control Act. *See* Gramm-Rudman-Hollings Act
Balancing test, **154–155**
    ballot access, 158
    *Barenblatt v. United States*, 163, 1595, 1596
    Blackmun application, 193–194
    clear and present danger move to, 115, 225, 427, 769–770
    Communist party witness testimony, 163, 1595
    conscientious objection, 2187
    for constitutional reason of state, 650
    dormant commerce clause, 806
    drug testing, 824, 826
    and drug trafficking, 680
    Federal Election Campaign Acts, 260
    fighting words, 1043
    Fourth Amendment activity, 1095–1096
    freedom of association, 1193
    freedom of speech, 17, 1043, 1129–1130, 1133
    free exercise clause, 1049, 2186–2187
    libel and First Amendment, 1146, 1285
    low-value test, 1646–1647
    peyote sacramental use, 822, 823
    search and seizure, 2331, 2340, 2341, 2342
    speedy trial, 163, 2256
    state regulation of commerce, 2517–2518
    warrantless searches, 2337
Baldus study, 1702
Ballot access, **158**
    established parties, 1941–1942
    initiative, 1939
    party fusion ban upheld, 1938
    restrictions to, 2701
    voting rights, 2813
    write-in votes, 265
Ballot initiative. *See* Direct democracy; Initiative; Referendum
Bank Holiday of 1933. *See* Emergency Bank Act
Bank of the United States Acts (1791, 1816), **159–160**
    broad construction, 250
    charter, 547
    Federalist advocacy, 1015–1016
    and implied powers, 160, 250, 1259

Bank of the United States Acts (1791, 1816) (continued)
  Jacksonian opposition, 1408, 1412, 1413, 1414, 1583–1584
  Jackson's veto, 1414
  judicial policymaking, 1461
  *McCulloch v. Maryland*, 1583, 1585, 1587, 1611, 1674, 1688, 1705–1707
  and Panic of 1819, 555
  veto of second, 1408, 1412, 1414
  Washington's signing of first, 2861
Bankruptcy Act (1938), **160**
Bankruptcy power, **160–161**
  bankruptcy law, 160, 161
  economic conditions and, 851
  Frazier-Lemke Acts (farm bankruptcy), 1105, 1644–1645, 2932
  Municipal Bankruptcy Act as unconstitutional under, 127
  and obligation of contracts, 1848–1849
  state debtor relief, 1300–1301
  substantive due process and, 1645
Bankruptcy Reform Act (1978), **161**
  bankruptcy judges, 1828
  bankruptcy power, 160
Becker Amendment, **167**
Benign racial classification, **169**
  discrete and insular minorities, 794
  neutrality principle, 2165
  racial quotas, 2146
Bias crime. *See* Hate crime
Bible reading. *See* Religion in public schools; Religious fundamentalism
Bicameralism, **171–173**
  as constitutional fundamental, 1947
  constitutionalism and, 643
  one-house legislative veto and, 762, 1333, 1599
  as Senate origin, 2357
  and separation of powers, 1948
  Wilson's (James) arguments for, 2909–2910
Bill of attainder, **174**
  Attorney General's List as, 138
  *Brown v. United States*, 257
  *Lovett, United States v.*, 1645
  loyalty oath, 1648
  and rule of law, 2298
  and standard of review, 2471
  women's disfranchisement as, 2918
Bill of credit, **174**
  borrowing power, 211
  *Craig v. Missouri*, 704
  as legal tender, 216–217
  and monetary power, 1751
  Taney Court on, 174, 2651

Bill of Rights (English), **174**
  bail, 148, 174
  and British constitution, 245
  cruel and unusual punishment prohibition, 729
  Fourteenth Amendment transformation of, 1091–1092
  freedom of debate, 501
  freedom of petition, 1125
  as parliamentary statute, 84
  quartering of troops, 2689
Bill of Rights (United States), **175–178**
  and American Civil Liberties Union principles, 78
  and American Indian status, 80–81
  Anti-Federalist advocacy of, 72, 101, 102, 1091
  application to states, 33, 178–180, 181, 1086, 1090–1092, 2217. *See also* Fourteenth Amendment; Incorporation doctrine
  as applying solely to federal government, 163, 1356
  Black's literal application of, 815, 816
  civil liberties embodied in, 375
  constitutional fictions on, 526
  and Court deference to armed forces, 117
  and Court's selective activism and restraint, 1445
  criminal justice and, 710, 718
  and criminal procedure, 2035–2036, 2043
  double standard, 1353–1354, 1356
  and drug regulation limitations, 821, 822, 823
  and economic liberties, 842
  and environmental regulation, 901–902
  and establishment of religion, 927–928
  exclusionary rule, 938
  extraterritoriality, 959–960
  and fair trial, 970–972
  federal actions limitation by, 1353–1354
  as federalism reinforcement, 998
  and foreign affairs, 1077
  fundamental rights, 1177, 1178, 2038
  importance in nation's founding, 546
  incorporation doctrine, 814–815, 1008, 1353–1356, 2293
  international human rights compared with, 1388
  as international influence, 1364
  Jefferson's advocacy, 1421
  and juvenile proceedings, 1523

Massachusetts Body of Liberties as precursor to, 374
  and natural rights, 1233
  Northwest Ordinance as precursor, 742
  penumbra theory, 1896
  and philosophy of Constitution, 1905
  and ratification of Constitution, 32, 177–178, 1045, 1421, 1611, 2118–2119
  selective incorporation, 2038, 2039
  selective judicial activism, 1447, 1448
  and social compact doctrine, 802
  and states' rights, 1091
  *See also* First Amendment; Fourth Amendment; Ninth Amendment; Second Amendment; Seventh Amendment; Tenth Amendment; Third Amendment
Bill of Rights in modern application, **178–180**
  and Fourteenth Amendment, 1090–1092
  use against state and local governments, 178
  *See also* Fourteenth Amendment
Birth control, **182–183**
  advertisement and sale of devices, 316
  as civil liberty, 376
  contraceptive sales to minors, 2204, 2208
  Douglas-Black clash, 816, 1233
  *Eisenstadt v. Baird*, 863
  equal protection grounds, 4, 182, 1118, 2204
  freedom of association, 1108
  freedom of intimate association, 1118, 1122
  *Griswold v. Connecticut*, 1120, 1122, 1233–1234, 1461, 2203
  and judicial policymaking, 1461, 1462
  minors' rights, 352
  penumbra theory, 1896
  as reproduction autonomy, 2203
  right of privacy, 4, 182, 1118, 1233–1234, 1461, 2203, 2242
  *See also* Abortion and the Constitution; Reproductive autonomy; Sterilization
Birthright citizenship, **183–184**
  aliens and, 65, 131, 183
  for children born to undocumented aliens, 368
  Fourteenth Amendment on, 1092
Bituminous Coal Act (1937), **184**
  *Carter v. Carter Coal Co.*, 321, 457–458
  unconstitutionality, 457, 2592

Black Codes, **189**
  Chase Court, 341
  and color of law, 444
  as dismantling of Civil Rights Act of 1866, 401, 402
  as equal protection violation, 908
  Freedmen's Bureau and, 1106
  *See also* Segregation
Blaine Amendment (1875), **197–198**
Blasphemy, **198**
  flag burning seen as secular equivalent, 1061
Block grants. *See* Federal grants-in-aid; Revenue sharing
Blood samples. *See* Testimonial and nontestimonial compulsion
Blue ribbon jury, **199–200**
  challenges, 1509
Body search, **205–206**
  intrusive, 1094–1095, 2283–2284
  and prisoners' rights, 205, 2013, 2244
  and right of privacy, 205–206, 1094, 1095, 2244–2245
  stop and frisk, 2552–2553
  *See also* Testimonial and nontestimonial compulsion
Boland Amendment, **206**
  and defense appropriations, 621, 622
  Reagan presidency and, 2128
Border search, **209**
  body search, 205
  for illegal alien workers, 1330
  probable cause, 71
  unreasonable, 2769
Bork nomination, **209–211**
  interpretivist position, 1393–1394
  judicial philosophy opponents, 50, 115, 210–211
  New Right jurisprudence, 1801
  and original intent, 2128
  and ratifier intent, 2121
  Reagan presidency and, 2127
  rejection of, 114, 115, 211
Borrowing power, **211**
  gold clause cases, 1201–1202
Boston Massacre, 26
Boycott, **214–215**
  advertisement for secondary disallowed, 1203–1204
  as antitrust violation, 1555
  civil rights, 1551, 1556
  picketing standards, 215, 1551
  Pitney and, 1911
  restriction of secondary, 1561, 1641
Brandeis brief, 219, **224–225**
  and legislative facts, 1590, 1591
  and social science research, 225, 2443
  women's maximum hours and

minimum wages, 35, 225, 1764, 2920
Breach of the peace, **227–228**
  clear and present danger, 1031
  and demonstration allowances, 767–768
  and freedom of assembly, 1107
  and picketing, 702
  and religious freedom, 299
Bricker Amendment, **243–244**
  Korean War, 1541, 1921
Brief, **244**
British Bill of Rights. *See* Bill of Rights (English)
British constitution, **245–246**
  and American colonies, 27, 31, 32, 779
  American constitutional divergence from, 84–85
  bicameralism, 171
  Declaration of Independence negating, 754
  Founders' view of, 1963
Broadcasting, **246–247, 247–249** (update 1), **249–250** (update 2)
  abandonment of scarcity premise, 1147
  affirmative action in licensing, 1723–1724, 2165
  cable television, 469–470, 1147–1148, 2739–2740
  cable television explicit programming, 1134
  Communications Act, 468–469
  Communications Decency Act, 471
  and community, 469
  and compelled speech, 475–476
  and corporate rights, 690–691
  and democracy, 470–471
  editorial advertisements, 445
  fairness doctrine, 246–249, 968–969, 1130, 1391, 2144
  First Amendment applications, 249, 445, 1147, 1391–1392
  free press/fair trial, 330, 1143
  licenses, 2009
  "must carry" law, 469–470, 1771–1772, 2739–2740
  rape victim's name liability, 702–703
  *Red Lion Broadcasting Co. v. Federal Communications Commission*, 968, 969, 2144
  restraints on vulgar words, 981, 1043, 1057, 1147, 1392
  right of reply, 1142
  Supreme Court coverage, 1439–1441
  televising of criminal trial, 330
  tort liability vs. free press, 1438–1439

*Turner Broadcasting System, Inc. v. FCC*, 2739–2740
  unconstitutional conditions, 2750
Broad construction, **250**
  Economic Opportunity Act, 843
  and enumerated powers, 1446
  Federalist, 1015, 1017, 1260
  of implied powers, 250, 1345, 1707
  internal improvements, 30, 250
  and judicial rule, 1484
  and living Constitution, 1632–1634
  by Story, 2554
  *See also* Liberal constitutional construction
Budget, **260–261**
  executive, 1999
  Office of Management and Budget, 1846–1847
  taxing and spending power, 994
  *See also* Budget process
Budget and Accounting Act (1921), **261**
  enactment, 260
  Reagan's use of, 262
Budget process, **261–263**
  balanced-budget amendment, 153–154
  balanced-budget amendment effects, 154
  budget initiation, 261
  Congressional Budget and Impoundment Control Act, 498–499, 1219
  Gramm-Rudman-Hollings Act, 214, 1219
  line-item veto, 1626–1627
  maximum deficit ceilings, 1219
  Office of Management and Budget, 1846–1847
Burden of proof, **264**
  evidence, 932
  harmless error, 1270
  and presumption of innocence in criminal cases, 718
  reasonable doubt, 1434, 2138–2139
Bureaucracy, **265–267, 267–269** (update)
  administrative agencies, 38, 39, 40, 42, 266–267
  appointments clause, 115
  and budget process, 261, 262
  Freedom of Information Act, 1117–1118
  *See also* Patronage; Public employees
Bureau of Indian Affairs, 82, 83
Bureau of the Budget, 260, 261, 262
Burger Court, **272–278**
  access to the courts, 23
  adequate state grounds, 34
  civil liberties, 380, 384

Burger Court (continued)
  civil rights, 400, 406
  commercial speech, 461
  conservative orientation of, 270
  equal protection, 2309, 2310
  expatriation, 957
  federalism, 1008
  Fourth Amendment activity, 1095
  freedom of speech and freedom of the
    press decisions, 369
  fundamental interests limitation, 1173
  habeas corpus review, 975, 1252, 1253,
    1254
  institutional litigation, 275–276, 2280
  liberal activism, 1615
  *Miranda* rules, 273, 276, 1927, 1928,
    1929
  public forum speech rights, 2167
  relationship to social change, 700
  *Roe v. Wade*, 270, 274, 277, 2163
  school desegregation, 65
  search and seizure, 2340
  separation of church and state, 2372
  solicitor general role in, 2451
  standing, 122
  state action, 2491
  state action cases and civil rights, 400
  state action limitation, 1063
  taxpayer suits, 1066–1067
Burke-Wadsworth Selective Training and
  Service Act. *See* Selective Service
  Acts
Burning of flag. *See* Flag desecration
Busing, school. *See* School busing

# C

Cabinet, **287–289**
  executive power, 948
  lack of constitutional status, 2000
  Senate advice and consent, 115
  Washington's inception of, 2861
Cable Act (1922), 594
Cable Communications Policy Act
  (1983), 248
Cable television
  community-building applications,
    469–470
  explicit programming, 1134
  First Amendment, 1147–1148
  "must carry" law, 469–470, 2739–
    2740
*Calvin's Case*, **294**
  citizenship, 363
Campaign finance, **294–296, 296–297**
  **(update 1), 297–298** (update 2)
  balancing test, 155, 1130

*Buckley v. Valeo*, 260, 295, 297, 298,
    1932, 1933, 1938, 1941, 1942, 2052,
    2893
  constitutional amendment proposals,
    76
  Court inconsistency, 139–140
  and electoral process First Amend-
    ment issues, 872
  Federal Election Campaign Acts, 260,
    986–987
  First Amendment and legislative limits
    on, 1047, 1052
  and government speech, 1215, 1216
  limits on contributions, 612
  limits upheld, 260
  Lobbying Disclosure Act, 1636
  minor political parties, 257, 1216
  political action committees, 1932–
    1933
  and property rights, 2052
  public employee prohibitions, 268
  soft money, 1938
  spending limits, 1941
Capital punishment, **299–304, 304–306**
  **(update 1), 306–307** (update 2)
  Antiterrorism and Effective Death
    Penalty Act, 103, 1254–1255
  Blackmun on unconstitutionality of,
    196
  Brennan on unconstitutionality of,
    236, 239
  Burger Court rulings, 272, 274, 700
  as civil liberties violation, 376
  as cruel and unusual punishment, 236,
    239, 300, 301–302, 307, 308, 721,
    729, 1070–1071, 1199, 1529, 1702–
    1703, 2257
  and double jeopardy, 812
  and drug traffickers, 680
  and elected judiciary, 864
  equal protection claims, 307, 915,
    1702–1703
  expedited federal collateral review,
    162
  and Fourteenth Amendment rights,
    307, 309, 1529
  *Furman v. Georgia*, 300–301, 302,
    303, 304, 306, 309–310, 721
  *Gregg v. Georgia*, 300, 301, 302, 303,
    305, 306, 308, 310–312, 732
  habeas corpus writs, 1254
  jury nullification, 1512
  of juveniles, 2475–2476
  *Lockett v. Ohio*, 303, 308
  of mentally incompetent, 2061
  *Payne v. Tennessee*, 1889
  *Penry v. Lynaugh*, 1895
  proportionate to culpability, 2369

racial discrimination. *See* Capital
    punishment and race
  rape case decision, 302, 440
  Rehnquist Court rulings, 382, 2169
  reversed in face of state's standardless
    imposition, 1199
  *Rosenberg v. United States*, 2294
  Scalia's views, 2316
  sentencing, 2366
  state constitutional law, 2498
  stay of execution, 2526
  Stevens's views, 2530, 2535
  Stewart's views, 2542
  victim impact statements, 208–209
Capital punishment and race, **307–309**
  discrimination implications, 300, 303,
    306, 307–309, 310, 732, 733, 1702–
    1703, 2087, 2106–2107
  *McCleskey v. Kemp*, 307–309, 396
Capital punishment cases of 1972, **309–
  310**
Capital punishment cases of 1976, **310–
  312**
Capitation taxes, **312**
  apportionment, 1324
  Chase Court decision, 341
  constitutionality of, 2470
  poll tax, 1961
Captive audience, **313**
  fairness doctrine, 445
  silent school prayer as, 2833
Career criminal sentencing laws, **316**
Cases and controversies, **322–324**
  and collusive suit, 443, 1464
  decision, 752
  doctrine application, 801
  *Hayburn's Case*, 1280
  on Indian lands, 1771
  judicial power, 1464–1467
  judicial power limitations, 122, 1222,
    1464
  judicial review, 1477
  judicial review of administrative acts,
    1481–1482
  standing, 2472–2473
  taxpayer suits, 1464–1465
  test case, 2676
*Cases on Constitutional Law* (Dowling),
  817
Categorical grants-in-aid. *See* Federal
  grants-in-aid
*Cato's Letters*, **324**
  on Lockean ideas, 512
Cease and desist order, **325**
  antitrust law, 104
Cellar-Kefauver Act (1950), 603
Censorship. *See* Prior restraint and
  censorship

Census, **326–327**
reapportionment, 2136, 2137
Central Intelligence Agency, 1256–1257
Certification, **327**
abstention doctrine, 20
Certiorari, writ of, **327–328**
appeal distinguished from, 108
Circuit Court of Appeals Act, 361
introduction of, 1490
rule of four, 2296
and writ of error, 327, 921
Chandler Act. *See* Bankruptcy Act
Charters, colonial. *See* Colonial charters
Chase Court, **337–342**
antislavery view, 567
ex post facto laws, 290
federal power issues, 340
Johnson (Andrew) impeachment, 338
judicial activism and, 335
*Milligan, Ex parte,* 338–339, 386, 402
Reconstruction issues, 338–340, 341
*Slaughterhouse* cases, 336, 341, 580
state regulatory and tax power issues,
340–341
Checks and balances, **342–343**
advice and consent as, 47
appointments clause, 115
and bureaucracy, 265, 266
cabinet subject to, 288, 289
constitutional commentary on, 449,
451
as constitutional fundamental, 1947
and constitutionalism, 637, 643
and constitutional theory, 654–655
economic analysis and, 834
for federalism, 995–996
House of Representatives and, 1305–
1306
impeachment powers, 1343
legislative power, 1597
limited government and, 1618–1619
Montesquieu as influence, 1755–1756
Paine as influence, 1874
as political philosophy of Constitution,
1944
presidential power seen superseding,
1996, 1997
in republican form of government,
2209, 2213
*See also* Separation of powers
Cherokee Indian Cases (1831–1832),
**343–345**
Jackson nullification, 1408
religious fundamentalist defense of
Cherokees, 2183
sovereign nation doctrine, 1535
Chief Justice, role of the, **346–348**
administrative duties, 2605

clerks, 429
Fuller's concept of, 1163, 1164
as presiding officer over presidential
impeachment trial, 346, 1340, 1343
Child benefit theory, **348–349**
Elementary and Secondary Education
Act, 876
same-race placement preferences as
contrary to, 46
Child custody
foster families, 1083–1084
and freedom of intimate association,
1119, 1123
issues in, 799–800
Child labor
*Bailey v. Drexel Furniture Company,*
151–152
Child Labor Tax Act, 349–350
Fair Labor Standards Act prohibition,
349, 594, 598, 1528
foreign commerce and, 1528
interstate commerce and, 349, 1528,
2048
Keating-Owen Child Labor Act, 1261–
1262, 1528
minimum wage, 35–36, 797, 1313,
1547
national police power and, 1777–1779
noxious products doctrine, 1830
Wagner Act cases, 349
White Court rulings, 2900
Child Labor Amendment, **349**
non-ratification of, 72, 73, 594, 598
ratification fight in Kansas, 441
*See also* Keating-Owen Child Labor
Act
Child Labor Tax Act, **349–350**
Child pornography, **350**
and First Amendment, 350, 351, 1802
and free speech, 375
as low-value speech, 1646
Children and the First Amendment,
**350–351**
bans on sales of sexually explicit
materials, 1194–1195
juvenile curfew laws, 1521–1522
Children's rights, **351–354**
abortion rights of minors, 6, 11, 192,
317, 352, 353, 1293, 1916, 2123,
2208
blood transfusion, 2191
child abuse, 774–775
child labor regulation, 349, 594, 598,
966, 1261–1262, 1528
contraceptive sales to minors, 2204,
2208
due process for delinquency proceedings, 1183–1184

exposure to sexually explicit materials,
1194–1195
gender rights, 2921
illegitimacy, 1325–1326
judicial activism and, 1448
minimum wage, 35–36, 797, 1313,
1547
parental conduct standards, 973–974
symbolic speech, 2702–2703
*Tinker v. Des Moines Independent
Community School District,* 2702–
2703
*See also* Education and the Constitution; Family and the Constitution; Juvenile proceedings
Child Support Recovery Act (1992), **354**
Chilling effect, **354–355**
computer data banks, 481–482
*Dombrowski v. Pfister,* 803
fairness doctrine, 248, 969
and freedom of the press, 1145, 1146
and free speech, 1056, 1134
and Internet free speech, 471
and libel suits, 1146
of sedition, 2351
Chinese Exclusion Act (1882), **355–356**
*Chae Chan Ping v. United States,* 328
legal challenges, 128, 130–131, 132,
1330
upheld, 1328
Chinese immigrants. *See* Asian Americans and the Constitution; Asian
immigrants and constitutional
history
Choice of law, **357–358**
*Allstate Insurance Co. v. Hague,* 357,
358
diversity jurisdiction, 798
Choice of law and constitutional rights,
**358**
Christian Right. *See* Religious fundamentalism
Church and state. *See* Establishment
clause; Establishment of religion;
Separation of church and state
Circuit courts, **359–361**
abolishment of appellate jurisdiction,
361
concurrent jurisdiction, 1495
*De Lovio v. Boit,* 360
federal judicial role, 1021, 1489–1490,
1497
Judiciary Act of 1789, 359, 1489, 1495,
1496, 2564, 2603
Judiciary Act of 1801, 1496–1497,
2564
Judiciary act of 1875, 1497
Judiciary Acts of 1802, 1498

Circuit Courts of Appeals Act (1891), **361**
  and contemporary federal judicial system, 1490
  Court jurisdictional control, 1498
  Evarts and, 931
  United States Courts of Appeals, 361, 2759–2760
Cities and the Constitution, **361–363**
  *Hunter v. Pittsburg*, 362
  municipal immunity, 1767–1768
  public purpose doctrine, 2076
  residential segregation, 2219–2222
Citizenship, **363–364** (historical development), **364–366** (theory), **366–367** (update 1), **367–369** (update 2)
  abolitionist constitutional theory, 2
  *Afroyim v. Rusk*, 59
  alien rights, 65, 131
  American Indians, 82, 587, 594
  Asian immigrants, 131, 1167, 1328, 2922
  as birthright, 183–184
  of blacks, 401, 820, 2143, 2354
  blacks' excluded from, 364, 819, 820, 1356, 2649
  *Calvin's Case*, 294, 363
  Chinese Exclusion Act, 356, 1328
  Civil Rights Act of 1866, 401
  coexisting state and federal, 989
  communitarians on, 472, 473
  corporate, 687–689, 798, 805
  denaturalization, 768–769
  deprivation of as cruel and unusual punishment, 309, 731
  District of Columbia residents, 796
  diversity jurisdiction, 798, 1468
  *Dred Scott v. Sandford* opinion, 364, 2649
  Emancipation Proclamation, 417
  expatriation and, 363, 956
  and fetal personhood, 8
  Fourteenth Amendment, 59, 129, 131, 168, 183–184, 364, 365, 366, 1085, 1087, 1090, 1092, 1167, 1357, 2305, 2497
  of freed slaves, 2143, 2354
  historical development, 363–364
  military relationship, 385
  *Minor v. Happersett*, 1740, 2918, 2919, 2920
  national vs. state, 1354
  and naturalization, 364–365, 366, 1785
  nondiscrimination as basic right of, 97
  *Paul v. Virginia*, 1888
  and petition right, 1125

  privileges and immunities protection, 364, 686, 1354, 2019, 2021
  race-based restrictions, 129, 130–131, 819, 820
  Reconstruction definition and basic rights of, 576, 578
  residents of territories, 2672
  revocation of, 59, 2733
  sex discrimination and, 2400
  *Slaughterhouse* cases, 1354, 2822
  state residence requirements, 2218–2219
  suffrage separated from, 68–69, 91, 2918
  theory, 364–366
  Thirteenth Amendment, 820, 2143, 2822
  voting privileges of, 2388
  Waite opinions, 2822
  as woman suffrage claim, 91, 370, 1740, 2477, 2918–2919, 2920
Citizens' suits. *See* Taxpayers' and citizens' suits
Civil disobedience, **369–372**
  abolitionist, 1183
  by anti-abortion movement, 93–94
  by civil rights movement, 369, 370–371, 1537
  draft card burning, 371, 817–818
  and freedom of speech, 371, 1135–1136
  by woman suffrage movement, 370
Civil forfeiture, **372–373**
  in drug regulation, 824
  Eighth Amendment limits, 985
  in federal criminal law, 985–986
  procedural due process, 2056
  and punitive damages, 2081–2082
Civil liberties, **373–380**, **380–382** (update 1), **382–384** (update 2)
  academic freedom, 21
  American Civil Liberties Union, 78–79
  amicus curiae briefs, 89
  ancient antecedents of, 374
  and antislavery controversy, 384–385
  bail, 148
  Bill of Rights, 175–178
  Blackstone on, 373
  Brennan commitment to, 229, 232, 234–236
  *Carolene Products Co., United States v.*, 382, 383
  and civil rights, 387
  Civil War restrictions, 416
  English antecedents of, 374
  Frank's judicial opinions, 1100
  Free Speech League and, 2324

  guilt by association and, 1236–1237
  Holmes's positions, 1296–1297
  Hughes Court and, 1311
  incorporation doctrine and, 2310–2311
  Japanese American cases, 131, 1416–1417, 2841
  Jeffersonian emphasis on, 1425
  Lincoln's Civil War record, 1620–1622, 1624
  Pennsylvania colonial charters, 1894
  Roosevelt Court and, 2293, 2302
  Roosevelt's (Franklin D.) record, 2290–2291
  Senate Subcommittee on Constitutional Rights, 2365
  subversive activity and, 2579
  Test Oath Cases, 2679
  Truman presidency and, 2734
  vagrancy laws and, 345
  Vietnam War issues, 2790
  Vinson Court rulings, 2793, 2795
  Warren Court rulings, 1616
  World War I and, 2928–2929
  World War II and, 2290–2291, 2929, 2930
  *See also* Natural rights and the Constitution; Slavery and civil liberties
Civil liberties and the antislavery controversy, **384–385**
  gag orders, 2, 31, 560, 2425, 2884
Civil-military relations, **385–387**
  and Korean War, 1541
Civil procedure. *See* Federal Rules of Civil Procedure
Civil rights, **387–394**, **394–398** (update 1), **399–401** (update 2)
  and Afrocentric schools, 58
  and age discrimination, 59
  and aliens, 65–66, 72
  and American Indians, 80–81, 82
  antidiscrimination legislation, 94–101
  and Asian Americans, 128–243
  as Bork nomination issue, 210, 211
  *Buchanan v. Warley*, 259
  cases and controversies, 323–324
  circuit court decisions, 360–361
  Civil War federal sovereignty over, 572, 573
  commentators on the Constitution on, 451
  compensation for unconstitutional criminal procedure, 714–715
  as constitutional aspiration, 664
  and critical legal studies, 724
  and critical race theory, 726
  and disabled people, 86–88
  disparate impact, 99, 100

domestic violence clause, 803
and education, 854
executive immunity from damages, 2922
expansion following World War II, 605
federal district courts caseload, 1491
federal enforcement, 200–201
and federalism, 1001–1002, 1007–1009
federal protection, 200–201, 1023–1027, 1070
fountainhead of modern doctrine, 1754
and Fourteenth Amendment framing, 1084–1087, 1088
Freedmen's Bureau, 1106
Fuller Court and, 1167–1168
Harlan's (1833–1911) dissents, 1267, 1268, 1918, 1919
Hughes's supportive opinions, 1310, 1311
injunction enforcement, 1372, 1373
institutional litigation, 1374
invidious discrimination, 1038
Johnson (Lyndon) legislative program, 1429, 1430
Justice Department Civil Rights Division activity, 136–137
*Monroe v. Pape*, 1754
noncriminal litigation, 2329
organizational memberships and compelled speech, 476
*Paul v. Davis*, 1888
pendent jurisdiction, 1891
and police misconduct, 2329
poll tax issue, 1961
and prisoners' rights, 653, 2011–2013
private conspiracy redress, 1230–1231
and private discrimination, 2015–2017
and public accommodations, 2062–2063
Republican party antebellum commitment, 2217
residential segregation challenges, 2219
Revised Statutes of the United States, 2227
Roosevelt Court and, 2293
school busing and, 2321
social rights distinction, 1038
states' rights and, 2519
*Strauder v. West Virginia*, 1038
Waite Court and, 2823, 2827
White Court and, 2900–2901
Wisdom's opinions, 2914, 2915
*See also* Civil rights movement; Reconstruction

Civil Rights Act of 1866 (framing), 94, 95, **401–402**
equal protection of the laws, 908
and Fourteenth Amendment, 1357
Johnson's (Andrew) veto of, 402, 578
racial discrimination targets, 2100
Civil Rights Act of 1866 (judicial interpretation), **402–404**
alien protections, 66
*Blyew v. United States*, 200–201
color of law usage, 444
constitutionality tests, 96
and constitutional remedies, 652
equal protection rights, 375
narrowing focus of, 98
*Patterson v. McLean Credit Union*, 1887
private property discrimination inclusion, 2063
and Revised Statutes of the United States (1875), 2227
twentieth-century open housing applications, 393, 2220, 2221
Civil Rights Act of 1875, 94, **404**
enforcement power, 1089
invalidation of, 95, 96, 217–218, 404, 408, 1437
public accommodations application, 2062
Civil Rights Act of 1957, 95, **404**
federal enforcement, 1025, 1026
and Justice Department Civil Rights Division, 411
Civil Rights Act of 1960, 95, **404–405**
federal enforcement, 1026
Civil Rights Act of 1964, 95
age discrimination and, 59, 60, 61
civil disobedience and, 371
and comparable worth, 474
Court rulings, 98, 1089
coverage, 97, 1026, 1089
disparate impact, 99
employment discrimination and, 100, 893–894
equal protection rights, 375, 911
and Fourteenth Amendment, 96
history of, 390
impact of, 412
interstate commerce restraints, 95
as national standard, 1008
and private discrimination, 2016
public accommodations provision, 168, 391–392, 2063
public accommodations provision upheld, 1282–1283
race-based adoption as violation of, 46
and racial discrimination, 2107
and racial preference, 2109

and racial quotas, 54
reflecting courts' reactions to social change, 700
regulatory agency, 2148
and Rehnquist Court, 2164
and school busing, 1459
and school desegregation implementation, 772
and Senate Subcommittee on Constitutional Rights, 2365
and sexual harassment, 100–101
Title VII applications, 100–101, 474, 1232, 1722
Civil Rights Act of 1968, 95, **407**
and housing discrimination, 393, 406, 407
as national standard, 1008
Title VIII open housing, 407, 1026, 1437, 1854, 2220, 2221
Civil Rights Act of 1991, **407–408**
and disparate impact claims, 99, 100
presumption against statutory retroactivity, 2225
as response to *Wards Cove* decision, 99–100
Civil Rights Cases (1883), **408–410**
badges of servitude, 409, 1437, 1919
and equal protection clause, 389, 909
and federal civil rights enforcement, 201
Harlan (1833–1911) dissent, 1267, 1919
invalidating antidiscrimination legislation, 95, 96, 1919, 2062
invalidating Civil Rights Act of 1875, 404
limiting federal civil rights enforcement, 201, 1089, 1293
and state jurisdictional rights, 1165
and Waite Court, 2828
Civil Rights Commission, **410**
Civil Rights Act of 1964, 405
creation of, 404
Civil Rights Division, **410–411**
establishment of, 404, 1025
Civil rights movement, **411–413**
boycott use, 1551, 1556
*Brown* decision as catalyst, 255, 1615
civil disobedience use, 369, 370–371, 1537
*Cox* test for demonstrations, 702
and Fourteenth Amendment-Bill of Rights incorporation, 179–180
indictment for murder of civil rights workers, 2006
and Justice Department, 136
and Kennedy administration, 1532, 1533

Civil rights movement (continued)
    King leadership, 1536–1537
    political trials, 1955
    public accommodations challenges,
      2062
    sit-ins, 2420
    states' rights challenges, 1008
    See also Desegregation; Race-
      consciousness; Racial
      discrimination; Racial preference
Civil rights practice, **413–414**
Civil rights removal, **414–415**
    and Civil Rights Act of 1866, 402,
      403
Civil Rights Repeal Act (1894), **415**
    antidiscrimination legislation, 94
    federal protection of civil rights, 1024
Civil service. See Public employees
Civil War, **415–418**
    and alien suffrage, 68
    and Compromise of 1850, 812–813
    Confiscation Acts, 134, 490–491,
      2432–2433
    conscientious objection, 2187
    conscription, 506
    constitutional results of, 571
    Dred Scott v. Sandford, 818–820
    Emancipation Proclamation, 417, 573,
      884–885
    federal judicial system changes, 1490
    federal jurisdiction, 1501
    Federal Test Acts, 1029–1030
    habeas corpus suspension, 1246, 1247,
      1256
    Homestead Act, 417, 1302
    and indestructibility of American
      federalism, 1007
    Legal Tender Cases, 1581
    Lincoln's conduct of, 415–417
    Lincoln's constitutional theory, 1620–
      1622, 1624
    Lincoln's war powers, 2840–2841
    loyalty oaths, 1647–1648, 1649, 2143
    Milligan, Ex parte, 2868
    as political question, 2022
    political trials, 1954, 1955
    Prize Cases, 2022
    rebel amnesties, 89
    Republican party, 2217
    and secession, 415, 1007
    Senate during, 2358
    slavery and, 2427, 2432
    sovereignty question, 415
    as state of war, 2505
    as undeclared war, 755
    unionism, 2688
    war powers, 2840–2841
    See also Reconstruction

Civil War amendments. See Fifteenth
    Amendment; Fourteenth Amend-
    ment; Thirteenth Amendment
Claims Court, **419–420**
    creation of new, 981
    Iranian hostage settlement, 741
    Tucker Act, 2737
    See also United States Court of
      Appeals for the Federal Circuit
Class action, **422–423**
    amicus curiae briefs, 89
    choice of law, 358
    doctrinal formula, 801
    federal courts litigation, 1491
    litigation strategy, 1630
    and mootness doctrine, 1464
    public interest law, 2071
    voting rights, 2320
Clayton Act (1914), **425–426**
    antitrust law, 104, 106
    injunctions, 831
Clean Air Act. See Environmental
    regulation and the Constitution
Clear and present danger, **426–428**
    bad tendency test, 146, 1129, 1198
    balancing test replacing, 115, 222,
      427, 769–770
    Brandenburg v. Ohio, 225–226, 1154,
      1353
    breach of the peace, 1031
    Chaplinsky v. New Hampshire, 331
    and criminal syndicalism statutes, 723
    Dennis v. United States, 1353, 1955
    "discounting" formula, 769–770
    Espionage Act, 15–16, 1156, 2929
    extremist speech, 961
    fighting words, 331, 1042
    and First Amendment rights, 146, 426,
      1050, 1051, 1149, 1299, 2318–2319,
      2901
    and freedom of assembly, 1107
    as free speech test, 15, 16, 17, 154–
      155, 769, 1129, 1149, 1955, 1990
    free speech vs. criminal advocacy,
      1154
    Hand (Learned) reformulation, 1264
    Herndon v. Lowry, 1285–1286, 1955
    Holmes's coining of phrase, 1050,
      1296, 1298, 1299, 2901
    and hostile audience, 1304–1305
    incitement to unlawful conduct as,
      1198, 1352, 1353
    and Jehovah's Witnesses cases, 2186,
      2188, 2189
    and political trials, 1955
    problems with, 2901
    Schenck v. United States, 426
    statement of, 1352

    and subversive activity, 426, 769, 1050,
      1298, 1352–1353
    and subversive advocacy, 2580
    Whitney v. California, 2901–2902
    World War I cases, 2901, 2928–2929
Clerks, **429**
    Supreme Court, 2604–2605
Closed shop, **434**
    Taft-Hartley ban, 2642
Cloture, **434**
    Civil Rights Act of 1964, 405
    filibuster, 1043–1044
    as temporal limit, 2664
Cocaine. See Crack cocaine and equal
    protection
Coefficient clause. See Necessary and
    proper clause
Coerced confession. See Police interro-
    gation and confessions
Coerced speech. See Compelled speech
Coercive acts. See Constitutional history
    before 1776; First Continental
    Congress, Declarations and
    Resolves of
Cold War
    Alien Registration Act, 67–68
    American armed forces abroad, 449
    Attorney General's List, 137–138
    Dennis v. United States, 769–770
    First Amendment absolutism, 17
    Internal Security Act, 1385–1386
    legislative investigation, 1595
    loyalty oaths, 1648
    loyalty-security programs, 1649–1650
    Marshall Plan, 1687
    McCarthyism, 1701–1702
    Mundt-Nixon bill, 1766–1767
    North Atlantic Treaty, 1827
    public employees' right-privilege
      distinction, 2065–2066
    State Department passport denials,
      1535
    See also Korean War; Vietnam War
Collateral attack, **441–442**
    jurisdiction, 1500
Collective bargaining, **442**
    antitrust implications, 1545
    and commerce clause, 456
    employee speech rights, 891
    and freedom of association, 4
    Wagner Act, 1545, 1548
    yellow dog contract, 2939
Collusive suit, **443**
    case or controversy doctrine, 322,
      1464
Colonial charters, **443–444**
    and colonist rights, 84
    and constitutionalism, 635–636

Colorado River Compact (1923), 1398, 1399
Color of law, **444–445**
  affirmative action and, 55–56
  in antidiscrimination law, 2092
  *Monroe v. Pape*, 1754
  police misconduct and, 2329
  primary elections test case, 423
  private actions in concert with state officials, 2006
Comity, judicial, **447**
  exhaustion of remedies, 975
  fugitive from justice, 1158
Comity clause. *See* Full faith and credit
Commander-in-chief, **448–449**
  and congressional war powers, 502–503
  and declaration of war, 755
  as enumerated presidential power, 1996, 1998
  Executive Order 10340, 945
  Polk's development of powers, 1959
  presidential plenary authority as, 1075, 2290
  presidential power to end wars, 494
  presidential war powers, 2844
  and undeclared war, 1242, 1541, 2841
*Commentaries on American Law* (Kent), 1534, 1535
*Commentaries on the Constitution of the United States* (Story), 559, 561–562, 1633, 2121, 2554
*Commentaries on the Laws of England* (Blackstone), 196, 197, 512, 1217, 1674, 2057, 2236
Commentators on the Constitution, **449–453**
  Arnold, Thurman, 453
  Bancroft, George, 159
  Beard, Charles A., 166–167, 452
  Bickel, Alexander M., 173, 453
  Boudin, Louis, 212, 453
  Brant, Irving, 226
  Burgess, John W., 452
  Calhoun, John C., 291–292, 451
  Chipman, Nathaniel, 356, 449
  Commager, Henry Steele, 447–448
  on Congress's jurisdiction-limiting authority, 1502–1503
  Cooley, Thomas McIntyre, 451, 680–681
  Corwin, Edward S., 452, 693–694, 1634, 2834
  Crosskey, William W., 453, 728–729, 1643
  Curtis, George Ticknor, 450, 736
  Cushman, Robert E., 738
  Davis, Jefferson, 451

Dillon, John Forrest, 451
Freund, Paul, 1155
Goodnow, Frank J., 1205
Haines, Charles G., 1257
Hamilton, Alexander, 449
Hamilton, Walton Hale, 1260–1261
Hildreth, Richard, 450
Jackson, Robert H., 452
Jay, John, 449
Kelly, Alfred H., 1528
Kent, James, 450, 1535
Kurland, Philip B., 1542–1543
Lee, Rex Edwin, 1574
and legal culture, 1577
Lieber, Francis, 451
Madison, James, 449
Murphy, Paul L., 1769–1770
Powell, Thomas Reed, 1980–1981
Progressive critiques, 2046–2047
on ratifier intent, 2120, 2121
Rawle, William, 450, 2124
St. George Tucker, Henry, 450
Schouler, James, 452
Smith, J. Allen, 2436
Stephens, Alexander H., 451
Story, Joseph, 450, 2554
Swisher, Carl Brent, 453, 2630
Taylor, John, 450
Thorpe, Francis N., 2700
Tiedeman, Christopher G., 451, 2701
Tucker, John Randolph, 451
Tucker, St. George, 2737
Von Holst, Hermann, 452
Willoughby, Westel W., 452, 2907–2908
Commerce
  Chief Justice Marshall's definition of, 1191
  *See also* Effects on commerce; Foreign commerce; Interstate commerce; Intrastate commerce; State regulation of commerce; State taxation of commerce; Stream of commerce doctrine; Subjects of commerce
Commerce clause, **453–460**
  *Adair v. United States*, 25–26
  age discrimination legislation, 59
  and American Indians, 80, 81, 82–83, 453–454
  Americans with Disabilities Act, 87
  antidiscrimination legislation tied to, 95, 1282
  and antitrust law, 103, 585, 1828
  Bituminous Coal Act upheld under, 184, 457
  broad construction of, 250, 1261, 1262

Burger Court use of, 276
child labor and, 350, 2048, 2049
Child Support Recovery Act and, 354
cities and, 362, 363
civil rights cases and, 390
and competition in interstate commerce, 1739
concurrent powers doctrine, 1534–1535
congressional power and, 2317
corporate charter vested rights, 2059–2060
dormant, 804–807
drug regulation, 821, 822, 823
and dual federalism, 827
economic equal protection, 840
*Edwards v. California*, 861, 2878
Embargo Acts, 885
environmental regulation, 900, 904
exclusive federal control over, 1425
extended to entire national economy, 850, 2932–2933
Fair Labor Standards Act upheld under, 743, 966
federal criminal law jurisdiction, 1567, 1568, 1570
federalism and shared powers, 1011–1012
federal regulation of private activity under, 991
federal treaty power superseding, 1389–1390
Food, Drug, and Cosmetic Act, 1069
foreign commerce and, 1072–1073, 1081
Frankfurter's views, 1003
freedom of contract and, 1114
and general welfare clause, 1186
*Gibbons v. Ogden*, 1189–1192, 1396, 1425, 1988
Hughes Court interpretation, 1314
interstate commerce and, 1396
interstate slave trade and, 1238
interstate transport of liquor and, 213–214
intrastate commerce and, 1396, 1399, 1918
jurisdiction to tax under, 1504–1505
limits tests, 1396
Marshall (John) treatise on, 1189–1190, 1191–1192
Marshall Court ruling, 1674, 1686
Minnesota rate cases, 1739–1740, 2899
National Industrial Recovery Act, 2288
navigation and waterways, 107, 454, 455

Commerce clause (continued)
  original meaning of "commerce"
    scholarship, 1643
  *Perez v. United States*, 1567, 1899
  *Philadelphia v. New Jersey*, 1904
  preemption, 1988
  and private-sector discrimination,
    2016
  and privileges and immunities, 2019–
    2020
  Public Utility Holding Act, 2079–2080
  railroads and their employees and,
    455, 456, 457
  rational basis standard of review, 2122
  Rehnquist Court and, 2169
  Roosevelt Court broad view of, 2293
  securities law and, 2350
  and segregated rail transport, 1918
  and segregated steamship transport,
    204
  selective exclusiveness doctrine, 681–
    682, 2356
  Sherman Antitrust Act and, 1828
  Shreveport doctrine and, 2415–2416
  as social and economic remedy, 330
  state and local government taxation
    and, 2493, 2494
  state import tax as violating, 256
  state police power, 1320
  state regulation of commerce curbs,
    1381
  state taxation of commerce, 2521
  state tax incentives and subsidies to
    business and, 2523
  stream of commerce doctrine, 1396,
    2470
  subjects of commerce and, 2565
  substantive due process and, 2574
  supremacy clause and, 2588
  Taft Court and, 2638
  Taney Court and, 455, 681, 1700, 2651
  treaty power superseding, 1390
  uniform preemptive national legisla-
    tion, 996
  vagrancy laws and, 2774
  Wagner Act cases, 2819–2821
  White Court and, 2899
  *Willson v. Black Bird Creek Marsh
    Co.*, 2908
  World War I, 2481
Commerce court, **460**
  establishment of, 590
Commercial speech, **460–461, 462**
  (update 1), **462–464** (update 2)
  alteration of doctrinal formula, 203–
    204
  attorney solicitation, 138–139, 165,
    1065

Blackmun doctrinal innovation, 190
*Board of Trustees of State University
  of New York v. Fox*, 203
Burger Court and, 275, 316
call for secondary boycott disallowed,
  1203–1204
*Central Hudson Gas & Electric Corp.
  v Public Service Commission*, 327
chilling effect and, 355
communitarians on, 473
First Amendment four-part test, 461,
  462–463, 464
First Amendment protection, 17, 138,
  139, 165, 327, 375, 1060, 1118,
  1133, 1135, 1556, 2351, 2800
First Amendment restriction on
  misleading, 1377
interest-balancing formula test, 1969
listeners' rights, 1628
as low First Amendment value, 1056,
  1128, 1133, 1646
*Posadas de Puerto Rico Associates v.
  Tourism Company*, 462
primary purpose test, 460, 461
"reduced protection," 830
"right of publicity" privacy cases,
  2014
standard of review, 2472
*Virginia Pharmacy Board v. Virginia
  Citizens Consumer Council*, 461,
  462
Committees of Correspondence, 32
Common law (Anglo-American), **465–
  466**
  affected with a public interest, 52–53
  against redelegation of power, 760
  antitrust law roots in, 104, 105
  arrest warrant, 119, 120, 121
  *Boyd* ruling, 2339
  breach of the peace, 227
  citizenship, 131
  and Civil Rights Cases, 409
  Coke's writings, 439–440
  collateral attack, 441
  conflict law as, 358
  and constitutional common law, 513
  damages, 739, 2741
  de facto/de jure, 759
  defendants' rights, 718
  *de minimis non curat lex*, 765
  doctrine stemming from, 801
  double jeopardy, 807–808
  evidence admissibility, 2872
  federal court jurisdiction, 1439
  feudal privileges, 1034
  freedom of contract, 1112, 1113
  full faith and credit, 1171
  and fundamental law, 1174

habeas corpus, 1245–1246
and higher law, 1571
human body property rights, 2057
jury nullification, 1512
jury size, 1516, 2727
jury unanimity, 2727
juvenile proceedings, 1522
labor activity restrictions, 1546, 1547,
  1554, 1555
libel, 1141, 1606, 1608
municipality liability, 1767
obscenity, 2747
official immunity, 1336
precedent, 1986
preferred freedoms, 1051
property, 2052, 2057, 2222
public law litigation vs., 2072
reasonable doubt, 264
right against self-incrimination, 1617–
  1618, 2233, 2234, 2236
rule of law, 2297, 2298
rules of liability, 1804
seditious libel, 16, 1138, 1606
slavery, 2451–2452
sovereign immunity, 2459
stare decisis, 2477
state constitutional law and, 2496
state police power, 2506
Story's views, 2556
suicide, 2267
women's status, 2920
writ of prohibition, 2050
Common law, constitutional. *See* Constitutional common law
Common law, federal. *See* Federal
  common law, civil; Federal common
  law of crimes
*Common Law, The* (Holmes), 1295,
  1296, 1308, 1315, 2712
*Common Sense* (Paine), 27, 537, 2297
Commonwealth status, **468**
  and federalism, 1004
  of Puerto Rico, 2081
Communications Act (1934), **468–469**
  broadcasting, 246, 247, 249
  Federal Communications Commission
    powers, 445–446
  wiretapping prohibition, 1853, 2913
Communications and community, **469–
  470**
Communications and democracy, **470–
  471**
  listeners' rights, 1628
Communications Decency Act (1996),
  **471–472**
  Internet restraints, 1392
Communism. *See* Cold War; Communist
  party; Loyalty-security program;

McCarthyism; Subversive activity; Subversive advocacy
Communist Control Act (1954), **472**
  McCarthyism, 606
  *Pennsylvania V. Nelson*, 1894
  subversive advocacy, 2581–2582
Communist party
  Attorney General's List, 138, 1436
  balancing test, 155, 770, 1595
  constitutionally protected activities vs. revolutionary incitements, 769, 770, 1353
  *Dennis v. United States*, 769–770, 1127, 1353
  First Amendment protections, 1127, 1595
  freedom of association, 1052, 1107, 1108–1109
  House Committee on Un-American Activities, 605, 1305
  and incitement to unlawful conduct, 1198–1199, 1353
  Internal Security Act, 1386
  labor union members, 257, 1561
  legislative investigations, 1595, 2866
  legislative investigation witness testimony, 1595–1596
  listeners' rights, 1560, 1628
  loyalty oath, 1648
  loyalty-security programs, 1649–1650, 1701–1702
  Mundt-Nixon Bill, 1766–1767
  Palmer raids, 2580
  restricted association rights, 1237
  right to travel appeal, 116
  *Robel v. United States*, 2280–2281
  subversive advocacy, 2581–2582
  *Yates* reversal of Smith Act convictions, 2938–2939
Communitarianism, **472–474**
Compact theory. *See* Social compact theory; Theories of the Union
Companion case, **474**
Comparable worth, **474–475**
  as sex discrimination issue, 2397
Compelled speech, **475–476**
  *Hurley v. Irish-American Gay, Lesbian, and Bisexual Group of Boston*, 1320
Compelling state interest, **477**
  in abortion, 5, 2204, 2284–2285
  in affirmative action, 33, 58, 848
  in afrocentric schools, 58
  in bail setting, 150–151
  and balancing test, 155
  in campaign finance, 295
  in dial-a-porn restraints, 778
  in family choices interference, 1123

  in First Amendment infringements, 155
  in gun control, 1243–1244
  overriding free association challenge, 1110
  *Paradise, United States v.*, 1877
  *Perry Education Association v. Perry Local Educators' Association*, 1899
  in public forum speech regulation, 2068
  in race- and sex-based antidiscrimination law, 2091, 2106
  in religious liberty infringement, 821, 1851, 2178, 2182, 2187, 2192, 2195
  in residency requirements, 2306
  in same-sex marriage, 147, 2308
  in suppressing instructions of violence, 1154
  *See also* Strict scrutiny
Competitive federalism, **477**
Comprehensive Drug Abuse Prevention and Control Act (1970), 821, 823
Comprehensive Forfeiture Act (1984), 680
Compromise of 1850, **477–478**
  Douglas's (Stephen) role in, 812–813
  fugitive slave laws, 1159, 1525
  Kansas-Nebraska Act, 1525, 1526
  Pierce administration and, 1908
  slavery and, 2430, 2431, 2435
  Webster statement on, 2885
  Whig party position, 2884, 2885
Compromise of 1877, **478–479**
  and antidiscrimination legislation, 94
Compulsory process, right to, **479–481**
  and capital punishment, 302
  for criminally accused, 2255–2256
  and right of confrontation, 491
Computers, **481–483**
  criminal justice technology, 711, 712–713
  Internet and free speech, 471, 1154, 1391–1392
  zoning technology, 2945
Concord town meeting resolutions (1776), **483**
  and constitutional conventions, 515–516
Concurrent jurisdiction, **483–484**
  abstention doctrine, 18
  habeas corpus, 1247
  Judiciary Act of 1789, 1495
  removal of cases, 2198–2199
  United States District Courts, 2762
Concurrent powers, **484**
  and doctrine of selective exclusiveness, 681
  as dormant, 807

  and federalism, 1012
  in interstate commerce, 1190
Concurrent resolution, **485**
  emergency powers, 886, 2842
  *Immigration and Naturalization Service v. Chadha*, 1219, 2843
  joint resolution vs., 1436–1437
  and war powers, 1998, 2838, 2843
Concurring opinion, **485**
  Brandeis on free speech, 222–23
  conference, 488
  grounds of opinion, 1235
Conditional spending, **485–488**
Confederate Constitution, **488**
  appellate jurisdiction, 109
  ban on alien suffrage, 68
  line-item veto, 1626
  provisions of, 575
  slave trade prohibition, 2050
Confederation Congress. *See* First Congress
Conference, **488**
  Supreme Court decision, 752
Confessions. *See* Police interrogation and confessions
*Confirmatio cartarum* (1297), **489**
Confirmation process, **489–490**
  judicial independence, 1456
  politicization of, 2325
  for Supreme Court justices, 112, 1018–1019
  *See also* Advice and consent; Advice and consent to Supreme Court nominations
Confiscation Acts (1861, 1862), **490–491**
  and attainder of treason, 134
  forfeiture of slaves by, 2432–2433
Conflict of laws. *See* Choice of law; Choice of law and constitutional rights
*Conflict of Laws* (Story), 2556
Conformity Act (1789), 1028
Confrontation, right of, **491, 491–493** (update)
  and administrative agency regulations, 39
  and capital punishment, 302
  in child abuse, 1691
  *Coy v. Iowa*, 703
  for criminally accused, 2255
  and fair trial, 971
  as fundamental in state and federal courts, 1921
  and hearsay evidence, 1282
  incorporation into criminal procedural due process, 2039
  in juvenile delinquency proceedings, 1183

Confrontation, right of (continued)
  lineup suspect, 1628
  and loyalty-security charges, 1650
  Scalia's views, 2316
Congress. *See* Continental Congress;
    First Congress; House of Represen-
    tatives; Senate; Legislative power;
    *specific headings below*
Congress and foreign policy, **493–496**
  Boland Amendment, 206, 2128
  commerce regulation, 1081
  declaration of war, 755–756
  delegation of power, 760, 761
  extraterritoriality, 959
  Iran-Contra affair, 1402
  powers and authority, 1073–1076,
    1078–1081
  and presidential treaty power, 1991–
    1993
  *See also* Advice and consent; Congres-
    sional war powers; Senate and
    foreign policy; Treaty power
Congress and the Supreme Court, **496–
    498**
  appellate jurisdiction, 108–109
  constitutional amending process, 73–
    74, 75
  Court's historical judicial restraint,
    1445–1446
  federal jurisdiction, 1501–1503
Congressional Budget and Impound-
    ment Control Act (1974), **498–499**
  and concurrent resolution, 485
  and congressional spending, 619–620
  as counter-impoundment measure,
    1349
  and executive power, 949
  Gramm-Rudman-Hollings Act
    amending, 1219
  as impairing presidential bureaucratic
    authority, 266
  as Nixon impoundment response, 610,
    615
  as reassertion of fiscal policymaking
    role, 260, 262
Congressional Budget Office, 260
Congressional contempt power. *See*
    Legislative contempt power
Congressional government, **499–500**
  delegation of power, 760–762
  Wilson (Woodrow) writings, 2911
Congressional investigation. *See* Legisla-
    tive investigation
Congressional membership, **500–501**
Congressional power. *See* Legislative
    power
Congressional privileges and immunities,
    **501–502**

*Congressional Record*, 2358
Congressional standing, **502**
Congressional veto. *See* Legislative veto
Congressional war powers, **502–503**
  concurrent resolution, 1998, 2843
  Confiscation Acts, 490
  constitutional and historical, 2835,
    2838–2844
  declaration of war, 455–456, 755–756,
    1080, 1998, 2836
  establishment of military forces, 386
  original intent and, 1080
  as restraints on presidential powers,
    449, 1075, 1998
  War Powers Resolution, 2838–2839
  World War I, 2927–2928
  *See also* Presidential war powers; War
    powers
Congress of Racial Equality, 412
Connecticut Compromise. *See* Great
    Compromise
Conquered provinces theory, **504–505**
Conscientious objection, **505–506**
  balancing test, 2187
  and civil disobedience, 371
  and conscription, 506
  exemption as right not privilege, 2187
  free exercise clause, 1049, 2187–2188
  Jehovah's Witness case, 2186
  naturalization eligibility, 1198
  religious beliefs definition, 2173, 2180,
    2188, 2193, 2353–2354
  *Seeger, United States v.*, 2353–2354
  state denial of, 1261
Conscription, **506–507**
  adoption of national, 571
  of aliens, 66, 68
  draft card burning, 817–818
  exclusion of women challenged, 2295–
    2296
  Selective Draft Law Cases, 506, 2173,
    2187, 2356, 2868–2869, 2928
  Selective Service Act, 2357
  Thirteenth Amendment-based invol-
    untary servitude challenge, 506,
    2187, 2356, 2928
  World War I, 506, 2356–2357, 2927
  World War II, 506, 2357
  *See also* Conscientious objection
Conscription Act (1917). *See* Selective
    Service Act
Conscription Acts (1863, 1940, 1948).
    *See* Selective Service Acts
Consent decree, **507**
  Packers & Stockyards Act, 1873
Consent search, **507**
  broadened conception, 1327–1328
  voluntary, 2334

Conservatism, **507–511**
  anti-abortion movement, 92–94
  Bork nomination, 209–211
  Burger Court, 270, 272, 273
  critique of liberalism, 1616
  devolution agenda, 775–778
  "Four Horsemen of Reaction," 2899
  liberal construction compared with,
    1612–1613
  New Right, 1801–1802
  obscenity views, 1838
  Progressive thought vs., 2048–2049
  Reagan presidency, 2124–2129
  of Rehnquist, 2155, 2156, 2158, 2159,
    2160
  of Rehnquist Court, 2161–2162,
    2168–2169
  religious fundamentalism, 2184–2185
  Republican party 1994 agenda, 775–
    776
  of Scalia, 2312–2314, 2315
  and welfare rights, 2875–2877
  of White (Edward), 2894–2895
  of White Court, 2899, 2900
Conspiracy law, **511–512**
  criminal conspiracy, 708–709
Constitution, **512–513**
  anti-retroactivity provisions, 2225
  bicameralism provision, 171
  Committee of Eleven's draft of, 287
  concept in Massachusetts Circular
    Letter, 1694
  concept of written, 84, 1174–1175,
    1364, 1419
  constitutional conventions framing of,
    514
  Declaration of Independence as basis,
    31, 534–535, 755, 1174, 1944, 1945,
    1946, 1985–1986
  as disinterested authority, 1046–2047
  English Bill of Rights influence, 175
  English roots, 1387
  Fourteenth Amendment transforma-
    tion of, 1090–1092
  as fundamental law, 1173–1174
  Fundamental Orders of Connecticut
    as first written, 1176
  fundamental principles, 1947
  gender-neutrality of original text,
    2920
  history of, 528–529
  impeachment grounds, 1336
  influence abroad, 1363–1368
  international human rights guarantees
    compared with, 1387–1389
  lack of gender distinctions in, 1185
  Madison as father of, 1656–1658,
    1659–1662

Massachusetts Constitution as classic, 1695
Montesquieu's influence, 1755–1756
natural, 1639
natural rights and, 1785–1787
nonjudicial interpretation of, 1821–1824
political philosophy of, 1944–1946, 1962–1963
and politics, 1956–1958
Preamble, 1985–1986
presidential powers enumeration, 1996
privileges and immunities clause, 2019–2022
on privileges and rights, 2251
public choice theory, 2063–2064
and republican form of government, 2209
right-privilege distinction, 2251–2252
supremacy of, 1963
textualism, 2682–2684
unwritten, 2770–2771
See also Bill of Rights; British Constitution; Commentaries on the Constitution; Constitutional history; Constitutionalism; Ratification of the Constitution; Ratifier intent; State constitutions
Constitutional amendments. See Amending process; Bill of Rights; specific amendments
Constitutional argument. See History in constitutional argumentation
Constitutional common law, 513–514
Constitutional convention, 514–516
and amending process, 74, 75, 77, 123–124, 2116
for balanced-budget amendment, 76, 123, 153, 618
as Concord town meeting resolution, 483
and constitutional reform, 651
for states returning to the Union, 2818
Constitutional Convention of 1787, 517–523
Adams (John) and, 28
amending process, 72, 74, 75, 77, 123–124
and Annapolis Convention, 90
Anti-Federalist arguments, 101–102
appointments clause, 48–49, 113–114
backgrounds of delegates, 1610–1611
and Bill of Rights, 175–176
bills of attainder prohibition, 174
bills of credit prohibition, 174
cases and controversies, 322

and commerce clause, 454, 804–805, 806
compromises and shared principles of, 1947
congressional privileges and immunities, 501
contract clause, 673
decisions of, 542
definition of American constitutionalism and, 636, 637
deliberative democratic aspirations of, 763
Dickinson's contribution, 780
District created as federal government seat, 795–796
domestic violence clause, 803
enumerated rights, 1045
Farran's compiled and edited records of, 975
Fitzsimons as delegate, 1061
Franklin as delegate, 1104, 1105
Gerry as delegate, 1187
Gorham as delegate, 1205
Great Compromise, 1228
Hamilton's contribution, 1258
House of Representatives inception, 1305
on impeachable offenses, 1337–1338
interest group theory, 1380
Johnson (William Samuel) as delegate, 1433–1434
on judicial power, 979–819
on judicial review, 1473, 1474
King as delegate, 1537
Langdon as delegate, 1561
Lansing as delegate, 1561
lawyers participating in, 1365, 1610
and Lecompton constitution, 1574
Madison's critical role in, 1656–1658, 1659–1663
Madison's notes, 1662–1663
and originalism, 1394
Pierce as delegate, 1908
Pinckney as delegate, 1909
Preamble drafting, 1985–1986
ratification of constitutional amendments, 2116
ratifier intent, 2120–2121
records of, 516–517, 975, 1662–1663
representation compromise, 2130, 2133
and republican form of government, 2209
Rutledge as delegate, 2301
Senate inception, 2357–2361
slave trade prohibitions, 2050
on Supreme Court justices' appointment method, 489

taxing and spending powers, 1998
theories of Union, 753–754, 997
on veto power, 1349
Virginia Plan, 2800
voting rights issue, 636
on war powers, 755, 1080
Wilson's (James) contributions, 2910–2911
Wythe as delegate, 2935
Yates as delegate, 2938
Constitutional Convention, records of, 516–517
Farran's compiled and edited notes, 975
Madison's notes, 1662–1663
Yates's notes, 2938
Constitutional court, 523–524
cases and controversies, 322
Court of Customs and Patent Appeals as, 696
Court of International Trade as, 696
as distinct from legislative courts, 1589, 1590, 1612
Farran's compiled and edited notes, 975
as federal court, 1017
federal judicial role, 1020–1023
federal question jurisdiction, 1027–1028
habeas corpus writs, 1248–1253
justiciability, 1519–1521
state nonimmunity to suits in, 1060
United States Court of Appeals for the Federal Circuit as, 981
Constitutional Dictatorship (Rossiter), 1996
Constitutional dualism, 524–525
deliberative democracy, 763–764
See also Amendment process (outside Article V); Constitutional theory
Constitutional federalism. See Federalism
Constitutional fictions, 525–528
Constitutional Government of the United States (Wilson), 1633, 2047
Constitutional history before 1776, 528–536
Massachusetts Body of Liberties, 149, 374, 531, 828, 1694
Stamp Act Congress, 2470–2471
Constitutional history, 1776–1789, 536–546
Adams (John) and, 27–29
American Revolution, 83–86
Anti-Federalist thought, 101–2, 101–102, 101–2
Articles of Confederation, 124–126, 537, 538, 539

Constitutional history (continued)
  civil-military relations, 385, 387
  Declaration of Independence, 752–
    755
  domestic violence clause, 803
  due process clause, 829
  equal protection, 907
  federalism, 997–999, 1011
  *Federalist, The,* 1013–1015
  First Congress, 1057–1059
  first election, 1934
  fundamental law, 1173–1174
  gender-neutrality of original text,
    2920
  Hamilton's views, 1257–1260
  judicial review, 1473–1474
  legislative power, 1596–1597
  liberal ideals, 1613–1614
  Lockean influence, 1640
  Madison's importance, 1656–1658,
    1659–1663
  Marshall (John) and, 1673
  Massachusetts Constitution of 1780,
    1695
  Northwest Ordinance, 1829
  and original intent, 1857
  political philosophy of Constitution,
    1944–1949
  popular sovereignty, 1962–1963
  postal power, 1970
  Preamble writing, 1985–1986
  property's importance, 2051, 2052–
    2053
  referendum, 763
  republican form of government, 2209
  republicanism, 2212–2213
  right against self-incrimination, 2236
  state precedent for judicial review,
    1298
  Washington's impact on, 2860–2861
  *See also* Constitutional Convention of
    1789
Constitutional history, 1789–1801, **546–**
    **550**
  amending process, 72, 74
  Bill of Rights, 178, 1091
  and Federalists, 1016
  federal jurisdiction over common law
    crimes, 980
  first act of Congress ruled unconstitu-
    tional, 1279–1280, 1324
  First Amendment, 1045
  Jay as first Chief Justice, 1418
  Jay' Treaty, 1419
  Judiciary Act of 1789, 1495–1497
  Madison and, 1658
  Washington's impact on, 546–549,
    2861–2862

Constitutional history, 1801–1829, **550–**
    **558**
  devolution cases, 777
  and federalism, 1000, 1011–1012
  and Federalists, 1017
  federal jurisdiction over common law
    crimes, 980–981
  Jefferson presidency, 550–553
  judicial review, 1473–1474
  Judiciary Act of 1801, 1496–1497
  Judiciary Acts of 1802, 1498
  labor organization, 1546
  liberal constitutional construction,
    1611–1612
  Madison presidency, 1658–1659
  *Marbury v. Madison,* 1667–1670
  Marshall Court, 1681–1687
  Marshall's (John) influence, 1673–
    1675
  *Martin v. Hunter's Lessee,* 1688–1691
  *McCulloch v. Maryland,* 1611, 1705–
    1707
  Missouri Compromise, 1747–1748
  Monroe (James) presidency, 554–555
  political parties, 1935
  unconstitutionality, 1293–1294
Constitutional history, 1829–1848, **558–**
    **564**
  and federalism, 1000–1001
  and Jacksonianism, 1412–1414
  Jackson presidency, 558–561
  labor organization, 1547
  political parties, 1935
  Polk presidency, 563
Constitutional history, 1848–1861, **564–**
    **570**
  Polk presidency, 565, 568
  republican form of government, 1652,
    2210
Constitutional history, 1861–1865, **570–**
    **576**
  Civil War, 415–418
  and federalism, 999, 1001
  Lincoln presidency, 415–417, 571–
    575
Constitutional history, 1865–1877, **576–**
    **582**
  amendment ratification, 72
  Bill of Rights, 178
  civil rights legislation, 94–96, 401–404
  and federalism, 191, 999, 1001
  Fifteenth Amendment, 1039–1042
  Fourteenth Amendment, 1084–1092
  Grant presidency, 580, 581
  Johnson (Andrew) presidency, 577–
    579
  Judiciary Act of 1875, 1497
  Legal Tender Cases, 1581–1582

Military Reconstruction Acts, 1728
  postal power, 1970
  Reconstruction's significance, 764
  Thirteenth Amendment, 2692–2693
Constitutional history, 1877–1901, **582–**
    **587**
  Asian immigrant legal challenges,
    130–131
  and Bill of Rights extension to states,
    178–179, 1090–1092
  and federalism, 1000, 1001, 1012
  freedom of contract, 1112
  Fuller Court, 1163–1170
  public purpose doctrine, 2073, 2075
Constitutional history, 1901–1921, **587–**
    **592**
  clear and present danger test, 1352–
    1353
  constitutional amendments, 72, 588,
    589
  and federalism, 1000, 1001, 1012
  and First Amendment rights, 1949–
    1050
  freedom of contract, 1112, 1116
  Fuller Court, 1163–1170
  Progressive thought, 2046–2048,
    2048–2050
  public purpose doctrine, 2073
  republican form of government, 2210
  Roosevelt (Theodore) presidency,
    589–590
  rule of reason doctrine, 2298–2299,
    2895
  Taft (William Howard) presidency,
    589–590
  White Court, 2897–2901
  Wilson (Woodrow) presidency, 590,
    591
Constitutional history, 1921–1933, **592–**
    **596**
  Asian immigrant court challenges, 131
  and Bill of Rights extension to states,
    179
  and federalism, 1001, 1008, 1012
  and First Amendment rights, 1050
  freedom of contract, 1116
  freedom of the press, 1138
  Harding (Warren) presidency, 593
  Hoover (Herbert) presidency, 595–
    596
  Judicial Conference of the United
    States, 1452
  Judiciary Act of 1925, 1497–1498
  Nineteenth Amendment, 1808–1809
  public purpose doctrine, 2073
Constitutional history, 1933–1945, **596–**
    **602**
  amendment ratification, 73

Asian American court challenges, 131
congressional investigations, 1595
Court-packing plan, 696–699, 1794, 2288–2289
and federalism, 1001, 1002
freedom of the press, 1138–1139
Hughes Court, 1312–1318
Japanese American cases' significance, 132
Judiciary Reform Act, 1498–1499
minimum wage legislation, 2881–2882
National Industrial Recovery Act, 1775–1776
New Deal legislative tests, 128, 2288–2289
New Deal's significance, 764
public purpose doctrine, 2073–2074, 2075–2076
Roosevelt (Franklin) presidency, 596–602
Roosevelt Court, 2292–2293
Constitutional history, 1945–1961, **602–608**
antidiscrimination legislation, 96–97
and Bill of Rights extension to states, 179
*Brown v. Board of Education*'s importance, 253
Eisenhower (Dwight) presidency, 605–607
and federalism, 1002
incorporation doctrine, 1355
North Atlantic Treaty, 1827
presidential powers decision, 1996
public purpose doctrine, 2076
secularist leanings, 1048
Truman (Harry) presidency, 603–605
Constitutional history, 1961–1977, **608–613**
amendment ratification, 73, 75, 608
Burger Court, 272–278
devolution and federalism issues, 777
and federalism, 1002–1003, 1008
and First Amendment rights, 1002–1003, 1008, 1051
freedom of the press, 1145–1146
free press/fair trial, 1150
*Griswold v. Connecticut* significance, 1233–1234
institutional litigation, 1375
Nixon presidency, 1815–1818
religious belief definitions, 2173–2174
Watergate scandal, 2864–2865
Constitutional history, 1977–1985, **613–617**
Burger Court, 272–277, 1008

and federalism, 1002–1003, 1008
feminist theory, 1032–1033
Reagan presidency, 617–622
Constitutional history, 1980–1989, **617–623**
conservative program, 776
delegation doctrine, 761, 762
devolution, 776–777
federalism, 1002, 1003
freedom of intimate association, 1119
freedom of speech cases, 1132–1135
Iran-Contra affair, 206, 1402–1403
Reagan (Ronald) presidency, 617–622
Constitutional history, 1989–1999, **623–626**
amendment ratification, 75
devolution, 776–777
freedom of the press, 1146
*Planned Parenthood v. Casey*, 1916
religious belief definition, 2174–2175
Constitutional interpretation, **626–633**
avoidance doctrine, 142
of Bill of Rights application, 1354
and Bork nomination rejections, 50, 115, 210
broad construction, 250
of commerce clause, 454, 1189–1192
communitarianism, 472
constitutionalism, 639, 1035
contemporary federalism rulings, 995
damages claims, 741
deconstructionist readings, 758–759
departmentalism, 1487
as doctrine, 801
Douglas-Black clash, 816
of due process clauses, 2043–2045
economics linkage, 1563–1566
and federal common law authority, 977–978
Federalist, 1015–1017
and federal judicial appointments, 1018
and federal jurisdiction, 1502
First Amendment expansion, 1049–1050
Fourth Amendment, 2340
free exercise clause, 2192–2193
fruit of the poisonous tree, 1158
Hamilton's views, 1260
Hughes Court, 1312, 1314, 1317
interpretivist, 1393–1394, 1480, 1860–1861
Jacksonian strict approach, 1412, 1413
Jeffersonianism, 1422
judicial function in, 1034, 1458–1459
judicial policymaking vs., 1462
judicial review, 1477–1478
judicial strategy, 1485

judicial supremacy in, 1475, 1476, 1487–1488
jurisprudence, 1505–1508
Justice Baldwin's views, 156–157
Justice Barbour's views, 162
Justice Blackmun's views, 190–196, 1291, 2204, 2284
Justice Black's views, 185–188, 815, 816, 1233, 2037, 2038
Justice Blair's views, 198
Justice Blatchford's views, 198–199
Justice Bradley's views, 216–218
Justice Brandeis's views, 219–225, 1633–1634
Justice Brennan's views, 229–240, 1458, 1459, 1480, 1634, 2214
Justice Brewer's views, 240–242
Justice Breyer's views, 242–243
Justice Brown's views, 252–253
Justice Burger's views, 269–272
Justice Burton's views, 279–280
Justice Butler's views, 283–284
Justice Byrnes's views, 285–286
Justice Campbell's views, 298
Justice Cardozo's views, 313–316, 2713
Justice Catron's views, 325
Justice Chase's views, 334–336
Justice Clark's views, 420–421
Justice Curtis's views, 735–736
Justice Cushing's views, 737–738
Justice Davis's views, 746, 746–747
Justice Day's views, 749
Justice Douglas's views, 813–816, 815, 1233, 1480
Justice Duvall's views, 832
Justice Ellsworth's views, 882–884
Justice Field's views, 1035–1036, 1035–1039
Justice Fortas's views, 1082–1083
Justice Frankfurter's views, 1101–1104, 2037–2038
Justice Fuller's views, 1161–1163
Justice Ginsburg's views, 1196–1197
Justice Goldberg's views, 1200
Justice Gray's views, 1226–1227
Justice Grier's views, 1229–1230
Justice Harlan's (1833–1911) views, 1265–1270
Justice Harlan's (1899–1971) views, 1268–1270, 2037–2038
Justice Holmes's views, 1296–1298, 1633
Justice Hughes's views, 1309–1312
Justice Hunt's views, 1319
Justice Iredell's views, 1404
Justice Jackson's (Howell E.) views, 1409

Constitutional interpretation (continued)
  Justice Jackson's (Robert H.) views,
      1410–1411, 2903
  Justice Jay's views, 1418
  Justice Johnson's views, 1425, 1433
  Justice Kennedy's views, 1529–1532
  Justice Lamar's (Joseph) views, 1558–
      1559
  Justice Lamar's (L. Q. C.) views, 1559
  Justice Lurton's views, 1651–1652
  Justice Marshall's (John) views, 1189–
      1192, 1458–1459, 1472, 1473,
      1611–1612, 1633, 1667–1669,
      1673–1675, 1682–1686, 1706–1707
  Justice Marshall's (Thurgood) views,
      1676–1681
  Justice Matthews's views, 1698
  Justice McKenna's views, 1709–1710
  Justice McKinley's views, 1710–1711
  Justice McLean's views, 1711–1712
  Justice McReynold's views, 1714–1715
  Justice Miller's views, 1731–1734
  Justice Moody's views, 1756
  Justice Murphy's views, 1768–1769
  Justice O'Connor's views, 1841–1846
  Justice Paterson's views, 1883–1884
  Justice Peckham's views, 1890–1891
  Justice Pitney's views, 1911–1912
  Justice Powell's views, 1975–1980
  Justice Reed's views, 2144–2145
  Justice Rehnquist's views, 2152–2160
  Justice Roberts's views, 2281–2282
  Justice Rutledge's (Wiley) views,
      2302–2303
  Justice Sanford's views, 2310–2311
  Justice Scalia's views, 2313–2316
  Justice Shiras's views, 2413–2414,
      2414
  Justice Souter's views, 2453–2456
  Justice Stevens's views, 2529–2539
  Justice Stewart's views, 2541–2542
  Justice Stone's views, 2543–2547
  Justice Story's views, 333, 2553–2557
  Justice Strong's views, 2563–2564
  Justice Sutherland's views, 2260,
      2626–2627
  Justice Swayne's views, 2628
  Justice Taft's views, 2634–2636
  Justice Taney's views, 333, 1652, 2210,
      2647–2650
  Justice Thomas's view, 2695–2696
  Justice Thompson's views, 2697–2698
  Justice Todd's views, 2704
  Justice Trimble's views, 2732
  Justice Van Devanter's views, 2780–
      2781
  Justice Vinson's views, 2791–2792
  Justice Waite's views, 2822–2824

  Justice Warren's views, 2849–2851
  Justice Washington's views, 2859
  Justice Wayne's views, 2867–2868
  Justice White's (Byron) views, 2885–
      2893
  Justice White's (Edward) views, 2894–
      2896
  Justice Whittaker's views, 2902–2903
  Justice Woodbury's views, 2923
  Justice Woods's views, 2923–2924
  legislative intent, 1592–1593
  liberal construction, 1610–1613
  Lincoln's view of, 1624
  and living Constitution, 1633–1634
  Madison's view of, 1659
  of New Right, 1801–1802
  noninterpretivist, 1480, 1820
  nonjudicial, 1821–1824
  original history, 628
  original intent, 1506, 1857–1859
  originalism, 1860–1865
  passivist, 1506
  "plain meaning rule" and textual
      approach, 627
  and political question doctrine, 1951–
      1952
  and postmodernism, 1971–1972
  Progressive, 1309, 2046–2047
  public understanding of, 2073
  ratifier intent, 2120–2121
  Reagan presidency, 2125–2126, 2127–
      2128
  retroactivity of decisions, 2224–2225
  right of association, 1107–1110
  Roosevelt Court, 2293
  and stare decisis, 1869
  of stream of commerce doctrine, 2559
  strict construction, 2560–2561
  by Supreme Court appointments,
      1485
  textualist, 1820, 2681–2684
  transformation of constitutional law
      and, 2712–2714
  See also Interpretivism; Noninterpre-
      tivism
Constitutionalism, 633–640
  in American Revolution period, 83–86
  bicameralism, 171–173
  British, 245–246
  broad construction vs., 250
  due process as core of, 2025
  ex post facto as mainstay, 958
  Federalist definition, 1015
  as Field's approach, 1035
  interest groups and, 1380–1382, 2063,
      2064
  Jeffersonian, 1423–1425
  and judicial review, 1472–1478

  and law of the land, 828
  limited government linked with,
      1618
  Lockean philosophy, 1639, 2051,
      2052
  Madisonian, 1659–1662
  of Marshall (John), 1674
  Montesquieu's influence, 1755–1756
  property's importance to, 2051–2057
  public choice theory, 2063–2064
  public interest law, 2071–2072
  public law litigation, 2072–2073
  public understanding of Court
      opinions, 2078
  in religious context, 665–666
  right to revolution and, 2248–2251
  and rule of law, 2297–2298
  taxation without representation and,
      2656
  Whig nationalism, 2884–2885
Constitutionalism and the American
      founding, 640–649
  liberal construction, 1611–1612
  right to revolution, 2248–2249
  Tocqueville's commentaries on, 2703–
      2704
Constitutionality. See Judicial review
Constitutional litigation. See Litigation
      strategy
Constitutional reason of state, 649–650
  and inherent powers, 1370–1371
Constitutional reform, 650–651
Constitutional remedies, 651–53, 653–
      54 (update)
  damages claims, 740–741
Constitutional rights, restrictions on. See
      Incidental burdens on constitutional
      rights; specific freedoms and rights
Constitutional rights of action. See
      Implied constitutional rights of
      action
Constitutional theory, 654–657, 657–
      661 (update)
  of Adams (John Quincy), 30–31
  and administrative agencies, 37, 38,
      40, 42
  and Bork nomination rejection, 209,
      210
  of bureaucracy, 268
  of Cardozo, 2901
  conservatism, 507–511
  constitutional dualism, 524–525
  constitutional interpretation vs., 657–
      658
  critical legal studies, 724–726
  democratic theory conflicts and recon-
      ciliations, 765–767
  dual federalism, 827

and economics theory, 1563–1566
historical background, 1387
of Hutchinson, 1323
and interest groups, 1380–1381
of Jefferson, 1419–1423, 1423–1425
jurisprudence, 1505–1508
and legal culture, 1576–1577
of Lincoln, 1620–1622, 1624, 2142
living Constitution as, 1632–1634
of Marshall (John), 1469–1470
of Montesquieu, 1755–1756
and ordered liberty, 1855
original intent, 1857–1859
originalism, 1859
pragmatism, 1982–194
Progressive thought, 2046–2048
ratifier intent, 2120–2021
representation, 2201–2203
republicanism and modern, 2213–2215
rights issues in historical perspective, 2252–2254
rights of counsel, 2260–2261
of Scalia, 2315–2316
on Union as indissoluble, 2142
of Webster, 2871, 2885
Whig party, 2885
of Wilson (James), 2909–2911
Constitution and civic ideals, **661–662**
and political philosophy of the Constitution, 1948–1949
Constitution as aspiration, **662–665**
Constitution as civil religion, **665–668**
Constitution as literature, **668–670**
feminist theory, 1032–1033
Contempt power, judicial, **670–671,
671–672** (update)
*Bridges v. California*, 244, 2076
evidence gathered through illegal electronic surveillance, 1184
executive privilege, 954
free press/fair trial, 1149–1150
public trial, 2076–2077
reporter's privilege, 1143
*Times-Mirror Co. v. California*, 244
Contempt power, legislative. *See* Legislative contempt power
Continental Association. *See* Association, The
Continental Congress, **672**
Adams (Samuel) as delegate, 32
Declaration of Independence adoption, 752
Declarations and Resolves of 1774, 26, 1059
Dickinson as delegate, 779
independence advocacy, 27, 32, 1003
Wilson (James) as delegate, 2909

Contraception. *See* Birth control; Reproductive autonomy
Contract clause, **672–678**
*Charles River Bridge v. Warren Bridge Company*, 332–333, 675
circuit courts and, 360
corporations under, 744, 2218
*Dartmouth College v. Woodward*, 673, 674, 675, 676, 690, 692, 744–746, 2218, 2285, 2871
debtors' relief legislation, 330
and duel federalism, 827
and economic liberties, 842
and economy, 850
and eminent domain, 2882–2883
expansion of, 1799
ex post facto laws and, 290
*Fletcher v. Peck*, 673, 674, 675
and Frazier-Lemke Act invalidity, 1645
and higher law, 1067–1068
*Home Building & Loan Association v. Blaisdell*, 1300–1301, 1645, 2218, 2226
inalienable police power as weakening, 211, 283, 1350
interstate compacts, 1228, 1399
King proposal, 1537
Legal Tender Act, 340
modern revival of, 70–71
Northwest Ordinance as precursor, 742
*Piqua Branch of the State Bank of Ohio v. Knoop*, 1910
and property protection, 2051
and protection of public health, 1829
as retroactivity of legislation limitation, 2225–2226
revision of, 2766
as right-to-work laws challenge, 2278
state reserved police power, 2218
and state taxation of banks, 801
and substantive due process, 2575
as temporal limit on lawmaking power, 2664
and vested rights, 1067, 2547
Webster's defense of, 2871
Webster's strict interpretation of, 2885
*West River Bridge Company v. Dix*, 2882–2883
Yazoo land grant, 1067, 1068, 1260
*See also* Freedom of contract; Obligation of contracts
Contract theory. *See* Social compact theory
Contract with America (1994), elements of, 775–776

Controlled-substance abuse, **678–680**
crack cocaine and equal protection, 703–704
*See also* Drug regulation
*Cooley* doctrine. *See* Selective exclusiveness
Cooperative federalism, **684**
as American federalism emphasis, 1006
competitive federalism vs., 477
federal environmental laws, 1009, 1010
federal grants-in-aid, 827, 1003
Copyright, **685–686**
First Amendment, 1377
intellectual property law, 1377–1378
patent, 1880–1881
protection of, 2326
Corporate citizenship, **687–689**
dual state decision, 798
privileges and immunities clause, 805
Corporate federalism (historical development), **689–690**
Corporate power, free speech, and democracy, **690–691**
Corporations and the Constitution, **691–693**
Brandeis's views, 220, 223–224
*Braswell v. United States*, 227
campaign finance, 139–140, 295, 296
charter vested rights limitation, 2059–2060
Chase Court on, 341
circuit courts and, 360
cities distinguished from, 361–362, 363
Civil Rights Cases, 409
congressional repeal of Mormon charter, 358–359
contract clause applicability, 744, 2218
corporate citizenship, 687–689, 798, 805
economy and, 850
Fourteenth Amendment protection and constitutional fictions, 526
freedom of contract, 687, 1112, 1116
freedom of speech rights, 1060
government-created, 1573–1574
institutional litigation, 1374
*Lebron v. National Railroad Passenger Corp.*, 1573–1574
limited immunity from legislative controls, 745–746
*Marshall v. Baltimore and Ohio Railroad*, 1230
*McCulloch v. Maryland*, 692
multinational, 1765–1766
out-of-state business transactions, 159

Corporations and the Constitution
    (continued)
  privatization of public functions,
    2017–2018
  and public policy issues of late
    nineteenth century, 583
  public purpose doctrine, 2074–2075
  rule of reason, 2049
  state action, 2482, 2490
  state reserved police power, 2218
  stockholder's suit, 2543
  Taney Court on, 298, 365
  See also Corporate citizenship; Corpo-
    rate federalism; Corporate power,
    free speech, and democracy
Corwin Amendment (1861), 694
Counsel, right to be represented by. See
    Right to counsel
Court-martial. See Military justice
Court of Claims. See Claims Court
Court of Customs and Patent Appeals,
    695–696
  as constitutional court, 419
  merged into new United States Court
    of Appeals, 981
Court of International Trade, 696
  as former United States Customs
    Court, 695
  Judicial Conference of the United
    States, 1452
Court of Military Appeals, 696
Court-packing plans, 696–699
  defeat of, 1313–1314
  and federal judicial system indepen-
    dence, 1494
  Judiciary Reform Act, 1498–1499
  Marbury v. Madison, 697, 1667–1668
  NLRB v. Jones Laughlin Steel Co.,
    1035
  rationale for, 1313, 1437–1438
  Roosevelt (Franklin D.) strategy, 697–
    699, 1794, 2288–2289
Courts and social change, 699–700 (I),
    700–701 (II)
  juvenile proceedings, 1522
  living Constitution, 1632–1634, 2712,
    2714
  public law litigation, 2072–2073
  selective judicial activism, 1447–1448
  sociological jurisprudence, 2445–2446
  transformation of constitutional law,
    2712–2714
  See also Social science research and
    Constitutional law
Courts of Appeals. See United States
    Courts of Appeals
Court system. See Judicial system,
    federal

Crack cocaine and equal protection,
    703–704
Creationism, 706–708
  balanced treatment statute, 2174,
    2327
  Epperson v. Arkansas, 2177, 2327
  establishment clause, 925
  religious fundamentalism and teaching
    of, 2184–2185, 2327
  Tennessee v. Scopes, 2666
Creation of the Presidency, 1775–1789
    (Thach), 947
Criminal code, federal. See Federal
    criminal law
Criminal conspiracy, 708–709
  conspiracy law, 511
  incitement cases, 1352
  to monopolize, 2413
Criminal Justice Act (1964), 709
  and right to counsel, 2260
Criminal justice and due process, 709–
    711
  bail, 147–151
  Bill of Rights incorporation, 815
  closed pretrial proceedings, 1181
  DNA sampling, 800
  double jeopardy, 807–812
  ex post facto crimes, 957
  fair trial, 970–972
  fruit of the poisonous tree, 1157–1158
  gag order, 1179–1180
  grand jury, 1220–1223
  habeas corpus, 1248–1252
  incompetency to stand trial, 2060–
    2061
  incorporation doctrine, 710, 1355,
    1615, 1666, 2039–2040
  insanity defense, 1718, 1719, 1720
  jury nullification, 1512–1514
  jury unanimity, 1517–1518
  police interrogation and confessions,
    1922–1932
  preventive detention, 2004–2006
  prisoners' rights, 2011–2013
  procedural due process, 2035–2045
  public trial, 2076–2077
  reasonable doubt, 2138–2139
  rights of criminally accused, 2254–
    2257
  right to counsel, 2260–2265
  See also Free press/fair trial; Race and
    criminal justice
Criminal justice and technology, 711–
    713
  DNA testing and genetic privacy, 800
  electronic eavesdropping, 872–876
  electronic media in courtroom, 1138,
    1147–1148

  unreasonable searches and seizures,
    721
  wiretapping, 2912–2913
Criminal justice system, 713–717
  federal-state relations in enforcement,
    1566–1571
  habeas corpus burdens, 1254
  racial discrimination, 2087, 2106. See
    also Capital punishment and race
  witness and juror sale of experiences
    to media, 2915–2916
  See also Capital punishment; Law
    enforcement and federal-state
    relations; Military justice
Criminal law. See Federal criminal law
Criminal procedure, 717–723
  arrest, 120
  and Bill of Rights, 2035–2036, 2043
  Brown v. Mississippi, 256
  burden of proof, 264
  and Burger Court, 380
  due process, 256
  due process clause as limitation on
    state, 1757
  and federal civil rights enforcement,
    200–201
  Federal Rules of Criminal Procedure,
    1029
  felony, 1031, 1032
  and Fourteenth Amendment, 200, 201
  fruit of the poisonous tree doctrine,
    1157–1158
  habeas corpus, 1252–1253
  harmless error, 1270–1271
  immunity grant, 1334–1335
  indictment, 1361–1362
  indigent right to counsel, 971, 1031,
    1083, 1193–1194, 1462, 1973
  information, 1369
  insanity defense, 2061
  insular cases, 1376
  jury nullification, 1513–1514
  law of the land, 828
  Miranda rules, 1742–1744, 1922,
    1926–1929, 2044
  national uniform standards, 1008
  presentment, 1991
  pretrial disclosure, 2004
  probable cause, 2023
  real evidence, 2130
  reasonable doubt, 2138–2139
  reporter's privilege, 2199–2200
  right against self-incrimination, 2234–
    2235
  right to counsel, 2260–2265
  Scalia's views, 2315
  strict construction of decisions, 2561
  subpoena, 2565–2567

unconstitutional conditions, 2749
waiver of constitutional rights, 2831
and Warren Court, 1927, 2848, 2855–2856
*See also* Law enforcement and federal-state relations; Police interrogation and confessions
Criminal syndicalism laws, **723–724**
  incitement to unlawful conduct, 1353
  injunction, 2940–2941
  Taney Court and, 2640
  *Younger v. Harris*, 2940–2941
Critical legal studies, **724–726**
  and critical race theory, 726
  critique of liberalism, 1616
  critique of rights, 725–726
  deconstruction, 756, 1616
  and indeterminacy thesis, 724–725
  and pragmatism, 1983
Critical race theory, **726–728**
  and civil rights, 401
  on difference and constitutional equality, 782
  on hate speech, 1277
Cross-examination, right of. *See* Confrontation, right of
Cruel and unusual punishment, **729–731, 731–732 (update 1), 732–733 (update 2)**
  and Bill of Rights (English), 175, 300
  capital punishment cases, 236, 239, 300, 301–302, 307, 308, 721, 729, 1070–1071, 1199, 1529, 1702–1703, 2257
  and career criminal sentencing laws, 316
  drug mandatory sentences challenged under, 822–823
  Eighth Amendment on, 2367, 2368, 2698–2699
  *Enmund v. Florida*, 896
  excessive penalties proportionate to the crime as, 2446–2447, 2873
  expatriation seen as, 2733, 2851
  federal criminal law, 985, 986
  forfeiture of property in drug trafficking cases as, 680
  juveniles and, 2475–2476
  paddling of students as, 1369–1370
  patients' rights and, 1885
  *Payne v. Tennessee*, 1889
  *Penry v. Lynaugh*, 1895
  protection incorporated into territories, 1376
  and rights of the criminally accused, 2257
  *Rummel v. Estelle*, 2299
  Scalia's views, 2316

social science research on, 2443
victim impact statements as conflict with, 208
Cults and the Constitution, **734**
  religious liberty in public places, 2189–2190
Cumberland Road bill. *See* Internal improvements
Curfew laws. *See* Japanese American cases; Juvenile curfew laws
Currency. *See* Monetary power
Curtilage. *See* Open Fields Doctrine
Curtis Act (1924), 594
Custodial interrogation. *See* Police interrogation and confessions
Customs Service
  employee drug testing, 825, 1096
  growth of, 1568

# D

Damages, **739–740**
  abstention clarification, 20
  and constitutional remedies, 651, 652–653
  executive immunity in civil rights actions, 2922
  by federal courts against state actions, 1493
  litigation strategy, 1631
  punitive, 2055–2056, 2081–2083
  tort, 2081–2083, 2706
  zoning, 2945
Damages claims, **740–741**
  "actual malice" libel, 1607, 1608, 1609, 2850
  constitutional, 740–741
  government wrongs, 1217–1218, 1344
  implied constitutional rights of action, 1344
  noncoverage of libelous parody, 1322
  official qualified immunity, 1336
  restrictions on presidential immunity, 1335
  and state sovereign immunity, 994–995
  *See also* Punitive damages
Darwinism
  and academic freedom, 21
  balanced treatment statute, 2174, 2327
  creationism teaching as alternative, 706–708
  and dynamic conception of constitutional law, 2712–2713
  and "living Constitution" phrase, 1632, 1633

*Tennessee v. Scopes*, 2666
*See also* Creationism
Death. *See* Euthanasia; Right to die
Death penalty. *See* Capital punishment; Capital punishment and race; Capital Punishment Cases of 1972; Capital Punishment Cases of 1976
Debate, freedom of. *See* Speech or debate clause
*Debates in the Several State Conventions, on the Adoption of the Federal Constitution, The* (Elliot), 2120
Decision, **752**
  dissenting opinion, 795
  grounds of opinion, 1235
  holding as basis, 1294
  opinion of the court, 1854–1855
  overruling, 1868
  plurality opinion, 1920
  *ratio decidendi*, 2121
  retroactivity of, 2223–2225
Declaration and Resolves of First Continental Congress. *See* First Continental Congress, Declaration and Resolves of
Declaration of Independence, **752–755**
  Adams (John) and, 27
  Adams (Samuel) and, 32
  as basis of Constitution, 31, 534–535, 755, 1174, 1944, 1945, 1946, 1985–1986
  Dickinson's abstention, 779
  on equal protection of the laws, 907
  Franklin and drafting of, 105
  higher law as basis, 754, 1174, 1286
  Jefferson authorship, 1419
  liberal ideals of, 1613
  Martin (Luther) and, 1687
  natural law basis, 1286, 2248
  and natural right of revolution, 2248–2249, 2250
  natural rights basis, 1387, 1419
  and petitionary power, 2273
  as popular sovereignty voice, 1962
  quartering of troops grievance, 2689
  race-consciousness, 2096
  separation of powers anticipated by, 1944–1945
  signers of, 336, 434, 1187, 2909
  slavery passage deletion, 2050
Declaration of Rights and Grievances (1765). *See* Stamp Act Congress, resolutions of
Declaration of war, **755–756**
  absence in Gulf War, 282, 1242–1243
  absence in Korean War, 1541, 1998
  absence in Vietnam War, 1242, 1998, 2790

Declaration of war (continued)
　constitutional provision, 2837
　five congressional instances, 1998,
　　2836
　by joint resolution, 1437
　and presidential use of armed forces,
　　449
　vs. initiating or deciding upon war,
　　1080
　See also State of war
Declaratory judgment, **756**
　abstention doctrine, 20
　advisory opinion, 51
　cases and controversies, 323, 1464
　equity, 920
　justiciability, 1520
　preenforcement challenges, 1464
　ripeness, 1464
Declaratory Judgment Act of 1934, 323
Deconstruction, **756–759**
　of liberalism, 1616
De facto/de jure, **759**
　Burger Court, 276
　desegregation litigation, 446–447
　and racial balance, 2098
　school busing, 1535–1536
　school desegregation, 1231
　school segregation, 706
　segregation, 276, 759, 1024, 2219–
　　2220, 2221
　wealth discrimination, 1362
Defamation. See Group libel; Libel and
　the First Amendment
*Defence of the American Constitution*
　(Adams), 28–29
Defendant's rights. See Rights of the
　criminally accused
Defense of Marriage Act. See Same-sex
　marriage
Deficits, budget. See Balanced-budget
　amendment; Budget; Budget
　process
Delegation of power, **760–761, 761–
　763** (update)
　to administrative agencies, 1935
　checks and balances, 343
　congressional relinquishment to presi-
　　dency, 1999, 2000
　*Curtiss-Wright Export Corporation,
　　United States v.,* 761
　Emergency Price Control Act upheld,
　　2937
　executive orders as, 944, 1999
　*Field v. Clark,* 1039
　in Gramm-Rudman-Hollings Act, 1219
　Hughes Court rulings, 1316
　implied powers, 1345
　inherent powers, 1370

　legislative, 2148, 2317
　legislative veto, 1333
　New Deal invalidations, 41, 1232,
　　2288, 2317–2318
　and presidential administrative
　　control, 266
　to regulatory agencies, 2148
　*Schechter Poultry Corp. v. United
　　States,* 2317–2318
　in sovereignty, 736
　tariff regulation, 1262
Deliberate speed. See All deliberate
　speed
Deliberative democracy, **763–765**
　public choice theory, 2064
　vs. direct democracy, 785
　See also Reapportionment; Represen-
　　tation
Demeanor evidence. See Confrontation,
　right of
*De minimis non curat lex,* definition, **765**
Democracy. See Communications and
　democracy; Corporate power;
　Deliberative democracy;
　Democratic theory and constitu-
　tional law; Direct democracy; Free
　speech and democracy
*Democracy and Distrust* (Ely), 318, 383
*Democracy in America* (Tocqueville),
　1365, 1955–1956
Democratic National Convention, 1837
Democratic Republicans. See Jeffersoni-
　anism
Democratic theory and constitutional
　law, **765–767**
　Field's jurisprudence, 1036
　judicial review tensions, 767, 1478–
　　1481, 2049
　jurisprudence impedances, 1506–1507
　popular sovereignty and, 1962–1963
　Progressive thought, 2049
　religion-secularism debate, 2173–2175
Demonstration, **767–768**
　anti-Vietnam War, 2319, 2790–2792
　civil rights, 389, 702
　in District of Columbia, 796
　draft card burning, 817–818
　First Amendment protection, 375,
　　1047, 1317
　and government regulation of free
　　speech, 1131
　injunction order, 2832
　permit fee based on public order
　　maintenance expenses, 1082
　public forum doctrine, 2068
　RICO application to, 1153
　as trespass, 34
　woman suffrage, 2918

　See also Civil disobedience; Incite-
　　ment to unlawful conduct
Denaturalization, **768–769**
　naturalized citizens and, 366
Department of Justice. See Attorney
　general and Department of Justice;
　Civil Rights Division; Solicitor
　general
Deportation, **770–771**
　and alien due process rights, 266,
　　1331
　of alien migrant workers, 1329, 1330
　of aliens, 65, 67, 128–129, 268–269,
　　365, 366, 770–771, 1330
　Antiterrorism and Effective Death
　　Penalty Act, 102, 1503–1504
　of Chinese immigrants, 128–129
　legislative veto, 1333, 1599
　Palmer raids, 65, 1875
　See also Expatriation
Desegregation, **771–774**
　all deliberate speed, 69, 255, 772
　all deliberate speed expiration, 1231
　of armed forces, 118, 605, 946
　artificiality of de facto/de jure distinc-
　　tion, 446–447
　*Bolling v. Sharpe,* 206–207
　*Brown v. Board of Education,* 253–
　　255, 273, 375, 383, 388, 389, 390,
　　391, 394, 399, 411, 446, 664, 771–
　　772, 854, 859, 2320, 2849, 2852–
　　2853
　Burger Court, 276
　Civil Rights Act of 1960, 405
　civil rights boycott, 1551, 1556
　and constitutional remedies, 652
　*Cooper v. Aaron,* 237–238, 683
　courts and social change, 700, 701
　of District of Columbia schools, 206–
　　207, 253, 254
　federal employees, 605
　federal enforcement, 1025–1026, 1747
　and federal grant conditions, 988
　first school case outside of South,
　　1535
　"freedom of choice" invalidated, 232,
　　1229
　goals of, 2320, 2627
　*Green v. County School Board of New
　　Kent,* 232, 237
　*Griffin v. County School Board of
　　Prince Edward County,* 1231
　housing discrimination, 1289
　injunction use, 1373
　institutional litigation, 1374
　judicial power, 1471–1472, 1475–1476
　judicial review, 1475–1476
　Justice Department actions, 136, 1025

*Keyes v. School District No. 1 of Denver*, 237, 1535–1536
liability standards, 773
military units to dispel violence, 1969
*Milliken v. Bradley*, 773, 774, 2321
of public schools in large cities, 1736–1737
racial balance remedies, 773, 774, 2098
school busing, 706, 2320
school implementation rulings, 65, 773
social science research data, 2441
Southern Manifesto, 2458
suit against Internal Revenue Service, 70
unconstitutionality of resistance legislation, 1231
Warren Court, 2848, 2852, 2853
"white flight," 1231
Developmentally Disabled Assistance and Bill of Rights Act (1975), **775**
as antidiscrimination legislation, 95
right to treatment, 789, 790
Devolution and federalism in historical perspective, **775–778**
Dial-a-porn, **778**
First Amendment rights, 1148
*Dicta. See Obita dicta*
Difference and constitutional equality, **780**
Direct and indirect taxes, **784–785**
Chase Court ruling, 340
constitutionality of, 2470
Field's judicial views, 1036
*Hylton v. United States*, 1324
import-export clause, 1348–1349
income tax, 1960, 1964, 2480
income tax invalidation, 1165, 1244, 1409, 1959–1960, 1964
intergovernmental tax immunities, 1383–1384
jurisdiction to tax, 1504–1505
out-of-state sale tax, 2907
*Pollock v. Farmers' Loan & Trust Co.*, 1959–1960, 1964
Populist view, 1964
property-tax financing of school districts, 1974–1975, 1977, 2309–2310, 2874
sales tax on religious materials upheld, 1427
Sixteenth Amendment, 784, 1165, 2421
*See also* Capitation taxes; Excise tax; State and local government taxation; State taxation of commerce

Direct democracy, **785–786**, **786–788** (update)
and deliberative democracy, 763
initiative as, 1371–1372
Progressive reforms, 2047
recall as, 2141
referendum as, 2146
and republican form of government, 1239, 1963
Wilson's (James) advocacy, 2909–2911
*See also* Initiative; Recall; Referendum
Direct elections, **788–789**
as Populist platform, 1964
Progressive advocacy, 2047
of senators, 72, 764, 788
Seventeenth Amendment, 2387–2388
Direct-mail solicitation. *See* Commercial speech
Disabilities, rights of persons with, **789–791**
affirmative action, 775
Americans with Disabilities Act, 86–88
*Cleburne v. Cleburne Living Center, Inc.*, 792
Developmentally Disabled Assistance and Bill of Rights Act, 775
educational mainstreaming, 791
Education of Handicapped Children Acts, 95, 790–791
federal protection, 1027
*O'Connor v. Donaldson*, 789–790
Rehabilitation Act, 2152
special educational provisions, 61, 95, 860–861, 1721
special school district creation, 202, 927, 2179–2180
Disability discrimination, **791–792**
Rehabilitation Act, 2152
Discovery, **793**
and fair trial, 971
pretrial disclosure, 2004
and right of confrontation, 492
Discrete and insular minorities, **793–795**
benign racial classification, 794
broadcasting license awards, 1723
Court protective role, 1311, 1381–1382
equal protection for, 375–376, 794, 910
as interest groups, 1381–1382
jury underrepresentation, 1509–1510, 1514–1515
litigation strategy, 1632
and neutrality principle, 2164
and preferred freedoms, 1990

race and sex in antidiscrimination law, 2092
race-consciousness, 794, 2095
reapportionment, 2136–2138
selective modern judicial activism, 1447, 1448
Stone footnote in *United States v. Carolene Products Company*, 317–318
Discrimination. *See* Age discrimination; Antidiscrimination legislation; Disability discrimination; Jury discrimination; Private discrimination; Race and sex in antidiscrimination law; Racial discrimination; Sex discrimination; Wealth discrimination
Discrimination remedy. *See* Due process of law; Equal protection of the laws
Dismissed time. *See* Released time
Disorderly conduct. *See* Breach of the peace
Dissenting opinion, **795**
abortion rights, 12, 13, 2699, 2872
*Abrams v. United States*, 16
affirmative action, 54, 56
Agricultural Adjustment Act, 285
antitrust, 2895
by Black and Douglas, 815
by Brandeis, 219–221, 1352
*Charles River Bridge v. Warren Bridge Company*, 333
clear and present danger standard, 15, 16, 1352
conference, 488
*Cruzan v. Director, Missouri Department of Health*, 2266
*Griswold v. United States*, 1462
grounds of opinion, 1235
by Holmes as "Great Dissenter," 1296, 1300, 1352, 1638, 2878
judicial social and economic predilections, 2882
as later overruling basis, 1462
*Lochner v. New York*, 1638, 2878
by Marshall (Thurgood), 1677–1678, 1680
and precedent, 1987
privacy rights, 1462
public understanding of, 2078
by Rehnquist, 2155–2156, 2157, 2160
by White (Byron), 2886, 2888, 2889, 2892–2893
District of Columbia, **795–796**, **796–797** (update)
abolition of slavery in, 31, 558
de jure segregation, 1024, 1086
diversity jurisdiction, 798

District of Columbia (continued)
  electoral votes, 73
  federal district court, 1491, 1492
  federal judiciary provisions, 1464
  home rule, 796, 797–798
  legislative court, 1589, 1590
  "midnight" judicial appointments,
     1667–1668
  minimum wage for women and
     minors, 35–36, 797, 2882, 2921
  representation, 796–797, 798
  restrictive covenant, 2222, 2223
  school desegregation ruling, 206–207,
     253, 254
  slavery in, 796
  welfare residency requirement, 2878–
     2879
District of Columbia Crime Control Act
     (1970), 796
District of Columbia Judicial Nomina-
     tion Commission, 798
District of Columbia Minimum Wage
     Law (1918), **797**
  *Adkins v. Children's Hospital*, 35–36,
     2921
  invalidation, 2921
  as model legislation, 796
District of Columbia Representation
     Amendment, **797**
  ratification failure, 614, 796
District of Columbia Self-Governing and
     Government Reorganization Act
     (1973), **797–798**
  mayor, council, and charter provisions,
     796
Diversity jurisdiction, **798–799**
  abstention doctrine, 20
  ancillary, 89
  chilling effect, 803
  choice of law and, 357
  circuit courts and, 360
  and civil federal common law, 977
  and concurrent jurisdiction, 483
  and conflicts law, 358
  District of Columbia residents' suits,
     796
  *Dred Scott v. Sandford*, 818, 1468
  *Erie Railroad Co. v. Tompkins*, 921
  and federal courts, 1468
  Federal Rules of Civil Procedure,
     1029
  and local government, 1638
  slavery and, 2431
  substantive due process, 2570
  United States Courts of Appeals,
     2759
  United States District Courts, 2762,
     2764

Divorce and the Constitution, **799–800**
  child custody, 799–800
  freedom of intimate association, 1121
  indigent access to the courts, 204, 799,
     1974, 2877
  jurisdiction, 799
  residence requirement, 799, 2219
DNA testing and genetic privacy, **800**
  experiment restriction, 2327
Doctrine, **801**
  act of state, 24–25
  affected with a public interest, 52–53
  Blackmun contributions, 190, 192–196
  changed circumstances, 2713
  common law, 465
  constitutional interpretation, 801
  economic regulation, 1189–1190
  extraterritoriality, 958
  fair return on fair value, 969–970
  federal plenary power in foreign
     affairs, 1072
  federal regulation of intrastate
     commerce, 2415–2416
  freedom of the press, 1144
  fruit of the poisonous tree, 1157–
     1158
  gender equality, 1196–1197
  inadmissible confessions, 1931
  inalienable police power, 1350, 2218
  irrebuttable presumption, 1404–1405
  judicial review and evolution of, 1481
  justiciability, 1520–1521
  libel, 1607–1609
  low-value speech, 1056
  nontolerance of prior restraint, 2010
  nullification repudiation, 1424
  official immunity, 1335
  original package, 1612, 1617, 1864–
     1865
  plain feel, 1912
  political question, 1652–1653, 1949–
     1953
  and precedent, 1986–1988
  preemption, 1989–1990
  property, 2051, 2052
  public forum, 1067–1071
  public purpose, 2073–2076
  reserved police power, 2218
  retroactive application, 2224–2225
  sovereignty, 1674–1675
  stare decisis, 2477–2478
  status of territories, 1358
  stream of commerce, 2559–2560
  *See also* Incorporation doctrine
Doctrine of vested rights. *See* Vested
     rights
*Documents in American History*
     (Commager), 447

Domestic commerce. *See* Intrastate
     commerce
Domestic violence clause, **803–804**
  and Fourteenth Amendment enforce-
     ment, 803–804
Dormant commerce clause, **804–806**,
     **806–807** (update)
  judicial enforcement of federalism-
     based limits, 990
  preemption of state laws under, 1390
Dormant powers, **807**
Dorr Rebellion (1842), 1652, 2210
Double jeopardy, **807–809**, **809–811**
     (update 1), **811–812** (update 2)
  and capital punishment, 302
  and career criminal sentencing laws,
     316
  and conspiracy law, 511
  and criminal procedure, 720, 722
  dual sovereignty rule, 1283
  expansion to states, 170, 2039
  federal appeal to increase criminal
     sentence not violation of, 893
  and federal criminal law, 982–983,
     985, 986
  and impeachable offenses, 1336
  and juvenile proceedings, 1523
  *Palko v. Connecticut*, 1874
  Racketeer Influenced and Corrupt
     Organizations Act (RICO), 2112
  and rights of criminally accused, 2256,
     2257
  and sexual predator laws, 2406
  state-federal cooperation as nonviola-
     tion of, 164, 1562
Draft. *See* Conscription
Draft card burning, **817–818**
  as civil disobedience act, 371, 817–
     818
  and conspiracy, 709
  and First Amendment, 1836
Driver's Privacy Protection Act, 993
Drug abuse. *See* Controlled-substance
     abuse; Drug regulation
Drug Enforcement Administration, 1568
Drug regulation, **821–822**, **822–823**
     (update 1), **823–824** (update 2)
  civil forfeiture, 824
  computer file of controlled substance
     prescriptions, 2883
  crack cocaine and equal protection,
     703–704
  federal criminal law, 983–984
  Food, Drug, and Cosmetic Act, 1069
  Harrison Act, 804, 1274, 1567
  jury nullification, 1512
  national police power, 804
  no-knock entry, 679, 1097

peyote sacramental use, 82, 679, 821–
822, 823, 2165–2166, 2181, 2192,
2194–2195
Posse Comitatus Act, 1569
right against self-incrimination and,
1572
right of privacy and, 2242–2243
*Whalen v. Roe,* 2242–2243
Drug testing, **824–826, 826–827**
(update)
balancing test, 824
of candidates for state offices, 330–
331
of Customs Service employees, 679,
1782–1783
latitude in, 823
mandatory, 2328, 2337, 2422–2423
of railway employees, 679
reasonable expectation of privacy and,
2337
in schools, 824–827, 2341
as search and seizure, 825, 826, 2337
suspicionless, 1096
as unreasonable search, 822, 823, 826
Drunk driving. *See* Alcohol
Dual federalism, **827**
in antebellum period, 567
and antitrust, 1539–1540
competitive federalism and, 477
congressional regulation of employment for state and municipal
workers, 1776
and contemporary federalism trends,
995–996, 1000, 1001
cooperative federalism vs., 1006
and exclusive jurisdiction, 1012
Field's approach, 1037
interstate commerce restriction, 1261
*Neagle, In re,* 2311
Shreveport doctrine, 2416
state immunity from federal law,
2503–2504
state police power, 1244
Taney Court and, 827, 1000–1001
Due process of law, **828–829**
abolitionist constitutional theory, 2, 3
abortion rights protection, 9, 11, 2057
*Adams v. Tanner* as violation, 32
administrative agencies, 37, 39
administrative law, 40, 41–42
alien entitlements, 131–132, 266,
1330, 1331, 1332
American Indian entitlements, 81
Antiterrorism and Effective Death
Penalty Act, 103
Attorney General's List as violation of,
138, 1436
bankruptcy power limitations, 161

bar admission, 2325
Black (Hugo) on, 329
burden of proof, 264
capital punishment, 299, 302, 307, 309
as civil liberty right, 373, 375
class action lawsuits, 422
coerced confessions, 256, 1280
Coke's origination of concept, 439
collateral attack, 441–442
commentators on the Constitution on,
451
communitarians on, 473
confrontation rights, 492
conspiracy law, 511
constitutional aspiration, 663
corporate citizenship, 805
corporations, 692
criminal justice, 709–711, 718, 722–
723
decency and fairness standards, 2284
deportment, 770
disability rights, 790, 791
discovery, 793
District of Columbia school segregation as violating, 206, 253
double jeopardy as violating, 807
*Dred Scott v. Sandford,* 2424
emergence as limitation on state
criminal procedure, 1757
entrapment, 898
evidence disclosure, 2255
*Evitts v. Lucey,* 935
ex post facto laws, 290, 958
eyewitness identification, 962
failure of pretrial disclosure, 2004
fair hearing, 265–266
fair trial, 970–972, 1142
as Fifth Amendment guarantee, 25,
33, 375, 828, 2306
First Amendment rights, 1126
first Court exposition of, 1771
first usage in American organic law,
1571
in foreign relations, 1077
Fourteenth Amendment clause, 375,
387, 760, 829, 970, 971, 1045, 1084,
1088, 1089–1090, 1091, 1288, 1355,
1572, 2036, 2317, 2318
freedom of assembly and association,
1107
freedom of contract, 25–26, 36, 70,
837–838, 1113, 1114, 1115, 1288,
2243
freedom of petition, 1125
fundamental rights, 1176–1177, 1233
*Goldberg v. Kelly,* 237
Harlan (1899–1971) conception, 1269
higher law, 1287

House Committee on Un-American
Activities as violating, 1305
*Hurtado v. California,* 1321–1322
immigration procedure, 1329
incorporation doctrine, 1354–1355,
2042–2045
involuntary confession, 1931
Japanese American cases as violating,
1416
judicial policymaking, 1471
jury exclusion cases, 1514–1515
jury nonunanimous verdicts, 1518
just compensation for property taken,
1519
just compensation incorporation, 1354
in juvenile proceedings, 1183–1184,
1522, 1523
labor activity, 1553–1554
and law of the land, 828, 1571, 1572,
2035
legal tender cases, 340
lineup suspect, 1627–1628
loitering, 345
loyalty oaths, 2467
loyalty-security programs, 1649–1650,
2365
Magna Carta, 439
Massachusetts Body of Liberties, 1694
and natural rights, 1233
nondelegation of powers, 760
and original intent, 1507–1508
in parental rights, 1750
in parental rights termination, 1524
*Parker v. Levy,* 1879
penumbra theory, 1896
*Planned Parenthood v. Casey,* 1915
plea bargaining, 1917–1918
pretrial confrontations, 1538–1539
preventive detention, 2005, 2006
property deprivation, 2316
property interest, 1697–1698
property rights, 2051–2052, 2055–
2056
punitive damage violations, 2082–
2083
race, reproduction, and constitutional
law, 2097
racial discrimination, 2099
*Railroad Retirement Board v. Alton
Railway Company,* 2115
*Railway Express Agency v. New York,*
2115
reasonable doubt, 264
as retroactive legislation limitation,
2225, 2226
right to counsel, 23, 1193–1194, 2260
right to die, 2266
right to privacy, 2242, 2284

Due process of law (continued)
  right to travel, 1535, 2276
  same-sex marriage, 2307
  Scalia's views, 2316
  self-incrimination protection, 33, 1930, 2039
  sentencing, 2367
  sex discrimination, 2391, 2398
  sex offender notification laws, 2401, 2406
  sinking fund cases, 2420
  speedy trial, 2465
  state action, 2487
  state police power, 2508
  substantive vs. procedural, 2025, 2032
  Sunday closing laws, 2584
  televising of criminal trial as violating, 330
  terrorist control measures, 2675
  ticket scalping, 2746
  tribal economic development, 2731
  vagrancy laws, 2774
  vested rights, 2783, 2934–2935
  voir dire, 2803
  voting rights, 2807
  Warren Court and, 1922
  wealth discrimination, 204
  women's status, 1740
  yellow dog contract restraints, 1547
  zoning, 2944–2945
  *See also* Economic due process;
    Procedural due process of law, civil;
    Procedural due process of law,
    criminal; Substantive due process

## E

Economic analysis and the Constitution, **834–837**
  Beard theory, 166–167, 2047
  checks and balances, 834
  commerce clause, 835–836
  due process, 834–836
  free market, 835
  interest-group legislation, 1381
  judicial review, 836
  just compensation, 836–837
  law and economics theory, 1563–1564
  Lockean liberalism as influence, 834
  monetary power, 834, 1751–1754
  Progressive thought, 2046–2047, 2048–2050
  state regulation of commerce, 835
  state taxation of commerce, 835
  taxing power, 834
  welfare benefits, 837

Economic due process, **837–839**
  economic liberties, 841
  and Fourteenth Amendment, 1007
  freedom of contract, 25–26, 36, 837–838
  interferences with free market, 838
  judicial power, 839
  *Lochner v. New York*, 838–839
  police power, 838
  property rights, 2051–2056
  *Young, Ex parte*, 2940
  *See also* Substantive due process
Economic equal protection, **839–841**
  commerce clause, 840
  comparable worth, 474–475
  economic due process, 839–840
  *Edwards v. California*, 2878
  interest group politics, 840–841
  for married women, 91
  welfare rights, 2251, 2874–2877, 2879–2880
  and welfare state, 2877–2881
  *See also* Property rights; Welfare benefits
*Economic Interpretation of the Constitution, An* (Beard), 166–167, 834, 2047
Economic liberties and the Constitution, **841–843**
  Bill of Rights, 842
  as civil liberties, 382, 383
  commercial powers of states, 841
  contract clause, 842
  economic due process, 837–839, 841
  and economic regulation, 841
  ex post facto laws, 841–842
  Fourteenth Amendment, 841–842
  freedom of contract, 842, 1111–1117
  and property rights, 2052
  substantive due process and, 2577
Economic Opportunity Act (1964), **843**
Economic regulation, **843–847, 847–848** (update)
  affected with a public interest doctrine, 52–53, 844, 2829–2830, 2917
  agricultural marketing, 62–63
  agricultural production controls, 62, 285
  *Allgeyer v. Louisiana*, 844–845
  American System, 88
  antitrust law vs., 104, 2413
  Brandeis brief, 225
  budget as presidential tool in, 262
  *Carolene Products Co., United States v.*, 1957–1958
  chain store price discrimination, 2283

collisions of federal/state powers, 845–846
congressional powers, 1191
contractual expectations as challenges basis, 71
Court's distinctive treatment of, 847
as denial of equal protection, 1800
and economic due process, 837
and economic liberties, 841
Economic Stabilization Act, 849–850
Elkins Act, 882
Emergency Bank Act, 885
Emergency Price Control Act, 887, 2937
and employment discrimination, 847
Federal Trade Commission Act, 1030–1031
Fourteenth Amendment and, 844, 2519
freedom of contract invalidating, 1735–1736
and freedom of the press, 1139
Full Employment Act, 1160
Fuller Court rulings, 1164–1167
fundamental interests vs., 1173
and general welfare clause, 1186–1187
*Granger* cases, 1224–1225, 2823
Holmes's views, 1296, 1638, 1990
Hughes Court rulings, 1312–1313
Hughes's opinions, 1309–1301
*Jacobs, In re*, 1414
just compensation incorporated into equal protection, 2130
laissez faire principles, 1414
legislation invalidation, 1288
liberal individualism vs., 1614, 1615
*Lochner v. New York*, 845, 1638–1639
majoritarian vs. minoritarian bias, 1957–1958
Marshall (John) doctrine, 1189–1192
Minnesota rate cases, 1739–1740, 2899
*Munn v. Illinois*, 2823
New Deal, 1313–1316
permissive approach, 1034
presumption of constitutionality, 1990
price controls, 885, 887
price setting, 843–844
production, 2046
and Progressivism, 2049
Public Utility Holding Company Act, 2079–2080
*Railway Express Agency v. New York*, 2115
rational basis test, 1990, 2121–2122
regulatory agencies, 2147–2148
reserved police power, 2218

rule of reason, 2298–2299
state law upheld, 2907
state police power, 1788–1789
state regulation of private business
  prices disallowed, 2230
Stewart's views, 2542
Stone's views, 2545
stream of commerce doctrine, 2470
substantive due process and, 845, 851,
  1034, 1639, 2292, 2437, 2571, 2575
tariff adjustment powers, 1262
tariff nullification, 1408, 1412
unfair competition, 1030
wartime legislation, 1605
wartime legislation extended into
  peacetime, 2924
World War I, 2927–2928
World War II, 2290, 2841, 2929–2930,
  2937
zoning laws, 2311
See also Labor and the Constitution;
  Monetary power
Economics of affirmative action, 848–
  849
Economic Stabilization Act (1970), 849–
  850
Economy, 850–853
  antitrust law, 103–107
  bankruptcy power, 851
  Charles River Bridge significance, 333
  Constitution and early economic
    growth, 850
  contract clause, 850
  and corporations, 850
  eminent domain, 851
  industrial (late nineteenth-century),
    584
  interstate commerce, 850
  Progressive Era, 852
  regulatory commissions, 852
  Sherman Antitrust Act, 852
  and substantive due process, 851
  Tenth Amendment, 850
  See also Commerce clause; Economic
    regulation
Education Amendments of 1972 (Title
  IX), 853
  as antidiscrimination legislation, 95,
    406, 853, 1027
Education and the Constitution, 854–
  858, 858–860 (update)
  academic freedom, 21–23, 855–856,
    1137
  affirmative action in higher education,
    759–760
  affirmative action in teacher hiring,
    2933–2934
  afrocentric schools, 58

alien rights, 1077, 1330, 1331, 1920
Amish refusal of schooling after age
  fourteen, 2187, 2914
Brown v. Board of Education. See
  under Desegregation
civil rights, 854
compulsory attendance, 858
contracting-out cases, 2018
corporal punishment, 369–370, 974
creationism teaching, 706–708, 2184–
  2185, 2327
de facto vs. de jure segregation, 759,
  1231
desegregation petitions, 771
desegregation rulings. See Desegregation
discrimination against non-English-
  speaking students, 1563
drug testing, 824, 825, 826–827, 2341
equal access for extracurricular
  student groups, 906
equal opportunity for disabled
  children, 790–791
equal protection, 771–772, 856–857,
  859
federal grants-in-aid, 854
First Amendment and, 855–856, 858–
  859
flag salute cases, 1064–1066, 2186
foreign-language teaching ban, 1724,
  2188
Fourteenth Amendment and, 854
Fourth Amendment and, 856
freedom of assembly and association,
  1108
freedom of speech, 170, 1126, 1134,
  1137, 1281
freedom of speech issues in high
  school shootings, 1154
free exercise of religion cases, 1724,
  2188, 2192
gun-free school zones, 1570–1571,
  1642–1643
home schooling, 2184
Morrill Act, 1761
"official English" laws, 1847–1848
paddling of students, 1369–1370
and parental rights, 974
private school racial discrimination,
  2017, 2299–2300
property ownership as basis for school
  district voting rights, 1542
property-tax financing challenge,
  1974–1975, 1977, 2309–2310, 2387,
  2874
public forum doctrine, 2069, 2070
Rehnquist Court decisions on civil
  liberties cases, 381

released time, 1703–1704, 2171–2172,
  2947
religious exercises, 804, 2176–2180
religious fundamentalism, 2184–2185
school board removal of objectionable
  library books, 202, 1216
school choice, 61, 2321–2322, 2814–
  2815
school district voting rights, 1542
segregated. See Segregation
single-sex education, 2417–2419
student free speech curbs, 170, 1281
student searches by school officials,
  1799
student suspension without due
  process, 1205
student symbolic speech, 2702–2703
tax-exempt status denial in face of
  racial discrimination, 204
teacher loyalty oaths, 1648
teaching of evolution, 2666
tuition grants, 2738–2739
vouchers, 2814–2815
Wisconsin v. Yoder, 2187
See also Government aid to religious
  institutions; Religion in public
  schools; School prayers
Education of Handicapped Children
  Acts, 860–861
  antidiscrimination legislation, 95, 790–
    791
  mainstreaming, 791
  mental retardation, 1721
EEOC. See Equal Employment Opportunity Commission
Effects on commerce, 861–862
  direct-indirect test, 1540
  Fair Labor Standards Act, 1548
  as federal criminal jurisdiction basis,
    1567
  intrastate commerce regulation, 744
  Jackson (Robert H.) rule, 2903
  as sole criterion of congressional
    power, 2933
  Wickard v. Filburn, 2903–2904
Eighteenth Amendment, 862
  attacks on, 2927
  Court rulings, 73
  ratification, 72, 593, 2050
  repeal of, 75, 594, 598, 2050, 2741
  Volstead Act enforcement, 2803–
    2804
  See also Prohibition
Eighth Amendment
  and Bill of Rights (English), 175
  cruel and unusual punishment prohi-
    bition, 175, 729, 2316, 2367, 2368,
    2698–2699

Eighth Amendment (continued)
　excessive bail prohibition, 148, 149,
　　150, 2005, 2306
　and execution of mentally incompe-
　　tent, 2061
　and execution of the insane, 1071
　forfeiture punishment limits, 983, 984
　proportional penalty in, 2368
　and punitive damages, 2055–2056,
　　2081–2083
　and rights of the criminally accused,
　　2254, 2257
　*Salerno, United States v.*, 2162
　*See also* Capital punishment
Elastic clause. *See* Necessary and proper
　　clause
Elected judiciary, **864–865**
Election finance. *See* Campaign finance
Elections, regulation of, **865–866**
　Federal Election Campaign Acts, 986–
　　987
　federal power, 423
　frequent vs. infrequent, 763
　polling place campaign-free zones, 279
　Seventeenth Amendment, 72, 500,
　　589, 2387–2388
　write-in votes, 264–265
Electoral College, **866–867**
　as deliberative democracy, 764
　and democratic theory, 765
　direct election proposals, 788, 789
　District of Columbia votes, 73
　multimember district, 1765
　not mentioned in Constitution, 1934
　political parties, 1934
　presidential election of 1800, 278
　presidential election of 1824, 30
　and presidential nationalism, 1948
　Twelfth Amendment, 866, 1940, 2740
Electoral districting, **867–869 (I), 869–**
　　**870 (II)**
　at-large system, 2286
　*Baker v. Carr*, 138, 152–153, 233,
　　237, 1470, 1951, 1952, 1953, 1987,
　　2131, 2132, 2227, 2228, 2849
　black-majority, 1735
　black representation, 2814
　census role, 326
　equal protection, 867–868, 917
　gerrymander, 867, 869, 1187–1189
　as justiciable controversy, 2133, 2137,
　　2203, 2227–2228
　majority-minority districts, 870
　multimember district, 1765
　new restrictions, 869
　one person, one vote, 868, 869, 1852–
　　1853, 2228, 2229
　and political parties, 868

population equality, 2881
　racial, 868
　racial discrimination, 2093–2094, 2408
　*Reynolds v. Sims*, 2227–2229
　three-fifths clause, 2700
　Voting Rights Act of 1965, 868–869,
　　870
　*See also* Reapportionment; Represen-
　　tation
Electoral districting, fairness, and
　　judicial review, **870–871**
　gerrymander, 871, 1187–1189
　landmark cases, 870–871
　one person, one vote, 871, 1852–1853
　reapportionment, 2130–2138
Electoral process and the First Amend-
　　ment, **871–872**
　campaign finance, 872
　rights of association, 872
Electronic eavesdropping, **872–876**
　executive inherent power claim, 2761–
　　2762
　by Federal Bureau of Investigation,
　　976
　First Amendment ramifications, 872–
　　873
　Fourth Amendment requirements,
　　170, 873–875, 1643, 2342, 2416,
　　2896–2897
　grounds for challenge, 64–65
　by Justice Department, 136
　*Katz v. United States*, 1093, 1527,
　　2139–2140
　legal requirements for, 170, 873, 1527
　as national security surveillance, 875
　*Olmstead v. United States*, 1849–1850
　Omnibus Crime Control and Safe
　　Streets Act, 170, 873–875, 1527,
　　2913
　protections against, 2416
　reasonable expectation of privacy and,
　　2139–2140
　as search, 872, 1850, 2139, 2140, 2141,
　　2333
　and self-incrimination, 873
　Senate Subcommittee on Constitu-
　　tional Rights and, 2365
　strict construction of, 2561
　third-party consent and, 2690–2691
　as unreasonable search, 2767
　upheld, 1405, 1849–1850, 2896–2897
　*White, United States v.*, 2896–2897
　*See also* Wiretapping
Electronic mail. *See* Internet
Electronic media freedoms. *See*
　　Freedom of the press
Electronic surveillance. *See* Electronic
　　eavesdropping

Elementary and Secondary Education
　　Act (1965), **876**
Eleventh Amendment, **876–878, 878–**
　　**879 (update 1), 879–882 (update 2)**
　admiralty and maritime jurisdiction,
　　879
　Age Discrimination Act, 881
　Americans with Disabilities Act, 87
　as Anti-Federalist concession, 12
　as *Chisholm v. Georgia* reaction, 356,
　　1418
　cities and, 362
　*Cohens v. Virginia*, 436–439
　*Edelman v. Jordan*, 853
　environmental regulation, 904
　and federalism, 994–995, 1010
　Fourteenth Amendment exceptions to,
　　877, 880
　governmental immunities under,
　　1470
　government wrongs and, 1217, 1218
　immunity of states from suit in federal
　　court, 133, 877, 1493, 1562
　intergovernmental immunity, 1382
　interstate compacts, 1399
　and judicial power, 1467–1468, 1470,
　　1493
　*Pennhurst State School & Hospital v.
　　Hadlerman*, 1893
　*Quern v. Jordan*, 2085
　*Seminole Tribe v. Florida*, 880–881
　sovereign immunity, 876, 2459
　validity upheld, 73
Elkins Act (1903), **882**
　as Interstate Commerce Act supple-
　　ment, 1397
Ellsworth Court. *See* Supreme Court,,
　　1789–1801
E-mail. *See* Internet and freedom of
　　speech
Emancipation Proclamation (1863),
　　**884–885**
　provisions of, 417, 573
　and Reconstruction, 1625
　and Thirteenth Amendment, 884
Embargo Acts (1807–1809), **885**
　constitutional issues, 553
Emergency Bank Act (1933), **885**
　gold clause cases, 1201
Emergency Court of Appeals, **885–886**
Emergency powers, **886–887**
　concurrent resolution, 886, 2842
　expansiveness of contemporary presi-
　　dential options, 1998
　growth of presidential, 886–887, 2842
　international economic transactions,
　　1386
　National Emergencies Act, 612, 887

Roosevelt's (F. D.) interpretation, 2290

and state milk price-controls, 1788–1789

steel seizure controversy, 2526–2527, 2941

*See also* War powers

Emergency Price Control Act (1942), **887**

delegation of power upheld, 2937

Emergency Court of Appeals, 885, 2937

rationing and price fixing, 887

Eminent domain, **887–889, 889–890** (update)

abstention doctrine, 19

civil forfeiture compared with, 372

congressional discretion, 889

and economic conditions, 851

and Fourteenth Amendment, 888–889

Hawaiian land reform, 1279

and just compensation, 888, 2646

Peckham and, 1890

police power and, 889

private property takings, 888–889, 2051–2052, 2055–2056, 2643, 2882–2883

public purpose doctrine, 2073, 2074, 2075, 2076

public use and, 2079, 2643

state action and, 2482

vested rights and, 888, 2783

*See also* Taking of property

Employee speech rights (private), **891–892**

First Amendment, 891

obscenity, 891

unions and collective bargaining, 891

workplace harassment, 891, 2925

Employee speech rights (public), **892**

low-First Amendment protection, 1551

Employers' Liability Acts (1906, 1908), **892–893**

Employers' liability cases, **893**

interstate commerce, 893

Employment. *See* Labor and the Constitution; Maximum hours and minimum wages legislation; Worker's compensation legislation; Workplace harassment and the First Amendment

Employment discrimination, **893–894**

of aliens, 1068

antidiscrimination legislation, 97, 99–101, 413, 2089

and civil rights, 396

Civil Rights Act of 1964, 392, 405, 406, 893–894

Civil Rights Act of 1991, 407–408

Civil Rights Act Title VII violation, 1232

comparable worth, 474

consent decrees, 507

disabled people, 86, 87, 791–792

disparate impact, 99, 100

and economic regulation, 847

Equal Employment Opportunity Act, 392

executive orders against, 1025

federal employee segregation, 605

and Fourteenth Amendment, 893

*Griggs v. Duke Power Co.*, 406

grounds for, 893

institutional litigation, 1374

*McDonnell Douglas Corp. v. Green*, 406

out-of-state residents, 1286

punitive damages, 99

Rehnquist Court rulings, 2164–2165

religious groups' exemption, 2175

religious liberty and, 2191, 2192, 2193

retirement age as, 59–60

sexual harassment, 100–101, 1722

and Thirteenth Amendment, 893

*Wards Cove Packing Co., Inc. v. Antonio*, 2164–2165

*See also* Race and sex in antidiscrimination law; Workplace harassment and the First Amendment

En banc, **895**

and appellate courts, 895

*Endo, Ex parte. See* Japanese American cases

Enforcement Acts. *See* Force Acts

Enfranchisement. *See* Voting rights; Woman suffrage

English Bill of Rights. *See* Bill of Rights (English)

English constitution. *See* British constitution

"English only" laws. *See* "Official English" laws

Entanglement test. *See* Government aid to religious institutions

Entitlement, **897–898**

budget process, 262

patients' rights, 1885

policy against unfunded, 777

as prison release, 897

procedural due process and, 897, 2027, 2028, 2032, 2033, 2880–2881

*See also* Welfare benefits; Welfare rights

Entrapment defense, **898–899**

Enumerated powers, **899–900**

Bill of Rights, 175, 1091

broad construction, 1446

and conditional spending, 485

Court's judicial deference, 1445, 1446

dual federalism, 827, 995–996, 1000

and federal criminal jurisdiction, 1567

and general welfare clause, 1186

as limited government, 1618

and living Constitution, 1633

as nonapplicable to foreign affairs, 1071–1072

of President, 1996

and private behavior regulatory laws, 991

taxing and spending, 2660

Tenth Amendment, 899

*See also* Implied powers; Inherent powers; National police power; Necessary and proper clause

Enumerated rights. *See* Bill of Rights

Environmental Protection Agency, 1009

as executive agency, 2147

Environmental Quality Improvement Act. *See* Environmental regulation and the Constitution

Environmental regulation and the Constitution, **900–903, 903** (update 1), **904–905** (update 2)

and Bill of Rights, 901–902

and commerce clause, 900, 904

consent decrees, 507

and Eleventh Amendment, 904

Endangered Species Act, 905

and federalism, 903–904

federalism-based invalidation of state laws, 990, 1009–1010

and Fourteenth Amendment, 905

and Fourth Amendment, 902–903

and interstate commerce, 904, 2564–2565, 2864

and just compensation for regulatory takings, 2150

land use regulation, 905

state police power, 1320

takings cases, 902–904

taxing and spending powers, 904–905

and Tenth Amendment, 901, 904

waste and pollution cases, 2864

Equal access, **906–907**

access to the courts, 23, 1231–1232

extracurricular student groups, 906

feminist theory, 1032

First Amendment, 906

freedom of speech, 906

private discrimination, 2063

public accommodations, 2063

public interest law, 2071

Equal access (continued)
  religion in public schools, 2178
  religious expression protection, 2185
  voluntary school prayer, 169, 203, 2323
Equal Employment Opportunity Commission, 406
  legislation establishing, 392
  limited authority, 2147–2148
Equality. *See* Difference and constitutional equality; Equal protection of the laws
Equal Pay Act (1964)
  as antidiscrimination legislation, 95
  comparable worth, 474
  difference and constitutional equality, 780–783
Equal protection of the laws, **907–914, 914–916** (update 1), **916–918** (update 2)
  abolitionist constitutional theory, 2
  abortion access, 12, 1615
  access to the courts, 23, 1232
  as affirmative action issue, 54, 55–56, 760, 912, 915–917
  and age discrimination, 59, 61
  and alienage discrimination, 66, 72, 190, 365, 1219, 1329, 1331
  and American Indians, 80
  and antimiscegenation laws, 1038, 1646, 1744–1745, 2827–2828
  as applying to illegal aliens, 1920
  and Asian Americans, 129, 130, 131–132
  and birth control access, 4, 182, 1118, 2204
  Black Codes violating, 189, 908
  Brennan opinions, 232–233, 237–238
  and *Brown v. Board of Education*, 909–910, 912
  Burger court views, 2309, 2310
  and capital punishment, 307, 915, 1702–1703
  choice of law and, 357
  cities and, 362
  civil liberties and, 375–376
  Civil Rights Act of 1866, 402, 907, 912–913
  Civil Rights Act of 1964, 405, 911, 913
  civil rights cases, 909
  Civil Rights Commission study, 410
  civil rights protection, 387, 388, 389, 394, 399–400, 909
  and comparable worth, 474
  and compelling state interest, 155, 477
  and conscription, 506, 2869
  and conscription exclusion of women, 2295–2296
  and constitutional aspiration, 663–664
  and controlled-substance abuse, 678
  and corporate citizenship, 805
  and crack cocaine possession or trafficking, 703
  critical race theory, 726
  decision maker's motive, 2862–2863
  Declaration of Independence on, 907
  and desegregation, 771–772
  difference and constitutional equality, 782
  and direct democracy, 787
  for disabled people, 790
  and discrete and insular minorities, 375–376, 794, 910
  discriminatory-intent test, 395–396
  and domestic violence clause, 803
  *Dred Scott v. Sandford*, 908–909, 912
  due process clause, 912
  early forerunner of, 1804
  economic, 839–840, 2879–2880
  economic regulation seen as denial of, 1800
  and education, 856–857
  and egalitarianism, 907, 912–913
  and electoral districting, 867–868, 917, 2228
  equal citizenship principle, 911
  as feminist basis for antipornography campaign, 1965–1967
  feminist theory, 1032
  and First Amendment, 1921–1922
  in foreign affairs, 1077
  Fourteenth Amendment guarantee, 46, 181, 206, 253, 368, 394, 401, 907–913, 916, 1085, 1086–1087, 1088, 1089–1090, 1092
  and freedom of contract, 1113, 1114, 1115
  and freedom of intimate association, 1121–1123
  and freedom of speech, 1130–1131
  and gender rights, 1185
  *Harper v. Virginia Board of Elections*, 1271–1272
  and housing discrimination, 393
  illegitimacy cases, 1325–1326, 1558
  and indigency, 817, 1362
  as initiative invalidations basis, 1372
  and invidious discrimination, 1038, 1401
  and involuntary sterilization, 2421–2422, 2528
  Japanese American cases, 1416
  and judicial activism, 910, 1448
  and judicial legislation, 1458, 1459
  and judicial policymaking, 1471
  and judicial review, 915
  and jury discrimination, 165, 1509, 1510, 1514, 2559
  just compensation incorporated into, 2130
  juvenile curfew laws challenges, 1521
  and legislative intent, 1593
  liberal extension of, 1615
  and nonmarital children, 917
  original intent interpretations, 1507–1508
  *Pace v. Alabama*, 1873
  *Palmer v. Thompson*, 1875
  *Paradise, United States v.*, 1877
  for parental rights, 1750
  *Perry Education Association v. Perry Local Educators' Association*, 1899
  *Personnel Administrator of Massachusetts v. Feeney*, 1902
  and plea bargaining, 1917–1918
  *Plessy v. Ferguson*, 909
  and political question doctrine, 1951–1952
  poll tax as denying, 1271
  in primary elections, 909, 2008
  prosecutorial discretion and, 2059
  in public accommodation access, 2063
  public interest law, 2071
  and race and reproduction, 2097
  and race and sex in antidiscrimination law, 2089
  and race as adoption factor, 46
  as racial discrimination test, 116, 909, 914–916, 2108
  racial quotas challenge, 1172, 2110, 2146
  *Railway Express Agency v. New York*, 2115
  in rape case, 1725
  rational basis, 914
  in reapportionment, 2132–2133
  as referendum challenge, 1415
  and religious services in park without permit, 1807
  and residence requirements, 2219
  and restrictive covenants, 909, 2219
  and rights of excluded jurors, 1514–1515
  and right to counsel, 23
  and right to travel, 2275
  and rule of law, 2298
  and same-sex marriage, 147, 2307, 2308
  school closures as denying, 1231
  as school desegregation basis, 206, 253, 254, 255
  and segregation, 2354

and sentencing, 2368

separate but equal argued as, 909, 1918

*Serrano v. Priest* and, 2387

and sex discrimination, 232–233, 910, 914–915, 917, 1156–1157, 1199, 1615, 2089, 2390, 2396–2397, 2398, 2921

and sexual orientation, 916, 917–918, 2287, 2401, 2403

sexual orientation, 787, 916, 2401, 2403

*Slaughterhouse* cases, 2423

and Social Security Act, 2445

standard of review, 914, 916, 2471

and state taxes, 1724

"stopping place" problem, 911–912

strict scrutiny, 910, 914, 916, 2562

substantive due process and, 2577

and Sunday closing laws, 2584

Taney Court rulings, 908–909

and Thirteenth Amendment, 908, 911

and torts, 2706

and unauthorized religious services in public park, 1807

and voting rights, 831, 2203, 2807

and vouchers, 2814

Warren Court expansion of, 274, 909–912, 1271–1272, 2853

*Washington v. Davis*, 2862–2863

and wealth discrimination, 1232, 2309–2310, 2869–2870

and welfare benefits, 917, 2305, 2408

and women's status, 1185, 2920. *See also* Sex discrimination

*Yick Wo v. Hopkins*, 2939–2940

and zoning, 2945

*See also* Due process of law

Equal representation. *See* One person, one vote

Equal rights amendment, **918–919**

and Fourteenth Amendment, 918

introduction and opposition, 594, 607, 2920

ratification failure, 614, 2117, 2921

and sex discrimination, 2392

Equitable restraint. *See* Abstention doctrine

Equity, **919–920**

and consent decree, 507

and injunction, 1373

judgment, 1442

jurisdiction, 920

in personam, 1374

Story's works on, 2556

Erdman Act (1898), **920–921**

Adamson Eight-Hour Act, 33, 921

interstate commerce, 25, 920

outlawing yellow dog contracts, 25, 684, 1547, 2939

violating Fifth Amendment due process, 1547

Error, writ of, **921–922**

appellate jurisdiction, 108

writs of certiorari compared with, 327, 921

Esch-Cummings Transportation Act (1920), **922**

upheld, 750

Espionage Act (1917), **923–924**

broad enforcement of, 2928

clear and present danger, 15–16, 1156, 2929

conspiracy, 709

*Debs v. United States*, 751

First Amendment and, 923

*Frohwerk v. United States*, 1156

incitement to unlawful conduct, 1352

prior restraint and censorship, 923

*Rosenberg v. United States*, 2294

*Schenck v. United States*, 1352, 2318–2319, 2928–2929

sedition, 2351

subversive advocacy, 2580, 2582

Establishment clause, **924–926**, **926–927** (update)

accommodation of religion, 926–927

"actual" vs. "avowed" secular purpose, 1602

*Agostini* revised test, 61, 1604, 2179–2180

Blaine Amendment, 197

*Board of Education of Kiryas Joel Village School District v. Grumet*, 927

child benefit theory, 348

*County of Allegheny v. American Civil Liberties Union*, 695

and creationism teaching, 706, 925

crèche display as part of seasonal exhibit allowed, 1653, 2166, 2198

crèche display invalidated, 1054–1055

cross erected in public forum, 312–313

*Epperson v. Arkansas*, 905

equal access, 906

expansive definitions of religion, 2173–2174

and First Amendment, 2378

freedom of religious speech, 2172–2173

freedom of speech, 926

government aid to religious institutions, 924, 1066, 1206–1208

governmental displays of religious symbols, 925

and intrachurch disputes, 2190

*Lemon* test, 203, 924, 925, 1206, 1560, 1562, 1602–1605, 2174, 2175, 2196

neutrality among religions, 926, 2166–2167, 2173–2174, 2187, 2188

neutrality vs. separationist view, 2294

Rehnquist restrictive interpretation, 2156–2157

released time challenges under, 1703–1704, 2171–2172

religious liberty interactions, 2175–2176, 2179, 2185, 2187, 2192

religious symbols in public places, 312–313, 1054–1055, 2196–2197, 2198

and sabbath laws, 2191, 2584–2585

sales tax on religious materials upheld, 1427

school choice, 2321

school prayers, 1, 168–169, 188, 1048–1049, 1207, 2176, 2179, 2322, 2323, 2324

secular humanism, 2177

and state churches, 1091

Warren Court and, 2856

*See also* Establishment of religion; Religious liberty; Separation of church and state

Establishment of religion, **927–929**

ambiguity and vagueness of, 2682

Becker Amendment, 167

Bill of Rights (United States), 927–928

broad vs. narrow view, 927

church vested with state veto power disallowed, 1562

and conscientious objection, 505

denominational discrimination disallowed, 1562–1563

*Engel v. Vitale*, 896

European precedents, 928

*Everson v. Board of Education*, 931

and First Amendment, 927–928, 1046, 1048–1049, 1054–1055

*Lemon v. Kurtzman (Lemon I and II)*, 1601–1602, 1603

Madison's "Memorial and Remonstrance" defining, 1662

Pennsylvania colonial charters, 1894

Rehnquist Court and, 2166–2167

religious test for public office, 2197

Stevens's views, 2529

subtly coercive school-sponsored prayers, 1575–1576

Sunday closing laws, 2584

taxpayer challenge suits, 1465, 2777

Ten Commandments classroom posting invalidated, 1602, 1603

Establishment of religion (continued)
  Toleration Act, 2704–2705
  tuition grants, 2738
  Vinson Court and, 2795
  Virginia Statute of Religious Freedom,
    928
  *See also* Government aid to religious
    institutions; Religion in public
    schools; Separation of church and
    state
Euthanasia, **930**
  and right of privacy, 2244, 2246
  and right to die, 930, 2266–2271
Evangelicals and the Constitution. *See*
    Religious fundamentalism
Evarts Act. *See* Circuit Courts of
    Appeals Act
Evidence, **932–934**
  acquittal against, 1512–1514
  admission of, 2726
  burden of proof, 932
  confession, 1923
  and confrontation right, 1921
  disclosure as right of criminally
    accused, 2255
  DNA testing and genetic privacy, 800
  and double jeopardy, 810
  electronic surveillance as source,
    1184, 1405
  exclusionary rule, 121, 936, 1666–
    1667, 1815, 2039, 2044, 2045, 2257,
    2872–2873
  ex post facto laws, 290
  eyewitness identification, 962
  and fair trial, 971–972
  and Fourteenth Amendment, 934
  and free press/fair trial, 1151
  fruit of the poisonous tree, 121, 1157–
    1158, 1928
  good faith exception, 1204–1205
  grand jury, 1220–1221
  harmless error, 1270
  hearsay, 933–934, 1282, 2345
  from illegal electronic surveillance,
    1184
  from illegal warrantless arrest, 121
  immunity grant, 1334–1335, 1526
  incriminating confession, 1931
  incriminating statements, 1931
  indictment based on inadmissible,
    1362
  inevitable discovery exception, 1815
  mere evidence rule, 1722, 2833–2834
  and *Miranda* rules, 2230
  pretrial disclosure, 2003–2004
  and probable cause, 2023
  as probable cause for search warrant,
    141, 294, 1092

real, 2130
  right to counsel, 242
  search and seizure, 932, 1092
  search incident to arrest, 2845
  search warrant based on informant's
    tip, 1327
  silver platter doctrine, 2416–2417
  and Sixth Amendment, 932
  in stop and frisk, 2552
  subpoena for, 2567
  from unconstitutional search, 2417
  unlawfully seized, 290, 2872–2873
  use immunity, 1526–1527
  *Weeks v. United States*, 2872–2873
  from wiretapping, 2913
Evidence against self. *See* Right against
    self-incrimination
Evidentiary privilege, **934–935**
  right of privacy, 935
  right to compulsory process, 480
Evolution, teaching of. *See* Creationism;
    Darwinism
Excessive fines. *See* Civil forfeiture;
    Punitive damages
Excise tax, **936**
  as agricultural subsidy, 294–285
  on gambling, 1670
  Hamilton constitutionality argument,
    1260
  on oleomargarine, 1704
  on products of child labor, 350
Exclusionary rule, **936–939**
  Bill of Rights, 938
  *Boyd* opinion, 2339
  Burger Court exception, 273
  and constitutional common law, 513
  and constitutional remedies, 652
  Court limits, 938
  and criminal due process revisions,
    2043–2044
  and drug trafficking, 679
  evidence obtained illegally, 2417
  evidence obtained in violation of, 936
  and exigent circumstances search, 937
  extension to the states, 722
  federal habeas corpus review, 1251
  Fourteenth Amendment and, 936,
    2917
  Fourth Amendment, 936
  Fourth Amendment and, 936, 2334,
    2335, 2336, 2338, 2339
  fruit of the poisonous tree doctrine,
    121, 936, 1157, 1815, 1928, 2336
  good faith exception, 1204–1205,
    2044
  harmless error, 1270, 2045
  inevitable discovery exception, 1815
  as judicial policymaking, 1462

limitations, 2044, 2045
  *Mapp v. Ohio*, 1666–1667, 2039
  probable cause, 938
  Reagan administration and, 2128
  real evidence, 2130
  rights of the criminally accused, 2257
  search and seizure, 936, 1535, 2334–
    2336, 2338
  search incident to arrest, 938
  in state criminal cases, 722, 1666–
    1667
  unlawfully seized evidence, 290
  *Weeks v. United States*, 2872–2873
  *Wolf v. Colorado*, 1666, 2039
Exclusive powers, **939**
  and doctrine of selective exclusive-
    ness, 681
  as dormant, 807
Executive agreements, **939–941, 941–
    942** (update)
  advice and consent, 939–941
  ambiguity and vagueness of, 2682
  Bricker Amendment, 243–244, 1541
  as domestic law, 737
  in foreign affairs, 1075, 1075–1076,
    2385
  North American Free Trade Agree-
    ment, 942
  *Pink, United States v.*, 1910
  preempting state law, 1390
  for settling American claims, 741,
    1078
  treaty power, 939
  World War II, 2929
Executive defiance of "unconstitutional"
    laws, **942–943**
  Anti-Federalist constitutional thought,
    943
  impoundment of funds as, 1349
  veto power, 942, 2784–2785
Executive immunity, **943–944**
  as absolute for official actions, 1335
  *Butz v. Economou*, 285
  from civil rights damages, 2922
  Clinton claims, 432
  for constitutional violations, 943
  expanded scope of, 1819
  of federal officials, 943–944
  good-faith defense, 944
  for nonconstitutional violations, 943
  non-immunity from civil damages
    litigation, 1335
  reasonable good-faith belief, 944
  of state officials, 943–944
  *Wood v. Strickland*, 2922
  *See also* Presidential immunity
Executive Office of the President, 260,
    262

Executive order, **944**
　affirmative action, 1026
　Committee on Fair Employment
　　Practices, 944
　as delegated legislative authority,
　　1999
　federal protection of civil rights, 944,
　　1025
　fund sequestration for estimated
　　budget deficit, 1219
　importance during wars, 944
　as ordinance-making power, 1995
　Reagan's (Ronald) use of, 619
　as regulation of government officials
　　and agencies, 944
　Roosevelt (Franklin D.) use of, 2929
　for strikes, 2526, 2757
　suspension of pending Iranian claims,
　　239
　Wilson's (Woodrow) use of, 2928
Executive Order 9066 and Public Law
　503 (1942), **944–945**
　Japanese American relocation, 944,
　　945, 1416, 2290, 2930
Executive Order 10340 (1952), **945**
　steel seizure, 945, 2526, 2734
　*Youngstown Sheet & Tube Co. v.
　　Sawyer*, 2941
Executive Order 11246 (1965), **945**
　affirmative action, 945, 1026
Executive Orders 9835 and 10450 (1947,
　1953), **945–946**
　antidiscrimination measures, 946
　Attorney General's List, 945
　loyalty-security programs, 945, 1649
Executive Orders 9980 and 9981 (1948),
　**946**
　armed forces desegregation, 605, 946
　federal employee desegregation, 605
Executive power, **946–949**
　advice and consent, 947
　ambiguity and vagueness of, 2682
　appointing and removal power, 109–
　　111, 948
　and appropriation of funds, 948
　and bureaucracy, 265–267
　of cabinet, 948
　and Civil War, 416
　Clay curtailment proposal, 424–425
　Clinton administration claims, 432
　as commander-in-chief, 448–449
　of Congress in foreign policy, 493–496
　Congressional Budget and Impound-
　　ment Control Act, 949
　and congressional government, 499
　and congressional war powers, 502–
　　503
　constitutional explicitness, 1471

and court-packing plans, 696
　delegation of power, 760–761, 762
　First Amendment, 948
　and Gulf War, 1243
　Hamilton's views of, 1258–1259, 1260
　implied powers, 947
　impoundment of funds, 948
　and legislative veto, 1599–1601
　line-item veto, 949, 1625–1627
　Lockean view of, 1640
　military, 385, 386–387
　presidential attempts to extend, 591,
　　600
　presidential emergency powers, 949
　presidential succession, 608–609
　Proclamation of Neutrality, 1259
　prosecutorial discretion, 2058
　Supreme Court justice appointments,
　　489, 490
　of unitary executive, 2755–2756
　and Vietnam War, 947
　war powers, 1080
　Wilson's (James) view of, 2910
　Wilson's (Woodrow) broad view of,
　　2911
　*Youngstown Sheet & Tube Co. v.
　　Sawyer*, 1995
　*See also* Presidential powers
Executive prerogative, **949–952**
　foreign affairs, 950
　in Iran-Contra affair, 950
　in Korean War, 951
　legislative power, 950
　noninterpretivist inroads seen on,
　　1393
　treaty negotiations opening, 1991
Executive privilege, **952–954**, **954–955**
　(update)
　Clinton claims, 432, 954
　*Clinton v. Jones*, 954
　"deliberative process" privilege, 955
　Freedom of Information Act exemp-
　　tions, 1118
　and impeachment, 953
　as implied power, 1346
　and independent counsel, 954, 1360
　and indictment, 953
　as inherent power, 1370
　judicial contempt power, 954
　and legislative investigation, 1596
　*Nixon, United States v.*, 952–954,
　　1816, 1955, 2865
　Nixon claims, 274, 952–954, 1816,
　　1955, 2312, 2865
　and presidential immunity in office,
　　954
　and right against self-incrimination,
　　954

and right to refuse to produce
　　documents, 952
　and secrecy of communications, 1215
　and Senate censure of Jackson, 1409
　Senate Subcommittee on Constitu-
　　tional Rights, 2365
　and separation of powers, 952, 955,
　　2384
　situational applications, 954–955
　and special prosecutor, 2463
　strict construction of, 2562
　Washington's claims, 1419
　as Watergate issue, 2312
　Watergate issues, 2864, 2865
Exhaustion of remedies, **955–956**
　and habeas corpus, 1249
Exigent circumstances search, **956**
　automobile search, 2332
　blood samples, 2319
　exclusionary rule, 937
　incident to arrest, 956, 2344
　*Payton v. New York*, 1889
　probable cause, 956
　search and seizure, 2332
　search incident to arrest, 956
　unreasonable search, 2767
　warrantless search, 956, 2846, 2881
Ex parte, **956**
　grand jury proceedings, 1221
Expatriation, **956–957**
　citizenship and, 363
　as cruel and unusual punishment,
　　2733, 2851
Exposition and protest (1828–1829),
　**957**
Ex post facto, **957–958**
　*Calder v. Bull*, 290
　as constitutional prohibition on retro-
　　active legislation, 2225
　and economic liberties, 841–842
　as mainstay of constitutionalism, 958
　Racketeer Influenced and Corrupt
　　Organizations Act (RICO), 2112
　and rule of law, 2298
　*See also* Retroactivity of legislation
Extradition. *See* Fugitive from justice
Extraterritoriality, **958–959**, **959–960**
　(update)
　and conduct compelled by foreign law,
　　960
　search and seizure, 960
　*See also* Territories of the United
　　States
Extremist speech, **960–962**
　hate speech, 1277–1279
　*See also* Clear and present danger;
　　Incitement to unlawful conduct;
　　Subversive advocacy

Eyewitness identification, **962–963**
  as evidence, 962
  lineup, 1627
  right of confrontation, 492
  right to counsel, 962, 1627

# F

Facial challenge. *See* Invalid on its face
Factions. *See* Interest groups
Fair comment. *See* Libel and fair
  comment
Fair Employment Practices Committee,
  1025
Fair hearing, **965–966**
  administrative law, 42
  for alien, 1077
  cease and desist orders, 325
  regulatory agencies, 2149
  rehearing, 2152
Fair Housing Act (1968), 393
Fair housing laws. *See* Open housing
  laws
Fair Labor Standards Act (1938), **966–
  968**
  child labor prohibition, 349, 594, 598,
    1528
  and commerce clause, 458, 459
  hours and wages legislation, 1699–
    1700
  invalidated for public employees,
    1549
  service and maintenance employee
    coverage, 1539
  upheld, 743, 1315, 1548, 2046, 2293
Fairness doctrine, **968**
  broadcasting, 246, 247, 248, 249, 445,
    968–969, 1130, 1391, 2144
  Communications Act, 468–469
  demise of, 249, 969, 1147, 2039
  freedom of speech and, 968–969,
    1130, 1147
  *Red Lion Broadcasting Company v.
    Federal Communications Commis-
    sion*, 968, 969, 2144
Fairness doctrine (historical development and update), **968–969**
  Frankfurter and Harlan argument
    against, 2037–2038
  yielding to selective incorporation,
    2039, 2040–2041
Fair return on fair value, **969–970**
  interstate commerce, 750
  utility rate setting, 1023
Fair trial, **970–972**
  balancing test, 155
  as basic right of the accused, 720

closed pretrial proceedings, 1181,
  1199, 1214
discovery, 793
grand jury leaks, 1221, 1223
indictment based on inadmissible
  evidence, 1362
jury discrimination, 1509–1511
jury unanimity vs. "heavy" majority,
  1434–1435
jury underrepresentations, 1514–1515
juvenile proceedings, 1522–1524
lineup suspect right to counsel, 1538–
  1539, 1627
military trials of civilians as violating,
  830
open trial, 2231–2232
Pennsylvania colonial charters, 1894
pre- and post-indictment identification, 1538
prejudicial publicity, 1150, 1405,
  2077
previous convictions, 1770
procedural criminal due process, 2039
public trial, 2076–2077
racial discrimination, 2088
right against self-incrimination, 2232–
  2241
right of confrontation, 1921
rights covered and not covered by
  Constitution, 714
right to counsel, 722, 1194, 1981,
  2259–2265
speedy trial, 2465–2466
speedy trial extended to states, 1539
venue, 2782
waiver of constitutional rights, 974
*See also* Access to the courts; Free
  press/fair trial; Trial by jury
Family and Medical Leave Act (1993),
  2400
Family and the Constitution, **972–974**
  child abuse, 774–775
  child custody awards, 799–800, 1083–
    1084, 1119, 1123
  children's rights, 351–354
  child's health protection, 2191
  Child Support Recovery Act, 354
  feudal privileges, 1035
  foster families, 1083–1084
  freedom of intimate association, 1118–
    1119, 1122–1124
  illegitimacy, 1325–1326, 1605–1606
  juvenile curfew laws challenges, 1521–
    1522
  juvenile proceedings, 1523–1524
  nonmarital children, 1824
  parental control of child's education
    rights, 2188

parental pre-abortion notification, 6,
  11, 193, 1293, 2208
parental rights termination, 1524
protection of family, 1756–1757
racial-preference in adoption, 45–47
welfare rights, 2875–2877
*See also* Divorce and the Constitution;
  Marriage and the Constitution
*Fanny Hill* (Cleland), 1716
Farm Mortgage Moratorium Act. *See*
  Frazier-Lemke Acts
FBI. *See* Federal Bureau of Investiga-
  tion
FCC. *See* Federal Communications
  Commission
FECA. *See* Federal Election Campaign
  Acts
Federal acts. *See key word*
Federal Budget. *See* Budget
Federal Bureau of Investigation, **975–
  977**
  damages claims against, 740
  electronic eavesdropping, 2139
  federal judicial nominee screening by,
    1019
  growth of, 1568
  Hoover (J. Edgar) directorship, 1303–
    1304
Federal common law, civil, **977–979**
  choice of law, 357
  circuit courts, 360
  seditious libel, 1016
Federal common law of crimes, **979–
  981**
  Federalist argument for, 1016
  Madison's denial of concept, 1658
Federal Communications Commission
  abandonment of scarcity premise,
    1147
  broadcast regulation, 246–247, 248,
    249
  community communications, 469
  delegated authority limits, 762
  delegated licensing authority, 2148
  dial-a-porn restrictions, 778
  establishment of, 468
  fairness doctrine, 968, 968–969, 969,
    1147, 2144
  minority station ownership, 1723, 2165
  offensive language regulation, 1147
  right of reply, 1141–1142
Federal constitutional rights. *See*
  Implied constitutional rights of
  action
Federal courts. *See* Circuit courts;
  Claims Court; Constitutional court;
  Federal judicial appointments,
  tenure, and independence; Jurisdic-

tion, federal; Supreme Court;
United States Court of Appeal for
the Federal Circuit; United States
Courts of Appeals; United States
District Courts

Federal Courts Improvement Act (1982),
**981**
abolishment of Court of Customs and
Patent Appeals, 696
Claims Court, 419
creation of United States Court of
Appeals for the Federal Circuit,
2758

Federal criminal law, **982–985, 985–
986** (update)
accusation notice, 2258
bias crimes, 1277
common law of crimes, 979–981
double jeopardy, 807–812, 982–983
federal-state enforcement, 1566–1571
*Grady* test, 982, 983
jurisdictional expansion, 1567
jury nullification, 1512–1514
jury size, 2255
jury unanimity, 1517, 2255
RICO cases, 982, 984
right against self-incrimination, 2237–
2238
right to counsel, 1193
sentencing, 984
*See also* Criminal justice and due
process; Criminal justice system;
Criminal procedure

Federal Election Campaign Acts (1971,
1974), **986–987**
balancing test, 260
*Buckley v. Valeo*, 260, 1932, 1933,
1941
political action committees, 1932–
1933
*See also* Campaign finance

Federal Elections Commission, 260, 987

Federal Farm Bankruptcy Act. *See*
Frazier-Lemke Acts

Federal grants-in-aid, **987–989**
conditional spending, 485–488
cooperative federalism, 684, 827, 1003
to education, 854
law enforcement, 1569
*Massachusetts v. Mellon*, 684
New Deal expansion of, 601
obiter dictum, 1157
revenue sharing, 2227
Sheppard-Towner Maternity Act,
2411, 2659

Federal Immunity Act (1954), **989**
testimony about subversive activity,
605

Federalism, **989–994**
avoidance doctrine, 142
capital district, 796
choice of law, 357–358
competitive, 477
conditional spending, 485–486
and constitutional common law, 514
and constitutional fictions, 526
as constitutional fundamental, 1947
and constitutionalism, 637–638
and constitutional theory, 654, 655
corporate, 689–690
devolution, 775–778
and divided sovereignty, 126
dormant commerce clause, 806, 990
dormant powers, 807
and Eleventh Amendment, 880, 881
environmental regulation, 903–904
exclusionary rule, 2917
and federal common law authority,
978
foreign affairs irrelevancy, 1071
and hate crime laws, 1276–1277
intergovernmental tax immunities,
1383–1384
interstate extradition, 1158
and judicial restraint, 1446
and judicial review, 990–992, 1473,
1490
jurisdiction, 1500
majoritarian bias concerns, 1956–1957
*Martin v. Hunter's Lessee*, 1688–1691
and political party system, 258, 1005–
1006, 1940
as political philosophy of the Constitution, 1944
Rehnquist Court, 2169
and representation, 2131
and seditious libel laws, 1607
and slavery, 417
state action as safeguard of, 1037,
2489, 2491
and state constitutions, 1004
state police power and, 2509
states' rights and, 2518–2519
supremacy clause and, 2586
theories of the Union and, 2685–
2688
treaty power, 2834
values of, 989–990, 998–999
and welfare right cases, 2876–2877
*See also* Cooperative federalism; Dual
federalism

Federalism, contemporary practice of,
**994–997**
*Gregory v. Ashcroft*, 1229
intergovernmental tax immunities,
1384

Jeffersonian views as neofederalism
basis, 1425
progressive centralization, 100
Report of the Conference of Chief
Justices on Federal-State relationships, 2200–2201
revenue sharing, 2227
*See also* Law enforcement and
federal-state relations

Federalism, history of, **997–1003**
Anti-Federalist constitutional thought,
101–102
Articles of Confederation, 124–125,
989, 997–998, 1010, 1013
Bill of Rights, 178, 1353–1354
Blackmun supporting opinion, 190,
191
Civil War changes in, 571
Clark (Tom) opinions, 420
devolution, 775–778
*Federalist* arguments for, 989, 995,
998, 999, 1010–1011, 1013–1015
feudal roots, 1035
First Continental Congress, 1059
as Frankfurter jurisprudence premise,
1102–1104
Fuller Court and, 1168–1169
and international influence of U.S.
Constitution, 1363
and Prohibition, 1168–1169
as Reagan tenet, 2125, 2126
Roosevelt's (Franklin) transformation
of, 597
Taft Court interpretation, 2641
Taney Court and, 2651
Virginia and Kentucky Resolutions,
1424
Waite Court and, 2822
wartime relaxation, 2927
Wilson's (James) arguments for,
2910

Federalism, theory of, **1003–1007**
inception, 997, 1003–1004
intergovernmental tax immunities,
1383–1384
Justice Rehnquist's views, 2153, 2155,
2156, 2160
Montesquieu's beliefs, 1755

Federalism and civil rights, **1007–1009**
Fourteenth Amendment, Section 5
enforcement, 1088, 1089–1089

Federalism and environmental law,
**1009–1010**
waste and pollution cases, 2864

Federalism and shared powers, **1010–
1013**
intergovernmental tax immunities,
1383–1384

Federalism in historical perspective. *See*
   Devolution and federalism in
   historical perspective; Federalism,
   history of
*Federalist, The,* **1013–1015**
   on advice and consent, 47
   on amending process, 74, 75
   on bicameralism, 172
   on bills of credit prohibition, 174
   on checks and balances, 342–343
   on commander-in-chief clause, 1997
   on common defense, 2835
   constitutional commentary, 449
   on constitutional supremacy, 1963
   on deliberative vs. direct democracy,
      763, 785
   on executive administration, 265
   exposition of constitutional system,
      1947
   on factions, 1380–1381, 1382, 1933,
      1947, 1956, 2063
   on federalism theory, 989, 995, 998,
      999, 1010–1011
   on general welfare clause, 1186
   Hamilton coauthorship, 1257, 1258–
      1259
   on impeachment, 1338, 1340
   on implied powers, 1344, 1346
   as international influence, 1365
   Jay essays, 1418
   on judicial independence, 1463
   on judicial power, 496–497, 1466,
      1467, 1469
   on judicial review, 1259, 1287, 1471,
      1473, 1475, 1487
   on judicial supremacy, 1487
   on limited government, 1618
   Madison's authorship, 1657, 1658,
      1659, 1660–1661
   on majoritarian and minoritarian
      biases, 1956
   on military powers, 386
   and original intent, 1394
   on popular consent, 1962, 1963
   on presidential removal power, 110
   on privileges and immunities, 2019
   ratification role, 2119
   on representation, 2201
   on republican government, 1963
   on right of revolution, 2249
   on source of Court's power, 1951
   on spending power, 2468
   on three-fifths clause, 2700
   on unenumerated rights, 2752–2753
Federalists, **1015–1017**
   Adams cabinet, 29
   Alien and Sedition Acts, 67, 1016,
      1424

and Bill of Rights, 176, 178
   deliberative democracy, 763
   Hamilton leadership, 1259–1260
   Hartford Convention, 1274
   and Jeffersonian constitutionalism,
      1424
   Judiciary Act of 1801, 1422, 1496–
      1497
   Judiciary Act repealed, 1498
   majoritarian bias concerns, 1956–1957
   "midnight judge" appointments, 697,
      1667–1668
   political philosophy, 1957
   theory of the Union, 2686–2687
Federal judicial appointments, tenure,
      and independence, **1017–1020**
   constitutional provisions, 1463
   forms of independence, 1455–1458
   good behavior clause, 111, 1018, 1020,
      1337–1338, 1454, 1456, 1948
   impeachment, 1020, 1336–1340, 1456
   Judicial Code, 1451
   nonapplicable to territories or District
      of Columbia, 1464
   tenure and salary provisions to ensure
      independence, 1463
   *See also* Judicial independence;
      Judicial power
Federal judicial role, **1020–1023**
   Judicial Code, 1451
Federal judicial system. *See* Judicial
   system, federal
Federal jurisdiction. *See* Jurisdiction,
   federal
Federal Mortgage Moratorium Act. *See*
   Frazier-Lemke Acts
Federal Power Commission, 2866
Federal protection of civil rights, **1023–
      1027**
   attorney general and Justice Depart-
      ment, 404, 410–411, 1024, 1025,
      1533
   and color of law, 444
   Force Acts, 1070
Federal question jurisdiction, **1027–1028**
   adequate state grounds, 34–35
   congressional power under Article III,
      1865
   declaratory judgment, 756
   Eleventh Amendment, 880
   federal judicial system, 653, 1489,
      1497
   habeas corpus powers, 1495
   Judiciary Act of 1801, 1497
   Judiciary Act of 1875, 1497
   *Pennhurst State School & Hospital v.
      Halderman,* 1893
   removal of cases, 2198–2199

Federal Rules of Civil Procedure, **1028–
      1029**
   choice of law rules, 798
   common law powers, 981
   federal question jurisdiction, 1027,
      1028
   jurisdiction, 1500
   Rule 11 sanctions and civil rights
      cases, 398
Federal Rules of Criminal Procedure,
      **1029**
   accusation notice, 2258
   denaturalization proceedings, 769
   federal felony definition, 1031
   indictment or information, 1369
   pretrial disclosure, 2004
   venue, 2782
Federal Test Acts (1862, 1865, 1868),
      318, **1029–1030**
Federal Tort Claims Act (1946), 419,
      **1030,** 1217–1218
   sovereign immunity waiver, 2459,
      2706, 2708
Federal Trade Commission Act (1914),
      **1030–1031**
   antitrust law, 104, 105, 106
   removal provision, 1318
   unfair competition provision, 1030
Felony, **1031–1032**
   accusation notice, 2258
   arrest, 119, 121, 1031
   criminal syndicalism laws, 723
   definition, 1031
   draft card burning as, 817–818
   due process, 828
   federal prosecutors, 1568
   incitement to, 1352
   indictment, 1361–1362, 1369
   infamy as conviction result, 1363
   misdemeanor distinction, 1031
   police pursuits and constitutional
      rights, 1932
   right to counsel, 23, 170, 1193–1194,
      2255, 2259, 2261–2262
   sterilization for habitual offenders
      invalidated, 2203
Feminist theory, **1032–1033**
   abortion rights, 5, 8–9, 2286
   attack on liberalism, 1616
   comparable worth, 474–475
   on difference and constitutional
      equality, 782
   on obscenity vs. pornography, 1838
   pornography as hate speech, 1277–
      1278
   pornography regulation, 1054, 1057,
      1134, 1965–1968
   pragmatism and, 1983

*See also* Woman suffrage; Woman suffrage movement
Fetal viability. *See* Person
Feudalism and the Constitution, **1034– 1035**
Fifteenth Amendment (framing and ratification), **1039–1041**
 amending process, 72
 as racial discrimination remedy, 387, 411, 578, 2099, 2480
 woman suffrage exclusion, 91, 370, 2918–2919
Fifteenth Amendment (judicial interpretation), **1041–1042**
 antidiscrimination legislation, 94, 95, 402
 circuit court decisions, 361
 city boundary delineations, 362
 constitutional circumvention, 2145– 2146
 enforcement limited to state abridgement of voting rights, 1089
 Force Acts, 1070, 1415
 gerrymander violation, 1203
 grandfather clauses, 2900
 literacy tests, 1242, 1629
 segregationist practices as nullifying, 1168
 as voting rights basis, 362, 2320, 2436, 2807, 2938
 Waite opinions, 2822–2823, 2826– 2827
 *See also* Voting rights
Fifth Amendment
 ambiguity and vagueness of, 2683
 challenges to police power, 2508
 due process clause, 25, 33, 375, 828, 2306, 2307
 just compensation and, 2646
 torts and, 2706
 *See also* Double jeopardy; Due process of law; Grand jury; Right against self-incrimination; Taking of property
Fighting words, **1042–1043**
 broadcasting restraints, 981, 1043
 chilling effect, 354
 clear and present danger, 331, 1042
 *Cohen v. California*, 435
 First Amendment absolutism, 17, 1047
 freedom of speech restrictions, 375, 1042–1043, 1057, 1128, 2855
 hate speech, 1278
 as low First Amendment value, 1056, 1057, 1133, 1646
 as nonapplicable to flag burning, 1062
Filibuster, **1043–1044**
 in Senate, 2359

Final judgment rule, **1044**
 federal question jurisdiction, 1027
 interlocutory, 1385
Firearms. *See* Gun control; Second Amendment
First Amendment, **1045–1052, 1053– 1055** (update 1), **1055–1057** (update 2)
 absolutism, 17, 815, 1047, 1051, 2931
 academic freedom, 21, 22
 accommodation of religion distinction, 24
 Alien and Sedition Acts as violation, 67, 1608
 alien rights under, 1330–1331
 ambiguity and vagueness of, 2683
 anonymous political speech, 90–91
 anti-abortion movement restraints, 93–94
 balancing tests, 154–155
 begging as speech protection, 1301
 Black-Douglas literal full protection theory, 815
 Black's "preferred" position doctrine, 187–188
 *Board of Education v. Pico*, 202, 1216
 Bork's controversial view of, 210
 Brandeis defense of, 221, 222–223
 Brennan analysis, 230–231, 234–235, 1062
 Brennan on central meaning of, 2214
 *Bridges v. California*, 1149
 broadcasting, 249, 445, 1147, 1392, 2739
 *Buckley v. Valeo*, 257, 1216
 Burger Court and, 270–271, 273
 cable television, 2739
 campaign finance, 295, 296, 297, 1932
 categories of speech excluded from, 1802
 as censorship bar, 1317
 child pornography, 350, 351, 1802
 children's issues, 350–351
 civil disobedience, 371
 civil liberties guaranteed by, 375
 clear and present danger test, 146, 426, 1050, 1051, 1149, 1299, 2318– 2319, 2901
 commercial speech, 17, 138, 139, 165, 460–464, 1118, 1133, 1135, 1556, 2351, 2800
 Communist party witness testimony, 1595–1596
 communitarians on, 472–473
 compelled speech, 475
 and compelling state interest, 155, 477
 computerized forms of information, 482

and constitutional aspiration, 663
content-based/content-neutral principle, 1053–1059, 1128–1129, 1132–1135, 1147–1148, 1320, 1351, 1646, 2199
copyright protection, 1377
corporate citizenship, 688
defamatory speech, 167, 1235, 1236
demonstrations, 767–768
and direct democracy, 787–788
distribution of literature in public forum, 1391
draft card burning, 1836
and education, 855–856, 858–859
and electoral process, 871–872
electronic eavesdropping, 872–873
employee speech rights (private), 891
and enumerated powers, 1091
and equal access, 906
and equal protection doctrine, 1921– 1922
Espionage Act, 923
essential rights construed as property, 2051
establishment clause, 2321, 2378
establishment of religion, 927–928
*Everson v. Board of Education*, 931
and executive power, 948
extremist speech, 960–961
fairness doctrine, 968–969
and fair trial, 972
and fighting words, 1042–1043, 1133, 1646
film censorship procedural requirements, 1106
flag desecration, 1061–1064
Fortas analysis, 1082–1083
Fourteenth Amendment's extension to states, 1045–1046
Framers' phrasing of, 177
freedom of association guarantee first recognized, 1773
free exercise clause, 1768
government-created corporations, 1573–1574
government secrecy, 1214–1215, 1257
government speech, 1215–1216
grand jury secrecy limits, 1223
group libel exclusion from, 167, 1236
as Hatch Act challenge, 268
and hate crimes, 1276
Holmes's changing view of, 1299
homeowner posting of "For Sale" or "Sold" signs, 1628
homeowner posting of political signs, 1556–1557
Hughes Court rulings, 1316–1317

First Amendment (continued)
  incitement to unlawful conduct, 1351–1353
  and incorporation doctrine, 179, 1008, 1353–1356
  initiative petitions, 1372
  intellectual property law, 1377–1378
  interaction between two religious clauses, 2174–2176
  interception of mail propaganda, 1560
  judicial activism and restraint, 1445
  labor activity, 1549–1556
  legislative investigations, 2866
  libel law, 1146, 1189, 1236, 1322, 1606–1608, 2067
  libelous publications, 1805
  libel plurality opinion, 829–830
  liberalism and, 1615
  lobbyist protection, 1636
  low-value speech doctrine, 1056–1057, 1128, 1133, 1646, 2940
  loyalty-security programs, 1649–1650
  Madisonian understanding of, 1658, 1662
  malicious libel, 1322
  and marketplace of ideas, 1136–1137, 1670–1671
  military power to restrict, 117
  minors' rights, 1195
  motion pictures, 1538
  *New York Times Company v. Sullivan*, 231, 234–235, 237
  as not mandating complete church-state separation, 1653
  nude dancing, 1830–1832
  obscenity prosecutions, 2318, 2476
  obscenity status, 1048, 1837–1839, 2296
  overbreadth doctrine, 250–251, 2317
  *Paul v. Davis*, 1888
  *Pell v. Procunier*, 1891
  *Perry Education Association v. Perry Local Educators' Association*, 1899
  picketing, 1550–1551, 1921–1922, 2414
  *Planned Parenthood v. Casey*, 1915
  political party rulings, 1938–1939, 1942–1943
  political speech shields, 1264
  pornography protections, 1965–1968
  as preferred freedoms, 1990–1991
  prior restraint and, 1788, 1805–1806, 2009–2011, 2351
  prisoners' rights, 2046
  privacy and, 2014–2015
  protection denial to alleged subversives, 79
  protection of private property, 1672

  public and nonpublic forums, 2068–2069
  public employee curbs, 268
  public employee protections, 36, 2066–2067, 2252
  public's access right to criminal trial, 2231–2232
  released time challenges, 2171–2172
  reporter's privilege, 226–227, 2413
  right to know, 2271, 2272
  school prayers, 2322, 2323, 2324
  scientific experimentation, 2327
  securities regulation, 2350, 2351
  seditious libel, 2353
  shopping center uses, 1308, 1672, 2060, 2414–2415
  Stewart's views, 2542
  and strict scrutiny, 1050–1051, 1990, 2562
  symbolic speech protection, 1061
  textualism problems, 2683
  two-level theory, 1837, 2744–2745
  Warren Court emphasis, 380, 2854–2855
  workplace harassment, 2925, 2926
  World War I cases, 1049–1050, 1126, 2901
  zoning ordinances, 2317
  *See also* Extremist speech; Freedom of assembly; Freedom of assembly and association; Freedom of petition; Freedom of speech; Freedom of the press; Religious liberty; Separation of church and state
First Congress, **1057–1059**
  Association and, 534, 672
  circuit court jurisdictions, 1489
  full faith and credit statute, 1170
  judicial removal, 1338
  Judiciary Act of 1789, 1495–1497
  right to petition debate, 2273
First Continental Congress, Declaration and Resolves of (1774), **1059–1060**
  Adams (John) role, 26
First World War. *See* World War I
Five Knights Case. *See* Petition of Right
Flag burning. *See* Flag desecration
Flag desecration, **1061, 1061–1064** (update)
  clear and present danger test, 427
  constitutional amendment proposal, 76
  and content neutrality doctrine, 1054, 1133
  as freedom of speech decision, 1133
  and incorporation doctrine, 179
  Scalia's views, 2315

  Stevens's views, 2538
  *Texas v. Johnson*, 382, 1062–1063, 1133
Flag Protection Act (1989), 1063
Flag salute cases, **1064–1066**
  clear and present danger test, 426, 2186, 2188, 2189
  First Amendment privilege, 1048
  free exercise vs. free speech applications, 2186
  Stone Court and, 2549–2550
  substantive due process and, 2574
FLSA. *See* Fair Labor Standards Act
FOIA. *See* Freedom of Information Act
Food, Drug, and Cosmetic Act (1938), **1069**
  as Pure Food and Drug Act extension, 2084
Food Stamp Act (1964), 2875
  amendment (1971), 770
Force Act (1833), **1069**
  as response to South Carolina nullification, 1408, 1413, 2457
Force Acts (1870, 1871), 94, **1070**
  and federalism, 994
  and Fifteenth Amendment, 1070, 1415
  and Fourteenth Amendment, 1088
  invoked in school desegregation violence, 1969
  and Ku Klux Klan, 733
  provisions, 181, 1070
  repeal of portions by Civil Rights Repeal Act, 415
Foreign affairs, **1071–1078, 1078–1081** (update)
  act of state doctrine, 24–25
  advice and consent, 47
  Boland Amendment, 206, 621, 622
  Bricker Amendment, 243–244
  constitutional provisions, 2834–2839
  crisis-based broad presidential powers, 741
  delegation of power, 761
  Embargo Acts, 885
  executive agreements, 939
  executive prerogative, 950
  extraterritoriality, 958–960
  free press/national security issue, 1140–1141
  immigration and alienage laws, 1330, 1332
  implied powers, 1345
  International Emergency Economic Powers Act, 1386
  international law and federal-state relations, 1389–1390
  Iran-Contra affair, 1402–1403, 2128

Jay's Treaty, 1419
Marshall Plan, 1687
Monroe Doctrine, 1755
North Atlantic Treaty, 1827
Panama Canal treaties, 1876
police action, 1921
as political question doctrine, 1950, 1953
presidential act of recognition, 168
presidential order upheld, 239
presidential powers, 1071, 1073–1076, 1078–1081, 1996–1997, 2836–2837
presidential war powers, 1997–1998, 2002–2003
Proclamation of Neutrality, 2045–2046
Roosevelt's (Franklin D.) policies, 2289–2290
Roosevelt's (Theodore) policies, 2291–2292
Senate role in, 47, 2361–2362
state limitations, 1072–1073, 1997
territorial incorporation theory, 1169
United Nations Charter, 603, 2757–2758
war powers, 2834–2844, 2840–2844
Washington presidency, 2861–2862
Washington's Farewell Address, 2863
*See also* Congress and foreign policy; Gulf War; Korean War; Senate and foreign policy; Treaty power; Vietnam War; World War I; World War II
Foreign commerce, **1081**
child labor prohibitions, 1528
and commerce clause, 1072–1073, 1081
drug regulation, 821, 823
import-export clause, 256, 1348–1349
North American Free Trade Agreement, 1826–1827
original package doctrine, 1864, 2923
Prohibition of Slave Trade Act, 2050
Pure Food and Drug Act, 2083–2084
selective exclusiveness, 2356
Foreign policy. *See* Congress and foreign policy; Congressional war policy; Foreign Affairs; Senate and foreign policy
Foreign Sovereign Immunities Act (1976), 25
Forfeiture. *See* Civil forfeiture
Foster families, **1083–1084**
intimate association value, 1124
same-race placement preference issue, 46
*Founders' Constitution, The* (Kurland and Lerner, eds.), 1543

Four-letter words. *See* Fighting words; Low-value speech; Obscenity
Fourteenth Amendment (framing), **1084–1087**
abolitionist constitutional theory, 2
Amnesty Act, 89
antislavery constitutional arguments, 1288
as Bill of Rights extension to states, 33, 39, 178–180, 197, 1045–1046, 1090–1092, 2917
Bingham's role, 181
citizenship clause, 59, 129, 131, 168, 183–184, 364, 365, 366, 1085, 1087, 1090, 1092, 1167, 2305, 2354, 2497
civil liberties guarantees, 375
civil rights guarantees, 387, 402, 411
due process clause, 375, 387, 760, 829, 970, 971, 1045, 1084, 1088, 1089–1090, 1091, 1288, 1355, 1572, 2036, 2317, 2318
due process connotation, 1572
and Eleventh Amendment, 877, 880
Fourth Amendment incorporations, 2917
and fundamental rights, 1037
and higher law, 1288
historical background, 1356–1357
immunities clause. *See subhead* privileges and immunities clause *below*
incorporation doctrine, 814–15, 830, 1008, 1045, 1086, 1353–1356
and individual rights, 2480
Johnson's (Andrew) public disapprobation of, 1428
Joint Committee on Reconstruction, 1436
"male" terminology first introduced into Constitution, 2477, 2918
privileges and immunities clause (second), 2020–2021
privileges and immunities clause, 96, 1087–1088, 1091, 1288, 2305
racial discrimination remedy, 186, 1084–1087, 1088
ratification, 72, 578
as rational basis for governmental classifications, 678
speedy trial coverage, 1539
state action coverage, 2329, 2482
as Thirteenth Amendment clarification, 2143
tort due process, 2706
trial by jury coverage, 830
as unenumerated rights protection, 33
women's initial exclusion, 91, 370, 1740, 2477, 2918, 2919, 2920

*See also* Due process of law; Equal protection of the laws; Incorporation doctrine
Fourteenth Amendment (judicial interpretation)
abortion decision, 5, 15, 2057
alien protection guarantee, 368
American Indians status, 79, 80, 82
Americans with Disabilities Act, 87, 88
anti-abortion movement citing, 92
antidiscrimination legislation, 94, 95, 96
antimiscegenation laws invalidation, 403, 1645–1646
arrest, 119, 120
and Asian Americans, 130, 131–132, 1331
capital punishment, 307, 309, 1529
Cardozo's common law approach to, 313–315
as censorship bar, 1317
Chase Court and, 338
citizenship of District of Columbia residents, 796
citizenship of women, 2919
Civil Rights Cases, 408–410
congressional remedial powers, 1527
controlled-substance abuse, 678
corporate citizenship, 688
corporate rights and privileges, 585
Court's selective activism and restraint, 1445
criminal justice and due process, 709–711
damages claims, 740
discrimination by private individuals, 1089
domestic violence clause enforcement, 803–804
due process incorporation into state criminal procedure, 2036–2042
economic due process, 1007
economic liberties, 841–842
economic regulation, 844, 2519
education applications, 854
eminent domain, 888–889
employment discrimination, 893
environmental regulation, 905
equal access, 2063
equal protection clause, 46, 206, 253, 387, 388, 389, 401, 780–783, 907–913, 916, 1084, 1086–1090, 1092, 1288, 1919, 2368, 2387, 2533
equal rights amendment, 918
*Euclid v. Ambler Realty Company*, 929
evidence, 934
exclusionary rule, 936

**Fourteenth Amendment** (continued)
expansive readings of, 626
and federalism, 989, 991, 992
Field incorporation theory, 1036–1038
Force Acts, 1088
freedom of contract, 1007, 1547, 1638, 2414
freedom of petition, 1125
freedom of speech, 2309–2310, 2311
freedom of the press, 1317
judicial activism, 1448
jury trial right, 157–158, 181, 1700
just compensation for property taken, 1519
juvenile curfew laws challenges, 1521
juvenile proceedings, 1523
and original intent, 178, 1086, 1088, 1091
peaceable assembly, 1107
*Pennhurst State School & Hospital v. Halderman*, 1893
*Pierce v. Society of Sisters*, 1908
as privacy right basis, 2246
private racially discriminative behavior, 1240–1241, 1437, 2063
and procedural due process, 64
property protection, 2051
public accommodation access, 168
public purpose definition, 2311
public use, 2079
race and sex in antidiscrimination law, 2089, 2091
racial discrimination, 186, 771, 1089, 1239–1241, 1437, 2093, 2099, 2101–2102, 2106, 2108
racial preference, 2109
racial quotas, 54
reapportionment, 152, 153
resident alien protections, 130
residential segregation, 2900
and restrictive covenants, 163
right against self-incrimination, 33, 1665–1666
right to counsel, 2260
right to life, 2329
same-sex marriage, 2307
separate but equal facilities, 771, 1918
sex discrimination, 218, 2398
*Slaughterhouse* cases, 2423–2424
state action limitation, 200, 280, 1037, 1063, 1064, 1411
state vs. private discrimination, 1089
vested rights protection, 1041–1042, 1225, 2203, 2783–2784, 2807
woman suffrage denial, 2477
*See also* Incorporation doctrine
**Fourteenth Amendment, Section 5 (framing), 1087–1091**

**Fourteenth Amendment, Section 5 (judicial construction), 1089–1090**
equal protection guarantee, 401
private discrimination, 2015, 2016
Waite opinions, 2822
**Fourteenth Amendment as a new Constitution, 1090–1092**
**Fourth Amendment, 1092–1097, 1097–1098 (update)**
administrative search, 42, 43
alien rights, 1330, 1332
arrest, 119, 120
arrest warrant, 120–121, 140, 141
Black's restrictive interpretation of, 186–187
civil liberties guarantees, 375
collective rights, 1091
consent search waiver, 507
criminal justice technology, 711–713
damages claims, 740
drug testing, 822–827, 2328
education application, 856
electronic eavesdropping require-ments, 170, 873–875, 1643, 2342, 2896–2897, 2913
environmental regulation, 902–903
exclusionary rule, 936, 2334, 2335, 2336, 2338, 2339
formalism of, 2339, 2340
Frankfurter championship, 1102
free press application, 1140, 1143, 1145
good faith exception, 1204–1205
habeas corpus, 2320
homeless persons' rights, 1302
implied damages action, 1344
incorporation doctrine, 1008, 2917
national security, 1781–1782
Paxton's Case, 1889
person concept, 1901
plain feel doctrine, 1912
plain view doctrine, 1914
pragmatism of, 2340, 2342, 2343
privacy guarantee, 2319
probable cause, 2022–2024, 2331, 2333, 2334, 2338, 2339
property definitions, 2339
property protection, 2051, 2052
reasonable expectation of privacy, 2139–2141
reasonableness requirement, 2337
right to privacy, 2334, 2337, 2342
search and seizure, 2333, 2338, 2344
search and seizure of innocent party's premises, 2948
search warrant based on informant's tip, 1327

search warrant requirement, 1092, 1099, 2343–2344
segregation and, 2354
seizure as witness against self, 2236
Stewart's views, 2542
stop and frisk, 2676
third-party consent, 2689
traffic stops, 2711
unreasonable search, 294, 330, 375, 822, 823, 1094–1095, 1097–1098, 1527, 2766–2768
waiver of constitutional rights, 2831
warrant clause, 2329, 2330, 2334
warrantless search, 2845, 2847, 2851
*Weeks v. United States*, 2872–2873
*Zurcher v. Stanford Daily*, 2947–2948
**Fourth Amendment, historical origins of, 1098–1099**
Franchise. *See* Voting rights; Woman suffrage
**Frazier-Lemke Acts (1934, 1935), 1105**
revision upheld, 2932
unconstitutionality, 1645
**Freedmen's Bureau, 1106**
Civil Rights Act of 1866, 402
economic support for freedmen, 416
federal civil rights enforcement, 1024
freedmen's rights, 578
Freedom of. . ., *See also headings begin-ning with* Right
**Freedom of assembly and association, 1106–1110**
Bill of Rights (English), 175
boycott, 215
campaign finance, 295
civil disobedience, 371
and content neutrality doctrine, 1053–1055
*Cox v. New Hampshire*, 702
demonstration, 702, 767
electoral process, 872
as First Amendment right, 1045, 1046, 1052, 1053
Fourteenth Amendment due process, 760, 1107
gay and lesbian St. Patrick's Day parade participation, 1320
juvenile curfew laws, 1521–1522
labor union organization, 1549, 1552
petition rights, 1125
political action committees, 1932–1933
and private discrimination, 2015, 2016–2017
public employee unionization, 1552
and public forum concept, 702, 1317
*Slaughterhouse* cases, 2424
state constitutions on, 1107

Freedom of association, **1110–1111**
balancing test, 1193
as civil liberty, 376, 377
for collective bargaining, 4
*Communist Party of the United States v. Subversive Activities Control Board,* 472
as First Amendment right, 1052
first Court recognition of, 1773
freedom of intimate association, 1108, 1118–1125
groups and, 1236–1237
and guilt by association, 1241–1242
judicial interpretation, 1107–1111
and labor union organization, 1549, 1552
and legislative investigations, 1052, 2866–2867
and loyalty-security program, 1650
and married couple contraceptive use, 1108
*NAACP v. Alabama,* 1773
and petition right, 1125
by political parties, 1937, 1938–1939, 1942–1943
and refusal to answer state bar admission questions, 1541
and right of privacy, 2243–2244
and secret societies, 1109
and sedition, 2351
and sex discrimination, 2016–2017
*See also* Freedom of intimate association

Freedom of contract, **1111–1117**
Adamson Act as noninterference, 33
affected with a public interest doctrine, 52, 53, 1115, 1166
*Allgeyer v. Louisiana,* 70, 1115, 2243
Chase Court and, 342
as civil liberty, 376, 382
corporations and, 687, 1112, 1116
due process clause, 25–26, 36, 70, 837–838, 2243
economic liberties, 842
equality of right, 25–26, 36
and Fourteenth Amendment, 1007, 2414
and fundamental interests, 1173
Holmes's dissent on, 1296
labor activity, 1547
maximum hour/minimum wage laws and, 35–36, 1638, 1764
Pitney and, 1911
as protected liberty, 1288
and public purpose doctrine, 2073
reaffirmed, 684
regulatory statute invalidated under, 1735–1736

Sherman Antitrust Act, 1165
*Slaughterhouse* cases, 2423
as subject to police power, 1294
substantive due process, 26, 687, 1114–1115, 1116, 2571, 2577
and ticket scalping, 2746
and vested rights, 1034
*See also* Obligation of contracts

Freedom of debate. *See* Speech or debate clause

Freedom of expressive association. *See* Freedom of association

Freedom of information. *See* Right to know

Freedom of Information Act (1966), **1117–1118**
applied to administrative agencies, 39
civil liberties and, 379
denouncement by Scalia, 2313
and government secrecy, 1215

Freedom of intimate association, **1118–1125**
antisodomy law, 213, 2247, 2891
*Bowers v. Hardwick,* 213, 2247, 2891
as child custody issue, 800
and contraceptive use, 1108, 1118, 1234
and divorce, 799
foster families, 1083–1084, 1124
as freedom of association guarantee, 1110
fundamental interests, 1173
and illegitimacy, 1326, 1558
and miscegenation, 1744–1745, 2097
penumbra theory, 1896
right of privacy basis, 1237, 2242, 2243, 2246–2247
and right to marry, 1671–1672
and same-sex marriage, 2308
and sexual orientation, 1124, 2403

Freedom of petition, **1125**
Bill of Rights (English), 175
and boycott, 215
and District of Columbia demonstrations, 796
as First Amendment right, 1046, 1052
*Slaughterhouse* cases, 2424
suppression of abolitionist petitions, 2, 31, 385, 2884

Freedom of religion. *See* Religious liberty

Freedom of speech, **1125–1132, 1132–1135** (update 1), **1135–1137** (update 2)
abortion counseling restraint, 2300
*Abrams v. United States,* 2901
absolutism, 17, 815
academic freedom, 21, 22

anonymous political speech, 90–91
anti-abortion protests, 93–94
antislavery suppressions, 2425–2426
bad tendency test, 146, 1129, 2311
balancing test, 154–155, 769, 1129–1130
and begging, 1301
Black-Douglas literal full protection theory, 815
and blasphemy, 198
as Bork nomination issue, 210
Brandeis on philosophical foundations of, 221, 222–223, 1050
breach of the peace vs., 227
broadcasting regulation, 246, 981, 1391–1392
Burger Court and, 380
and cable television, 2739
and campaign expenditure limitations, 260
and captive audience, 313
cases (1985–1989), 1132–1135
*Cato's Letters,* 324
children and, 351
chilling effect, 354, 471
civil disobedience and, 371, 1135–1136
civil liberties and, 375
clear and present danger test, 15, 16, 225–26, 426, 769, 961, 1129, 1352, 1955, 1990, 2318–2319, 2901
commercial speech restrictions, 1377
Communications Act, 469
communitarians on, 473
and computer technology, 481
and congressional investigation witnesses, 1595
for congressional members, 501
and conspiracy law, 511, 709
content-neutral/content-based doctrine, 1053–1059, 1128–1129, 1132–1135, 1215–1216, 1351, 1837, 2123, 2123–2124, 2167–2168, 2914
copyright and, 685–686, 1377
corporate rights, 690–691, 1060
and criminal syndicalism statutes, 723
degree and coverage scope, 1135–1137
and destruction of draft card, 818, 1836
economic implications, 1565–1566
employee speech, 891–892, 2925
employer speech, 1551–1552
and enhanced punishment of hate crimes, 1276
and equal access, 906
and espionage, 2318–2319
establishment clause, 926

Freedom of speech (continued)
  evolution teaching, 2666
  extremist speech, 960–962
  fairness doctrine, 968–969, 1147, 2230
  fighting words, 375, 1042–1043, 1057,
    1128, 2855
  as First Amendment right, 1045–1048,
    1053–1059
  flag desecration cases, 1054, 1061–
    1064
  and Fourteenth Amendment due
    process, 760
  and free access to media, 1725
  and freedom of association, 1110
  freedom of press distinctions, 1147
  Gitlow v. New York, 2901
  and government refusals to aid
    religious expression, 1208, 1209
  government subsidized speech, 1131–
    1132
  and group libel, 167, 1235–1236
  as hate crime challenge, 1276, 2913–
    2914
  and hate speech, 1277, 2123–2124
  Holmes's theory of, 1046, 1047, 1050,
    1296, 1298–1300
  homeowner posting of "For Sale" or
    "Sold" signs, 1628
  homeowner posting of political signs,
    1556–1557
  hostile audience, 1304–1305
  Hustler Magazine v. Falwell, 1133
  incidental burdens on, 1351
  incitement test, 1351–1353, 1696
  and incorporation doctrine, 179, 1008
  and intellectual property law, 1377–
    1378
  and Internet, 471, 1148, 1391–1392
  Jefferson's statement on, 1423
  and labor activity, 1549, 1551, 1553
  least restrictive means test, 1573
  and legislative investigation witnesses,
    1595
  listener's rights, 1628
  low-value speech doctrine, 1056–
    1057, 1128, 1132–1133, 1646–1647,
    2940
  Mill (John Stuart) on, 1730–1731
  movies protected under, 279
  murder manuals and instructions of
    violence, 1153–1154
  mythology of Holmes's championship,
    1298–1300
  O'Brien test, 1837
  obscenity restrictions, 161–162, 1128,
    2296
  offensive language restrictions, 981,
    1043, 1057, 1147

  "official English" laws, 1847–1848
  overt acts test, 1871
  parliamentary rights, 1880
  Pell v. Procunier, 1891
  Pennsylvania Constitution of 1776,
    1895
  Perry Education Association v. Perry
    Local Educators' Association, 1900
  picketing rulings, 1550, 1907
  and political parties, 1937
  political speech, 871
  polling place restrictions, 279
  pornography ordinances and, 1966–
    1967
  as preferred freedom, 1990
  prior restraint and censorship, 2009–
    2011
  protected from unprotected but
    related conduct, 2855
  of public employees, 22, 892, 1134,
    1137, 1782, 2866
  public forum doctrine, 34, 203, 369,
    1131, 1134, 2009, 2067–2071, 2167
  religious groups' rights, 1560, 2172–
    2173, 2186, 2194, 2198, 2904
  in "restricted environments," 1133–
    1134
  and RICO Act, 1152–1153
  and right against self-incrimination,
    2235
  right-privilege rejection, 234
  Schenck v. United States, 2318–2319
  scientific speech and, 2326
  secondary boycott advertisement disal-
    lowed, 1203–1204
  and seditious libel, 16, 1016, 1606–
    1607, 2353
  shopping centers, 1131, 1308, 1566,
    2414–2415
  soundtrucks and amplifiers and, 2452–
    2453
  special-use public property limitation,
    34
  standard of review, 2471
  Stevens's views, 2538
  Stewart's views, 2542
  street-corner preaching, 1542
  strict scrutiny, 2562
  student curbs, 170, 1281
  student on-campus worship group
    denial, 203
  subsidized speech, 2567–2568
  and subversive advocacy, 2580
  symbolic speech, 1061, 1062, 2630–
    2632
  Tennessee v. Scopes, 2666
  Texas v. Johnson, 1133
  two-level theory, 2744–2745

  unconstitutional conditions, 2749–
    2750
  unprotected areas, 2855
  value pluralism and, 2778
  Vinson Court and, 2794
  and violence advocacy or instruction,
    1153–1154
  Warren Court and, 2854–2855
  Whitney v. California, 2901–2902
  and witness and juror personal experi-
    ences sales to media, 2915–2916
  and workplace harassment, 2925, 2926
  World War I cases, 1606–1607
  See also Freedom of the press; Libel
    and the First Amendment
Freedom of speech, legislator's. See
    Legislative immunity; Speech or
    debate clause
Freedom of the press, 1138–1144,
    1144–1147 (update 1), 1147–1149
    (update 2)
  absolutism, 17
  actual malice rule, 1141, 1146, 1322,
    1607, 1608–1609, 2067, 2850
  ambiguity and vagueness of, 2683
  and antislavery statements suppres-
    sion, 2426
  Bork controversial view of, 210
  broadcasters and, 469, 691
  Burger opinions, 271
  cable television, 1147–1148
  Cato's Letters, 324
  Cohen v. Cowles Media Co., 436
  and computer technology, 481, 482–
    483
  and conspiracy law, 709
  content-based/content-neutral regula-
    tion, 1054, 1055
  copyright and, 685–686
  corporate rights and, 690–691
  electronic media and, 1138, 1147–
    1148
  and fair trial. See Free press/fair trial
  as First Amendment right, 1046, 1051,
    1051–1052, 1054, 1055, 1138, 1144,
    2351
  Freedom of Information Act, 1117
  freedom of speech distinctions, 1147
  free newspaper space for political
    rebuttal disallowed, 1725
  Grosjean v. American Press Co., 1138–
    1139, 1317
  incidental burdens on, 1351
  and incorporation doctrine, 179
  and Internet, 1148
  libel restrictions. See Libel and the
    First Amendment
  Madison's view of, 1658

Milton (John) on, 1737–1739
and national security, 1129, 1139, 1140, 1145
*Near v. Minnesota*, 1138, 1145, 1317
*New York Times Co. v. United States*, 1438–1439, 1805–1807, 2009
and original intent, 1607
and Pentagon Papers publication, 1129, 1139, 1140, 1145, 1438–1439, 1805–1807, 2009
*People v. Croswell*, 1897
as preferred freedom, 1990
prior restraint and censorship, 1438–1439, 1805–1807, 2009–2011
privacy rights vs., 1142, 2014
and public property, 369
reporter's privilege, 226–227, 1143, 2413
and right against self-incrimination, 2236
and right to know, 1143–1144, 2271–2272
right to privacy vs., 2244
right to reply invalidations, 1142, 1144–1145, 1725
Sedition Act (1798) convictions, 67
seditious libel and, 1138, 1139, 2351, 2353
source disclosure, 1143
state action and, 2310
Stewart's views, 2542
student newspaper curbs, 1281
subsidized speech, 2568
and subversive advocacy, 2580
"taxes on knowledge" held unconstitutional, 1234
and tort liability, 1069, 1438–1439
Vinson Court and, 2794
Zenger's case, 1512, 2944
Free exercise clause. *See* Religious liberty
Freeport Doctrine (1858), **1148–1149**
slavery in territories, 813, 1625, 2436
Free press/fair trial, **1149–1152, 1152** (update)
broadened open proceedings, 1199
closed pretrial proceedings, 1181, 1214, 2077
and electronic equipment, 330, 1142–1143, 1152
*Estes v. Texas*, 929
and First Amendment rights, 972, 1142, 1145–1446
gag order, 1138, 1142, 1144, 1145, 1151, 1152, 1179–1180, 1789, 2077
prejudicial publicity, 1150, 1405, 2077
prior restraint on pretrial publicity, 1789

public access to criminal trials, 2231–2232
*Richmond Newspapers, Inc. v. Virginia*, 2231–2232, 2271–2272
televising of trial, 330
tort liability, 1438–1439
Free-Soil parties, 3, 31, 1848, 2435
Free speech and RICO, **1152–1153**
Free Speech League, 2324
Free speech, murder manuals, and instruction of violence, **1153–1154**
Columbine High School shootings, 1154
Free trade. *See* Commerce clause
French and Indian War, 755
French Revolution, 29
Fries' Rebellion, **1156**
Fruit of the poisonous tree, **1157–1158**
direct and indirect evidence, 2336
exclusionary rule, 121, 936, 1157, 1815, 1928, 2336
inevitable discovery, 1815
oral incrimination in wake of illegal arrest, 2922
FTC. *See* Federal Trade Commission Act
FTCA. *See* Federal Tort Claims Act
Fugitive from justice, **1158–1159**
Articles of Confederation clause, 540
Fugitive Slave Acts (1793, 1850)
Abolitionist constitutional theory, 2, 3, 4
abolitionist legal challenge, 2432
civil liberties denials, 2425, 2431
Compromise of 1850, 477, 478
preemption doctrine, 2555
as property protection, 2427, 2428, 2430
upheld, 2006, 2417
Fugitive slavery, **1159–1160**
abolitionist constitutional theory, 2, 3, 4, 2432
civil disobedience and, 370
Compromise of 1850, 477, 478
constitutional clauses on, 2, 409
denial of trial rights, 2425, 2431
federal law of 1793 upheld, 2006
habeas corpus, 1248
personal liberty laws, 3, 4, 1159, 1901, 2006
political trials, 1955
property protection, 2427, 2428, 2430
*Sims' case*, 2417
*Somerset's case*, 2452
taking of property application, 2054
Full Employment Act (1946), **1160**
as post-World War II measure, 603

Fuller Court, **1163–1170**
new judicialism, 1160, 1161–1162
separate but equal doctrine, 1160
Full faith and credit, **1170–1171, 1171–1172** (update)
Articles of Confederation clause, 540
and collateral attack, 441
and comity, 447, 2019
jurisdiction, 1500
Nevada-domiciled divorces, 799
Fundamental interests, **1172–1173**
*Brown v. Board of Education*, 2309–2310
constitutional justification, 1505
education as, 2309, 2309–2310, 2310
and fundamental law, 1175
involuntary sterilization, 2528
litigation strategy, 1632
marriage as, 1671, 2943
as preferred freedoms, 1991
preventive detention, 2317
and privileges and immunities, 2020
reproduction autonomy, 2284, 2528
and strict scrutiny, 2562
voting rights as, 1401, 2228
welfare benefits, 742, 2408
*See also* Fundamental rights; Natural rights and the Constitution
Fundamentalists and the Constitution. *See* Religious fundamentalism
Fundamental law (history), **1173–1174**
Bill of Rights (English), 174
and constitutional conventions, 514
and constitutional history before 1776, 529
as higher law, 1286–1289
law of the land as, 1571–1572
Locke's philosophy, 1639
Madison's respect for, 1658, 1659
Massachusetts Circular Letter, 1694
taxation without representation as violation, 2656
written constitution as, 84, 1173, 1174, 1419
Fundamental Laws of West New Jersey. *See* New Jersey Colonial Charters
Fundamental law and the Supreme Court, **1174–1175**
Constitution as basis, 1674
Fundamental Orders of Connecticut (1639), **1176**
freedom of debate, 501
as genesis of written constitution, 1364
as social compact, 1303
Fundamental rights, **1176–1177**
Cardozo definition, 1176, 1990
Court's definition of waiver, 1436

Fundamental rights (continued)
　Courts' protective role, 655–657
　Declaration of Independence on, 752–
　　755
　definitions, 1176, 1990, 2339
　due process protection, 1176–1177,
　　1233
　educational quality not seen as, 1974–
　　1975, 1977
　and Fourteenth Amendment, 1037
　Frankfurter definition, 1176
　habeas corpus, 1245, 1255
　and incorporation doctrine, 1355
　Insular cases dichotomy, 1176–1177
　and international human rights, 1386–
　　1388
　as Jeffersonian constitutionalism
　　element, 1423
　loyalty oaths and, 2467
　no benefits from violations of, 1157
　*Palko v. Connecticut*, 1874
　as preferred freedoms, 1990
　and privileges and immunities, 1354
　property linked with, 2051
　reproductive autonomy, 2203, 2204
　rights of accused persons and, 2744
　same-sex marriage and, 2307, 2308
　sex discrimination and, 2390, 2399
　*Slaughterhouse* cases and, 2424
　speedy trial as, 1539
　voting as, 2879
　Warren Court and, 1177
　welfare aid not seen as, 2251, 2874–
　　2875, 2879
　*See also* Bill of Rights; Civil rights;
　　First Amendment; Natural rights
　　and the Constitution

# G

Gag order, **1179–1180**
　abolitionist petitions, 2, 31, 560, 2425,
　　2884
　constitutionality in murder case,
　　1789
　and First Amendment, 1051, 2010
　free press/fair trial, 1138, 1142, 1144,
　　1145, 1151, 1152, 1181, 2077
　*Nebraska Press Association v. Stuart*,
　　1179, 1789, 2010
　shield laws, 2413
Gag rule. *See* Civil liberties and the
　　antislavery controversy; Freedom of
　　petition; Slavery and the Constitu-
　　tion
Gambling, 1777, 1779, 2416
　Puerto Rican statute, 1969

and right against self-incrimination,
　　1670
Gay rights. *See* Same-sex marriage;
　　Sexual orientation; Sexual prefer-
　　ence and the Constitution
Geary Act (1892), 128
Gender discrimination. *See* Sex discrimi-
　　nation
Gender rights, **1185**
　abortion as, 5, 12–13, 14, 192
　birth control as, 4, 182, 182–183
　classification on basis of sex disal-
　　lowed, 2921
　in constitutional history, 2920–2921
　difference and constitutional equality,
　　781–782
　feminist theory, 1032–1033
　feudal privileges, 1034, 1035
　Fourteenth Amendment, 2477, 2918
　freedom of contract equality, 36, 1112
　Ginsburg cases, 1195, 1196–1197
　judicial activism, 1448
　male feudal privileges, 1034, 1035
　married women's contract rights,
　　1112
　Seneca Falls Convention, 2365–2366
　single-sex education, 2417–2419
　in Social Security benefits, 293
　woman suffrage, 2917–2919
　women's rights movement,
　　nineteenth-century, 91–92
　*See also* Equal rights amendment;
　　Race and sex in antidiscrimination
　　law; Reproductive autonomy; Sex
　　discrimination
General Accounting Office, 261
General Appropriation Act (1907), 288
General Laws and Liberties of Massa-
　　chusetts. *See* Massachusetts General
　　Laws and Liberties
General warrant, **1185–1186**
　Fourth Amendment repudiation, 1092,
　　1098, 1099
　historical background, 1098–1099
　Paxton's case, 1888
　Pitt and, 1912
　probable cause, 2330
　writ of assistance, 132, 1186
General welfare clause, **1186–1187**
　broad construction, 250
　and federal grants-in-aid, 987
　and federal power boundaries, 998
　and inalienable police power, 283,
　　1350
　as internal improvements basis, 1385
　and public policy doctrine, 2076
　supremacy clause and, 2587
　Tennessee Valley Act, 2667

Genetic privacy. *See* DNA testing and
　　genetic privacy
Gerrymander, **1187–1188**, **1188–1189**
　　(update)
　census and control of, 326
　electoral districting, 867, 869, 871
　Fifteenth Amendment violation ruling,
　　1203
　"incumbent survival," 2135
　partisan, 1306, 2135
　political question doctrine, 1952,
　　1953
　racial, 392, 1188, 1783, 2093, 2136,
　　2137, 2814
　as reapportionment result, 153, 2135,
　　2136
Global markets and the Constitution. *See*
　　Multinational corporations, global
　　markets, and the Constitution
Glorious Revolution (1688–1689), 175,
　　208, 1571–1572
Gold clause cases, **1201–1202**
　Court ruling, 2288
　Gold Reserve Act, 1202–1203
　necessary and proper clause, 1751
Gold Reserve Act (1934), **1202–1203**
　gold clause cases, 1201–1202
Good behavior, **1204**
　ensuring nonpartisan judiciary, 1948
　as federal judicial tenure basis, 111,
　　1018, 1020, 1337–1338, 1454, 1456
　judicial deviation as misdemeanor,
　　2284
　public employees, 268
Good faith exception, **1204–1205**
　as exclusionary rule limitation, 2044
　search and seizure, 2338
Government aid to religious institutions,
　　**1206–1207**, **1207–1208** (update 1),
　　**1208–1209** (update 2)
　Blaine Amendment prohibition, 197–
　　198, 587
　establishment clause, 924
　invidious discrimination, 1048
　*Lemon* test, 1602–1604
　loan of state-purchased textbooks, 202
　*Mueller v. Allen*, 1763
　neutrality vs. separationist view, 2294
　on-site special education services in
　　sectarian schools, 61, 63, 2179
　religion as "viewpoint" decision,
　　1559–1560
　school choice and, 2321
　secular instruction materials, 1604
　secular purposes requirement, 1601–
　　1602
　separation of church and state, 2376,
　　2378

specifically created school district for special education children, 202, 927, 2179–2180

tax deductions for expenses, 1763

taxpayer suit standing, 1066, 2777

textbook loans to racially discriminative private schools, 2017

tuition grants, 2738–2739

vouchers, 1208, 2814–2815

*Walz v. Tax Commission*, 2833

*Witters v. Washington Department of Services for the Blind*, 2916–2917

*Wolman v. Walter*, 2917

*See also* Religion in public schools

Government arts funding. *See* Government speech

Government as proprietor, **1209–1214**

*Government by Judiciary* (Boudin), 212

Government employees. *See* Public employees

Government instrumentality, **1214**

Government regulation of the economy. *See* Economic regulation

Government secrecy, **1214–1215**

and First Amendment, 1257

Freedom of Information Act, 1117–1118, 1215

right to know, 2271–2272

*See also* Free press/fair trial

Government speech, **1215–1217**

*Board of Education v. Pico*, 202, 1216

as constitutional puzzle, 202

*Epperson v. Arkansas*, 906

and freedom of speech, 1131, 1136

and minor political parties, 257, 1216

*Planned Parenthood v. Casey*, 1915

and privacy rights, 2244

and public forum, 2070

Government wrongs, **1217–1218**

Gramm-Rudman-Hollings Act (1985), **1219**

balanced-budget amendment, 618

constitutionality challenges, 214, 615

as deficit reduction measure, 262

Scalia unconstitutionality opinion, 2313

Grandfather clause, **1219–1220**

Fifteenth Amendment application, 2900

*Gunn v. United States* invalidation, 1219

literacy test exemptions, 129, 392, 1242, 1629, 2808

Grand jury, **1220–1222, 1222–1224** (update)

exclusionary rule, 290

felony, 1031

Fifth Amendment guarantee, 1091, 1222

and illegal electronic surveillance evidence, 1184

immunized testimony, 989, 1221, 1335, 1526, 1527

indictment, 1361–1362, 2256, 2258

indictment arrest warrant, 121

indictment excluded from incorporation doctrine, 1356

judicial review, 1222–1223

juror racial discrimination, 1510–1511

presentment, 1991

refusal to testify, 2747

reporter's privilege, 226–227, 1051, 1438, 2200

secrecy, 1222–1223

single judge as, 1849

state constitutional law, 2496

witness immunity grants, 989, 1526, 1527

*Granger* cases, **1224–1225**

affected with a public interest, 52, 53, 1224, 2823

Grants-in-aid. *See* Federal grants-in-aid

Great Compromise, **1228**

bicameralism arrangement, 172

and Constitutional Convention of 1787, 521, 543

federalism and shared powers, 1011

Gerry role, 1187

House of Representatives provision, 1305

Johnson (William Samuel) role, 1433

Paterson's role, 1882

Senate provision, 1305, 2358

Sherman's introduction of, 2412

three-fifths clause, 2700

Great Depression

Bankruptcy Act, 160

budget and fiscal policy, 262

commerce clause use, 2481

Fair Labor Standards Act, 967

farm bankruptcy acts, 1105

Hughes Court, 1311

invalidated legislation, 127–128

public programs, 40

public purpose doctrine, 2075–2076

state debtor relief, 1300–1301

Sutherland's obiter dictum on social legislation, 2882

*See also* New Deal

Greenback Act (1862), 417

Greenback issuance. *See* Legal tender cases

Grounds of opinion, **1235**

Group conflict and the Constitution. *See* National unity, group conflict, and the Constitution

Group libel, **1235–1236**

*Beauharnais v. Illinois*, 167, 1235, 1236

excluded from First Amendment, 167

and freedom of speech, 1130

Groups and the Constitution, **1236–1238**

amicus curiae, 89

class action suits, 422

guilt by association, 1241–1242

interest group litigation, 1378–1379

*See also* Freedom of assembly and association; Freedom of association

*Growth of American Law, The: The Law Makers* (Hurst), 1321

*Growth of the American Republic, The* (Commager), 447

Guarantee clause, **1238–1239, 1239** (update)

initiative and referendum challenges under, 789, 1238–1239, 1372

legitimacy of state government, 1652

republican form of government, 2209

Guilt by association, **1241–1242**

Hughes's argument against, 1241

individual rights restrictions, 1236–1237

Gulf of Tonkin Resolution (1964), **1242**

Vietnam War, 2789, 2790

Gulf War, **1242–1243**

Bush conduct of, 281, 282, 1242, 2002, 2043

Clinton actions in postwar period, 2002–2003

Gun control, **1243–1244**

background checks on prospective handgun purchasers, 624

federal criminal prosecution, 1570–1571

gun-free school zones, 1570–1571, 1642–1643

*López, United States v.*, 624, 1570–1571, 1642–1643

radical Populist constitutional interpretation vs., 2113–2114

Second Amendment arguments, 2113–2114, 2250, 2347

Gun-Free School Zones Act (1990), 1570, 1642–1643

# H

Habeas corpus, **1245–1252, 1252–1253** (update 1), **1254–1255** (update 2)

abstention doctrine, 18

**Habeas corpus** (continued)
   access to the courts, 23
   adequate state grounds, 35, 2821
   Antiterrorism Act restrictions on, 103,
      1254–1255, 1503, 1504
   appeals, 1701
   *Brown v. Allen*, 1250
   capital punishment, 302, 305, 306–307
   in capital punishment review, 1254–
      1255
   Chase Court and, 338, 339
   and Civil Rights Act of 1866, 402
   and collateral attack, 441, 442
   as constitutional remedy, 651, 652,
      653
   in criminal procedural due process,
      1100–1101
   and excessive bail, 148, 175
   federal court power to try facts anew,
      975
   federal question jurisdiction, 1495
   Force Acts suspension of, 1070
   Fourth Amendment and, 2320
   Frankfurter commentary, 1245
   fugitive slaves and, 2417
   as fundamental interest, 1172
   legislation, 1255–1256
   Lincoln suspension of, 181, 416, 572
   *Merryman, Ex parte*, 2841
   *Milligan, Ex parte*, 1246, 1247
   *Penry v. Lynaugh*, 1895
   and personal liberty laws, 1901
   prisoner claims for, 654, 1434, 2547–
      2548
   as privilege, 2241, 2251
   *Quirin, Ex parte*, 2085
   scope of, 1252–1253, 2044
   *Slaughterhouse* cases, 2424
   state criminal process through, 1757
   subversive advocacy and, 2580
   waiver of rights, 2831
   war powers, 2840
   written law as basis of federal court
      power of, 207
**Habeas Corpus Act of 1679, 1255**
   application in colonies, 1456
   bail, 148, 175
   as statute, 84
**Habeas Corpus Act of 1863, 1256**
   and Union internal security policy,
      572
**Habeas Corpus Act of 1867, 1267**
   and constitutional remedies, 652
   federal courts' writs for state
      prisoners, 1248, 1254
**Harassment.** *See* Hate speech; Sex
   discrimination; Workplace harassment and the First Amendment

**Harmless error, 1270–1271, 1271**
   (update)
   limitation in appeal, 2045
**Harrison Act (1914), 1274**
   as national police power, 804, 1567
   upheld, 804
**Hartford Convention, 1274–1275**
   Adams (John Quincy) essay on, 30
   New England state secession
      advocates, 2480
   three-fifths clause abrogation demand,
      2700
   and War of 1812, 1017
**Hatch Act (1940), 1275**
   political activity prohibitions, 268
   relaxation of, 2845
   right-privilege distinction, 2252
**Hate crimes, 1275–1277**
   speech vs. conduct distinction, 1276,
      2914
   *Wisconsin v. Mitchell*, 2913–2914
**Hate speech, 1277–1279**
   bias-motivated conduct vs., 1276
   definition and characterization, 1056–
      1057
   and freedom of speech, 1127–1128
   group libel and, 1235–1236
   overbreadth of legislation, 2123
   *R. A. V. v. City of St. Paul*, 2123–
      2124, 2913–2914, 2926
   regulation efforts, 470
   workplace harassment, 2926
**Hawaiian sovereignty.** *See* Native
   Hawaiian sovereignty movements
**Health Insurance for the Aged Act
   (Medicare) (1965), 1281**
**Health violations.** *See* Administrative
   search
**Hearing.** *See* Fair hearing; Rehearing
**Hearsay rule, 1282**
   of co-conspirators, 708
   compulsory process right, 480
   confrontation right, 492
   credible, 2330
   evidence, 933–934
   and fair trial, 971
   grand jury indictment, 1362
   informant's tip, 1327
   probable cause, 818
**Hepburn Act (1906), 1284–1285**
   as Interstate Commerce Act supple-
      ment, 1397, 1398
   Roosevelt (Theodore) proposal, 2292
**Higher law, 1286–1289**
   as attack on writ of assistance, 1099
   and contract clause, 1067–1068
   as Declaration of Independence basis,
      754, 1174, 1286

   inherent power distinguished from,
      1370–1371
   law of the land as, 1571
   as legislative power limitation, 1596
   *Loan Association v. Topeka*, 1636
   New Right opposition, 1801
   philosophy of, 262, 1286–1287
   slavery and, 2389
   *Terrett v. Taylor*, 1636
   vested rights and, 290
   written constitutions as, 1174, 1474
**History in constitutional argumentation,
   1290–1292**
   Bill of Rights application, 1353
   and interpretivism, 1394
   Wisconsin school of legal history,
      1321
*History of the United States During the
   Administrations of Jefferson and
   Madison* (Adams), 26
**Holding, 1294**
   campaign finance, 296
   and common law, 465
   stare decisis, 2477
**Holmes and free speech, 1046, 1047,
   1050, 1296, 1298–1300**
**Homelessness and the Constitution,
   1301–1302**
   judicial scrutiny of mental illness and,
      1720
**Homestead Act (1862), 1302**
   and Civil War economy, 417
**Homosexuality.** *See* Same-sex marriage;
   Sexual orientation; Sexual preference and the Constitution
**Hostile audience, 1304–1305**
   and breach of the peace, 228
   and demonstration rights, 768
   and free speech restriction, 1055
**Hot pursuit.** *See* Exigent circumstances
   search
**Hours of work legislation.** *See* Adamson
   Eight-Hour Act; Maximum hours
   and minimum wages legislation
**House Committee on Un-American
   Activities, 1305**
   activities of, 605
   bill of attainder, 1645
   contempt conviction upheld, 162–
      163
   Dies Committee as forerunner, 780
   permanent committee status
      conferred on, 604
**House of Representatives, 1305–
   1307**
   abolitionist petitions gag order, 560,
      2425
   apportionment, 172

constitutional amendment proposals, 76
in constitutional history, 1789–1801, 546
Dies Committee, 780
District of Columbia limited-voting delegate, 797
exclusive powers, 1307
First Congress, 1058
first members elected to, 319
impeachment articles of Andrew Johnson, 126, 1429
impeachment articles of Richard Nixon, 126–127
impeachment articles of William J. Clinton, 127, 1360
impeachment of federal judges, 1454
impeachment power, 111, 1307, 1336, 1340
investigative powers, 1594
joint Iran-Contra hearings, 1401–1403
legislative process, 1597–1599
member qualifications, 500, 1306
members' official immunity, 1335
and presidential tied vote, 1934
Speaker authority, 589
Speaker in presidential succession, 2002
Speaker qualifications, 1307
speech or debate clause, 2464
supermajority rules, 2585
and three-fifths clause, 2700
vacancy special-election requirement, 1307
Wilson's (James) founding influence, 2909–2910
Housing. See Open housing laws; Residential segregation; Restrictive covenant
Housing and Rent Act (1947), 603
HUAC. See House Committee on Un-American Activities
Hughes Court, 1312–1318
civil liberties, 1311
Great Depression, 1311
New Deal, 1312–1318
Human body. See Body search; Property rights and the human body; Reproductive autonomy
Human life. See Person
Human Life Statute, 92
Human rights. See Fundamental rights; International human rights; Natural rights and the Constitution
Hyde Amendment, 1324
ban on Medicaid-funded abortion, 6, 7, 2205–2206

I

ICC. See Interstate Commerce Commission
IIRAIRA. See Illegal Immigration Reform and Immigrant Responsibility Act
Illegal aliens. See Alien; Immigration and alienage
Illegal Immigration Reform and Immigrant Responsibility Act (1996), 1235
and Antiterrorism and Effective Death Penalty Act, 103
government benefits distinctions, 1332
legislative veto question, 1333
Illegitimacy, 1325–1327
as discrimination basis, 1824
and equal protection, 1122, 1558
and freedom of intimate association, 1122
fundamental interests, 1173
heightened scrutiny, 1605, 1606
immigration law, 1331
as invidious discrimination, 1401
Levy v. Louisiana, 1401
standard of review, 1326, 1605–1606
as suspect classification, 2732
See also Nonmarital children
Immigration and alienage, 1328–1330, 1330–1332 (update), 1332–1333 (update)
Alien and Sedition Acts, 67
Alien Registration Act, 68
alien status, 65–66
alien suffrage, 68–69
amnesty for resident aliens, 1333
Antiterrorism Act deportation provisions, 103
birthright citizenship, 183
Chinese Exclusion Act, 128, 1328, 1330
citizenship and, 368
discrete and insular minorities, 794
equal protection for undocumented aliens, 1920
expatriation, 956–957
Fuller Court and, 1167
head tax upheld, 1328–1329
Illegal Immigration Reform and Immigrant Responsibility Act, 1325, 1332
Immigration Act quotas, 595
Immigration Reform and Control Act, 1333
legislative veto, 1333

literacy test, 1329
nativism, 1328–1329
race-based restrictions, 128, 1328–1329
as suspect classification, 66, 72
terrorism control, 2674
visas, 2801–2802
See also Asian Americans and the Constitution; Asian immigrants and constitutional history
Immigration and Nationality Act (1952)
denaturalization, 768
deportation grounds, 770–771
Immigration Reform and Control Act (1986), 1333
Immunities. See Privileges and immunities
Immunity. See Executive immunity; Immunity of public officials; Intergovernmental immunity; Judicial immunity; Legislative immunity; Presidential immunity: Sovereign immunity; Speech or debate clause; State immunity from federal law
Immunity grant (self-incrimination), 1334–1335
and compulsory process right, 480
Counselman v. Hitchcock, 694–695
Federal Immunity Act, 989
grand jury, 989, 1221, 1335, 1526, 1527
and right against self-incrimination, 2237
supplanting Fifth Amendment right, 257, 1526
use immunity, 1526–1527
Immunity of public officials, 1335–1336
civil liability and unofficial presidential acts, 625
Stevens's views, 2537
waiver for unofficial communication, 1324
Impeachment, 1336–1340, 1340–1343 (update)
articles of impeachment of Andrew Johnson, 110, 126, 139, 181, 288, 579, 1339, 1340, 1429, 2476, 2669, 2751
articles of impeachment of Richard M. Nixon, 126–127, 338, 609, 1339, 1341, 2865
articles of impeachment of William J. Clinton, 127, 431, 433–434, 625, 1340, 1341–1342, 1360
censure by Senate vs., 1342
as checks and balances power, 342
Chief Justice as presiding officer, 346, 1340, 1343

Impeachment (continued)
  executive privilege, 953
  grounds for removal, 1336
  House of Representatives role, 111,
    1307, 1336, 1340
  independent counsel (special prose-
    cutor) and, 1360, 2463
  judicial, 111, 337, 552, 1020, 1337–
    1341, 1454, 1456, 1669, 1684, 1953,
    2763
  legislative supremacy in, 1945
  recall vs., 2141
  Senate trial, 1336, 1340, 1953, 2360,
    2363
  special prosecutor (independent
    counsel) and, 1630, 2463
*Imperial Presidency* (Schlesinger), 1996
Implied constitutional rights of action,
    **1343–1344**
  *Bivens v. Six Unknown Named Agents
    of the Federal Bureau of Narcotics*,
    185, 1344
  damages claims, 740–741, 1344
  Rehnquist Court and, 2162–2163
  violations by federal officials, 185
  *Young, Ex parte*, 1343–1344
Implied powers, **1344–1348**
  Bank of the United States Acts, 159–
    160, 160, 250, 1259, 1461, 2861
  broad construction, 250, 1345, 1707
  Court's substantive interpretations,
    1445
  executive power, 947
  and federalism, 1006
  incidental, 1346–1347
  and inherent powers, 1344, 1346,
    1370
  Jeffersonian rejection of concept, 1425
  and living Constitution, 1633
  Madison's theory of, 539
  Marshall (John) on, 900
  *McCulloch v. Maryland*, 744, 1461,
    1633, 1685, 1706–1707
  monetary, 1751–1754
  supremacy clause, 2587
  Tenth Amendment, 1011
  Waite Court and, 2825
  *See also* Enumerated powers
Import-export clause, **1348–1349**
  original package doctrine, 1864
  state property tax, 1725
  state violation, 256
Impost, **1349**
  definition, 1349
  import-export clause, 1348–1349
  original package doctrine, 1864
  *See also* Excise tax; State taxation of
    commerce

Impoundment of funds, **1349–1350**
  balanced-budget amendment as justi-
    fying, 154
  Congressional Budget and Impound-
    ment Control Act, 498–499, 610,
    1349
  congressional control over, 266
  and delegation of power, 1999
  executive power, 948
  as Nixon policy, 610
Inalienable police power, **1350**
  backing claims against commerce
    clause, 1350
  *Boston Beer Company v. Massachu-
    setts*, 211–212
  primacy over vested rights claim, 283,
    1350
Incidental burdens on constitutional
    rights, **1350–1351**
  and religious liberty, 2181–2182
Incitement to unlawful conduct, **1351–
    1353**
  bad tendency test, 146, 1646
  clear and present danger rule, 770,
    1198, 1352
  freedom to advocate ideas vs., 1538
  hate speech, 1278
  *Herndon v. Lowry*, 1285–1286
  Holmes's *Gitlow* dissent, 1198–1199
  as low First Amendment value, 1056,
    1646–1647
  *Schenck v. United States*, 1352
  vagueness doctrine, 1285–1286
Income tax. *See* Direct and indirect
    taxes; Sixteenth Amendment
Incorporation doctrine, **1353–1356**
  Bill of Rights and Fourteenth Amend-
    ment, 33, 178–180, 186, 197, 760,
    814, 815, 1005, 1045, 1051, 1086,
    1091–1092, 1353
  Black applications, 185–186, 814–815,
    1086, 1355, 2037, 2038
  Cardozo's hierarchy of rights, 1990
  civil liberties and, 2310–2311
  and criminal procedural due process,
    710, 1355, 1615, 1666, 2039, 2039–
    2040
  Douglas application, 814–815
  and due process clauses of Fifth and
    Fourteenth Amendment, 2042–
    2045
  earliest judicial rejection, 2832
  and federalism, 1008
  Field theory, 1036–1038, 1354
  Fourth Amendment rights, 2917
  Frankfurter-Black debate on, 33,
    1101–1102
  of freedom of assembly, 760

  of freedom of speech, 760, 1046, 1788,
    2186
  *Gitlow v. New York*, 1198, 1354, 2186,
    2310
  Harlan (1833–1911) theory, 1267
  Harlan (1899–1911) theory, 1269
  Holmes's dissent, 1300
  and judiciary policymaking, 1462
  and just compensation, 2130
  *Near v. Minnesota* as adoption of,
    1788
  *Palko v. Connecticut*, 1355, 1874,
    1990, 2293
  privileges and immunities, 2021
  rationalization of rights incorporated,
    1355
  Sanford acknowledgement of, 2310–
    2311
  Second Amendment status, 1243
  selective, 1462, 2038–2045, 2293,
    2856
  trial by jury, 830
  and Warren Court, 169–170, 380, 715
Incorporation doctrine and original
    intent, **1356–1358**
Incorporation of territories, **1358**
  insular cases, 1376
Indecent speech. *See* Low-value speech
Independence of judiciary. *See* Judicial
    independence
Independent counsel, **1358–1360,
    1360–1361** (update)
  congressional creation of office, 115,
    620
  executive privilege, 954
  impeachment articles of William J.
    Clinton, 127, 625
  investigation of Clinton administra-
    tion, 1360–1361
  *See also* Special prosecutor
Independent state grounds. *See*
    Adequate state grounds
Indian Bill of Rights (1968), 2365
Indian Civil Rights Act (1968), 80–81,
    82, 607
Indian tribes. *See* American Indians and
    the Constitution; Tribal Economic
    Development and the Constitution
Indictment, **1361–1362**
  as accusation notice, 2258
  arrest warrant, 121
  executive privilege, 954
  felony, 1361–1362, 1369
  grand jury, 1220, 1221, 1222
  impeachable offense vs., 1336, 1337,
    1429
  incorporation doctrine exclusion, 1356
  law of the land, 828

presentment, 1991
  as right of criminally accused, 2256
  right to counsel prior to, 1538, 2263–
    2264
Indigent, **1362–1363**
  abortion funding restriction, 1272–
    1273, 1324, 1974
  access to the courts, 204, 380, 799,
    817, 1231–1232, 2877, 2879
  Criminal Justice Act, 709
  *Edwards v. California*, 861, 2878
  equal protection rights, 817
  homelessness, 1301–1302
  *in forma pauperis*, 1368–1369
  insanity defense right, 1719
  poverty law, 1972–1975
  public interest law, 2071
  rights of criminally accused, 2255
  right to counsel, 709, 971, 1031, 1083,
    1193–1194, 1462, 1973, 2260,
    2262–2263, 2265, 2877
  right to counsel limitation, 2295
  school finance, 2309–2310
  Social Security Act, 2445
  subpoena use, 2567
  welfare rights, 2252, 2874–2875
  welfare state, 2877–2871
  *See also* Wealth discrimination
Indirect taxes. *See* Direct and indirect
  taxes
Industrial Workers of the World (IWW),
  723, 1954, 1955, 2580
Inevitable discovery, 2338
Infamy, **1363**
Influence of the American Constitution
  abroad, **1363–1366, 1366–1368**
  (update)
  international human rights, 1386–
    1388, 1389
Informant's tip, **1368**
  from electronic eavesdropping, 2896–
    2897
  Jencks Act, 1426
  and probable cause, 2024, 2469
  as search warrant basis, 1327, 1368,
    2024, 2469
  stop and frisk, 2552
*In forma pauperis*, **1368–1369**
  *Gideon v. Wainwright*, 1193, 1369
Information, **1369**
  Freedom of Information Act, 1117–
    1118
  government secrecy vs. right to, 1214–
    1215
  *See also* Marketplace of ideas; Right to
    know
Inherent powers, **1370–1371**
  abstention doctrine, 18

executive electronic surveillance
  claim, 2761–2762
and implied powers, 1344, 1346, 1370
of President, 1996, 2841
sovereignty and, 1006
and steel mill seizure, 2839
*Youngstown Sheet & Tube Co. v.
  Sawyer*, 2839
Inherited hierarchy. *See* Feudalism and
  the Constitution
Initiative, **1371**, **1371–1372** (update)
  campaign finance and, 295, 297
  deliberative democracy vs., 763–764
  as direct democracy, 785, 787–788,
    1371–1372
  as direct legislation, 788
  guarantee clause challenges, 789,
    1238, 1239, 1372
  paid circulators disallowed, 1939
  physician-assisted suicide, 2270–2271
  proposed jurisdictional reform, 1504
  for state encouragement of private
    discrimination, 2170–2171
  *See also* Referendum
Injunction, **1372–1373**
  abstention doctrine, 20, 1373
  against labor, 750–751, 831, 1192,
    1373, 1545, 1547, 1553, 1555–1556,
    1641, 1825, 2757
  against picketing, 1192, 1373, 1547,
    2733
  against publication, 1788, 1806, 2009
  against sale of allegedly obscene
    materials, 1538
  against same-sex marriage, 147
  anti-abortion protests, 94
  Cherokee Indian Cases, 344
  civil rights demonstration, 2832
  Clayton Act, 831
  and constitutional remedies, 652
  and contempt power, 670
  criminal syndicalism laws, 2940–2941
  as curb on governmental official
    future constitutional violations, 740
  expressive activity, 319
  by federal court against state action,
    1343–1344, 1493, 1750, 2940
  final judgment rule, 1044
  free press/fair trial issues, 1140, 1145,
    1150–1151, 2077
  in institutional litigation, 1373, 1374
  jurisdiction, 1500
  justiciability, 1520
  national security, 1140, 1145
  as offensive assertion of federal right,
    1343–1344
  *Osborn v. Bank of the United States*,
    740

three-judge court approval, 1499
  as yellow dog contract enforcement,
    1292
  *Young, Ex parte*, 1373, 2940
  zoning, 2945
  *See also* Gag order
In personam, **1734–1735**
In re, **1374**
In rem, **1374**
Insanity defense. *See* Mental illness and
  the Constitution
Inspections. *See* Administrative search
*Institutes* (Coke), 439–440
Institutional litigation, **1374–1375**
  Burger Court and, 275–276, 2280
  doctrinal formula, 801
  injunctive relief, 1373, 1374
  pattern of official treatment, 2280
  prisoners' rights, 2011–2012
  residential segregation, 2221
  school desegregation, 1231
  *See also* Public law litigation
Insular cases, **1375–1376**
  federalism issue, 1169
  Fuller dissent, 1161
  fundamental rights dichotomy, 1176–
    1177
  status of territories, 1358, 1376
Insularity. *See* Judicial independence
Integration. *See* Desegregation; Segregation
Integration of the federal government.
  *See* Executive Orders 9980 and
  9981
Intellectual property law and the First
  Amendment, **1377–1378**
  copyright, 685–686
  patent, 1882
Intelligence Identities Protection Act
  (1982), 1140
Intent. *See* Original intent; Ratifier
  intent
Interest group litigation, **1378–1380**
  as constitutionally protected political
    activity, 1773
  denial of standing, 1651
  test case legality, 1773
Interest groups, **1380–1382**
  and Bork nomination, 1393
  and economic due process, 840–841
  and federalism, 1006, 1956–1957
  and Japanese American internment,
    1415–1416
  public choice theory, 2063–2064
  statutory interpretation, 2525
  sustaining separation of powers,
    1947
  and term limits, 2669

Intergovernmental immunity, **1382–
 1383**
 dual federalism, 827
 Stone's views, 2544
Intergovernmental tax immunities,
 **1383–1384**
 *Graves v. New York ex rel. O'Keefe*,
 1226, 1384
 *Weston v. City Council of Charleston*,
 2882
Interlocutory, **1385**
 final judgment rule, 1044, 1385
Internal commerce. *See* Intrastate
 commerce
Internal improvements, **1385**
 American System, 88, 1385
 broad construction justifying, 30,
 250
 *Charles River Bridge v. Warren
 Bridge Company*, 331–333
 Jacksonian opposition, 1408, 1412,
 1413
 Maysville Road Bill, 1700–1701
 spending power and, 2468
Internal Revenue Act (1862), 2539
Internal security. *See* Loyalty oath;
 Loyalty-security program; Subver-
 sive activity; Subversive advocacy
Internal Security Act (1950), **1385–
 1386**, 1950
 passage over Truman veto, 604–605,
 1702
 Subversive Activities Control Board,
 2578
International Covenant on Civil and
 Political Rights, 1388
International Emergency Economic
 Powers Act (1977), **1386**
International human rights, **1386–
 1389**
 treaty ratification and federal-state
 relations, 1390
International law and federal-state
 relations, **1389–1390**
 citizenship and, 368
 executive branch deficiencies, 71,
 1390
International trade. *See* Foreign
 commerce
Internet and freedom of speech, **1391–
 1392**
 Columbine High School shootings,
 1154
 Communications Decency Act, 471
 *Reno v. American Civil Liberties
 Union*, 1148
Internet and freedom of speech.
 indecent speech prohibition, 1057

Interposition, **1392**
 as *Brown v. Board of Education*
 reaction, 2458
 Madison's opposition to, 1659
 secession and, 2346
 South Carolina ordinance of secession
 and, 2457
 Webster-Hayne debates of 1830, 559
Interpretation, constitutional. *See*
 Constitutional interpretation
Interpretivism, **1393–1396**
 counterpart to, 1820
 judicial review, 1477–1478, 1480
 and originalism, 1860–1861
Interstate comity. *See* Full faith and
 credit; Privileges and immunities
Interstate commerce, **1396**
 Adamson Eight-Hour Act, 33, 2912
 agricultural production, 62, 63
 Americans with Disabilities Act, 87
 bituminous coal regulation, 184
 Chase Court decision, 341
 child labor and, 349, 1528, 2048
 Child Support Recovery Act and, 354
 and civil rights, 392
 Civil Rights Act of 1964, 95, 405
 competition in, 1739
 congressional regulatory power, 750,
 1261–1262, 1570–1571
 definition, 2513
 discrimination against, 2514, 2515
 and dormant commerce clause, 805,
 806
 drug regulation, 821, 822, 823, 1274
 economic factors, 850
 effects on commerce, 861
 Employers' Liability Acts, 893, 2899
 employers' liability cases, 893
 environmental regulation, 904, 1320,
 2564–2565, 2864
 Erdman Act, 920
 Fair Labor Standards Act, 966, 1315,
 1539, 1548, 2046
 Federal Bureau of Investigation
 duties, 976
 federal criminal jurisdiction, 1567,
 1568, 1570–1571
 federal protective powers, 750–751
 Food, Drug, and Cosmetic Act, 1069
 and fugitive from justice, 1159
 Gun-Free School Zones Act, 1642–
 1643
 Hepburn Act, 1284–1285
 Hughes Court and, 1314–1315
 import-export clause, 1348, 1349
 insurance as, 2458
 internal improvements and, 1385
 Interstate Commerce Act, 1396–1397

intrastate rates competition, 1308
and labor union activity, 25, 167, 1561,
 1641–1642
least restrictive means test, 1573
license cases, 1617
local environmental regulation, 1320
Mann Act, 1666
Mann Act sustained, 1294, 2899
minimum wage regulation, 743–744,
 1315
national police powers, 1261–1262,
 1294, 1777–1779
noxious products doctrine, 1830
original package doctrine, 256, 1348,
 1612, 1617, 1864–1865, 2923
*Panama Refining Co. v. Ryan*, 1877
*Pensacola Telegraph Co. v. Western
 Union Telegraph Co.*, 1896
*Philadelphia & Reading Railroad Co.
 v. Pennsylvania*, 1904
privileges and immunities, 2020
production distinction, 1536, 1539–
 1540
Pure Food and Drug Act, 1290, 2083–
 2084, 2899
railroads and, 584
rational basis standard of review,
 2122
regulatory agency, 1396–1397, 2147
restraint of, 2757
and securities law, 2350
segregation disallowance, 1257, 2063
separate but equal doctrine, 1645
service and maintenance employees
 coverage, 1539
slave trade, 1238
*Southern Pacific Co. v. Arizona*, 2458–
 2459
state discrimination based on proprietary prerogative, 1212
state highway regulation as unconstitutional, 2124
state liquor prohibition statutes, 1601
state regulation limitations, 750,
 1189–1192, 2060, 2512, 2516
state taxation of commerce, 2521
Stone Court and, 2549
stream of commerce doctrine, 2559
subjects of commerce, 2565
Sugar Trust Case, 1539–1540, 1642
Sunday closing laws, 2584
Taney Court and, 2652
waste disposal across state line, 2864
Whig constitutional nationalism,
 2885
White Court and, 2899
*See also* Excise tax; Interstate
 compact; Intrastate commerce

Interstate Commerce Act (1887), **1396–1397**
and administrative law, 1001
and commerce clause, 455
long haul/short haul provision, 1642
and national railroad regulation, 584
Water Power Act, 2866
Interstate Commerce Commission
creation of, 1397, 2147
denial of rate-setting authority, 1397–1398
Mann-Elkins Act, 1666
and quasi-judicial bodies, 1464
and railroads, 1709
rate-making powers, 1285
regulatory activities, 2049
Interstate compact, **1398–1399**
contract clause extension, 1228
proprietary adjustments, 1212–1213
sovereignty and, 2461
Interstate travel. *See* Right to travel
Intimate association. *See* Freedom of intimate association
Intolerable Acts. *See* First Continental Congress, Declaration and Resolves of
Intrastate commerce, **1399**
and commerce clause, 1396
exempted from Interstate Commerce Act, 1397
federal regulation, 2415–2416
interstate rates competition, 1308
Minnesota rate cases, 1739–1740, 2899
regulation validity, 744
reserved to state governance, 1191
segregation upheld, 1918
Shreveport doctrine, 2415–2416
state regulation of commerce, 2513
state taxation of commerce, 2521
stream of commerce doctrine, 2559
Invalid on its face, **1399–1400**
chilling effect, 354
municipal ordinance, 1645
Invasion of privacy. *See* Right of privacy
Inverse condemnation, **1400–1401**
just compensation, 2643
Investigative power. *See* Legislative investigation
Investment Advisers Act (1940), 2351
Invidious discrimination, **1401**
benign racial classification vs., 794
Douglas's use of term, 1401
and establishment of religion, 1048
Field's first impression decision, 1038
*Ho Ah Kow v. Nunan*, 1038
residential segregation, 2219

Involuntary servitude. *See* Peonage; Slavery and the Constitution
Iran-Contra affair, **1401–1403**
Boland Amendment, 206, 2128
Bush comment on, 281
executive prerogative, 950
independent counsel investigation, 1361
and presidential and congressional powers in foreign policy, 621–622
Reagan presidency and, 2128
Senate and, 2360
Iranian Hostages Agreement, 741, 1078
Irrebuttable presumption, **1404–1405**
mandatory maternity leave, 430
Item veto. *See* Line-item veto

# J

Jacksonianism, **1411–1413**
and judicial review, 1474–1475
and judicial supremacy, 1583–1584
Marshall (John's) dislike of, 1675
as Polk political theme, 1958
Whig Party opposition, 2884
Jackson's Proclamation to the People of South Carolina, **1413–1414**
as nationalistic, 1408, 1409
Jackson's veto of the Bank of the United States Bill, **1414**
based on presidential independency doctrine, 1408
based on separation of powers, 160
based on states' rights, 1412
Taney contribution, 2647
Japanese American cases (1943–1944), **1415–1417**
and alien subversion fears, 65
as civil liberties infringement, 2841
constitutionality challenges, 129–130, 131, 1247, 2930–2931
constitutional significance, 132
executive order, 944, 945, 2290
as guilt by association, 1237, 1241
habeas corpus suspension, 1247
and presidential war powers, 1998, 2839
state of war rationale, 2505
Stone Court and, 2550
and war powers, 2841, 2842, 2930–2931
Japanese American relocation. *See* Executive Order 9066 and Public Law 503; Japanese American cases
Japanese Americans. *See* Asian Americans and the Constitution; Asian

immigrants and constitutional history; Japanese American cases
Jay Court. *See* Supreme Court, 1789–1801
Jay's Treaty, 1417, **1419**
constitutional debate, 548–549
treaty power issues, 1259–1260, 2834, 2861–2862
Jeffersonianism, **1423–1425**
Adams (John) conflicts with, 29
and judicial review, 1474–1475
Madison's defense of, 1658–1659
Marshall's (John) dislike of, 1675
repeal of Federalist Judiciary Act of 1801, 1422, 1498
*See also* Anti-Federalist constitutional thought
Jehovah's Witnesses cases
blood transfusion, 2191
door-to-door pamphlet distribution, 1410–1411
flag salute refusal, 1065–1066, 2186, 2188
free speech basis, 2186, 2188
minors' street sale of merchandise, 2008
religion and free speech, 2172–2173, 2188
and religious liberty, 2188–2189, 2192
religious use of state property, 2198
Jencks Act (1957), **1426**
Jim Crow. *See* Black Codes: Segregation; Separate but equal doctrine
Joint Committee on Reconstruction, **1436**
Fourteenth Amendment framing, 1085
Joint resolutions, **1436–1437**
annexation of Texas, 90
international agreement approval, 1992
*See also* Concurrent resolution
Journalistic practices, tort liability, and the freedom of the press, **1438–1439**
*Food Lion, Inc. v. American Broadcasting Co. (ABC)*, 1069
*See also* Free press/fair trial
Journalists and the Supreme Court, **1439–1441**
Judges' Bill (1925), 1490
Judgment, **1442**
decision, 752
full faith and credit, 1170, 1171–1172
stay of execution, 2526
*See also* Final judgment rule; Habeas corpus; Res judicata

Judicial activism and judicial restraint, **1442–1449, 1449–1450** (update)
  in abortion decisions, 5, 11
  activism's rise in late nineteenth century, 582–583
  affected with a public interest, 53
  areas of, 1447–1448
  avoidance doctrine, 142
  Blackmun approach, 192
  as Bork nomination issue, 2127
  Brandeis approach, 2313
  Chase Court, 338
  civil liberties, 383–384
  conservative agenda, 776
  equal protection of the laws, 910
  Field's activism, 1035–1036
  Frankfurter approach, 1101, 1450, 1458, 2313
  Fuller approach, 1161
  Hand (Augustus and Learned) restraint philosophies, 1263
  hidden, 2325
  Holmes's restraint, 1296, 1446
  interpretivism, 1393–1394, 1395, 1480
  judicial interpretive/noninterpretive review, 1477–1478
  judicial legislation, 1458, 1459–1460
  judicial policymaking, 1460–1463
  judicial role, 1482–1485
  and living constitution, 1632–1634
  *Marbury v. Madison,* 1444–1445
  Marshall approach, 1445
  and original intent, 2127–2128
  and particularism, 1197
  and political philosophy of the Constitution, 1945
  procedural vs. substantive, 1444–1446, 1450
  restraint in wealth discrimination cases, 2869–2870
  and social legislation, 2882
  and standing, 2473
  Taft approach, 2314
  Thayer's rule, 1446, 1449
  Thomas approach, 2695
  Warren Court, 2853, 2857–2858
  Warren Court vs. Burger Court, 272, 274, 277
  *See also* Constitutional theory
Judicial appointments. *See* Appointment of Supreme Court justices; Confirmation process; Federal judicial appointments, tenure, and independence; Senate and judicial appointments
Judicial Code, **1451**
  abolishment of circuit courts, 361
  amendment (1937), 1499

Judicial collegiality, **1451–1452**
Judicial conference of the United States, **1452–1453**
  Chief Justice as presiding officer, 347
Judicial contempt power. *See* Contempt power, judicial
Judicial immunity, **1453–1454**
  *Butz v. Economou,* 285
  Court cases upholding, 1335
  sterilization cases, 2565
Judicial impeachment, **1454–1455**
  Chase acquittal, 1339, 1340
  as congressional process, 1340
  historical debate, 1337–1339
  *Marbury v. Madison,* 1669, 1684
  *Nixon v. United States,* 1953
  offenses, 1341
  political elements, 1456
Judicial independence, **1455–1457**
  federal appointments and tenure, 1017, 1019–1020, 1463
  and good behavior, 1204, 1948
  Jay's advocacy, 1418
  Jefferson's advocacy, 1422
  as judicial appointment/confirmation criteria, 50–51
  and political question avoidance, 1950–1951
  and separation of powers, 1418
  *See also* Federal judicial appointments, tenure, and independence
Judicial legislation, **1457–1460**
  *Baker v. Carr,* 1458
  Bork's views on, 210
  *Brown v. Board of Education,* 1458, 1471
  *Cooper v. Aaron,* 1458
  *Gideon v. Wainwright,* 1458
  judicial policymaking, 1460–1463
  and statutory interpretation, 1459
  taxpayer spending challenges, 1464–1465
Judicial policymaking, **1460–1463**
  double jeopardy, 808
  and interpretivism, 1480
  and judicial power, 1471
  and political question doctrine, 1951–1952
  rule of reason, 2298
  *See also* Judicial legislation
Judicial power, **1463–1470**
  admiralty and maritime jurisdiction, 44–45, 1466–1467
  antidisability discrimination legislation, 791
  Anti-Federalist view of, 102
  as apolitical, 1950–1951
  appellate jurisdiction, 108–109

Article III specifications, 122, 979, 1463–1464, 1465, 1489
cases and controversies, 322, 1464–1467
civil liberties and civil rights, 380
congressional transfer of jurisdiction, 1827–1828
constitutional court jurisdiction, 523
as distinct from legislative power, 1596, 1597
diversity jurisdiction, 798–799
economic due process, 839
federal civil rights enforcement, 1007
as federalism check, 995, 996–997
federal judicial role, 1020–1023
federal judicial system, 1489–1498
federal question jurisdiction, 653, 1027–1028
*Flast v. Cohen* landmark decision, 1066–1067, 1465
and foreign affairs, 1071
judicial legislation, 1458–1460
Judiciary Act of 1789, 1495–1496
justiciability, 1519–1521
legitimacy debates, 1472
and local government, 1638
*Osborn v. Bank of the United States,* 1466
overstepped constitutional bounds, 1479–1480
Peters and, 1902
substantive due process and, 2577
Warren Court expansive view of, 2714
*See also* Federal judicial appointments, tenure, and independence; Judicial activism and judicial restraint; Judicial review
Judicial power and legislative remedies, **1470–1472**
Judicial Reform Act (1998), 1504
Judicial restraint. *See* Judicial activism and judicial restraint
Judicial review, **1472–1478**
  of abortion rights, 2285–2286
  abstention doctrine, 19
  of academic freedom, 22
  Ackerman's dualist theory of, 524
  of administrative acts, 1481–1482
  alien deportation limitations, 1503
  of alien proceedings, 1325, 1331, 1332
  amending process, 73
  Antiterrorism and Effective Death Penalty Act features, 103
  and appellate jurisdiction, 109
  areas for judicial activism, 1447–1448
  avoidance doctrine, 142
  *Bonham's Case* as precedent, 207–208
  Boudin history of, 212

of bureaucracy, 266
cases and controversies, 322
by Chase Court, 338
checks and balances, 342
of civil liberties, 378–379, 380
of civil rights acts, 1026
classic justification, 1472, 1583
commentators on the Constitution on, 453
*Commonwealth v. Caton* as disputed precedent for, 467
of congressional contempt and investigative powers, 1536, 1594
as constitutional enforcement measure, 740
and constitutional fictions, 526
and constitutional interpretation, 632
and constitutionalism, 638
and constitutional theory, 654, 655–657
countermajoritarian potential, 767
and democratic theory, 1036
democratic theory's potential conflicts with, 765, 767
*Eakin v. Raub*, 833
of economic policy, 836
of electoral districting, 870–871
of equal protection of the laws, 915
facial challenges, 1399–1400
of federal criminal law, 983
of federalism issues, 989, 990–992, 993, 995, 996–997, 1473
*Federalist* justification, 1259, 1287, 1471
Federalist vs. Jeffersonian views of, 1498
federal question jurisdiction, 1027
first alleged state precedent, 1298
first reported instances, 165–166, 1324, 2301
and fundamental law, 1174–1175
of grand jury, 1222–1223
Hamilton espousal, 1259, 1260, 1287
Hand (Learned)-Wechsler debate, 1476, 1478
and higher law, 1287
inception of, 86, 165–166
of independent counsel removal, 1359
interpretive vs. noninterpretive, 1477–1478
interpretivism, 1393–1394
Jefferson's view, 1422, 1474
as judicial independence insurance, 50
and judicial legislation, 1458
and judicial power, 1489
judicial supremacy vs., 1487–1488
Judiciary Act of 1789 provisions, 1496, 2589–2590

and "law of the land," 1571
and legislative motivation, 1585–1589
limited government and, 1618–1619
*Marbury v. Madison*, 266, 740, 1287, 1424, 1469–1470, 1472, 1474, 1475, 1477, 1487, 1489, 1583, 1667–1670, 1673, 1675, 1986, 2589–2590
as Marshall Court legacy, 1686
Marshall's (John) views, 1472, 1473, 1474, 1475, 1477, 1583
*Martin v. Hunter's Lessee*, 1689–1690
Paterson's views, 1883
Peckham's views, 1890
philosophical theories, 1905
political questions outside scope of, 1454, 1949, 1952, 1953
and precedent, 1986
of punitive damages excesses, 2082–2083
rational basis standard, 2120–2122, 2123
rule of reason, 2299
*Rutgers v. Waddington* as early precedent, 2301
and sovereignty of the people, 1963
state police power and, 2507
state precedents for, 2723
state sovereignty and, 1181
strict scrutiny and, 2562
substantive due process and, 2049
as supremacy of federal law, 1490
Taft Court, 2637
of taxpayers suits, 1066
two-prong theory of, 2857
and unconstitutionality, 2752
U.S. constitutional example, 1367
value pluralism implications, 2778
Warren Court, 2857
Judicial review and democracy, **1478–1481**
Progressive arguments, 2049
tensions between, 767, 1478–1481, 1494, 1506–1507
Judicial review of administrative acts, **1481–1482**
and administrative agencies, 37, 39, 40, 41
Judicial role, **1482–1485**
in protecting state autonomy, 1803
Judicial strategy, **1485–1487**
Judicial supremacy, **1487–1488**
Brennan arguments, 1458
in constitutional interpretation, 1475, 1476
*Cooper v. Aaron*, 1458
as deterrent against unconstitutional legislative drafts, 1583–1584
federal over state law, 1490

Fugitive Slave Act, 2
judicial review, 1472–1482, 1490
*Marbury v. Madison*, 1458–1459
*Martin v. Hunter's Lessee*, 1690
and nonjudicial interpretation of Constitution, 1821–1822
republican thought in conflict with, 2214–2215
Stewart's views, 2542
*See also* Judicial legislation
Judicial system, federal, **1489–1498**
caseload explosion, 1492–1493, 1494
federal question jurisdiction, 1027–1028, 1489, 1495, 1497
Judicial Code, 1451
Judiciary Act of 1789, 1495–1497
Judiciary Act of 1801, 1496–1497
jurisdiction, 1501–1504
justiciability, 1519–1521
public law litigation, 2072–2073
special tribunals, 1492
structural problems, 1493–1494
witness and juror financial profits from media sales, 2915–2916
*See also* Supreme Court *headings*
Judiciary Act of 1789, **1495–1496**
appellate jurisdiction, 108
and Article III provisions, 546, 2589
attorney general post, 134
basic right to bail, 148, 149
circuit court system, 359, 1489, 1495, 1496, 2564, 2603
federal judicial system, 1463, 1489–1490
habeas corpus, 1254, 1256
Judicial Code, 1451
judicial review, 1496, 2589–2590
Paterson and, 1882
Posse Comitatus Act revision, 1969
provision for Supreme Court, 2589
removal powers, 1497, 2199
writ of prohibition, 2050
Judiciary Act of 1801, **1496–1497**
circuit court system, 359, 2759
Jefferson's attack on, 551
partisan federal courts and judges, 29, 1667, 1684
Paterson and, 1883
repeal of, 1422, 1498, 1667, 1684, 2759
repeal upheld, 2564
Judiciary Act of 1837. *See* Circuit courts
Judiciary Act of 1869. *See* Circuit courts
Judiciary Act of 1875, **1497**
federal judicial system, 1490
Judiciary Act of 1891. *See* Circuit Courts of Appeals Act
Judiciary Act of 1911. *See* Judicial Code

Judiciary Act of 1925, 348, **1497–1498**
Judiciary Acts of 1802, **1498**
   as repeal of Federalist 1801 Judiciary
     Act, 1422, 1498, 1667, 2564
Judiciary Reform Act (1937), **1498–
     1499**
Jurisdiction, **1499–1501**
   abstention doctrine, 17–20
   by administrative agencies, 41
   admiralty and maritime, 44–45
   American Indian tribal, 81
   ancillary, 89–90
   appeal, 107–108
   appellate, 108–109
   automobile search, 141
   bankruptcy courts, 161
   birthright citizenship, 183
   Cherokee Indian Cases, 344
   of civil court over military, 1736
   concurrent, 483–484
   congressional transfer from judiciary,
     1827–1828
   of constitutional law, 1674
   declaratory judgment, 756
   diversity, 798–799
   divorce, 799
   and double jeopardy, 810–811, 1562
   and dual federalism, 1012
   equity, 920
   and fair trial, 970
   federal civil rights cases, 2227
   federal-state law enforcement, 1566–
     1571
   fugitive from justice, 1158–1159
   Fugitive Slave Act, 2
   habeas corpus, 1248–1250, 1256
   of independent counsel, 115
   Judicial Code, 1451
   Judiciary Act of 1801, 1496–1497
   juvenile proceedings, 1522
   legislative court, 1590
   military justice, 2937
   personal, 1500
   religion in public schools, 1049
   sovereignty and, 2461
   status of forces agreement and, 2524
   in stockholder' suit, 801
   of Supreme Court, 722, 1184, 1498
   territorial, 1499
   of United States Courts of Appeals,
     1491–1492, 2759
   writ of prohibition, 2050
   zoning, 2945
   *See also* Original jurisdiction; Pendant
     jurisdiction
Jurisdiction, federal, **1501–1503, 1503–
     1504** (update)
   *Bollman* as precedent, 207

Chase Court, 338
   civil liberties, 379
   *Erie Railroad Co. v. Tompkins*, 1439
   foreign affairs, 1076–1077
   Judiciary Act of 1875 widening of,
     1497
   Judiciary Acts of 1802, 1498
   legislative policy-limiting measures,
     1503–1504
   *See also* Appellate jurisdiction;
     Federal question jurisdiction
Jurisdiction and Removal Act. *See*
     Judiciary Act of 1875
Jurisdiction to tax, **1504–1505**
   intergovernmental tax immunities,
     1383–1384
Jurisprudence and constitutional law,
     **1505–1508**
   feminist theory, 1032–1033
   jury composition, 1509–1512
   mechanical, 1715
   and ratifier intent, 2120
   sociological, 2445–2446
Jurors and freedom of speech. *See*
     Witnesses, jurors, and freedom of
     speech
Jury. *See* Blue ribbon jury; Grand jury;
     Petit jury; Trial by jury
Jury challenges. *See* Peremptory
     challenges
Jury discrimination, **1509–1511, 1511–
     1512** (update)
   blue ribbon jury, 199–200, 1509
   and fair trial, 970–971
   improper exclusions, 1509–1510
   invidious discrimination, 1038
   loyalty oath, 1029–1030
   peremptory challenges, 1510, 1511,
     1898–1899, 2088, 2170
   racial, 165, 189, 253, 1038, 1509,
     1510–1511, 1787, 1825, 2558–2559,
     2907
   religious exemption, 2192
   service as political right, 1509, 1514–
     1515
   *Strauder v. West Virginia*, 388
   voir dire potential, 2803
   wealth discrimination, 253
   *William v. Mississippi*, 2906–2907
Jury nullification, **1512–1514**
   capital punishment, 300
Jury service as a political right, **1514–
     1515**
   citizen's obligation, 368
   underrepresented groups, 1509–1510
Jury size, **1515–1517**
   exclusion from incorporation doctrine,
     1356

   five-person unconstitutionality, 157–
     158, 1516, 1517
   jury unanimity, 1517, 1518
   *Patton v. United States*, 1887
   six-member state criminal jury, 2255
   six-person minimum, 264, 1516–1517,
     2727, 2906
   twelve on federal criminal jury, 2255
Jury trial. *See* Trial by jury
Jury unanimity, **1517–1518, 1518–1519**
   (update)
   for federal criminal jury, 710, 1517,
     2255
   nonunanimous verdicts upheld, 1434–
     1435, 1510, 1518
   reasonable doubt diminished, 1434
   as traditional common law feature,
     2727
*Jus dare*, **1519**
*Jus dicere*, **1519**
Just compensation, **1519**
   American Indian property, 80, 82
   *Charles River Bridge v. Warren
     Bridge Company*, 332
   Claims Court, 419
   economic analysis, 836–837
   eminent domain, 888, 2646
   Fifth Amendment and, 2646
   foreign affairs, 1077–1078
   government acquisition of property,
     2643
   incorporated into due process clause,
     1354
   incorporated into equal protection
     clause, 2130
   inverse condemnation, 1400–1401
   Railroad Control Act, 2114
   for regulatory takings, 2150–2151
   for taking of property, 345, 1113,
     1519, 1564, 2150, 2437, 2534, 2643,
     2946
   tribal economic development and,
     2731
Justice Department. *See* Attorney
     general and Department of Justice;
     Civil Rights Division; Solicitor
     general
Justiciability, **1519–1521**
   avoidance doctrine, 142
   as bar to direct democracy rulings,
     785
   and common law, 466
   federal judicial system, 1491
   guarantee clause, 1239
   one person, one vote rule, 326
   and political question doctrine, 1653
   reapportionment, 152–153, 2133,
     2137, 2203, 2227

resting on nature of legal wrong, 1953
standing as barrier, 122
Juvenile curfew laws, **1521–1522**
Juvenile proceedings, **1522–1524**
  capital punishment, 2475–2746
  double jeopardy attachment proceedings, 808
  *Gault, In re*, 1183, 1523, 1524, 2265
  legal fictions in, 2317
  McKeiver v. Pennsylvania, 1523, 1524
  minors' rights, 352
  preventive detention, 2005, 2317
  reasonable doubt standard, 1523, 2912
  right to counsel, 1183, 1523, 2263, 2265
  trial by jury, 1709

# K

Kansas-Nebraska Act (1854), **1525–1526**
  Lecompton constitution, 1526, 1574
  Lincoln opposition, 1620
  Pierce policy, 1908
  popular sovereignty, 1962
  provisions, 813
  and Republican party formation, 3, 2216
  and slavery in the territories, 2427
  and territorial sovereignty, 2435
Keating-Owen Child Labor Act (1916), **1528**
  invalidation, 1261–1262, 1528
Kentucky Resolution. *See* Virginia and Kentucky Resolutions
Kerner Commission, 2220
Klan Act. *See* Force Acts
Korean War, **1541–1542**
  Bricker Amendment, 243–244, 1541, 1921
  conscientious objection, 505
  conscription, 2357
  executive prerogative, 951
  loyalty-security programs, 1541, 1650
  McCarthyism, 1541, 1701–1702
  military desegregation, 118
  as police action, 603, 1541–1542, 1921
  presidential plenary authority, 1075
  Senate and, 2360
  as state of war, 2505
  steel seizure controversy, 946, 2448, 2526–2527
  Subversive Activities Control Act, 2581
  Truman policies, 2448, 2734
  as undeclared war, 755, 1541, 1998
Ku Klux Klan
  advocacy vs. incitement, 225–226

court victories for, 225–226, 733, 1272, 1955
Force Acts, 733, 1070
hate speech, 1277, 1278
incitement to unlawful conduct, 1353
symbol display in public square, 312–313, 2173
voting rights infringement conviction, 2938
Ku Klux Klan Act. *See* Force Acts

# L

Labor and the antitrust laws, **1545–1546**
  applications, 70, 107, 167–168, 1555, 1641
  Clayton Act, 425–426
  injunction, 831, 1545
  *Loewe v. Lawlor*, 1545, 1641–1642
Labor and the Constitution, **1546–1553, 1553–1554** (update)
  Adamson Eight-Hour Act, 33, 2912
  alien temporary workers, 1329–1330
  alien unauthorized workers, 1333
  boycott, 215
  Brandeis opinions, 219–220, 223
  Child Labor Amendment, 72, 73, 349, 594, 598
  Child Labor Tax Case, 151–152
  Clayton Act, 425–426, 831
  *Debs* cases, 750–751
  domestic violence clause, 803
  economic vs. political activity distinction, 1549, 1551
  Erdman Act, 25, 1547
  Fair Labor Standards Act, 349, 458, 459, 594, 598, 966–967, 1548
  and feudal privileges, 1034–35
  freedom of contract, 1112
  injunctions. *See under* Labor movement
  Keating-Owen Child Labor Act, 1261, 1528
  Landrum-Griffin Act, 603, 1560–1561
  legal services right, 1109
  *Lochner v. New York*, 1547, 1548, 1552–1553, 1638–1639
  *Loewe v. Lawlor*, 1545, 1641–1642
  maximum hour and minimum wage laws, 33, 35–36, 1638–1639, 1764
  public employees, 1552
  right-to-work laws, 2277–2278
  *Schechter Poultry Corp. v. United States*, 2819, 2820
  strike limitations, 1549–1550, 1553

Taft-Hartley Act, 79, 2277–2278
union employees' speech rights, 891
Wagner Act, 442, 458, 603, 1547, 1547–1548, 2289, 2293
Wagner Act cases, 349, 1548, 2819–2821
women's protection laws, 2920–2921
workplace harassment and First Amendment, 2925–2926
*See also* Child labor; Labor and the antitrust laws; Labor movement; Maximum hours and minimum wages legislation
Labor and the Constitution, Taft-Hartley Act, 79, 442, 603
Labor Board cases. *See* Wagner Act cases
Labor Management Reporting and Disclosure Act. *See* Landrum-Griffin Act
Labor movement, **1554–1556**
  bill of attainder, 257
  boycott strikes, 215
  closed shop, 434
  collective bargaining, 442, 1545, 1548
  constitutional aspiration, 664
  freedom of contract, 25–26
  injunction to enforce yellow dog contract, 1292
  injunction use against, 750, 750–751, 831, 1192, 1373, 1545, 1547, 1553, 1555–1556, 1641, 1825, 2757
  New Deal policy, 2293, 2818–2821
  picketing, 1907
  and political trials, 1954–1955
  right-to-work laws, 2277–2278
  self-regulation measures, 1561
  workers' compensation legislation, 2924–2925
  yellow dog contract, 1292, 2900
Land Ordinance of 1784. *See* Ordinance of 1784
Landrum-Griffin Act (1959), **1560–1561**
  federal authority over internal union affairs, 603
Land use
  controls, 2644
  delegation of power, 1232
  environmental regulations, 905
  Hawaiian feudal tenure system, 1279
  Homestead Act, 1302
  just compensation for restrictions, 2150
  restriction as economic value deprivation, 2055, 2150–2151
  Yazoo land grant, 1067, 1068, 1260
  *See also* Eminent domain; Zoning

Law and economics theory, **1563–1566**
   *Lochner v. New York* dissent, 1638
   pragmatism and, 1983
Law enforcement and federal-state
   relations, **1566–1570, 1570–1571**
   (update)
   commerce-based federal criminal
     legislation, 1568, 1570
   examples of crimes, 1568
   Federal Bureau of Investigation, 975–
     977
   *López, United States v.*, 1570–1571
   national police force, 1566, 1569–
     1570
   *Perez v. United States*, 1567
   *Rewis v. United States*, 1570
   statutory interpretation, 1570–1571
   *See also* Police interrogation and
     confessions
*Law of Nations or the Principles of*
   *Natural Law, The* (Vattel), 633, 637,
   941, 2781
Law of the land, **1571–1572**
   constitutional commentary on, 449
   and due process, 828, 1571, 1572,
     2035
   and higher law, 1287
   and rule of law, 2297
*Leading Constitutional Decisions*
   (Cushman, ed.), 738
Least restrictive means test, **1573**
   and compelling state interest, 477
   legislative intent, 1593
   in regulating commercial advertising,
     203–204
   and religious liberty, 2182
Lecompton Constitution, **1574**
   Douglas (Stephen) opposition, 813
   and Kansas-Nebraska Act, 1526, 1574
*Legacy of Suppression* (Levy), 1607
Legal assistance. *See* Right to counsel
Legal culture, **1576–1578**
Legal positivism. *See* Philosophy and the
   Constitution
Legal pragmatism. *See* Pragmatism
Legal process, **1578–1580**
   access to the courts, 23
*Legal Process, The: Basic Problems in*
   *the Making and Application of Law*
   (Hart and Sacks), 1578
Legal realism, **1580–1581**
   critical legal studies, 724
   deconstruction, 756–759
   Douglas as central to movement, 814,
     1581
   interest group litigation, 1378
   Laski influence, 1563
   social science research, 2442–2443

Legal representation. *See* Right to
   counsel
Legal Service Corporation, 1378
Legal tender cases, **1581–1582**
   Chase Court, 340
   Waite Court, 2825
Legislation, **1582–1589**
   advisory opinion on, 51
   constitutionality. *See* Judicial review
   Constitution as paramount to, 1583
   District of Columbia experiments with
     "model," 796
   and dormant powers, 807
   ex post facto application, 957
   federal environmental, 1009–1010
   filibuster, 1043–1044
   First Congress, 1058
   full faith and credit, 1172
   judicial, 1457–1460
   judicial activism and restraint, 1446–
     1447
   judicial review superseding, 740, 1583,
     2389
   judicial supremacy, 1458
   legislative intent, 1592–1593
   legislative power, 1596–1597
   narcotics laws, 821–822
   overbreadth, 1866–1868
   pocket veto, 1920–1921
   poverty programs, 1973
   preemption of federal over state,
     1988–1990
   presidential influence on, 1999
   presidential ordinance-making power,
     1994–1995
   procedural review, 1585
   process in Congress, 1597–1599
   purposes and motives, 1597–1599
   rational basis test, 2121–2123
   retroactivity of, 2225–2226
   Revised Statutes of the United States
     (1875), 2227
   ripeness of challenge, 279
   statutory interpretation and, 2525
   and sufferance federalism, 996
   supermajority rules, 2585–2586
   and term limits, 2670
   *See also* Antidiscrimination legislation;
     Antitrust law; Race and sex in
     antidiscrimination law; *specific acts*
Legislative contempt power, **1589**
   limited by judicial review, 1536, 1594
   parliamentary privilege, 1888
   upheld by Marshall Court, 1433
Legislative court, **1589–1590**
   Claims Court as, 419, 981
   constitutional distinguished from, 523
   constitutional legitimacy, 1019

   Federal Rules of Civil Procedure,
     1028
   judicial appointments and tenure,
     1019
   and judicial power, 1463–1464, 1612
   as Marshall (John) invention, 1612
   as territorial court, 83
Legislative facts, **1590–1591**
   Brandeis brief, 225
   and school desegregation ruling, 254,
     255
Legislative immunity, **1591**
   as Articles of Confederation provision,
     540
   exclusion of unofficial communication,
     1324
Legislative intent, **1591–1592**
   clear statement rule, 1229
   and double jeopardy, 809–810
   and federal common law authority,
     978–979
   language of law and, 2316
   least restrictive means test, 1573
   and severability, 2388–2389
Legislative investigation, **1593–1596**
   and freedom of association, 1052,
     2866–2867
   House Committee on Un-American
     Activities, 1305
   as implied power, 1346
   Iran-Contra affair, 1401–1403
   limited by judicial review, 1536
   of loyalty and security, 605
   McCarthyism, 1701–1702
   right against self-incrimination, 2866
   *Sweezy v. New Hampshire*, 2867
   Watergate scandal, 922, 2360, 2365,
     2865
   *Watkins v. United States*, 2866–2867
Legislative power, **1596–1597**
   administrative agencies, 40–42, 1482,
     1935
   bicameralism, 171
   Civil War expansion of, 416
   under commerce clause, 1396
   constitutional explicitness on, 1471,
     1945
   delegation of, 2148, 2317
   economic regulation curbs, 1414
   executive power vs., 214
   executive prerogative and, 950
   federal elections regulation, 1940–
     1941
   federal primary elections regulation,
     2007
   in foreign affairs. *See* Congress and
     foreign policy; Senate and foreign
     policy

immigration and naturalization, 2801–
2802
*McCulloch v. Maryland* broadening,
1425
under necessary and proper clause,
1058–1059, 1425
noninterpretivist inroads seen on,
1393
as popular sovereignty, 497
postal power, 1970–1971
pre-1937 judicially implied limitations,
2934–2935
preeminence under Jeffersonian
constitutionalism, 1423
preemption, 1989–1990
privilege from arrest, 2019
Reconstruction policy, 2142–2143
regulatory agencies creation, 2148
Rehnquist Court challenges, 2169
of states, 1835
taxing and spending, 1998, 2000,
2658–2661
Legislative purposes and motives, **1597–
1599**
canons of construction, 1598
for congressional investigation, 1708
Legislative Reorganization Act (1946),
266, 494, 2360
Legislative veto, **1599–1601**
and administrative agencies, 38, 269
Burger Court and, 380
checks and balances, 343
and concurrent resolution, 485
and constitutional theory, 654
and delegation doctrine, 762
and foreign policy, 495
invalidation of, 172, 762, 1386, 1460,
1599–1600, 2129, 2148
one-house status, 762, 1333, 1599,
1600, 2148
as power over executive policymaking,
611–612
and regulatory agencies, 2148
*Lemon* test, **1602–1603, 1603–1604**
(update)
actual purpose and effect components,
1602, 2196
*Agostini* revision, 61, 1604
*Board of Education of the Westside
Community Schools v. Mergens*,
203, 1207
establishment clause, 203, 924
government aid to religious institutions, 1207
*Lemon v. Kurtzman* as basis, 1601–
1602
neutrality principle ascendancy, 1207,
1208, 1209, 2176

and religious liberty, 2175–2176
replacement suggestions, 2176
Scalia critiques, 1560, 1602
Lend-Lease Act (1941), 2290, 2841
Lesbianism. *See* Same-sex marriage;
Sexual orientation; Sexual prefer-
ence and the Constitution
*Letter concerning Toleration* (Locke),
1639
"Letters from a Farmer in Pennsylvania"
(Dickinson), 779, 1174
*Letters from Birmingham Jail* (King),
369
Letters of marque and reprisal, **1605**
congressional power to grant, 385
Lever Food and Drug Control Act
(1917), **1605**
Libel and the First Amendment, **1606–
1608, 1608–1610** (update)
absolutism, 17
actual malice standard, 1062, 1141,
1146, 1189, 1285, 1322, 1607, 1608–
1609, 2067, 2850
*Curtis Publishing Company v. Butts*,
2067
false statement of facts as low-value
speech, 1646, 1647
freedom of speech and, 1128,
1130
freedom of the press and, 1139,
1141–1142, 1146, 1729–1730
*Gertz v. Robert Welch, Inc.*, 1189
group libel, 1235–1236
*Herbert v. Lando*, 1285
*Hustler Magazine and Larry Flynt v.
Jerry Falwell*, 1322
and interpretivism, 1861
and liberal media licensing laws, 470
*Masson v. New Yorker Magazine*,
1696–1697
*New York Times Co. v. Sullivan*, 234–
235, 237, 1134, 1141, 1146, 1150,
1236, 1607, 1608, 1609, 1804–1805,
2014, 2067, 2850, 2855
plurality opinion, 829–830
press protections, 2313
and private person's recovery
standard, 1607–1608
and public figure's status, 1052, 1609,
2067
and right to privacy, 2244
truth as evidentiary factor, 1260
Warren Court and, 2848, 2850
*See also* Seditious libel
Liberal constitutional construction,
**1610–1613**
and living Constitution, 1632–1635
Marshall (John) exemplifying, 1611

Liberalism, **1613–1617**
and communitarianism, 472
and limited government, 1619
Lockean, 834
obscenity views, 1838
and value pluralism, 2778
of Warren Court, 1615, 1616, 2312,
2315, 2853, 2855–2858
Libertarianism, 16
Liberty of contract. *See* Freedom of
contract
Liberty party, 3, 182
License cases, **1617**
dual federalism, 827
liquor, 1229–1230, 1617
original package doctrine, 256, 1348,
1612
state bar on imported liquor, 1601
Licenses
broadcasting, 247, 248–249, 968, 969,
1723–1724, 2009, 2165
and freedom of expression, 2009
liquor sales, 1617
motion pictures, 1106, 1538
oil import fees, 987
Life, definition of. *See* Person
Life-sustaining treatment. *See* Right to
die
Limited government, **1618–1619**
broad construction vs., 250
contemporary limitations, 1995
Declaration of Independence on, 754
and federalism, 1001
Jeffersonian, 1425
judicial review seen as subversion of,
1498
as liberal agenda, 1613, 1619
Magna Carta as symbol of, 1663–1664
as political philosophy of Constitution,
1944, 1946
republican form of government, 2209
three specific connotations, 1618
Vattel as theorist, 2781
written constitutions and, 1474
Lincoln and constitutional theory, 1620–
1622, **1624–1625,** 2142
Lincoln-Douglas debates, **1625**
binding Supreme Court decisions,
1475
criticism of *Dred Scott* decision, 1620
Freeport Doctrine, 1148
popular sovereignty, 1963
Lincoln's plan of Reconstruction, **1625**
Line-item veto, **1625–1626, 1626–1627**
(update)
constitutional amendment proposal,
76, 2129
executive power, 949

Line-item veto (continued)
  Line Item Veto Act, 626
  unconstitutionality ruling, 1627, 2169
Line Item Veto Act (1996), 1626–1627
Lineup, 1627–1628
  right to counsel at, 1538–1539, 1627–
    1628, 2264–2265, 2818
  testimonial and nontestimonial
    compulsion, 2677
Liquor. See Alcohol; Prohibition
Listeners' rights, 1628–1629
  fairness doctrine, 968
  First Amendment, 1046, 1560
  and mail propaganda, 1560, 1628
  religion as viewpoint ruling, 1559–
    1560
  right to know, 1143, 1628, 2271
  subsidized speech and, 2567–2568
Literacy test, 1629
  Civil Rights Act of 1964, 405
  congressional ban, 1629
  effect on blacks, 392
  grandfather clause, 129, 392, 1242,
    1629
  for immigrants, 1329
  non-English schooling-level equiva-
    lence, 1527
  voting rights, 1041, 1042, 1089–1090,
    1629, 2808
  Voting Rights Act of 1965, 1629
Litigation. See Class action; Institutional
    litigation; Public law litigation
Litigation strategy, 1629–1632
Litvinov Assignment, 168
Living Constitution, 1632–1635
  as Brennan interpretive principle, 239,
    240
  expressed in McCulloch v. Maryland,
    1633
  as transformation of constitutional law,
    2712–2714
Lobbying Disclosure Act (1995), 1636
Local government, 1637–1638
  District of Columbia, 796, 797–798
  law enforcement responsibilities,
    1566, 1569
  liability limitations, 1217
  multimember districts, 1765, 2135
  municipal immunity, 1767–1768
  nonliability for employee violations,
    1751
  ordinance invalid on its face, 1645
  proprietary-rights exception, 1210–
    1211, 1212
  See also State and local government
    taxation
Long haul-short haul rate discrimination,
  1642

Interstate Commerce Act provision,
    1397, 1398
Loose construction. See Broad construc-
    tion
Louisiana Purchase Treaty (1803), 1644
  constitutional issues, 83, 228, 552,
    1422, 1644
  slavery issue, 2434
Low-value speech, 1646–1647
  broadcasting restraints on vulgar
    words, 981, 1043, 1057, 1147, 1392
  Chaplinsky v. New Hampshire, 1056
  content-based free speech restrictions,
    1056–1057, 1132–1133
  obscenity-pornography distinction as,
    1968
Loyalty oath, 1647–1648
  American Civil Liberties Union cases,
    157
  Civil War, 1647–1648, 1649, 2143
  electoral process and the First
    Amendment, 872
  Elfbrandt v. Russell, 882
  Federal Test Acts, 1029–1030
  public employees, 2066, 2904
  subversive activity definition, 1187
  Test Oath Cases, 2679
  Wieman v. Updegraff, 1649–1650
Loyalty-security programs, 1649–1650
  Attorney General's List, 138, 604,
    1436
  Court restrictions, 1536
  McCarthyism, 1702

M

Madisonian Constitution, 1657–1658,
  1659–1662
Madison's "Memorial and Remonstrance" (1785), 1662
Madison's Notes of the Debates, 1662–
  1663
  and abolitionist constitutional theory,
    3
Mafia. See Organized Crime Control Act
Magna Carta, 1663–1664
  and British constitution, 245
  civil liberties, 374, 375
  constitutionalism, 634
  due process, 439, 828, 2035
  freedom of petition, 1125
  general search, 1098, 1099
  law of the land, 1571, 1572, 2035
  reconfirmation, 489
  right to petition, 2272
  rule of law, 1663–1664, 1945, 2234,
    2297

Mail service. See Postal power
Majority opinion. See Opinion of the
  court
Malapportionment. See Reapportion-
  ment
Malice aforethought. See Libel and the
  First Amendment
Mandamus, writ of, 1666
  and Marbury v. Madison, 1668, 1669
  and original jurisdiction, 1668, 1669
  United States Courts of Appeals, 2760
Mann Act (1910), 1666
  as polygamy conviction basis, 1961
  sustained, 1294, 2899
Mann-Elkins Act (1910), 1666
  as Interstate Commerce Act supple-
    ment, 1397, 1398
Market economy. See Economic liberty
  and the Constitution; Economy;
  Law and economics theory
Marketplace of ideas, 1670–1671
  and corporate social responsibility,
    688
  freedom of speech, 1136–1137, 1299
  hate speech, 1277
  listener's rights, 1628
  right to know, 2271
  and value pluralism, 2778
Marriage and the Constitution, 1671–
  1672
  birth control rights, 182, 1233–1234,
    2203–2204
  citizenship and, 368
  equal protection, 1156–1157
  freedom of intimate association, 1118–
    1119, 1120, 1121, 1123
  as fundamental interest, 1671, 2943
  husband's feudal privileges, 1034,
    1035
  miscegenation laws, 189, 403
  miscegenation laws held invalid,
    1645–1646
  polygamy restriction, 1961–1962,
    2186, 2229
  privacy rights, 1233, 1234, 2052, 2242,
    2243, 2247, 2943
  rights issues in historical perspective,
    2252–2253
  same-sex, 147, 2307
  spousal abortion consent, 6, 2206
  women's economic rights, 91, 1112
  women's historical coverture, 2920
  Zablocki v. Redhail, 1671, 1672, 2943
  See also Divorce and the Constitution;
    Family and the Constitution
Marshall Court, 1681–1687
  American Indian decisions, 81
  appellate jurisdiction, 436–437

on bills of credit, 174
on commerce clause, 454
on contract clause, 673, 674, 675, 677, 692
on corporations, 692
doctrinal contributions, 801
and dual-sovereignty system of federalism, 570
and implied powers, 900
Justice Johnson's independence, 1433
Justice Livingston's inactivity, 1635
Justice Marshall's leadership, 1673–1675, 1681–1682
*Marbury v. Madison*, 1667–1670, 1673, 1683–1684
*McCulloch v. Maryland*, 1705–1707
nationalistic decisions, 1000, 1001, 1017
Roane critiques, 2280
on state police power, 2556
Marshall Plan, **1687**
Martial law. *See* Civil-military relations
Maryland Toleration Act (1649), **1691**
Massachusetts Bay, Colonial Charters of (1629, 1691), **1693**
and constitutionalism, 635
Massachusetts Body of Liberties (1641), **1694**
bail, 149
civil liberties, 374
as constitutional influence, 531
due process, 828
Massachusetts Circular Letter of 1768, **1694–1695**
Adams (Samuel) arguments, 31
and American constitutionalism, 643
Massachusetts Constitution (1780), **1695–1696**
abolishment of slavery in Massachusetts, 1623
Adams (Samuel) as convention delegate, 32
bicameralism, 171
framed at first constitutional convention in world history, 516
political theory underlying, 27–28, 29
rule of law, 2297
as state constitution model, 540
Massachusetts General Laws and Liberties, **1696**
Massachusetts Resolutions. *See* Embargo Acts
Mass demonstrations. *See* Demonstration
Master, special. *See* Special master
Maximum hours and minimum wages legislation, **1699–1700**
Adamson Eight-Hour Act, 33, 2912

*Adkins v. Children's Hospital*, 36, 797, 1313, 2882, 2921
*Adkins* voiding minimum wage laws, 36
Brandeis brief, 35, 219, 225, 1746, 2443, 2920
*Bunting v. Oregon* upholding, 263, 1639
and commerce clause, 456
constitutionality history, 2881–2882
District of Columbia Minimum Wage Act, 35, 797, 2882, 2921
and due process, 36, 2049
Fair Labor Standards Act, 966–967
and freedom of contract, 36, 1547, 1735–1736
interstate commerce, 1315
and interstate commerce, 2566
invalidations, 1641, 2288
*Lochner v. New York*, 1547, 1548, 1552–1553, 1638–1639, 2049
*Loewe v. Lawlor*, 1641
for manufactures, 744
*Muller v. Oregon*, 1764
and religious liberty, 2192
and states' rights, 1760
*Stettler v. O'Hara*, 2529
sustained for women, 2529
upheld, 2289
*West Coast Hotel Company v. Parrish*, 2289, 2881–2882, 2921
women and children minimum wage, 35–36, 1313, 1547
women's minimum wages, 35–36, 1547, 2921
women's working hours, 225, 1764, 2920–2921
Mayflower Compact, 531
Maysville Road Bill (1830), **1700–1701**
internal improvements halt, 1385
Jackson (Andrew) veto, 1408
McCarran Act. *See* Internal Security Act
McCarran-Walter Act. *See* Immigration and alienage
McCarthyism, **1701–1702**
academic freedom, 21–22
Alien Registration Act, 67–68
and avoidance doctrine, 142
Communist Control Act, 606
and Federal Bureau of Investigation, 976
and Korean War-inspired anticommunism, 1541
legislative investigations, 1595
loyalty oaths, 1648
loyalty-security programs, 1649
right against self-incrimination, 1233

McNabb-Mallory Rule, **1713–1714**
Federal Rules of Criminal Procedure, 1029
Mechanical jurisprudence, **1715**
Media. *See* Broadcasting; Communications and community; Communications and democracy; Freedom of the press; Free press/fair trial; Journalistic practices, tort liability, and the freedom of the press; Reporter's privilege
Medicaid-funded abortions
constitutionality of state denial, 2880
*Harris v. McRae*, 1272–1273
Hyde Amendment, 6, 67, 1325, 2205, 2205–2206
*Maher v. Roe*, 1272, 1665, 2205, 2286, 2870, 2872
Medicare. *See* Health Insurance for the Aged Act
Meese Commission, **1715–1716**
Megan's Law. *See* Sex offender notification laws
Memorandum order, **1717**
Mental illness and the Constitution, **1717–1720**, **1720** (update)
capital punishment as cruel and unusual punishment, 1070–1071
indigent's right to insanity defense, 64
insanity defense, 2061
and involuntary confinement, 1846
involuntary sterilization, 2528
prisoner's rights, 2863
psychiatric legal limitations, 2060–2062
right to treatment/right to refuse treatment, 789–790
sexual predator laws, 2406, 2407
Mental retardation and the Constitution, **1720–1722**
capital punishment, 2061
civil rights guarantees, 789, 792
Developmentally Disabled Assistance and Bill of Rights Act, 775, 789, 790
involuntary sterilization, 259, 284, 789, 791–792, 1297, 2528
involuntary commitment, 2061
not recognized as discrete and insular minority, 1382
rational basis scrutiny, 790, 792
right to die, 2268
Mercy killing. *See* Euthanasia; Right to die
Mere evidence rule, **1722**
search warrants, 2345
unreasonable search, 2767
*Warden v. Hayden*, 2833–2834

Mexican War
    as declared war, 755, 1998
    Spot Resolutions, 2469–2470
    Treaty of Guadalupe Hidalgo, 2720
    Whig opposition, 2884
Military. *See* Armed forces
Military justice, **1726–1727**
    Chase Court and, 338–339
    civilian trials, 746, 747, 830, 1464,
        1955, 2170
    civil-military relations, 385–387
    Civil War, 2841
    constitutional recognition as separate
        system, 117, 1464
    court-martials, 603
    Court of Military Appeals, 696
    habeas corpus, 1247
    jurisdiction and due process, 2937
    jurisdiction of civil court over military,
        1736
    *Milligan, Ex parte*, 338–339, 386, 402,
        448
    *Parker v. Levy*, 1879
    and political trials, 1054
Military Justice Act (1968), 2365
Military Reconstruction Acts (1867),
    **1728**
    Chase Court and, 339
    enforcement of, 1745
    Joint Committee on Reconstruction,
        1436
    and Omnibus Act, 1851–1852
    Stevens's sponsorship, 2540
Military Selective Service Act (1967),
    2357
Militia Act (1795), 416
Militia Act (1862), 571
Militias. *See* Second Amendment
Militias, modern, **1728–1729**
    constitutional controversy, 553, 2249–
        2250
Mill and freedom of expression, **1730–
    1731**
Milton and freedom of expression,
    **1737–1739**
Minimum wage. *See* Maximum hours
    and minimum wages legislation
Ministerial Act, **1739**
    fugitive from justice, 1158
    and President's discretionary power,
        289
Minnesota rate cases, **1739–1740**
    closed loophole with federal regula-
        tion, 2899
Minorities. *See* Asian Americans and the
    Constitution; American Indians and
    the Constitution; Discrete and
    insular minorities; Immigration and

alienage; Race-consciousness; Racial
    discrimination
Minors. *See* Children and the First
    Amendment; Children's rights;
    Juvenile curfew laws; Juvenile
    proceedings
*Miranda* rules, **1742–1743, 1743–1744**
    (update)
    Burger Court and, 273, 276, 1927,
        1928
    *Edwards v. Arizona*, 861, 1928
    exceptions to, 273, 276, 1327, 1802–
        1803, 1856, 1927, 1928, 1930
    "interrogation" definition, 2229–2230
    *Oregon v. Bradshaw*, 861
    police interrogation, 1922, 1926–1929,
        1930, 2256
    prisoner waiver of, 1926, 1930–1931,
        2240
    Rehnquist Court restrictions, 2169
    requirement for, 2319
    right to counsel, 1926, 1927, 1930,
        2255, 2263–2264
    self-incrimination warning, 1742–
        1744, 1865, 1922, 1926–1929, 2238,
        2239–2240
    undercover agent exception, 1327,
        1930
    violation of, 1865
    waivers of, 1926, 2240
    Warren Court and, 2850
    weakening of, 1273, 1927–1928,
        2169
    White (Byron) dissent, 2886, 2889,
        2892
Miscegenation, **1744–1745**
    antimiscegenation laws argued as
        equal treatment, 1038, 2827–2828
    antimiscegenation laws held invalid,
        1645–1646, 2309
    Black Codes, 189
    *Loving v. Virginia*, 403, 1645–1646,
        2307, 2309
    *Pace v. Alabama*, 1873, 2827–2828
    race and constitutional law, 2097
    same-sex marriage legal issues
        compared with, 2307, 2309
Misdemeanor, **1745**
    due process, 828
    felony distinction, 1031
    as impeachable offense, 1336, 1337,
        1340, 1341, 1343
    and impeachment of Presidents,
        609
    information, 1369
    and jury trial, 157, 157–158
    right to counsel, 116, 2255
    warrantless arrest, 120, 121

Missouri Compromise (1820), **1747–
    1748**
    antislavery resolution of, 568, 569
    constitutional issues, 556
    Kansas-Nebraska Act as voiding, 813,
        1525, 1526
    Pinkney and, 1910
    slavery issues, 2427, 2430, 2555
    unconstitutionality ruling, 819, 820
Monetary power, **1751–1754**
    Emergency Bank Act, 885
    gold clause cases, 1201–1202, 1751,
        2288
    Gold Reserve Act, 1202–1203
    Legal Tender Cases, 1581–1582
    *McCulloch v. Maryland*, 1583, 1585,
        1587, 1611, 1705–1707, 1751
    printing of money, 834
    *See also* Bank of the United States
        Acts; Taxing and spending powers
Monopolies. *See* Antitrust law;
    Commerce clause
Monroe Doctrine, **1755**
    Adams (John Quincy) authorship, 30
    Monroe's cabinet and crafting of, 288
    Roosevelt (Theodore) corollary, 2292
Mootness, **1758–1759, 1759–1760**
    (update)
    *Carroll v. President of Commissioners
        of Princess Anne*, 319
    *DeFunis v. Odegaard*, 759–760
    and judicial power, 1464
    and justiciability, 1520
Moral relativism. *See* Value pluralism
    and the Constitution
Morrill Act (1862), 417, **1761**
Multimember district, **1765**
    nonpurposeful racial discrimination,
        393, 1751, 1765, 2135
    reapportionment, 2135
Multinational corporations, global
    markets, and the Constitution,
    **1765–1766**
Multistate compacts. *See* Interstate
    compact
Mundt-Nixon bill (1948–1949), **1766–
    1767**
    features in Internal Security Act, 1385
    House Committee on Un-American
        Activities backing, 1305
Municipal Bankruptcy Act (1936), **1767**
    invalidation, 127
Municipal government. *See* Local
    government
Municipal immunity, **1767–1768**
    *Monroe v. Pape*, 1754
    nonliability for employee violations,
        1751

Muscle Shoals Bill (1931), 596
"Must carry" law, **1771–1772**
  broadcasting, 1147–1148, 2739–2740
  communications and community, 469–470

# N

NAACP Legal Defense & Educational Fund, **1774**
  *Brown v. Board of Education*, 253, 255, 772, 1528
  civil rights movement litigation, 411
  freedom of association in Alabama suit, 1773
  Marshall (Thurgood) contribution, 1676, 1678
  public interest law, 2071
  restrictive covenant, 2222–2223
  school desegregation, 772, 773–774
  test cases as protected political activity, 1773
NAFTA. *See* North American Free Trade Agreement
Narcotics. *See* Controlled-substance abuse; Crack cocaine and equal protection; Drug testing; Drug regulation
Nashville Convention Resolutions (1850), **1774–1775**
  slavery in the territories, 2435
National American Woman Suffrage Association, 2919
National Association for the Advancement of Colored People. *See* NAACP Legal Defense & Educational Fund
National Association of Broadcasters, 968
National Association of Colored Women, 2919
National Association of Manufacturers, 349
National Defense Act (1916), 2356
National Emergencies Act. *See* Emergency powers
National Environmental Policy Act. *See* Environmental regulation and the Constitution
National Firearms Act (1934), 2452
National Industrial Recovery Act (1933), **1775–1776**
  aims under commerce clause, 457–458
  delegation of powers, 41, 2288, 2317–2318

"Little NIRA" bituminous coal case, 321
*Panama Refining Co. v. Ryan,* 1877
*Schechter Poultry Corp. v. United States,* 2317–2318, 2592, 2819, 2820
  unconstitutionality, 457, 599, 697, 2288, 2317–2318, 2592
  Wagner Act, 2818–2819
  Wagner Act cases, 2819–2820
Nationality Act (1940), 2733
National Labor Relations Acts. *See* Taft-Hartley Labor Relations Act; Wagner Act
National Labor Relations Board, 1548–1549
  and antitrust laws, 1545
  judicial function, 2147
  upheld, 1548, 2289
  Wagner Act cases, 2819–2821
  as Wagner Act provision, 2819
National Organization for Women, 379
National police power, **1777–1780**
  armed forces excluded from, 1969
  Chase Court decision, 340
  drug traffic regulation, 804
  in employment relations, 1548
  expansion of, 1704
  general welfare clause, 1186–1187
  *Hammer v. Dagenhart,* 1261–1262
  interstate commerce restrictions, 1261–1262, 1294
  Pure Food and Drug Act, 1001, 2083–2084
  White Court expansion of, 2899
  *See also* Police power; State police power
National Prohibition cases. *See* Amending process; Eighteenth Amendment
National Rifle Association, 1243
National Security Act (1947), **1781**
National Security Agency, 2326
National security and the Fourth Amendment, **1781–1782**
  communications and democracy, 470
  and constitutional reason of state, 649
  electronic eavesdropping, 875
  freedom of speech, 1129
  freedom of the press, 1140, 1145
  Jencks Act, 1426
  loyalty-security programs, 1649–1650
  right to travel, 1257
  and scientific speech, 2326
  and terrorism control, 2675
  wiretapping provision, 2913
  *See also* Subversive activity
National unity, group conflict, and the Constitution, **1783**

National Voter Registration Act, 2812
Native American Church, 821–822, 823
Native Americans. *See* American Indians and the Constitution
Native Hawaiian sovereignty movements, **1784–1785**
Naturalization, **1785**
  and Alien Act, 67
  citizenship and, 364–365, 366, 1785
  common law and *Calvin's Case,* 294, 363
  conscientious objector eligibility, 1195
  denaturalization, 768–769
  and Internal Security Act, 1386
  pacifism and, 2325–2326
  racial restrictions, 129, 130–131, 1167
  Senate Judiciary Committee and, 2364
  visas and, 2801
  *Wong Kim Ark, United States v.,* 2922
  World War II cases, 2930
  wrongful, 367
Natural law. *See* Higher law; Natural rights and the Constitution
Natural rights and the Constitution, **1785–1787**
  Americans with Disabilities Act, 87
  *Boyd* opinion, 2339
  civil disobedience, 1537
  as constitutional fundamental, 1947
  as Declaration of Independence basis, 1419
  due process, 1233
  fundamental interests, 1172–1173
  insular cases, 1376
  and international human rights, 1387
  Lockean philosophy, 1640, 2051, 2052, 2248
  as not applied to territories, 1376
  philosophy and the Constitution, 1904
  privileges and immunities, 2019
  procedural or remedial rights vs., 1376
  property, 2051, 2052, 2053
  representation, 2201
  revolution based on, 2248, 2249–2250
  slavery abrogating, 1947, 2210
  social compact theory, 2439
  as unenumerated rights, 2753
*Nature of the Judicial Process, The* (Cardozo), 313, 314, 2901
Nazi war criminals, denaturalization proceedings, 769
Necessary and proper clause, **1790–1791**
  and American Indians, 80, 81
  amnesty, 89
  and broad construction, 250
  congressional power over federal elections, 1940

Necessary and proper clause (continued)
  congressional powers under, 1058–
    1059, 1425
  enumerated powers, 1751
  and federal power boundaries, 998,
    1011
  implied incidental powers doctrine,
    1347
  and inherent powers, 1370–1371
  intergovernmental immunity, 1382
  and judicial policymaking, 1461
  as liberal latitude to exercise specific
    powers, 1259
  and living Constitution, 1633
  *McCulloch v. Maryland*, 1674, 1685,
    1706–1707
  and monetary power, 1751
Negligence. *See* Damages claims;
  Government wrongs
*Negro and the First Amendment, The*
  (Kalven), 1525
Neutral principles, **1792–1793**
New Christian Right. *See* Religious
  fundamentalism
New Deal (constitutional significance),
  **1797–1798**
  as "constitutional moment," 764
New Deal, **1793–1797**
  administrative agencies, 40, 41
  agricultural production controls, 62–
    63
  brain trust, 2738
  bureaucracy, 266
  congressional investigations, 1595
  constitutionality defense, 226
  Court invalidations, 41, 284, 1232,
    1313, 1437–1438, 1547, 2288
  Court-packing plan, 113, 600, 697–
    699, 1437, 1794, 2288–2289
  Court tests, 2288–2289, 2819–2821
  and delegation of power challenges,
    41, 1232, 2288, 2317–2318
  devolution and federalism issues, 777
  Emergency Bank Act, 885
  and federalism, 1002
  Frankfurter supportive rulings, 1103
  gold clause cases, 1201–1202
  Gold Reserve Act, 1202–1203
  Hughes Court rulings, 1312–1316
  Hughes invalidation rulings, 1311–
    1312
  labor activity, 1546, 1547–1548, 1555
  liberalism of, 1615, 1616
  and living Constitution, 1634
  National Industrial Recovery Act aims
    and unconstitutionality, 457, 599,
    697, 1775–1776, 2288, 2317–2318,
    2592

and political parties, 1935
  Progressive agenda, 2884
  Public Utility Holding Company Act,
    2079–2080
  rational basis test, 2123
  Reed's role in, 2144
  reforms, 599
  regulatory agencies, 2147
  Roosevelt (F.D.) policies, 2288–2291
  Roosevelt Court, 2292–2293
  *Schechter Poultry Corp. v. United
    States*, 2317–2318, 2592, 2819, 2820
  Tennessee Valley Authority Act,
    2666–2667
  Wagner Act, 2818–2819
  Wagner Act cases, 2819–2821
New Jersey Colonial Charters, **1799–
  1800**
New Jersey Plan, **1800**
  and federalism, 1011
  as framework for discussion of Consti-
    tution, 519–520
  Paterson and, 1882
  as Virginia Plan alternative, 542–543
*New Republic* (periodical), 2047
New Right, **1801–1802**
Newsman's privilege. *See* Reporter's
  privilege
New York Charter of Liberties and Privi-
  leges (1683), **1804**
New York Port Authority Compact
  (1921), 1398–1399
Nineteenth Amendment, **1808–1809**
  Court rulings, 73
  ratification, 72, 92, 593
  woman suffrage, 2389, 2808, 2917–
    2918, 2919
  women's minimum wage effect, 2920–
    2921
Ninth Amendment, **1809–1813, 1813–
  1815** (update)
  on rights retained to the people, 1091
  unenumerated rights, 2752, 2754
NLRB. *See* National Labor Relations
  Board
No-knock entry, **1820**
  in drug search, 679, 1097
Nolo contendere, **1820**
Noninterpretivism, **1820**
  and democracy, 1480–1481
  dispute with interpretivism, 1393,
    1394, 1395–1396
  judicial review, 1478–1479, 1480
  as nonoriginalism, 1394
  as replacing broad construction, 250
Nonjudicial interpretation of the Constitution, **1821–1823, 1823–1824**
  (update)

by Lincoln, 1620–1622, 1624
  and living Constitution, 1632–1634
  original meaning of "commerce," 1643
  value pluralism, 2778–2779
  *See also* Commentators on the Consti-
    tution
Nonmarital children, **1824**
  adoption and race, 45–46
  citizenship of, 367
  equal protection of the laws, 917
  illegitimacy, 1325–1326
  immigration law, 1331
Nontestimonial compulsion. *See* Testimonial and nontestimonial
  compulsion
Norris-LaGuardia Act (1932), **1825–
  1826**
  antitrust applied to unions, 1545
  injunction in labor dispute, 1373
  provisions of, 596
  and Taft Court, 2638
North American Free Trade Agreement,
  **1826–1827**
  as executive agreement, 942
  and federal-state relations, 1390
North Atlantic Treaty (1949), **1827**
Northwest Ordinance (1787), **1829**
  alien suffrage, 68
  bail, 149
  King (Rufus) authorship, 1537
  "law of the land" usage, 828, 1571
  representation, 2130
  republican form of government, 2209
  rights guarantees, 742
  slavery and, 2427, 2434, 2557
  as territory governance model, 2479,
    2673
Notice, **1830**
  of accusation, 2258–2259
  administrative law, 42
  ex parte, 956
  in juvenile proceedings, 1183
  by regulatory agency, 2149
  waiver of rights, 2831
Notice clause. *See* Right to be informed
  of accusation
Noxious products doctrine, **1830**
Nuclear technology. *See* Atomic Energy
  Act
Nude dancing, **1830–1832**
Nullification, **1832–1833**
  and American System, 88
  Calhoun theory, 292
  Calhoun-Webster debate, 2871
  commentators on the Constitution on,
    450
  Exposition and Protest, 957
  Force Act, 1069, 1408, 1413–1414

as interposition, 1392
Jackson's Proclamation to the People
of South Carolina, 1408, 1409,
1413–1414
*Judge Peters, United States v.*, 1441–
1442
Madison's opposition, 1659
Pennsylvania case, 1441–1442
secession and, 2346
South Carolina ordinance, 1424, 2457
states' rights and, 2519
Tariff Act of 1828, 559, 1069, 2480
theories of the Union and, 2687
Virginia and Kentucky Resolutions,
1424
Nullification, jury. *See* Jury nullification

# O

Obiter dictum, **1835**
free press/fair trial, 1149
grants-in-aid, 1157
on Missouri Compromise unconstitutionality, 819
political question doctrine, 2202
public forum doctrine, 2067–2068
scientific speech and, 2326
Obligation of contracts, **1835–1836**
and economic liberties, 841
economic regulation as challenge to,
70–71
gold clause cases, 1201
Legal Tender Act, 340
limitations on state impairments of,
801
and state bankruptcy acts, 1848–1849
state charters for corporations, 745
and temporal limits on lawmaking
powers, 2664
unconstitutional repeal of, 2766
*See also* Contract clause; Freedom of
contract
*O'Brien* formula, **1837**
Obscenity, **1837–1839**
Brennan opinions, 235
broadcasting prohibitions, 469
*Brockett v. Spokane Arcades, Inc.*,
251, 1968
*Butler v. Michigan*, 285
child pornography, 350, 351
child-protection rationales, 351
constitutional tests for, 1716–1717,
1734–1735, 2296, 2747
definition adjustments, 251, 1048,
1130, 1194, 1414, 1734–1735, 1839,
1967, 2747–2748, 2855
dial-a-porn, 778

employee speech rights (private), 891
and fighting words, 1043
First Amendment absolutism, 17
First Amendment and, 2476
First Amendment limitations, 1047–
1048, 1128
and freedom of speech, 375
freedom of speech restrictions, 1128,
1130, 1134
injunction against sale, 1538
Lockhart articles on, 1640
as low-value speech, 1056, 1057, 1133,
1646, 1968, 2940
*Miller* test, 1130, 1734–1735, 1839,
1967, 2833
national standard over community
standard, 1414
*Paris Adult Theater I v. Slaton*, 1734–
1735, 1839
pornography definition vs., 1967,
1968
postal power over, 1970
prior restraint on film showing, 1106
procedural safeguards, 161–162
RICO Act application, 1153
*Roth v. United States*, 235, 1837, 1838,
1968, 2855
sales to minors, 1194–1195
search warrant and, 2476
standards for, 2747–2748
Stevens's views, 2534
*Ulysses* case, 2747–2748
Warren's views, 2850
"without redeeming social importance" standard, 1414, 1838
*See also* Pornography
Occupational Safety and Health Act, 44
Ocean law and the Constitution, **1840–
1841**
*See also* Admiralty and maritime jurisdiction
Office of Management and Budget,
**1846–1847**
growth and power of, 1999
increased controls of, 260
required annual deficits report, 1219
as unit of the President's Executive
Office, 289
"Official English" laws, **1847–1848**
Official immunity. *See* Executive
immunity; Immunity of public
officials; Judicial immunity; Legisla-
tive immunity; Municipal immunity;
Presidential immunity; Sovereign
immunity
OMB. *See* Office of Management and
Budget
Omnibus Act (1868), **1851–1852**

Omnibus Crime Control and Safe
Streets Act (1968), **1852**
electronic surveillance requirements,
170, 873–875, 1527, 2913
Shreveport doctrine, 2416
One person, one vote, **1852–1853**
*Avery v. Midland County*, 142
census and, 326
*Colegrove v. Green*, 440–441
electoral districting, 868, 869, 871
equal representation, 153, 2228, 2229
*Gray v. Sanders*, 1227–1228
primary elections, 2007
*On Liberty* (Mill), 1730–1731
Open fields doctrine, **1853**
warrantless investigation to seize
evidence, 1849
Open housing laws, **1853–1854**
Civil Rights Act of 1968, 407, 1026,
1437, 1854, 2220, 2221
disabled persons coverage, 791
initiation of, 2220, 2221
private racial discrimination, 1437,
2221
referendum requirement overruled,
1320
state initiative overturning, 2170–2172
zoning and, 2947
Operation Rescue. *See* Anti-abortion
movement
Opinion of the Court, **1854–1855**
Chief Justice and, 346
concurring opinion, 485
conference, 488
decision vs., 752
Marshall Court innovation, 1683
obiter dictum, 1835
plurality opinion vs., 1920
precedent, 1986–1987
public understanding of, 2078
*ratio decidendi*, 2121
seriatim, 2387
*See also* Dissenting opinion
Oral argument, **1855**
Chief Justice's role, 347
decision following, 742
Ordered liberty, **1855**
and criminal procedural due process,
2036–2037
fundamental rights, 1176
and substantive due process, 2572
Ordinance of 1784, **1856**
slavery and, 2427
territories and, 2479
Organized Crime Control Act (1970),
**1857**
immunity grant, 1335
review of sentence, 809

Organized Crime Control Act (1970)
(continued)
  upheld, 783
  use immunity, 1526
Original intent, **1857–1859**
  Bill of Rights, 1353–1354
  as Bork nomination issue, 210, 211, 2127
  congressional war powers, 1080
  as conservative agenda, 776
  constitutional interpretation, 1506
  devolution as, 776
  of Fourteenth Amendment, 178, 1086, 1088, 1091
  incorporation doctrine, 1356–1357
  interpretivism, 1393–1396
  as jurisprudence issue, 1506–1508
  living Constitution vs., 1632
  as New Right jurisprudence, 1801
  radical Populist constitutional interpretation, 2113
  ratifier intent, 2120–2021
  scant evidence of, 1611
  seditious libel, 1606–1607
  textualism vs., 2315, 2681
  See also Judicial activism and judicial restraint
Originalism, **1859–1863**
  and constitutional theory, 655–656
  historical citations in constitutional argumentation, 1291
  and judicial restraint, 1450
  ratifier intent, 2120–2121
  Rehnquist defense of, 2159–2160
  of Scalia, 2314, 2315, 2316
  shift from, 2712, 2713
  as successor term for interpretivism, 1394
Original jurisdiction, **1863–1864**
  appellate jurisdiction vs., 1468
  Article III provision, 356, 1468
  Cherokee Indian Cases, 344
  circuit courts and, 360
  Judiciary Act of 1789 provision, 1489, 1496
  Marbury v. Madison, 1444–1445, 1468–1469, 1669, 1684
  removal of cases, 2198–2199
  special master, 2462
  Supreme Court and, 2588
  and writ of mandamus, 1668, 1669
Original package doctrine, **1864–1865**
  Brown v. Maryland, 1612
  Chase Court decision, 341
  License cases, 1617
  limited to foreign commerce, 2923
  and state import tax, 256, 1348
  Webb-Kenyon Act, 2870

Overbreadth, **1866–1868**
  breach of the peace statutes, 227
  Brennan as doctrine architect, 234, 238, 251
  Broadrick v. Oklahoma, 250–251
  Brockett v. Spokane Arcades, Inc., 251
  and chilling effect, 354, 803
  and freedom of speech, 1131, 1317, 2854
  Hatch Act challenge, 1275
  hate crime law, 2123
  invalid on its face, 1400
  as litigation strategy, 1631
  loyalty oaths, 2066
  loyalty-security programs, 1536
  and sedition, 2352
  vagueness vs., 2775
Overruling, **1868–1870**
  of affirmative action intermediate scrutiny, 33
  establishment clause, 926
  expectations for Roe v. Wade, 12, 92–93
  judicial policymaking, 1462
  by Rehnquist Court, 2168
  See also Retroactivity of judicial decisions
Overt acts test, **1870–1871**
Overtime. See Maximum hours and minimum wages legislation

**P**

Pacifism. See Conscientious objection
Packers & Stockyards Act, **1873**
  consent decree, 1873
PACs. See Political action committees
Palmer raids, **1875**
  deportations of aliens, 65
  and Justice Department, 135
  and subversive advocacy, 2580
  on suspected aliens and radicals, 1875
Panama Canal Treaties, **1876**
  as Bush justification for troops in Canal Zone, 2002
  Canal Zone abolished, 1876
  Carter (Jimmy) and ratification of, 320
  and congressional power, 1876
  Roosevelt (Theodore) presidency, 2292
Panic of 1819, 555
Pardoning power, **1878**
  amnesty, 89
  Confederate amnesties, 1625
  executive discretion as absolute, 1235
  Ford pardon of Nixon, 1070, 1339, 1878, 2864, 2865

  and impeachment, 1878
  and judicial review, 467
  limits of, 2319
  as presidential power, 1235, 1878, 1996
  and Sedition Act victims, 67, 1422
  as unlimited, 1770
Parent-child relationships. See Family and the Constitution
Parliamentary privilege, **1880**
  Pitt and, 1912
  power to punish for contempt, 1880
  speech or debate clause, 2464
Parochial schools. See Government aid to religious institutions
Parody
  First Amendment coverage problems, 1377
  noncoverage by libel law, 1322
Partial-birth abortion, 13, 14–15
Passenger cases, **1880**
Passport restrictions. See Right to travel
Patent, **1880–1882**
  copyright, 1880–1881
  Court of Customs and Patent Appeals, 695–696
  Grier opinions, 1230
  intellectual property, 1337–1338, 1882
  protection of, 2326
  states' immunity from damage suits, 777
  trademark and copyright vs., 1881
Paterson Plan. See New Jersey Plan
Patients' rights, **1884–1885**
  right to die, 2266–2271
  and smallpox vaccination, 1884
  treatment refusal, 1884
Patronage, **1885–1887**
  antipatronage doctrine, 1939
  Branti v. Finkel, 226, 1939
  and bureaucracy, 268
  Elrod v. Burns, 226, 1885–1886, 1939, 1940
  merit system vs., 1892
  Pickering v. Board of Education, 1886
  Rutan v. Republican Party of Illinois, 1939, 2300–2301
Paxton's case, **1888–1889**
  general warrant, 1888
  and Otis, 1865
  writ of assistance, 132, 1099, 1888
Pendent jurisdiction, **1891**
  ancillary jurisdiction vs., 90
  Federal Rules of Civil Procedure, 1028–1029
  Pennhurst State School & Hospital v. Halderman, 1893

Pendleton Act, **1892**
  merit system for selecting U.S. employees, 1892
Pennsylvania Colonial Charters, **1894**
  bail, 151
  colonial constitutions, 1894
  and constitutionalism, 635–636
Pennsylvania Constitution of 1776, **1894–1895**
  as model for other state constitutions, 540
  Paine contribution, 27
  right against self-incrimination, 2235
  right of revolution, 2248
Pentagon Papers case
  *Gravel v. United States,* 1226
  national security vs. free press, 1129, 1139, 1140, 1145
  *New York Times Co. v. United States,* 1438–1439, 1805–1807, 2009
Penumbra theory, **1896**
  birth control, 1896, 2242
  freedom of intimate association, 1896
  right of privacy, 1810, 1896
Peonage, **1896–1897**
  *Bailey v. Alabama,* 151, 1310, 2900
  Black Codes, 189
  ruling against debt peonage ruling, 1960–1961
  as substitute for black slavery, 1896–1897
  Thirteenth Amendment and, 1960, 1961, 2900
Per curiam, **1898**
Peremptory challenges, **1898–1899**
  *Batson v. Kentucky,* 1898–1899
  and fair trial, 971
  and jury discrimination, 1510, 1511, 2088, 2170
Persian Gulf War. *See* Gulf War
Person, **1900–1901**
  abortion viability testing, 2872
  constitutional references to, 1900
  corporation as, 691, 692, 1900
  doctrines of standing, 1900
  fetus as, 5, 7, 8–9, 10, 11, 12, 14–15, 92, 1900, 2126, 2206, 2285, 2872
  Fourth Amendment concept, 1901
  property rights and human body, 2057–2058
  right of privacy, 1901
  right to die, 2267
  substantive rights of, 1901
Personal liberty laws, **1901–1902**
  as anti-fugitive slave laws device, 3, 4, 1159, 1901, 2006
  habeas corpus, 1901

  as interposition, 1392
  secession and, 2346
Personal relationships. *See* Freedom of intimate association
Personal Responsibility and Work Opportunity Reconciliation Act (1996), 2875, 2876, 2877
Petition for Redress of Grievances. *See* Freedom of petition
Petition of Right (1628), **1903**
  on bail, 148
  *Darnel's Case,* 1903
  due process, 828
  on "law of the land" and "due process," 1571
  quartering of troops, 2689
  rule of law, 1903
  sovereignty, 1903
  as statute, 84
  Third Amendment and, 1903
Petition rights. *See* Freedom of petition
Petit jury, **1903**
  juror service as political right, 1514–151
  jury size, 1515–1517
  as right of the criminally accused, 2255
  Sixth Amendment protection, 1091
  trial jury, 1903
  *See also* Jury discrimination
Philosophy and the Constitution, **1904–1906**
  Bill of Rights (United States), 1905
  constitutional jurisprudence, 1505–1506
  individual autonomy or majoritarian democracy, 1906
  legal culture, 1576–1578
  legal process school, 1578–1579
  Lockean doctrines, 1639–1640
  natural rights, 1904
  original intent, 1506–1508, 1857–1859, 2127–2128
  postmodern interpretation, 1971–1972
  pragmatism, 1982–1984
  and Reconstruction, 1905
  separation of powers, 1904
  theories of judicial review, 1905
  *See also* Political philosophy of the Constitution
Physician-assisted suicide. *See* Right to die
Picketing, **1906–1908**
  and boycott, 215, 1551
  and breach of peace, 702
  as civil disobedience act, 370
  civil rights boycott, 1551, 1556

  clear and present danger test, 426
  "content control," 1907
  First Amendment protection, 375, 1047, 1556, 1921–1922
  freedom of speech and, 1550, 1907
  handbilling vs., 1553, 1906
  individual residence ban, 1156
  injunction, 1192, 1373, 1547, 2733
  labor movement, 1906
  regulation of, 1550–1551, 1561
  in shopping centers, 1308, 2414
  *Thornhill v. Alabama,* 1555
  "unlawful objective test," 1907
  upholding of peaceful, 1548, 1555, 1556
Pinckney Plan, **1909**
Plain feel doctrine, **1912–1913**
Plain view doctrine, **1913, 1913–1914** (update)
  and open fields doctrine, 1853
  plain feel doctrine, 1912
  search and seizure, 1913, 2680
Plea bargaining, **1917–1918**
  consent decree, 507
  sentencing, 2367
  speedy trial, 2465
  unconstitutional conditions, 2749
  waiver of constitutional rights, 2831
  Warren Court and, 716
Plurality opinion, **1920**
  libel and, 829–830
  as precedent, 1987
Plural marriage. *See* Polygamy
Pocket veto, **1920–1921**
  first employment, 1409
  uses, 2784–2785
Pocket Veto Case, **1921**
Police action, **1921**
  arrest, 120
  Bricker Amendment, 243–244
  declaration of war, 755–756
  Korean War, 603, 1541–1542, 1921
  and war powers, 2843, 2844
Police interrogation and confessions, **1922–1930, 1930–1931** (update 1), **1931–1932** (update 2)
  *Brown v. Mississippi,* 256, 1923, 1924
  Burger Court and, 1929
  coerced confessions, 329, 2237
  defendant's state of mind, 2062
  due process test, 1280
  *Escobedo v. Illinois,* 1925, 1926, 2263, 2264, 2856
  inadmissible confession, 1931
  "interrogation" definition, 2229–2230
  juvenile proceedings, 1522
  *Massiah v. United States,* 1925, 1929
  McNabb-Mallory Rule, 1713–1714

Police interrogation and confessions
  (continued)
  *Miranda* rules, 716, 1138, 1742–1744,
    1922, 1923, 1926–1929, 1930, 2238,
    2239–2240, 2263–2264, 2850, 2856
  *Miranda* rules waiver, 1930–1931
  Omnibus Crime Control and Safe
    Streets Act, 1852
  right against self-incrimination, 2238,
    2239–2240
  rights of criminally accused, 2256,
    2856
  right to counsel, 1923, 1926, 1927,
    1930, 1931, 2263
  untrustworthiness rationale, 1924,
    1929
  voluntariness test, 1742–1743, 1924–
    1925, 1926, 1929, 1930, 2062, 2286
Police power, **1932**
  abuse of, 720
  and affected with a public interest
    doctrine, 52, 1788–1789
  and American Indians, 80, 81
  commentators of the Constitution on,
    451
  constitutionalism and, 642
  definition, 1932
  and District of Columbia, 35
  drug regulation, 823
  economic due process, 838
  and eminent domain, 889
  freedom of contract subject to, 1294
  Freund (E.) exposition of, 1154–1155
  governmental assistance to children,
    348
  inalienable, 211–212, 1350
  postal regulation, 1970
  rate regulation, 1023
  reserved power, 2218
  vaccination and, 1415
  vested rights and, 2783
  zoning as, 2944–2945, 2946
  *See also* National police power;
    Reserved police power; State police
    power
Police pursuits and constitutional rights,
  **1932**
Political action committees, **1932–1933**
  campaign finance, 296
Political parties, **1933–1937, 1937–**
  **1938** (update)
  bipartisan foreign policy, 1076
  direct primaries, 788, 789
  Electoral College, 2740
  electoral districting, 868
  and federalism, 258, 1005–1006,
    1940
  Federalists, 1015–1017, 2861

federal judiciary appointments, 1019–
  1020
first demarcation of, 2861
freedom of association, 1108
gerrymander, 1188–1189, 1306
minor parties' status, 257, 1216, 1938
one-party primaries, 1041
patronage, 268, 1885–1886, 1939,
  2300–2301
and presidential impeachment, 1342
presidential nominating conventions,
  1934–1936
primary election, 2006–2008
public employee restrictions, 2066
reapportionment, 2136, 2137
shifts during 1850's, 564, 575–576
soft money spending, 1938
*Timmons v. Twin Cities Area New*
  *York*, 1938
two-party system, 1940
Washington's warning against, 1934
*See also* Campaign finance; Republican party; Whig party
Political parties, elections, and constitutional law, **1938–1940**
  abortion issue, 11, 2872
  affirmative action backlash, 56
  antidiscrimination legislation, 98
  control over nominating process, 1938
  electoral districting, 868
  presidential election of 1796, 549
  presidential election of 1800, 549–550
  as second and unofficial government,
    258
  *See also* Ballot access; Campaign
    finance
Political parties in constitutional law,
  **1940–1944**
  *Elrod v. Burns*, 226, 1939, 1940
  *Terry v. Adams*, 1941
Political philosophy of the Constitution,
  **1944–1947, 1947–1949** (update)
  critics of, 1957
  deconstruction of, 756–759
  interest groups, 1380–1382, 1947
  liberal construction and, 1610–1613
  liberalism and, 1613–1617
  liberty emphasized over virtue, 1948–
    1949
  Montesquieu's influence, 1755
  pragmatism, 1982–1984
  property linked with liberty, 2051
  and questions of constitutional juris-
    prudence, 1507
  ratifier intent, 2120
  republicanism, 2211–2213
  republicanism and modern theory,
    2213–2215

selective judicial activism, 1447–1448
*See also* Interpretivism; Original
  intent; Originalism; Philosophy and
  the Constitution
Political question doctrine, **1949–1951,**
  **1951–1953** (update 1), **1953**
  (update 2)
  *Baker v. Carr*, 138, 152–153, 233,
    237, 1470, 1951, 1952, 1953
  Civil War blockade decision as, 2022
  *Field v. Clark* precedent, 1039
  foreign affairs, 1076
  guarantee clause, 1239
  hearing of evidence against impeached
    judge, 1819
  and judicial restraint, 1450
  and justiciability, 1520, 1653, 1955
  as liberal constitutional construction,
    1612
  Lincoln's affirmation of, 1624
  *Luther v. Borden*, 1652–1653, 2210
  *Nixon v. United States*, 1953
  as precluding judicial review, 1454,
    1470
  and representation, 2202–2203
  state action, 1652–163
  Taney's reinforcement, 2650
Political speech. *See* Anonymous
  political speech; Campaign finance;
  Electoral process and the First
  Amendment; First Amendment;
  Freedom of speech; Subversion
  advocacy
Political trials, **1953–1956**
Politics, **1956–1958**
  and judicial independence, 1455–1457
  majoritarian vs. minoritarian bias,
    1956–1957
  and Supreme Court appointments,
    1615
  *See also* Conservatism; Federalists;
    Jacksonianism; Jeffersonians; Liber-
    alism; Political parties; Political
    question doctrine; Populism;
    Progressivism; Republican party;
    Whig party
Poll tax, **1961**
  *Breedlove v. Suttles*, 228, 1961
  Court denial of, 1271–1272
  Court upholding of, 228
  as equal protection denial, 1271
  as invidious discrimination, 1401
  Twenty-Fourth Amendment abolish-
    ment of, 73, 377, 1306, 1961, 2741
  voting rights and, 392, 2808
  as wealth discrimination, 1362, 1974,
    2879
  *See also* Capitation taxes

Pollution. *See* Environmental regulation and the Constitution; Federalism and environmental law; Waste, pollution, and the Constitution

Polygamy, **1962–1962**
beliefs vs. practices distinction, 2186, 2229
free exercise clause, 748, 1048, 1049
petition campaign, 2273
*Reynolds v. United States*, 2180, 2186, 2229

Popular consent. *See* Popular sovereignty in democratic political theory

Popular sovereignty, **1962**
Kansas-Nebraska Act, 1525, 1526
Lincoln-Douglas debates, 1620, 1963
slavery in territories, 812, 1525, 1526, 1627, 1962, 2435
Taney Court and, 820
Wilmot Proviso and, 563, 1962, 2908

Popular sovereignty in democratic political theory, **1962–1964**
Adams (John) reservations, 27
and amending process, 76, 77, 78
as constitutional political philosophy, 1945
and constitutional theory, 766
and Declaration of Independence, 752, 1962, 2248
and deliberative democracy, 763–764
and direct democracy, 785, 786
Framers' distrust of, 785
freedom of speech, 1126–1127
guarantee clause, 1238
Jacksonian, 1411–1413
Jeffersonian, 1423
through legislative power, 497
New Right jurisprudence, 1801
republican form of government, 2209
and right of revolution, 2248–2249
seditious libel and, 2352–2353

Populism, **1964–1965**
constitutional amendments, 72
direct democracy, 785–785, 787–788
republican government vs., 1963
*See also* Popular sovereignty in democratic political theory

Populist constitutional interpretation. *See* Nonjudicial interpretation of the Constitution; Radical Populist Constitutional interpretation

Pornography, **1965–1967**
child pornography, 350, 351, 375, 1646, 1802
content-neutral vs. content-based regulation, 1054, 1057
dial-a-porn, 778, 1148

First Amendment protections, 1965–1968
as hate speech, 1277–1278
Indiana ordinance unconstitutionality, 1966–1968
Internet, 1391
as low-value speech, 1134, 1646
Meese Commission, 1715–1716
as sex discrimination, 1134, 1965–1966, 1966–1968
Stevens's views, 2530
Stewart's "know it when I see it" aphorism, 1414, 1965
workplace harassment, 2926
*See also* Obscenity

Pornography and feminism, **1966–1969**
gender inequality argument, 1965–1966
hate speech theory, 1277–1278
regulation advocacy, 1054, 1057, 1134

Pornography over the telephone. *See* Dial-a-porn

Posse Comitatus Act (1878), **1969**
military enforcement of domestic law, 1568–1569
and President's use of armed forces, 448

Postal power, **1970–1971**
Espionage Act powers, 2352
as federal criminal jurisdiction basis, 1567
mail refusal for antislavery literature, 384, 2425
over alleged foreign subversive propaganda, 1560, 1628

Postmodernism and constitutional interpretation, **1971–1972**
deconstruction, 756–759, 1616
pragmatism, 1983

Poverty. *See* Indigent; Wealth discrimination; Welfare benefits

Poverty law, **1972–1975**
*Edward v. California*, 1973
welfare state, 2874–2875, 2877–2881
*See also* Welfare benefits; Welfare rights

Pragmatism, **1982–1983, 1983–1984** (update)
abortion decisions, 11
academic freedom, 21
of Clinton administration, 432
deconstruction, 756–759
formalist ideas supplanted by, 2339, 2342, 2343
as Holmes's approach, 1983
legal realism, 1580–1581
and living Constitution, 1632, 1633

Prayers in school. *See* Religion in public schools; School prayers

Preamble, **1985–1986**
and amendment process (outside Article V), 78
deconstructionist readings of, 758

Precedent, **1986–1988**
abortion rights, 12
affirmative action, 1304
campaign finance, 296
and common law, 465
and constitutional theory, 656
and interpretivism, 1395
and judicial activism and restraint, 1450
*Marbury v. Madison* as, 1669–1670
in New Deal, 1798
and opinion of the Court, 1854
and originalism, 1862
and overruling, 1868
Rehnquist Court overrulings, 2168
stare decisis, 2477–2478

Preemption, **1988–1989, 1989–1990** (update)
and air traffic regulation, 263
and aliens, 66
and concurrent powers of federal and state governments, 484
and federalism, 996, 1010, 1289–1290
Fugitive Slave Act (1793) enforcement, 2555
and labor activity, 1554
legislative intent, 1593

Preferred freedoms, **1990–1991**
Court's special role, 1311
and First Amendment-Fourteenth Amendment incorporation, 1051
fundamental rights, 1176
Rutledge endorsement, 2302
*See also* First Amendment; *specific freedoms*

Presentment, **1991**
grand jury, 1220
law of the land, 828
line-item veto act violating, 1627

President and the treaty power, **1991–1994**
as enumerated power, 1996
as foreign affairs power, 1071, 1074
Senate advice and consent, 47, 1073

Presidential Election Campaign Fund Act. *See* Federal Election Campaign Acts

Presidential immunity, **1994**
as absolute for official actions, 1335
*Clinton v. Jones*, 433–434, 1335, 1994
*Nixon, United States v.*, 1818, 1994
*Nixon v. Fitzgerald*, 1335, 1994

Presidential ordinance-making power, **1994–1995**
and concurrent resolution, 485
Presidential powers, 949, **1995–2000**
appointing and removal, 109–111
Boland Amendment, 206
budget preparation and submission, 260, 261–62
congressional war powers vs., 755–756
crisis-enhanced, 741, 2290
differentiated from legislative power, 214
domestic violence clause, 803
emergency, 886–887
executive orders, 239
executive power, 946–949
expansive vs. narrow view of, 1995–1996
federal judicial appointments, 1018, 1019–1020
foreign affairs, 1071, 1073–1076, 1078–1081, 1996–1997, 2289–2290, 2836–2837
Hamilton's theory of, 2836–2837
implied, 1346
and impoundment of funds, 1349
independent counsel and judicial restrictions of, 1360
inherent, 1996, 2841
International Emergency Economic Powers Act, 1386
Jacksonian magnification of, 1409
Johnson's (Lyndon) concept of, 1430
judicial appointments, 1455–1456
judicial review vs., 1474–1475
Justice Jackson's sliding scale, 1996
Justice Story's views, 2554
Korean War, 1541
line-item veto proposals, 1625, 1626–1627
pardoning power, 1235, 1878, 1996
Prize Cases, 2866
Proclamation of Neutrality, 1259, 2045–2046
regulatory agencies, 2148–2149
Rehnquist Court restrictions, 2169
Roosevelt's (Theodore) broad view of, 1995, 2291
spending, 2000–2001
steel seizure controversy, 2526–2527, 2839, 2941
Supreme Court justice appointments, 111–112, 1018–1019, 1485
treaty power, 1991–1994
Truman's view of, 2734–2735
veto power, 196, 322, 547, 1999, 2784–2785

war powers. *See* Presidential war powers
*Youngstown Sheet & Tube Co. v. Sawyer*, 2941
Presidential removal. *See* Impeachment
Presidential spending power, **2000–2001**
impoundment of funds, 1349–1340, 1999
Presidential succession, **2001–2002**
Twentieth Amendment, 2741
Twenty-Fifth Amendment, 73, 608–609, 2002, 2741
by vice president, 2786
Presidential war powers, **2002–2003**
authority as commander-in-chief, 1075, 1996, 1997, 1998, 2844
based on practice and precedent, 1997–1998
Bush approach, 2002, 2843
Clinton approach, 1079, 2002–2003, 2844
concurrent resolution, 1998, 2838, 2843
for ending war, 494
Hamiltonian views of, 2836–2837
for initiating war, 1080
limitations, 2839
Lincoln's view of, 574, 1620–1621, 2840–2841
Prize Cases, 2022
Roosevelt's (F. D.) use of, 2290–2291
Truman's use of, 603
undeclared wars, 756, 1075
War Powers Acts, 1998
War Powers Resolution, 610–611, 1998, 2838–2839, 2843
in World War I, 2927–2928
*See also* Congressional war powers; War powers
Press freedom. *See* Freedom of the press; Free press/fair trial
Presumption of constitutionality. *See* Rational basis; Standard of review
Pretrial disclosure, **2003–2004**
accusation notice, 2259
confrontation right, 492
and fair trial, 972
Preventive detention, **2004–2006**
bail, 149, 150, 2005
Burger Court and, 273
Internal Security Act provisions, 1385–1386
Japanese American cases, 1415–1417
of juvenile offenders, 2005, 2317
punitive nature of, 2317
Racketeer Influences and Corrupt Organizations Act (RICO), 2306

Rehnquist's views, 2317
*Salerno, United States v.,* 2162
Price controls. *See* Economic regulation; Police action; State police action
Price-fixing. *See* Antitrust law; Economic regulation
Primary election, **2006–2007, 2007–2008** (update)
as Article I voting right, 1941
black voter exclusion, 1041–1042, 1238, 2436
black voter participation, 392, 411
closed to independents, 1942
as direct democracy, 764
as direct elections, 788, 789, 1557
equal protection, 909
and independent voters, 1938, 1942
literacy test, 2485
opened to independents, 1938
party autonomy, 1938–1939
Populist platform, 1964
Progressive advocacy, 2047
racial discrimination, 1818, 1819
state action and, 1942, 2485
test case, 410, 423
white primary cases, 1941
Prior restraint and censorship, **2009–2011**
demonstration rights, 768
Espionage Act, 923
First Amendment rights, 1049, 1317, 1788
Fourteenth Amendment rights, 1317
freedom of assembly, 1107
freedom of the press, 1138, 1139, 1144, 1145, 1438
free press/fair trial, 1150–1151
gag law, 1138, 1142
journalistic tort claims, 1438–1439
listeners' rights, 1628
motion pictures, 1106
*Near v. Minnesota,* 1788, 1806, 2009
*Nebraska Press Association v. Stuart,* 1789, 2010
Pentagon Papers case, 1438–1439, 1805–1807, 2009
religious services in park without permit, 1807
World War I, 2927
Prior testimony. *See* Confrontation, right of
Prisoners' rights, **2011–2012, 2012–2013** (update 1), **2013** (update 2)
access to the courts, 23, 212, 2046
and body search, 205, 2013, 2244–2245
Burger Court on, 272

Civil Rights of Institutionalized
Persons Act, 653
constitutional violations and remedies,
654
correspondence censorship, 2046
cruel and unusual punishment, 654,
730, 731
drug testing, 824
freedom of speech regulation, 1134
habeas corpus, 1246–1255, 1434
lack of constitutional guarantees, 715
medical needs, 721
mental illness treatment with antipsychotic drugs, 2863
*Pell v. Procunier*, 1891
and privacy rights, 2244–2245
psychiatric treatment refusal, 2061
public forum doctrine, 2069
religious free expression, 1851, 2190
remedial litigation restraints, 1504
Stevens's views, 2529
voluntary self-incrimination, 1327
writ-writing assistance, 1434
Prison Litigation and Reform Act (1995),
1504
Privacy. *See* Reasonable expectation of
privacy; Right of privacy
Privacy Act (1974), **2013–2014**
restricting flow of loyalty-security
information, 1650
Senate Subcommittee on Constitutional Rights, 2365
Privacy and the First Amendment,
**2014–2015**
Private contract. *See* Freedom of
contract
Private discrimination, **2015–2017**
and antidiscrimination legislation,
413
and Civil Rights Act of 1866, 403
equal access laws, 2063
*Reitman v. Mulkey*, 2170–2171
residential discrimination, 2221
restrictive covenant, 2222–2223
*Runyon v. McCrary*, 2299–2300
state initiative supporting, 2170–
2172
state laws vs., 1089
voting rights, 1415, 2938
*Yarbrough, Ex parte*, 2938
Privatization and the Constitution,
**2017–2018**
Privilege, evidentiary. *See* Evidentiary
privilege
Privilege against self-incrimination. *See*
Right against self-incrimination
Privileged comment. *See* Libel and the
First Amendment

Privilege from arrest, **2019**
congressional privileges and immunities, 501
Privilege-right distinction. *See* Right-
privilege distinction
Privileges and immunities, **2019–2022**
abortion residency requirement, 2285
alien claims, 65
analysis for applying, 1798–1799
and antidiscrimination legislation, 96,
2021
Articles of Confederation clause, 540
and choice of law, 357
of citizens, 364, 686, 1354, 2019, 2021
congressional, 501–502
and federalism, 998
Fourteenth Amendment protection,
181, 1084, 1087–1088, 1091, 1125,
1357, 2020–2021, 2305
fundamental interests, 1172
and interstate commerce, 805, 806
interstate discrimination prohibitions,
1211–1212
nonresident employment ban as
violating, 1286, 2020
privileges as distinct from immunities,
2251
and racial discrimination, 3
and search and seizure, 215–216
*Slaughterhouse* cases, 1091, 1354,
2021
state nonresident discrimination, 1286,
2020, 2218
substantive due process and, 2570,
2577
vested rights, 2784
voting rights and, 2388
women's claims, 218, 2920
Privy council, **2022**
Prize Cases (1863), **2022**
constitutionality upheld, 1230, 2868
and constitutional reason of state, 649
legality of blockade around seceding
states, 415
Probable cause, **2022–2024**
for administrative search, 43–44, 1095
*Aguilar v. Texas*, 2330, 2331
arrest, 120
arrest warrant, 120, 121
automobile search, 140, 244, 319, 329,
2169, 2846
civil forfeiture, 372–373
DNA forensic samples, 800
*Draper v. United States*, 2330
drug testing, 822, 825, 826, 827
dwelling inspections, 294
exclusionary rule, 938
exigent circumstances search, 956

fixed/variable, 2331
flight from officer not basis for, 2922
Fourth Amendment and, 2022–2024,
2331, 2333, 2334, 2338, 2339
grand jury, 1220, 1222
hearsay, 818
indictment, 1361
informant's tip, 1327, 1368
no-knock entry, 1820
plain view doctrine, 1913
prosecutorial discretion, 2058
real evidence, 2130
search and seizure, 1095, 2139
search warrant, 141, 1092, 1098, 1725,
2469, 2948
*Spinelli v. United States*, 2330
stop and frisk rule, 2552, 2675, 2939
third-party consent, 2689
traffic stops, 2711
unreasonable search, 71, 2022–2023,
2767
vagrancy laws, 2774
warrantless search, 140, 2329, 2846
wiretapping approval, 2913
Procedural activism/restraint. *See*
Judicial activism and judicial
restraint
Procedural due process of law, civil,
**2024–2031, 2031–2034** (update 1),
**2034–2035** (update 2)
administrative, 266, 1481–1482
alien removal, 1325
*Bishop v. Wood*, 184
and civil forfeiture, 2056
computer technology, 481
criminal due process vs., 709
damages, 739
deportation, 770
entitlement, 897, 2880–2881
failure to rehire nontenured college
teacher, 203
freedom of intimate association, 1121
*Hurtado v. California*, 1321–1322
indigency, 1362
involuntary sterilization, 2422
and irrebuttable presumption, 1404
judicial review of administrative acts,
1481–1482
juvenile curfew laws, 1521
juvenile proceedings, 1523–1524
and law of the land, 828
mandatory maternity leave, 430
paddling of students, 1370
*Parham v. J. R.*, 1878
*Paul v. Davis*, 1887–1888
property cases, 1749, 2053
public employees protections, 2066–
2067

Procedural due process of law, civil (continued)
punitive damages, 2082–2083
railroad rates, 346
by regulatory agencies, 2149
Social Security Act, 2445
student suspension, 1205
student termination, 201
taking of property, 2052
tort law, 2706
Procedural due process of law, criminal, **2035–2042, 2042–2045** (update)
bail, 147–151
civil due process vs., 709
exclusionary rule, 1666–1667, 2039
habeas corpus, 1100–1101, 1246–1255
indigent's right to prepare insanity defense, 64
irrebuttable presumption, 1404
jury service rights, 1514–1515
*Moore v. Dempsey*, 1758
police interrogation and confession, 1922–1932
preventive detention, 2306
prisoners' rights, 2013, 2863
public trial, 2076–2077
reasonable doubt, 2138–2139
sentencing, 2366, 2367
Warren Court and, 380
Process theory. *See* Legal process
Prochoice commentary. *See* Abortion and the Constitution
Proclamation of Neutrality (1793), **2045–2046**
cabinet participation, 288
executive power, 1259
Washington's issuance, 2861
Proclamations. *See* Presidential ordinance-making power
Production, **2046**
commerce and, 2560
Fair Labor Standards Act coverage, 966–967, 1539
interstate commerce distinction, 1536, 1539–1540
New Deal agricultural controls, 62
Progressive constitutional thought, **2046–2048**
Darwinism and, 2713
judicial review and, 383
Wilson (Woodrow) theory, 2911
Progressivism, **2048–2050**
child labor regulation, 2900
civil service statutes, 268
constitutional amendments, 72
constitutional interpretation, 1309
constitutional theory, 2046–2048

Declaration of Independence citations, 754
devolution and federalism issues, 777
direct election, 788
direct primary, 1557
economy and, 852
and federalism, 1008
initiative, 785, 1371
Justice Brandeis's views, 219, 223–224
Justice Day's views, 749
Justice Hand's (Learned) views, 1263
Justice Hughes's views, 1309–1310
LaFollette-Wheeler presidential ticket, 1557, 2884
national executive budget system, 261
and Populism, 1964
as prohibition movement ally, 2050
Pure Food and Drug Act, 2083–2084
recall, 2141
referendum, 785, 1557, 2146
representation reforms, 2202
as Roosevelt (Theodore) influence, 2292
White Court rulings, 2900
woman suffrage advocacy, 2918
Prohibition, **2050**
and American Indians, 82
Eighteenth Amendment, 72, 75, 593, 598, 862
and federalism, 1168–1169
petition campaign, 2273
repeal of, 75, 594, 598, 2050, 2741
and state regulation of commerce, 1601, 2870
Taft Court and, 2641
Twenty-First Amendment, 73, 74–75, 594, 598
Volstead Act, 2803–2804
and woman suffrage movement, 2919
World War I, 2927
Prohibition, writ of, **2050**
United States Courts of Appeals, 2050, 2760
Prohibition of Slave Trade Act (1807), **2050**
as compromise, 2429
Prolife movement. *See* Anti-abortion movement
Proof standard. *See* Burden of proof; Reasonable doubt
Property, **2051**
alien ownership limitations, 129, 131
antiredistributive principle, 2051–2052
civil forfeiture, 372
constitutional respect for, 1945–1946, 2051
deprivation of, 2316

and due process, 1697
eminent domain, 2643
environmental regulation of private lands, 903
forfeiture in drug trafficking cases, 680
and homeless people, 1302
jurisdiction to tax, 1504–1505
just compensation, 1113, 1519
legal meaning, 2053, 2057, 2646
public forum criteria, 2068–2069
regulatory takings, 2149–2150, 2646
restrictive covenant, 2222–2223
and right of privacy, 2243
school district voting rights, 1542
as school finance basis, 1974–1975, 1977, 2309–2310, 2387, 2874
slaves as, 2426–2427
as voting requirement, 2052–2053, 2806
zoning, 2944–2946
*See also* Public forum; Taking of property
Property rights, **2051–2055, 2055–2057** (update)
of American Indians, 80, 82
*Charles River Bridge v. Warren Bridge Company*, 331–333
and contract clause, 673
of corporations, 687
*Granger* cases, 1224–1225
inheritance by illegitimate children, 1325–1326
intellectual property law, 1377–1378
investment-backed expectations and, 1564
as issue in free speech challenges, 1566
legislation adversely affecting, 2781
married women's coverture, 2920
procedural due process, 2035
racial equality in, 259
Rehnquist Court and, 2055–2056
sex discrimination, 36, 1112, 2920
slavery and, 2427
Stevens's views, 2532
substantive due process protection, 212, 259, 2048–2049, 2052, 2055–2056
Third Amendment affirmation, 2689
third-party consent, 2690
vested rights, 2782–2784
zoning infringement, 2946
Property rights and the human body, **2057–2058**
organ transplants and sales, 2057–2058
tort protections, 2057

Proprietary prerogatives. *See* Government as proprietor
Prosecutorial discretion and its constitutional limits, **2058–2059**
    double jeopardy, 807–811
    evidence disclosure, 972, 2004
    fair trial, 971–972
    federal felony, 1568
    immunity from suit, 1328
    independent counsel, 1359–1360
    jury nullification, 1512
    pretrial disclosure, 2004, 2259
    probable cause, 2023
    racial discrimination, 2058, 2059, 2088
    rights of the criminally accused, 2254–2257
Protests. *See* Civil disobedience; Demonstration
Psychiatry and constitutional law, **2060–2062**
Public accommodations, **2062–2063**
    Americans with Disabilities Act, 86, 87
    antidiscrimination legislation, 97, 168, 413, 1089
    civil liberties and, 379
    Civil Rights Act of 1875, 404, 1089, 1437, 2062
    Civil Rights Act of 1964, 405, 1282–1283
    medical facility abortion restrictions, 7–9, 12
    *Plessy v. Ferguson* legitimizing segregation, 1919
    segregation in, 253, 2354, 2415, 2420, 2486, 2693
    separate but equal doctrine, 1918, 1919
    sexual preference discrimination, 1320
    sit-ins, 168, 2420
Public assistance. *See* Welfare benefits; Welfare rights
Public choice theory and constitutional jurisprudence, **2063–2064**
    Article III and, 122
Public employees, **2065–2067**
    affirmative action, 57
    alien exclusions, 1065, 1077, 1262, 1331
    civil service statutes, 268
    compensation for outside speeches or articles, 1782
    congressional regulation of state and municipal, 1776
    damages claims against, 740
    discharge for criticizing superior upheld, 2866
    drug testing of, 824–827, 1096

Fair Labor Standards Act application, 967, 1549
Federal Bureau of Investigation investigations of, 976
federal rights violation suit, 1751
federal segregation, 1025, 2911
federal segregation ended, 605
and First Amendment, 36, 2252
free speech rights, 22, 892, 1134, 1137, 2866
Hatch Act, 251, 268, 1275
intergovernmental taxation, 1226, 1384
labor relations rights, 1552
liabilities for wrongs, 1217–1218
loyalty oath, 1187, 1648, 2904
loyalty-security programs, 1649–1650
merit system, 1892
overbreadth doctrine, 150–251
patronage, 226, 268, 1885–1887, 1939
Pendleton Act, 1892
political activity prohibition, 251, 268, 1275
right-privilege distinction, 22, 36, 2065–2066, 2252
Public facilities. *See* Public accommodations
Public figure, **2067**
    defamation vs. freedom of the press, 1133, 1141, 1146, 2014
    libel as actual malice, 1062, 1189, 1285, 1322, 1607, 1609, 2067, 2850, 2855
    nonrecovery of defamation damages, 1133, 1322
Public forum, **2067–2068, 2068–2069** (update 1), **2069–2071** (update 2)
    access to, 369
    airport terminals, 1391
    Burger Court and, 2167
    captive audience, 313
    children's speech rights, 351
    *Cornelius v. NAACP Legal Defense and Educational Fund, Inc.,* 686–687
    *Cox v. Louisiana,* 702
    *Cox v. New Hampshire,* 702
    criteria, 2068–2069
    demonstrations, 702, 767
    distribution of literature, 1283, 1317, 1391
    freedom of assembly, 702, 1107, 1317
    freedom of speech limitations, 34, 203, 369, 1131, 1134, 2009, 2067, 2167
    hostile audience, 1304–1305
    Hughes Court ruling, 1317

nonpublic forum distinction, 2068–2069
*Perry Education Association v. Perry Local Educators' Association,* 1899
picketing standards, 702, 1550–1551
posting of political campaign signs, 369
property rights vs. free speech, 1565–1566
Rehnquist Court and, 2167
religion as "viewpoint" ruling, 1560
religious speech, 2173, 2189–2190, 2194, 2904
religious symbols displays, 312, 1054–1055, 1653, 2166, 2196–2197
religious use of state property, 2198
shopping centers, 476, 1131, 1308, 1566, 1672, 2060, 2414–2415
speeches, parades, and meetings, 702
Public interest law, **2071–2072**
    Brandeis influence on, 219, 223–224
    standard of review, 1588
    *See also* Judicial legislation; Judicial strategy; Public law litigation
Publicity. *See* Commercial speech; Intellectual property law and the First Amendment
Public law litigation, **2072–2073**
    and legal process school, 1578
Public purpose doctrine, **2073–2076**
    Dillon as leading advocate, 783–784
    narrow interpretations of, 2311
    regulatory takings, 2151
    taking of property, 2055, 2074–2076
Public relief. *See* Welfare benefits
Public school desegregation. *See* Desegregation
Public schools. *See* Education and the Constitution; Religion in public schools
Public trial, **2076–2078**
    closed pretrial proceedings, 1181, 1214, 2077
    free press/fair trial, 1142, 2077
    *Richmond Newspapers, Inc. v. Virginia,* 2231–2232, 2271–2272
    as right of criminally accused, 2256
Public understanding of Supreme Court opinions, **2078–2079**
    journalists' coverage of proceedings, 1439–1441
Public use, **2079**
    affected with a public interest, 2917
    just compensation for property taken, 1519
    Peckham's views, 1890
    public purpose doctrine, 2074–2075

Public utilities regulation. *See* Economic regulation

Public Utility Holding Company Act (1935), **2079–2080**
  securities law, 2350

Public works. *See* Internal improvements; New Deal

Puerto Rico, **2080**
  commonwealth status, 468
  emigrant voting rights, 1527, 1629
  federal district court, 1491, 1492
  gambling statute, 1969
  legislative court, 1589
  territorial status, 2672

Puerto Rico, constitutional status of, **2080–2081**
  insular cases, 1375–1376

Punishment. *See* Capital punishment; Cruel and unusual punishment; Sentencing

Punitive damages, **2081–2082, 2082–2083** (update)
  and antidiscrimination legislation, 99, 100
  excessive as due process violations, 2055–2056
  *Pacific Mutual Life Insurance Co. v. Haslip*, 2314
  Scalia's views, 2314, 2315
  *Smith v. Wade*, 739
  tort, 2081–2083

Pure Food and Drug Act (1906), **2083–2084**
  Food, Drug, and Cosmetic Act revision of, 1069
  and interstate commerce, 1290, 2083
  as national police power, 1001, 2083
  upheld, 2899

**Q**

Quasi-public corporations. *See* Privatization and the Constitution

Quotas, racial. *See* Racial quotas

**R**

Race and criminal justice, **2087–2089**
  capital punishment, 2087–2088
  crack cocaine regulation, 703

Race and sex in antidiscrimination law, **2089–2093**
  Civil Rights Act of 1991, 99–100
  color of law, 2092
  compelling state interest, 2091
  "compounded identities," 2090

*Degraffenreid v. General Motors Assembly Division*, 2089–2091
  disparate impact, 99, 100
  employment discrimination, 99, 100–101, 1232, 2089
  and Fourteenth Amendment, 2089, 2091
  *Jefferies v. Harris County Community Action Association*, 2090–2091
  standard of review, 2092
  strict scrutiny, 2091

Race and voting, **2093–2094**
  gerrymander, 392, 1783, 2093, 2136, 2137, 2814
  multimember district, 1751, 1765, 2135
  reapportionment, 1735, 2093, 2136–2137, 2756
  *See also* Electoral districting; Poll tax; Voting rights; Voting Rights Act of 1965 and its amendments

Race-consciousness, **2094–2096**
  adoption same-race preferences, 46
  affirmative action, 52–58, 2094–2095, 2230–2231
  afrocentric schools, 58
  and antidiscrimination legislation, 99–100
  benign racial classification, 169
  broadcasting license awards, 1723, 2165
  child custody, 799–800
  discrete and insular minorities, 794, 2095
  employer speech restrictions, 1552
  gerrymander, 392, 1188, 1783, 2093, 2136, 2137, 2814
  judicial activism, 1448
  jury discrimination, 1511–1512
  minority business enterprises, 1172, 2230–2231
  racial preference, 2146–2147
  racial proportionality, 2095
  reapportionment, 2136–2137, 2756
  strict scrutiny, 2170

Race, reproduction, and constitutional law, **2096–2098**
  abortion-access restrictions, 7–9, 2097

Racial balance, **2098–2099**
  busing for, 2320

Racial classification. *See* Benign racial classification; Invidious discrimination; Racial discrimination; Suspect classification

Racial discrimination, **2099–2105, 2105–2107** (update 1), **2108** (update 2)

in adoption policies, 46
affirmative action as remedy, 55–56, 2103–2105
affirmative action distinction, 232
and afrocentric schools, 58
against American Indians, 83
against Asian Americans, 128–132, 1328–1331, 2939–2940. *See also* Japanese American cases
alien rights, 1331
by armed forces, 117–118
badges of servitude, 145–146
benign and ameliorative, 169, 794, 2106, 2146, 2165
Black Codes, 189
*Brown v. Board of Education*, 253–255, 771–772, 2099–2100
*Buchanan v. Warley*, 259
on buses, 1761
in capital punishment, 300, 303, 306, 307–309, 310, 732, 733, 1702–1703, 2087, 2106–2107
in citizenship denial, 129, 130–131, 819, 820
civil disobedience against, 371
civil liberties and, 377
Civil Rights Act of 1866, 403, 2100
Civil Rights Act of 1964, 405, 2107
class action lawsuits, 422
and commerce clause, 459
and compelling state interest, 2106
constitutional colorblindness, 2105, 2108
in criminal justice system, 2087–2089, 2106, 2107
and critical legal studies, 724
and critical race theory, 726–728
difference and constitutional equality, 780–781
*Dred Scott v. Sandford*, 818–820, 2099
effects test, 2101–2104
in electoral districting, 868, 2286
and equal protection clause, 116, 909, 915–916, 2108
fighting words, 1057
Fourteenth Amendment protections, 186, 771, 1084–1089, 1239–1241, 1437, 2093, 2099, 2101–2102, 2106, 2108
Fuller Court and, 1167–1168
group libel and, 1235–1236
*Guest, United States v.*, 1239–1241, 1437
and hate crime, 1275–1277
and hate speech, 1277, 1278
in housing, 1289
and illegitimacy inheritance, 1605

in immigration and alienage, 1328–1329

and institutional tax-exempt status, 204

interstate commerce, 1257

invidious discrimination, 1038, 1401

Japanese American cases, 131, 1415–1417, 1871, 2107, 2930–2931

*Jones v. Alfred H. Mayer Co.*, 1437

and judicial power, 1471–1472

in jury composition, 165, 189, 253, 1038, 1509, 1510–1511, 1787, 1825, 2558–2559, 2907

Justice Department civil rights actions, 136, 410–411

King's leadership of civil rights movement, 1536–1537

in land ownership, 1871

literacy tests, 1090, 1629

in local government, 1637, 1638

miscegenation laws, 1645–1646

multimember districts, 1751, 1765, 2135, 2136

neutrality principle, 2164, 2165, 2166

*Pace v. Alabama*, 1873

*Plessy v. Ferguson*, 253, 771, 1167, 1918–1919

political trials, 1955

poll tax, 1961

in primary elections, 1238, 1941, 2007, 2008, 1818, 1819

private, 1240–1241, 1437, 2015–2017

by private club, 1758

and private contracts, 407

by private religious schools, 2017

by private schools, 2299–2300

and property rights, 259

prosecutorial discretion and, 2058, 2059

in public accommodations, 168, 1282–1283, 2062–2063

purposeful, 2627

racial quota remedy, 1172, 2110–2111

and reapportionment, 2756

Reconstruction era, 578

*Regents of University of California v. Bakke*, 2104–2105

Rehnquist court and, 2164–2167

and republican form of government, 2210

residential segregation, 2219–2222

restrictive covenants, 2222–2223, 2410–2411

ripeness of protest action, 1865

separate but equal doctrine, 253, 1167, 2369–2370

sit-ins against, 2420

social science research, 2441, 2443–2444

state action, 280, 2491

strict scrutiny, 1417, 1448, 2106, 2108, 2170

suspect classification, 169, 186, 780–781, 1416, 1646, 2842

Vinson Court and, 2792, 2793

Warren Court and, 380, 2853–2854

White Court and, 2900–2901

workplace harassment as, 2926

zoning, 2220–221, 2945

*See also* Antidiscrimination legislation; Civil rights; Civil rights movement; Desegregation; Fifteenth Amendment; Segregation; Slavery and civil liberties; Slavery and the Constitution; Thirteenth Amendment; Voting rights

Racial intermarriage. *See* Miscegenation

Racial preference, **2109–2110**

adoption placement, 45–47

aid to religious schools, 2110

*Bakke* decision, 2146–2147

Civil Rights Act of 1964, 2109

in state university acceptance, 2146–2147

*See also* Affirmative action; Race-consciousness; Racial quotas

Racial quotas, **2110–2111**

and affirmative action, 53, 54, 57

as badge of servitude, 2110

as benign racial classification, 169

*Croson* justification standard, 2165

and discrete and insular minorities, 794

immigration, 1329

minority business enterprises validity, 1172

*Regents of University of California v. Bakke*, 2110–2111

state university admissions, 2146

Racketeer Influenced and Corrupt Organizations Act (RICO), **2111–2113**

for anti-abortion violence, 13, 93, 2112

and criminal conspiracy, 708

as federal criminal law, 982, 984, 1568

and freedom of speech, 1152–1153

and preventive detention, 2306

Radical Populist constitutional interpretation, **2113–2114**

Radio. *See* Broadcasting

Railroad Control Act (1918), **2114**

Railroad regulation. *See* Economic regulation

Railroad Retirement Act (1934), **2114–2115**

Railroads

employee drug testing, 679

employee retirement, 2114–2115

interstate commerce, 584

just compensation, 345

procedural due process, 346

Railroad Control Act, 2114

rate-setting. *See* Economic regulation

state taxation of commerce, 584

substantive due process, 346

taking of property, 345

Webb-Kenyon Act upheld, 421

Railway Labor Act, 392, 596

Rate regulation. *See* Economic regulation

Ratification of constitutional amendments, **2116–2118**

District of Columbia representation failure, 796, 797

Eighteenth Amendment, 72, 862

equal rights amendment failure, 614, 2117, 2921

Fifteenth Amendment, 1040

Fourteenth Amendment, 1085, 2143

history of, 72–76

Nineteenth Amendment, 2917–2918

rescission debate, 74

Ratification of the Constitution, **2118–2119**

Anti-Federalist opposition, 101–102, 1421, 1561, 1575, 1688, 2938

Bill of Rights inclusion, 32, 176–178, 1045, 1421, 1611, 2118–2119

campaign for, 523

Dickinson essays supporting, 780

and dual federalism, 995

due process clause, 829

*Federalist* arguments for, 1013–1015, 1258–1259, 1947, 2119

Federalists' strategy for, 2118

Hamilton's contribution, 1258–1259

Madison's contribution, 1657–1658

Pendleton's role, 1892

Pinkney's role, 1910

Randolph's (Edmund) role, 2116

Sherman's role, 2412

Washington's stature and, 2119

Wilson's (James) contribution, 2909

Yates's "Brutus" letters, 2938

Ratifier intent, **2120–2121**

*Ratio decidendi*, **2121**

grounds of opinion, 1235

opinion of the Court, 1854

Rational basis, **2121–2122, 2122–2123** (update)

in age discrimination, 59

in alienage disqualification, 66, 72

census and, 326

Rational basis (continued)
  difference and constitutional equality,
    781–782
  economic regulations, 1990
  equal protection, 914
  in fetal viability tests, 8, 9
  in governmental classification, 678
  group homes for mentally retarded,
    790, 792
  Japanese American cases, 1416–1417
  least restrictive means test vs., 1573
  as legislation standard, 1588
  legislative facts, 1590
  legislative intent, 1593
  public use, 2079
  in school finance, 2309
  in sex discrimination, 2390, 2399
  in voting rights, 1271–1272
  in wealth discrimination, 741, 742
  in zoning cases, 428, 2945
Real evidence, 2130
Reapportionment, 2130–2136, 2136–
    2138 (update)
  Baker v. Carr, 138, 152–153, 233,
    237, 1470, 1951, 1952, 1953, 1987,
    2131, 2132, 2227, 2228, 2849
  black-majority congressional districts,
    1735
  Burger Court and, 273–274
  census's role in, 326, 2136, 2137
  electoral districting, 869
  gerrymander, 153, 1187–1189, 1952,
    2135
  judicial authority dissent, 1470
  judicial policymaking, 1461
  justiciability, 2133, 2137, 2203, 2227
  liberalism and, 1615
  Mahan v. Howell, 1664–1665
  O'Connor opinion, 1783
  one person, one vote, 1852–1853
  political question doctrine, 1951,
    1952
  precedent case, 1987
  race-conscious, 2136–2137, 2756
  racial, 1735, 2093
  racial discrimination, 2756
  representation reform, 2202
  Reynolds v. Sims, 273, 2133, 2134,
    2854
  Warren Court and, 273, 1615, 2849,
    2854, 2857
  Wesberry v. Sanders, 1461, 2133–
    2134
  See also One person, one vote
Reasonable doubt, 2138–2139
  and Attorney General's List, 138
  and burden of proof, 264, 1434
  and capital punishment, 302, 311

  and evidence disclosure, 972
  and fair trial, 972
  and grand jury, 1222
  and guilt establishment, 718
  and harmless error, 1270
  and jury nullification, 1512–1514
  in juvenile proceedings, 1523, 2912
  and nonunanimous jury, 1434, 1518
  as right of criminally accused, 2254,
    2255
Reasonable expectation of privacy,
    2139–2141
  and drug testing, 825, 826–827, 2337
  and electronic eavesdropping, 1527,
    2139
  and Fourth Amendment, 1093–1094
  and grand jury, 1220, 1221, 1222,
    1223
  Katz v. United States, 1093, 1527,
    2139–2140, 2141
  Miller, United States v., 2140
  and open fields doctrine, 1853
  and property rights, 2052
  Smith v. Maryland, 2140–2141
  and trash search, 294
  and unreasonable search, 2768
  and unwarranted search, 141, 1527
  See also Privacy Act; Privacy and the
    First Amendment; Right of privacy;
    Unreasonable search
Reason of state. See Constitutional
    reason of state
Recall, 2141
  direct, 788
  Progressive advocacy, 2047, 2292
Reciprocal tax immunities. See Intergov-
    ernmental tax immunities
Reconstruction, 2142–2144
  amendments, 72, 73–74, 577, 578
  Bill of Rights amendments, 577, 578
  Bill of Rights-Fourteenth Amendment
    incorporation, 178, 179–180. See
    also Incorporation doctrine
  black franchise, 1039
  Chase Court, 338–340
  civil rights activity during, 394
  and conquered provinces theory, 504
  as "constitutional moment," 764
  Court-packing plan, 697
  federal enforcement of civil rights,
    1024
  federal jurisdiction, 1501
  Force Acts, 1070
  Freedmen's Bureau, 1106
  guarantee clause, 1238
  habeas corpus, 1252, 1256
  and individualistic rights, 1091–
    1092

  Johnson (Andrew) policy, 2142, 1428.
    See also Articles of impeachment of
    Andrew Johnson
  Joint Committee on Reconstruction,
    1436
  Judiciary Act of 1875, 1497
  Justice Davis's views, 746
  Lincoln's plan, 1625, 2142, 2818
  Military Reconstruction Acts, 1436,
    1728
  Omnibus Act, 1851–1852
  philosophy of the Constitution and,
    1905
  Posse Comitatus Act, 1969
  republican form of government and,
    2210
  state suicide theory, 2520
  Supreme Court and, 2591
  Wade-Davis bill, 2818
  Waite Court, 2822–2823
  woman suffrage denial, 69, 1740,
    2477, 2807–2808, 2918, 2919,
    2920
Reconstruction amendments. See
    Fifteenth Amendment; Fourteenth
    Amendment; Thirteenth Amend-
    ment
Records of the Federal Convention
    (Farrand, ed.), 975
Redistricting. See Reapportionment
Redress of grievances. See Freedom of
    petition
Red Scare. See Communist party;
    Palmer raids; Subversive activity
Referendum, 2146
  campaign finance and, 295
  deliberative democracy vs., 763–764
  as direct democracy, 785, 787–788
  as direct legislation, 788
  equal protection attack, 1415
  guarantee clause challenges, 789,
    1238, 1239
  Lecompton constitution, 1574
  Progressive advocacy, 1557, 2047
  regulation, 866
  See also Initiative
Regulation. See Economic regulation
Regulatory agencies, 2147–2149
  broadcasting, 246–247, 249, 968–969,
    1147, 2148
  cable television explicit programming,
    1134
  cease and desist orders, 325
  commissions' purposes, 2049
  conservative deregulation, 776
  and the economy, 852
  environmental law, 1009–1010
  and fair return on fair value, 969–970

Federal Trade Commission Act, 1030–1031

Food, Drug, and Cosmetic Act, 1069

and freedom of contract, 1116–1117

and interstate commerce, 805, 1397–1398, 2147–2148

and legislative veto, 1599

state police power, 1023

Water Power Act, 2865–2866

Regulatory takings, 2149–2152

*Eastern Enterprises v. Apfel*, 2226

economic viability test, 2055, 2150–2151

first application of takings clause, 2646

just compensation, 2150

*Lucas v. South Carolina Coastal Council*, 1651, 2149, 2150

and retroactivity of legislation, 2226

Rehabilitation Act (1973), **2152**

as antidiscrimination legislation, 95, 406, 791, 1027

Rehearing, **2152**

Rehnquist Court, **2160–2168, 2168–2170** (update)

abortion rights, 2872

capital punishment, 281, 2169

case-specific decisions, 2866

civil liberties, 380–381, 384

and critical race theory, 727

devolution, 776

as doctrinally splintered, 2161–2162

Fourth Amendment activity, 1095–1098

habeas corpus review, 1252, 1253, 1254

Kennedy as swing vote, 1530–1532

neutrality principle, 2164–2167, 2169–2170

political parties, 1938

preventive detention, 2317

property rights, 2055–2056

reapportionment, 2137–2138

reasonable expectation of privacy, 1093–1094

Rehnquist flexibility, 2158

search and seizure, 2340

sex discrimination, 2395

and social change, 700

solicitor general's role in, 2451

standard of review, 2472

standing, 122

state action cases, 400, 2487, 2492

unconstitutional conditions, 2750–2751

Released time, **2171–2172**

college students' religious use of state university property vs., 2198

*McCollum v. Board of Education*, 1703–1704, 2171, 2176

off-premise allowed, 2171–2172, 2947

on-premise denied, 1703–1704, 2171

separation of church and state, 2371

*Zorach v. Clausen*, 2171–2172, 2947

Religion and fraud, **2172**, 2194

Religion and free speech, **2172–2173**

equal access, 2185

Jehovah Witnesses cases, 1410–1411, 2172–2173, 2186

in public forum, 2194

religion as "viewpoint" ruling, 1559–1560

religious use of state property, 2198

school facilities for student groups, 2178, 2179, 2185

teacher statements of own beliefs, 2178

unpopular sects, 2189–2190

*See also* School prayers

Religion and secularism in constitutional interpretation and democratic debate, **2173–2174**

conscientious objection, 2188

crèche and menorah as elements in secular holiday displays, 2196–2197, 2198

public school curriculum, 2177–2178

religious diversity, 2180–2181

Religion clauses in interaction, **2175–2176**

constitutional provisions, 2185

school-sponsored religious exercises, 2179

Religion in public schools, **2176–2177, 2177–2178** (update 1), **2179–2180** (update 2)

Bible reading, 587

constitutional issues, 854–855

creationism teaching, 706–708, 2177

equal access rationale, 2185

and establishment clause, 1, 1048–1049, 2176

fundamentalist objectives, 706–708, 1049, 2177–2178, 2184–2185

and *Lemon* test, 203, 1206, 1208, 1209

outside school hours, 2178, 2179, 2185

private religious speech, 2179

Reagan's views, 2125–2126

released time, 1703–1704, 2171–2172, 2176, 2947

and separation of church and state, 2370

student on-campus worship meeting, 203

Ten Commandments posting, 2177

Warren Court and, 2856

*See also* Government aid to religious institutions; School prayers

Religious diversity and the Constitution, **2180–2181**

Religious freedom. *See* Religious liberty

Religious Freedom Restoration Act (1993), **2181–2183**

compelling state interest test, 625, 2195

and Fourteenth Amendment powers, 991

invalidation of state law cases, 2169, 2181, 2182, 2195

Religious fundamentalism, **2183–2185**

creationism teaching, 706–708, 2184–2185

objections to public school curricula, 2177–2178, 2184–2185

and rulings against school prayer and Bible reading, 1049

*Tennessee v. Scopes*, 2666

Religious institutions and government aid. *See* Government aid to religious institutions

Religious liberty, **2185–2192, 2192–2194** (update 1), **2194–2195** (update 2)

accommodation of religion, 24, 2194–2195

American Indian cases, 82, 1653, 2181. *See also subhead* peyote sacramental use *below*

Amish school-leaving age, 2187, 2914

bad tendency test, 1177

belief and action distinction, 2186, 2187, 2192, 2229, 2914

Burger Court and, 273

censorship of alleged sacrilegious films, 279

and child custody, 799–800

as civil liberty, 373

communitarians on, 473

compelling state interest test, 821, 2178, 2182, 2187

and conscientious objection, 505–506, 2187–2188

content-neutral and content-based regulation, 1053, 1054–1055

delineation of constitutional protection, 1049, 2192

*Employment Division, Department of Human Resources of Oregon v. Smith*, 2182, 2184

establishment clause interaction, 2175–2176, 2185, 2187, 2192

and expansive definitions of religion, 2173–2174

federalism and, 624

Religious liberty (continued)
First Amendment and, 187–188, 389, 1045, 1046, 1047, 1053, 1768, 2186
flag salute in schools case, 1065, 2186
fraud protection vs., 2172, 2190
incidental burdens on, 1351
and incorporation doctrine, 179, 1008, 2186
as Jeffersonian constitutionalism element, 1423–1424
Maryland Toleration Act, 1691
and Mormon charter repeal, 358–359
nonapplicable to exemption from neutral law, 2175
off-premises released time, 2172
Penn's advocacy, 1892, 1894
peyote sacramental use, 821–822, 823, 1207, 2165–2166, 2181, 2182, 2184, 2192, 2194–2195
*Pierce v. Society of Sisters*, 1908
polygamy's nonprotection, 1961, 2180, 2186
as preferred freedom, 1990
prisoners' rights, 1851, 2190
religious diversity, 2180–2181
Religious Freedom Restoration Act, 2181–2182
religious fundamentalism and, 2183–2185
Rhode Island and Providence Plantations, Charter of, 2230
and right against self-incrimination, 2235
Sabbatarian cases, 1105, 2191, 2192, 2195, 2584
school curriculum objections, 2177–2178, 2184
secular regulation of, 748, 2008
separation of church and state and, 2371
slavery and, 2426
of solicitors, 299, 461
street-corner preaching and, 1542
strict scrutiny, 1575
Sunday closing laws, 2584
symbols in public places, 1054–1055, 1653, 2166, 2196–2197, 2198
Toleration Act, 2704–2705
value pluralism and, 2778
Virginia Statute of Religious Freedom, 2801
Williams (Roger) advocacy, 2906
yarmulke prohibition, 1292, 2192
*See also* Establishment clause; Establishment of religions; Government aid to religious institutions; Religion in public schools; Separation of church and state

Religious schools. *See* Government aid to religious institutions
Religious symbols in public places, **2196–2197**
*Capitol Square Review and Advisory Board v. Pinette*, 312–313
*County of Allegheny v. American Civil Liberties Union*, 695
crèche display invalidated, 1054–1055
crèche or menorah display as part of seasonal exhibit, 1653, 2166, 2196
government endorsement test, 2196
use of state property, 2198
Religious test for public office, **2197–2198**
Adams (John) advocacy, 27
Article IV prohibition, 2192
Religious use of state property, **2198**
Remand, **2198**
Remedies. *See* Constitutional remedies; Exhaustion of remedies
Removal of cases, **2198–2199**
Chase Court, 338
civil rights, 402, 403, 414–415
and color of law, 445
and concurrent jurisdiction, 483
Judiciary Act of 1875, 1497, 2199
from state to federal courts, 414
Removal power. *See* Appointing and removal power, presidential
Rendition. *See* Fugitive from justice; Fugitive slavery
Repeal Act (1894). *See* Civil Rights Repeal Act
Reporter's privilege, **2199–2200**
and contempt of court, 1143, 1150
and freedom of the press, 1143
and grand jury testimony, 226, 1051, 1438, 2200
shield laws, 2413
and tort liability, 1438–1439
Report of the Conference of Chief Justices on Federal-State Relationships (1958), **2200–2201**
Representation, **2201–2203**
agency relationship, 2063–2064
Anti-Federalist view of, 102, 763
bicameralism, 171–173
and black disenfranchisement, 1092, 2093
British denial to American colonies, 27
census requirement, 326
and deliberative democracy, 763
District of Columbia denial of, 796–797, 798
*Federalist* definition, 1015
Federalists' view of, 763

filter theory of, 763
gerrymander, 1187–1188
Great Compromise, 1228
guarantee clause, 1238
in House of Representatives, 1305, 1306
multimember districts, 1765, 2135
Paine on, 1874
Puerto Rico, 2080
reapportionment, 152–153, 2130–2138, 2202, 2857
and republican government, 1963
in Senate, 172, 2357
three-fifths formula, 545, 2700
*See also* Electoral districting
Reproductive autonomy, **2203–2209**
abortion, 5–11, 196
for adolescents, 193, 212, 317, 1293, 2204
birth control, 182, 1122, 1233–1234, 2203–2204
as civil liberty, 376, 380
DNA sampling excluded from, 800
and freedom of intimate association, 1119, 1120, 1122
*Harris v. McRae*, 1272–1273
and implied rights, 2163
involuntary sterilization, 2528
and judicial policymaking, 1461–1462
*Maher v. Roe*, 1665, 2205
property rights in the human body, 2057
race discrimination and, 2096–2098
right of privacy, 1289, 2052, 2242, 2243
*Roe v. Wade* and *Doe v. Bolton* significance, 2284–2286, 2921
sex discrimination and, 2394
substantive due process and, 2573–2574
*Webster v. Reproductive Health Services*, 2872
*See also* Abortion and the Constitution; Birth control; Race, reproduction, and Constitutional law; Sterilization
Republican form of government, **2209–2211**
Anti-Federalist definition of, 102, 1412
Constitution as embodiment, 1633
deliberative democracy, 763–764
federalism and, 998
first judicial exposition (1849), 1652, 2210
guarantee clause, 703, 1238–1239
initiative and, 785
initiative seen contrary to, 1371

Jacksonianism and, 1412–1413
liberalism and, 1614
political question doctrine, 1949–1950
and popular consent, 1962–1963
populism vs., 1963
as requirement for Confederate state's
return to Union, 2818
and sanction of slavery, 1947
Republicanism, **2211–2213**
Anti-Federalists and, 1957
guarantee clause, 1239
modern application of traditional
thought, 2215
Republicanism and modern constitutional theory, **2213–2216**
Republican party, **2216–2217**
on Bill of Rights protections, 1357
contemporary political agenda, 2161
devolution agenda, 775–776
Fifteenth Amendment, 1039–1041
Fourteenth Amendment, 1084–1085,
1088
Lincoln leadership, 1620
Reconstruction policy, 2210
slavery in the territories issue, 3,
2216–2217, 2425, 2425–2426
Stevens (Thaddeus) power, 2539–
2540
theory of the Union, 30
as Whig party successor, 1526, 2884
Republicans, Jeffersonian. *See* Jeffersonianism
Reserved police power, **2218**
contract clause, 744–746, 1301, 1645,
2218
Reserve powers of states and people. *See*
Tenth Amendment
Residence requirements, **2218–2219**
abortion, 2285
divorce, 799, 2219
hunting license fees, 157
privileges and immunities scrutiny,
1286, 2020, 2218
and right to travel, 2275–2276, 2277
state automobile tax, 2907
state law discrimination against out-of-
staters, 2020
voting rights, 830–831, 2219, 2813
welfare assistance, 1973, 2218, 2219,
2275, 2873, 2874, 2877, 2878–2879
*Zobel v. Williams*, 2275–2276, 2277
Residential segregation, **2219–2222**
Civil Rights Act of 1866 application,
393, 2220, 2221
Civil Rights Act of 1968 application,
393, 406, 407
class action suit against street closing,
1717

Fourteenth Amendment application,
2900
open housing laws, 1853–1854
restrictive covenant, 2222–2223
"white flight," 1231
zoning, 2947
Res judicata, **2222**
Restrictive covenant, **2222–2221**
and civil liberties, 377
*Corrigan v. Buckley*, 693
equal protection, 909
and Fourteenth Amendment, 163, 389
indirect enforcement, 163–164
as racial discrimination, 2410–2411
residential segregation cases, 2219
as segregation, 2355
and state action, 2484, 2485
unconstitutionality of, 2751
Vinson Court and, 2795
Retirement. *See* Age discrimination
Retroactivity of judicial decisions, **2223–
2225**
Retroactivity of legislation, **2225, 2225–
2226** (update)
antidiscrimination law, 99–100
Antiterrorism and Effective Death
Penalty Act, 103
*Eastern Enterprises v. Apfel*, 2226
ex post facto, 957–958
Revenue sharing, **2226–2227**
as federal grants-in-aid, 987
and federalism, 1003
Reverse discrimination. *See* Affirmative
action; Race-consciousness; Racial
preference; Racial quotas
Revised Statutes of the United States
(1875), **2227**
Judiciary Code, 1451
Revolution, right of. *See* Right of revolution
Revolutionary War. *See* American
Revolution and constitutional theory
RFRA. *See* Religious Freedom Restoration Act
Rhode Island and Providence Plantations, Charter of (1663), **2230**
RICO. *See* Racketeer Influenced and
Corrupt Organization Act
Right
argument for subsistence as, 2874–
2875
privilege distinction, 2251–2252
*See also* Fundamental rights; *headings
beginning with* Freedom of *and
those beginning with* Right
Right against self-incrimination, **2232–
2239, 2239–2241** (update)
adverse comment, 1231

alcohol testing refusal, 2458
blood samples, 2319
body search as non-violation of, 205
*Boyd v. United States*, 215–216, 2236
capital punishment and, 302
coerced confessions, 256, 329, 1183
collective entity rule, 2241
and common law, 1617–1618
and Communist Control Act (1954),
472
and compulsory process, 64, 470
corporate records, 227
DNA samples excluded from, 800
and due process, 828, 2039
electronic eavesdropping, 873
*Estelle v. Smith*, 929
executive privilege, 954
failure to pay federal marijuana tax,
1572
Federal Immunity Act, 989
Fifth Amendment protection, 721
forced vomiting of drug capsules,
2283–2284
Fourteenth Amendment protection,
33, 722, 1665–1666
and gambling, 1670
in government-linked coercion, 444
government undercover informant,
1930
immunity grant, 257, 1334–1335,
1526–1527
involuntary confession, 444
juvenile delinquency proceedings,
1183
legislative investigations, 1595, 2866
Lilburne as catalyst, 1617–1618
and McCarthyism, 1233, 1649
*Miranda* rules, 1742–1744, 1865,
1922, 1926–1929, 2238, 2239–2240
*Miranda v. Arizona*, 1741–1742
nonapplicable to mental illness
commitment proceedings, 1720
police interrogation and confessions,
1922–1929, 1930–1932, 2238–
2239
prearrest silence, 1426
prisoner voluntary self-incrimination,
1327, 1930
required registration of Communist
organizations, 2581
as right of criminally accused, 2255,
2256
and right to counsel, 2234–2235,
2238, 2263, 2264
subpoena and, 2567
testimonial and nontestimonial
compulsion, 2677–2678
textualism problem, 2683

Right against self-incrimination
   (continued)
   two-sovereignties rule, 2237, 2745–
      2746
   unconstitutional conditions, 2749
   United States District Courts, 2764
   unreasonable search, 216
   use immunity, 1526–1527
   voice sample allowed, 784
   waiver of, 2831
Right of association. *See* Freedom of
   association
Right of confrontation. *See* Confrontation, right of
Right of privacy, **2241–2245, 2245–**
   **2248** (update)
   in abortion, 5, 8, 10–11, 12, 92, 94,
      274, 1118, 2242, 2284, 2285, 2921
   and administrative search, 42, 43
   balancing test, 155
   in birth control, 4, 182, 1118, 1121,
      1233–1234, 1461, 2203, 2242
   and body search, 205–206, 1094,
      1095, 2244–2245
   as Bork nomination issue, 210, 211
   and captive audience, 313
   communitarians on, 473
   and computer technology, 481, 482
   constitutional recognition of, 1615,
      2052
   construction of, 2052
   dissent argument, 1462
   in DNA testing, 800
   evidentiary privilege, 935
   "false light" privacy, 2014
   and First Amendment, 2014–2015
   and freedom of intimate association,
      1121–1122, 1237
   and freedom of speech, 1130
   and freedom of the press, 1142, 1145,
      2014
   *Griswold v. Connecticut*, 1120, 1122,
      1233–1234, 1461, 1480, 1810–1812,
      2242, 2243, 2246, 2247
   by homeless people, 1302
   and involuntary sterilization, 2528
   and judicial policymaking, 1461–1462,
      1480
   as marriage protection, 2943
   and Ninth Amendment, 1810–1812
   and open fields doctrine, 1853
   penumbra theory, 1896
   as person, 1901
   *Planned Parenthood v. Casey*, 1915
   primary elections challenged as
      violating, 2007
   prisoners' rights, 2013
   Rehnquist Court rulings, 381

   and right not to hear, 1628
   "right" of publicity vs., 2014–2015
   in right to die, 2266, 2268
   in same-sex marriage, 2308
   and search and seizure, 2334
   Senate subcommittee investigation of
      Nixon administration abuses, 2365
   and sex offender notification laws,
      2401
   in sexual orientation and preference,
      2244, 2247, 2401, 2403, 2407
   sound truck ban, 1542
   Stewart's views, 2542
   and substantive due process, 1289,
      2573, 2575–2576
   and unreasonable searches and
      seizures, 721
   and warrantless search, 2847
   Warren and Brandeis *Harvard Law*
      *Review* article, 2247
   *Whalen v. Roe*, 2242–2243, 2245
   *See also* Reasonable expectation of
      privacy
Right of property. *See* Property rights
Right of revolution, **2248–2249, 2249–**
   **2251** (update)
   federal suppression of Whiskey Rebel-
      lion, 2885
   and gun control, 1243–1244
   as Lockean extraconstitutional right,
      1640, 2248
   radical Populist constitutional inter-
      pretation, 2113
Right-privilege distinction, **2251–2252**
   academic freedom, 22
   Brennan rejection of, 234
   Holmes's rhetorical use of, 2251–2252
   public employees, 22, 36, 2065–2066,
      2252
   *Speiser v. Randall*, 234
   welfare cases, 1974
Rights. *See* Bill of Rights; Fundamental
   rights; Natural rights and the
   Constitution; Waiver of constitutional rights; *specific rights found*
   *under headings beginning with*
   Freedom *and* Right
Rights issues in historical perspective,
   **2252–2254**
Rights of the criminally accused, **2254–**
   **2257**
   accusation notice, 2258–2259
   against double jeopardy, 807–812,
      2256, 2257
   against self-incrimination, 2232–2241,
      2255, 2256
   ambiguity and vagueness of, 2683
   bail, 147–151, 2257

   constitutional delineation, 714–716
   *Miranda* rules, 1742–1744, 2255,
      2256, 2850
   police interrogation and confessions,
      1922–1931, 2256
   public trial, 2076–2078, 2256
   Rehnquist Court contraction of, 2162,
      2169
   speedy trial, 2465–2467
   textualism problems, 2683
   Warren Court's expansion of, 975,
      1927, 1928, 2850, 2856
   *See also* Fair trial; Right to counsel;
      Speedy trial; Trial by jury
Right to bail. *See* Bail
Right to bear arms. *See* Gun control;
   Right of revolution; Second Amend-
   ment
Right to be informed of accusation,
   **2258–2259**
   and fair trial, 971
Right to confront witnesses. *See*
   Confrontation, right of
Right to counsel, **2259–2265**
   as access to the courts, 23
   *Argersinger v. Hamlin*, 116, 2262
   *Betts v. Brady*, 2261
   capital punishment and, 302
   in criminal cases, 720, 722
   Criminal Justice Act, 709
   and due process, 828, 1538–1539,
      2045
   *Escobedo v. Illinois*, 923, 1200, 2263,
      2264, 2856
   evidence and, 242
   expansion of, 116, 170
   eyewitness identification, 962
   and fair trial, 971
   felony cases, 1031
   *Gideon v. Wainwright*, 1193, 1462,
      2261–2262, 2856
   incorporation doctrine, 1355
   indigent limitation, 2295
   by indigents, 1031–1032, 1083, 1362,
      1462, 1973, 2260, 2262–2263, 2265,
      2877
   and indigent's insanity defense, 64
   and "interrogation" definition, 2230
   *Johnson v. Zerbst*, 1436, 2260, 2261
   juvenile proceedings, 1183, 1523, 2263
   at lineup, 1538–1539, 1627–1628,
      2264–2265, 2818
   *Massiah v. United States*, 1696, 2264
   *Miranda* rules, 1923, 1926, 1927,
      1930, 1931, 2230, 2255, 2263–2264
   *Palko v. Connecticut*, 1875
   police interrogation and confessions,
      1923, 1926, 1927, 1930, 1931, 2263

*Powell v. Alabama*, 1981, 2260–2261, 2263
pretrial procedures, 1538–1539
preventive detention, 2306
public interest law and, 2071–2072
quality of representation, 2265
race and, 2087
and right against self-incrimination, 2234–2235, 2238, 2263
as right of criminally accused, 1923, 1925, 2255
*Scott v. Illinois*, 2262
sentencing and, 2367
in summary courts-martial, 1726–1727
and waiver of constitutional rights, 974
Right to die, **2266–2267, 2267–2271** (update)
assisted suicide, 2269–2270
communitarians on, 473
*Cruzan v. Director of Missouri Department of Health*, 790, 2163, 2266, 2267, 2268–2269
euthanasia, 930
and property rights in the human body, 2057
*Quinlan, In re*, 2268
refusal of treatment, 790, 930
Rehnquist Court and, 2163, 2170
and right of privacy, 2244, 2246, 2268
Scalia's views, 2314
and substantive due process, 2577–2578
Right to jury trial. *See* Trial by jury
Right to know, **2271–2272**
Freedom of Information Act, 1117
and freedom of speech, 1132
and freedom of the press, 1143–1144, 1145–1146
government secrecy, 1214–1215
and listeners' rights, 1143, 1628
prior restraint vs., 2010
Privacy Act, 2012–2013
*Richmond Newspapers, Inc. v. Virginia*, 2231–2232, 2271–2272
Right to petition, **2272–2274**
and initiatives, 1371, 1372
lobbyist, 1636
state constitutional guarantees, 1107
*See also* Civil liberties and the antislavery controversy; Gag order
Right to privacy. *See* Right of privacy
Right to remain silent. *See* Right against self-incrimination
Right to travel, **2274–2276, 2276–2277** (update)
as civil liberty, 376
components of, 2305
Court approaches, 137, 1950

divorce and, 2452
facial challenges, 1400
Fifth Amendment due process protection, 1535
international, 2276
interstate, 2274–2275
and national security, 1141, 1257
passport denials, 1535, 2146, 2943
and privileges and immunities, 2021
restriction on indigents, 861, 2878
restrictions on suspect subversives, 116, 1109
*Saenz v. Roe*, 2305
*Slaughterhouse* cases, 2424
substantive due process and, 1077, 2306, 2574, 2577
visas, 2801–2802
and welfare rights, 2408, 2877, 2878–2879
*See also* Residence requirements
Right to vote. *See* Voting rights
Right-to-work laws, **2277–2278**
Ripeness, **2278–2279, 2279–2280** (update)
abstention doctrine, 19
as administrative agency challenge, 41
chilling effect, 355
declaratory judgment, 756
judicial power, 1464
of racial discrimination protest, 1865
Robinson-Patman Act (1936), **2283**
Roosevelt Court, **2292–2294**
Rucker Act (1887), 2459
Rule of four, **2296**
and appeal, 108
and certiorari, 108, 2296
Rule of law, **2297–2298**
arrest, 119
Bill of Rights (English), 175
capital punishment, 299
and constitutionalism, 633, 641
as constitutional political philosophy, 1945
and critical race theory, 726
difference and constitutional equality, 780
immunity doctrine tension with, 2459
jury nullification as undermining, 1514
Magna Carta, 1663–1664, 1945, 2234, 2297
*Marbury v. Madison* establishing, 1673
Petition of Right, 1903
and popular sovereignty, 1945
and presidential powers, 1996
Progressivism and, 2049
and retroactivity of legislation, 2225

and sovereign immunity, 2459, 2460
Story's views, 2555
Rule of reason, **2298–2299**
antitrust law, 2472
corporation restraints, 1642, 2049
Sherman Antitrust Act, 2298–2299, 2314, 2895, 2898
as White (Edward) doctrine, 2895, 2898
Rules Enabling Act (1934), 1028
Rule-skepticism. *See* Legal realism
Runaway slaves. *See* Fugitive slavery
Rutledge Court. *See* Supreme Court, 1789–1801

## S

Safety inspection. *See* Administrative search
Same-sex marriage, **2307–2308 (I), 2308–2309 (II)**
*Baehr v. Lewin*, 147
Defense of Marriage Act condemning, 432
due process and, 2307
equal protection and, 147, 2307, 2308
freedom of intimate association, 1124
full faith and credit, 1172
fundamental rights and, 2308
right of privacy and, 2308
right to marry and, 2308
sex discrimination and, 147, 2307, 2309
sexual orientation and, 2404
School busing, **2320–2321**
Court affirmation, 1535
de facto/de jure segregation, 759
for desegregation, 391, 773
and federal judiciary equity powers, 1459
federal protection, 1026
local government and, 1638
Nixon's views, 2320
prohibitive initiative invalidation, 785–786
for racial balance, 2320, 2321
segregation maintenance and, 2320–2321
state effort to limit, 706
School choice, **2321–2322**
voucher programs, 61, 2814–2815
School desegregation. *See* Desegregation
School prayers, **2322–2323, 2323–2324** (update)
communitarians on, 473
constitutional amendment proposal, 76, 123, 2125–2126, 2127

School prayers (continued)
  daily Old Testament readings, 804
  denial of student on-campus worship
    meeting, 203
  *Engel v. Vitale*, 188, 2176–2177,
    2856
  and establishment clause, 1, 168–169,
    188, 1048–1049, 1207, 2179
  First Amendment and, 2322, 2323,
    2324
  "moment of silence" invalidated,
    2174, 2323, 2832–2833
  prohibition of, 380
  and separation of church and state,
    2371, 2372, 2373
  student-initiated, 2179
  subtle coercive pressure ruling, 1575–
    1576, 1603
  unconstitutionality, 2176
  voluntariness as immaterial, 2176
  voluntary, 2322, 2323
  Warren Court and, 2856
Science, technology, and the Constitu-
    tion, **2326–2329**
  Atomic Energy Act, 133, 2326
  computers, 481–483
  criminal justice, 711–713, 800
  drug testing, 2328
  patents, 1881
  *See also* Electronic eavesdropping;
    Wiretapping
Scientific creationism. *See* Creationism
Scopes trial, 2666
Scott Act (1888), 128
Scottsboro trials, 1981, 2260
Search, unreasonable. *See* Unreasonable
  search
Search and seizure, **2329–2336, 2336–
    2338** (update 1), **2338–2343**
    (update 2)
  aerial searches, 2337, 2343, 2768
  automobile searches, 140–141, 2332
  balancing test and, 2331, 2340, 2341,
    2342
  border search, 209
  *Boyd v. United States*, 215–216
  Burger Court and, 276, 2162, 2340
  drug regulation, 821, 823–824
  drug testing, 825, 826, 2337
  electronic eavesdropping, 872, 1850,
    2139, 2140
  evidence, 932
  exclusionary rule, 936
  expectation of privacy and, 2334
  extraterritoriality, 960
  Fourteenth Amendment/Fourth
    Amendment coextensive protec-
    tions, 1535, 2917

  Fourth Amendment, 1092–1096,
    1097–1098, 1099
  freedom of the press, 1143
  general warrant, 1098–1099, 1185–
    1186
  good faith exception, 1204–1205,
    2338
  habeas corpus review, 1251
  hearsay evidence, 2330
  from innocent party, 2948
  limits on, 2331
  no-knock entry, 679, 1097, 1820
  nonapplicable to welfare caseworker
    home visit, 2934
  open fields doctrine, 1853
  of persons, 2331
  plain view doctrine, 1913, 2680
  probable cause, 2023, 2024, 2329,
    2330, 2331, 2333
  public, 2332, 2333
  public surveillance and, 2337, 2343
  reasonable expectation of privacy,
    2139–2141
  reasonable grounds for, 2337
  Rehnquist Court, 2162, 2169, 2340
  right against self-incrimination linked
    with, 2236
  right of the criminally accused, 2254
  silver platter doctrine, 2416–2417
  sobriety checkpoints, 1726
  state-federal single standard, 1535
  stop and frisk clause, 2331, 2341
  student searches by school officials,
    1799
  and surveillances, 711
  third-party consent, 2689–2691
  unconstitutionality of, 2751
  warrantless search, 2845–2847
  warrants, 2330, 2332, 2333
  *See also* Exigent circumstances search;
    Unreasonable search
Search incident to arrest, **2343–2344**
  exclusionary rule, 938
  exigent circumstances, 956, 2344
  extended to premises, 61
  limits to person of the arrestee and his
    immediate environs, 355
  plain view doctrine, 1913
  search warrant and, 2343
  unreasonable search and, 2329, 2766,
    2769
  as warrantless search, 2845–2846
Search warrant, **2344–2345**
  and administrative search, 42, 43
  *Aguilar* affidavit, 63–64
  arrest warrant parallel, 120–121
  automobile search, 140, 141, 329–330
  for computerized matching, 482

  conflict of interest in issuance, 2345
  drug search, 679, 1097
  expansions, 2336, 2337
  Fourth Amendment requirement,
    1092, 1099, 2343–2344, 2344
  hearsay evidence and, 2345
  informant's tip as basis, 1327, 1368,
    2024
  invalid, 682–683
  issuance of, 2344–2345
  mere evidence rule and, 2345
  no-knock entry, 1097
  not required for consent search, 507
  obscene materials and, 2476
  Paxton's case, 1888
  for premises of nonsuspects, 2948
  probable cause, 1098, 2024, 2330,
    2345, 2469, 2948
  and property interest, 2339
  and reasonable expectation of privacy,
    141
  *Steagald v. United States*, 2526
  unreasonable search defined by, 2766
  and writ of assistance, 132
  *See also* Warrantless search
Secession, **2345–2346**
  blockade legality, 415, 1230, 2022,
    2868
  Chase Court on, 339
  and Civil War inception, 415
  Compromise of 1850 halting, 813
  and conquered provinces theory, 504
  constitutional commentary on, 450
  Corwin Amendment, 694
  Exposition and Protest, 957
  Force Act, 1069
  and indestructibility of American
    federalism, 1007
  and interposition, 2346
  Lincoln's Constitution-based rejection
    of, 1624
  Lincoln's election and, 1620
  and nullification, 1413, 1424, 2346
  and personal liberty laws, 2346
  Republican party rejection of, 2217
  South Carolina ordinance of, 2457
  and sovereignty, 2346
  and states' rights, 747, 1413, 2346,
    2519
  and view of the Union, 1621
  *See also* Civil War; Confederate
    Constitution
Second Amendment, **2346–2347, 2347–
    2348** (update)
  ambiguity and vagueness of, 2684
  civil-military provision, 385
  Civil War militias, 574
  federal power over militias, 1691

gun control and, 574, 1243–1244, 2347
militias and, 2347, 2348
presidential power over state militias, 1691
radical Populist constitutional interpretation, 2113–2114
Reconstruction era view of right to firearms, 1091
and right of revolution, 2249–2250
on rights of the people, 1091
on right to bear arms and, 2250, 2346, 2347, 2348
states' rights and, 2347, 2348
Secondary boycott. *See* Boycott
Second Continental Congress. *See* Continental Congress
*Second Treatise* (Locke), 1639–1640, 1962, 2297
Second World War. *See* World War II
Secret Service, 1568
Section 1983, Title 42, United States Code (judicial interpretation), **2349–2350**
abstention doctrine and, 18
as constitutional remedy, 652, 653, 654
damage claims under, 739, 740
federal civil rights enforcement, 1025
federal court jurisdiction over civil rights cases, 2227
Force Acts as foundation, 1070
implied constitutional rights of action, 1344
judicial immunity, 1453–1454
as limitation on state and local government wrongs, 1217, 1344
*Monell v. Department of Social Services*, 1751, 1754
*Monroe v. Pape*, 1754, 1767
municipal immunity, 1751, 1754, 1767–1768
prosecutorial immunity from suit, 1328
state legislative officials' damages immunity, 2667
workplace hazards in municipalities, 442
zoning damages, 2945
Securities Act (1933), 2350
Securities Exchange Act (1934), 2350
Securities law and the Constitution, **2350–2351**
Security. *See* National security and the Fourth Amendment
Sedition, **2351**
Alien Registration Act, 68
chilling effect of, 2351

clear and present danger test, 426
Palmer raids, 1875, 2929
*Pennsylvania v. Nelson*, 1894
Sedition Act (1798). *See* Alien and Sedition Acts
Sedition Act (1918), **2351–2352**
repeal of, 2581
and subversive advocacy, 2580
Seditious libel, **2352–2353**
anonymous political speech, 91
bad tendency test, 146
content-based restrictions, 1132
English law, 16, 1138, 1606
federal common law, 1016
First Amendment and, 2353
and freedom of speech, 16, 1126, 1606–1607
and freedom of the press, 1138, 1139, 2351, 2353
jury nullification, 1512
*People v. Croswell*, 1897
political trial, 1954
and popular sovereignty, 2352–2353
and subversive advocacy, 2579–2580
wartime applications, 1606–1607
World War I, 2928
Zenger's case, 1512, 2944
Segregation, **2354–2355**
in armed forces, 117, 118, 946
Asian Americans, 129, 586
as badge of servitude, 1918, 1919
Black Codes, 189, 341, 401
*Bob-Lo Excursion Company v. Michigan*, 204
*Brown v. Board of Education*, 253–255
*Buchanan v. Warley*, 259
civil disobedience and, 370
civil rights and, 388–389
commerce clause and, 459
de facto/de jure distinction, 276, 759, 1024, 2320, 2321
in District of Columbia, 1086
equal protection and, 2354
*Evans v. Abney*, 930
Executive Orders 9980 and 9981, 605, 946
in federal employment, 1025, 2911
and federal tax-exempt status of schools, 24
and Fourteenth Amendment, 1086
in housing, 1853–1854
in interstate commerce, 1257, 1645
Jim Crow law and, 2354
in late nineteenth century, 586–587
*McLaurin v. Oklahoma State Regents*, 2628–2629
NAACP litigation, 1676, 1678

open housing laws, 1853–1854
*Plessy v. Ferguson*, 253, 388, 399, 411, 771, 1918–1919, 2354
in public accommodations, 168, 253, 1167, 2062–2063
public accommodations and, 2354, 2415, 2420, 2486, 2693
racial balance and, 2098
racial discrimination and, 2354–2355, 2369
residential, 1853–1854, 2219–2222, 2355, 2411
restrictive covenants and, 2355
*Roberts v. City of Boston*, 2282–2283
in schools, 253–255, 2320–2321, 2355
separate but equal doctrine, 253, 771, 1167, 1918–1919, 2062, 2282–2283
social science research, 399, 2443
state action and, 2483–2484, 2486
states' rights and, 1204, 2519
*Sweatt v. Painter*, 2628–2629
in transportation, 1761
urban residential, 2321
voter restrictions, 1041, 1042
zoning ordinances, 2354
*See also* Desegregation; Racial discrimination
Selective Draft Law Cases (1918), **2356**
conscientious objection, 2173
constitutionality upheld, 506, 2928
involuntary servitude argument denied, 2187, 2928
Selective exclusiveness, **2356**
and commerce clause, 681–682, 2356
and state vs. national commerce powers, 1192
Selective incorporation. *See* Incorporation doctrine
Selective prosecution. *See* Prosecutorial discretion and its constitutional limits
Selective Service Act (1917), **2356–2357**
World War I, 2927
Selective Service Acts (1863, 1940, 1948), **2357**
and civil disobedience, 371
and conscientious objection, 505
denominational exemptions, 2187
and draft card destruction, 1836
Vietnam War, 2790
Self-incrimination. *See* Right against self-incrimination; Immunity grant
Self-representation, right to. *See* Waiver of constitutional rights

Senate, **2357–2361**
  advice and consent function, 47, 109, 114–116, 2358, 2359, 2363
  advice and consent to federal judicial appointments, 1018
  advice and consent to presidential appointing and removal power, 109–111
  advice and consent to presidential treaty power, 1991–1993, 1996
  Bork nomination rejection, 209
  committees, 2360
  confirmation process, 2325
  constitutional amendment proposals, 76
  and democratic theory, 765
  direct election amendment, 72, 764, 788, 1306, 1964
  disciplinary measures in, 2358
  election to, 2358
  equal representation in, 172
  filibuster, 1043–1044, 2359
  First Congress, 1058, 1059
  Great Compromise and, 1305, 2358
  impeachment trial of Andrew Johnson, 126, 1429
  impeachment trial of William J. Clinton, 127
  impeachment trial powers, 111, 1336, 1340, 1342, 1819, 1953, 2360, 2363
  impeachment trials of federal judges, 1454, 1953
  investigative powers, 1594–1596
  joint Iran-Contra hearings, 1401–1403, 2360
  legislative process, 1597–1599
  line-item authority, 1627
  membership and powers, 500, 546, 547
  members' official immunity, 1335
  partial-birth abortion ban, 13
  presidential censure by, 1342, 1409
  Seventeenth Amendment and, 2387–2388
  speech or debate clause, 2464
  supermajority rules, 2585
  Twentieth Amendment and, 2359
  vice-president as president of, 2358
  Watergate hearings, 922, 2360, 2365
Senate and foreign policy, **2361–2363**
  appointment approval, 2361, 2362
  increase in powers during Clinton presidency, 1078–1079
  Senate Foreign Relations Committee, 1078, 1079
  treaty power, 1978, 1991–1993, 1996, 2359, 2361, 2362
  Vietnam War, 2789

Senate and judicial appointments, **2363–2364**
  advice and consent to federal judicial appointments, 1017–1018, 1019–1020
  advice and consent to Supreme Court justice nominations, 47–51, 111–112, 114, 1018–1019, 2364
  appointment clause, 114–115
  federal judges, 2363
  impeachment powers, 111
  reasons for rejections, 114–115
  Senate Judiciary Committee and, 2363
Senate Foreign Relations Committee, 1078, 1079
Senate Judiciary Committee, **2364–2365**
  and Bork nomination, 209–210, 211
  and naturalization, 2364
  Subcommittee on Constitutional Rights, 2365
  subcommittees, 2364
  and Supreme Court justice nominees, 112, 113
  Thomas confirmation hearings, 2695
Senate Subcommittee on Constitutional Rights, **2365**
  Ervin as chair, 922, 2365
Seneca Falls Convention (1848), **2365–2366**
  civil disobedience and, 370
  inclusion of suffrage, 1808, 2918, 2919
  Stanton and, 2477
  women's rights manifesto, 562
Sentencing, **2366–2369**
  capital punishment and, 2366
  career criminal, 316
  for crack cocaine possession or trafficking, 703
  culpability and, 2368–2369
  discretionary, 2366
  disparity in federal sentencing, 984, 985
  disproportionate, 2299
  and double jeopardy protections, 810, 811–812
  due process and, 2367
  ex post facto applications, 2225
  for federal crime, 984, 985, 1749–1750
  indeterminate, 2366
  mandatory, 2366
  *Mistretta v. United States*, 984
  parole and, 2366, 2367
  plea bargaining and, 2367
  procedural due process and, 2367
  and right to counsel, 2367
  victim impact statements, 208–209

Sentencing Reform Act (1984), 984, 1749
Separate but equal doctrine, **2369–2370**
  *Brown v. Board of Education* as response to, 2369, 2370
  and civil vs. social rights distinction, 1038
  constitutionality debate, 254, 771
  equal protection of the laws, 909
  Fuller Court ruling, 1160, 1167–1168
  Jim Crow laws, 2369
  Justice Harlan (1833–1911) dissent, 1167, 1267
  Justice Hughes opinion against, 1311
  minimum content within, 1748–1749
  as not burdening interstate commerce, 1645
  *Plessy v. Ferguson*, 253, 388, 399, 411, 771, 1918–1919, 2354
  public accommodation, 2062
  *Roberts v. City of Boston*, 2282–2283
  single-sex education and, 2418
  unconstitutionality, 2849, 2852
  *See also* Segregation
Separation of church and state, **2370–2378, 2378–2381** (update)
  accommodation of religion distinction, 24
  aid to church-related schools, 2373–2376
  Bible reading in schools challenge, 804
  Bill of Rights and, 2370
  Burger Court and, 273
  Butler Act and, 2666
  and creationism teaching, 706–708
  establishment clause and, 924, 2371, 2372, 2378, 2379
  establishment clause-religious liberty interactions, 2175–2176, 2187
  First Amendment and, 2377, 2378
  First Amendment limitations seen, 1653
  government aid to religious institutions, 1206–1209
  holiday displays, 2376–2377
  in Jeffersonian constitutionalism, 1423–1425
  legislative chaplaincies constitutionality, 1672
  Locke espousal, 1639
  Madison's "Memorial and Remonstrance" advocating, 1662
  *Mueller v. Allen*, 1763
  neutrality vs. separationist view, 2294
  and public forum doctrine, 2070, 2073
  Reagan's views, 2125–2126

rejection of religious test for public office, 2197
released time and, 1704, 2171, 2371
religion as "viewpoint" entitlements, 1559–1560
and religious free speech, 2173
religious fundamentalism and, 2184–2185
and religious legal exemptions, 2180–2181
religious liberty and, 2371
religious test for public office, 2192, 2197–2198
Rhode Island and Providence Plantations, Charter of, 2230
school prayers and, 2371, 2372, 2373
state tax deductions for both secular and parochial school expenses, 1763
Stevens's views, 2534
Sunday closing laws, 2372, 2373, 2585
tax exemptions and, 2680–2681
*Tennessee v. Scopes*, 2666
Virginia Statute of Religious Freedom, 2801
Warren Court and, 2856
Williams (Roger) advocacy, 2906
*See also* Establishment clause; Establishment of religion; Government aid to religious institutions; Religion in public schools; Religious liberty; School prayers
Separation of powers, **2381–2385, 2385–2387 (update)**
act of state doctrine, 25
Adams (John) advocacy, 27
Adams (Samuel) concerns, 32
and administrative agencies, 37–38, 40, 41, 267, 269
and administrative law, 40, 41
advice and consent as, 47
and appellate jurisdiction, 108
and appointments clause, 115
avoidance doctrine, 142
balanced-budget amendment effect on, 153–154
*Bowsher v. Synar*, 214
and budget process, 260, 261, 262
and bureaucracy, 265, 266, 267, 269
Burger Court and, 380
cabinet subject to, 288, 289
cases and controversies, 322
checks and balances compared with, 342, 2381
and common law, 466
as constitutional fundamental, 1947
and constitutionalism, 637
and constitutional theory, 654
and declaration of war, 755–756

and executive agency, 2147
executive power vs. legislative, 214
executive privilege, 952, 955, 2384
executive veto power, 2383
and federal common law authority, 978
and federalism, 1010
and federalism in contemporary practice, 994–997
federal judiciary and legislative functions, 1749
federal jurisdiction, 1502–1503
in foreign affairs, 1071–1078, 1078–1081
guarantee clause, 1238
*Immigration and Naturalization Service v. Chadha*, 1219
in impeachment proceedings, 1336, 1340
and independent counsel, 115, 1359
and interdependencies, 1944
and interest groups, 1380, 1947
and judicial immunity, 1454
and judicial independence, 50–51, 1418, 1455–1457
and judicial review, 1474, 1481
and judicial supremacy, 1487–1488
and law of the land, 1572
legislative/executive/judicial branches in, 2381
legislative remedies for judicial power, 1470–1473
as limiting government, 1944
Lincoln's affirmation of, 1624
Marshall Court and, 1433
Montesquieu's influence in, 1755
nondelegation of power implicit in, 760–761
one-house legislative veto and, 1333
origin of, 2381–2383
*Panama Refining Co. v. Ryan*, 1877
and political parties, 258, 1935
as political philosophy of the Constitution, 1904, 1944, 1948
and political question identification, 1951
practical effects of, 2383
presidential power seen superseding, 1996
and regulatory agencies, 2147, 2148
in republican form of government, 2209, 2213
Scalia's views, 2313
and sovereign immunity, 2460
and special prosecutor, 2462, 2463–2464
and standing, 2475
in state constitutions, 2500

statutory interpretation and, 2525
Supreme Court and, 2383
taxpayers' and citizens' suits, 2661–2662
and taxpayer standing, 1066–1067
and vested rights, 1034
veto power and, 2784
Vinson Court and, 2793
and Watergate issues, 2864–2865
White (Byron) dissents, 2889, 2893
Wilson (Woodrow) arguments, 2909
*See also* Executive power; Judicial power; Legislative power; Presidential powers
Seriatim, **2387**
Seventeenth Amendment, **2387–2388**
and constitutional reform, 650
direct election of senators, 500, 764, 788, 1306, 1964
ratification, 72, 589
regulation of elections, 865
Seventh Amendment, **2388**
and civil juries, 1091
and jury size, 1516
and jury unanimity, 1517
property protection, 2051
and trial by jury, 2388
Severability, **2388–2389**
legislative intent, 2388–2389
Sex discrimination, **2389–2396, 2396–2398 (update 1), 2398–2400 (update 2)**
affirmative action to correct "manifest imbalance," 1435
antidiscrimination legislation, 97, 406, 791, 1027, 2089–2093
by armed forces, 117–118
*Bradwell v. Illinois*, 218
Burger Court and, 272–273, 274–275
citizenship laws and, 2400
comparable worth and, 474, 2397
Court endorsement of, 218
death benefit exceptions for widowers, 2881
direct private damage actions, 748
draft registration exclusion of women, 2295–2296
due process and, 2391, 2398
in education, 400
Education Amendments of 1972 (Title IX), 853
and equal protection, 232–233, 910, 914–915, 917, 1615, 2390, 2396–2397, 2398, 2921
equal protection rejections for, 1199, 2921
equal rights amendment, 918–919
federal protection, 1027

Sex discrimination (continued)
feminist theory, 1032–1033, 1134
fighting words, 1057
freedom of association argument, 1110–1111, 2016–2017
fundamental rights and, 2390, 2399
Ginsburg judicial approach, 1196–1197
hate speech as, 1277, 1278
illegitimacy and, 799, 1404–1405
irrebuttable presumption analysis, 1404–1405
*Lockwood, In re,* 2920
male exclusion from nursing profession, 1746
neutrality principle, 2165
nonmarital children and, 1325, 1326, 1331
paternalism and, 2391
*Personnel Administrator of Massachusetts v. Feeney,* 1902
pornography as, 1134, 1965–1966, 1966–1968
pregnancy and, 2394, 2395, 2397
racial discrimination precedent, 2392
in rape case, 1725
rational basis test, 428, 2390, 2399
Reconstruction-era legitimacy, 2920
Rehnquist Court and, 2165, 2170
and same-sex marriage prohibitions, 147, 1124, 2307, 2309
and social change, 700
Social Security Act and, 2391–2392, 2397
standard of review, 273, 704, 2390, 2471
statutory rape and, 2399
strict scrutiny and, 2399
Title VII and, 2393, 2395, 2399
Violence Against Women Act, 2797
welfare benefits, 293–294
women's historical coverture, 2920
*See also* Race and sex in antidiscrimination legislation; Reproductive autonomy; Woman suffrage movement; Women in Constitutional history; Workplace harassment and the First Amendment
Sex offender notification laws, **2400–2401**
Sexual harassment. *See* Workplace harassment and the First Amendment
Sexual orientation, **2401–2403, 2403–2405** (update)
*Bowers v. Hardwick,* 213, 381, 400
and child custody, 800

and civil rights, 394, 400
Clinton administration rights policy, 432
communitarians on, 473
and constitutional aspiration, 665
discrimination and, 2401, 2402, 2403, 2404
equal protection, 787, 916, 917–918, 2287, 2401, 2403
and freedom of intimate association, 1124, 2403
and hate crime, 1276
and hate speech, 1277
and right of privacy, 2244, 2247, 2401, 2403, 2407
*Romer v. Evans,* 383, 400, 2286–2287
same-sex marriage, 147, 432, 2307, 2404
substantive due process and, 2401, 2403
*See also* Gender rights; Sexual preference and the Constitution
Sexual orientation and the armed forces, **2405–2406**
Clinton administration policy, 432
discriminatory practices, 117, 118
Sexual predator laws, **2406–2407**
*See also* Sex offender notification laws
Sexual preference and the Constitution, **2407–2408**
antisodomy law, 213, 2247, 2401, 2403, 2891–2892
*Bowers v. Hardwick,* 213, 381, 400
freedom of intimate association, 1124, 2403
public accommodation rights, 1320
right of privacy, 2244, 2247, 2401, 2403, 2407
*Romer v. Evans,* 383, 407, 2286–2287
St. Patrick's Day Parade participation, 1320
*See also* Sexual orientation
Shays' Rebellion, **2410**
and Annapolis Convention, 90
as constitutional concern, 28, 32
and domestic violence clause, 803
Sheppard-Towner Maternity Act (1921), **2411**
federal grants to state, 2659
Sherman Antitrust Act (1890), **2412–2413**
antitrust law, 103, 104, 105, 106, 107
application to unions, 70, 107, 1545, 1641–1642
and commerce clause, 455, 585
constitutionality as applied to holding companies, 1828
and the economy, 852

extraterritoriality, 959
Fuller construction, 1162
Fuller Court applications, 1165–1166
*Loewe v. Lawlor,* 1641
as nonapplicable to production monopolies, 2046
Olney's antipathy to, 1850–1851
*Parker v. Brown,* 1879
prosecution under, 1540
Roosevelt (Theodore) use of, 2292
rule of reason underpinnings, 2298–2299, 2314, 2895
Sugar Trust ruled as outside interstate commerce, 1539–1540, 1642, 2048
Shield laws, **2413**
Shopping centers, **2414–2415**
and compelled speech, 476
First Amendment rights, 1308, 1672, 2060
and freedom of speech, 1131, 1308
picketing cases, 1308, 2414
property rights vs. free speech, 1566
Shreveport doctrine, **2415–2416**
invoked in *Schechter Poultry Corp. v. United States,* 2317
Silver platter doctrine, **2416–2417**
*Elkins v. United States,* 882
seizure of evidence and, 2416
Simpson-Mazzoli Act (1986), 2364
Single-sex education, **2417–2419**
Sinking fund cases, **2419–2420**
Sit-in, **2420**
*Bell v. Maryland,* 168
as civil disobedience act, 371
civil rights movement, 389, 414
First Amendment protection, 1047
public accommodations, 2062
state action and, 2486
Sixteenth Amendment, **2421**
direct and indirect taxes, 784, 1165
*Eisner v. Macomber,* 863–864
income tax, 1960, 1964, 2480
ratification, 72, 784, 1960
Sixth Amendment
ambiguity and vagueness of, 2683
evidence and, 932
speedy trial and, 1655, 2465–2467
subpoena and, 2567
textualism problems, 2683
venue and, 2782
*See also* Fair trial; Petit jury; Public trial; Rights of the criminally accused; Right to counsel; Speedy trial; Trial by jury
Slander. *See* Libel and the First Amendment
SLAPPS. *See* Strategic lawsuits against public participation in government

*Slaughterhouse* cases, **2423–2422**
  Chase Court decision, 336, 341, 580
  and constitutional fictions, 527
  and federal civil rights enforcement,
    201, 402
  privileges and immunities, 1091, 1354
  Waite Court and, 2827
Slavery and civil liberties, **2424–2426**
  abolitionist constitutional theory, 2–3
  antislavery controversy, 384–385
  badges of servitude, 145–146
  *Dred Scott v. Sandford*, 374, 387, 402,
    566
  due process and, 2425
  federalism and, 1007
  freedom of speech and, 2425–2426
  freedom of the press and, 2426
  fugitive slave laws, 2, 3, 1159–1160
  inconsistency with Declaration of
    Independence, 1613
  personal liberty laws, 3, 4, 1159, 1901,
    2006
  religious liberty and, 2426
  trial by jury rights, 2425, 2431
  *See also* Black Codes; Fugitive slavery
Slavery and property, **2426–2427**
  District of Columbia slave trade, 796
  *Dred Scott v. Sandford*, 2054
  Emancipation Proclamation, 884–885
  fugitive slave laws, 2, 3, 4, 1159–1160
  higher law invocation, 1287
  interstate slave trade, 3, 1238
  Lincoln's views, 1622–1623
  property rights in the human body,
    2057
  slave trade prohibition, 545, 2050
  taking of property application, 2054
  *See also* Thirteenth Amendment
Slavery and the Constitution, **2427–
  2434**
  abolitionist constitutional theory, 2–4
  abolition of slave trade, 545, 2050
  antebellum period, 566, 567–568
  Corwin Amendment, 694
  Declaration of Independence, 753,
    754, 2050
  *Dred Scott v. Sandford*, 754, 818–820
  Emancipation Proclamation, 1625
  fugitive slavery, 1159–1160
  fugitive slavery and Article IV, 545
  as major issue at Constitutional
    Convention of 1787, 521
  Prohibition of Slave Trade Act, 2050
  proslavery jurisprudence, 558
  protective clauses, 2
  republican ideals vs. sanctioned
    slavery, 1947, 2210
  right to trial by jury and, 2431

slave trade and, 2429, 2430
  sojourner slaves, 466–467
  state and federal sovereignty, 298
  Taney Court and, 2649, 2654–2655
  Thirteenth Amendment prohibition,
    2057, 2691
  three-fifths clause, 545, 2700
  Whig view as moral evil, 31
Slavery in the territories, **2434–2436**
  abolitionist constitutional theory, 2, 3
  annexation of Texas and, 90
  antebellum solutions, 569
  Compromise of 1850, 477
  Douglas (Stephen) policies, 812–813
  *Dred Scott v. Sandford*, 818–820,
    2216, 2436, 2647, 2649–2650
  Freeport Doctrine, 813, 1148–1149,
    1625, 2436
  Homestead Act, 1302
  Kansas-Nebraska Act, 1525–1526,
    1620, 2427, 2435
  Lecompton constitution, 1574
  Lincoln-Douglas debates, 812–813,
    1620, 1625
  Lincoln opposition, 1622
  Missouri Compromise, 1747–1748
  Nashville Convention Resolutions,
    1774–1775, 2435
  Northwest Ordinance prohibition, 742
  popular sovereignty, 812, 1525, 1526,
    1627, 1962, 2435
  Republican party "Free Soil" tenets,
    2216–2217
  Whig opponents, 31, 2884–2885
  Wilmot Proviso, 3, 477, 563, 568, 569,
    2908
Smith Act. *See* Alien Registration Act
Sobriety checkpoints. *See* Traffic stops
Social choice theory. *See* Article III and
  public choice theory
Social compact theory, **2438–2440**
  and Concord town meeting resolu-
    tions, 483
  and constitutional conventions, 514
  and constitutionalism, 641–642
  Declaration of Independence, 752
  and equality doctrine, 802
  Fundamental Orders of Connecticut,
    1176, 1303
  and higher law, 1636
  and limited government, 1618
  Mayflower Compact, 531
  and natural rights, 2439
  and preservation of private property,
    2782
  state linked with, 2478
  unenumerated rights, 2753
  and vested rights, 2782–2783

Social programs. *See* Entitlement;
  Welfare state
Social science in constitutional litigation,
  **2440–2442**
Social science research and constitutional law, **2442–2444**
  Brandeis brief, 225, 2443
  *Brown v. Board of Education*, 2443
  capital cases, 2443
  constitutional litigation and, 2440–
    2442
  cruel and unusual punishment, 2443
  jury size, 1516
  jury unanimous vs. nonunanimous
    verdicts, 1518
  legal realism, 2442–2443
  obscenity laws, 2443
  *Plessy v. Ferguson*, 2443
  pragmatism, 1983, 1984
  racial discrimination, 2443–2444
  segregated education, 399, 2443
  voting rights cases, 414
Social Security Act (1935), **2444–2445**
  *Califano v. Goldfarb*, 293
  Medicare (Health Insurance for the
    Aged Act), 1281
  objection on religious ground, 1575
  *Railroad Retirement Board v. Alton
    Railway Company*, 2115
  sex discrimination, 2391–2392, 2397
  taxing and spending powers, 2659,
    2660
  unemployment compensation
    challenge, 2540–2541
  upheld, 1283–1284, 2289, 2821
  welfare programs, 2444, 2445
Sociological jurisprudence, **2445–2446**
  Brandeis brief, 225, 2443
  interest group litigation, 1378
  legal realism, 1580
  Pound's formative role, 1972
  pragmatism, 1982
  selective judicial activism, 1448
Sodomy. *See* Freedom of intimate
  association; Sexual preference and
  the Constitution
Solicitor general, **2447–2451**
  Supreme Court role, 2448, 2449–
    2450, 2612
Solid waste disposal. *See* Waste, pollution, and the Constitution
Somerset's Case (1772), **2451–2452**
Soundtrucks and amplifiers, **2452–
  2453**
  ban on "loud and raucous," 1542
  as breach of the peace, 227
  content-neutral ban, 1351
  and freedom of speech, 1131

South Carolina Exposition and Protest. *See* Exposition and Protest

South Carolina Ordinance of Nullification (1832), **2457**
and Cherokee Indian Cases, 345
and compact theory, 1424
and Force Act, 1069, 1408, 1413–1414
Jackson's Proclamation to the People of South Carolina, 1408, 1409, 1413–1414
and Tariff Act, 559, 1069, 2480, 2519

South Carolina Ordinance of Secession (1860), **2457**

Southern Christian Leadership Council, 411, 412

Southern Manifesto (1956), **2458**
and civil rights, 390

Sovereign immunity, **2459, 2459–2460** (update)
act of state doctrine, 25
and Americans with Disability Act, 87–88
Eleventh Amendment prohibitions, 876, 1562
and federalism, 994–995, 1010
Federal Tort Claims Act, 1030, 2459, 2706, 2707
injunctive relief, 1373
judicial power, 1467–1468
*Larson v. Domestic and Foreign Commerce Corporation*, 1562
municipalities, 1767–1768
*Osborn vs. Bank of the United States*, 1467–1468
*Pennhurst State School & Hospital v. Halderman*, 1893
of states from congressional regulation, 1181–1182
suit against United States distinguished from suit against extraofficial acts or unconstitutional behavior, 1562

Sovereignty, **2460–2462**
and amending process, 76, 77, 78
American Indian tribal, 82, 1535, 1612, 2731
American redefinition of, 246
Articles of Confederation, 125–126
Bill of Rights, 1091
citizenship and, 365
Civil War and, 415
and constitutionalism, 636
corporate challenges to state, 692
and Court federalism rulings, 992–993
*Curtiss-Wright Export Corporation, United States v.*, 2289

delegation of power, 736
and double jeopardy, 808–812, 1283
external, 2289
and federal environmental laws, 1009–1010
in federalism system, 570, 997, 1006
government-proprietor distinction, 1210, 1211, 1212
guarantee clause, 1239
and immigration laws, 1330, 1332
*Martin v. Hunter's Lessee*, 1689–1690
*McCulloch v. Maryland*, 1674–1675
native Hawaiian movements, 1784–1785
and nullification, 1832
*Pennsylvania v. Nelson*, 1894
of the people. *See* Popular sovereignty in democratic political theory
Petition of Right, 1903
*Piqua Branch of the State Bank of Ohio v. Knoop*, 1911
and political philosophy of the Constitution, 1945
and political question doctrine, 1950
and presidential powers, 1997
and secession, 2346
and separation of powers, 32
state, 449, 450, 558–559, 2478–2479, 2555
states' rights and, 2519
supremacy clause and, 2587
over territories, 1358
tribal economic development and, 2731
as Voting Rights Act challenge, 2456–2457
war and foreign affairs, 2834–2839
westward expansion of, 564
*See also* Popular sovereignty

Spanish American War
as declared war, 755, 1998
as federalism issue, 1169
Puerto Rico acquisition, 2080

Special interest groups. *See* Interest group litigation; Interest groups

Special master, **2462**
institutional litigation, 1375
Supreme Court and, 2593

Special prosecutor, **2462–2464**
appointment of, 2463
impeachment and, 2463
independent counsel appointment, 115
Reagan presidency, 2128–2129
in Watergate scandal, 209, 1359, 2463, 2865
*See also* Independent counsel

Speech freedom. *See* Freedom of speech

Speech or debate clause, **2464**
Burger Court and, 274
congressional privileges and immunities, 501
*Gravel v. United States*, 1226
legislative immunity, 1591
member absolute immunity, 1335
nonimmunity for unofficial communication, 1324

Speedy trial, **2465–2466, 2466–2467** (update 1), **2467** (update 2)
balancing test, 163
*Barker v. Wingo*, 163
denial of, 2465
pre-accusal period not covered, 1633
rights of criminal defendant, 2256, 2466
as Sixth Amendment right, 1655, 2465
states' application of, 1539

Speedy Trial Act (1974), 2466, 2467

Spending power, **2468–2469**
deficit spending and, 2468
internal improvements, 2468

*Spirit of American Government, The* (Smith), 2046–2047

*Spirit of the Laws, The* (Montesquieu), 1470, 1755

Spoils system. *See* Patronage

Spot Resolutions (1847), **2469–2470**

Stamp Act Congress, Resolutions of (1765), 531, **2470–2471**
Dickinson's role, 779

Standard of proof. *See* Reasonable doubt

Standard of review, **2471–2472**
abortion rights, 11, 1293
age discrimination, 59
alienage, 368
burden of proof, 264
capital punishment, 307
children of illegal aliens, 1920
commercial speech, 2472
and compelling state interest, 477
and constitutional limitations on government, 2471
equal protection, 914, 916, 2471
freedom of speech, 2471
illegitimacy cases, 1326, 1605
judicial activism or restraint, 1445
least restrictive means test, 1573
legislative facts, 1590–1591
legislative intent, 1593
race and sex in antidiscrimination law, 2092
rational basis, 1588, 2121–2123
religious liberty, 1575
sex discrimination, 273, 704, 2390, 2471
two bases, 741–742

Standing, **2472–2474, 2474–2475** (update)
  as administrative agency challenge, 37, 41
  Article III, 122, 1066
  Burger Court, 122
  cases and controversies, 322, 2472–2473
  chilling effect, 355
  criteria, 2472–2474
  interest group litigation, 1378, 1651
  invalid on its face, 1399–1400
  judicial legislation, 1460
  judicially broadened criteria, 776
  judicial power, 1464
  judicial restraint, 1450
  jury discrimination, 1511–1512
  as justiciability barrier, 122
  lack of injury in fact, 1651
  person, 1900
  public choice theory, 122
  Rehnquist Court, 122
  *Roe v. Wade*, 2284
  taxpayer suits, 1066–1067, 2777
Stare decisis, **2477, 2477–2478** (update)
  and abortion cases, 15, 2208
  and capital punishment cases, 306
  and judicial independence, 1455
  and opinion of the Court, 1854
  and overruling, 1868–1869
  public choice theory, 122
  Stevens's views, 2532
  Stewart's views, 2541
State, **2478–2482**
  authority of, 2480
  autonomy, 1803
  and cities, 361–363
  constitutional reason of, 649–650
  corporate citizenship, 798
  dual federalism, 827
  immunity from damages, 2667
  initiatives and referenda, 786, 787–788
  interstate compacts, 2479
  limitation on legislative power of, 2766
  loyalty to, 2480
  power delegated to, 2479
  power to define and punish crimes, 721
  senators allotted, 2479
  as social compact, 2478
  sovereignty, 2478–2479, 2555
  supremacy clause and, 2479
  voter qualifications, 68, 69, 1740
State action, **2482–2488, 2488–2490** (update 1), **2490–2491** (update 2)
  abstention doctrine, 17–20
  academic freedom, 21

adequate state grounds, 34–35
administrative agencies, 40, 42
alien restrictions, 1330, 1332–1333
antidiscrimination legislation, 95, 96
arrest warrants, 2488–2489
captive audience, 313
and civil liberties, 377
and civil rights, 389–390, 399
clear statement rule, 1229
and color of law, 444, 445
common law rights, 2489
compelling state interest, 2187
corporations and, 2482, 2490
criminal double jeopardy, 808
criminal procedural due process, 2036–2042
critical legal studies, 724
devolution policy, 777
direct-ballot process, 287–288
discrimination against aliens, 66, 1331
due process, 2036, 2487
economic due process, 839
eminent domain, 2482
federal court suits, 1060
federalism boundaries, 998, 1007, 1037, 2489, 2491
federal regulation of, 990–992, 996, 1493
foreign affairs exclusions and limitations, 1072–1073, 1997
Fourteenth Amendment and, 1088, 2036, 2329, 2482
as Fourteenth Amendment limitation, 200, 280, 1037, 1063, 1064, 1411
Fourteenth Amendment restrictions of, 816, 1037, 1089, 1090–1092
freedom of contract, 1113–1114
freedom of the press, 2310
full faith and credit, 1171–1172
Holmes's support for, 1296
incorporation doctrine, 33, 178–180, 186, 197, 760, 814–815, 1353–1356
individual's rights vs. *See* Compelling state interest
initiative, 1371–1372
intent and procedural due process claim, 2032
interposition, 1392–1393
interstate compact, 1398–1399
judicial activism and judicial restraint, 1446–1447
jury discrimination, 1511
legislative investigation, 1594
liability for government wrongs, 1217
local government, 1637–1638
no-fault divorce, 799
political party primary laws, 2007–2008

political party regulation, 1940, 1941–1942
political philosophy of the Constitution, 1944
political question doctrine, 1652–1653, 1949–1951
preemption of federal law, 1988–1990
primary elections, 2485
in private conduct, 2492
in private discrimination, 280, 2015
privatization, 2017
and privileges and immunities clause, 2020
proprietary commercial benefits, 1211
public function of, 2675
public purpose doctrine, 2073–2076
residence requirements, 2218–2219
restrictive covenant, 2484, 2485
retroactivity of legislation, 2225–2226
search and seizure protections, 1535
segregation, 2483–2484, 2486
state residents preference laws, 2020
substantive due process and, 2569
tuition grants, 2738
voting rights, 2484–2485
vs. state inaction, 775
woman suffrage provisions, 2919
women's exclusion from political process, 2920
  *See also* State police power
State action—beyond race, **2491–2493**
  and liberalism, 1616
State aid to parochial schools. *See* Government aid to religious institutions
State and Local Fiscal Assistance Act. *See* Revenue sharing
State and local government taxation, **2493–2494, 2494–2495** (update)
  automobile tax residency requirement, 2907
  church-owned real estate, 2191
  commerce clause, 2493, 2494
  direct taxes, 784
  economic analysis, 834
  intergovernmental immunities, 1383–1384, 2493
  jurisdiction to tax, 1504–1505
  out-of-state sales tax, 2907
  privileges and immunities clause, 2493
  public purpose doctrine, 2073–2075
  restraints on, 2493
  *See also* State taxation of commerce
State constitutional law, **2495–2499**
  amendment process (outside Article V), 77
  Article V conventions clause, 123–124
  bicameralism, 172

State constitutional law (continued)
  capital punishment, 2498
  common law and, 2496
  equal rights, 2498
  grand juries, 2496
  individual rights, 2496
  interpretation of, 2498
  and Jeffersonianism, 1425
  privileges or immunities in, 2495
  rational basis standard, 2122
  revision of, 2495, 2496
State constitutions, **2499–2503**
  amendments to, 2501
  and American founding, 540–541,
    642–643, 2501
  in antebellum period, 566–567
  assembly and petition rights, 1197
  bicameralism, 172
  contract clause, 673
  criminal justice, 2502
  due process clauses, 828–829
  economic regulation, 2502
  education, 2502
  elections, 2500
  English Bill of Rights as resource, 175
  environmental protection, 2502
  and federalism, 1004
  first permanent, 540
  as fundamental and written, 85–86,
    1174
  judicial systems, 2500
  "law of the land" usage, 828, 829,
    1571, 1572
  legislative purpose, 1599
  Massachusetts Constitution (1780),
    27–29, 1695–1696
  New York, 562
  omissions of specific rights, 176
  Pennsylvania Constitution of 1776,
    540, 1894–1895
  privacy guarantees, 2245
  privilege from arrest, 2019
  reapportionment requirements, 2132
  religious liberty provisions, 2186
  republican form of government, 2209–
    2210
  for return to Union, 2818
  revisions to, 2501
  Rhode Island Dorr rebellion, 1652
  separation of powers in, 2500
  spending power, 2468
  variety in, 2500
  Vermont Constitution of 1777, 2782
  Virginia Constitutional Convention of
    1829–1830, 558
  Virginia Declaration of Rights and
    Constitution of 1776, 540, 2799–
    2800

State immunity from federal law, **2503–
    2505**
  dual sovereignty and, 2503, 2504
  Eleventh Amendment, 133, 877
  *Tenney v. Brandhove*, 2667
State legislatures. *See* Reapportionment;
    Representation
*Statement of Principles on Academic
    Freedom and Tenure* (1940), 21, 22
State of emergency. *See* Emergency
    powers
State of war, **2505**
  federal government food and fuel
    controls, 1605
  joint resolution ending, 1437
  police action vs., 1921
  *See also* Declaration of war
State police power, **2505–2512**
  and commerce clause, 1320
  commerce regulations, 1191
  common law and, 2506
  constitutionality of, 2509
  dual federalism, 1244
  due process and, 2508
  *Euclid v. Ambler Realty Company*,
    929
  federalism and, 2509
  Fourteenth Amendment and, 929
  as inalienable, 1350, 2507, 2547
  Johnson's (Andrew) vetoes upholding,
    1428
  judicial review and, 2507
  in late nineteenth century, 585–586
  law enforcement and federal relations,
    1566–1571
  limitations on, 2509, 2510
  limiting freedom of contract, 1547
  milk price-control program, 1788–
    1789
  narrow interpretations of, 2311
  and political parties, 1940
  preemption, 2511–2512
  private economic rights and, 2511
  prohibition statutes, 2050
  regulatory commissions, 1023
  reserved, 2218
  restraints on, 2511
  restricted by freedom of contract
    doctrine, 684
  rights of property and, 2508
  rights of the public and, 2507
  state action and, 2489
  Story's views, 2555
  subjects of commerce and, 2566
  substantive due process and, 1764,
    2509, 2571
  supremacy clause and, 2587
  Taney Court and, 2556

  upheld by Justice Day, 749
  use of deadly force, 2665
  and vested rights, 1225, 2507
  Waite Court on, 676
  zoning and, 2510
State regulation of commerce, **2512–
    2515, 2515–2517** (update 1),
    **2517–2518** (update 2)
  alcohol bans, 1601, 2870
  balancing test, 2517–2518
  closed loophole with federal regula-
    tion, 2899
  commerce clause curbs, 455, 1381,
    1396
  constitutional economic liberties, 841
  discrimination against out-of-state
    interests, 2515–2517
  dormant commerce clause, 804–807
  economic analysis, 835
  extraterritoriality issue, 2517
  federal limits on, 2274
  and freedom of contract, 1112
  geographical terminology of, 2517–
    2518
  importation of goods, 2514
  and interstate commerce, 1189–1190,
    1396, 2060, 2512, 2516
  and intrastate commerce, 2513
  and just compensation, 2129–2130
  least restrictive means test, 1573
  limits clarification, 750
  "massive" burden invalidation, 171
  Minnesota rate cases, 1739–1740,
    2899
  and privileges and immunities, 2019–
    2020
  production and trade, 2514
  rational basis standard of review,
    2122
  substantive due process and, 2547
  Taft Court and, 2641
  taxation of banks, 801
  *Wabash, St. Louis & Pacific Railway
    v. Illinois*, 2817
  Webb-Kenyon Act, 2870
States' rights, **2518–2520**
  Bill of Rights on, 1091
  civil rights and, 2519
  as Civil War issue, 549, 571
  and commerce clause, 454–455
  and conditional spending, 486
  conservatism and, 776–777, 1005
  devolution and, 776–777
  domestic violence clause and, 803
  Eleventh Amendment and, 356
  federalism and, 2518–2519
  and federal protection of civil rights,
    1008, 1023–1024

*Garcia v. San Antonio Metropolitan Transit Authority*, 1181–1182
immunity from congressional regulation, 1181–1182
interposition, 1392–1393
Jacksonianism and, 1412, 1413
Jeffersonian and, 1421–1422, 1424
and judicial supremacy, 1488
Lincoln's view of, 1622
nullification and, 2519
nullification crisis, 1408, 1409, 1412–1413
Randolph (John) advocacy, 2116
Roane advocacy, 2280
secession as, 747, 2346, 2519
Second Amendment and, 2347, 2348
sectional rivalry and, 2519
segregation under, 1204, 2519
sovereignty and, 2519
Taft Court support for, 2641
Taney Court on, 298, 2651
Tenth Amendment and, 178, 2667–2668
theories of the Union and, 2519
twentieth-century causes, 1424
and wages and hours legislation, 1760
States' rights amendments, **2520**
State suicide theory, **2520–2521**
State taxation of commerce, **2521–2523**
in banking, 1655
and commerce clause, 2521
and contract clause, 801
dormant commerce clause litigation, 806
economic analysis, 835
import-export clause, 256, 1349, 1725
impost, 1349
in insurance, 1724
interstate commerce, 2521
intrastate commerce, 2521
Lockhart articles on, 1640
Multistate Tax Compact, 2523
original package doctrine, 1864
railroads, 584
Stone's views, 2544
Taft Court and, 2641
State tax incentives and subsidies to business, **2523–2524**
Status of forces agreement, **2524**
North Atlantic Treaty, 1827
Statutory construction. *See* Legislation
Statutory interpretation, **2525**
capital punishment, 307
census, 326
federal-state criminal enforcement relations, 1570–1571
interest group legislation, 2525
judicial legislation, 1459

legislative intent, 1229
Scalia's views, 2316
and vested rights, 1034
Stay of execution, **2526**
*Rosenberg v. United States*, 2294
Steel seizure controversy, **2526–2527**
Executive Order 10340, 945
and presidential inherent powers, 2839
and solicitor general, 2448
Truman rationale, 2734–2735
unconstitutionality ruling, 2941
*Youngstown Sheet & Tube Co. v. Sawyer*, 2839, 2941
Sterilization, **2528–2529**
*Buck v. Bell*, 259, 284, 789, 791–792, 1297, 2528
constitutionality of, 2421–2422
fundamental interests and, 2528
habitual offenders statute invalidated, 2203, 2421–2422
immunity from damage suits, 2565
as instrument of genocide, 2528
*Skinner v. Oklahoma*, 2421–2422
substantive due process and, 2573
Stockholder's suit, **2543**
Minnesota rate cases, 1739–1740
Supreme Court jurisdiction, 801
Stone Court, **2548–2551**
flag salute cases, 2549–2550
Japanese American cases, 2550
lack of unity on, 2548
Stop and frisk, **2552–2553**
airport, 2553
circumstantial evidence and, 2552
Fourth Amendment and, 2676
motivation for, 2676
probable cause, 2552, 2675, 2939
reasonable cause, 1095–1096
requirements for, 2552
search and seizure, 2331, 2341
susceptibility to abuse, 2676
unreasonable search and, 2767, 2769
Strategic lawsuits against public participation in government, **2557–2558**
Stream of commerce doctrine, **2559–2560**
Agricultural Marketing Agreement Act definition, 63
commerce clause limits, 1396, 2470
economic regulation, 2470
Fuller articulation, 1162–1163
interstate commerce and, 2559
intrastate commerce and, 2559
labor antitrust ruling, 1642
Marshall's (John) commerce power exposition foreshadowing, 1191
trade practices and, 2317

Strict construction, **2560–2562**
Burger Court and, 380
of commerce power, 1190–1191
of free exercise clause, 2193, 2194
internal improvements as exceeding, 30
and Jackson presidency, 1409
and judicial role, 1484
liberal construction vs., 1611
as Rehnquist doctrine, 2154, 2155
Taney Court of contract clause, 675
textualism vs., 2315–2316
Strict scrutiny, **2562–2563**
abortion rights, 11–12, 1293
affirmative action, 33–34, 57, 58
of alienage classification, 66, 72, 368, 1219
and compelling state interest, 477
content-based restrictions on high-value speech, 1133
durational residence voting requirements, 831
education denial to children of illegal aliens, 1920
equal protection of the laws, 910, 914, 916, 2562
and First Amendment rights, 1050–1051, 1990, 2562
and fundamental rights, 1176, 1177
illegitimacy, 1326
legislative facts, 1590–1591
*Palmore v. Sidoti*, 1876
preferred freedoms doctrine, 1990
public-nonpublic forum distinction, 2068–2069
race and sex in antidiscrimination law, 2091
of racial criteria, 46, 58, 1417, 1448, 2170
racial discrimination and, 2106, 2108
rational basis standard, 2123
same-sex marriage and, 2307
school finance and, 2387
sex-based classifications, 233, 273, 1157
sex discrimination and, 2399
of voting rights cases, 1271, 1272, 1401, 2203, 2228
of wealth discrimination, 741, 742
welfare benefits and, 2305
*See also* Compelling state interest
Strip search. *See* Body search
Student Nonviolent Coordinating Committee, 411, 412
Subjects of commerce, **2565–2566**
Agricultural Marketing Agreement Act, 62–63
farm bankruptcy acts, 1105

Subjects of commerce (continued)
  *Granger* cases, 1224–1225
  Interstate Commerce Act, 1396–1397
  limitation on congressional regulation, 1190
  Marshall (John) definition, 1191
  *See also* Commerce clause; Foreign commerce; Interstate commerce; Intrastate commerce; State regulation of commerce
Subpoena, **2566–2567**
  enforcement of, 2339
  right to compulsory process and, 479
Subsidies to business. *See* State tax incentives and subsidies to business
Subsidized speech, **2567–2568**
  abortion and, 2568
  freedom of speech and, 2567
  freedom of the press and, 2568
  by government, 1131–1132
Substantive activism/restraint. *See* Judicial activism and judicial restraint
Substantive due process, **2569–2575**, **2575–2576** (update 1), **2576–2578** (update 2)
  abolitionist constitutional theory, 2, 829
  in abortion, 4–6, 12
  antimiscegenation laws, 1646
  bankruptcy power, 1645
  in birth control, 182, 1233–1234
  Bork's views, 210
  Burger Court and, 274
  Chase Court and, 338
  and compelling state interest, 155, 477
  contract clause, 2575
  corporations and, 692
  and criminal justice due process, 710
  to defend personal liberties, 1724
  diversity jurisdiction and, 2570
  as economic regulation challenge, 845, 851, 1034, 1639, 2292, 2437, 2571, 2575
  Evarts and, 931
  excessive punitive damages, 2055
  fair return on fair value, 970
  federalism and shared powers, 1012
  in flag salute cases, 2574
  and foreign affairs, 1077
  in freedom of contract, 26, 687, 1114–1115, 1116, 2571, 2577
  in freedom of intimate association, 1237
  fundamental interests, 1173
  guarantee of personal freedoms and, 2421

historical jurisprudence background, 1291
and hours and wages legislation, 1699
inalienable police power, 1350, 2218
inception, 1287
incorporation, 1354
involuntary sterilization and, 2421–2422, 2528, 2573
judicial power and, 2577
juvenile curfew laws challenges, 1521
*Lochner v. New York*, 692
neutrality, 24
ordered liberty and, 2572
Peckham's views, 1890
as personal liberties guarantee, 255, 1123, 1724
*Pierce v. Society of Sisters*, 1908
preventive detention and, 2306
and prisoner's rights, 2863
privacy rights, 1289
procedural due process vs., 2025, 2032
as property protection, 212, 2048–2049, 2052, 2055–2056
property rights protection, 212, 259, 2048–2049, 2052, 2055–2056
punitive damages excesses and, 2082–2083
in rate regulation, 346, 2437
in reproductive autonomy, 2573–2574
reserved police power, 2218
restraints on government power, 2569, 2577
right of privacy and, 2573, 2575–2576
right to die and, 2577–2578
right to marry and, 1118
right to travel and, 2306, 2574, 2577
same-sex marriage and, 2307
Scalia's views, 2316
sexual orientation and, 2401, 2403
sinking fund cases, 2420
*Slaughterhouse* cases and, 2423, 2570
standard of review, 2471
state action and, 2569
state case predating Court's acceptance, 2934–2935
in state police power, 1764, 2509, 2571
in state regulation of commerce, 2547
state vs. private action, 775
strict scrutiny and, 2562
vested rights and, 2052, 2784, 2934–2935
in voting rights, 2577
as weapon against police power, 1350
White's (Byron) views, 2893
*Wynehamer v. People of New York*, 2934–2935
yellow dog contracts and, 2571

Suburbanization. *See* Residential segregation
Subversive Activities Control Act (1950), 472, 2581
Subversive Activities Control Board, **2578**
  Communist Control Act, 472
  executive order rejuvenating, 1995
  and First Amendment rights, 1050
  Internal Security Act, 1385
  registration as violation of self-incrimination rights, 64, 1385
Subversive activity, **2578–2579**
  Alien Registration Act, 68, 769
  Alien Registration Act convictions reversals, 2938–2939
  aliens as suspects, 65
  Attorney General's List, 137–138, 604
  bad tendency test, 146
  balancing test, 154–155
  bills of attainder, 174, 1645
  *Brandenburg v. Ohio*, 2353
  civil liberties and, 2579
  clear and present danger test, 426, 769, 1050, 1298, 1352–1353, 2580
  denaturalization, 768
  deportation, 770
  Dies Committee, 780
  Federal Bureau of Investigation monitoring of, 976
  First Amendment absolutism, 17
  freedom of association, 1108–1109
  freedom of speech, 1127–1128
  House Committee on Un-American Activities, 162–163, 1305
  implied self-preservation powers against, 1347–1348
  incitement/abstract doctrine distinction, 769, 1109, 1187, 1198, 1199, 1353, 2280, 2938–2939
  Internal Security Act, 604–605, 1385–1386, 1950
  labor unions, 79
  legislative investigations, 1595
  loyalty oaths, 1187, 1648
  loyalty-security programs, 1536, 1649–1650
  McCarthyism, 1701–1702
  Mundt-Nixon bill, 1766–1767
  Palmer raids, 1875, 2580
  political trial, 1954
  public employees' right-privilege distinction, 2065–2066
  right to travel restriction, 116, 1535
  *Rosenberg v. United States*, 2295
  seditious libel charges, 2353
  Subversive Activities Control Board, 2578

World War II policies, 2290
*Yates v. United States*, 2938–2939
*See also* Espionage Act; Sedition;
  Treason
Subversive advocacy, **2579–2582**
  clear and present danger, 2580
  extremist speech, 961
  freedom of speech and, 2580
  freedom of the press and, 2580
  habeas corpus and, 2580
  incitement restrictions, 1352–1353
  national security and, 2579
  Palmer raids, 1875, 2580
  right against self-incrimination, 2581
  *See also* Communist party; National
    Security and the Fourth Amend-
    ment; Right to revolution;
    Subversive activity
Sufferance federalism. *See* Federalism,
  contemporary practice of
Suffrage. *See* Alien suffrage; Woman
  suffrage; Woman suffrage
  movement; Voting rights
Sugar Act (1764), 2470
Suicide, assisted. *See* Right to die
Sunday closing laws, **2584–2585**
  establishment of religion and, 1048,
    2191, 2584
  interstate commerce and, 2584
  separation of church and state, 2372,
    2373, 2585
Supermajority rules, **2585–2586**
  amending process, 75, 765
  filibuster, 1043–1044
  public choice theory, 2064
Supremacy clause, **2586–2587**
  and air traffic regulation, 263
  ambiguity and vagueness of, 2682
  and American Indians, 80
  *Chisholm v. Georgia*, 1418
  and comity, 447
  and constitutional supremacy, 1458,
    1471
  Constitution as "law of the land,"
    1571–1572
  and dormant powers, 807
  dual federalism, 827
  and federal grants-in-aid, 988–989
  and federalism, 1011, 2586
  and federal law, 1467
  and general welfare, 2587
  implied powers, 2587
  intergovernmental tax immunities,
    1383, 1384
  interpretation problems, 2586–2587
  and judicial legislation, 1458–1459
  and judicial review, 1472–1473
  and Paterson Plan, 543

preemption cases, 1988–1990
  sovereignty and, 2587
  state police power, 2587
  states and, 2479
  taxing and spending powers, 2661
  torts and, 2706
  treaty power, 2834
Supreme Court (history), **2588–2595**
  advice and consent to justice nomina-
    tions, 47–51
  advisory opinion refusal by, 51, 288
  amicus curiae briefs, 89
  anti-abortion movement, 92–93
  antidiscrimination legislation, 97–98
  antitrust law, 106–108
  appointment of justices, 111–113
  appointments clause, 114–115
  avoidance doctrine, 142
  Bork nomination, 209–211
  *Brown v. Board of Education* signifi-
    cance, 253
  confirmation process, 489–490
  constitutional creation of, 1020, 1021
  Court-packing attempts, 113, 600,
    697–699
  creation of contemporary federal
    judiciary system, 1490
  Declaration of Independence and, 754
  doctrinal development, 801
  dormant commerce clause, 805–807
  Douglas as longest-serving justice, 813
  Field as second longest-serving
    justice, 1035
  first black justice, 1429, 1676–1681
  first woman justice, 1841–1846
  former attorney generals as justices,
    134
  fundamental law, 1174–1175
  great dissenters, 795
  higher law applications, 1286–1289
  impeachment of justices, 552
  increase in number of justices, 1581
  Jay as first Chief Justice, 1418
  judicial leadership, 1485–1486
  judicial supremacy claim, 1488
  Judiciary Act of 1789, 1489, 1495–
    1497
  Judiciary Act of 1801, 1496–1497
  Judiciary Act of 1875, 1497
  Judiciary Act of 1925, 1497–1498
  Judiciary Acts of 1802, 1498
  Judiciary Reform Act (1937), 1498–
    1499
  justice composite type, 112
  justice selection motivations, 112–113,
    114
  and legal culture, 1577
  Legal Tender Cases, 1581–1582

litigation strategy, 1629–1632
  nominations to, 2359
  as only tribunal constitutionally
    required, 1463
  original jurisdiction, 1489
  and Progressivism, 2047, 2048–2050
  review of state judgments, 1490
  role and authority, 557
  second woman justice, 1195–1198
  *See also* Appointment of Supreme
    Court justices
Supreme Court (role in American
  government), **2595–2600**
  appellate jurisdiction, 108–109, 436–
    437, 546, 2588, 2592, 2596, 2616,
    2617, 2618
  appellate jurisdiction limitation, 1503,
    1504
  braking decisions, 2597–2598
  Circuit Courts of Appeals Act, 361
  congressional relations, 496–498
  constitutional interpretation, 629, 630,
    631
  as court of last resort, 1463
  decision, 752
  dissenting opinion, 795
  essential functions, 2593
  federal jurisdiction, 1502–1503
  federal question jurisdiction, 1027–
    1028
  Federal Rules of Criminal Procedure,
    1029
  interpretation of presidential powers,
    2384
  Judicial Code, 1451
  judicial review, 1472–1478
  judicial role, 1482–1485
  judicial strategy, 1482–1485
  original jurisdiction, 356, 2588, 2596,
    2616, 2617
  relation to state courts, 2588, 2590
  *See also* Constitutional interpretation
Supreme Court, 1789–1801, **2600–2603**
  Jay as Chief Justice, 1418
  prior judicial review instances, 165–
    166
  Rutledge as Chief Justice, 2301
Supreme Court at work, **2603–2610**
  appellate jurisdiction, 1494, 1502
  caseload, 2606, 2623–2624
  Chief Justice's duties, 346–348, 2605
  circuit court duty, 2589, 2603
  clerks, 429, 2604–2605
  conference, 488, 2607, 2620–2621
  content and scope, 1493
  decision announcements, 2607
  denial of review, 2606
  journalistic coverage, 1439–1441

Supreme Court at work (continued)
  judicial strategy, 1485–1487
  legitimizing decisions, 2597, 2598
  lower court compliance with, 2609
  Office of Marshal, 2605
  opinion assignment, 2607–2607
  oral argument, 1855, 2607, 2621
  period of terms, 2588, 2619–2620
  plurality opinion, 1920
  retroactivity of decisions, 2223–2225
  ripeness, 2278–2280
  special master appointments, 2462, 2593
  tenure, 2588
  term, 2669
  Wheat as first official reporter, 2883
Supreme Court bar, **2610–2613**
  admission to, 2610, 2611
  solicitor general and, 2612
Supreme Court decisions, impact of, **2613–2616**
  *Brown v. Board of Education*, 253–255
  on civil rights, 2613
  on corporations, 692
  on desegregation, 2613
  *Dred Scott v. Sandford*, 820
  on economy, 2613
  on federalism, 2613
  *Griswold v. Connecticut*, 1120, 1122, 1233–1234
  on legislative investigations, 2614
  *Marbury v. Madison*, 1667–1670
  *McCulloch v. Maryland*, 1705–1707
  *Plessy v. Ferguson*, 1918–1919
  on public opinion, 2614
  public understanding, 2078
  on regulatory commissions, 2614
  *Roe v. Wade/Doe v. Bolton*, 2284–2286, 2921
  on states and local communities, 2614
  *See also* Judicial legislation; Judicial policymaking
Supreme Court opinions. *See* Advisory opinion; Concurring opinion; Dissenting opinion; Grounds of opinion; Opinion of the Court; Plurality Opinion; Public Understanding of Supreme Court opinions
Supreme Court practice, **2616–2623**
  test case, 2676–2677
Supreme Court's work load, **2623–2624**
  caseload explosion, 1492–1493
  Judiciary Act of 1925, 1498
Suspect classification, **2624–2625**
  alienage as, 66, 72, 1219
  and fundamental rights, 1177
  illegitimacy as, 1326, 2732
  and least restrictive means test, 1573

  poverty not seen as, 2879
  race as, 169, 186, 781, 1416, 1646, 2842
  sex as, 1157
  strict scrutiny, 1177
  wealth discrimination, 742, 2309
Suspect's rights. *See Miranda* rules; Rights of the criminally accused
Symbolic speech, **2630–2632**
  clear and present danger test, 427
  First Amendment protection, 375
  flag desecration, 1061, 1062
  freedom of speech and, 2630
  Ku Klux Klan, 312–313, 2173
  *Tinker v. Des Moines Independent Community School District*, 2702–2703
  *See also* Religious symbols in public forums

**T**

Taft Court, **2637–2642**
  goals of, 2634–2635
  inconsistencies in, 2638–2639
  interpretation of federalism, 2641
  judicial review, 2637
Taft-Hartley Labor Relations Act (1947), **2642**
  antisubversion provisions, 79
  collective bargaining, 442
  right-to-work laws, 2277–2278
  steel seizure controversy, 2526
  strike injunction, 1553
  union membership, 1554
  as Wagner Act successor, 2642, 2819
Taking of property, **2643–2644**, **2644–2646** (update 1), **2646–2647** (update 2)
  building permit issuance, 802–803
  cable television installation, 1643–1644
  due process, 2534
  and economics theory, 1563–1566
  eminent domain, 888–889, 2051–2052, 2055–2056, 2882–2883
  environmental regulation and, 902–904
  executive agreement, 239
  fair return on fair value, 750, 969–970
  Frazier-Lemke Act voided as, 1105
  fugitive slaves as, 2054, 2427, 2428, 2430
  inverse condemnation, 1400–1401
  just compensation, 345, 1113, 1519, 1564, 2150, 2437, 2534, 2643, 2946

  nonphysical effects on value, 1651, 2055
  *Penn Central Transportation Co. v. New York City*, 1892
  per se rule for total, 1651, 2149–2150
  procedural due process, 2053, 2054
  property definition, 2646
  and property rights, 2054–2055
  public purpose doctrine, 2055, 2074–2076
  public use restriction, 2079
  Railroad Control Act, 2114
  rate regulation and, 2437
  regulatory takings, 1651, 2149–2150
  as retroactive legislation limitation, 2225, 2226
  zoning damages, 2945, 2946
Taney Court, **2651–2656**
  on bills of credit, 174, 2651
  on commerce clause, 455, 681, 1700, 2651
  on contract clause, 675–676
  on corporations, 325
  *Dred Scott* decision, 819–820, 2436, 2647, 2649–2650
  dual federalism, 827, 1000–1001
  equal protection of the laws, 908–909
  federalism and, 2651
  first case on commerce clause, 1700
  instrumentalist tone of, 2653
  on interstate commerce, 2652
  landmark cases, 2647–2650
  selective exclusiveness approach, 2652
  on slavery, 568, 569–570, 2649, 2654–2655
  on state police power, 2556
  on states' rights, 298, 2651
Tariff Act (1828), **2656**
  Exposition and Protest, 957
  South Carolina nullification, 559, 1069, 2480, 2519
Taxation without representation, **2656–2657**
  Adams (Samuel) protests, 31
  and Bill of Rights (English), 175
  colonial claims, 2201
  and confirmatio cartarum, 489
  constitutionalism and, 2656
  Declaration of Independence charge of, 754
  Declarations and Resolves of First Continental Congress, 1059
  Dickinson commentary, 779
  in District of Columbia, 796, 797
  Henry (Patrick) protest, 1284
  Townsend Acts as, 779, 2711
  unconstitutionality, 2751
  as violation of fundamental law, 2656

Tax Court of the United States, **2657**
Tax credits and religious schools. *See* Government aid to religious institutions
Taxing and spending powers, **2658– 2660, 2660–2661** (update)
  as antidiscrimination law basis, 95, 204
  belonging solely to Congress, 1998
  Boland Amendment, 206
  budget process, 260, 261
  child labor and, 151–152, 350, 1777– 1779
  Child Labor Tax Case, 151–152
  commerce clause, 455
  concurrent powers of federal and state governments, 484
  conditional spending, 485–488
  congressional agencies, 266
  constitutional questions on, 2659
  direct and indirect taxes, 784–785
  drug regulation, 804, 821
  and dual federalism, 827
  Economic Opportunity Act, 843
  enumerated powers and, 2660
  environmental regulation, 904–905
  establishment clause as limit, 1066
  as federal criminal jurisdiction basis, 1567
  and federal grants-in-aid, 987
  and federalism, 994, 1010
  and freedom of contract, 1117
  general welfare clause, 1186–1187, 2659
  Hamiltonian broad construction advocacy, 250
  of House of Representatives, 1307
  import-export clause, 1348–1349
  for internal improvements, 1385
  limits on, 2658
  and line-item veto, 1626
  New Deal, 1315
  presidential impoundment, 1349
  presidential spending power, 2000– 2001
  regulatory function of, 2658, 2659
  revenue sharing, 2227
  Social Security and, 2659, 2660
  spending power, 2468–2469
  standing and, 1464–1465
  state and local governments, 1211
  strict construction of, 2561
  supremacy clause and, 2661
  taxpayer challenges to spending programs, 1464–1465
  *See also* Budget process; Direct and indirect taxes; Intergovernmental tax immunities; State and local government taxation

Tax Injunction Act (1937), 447
Taxpayers' and citizens' suits, **2661– 2662**
  cases and controversies, 1464–1465
  federal funds to religious schools, 1066, 2777
  federal spending challenges, 164– 165
  *Flast v. Cohen,* 1066–1067
  personal stake in outcome of, 2661
  separation of powers and, 1066–1067, 2661–2662
  standing, 1066–1067, 2777
Technology and the Constitution. *See* Science, technology, and the Constitution
Telecommunications Act (1996), 471, 2489
Telephone pornography. *See* Dial-a-porn
Telephone tapping. *See* Wiretapping
Television. *See* Broadcasting; Cable television
Temperance. *See* Prohibition
Temporal limits on lawmaking powers, **2663–2665**
  cloture rule, 434, 2664
Temporary Assistance for Needy Families, 2875–2876
Tennessee Valley Authority Act (1933), **2666–2667**
  constitutionality challenges, 128
Ten Pound Act Cases (1786–1787), **2667**
  as first judicial review instances, 165– 166
Tenth Amendment, **2667–2669**
  age discrimination extension to state and local governments, 59
  child labor regulation seen violating, 1528
  Child Labor Tax Act and, 350
  cities and, 362
  devolution and, 776
  dual federalism and, 827
  economy and, 850
  enumerated powers, 744, 899, 1011
  and environmental regulation, 901, 904, 1009–1010
  implied powers, 1011
  and intergovernmental immunity, 1382
  and judicial power, 1465
  Municipal Bankruptcy Act as violation of, 127–128
  on rights retained to the people, 1091
  on states' rights, 178, 2533, 2667– 2668

Tenure of Office Act (1867), **2669**
  violation as Johnson (Andrew) impeachment charge, 110, 126, 288, 579, 1339, 1428–1429, 2476, 2669
Term (Supreme Court), **2669**
Term limits, **2669–2671**
  Anti-Federalist advocacy, 763
  in state and local government, 2671
  Stevens's views, 2537
  Twenty-Second Amendment, 73, 2741–2742
  Washington's Farewell Address precedent, 2862, 2863
Territorial Court, **2671–2672**
  slavery and, 2435
Territories of the United States, **2672– 2673**
  acquisition authorization, 83
  citizenship in, 2672
  colonialism constitutionality, 1169
  commonwealth status of, 468
  constitutional guarantees, 830
  diversity jurisdiction, 798
  extraterritoriality, 959
  federal judiciary provisions, 1464
  incorporation, 1358
  incorporation theory, 1169
  insular cases, 1375–1376
  legislative court, 1589–1590
  Missouri Compromise, 1747–1748
  Ordinance of 1784, 1856
  republican form of government, 2209
  as statehood probation, 2479
  Treaty of Guadalupe Hidalgo, 2720
  *See also* Northwest Ordinance; Slavery in the territories
Territory, **2673–2674**
  court, 2671–2672
  and federalism, 1005
  incorporation of, 2673–2674
  Louisiana Purchase Treaty, 1644
  Northwest Ordinance, 1829, 2479, 2673
  Puerto Rico status, 2080–2081
Terrorism control and the Constitution, **2674–2675**
  Antiterrorism and Effective Death Penalty Act, 101–102, 1503
  free speech vs. advocacy of force, 1154
  immigration law, 2674
  and limitation of federal jurisdiction, 1503
Test Acts. *See* Federal Test Acts
Test case, **2676–2677**
  abortion rights, 2284–2286, 2921
  birth control, 1233–1234
  cases and controversies clause, 2676

Test case (continued)
  Cherokee Indian Cases, 344
  and civil rights legislation, 410
  collusive suit, 443
  as constitutionally protected political activity, 1773
  on Indian lands, 1771
  interest group litigation, 1378–1379
  litigation strategy, 1630
  Rhode Island Dorrite constitution, 1652
  segregation ordinances, 259
  separate but equal facilities, 1918–1917
  voting rights in primary elections, 410, 423
  woman suffrage, 1740, 2807–2808
Testimonial and nontestimonial compulsion, **2677–2679**
  alcohol-level blood test from unconscious person, 229
  blood samples, 2319, 2677
  drunk-driving blood test, 205
  Fifth Amendment applications, 2237–2238, 2240–2241
  right against self-incrimination and, 2677–2678
Testimonial immunity. *See* Immunity grant
Test oath cases (1867), **2679–2680**
  and amnesty, 89
  attorney loyalty oath ruling, 1030
  and bill of attainder, 174, 1648
  Chase Court and, 335, 339
  civil liberties and, 2679
  and First Amendment privilege, 1048
Texas annexation. *See* Annexation of Texas
Textualism, **2681–2684**
  ambiguity and vagueness of, 2682–2684
  and judicial restraint, 1450
  noninterpretivism, 1820
  original intent and, 2315, 2681
  "plain meaning" rule, 627
  reliance on language of Constitution, 2681
  of Scalia, 2315, 2316
  strict constructionism vs., 2316
  *See also* Transformation of constitutional law
Theories of the Union, **2685–2689**
  of Adams (John Quincy), 30
  compact theory, 2687, 2688
  Constitutional Convention of 1787, 753–754
  creation of states, 2685
  federalism and, 2686

Federalist-Whig doctrine, 2686–2687, 2885
  interposition, 1392–1393
  of Lincoln, 1620–1621
  Louisiana Purchase Treaty, 1644
  nullification and, 2687
  separation of powers and, 2685
  states' rights and, 2519, 2686–2687
  territorial problems and, 2685
  of Webster (Daniel), 2871
Third Amendment, **2689**
  civil-military provision of, 385
  Petition of Right, 1903
  property rights and, 2052
Third-party consent, **2689–2691**
  actual authority basis, 1327–1328
  electronic eavesdropping and, 2690–2691
  probable cause and, 2689
  property rights and, 2690
  unreasonable search and, 2690
Thirteenth Amendment (framing), **2691–2693**
  abolitionist constitutional theory, 2691
  African American citizenship, 820, 2143, 2822
  "badges and incidents" theory, 201
  badges of servitude, 201, 1918, 1919, 2016
  Emancipation Proclamation, 884
  Freedmen's Bureau, 1106
  as peonage protection, 1960, 1961, 2900
  ratification, 72, 577
  Reconstruction policy, 2412–2143
  slavery abolishment, 2057, 2480, 2497, 2691
  three-fifths clause, 2692
Thirteenth Amendment (judicial interpretation), **2693–2695**
  and antidiscrimination legislation, 94, 95, 96, 401–402, 403
  and badges of servitude, 146, 1437
  and Civil Rights Act of 1866, 403
  Civil Rights Cases, 408–410
  and color of law, 445
  conscription as involuntary servitude argument, 506, 2187, 2356, 2928
  employment discrimination, 893
  equal protection of the laws, 908, 911
  as nonapplicable to group violence against blacks, 1293
  as nonapplicable to Selective Draft Law Cases, 2187, 2928
  *Patterson v. McLean Credit Union*, 1887
  peonage, 1897

private racial discrimination, 1241, 1283, 1293, 1437, 2015, 2016, 2063, 2099, 2290
  property rights in human body prohibition, 2057
  and rights of individual employee, 1549
  *Slaughterhouse* cases, 2423
  and voting rights, 2806
*Thoughts on Government* (Adams), 27
Three-fifths clause, **2700–2701**
  representation, 545
  Thirteenth Amendment, 2692
Three-judge court, **2701**
  injunction approval, 1499
"Three strikes" laws. *See* Career criminal sentencing laws
Timber Culture Act. *See* Environmental regulation and the Constitution
Title IX. *See* Education Amendments
Titles of nobility, **2703**
Toleration Act (1689), **2704–2705**
  Bill of Rights (English), 175
Tonkin Gulf Resolution. *See* Gulf of Tonkin Resolution
Tort Claims Act. *See* Federal Tort Claims Act
Torts, **2706–2710**
  Federal Tort Claims Act, 419, 1030, 1217–1218
  Fifth Amendment and, 2706
  Fourteenth Amendment and, 2706
  journalistic liability, 1069, 1438–1439
  litigation strategy, 1631
  physical contact protection, 2057
  procedural due process and, 2706
  punitive damages, 2081–2083
  sovereign immunity, 1030, 2459, 2706, 2707
  supremacy clause and, 2706
  worker's compensation replacing, 2924–2925
  *See also* Damages; Damages claims
*To Secure These Rights* (report of the Committee on Civil Rights), 318
Townshend Acts (1767), **2711**
  as taxation without representation, 779
  writ of assistance, 1099
Trade. *See* Commerce clause; Foreign commerce; Interstate commerce; Intrastate commerce; State regulation of commerce; State taxation of commerce
Trademark law. *See* Intellectual property law and the First Amendment
Trade unions. *See* Labor and the Constitution

Traffic stops, **2711–2712**
   automobile search, 209, 2711
   Fourth Amendment and, 2711
   sobriety checkpoints, 1096, 1726
Transactional immunity. *See* Immunity grant
Transformation of constitutional law, **2712–2714**
   living constitution, 1632–1634, 2712, 2714
   originalism, 2712
   progressive constitutional thought, 2713
Travel. *See* Right to travel
Travel Act (1961), 1568, 1670
Treason, **2715–2720**
   attainder of, 133–134
   as breach of allegiance, 2716
   Burr trial, 207, 278, 552, 2913
   citizenship theory and, 364
   conspiracy vs., 207, 278
   constitutional provisions, 2840
   conviction for, 2717
   *Cramer v. United States*, 705
   Davis (Jefferson) indictment, 747
   dual nationality and, 2716–2717
   Fries' Rebellion, 1156
   Hartford Convention, 30
   as impeachment ground, 609, 1336, 1337
   political trials, 1954, 1955
   right to counsel, 2259
   in state constitutions, 2715
   Whiskey Rebellion conviction and pardon, 2861, 2885
   witness testimony, 2718
   World War II cases, 2931
*Treatise on Evidence* (Wigmore), 2904–2905
*Treatise on the Constitutional Limitations Which Rest upon the Legislative Power of the States of the American Union* (Cooley), 680
Treaty of Guadalupe Hidalgo (1850), **2720**
Treaty on the Execution of Penal Sentences (1977), **2720–2721**
Treaty power, **2721–2722**
   and American Indians, 79, 81
   Bricker Amendment, 243–244, 1541
   and drug regulation, 821
   executive agreements, 939
   executive branch obligation deficiencies, 71
   First Congress, 1059
   and foreign affairs, 1076
   Jay's Treaty, 1259–1260, 1419, 2861–2862

Louisiana Purchase Treaty, 1644
*Missouri v. Holland*, 1081
   and political question doctrine, 1953
   as preempting state law, 1389–1390, 2834
   self-executing and non-self-executing treaties, 1080
   Senate, 1978, 1991–1993, 1996, 2359, 2361, 2362
   Senate advice and consent, 47, 1073, 1991
   Senate's strengthened role under, 1978
   supermajority rule, 2585
   as supreme law, 1746
   termination, 1993
   territory acquisition, 83
   *Ware v. Hylton*, 2834
   *See also* President and the treaty power
Trespass, **2722–2723**
   civil disobedience and, 371
   civil rights and, 389
   demonstration restrictions, 34
   informant electronic eavesdropping, 2896
   labor activity, 1554
   and open fields doctrine, 1849
Trial by jury, **2724–2730**
   applicable to territory, 1376
   Bill of Rights, 1091
   blue ribbon jury, 199–200
   *Bushell's Case*, 282–283
   in capital punishment cases, 302
   Civil Rights Act of 1957, 404
   compulsory process right, 479–481
   confrontation right, 491–492
   contempt power used to deny, 671
   criminal case guarantee, 721, 722
   in criminal contempt case, 435
   declaratory judgment, 756
   double jeopardy, 807–812
   and due process, 828, 2039
   evolution of, 2724–2725
   fair trial, 970
   felony, 1032
   and fugitive slaves, 2425, 2431
   and grand jury, 1220–1221
   incorporation doctrine, 830, 2832
   and incriminating statements, 1696
   in injunction violation prosecutions, 596
   judicial discretion, 166
   jurors' rights, 1514–1515
   jury nullification, 1512–1514
   jury selection, 2727
   jury size, 157–158, 264, 1515–1517, 2727, 2906

jury unanimity, 1434–1435, 1510, 1517–1518, 2727
juvenile proceedings, 353, 1523, 1709
for misdemeanors, 157, 157–158
*Palko v. Connecticut*, 1875
prejudicial publicity, 1150, 1405, 2077
*Quirin, Ex parte*, 2085
reasonable doubt, 2138–2139
   as right of the criminally accused, 2255
Sixth Amendment and, 2724
Ten Pound Act Cases, 2667
venue, 2782
vicinage, 2786–2787
and victim impact statements, 208–209
voir dire, 2803
waiver of constitutional rights, 2830
Warren Court on, 716
*See also* Fair trial; Jury discrimination; Public trial; Speedy trial; Witness, jurors, and the freedom of speech
Trials. *See* Fair trial; Impeachment; Military justice; Political trials; Public trial
Tribal economic development and the Constitution, **2731–2732**
Tucker Act (1887), **2737–2738**
Tuition grants, **2738–2739**
   enjoinment, 1231
   establishment of religion and, 2738
   state action and, 2738
   *See also* Vouchers
TVA. *See* Tennessee Valley Authority Act
Twelfth Amendment, **2740**
   as Anti-Federalist concession, 72
   Electoral College, 866, 1940
   elector selection, 1940
   Jefferson approval, 1423
   separate presidential and vice-presidential ballots, 550
Twentieth Amendment, **2740–2741**
   presidential succession, 2741
   ratification, 73, 594, 598, 2741
   Senate and, 2359
   term commencement, 2741
Twenty-Fifth Amendment, **2741**
   presidential incapacity, 1342, 1343
   presidential succession, 2002
   ratification, 73, 608
Twenty-First Amendment, **2741**
   as Prohibition repeal, 2050
   ratification, 73, 74–75, 594, 598
Twenty-Fourth Amendment, **2741**
   capitation taxes, 312
   poll tax abolition, 73, 377, 1306, 1961, 2741

Twenty-Fourth Amendment (continued)
ratification, 73, 608
voting rights, 2809
Twenty-Second Amendment, 2741–2742
constitutional reform, 650
presidential two-term limit, 73, 2741–2742
ratification, 73, 602
Twenty-Seventh Amendment, 2742–2743
ratification, 73, 75–76
Twenty-Sixth Amendment, 2743
ratification, 73, 75, 608
voting age, 377, 1090, 1306
Twenty-Third Amendment, 2743–2744
District of Columbia presidential electors, 796
ratification, 73, 608
Two-level theory, 2744–2745
clear and present danger test, 331
obscenity and, 1837
Two-sovereignties rule, 2745–2746
as Fifth Amendment restriction, 2237
*Two Treatises of Government* (Locke), 1639–1640

## U

UCMJ. *See* Uniform Code of Military Justice
Ultra vires, 2747
Unconstitutional conditions, 2748–2749, 2749–2751 (update)
Unconstitutionality, 2751–2752
earliest rulings, 1279–1280, 1294
justiciability showing, 1521
Unenumerated rights, 2752–2754
abortion seen as, 10–11
as Bork nomination issue, 210, 211
Fourteenth Amendment protection, 33
natural rights and, 2753
Ninth Amendment and, 2752, 2754
social compact and, 2753
as statute invalidation vehicle, 11
*See also* Freedom of assembly and association; Freedom of intimate Association; Right of privacy
Uniform Code of Military Justice, 1726–1727
Union. *See* Civil War; Theories of the Union
Unions. *See* Labor and antitrust laws; Labor and the Constitution; Labor movement
Unitary executive, 2755–2756

United Colonies of New-England Commissioners, 997
United Nations Charter, 2757–2758
International human rights, 1387
and U.S. Korean War involvement, 1075, 1541, 1921
U.S. participation issues, 603
United Nations Convention Relating to the Status of Refugees, 71
United States Court of Appeals for the Federal Circuit, 2758
creation of, 981, 1492
Judicial Conference of the United States, 1452
jurisdiction of Claims Court transferred to, 419, 2758
jurisdiction of Court of Customs and Patent Appeals transferred to, 696, 2758
review of Court of International Trade decisions, 696
United States Courts of Appeals, 2758–2761
in basic judiciary system, 1463
certification and, 327
diversity jurisdiction and, 2759
empowerments, 2760
established by Circuit Courts of Appeals Act, 361
functions, 2758–2759
Judicial Conference of the United States, 1452
jurisdiction and caseloads, 1491–1492, 2759
original jurisdiction, 2759
relationship to Supreme Court, 2760–2761
writ of mandamus, 2760
writ of prohibition, 2050, 2760
United States District Courts, 2762–2765
admiralty and maritime jurisdiction, 45, 1495
in basic judiciary system, 1463
caseload, 2764
concurrent jurisdictions, 2762
diversity jurisdiction, 2762, 2764
functions of, 2763
immunity grants by, 989
Judicial Code, 1451
Judicial Conference of the United States, 1452
statutory jurisdiction, 1490–1491
workload, 1491, 2763
Universal Declaration of Human Rights, 1387–1388
Universal Military Training and Service Act. *See* Selective Service Acts

Universities. *See* Academic freedom; Affirmative action; Education and the Constitution
Unmarried cohabitation. *See* Freedom of intimate association
Unreasonable search, 2766–2768, 2768–2770 (update)
aural and visual surveillance, 1527
*Chandler v. Miller*, 330
drug testing as, 294, 822, 823, 826, 1096
exclusion of evidence gained by, 722
Federal Bureau of Investigation break-ins, 976
Fourth Amendment protection, 294, 330, 375, 822, 823, 1094–1095, 1097–1098, 1527, 2766–2768
and freedom of speech, 1131
harmless error, 1270
*Katz v. United States*, 1527
physical intrusion requirement, 1527
probable cause, 71, 2022–2023, 2767
prohibition on, 2330
reasonable expectation of privacy and, 2768
and right against self-incrimination, 216
and right of privacy, 721
rights of criminally accused, 2257
search incident to arrest and, 2329, 2766, 2769
stop and frisk, 2767, 2769
waiver of constitutional rights, 2831
warrantless searches and, 2766–2767, 2768, 2847
*See also* Exclusionary rule
Unwritten Constitution, 2770–2772
and higher law, 1287
and limited government, 1618–1619
Unwritten law. *See* Higher law
Urban areas. *See* Cities and the Constitution; Public purpose doctrine; Residential segregation
Urine testing. *See* Drug testing
Use immunity. *See* Immunity grant
Utility regulation. *See* Economic regulation

## V

Vaccination, 2773
patients' rights, 1884
religious liberty conflict, 2190
and right of privacy, 2244
as under police power, 1415
Vagrancy laws, 2774–2775
*Papachristou* decision, 816

street gang loitering ordinance, 345
vagueness doctrine and, 345, 2774
Vagueness, **2775–2777**
breach of the peace statutes, 227
*Chicago v. Morales*, 345
chilling effect and, 354
civil rights cases and, 390
drug laws, 678–679
freedom of speech, 1131
free speech and RICO Act, 1152–1153
harassment law, 2925
incitement to unlawful conduct, 1285–1286
interpretive latitude and, 2775
invalid on its face, 1399
juvenile curfew laws, 1521
juvenile proceedings, 1523
as litigation strategy, 1631
loyalty oaths, 2066
loyalty-security programs, 1536
overbreadth vs., 1866–1867, 2775
partial-birth abortion bans, 13
*Planned Parenthood of Central Missouri v. Danforth*, 1916
vagrancy laws, 345, 2774
Value pluralism and the Constitution, **2778–2779**
association with liberalism, 2778
freedom of speech and, 2778
marketplace of ideas and, 2778
New Right jurisprudence rejection of, 1801
VAWA. *See* Violence Against Women Act
Vehicular pursuits. *See* Police pursuits and constitutional rights
Venue, **2782**
change of, 2782
free press/fair trial, 1142
Judicial Code, 1451
Sixth Amendment and, 2782
vicinage vs., 2786–2787
Vermont Constitution of 1777, **2782**
Vested rights, **2782–2784**
*Calder v. Bull*, 290
*Charles River Bridge v. Warren Bridge Company*, 332–333
and contract clause, 1068, 2547
corporate charter, 2059–2060
*Dartmouth College v. Woodward*, 2871
due process and, 2783, 2934–2935
eminent domain and, 888, 2783
and feudalism, 1034
Fourteenth Amendment protection, 1041–1042, 1225, 2203, 2783–2784, 2807

and freedom of contract doctrine, 744, 745
inalienable policy power supremacy over, 283, 1350
Paterson ruling, 360, 1883
police power and, 2783
privileges and immunities, 2784
and public purpose doctrine, 2073
reserved police power and, 2218
state police power and, 1225, 2507
and substantive due process, 2052, 2784, 2934–2935
*See also* Contract clause
Veto power, **2784–2785**
checks and balances, 342
executive defiance of "unconstitutional" laws, 942
Ford's extensive use of, 1070
impoundment of funds as, 1349
Jackson's extensive use of, 1408, 1409, 1412, 1414
Johnson's (Andrew) enlargement of, 1428
joint resolution subject to, 1436–1437
line-item veto, 1625–1627
pocket veto, 1920–1921, 2784–2785
and political philosophy of Constitution, 1945
presidential first use of, 547
as presidential power, 322, 547, 1996, 1999
separation of powers and, 2383, 2784
Vice-presidency, **2785–2786**
and presidency of Senate, 2358
separate ballot for, 550
Vicinage, **2786–2787**
Vietnam War, **2787–2791**
amnesty, 89, 1070
antiwar demonstrations, 2319, 2790–2792
antiwar demonstrations in District of Columbia, 796
antiwar movement, 1431
antiwar suit against Army surveillance, 1557
Calley court-martial as political trial, 1954, 2360
congressional leadership in ending, 494
conscientious objection, 505, 506, 2188, 2193
conscription, 2357
and critical legal studies, 724
draft card burning, 817–818
executive power, 947
Gulf of Tonkin Resolution, 1242
interposition, 1392

Johnson's (Lyndon) strategy, 1430–1431
*Massachusetts v. Laird*, 1692
*Parker v. Levy*, 1879
Pentagon Papers case, 1129, 1139, 1140, 1145, 1805–1807, 2009
as police action, 1921
political question doctrine, 1470, 1955
presidential plenary authority, 1075
presidential war powers controversy, 494, 610
Senate antiwar policies, 2360
state of war, 2505
symbolic speech, 2703
as undeclared war, 755, 1242, 1998, 2360, 2787
War Powers Resolution, 485, 494, 610–611, 2838–2839, 2842, 2843
wiretapping, 2761–2762
Vinson Court, **2792–2797**
alien hearings, 2408
*Brown v. Board of Education* arguments before, 2852
civil liberties rulings, 380, 2793, 2795
commentators on the Constitution on, 452
freedom of speech and, 2794
Justices of, 420
*Rosenberg v. United States*, 2294
Violence Against Women Act (1994), **2797**
and constitutional aspiration, 665
Virginia and Kentucky Resolutions (1798–1799), **2798–2799**
constitutional theory, 1412, 1421
as interposition, 1392
Jefferson and Madison authorship, 1421–1422, 1424
as response to Alien and Sedition Acts, 65, 67, 228, 1016, 1049, 1421, 1424
Virginia Charter of 1606, **2799**
Virginia Declaration of Rights and Constitution of 1776, **2799–2800**
bail clause, 158
civil liberties, 376
as first permanent state constitution, 540
as influence on French *Declaration of Rights*, 1366
and Jeffersonian constitutional theory, 1419–1420
Madison's role in, 1656
omitted rights, 176
property linked with liberty, 2051
republican form of government, 2209
right against self-incrimination, 2235

Virginia Plan, **2800**
  and bicameralism, 172
  and federalism, 1011
  as framework for discussion of Constitution, 518, 519, 521, 542
  and judicial appointments, 48
  Madison's contributions, 1657
  Paterson and, 1882
  Pinckney Plan, 1909
  Randolph (Edmund) and, 2116
  three-fifths formula, 2700
Virginia Statute of Religious Freedom (1786), **2801**
  and constitutional religious liberty guarantee, 2185
  on establishment of religion, 928
  Madison's "Memorial and Remonstrance" and, 1662
  rejection of religious test for public office, 2197
Virtual representation. *See* Representation; Taxation without representation
Visas, **2801–2802**
Voice samples. *See* Testimonial and nontestimonial compulsion
Void for vagueness. *See* Vagueness
Voir dire, **2803**
  and fair trial, 970
  and free press/fair trial, 1152
Volstead Act (1919), **2803–2804**
Voluntariness. *See* Police interrogation and confessions
Voting rights, **2811–2812** (update),
  **2811–2812** (update)
  alien, 68–69
  amendments broadening scope of, 1306
  in antebellum period, 566
  ballot access, 158, 2813
  black disenfranchisement, 1168, 2202
  of black males, 1039–1041, 1070, 1090, 1092, 1728
  capitation taxes and, 312
  citizenship separated from, 68–69, 91, 2918
  city boundary delineations and, 362
  Civil Rights Act of 1957, 404
  Civil Rights Act of 1960, 405
  Civil Rights Commission investigation of, 410
  civil rights movement and, 1026
  class actions, 2320
  as Constitutional Convention of 1787 issue, 636
  Court invalidations, 1041
  in deliberative democracy, 764

District of Columbia disenfranchisement, 608, 796, 797
  due process and, 2807
  eighteen-year-old vote, 73, 608, 1090, 2743
  electoral districting, 152–153, 867–870, 2227–2229, 2814
  Fifteenth Amendment and, 2436, 2807, 2938
  Fifteenth Amendment enforcement, 1089
  Fifteenth Amendment non-protection of private abridgement, 1415, 2938
  Fifteenth Amendment non-protection of women, 2918
  Fifteenth and Nineteenth Amendment guarantees, 375, 387, 392
  first case under Fifteenth Amendment, 2145
  Force Acts, 1070
  and Fourteenth Amendment framing, 1084–1085, 1086, 1087, 1090
  as fundamental interest, 1401, 2228
  gerrymander effects, 1187–1189, 1203, 2814
  grandfather clause, 1219, 1242, 1629, 2808
  homeless people and, 1302
  jury service linkage, 1515
  Lincoln's Reconstruction plan, 1625
  literacy test, 1041, 1042, 1089–1090, 1629, 2808
  Military Reconstruction Acts, 1728
  multimember districts, 1751, 1765, 2135
  non-English literacy equivalent, 1527
  one person, one vote, 440, 1852–1853
  poll tax abolishment, 73, 1271–1272, 1961
  poll tax upheld, 228, 1961
  primary election exclusions, 1238, 2808
  primary elections, 423, 1941, 2007, 2008
  primary election test case, 410, 423
  property requirements, 2052–2053, 2806
  punishment of private interference upheld, 2938
  racial discrimination, 392–393, 1751, 2480, 2811, 2906–2907
  and reapportionment, 152–153, 2130–2138
  *Reese, United States v.*, 2822–2823
  *Reese v. United States*, 2145–2146, 2827
  residence requirements, 830–831, 2219, 2813

rights violations investigation, 607
  school district limitation, 1542
  *South Carolina v. Katzenbach*, 2456–2457
  state action and, 2484–2485
  Stone Court and, 2550–2551
  strict scrutiny, 1271, 1272, 1401, 2203, 2228
  substantive due process and, 2577
  Thirteenth Amendment and, 2806
  *Thornburg v. Gingles*, 2136
  Twenty-Fourth Amendment, 2741, 2809
  Twenty-Sixth Amendment, 2743
  understanding clause, 2320
  Waite opinion, 2822–2823
  Warren Court decisions, 380
  wealth discrimination, 1271–1272, 1362, 1974, 2053
  "white primary" and, 2808
  write-in votes, 264–265
  *See also* Fifteenth Amendment; Race and voting; Representation; Woman suffrage; Woman suffrage movement
Voting Rights Act of 1965 and its amendments, **2812–2813, 2813–2814** (update)
  amendments (1970), 2743
  and black-majority districts, 1735
  as broadening voter eligibility, 1306
  and civil liberties, 377, 379
  and civil rights, 392–393
  constitutionality upheld, 2456–2457
  electoral districting, 868–869, 870, 2093
  enactment and provisions, 1026, 1042, 2810
  gerrymander, 1188
  impact of, 412
  literacy equivalency provision, 1527, 1629
  literacy tests suspension, 1090, 1629
  multimember districts remedy, 1765, 2135
  as national standard, 1008
  *Oregon v. Mitchell*, 1856
  primary elections, 2008
  race-conscious reapportionment, 2756
  reapportionment, 1765, 2135, 2136
Vouchers, **2814–2815**
  *Agostini v. Felton* supporting, 61, 1604
  government aid to religious institutions and, 1208, 2814–2815
  and religious objections to public school teachings, 2178
  tuition grants, 2738–2739

Vulgarities. *See* Fighting words; Low-value speech

# W

Wade-Davis Bill (1864), **2818**
  Lincoln-congressional clash over, 1625
  Lincoln veto, 2142
Wadsworth Act (1940), 2357
Wage and hour law. *See* Adamson Eight-Hour Act; Fair Labor Standards Act; Maximum hours and minimum wages legislation
Wagner Act (1935), **2818–2819**
  boycott, 215
  child labor, 349
  collective bargaining, 442, 1545
  commerce clause, 458
  employer speech, 1551
  Shreveport doctrine test, 2415
  union membership, 1553–1554
  upheld, 1547, 2289
  *See also* Taft-Hartley Labor Relations Act
Wagner Act cases (1937), **2819–2821**
  and child labor, 349
  employer treatment of unions, 1548
Waite Court, **2824–2830**
  Civil Rights Cases, 2828
  Fourteenth and Fifteenth Amendment opinions, 2822–2823, 2826–2827
  Legal tender cases, 1581–1582
  state action doctrine, 1037–1038
  on state police power, 676
Waiver of constitutional rights, **2830–2832**
  *Faretta v. California*, 974
  *Johnson v. Zerbst*, 1436
  *Miranda* rules, 1926, 1930–1931, 2240
  plea bargaining as, 1917–1918
  right to counsel, 2260
  voluntariness of, 2710
War, declaration of. *See* Declaration of war
War, foreign affairs, and the Constitution, **2834–2840**
  Congress and foreign policy, 494–495
  Senate and foreign policy, 2361–2363
War of 1812
  as declared war, 755, 1998
  and Federalists, 1017
  Hartford Convention protest, 1017, 2480
  interposition, 1392
  Madison's conduct of, 1659

War powers, **2840–2842, 2842–2844** (update 1), **2844** (update 2)
  and American hostage crisis in Tehran, 614–615
  Clinton administration on, 432
  commentators on the Constitution on, 451
  concurrent resolution, 1998, 2838
  congressional, 502–503
  constitutional provisions, 2835
  declaration of war, 755–756, 1080, 1998
  emergency powers, 886
  government price regulation, 1605
  Gulf War, 1243
  historical background, 2834–2839
  International Emergency Economic Powers Act, 1386
  Japanese American cases, 131, 2930–2931
  Korean War, 1541
  legislation continued in peacetime, 2924
  National Security Act, 1781
  Story's views, 2554
  territory acquisition, 83
  War Powers Resolution (1973), 485, 494, 610–611, 2838–2839, 2842, 2843
  wartime dislocations legislation, 603
  World War I, 2927–2929
  World War II, 2929–2931
  *See also* Congressional war powers; Presidential war powers; War, foreign affairs, and the Constitution
War Powers Acts (1941, 1942), **2844–2845**
  presidential powers, 1998
War Powers Resolution (1973), 610–611, 2838–2839, 2842, 2843
  and concurrent resolution, 485
  congressional override of Nixon's veto of, 494
Warrant. *See* Arrest warrant; General Warrant; Search warrant
Warrantless search, **2845–2847**
  administrative search, 43, 44
  automobile, 140, 141, 244, 329, 1427, 2295, 2846, 2847
  balancing test and, 2337
  benign forms of, 2847
  blood samples and, 2319
  body search as, 205
  border search as, 209
  drunk-driving blood test, 205
  of employment facilities voided, 1681
  exigent circumstances, 956, 2846
  exigent circumstances rejected, 2881

  Fourth Amendment prohibition, 2881
  general search, 1098–1099
  general warrant, 1185–1186
  homeless shelters protected from, 1302
  plain feel doctrine, 1912
  plain view doctrine, 1913
  probable cause, 140, 2329, 2846
  seizures in, 2339
  third-party consent, 2689–2691
  trash search, 294
  unreasonable search, 2766–2767, 2768, 2847
  vessel search, 319
  Warren Court approach, 1095
Warren Court, **2851–2858**
  access to the courts, 23
  antidiscrimination legislation, 94
  Brennan role in, 229–231, 232–236, 238–239
  *Brown v. Board of Education*, 254–255, 273, 771–772, 2849, 2852–2853
  Burger Court outlook vs., 270, 272, 273, 274, 275, 276, 277
  capital punishment, 302
  civil liberties expansion, 379, 380, 2414, 2594
  commentators on the Constitution on, 452
  conservative backlash, 776, 1291, 1315, 1801
  constitutionalism, 382–383, 658, 2072
  criminal defendant's rights, 975, 1927, 1928, 2263
  criminal procedure, 715–716, 1927, 2848, 2855–2856
  double jeopardy, 169–170
  draft card burning, 818
  due process decisions, 722
  dynamic and changing Constitution view, 2713–2714
  electoral districting, 2227–2229
  equal protection, 274, 909–912, 1271–1272, 2853
  equal protection clause expansion, 1271, 1272, 2853
  federalization of state criminal procedure, 2039
  force of Warren's leadership, 1485–1486, 2848–2851, 2851–2852
  freedom of the press, 271–272
  fundamental interests, 1173
  fundamental rights, 1177
  habeas corpus expansion, 1252, 1253, 1254
  incorporation doctrine, 169–170, 179, 715, 1267

Warren Court (continued)
  individual rights, 725
  judicial activism, 607–608, 1448,
    2853, 2857–2858
  judicial power, 1066–1067
  Justice Goldberg's record, 1200
  Justice Marshall's (Thurgood)
    opinions and dissents, 1676–1682
  Justices of, 420
  landmark decisions, 273
  legal process school as reaction to,
    1578, 1579
  legislative investigations, 2866–
    2867
  libel laws, 2850, 2855
  liberalism of, 607–608, 1615, 1616,
    2853, 2855–2858
  libertarianism of, 2312, 2315, 2340,
    2549
  *Miranda* rules, 1922, 1926, 2850
  New Right backlash, 1801
  originalism reaction to perceived
    excesses, 1291
  overbreadth doctrine, 250
  pragmatist legacy, 1983
  probable cause, 1095
  protections for public employees,
    2066
  race-related legislation, 1448
  reapportionment, 152–153, 273,
    1615, 2849, 2854, 2857
  *Reynolds v. Sims*, 273, 2227–2229
  scholarly critics, 1542
  selective incorporation of Bill of
    Rights, 2039, 2041
  self-incrimination cases, 64
  as social change agent, 700
  solicitor general role in, 2451
  standard of review, 2471
  state action and, 400, 2491
  states' rights, 2520
  strict scrutiny, 2562
  suspect classification, 2625
  taking of property, 2646
  three themes of, 2853
  voting rights, 2804
  welfare benefits, 2408
Washington, D.C. *See* District of
  Columbia
Washington's Farewell Address (1796),
  2862, **2863**
Waste, pollution, and the Constitution,
  **2864**
Watergate and the Constitution, **2864–
  2865**
  attorney general and Justice Depart-
    ment, 134, 135
  Burger Court and, 274

Ervin as chair of Senate investigative
    committee, 922, 2365
  executive privilege claim, 1955
  final judgment rule, 1044
  impeachment articles of Richard
    Nixon, 126–127, 609, 1339
  Iran-Contra comparisons, 1402
  issues involved, 609–610
  *Nixon, United States v.*, 1817–1818
  Nixon pardon, 1070, 1339, 2864
  Nixon refusal to surrender tapes,
    1816
  political trials, 1954
  presidential immunity ruling, 1994
  Senate select committee investiga-
    tion, 2360, 2365
  special prosecutor, 1359, 2463
Water Pollution Control Act. *See*
  Environmental regulation and the
  Constitution
Water Power Act (1920), **2865–2866**
Water Quality Improvement Act. *See*
  Environmental regulation and the
  Constitution
Wealth discrimination, **2869–2870**
  in abortion access, 6, 7, 8–9, 1324,
    1665, 1974, 2205, 2286, 2870,
    2872
  in access to the courts, 23, 204, 1232,
    1974
  in bail-setting, 149, 716
  due process, 204
  equal protection guarantees, 2309–
    2310
  guarantees against, 2309
  and income tax unconstitutionality,
    1960, 1964
  indigency, 1362
  jury selection from property tax rolls,
    253
  poll tax as, 1362, 1974, 2879
  property-tax financing of school
    districts, 1974–1975, 2309–2310,
    2387
  right to counsel, 2262
  *San Antonio Independent School
    District v. Rodriguez*, 2309–2310
  strict scrutiny vs. rational basis
    standard, 741–742
  as suspect classification, 472
  in voting rights, 1271–1272, 1362,
    1974, 2053, 2879
  in welfare benefits, 741, 742, 2408,
    2869, 2873
  in zoning, 2947
*Wealth of Nations* (Smith), 834
Webb-Kenyon Act (1913), **2870**
  upheld, 421, 1169

Welfare benefits, **2873**
  abortion funding restriction, 5, 6, 8–
    9, 1665, 2205
  alienage restrictions, 66, 1218–1219,
    1332–1333
  alienage rights, 190, 1077, 1331
  *Califano v. Westcott*, 293–294
  Contract with America (1994) opposi-
    tion, 776
  Court deference to legislative
    judgments, 2876–2877
  *Dandridge v. Williams*, 741–742,
    2873, 2874, 2876, 2879–2880
  denied access to the courts, 23
  devolution, 778
  due process, 1697–1698
  economic analysis, 837
  entitlement, 897, 2880
  equal protection, 917, 2305, 2408
  fair hearing, 965–966
  federal grants-in-aid, 988
  food stamp program, 770, 2874–2875,
    2876
  and freedom of intimate association,
    1119, 1120, 1122, 1123–1124
  home visit by caseworker allowed,
    2934
  Johnson (Lyndon) administration,
    1430
  poverty law, 1973–1975
  procedural due process, 1200–1201
  residence requirements, 1973, 2218,
    2219, 2275, 2873, 2874, 2877,
    2878–2879
  right-privilege distinction, 2252
  *Saenz v. Roe*, 778, 2305
  *Shapiro v. Thompson*, 2305, 2408
  Social Security Act, 2445–2446
  standard of review, 741–742
  waiting period, 2408
  wealth discrimination, 741, 742, 2408,
    2869, 2873
Welfare rights, **2874–2875**, **2875–
  2877** (update)
  international human rights guaran-
    tees, 1388
  *Lochner v. New York*, 1638, 2878
  nonmandated, 2877
  privilege distinction, 2252
  reform bill (1996), 777
  *See also* Medicaid-funded abortions
Welfare state, **2877–2881**
  Economic Opportunity Act, 843
  Health Insurance for the Aged Act
    (Medicare), 1281
  Sheppard-Towner Maternity Act,
    2411, 2659
  welfare rights, 2874–2875

*See also* Maximum hours and
  minimum wages legislation; New
  Deal; Social Security Act
*We, the People* (Ackerman), 524
Whig party, **2884–2885**
  Adams (John Quincy) theory develop-
    ment, 30–31
  constitutional nationalism, 2885
  development of mass electioneering
    techniques, 559
  theory of the Union, 2686–2687,
    2885
  Webster and, 2885
Whiskey Rebellion (1794), **2885**
  guarantee clause, 1238
  militia response, 2861
White Court, **2897–2901**
  Justices of, 421
Wilkes Cases, **2905**
  right against self-incrimination, 2236
Williams Act (1934), 2350
Wilmot Proviso (1846), **2908**
  abolitionist free-soiler support, 3
  Douglas (Stephen) opposition, 812
  as popular sovereignty alternative,
    563, 1962
  on slavery in the territories, 2435
Wiretapping, **2912–2913**
  Black opinion on, 187
  challenge rights, 64–65
  electronic eavesdropping laws, 873
  by federal agents, 1774
  Federal Bureau of Investigation
    activities, 976, 2139
  and interrogation by informers, 1853
  Justice Department use of, 136
  and lawlessness by public officials,
    719
  laws and, 873
  and living Constitution, 1633–1634
  *Olmstead v. United States*, 711,
    1849–1850, 2913
  Omnibus Crime Control and Safe
    Streets Act, 1852, 2913
  presidential inherent power claim,
    2761–2762
  search and seizure, 1850, 2139, 2140
  Senate Subcommittee on Constitu-
    tional Rights investigation, 2365
  *See also* Electronic eavesdropping
Witnesses, jurors, and the freedom of
  speech, **2915–2916**
  confrontation right, 2255
  cross-examination, 2255
  federal immunity, 989
  fruit of the poisonous fruit, 1158
  grand jury, 1221
  legislative investigations, 1595

*See also* Right against self-incrimination
Woman's Christian Temperance Union,
  2919
Woman's Party, 2919
Woman suffrage, **2917–2918**
  citizenship basis, 91, 370, 1740, 2477,
    2918–2919, 2920
  constitutional aspiration, 664
  and Fifteenth Amendment, 91, 2736,
    2807–2808
  and Fourteenth Amendment, 1092,
    1740, 2807
  *Minor v. Happersett* denial of, 1740,
    2807–2808, 2918, 2919, 2920
  Nineteenth Amendment, 72, 73, 92,
    593, 1306, 1808–1809, 2389, 2808,
    2917–2918, 2919
  post–Civil War denial, 69
  Progressive advocacy, 2047
  Reconstruction-era denial, 69, 1740,
    2477, 2807–2808, 2918, 2919,
    2920
  and state law, 1740
Woman suffrage movement, **2918–
  2920**
  Anthony's work, 91–92
  civil disobedience and, 370
  petition campaign, 2273
  Seneca Falls Convention, 562, 2365–
    2366, 2804
  split over Fifteenth Amendment, 91
  Stanton's work, 2476–2477, 2806
  Truth's arguments, 2736
Women in constitutional history, **2920–
  2922**
  abortion rights, 4–15, 190, 191, 192,
    196, 2204
  Anthony and Stanton women's rights
    leadership, 91–92, 2476–2477,
    2806
  birth control rights, 4, 182–183, 2204
  Brandeis brief, 224–225, 1764, 2920
  equal rights amendment, 918–919
  feminist theory, 1032–1033
  freedom of intimate association,
    1118–1119
  gender rights, 1185
  husband's feudal privileges, 1034,
    1035
  maximum hours and minimum wages
    laws, 35–36, 797, 1764
  Seneca Falls Convention, 2365–2366
  Supreme Court justices, 1195–1197,
    1841–1846
  Truth's contributions, 2736
  woman suffrage movement, 2918–
    2919

*See also* Marriage and the Constitu-
  tion; Race and sex in
  antidiscrimination law; Reproductive autonomy; Sex discrimination
Women's rights movement. *See*
  Feminist theory; Gender rights;
  Woman suffrage movement
Women's suffrage. *See* Woman suffrage;
  Woman suffrage movement
Workers' compensation legislation,
  **2924–2925**
  and commerce clause, 456
  graduated scale of compensation,
    1804
  Pitney and, 1911
Workplace harassment and the First
  Amendment, **2925–2926 (I),
  2926 (II)**
  employee speech rights (private),
    891, 2925
  and freedom of speech, 1136
  and hate speech, 1278
  sexual harassment as Title VII viola-
    tion, 100–101, 1722
World Trade Organization, 1766
World War I, **2926–2929**
  Budget and Accounting Act
    following, 261
  clear and present danger doctrine,
    1299, 1955
  commerce clause use, 2481
  conscription, 506, 2356–2357, 2927
  conspiracy cases, 708
  criminal syndicalism laws, 723–724
  as declared war, 755, 1998
  espionage, 2351
  Espionage Act, 15–16, 751, 923–924
  and First Amendment rights, 1049–
    1050, 1126, 2901, 2928
  free speech cases, 1606–1607
  Lever Food and Drug Control Act,
    1605
  loyalty-security programs, 1649
  nativism, 1329
  political trials, 1954, 1955
  seditious libel, 2353
  Selective Service Act, 2927
  war powers, 2841, 2927–2929
  Wilson (Woodrow) policies, 2911–
    2912, 2927, 2928
World War II, **2929–2931**
  alien detentions, 65
  Bracero Program, 1330
  conscientious objection, 505
  conscription, 506, 2357
  as declared war, 755, 1998
  Emergency Price Control Act, 887,
    2937

World War II (continued)
  group libel statutes following, 1235
  habeas corpus suspension, 1246, 1247
  *Haupt v. United States,* 1279
  international human rights inception, 1387
  Japanese American cases, 65, 129–130, 132, 1241, 1415–1417, 2290, 2930–2931
  legislative investigation, 1595
  loyalty-security programs, 1649, 2581
  political trials, 1954
  postwar Marshall Plan, 1687
  presidential broad war powers, 1998
  Roosevelt (Franklin D.) policies, 2290–2291, 2841, 2929–2931
  segregation, 2355
  Senate bipartisanship, 2360
  as social change agent, 2390
  subversive advocacy cases, 2580, 2581
  treason cases, 2931
  U.S. constitutional influence on occupation of Germany and Japan, 1365, 1367
  war powers, 2841
  War Powers Acts, 2844–2845
World Wide Web. *See* Internet
Writ of assistance. *See* Assistance, writ of
Writ of certiorari. *See* Certiorari, writ of
Writ of error. *See* Error, writ of
Writ of habeas corpus. *See* Habeas corpus
Writ of prohibition. *See* Prohibition, writ of
Writs of assistance. *See* Paxton's Case

**Y**

Yellow dog contract, **2939**
  *Coppage v. Kansas,* 2900
  Erdman Act prohibiting, 25, 1547, 2939
  injunction as enforcement, 1292
  Norris-LaGuardia Act, 596
  upheld, 684
Youth curfew laws. *See* Juvenile curfew laws

**Z**

Zenger's case, **2944**
  freedom of the press, 1138
  jury nullification, 1512
  seditious libel, 2352–2353
Zoning, **2944–2945, 2946–2947** (update)
  adult bookstore, 2317
  adult movie theaters, 1054, 1057, 1133, 2199, 2529, 2940
  controls, 2644
  family-based restrictions, 973, 1124
  First Amendment and, 2317
  grandfather clause, 1219–1220
  *Penn Central Transportation Co. v. New York City,* 1893, 2946
  racial exclusionary, 2219, 2220–2221, 2222, 2354, 2484
  rational basis review, 428, 2022
  regulatory takings, 2150, 2151
  Rehnquist Court rulings, 381
  state police power, 2510
  *See also* Restrictive covenant